CANADIAN
ORGANIZATIONAL
BEHAVIOUR

Fourth Edition

Steven L. McShane

McGraw-Hill Ryerson

Toronto   Montréal   Boston   Burr Ridge, IL   Dubuque, IA   Madison, WI   New York   San Francisco   St. Louis
Bangkok   Beijing   Bogotá   Caracas   Kuala Lumpur   Lisbon   London   Madrid   Mexico City   Milan   New Delhi
Santiago   Seoul   Singapore   Sydney   Taipei

McGraw-Hill Ryerson Limited
A Subsidiary of The McGraw-Hill Companies

CANADIAN ORGANIZATIONAL BEHAVIOUR
Fourth Edition

ISBN: 0-07-087180-9

1 2 3 4 5 6 7 8 9 10 VH 0 9 8 7 6 5 4 3 2 1 0

Care has been taken to trace ownership of copyright material contained in this text; however, the publisher will welcome any information that enables them to rectify any reference or credit for subsequent editions.

Canadian Cataloguing in Publication Data

McShane, Steven Lattimore
    Canadian organizational behaviour

Triennial.
[1st ed.]-
Vols. for 1998-   accompanied by: Instructor's manual, Test bank, and computer disks (9 cm).
Published in: Toronto, 1995-   ; published by: McGraw-Hill Ryerson, 1998-   .
ISBN 0-07-087180-9 (4th ed.)

1. Organizational behavior. 2. Organizational behavior – Canada. I. Title.

HD58.7.M33   658.3   C98-300627-X rev.

Vice President and Editorial Director: Pat Ferrier
Sponsoring Editor: Susan Calvert
Developmental Editor: Kim Brewster
Senior Marketing Manager: Jeff MacLean
Manager, Editorial Services: Kelly Dickson
Senior Supervising Editor: Margaret Henderson
Copy Editor: Susan Broadhurst
Production Coordinator: Brad Madill
Composition: Valerie Bateman & Carlos Reyes/ArtPlus Limited
Interior Design: Dianna Little
Cover Design: Dianna Little
Cover Photos: Large photo: Daryl Benson. Small photos (1–r): Bill Frymire; Nora Good; Paul Eekhoff; Mark Tomalty; Masterfile; Bill Frymire. ALL MASTERFILE.
Printer: Von Hoffmann Press, Inc.

*Dedicated with love and devotion to Donna,
and to our wonderful daughters,
Bryton and Madison*

ABOUT THE AUTHOR

Steven L. McShane is Professor of Management in the Graduate School of Management at the University of Western Australia (UWA). He has also served on the business faculties at Simon Fraser University in Vancouver and Queen's University in Kingston. Steve receives high teaching ratings from MBA and doctoral students both in Perth, Australia, and in Singapore, where he also teaches for UWA. He is also a popular course instructor in executive development programs, where he has worked with the leading employers in Western Australia.

Steve earned his Ph.D. from Michigan State University, a Master of Industrial Relations from the University of Toronto, and an undergraduate degree from Queen's University at Kingston. He has served as President of the Administrative Sciences Association of Canada and Director of Graduate Programs in the business faculty at Simon Fraser University. Steve has published several dozen articles and conference papers on diverse issues, such as the socialization of new employees, gender bias in job evaluation, wrongful dismissal, and media bias in business magazines. His work has appeared in equally diverse journals, including *Industrial and Labor Relations Review*, *Journal of Rehabilitation*, *Canadian Journal of Administrative Sciences*, and *Journal of Occupational and Organizational Psychology*. Steve recently co-authored *Organizational Behavior* (McGraw-Hill/Irwin, 2000) with Mary Ann von Glinow, which has become required reading in major universities on three continents.

Along with teaching and writing, Steve enjoys his leisure time swimming, body surfing, canoeing, skiing, and travelling with his wife and two daughters.

CONTENTS

PART FIVE

PREFACE

There's a revolution going on in the workplace. Knowledge is replacing infrastructure. Self-leadership is replacing direct supervision. Networks are replacing hierarchies. Virtual teams are replacing committees. Companies are looking for employees with emotional intelligence, not just technical smarts. Globalization has become the mantra of corporate survival. Coworkers aren't down the hall; they're at the other end of an Internet connection located somewhere else on the planet.

Canadian Organizational Behaviour, Fourth Edition, is written with this revolution in mind. This book describes organizational behaviour (OB) theories and concepts in the context of current and emerging workplace realities. For example, we learn how employees control their own motivation and behaviour through self-leadership; how clashing corporate cultures can sink a global merger; and how the Internet is driving fundamental changes in the way organizations are structured. We also discuss several emerging concepts that are reshaping the field of organizational behaviour, such as knowledge management, emotional intelligence, and appreciative inquiry. Throughout this book, we emphasize that these organizational behaviour ideas are for everyone, not just managers.

CANADIAN ORIENTATION

Canadian Organizational Behaviour, Fourth Edition, is written by a Canadian for Canadians. This book includes several Canadian cases and makes solid use of Canadian scholarship in organizational behaviour. The Canadian orientation is most apparent in the Canadian examples scattered throughout this textbook. For example, you will read about a virtual team led by a Web designer in Dawson Creek, British Columbia; about the infectious good cheer of a Tim Hortons' employee in Cambridge, Ontario; about the motivation of Frantic Films' founders in Winnipeg; and about the leadership competencies of an Air Nova executive in Halifax.

Without losing its Canadian orientation, *Canadian Organizational Behaviour* also serves up plenty of international material. For instance, you will learn how Nokia in Finland has adapted to change over the past century; how Singapore Airlines and HKT (Hong Kong's telephone company) are rewarding employees with share options; how British advertising firm St. Luke's has created an ultra-flat organizational structure; how an executive in New Zealand tries to avoid office politics by telecommuting; and how Oakley Inc., the maker of ultrahip eyewear and footwear, has built a quirky headquarters in California that symbolizes its warlike corporate culture.

LINKING THEORY WITH REALITY

Every chapter of *Canadian Organizational Behaviour,* Fourth Edition, is filled with real-life examples to make OB concepts more meaningful and reflect the relevance and excitement of this field. For example, you will read how team cohesiveness led Mitel employees in Ottawa to create a beach resort out of a coworker's cubicle; how Sears Canada applies the relationship between employee satisfaction and customer satisfaction; how escalation of commitment at B.C. Ferries resulted in the PacifiCat fiasco; how software engineers fulfil their needs through hidden "Easter eggs" in software programs; and how Nortel Networks is moving "at Web speed" to become a leading maker of Internet gear.

These real-life stories appear in many forms. Every chapter of *Canadian Organizational Behaviour* is filled with photo captions and in-text anecdotes about work life in this new millennium. Each chapter also includes *Connections*, a special feature that "connects" OB concepts with real organizational incidents. Case studies and video case studies in each chapter also connect OB concepts to the emerging workplace realities. The organizations described throughout this book have a balanced regional representation throughout Canada and around the planet. Moreover, they cover a wide range of industries—from software to city government—and from small businesses to the *Financial Post 500*.

ORGANIZATIONAL BEHAVIOUR KNOWLEDGE FOR EVERYONE

A distinctive feature of *Canadian Organizational Behaviour* is that it is written for everyone in organizations, not just "managers." The philosophy of this book is that everyone who works in and around organizations needs to understand and make use of organizational behaviour knowledge. The new reality is that people throughout the organization—systems analysts, production employees, accounting professionals—are assuming more responsibilities as companies remove layers of bureaucracy and give teams more autonomy over their work. This book helps everyone to make sense of organizational behaviour and provides the tools to work more effectively in the workplace.

CONTEMPORARY THEORY FOUNDATION

Canadian Organizational Behaviour, Fourth Edition, has a solid foundation of contemporary and classic scholarship. You can see this in the references. Each chapter is based on dozens of articles, books, and other sources. The most recent literature receives thorough coverage, resulting in what we believe is the most up-to-date organizational behaviour textbook available. These references also reveal that we reach out to information systems, marketing, and other disciplines for new ideas. At the same time, this textbook is written for students, not the scholars whose work is cited. Consequently, you won't find detailed summaries of specific research studies. Also, the names of researchers or their affiliations are rarely mentioned in the text. The philosophy of this textbook is to present OB scholarship in ways that students will remember long after the final examination.

Along with recent literature, *Canadian Organizational Behaviour* carefully integrates four emerging workplace realities: globalization, information technology, knowledge management, and ethics.

- *Globalization* This book emphasizes globalization through frequent discussion of diversity and cross-cultural issues. It also adopts a global perspective because the most interesting examples are found anywhere in the world, not just in Montreal or Vancouver.

- *Information technology* The Internet, computer systems, and other emerging forms of information technology now play an integral role in organizational life, so it is integrated at the same level in *Canadian Organizational Behaviour*. For instance, you will learn how information technology leads to technostress, improves and hinders communication, alters team dynamics, and leverages the potential for new forms of organizational structure.

- *Knowledge management* Knowledge management argues that effective organizations have a high capacity to acquire, share, and use knowledge. This emerging and increasingly popular way of viewing organizations is discussed at the beginning of this book (Chapter

1), and is discussed in the context of employee behaviour (Chapter 2), communicating across work units (Chapter 8), involving employees (Chapter 10), improving creativity (Chapter 11), and several other topics.

- *Business ethics* This book also recognizes the importance of ethical issues in various organizational behaviour topics. Along with an overview of business ethics in Chapter 1 and Chapter 7, we will look at the ethical implications of specific topics, such as monitoring employee performance, stereotyping employees, engaging in organizational politics, applying organization development practices, and influencing organizational culture.

CONTINUOUS DEVELOPMENT

Year 2000 marked the launch of *Organizational Behavior,* the American and international textbook that I co-authored with Mary Ann Von Glinow. This book was built on the foundation of *Canadian Organizational Behaviour,* apparently the first time that a major Canadian textbook has been adopted for the American and international audience.

But *Canadian Organizational Behaviour* won't become another "Canadianized" version of a U.S. textbook. Instead, it embraces the practice of "continuous development" in which every variation of this book thoroughly updates the previous variation. This continuous development is possible because I am the lead author in each book. For example, this Canadian edition offers plenty of new concepts and issues that aren't found in the most recent U.S. edition. The next variation of this textbook will update this Canadian edition, and so on. This is significantly different from "Canadianized" books in which local authors add Canadian examples but have less freedom to update content from the older U.S. book. In short, continuous development ensures that Canadians have the latest organizational behaviour concepts, issues, and examples. The next section highlights the results of this continuous development process.

CHANGES TO THE FOURTH EDITION

Canadian Organizational Behaviour, Fourth Edition, has more improvements than any edition since the book was first published. Concepts have been updated and there are numerous changes in the examples, features, photos, and classroom activities. Instructors will notice that some chapters have been reorganized so that the book is more closely aligned with their preferred sequence of topics. For instance, creativity and team decision making has its own chapter, reflecting the growing interest in this area. Employment relations and career dynamics is now the final chapter to launch students from this book to their future. Every chapter has been substantially updated with new conceptual and anecdotal material. Almost all of the chapter-opening vignettes and *Connections* (previously called *Perspectives*) features are new. Over 80 percent of the photographs are also new to this edition.

Based on a substantial literature search and comments from many reviewers, *Canadian Organizational Behaviour,* Fourth Edition, has numerous content changes and significantly updated references in every chapter. Here are some of the more significant changes to this edition:

- *Chapter 1: Introduction to the Field of Organizational Behaviour* – The emerging trends in OB have been expanded, including new coverage of telecommuting, business ethics, and globalization. Emerging disciplines are identified in the multidisciplinary anchor. The open systems section includes a discussion of stakeholders. This chapter updates information on intellectual capital and knowledge management.

- *Chapter 2: Individual Behaviour and Learning in Organizations* – This chapter updates conceptual issues in behaviour modification. It also adds new information on 360-degree feedback, the ethics of employee monitoring, experiential learning, and action learning.

- *Chapter 3: Foundations of Employee Motivation* – McClelland's theory of learned needs receives more coverage in this edition. Revised and updated information is provided on equity theory. The ethics of equity is introduced.

- *Chapter 4: Applied Motivation Practices* – The meaning of money in the workplace is a new addition to the section on rewards. The topic of organizational rewards receives more coverage, including new material on share ownership. We also introduce a section on improving the effectiveness of performance-based rewards. The emerging topic of self-leadership is updated.

- *Chapter 5: Stress Management* – This edition introduces several emerging stressors, including technostress, sexual harassment, and workplace violence. The section on the consequences of distress is significantly updated. The emerging concept of work-life balance is discussed. Information on the various ways to manage stress has been updated.

- *Chapter 6: Perception and Personality in Organizations* – This chapter introduces the concept of splatter vision and updates information on mental models. Social identity theory was introduced in the previous edition and is updated here due to the rapidly growing OB literature on this subject. Stereotyping, attribution theory, and the Johari Window have been updated. There is more discussion of diversity management and new material on the Myers-Briggs Type Indicator.

- *Chapter 7: Workplace Emotions, Values, and Ethics* – The previous edition (1998) was apparently the first OB text to discuss workplace emotions in depth, including emotional intelligence and emotional labour. This edition further updates and expands these emerging concepts. We also add or expand discussion of humour at work, job satisfaction across cultures, the link between job satisfaction and customer satisfaction, and emotional dissonance. The section on ethical values and behaviour has been revised with new material on moral intensity and ethical sensitivity.

- *Chapter 8: Communicating in Organizational Settings* – Communication competence and the purposes of communication in organizations have been added or revised. We added new information on emoticons, netiquette, and other issues in electronic mail. There is also new material on workspace design, newsletters, and e-zines. The section on active listening was revised around new research from the field of marketing.

- *Chapter 9: Team Dynamics* – This edition updates information on virtual teams, skunkworks, team cohesiveness, and team building. We also revise the team effectiveness model and introduce discussion of team roles.

- *Chapter 10: Decision Making and Employee Involvement* – This completely revised chapter recognizes the natural integration of employee participation in the decision-making process. The decision-making material is more solution-oriented. It also adds information on intuition and scenario planning, and updates the section on escalation of commitment. The employee involvement section adds more information about codetermination, introduces the concept of communities of practice, and provides a more complete discussion of sociotechnical systems and self-directed work teams. We also add the Vroom-Jago model.

- *Chapter 11: Creativity and Team Decision Making* – This completely revised chapter recognizes the rapidly growing popularity of creativity in the workplace. We give students the latest details on creativity, apparently more than any other OB textbook. This includes discussion of the creative process, personal and work environment conditions supporting creativity, and practices that further leverage the creative potential. Creativity is integrated with team decision making, including updated information on brainstorming and electronic brainstorming.

- *Chapter 12: Organizational Power and Politics* – This edition adds new information on sexual harassment as an abuse of power. It also introduces the emerging topic of office romance from the perspective of organizational power. The topics of legitimate power and types of political activity are updated.

- *Chapter 13: Organizational Conflict and Negotiation* – The conflict process is revised with further distinction between task-related and socioemotional conflict. The interpersonal conflict-management styles section and some material on structural approaches to conflict management are also revised. This edition introduces drum circles and relationship restructuring strategies to manage conflict. Alternative dispute resolution is introduced in the section on third-party conflict resolution.

- *Chapter 14: Organizational Leadership* – This edition recognizes the trend toward leadership competencies (rather than the historical perspective of leader traits) and integrates emotional intelligence as a leadership competency. It links the concept of servant leadership to path–goal theory and recognizes the role of self-leadership as a leadership substitute. The emerging topic of transformational leadership is updated, as is the topic of gender issues in leadership.

- *Chapter 15: Organizational Change and Development* – This edition takes a closer look at the powerful forces for organizational change and places more emphasis on creating an urgency to change. We have updated the discussion on reducing the restraining forces and added the topic of search conferences as a change management strategy. The emerging topic of appreciative inquiry has been updated to reflect key terms in the recent literature.

- *Chapter 16: Organizational Structure and Design* – This chapter includes fuller discussion on coordinating work activities. The section on matrix structures has been revised. The emerging topic of network structures is updated and revised.

- *Chapter 17: Organizational Culture* – Several parts of this popular chapter have been revised and updated, including discussion of organizational culture artifacts, performance, and mergers. We also add new material on adaptive cultures, corporate cults, and the relevance of business ethics in corporate culture.

- *Chapter 18: Employment Relationship and Career Dynamics* – This chapter has been moved so that the book finishes with the student's career launch (even for students who are in mid-career). You will also find plenty of changes, including updated information on psychological contracts, employability, socialization agents, and lateral careers. Equally important are the new topics on Holland's theory of occupational choice and boundaryless careers. This book finishes with a new section on advice for personal career development.

SUPPORTING THE LEARNING PROCESS

The changes described above refer only to the text material. *Canadian Organizational Behaviour,* Fourth Edition, has also changed more than any previous edition in terms of cases, videos, team exercises, and self-assessments.

Video cases

Every chapter in *Canadian Organizational Behaviour,* Fourth Edition, includes a video case related to the chapter. Most are from the Canadian Broadcasting Corporation, including *Venture, The National Magazine*, and *Undercurrents*. These video cases focus on critical issues in the textbook, such as transformational leadership at IBM (Chapter 14), the competitive dynamics between Nortel Networks and Cisco Systems (Chapter 1), and a special feature program on how Canadians are becoming overstressed at work (Chapter 5).

Chapter cases and additional cases

Every chapter includes one short case that challenges students to diagnose issues and apply ideas from that chapter. Additional cases appear at the end of the book. Many cases are new to this book and are written by Canadian instructors from Halifax to Vancouver. Others, such as Arctic Mining Consultants, are classics that have withstood the test of time.

Team exercises and self-assessments

Experiential exercises and self-assessments represent an important part of the active learning process. *Canadian Organizational Behaviour* facilitates that process by offering one or two team exercises as well as a self-assessment exercise in every chapter. Many of these learning activities are not available in other organizational behaviour textbooks, such as Budget Deliberations (Chapter 12), Where in the World are We? (Chapter 10), A Not-so-Trivial Cross-Cultural Communication Game (Chapter 8), and Assessing Your Self-Leadership Skills (Chapter 4).

Student online learning centre
<www.mcgrawhill.ca/college/mcshane4>

Canadian Organizational Behaviour first introduced Web-based support for students in 1995 and continues that tradition with a comprehensive and user-friendly online learning centre. The site includes practice questions similar to those found in the test bank, online self-assessments, links to relevant external Web sites, and other valuable resources for students.

Indexes, margin notes, and glossary

Canadian Organizational Behaviour tries to avoid unnecessary jargon, but the field of organizational behaviour (as with every other discipline) has its own language. To help you learn this language, key terms are highlighted in bold and brief definitions appear in the margin. These definitions are also presented in an alphabetical glossary at the end of the text. We have also developed a comprehensive index of content, names, and organizations described in this book.

INSTRUCTOR SUPPORT MATERIALS

Canadian Organizational Behaviour includes a variety of supplemental materials to help instructors prepare and present the material in this textbook more effectively. Some restrictions may apply, so please consult your McGraw-Hill Ryerson sales representative regarding these resources.

Instructor online learning centre

Along with the Student OLC (see above), *Canadian Organizational Behaviour* includes a password-protected Web site for instructors. The site offers downloadable supplements, sample syllabi, links to OB news, regular updates on concepts and stories discussed in this book, and other resources.

Microsoft® PowerPoint® powernotes

Canadian Organizational Behaviour was apparently the first OB textbook (in 1995) to introduce a complete set of PowerPoint files. This resource is now more sophisticated than ever. Each PowerPoint file has more than a dozen slides relating to the chapter, and most files display one or more photographs from the textbook.

Instructor's resource manual

The *Instructor's Resource Manual* is written entirely by the textbook author to ensure that it represents the textbook's content and supports instructor needs. Each chapter in the *Instructor's Guide* includes the learning objectives, glossary of key terms, a chapter synopsis, complete lecture outline in larger typeface with thumbnail images of corresponding PowerPoint Powernotes, solutions to the end-of-chapter discussion questions, and comments on photo caption critical-thinking questions. It also includes teaching notes for the chapter case, additional cases, video case, team exercises, and self-assessments. Many chapters include supplemental lecture notes and suggested videos. The *Instructor's Resource Manual* also includes a very large set of transparency masters and notes for the end-of-text cases.

Test bank and computerized test bank

The *Test Bank* manual includes more than 2,000 multiple choice, true/false, and essay questions. The textbook author wrote all questions and the majority of them have been tested in class examinations. Each question identifies the relevant page reference and difficulty level. The entire *Test Bank* manual is also available in a computerized version. Instructors receive special software that lets them design their own examinations from the test bank questions. It also lets instructors edit test items and add their own questions to the test bank.

ACKNOWLEDGEMENTS

Canadian Organizational Behaviour, Fourth Edition, symbolizes the power of teamwork. More correctly, it symbolizes the power of a *virtual team* because I wrote this book from the opposite side of the planet! Allow me to explain: In 1998, I accepted a professorship at the Graduate School of Management at the University of Western Australia, one of top-ranked universities in the Asia-Pacific region. For several years in Canada, I had been writing about globalization but hadn't really practised it. By moving to Perth, Australia, my family and I have the opportunity to understand Canada and the rest of this world from a different view. The Aussies call it a "walkabout." My walkabout now includes teaching in Perth and Singapore, as well as treks with my family once or twice each year back home to Canada. So, you can see why this book illustrates the power of virtual teams.

Of course, superb virtual teams require equally superb team members. Sponsoring Editor Susan Calvert led the way with unwavering support, while solving the behind-the-scenes challenges to make my life much easier. Kim Brewster, my developmental editor, is equally amazing. Kim joined us later in the project but landed in the position with her feet running. As a result, she completed the impossible workload in half the time. The keen copy editing skills of Susan Broadhurst made *Canadian Organizational Behaviour*, Fourth Edition, incredibly error-free. Margaret Henderson, our senior supervising editor, flawlessly reduced production time by introducing virtual page proofing. Dianna Little provided an excellent design and was responsive to our minor suggestions. Thanks to you all. This has been an exceptional team effort!

Several instructors from colleges and universities across Canada carefully reviewed *Canadian Organizational Behaviour*, Fourth Edition, and provided valuable feedback and suggestions. Their compliments were energizing and their suggestions significantly improved the final product:

- Wilf Ratzburg, British Columbia Institute of Technology

- Ron Burke, York University

- Beverly Linnell, Southern Alberta Institute of Technology

- Alvin Turner, Brock University

I would also like to extend my sincerest thanks to the instructors who contributed cases and exercises to this edition of *Canadian Organizational Behaviour*. Their names and affiliations are appropriately acknowledged throughout this book.

Canadian Organizational Behaviour is continually updated, but the ideas provided by these reviewers of previous editions of this book are still apparent and appreciated: Brenda Bear, Donna Bentley, Ron Burke, Robert Cameron, Joan Condie, Claude Dupuis, Susan FitzRandolph, Richard Foggo, Beth Gilbert, Kristi Harrison, Brian Harrocks, Jack Ito, Patsy Marshall, Anwar Rashid, John Redston, Yaghoub Safai, Barbara Shannon, Pat Sniderman, Eileen Stewart, Paul Tambeau, Verlie Thomas, Judy Wahn, and Judith Zacharias.

Canadian Organizational Behaviour, Fourth Edition, was further strengthened by the development of the U.S. and international edition. Along with excellent feedback and suggestions from 15 reviewers, I am grateful to John Biernat, Christine Scheid, Ellen Cleary, Marc Mattson, Glenn Turner, and other people associated with McGraw-Hill/Irwin. I am particularly honoured to have Mary Ann Von Glinow work with me on the U.S. edition of this text-book. Finally, my eternal thanks are extended to Rod Banister, who planted the original seed that became the first edition of *Canadian Organizational Behaviour*.

My students deserve special recognition for sharing their learning experience and assisting with the development of *Canadian Organizational Behaviour*. These include undergraduate students at Simon Fraser University in Canada, Master of Business Administration students at the University of Western Australia, and officers attending the command and staff college in the Singapore Armed Forces. They have been warmly receptive to emerging OB concepts, cases and exercises, examination questions, and other pedagogical features of this book. I also thank my colleagues at the University of Western Australia's Graduate School of Management for their support, as well as to colleagues at Simon Fraser University in Vancouver, Canada. I am particularly grateful to SFU's business faculty for extending my library account while I adjusted to life in a different part of the world.

Finally, I am forever indebted to my wife Donna McClement and to our wonderful daughters, Bryton and Madison. Their love and support give special meaning to my life.

For the Student

ONLINE QUIZZING

Do you understand the material? You'll know after taking an Online Quiz! Try the Multiple Choice and True/False questions for each chapter. They're auto-graded with feedback and you have the option to send results directly to faculty.

WEB LINKS

This section references various Web sites including all company Web sites linked from the text.

SELF-ASSESSMENTS

What type of personality are you? How well do you cope with stress? Try these interactive self-assessments to learn more about your own behaviour and personally put the theories from each chapter to the test.

CHAPTER REVIEW FEATURES

A chapter Outline and a chapter Summary that has key vocabulary links to the glossary provide all you need for a quick review.

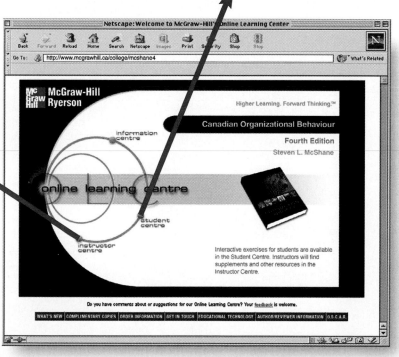

Your Internet companion to the most exciting educational tools on the Web!

The Online Learning Centre can be found at:
www.mcgrawhill.ca/college/mcshane4

EDUCATIONAL CONTENT

CHAPTER ONE

Introduction to the Field of Organizational Behaviour

LEARNING OBJECTIVES

After reading this chapter, you should be able to:

- Define organizational behaviour.
- Identify three reasons for studying organizational behaviour.
- List six emerging trends in organizational behaviour.
- Identify the five anchors on which organizational behaviour is based.
- Diagram an organization from an open systems view.
- Define knowledge management and intellectual capital.
- Identify three common ways that organizations acquire knowledge.

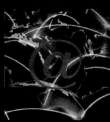

Left: Reprinted with permission from the *Globe & Mail* (T. Kolley). Right: Dave Chan. *The Ottawa Citizen.*

CEO John Roth (left) has leveraged the power of organizational behaviour to make Nortel Networks one of the world's leading high-technology companies. Mary Young (right) and other Nortel employees say they are ready to move at "Web speed."

In just two years, Nortel Networks has become one of the hottest developers of fibre optic Internet gear. CEO John Roth removed layers of management, decentralized decision making, outsourced or sold off its Old Economy telephone equipment plants, and spent billions of dollars acquiring several Net-savvy businesses.

To succeed in this hyperfast Internet world, Roth is quickly replacing Nortel's bureaucratic corporate culture with what he calls a "culture of speed." Many Nortel employees have already adapted. "I like the pace," says Mary Young, a microchip engineer at one of Nortel's research centres in Ottawa. "The pace is hectic and I like that. I'm not good at sitting still."

Nortel's emerging culture also values knowledge, competencies, and communication. "Nortel runs on talent," says Nortel vice-president Rosemary McCarney. The company's headquarters in Brampton, Ontario, is designed as an open cityscape to encourage communication and teamwork. Nortel also uses technology to connect employees who work at home and other places away from the office. Further afield, 2000 Nortel employees spread throughout Latin America and the Caribbean participate in monthly hour-long videoconference sessions that are in a talk-show format.

"It's not just about arranging formal meetings across distance and time zones," says McCarney. "It's about teaming up with people, bouncing off ideas, improvising and really doing spontaneous and creative day-to-day work as well."

Nortel is quickly adapting to the chaotic world of the Internet. The company is challenging rivals Cisco Systems and Lucent Technologies and is poised for rapid growth as electronic commerce takes off. "We're firing on all cylinders," says Roth. Nortel now "moves at Web speed."[1]

www.nortelnetworks.com

Nortel Networks has leveraged the power of the Internet, but its real power comes from the effective application of organizational behaviour theories and concepts. More than ever, organizations are relying on these ideas and practices to remain competitive. For example, Nortel is changing its organizational culture to keep pace with the emerging Internet environment. The company's reward system, organizational structure, and John Roth's leadership are quickly aligning employees with these values. Nortel's smooth acquisition of Bay Networks and other companies is also due, in part, to effective communications, team development, and other organizational behaviour practices.[2]

This book is about people working in organizations. Its main objective is to help you understand behaviour in organizations and to work more effectively in organizational settings. Organizational behaviour knowledge is not only important for managers and leaders. It is relevant and useful to anyone who works in and around organizations. In this chapter, we introduce you to the field of organizational behaviour, outline the main reasons why you should know more about it, describe the fundamental perspectives behind the study of organizations, and introduce the concept that organizations are knowledge and learning systems.

THE FIELD OF ORGANIZATIONAL BEHAVIOUR

• **Organizational behaviour (OB)**
The study of what people think, feel, and do in and around organizations.

Organizational behaviour (OB) is the study of what people think, feel, and do in and around organizations. OB scholars systematically study individual, team, and structural characteristics that influence behaviour within organizations. By saying that organizational behaviour is a field of study, we mean that scholars have been accumulating a distinct knowledge about behaviour within organizations—a knowledge base that is the foundation of this book.

By most estimates, OB emerged as a distinct field around the 1940s.[3] However, its origins can be traced much further back in time. The Greek philosopher Plato wrote about the essence of leadership. Aristotle, another respected philosopher, addressed the topic of persuasive communication. The writings of sixteenth-century Italian philosopher Niccolo Machiavelli laid the foundation for contemporary work on organizational power and politics. In 1776, Adam Smith advocated a new form of organizational structure based on the division of labour. One hundred years later, German sociologist Max Weber wrote about rational organizations and initiated discussion of charismatic leadership. Soon after, Frederick Winslow Taylor introduced the systematic use of goal setting and rewards to motivate employees. In the 1920s, productivity studies at Western Electric's Hawthorne plant reported that an informal organization—employees casually interacting with others—operates alongside the formal organization. OB has been around for a long time; it just wasn't organized into a unified discipline until after the Second World War.

WHAT ARE ORGANIZATIONS?

Organizations have existed for as long as people have worked together. Archaeologists have discovered massive temples dating back to 3500 BC that were constructed through the organized actions of many people. The fact that these impressive monuments were built suggests not only that complex organizations existed, but that the people in them cooperated reasonably well.[4] We have equally impressive examples of contemporary organizations, such as the Confederation Bridge that links Prince Edward Island and New Brunswick, Hong Kong's new island airport at Chek Lap Kok, and the people who coordinate that complex computer network that we call the Internet.

Copyright © Barrett and MacKay photo.

Confederation Bridge is a testament to the power of organizations. The 13-kilometre connection between Prince Edward Island and New Brunswick is the world's longest bridge across ice-covered water and was recently named one of the five most significant Canadian engineering achievements of the twentieth century. An army of 1500 workers built dozens of piers and girders weighing up to 7500 tonnes each. The world's largest self-propelled floating crane transported each precast piece to the bridge site. All of this occurred in a gruelling 44-month schedule with an alliance of several companies and over 1000 support businesses. The project was so daunting that many people didn't believe it could be accomplished. "We had to make believers out of our own workforce," says project director Paul Giannelia.[8] In your opinion, what organizational behaviour concepts described in this book would have the greatest influence on the success of the Confederation Bridge and other mammoth projects?

"[A] company is one of humanity's most amazing inventions," says Steven Jobs, CEO of Apple Computer and Pixar Animation Studios. "It's totally abstract. Sure, you have to build something with bricks and mortar to put the people in, but basically a company is this abstract construct we've invented, and it's incredibly powerful."[5]

So, what are these powerful constructs that we call **organizations?** They are groups of people who work interdependently towards some purpose.[6] Organizations are not buildings or other physical structures. Rather, they consist of people who interact with each other to achieve a set of goals. Employees have structured patterns of interaction, meaning that they expect each other to complete certain tasks in a coordinated way—in an *organized* way.

Organizations have a purpose, whether it's building a bridge to Prince Edward Island or selling books on the Internet. Some organizational behaviour scholars are skeptical about the relevance of goals in a definition of organizations.[7] They argue that an organization's mission statement may be different from its true goals. Also, they question the assumption that all organizational members believe in the same goals. These points may be true, but imagine an organization without goals: it would consist of a mass of people wandering around aimlessly without any sense of direction. Overall, organizations likely have a collective sense of purpose, even though it is not fully understood or agreed upon.

Organization A group of people who work interdependently towards some purpose.

www.confederationbridge.com

WHY STUDY ORGANIZATIONAL BEHAVIOUR?

You are probably reading this book as part of a course in organizational behaviour. Aside from diploma or degree requirements, why should you or anyone else study OB? After all, who ever heard of a career path leading to "Vice-President of OB" or "Chief OB Officer"?

The main reason for studying organizational behaviour is that most of us work in organizations, so we need to understand, predict, and influence the behaviours of others in organizational settings (see Exhibit 1.1). Marketing students learn marketing concepts and computer science students learn about circuitry and software code. But all of us need organizational behaviour knowledge to address people issues when we try to apply marketing, computer science, and other ideas.

EXHIBIT 1.1 Reasons for Studying Organizational Behaviour

Satisfying the need to understand and predict

Every one of us has an inherent need to know about the world in which we live. This is particularly true in organizations because of their profound effect on our lives. We feel more comfortable when we can understand why organizational events occur and accurately anticipate future events.[9] The field of organizational behaviour uses systematic study to help us understand and predict organizational life. OB's crystal ball isn't perfectly clear because human behaviour is influenced by a complex combination of factors. Nevertheless, OB helps us to make sense of the workplace and, to some extent, predict what people will do under various conditions.

The OB knowledge presented in this book also gives you the opportunity to question and rebuild your personal theories that have developed through observation and experience. For example, what theories do you hold about effective leadership? Look at the "It All Makes Sense?" self-assessment exercise at the end of this chapter. How many of these theoretical statements are true? Even if you answer most of them correctly, the information you will read in this book can further develop and crystallize your personal beliefs so that they more accurately model and predict organizational behaviour.

Influencing organizational events

It's nice to understand and predict organizational events, but most of us want to influence the environment in which we live. Whether you are a marketing specialist or a computer programmer, you need to know how to communicate effectively with others, manage conflict, make better decisions, build commitment to your ideas, help work teams operate more effectively, and so on. OB knowledge will help you to influence organizational events. Most organizational behaviour scholars take this prescriptive view by concluding their systemic research with specific recommendations for organizational action.[10]

This book takes the view that organizational behaviour knowledge is for everyone—not just managers. Indeed, as organizations reduce layers of management and delegate more responsibilities to the rest of us, the concepts described in this book will become increasingly important for anyone who works in and around organizations. We all need to understand organizational behaviour and to master the practices that influence organizational events. That's why you won't find very much emphasis here on "management." Yes, organizations will continue to have managers. However, their roles have changed and, more importantly, the rest of us are now expected to manage ourselves. As one forward-thinking OB scholar wrote many years ago: everyone is a manager.[11]

EMERGING TRENDS IN ORGANIZATIONAL BEHAVIOUR

There has never been a better time to learn about organizational behaviour. The pace of change is accelerating, and most of the transformation is occurring in the workplace.[12] Let's take a brief tour through a few of the emerging organizational behaviour issues discussed in this textbook: globalization, the changing workforce, emerging employment relationships, information technology, work teams, and business ethics.

GLOBALIZATION

William Cornelius Van Horne, the Canadian Pacific Railway CEO who built the legendary Banff Springs Hotel in 1888, once said: "If we can't export the scenery, we'll import the tourists."[13] Van Horne knew that international business would build the Canadian economy, but he would not have imagined the extent to which Canadian organizations have globalized today. **Globalization** occurs when an organization extends its activities to other parts of the world, actively participates in other markets, and competes against organizations located in other countries.[14]

Globalization Occurs when an organization extends its activities to other parts of the world, actively participates in other markets, and competes against organizations located in other countries.

Nortel Networks, described in the opening vignette of this chapter, is a case in point. The Canadian company's main competitors are Cisco Systems and Lucent Technologies in the United States, Alcatel in France, Ericsson in Sweden, and Siemens in Germany. Nortel operates in a global economy and employs people in almost every part of the planet. "I've got 75,000 employees all around the world," explains Nortel CEO John Roth. "[As] head of a global corporation who happens to reside in Canada, I have global obligations, not Canadian obligations."[15]

Implications for organizational behaviour

Globalization is related to several organizational behaviour issues—some good, some not so good. Globalization requires new organizational structures and different forms of communication to extend around the planet. It often creates new career opportunities and potentially brings in new knowledge to improve the organization's competitive advantage. However, globalization also increases competition, which leads to continuous change and restructuring. This sometimes results in downsizing (layoffs and other forms of workforce reduction), mergers, and other events that produce stress and dissatisfaction among employees.[16]

Globalization also affects how we apply organizational behaviour concepts and practices. For the past 40 years, OB scholars have warned that organizational practices in one country may not be applicable elsewhere because of cultural and historical differences.[17] We cannot assume that work teams, employee involvement, share options, or other organizational behaviour practices that work in Canada will work as well in Europe, Asia, or other parts of the world.[18] This doesn't mean that we have to reinvent organizational behaviour. Rather, globalization emphasizes the need to recognize the contingencies of effective OB practices in different cultures. (The contingency anchor of OB is discussed later in this chapter.)

Photo by Pierre-Louis Mongeau.

Thanks to the Internet, Ryan & Deslauriers is a global marketing agency with only 20 employees in Montreal (shown in photo) and in the resort community of Mont-Tremblant, Quebec. After producing a successful direct-marketing campaign for condominiums in Mont-Tremblant, the agency began receiving calls from resorts in the United States that wanted the agency to provide similar services. One-half of Ryan & Deslauriers's clients are now outside of Canada, some of them as far away as Mexico and Europe. Company president David Harries spends a lot of time visiting clients, but his firm mainly depends on Web-based communication to maintain a global presence. "Laptop computers, e-mails, and electronic transfers of sketches become part of your daily life," says Harries.[19] What issues in communication and team dynamics should Ryan & Deslauriers employees consider as they use the Internet to work with each other and with clients in other countries?

www.thealternateroute.com

William R. Hill, CEO of OAO Technology Solutions, discovered the need for global sensitivity when the American personally expanded operations into Canada. Sales were much slower than anticipated, so Hill replaced himself with a Canadian who was more attuned to the Canadian culture. Soon after, sales exceeded expectations. "You may not think of Canada as international and we didn't either—but certainly do now," says Hill. "You don't see the business and cultural differences unless you actually live somewhere and experience it."[20]

Globalization also has important implications for how we learn about organizational behaviour. The best-performing companies may be in Hong Kong, Finland, or Germany, not just in Vancouver or Montreal. That's why you will encounter numerous examples of international businesses in this book. We want you to learn from the best, no matter where their headquarters is located.

THE CHANGING WORKFORCE

You don't have to visit a global organization to find employees from diverse backgrounds. Most companies operating exclusively within Canada have a multicultural workforce because of the country's increasing demographic diversity. Exhibit 1.2 illustrates the primary and secondary dimensions of this diversity. The primary categories—gender, ethnicity, age, race, sexual orientation, and mental/physical qualities—represent personal characteristics that influence an individual's socialization and self-identity. The secondary dimensions are those features that we learn or have some control over throughout our lives, such as education, marital status, religion, and work experience.

EXHIBIT 1.2	Primary and Secondary Dimensions of Workforce Diversity

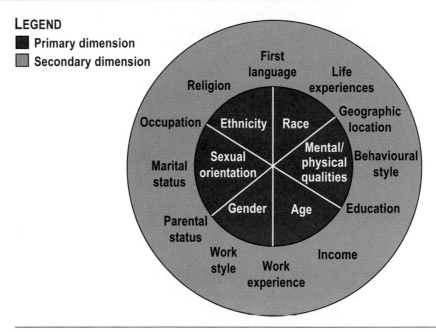

Sources: Adapted from M. Loden, *Implementing Diversity* (Chicago: Irwin, 1996); S. Bradford, "Fourteen Dimensions of Diversity: Understanding and Appreciating Differences in the Workplace," in J.W. Pfeiffer (ed.), 1996 *Annual: Volume 2 Consulting* (San Diego: Pfeiffer and Associates, 1996), pp. 9–17.

Employees in Canadian organizations have significantly increased many of these primary and secondary dimensions of diversity. For instance, more than one-half of all immigrants to Canada currently come from Asia, compared to only 3 percent a few decades ago. At the same time, the percentage of immigrants from Europe and the United States has fallen to 25 percent. The result is an increasing population mosaic that is reflected in the Canadian workplace. Cultural diversity is particularly apparent in Metropolitan Toronto, where racial minorities represent almost one-half of the population.[21]

The participation of women in the labour force has also surged since the 1950s. Sixty percent of Canadian women currently participate in the paid workforce, compared to only 20 percent a few decades ago. Moreover, gender-based shifts are occurring within occupations. For example, Canadian medical schools now graduate more women than men each year. This is quite a transformation from the 1960s, when 90 percent of medical school graduates were men and medical economics journals were debating whether medical training was wasted on women![22]

Age cohorts represent another primary dimension of diversity in the workplace. Baby boomers—people born between 1946 and 1964—are entering the latter half of their careers, whereas Generation-X employees—those born between 1965 and 1977[23]—are in the early stages of career development. Several writers point out that each generation was raised with different experiences, different skills, and, consequently, a different set of values. At each stage of life, they may also have different needs to fulfil.[24]

Implications for organizational behaviour

Diversity presents both opportunities and challenges within organizations. It can become a competitive advantage by improving decision making and team performance on complex tasks.[25] For many businesses, a diverse workforce is also necessary to provide better customer service in the global marketplace. "We go out of our way to recruit from a melting pot of nationalities," says an executive at Amadeus, a developer of worldwide airline reservation software located near Nice, France. "We believe that our product is superior because of the different cultures of the people developing it."[26]

Workforce diversity also brings new challenges. For instance, women have represented a large portion of the workforce for the past two decades, yet they are still underrepresented in senior positions.[27] Diversity issues such as perceptual distortions and organizational politics (discussed in Chapter 6 and Chapter 12) largely explain this discrepancy. Diversity also influences team development (Chapter 9) and the potential for conflict among employees (Chapter 13). Organizations need to address these potential problems and adapt to emerging workforce needs.

General Motors of Canada is addressing some of these problems through a task force that recommends ways to make women an integral part of the automaker's workforce, up and down the organization. For instance, one initiative allows women to enter GM's manufacturing occupations, which gives them the experience and competencies for faster promotions to senior jobs.[28] Other organizations are providing better work–life balance and involving employees more fully in organizational decisions.[29]

Unfortunately, surveys suggest that Canadian companies aren't adjusting quickly enough to expectations of the emerging workforce. For example, only 58 percent of Generation-X employees are somewhat or very satisfied with their jobs, compared with over 90 percent of baby boomers. Only 2 percent of the younger generation feel that their work provides an opportunity to get ahead.[30] "[Generation Xers] want to have meaning in their work at an entry level, rather than waiting 10 or 15 years for it," explains Robert Barnard, co-founder of D-Code, a Toronto-based consulting firm that specializes in the under-35 market.[31]

EMERGING EMPLOYMENT RELATIONSHIPS

Canada's workforce isn't the only thing that's changing. After more than 100 years of relative stability, employment relationships are being redefined. Replacing the job-for-life contract is a "new deal" called **employability**. Employees perform a variety of work activities rather than hold specific jobs, and they continuously learn skills that will keep them employed. Corporate leaders claim that employability is necessary so organizations can adapt to the rapidly changing business environment. However, as we shall learn throughout this book, employability also has implications for job design, organizational loyalty, career dynamics, and workplace stress.[32]

Employability The "new deal" employment relationship in which the job is viewed as a temporary event, so employees are expected to keep pace with changing competency requirements and shift to new projects as demand requires.

Another employment shift is the increasing percentage of the workforce in **contingent work.** This includes any job in which the individual does not have an explicit or implicit contract for long-term employment, or one in which the minimum hours of work can vary in a nonsystematic way. According to Statistics Canada, more than 12 percent of the Canadian workforce is employed in some sort of "nonpermanent" work arrangement.[33]

Contingent work Any job in which the individual does not have an explicit or implicit contract for long-term employment, or one in which the minimum hours of work can vary in a nonsystematic way.

Some experts predict that this trend will continue. "We are moving into the age of contractualization where everyone is their own boss," claims one consultant, who argues that the concept of "employee" is a throwback to Industrial Revolution servitude.[34] A new breed of "free agents" is thriving on the independence and reliance on knowledge that contingent work demands.[35] At the same time, many contingent workers would rather be employed in stable, well-paying jobs. We will learn that contingent work affects organizational loyalty, career dynamics, and other aspects of organizational behaviour.

Telecommuting

Telecommuting (also called *teleworking*)
Working from home or another location away from the office, usually with a computer connection to the office.

Another dramatic change in the employment relationship is **telecommuting** (also called *teleworking*)—working from home or another location away from the office, usually with a computer connection to the office.[36] More than 1.5 million Canadians are already telecommuters. As we move from an industrial economy to a knowledge-based economy, the number of people who take the information highway to work each day will continue to increase. Moreover, technology has untethered some employees so completely from the employer's physical workspace that clients and co-workers are oblivious to their true locations.

Telecommuting poses a number of organizational behaviour challenges.[37] Employers that previously evaluated employees for their "face time"—the amount of time they were physically in the workplace—need to develop outcome-based measures of performance. Employees accustomed to direct supervision need to learn how to manage themselves through self-leadership (see Chapter 4). They also need to adjust to increased isolation and lack of political networking. As telecommuting increases, employees must also learn how to get things done through **virtual teams**—cross-functional groups that operate across space, time, and organizational boundaries with members who communicate mainly through electronic technologies.[38]

Virtual teams Cross-functional teams that operate across space, time, and organizational boundaries with members who communicate mainly through electronic technologies.

As organizations and employees address these issues, the benefits of telecommuting are becoming apparent. Employers are discovering that telecommuting reduces real estate costs and increases employee flexibility. "It's surprising the number of engineers who will respond to a question at 11:00 on a Saturday night," says an executive at Cisco Systems, a leading provider of Internet hardware. Telecommuting has also made believers out of many employees. A survey of Canadian employees recently found that working from home is the second most valuable benefit among those with this option.[39] As Connections 1.1 describes, employees appreciate the convenience and flexibility that this employment relationship provides.

INFORMATION TECHNOLOGY AND OB

Information technology is shaking up organizations and forcing OB scholars to re-examine their concepts in light of these revolutionary changes. We have already noted how this technology has given rise to virtual teams and telecommuting, and has made it possible for small businesses such as Ryan & Deslauriers to compete in the global marketplace. More generally, information technology challenges traditional business logic regarding how employees interact, how organizations are configured, and how they relate to customers.

Consider a recent experience at Karo Marketing Design. The Calgary-based marketing and graphic design firm completed several creative pieces for the Fairmont Hamilton Princess hotel, including a brochure, menus, posters, and print advertisements. There was nothing unusual about this, except that the hotel is located in Bermuda! Karo relied on photographs of the hotel's site and used the Internet to show the hotel manager sketches of the designs before the final work was completed.[40] These virtual client relationships at Karo Marketing Design affect how employees communicate, maintain team dynamics, make decisions, and so forth.

"Can't talk now. I'm in a seminar about improving communication with technology."

© 1996 Ted Goff. www.tedgoff.com

CONNECTIONS 1.1

The Telecommuting Revolution

Donna Phillips would have to commute more than two hours each day from her home in Camrose, Alberta, to the consulting firm where she works in St. Albert. Fortunately, she has been able to cut that time down to about ten seconds. Phillips is one of the 1.5 million Canadians who have become telecommuters.

"It gives me the opportunity to work in my field without having to commute," says Phillips, who has worked for Bradley Wells Consulting for the past two years from her home office. "It's certainly far more desirable for me."

Thanks to advances in information technology, most knowledge workers can now complete their tasks from home rather than in the office, often without clients knowing it. For instance, some employees at the VAS call centre in Sussex, New Brunswick, have client calls routed to their home. "It's so convenient," says Jennifer Coone, one of the first VAS customer care representatives to initiate telecommuting in New Brunswick. "It's nice to be able to go right to work without warming up my car or shovelling snow."

In spite of its advantages, many employees who telecommute full-time admit that they miss socializing with co-workers. "I'm still struggling with that," admits Donna Phillips. "I moved to a new community at the same time I started teleworking, so I didn't have a network of acquaintances or co-workers."

Sources: E. Robb, "Call Centre in the Home," *Moncton Times and Transcript,* December 21, 1999, p. C2; D. Quigley, "Plugged In! Computers Let Millions of Canadians Punch a Clock at Home," *Edmonton Sun,* December 12, 1999, p. SE4; T. Belford, "Driving to Work by Phone," *National Post,* April 5, 1999, p. C14.

Network organization
An alliance of several organizations for the purpose of creating a product or serving a client.

Information technology also makes it easier to create a **network organization**—an alliance of several organizations for the purpose of creating a product or serving a client. Cisco Systems, a direct competitor of Nortel Networks, is really a constellation of suppliers, contract manufacturers, assemblers, and other partners connected through an intricate web of information technology. Cisco's network springs into action as soon as a customer places an order (usually through the Internet). Suppliers send the required materials to assemblers who ship the product directly to the client, usually on the same day. Seventy percent of Cisco's product is outsourced this way. In many cases, Cisco employees never touch the product.[41] Some writers predict that skyscrapers will become obsolete as information technology forms more durable and flexible network organizations around the globe.[42]

TEAMS, TEAMS, AND MORE TEAMS

Visit Kemet Electronics Corp's ceramic capacitors plant in Monterey, Mexico, and you will soon discover that people don't work alone. "We have 2000 employees and 2000 teams," explains plant manager Ed Raygada. "But they aren't one-person teams. Most of our employees participate in multiple teams. You can be a leader of one team and a member of another team. Our goal is to have every employee serving on five teams."[43]

At Kemet and many other companies, teams are replacing individuals as the basic building blocks of organizations. According to a survey of Canadian human resource executives, the introduction of project- and team-based work will continue to be a leading source of organizational change over the next few years. For example, one of the most dramatic changes at TRW Canada's plant in Tillsonburg, Ontario, was the introduction of self-directed work teams. These teams have a high degree of responsibility for their work activities at the automobile parts manufacturer. Supervisors have become advisers—providing coaching support when the team asks for it.[44]

Organizational behaviour scholars have long argued that teams can be more effective than individuals working alone in many situations. Diverse work groups can potentially resolve complex problems more creatively than if those team members had worked individually. Moreover, by giving teams direct responsibility for coordination and control of work activities, companies can increase responsiveness and remove unnecessary layers of management. However, teams are not appropriate in every situation. Team dynamics and team decision making are the focus of attention in Chapters 9, 10, and 11.

BUSINESS ETHICS

Check out your favourite newspaper or Internet news site and you will almost certainly read about incidents of unethical business conduct. For example, five international drug companies recently pleaded guilty to fixing prices and divvying up the market for vitamins in Canada. Executives at Livent Inc., a Toronto-based entertainment company, allegedly engaged in fraudulent financial reporting. Perhaps the most devastating for Canada's international reputation were three separate incidents (including the famous Bre-X scandal) where Canadian mining company executives profited from inflated share prices by falsifying data about their drilling results.[45]

Ethics refers to the study of moral principles or values that determine whether actions are right or wrong and whether outcomes are good or bad. We rely on our ethical values to determine "the right thing to do." One of the dilemmas organizational leaders face is that the distinction between ethical and unethical behaviour is not black and white. Instead, it depends on several factors, such as the person's reason for engaging in the behaviour, specific conditions in that culture, the influence of external factors on the behaviour, and so forth.

Throughout this book you will discover numerous topics that relate to business ethics, such as monitoring employee performance, rewarding people equitably, stereotyping employees, using peer pressure, engaging in organizational politics, and applying organization development practices. We will also cover the topic of ethical values and behaviour more fully in Chapter 7.

> **Ethics** The study of moral principles or values that determine whether actions are right or wrong and whether outcomes are good or bad.

THE FIVE ANCHORS OF ORGANIZATIONAL BEHAVIOUR

Globalization, the changing workforce, emerging employment relationships, information technology, work teams, and business ethics are just a few of the issues that we will explore in this textbook. To understand these and other topics, organizational behaviour scholars rely on a set of basic beliefs or knowledge structures (see Exhibit 1.3). These conceptual anchors represent the way that OB researchers think about organizations and how they should be studied. Let's look at each of these five beliefs that anchor the study of organizational behaviour.

THE MULTIDISCIPLINARY ANCHOR

Organizational behaviour is anchored around the idea that the field should develop from knowledge in other disciplines, not just from its own isolated research base.[46] In other words, OB should be multidisciplinary. The upper part of Exhibit 1.4 identifies the traditional disciplines from which organizational behaviour knowledge has developed. For instance, the field of psychology has aided our understanding of most issues relating to individual and

EXHIBIT 1.3   Five Conceptual Anchors of Organizational Behaviour

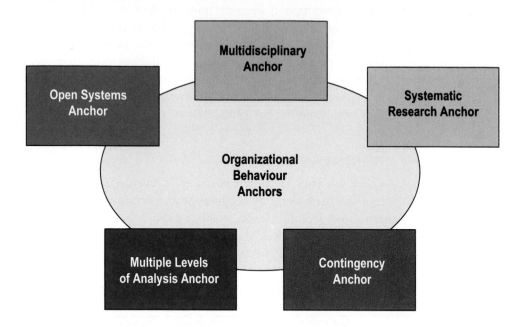

interpersonal behaviour. Sociologists have contributed to our knowledge of team dynamics, organizational socialization, organizational power, and other aspects of the social system.

The bottom part of Exhibit 1.4 identifies some of the emerging fields from which organizational behaviour knowledge is acquired. The communications field helps us to understand the dynamics of knowledge management, electronic mail, corporate culture, and employee socialization. Information systems scholars are exploring the effects of information technology on team dynamics, decision making, and knowledge management. Marketing scholars have enhanced our understanding of knowledge management, creativity, and decision making related to their field. Women's studies scholars are studying power relations between men and women in organizations, as well as perceptual biases.

The true test of OB's multidisciplinary anchor is how effectively OB scholars continue to transfer knowledge from traditional and emerging disciplines. History suggests that fields of inquiry tend to become more inwardly focused as they mature.[47] Hopefully, OB will avoid this tendency by continuing to recognize ideas from other disciplines.

THE SYSTEMATIC RESEARCH ANCHOR

A second anchor is that organizational behaviour researchers believe in the systematic collection of data and information about organizations. In other words, they rely on a set of principles and practices that minimize personal biases and distortions about organizational events. For the most part, they rely on the **scientific method** by forming research questions, systematically collecting data, and testing hypotheses against those data. OB scholars are also turning to qualitative research methods to make sense of organizations. Qualitative researchers also rely on systematic practices (grounded theory, triangulation, etc.) to ensure that they document shared meaning of organizational events. Appendix A at the end of this book provides an overview of research design and methods commonly found in organizational behaviour studies.

Scientific method A set of principles and procedures that help researchers to systematically understand previously unexplained events and conditions.

EXHIBIT 1.4   Multidisciplinary Anchor of Organizational Behaviour

Disciplines	Relevant OB Topics
Traditional	
Psychology	Motivation, perception, attitudes, personality, job stress, job enrichment, performance appraisals, leadership
Sociology	Team dynamics, roles, socialization, communication patterns, organizational power, organizational structure
Anthropology	Corporate culture, organizational rituals, cross-cultural dynamics, organizational adaptation
Political Science	Intergroup conflict, coalition formation, organization environments
Economics	Decision making, negotiation, organizational power
Industrial Engineering	Job design, productivity, work measurement
Emerging	
Communications	Knowledge management, electronic mail, corporate culture, employee socialization
Information Systems	Team dynamics, decision making, knowledge management
Marketing	Knowledge management, creativity, decision making
Women's Studies	Organizational power, perceptions

THE CONTINGENCY ANCHOR

"It depends" is a phrase that OB scholars often use to answer a question about the best solution to an organizational problem. The statement may frustrate some people, yet it reflects an important way of understanding and predicting organizational events, called the **contingency approach**. This anchor states that a particular action may have different consequences in different situations. In other words, no single solution is best in all circumstances.[48]

Many early OB theorists have proposed universal rules to predict and explain organizational life, but there are usually too many exceptions to make these "one best way" theories useful. For example, in Chapter 14 we will learn that leaders should use one style (e.g., participation) in some situations and another style (e.g., direction) in other situations. Thus, when faced with a particular problem or opportunity, we need to understand and diagnose the situation, and select the strategy most appropriate *under those conditions*.[49]

Although contingency-oriented theories are necessary in most areas of organizational behaviour, we should also be wary about carrying this anchor to an extreme. Some contingency models add more confusion than value over universal ones. Consequently, we need to balance the sensitivity of contingency factors with the simplicity of universal theories.

• Contingency approach The idea that a particular action may have different consequences in different situations; that no single solution is best in all circumstances.

THE MULTIPLE LEVELS OF ANALYSIS ANCHOR

Organizational events are usually studied from three common levels of analysis: individual, team, and organization (see Exhibit 1.5). The individual level includes the characteristics and behaviours of employees as well as the thought processes that are attributed to them, such as motivations, perceptions, personalities, attitudes, and values. The team level of analysis looks at the way people interact. This includes team dynamics, decisions, power, organizational politics, conflict, and leadership. At the organizational level, we focus on how people structure their working relationships and on how organizations interact with their environments.

Although an OB topic is typically pegged into one level of analysis, it usually relates to all three levels.[50] For instance, communication includes individual behaviours and interpersonal (team) dynamics. It also relates to the organization's structure. Therefore, you should try to think about each OB topic at the individual, team, and organizational levels, not just at one of these levels.

THE OPEN SYSTEMS ANCHOR

Phil Carroll likes to think of himself as an ecologist for the organization. The recently retired CEO of Shell Oil believes that all executives are responsible for how well their organizations interact with the external environment. "We must learn how to see the company as a living system and to see it as a system within the context of the larger systems of which it is a part," Carroll explains.[51]

Phil Carroll is describing the fifth anchor of organizational behaviour—the view that organizations are **open systems.** Organizations are open systems because of their interdependence with the external environment. Their survival and success depends on how well employees sense environmental changes and alter their patterns of behaviour to fit those emerging conditions.[52] In contrast, a closed system has all the resources needed to survive without dependence on the external environment. Organizations are never completely closed systems, but monopolies operating in very stable environments can ignore customers and others for a fairly long time without adverse consequences.

As Exhibit 1.6 illustrates, organizations acquire resources from the external environment, including raw materials, employees, financial resources, information, and equipment. Inside the organization are numerous subsystems, such as processes (communication and reward systems), task activities (production, marketing), and social dynamics (informal groups,

Open systems
Organizations and other entities with interdependent parts that work together to continually monitor and transact with the external environment.

EXHIBIT 1.5   Three Levels of Analysis in Organizational Behaviour

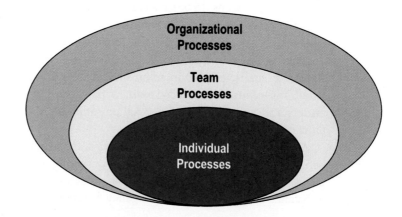

EXHIBIT 1.6   Open Systems View of Organizations

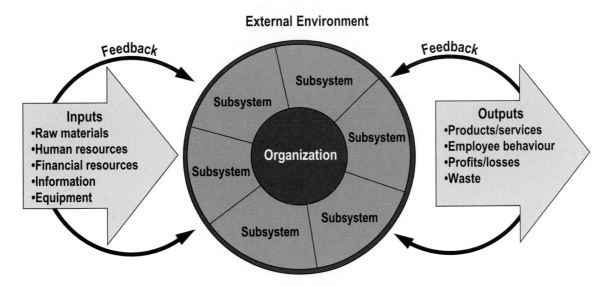

power dynamics). With the aid of technology (such as equipment, work methods, and information), these subsystems transform inputs into various outputs. Some outputs (e.g., products and services) may be valued by the external environment, whereas other outputs (e.g., stressed employees, pollution) have adverse effects. The organization receives feedback from the external environment regarding the value of its outputs and the availability of future inputs. This process is cyclical and, ideally, self-sustaining, so that the organization may continue to survive and prosper.

External environment and stakeholders

The external environment consists of the natural and social conditions outside the organization. For example, companies depend on physical space, natural resources, and a knowledgeable workforce. Probably the most important component of the external environment is the organization's **stakeholders.** These are the shareholders, customers, suppliers, governments, and any other groups with a vested interest in the organization.[53] Stakeholders influence the firm's access to inputs and ability to discharge outputs. For example, how well the organization treats the community and natural environment affects its right to operate in that environment. "If we don't act responsibly, we will lose our right to operate and grow," warns Rick George, CEO of Calgary-based Suncor Energy Inc. "But if this company pays attention to the environmental and social needs of our stakeholders, we will not only succeed, we will have a distinct competitive advantage."[54]

Any executive will tell you that organizations operate in a much more turbulent environment than they did a few decades ago. This means that the environment is so complex and is changing so rapidly that careful analysis of corporate decisions may be a waste of precious time.[55] Rather than focus on strategic planning, companies must become adaptable and responsive to the turbulent environment. This includes giving employees more freedom to make decisions, allowing them to experiment, and viewing mistakes as learning opportunities.

Systems as interdependent parts

Organizational systems consist of many internal subsystems that need to be continuously aligned with each other. As companies grow, they develop more and more complex subsystems

Stakeholders Shareholders, customers, suppliers, governments, and any other groups with a vested interest in the organization.

that must coordinate with each other in the process of transforming inputs to outputs.[56] These interdependencies can easily become so complex that a minor event in one subsystem may amplify into serious unintended consequences elsewhere in the organization.

Discovery Toys experienced this when it tried to branch out from toys into children's clothing. The company focused on clothing design and market research, but did not foresee the huge problems in warehousing and inventory control that followed. These problems, in turn, frustrated Discovery Toys' independent sales reps. One year later, Discovery Toys discontinued the clothing line at a significant loss.[57]

Companies can try to minimize unintended consequences by encouraging employees to think through the implications of their decisions and actions. British Airways does this with a computer simulation that challenges employee teams to make "Granny" a happy British Airways passenger while getting her from London, England, to Toronto. It isn't as easy as it sounds. When participants use bonus air miles to lure Granny onto a particular flight, the computer program quickly points out that this action affects other customers and requires the marketing department to communicate the bonus plan. Through this exercise, British Airways employees learn how decisions and actions in one subsystem affect not just Granny, but also people in other parts of the organization.[58]

The open systems approach is an important way of viewing organizations. However, it has traditionally focused on physical resources that enter the organization and are processed into physical goods (outputs). This was representative of the industrial economy, but not of the "new economy" where the most valued input is knowledge. The final section of this chapter introduces the key features of this emerging perspective in organizational behaviour.

KNOWLEDGE MANAGEMENT

Knowledge management Any structured activity that improves an organization's capacity to acquire, share, and use knowledge in ways that improve its survival and success.

Intellectual capital The knowledge that resides in an organization, including its human, structural, and relationship capital.

Organizational behaviour scholars have built on the open systems anchor to create an entire subfield of research dedicated to the dynamics of **knowledge management**. Knowledge management is any structured activity that improves an organization's capacity to acquire, share, and use knowledge in ways that improve its survival and success.[59] The knowledge that resides in an organization is called its **intellectual capital.** Intellectual capital is the sum of an organization's human capital, structural capital, and relationship capital:[60]

- *Human capital*—This is the knowledge that employees possess and generate, including their skills, experience, and creativity.

- *Structural capital*—This is the knowledge captured and retained in an organization's systems and structures. It is the knowledge that remains after the human capital has gone home.

- *Relationship capital*—This is the value derived from an organization's relationships with customers, suppliers, and other external stakeholders who provide added value for the organization. For example, this includes customer loyalty as well as mutual trust between the organization and its suppliers.[61]

KNOWLEDGE MANAGEMENT PROCESSES

Knowledge management has become such an important part of contemporary OB thinking that you will read about it with regards to various topics throughout this book. At this point, you should understand that knowledge management includes several strategies for knowledge acquisition, sharing, and use.

In the hyperfast Internet world, PMC-Sierra Inc. can't acquire enough knowledge through research. So the Burnaby, B.C., semiconductor company also buys start-up firms with leading-edge knowledge. For example, PMC recently bought Ottawa-based Extreme Packet Devices for $600 million. Extreme was just one year old with no sales or customers, but its four founders (shown in photo) and 50 employees had developed technology that managed Internet traffic faster than that of any other company. That unique knowledge kept PMC-Sierra ahead of the competition and made millionaires out of half of Extreme's employees.[62] Along with buying entire companies, how else might PMC-Sierra acquire knowledge?

www.pmc-sierra.com
www.extremepacket.com

Grafting The process of acquiring knowledge by hiring individuals or buying entire companies.

Knowledge acquisition

Knowledge acquisition includes the organization's ability to extract information and ideas from its environment as well as through insight. One of the fastest and most powerful ways to acquire knowledge is through **grafting**—hiring individuals or acquiring entire companies.[63] For instance, Nortel Networks quickly became a leader in fibre optic networks by acquiring Bay Networks, Qtera Corp., and other organizations with leading-edge knowledge. Knowledge also enters the organization when employees learn about the external environment, such as discovering what the competition is doing or how customer needs are changing. A third knowledge acquisition strategy is through experimentation. Companies receive knowledge through insight as a result of research and other creative processes (see Chapter 11).[64]

Knowledge sharing

Communities of practice Informal groups bound together by shared expertise and passion for a particular activity or interest.

Nearly half of Canadian executives say their companies are poor at transferring knowledge to other parts of the organization.[65] To improve knowledge sharing, organizations need to improve communication (see Chapter 8). For example, lawyers at McMillan Binch in Toronto share all of their old and current precedents through a common database.[66] Larger companies further encourage knowledge sharing through **communities of practice.** These are informal groups bound together by shared expertise and passion for a particular activity or interest.[67]

• **Organizational memory**   The storage and preservation of the organization's knowledge (i.e., its intellectual capital).

www.city.ottawa.on.ca

Andersen Consulting and Buckman Labs further improve knowledge sharing by awarding bonuses to employees who regularly contribute to the company's knowledge database and online forums.[68]

Knowledge use

Acquiring and sharing knowledge are wasted exercises unless knowledge is effectively put to use. "Companies are finding they need better ways of leveraging the knowledge that they already have," says an executive at Open Text Corp. in Toronto.[69] To do this, employees must realize that the knowledge is available and that they have enough freedom to apply it. This requires a culture that supports experiential learning (see Chapter 2).

ORGANIZATIONAL MEMORY

Intellectual capital can be lost as quickly as it is acquired. Corporate leaders need to recognize that they are the keepers of an **organizational memory.** This unusual metaphor refers to the storage and preservation of intellectual capital. It includes information that employees possess as well as knowledge embedded in the organization's systems and structures. It includes documents, objects, and anything else that provides meaningful information about how the organization should operate.

How do organizations retain intellectual capital? One method is to keep good employees. "Our assets go home at night," explains a Microsoft executive. "If enough of them don't come back in the morning, the corporation is in danger."[70] A second strategy is to transfer knowledge systematically before employees leave. For instance, many employees at New Flyer Industries are getting close to retirement, so executives at the Winnipeg bus manufacturer anticipate the need for consultants who work exclusively at transferring knowledge from retiring employees to younger ones.[71]

A third organizational memory strategy is to transfer knowledge into structural capital.[72] This includes bringing out hidden knowledge, organizing it, and putting it in a form that can be made available to others. DecisionOne Corp., a provider of computer maintenance and technology support services, has "knowledge architects" at each site that document best practices and other information from call centre operators. This information will then be available to everyone long after a particular call centre expert leaves.[73]

Before leaving the topic of organizational memory and knowledge management, you should know that successful companies also *unlearn.* Sometimes it is appropriate for organizations to selectively forget certain knowledge.[74] This means that they should cast off the routines and patterns of behaviour that are no longer appropriate. Employees need to rethink their perceptions, such as how

S.L. McShane

Three years of employee buyouts and early retirements have left Ottawa's City Hall with a bad case of corporate amnesia. The municipality started receiving more complaints about snowplow operators who had damaged homeowners' lawns with their equipment. The reason? Several experienced employees had taken early retirement without teaching rookie snowplow operators about snow removal on specific streets in Ottawa. City councillors also had to reopen budget deliberations because they weren't notified of a $1.4 million debt to the Province of Ontario. An audit found that employees who knew about the money had left the company due to downsizing. "When the city loses a long-term employee, it loses a piece of its corporate memory," said the consultant who audited these incidents.[75] What strategies could the City of Ottawa apply to minimize this loss of organizational memory?

they should interact with customers and which is the "best way" to perform a task. As we shall discover in Chapter 15, unlearning is essential for organizational change.

THE JOURNEY BEGINS

This chapter gives you some background about the field of organizational behaviour. But it's only the beginning of our journey. Throughout this book, we will challenge you to learn new ways of thinking about how people work in and around organizations. We will also rely on a broad range of firms across Canada and around the planet. You will recognize some companies—such as Nortel Networks, Four Seasons Hotels and Resorts, and Nokia. But we also introduce you to many firms that you probably haven't heard about. Some, such as Research in Motion and Ballard Power, are emerging forces in today's fast-paced world of work. Still others, such as Stratford Internet Technologies and Ryan & Deslauriers, are small organizations. Chances are that you will work in a small business, so it makes sense that we should learn about organizational behaviour in these operations as well.

CHAPTER SUMMARY

- Organizational behaviour is a relatively young field of inquiry that studies what people think, feel, and do in and around organizations. Organizations are groups of people who work interdependently towards some purpose.

- OB concepts help us to predict and understand organizational events, adopt more accurate theories of reality, and control organizational events more effectively. They let us make sense of the work world, test and challenge our personal theories of human behaviour, and understand ways to manage organization activities.

- There are several emerging issues and changes in organizational behaviour. Globalization requires corporate decision makers to be more sensitive to cultural differences. The workforce is becoming increasingly diverse. Companies and employees must adjust to emerging employment relationships. Information technology has created virtual teams and network organizations. Employees are expected to work in teams rather than alone. Companies are coming under increasing scrutiny for their ethical practices.

- Organizational behaviour scholars rely on a set of basic beliefs to study organizations. These anchors include beliefs that OB knowledge should be multidisciplinary and based on systematic research, that organizational events usually have contingencies, that organizational behaviour can be viewed from three levels of analysis (individual, team, and organization), and that organizations are open systems.

- The open systems anchor suggests that organizations have interdependent parts that work together to continually monitor and transact with the external environment. They acquire resources from the environment, transform them through technology, and return outputs to the environment. The external environment consists of the natural and social conditions outside the organization. This includes stakeholders—any group with a vested interest in the organization. External environments are generally much more turbulent today, so organizations must become adaptable and responsive.

- Knowledge management develops an organization's capacity to acquire, share, and use knowledge in ways that improve its survival and success. Intellectual capital is knowledge that resides in an organization, including its human capital, structural capital, and relationship capital. It is a firm's main source of competitive advantage.

- Organizations acquire knowledge through grafting, individual learning, and experimentation. Knowledge sharing occurs mainly through communication. Knowledge use occurs when employees realize that the knowledge is available and that they have enough freedom to apply it. Organizational memory refers to the storage and preservation of intellectual capital.

KEY TERMS

Communities of practice, p. 19

Contingency approach, p. 16

Contingent work, p. 10

Employability, p. 10

Ethics, p. 13

Globalization, p. 7

Grafting, p. 19

Intellectual capital, p. 18

Knowledge management, p. 18

Network organization, p. 12

Open systems, p. 16

Organization, p. 5

Organizational behaviour (OB), p. 4

Organizational memory, p. 20

Scientific method, p. 14

Stakeholders, p. 17

Telecommuting, p. 11

Virtual teams, p. 11

DISCUSSION QUESTIONS

1. A friend suggests that organizational behaviour courses are only useful to people who will enter management careers. Discuss the accuracy of your friend's statement.

2. Look through the list of chapters in this book and discuss how information technology could influence each organizational behaviour topic.

3. "Organizational theories should follow the contingency approach." Comment on the accuracy of this statement.

4. Employees in the City of Calgary's water distribution unit were put into teams and encouraged to find ways to improve efficiency. The teams boldly crossed departmental boundaries and areas of management discretion in search of problems. Employees working in other parts of the City of Calgary began to complain about these intrusions. Moreover, when some team ideas were implemented, the city managers discovered that a dollar saved in the water distribution unit may have cost the organization two dollars elsewhere. Use the open systems anchor to explain what happened here.

5. After hearing a seminar on knowledge management, an oil company executive argues that this perspective ignores the fact that oil companies could not rely on knowledge alone to stay in business. They also need physical capital (such as pumps and drill bits) and land (where the oil is located). In fact, these two may be more important than what employees carry around in their heads. Discuss the merits of the oil executive's comments.

6. Fully describe intellectual capital, and explain how an organization can retain this capital.

7. An information technology consultant recently stated that over 30 percent of U.S. companies use software to manage documents and exchange information, whereas Canadian firms are just beginning to adopt this technology. Based on this, he concluded that "knowledge management in Canada is at its beginning stages"; in other words, that few Canadian firms practise knowledge management. Comment on this consultant's statement.

8. BusNews Ltd. is the leading stock market and business news service. Over the past two years, BusNews has experienced increased competition from other news providers. These competitors have brought in Internet and other emerging computer technologies to link customers with information more quickly. There is little knowledge within BusNews about how to use these computer technologies. Based on the knowledge acquisition processes for knowledge management, explain how BusNews might gain the intellectual capital necessary to become more competitive in this respect.

Case Study

ACTIVITY 1.1
The Great Idea That Wasn't
By Fiona McQuarrie, University College of the Fraser Valley

Irina cradled her baby daughter in her arms and looked at the piles of unfinished work covering her desk. She wondered how such a great idea—telecommuting to her job from home—had gone so wrong in only three months.

Irina is a mortgage officer at a large Canadian bank. She joined the bank 12 years ago, and worked her way through successively more responsible jobs until she achieved her current position four years ago. She enjoys the work, assisting clients in completing mortgage applications and then processing and approving or rejecting the applications. Irina finds it very satisfying to help her clients achieve their dreams of owning their own homes or businesses. However, the real estate market in her city had become increasingly competitive, and her employer had responded to the greater demand for mortgages by promising better customer service than the other banks. This resulted in the mortgage officers working longer or different hours—sometimes as many as 80 hours a week—to be more available to potential clients.

When Irina and her husband discovered that their first child was on its way, they were delighted. But Irina saw that there would be problems once the baby was born. Obtaining full-time daycare for a new baby would be nearly impossible, not to mention expensive. She certainly could not continue to work 80 hours a week, and her husband would not be able to alter his work schedule to stay home and care for the baby.

So Irina went to her supervisor, David, and her department head, Ottavio, and made a proposal. She offered to continue working full-time once the baby was born, but she wanted to telecommute from home. "Much of my work is on the phone, which I can do from home as well as I can at work," she told them. "And if I have a computer at home, I can do most of the processing of the applications there as well. I can also work outside regular office hours, because I won't have to leave when the building closes." David agreed to the idea, as long as Irina would come into the office once a week for the regular mortgage officers' meeting. Ottavio was more reluctant, pointing out that a similar scheme had been tried several years ago and had proved unsuccessful. However, because Irina had an exceptional work record, Ottavio eventually also agreed to her proposal.

Irina took a month off of work when Sarah was born, but then eagerly returned to work as a telecommuter. The company provided her with a computer, modem, and printer at home similar to what she had had in her office and arranged for a courier to deliver

ACTIVITY 1.1 CONTINUED

and pick up mortgage applications once a day. At first, the telecommuting arrangement worked well. Irina did not have to get dressed up for work, she did not have to fight traffic or find a parking space, and she was able to work while spending time with her new daughter.

The first major problem Irina encountered was in trying to find a suitable place to work in her home. With Sarah's arrival, baby furniture and supplies had occupied most of the free space in the house. For the first few weeks, Irina tried working at the kitchen table, but she found that the computer was too bulky to move on and off the table at every mealtime. She eventually purchased a second-hand desk and set it up in a corner of the living room, right next to the television. While this arrangement allowed her to keep all of her work in one place, it also meant that the work was always visible, even when she was trying to relax and watch TV.

Irina then discovered that caring for an infant was far more demanding than she had expected. Sarah was a good baby, but frequently she would cry when the phone rang and then continue to cry even after the phone was answered. Irina also found it difficult to arrange times to call clients back, since she had to fit those calls around Sarah's feeding schedule. And since Irina often had to get up in the night to take care of Sarah, she frequently felt exhausted during the day. Although Irina had arranged to be available to clients outside of regular office hours, she often found that she was so tired, especially in the evenings, that she was not very productive during those times.

Once a week, as agreed, Irina went to the office for the regular mortgage officers' meeting. She enjoyed seeing her co-workers, but she was somewhat disturbed by the remarks they made about her new work arrangement: "So what's happening on all the soap operas on TV? I bet you can watch those whenever you want!" "It must be nice to not have to work as hard as we do here." Irina also found that while the meetings were informative, there was a lot at work that she was missing out on. Frequently discussion would focus on someone she didn't know, and only after she asked would she be told that the person had just been hired. People would also leave or be transferred to new positions, and Irina would

not know about that unless it came up in the discussion. Irina also found that the mortgage officers who worked in the office were getting many more clients than she was, simply because they were available to help new clients visiting the bank's offices.

After last week's meeting, David asked to see Irina privately in his office. He told her that he had received several phone calls from clients complaining about a baby crying in the background while they were talking to Irina. He also said that Ottavio had expressed concern about Irina's level of productivity since she had started telecommuting. Irina asked what the problem with her productivity was. David told her that since she did not have to spend time driving to and from work and dealing with distractions in the office, the bank expected her to be more productive than the other mortgage offices. In fact, David said, Ottavio had even wondered if Irina was working the hours she had promised, since her productivity did not seem to match the hours she claimed to be working.

"Well, David," Irina responded, "I am working as hard as I ever did, and I am doing what I agreed to do, including coming into the office once a week. The company is saving money by not having to provide an office for me here at work, and I am making myself available to clients outside regular office hours as I promised. I don't know what else I can do."

"All I can say," said David, "is that Ottavio is very concerned about your productivity and the image you are communicating to clients. In fact, Ottavio said that these were the same problems the company encountered before when they allowed people to telecommute. If things don't improve within the next month or so, we will have to ask you to return to your regular hours at the office."

Discussion Questions

1. What are the major problems in this tele-commuting arrangement?

2. Is it Irina's or the bank's responsibility to solve these problems?

3. What solutions can you suggest to the problems that you have identified?

Video Case Study

ACTIVITY 1.2
Nortel versus Cisco

In one corner is Nortel Networks, a Canadian champion. In the other corner is Cisco Systems, an American giant. In the arena of communications, it's a clash of titans. Both companies are battling it out to become the number-one maker of Internet gear.

"We're no longer competing against other companies in Canada. We're competing against the best people in the world," says John Roth, CEO of Nortel Networks. The global company has been making telephone equipment since 1895. Now Roth is quickly turning the old Northern Telecom into Nortel Networks—a savvy designer of fibre optic communications systems for the Internet.

Cisco Systems is much younger, but it has a head start on the Internet business. Cisco started in 1984 when a husband-and-wife team created technology to hook up Stanford University's computer network. Their invention got computers talking to each other and Cisco took off, hooking up computer networks inside corporations everywhere. Cisco became the leader in routers, the little boxes that act like traffic cops, telling all of those data streams on the Internet where to go and when to get there. Now it wants to enter the fibre optic business, while Nortel is entering Cisco's router business.

One of the hot zones of the Nortel–Cisco battle is in Ottawa, Ontario. Most of Nortel's research operations are in Ottawa, where high-tech employees are always in short supply. Cisco bought an Ottawa-based company named Skystone and immediately slapped a huge billboard directly across from Nortel inviting Nortel employees to join Cisco. Nortel then opened a recruiting office next door to Cisco's plant in Ottawa.

While competing for the same employees, the two companies seem to have different corporate cultures. Roth calls Nortel's culture leading edge, trustworthy, and responsive. Cisco executives say their company is Internet savvy, aggressive, and customer focused.

In fact, culture clash killed a potential Nortel–Cisco partnership a couple of years ago.

The partnership may have failed, but Nortel is practising Cisco's method of growth by spending billions to acquire smaller companies. Nortel got into routers in 1998 by acquiring Bay Networks of California. It recently bought Qtera, a high-performance fibre optic company in Florida, for more than $3 billion. Cisco also wanted Qtera, but Nortel won out.

So who's the winner in this battle? "Market share speaks for itself," says Don Listwin, the Saskatchewan-born executive vice-president at Cisco Systems. "And if you take a look at the market shares across the product categories by one measure, we are clearly in the number-one or number-two position in 21 product categories." Cisco does clobber Nortel in all of the categories that relate to Internet routers. Nortel however, is number one in fibre optics, and you can't run the Internet without that. You could say they're both champions, but in different weight divisions.

Listwin also points out that the Internet is about moving quickly, whereas the telephony that Nortel comes from is slow and predictable. But Roth claims that Nortel is already revving up to Web speed. "Nortel is a different company today than we were six months ago," says Roth. "We're a very different company than we were 12 months ago. We're going to be a very different company in another six months. Because we know what we have to do differently."

Discussion Questions

1. What organizational behaviour topics stand out in this video program as the most important ingredients in the success of Nortel Networks and Cisco Systems?

2. Use the open systems anchor to describe why Nortel is changing from its previous Northern Telecom days.

Source: Based on "Nortel versus Cisco," *Venture* 733 (January 4, 2000).

TEAM exercises

ACTIVITY 1.3
HUMAN CHECKERS

Purpose: This exercise is designed to help students understand the importance and application of organizational behaviour concepts.

Materials: None, but the instructor has more information about the team's task.

Instructions:

Step 1: Form teams with six students each. If possible, each team should have a private location where team members can plan and practise the required task without being observed or heard by other teams.

Step 2: All teams will receive special instructions in class about the team's assigned task. All teams have the same task and will have the same amount of time to plan and practise the task. At the end of this planning and practice, each team will be timed while completing the task in class. The team that completes the task in the least amount of time wins.

Step 3: Other than chairs, no special materials are required or allowed for this exercise. Although the task is not described here, students should learn the following rules for planning and implementing the task:

- Rule #1: You cannot use any written form of communication or any props other than chairs to assist in the planning or implementation of this task.

- Rule #2: You may speak to other students in your team at any time during the planning and implementation of this task.

- Rule #3: When performing the task, you must move only in the direction of your assigned destination. In other words, you can only move forward, not backwards.

- Rule #4: When performing the task, you can move forward to the next space, but only if it is vacant (see Exhibit 1).

- Rule #5: When performing the task, you can move forward two spaces, if that space is vacant. In other words, you can move around a student who is one space in front of you to the next space if that space is vacant (see Exhibit 2).

Step 4: When all teams have completed their task, the class will discuss the implications of this exercise for organizational behaviour.

EXHIBIT 1   **EXHIBIT 2**

Discussion Questions

1. Identify the organizational behaviour concepts that the team applied to complete this task.

2. What personal theories of people and work teams were applied to complete this task?

3. What organizational behaviour problems occurred and what actions were (or should have been) taken to solve them?

ACTIVITY 1.4
DEVELOPING KNOWLEDGE FROM MISTAKES

Purpose: The problem that people make from their mistakes isn't so much the mistakes themselves. Rather, it's that they do not take the time to learn from those mistakes. This exercise is designed to help you understand how to gain knowledge from past mistakes in a specific situation.

Instructions:

Step 1: The class will be divided into small teams (four to six people). The instructor will identify a situation that students would have experienced and, therefore, at which they probably have made mistakes. This could be the first day at work, the first day of a class, or a social event such as a first date.

Step 2: After the topic has been identified, each team member writes down an incident in which something went wrong in that situation. For example, if the topic is the first day of classes, someone might note how they were late for class because they forgot to set their alarm clock.

Step 3: Each student describes the mistake to other team members. As an incident is described, students should develop a causal map of the incident. They should ask why the problem happened, what were the consequences of this incident, did it happen again, and so on. This knowledge might not be as obvious as you think. For example, in the incident of being late, the learning might not be that we should ensure that the alarm clock is set. It may be a matter of changing routines (going to bed earlier), rethinking our motivation to enrol in a program, and so on.

Step 4: As other incidents are analyzed, the team should begin to document specific knowledge about the incident. Think of this knowledge as a road map for others to follow when they begin their first day of class or first day at work, go on a first date, etc.

Source: This exercise was developed by Steven L. McShane, based on ideas in P. LaBarre, "Screw Up, and Get Smart," *Fast Company*, 19 (November 1998), p. 58.

ACTIVITY 1.5
IT ALL MAKES SENSE?

Purpose: This exercise is designed to help you understand how organizational behaviour knowledge can help you to understand life in organizations.

Instructions: Read each of the statements below and circle whether each statement is true or false, in your opinion. The class will consider the answers to each question and discuss the implications for studying organizational behaviour. After reviewing these statements, the instructor will provide information about the most appropriate answer. (Note: This activity may be done as a self-assessment or as a team activity.)

1. True False   A happy worker is a productive worker.

2. True False   Decision makers tend to continue supporting a course of action even though information suggests that the decision is ineffective.

3. True False   Organizations are more effective when they prevent conflict among employees.

4. True False   It is better to negotiate alone than as a team.

5. True False   Companies are most effective when they have a strong corporate culture.

6. True False   Employees perform better when they don't experience stress.

7. True False   The best way to change an organization is to get employees to identify and focus on its current problems.

8. True False   Female leaders involve employees in decisions to a greater degree than do male leaders.

9. True False   Male business students today have mostly overcome the negative stereotypes of female managers that existed 20 years ago.

10. True False   Top-level executives tend to exhibit a Type A behaviour pattern (i.e., hard-driving, impatient, competitive, short-tempered, strong sense of time urgency, rapid talkers).

11. True False   Employees usually feel overreward inequity when they are paid more than co-workers who perform the same work.

CHAPTER TWO

Individual Behaviour and Learning in Organizations

LEARNING OBJECTIVES

After reading this chapter, you should be able to:

- Describe the four factors that influence individual behaviour and performance.
- Identify five types of work-related behaviour.
- Define learning.
- Describe the A-B-C model of organizational behaviour modification.
- Explain how feedback influences individual behaviour and performance.
- Identify five elements of effective feedback.
- Describe the three features of social learning theory.
- Discuss the value of learning through experience.

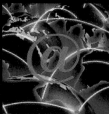

Réno-Dépôt Vice-President Richard Blain holds some of the job applications filled out during the World Skills Competition in Montreal.

Réno-Dépôt is obsessed with providing exceptional customer service. Quebec's leading home improvement retailer is particularly keen on recruiting and keeping experienced tradespeople from the building industry because they can answer tough questions from do-it-yourself customers.

To recruit more of this talent, Réno-Dépôt recently held a successful recruiting blitz during a World Skills Competition in Montreal. The company is a major sponsor of the event, in which carpenters, cabinet-makers, and other tradespeople demonstrate their skills. The recruiting blitz produced a boatload of application forms submitted by participants and spectators alike.

As Réno-Dépôt expands into Ontario (under the name Building Box), it will face Home Depot Canada, another home improvement juggernaut that practically wrote the book on hiring and developing a skilled workforce. Before they ever speak to a customer, new recruits in Home Depot stores across Canada complete a full week of training in Toronto. Some learn the intricacies of operating a cash register; others learn how to help customers design kitchens. Once in the stores, they are expected to attend four hours of training each month, ranging from seminars on paint chemistry to designing in-store signage.

"We just keep raising the bar," says Home Depot Canada President Annette Verschuren. "Our objective is to continually improve customer service levels and never let them diminish. The way to do that is to attract people, motivate people, and to invest in people."[1]

www.renodepot.com
www.homedepot.com

Réno-Dépôt and Home Depot Canada recognize that customer service primarily depends on the four drivers of individual behaviour: motivation, ability, role perceptions, and situational factors. This chapter introduces these concepts as part of the dynamics of individual behaviour and learning in organizations. We begin by introducing a model of individual behaviour and performance as well as the main types of work-related behaviour. Most elements of the individual behaviour model are influenced by individual learning, so the latter part of this chapter discusses the concept of learning and describes four perspectives of learning in organizational settings: reinforcement, feedback, observation, and experience.

MARS MODEL OF INDIVIDUAL PERFORMANCE

Réno-Dépôt and Home Depot Canada depend on employees to satisfy customers and fulfil other organizational objectives. How can organizations ensure that all employees provide exceptional customer service and fulfil their other work obligations? To answer this question, let's begin with the MARS model of individual performance. Exhibit 2.1 illustrates the MARS model, which represents the four factors that directly influence an employee's voluntary behaviour and resulting performance: motivation, ability, role perceptions, and situational factors. These four factors are represented by the acronym MARS.

The MARS model shows that these four factors have a combined effect on individual performance. If any factor weakens, employee performance will decrease. For example, highly qualified salespeople who understand their job duties and have sufficient resources will not perform their jobs as well if they are not motivated to market the company's products or services. Let's briefly examine these four influences on individual behaviour and performance.

EMPLOYEE MOTIVATION

Motivation The internal forces that affect the direction, intensity, and persistence of a person's voluntary choice of behaviour.

Motivation represents the forces within a person that affect his or her direction, intensity, and persistence of voluntary behaviour.[2] *Direction* refers to the fact that motivation is goal-oriented, not random. People are motivated to arrive at work on time, finish a project a few hours early, or aim for many other targets. *Intensity* is the amount of effort allocated to the

---

EXHIBIT 2.1 MARS Model of Individual Behaviour and Performance

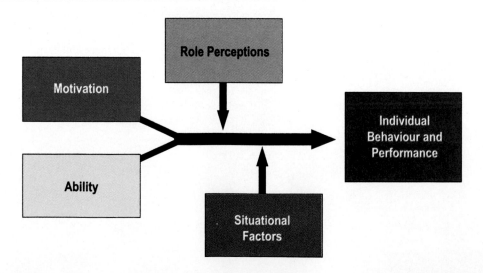

goal. For example, two employees might be motivated to finish their project a few hours early (direction), but only one of them puts forth enough effort (intensity) to achieve this goal. Finally, motivation involves varying levels of *persistence*; that is, continuing the effort for a certain amount of time. Employees sustain their effort until they reach their goal or give up. Chapter 3 looks more closely at the conceptual foundations of employee motivation, while Chapter 4 presents some applied motivation practices.

ABILITY

A second influence on individual behaviour and performance is the person's ability. **Ability** includes both the natural aptitudes and the learned capabilities required to complete a task successfully. *Aptitudes* are the natural talents that help employees learn specific tasks more quickly and perform them better. For example, you cannot learn finger dexterity; rather, some people have a more natural ability than others to manipulate small objects with their fingers. There are many different physical and mental aptitudes, and our ability to acquire skills is affected by these aptitudes. *Learned capabilities* refer to the skills and knowledge that you have actually acquired. These include the physical and mental skills you possess as well as the knowledge you acquire and store for later use.

- **Ability** The natural aptitudes and learned capabilities required to successfully complete a task.

Employee competencies

The external environment is changing so rapidly that many organizations prefer to hire people for their generic competencies rather than their job-specific skills. **Competencies** are the characteristics of people that lead to superior performance.[3] Along with natural and learned abilities, competencies include the person's values and personality traits.

- **Competencies** The abilities, individual values, personality traits, and other characteristics of people that lead to superior performance.

Many Canadian firms have identified generic competencies that distinguish outstanding performers across the organization or broad job groups. These competencies are then used to select job applicants for a wide variety of jobs. For instance, the Royal Bank of Canada looks for people with a strong customer orientation, social skills, willingness to learn, and need for achievement.[4]

Person–job matching

Whether an organization relies on broad competencies or on job-specific skills, there are basically three ways to match individuals with job requirements.[5] One strategy is to select applicants whose existing competencies best fit the required tasks. This includes comparing each applicant's competencies with the requirements of the job or work unit. A second approach is to provide training so employees develop required skills and knowledge. For instance, Canadian Tire estimates that $50 invested in customer service and related training programs can yield paybacks of $500 a year in increased profits. This is consistent with academic research on the benefits of job-related training.[6]

The third person–job matching strategy is to redesign the job so employees are only given tasks within their capabilities. MediaOne recently did this after introducing e-mail as a form of customer communication at its call centres. Executives at the U.S. cable television systems company realized that call centre staff with strong verbal communication skills aren't necessarily good at written communication. "Many people who can carry on a good conversation on the phone could not put a cogent thought down in writing if they tried," says a MediaOne executive. The company identified employees with strong written communication skills and redesigned their tasks so they would be responsible for answering e-mail questions.[7]

Ron Long. Courtesy of Simon Fraser University.

Crew members of a B.C. Ferries vessel were so disorganized during one safety exercise that they couldn't find a simulated fire, let alone put it out! One shipmate heard the fire alarm and ran to the alarm station, but didn't look for the fire. A catering attendant knew the fire's location, but watched the drill without saying anything. The problem in this potentially dangerous incident was that crew members had poor role perceptions. They didn't know their tasks or priorities during a fire or emergency.[8] How should B.C. Ferries and other organizations minimize inaccurate or ambiguous role perceptions?

www.bcferries.bc.ca

ROLE PERCEPTIONS

Role perceptions A person's beliefs about what behaviours are appropriate or necessary in a particular situation, including the specific tasks that make up the job, their relative importance, and the preferred behaviours to accomplish those tasks.

Role perceptions are a person's beliefs about what behaviours are appropriate or necessary in a particular situation. Employees have accurate role perceptions when they understand the specific tasks assigned to them, the relative importance of those tasks, and the preferred behaviours to accomplish those tasks. Sales staff at a clothing store might understand that they serve customers and stock shelves, but they might have poor role perceptions regarding the relative importance of these tasks.

One Canadian survey reported that less than half of the employees interviewed said their managers described their goals and assignments clearly. This is unfortunate because inaccurate role perceptions cause employees to exert effort towards the wrong goals, and ambiguous role perceptions lead to lower effort.[9] These misperceptions occur when employees receive no information or conflicting information about task responsibilities and the relative importance of those responsibilities. More accurate role perceptions develop when the required tasks are described clearly, employees are trained in the most appropriate way to accomplish those tasks, and they receive frequent and meaningful performance feedback.

SITUATIONAL FACTORS

Job performance depends not just on motivation, ability, and role perceptions. It is also affected by the situation in which the employee works. Situational factors include conditions beyond the employee's immediate control that constrain or facilitate his or her behaviour and performance.[10] Some factors—such as time, people, budget, and physical work facilities—are controlled by others in the organization. Corporate leaders need to arrange these conditions carefully so employees can achieve their performance potential. Lockheed Martin's jet fighter production facility does this by asking employees to identify obstacles created by management that prevent them from performing effectively.[11]

Other situational characteristics—such as consumer preferences and economic conditions—originate from the external environment and, consequently, are beyond the employees' and organization's control. For instance, a sales representative may have more difficulty selling the product or service when the economy enters a recession or where demographics of the sales area result in fewer people purchasing the item. Rather than create a defeatist attitude, some companies encourage employees to focus on things they can control, rather than on these external situational factors.

Motivation, ability, role perceptions, and situational factors affect all conscious workplace behaviours and their performance outcomes. In the next section, we introduce the five categories of behaviour in organizational settings.

TYPES OF WORK-RELATED BEHAVIOUR

People engage in many different types of behaviour in organizational settings. Exhibit 2.2 highlights five types of behaviour discussed most often in the organizational behaviour literature: joining the organization, remaining with the organization, maintaining work attendance, performing required tasks, and exhibiting organizational citizenship.

JOINING THE ORGANIZATION

Success doesn't sound like a cash register at Dell Computer Corp. It sounds more like the "clang! clang! clang!" of a cow bell. Whenever someone with valuable knowledge or experience joins Dell's headquarters, employees ring a bell that symbolically signals the good news. Dell employees celebrate the arrival of key employees because they and other organizations need qualified people to perform tasks and acquire knowledge. In fact, attracting and retaining talented employees is one of the top five (from a list of 39) nonfinancial factors used by Wall Street's decision makers when picking stocks.[12]

The importance of hiring qualified people is obvious when we consider the consequences of a business failing to find enough of the right people. Montreal's Children's Hospital faces this problem. There are so few nurses available to staff the intensive-care unit (ICU) that doctors

EXHIBIT 2.2   Types of Work-Related Behaviour

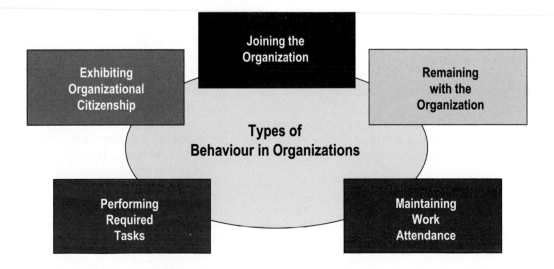

routinely close the unit to new patients and divert them to another hospital. Ideally, the ICU should have about 70 nurses; instead, it is struggling with fewer than 50.[13]

Motivation seems to be the most important influence (among the four factors in the MARS model) on joining an organization. As Connections 2.1 discusses, high-tech firms in Ottawa are going to extreme lengths to lure employees away from competitors. The recruitment strategies described in this feature might motivate applicants to join the organization. However, fostering unrealistic expectations about the job may result in job dissatisfaction and reduced organizational loyalty (see Chapter 18). Eventually, companies may face problems with the second type of organizational behaviour: remaining with the organization.

www.cisco.com
www.alcatel.com

CONNECTIONS 2.1

Open Season for Ottawa's High-Tech Talent

It's open season for Ottawa's workforce. High-technology companies are expanding or moving into this digital hot spot, but there aren't enough employees to go around. Cisco Systems is using offbeat recruiting practices to hire over 2000 people for its Ottawa operations. For example, the California-based Internet equipment firm placed a large billboard on its property across from Nortel Networks, inviting Nortel employees to join Cisco. It also uses more subtle recruiting tactics, such as sponsoring the Ultimate Frisbee Tournament.

Nortel is fighting back with its own aggressive recruiting strategies. Ottawa's largest high-tech employer is expanding, and is offering $2000 to each employee who recruits new talent. Nortel also opened a "high-speed" (from application to hiring in one day) recruiting centre near the Canadian operations of Alcatel (formerly Newbridge Networks). Nortel executives say they aren't targeting Alcatel employees, but admit that Nortel intends to lure people away from other companies.

Alcatel is vulnerable to talent poaching as this French-owned firm digests the recent merger with Newbridge. To minimize the exodus,

Cisco Systems' Human Resource Manager Randy Baker uses Frisbee competitions and other offbeat strategies to recruit Ottawa's high-tech talent.

Alcatel increased all employees' salaries by 5 percent and is offering a 10 percent "loyalty bonus" to employees who are still with the company one year from now.

Alcatel also offers its employees up to $8000 after tax for recommending friends who successfully join the company. "[Alcatel's internetworking division] is projected to be the fastest-growing division within the whole Alcatel company," says Pearse Flynn, who heads the division. "So I need to take [people] from Nortel. I need to take people from Cisco. And I will get them."

Sources: C. Guly, "Cars, Cash and Cruises," *Ottawa Citizen*, June 17, 2000; B. Hill, "Newbridge Has the Inside Track," *Ottawa Citizen*, March 19, 2000; P. Tam, "Hands Off Our Talent," *Ottawa Citizen*, March 4, 2000; B. Hill and J. Campbell, "Open Season," *Ottawa Citizen*, February 21, 2000; D. Buckner, "Nortel versus Cisco," *CBC Venture*, January 4, 2000; K. Goff, "Nortel Opens 'High-Speed' Recruiting Centre in Kanata," *Ottawa Citizen*, November 30, 1999.

REMAINING WITH THE ORGANIZATION

Organizations need to do more than hire employees; they also need to keep them. As we learned in Chapter 1, the knowledge that employees carry in their heads represents a large portion of an organization's intellectual capital. Long-service employees have valuable knowledge about work processes, corporate values, and customer needs. Thus, knowledge management involves ensuring that valuable employees stay with the organization. "At 5 p.m., 95 percent of our assets walk out the door," says an executive at SAS Institute, a leading statistics software firm. "We have to have an environment that makes them want to walk back in the door the next morning."[14]

Job satisfaction
A person's attitude (beliefs, assessed feelings, and behavioural intentions) regarding the job and work context.

Why do people quit their jobs? **Job satisfaction**—a person's evaluation of his or her job and work context—is a major influence on turnover (see Chapter 7). Employees become dissatisfied with their employment relationship, which motivates them to search for and join another organization with better conditions.[15] The labour market is another factor. Even if employees are dissatisfied with their jobs, they often remain until another job offer comes along.

MAINTAINING WORK ATTENDANCE

Along with attracting and retaining employees, organizations need to ensure that everyone shows up for work at scheduled times. Statistics Canada reports that during any given week, more than 500,000 employees—almost 6 percent of the full-time workforce—are absent from work due to illness or personal reasons. Absenteeism, including work delays and shutdowns, costs the Canadian economy around $10 billion each year. Toronto's fire department faces this problem. Absenteeism is so high in some parts of the organization that fire vehicles are pulled out of service up to 500 times per month due to staff shortages. In Scarborough, the average firefighter is absent from scheduled work almost 14 days per year.[16]

What causes people to be absent from work? Situational factors—such as a snowstorm or a car breakdown—certainly influence work attendance.[17] Family responsibilities account for one-quarter of all absences.[18] Ability is also a source of absenteeism, such as when employees are incapacitated by illness or injury. Motivation is a third factor. Employees who experience job dissatisfaction or work-related stress are more likely to be absent or late for work because taking time off is a way to temporarily withdraw from stressful or dissatisfying conditions. Absenteeism is also higher in organizations that offer generous sick leave because this benefit limits the negative financial impact of taking time off from work.[19]

PERFORMING REQUIRED TASKS

Task performance
Goal-directed activities that are under the individual's control.

People are hired to perform tasks above a minimum standard. **Task performance** refers to goal-directed activities that are under the individual's control.[20] These include physical behaviours as well as mental processes leading to behaviours. For example, foreign exchange traders at the Canadian Imperial Bank of Commerce make decisions and take actions to exchange currencies. These traders have certain *performance standards*; that is, their behaviours and the outcomes of those behaviours must exceed a minimum acceptable level.

In most jobs, employees are evaluated on several performance dimensions.[21] Foreign exchange traders, for example, must be able to identify profitable trades, work cooperatively with clients and co-workers in a stressful environment, assist in training new staff, and work on special telecommunications equipment without error. Each of these performance dimensions requires specific skills and knowledge. Some are more important than others, but only by considering all performance dimensions can we fully evaluate an employee's contribution to the organization.

EXHIBITING ORGANIZATIONAL CITIZENSHIP

Rick Boomer, head porter at the Empress Hotel in Victoria, B.C., happened to be in the hotel on his day off when a tour departed for Whistler, leaving behind 100 pieces of luggage. Boomer rented a truck, loaded it himself, took the 90-minute ferry ride across Georgia Strait, fought Vancouver's rush-hour traffic, negotiated twisting mountain roads, and delivered the luggage to Whistler. He took a quick nap, then returned to Victoria for his regular work shift![22]

For the past 50 years, management writers have known that organizations depend on employees like Rick Boomer to perform beyond their standard job duties. **Organizational citizenship** behaviours go further than the job requires.[23] They include avoiding unnecessary conflicts, helping others without selfish intent, gracefully tolerating occasional impositions, being involved in organizational activities, and performing tasks that extend beyond normal role requirements.[24] For example, good organizational citizens work cooperatively with co-workers and share resources. They forgive others for mistakes and help co-workers with their problems.

How do employees become good organizational citizens? Rewards and recognition may encourage these behaviours, but research has identified two conditions that are essential for organizational citizenship. One of these is the perceived fairness of the company's treatment of employees. Organizations encourage organizational citizenship by correcting perceptions of injustice in the workplace. Employees feel a higher sense of obligation to "walk the extra mile" when organizations distribute rewards fairly and have a process in place to correct problems when employees feel unfairly treated. One way to improve organizational citizenship through perceived fairness is to involve employees in decisions that affect them.[25]

The second condition is the degree to which employees hold strong ethical values, particularly a sense of social responsibility.[26] **Social responsibility** refers to a person's or an organization's moral obligation towards others who are affected by its actions. People with a strong social responsibility norm are more highly motivated to assist others, whether this assistance will ever be repaid, and avoid behaviours that interfere with others' goals. It is a value learned through lifelong socialization, so organizations might try to hire people with this value.

The five types of workplace behaviour and the MARS model of individual performance are related to many topics in this book. One of the more important topics is individual learning because it affects employee ability, role perceptions, and motivation. The rest of this chapter examines the topic of learning in organizational settings.

LEARNING IN ORGANIZATIONS

Most employees appreciate a good paycheque, but an increasing number of them place at least as much value on the opportunity to learn new things at work. "I'm here because I keep learning," says John Waterman, a thirtysomething employee. "Whenever I start to get a little bored, a new project comes along with opportunities for learning."[27] **Learning** is a relatively permanent change in behaviour (or behaviour tendency) that occurs as a result of a person's interaction with the environment.[28] Learning occurs when the learner behaves differently. For example, we can see that you have learned computer skills by operating the keyboard and windows more quickly than before. Learning occurs when behaviour change results from interaction with the environment. This means that we learn through our senses, such as through study, observation, and experience.

Learning influences individual behaviour and performance through three elements of the MARS model. First, people acquire skills and knowledge through learning opportunities,

Organizational citizenship Employee behaviours that extend beyond the usual job duties. They include avoiding unnecessary conflicts, helping others without selfish intent, gracefully tolerating occasional impositions, being involved in organizational activities, and performing tasks that extend beyond normal role requirements.

Social responsibility A person's or an organization's moral obligation towards others who are affected by its actions.

Learning A relatively permanent change in behaviour (or behaviour tendency) that occurs as a result of a person's interaction with the environment.

which gives them the competencies to perform tasks more effectively. Second, learning clarifies role perceptions. Employees develop a better understanding of their tasks and the relative importance of work activities. Third, learning motivates employees. Employees are more motivated to perform certain tasks because they learn that their effort will result in desired performance. Moreover, learning generates feelings of accomplishment and other forms of need fulfilment (see John Waterman's comments in the previous paragraph). A Canadian study revealed that continuous skill development is one of the most important features that employees consider in their employment.[29]

Learning is also essential for **knowledge management**—the organization's capacity to acquire, share, and use knowledge in ways that improve its survival and success (see Chapter 1).[30] Réno-Dépôt and Home Depot Canada provide superior customer service by giving employees opportunities to learn new skills and encouraging them to share knowledge throughout the organization.[31] This learning is critical for an organization's **absorptive capacity**.[32] This unusual phrase means that employees must have a sufficient level of related knowledge to be aware of and make sense of information outside the organization. Without basic knowledge of wireless technology, for example, employees would have difficulty understanding and acquiring new information from a technical seminar on this topic.

The main point here is that acquiring new knowledge from the environment requires an absorptive capacity, which depends on how much employees have already learned. "If we don't learn from the environment in which we work, we'll very soon become obsolete," warns Hubert Saint-Onge, an executive at Mutual Group in Waterloo, Ontario, and a Canadian pioneer in knowledge management.[33]

- **Knowledge management** Any structured activity that improves an organization's capacity to acquire, share, and use knowledge in ways that improve its survival and success.

- **Absorptive capacity** Employees must have a sufficient level of related knowledge to be aware of and make sense of information outside the organization.

LEARNING EXPLICIT AND TACIT KNOWLEDGE

When employees learn, they acquire both explicit and tacit knowledge. Explicit knowledge is organized and can be communicated from one person to another. The information you receive in a lecture is mainly explicit knowledge because the instructor packages and consciously transfers it to you. Explicit knowledge can be written down and given to others. However, explicit knowledge is really only the tip of the knowledge iceberg. Most of what we know is **tacit knowledge**.[34] You have probably said to someone: "I can't tell you how to do this, but I can show you." Tacit knowledge is subtle, complex, and not completely understood, so it cannot be verbally communicated. And because tacit knowledge isn't documented, it is quickly lost when employees leave the organization.

- **Tacit knowledge** Subtle information, acquired through observation and experience, that is not clearly understood and therefore cannot be explicitly communicated.

Tacit knowledge is acquired through observation and direct experience.[35] For example, airline pilots do not learn how to operate a commercial jet through lectures. They master the necessary skills by watching the subtle details as others perform the tasks, and by directly experiencing this complex interaction of behaviour with the machine's response. Most knowledge in organizations is tacit, but this does not mean that it should remain so. An important challenge in knowledge management is to make tacit knowledge more explicit so that it may be more easily stored and shared.

Learning tacit and explicit knowledge occurs in many ways. The rest of this chapter introduces four perspectives of learning: reinforcement, feedback, social learning (observation), and direct experience. These activities are not completely different (for example, feedback can be viewed as a form of reinforcement). Rather, they provide different views of the learning process. By understanding each of these perspectives, we can more fully appreciate the dynamics of learning.

BEHAVIOUR MODIFICATION: LEARNING THROUGH REINFORCEMENT

Behaviour modification (also known as *operant conditioning* and *reinforcement theory*) A theory that explains learning in terms of the antecedents and consequences of behaviour.

One of the oldest perspectives of learning, called **behaviour modification** (also known as *operant conditioning* and *reinforcement theory*), takes the rather extreme view that learning is completely dependent on the environment. Behaviour modification does not question the notion that thinking is part of the learning process, but views human thoughts as unimportant and intermediate stages between behaviour and the environment.[36] Our experience with the environment teaches us to alter our behaviours so that we maximize positive consequences and minimize adverse consequences.[37]

Behaviour modification emphasizes voluntary behaviours. Researchers call them *operant behaviours* because they "operate" on the environment—they make the environment respond in ways that we want.[38] For example, you put a certain amount of money in a machine and press a certain button so that a particular can of soft drink comes out. You have learned from past experience how to cause the environment (the soft drink machine) to deliver that brand of soft drink. Operant behaviours are different from *respondent behaviours*. Respondent behaviours are involuntary responses to the environment, such as automatically withdrawing your hand from a hot stove or automatically contracting your eyes when you turn on a bright light. This book focuses on operant behaviours because most learned behaviours in organizational settings are voluntary.

A-B-Cs OF BEHAVIOUR MODIFICATION

Behaviour modification recognizes that behaviour is influenced by two environmental contingencies: the antecedents that precede behaviour and the consequences that follow behaviour. These principles are part of the A-B-C model of behaviour modification shown in Exhibit 2.3. The central objective of behaviour modification is to change behaviour (B) by managing its antecedents (A) and consequences (C).[39]

EXHIBIT 2.3   A-B-Cs of OB Modification

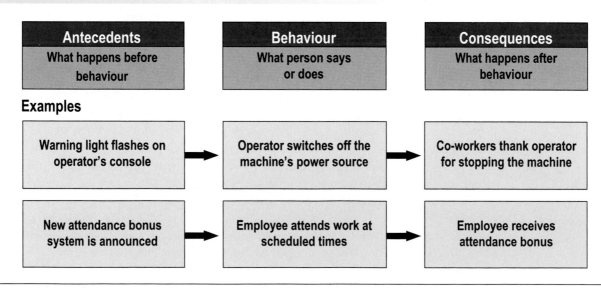

Sources: Adapted from T.K. Connellan, *How to Improve Human Performance* (New York: Harper & Row, 1978), p. 50; F. Luthans and R. Kreitner, *Organizational Behavior Modification and Beyond* (Glenview, IL: Scott, Foresman, 1985), pp. 85–88.

Antecedents are events preceding the behaviour that inform employees that certain behaviours will have particular consequences. An antecedent may be a sound from your computer signalling that an e-mail has arrived, or a request from your supervisor to complete a specific task by tomorrow. These antecedents let employees know that a particular action will produce particular consequences. Notice that antecedents do not cause operant behaviours. The computer sound doesn't cause us to open our e-mail. Rather, the sound is a cue telling us that certain consequences are likely to occur if we engage in certain behaviours.

Although antecedents are important, behaviour modification mainly focuses on the *consequences* of behaviour. Consequences are events following a particular behaviour that influence its future occurrence. This concept is based on the **law of effect**, which states that the likelihood that an operant behaviour will be repeated depends on its consequences. If behaviour is followed by a pleasant experience, the person will probably repeat the behaviour. If the behaviour is followed by an unpleasant experience or by no response at all, the person is less likely to repeat it. The law of effect explains how people learn to associate behaviours with specific environmental responses. OB scholars have identified four types of consequences and five schedules to administer these consequences.

Law of effect States that the likelihood that an operant behaviour will be repeated depends on its consequences.

CONTINGENCIES OF REINFORCEMENT

Behaviour modification identifies four types of consequences, collectively known as the *contingencies of reinforcement,* that strengthen, maintain, or weaken behaviour. As shown in Exhibit 2.4, these contingencies are positive reinforcement, negative reinforcement, punishment, and extinction:[40]

EXHIBIT 2.4   Contingencies of Reinforcement

	Consequence Is Introduced	No Consequence	Consequence Is Removed
Behaviour Increases or Is Maintained	**Positive Reinforcement** — Example: You receive a bonus after successfully completing an important project.		**Negative Reinforcement** — Example: Supervisor stops criticizing you when your job performance improves.
Behaviour Decreases	**Punishment** — Example: You are threatened with demotion or dismissal after treating a client badly.	**Extinction** — Example: Co-workers no longer praise you when you engage in dangerous pranks.	**Punishment** — Example: You give up your "employee of the month" parking spot to this month's winner.

Positive reinforcement Occurs when the introduction of a consequence increases or maintains the frequency or future probability of the behaviour preceding that event.

Negative reinforcement Occurs when the removal or termination of a consequence increases or maintains the frequency or future probability of the behaviour preceding that event.

Punishment Occurs when the introduction of a consequence decreases the frequency or future probability of the behaviour preceding that event.

Extinction Occurs when the removal or withholding of a consequence decreases the frequency or future probability of the behaviour preceding that event.

- *Positive reinforcement*—**Positive reinforcement** occurs when the *introduction* of a consequence *increases or maintains* the frequency or future probability of a behaviour. Receiving a bonus after successfully completing an important project usually creates positive reinforcement because it typically increases the probability that you use those behaviours in the future.

- *Negative reinforcement*—**Negative reinforcement** occurs when the *removal or avoidance* of a consequence *increases or maintains* the frequency or future probability of a behaviour. Supervisors apply negative reinforcement when they stop criticizing employees whose substandard performance has improved. When the supervisor withholds criticism, employees are more likely to repeat behaviours that improved their performance.[41] Negative reinforcement is sometimes called avoidance learning because employees engage in the desired behaviours to avoid unpleasant consequences (such as being criticized by your supervisor or being fired from your job).

- *Punishment*—**Punishment** occurs when a consequence *decreases* the frequency or future probability of a behaviour. It may occur by introducing an unpleasant consequence or removing a pleasant consequence (see Exhibit 2.4). An example of the former would be where an employee is threatened with a demotion or dismissal after treating a client badly. The latter form of punishment would occur when a salesperson is forced to give a cherished parking spot to another employee who has higher sales performance for the month.

- *Extinction*—**Extinction** occurs when the target behaviour decreases because no consequence follows it. For example, if an employee makes practical jokes that are potentially dangerous or costly, this behaviour might be extinguished by discouraging others from praising the employee when he or she engages in these pranks. Behaviour that is no longer reinforced tends to disappear; it becomes extinct. In this respect, extinction is a do-nothing strategy.[42]

Comparing reinforcement contingencies

In most situations, positive reinforcement should follow desired behaviours and extinction (do nothing) should follow undesirable behaviours. This is because there are fewer adverse consequences when applying these contingencies compared with punishment and negative reinforcement. However, some form of punishment (dismissal, suspension, demotion, etc.) may be necessary for extreme behaviours, such as deliberately hurting co-workers or stealing inventory. Indeed, research suggests that punishment maintains a sense of equity.[43] Co-workers are often eager to hear about an employee's discipline because it fulfils their need for social justice.

Unfortunately, organizations tend to be inconsistent in their administration of punishment, so justice through discipline is an elusive goal.[44] Moreover, punishment is usually an emotionally charged event that creates negative feelings and undermines the employee's ability to learn from the punishment.[45] In extreme cases, employees develop hostilities towards the organization that may result in aggression and other forms of dysfunctional behaviour.

SCHEDULES OF REINFORCEMENT

Along with the types of consequences, behaviour modification identifies the schedule that should be followed to maximize the reinforcement effect. In fact, there is some evidence that the reinforcement schedule affects learning more than the size of the reinforcer.[46] Behaviour

Continuous reinforcement A schedule that reinforces behaviour every time it occurs.

Fixed interval schedule A schedule that reinforces behaviour after it has occurred for a fixed period of time.

Variable interval schedule A schedule that reinforces behaviour after it has occurred for a variable period of time around some average.

Fixed ratio schedule A schedule that reinforces behaviour after it has occurred a fixed number of times.

Variable ratio schedule A schedule that reinforces behaviour after it has occurred a varying number of times around some average.

modification theorists have identified five schedules of reinforcement. One of these is **continuous reinforcement**—reinforcing every occurrence of the desired behaviour. Continuous reinforcement is most effective for learning new behaviours. Employees learn desired behaviours quickly and, when the reinforcer is removed, extinction also occurs very quickly.

The other four reinforcement schedules are intermittent. They apply the reinforcer after a fixed or variable time (interval) or number of target behaviours (ratio). As illustrated in Exhibit 2.5, a fixed schedule means that the reinforcer occurs after the same number of behaviours or time units, whereas a variable schedule means that the reinforcer varies randomly around an average number of behaviours or time units.

The **fixed interval schedule** occurs when behaviour is reinforced after a fixed time. Most people get paid on a fixed interval schedule because their paycheques are received every week or two weeks. As long as the job is performed satisfactorily, a paycheque is received on the appointed day. The **variable interval schedule** involves administering the reinforcer after a varying length of time. Promotions typically follow this schedule because they occur at uneven time intervals. The first promotion might be received after two years of good performance, the next after four more years, the third after 18 more months, and so on.

The **fixed ratio schedule** reinforces behaviour after a fixed number of target behaviours. Some piece rate systems follow this schedule; employees are paid after they produce a fixed number of units. The **variable ratio schedule** reinforces behaviour after a varying number of target behaviours. Salespeople experience variable ratio reinforcement because they make a successful sale (the reinforcer) after a varying number of client calls. They might make four unsuccessful calls before receiving an order on the fifth call. This may be followed by 15 unsuccessful sales calls before another sale is made. One successful sale might be made per ten calls, on average, but this does not mean that every tenth call will be successful.

EXHIBIT 2.5   Schedules of Reinforcement

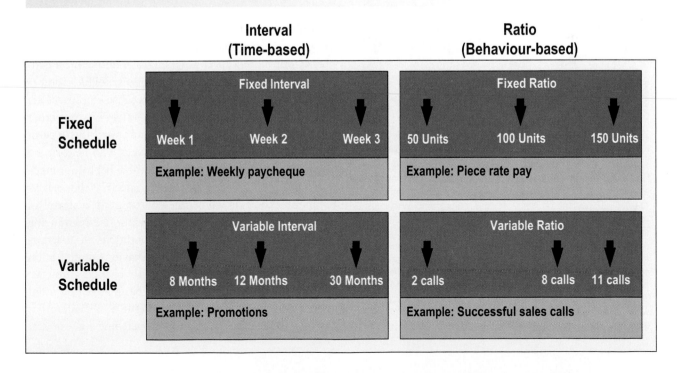

The variable ratio schedule is a low-cost way to reinforce behaviour because employees are rewarded infrequently. It is also highly resistant to extinction. Suppose that your boss approaches your work area at varying times during the day. Chances are that you would work better and more consistently throughout the day than if your boss visited at exactly 11 a.m. every day. If your boss doesn't approach you at all on a particular day, you would still expect a visit right until the end of the day if previous visits had been random.

BEHAVIOUR MODIFICATION IN PRACTICE

www.novachemicals.com

Research has generally found that behaviour modification significantly improves learning and task performance in work settings.[47] There are also many industry examples where behaviour modification has been effective. Moncton, N.B.–based Marine Atlantic Inc. successfully applied behaviour modification to reduce costs and improve customer service. Supervisors at the Atlantic Canada ferry service learned how to measure and graph team performance and give positive reinforcement. Auto parts manufacturer Dana Corp. relies on behaviour modification through a game called safety bingo to reinforce safe work behaviours. Employees can draw a number for their bingo card for every day that the plant has no accident. The employee who fills a bingo card first wins a television set.[48]

Limitations of behaviour modification

In spite of these favourable results, behaviour modification is more difficult to apply to conceptual activities than to observable behaviours. For example, it's much easier to reward employees for good work attendance than for good problem solving.[49] A second problem is "reward inflation," in which the reinforcer either is quickly forgotten or is eventually considered an entitlement. A bonus that was once an unexpected surprise becomes an expected part of the employment relationship. Withholding the reinforcer may represent extinction, but it feels like punishment![50]

Behaviour modification programs also raise ethical concerns. One issue is that the variable ratio schedule is sometimes viewed as a form of gambling, because employees are essentially betting that they will win a lottery or some other reinforcer. A forest products firm that applied this type of schedule discovered that some employees who held strong anti-gambling beliefs were upset with these behaviour modification practices.[51] The other ethical concern is that behaviour modification is sometimes viewed as a form of manipulation. It alters human behaviour by rearranging incentives and other environmental conditions while ignoring human thoughts and feelings.[52] Behaviour modification experts point out that any attempt to change employee behaviour is a form of manipulation. No matter how valid this counter-argument may be, behaviour modification has an image problem that is difficult to overcome.

Courtesy of Nova Chemicals.

Nova Chemicals introduced a $1 million "Recruitment and Retention Program" to reinforce good attendance and continued employment at its Joffre, Alberta, construction site. Absenteeism reached 20 percent on some Fridays before long weekends, threatening the project's completion deadline. Nova Chemicals' solution was to reward employees who achieved perfect attendance with a chance to win one of ten $2000 prizes each week. A final draw of four $100,000 grand prizes encouraged employees to stay until the end of their contracts. Nova's behaviour modification program cut absenteeism rates by 25 percent and dramatically improved employment levels.[53] Would this type of reinforcement work as effectively for employees in long-term jobs, such as assembly line workers?

LEARNING THROUGH FEEDBACK

Feedback Any information that people receive about the consequences of their behaviour.

When the Conference Board asked human resource executives to identify the primary causes of poor performance, the top-ranked problem was poor or insufficient feedback to employees.[54] **Feedback** is any information that people receive about the consequences of their behaviour. Feedback may be an antecedent or a consequence, if we look at it from a behaviour modification perspective. However, our discussion of learning through feedback will take a broader view by considering the effects on employee thoughts as well as behaviours.

Feedback influences behaviour and task performance through role perceptions, ability, and motivation.[55] Feedback clarifies role perceptions by communicating what behaviours are appropriate or necessary in a particular situation. It improves ability by frequently providing information to correct performance problems.[56] This is known as corrective feedback, because it makes people aware of their performance errors and helps them correct those errors quickly. Lastly, feedback is a source of motivation. It fulfils personal needs and makes people more confident that they are able to accomplish certain tasks (see Chapter 3).

FEEDBACK SOURCES

Feedback can originate from social or nonsocial sources. Social sources include supervisors, clients, co-workers, and anyone else who provides information about an employee's behaviour or results. B.C. Gas, Consumers Gas, Federal Express, and Nortel Networks are some of the Canadian firms that use multi-source feedback, in which employees receive performance feedback from several people.[57] This is often called **360-degree feedback**, because feedback is received from a full circle of people around the employee (see Exhibit 2.6).[58] In some organizations, the feedback is submitted to a more senior person who combines the results into a single performance appraisal report. In other organizations, evaluators complete an intranet-based feedback form that automatically transmits the combined results to the employee.

360-degree feedback Performance feedback is received from a full circle of people around the employee.

EXHIBIT 2.6   360-Degree Feedback

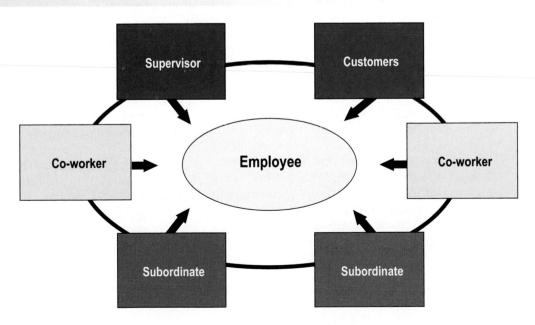

Research suggests that multi-source feedback provides more complete and accurate information than feedback from a supervisor alone.[59] Connections 2.2 describes how Canadian companies are discovering the benefits of 360-degree feedback. Employees who work away from the office and on projects with different team leaders need performance information from a variety of sources. However, multi-source feedback is expensive and works best when the results are used for employee development, not for determining pay bonuses. With multiple opinions, the 360-degree process can also produce ambiguous and conflicting feedback, so employees may require guidance to interpret the results.[60]

Along with social sources, employees usually receive nonsocial sources of feedback. With a click of the computer mouse, a marketing manager at Xerox Canada can look at the previous day's sales and compare them with past results. The job itself can also be a source of feedback. Many employees see the results of their work effort while they are making a product.

The preferred feedback source depends on the purpose of the information. To learn about their progress towards goal accomplishment, employees usually prefer nonsocial feedback sources, such as computer printouts or feedback directly from the job.[61] This is because information from nonsocial sources is considered more accurate than from social sources. Corrective feedback from nonsocial sources is also less damaging to self-esteem. This is probably just as well because social sources tend to delay negative information, leave some of it out, and distort the bad news in a positive way. [62]

When employees want to improve their self-image, they seek out positive feedback from social sources. It feels better to have co-workers say that you are performing the job well than to discover this from a computer printout.[63] Positive feedback from co-workers and other

www.petro-canada.ca

CONNECTIONS 2.2

Feedback Sources Are All Around

Once each year, Tom Miles is summoned to corporate headquarters where his boss provides feedback on his personal skills, teamwork, and other factors. The trouble is that the computer programmer works in clients' offices or from his home in Mississauga, Ontario. Miles and his boss communicate mostly through e-mail. "[My boss] was the first to admit he couldn't evaluate me because he never saw me," says Miles.

How do companies provide accurate feedback in an era when employees work away from the office or have several projects with different bosses? Petro-Canada, Intrawest, B.C. Gas, and other Canadian companies rely on 360-degree feedback. Subordinates, peers, superiors, customers, and others submit con-

fidential ratings to the employee's supervisor. The result is a more complete picture of the employee's performance.

Some companies let employees choose the people who will evaluate them. Choosing friends doesn't guarantee a glowing evaluation, however. Disney Corp. tested the 360-degree system with teams picked by bosses and teams picked by the person being evaluated. Friends were tougher.

"[Friends are] trying to help you," explains Murray Lonseth, of Right Management Consultants in Calgary. "People who aren't your friends are more inclined to say politically correct things whereas friends tend to be more honest with you."

Sources: L. Ramsay, "Time to Examine the Exam," *National Post*, October 18, 1999, p. C15; V. Barnett, "Judged by Your Peers," *Montreal Gazette*, March 29, 1999, p. E2.

social sources mainly motivates because it fulfils social (relatedness) as well as growth needs (see Chapter 3).

GIVING FEEDBACK EFFECTIVELY

Whether feedback is received from a supervisor or a computer printout, it should be specific, sufficiently frequent, timely, credible, and relevant:

- *Specific feedback*—Feedback should include specific information such as "you exceeded your sales quota by 5 percent last month" rather than subjective and general phrases such as "your sales are going well." This helps employees redirect their effort and behaviour more precisely and gives them a greater sense of accomplishment when the feedback is positive. Also, notice that specific feedback is focused on the task, not on the person. This reduces the person's defensiveness when receiving negative feedback.

- *Frequent feedback*—Ideally, employees should be able to monitor their own performance from nonsocial feedback sources. If this isn't possible, the feedback provider needs to consider the employee's task cycle (how long it takes to complete each task) and task experience. Cashiers have very short cycles (they finish working with a customer within a few minutes) so they should receive feedback more often than people with long cycles (executives, salespeople). Employees working on new tasks should also receive more frequent feedback because they require more behaviour guidance and reinforcement.

- *Timely feedback*—Feedback should be available as soon as possible so that employees make a clear association between their behaviour and its consequences. For instance, when Nissan Canada receives negative feedback from customers, it forwards the information the same day to the dealership where the complaint originated.[64]

- *Credible feedback*—Employees are more likely to accept feedback (particularly corrective feedback) from trustworthy and credible sources.[65] Multi-source feedback has higher credibility because it comes from several people. Employees are also more likely to accept corrective feedback from nonsocial sources (e.g., computer printouts, electronic gauges) because it is not as judgmental.

- *Relevant feedback*—Feedback must relate to the individual's behaviour rather than to conditions beyond the individual's control. This ensures that the feedback is not distorted by situational factors.[66] Feedback is also relevant when it is linked to goals. Goals establish the benchmarks (i.e., what ought to be) against which feedback is judged.

SEEKING FEEDBACK

So far, we have presented the traditional view that supervisors and others give feedback to employees. However, employees do not just passively receive feedback; they actively seek it as well.[67] The most obvious way to do this is through *inquiry*—asking other people about their performance and behaviour. This feedback-seeking tactic tends to be used when individuals have high self-esteem, expect to receive positive feedback, and work in an organization that values openness.

Direct inquiry is a powerful form of feedback in a private setting and when the person providing the feedback communicates the information clearly and diplomatically. However, many people have difficulty with direct inquiry when someone has performed a task poorly. Supervisors and co-workers tend to provide inaccurate feedback when the information is negative. Moreover, it is more difficult to save face when receiving negative feedback in response to a direct request. A third problem is that inquiry is only possible when someone else is available and has time to answer questions.

Thus, employees often use other feedback-seeking tactics. The most common of these is *monitoring*. This involves scanning the work environment and the behaviour of others for information cues. Executives monitor corporate data to determine whether their strategies have worked. Salespeople monitor the nonverbal cues of customers during a transaction. Monitoring usually occurs at any time and can be more efficient than relying on others to transmit the information. For instance, production employees can continuously monitor the quality of their work quickly and independently. And although monitoring nonverbal cues of clients and co-workers creates the risk of misinterpreting meaning (see Chapter 8), it has the advantage of avoiding problems with having to save face.

ETHICS OF EMPLOYEE MONITORING

From the time you wake up to the time you retire for the day, you leave behind a trail of data for others to gather, merge, analyze, massage, and even sell—often without your knowledge or consent. That warning from Canada's Privacy Commissioner applies not just to consumers, but to employees in most organizations. Nearly two-thirds of large and mid-size companies monitor employee telephone conversations, transactions, keystrokes, Web hits, e-mail messages, and other forms of behaviour on the job.[68]

Canadian National Railway Co. (CN) warns employees that e-mail messages transmitted on its computers are company property and may be viewed by CN officials. Canadian discount brokerage firm TD Waterhouse hires a team of industrial psychologists to listen in on telephone conversations between clients and customer-service representatives. The consultants then work with TD's employees to improve their communication skills. As part of a work efficiency project, consultants outfitted employees at the Ontario Ministry of Social Services with a device that monitored their behaviour throughout the day. Several government and private sector companies in Canada use special software to monitor employee phone calls, e-mail, Internet connections, and computer files. One company in the United States takes employee monitoring to an extreme by requiring employees to use specific log-off codes whenever they go to the bathroom or otherwise leave their desks.[69]

Critics argue that monitoring is an invasion of employee privacy. It symbolizes a lack of trust that undermines the employment relationship. Employers, on the other hand, point out that they have a legal right to engage in most forms of monitoring to protect company assets, provide a safer work environment, and give employees more accurate feedback about their performance.[70] Some research indicates that employees see monitoring as a necessary evil. Although concerned about invasion of privacy, most employees are willing to be monitored when the information is used only for developmental feedback.[71] Still, as technology leads to more sophisticated surveillance, debate about the ethics of employee monitoring will become more intense.

"It's a wasted-motion sensor."

© Ted Goff. www.tedgoff.com

SOCIAL LEARNING THEORY: LEARNING BY OBSERVING

Feedback and behaviour modification mainly consider learning through direct experience with the environment. However, we also learn by observing the behaviours and consequences of other people. **Social learning theory** states that much learning occurs by observing others and then modelling the behaviours that lead to favourable outcomes and avoiding behaviours that lead to punishing consequences.[72] There are three related features of social learning theory: behavioural modelling, learning behaviour consequences, and self-reinforcement.

Social learning theory A theory stating that learning mainly occurs by observing others and then modelling the behaviours that lead to favourable outcomes and avoiding behaviours that lead to punishing consequences.

BEHAVIOURAL MODELLING

People learn by observing the behaviours of a role model on the critical task, remembering the important elements of the observed behaviours, and then practising those behaviours.[73] Behavioural modelling works best when the model is respected and the model's actions are followed by favourable consequences. For instance, recently hired college graduates should learn by watching a previously hired college graduate who successfully performs the task.

Behavioural modelling is a valuable form of learning because tacit knowledge and skills are mainly acquired from others in this way. Earlier in this chapter, we explained that tacit knowledge is the subtle information about required behaviours, the correct sequence of those actions, and the environmental consequences (such as a machine response or customer reply) that should occur after each action. The adage that a picture is worth a thousand words applies here. It is difficult to document or verbally explain how a master baker kneads dough better than someone less qualified. Instead, we must observe these subtle actions to develop a more precise mental model of the required behaviours and the expected responses. Behavioural modelling also guides role perceptions. Leaders model the behaviour that they expect from others, for example.

Behaviour modelling and self-efficacy

Behavioural modelling is also valuable because it enhances the observer's **self-efficacy**. Self-efficacy refers to a person's belief that he or she has the ability, motivation, and resources to complete a task successfully.[74] People with high self-efficacy have a "can-do" attitude towards a specific task and, more generally, with regards to other challenges in life.

Self-efficacy A person's belief that he or she has the ability, motivation, and resources to complete a task successfully.

Behavioural modelling increases self-efficacy because people gain more self-confidence after seeing someone else do it than if they are simply told what to do. This is particularly true when observers identify with the model, such as someone who is similar in age, experience, gender, and related features. You might experience this when working in a student support group. You form a "can-do" attitude when another student similar to you describes how he or she was able to perform well in a course that you are now taking. You learn not only what has to be done, but that others like you have been successful at this challenge.

Self-efficacy is also affected by initial experiences when practising the previously modelled behaviour. Observers gain confidence when the environmental cues follow a predictable pattern and there are no unexpected surprises when practising the behaviour.[75] For example, computer trainees develop a stronger self-efficacy when they click the mouse and get the same computer response as the model did when performing the same behaviour. The expected response gives trainees a greater sense of control over the computer because they can predict what will happen following a particular behaviour.

LEARNING BEHAVIOUR CONSEQUENCES

A second element of social learning theory states that we learn the consequences of behaviour in ways other than through direct experience. In particular, we learn by logically thinking through the consequences of our actions and by observing the consequences that other people experience following their behaviour. On the first point, we often anticipate desirable or adverse consequences through logic. We expect either positive reinforcement or negative reinforcement after completing an assigned task and either punishment or extinction after performing the job poorly because it is a logical conclusion based on ethical values.

We also learn to anticipate consequences by observing the experiences of other people. Civilizations have relied on this principle for centuries, by punishing civil disobedience in public to deter other potential criminals.[76] Learning behaviour consequences occurs in more subtle ways in contemporary organizations. Consider the employee who observes a co-worker receiving a stern warning for working in an unsafe manner. This event would reduce the observer's likelihood of engaging in unsafe behaviours because he or she has learned to anticipate a similar reprimand following those behaviours.[77]

SELF-REINFORCEMENT

The final element of social learning theory is *self-reinforcement*. Self-reinforcement occurs whenever an employee has control over a reinforcer but doesn't "take" the reinforcer until completing a self-set goal.[78] For example, you might be thinking about taking a work break after you finish reading the rest of this chapter—and not before! You could take a break right now, but you don't use this privilege until you have achieved your goal of reading the chapter. The work break is a form of positive reinforcement that is self-induced. You use the work break to reinforce completion of a task. Numerous consequences may be applied in self-reinforcement, ranging from raiding the refrigerator to congratulating yourself for completing the task.[79] Self-reinforcement has become increasingly important because employees are given more control over their working lives and are less dependent on supervisors to dole out positive reinforcement and punishment.

LEARNING THROUGH EXPERIENCE

Brigitte Shim learned plenty of architectural knowledge at school, but her co-op education provided most of her insight about running a practice. "Nobody teaches you at school to design a practice," says the award-winning Toronto architect. Shim's architectural program included stints at several architectural firms, including that of famed architect Arthur Erickson in Vancouver. These jobs taught Shim explicit knowledge, but they also transferred tacit knowledge that can't be taught in the classroom. As Shim explains: "The actual task is secondary to the osmosis."[80]

Whether through co-op education programs or real-time training in the forest, many organizations are discarding the notion that learning is measured by the number of hours employees spend in the classroom. Classrooms convey explicit knowledge that has been documented, but most tacit knowledge and skills are acquired through experience as well as through observation. Much of what we learn in organizations takes place while practising new behaviours and watching the environmental responses to our actions.[81]

Experiential learning is related to the concept of **implicit learning.** Implicit learning occurs when we acquire information about relationships in the environment without any

Implicit learning
The experiential phenomenon of acquiring information about relationships in the environment without any conscious attempt to do so.

Courtesy of International Forest Products Ltd.

The classroom is surrounded by trees at International Forest Products (Interfor). The British Columbia forest products company introduced a peer training program in which specially trained employees provide hands-on, just-in-time learning to co-workers right in the forest. Rather than going to off-site lectures, Interfor employees can now learn a new skill on the job when they need it from a peer trainer. As a result, Interfor has less downtime and its employees receive a more thorough understanding of the training topic through direct experience.[83] What concepts about learning presented earlier in this chapter help to explain why Interfor's employees tend to learn more effectively in the woods rather than in the classroom?

conscious attempt to do so.[82] In other words, we aren't even aware of much of the information we acquire. Most implicit learning occurs when we interact with the environment, such as when we work with customers or operate a machine. Less implicit learning occurs off the job because knowledge about the environment is indirect.

PRACTISING LEARNING THROUGH EXPERIENCE

Learning through experience must occur within a learning culture. The organization or immediate work unit must value the process of individual and team learning. It does this by establishing an environment that rewards experimentation and recognizes mistakes as a natural part of the learning process. Without these conditions, mistakes are hidden and problems are more likely to escalate or re-emerge later. It's not surprising, then, that one of the most frequently mentioned lessons from North America's best-performing manufacturers is to expect mistakes. "[Mistakes] are a source of learning and will improve operations in the long run," explains an executive at Lockheed Martin. "[They] foster the concept that no question is dumb, no idea too wild, and no task or activity is irrelevant."[84]

Action learning

Action learning A form of on-site, experiential-based learning in which participants investigate an organizational problem or opportunity and possibly implement their solution.

The fastest-growing form of experiential learning in the workplace is called **action learning**. Action learning refers to a variety of experiential-based learning activities in which employees solve real-life problems, usually in teams, with immediate relevance to the company. For example, an action learning team at Carpenter Technology was challenged to investigate the steel manufacturer's strategy for entry into India. A typical team consists of people from various parts of the organization who investigate the organizational problem or opportunity, write up their recommendations, and meet with senior executives to discuss their results.[85]

Action learning is considered to be one of the most important ways to develop executive competencies.[86] It involves both tacit and explicit learning, forces employees to diagnose new situations, and makes them rethink current work practices. At the same time, the results of action learning potentially add value to the organization in terms of a better work process or service. For example, one of Motorola's action learning teams spent several months learning how to create and manage a software business.[87]

Action learning and other forms of experiential learning will become more important as organizational leaders recognize the value of knowledge acquisition and sharing for corporate competitiveness. However, knowledge does not provide value unless it is translated into action, so we must consider all four drivers of individual behaviour: motivation, ability, role perceptions, and situational factors. The next two chapters look at the conceptual foundations and applied strategies of employee motivation.

CHAPTER SUMMARY

- Individual behaviour is influenced by motivation, ability, role perceptions, and situational factors (MARS). Motivation consists of internal forces that affect the direction, intensity, and persistence of a person's voluntary choice of behaviour. Ability includes both the natural aptitudes and learned capabilities to perform a task. Role perceptions are a person's beliefs about what behaviours are appropriate or necessary in a particular situation. Situational factors are environmental conditions that constrain or facilitate employee behaviour and performance.

- These four factors influence various types of behaviour, including joining the organization, remaining with the organization, maintaining work attendance, performing required job duties, and exhibiting organizational citizenship.

- Learning is a relatively permanent change in behaviour (or behaviour tendency) that occurs as a result of a person's interaction with the environment. Learning influences ability, role perceptions, and motivation in the MARS model of individual performance. The four main perspectives of learning in organizations are behaviour modification (reinforcement), feedback, social learning, and direct experience.

- The behaviour modification perspective of learning states that behaviour change occurs by altering its antecedents and consequences (the A-B-C model). Antecedents are environmental stimuli that provoke (not necessarily cause) behaviour. Consequences are events following behaviour that influence its future occurrence. Consequences include positive reinforcement, negative reinforcement, punishment, and extinction. The schedules of reinforcement also influence behaviour.

- Feedback is any information that people receive about the consequences of their behaviour. It affects role perceptions, learning (through corrective feedback), and employee motivation. Employees prefer nonsocial sources of feedback to learn about their goal progress. They prefer positive feedback from social sources to improve their self-image. Employees seek out feedback, rather than just passively receive it. Although employee monitoring is sometimes necessary for feedback, it raises ethical concerns.

- Effective feedback is specific, frequent, timely, credible, and relevant.

- Social learning theory states that much learning occurs by observing others and then modelling those behaviours that seem to lead to favourable outcomes and avoiding behaviours that lead to punishing consequences. It also recognizes that we often engage in self-reinforcement. Behavioural modelling is effective because it transfers tacit knowledge and enhances the observer's self-efficacy.

- Many companies now use peer training, action learning, and other experience-based methods of employee learning. Learning through experience is an effective way to acquire tacit knowledge and skills and is consistent with the implicit learning process.

KEY TERMS

360-degree feedback, p. 45

Ability, p. 33

Absorptive capacity, p. 39

Action learning, p. 51

Behaviour modification, p. 40

Competencies, p. 33

Continuous reinforcement, p. 43

Extinction, p. 42

Feedback, p. 45

Fixed interval schedule, p. 43

Fixed ratio schedule, p. 43

Implicit learning, p. 50

Job satisfaction, p. 37

Knowledge management, p. 39

Law of effect, p. 41

Learning, p. 38

Motivation, p. 32

Negative reinforcement, p. 42

Organizational citizenship, p. 38

Positive reinforcement, p. 42

Punishment, p. 42

Role perceptions, p. 34

Self-efficacy, p. 49

Social learning theory, p. 49

Social responsibility, p. 38

Tacit knowledge, p. 39

Task performance, p. 37

Variable interval schedule, p. 43

Variable ratio schedule, p. 43

DISCUSSION QUESTIONS

1. An insurance company has high levels of absenteeism among the office staff. The head of office administration argues that employees are misusing the company's sick leave benefits. However, some of the mostly female staff members have explained that family responsibilities interfere with work. Using the MARS model, as well as your knowledge of absenteeism behaviour, discuss some of the possible reasons for absenteeism here and how it might be reduced.

2. Organizational citizenship behaviours occur in a variety of settings. Identify specific organizational citizenship behaviours that you have encountered when working with other students on team projects and assignments.

3. You notice that sales representatives in eastern Ontario made 20 percent fewer sales to new clients over the past quarter than salespeople located elsewhere in Canada. Use the MARS model to explain why the eastern Ontario sales reps' performance may have been lower than elsewhere.

4. Customer service representatives at Cisco Systems receive 50 points every time they convince a client to click through an online demonstration rather than place an order over the telephone. If the employees reach a minimum number of sales, they receive at least 1500 points. These points are later traded for music CDs (900 points), coffee makers (2500 points), and other rewards. What contingency and schedule of reinforcement is Cisco Systems using here?

5. When do employees prefer feedback from nonsocial rather than social sources? Explain why nonsocial sources are preferred under those conditions.

6. Senior officials in a manufacturing firm are increasingly concerned about the liability they face if any of their supervisory staff engage in sexual harassment. The company's lawyer

says that monitoring supervisory staff with hidden cameras may minimize this risk. Discuss the dilemmas that this company faces with regards to employee monitoring in this situation. What is the best solution here?

7. The person responsible for training and development in your organization wants to build a new training centre where all employees can receive classroom instruction in new skills and knowledge. Why might this idea be an ineffective approach to learning?

8. A consulting firm has recommended that Big Rock Mining Co. rely on action learning to prepare its technical staff for leadership positions in the organization. The executives complain that action learning takes too long, whereas consultants could provide several classroom sessions in less time and at less expense. Discuss their arguments against action learning.

 Case Study

ACTIVITY 2.1
Vêtements Ltée

Vêtements Ltée is a chain of men's retail clothing stores located throughout the province of Quebec. Two years ago, the company introduced new incentive systems for both store managers and sales employees. Store managers in each store receive a salary with annual merit increases based on sales above targeted goals, store appearance, store inventory management, customer complaints, and several other performance measures. Some of this information (e.g., store appearance) is gathered during visits by senior management, while other information is based on company records (e.g., sales volume).

Sales employees are paid a fixed salary plus a commission based on the percentage of sales credited to that employee over the pay period. The commission represents about 30 percent of a typical paycheque and is intended to encourage employees to actively serve customers and to increase sales volume. Because returned merchandise is discounted from commissions, sales staff are discouraged from selling products that customers do not really want.

Soon after the new incentive systems were introduced, senior management began to receive complaints from store managers regarding the performance of their sales staff. They observed that sales employees tended to stand near the store entrance waiting to "tag" customers as their own. Occasionally sales staff would argue over "ownership" of the customer. Managers were concerned that this aggressive behaviour intimi-

dated some customers. It also tended to leave some parts of the store unattended by staff.

Many managers were also concerned about inventory duties. Previously, sales staff would share responsibility for restocking inventory and completing inventory reorder forms. Under the new compensation system, however, few employees were willing to do these essential tasks. On several occasions, stores had faced stock shortages because merchandise was not stocked or reorder forms were not completed in a timely manner. Potential sales have suffered due to empty shelves when plenty of merchandise was available in the back storeroom or at the warehouse. The company's new automatic inventory system could reduce some of these problems, but employees must still stock shelves and assist in other aspects of inventory management.

Store managers have tried to correct the inventory problem by assigning employees to inventory duty, but this has created resentment among the employees selected. Other managers have threatened sales staff with dismissals if they do not do their share of inventory management. This strategy has been somewhat effective when the manager is in the store, but staff members sneak back onto the floor when the manager is away. It has also hurt staff morale, particularly relations with the store manager.

To reduce the tendency of sales staff to hoard customers at the store entrance, some managers have assigned employees to specific areas of the store. This has also created some resentment among employees stationed in areas with less traffic or lower-priced merchandise. Some staff members have

ACTIVITY 2.1 CONTINUED

openly complained of lower paycheques because they have been placed in a slow area of the store or have been given more than their share of inventory duties.

Discusssion Questions

1. Describe the new reward system at Vêtements Ltée in terms of behaviour modification. In particular, what contingency and schedule of reinforcement were applied here?

2. Using the A-B-C model of behaviour modification, explain why the following behaviours occurred: (a) standing near the store entrance, and (b) sneaking onto the sales floor when posted to inventory duties.

3. What actions should the organization take to correct these problems?

© Copyright Steven L. McShane.

 Video Case Study

ACTIVITY 2.2
Workplace Perks

Earl Knight puts in ten-hour workdays at Cigna Insurance Company. The last thing that either he or his working wife wants to do at the end of the day is cook. However, at Cigna, ordering takeout is not exactly what you think. For $10 per dinner, the company chef cooks for the family.

With working hours up and job security down, many companies offer a range of attractive and unusual benefits from on-site dry cleaning to lactation rooms for nursing mothers. For example, Patty Carter takes her laundry to her $7 per hour assembly line job at the Connor Packaging Company. That's because her company does the laundry for her. Connor Packaging also likes to give money away—$15 dollars a week per child, for example, for daycare.

Is this good business? Wilton Connor, owner of Connor Packaging, thinks so. He says, "Absolutely it's good business. It's good hard-nosed business. Treat people as if they are human beings with needs and concerns and you will get back loyalty and good work." Hattie Carter, a Connor Packaging employee, supports Connor's comments: "We try to make him as happy in every way we can because he's been very good to us."

Andersen Consulting has a concierge to take care of life's small tasks. Employees pay just $5 per day for the service. The company says that this is a cost-effective way of keeping busy employees happy and more focused on their work.

The Centers for Disease Control and Prevention in Atlanta keep employees with the organization by sponsoring a fitness program. Employees enjoy this benefit, but it also reduces absenteeism and health care costs. Coca-Cola also discovered this. "We did find that employees that participate in our fitness centre have less health care costs. Something like $500 dollars a year less," says Arlene Kirchoffer, Coke's health promotion manager. That adds up to savings of $1.2 million a year at Coke's headquarters in Atlanta alone.

Many employees now consider fitness programs to be an important fringe benefit. And the companies that provide them are finding that they not only save money but also win the appreciation and loyalty of employees.

Discussion Questions

1. According to research, 53 percent of employees expect to leave their jobs voluntarily in the next five years. Do you think that Connor Packaging Company can keep its employees for longer than that? Explain.

2. Do you think that employees who have benefits similar to those at Cigna or the Centers for Disease Control and Prevention will exhibit higher levels of organizational citizenship than employees in firms that don't offer such benefits? Explain.

Source: NBC Archives.

ACTIVITY 2.3
A QUESTION OF FEEDBACK

Purpose: This exercise is designed to help you understand the importance of feedback, including problems that occur with imperfect communication in the feedback process.

Materials: The instructor will distribute a few pages of exhibits to one person on each team. The other students will require a pencil with an eraser and blank paper. Movable chairs and tables in a large area are helpful.

Instructions:

Step 1: The class is divided into pairs of students. Each pair is ideally located in a private area, away from other students and where one person can write. One student is given the pages of exhibits from the instructor. The other student is not allowed to see these exhibits.

Step 2: The student holding the materials will describe each of the exhibits and the other student's task is to accurately replicate each exhibit with pencil and paper. The pair of students can compare the replication with the original at the end of each drawing. They may also switch roles for each exhibit if they wish. If roles are switched, the instructor must distribute exhibits separately to each student so that the other person does not see them. Each exhibit has a different set of limitations, as described below:

- Exhibit 1: The student describing the exhibit cannot look at the other student or his or her diagram. The student drawing the exhibit cannot speak or otherwise communicate with the person describing the exhibit.

- Exhibit 2: The student describing the exhibit may look at the other student's diagram. However, he or she may only say "yes" or "no" when the student drawing the diagram asks a specific question. In other words, the person presenting the information can only use these words and only when asked a question by the writer.

- Exhibit 3 (optional—if time permits): The student describing the exhibit may look at the other student's diagram and may provide any feedback at any time to the person replicating the exhibit.

Step 3: The class will gather to debrief this exercise. This may include discussion on the importance of feedback, the characteristics of effective feedback for individual learning, and how feedback is a form of reinforcement in behaviour modification.

ACTIVITY 2.4
TASK PERFORMANCE EXERCISE

Purpose: This exercise is designed to help you understand how specific behaviours are associated with job performance and how people may have different standards or expectations about which behaviours constitute good performance.

Instructions: The instructor will identify a job that all students know about, such as a bank teller or course instructor. Students will focus on one performance dimension, such as service skills among cafeteria cashiers, technical skills of computer lab technicians, or lecture skills of instructors. Whichever performance dimension or job is chosen for your team, the following steps apply:

Step 1: The instructor identifies a specific job and students are placed into teams (preferably of four or five people).

Step 2: Working alone, each student writes down five specific examples of effective or ineffective behaviour for the selected job and performance dimension. Each incident should clearly state the critical behaviour that made it effective or ineffective (e.g., "Instructor sat at desk during entire lecture"; "Bank teller chewed gum while talking to client"). The statements should describe behaviours, not attitudes or evaluations.

Step 3: Members of each team jointly number each statement and delete duplicates. Each behaviour statement is read aloud to the team and, without any discussion, each team member privately rates the statement using the seven-point behaviourally anchored rating scale that accompanies this exercise. When all statements have been rated, the ratings for each statement are compared. Discard statements about which team members significantly disagree (such as when ratings are two or three points apart).

Step 4: Average the ratings of the remaining statements and write them at the appropriate location on the seven-point behaviourally anchored rating scale. An arrow or line should point to the exact place on the scale where the statement's average score is located. (You may want to put the seven-point rating scale and your results on an overhead transparency or flip chart if your results will be shown to the class.)

Step 5: Each team presents its results to the class and describes areas of disagreement. Other class members discuss their agreement or disagreement with each team's results, including the quality of the statements (e.g., behaviour-oriented) and their location on the performance scale.

BEHAVIOURALLY ANCHORED RATING SCALE

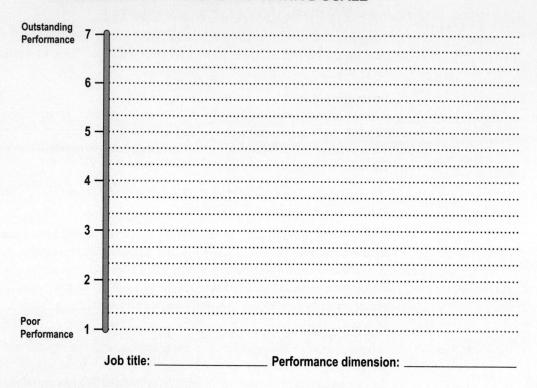

Outstanding Performance 7

6

5

4

3

2

Poor Performance 1

Job title: _____ Performance dimension: _____

ACTIVITY 2.5
ASSESSING YOUR SELF-EFFICACY

Purpose: This exercise is designed to help you understand the concept of self-efficacy and to estimate your general self-efficacy.

Overview: Self-efficacy refers to a person's belief that he or she has the ability, motivation, and situational resources to complete a task successfully. Self-efficacy is usually conceptualized as a situation-specific belief. You may believe that you can perform a certain task in one situation, but are less confident about performing that task in another situation. However, there is also evidence that people develop a more general self-efficacy that influences their beliefs in many situations. This exercise helps you to estimate your general self-efficacy.

Instructions: Read each of the statements in the scale and circle the response that best fits your personal belief. Then use the scoring key in Appendix B of this book to calculate your results. This self-assessment is completed alone so that students can rate themselves honestly without concerns of social comparison. However, class discussion will focus on the meaning of self-efficacy, how this scale might be applied in organizations, and the limitations of measuring self-efficacy in work settings.

GENERAL SELF-EFFICACY SCALE

To what extent does each statement describe you? Indicate your level of agreement by marking the appropriate response on the right.	Strongly Agree	Agree	Neutral	Disagree	Strongly Disagree
1. When I make plans, I am certain I can make them work.	❏	❏	❏	❏	❏
2. One of my problems is that I cannot get down to work when I should.	❏	❏	❏	❏	❏
3. If I can't do a job the first time, I keep trying until I can.	❏	❏	❏	❏	❏
4. When I set important goals for myself, I rarely achieve them.	❏	❏	❏	❏	❏
5. I give up on things before completing them.	❏	❏	❏	❏	❏
6. I avoid facing difficulties.	❏	❏	❏	❏	❏
7. If something looks too complicated, I will not even bother to try it.	❏	❏	❏	❏	❏
8. When I have something unpleasant to do, I stick to it until I finish it.	❏	❏	❏	❏	❏
9. When I decide to do something, I go right to work on it.	❏	❏	❏	❏	❏
10. When trying to learn something new, I soon give up if I am not initially successful.	❏	❏	❏	❏	❏
11. When unexpected problems occur, I don't handle them well.	❏	❏	❏	❏	❏
12. I avoid trying to learn new things when they look too difficult for me.	❏	❏	❏	❏	❏
13. Failure just makes me try harder	❏	❏	❏	❏	❏
14. I feel insecure about my ability to do things.	❏	❏	❏	❏	❏
15. I am a self-reliant person.	❏	❏	❏	❏	❏
16. I give up easily.	❏	❏	❏	❏	❏
17. I do not seem capable of dealing with most problems that come up in life.	❏	❏	❏	❏	❏

Source: M. Sherer, J.E. Maddox, B. Mercandante, S. Prentice-Dunn, B. Jacobs, and R.W. Rogers, "The Self-Efficacy Scale: Construction and Validation," *Psychological Reports*, 51 (1982), pp. 663–71.

CHAPTER THREE

Foundations of Employee Motivation

LEARNING OBJECTIVES

After reading this chapter, you should be able to:

- Define motivation and distinguish between content and process theories.
- Compare the four content theories of motivation.
- Discuss the practical implications of content motivation theories.
- Explain how each component of expectancy theory influences work effort.
- Discuss the practical implications of expectancy theory.
- Explain how employees react to inequity.
- Describe the five characteristics of effective goal setting.

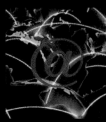

Chris Bond and Ken Zorniak are motivated by impossible challenges. They have a lot of opportunity to fulfil that need at Frantic Films, their Winnipeg-based visual effects company.

Chris Bond and his staff at Frantic Films thrive on tough challenges. "I like pushing it," says Bond, who founded the Winnipeg-based visual effects animation firm with Ken Zorniak in the late 1990s. "The bigger the project, the more difficulty there is, the more interesting it is to work on."

Joan Stephens, marketing director for Manitoba Theatre Centre, agrees that Frantic's ten employees are extremely motivated. "They're young, eager, and enthusiastic, and they seem not to need any sleep," says Stephens, who has used Frantic for several TV commercials.

The barely 30-year-old Bond and Zorniak have already been nominated for an Emmy award and have received several Canadian awards for their work. These Generation Xers want to do more than make a good living; they want to make a difference. And they don't want to wait several years before experiencing those opportunities.

Gord Mawhinney, a partner in Calgary-based CSB Systems, thinks he understands what motivates the new generation: "First off, young people have very high expectations of what they can accomplish," he advises. "The other thing is that young people really want empowerment; they want to be in on and making decisions, and they want to be challenged."

The challenge for corporate Canada is to bring these conditions into larger businesses. JC Penney, the giant U.S. retailer, thinks it has the answer. "It occurred to us that Gen-Xers will work 90 hours a week if they have their own business," explains a JC Penney executive. "So we teach managers how to allow them a little flexibility and creativity. You want to be a resource for them, but you don't want to detail everything for them."[1]

Motivation The internal forces that affect the direction, intensity, and persistence of a person's voluntary choice of behaviour.

www.franticfilms.com
www.mtc.mb.ca
www.csbsystems.com
www.jcpenney.com

Content theories of motivation Theories that explain the dynamics of employee needs, such as why people have different needs at different times.

Process theories of motivation Theories that describe the processes through which need deficiencies are translated into behaviour.

Motivation is critical to work performance and productivity. Even when people have clear work objectives, the right skills, and a supportive work environment, they won't get the job done without sufficient motivation to achieve those work objectives. **Motivation** refers to the forces within a person that affect his or her direction, intensity, and persistence of voluntary behaviour.[2] Motivated employees are willing to exert a particular level of effort (intensity) for a certain amount of time (persistence) towards a particular goal (direction).

Motivating employees has never been more challenging. One reason, as we read in the opening story, is that the workforce is changing. Generation-X employees bring different needs and expectations to the workplace than do their baby boomer counterparts.[3] Meanwhile, baby boomers' needs are shifting as they enter new stages of their lives. There is some evidence that companies have not yet adjusted to these changes. One survey indicates that only 37 percent of employees feel that their bosses know what motivates them.[4]

Motivating employees is also more challenging at a time when firms have dramatically changed the jobs that people perform, reduced layers of hierarchy, and jettisoned large numbers of employees throughout the process. These actions have significantly damaged the levels of trust and commitment necessary for employees to put out effort beyond the minimum requirements. Some organizations have completely given up on motivation from the heart and, instead, rely on financial incentives. These strategies may have some effect (both positive and negative), but they do not capitalize on the employee's motivational potential.

Lastly, as companies flatten hierarchies to reduce costs, they can no longer rely on supervisors to practise the old "command-and-control" methods of motivating employees. This is probably just as well because the traditional approach to motivating employees through close supervision is becoming less acceptable to people entering the workforce.[5] Still, many businesses have not discovered other ways to motivate employees.

In this chapter, we look at the foundations of employee motivation. Motivation theories fall into two main categories: content theories and process theories. **Content theories of motivation** explain the dynamics of employee needs, such as why people have different needs at different times. By understanding an employee's needs, we can discover the conditions that motivate that person. **Process theories of motivation** do not directly explain how needs emerge. Instead, they describe the processes through which needs are translated into behaviour. Process theories of motivation help to explain why people behave the way they do. In doing so, they help us to understand, predict, and influence employee performance, attendance, work satisfaction, and other outcomes.

CONTENT THEORIES OF MOTIVATION

Needs Deficiencies that energize or trigger behaviours to satisfy those needs.

Most contemporary theories recognize that motivation begins with individual needs. **Needs** are deficiencies that energize or trigger behaviours to satisfy those needs. At some point in your life, you might have a strong need for food and shelter. At other times, your social needs may be unfulfilled. Unfulfilled needs create a tension that makes us want to find ways to reduce or satisfy those needs. The stronger your needs are, the more motivated you are to satisfy them. Conversely, a satisfied need does not motivate.[6] In this section, we will look at the four content theories of motivation that dominate organizational thinking today.

NEEDS HIERARCHY THEORY

Needs hierarchy theory Maslow's content motivation theory of five instinctive needs arranged in a hierarchy, whereby people are motivated to fulfil a higher need as a lower one becomes gratified.

One of the earliest and best-known content theories is **needs hierarchy theory**. Developed by psychologist Abraham Maslow, this theory condenses the numerous needs that scholars have identified into a hierarchy of five basic categories.[7] At the bottom are *physiological needs,* which include the need to satisfy biological requirements for food, air, water, and shelter. Next come *safety needs*—the need for a secure and stable environment and the absence of pain, threat, or illness. *Belongingness* includes the need for love, affection, and interaction with other people. *Esteem* includes self-esteem through personal achievement as well as social esteem through recognition and respect from others. At the top of the hierarchy is *self-actualization,* which represents the need for self-fulfilment—a sense that the person's potential has been realized.

Satisfaction-progression process A process whereby people become increasingly motivated to fulfil a higher need as a lower need is gratified.

Maslow recognized that an employee's behaviour is motivated simultaneously by several need levels, but he believed that behaviour is mostly motivated by the lowest unsatisfied need at the time. As the person satisfies a lower-level need, the next higher need in the hierarchy becomes the primary motivator. This is known as the **satisfaction-progression process**. Even if a person is unable to satisfy a higher need, he or she will be motivated by it until it is eventually satisfied. Physiological needs are initially the most important and people are motivated to satisfy them first. As they become gratified, safety needs emerge as the strongest motivator. As safety needs are satisfied, belongingness needs become most important, and so forth. The exception to the satisfaction-progression process is self-actualization; as people experience self-actualization, they desire more rather than less of this need.

Maslow's needs hierarchy is one of the best-known organizational behaviour theories, but the model is much too rigid to explain the dynamic and unstable characteristics of employee needs.[8] Researchers have found that individual needs do not cluster neatly around the five categories described in the model. Moreover, gratification of one need level does not necessarily lead to increased motivation to satisfy the next higher need level. Although Maslow's model may not predict employee needs as well as scholars initially expected, it provides an important introduction to employee needs and has laid the foundation for Alderfer's ERG theory, which has better research support.

ERG THEORY

ERG theory Alderfer's content motivation theory of three instinctive needs arranged in a hierarchy, in which people progress to the next higher need when a lower one is fulfilled, and regress to a lower need if unable to fulfil a higher need.

ERG theory was developed by organizational behaviour scholar Clayton Alderfer to overcome the problems with Maslow's needs hierarchy theory.[9] ERG theory groups human needs into three broad categories: existence, relatedness, and growth. (Notice that the theory's name is based on the first letter of each need.) As Exhibit 3.1 illustrates, existence needs correspond to Maslow's physiological and safety needs. Relatedness needs refer mainly to Maslow's belongingness needs. Growth needs correspond to Maslow's esteem and self-actualization needs.

Existence needs A person's physiological and physically related safety needs, such as the need for food, shelter, and safe working conditions.

Relatedness needs A person's need to interact with other people, receive public recognition, and feel secure around people (i.e., interpersonal safety).

Growth needs A person's self-esteem through personal achievement as well as self-actualization.

Existence needs include a person's physiological and physically related safety needs, such as the need for food, shelter, and safe working conditions. **Relatedness needs** include a person's need to interact with other people, receive public recognition, and feel secure around people (i.e., interpersonal safety). **Growth needs** consist of a person's self-esteem through personal achievement as well as the concept of self-actualization presented in Maslow's model.

ERG theory states that an employee's behaviour is motivated simultaneously by more than one need level. Thus, you might try to satisfy your growth needs (such as by completing an assignment exceptionally well) even though your relatedness needs aren't completely satisfied. However, ERG theory applies the satisfaction-progression process described in Maslow's needs hierarchy model, so one need level will dominate a person's motivation more than others. As existence needs are satisfied, for example, relatedness needs become more important.

EXHIBIT 3.1   Content Theories of Motivation Compared

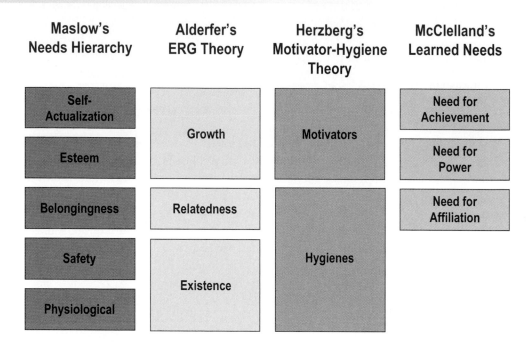

Maslow's Needs Hierarchy	Alderfer's ERG Theory	Herzberg's Motivator-Hygiene Theory	McClelland's Learned Needs
Self-Actualization	Growth	Motivators	Need for Achievement
Esteem			Need for Power
Belongingness	Relatedness	Hygienes	Need for Affiliation
Safety	Existence		
Physiological			

- **Frustration-regression process** Process whereby people who are unable to satisfy a higher need become frustrated and regress to the next lower need level.

Unlike Maslow's model, however, ERG theory includes a **frustration-regression process** whereby those who are unable to satisfy a higher need become frustrated and regress back to the next lower need level. For example, if existence and relatedness needs have been satisfied, but growth need fulfilment has been blocked, the individual will become frustrated and relatedness needs will again emerge as the dominant source of motivation.

Although not fully tested, ERG theory seems to explain the dynamics of human needs in organizations reasonably well.[10] It provides a less rigid explanation of employee needs. Human needs cluster more neatly around the three categories proposed by Alderfer than the five categories in Maslow's hierarchy. The combined processes of satisfaction-progression and frustration-regression also provide a more accurate explanation of why employee needs change over time. Overall, it seems to come closest to explaining why employees have particular needs at various times.

MOTIVATOR-HYGIENE THEORY

- **Motivator-hygiene theory** Herzberg's theory proposes that employees are primarily motivated by growth and esteem needs such as recognition, responsibility, advancement, achievement, and personal growth.

Frederick Herzberg's **motivator-hygiene theory** differs from Maslow's and Alderfer's needs hierarchy models because it does not suggest that people change their needs over time. Instead, Herzberg proposes that employees are primarily motivated by growth and esteem needs such as recognition, responsibility, advancement, achievement, and personal growth. These factors are called *motivators* because employees experience job satisfaction when they are received and are therefore motivated to obtain them. **Job satisfaction** represents a person's evaluation of his or her job and work context.[11] In contrast, factors extrinsic to the work, called *hygienes*, affect the extent to which employees feel job dissatisfaction. Hygienes include job security, working conditions, company policies, co-worker relations, and supervisor relations. Improving hygienes will reduce job dissatisfaction, but will have almost no effect on job satisfaction or employee motivation.[12]

- **Job satisfaction** A person's attitude (beliefs, assessed feelings, and behavioural intentions) regarding the job and work context.

A unique characteristic of motivator-hygiene theory is that it does not view job satisfaction and job dissatisfaction as opposites. Improving motivators increases job satisfaction, but does not decrease job dissatisfaction. Improving hygienes reduces job dissatisfaction, but does not increase job satisfaction. Moreover, job satisfaction is produced by growth fulfilment and other work content outcomes, whereas job dissatisfaction is produced by the work context. Thus, Herzberg's theory differs from Maslow's and Alderfer's hierarchy models by suggesting that growth needs represent the only source of motivation.

Limitations of motivator-hygiene theory

Motivator-hygiene theory provides a unique perspective of employee motivation, but many scholars have concluded that Herzberg's findings are mainly due to problems with the methodology he used. Other studies relying on more appropriate methods don't support Herzberg's hypothesis that work content and recognition are the only sources of employee motivation.[13]

Contrary to Herzberg's findings, hygiene factors are widely used to motivate people to join the organization, attend work on time, perform their jobs better, and learn new skills. For example, many high-technology firms have found that younger recruits are motivated as much by a "cool" work environment as by the work they will perform. The work must be interesting, but so should the workplace. Thus, many companies provide game rooms, free pizza, and plenty of opportunity for employees to customize their workspace.[14]

So, why mention Herzberg's theory here? Motivator-hygiene theory casts a spotlight on job content as a dominant source of employee motivation. Before Herzberg's work was published, many researchers were preoccupied with the physical and social contexts of work. Few writers had addressed the idea that employees may be motivated by the work itself. Motivator-hygiene theory changed this view and has led to considerable study into the motivational potential of jobs.[15] We will look more closely at motivational aspects of job design in Chapter 4.

MCCLELLAND'S THEORY OF LEARNED NEEDS

The content motivation models described so far look at the individual's primary or instinctive needs and their relative importance in life. However, people also have secondary needs or drives that are learned and reinforced through childhood learning, parental styles, and social norms. Several learned needs can motivate us at the same time. Psychologist David McClelland devoted his career to studying three secondary needs that he considered to be particularly important sources of motivation: need for achievement, need for affiliation, and need for power.

Need for achievement (nAch)

Need for achievement (nAch) A learned need that causes people to want to accomplish reasonably challenging goals through their own efforts.

The most widely studied learned need is **need for achievement (nAch)**. People with a high nAch want to accomplish reasonably challenging goals through their own efforts. They prefer working alone rather than in teams because of their strong need to assume personal responsibility for tasks. High-nAch people tend to choose tasks with a moderate degree of risk. When given a choice, they do not want work that is either too easy or nearly impossible to complete. High-nAch people also have a strong need for unambiguous feedback and recognition for their success.[16]

Research indicates that high-nAch people are mainly motivated by the expectation of satisfying their need for achievement. Money is a relatively weak motivator for them, except to the extent that it provides feedback and recognition. In contrast, employees with a low nAch perform their work better when money is used as a financial incentive.

K. Morison, Calgary Herald

www.intervisual.com

Pamela Grof is a successful entrepreneur with a strong need for achievement. Starting at the age of 12, Grof built a series of Calgary-based businesses—ranging from house cleaning to art sales—before launching InterVisual, a Web design firm. InterVisual quickly developed a blue-chip client list, expanded into Toronto, and is moving into the United States and United Kingdom. Where did Grof develop her strong need for achievement? "I come from an entrepreneurial family," Grof explains. "I have two brothers and my father who are all in business for themselves. I very much have that business side within me."[17] If need for achievement is learned, how might this need be developed later in life?

A substantial body of research has found that successful entrepreneurs tend to have a high nAch. This is possibly because high-nAch people establish challenging goals for themselves and thrive on competition.[18] Corporate and team leaders should have a somewhat lower nAch because they must delegate work and build support through involvement (characteristics not usually found in high achievers). However, high-nAch people may perform well in large companies where they are given considerable independence—as though they are running their own businesses.[19]

One of the most fascinating streams of research on need for achievement has been its effect on the economic growth and decline of civilizations. One study measured nAch in stories in children's primary-school readers and found that nAch scores were associated with economic growth in those countries over the next 20 years. Another study that estimated nAch in popular literature in Europe between 1400 and 1830 found that a rise in nAch preceded economic growth by as much as 50 years. A third study reported that nAch (as measured by fourth-grade readers) predicted the number of patents recorded in the United States between 1800 and 1950.[20] Overall, there is convincing evidence that need for achievement is learned, and that this need has a powerful influence on the success of organizations and societies.

Need for affiliation (nAff)

> **Need for affiliation (nAff)** A desire to seek approval from others, conform to their wishes and expectations, and avoid conflict and confrontation.

Need for affiliation (nAff) refers to a desire to seek approval from others, conform to their wishes and expectations, and avoid conflict and confrontation. People with a strong nAff want to form positive relationships with others. They try to project a favourable image of themselves and take other steps to be liked by others. Moreover, high-nAff employees actively support others and try to smooth out conflicts that occur in meetings and other social settings. As Exhibit 3.1 (see page 64) illustrates, need for affiliation is similar to Maslow's belongingness need and Alderfer's relatedness need. The main difference is that need for affiliation is learned rather than instinctive.

High-nAff employees tend to be more effective than those with a low nAff in coordinating roles, such as helping diverse departments work on joint projects. They are also more effective in sales positions where the main task is cultivating long-term relations with prospective customers. More generally, employees with high nAff prefer working with others rather than alone, tend to have better attendance records, and tend to be better at mediating conflicts.

Although people with a high nAff are more effective in many jobs requiring social interaction, they tend to be less effective at allocating scarce resources and making other decisions that potentially generate conflict. For example, research has found that executives with a high nAff tend to be indecisive and are perceived as less fair in the distribution of resources. Thus, people in decision-making positions must have a relatively low need for affiliation so that their choices and actions are not biased by a personal need for approval.[21]

Need for power (nPow)

Need for power (nPow) A desire to control one's environment, including people and material resources.

Need for power (nPow) refers to a desire to control one's environment, including people and material resources. People with a high nPow want to exercise control over others and are concerned about maintaining their leadership position. They frequently rely on persuasive communication (see Chapter 8), make more suggestions in meetings, and tend to publicly evaluate situations more frequently. Some people have a high need for *personalized power*. They enjoy their power for its own sake and use it to advance their career and other personal interests. Others mainly have a high need for *socialized power*. They want power as a means to help others, such as by improving society or increasing organizational effectiveness.[22]

Some corporate leaders claim to have a socialized need for power, but they privately view the power of their position as a reward. It is a status symbol and a tool to fulfil personal needs more than a delicate instrument to serve stakeholders.[23] You can see personalized power in action when supervisors and senior executives are reluctant to involve employees in decisions or otherwise share power with them. In more extreme cases, a personal need for power leads to illegal diversion of corporate resources as well as the psychological and sexual abuse of subordinates (see Chapter 12).[24]

Corporate and political leaders have a high nPow because this motivates them to influence others—an important part of the leadership process (see Chapter 14).[25] However, McClelland argues that effective leaders should have a high need for socialized rather than personalized power. These leaders have a high degree of altruism and social responsibility and are concerned about the consequences of their own actions on others. In other words, leaders must exercise their power within the framework of moral standards. The ethical guidance of their need for power develops follower trust and respect for the leader, as well as commitment to the leader's vision.[26]

Learned needs

McClelland argued that achievement, affiliation, and power needs are learned rather than instinctive. Accordingly, he developed training programs that strengthen these needs. In his achievement motivation program, trainees practise writing achievement-oriented stories after reading others and practise achievement-oriented behaviours in business games. They also complete a detailed achievement plan for the next two years and form a reference group with other trainees to maintain their new-found achievement motive style.[27]

These programs seem to work. For example, need achievement course participants in India subsequently started more new businesses, had greater community involvement, invested

Barbara Moses shakes her head at some of the half-baked ideas that employers have come up with to motivate staff. The Toronto-based workplace consultant and best-selling author of *The Good News About Careers: How You'll Be Working in the Next Decade* (Stoddart, 1999) recalls what happened when one company awarded an alarm clock bearing the company's logo to a few select employees. "It completely turned them off," Moses says. "People were saying: 'I work for them, I don't want to wake up to them.'" Moses argues that the problem isn't just the choice of awards; it's giving the same reward to everyone. The best thing for an employer to do, she suggests, "is be savvy in not using a one-size-fits-all approach."[28] How can employers ensure that employees receive valued rewards for their performance?

www.bbmcareerdev.com

more in expanding their businesses, and employed twice as many people as nonparticipants. Research on similar achievement-motive courses for North American small business owners reported dramatic increases in the profitability of the participants' businesses.

PRACTICAL IMPLICATIONS OF CONTENT MOTIVATION THEORIES

Content theories of motivation suggest that different people have different needs at different times. Some employees are ready to fulfil growth needs, whereas others are still struggling to satisfy their minimum existence needs. Needs change as people enter new stages of their lives.

Most organizations distribute the same reward, such as a salary increase or paid time off, to all employees with good performance. But rewards that motivate some people have less effect on others. Thus, content motivation theories advise organizations to offer employees a choice of rewards. This is what Nortel Networks does when rewarding length of service. At each five-year service level, employees are offered a choice of awards, including fine art and sculptures, jewellery, timepieces, luggage, and leather portfolios. Moreover, the Canadian maker of Internet gear includes a survey with the award, asking employees how future awards can meet their needs better.[29]

Content theories of motivation also warn us against relying too heavily on financial rewards as a source of employee motivation.[30] Chapter 4 will describe how money does motivate employees to some extent. At the same time, there are potentially more powerful sources of motivation, such as challenging assignments, learning opportunities, and praise from colleagues and corporate leaders. For instance, most software programmers make good money, but their real reward seems to be the respect and fun of hiding Easter eggs in their software. As Connections 3.1 describes, these nuggets of graphical graffiti satisfy a programmer's need for recognition by peers or users. The point here is that organizations must recognize nonfinancial as well as financial sources of motivation.

PROCESS THEORIES OF MOTIVATION

At the beginning of this chapter we distinguished the content theories presented above from process theories of motivation. Content theories explain why people have different needs at different times, whereas process theories describe the processes through which need deficiencies are translated into behaviour. Three of the most popular process theories of motivation are expectancy theory, equity theory, and goal setting.

CONNECTIONS 3.1

Fulfilling Needs Through Cyber Easter Eggs

7.5.3 Core Project Team: Bala Akella, Wendy Chiou, Doug Clarke, Mike Crawford, Michael...

Hidden in one version of the Macintosh operating system is an elaborate Easter egg showing Apple's headquarters.

Computer programmers like a good paycheque, but they love the recognition found in Easter eggs. Easter eggs are nuggets of graphical graffiti left behind by programmers in most software programs. Click in the right place or type in a special command and a special message or image will appear.

Some Easter eggs are the inspiration of individual programmers who gain respect by cleverly sneaking them by the quality inspectors. Others are created by the entire development team to fulfil its need for public recognition.

Excel 97, Microsoft's popular spreadsheet package, has a hidden flight simulator. Fly across its landscape to the right mountain and you can see a list of the programmers' names.

One version of the Macintosh operating system had perhaps the most elaborate Easter egg ever created. By dragging a special phrase onto the desktop, the operating system revealed a virtual-reality image of Apple's headquarters, complete with a flag that waved in the direction of the user's mouse. The names of Apple Computer employees scrolled across the bottom of the image.

In spite of the popularity of cyber Easter eggs, software companies are forcing programmers to fulfil their needs in other ways. Microsoft's Windows 2000 operating system is so businesslike that programmers are strictly forbidden from adding Easter eggs to the software. Apple is also discouraging Easter eggs and has banned the practice of listing everyone's name in the company's products.

"Just as the rainbow of colours have been drained out of the original Apple logo, some of the spirit has drained of the teams who took comfort in the credit they received at the end of a project," warns a software industry observer.

Sources: L. Kahney, "Taking the Fun Out of Win2000," *Wired News,* February 16, 2000 (online); "Cracking Open the Eggs," *The Economist,* December 18, 1999; D. Claymon, "Apple Tradition Dies as Named Credits End," *Arizona Republic,* December 6, 1999, p. E5; L. Gornstein, "Software Harbors Treasures," *Arizona Republic,* March 9, 1998, p. E1; T. Standage "Easter Eggs Beyond a Joke," *Daily Telegraph* (London), February 19, 1998, p. 4. Some information was also collected from the Web site http://www.eeggs.com.

EXPECTANCY THEORY OF MOTIVATION

Expectancy theory A process motivation theory stating that work effort is directed towards behaviours that people believe will lead to desired outcomes.

Expectancy theory is a process motivation theory based on the idea that work effort is directed towards behaviours that people believe will lead to desired outcomes.[31] Through experience, we develop expectations about whether we can achieve various levels of job performance. We also develop expectations about whether job performance and work behaviours lead to particular outcomes. Finally, we naturally direct our effort towards outcomes that help us fulfil our needs.

EXPECTANCY THEORY MODEL

The expectancy theory model is presented in Exhibit 3.2. The key variable of interest in expectancy theory is *effort*—the individual's actual exertion of energy. An individual's effort level depends on three factors: effort-to-performance (E→P) expectancy, performance-to-outcome (P→O) expectancy, and outcome valences (V). Employee motivation is influenced by all three components of the expectancy theory model. If any component weakens, motivation weakens.

E→P expectancy

Effort-to-performance (E→P) expectancy An individual's perceived probability that a particular level of effort will result in a particular level of performance.

The **effort-to-performance (E→P) expectancy** is the individual's perception that his or her effort will result in a particular level of performance. Expectancy is defined as a *probability*, and therefore ranges from 0.0 to 1.0. In some situations, employees may believe that they can unquestionably accomplish the task (a probability of 1.0). In other situations, they expect that even their highest level of effort will not result in the desired performance level (a probability of 0.0). For instance, many people aren't motivated to try some of the black diamond ski runs at Whistler Mountain because even their best effort won't get them down the hill feet first! In most cases, the E→P expectancy falls somewhere between these two extremes.

P→O expectancy

Performance-to-outcome (P→O) expectancy An individual's perceived probability that a specific behaviour or performance level will lead to specific outcomes.

The **performance-to-outcome (P→O) expectancy** is the perceived probability that a specific behaviour or performance level will lead to specific outcomes. This probability is developed from previous learning. For example, students learn from experience that skipping class for a particular course either ruins their chance of a good grade or has no effect at all. In extreme

EXHIBIT 3.2 Expectancy Theory of Motivation

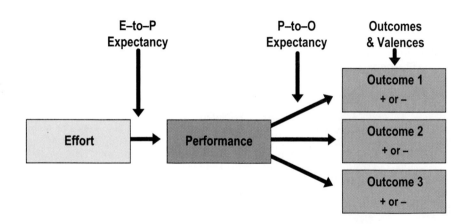

cases, employees may believe that accomplishing a particular task (performance) will *definitely* result in a particular outcome (a probability of 1.0), or they may believe that this outcome will have *no effect* on successful performance (a probability of 0.0). More often, the P→O expectancy falls somewhere between these two extremes.

One important issue in P→O expectancies is which outcomes do we think about? We certainly don't evaluate the P→O expectancy for every possible outcome. There are too many of them. Instead, we only think about outcomes of interest to us at the time. One day, your motivation to complete a task may be fuelled mainly by the likelihood of getting off work early to meet friends. Other times, your motivation to complete the same task may be based more on the P→O expectancy of a promotion or pay increase. The main point is that your motivation depends on the probability that a behaviour or job performance level will result in outcomes that you think about.

Outcome valences

Valence The anticipated satisfaction or dissatisfaction that an individual feels towards an outcome.

The third element in expectancy theory is the **valence** of each outcome that you consider. Valence refers to the anticipated satisfaction or dissatisfaction that an individual feels towards an outcome. It ranges from negative to positive. (The actual range doesn't matter; it may be from −1 to +1, or from −100 to +100.) An outcome valence is determined by the strength of the person's basic needs that are associated with the outcome. Outcomes have a positive valence when they directly or indirectly satisfy our needs, and have a negative valence when they inhibit need fulfilment. If you have a strong relatedness (social) need, for example, you would value group activities and other events that help to fulfil that need. Outcomes that move you further away from fulfilling your social need—such as working alone in your home—will have a strong negative valence.

Notice that some outcomes directly fulfil personal needs, whereas other outcomes indirectly fulfil those needs. You might be motivated to achieve the highest sales in your company this month because "it feels great." This is the direct outcome of growth need fulfilment. At the same time, you might want to be the top salesperson because you will be mentioned in the company magazine, thereby indirectly fulfilling your social needs.

EXPECTANCY THEORY IN PRACTICE

One of the appealing characteristics of expectancy theory is that it provides clear guidelines for increasing employee motivation by altering a person's E→P expectancies, P→O expectancies, and/or outcome valences.[32] Several practical implications of expectancy theory are listed in Exhibit 3.3 and described below.

Increasing E→P expectancies

E→P expectancies are based on self-esteem and previous experience in that situation.[33] Consequently, employees should be given the necessary competencies, clear role perceptions, and sufficient resources to reach the desired levels of performance so that they form higher E→P expectancies. This involves properly matching employees to jobs based on their abilities, clearly communicating the tasks required for the job, and providing sufficient resources for them to accomplish those tasks.

Even when employees have the capacity and resources to perform the work, they may have low E→P expectancies because of low self-efficacy. Counselling and coaching may help employees develop confidence that they already possess the skills and knowledge to perform the job. Similarly, E→P expectancies are learned, so positive feedback typically strengthens

EXHIBIT 3.3   Practical Applications of Expectancy Theory

EXPECTANCY THEORY COMPONENT	OBJECTIVE	APPLICATIONS
E→P Expectancies	To increase the belief that employees are capable of performing the job successfully	• Select people with the required skills and knowledge. • Provide required training and clarify job requirements. • Provide sufficient time and resources. • Assign simpler or fewer tasks until employees can master them. • Provide examples of similar employees who have successfully performed the task. • Provide counselling and coaching to employees who lack self-confidence.
P→O Expectancies	To increase the belief that good performance will result in certain (valued) outcomes	• Measure job performance accurately. • Clearly explain the outcomes that will result from successful performance. • Describe how the employee's rewards were based on past performance. • Provide examples of other employees whose good performance has resulted in higher rewards.
Valences of Outcomes	To increase the expected value of outcomes resulting from desired performance	• Distribute rewards that employees value. • Individualize rewards. • Minimize the presence of countervalent outcomes.

employee self-efficacy.[34] Positive reinforcement and behavioural modelling also tend to increase E→P expectancies in many situations.

Increasing P→O expectancies

The most obvious ways to improve P→O expectancies are to measure employee performance accurately and distribute more valued rewards to those with higher job performance. Many organizations have difficulty putting this straightforward idea into practice. Some executives are reluctant to withhold rewards for poor performance because they don't want to experience conflict with employees. Others don't measure employee performance very well. For instance, the Canadian government's Human Resources Development Department consistently paid its managers and executives performance bonuses even though a scathing audit revealed dismal record keeping and mismanagement of $1 billion in job creation funds.[35] Chapter 4 looks in more detail at reasons why rewards aren't connected to job performance.

For most of this century, Japanese employees have had lifetime employment and a seniority-based pay system. Expectancy theory suggests that this reward system won't motivate employees. However, this system, along with Japanese cultural values, creates loyalty, which motivates employees to work long hours. Now, some Japanese firms are questioning the value of rewarding employees for their age. During Japan's recent economic recession, NEC, Fujitsu, and other companies introduced performance-based incentives for most employees. "The times of endless growth are over, and so are the lifetime employment and seniority wage systems that took growth for granted," says an executive at Toyota Motor company.[37] Do you think that performance-based pay will motivate Japanese employees more or less than the system of lifetime job security and seniority-based pay?

P→O expectancies are perceptions, so employees should *believe* that higher performance will result in higher rewards. Having a performance-based reward system is important, but this fact must be communicated. When rewards are distributed, employees should understand how their rewards have been based on past performance. More generally, companies need to regularly communicate the existence of a performance-based reward system through examples, anecdotes, and public ceremonies.

Increasing outcome valences

Performance outcomes influence work effort only when they are valued by employees.[36] This brings us back to a conclusion of the content theories of motivation, namely, that companies must pay attention to the needs and reward preferences of individual employees. They should develop more individualized reward systems so that employees who perform well are offered a choice of rewards.

Expectancy theory also emphasizes the need to discover and neutralize countervalent outcomes. These are performance outcomes that have negative valences, thereby reducing the effectiveness of existing reward systems. For example, peer pressure may cause some employees to perform their jobs at the minimum standard even though formal rewards and the job itself would otherwise motivate them to perform at higher levels.

DOES EXPECTANCY THEORY FIT REALITY?

global.toyota.com

Expectancy theory has been a difficult model to test because it must recognize almost every possible performance level and outcome that employees could imagine. Most of the early studies also suffered from measurement and research design problems.[38] Some critics have suggested that expectancy theory is an imperfect theory because it doesn't predict spontaneous behaviours (such as making a rude remark to a co-worker).[39] One could argue that expectancy theory accounts for spontaneous behaviours because they are learned from past experience, but expectancy theory requires further clarification on this point.

In spite of its limitations, expectancy theory offers one of the best models available for predicting work effort and motivation. For example, expectancy theory predicts a person's motivation to use a decision support system, leave the organization, and work with less effort in a group setting.[40] All three components of the model have received some research support. There is particularly good evidence that P→O expectancies influence employee motivation.

EQUITY THEORY

Barb Nuttall felt that she wasn't being paid fairly as a Canada Safeway cashier in Regina, Saskatchewan. Nuttall noticed that most of the food retailer's cashiers are women and that they are paid about 35 cents an hour less than the mostly male food clerks. Both jobs have similar value and require a lot of lifting. In fact, cashiers handle money, so this higher responsibility should make their job worth more to Safeway. With these concerns in mind, Nuttal and other Safeway cashiers fought to have their pay increased to the same level as food clerks. The Saskatchewan Human Rights Commission became involved and Canada Safeway recently negotiated a collective agreement that would raise cashier salaries in line with those of food clerks.[41]

Canada Safeway's cashiers experienced the emotional tension created by feelings of inequity, which motivated them to act on those emotions. **Equity theory** explains how people develop perceptions of fairness in the distribution and exchange of resources. As a process theory of motivation, it explains what employees are motivated to do when they feel inequitably treated. At Canada Safeway, perceived inequities motivated cashiers to complain and try to change the source of the perceived inequity. Let's look more closely at the four main elements of equity theory: outcome/input ratio, comparison other, equity evaluation, and consequences of inequity.[42]

> • **Equity theory** A process motivation theory that explains how people develop perceptions of fairness in the distribution and exchange of resources.

OUTCOME/INPUT RATIO

The outcome/input ratio is the value of the outcomes you receive divided by the value of inputs you provide in the exchange relationship. Inputs include skills, effort, experience, amount of time worked, performance results, and other employee contributions to the organization. Employees see their inputs as investments into the exchange relationship. For Canada Safeway cashiers, these inputs included their level of responsibility, amount of lifting, and other factors. Outcomes are the things employees receive from the organization in exchange for the inputs, such as pay, promotions, recognition, or an office with a window.

Both inputs and outcomes are weighted by their importance to the individual. These weights vary from one person to the next. To some people, seniority is a valuable input that deserves more organizational outcomes in return. Others consider job effort and performance to be the most important contributions in the exchange relationship, and give seniority relatively little weight. Similarly, equity theory recognizes that people value outcomes differently because they have different needs. For example, it accepts that some employees want time off with pay whereas others consider this to be a relatively insignificant reward for job performance.

COMPARISON OTHER

Equity theory states that we compare our situation with a comparison other.[43] However, the theory does not identify the comparison other. It may be another person, a group of people, or even you in the past. It may be someone in the same job, another job, or another organization. Most of the time, we tend to compare ourselves with others who are nearby, in similar positions, and with similar backgrounds.[44] In our earlier example, Canada Safeway cashiers in Saskatchewan compared themselves with food clerks, who work near the cashiers. This probably occurs because it is easier to get information about co-workers than about people working elsewhere.

People in more senior positions compare themselves more with their counterparts in other organizations. Chief executive officers have no direct comparison within the firm, so they tend to compare themselves with CEOs in other organizations. This explains why one-third of Canadian executives state that they are underpaid whereas many of us would disagree with that view![45] They compare themselves to other CEOs, including their higher-paid counterparts

"I'm paid $4,000,000 a year. You're paid $40,000. The only difference is a few zeros. Everyone knows that zero equals nothing. So what's the problem?"

in the United States, whereas we might compare their salaries to ours. Some research suggests that employees frequently collect information on several referents to form a "generalized" comparison other.[46] For the most part, however, the comparison other varies from one person to the next and is not easily identifiable.

EQUITY EVALUATION

We form an equity evaluation after determining our own outcome/input ratio and comparing this with the comparison other's ratio. Let's consider the Canada Safeway cashiers again. The cashiers feel *underreward inequity* because the food clerks receive higher outcomes (pay) for inputs that are, at best, comparable to what the cashiers contribute. This condition is illustrated in Exhibit 3.4(a).

In the *equity condition*, the cashiers would believe that their outcome/input ratio is similar to the food clerks' ratio. If the cashiers feel that they provide the same inputs as the clerks, they would feel equity if both job groups received the same pay and other outcomes (see Exhibit 3.4(b)). If the cashiers claim they make a greater contribution because they have more responsibility, they would have feelings of equity only if they receive proportionally more pay than the food clerks receive.

Lastly, it is possible that some Canada Safeway food clerks experience *overreward inequity* (see Exhibit 4.3(c)). The food clerks feel that their jobs have the same value as the cashiers, yet they earn more money. However, as we learn next, overreward inequity isn't as common as underreward inequity.

The equity theory model recognizes that you make more complex equity evaluations where you and the comparison other have different outcomes and inputs. By comparing outcome/input *ratios*, the model states that equity occurs when the amount of inputs and outcomes are

EXHIBIT 3.4   Equity Theory Model

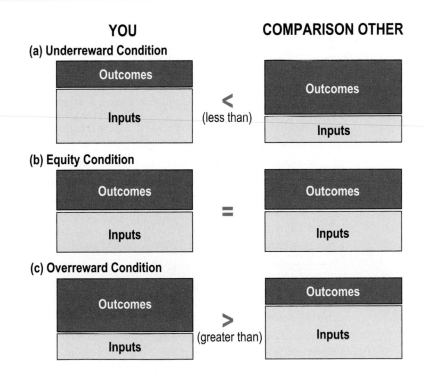

proportional. They don't necessarily have the same amount. For instance, we feel equitably treated when we work harder than the comparison other and receive proportionally higher rewards as a result.

CONSEQUENCES OF INEQUITY

What happens when people feel inequity in the workplace? Canada Safeway cashiers in Saskatchewan successfully reduced the uncomfortable tension by putting pressure on the company to increase their pay to the level of food clerks. This is one of six possible ways to reduce feelings of inequity:[47]

- *Changing inputs*—Underrewarded workers tend to reduce their effort and performance if these outcomes don't affect their paycheques. Overpaid workers sometimes (but not very often) increase their inputs by working harder and producing more.

- *Changing outcomes*—People experiencing underreward inequity might ask for more desired outcomes, such as a pay increase. If this does not work, some are motivated to join a labour union and demand these changes at the bargaining table.[48] Others misuse sick leave for more paid time off. At the extreme, some people steal company property or use facilities for personal use as ways to increase their outcomes.[49]

- *Changing perceptions*—Employees may distort inputs and outcomes to restore equity feelings.[50] Overrewarded employees typically follow this strategy because it's easier to increase their perceived inputs (seniority, knowledge, etc.) than to ask for less pay! As Canadian author Pierre Burton once said: "I was underpaid for the first half of my life. I don't mind being overpaid for the second half."[51]

- *Leaving the field*—Some people try to reduce feelings of inequity by getting away from the inequitable situation. Thus, equity theory explains some instances of employee turnover and job transfer. It also explains why an underrewarded employee might take more time off work even though he or she is not paid for this absenteeism.

- *Acting on the comparison other*—Equity is sometimes restored by changing the comparison other's inputs or outcomes. If you feel overrewarded, you might encourage the referent to work at a more leisurely pace. If you feel underrewarded, you might subtly suggest that the overpaid co-worker should be doing a larger share of the workload.

- *Changing the comparison other*—If we can't alter the outcome/input ratio through other means, we might eventually replace the comparison other with someone having a more compatible outcome/input ratio. As was mentioned earlier, we sometimes rely on a generalized comparison other, so adjusting the features of this composite referent may reduce feelings of inequity fairly easily.

The ethics of inequity

Inequity in the workplace extends beyond employee motivation to the organization's ethical conduct. In fact, a fundamental ethical principle, called the *distributive justice rule*, applies to the concept of equity and equality.[52] Specifically, this principle suggests that inequality is acceptable if (1) everyone has equal access to the more favoured positions in society, and (2) the inequalities are ultimately in the best interest of the least well off in society. The first part means that everyone should have equal access to higher-paying jobs and other valued positions in life. The second part says that some people can receive greater rewards than others if this benefits those who are less well off. Employees in risky jobs should be paid more if this benefits others who are less well off.

Applying the distributive justice rule is challenging because it is difficult to determine how much "the least well off" benefit from those who receive higher rewards. Consider the business jet and US$200 million bonus that Steve Jobs received for turning around Apple Computer. If Jobs hadn't stepped in as CEO, Apple might be history today. Instead, it grew faster than most other computer makers. Does this make Jobs' bonus fair or ethical? The same question can be asked about the paycheques of Canadian bank executives. As Connections 3.2 explains, some people claim that Canada's bank executives are paid too much. Bankers, on the other hand, say they are fairly paid because they earn less than American bank executives.

EQUITY THEORY IN PRACTICE

Equity theory has received considerable support in research and practice. Organizational behaviour researchers have applied the equity theory model to explain why baseball players change teams, why employees steal from their employer, why people become hostile at work, and why employees engage in numerous other behaviours.[53] One of the clearest lessons from equity theory is that we continually need to treat people fairly in the distribution of organizational rewards. If feelings of inequity are sufficiently strong, employees may put less effort into the job, leave the organization, steal resources or time (e.g., absenteeism), or join a labour union to correct these inequities.

www.caldwellsecurities.com
www.bankofmontreal.com www.royalbank.com

CONNECTIONS 3.2

Ethics of Fair Pay Among Canada's Bank Executives

Matthew Barrett is widely recognized for turning the Bank of Montreal into one of the best-performing financial institutions in Canada. But the $21 million payout he received after quitting as CEO has left some people wondering about the ethics of bank executive pay. "[Matthew Barrett has] done a good work," says Tom Caldwell, president of Toronto-based investment firm Caldwell Securities. "Whether the man should be canonized or not, that's another matter."

What is a fair level of pay for corporate executives? Plato, the Greek philosopher, felt that no one in a community should earn more than five times the salary of the lowest paid worker. In the 1970s, management guru Peter Drucker suggested that 20 times the lowest worker's earnings was more reasonable. Bankers cherish Drucker's wisdom on many issues, but not on the ethics of fair pay. Royal Bank of Canada CEO John Cleghorn recently took home $6.7 million—well over 100 times the average (not the lowest) bank employee salary.

Quebec politician and retired journalist Yves Michaud has tried unsuccessfully to have shareholders limit bank executive salaries to 20 times that of the average bank employee. But Cleghorn and other bankers argue that they are paid fairly. "We look at the market," Cleghorn explains. "And if we didn't pay market value, we wouldn't be able to attract, let alone keep talent—and I'm no different."

Sources: R. Blackwell, "Banks Give Shareholders a Voice," *Globe and Mail*, March 3, 2000, p. B10; J. Stevenson, "Royal Bank Chairman Faces Tough Day of Questioning Despite Record Quarterly Profits," *Vancouver Sun*, February 24, 2000; J. Stevenson, "Barrett's Golden Handshake," *Halifax Chronicle-Herald*, January 12, 2000; T. Fennell, "Battling the Banks," *Maclean's*, January 27, 1997, p. 52.

Unfortunately, maintaining feelings of equity is not an easy task. Employees have different opinions regarding which inputs should be rewarded (e.g., seniority versus performance) and which outcomes are more valuable than others.[54] Moreover, as the workplace becomes more diverse, organizations are developing customized employment relationships. For example, many firms give employees with family obligations more flexible work hours. However, some people who do not have families feel that this privilege is unfair to them. We can try to improve equity perceptions by telling employees how rewards are distributed, but we also need to understand the inputs and outcomes that are most important to people.

GOAL SETTING

Goals The immediate or ultimate objectives that employees are trying to accomplish from their work effort.

Goal setting The process of motivating employees and clarifying their role perceptions by establishing performance objectives.

Management-by-objectives (MBO) A formal, participative goal-setting process in which organizational objectives are cascaded down to work units and individual employees.

Mitel Corp, the Ottawa-based maker of telephone network gear, has a secret weapon to keep project deadlines on time. An enormous digital clock—two metres long and 30 centimetres tall—placed in the cafeteria measures everything from tenths of a second to days in a year. Beside the clock is a whiteboard that lists interim deadlines for all major projects. Whenever a team misses a deadline, Stephen Quesnelle, Mitel's head of quality programs, puts a red slash through the date for everyone to see. "If you miss your deadline, it goes on the board," warns Quesnelle. Employees initially complained, but the results have silenced the critics. Mitel's average length of product development has dropped from 70 to 50 weeks.[55]

Mitel and other organizations have discovered that goal setting is one of the most effective theories of motivation in organizations.[56] **Goals** are the immediate or ultimate objectives that employees are trying to accomplish with their work effort. **Goal setting** is the process of motivating employees and clarifying their role perceptions by establishing performance objectives. Notice that goal setting potentially improves employee performance in two ways: (1) by stretching the intensity and persistence of effort, and (2) by giving employees clearer role perceptions so that their effort is channelled towards behaviours that will improve work performance.

Some companies apply goal setting through a formal process known as **management-by-objectives (MBO)**. There are a few variations of MBO programs, but they generally identify organizational objectives, then cascade them down to work units and individual employees.[57] Employees are actively involved with their supervisors in goal formation as well as clarifying the means to reach the agreed-upon goals. MBO also includes periodic review and feedback. Although the process frequently creates too much paperwork, MBO can be an effective application of goal setting in some parts of the organization.

CHARACTERISTICS OF EFFECTIVE GOALS

Goal setting is more complex than simply telling someone to "do your best." Instead, organizational behaviour scholars have identified five conditions, shown in Exhibit 3.5, necessary to maximize task effort and performance.[58]

Specific goals

Employees put more effort into a task when they work towards specific goals rather than "do your best" targets. Specific goals have measurable levels of change over a specific time, such as "reduce scrap rate by 7 percent over the next six months." Specific goals communicate more precise performance expectations, so employees can direct their effort more efficiently and reliably.

Results-oriented goals

Results-oriented goals improve work performance more than process-oriented goals. A results-oriented goal is one that directly refers to the person's job performance, such as the number of

Bud Kanke, founder of Kanke Seafood Restaurants, doesn't rely on incentives alone to motivate staff. Instead, he talks a lot about "stretching" his 250 staff members by setting challenging goals. For example, every manager and chef at the Vancouver restaurant group (which owns Joe Fortes restaurant) fills out a two-page goal planner that motivates them to achieve corporate goals. "Setting and achieving goals is the highest and most effective form of self-motivation that exists," says Kanke. Reaching your goals, he argues, generates self-satisfaction and confidence, which spills over to co-workers.[61] What conditions are necessary to make the goal-setting process at Kanke Seafood Restaurants work effectively?

customers served per hour. Process-oriented goals refer to the work processes used to get the job done, such as finding ways to reduce the number of errors in an application form. Research indicates that process-oriented goals encourage employees to think about different ways to get the job done, but seem to block them from choosing one method and getting on with the job. Therefore, results-oriented goals tend to be more effective.

Challenging goals

Employees tend to have more intense and persistent work effort when they have challenging rather than easy goals. Challenging goals also fulfil a person's need for achievement or growth needs when the goal is achieved.[59] Many organizations use "stretch" goals—goals that are challenging enough to stretch the employee's abilities and motivation towards peak performance. "We set stretch goals that many people thought to be impossible, and we made those goals part of our culture," explains John Chambers, CEO of Cisco Systems. Stretch goals are effective if employees receive the necessary resources to accomplish them and do not become overstressed in the process.[60]

Goal commitment

Of course, there are limits to challenging goals. At some point, a goal becomes so difficult that employees are no longer committed to achieving it. At that point, work effort falls dramatically, as we see in Exhibit 3.6. This is the same as the E→P expectancy that we learned about in the section on

---

EXHIBIT 3.5   Characteristics of Effective Goal Setting

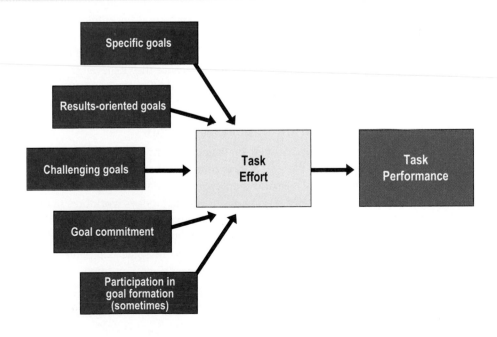

EXHIBIT 3.6 Effect of Goal Difficulty on Performance

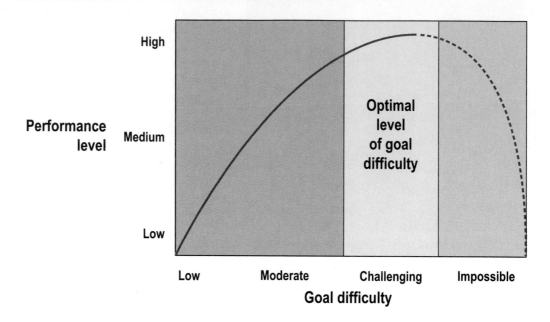

Performance level

High

Medium

Low

Optimal level of goal difficulty

Low   Moderate   Challenging   Impossible

Goal difficulty

expectancy theory.[62] The lower the E→P expectancy that the goal can been accomplished is, the less committed (motivated) the employee is to the goal.

The optimal level of goal difficulty is the area in which it is challenging but employees are still committed to achieving the goal.[63] John Westrum, founder and CEO of Westrum Development Co., tries to maintain this balance between challenge and commitment by establishing intermediate goals. When the initial goals are accomplished for two years in a row, then employees at the home-building firm agree to "raise the bar" by moving to more challenging goals. "If you set unrealistic goals in the beginning, people will be discouraged," advises Westrum.[64]

Another influence on goal commitment is the employee's **self-efficacy**. Recall from Chapter 2 that high self-efficacy employees have a "can-do" attitude. They are confident that they can perform the tasks facing them. There is some evidence that high self-efficacy employees are more likely to accept their goals because they believe they can choose successful strategies to reach those goals.[65] Those with low self-efficacy, on the other hand, tend to be in a panic when given a unique goal where the means to achieve that goal isn't obvious.

Self-efficacy A person's belief that he or she has the ability, motivation, and resources to complete a task successfully.

Participation in goal formation

Another way to build or maintain commitment to goals is to ensure that employees are involved in the goal-setting process.[66] Participation in goal formation tends to increase goal commitment because employees take ownership of the goal, compared to goals that are merely assigned by supervisors. In fact, today's workforce increasingly expects to be involved in goal setting and other decisions that affect them. Participation may also improve goal quality, because employees have valuable information and knowledge that may not be known to those who initially formed the goal. In some companies, for example, employees review future goals to identify resource needs and conditions that may interfere with goal accomplishment. This process ensures that employees buy into those goals and have the competencies and resources necessary to accomplish them.

As part of its goal-setting process, employees at Raytheon Corp.'s Defense Systems and Electronics Group engage in a form of "catchball" to ensure that the goals are appropriate and employees are committed to them. After a team proposes a goal (such as improving product reliability), each person in the work process "receives" the goal and decides whether it is acceptable. Any barriers to goal accomplishment are documented and sent along with the goal to the next person in the work process. The team that developed the goal receives the final documentation and determines whether the goal will be adjusted.[68] When is this "catchball" process most important in goal setting?

Implicit learning The experiential phenomenon of acquiring information about relationships in the environment without any conscious attempt to do so.

Goal feedback

Feedback is another necessary condition for effective goal setting. As we discussed in Chapter 2, feedback is a powerful source of learning. In terms of goal setting, feedback lets us know whether we have achieved the goal or are properly directing our efforts towards it. Feedback is also an essential ingredient in motivation because our growth needs cannot be satisfied unless we receive information on goal accomplishment.

GOAL SETTING APPLICATIONS AND LIMITATIONS

Goal setting is one of the "tried and true" theories in organizational behaviour. It is widely supported by research and is generally successful in practice. However, we must keep the contingency approach to organizational behaviour in mind. Goal setting does not work for everyone in every situation.

One problem with goal setting is that when goals are tied to monetary incentives, some employees are motivated to select easy rather than difficult goals.[67] In some cases, employees have negotiated goals with their supervisors that have already been completed! Employees with high self-efficacy and need for achievement tend to set challenging goals whether or not they are financially rewarded for their results. However, employers should typically separate goal setting from the pay-setting process.[69]

A second concern is that goal setting can interfere with job performance on new or complex tasks.[70] The best explanation we have for this is that working on a new or complex task requires a large amount of **implicit learning** (as we discussed in Chapter 2). We use our unconscious learning strategies to sort out the best work processes for these tasks. Unfortunately, goal setting interferes with implicit learning by shifting our attention to more explicit (and cumbersome) learning processes. Goal setting is effective for simple or routine tasks, on the other hand, because the best work processes are already known or are quickly learned without much thought.[71]

COMPARING MOTIVATION THEORIES

Exhibit 3.7 summarizes the central ideas behind the four content and three process theories of motivation presented in this chapter. As you can see, each of the process theories provides a unique perspective of employee motivation. Each looks at different variables in the workplace and the minds of employees. As for the content theories, Alderfer's ERG theory builds on Maslow's needs hierarchy theory. McClelland's learned needs theory is somewhat more distinctive because it suggests that some needs are acquired (learned) rather than instinctive.

ARE MOTIVATION THEORIES CULTURE BOUND?

Are the motivation theories presented throughout this chapter culture-bound? A few scholars think so. They argue that most theories of motivation were developed and tested in North America, so they don't readily apply in cultures with different values.[72]

EXHIBIT 3.7   Comparing Employee Motivation Theories

MOTIVATION THEORY	TYPE	CENTRAL IDEA
Maslow's Needs Hierarchy	Content	People try to satisfy higher need when lower need is fulfilled (satisfaction-progression).
Alderfer's ERG Theory	Content	Satisfaction-progression (above), and people focus on lower need if unable to satisfy higher need (frustration-regression).
Herzberg's Motivator-Hygiene Theory	Content	Motivators (job content, recognition) motivate and satisfy, whereas hygiene factors (work relations, work environment) create dissatisfaction but do not motivate.
McClelland's Learned Needs	Content	Some needs are learned rather than instinctive, and more than one need can motivate at the same time.
Expectancy Theory	Process	Motivation is determined by perceived expectancies, outcome values, and a rational decision-making process.
Equity Theory	Process	Perceived equity is formed from outcome/input ratios with a comparison other, and people are motivated to reduce perceived inequities.
Goal Setting	Process	Clear, relevant goals increase motivation and performance by stretching the intensity and persistence of effort and by clarifying role perceptions.

Some of this criticism has focused on older content theories (e.g., Maslow's needs hierarchy) that were rejected by organizational behaviour theorists long ago. It doesn't make sense to complain about the relevancy of motivation theories abroad if they don't work in North America, either. Another criticism has been that people in other cultures have different needs. However, research has revealed that feelings of achievement and interesting work are the two most important motivating factors in several cultures (China, Germany, United States, etc.). Employees in different cultures may have different absolute levels of need for achievement, for example, but their relative strength is similar. Moreover, the conceptual structure of need for achievement is consistent across several different cultures, suggesting that its meaning is relevant in other societies.[73]

Expectancy theory has also been criticized as culture-bound.[74] Some critics argue that expectancy theory only works in Canada and other cultures where people have strong feelings of personal control. Others claim that expectancy theory applies to individual motivation and, consequently, doesn't work in cultures where people place a higher value on group membership. In reality, expectancy theory requires neither of these conditions. First, expectancy theory does not assume that people feel that they have complete control over their lives; on the contrary, the E→P expectancy directly varies with the employee's perceived control over the work situation. Second, expectancy theory applies to team and organizational outcomes, not just to individual performance. Research indicates that expectancy theory predicts employee motivation in different cultures.[75]

Equity theory also allows for individual differences and, consequently, seems to apply equally well to other cultures. We know that people in some cultures are more sensitive to perceived inequities than those in other cultures. For example, some cultures value equality more than equity. However, feelings of inequity exist even in more egalitarian cultures. Equity theory also allows for the fact that the most important inputs and outcomes can vary from one culture to the next.[76]

The debate over the cross-cultural relevance of motivation theories will continue for some time. Certainly, we must not automatically assume that a theory successfully tested here will apply equally well in other societies. We need to continuously evaluate motivation theories and other organizational behaviour concepts in other cultures. Hopefully, future research will throw more light on the topic by evaluating the cross-cultural relevance of expectancy, goal-setting, and other contemporary motivation theories. In the meantime, it is not clear (at least, not as clear as the critics believe) that contemporary motivation theories are culture-bound.

CHAPTER SUMMARY

- Work motivation refers to the forces within a person that affect his or her direction, intensity, and persistence of voluntary behaviour in the workplace. Companies need to rethink their motivational practices because of an increasingly diverse workforce, turbulent changes in employment relationships, and flatter organizational structures that require less reliance on direct supervision to control employee behaviour. Content motivation theories explain why people have different needs at different times. Process theories of motivation describe the processes through which needs are translated into behaviour.

- According to Maslow's needs hierarchy, the lowest needs are initially most important, but higher needs become more important as the lower ones are satisfied. Alderfer's ERG theory groups human needs into a hierarchy of three broad categories: existence, relatedness, and growth. Herzberg's motivator-hygiene theory suggests that people are only motivated by characteristics of the work itself. McClelland studied need for achievement, need for power, and need for affiliation. These needs are learned rather than instinctive, and more than one need may motivate a person at the same time.

- Content motivation theories advise organizations to offer employees a choice of rewards. They also encourage organizations to recognize nonfinancial as well as financial sources of motivation.

- Expectancy theory states that work effort is determined by the perception that effort will result in a particular level of performance (E→P expectancy), the perception that a specific behaviour or performance level will lead to specific outcomes (P→O expectancy), and the valences that the person feels for those outcomes.

- The E→P expectancy increases by improving the employee's ability and confidence to perform the job. The P→O expectancy increases by measuring performance accurately, distributing higher rewards to better performers, and showing employees that rewards are performance-based. Outcome valences increase by finding out what employees want and using these resources as rewards.

- Equity theory explains how people develop perceptions of fairness in the distribution and exchange of resources. The model includes four elements: outcome/input ratio, comparison other, equity evaluation, and consequences of inequity. The theory also explains what people are motivated to do when they feel inequitably treated.

- Goal setting is the process of motivating employees and clarifying their role perceptions by establishing benchmarks against which growth needs are fulfilled. Goals are more effective when they are specific, results-oriented, challenging, accepted by the employee, and accompanied by meaningful feedback. Participative goal setting is important in some situations. Goal setting is usually less effective when tied to financial rewards and when applied to new or complex tasks.

- We must not automatically assume that an employee motivation theory successfully tested in North America will apply equally well in other cultures. However, there is increasing support for the cross-cultural relevance of the motivation theories described here.

KEY TERMS

Content theories of motivation, p. 62

Effort-to-performance (E→P) expectancy, p. 70

Equity theory, p. 74

ERG theory, p. 63

Existence needs, p. 63

Expectancy theory, p. 70

Frustration-regression process, p. 64

Goal setting, p. 78

Goals, p. 78

Growth needs, p. 63

Implicit learning, p. 81

Job satisfaction, p. 64

Management-by-objectives (MBO), p. 78

Motivation, p. 62

Motivator-hygiene theory, p. 64

Need for achievement (nAch), p. 65

Need for affiliation (nAff), p. 66

Need for power (nPow), p. 67

Needs, p. 62

Needs hierarchy theory, p. 63

Performance-to-outcome (P→O) expectancy, p. 70

Process theories of motivation, p. 62

Relatedness needs, p. 63

Satisfaction-progression process, p. 63

Self-efficacy, p. 80

Valence, p. 71

DISCUSSION QUESTIONS

1. This chapter begins by saying that motivating employees has never been more challenging. Do you agree with this statement? Are there any other reasons why employees might be more (or less) difficult to motivate today than, say, 20 years ago?

2. Think about your personal level of need for achievement, affiliation, and power. What factors in your past have caused you to experience high, moderate, or low levels of each? Which of these would you like to increase or decrease in the future?

3. As a team leader, you notice that one employee isn't putting a lot of effort into the team project because she doesn't believe she has the ability to contribute anything valuable. Using your knowledge of expectancy theory's E→P expectancy, identify four ways that you might increase this person's motivation to contribute to the team.

4. Use all three components of expectancy theory to explain why some employees are motivated to show up for work during a snowstorm whereas others don't make any effort to leave their homes.

5. Several service representatives are upset that the newly hired representative with no previous experience will be paid $1000 a year above the usual starting salary on the pay range. The department manager explained that the new hire would not accept the entry-

level rate, so the company raised the offer by $1000. All five reps currently earn salaries near the top of the scale ($10,000 higher), although they all started at the minimum starting salary a few years earlier. Use equity theory to explain why the five service representatives feel inequity in this situation.

6. Inequity occurs in the classroom as well as in the workplace. Identify classroom situations in which you had feelings of inequity. How might course instructors minimize these inequitable situations?

7. In at least one African country, many employees believe that pay levels should be partly determined by the number of children in the employee's family. The argument is that employees with more children need more money to support their families. Discuss this idea in the context of the equity theory model.

8. Last year, Prairie Cellular Ltd. introduced a goal-setting program to improve motivation and performance among its salespeople. In January of each year, salespeople are assigned a set of specific goals to improve work processes (e.g., submitting sales notes on time; saying the customer's last name in conversations, etc.). After the first year, however, senior management decided to cancel the goal-setting program because sales did not improve even though competitors did well. Use your knowledge of the characteristics of effective goals to explain why goal setting may not have been effective at Prairie Cellular.

Case Study

ACTIVITY 3.1
Perfect Pizzeria

Perfect Pizzeria in Southville, Illinois, is the chain's second-largest franchise. The headquarters is located in Phoenix, Arizona. Although the business is prospering, it has employee and managerial problems.

Each operation has one manager, one assistant manager, and two to five night managers. The managers of each pizzeria work under an area supervisor. There are no systematic criteria for being a manager or becoming a manager trainee. The franchise has no formalized training period for managers. No college education is required. The managers for whom the case observer worked during a four-year period were relatively young (ages 24 to 27), and only one had completed college. They came from the ranks of night managers, assistant managers, or both. The night managers were chosen for their ability to perform the duties of the regular employees. The assistant managers worked a two-hour shift during the luncheon period five days a week to gain knowledge about bookkeeping and management. Those becoming managers remained at that level unless they expressed interest in investing in the business.

The employees were mostly college students; a few high school students performed the less-challenging jobs. Because Perfect Pizzeria was located in an area with few job opportunities, it had a relatively easy task of filling its employee quota. All the employees, with the exception of the manager, were employed part-time. Consequently, they earned only the minimum wage.

The Perfect Pizzeria system is devised so that food and beverage costs and profits are set up according to a percentage. If the percentage of food unsold or damaged in any way is very low, the manager gets a bonus. If the percentage is high, the manager does not receive a bonus; rather, he or she receives only his or her normal salary.

There are many ways in which the percentage can fluctuate. Because the manager cannot be in the store 24 hours a day, some employees make up for their low paycheques by helping themselves to the food. When a friend comes in to order a pizza, extra

ACTIVITY 3.1 CONTINUED

ingredients are put on it. Occasional nibbles by 18 to 20 employees throughout the day at the meal table also raise the percentage figure. An occasional bucket of sauce may be spilled or a pizza accidentally burned. Sometimes the wrong size of pizza may be made.

In the event of an employee mistake or a burned pizza by the oven person, the expense is supposed to come from the individual. Because of peer pressure, the night manager seldom writes up a bill for the erring employee. Instead, the establishment takes a loss and the error goes unnoticed until the end of the month when inventory is taken. That's when the manager finds out that the percentage is high and that there will be no bonus.

In the present instance, the manager took retaliatory measures. Previously, each employee was entitled to a free pizza, salad, and all the soft drinks he or she could drink for every six hours of work. The manager raised this figure from 6 to 12 hours of work. However, the employees had received these six-hour benefits for a long time. Therefore, they simply took advantage of the situation whenever the manager or assistant manager was not in the building. Although the night managers theoretically had complete control of the operation in the evenings, they did not command the same respect that the manager or assistant manager did because night managers received the same pay as the regular employees, could not reprimand other employees, and were basically the same age as or sometimes even younger than the other employees.

Thus, apathy grew within the pizzeria. There seemed to be a further separation between the manager and his workers, who started out as a closely knit group. The manager made no attempt to alleviate the problem, because he felt it would iron itself out. Either the employees that were dissatisfied would quit or they would be content to put up with the new regulations. As it turned out, there was a rash of employee dismissals. The manager had no problem filling the vacancies with new workers, but the loss of key personnel was costly to the business.

Because of the large turnover, the manager found he had to spend more time in the building, supervising and sometimes taking the place of inexperienced workers. This was in direct violation of the franchise regulations, which stated that a manager would act as a supervisor only and at no time would take part in actual food preparation. Employees were placed under strict supervision when the manager worked alongside them. The operation no longer worked smoothly because of differences between the remaining experienced workers and the manager concerning the way in which a particular function should be performed.

Within a two-month period, the manager was again free to go back to his office and leave his subordinates in charge of the entire operation. During this two-month period, in spite of the differences between experienced workers and the manager, the unsold/damaged food percentage had returned to the previous low level and the manager received a bonus each month. The manager felt that his problems had been resolved and that conditions would remain the same, since the new personnel had been properly trained.

It didn't take long for the new employees to become influenced by the other employees. Immediately after the manager had returned to his supervisory role, the unsold/damaged food percentage began to rise. This time the manager took a bolder step. He cut out all benefits—no free pizzas, salads, or drinks. With the job market even worse than usual, most employees were forced to stay. The appointment of a new area supervisor made it impossible for the manager to "work behind the counter," because the supervisor was centrally located in Southville.

The manager tried still another approach to alleviate the rising unsold/damaged food percentage and maintain his bonus. He placed a notice on the bulletin board stating that if the percentage remained at a high level, a lie detector test would be given to all employees. All those found guilty of taking or purposefully wasting food or drinks would be terminated immediately. This threat did not have the desired effect on the employees, because they knew that if they were all subjected to the test, they would all be found guilty. The manager would have to dismiss all of them and this would leave him in a worse situation than ever.

ACTIVITY 3.1 CONTINUED

Even before the following month's unsold/damaged food percentage was calculated, the manager knew it would be high. He had evidently received information from one of the night managers about the employees' feelings towards the notice. What he did not expect was that the percentage would reach an all-time high. That is the state of affairs at the present time.

Discussion Questions

1. Use expectancy theory to explain why the food wastage remained high at Perfect Pizzeria. Your answer should also explain the motivation of the night manager in failing to report the misuse of food.

2. Would goal setting reduce the food wastage problem? Why or why not?

3. Recommend ways to reduce food wastage at Perfect Pizzeria.

Source: J.E. Dittrich and R.A. Zawacki, *People and Organizations* (Plano, TX: Business Publications, 1981), pp. 126–28. Used by permission of McGraw-Hill/Irwin.

Video Case Study

ACTIVITY 3.2
Who Wants to be a Billionaire?

Jim Bosley and Mike Lazaretis have built Research In Motion (RIM) into a company worth about 12 billion dollars. This global powerhouse isn't in Silicon Valley. RIM dominates a small industrial park in Waterloo, Ontario. But don't be fooled by the small community setting or Bosley's and Lazaretis' laid-back style. They can compete with the best of obsessive, high-tech entrepreneurs.

"I think the technology industry draws obsessive people," says Bosley. Lazaretis adds that, although it's nice to go home and see the kids after a full day at the office, he has a strong need to come back to the office a few hours later. RIM's co-CEOs also explain that they aren't motivated by the perks of success. Says Bosley: "If what's important to you is the fast buck ... then you should move to the U.S."

Bill Lipson is a Canadian entrepreneur who moved to Silicon Valley to keep up with the fast buck and the fast pace. "Right now, this is very much like the gold rush days," Lipson explains. "What you're trying to do, it's a land-grab. You want to capture as much of the market, whether that's customers, revenue, or a combination."

So what motivates Lipson? "It is the excitement of being down here, which is extremely positive. It's also a bit of paranoia in that you don't know what's down the next curve."

University of Waterloo engineering students have a lot of career choices in these boom days, such as whether they are motivated to join a company, move to the United States, or start their own business. Some students have already started their own firms. Others, like Marnie Andrews, are less confident about starting a business. "So I wonder if there are other ways I can become a billionaire?" asks Andrews.

Discussion Questions

1. Looking at ERG Theory or Maslow's Needs Hierarchy, which needs dominate the motivation of Jim Bosley and Mike Lazaretis? Are their needs different from those of Bill Lipson?

2. This video program makes several references to "becoming a billionaire." To what extent are the people interviewed in this program motivated by money? (You may want to read the first part of Chapter 4 before discussing this topic.)

Source: Based on "Who Wants To Be A Billionaire?" *The National Magazine* (April 10, 2000).

TEAM exercise

ACTIVITY 3.3
BONUS DECISION MAKING

Purpose: This exercise is designed to help you understand the elements of equity theory and how people differ in their equity perceptions.

Instructions: Four managers in a large national insurance company are described below. The national sales director of the company has given your consulting team (first individually, then together) the task of allocating $100,000 in bonuses to these four managers. It is entirely up to your team to decide how to divide the money among these people. The only requirements are that all of the money must be distributed and that no two branch managers can receive the same amount. The names and information are presented in no particular order. You should assume that economic conditions, client demographics, and other external factors are very similar for these managers.

Step 1: Students will form teams of four or five people. Working alone, read the information about the four managers. Then fill in the amount you would allocate to each manager in the "Individual Decision" column.

Step 2: Still working alone, fill in the "Equity Inputs Form." First, in the "Input Factor" column, list in order of importance the factors you considered when allocating the bonus amounts (e.g., seniority, performance, age, etc.). The most important factor should be listed first and the least important one listed last. Next, in the "Input Weight" column, estimate the percentage weight that you assigned to this factor. The total of this column must add up to 100 percent.

Step 3: After individually allocating the bonus money and determining the input factors and weights, team members will compare their results and note any differences. Then, team members will reach a consensus on the bonus amount that each manager should receive. These amounts will be written in the "Team Decision" column.

Step 4: The instructor will call the class together to compare team results and note differences in inputs and input weights used by individual students. Discussion of these results in terms of equity theory will follow.

Manager Profiles:

Bob B.—Bob has been in the insurance business for over 27 years and has spent the past 21 years with this company. A few years ago, Bob's branch typically made the largest contribution to regional profits. More recently, however, it has brought in few new accounts and is now well below average in terms of its contribution to the company. Turnover in the branch has been high and Bob doesn't have the same enthusiasm for the job as he once did. Bob is 56 years old and is married with five children. Three children are still living at home. Bob has a high-school diploma as well as a certificate from a special course in insurance management.

Edward E.—In the two years that Edward has been a branch manager, his unit has brought in several major accounts and now stands as one of the top units in the country. Edward is well respected by his employees. At 29, he is the youngest manager in the region and one of the youngest in the country. The regional director initially doubted the wisdom of giving Edward the position of branch manager because of his relatively young age and lack of experience in the insurance industry. Edward received an undergraduate business degree from the

University of Prince Edward Island and worked for five years as a sales representative in Kitchener, Ontario, before joining this company. Edward is single and has no children.

Lee L.—Lee has been with this organization for seven years. Her first two years were spent as a sales representative in the office that she now manages. According to the regional director, Lee rates about average as a branch manager. She earned an undergraduate degree in geography from the University of Calgary and worked in Alberta as a sales representative for four years with another insurance company before joining this organization. Lee is 40 years old, divorced, and has no children. She is a very ambitious person but sometimes has problems working with her staff and other branch managers.

Sandy S.—Sandy is 47 years old and has been a branch manager with this company for 17 years. Seven years ago, her branch made the lowest contribution to the region's profits, but this has steadily improved and is now slightly above average. Sandy seems to have a mediocre attitude towards her job but is well liked by her staff and other branch managers. Her experience in the insurance industry has been entirely with this organization. She previously worked in nonsales positions, and it is not clear how she became a branch manager without previous sales experience. Sandy is married and has three school-aged children. Several years ago, Sandy earned a diploma in business from a nearby community college by taking evening courses.

BONUS ALLOCATION FORM

Name	Individual Decision	Team Decision
Bob B.	$ _____	$ _____
Edward E.	$ _____	$ _____
Lee L.	$ _____	$ _____
Sandy S.	$ _____	$ _____
TOTALS:	$ 100,000	$ 100,000

EQUITY INPUTS FORM

Input Factor*	Input Weight**
_____	_____ %
_____	_____ %
_____	_____ %
_____	_____ %
_____	_____ %
TOTAL:	100 %

* List factors in order of importance, with most important factor listed first.

** The weight of each factor is a percentage ranging from 1 to 100. All factor weights together must add up to 100 percent.

© 1997, 1983 Steven L. McShane

Self-Assessment **exercise**

ACTIVITY 3.4
MEASURING YOUR GROWTH NEED STRENGTH

Purpose: This self-assessment is designed to help you estimate your level of growth need strength.

Instructions: People differ in the kinds of jobs they would most like to hold. The questions in this exercise give you a chance to say just what it is about a job that is most important to you. For each question, two different kinds of jobs are briefly described. Please indicate which of the two jobs you personally would prefer if you had to make a choice between them. In answering each question, assume that everything else about the jobs is the same. Pay attention only to the characteristics actually listed. After circling each answer, use the scoring key in Appendix B of this book to calculate your results for this scale. This exercise is completed alone so students can assess themselves honestly without concerns of social comparison. However, class discussion will focus on the growth need strength concept and its implications.

GROWTH NEED STRENGTH SCALE

JOB A	Circle the number indicating the degree to which you prefer Job A or Job B					JOB B
1. A job where the pay is very good.	1 Strongly Prefer A	2 Slightly Prefer A	3 Neutral	4 Slightly Prefer B	5 Strongly Prefer B	A job where there is considerable opportunity to be creative and innovative.
2. A job where you are often required to make important decisions.	1 Strongly Prefer A	2 Slightly Prefer A	3 Neutral	4 Slightly Prefer B	5 Strongly Prefer B	A job with many pleasant people to work with.
3. A job in which greater responsibility is given to those who do the best work.	1 Strongly Prefer A	2 Slightly Prefer A	3 Neutral	4 Slightly Prefer B	5 Strongly Prefer B	A job in which greater responsibility is given to loyal employees who have the most seniority.
4. A job in a firm that is in financial trouble and might have to close down within the year.	1 Strongly Prefer A	2 Slightly Prefer A	3 Neutral	4 Slightly Prefer B	5 Strongly Prefer B	A job in which you are not allowed to have any say whatever in how your work is scheduled, or in the procedures to be used in carrying it out.

5. A very routine job.	──1── Strongly Prefer A	──2── Slightly Prefer A	──3── Neutral	──4── Slightly Prefer B	──5── Strongly Prefer B	A job where your co-workers are not very friendly.
6. A job with a supervisor who is often very critical of you and your work in front of other people.	──1── Strongly Prefer A	──2── Slightly Prefer A	──3── Neutral	──4── Slightly Prefer B	──5── Strongly Prefer B	A job that prevents you from using a number of skills that you worked hard to develop.
7. A job with a supervisor who respects you and treats you fairly.	──1── Strongly Prefer A	──2── Slightly Prefer A	──3── Neutral	──4── Slightly Prefer B	──5── Strongly Prefer B	A job that provides constant opportunities for you to learn new and interesting things.
8. A job where there is a real chance you could be laid off.	──1── Strongly Prefer A	──2── Slightly Prefer A	──3── Neutral	──4── Slightly Prefer B	──5── Strongly Prefer B	A job with very little chance to do challenging work.
9. A job in which there is a real chance for you to develop new skills and advance in the organization.	──1── Strongly Prefer A	──2── Slightly Prefer A	──3── Neutral	──4── Slightly Prefer B	──5── Strongly Prefer B	A job that provides lots of vacation time and an excellent benefits package.
10. A job with little freedom and independence to do your work in the way you think best.	──1── Strongly Prefer A	──2── Slightly Prefer A	──3── Neutral	──4── Slightly Prefer B	──5── Strongly Prefer B	A job where working conditions are poor.
11. A job with very satisfying teamwork.	──1── Strongly Prefer A	──2── Slightly Prefer A	──3── Neutral	──4── Slightly Prefer B	──5── Strongly Prefer B	A job that allows you to use your skills and abilities to the fullest extent.
12. A job that offers little or no challenge.	──1── Strongly Prefer A	──2── Slightly Prefer A	──3── Neutral	──4── Slightly Prefer B	──5── Strongly Prefer B	A job that requires you to be completely isolated from co-workers.

Source: Developed by J.R. Hackman and G.R. Oldham as part of the Job Diagnostic Survey instrument. The authors have released any copyright ownership of this scale. See J.R. Hackman and G. Oldham, *Work Redesign* (Reading, MA: Addison-Wesley, 1980), p. 275.

CHAPTER FOUR

Applied Motivation Practices

LEARNING OBJECTIVES

After reading this chapter, you should be able to:

- Explain how money and other financial rewards affect our needs and emotions.
- Discuss the advantages and disadvantages of the four types of rewards.
- Identify four commonly applied team- or organizational-level performance-based rewards.
- Describe five ways to improve reward effectiveness.
- Discuss the advantages and disadvantages of job specialization.
- Diagram the job characteristics model of job design.
- Identify three strategies to enrich jobs.
- Describe the five elements of self-leadership.
- Explain how mental imagery improves employee motivation.

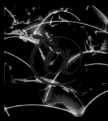

Stephen Benson, an IKEA employee in Calgary, used the company's $2500 "Big Thank You Bonus" to reduce payments on his motorcycle. "It's the bike that IKEA bought," Benson says proudly.

On a recent Saturday in October, Calgary IKEA employee Stephen Benson went home very happy. So did 44,000 other employees at IKEA's 152 stores around the globe. The Scandinavian home furnishings retailer held a special "Big Thank You Bonus" by pledging the entire day's sales revenue to employees. The idea was to thank staff members for their hard work and loyalty. Customers were also rewarded with special prices, entertainment, and, not surprisingly, exceptional service from employees.

The unique reward exceeded everyone's expectations. Customers rang up $118 million in sales, nearly doubling IKEA's previous one-day record. In Canada, the resulting bonus amounted to more than $2500 for each full-time employee and a pro-rated amount for part-time staff. Consistent with the company's egalitarian values, everyone from cashiers to the company president received the same amount. Similar bonuses were distributed to employees in other countries, up to a maximum of three months' salary.

"Saturday proved to be an overwhelmingly positive day for everyone at IKEA," said Luc Lauwers, president of IKEA Canada. "IKEA employees worked tirelessly throughout the day and well into the night, showing the same enthusiasm that has helped make the company so successful."

Stephen Benson certainly appreciates the reward. Benson used his bonus to reduce the amount owing on the Yamaha Virago motorcycle that he recently bought. "It's the bike that IKEA bought," says Benson.[1]

IKEA didn't become the world's largest home furnishings retailer by paying big bonuses and salaries. The company doesn't pay sales commissions and its basic pay rate is about $14 per hour for staff and a little more for junior management.[2] Yet, the "Big Thank You Bonus" suggests that *money does matter* to IKEA's employees. The first part of this chapter looks at the complex dynamics of reward systems. We look at the meaning of money and other financial rewards, the different types of rewards and their objectives, and the characteristics of effective reward implementation.

Of course, reward systems are not the only way to motivate employees. Thus, we consider two other applied motivation practices: job design and self-leadership. The second part of this chapter examines the dynamics of job design, specific job design strategies to motivate employees, and the effectiveness of recent job design interventions. The final part of this chapter introduces the emerging concept of self-leadership. This final section explains how employees motivate themselves through personal goal setting, constructive thought patterns, designing natural rewards, self-monitoring, and self-reinforcement.

THE MEANING OF MONEY IN THE WORKPLACE

Money and other financial rewards are a fundamental part of the employment relationship.[3] Organizations distribute money and other benefits in exchange for the employee's availability, competencies, and behaviours. Rewards try to align individual goals with corporate objectives and to provide a return to the individual's contribution. This concept of economic exchange can be found across cultures. The word for "pay" in Malay and Slovak means to replace a loss; in Hebrew and Swedish it means making equal.[4]

Courtesy of ARCNET.

Most of the cars in ARCNET's employee parking lot look alike. That's because the New Jersey architectural engineering firm gives every employee—from secretaries to the president—keys to a new BMW after one year of employment. ARCNET's CEO, Al Galdi (shown here being interviewed) offers this dreamy perk as a way to motivate employees to stay with the company. Each vehicle is leased for about US$9000 per year, including insurance. Galdi frequently asks employees if they would rather have the cash, but most prefer the BMWs. "I see the effect already," says Galdi. "My employees want to work harder and it's a benefit when it comes to recruiting."[5] Would a luxury car satisfy the same needs as a cash reward?

But money is not just an economic medium of exchange in the employment relationship. It has much deeper meaning to most people.[6] It affects our needs, our emotions, and our self-identities. As one scholar wrote: "Money is probably the most emotionally meaningful object in contemporary life: only food and sex are its close competitors as common carriers of such strong and diverse feelings, significance, and strivings."[7]

MONEY AND EMPLOYEE NEEDS

Money is a complex symbol that fulfils a variety of needs. Money is strongly linked to the fulfilment of existence needs because it allows us to buy food and shelter. Some people also see money as a symbol of respect and status, thereby fulfilling some social needs. For others, money symbolizes personal accomplishments. People with a high need for achievement are not motivated primarily by money (see Chapter 3), but they do value money as a source of feedback and a representation of goal achievement. Thus, money helps to fulfil growth needs.

Money is also valued as a symbol of power. Those who possess money are often viewed as being more powerful, so people with a strong need for power are motivated to acquire more money and to make their wealth known. This wealth is then used to influence others. Some writers suggest that men are more likely to believe that money equals power and that power is the path to respect. Other research suggests that women are more likely to use money as a source of power when conflicts arise.[8]

MONEY ATTITUDES AND SELF-IDENTITY

Money generates a variety of emotions. Some individuals view money as the root of all evil. Others are nervous with money and its responsibilities. Money is associated with greed, avarice, and, occasionally, generosity. People also tend to identify themselves in terms of how much money they have acquired and dispersed. One stream of research examines the "money ethic," that is, the extent to which people believe that money is not evil, is a representation of their success, and should be budgeted carefully.[9] Men and women differ in their attitudes towards money. One survey of money attitudes reported that men attach more importance or value to money than do females in 40 of the 43 countries studied.

The bottom line is that money and other financial rewards do much more than pay employees back for their contributions. They fulfil a variety of needs, influence emotions, and shape a person's self-identity. This is important to remember when distributing rewards in the workplace. Over the next several pages, we look at various types of rewards and how to improve the implementation of performance-based rewards.

TYPES OF REWARDS AND THEIR OBJECTIVES

Organizations reward employees for their membership and seniority, job status, competencies, and performance. Each reward objective has advantages and disadvantages, as Exhibit 4.1 summarizes.

MEMBERSHIP AND SENIORITY-BASED REWARDS

The largest portion of most paycheques is based on membership and seniority. Employees receive fixed hourly wages or salaries, and many benefits are the same for everyone in the firm. Other rewards increase with seniority, such as the amount of paid vacation time. Base pay sometimes increases with the number of years in a job. Large Japanese firms typically increase every employee's pay rate for each year on the job or age. Stelco, the Hamilton-based steel manufacturer, rewards long-term employees with a quarter-century banquet.[10]

EXHIBIT 4.1 Reward Objectives: Advantages and Disadvantages

Reward Objective	Advantages	Disadvantages
Membership/Seniority	• May attract applicants • Minimizes stress of insecurity • Reduces turnover	• Doesn't directly motivate performance • May discourage poor performers from leaving • Golden handcuffs may undermine performance
Job status	• Tries to maintain internal equity • Minimizes pay discrimination • Motivates employees to compete for promotions	• Encourages political tactics to increase job worth • Creates psychological distance between employees and executives
Competencies	• Improves workforce flexibility • Tends to improve quality • Consistent with employability	• Subjective measurement of competencies • Skill-based pay plans are expensive • Employees reach top of pay scale even when skills are unused
Task performance	• Motivates task performance • Attracts performance-oriented applicants • Organizational rewards create an ownership culture • Pay variability may avoid layoffs during downturns	• May weaken motivation of the job itself • May distance the reward giver from the receiver • May discourage creativity • Viewed as quick fixes, but don't solve root causes

Advantages and disadvantages

Membership-based rewards may attract job applicants, particularly when the size of the reward increases with seniority. They also provide a level of security that minimizes stress and builds loyalty.[11] Seniority-based rewards reduce turnover because the cost of quitting increases with the employee's length of service. However, membership-based rewards do not directly motivate job performance. Membership-based rewards also discourage poor performers from quitting because they seldom have better job offers. Instead, the good performers are lured to better-paying jobs. Lastly, we will learn in Chapter 7 that some rewards become golden handcuffs—financial incentives that discourage people from leaving the organization—that can undermine job performance.

JOB STATUS-BASED REWARDS

Job evaluation
Systematically evaluating the worth of jobs within the organization by measuring their required skill, effort, responsibility, and working conditions. Job evaluation results create a hierarchy of job worth.

Almost every organization rewards employees for the status of their jobs in the organization. This is particularly true in Canada where job status is rewarded more than in the United States.[12] **Job evaluation** systematically evaluates the worth of each job within the organization by measuring its required skill, effort, responsibility, and working conditions.[13] Jobs that require more skill and effort, have more responsibility, and have difficult working conditions would have more value and, consequently, would be placed in higher pay grades. Organizations that don't rely on job evaluation still tend to reward job status based on pay survey information about the external labour market. People in some higher-status jobs are also rewarded with larger offices, company-paid vehicles, and exclusive dining rooms.

Advantages and disadvantages

Job evaluation systems try to maintain internal equity, that is, they try to make pay levels fair across different jobs within the organization. This process also minimizes pay discrimination by ensuring that jobs dominated by women receive similar pay as jobs dominated by men in the organization.[14] Pay surveys generally try to maintain external equity, that is, ensure employees feel their pay is fair when compared to how much people in other organizations are paid. Job status-based rewards also motivate employees to compete for positions further up in the organizational hierarchy.

Despite these advantages, job status-based rewards have received much criticism. They motivate employees to increase their job's worth by exaggerating job duties and hoarding resources. These political behaviours may increase the job's pay rate through a job evaluation system, but they don't help the organization.[15] Job evaluation also tends to motivate technical employees to move into higher-valued management positions, even though they would prefer to stay in technical positions. Job status-based benefits, such as executive dining rooms and golf memberships, create a psychological distance between employees and management, thereby inhibiting communication across these groups. Some companies try to minimize these problems by closing executive dining rooms and removing other status-based benefits. There is also a strong trend away from rewarding employees for their job status and towards competency-based rewards.

COMPETENCY-BASED REWARDS

Competencies The abilities, individual values, personality traits, and other characteristics of people that lead to superior performance.

Competencies are the skills, knowledge, and other underlying characteristics that lead to superior performance (see Chapter 2).[16] Competency-based pay rewards employees for their skills, knowledge, and traits that lead to desired behaviours. For instance, providing superior customer value is one of several competencies employees are expected to possess at Bell Sygma. The Bell Canada subsidiary assesses how well each employee identifies customer requirements, meets commitments on schedule, is responsive to customer problems, and provides quality products and services.[17]

How do Bell Sygma and other firms reward employees for their competencies rather than their status? They flatten the organizational hierarchy, reduce the number of pay grades, and reward employees for their demonstrated competencies. Employees work in a variety of jobs, but are not paid for the status of each job. Rather, pay is determined more by what employees possess—their competencies—than what specific position they hold.[18] This motivates employees to acquire skills and knowledge by moving laterally through several jobs, rather than waiting for promotion within a tall career ladder.

Skill-based pay (SBP) Pay structures in which employees earn higher pay rates with the number of skill modules they have mastered, even though they perform only some of the mastered tasks in a particular job.

Skill-based pay (SBP) plans represent a variation of competency-based pay. In SBP plans, employees earn higher pay rates with the number of skill modules they have mastered.[19] Through special training and job rotation, employees learn how to operate another machine or complete another set of tasks. The employee's pay rate depends on the number of skill modules that he or she has mastered, not on the specific job performed on a particular day. Approximately 10 percent of Canadian companies—including Shell Canada and GE Canada—use skill-based plans, mostly for production employees.

Advantages and disadvantages

Competency-based rewards improve workforce flexibility because employees possess a variety of skills to move into different jobs as demands require. Product or service quality tends to improve because employees with multiple skills are more likely to understand the work process and know how to improve it.[20] Competency-based rewards are also consistent with **employability**. This is the emerging view that employees are not hired to perform a specific job for life. Rather, they perform a variety of tasks and therefore must continuously learn skills that will keep them employed (see Chapter 1).

Employability The "new deal" employment relationship in which the job is viewed as a temporary event, so employees are expected to keep pace with changing competency requirements and shift to new projects as demand requires.

One potential problem with competency-based pay is that measuring competencies can be subjective, particularly where they are personality traits or values.[21] Skill-based pay systems measure specific skills, so they are usually more objective and accurate. However, SBP plans are expensive because they motivate employees to spend time learning new tasks. Also, it's not uncommon to have most employees eventually reach the highest pay rate because few firms have established ways to reduce pay rates when employees become rusty on specific skills.

PERFORMANCE-BASED REWARDS

Yo! Sushi pays its servers more than a fixed hourly rate. The Japanese restaurant chain sets individual- and restaurant-level performance targets, then awards bonuses of up to 20 percent of annual salary based on how well employees have achieved their objectives.[22] Yo! Sushi is following the trend towards performance-based rather than purely membership- and seniority-based rewards. Canadian and U.S. firms have applied performance-based rewards for several decades, but Yo! Sushi and other Asian employers are also quickly shifting away from traditional pay systems that reward membership, age, and seniority. Performance-based rewards are most popular in Thai companies and least likely to be found in Indonesian firms.[23]

Performance-based rewards are not new, but they now come in more flavours than ever before. Exhibit 4.2 lists the most common types of individual, team, and organization-wide performance-based rewards.

Individual rewards

Individual rewards have existed since Babylonian days in the twentieth century BC.[24] The oldest of these is the *piece rate*, which calculates pay by the number of units the employee produces. *Commissions* pay people based on sales volume rather than the number of units produced. Many real estate agents and automobile salespeople are paid straight commission. *Royalties* pay individuals a percentage of revenue from the resource or work ascribed to them. Some mining companies pay their exploration geologists royalties from the mineral deposits they discover.

Merit pay—increasing the individual's pay based on performance appraisal results—was common during times of high inflation. However, many firms have replaced merit pay with *bonuses* for accomplishing specific tasks or achieving certain goals. For example, Bombardier

EXHIBIT 4.2   Types of Performance-Based Rewards

recently introduced a bonus for managers who implement a special quality management process (Six Sigma) and another bonus for success resulting from that process.[25]

Team rewards

Canadian organizations are introducing team-based rewards as they place more emphasis on team-based work structures (see Chapter 9).[26] Some firms give bonuses or special awards to teams or larger groups of employees. Consumers Glass, the Canadian manufacturer of various glass products, awards a President's Trophy to the plant with the lowest accident frequency. It recently awarded 200 Wittnauer commemorative wristwatches to employees at its Scoudouc, New Brunswick, plant for achieving 1 million hours of work without a lost-time accident.[27]

One of the most popular team-based rewards is the **gainsharing plan.** Gainsharing motivates team members to reduce costs and increase labour efficiency in their work process. Typically, the company shares the cost savings with employees for one or two years. The City of Waterloo, Ontario, has a gainsharing plan called "Winshare" that recently distributed $215,000 to employees based on a $1.3 million budget surplus. Clerical employees at University Hospital in Edmonton collectively receive a gainsharing bonus for suggestions that reduce waste.[28]

Gainsharing plans tend to improve team dynamics and pay satisfaction. They also create a reasonably strong effort-to-performance expectancy (see expectancy theory in Chapter 3) because much of the cost reduction and labour efficiency is within the team's control. In other words, team members quickly learn that their work efficiencies increase the size of the gainsharing bonus.[29] One concern, however, is that gainsharing plans may increase workloads and reduce customer service in the long run as employees find ways to cut costs in the short term.

Organizational rewards

IKEA's "Big Thank You Bonus" is typical of the emerging trend towards organization-wide rewards. Gainsharing plans can apply to the entire organization rather than to one team or work unit. However, the most common organization-wide reward systems are employee share ownership plans, share options, and profit-sharing plans:

- **Employee share ownership plans (ESOPs).** Approximately one-third of publicly traded firms in Canada encourage employees to buy company shares, usually by offering

---

Gainsharing plan A reward system usually applied to work teams that distributes bonuses to team members based on the amount of cost reductions and increased labour efficiency in the production process.

Employee share ownership plan (ESOP) A reward system that encourages employees to buy shares of the company.

these shares at a discount from the current stock market price. Employees are subsequently rewarded through dividends and market appreciation of those shares.[30] For example, more than 75 percent of employees at Procter & Gamble (P&G) Canada participate in the company's ESOP plan. The household goods manufacturer gives one share each to new employees, then encourages them to buy more shares by paying half of the cost. "[T]he interests of the employee and the company are inseparable," explains a P&G Canada executive. "To give employees the chance to own shares in the company reenforces that principle."[31]

Share options A reward system that gives employees the right to purchase shares from the company at a future date at a predetermined price.

- **Share options.** Share options give employees the right to purchase shares from the company at a future date at a predetermined price.[32] For example, your employer might offer you the right to purchase 100 shares at $50 two years or more from now. If the share price on the Toronto Stock Exchange two years from now is above $50, you could "exercise" your options by purchasing the shares from the company at $50 and selling them at a profit. If the price is below $50, you could wait until the share price rises above that amount. JDS Uniphase, Nortel Networks, and other Canadian high-technology firms prefer share options over ESOPs because they instantly connect new employees to the organization's success. As Connections 4.1 describes, share options have become one of the hottest forms of performance-based pay in Canada and elsewhere.

Profit sharing A reward system in which a designated group of employees receives a share of corporate profits.

- **Profit sharing.** This organizational-level reward pays bonuses to employees based on the previous year's level of corporate profits. These plans are most often found in firms that use teams and face plenty of competition.[33] Dofasco is one of those organizations. The Hamilton-based steel maker annually distributes 14 percent of its pre-tax profit equally to its employees. In a recent record-breaking year, this amounted to a profit-sharing bonus of nearly $8000 per employee.[34]

How effective are these organization-wide rewards? The evidence is mixed. The positive news is that ESOPs and share options tend to align employee behaviours more closely to organizational objectives. In other words, they create an "ownership culture" in which employees feel aligned with the organization's success. According to one study, productivity rises by 4 percent annually at ESOP firms, compared to only 1.5 percent at non-ESOP firms. Profit sharing tends to create less of this ownership-culture effect. However, it has the advantage of automatically adjusting employee compensation with the firm's prosperity, thereby reducing the need for layoffs or negotiated pay reductions during recessions.[35]

The main problem with these organizational-level rewards is that employees often perceive a weak connection between individual performance and corporate profits or the value of company shares. Even in small firms, the company's share price or profitability is influenced by economic conditions, competition, and other factors beyond the employee's immediate control. Another concern is that these organizational-level rewards fail to motivate employees during recessions when profits are negligible or during "bear" markets when share prices decline. Indeed, morale may be lower in companies that offer these plans.

IMPROVING REWARD EFFECTIVENESS

Performance-based rewards have been criticized for a variety of reasons.[36] One concern is that they distract employees from the motivation that comes from serving customers or achieving challenging objectives. Rewards also potentially create a psychological distance between the persons giving and receiving the reward. Another concern is that rewards discourage

CONNECTIONS 4.1

Soggies Take the Risk and Reward of Share Options

Share options (also called stock options) are the currency of employment in the emerging knowledge-based economy. Share markets can fall as fast as they rise, but that doesn't seem to discourage "Soggies" (the share-options generation) from giving up some of their fixed salaries for the greater potential of share options.

JDS Uniphase has a lot of Soggies. The fibre optics company's 6300 employees collectively hold more than 22 million share options worth an average of $675,000 per employee. Executives have a higher portion of those shares, but assembly line staff have received enough share options over the past two years to be the equivalent of one year's salary.

"We want to allow JDS employees to continue to participate in the growth of the company," says an executive at JDS's headquarters in Ottawa. "It's all about attracting, motivating, and retaining employees and creating a pride of ownership."

The share options boom is not restricted to North America. Singapore Press Holdings and Singapore Airlines, two of the island-

Courtesy of Singapore Airlines.

Singapore Airlines represents the trend in Asia of rewarding employees with share options.

state's largest companies, recently started company-wide share options programs. HKT, Hong Kong's telephone company, did the same a few years ago to replace the "thirteenth-month" paycheque that all employees traditionally received. At the time, HKT's employees complained about losing their guaranteed bonus. Now employees are seeking more share options. "[HKT employees] will be actively seeking stock options—unlike our passive response before," says a representative of the Hong Kong Telecom Employees Union.

Sources: Y. Ghahremani, "In the Company of Millionnaires," *Asiaweek,* March 17, 2000, p. 42; J. Bagnall, "High-Tech Firms Share the Wealth," *Ottawa Citizen,* October 17, 1999; P. Caulfield, "Employee Share Ownership Plans Help BC Tech Firms Keep Their Best and Brightest," *Silicon Valley North,* October 1999.

creativity and risk-taking because employees are less likely to explore new opportunities outside the realm of rewarded behaviour or results. Lastly, many corporate leaders use rewards as quick fixes, rather than carefully diagnosing the root cause of the undesirable behaviour. For example, one company hands out cash to employees who arrive early at company meetings and fines those who arrive late.[37] This company would be better off identifying the causes of lateness and changing the conditions, rather than using money to force a solution to the problem.

Financial rewards are certainly imperfect, but this does not necessarily mean that we should abandon performance-based pay. On the contrary, evidence indicates that the top-performing companies in Canada and elsewhere are more likely to have performance-

based rewards.[38] Reward systems do motivate most employees, but only under the right conditions. Here are some of the more important strategies to improve reward effectiveness.

Link rewards to performance

Employees with better performance should receive more rewards than poorer performers.[39] This simple principle is a logical conclusion of both behaviour modification (Chapter 2) and expectancy theory (Chapter 3), yet it seems to be unusually difficult to apply. A recent survey reported that one-third of the 770 Canadian and U.S. firms studied paid rewards to people who didn't meet minimum performance standards. The Canadian government might be included in that list. An auditor's report recently found that government managers responsible for mishandling $1 billion in job creation funds were paid bonuses for "satisfactorily" doing their jobs![40] Not surprisingly, another survey found that only 36 percent of Canadian employees believed that top performers receive more money and recognition than average or poor performers.[41]

How can we improve the pay-for-performance linkage? First, there is plenty of evidence that pay decisions are often biased by favouritism and political tactics.[42] This bias is minimized in gainsharing, share ownership, and other plans that rely on objective performance measures. Second, where subjective measures of performance are necessary, companies should rely on multiple sources of information. In other words, they should use 360-degree feedback to minimize biases from any single source (see Chapter 2). Third, surveys indicate that most Canadians don't understand how their paycheque is related in any way to their performance ratings.[43] This partly occurs because companies reward employees too long after they received the favourable performance feedback. The solution is to apply rewards soon after the performance and in a large enough dose (such as a bonus rather than a pay increase) that employees can see the reward.[44]

Ensure that rewards are relevant

Companies need to align rewards with performance within the employee's control. The more employees see a "line of sight" between their daily actions and the reward, the more they are motivated to improve performance.[45] For example, Sears Canada rewards senior executives for corporate performance because they have some control over the company's overall success. Bonuses for department sales managers, on the other hand, are based on profits and customer satisfaction in their departments but not on Sears' overall corporate performance.[46] Reward systems also need to correct for situational factors. Salespeople in one region may have higher sales because the economy is stronger there than it is elsewhere, so sales bonuses need to be adjusted for these economic factors.

Use team rewards for interdependent jobs

Organizations should use team (or organizational) rewards rather than individual rewards when employees work in highly interdependent jobs.[47] One reason for this is that individual performance is difficult to measure in these situations. For example, you can't judge how well one employee in a chemical processing plant contributes to the quality of the liquid produced. It is a team effort. A second reason is that team rewards tend to make employees more cooperative and less competitive. People see that their bonuses or other incentives depend on how well they work with co-workers, and they act accordingly.

A third reason for having team rewards is that they support employee preferences for team-based work arrangements. This was found in a study of Xerox customer service representatives. The Xerox employees assigned to teams with purely team bonuses eventually accepted and preferred a team structure, whereas those put in teams without team rewards did not adapt as well to the team structure.[48]

Ensure that rewards are valued

It seems obvious that employees should value the rewards that they receive. Yet companies sometimes make false assumptions about what employees want, with unfortunate consequences. Consider the British firm that asked staff to choose an employee of the month. Everyone thought that the incentive was so tacky that they chose the worst employees for the award. "The company was surprised at the choices," explains a consultant familiar with the case, "but it didn't dawn on them what was going on."[49] Executives thought that the recognition would motivate employees, whereas the "uncool" nature of this reward had the opposite effect.

The solution, of course, is to ask employees what they value. Campbell Soup's Canadian distribution centre did this a few years ago. Executives thought that the employees would ask for more money in a special team reward program. Instead, distribution staff said that the most valued reward was a leather jacket with the Campbell Soup logo on its back.[50] Making rewards interesting also creates value. The Hong Kong office of DHL International gave sales staff miniature air cargo containers to put on their desks. Each month, those who exceeded their sales target at the courier company received small blocks that would be put into the containers. Travel prizes were awarded to those who filled their containers. This visual incentive was so successful that most sales staff exceeded their targets by 40 percent. Now, sales staff at DHL's offices in Taiwan and China want a similar incentive plan.[51]

Watch out for unintended consequences

Performance-based reward systems sometimes have an unexpected—and undesirable—effect on employee behaviour.[52] Employee behaviour is a complex combination of needs, competencies, role perceptions, and situational factors, so it is often difficult to foresee the unexpected results when reward systems are introduced. Consider the pizza company that decided to reward its drivers for on-time delivery. The plan got more hot pizzas to customers on time, but it also increased the accident rates of its drivers because the incentive motivated them to drive recklessly.[53] Connections 4.2 describes a few other examples where reward systems had unintended consequences. The solution here is to carefully think through the consequences of rewards and, where possible, test incentives in a pilot project before applying them across the organization.

CONNECTIONS 4.2

www.donnelly.com www.aesc.com
www.toyota.com www.inco.com

When Rewards Go Wrong

There is an old saying that "what gets rewarded gets done." But what companies reward isn't always what they had intended for employees to do. Here are a few dramatic examples:

John Thoening.

Customer service incentives may have rewarded the wrong behaviours at Toyota dealerships.

• Toyota rewards its dealerships based on customer satisfaction surveys, not just on car sales. What Toyota discovered, however, is that this motivates dealers to increase satisfaction scores, not customer satisfaction itself. One Toyota dealership received high ratings because it offered free detailing to every customer who returned a "very satisfied" survey. The dealership even had a special copy of the survey showing clients which boxes to check off. This increased customer ratings, but not customer satisfaction.

• Donnelly Mirrors, the automobile parts manufacturer, introduced a gainsharing plan that motivated employees to reduce labour costs but not material costs. Employees knew that they worked faster with sharp grinding wheels, so they replaced the expensive diamond wheels more often. This action reduced labour costs, thereby giving them the gainsharing bonus, but these labour savings were easily offset by much higher costs for diamond grinding wheels.

• Soon after it purchased the majority share of Tisza Power in Hungary, AES Corp. wanted to cut the workforce by one-half. To do this, all employees who voluntarily quit were offered a cash reward and severance package. Unfortunately, someone miscalculated the value of this incentive. Over two-thirds of the employees signed up for the buyout package, leaving Tisza's operations short by 1000 staff members. At one point, AES management convened a meeting to persuade some employees to stay.

• A miner at Inco's mine in Garson, Manitoba, died when some of the roof supports he installed fell apart. The miner's work significantly affected everyone's safety (the supports prevented the mine from caving in), yet an inquiry learned that nearly half of his pay was based on bonuses for working faster. The company did not have a bonus for proper construction of the roof supports. Other inquiries into Canadian mining accidents have also concluded that productivity bonuses unintentionally motivate miners to bypass safety procedures.

Sources: M.S. Gaspar and J. O'Leary, "Power Co. Golden Parachute Works Too Well," *Budapest Business Journal*, January 27, 1997, p. 3; F.F. Reichheld, *The Loyalty Effect* (Boston, MA: Harvard University Press, 1996), p. 236; D.R. Spitzer, "Power Rewards: Rewards That Really Motivate," *Management Review*, May 1996, pp. 45–50; E.E. Lawler III, *Strategic Pay* (San Francisco: Jossey-Bass, 1990), p. 120; T. Pender, "Miners' Bonus Wage System Comes Under Ontario Scrutiny," *Globe and Mail*, August 25, 1986, p. A16.

BEYOND MONEY AND FINANCIAL REWARDS

At the beginning of this chapter, we said that money and other financial rewards have a complex effect on the needs, emotions, and self-identities of employees. Money also seems to have become a top priority when forming the employment relationship. "Show me the money"—the often-repeated phrase from the film *Jerry Maguire*—captures this emerging reality as companies offer more signing bonuses, share options, and BMWs. "There is definitely the monetary side," explains an employee at PMC-Sierra in Burnaby, B.C. "You have a stock purchase plan and bonuses, raises—they keep you happy."

But money isn't the only thing that motivates people to join an organization and perform effectively. "Money does matter," says an executive at Toronto computer graphics company Alias/Wavefront. "But so does the reputation of the company in the marketplace. My ability to attract top people depends on how much creative freedom and job challenge I can give them."[54] Consistent with this view, some recruiters steer clear of applicants who are interested mainly in monetary gain. "Greed is not the right reason to come and work in a startup," warns Bruce Gregory, CEO of Extreme Packet Devices Inc. in Kanata, Ontario. "It's passion for what we're doing that drives us."[55]

JOB DESIGN

Job design The process of assigning tasks to a job and distributing work throughout the organization.

Financial rewards can motivate, but OB scholars generally agree that the deepest "passion" for performing a job well comes from the work itself. **Job design** refers to the process of assigning tasks to a job, including the interdependency of those tasks with other jobs. A job is a set of tasks performed by one person.[56] Some jobs have very few tasks, each of which requires limited skill or effort. Other jobs include a very complex set of tasks and can be accomplished by only a few highly trained tradespeople or professionals.

The characteristics of jobs are being transformed by information technology. Computer networks can offer employees more responsibility and autonomy, such as improving access to information databases so that employees can complete their work without asking permission for information. Yet these same computer networks can also reduce personal control on the job where the technology monitors employee actions, keystrokes, and whereabouts. It all depends on how the technology is implemented.[57] Employability is also changing our idea about work and jobs. Employees are no longer hired into specific, narrowly defined jobs. Instead, they hold generic titles (associates, team members) and are expected to perform several clusters of tasks.[58]

Whether the change occurs through information technology or workforce flexibility, job design often produces an interesting conflict between the employee's motivation and ability to complete the work. To understand this issue more fully, we begin by describing early job design efforts aimed at increasing work efficiency through job specialization.

JOB DESIGN AND WORK EFFICIENCY

Job specialization The result of division of labour in which each job now includes a narrow subset of the tasks required to complete the product or service.

Mary Strang sees plenty of windshields, about 72 of them every hour. Mary and her assembly line partner mount one windshield onto a Chrysler Neon every 45 seconds. That's more than 500 windshields on each work shift, five days each week, plus a couple of Saturdays every month.[59] Mary works in a job with a high degree of **job specialization**. Job specialization occurs when the work required to build a Neon car—or produce any other product or service—is subdivided into separate jobs assigned to different people. Each resulting job includes a very narrow subset of tasks, usually completed in a short "cycle time." Cycle time is the time required to complete the task before starting over with a new work unit. For Mary, the cycle time is less than one minute.

EXHIBIT 4.3   Horizontal and Vertical Job Specialization

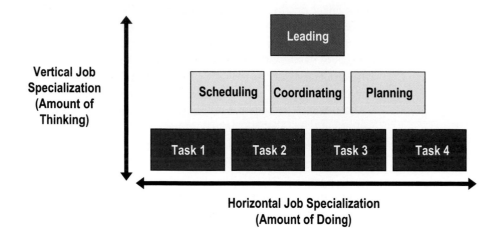

The economic benefits of job specialization were popularized over 200 years ago in Adam Smith's famous example of pin manufacturing.[60] There are several distinct operations in pin manufacturing, such as drawing out the wire, straightening it, cutting it, sharpening one end, grinding the other end, putting on the head, and whitening the head. If ten people made their own pins separately and independently, they would each produce 100 to 200 pins per day. But in a factory where each specialized task was assigned to a different person, Smith reported that these ten employees collectively produced almost 4800 pins per day!

Why does job specialization potentially increase work efficiency? One reason is that employees have fewer tasks to juggle and therefore spend less time changing activities. They also require fewer physical and mental skills to accomplish the assigned work, so less time and resources are needed for training. A third reason is that employees practise their tasks more frequently with shorter work cycles, so jobs are mastered quickly. Lastly, work efficiency increases because employees with specific aptitudes or skills can be matched more precisely to the jobs for which they are best suited.[61]

Adam Smith was mainly writing about *horizontal job specialization*, in which the basic physical behaviours required to provide a product or service are divided into different jobs (see Exhibit 4.3). With horizontal job specialization, employees perform fewer tasks. *Vertical job specialization*, on the other hand, refers to separating physical tasks from the administration of these tasks (planning, organizing, scheduling, etc.). In other words, vertical job specialization divorces the "thinking" job functions from the "doing" job functions.

Scientific management The process of systematically determining how work should be partitioned into its smallest possible elements and how the process of completing each task should be standardized to achieve maximum efficiency.

SCIENTIFIC MANAGEMENT

One of the strongest advocates of job specialization was Frederick Winslow Taylor, an industrial engineer who introduced the principles of **scientific management** in the early 1900s.[62] Scientific management involves systematically partitioning work into its smallest elements and standardizing tasks to achieve maximum efficiency. Taylor advocated vertical job specialization so that detailed procedures and work practices are developed by engineers, enforced by supervisors, and executed by employees. He also applied horizontal job specialization, such as narrowing the supervisor's role to such a degree that one person manages operational efficiency, another manages inspection, and another is the disciplinarian. Through scientific management, Taylor also popularized many organizational practices that are commonly found today, such as goal setting, employee training, and incentive systems.

There is ample evidence that scientific management has improved efficiency in many work settings. One of Taylor's earliest interventions was at a ball bearing factory where 120 women each worked 55 hours per week. Through job specialization and work efficiency analysis, Taylor increased production by two-thirds using a workforce of only 35 women working fewer than 45 hours per week. Taylor also doubled the employees' previous wages. No doubt, some of the increased productivity can be credited to improved training, goal setting, and work incentives, but job specialization has also contributed to the success of scientific management.

PROBLEMS WITH JOB SPECIALIZATION

Job specialization tries to increase work efficiency, but it doesn't necessarily improve job performance. The problem is that job specialization ignores the effects of job content on employees.[63] One effect is that highly specialized jobs are usually tedious, trivial, and socially isolating. "Specialization is the root of a lot of boredom," explains Dennis Bakke, co-founder of AES Corp., an American electrical power company that takes pains to avoid specialized jobs.[64]

Job specialization was supposed to allow companies to buy cheap, unskilled labour. Instead, many companies must offer higher wages—some call it *discontentment pay*—to compensate for the job dissatisfaction of narrowly defined work.[65] Job specialization also costs more in terms of higher turnover, absenteeism, sabotage, and mental health problems. Work quality is often lower with highly specialized jobs because employees see only a small part of the process. As one observer of General Motors' traditional assembly line reported: "Often [employees] did not know how their jobs related to the total picture. Not knowing, there was no incentive to strive for quality—what did quality even mean as it related to a bracket whose function you did not understand."[66]

Perhaps the most important reason why job specialization has not been as successful as expected is that it ignores the motivational potential of jobs. As jobs become specialized, the work tends to become easier to perform but is less motivating. As jobs become more complex, work motivation increases but the ability to master the job decreases. Maximum job performance occurs somewhere between these two extremes, where most people can eventually perform the job tasks efficiently, yet the work is interesting.

JOB DESIGN AND WORK MOTIVATION

Industrial engineers may have overlooked the motivational effects of job characteristics, but this is now the central focus of many job design changes.[67] Frederick Herzberg is credited with casting more of the spotlight on job content as a dominant source of employee motivation (see Chapter 3).[68] It might seem rather obvious to us today that the job itself is a source of motivation, but this was radical thinking when Herzberg proposed the idea in the 1950s.

• **Job characteristics model** A job design model that relates five core job dimensions to three psychological states and several personal and organizational consequences.

Herzberg's writing led to considerable study into the motivational potential of jobs.[69] Out of that research has emerged Hackman's and Oldham's **job characteristics model.** This model, shown in Exhibit 4.4, details the motivational properties of jobs as well as specific personal and organizational consequences of these properties.[70] The job characteristics model identifies five core job dimensions that produce three psychological states. Employees who experience these psychological states tend to have higher levels of internal work motivation (motivation from the work itself), job satisfaction (particularly satisfaction with the work itself), and work effectiveness.

EXHIBIT 4.4 The Job Characteristics Model

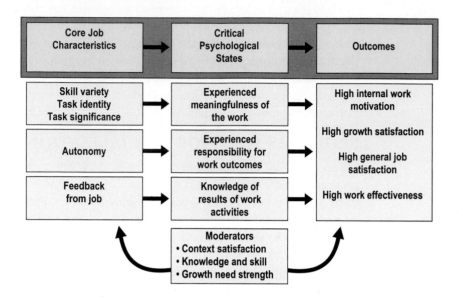

Source: J.R. Hackman and G. Oldham, *Work Redesign* (Reading, MA: Addison-Wesley, 1980), p. 90. Used with permission.

CORE JOB CHARACTERISTICS

Hackman and Oldham have identified five core job characteristics (see Exhibit 4.4). Desirable work outcomes increase when jobs are redesigned such that they include more of these characteristics.

- *Skill variety*—**Skill variety** refers to using different skills and talents to complete a variety of work activities. For example, sales clerks who normally only serve customers might be assigned the additional duties of stocking inventory and changing storefront displays.

- *Task identity*—**Task identity** is the degree to which a job requires completion of a whole or identifiable piece of work, such as doing something from beginning to end, or where it is easy to see how one's work fits into the whole product or service. An employee who assembles an entire computer modem rather than just solders in the circuitry would develop a stronger sense of ownership or identity with the final product.

- *Task significance*—**Task significance** is the degree to which the job has a substantial impact on the organization and/or larger society. For instance, 96 percent of Canadian government employees believe that their work is important.[71] Some have high task significance because their work keeps Canada running; others keep the country safe; still others have high task significance because they help people in need.

- *Autonomy*—Jobs with high levels of **autonomy** provide employees with freedom, independence, and discretion in scheduling the work and determining the procedures to be used to complete the work. In autonomous jobs, employees make their own decisions rather than rely on detailed instructions from supervisors or procedure manuals.

Skill variety The extent to which a job requires employees to use different skills and talents to complete a variety of work activities.

Task identity The degree to which a job requires completion of a whole or identifiable piece of work.

Task significance The degree to which the job has a substantial impact on the organization and/or larger society.

Autonomy The degree to which a job gives employees the freedom, independence, and discretion to schedule their work and determine the procedures to be used to complete the work.

Ian Lindsay, *Vancouver Sun.*

James Walton has a lot of motivational potential in his job. That's partly because the founder of Vancouver-based Storm Brewing Ltd. does most of the work—from brewing his "Black Plague Stout" to developing the gruesome marketing strategy that features a dead rat. Walton can also tell how well he is doing by tasting and smelling his popular brews and watching sales increase. Most of Walton's products are sold to local pubs and restaurants, so he also notices his respect gaining as a specialized brewer in western Canada. "[Walton's] brewing Lambic beer in bourbon casks, and he's the only one doing that as far as I know," says a brewer in North Vancouver. "Some of his stuff has been exceptional."[72] Based on the job characteristics model, why is James Walton highly motivated by his work?

Job feedback The degree to which employees can tell how well they are doing based on direct sensory information from the job itself.

- *Job feedback*—**Job feedback** is the degree to which employees can tell how well they are doing based on direct sensory information from the job itself. Airline pilots can tell how well they land their aircraft and physicians can see whether their operations have improved the patient's health.

CRITICAL PSYCHOLOGICAL STATES

The five core job characteristics affect employee motivation and satisfaction through three critical psychological states.[73] One of these is *experienced meaningfulness*—the belief that one's work is worthwhile or important. James Walton, the founder of Vancouver-based Storm Brewing Ltd., probably experiences a high level of meaningfulness because his job involves a lot of skill variety, task identity, and task significance. In contrast, meaningfulness drops as a job loses one or more of these characteristics.

Work motivation and performance increase when employees feel personally accountable for the outcomes of their efforts. Autonomy directly contributes to this feeling of *experienced responsibility*. Employees must be assigned control of their work environment to feel responsible for their successes and failures. The third critical psychological state is *knowledge of results*. Employees want information about the consequences of their work effort. Knowledge of results can originate from co-workers, supervisors, or clients. However, job design focuses on knowledge of results from the work itself.

INDIVIDUAL DIFFERENCES

Job redesign doesn't increase work motivation for everyone in every situation. Employees must have the required skills and knowledge to master the more challenging work. Otherwise, job redesign tends to increase stress and reduce job performance. A second condition is that employees must be reasonably satisfied with their work environment (e.g., working conditions, job security, salaries) before job redesign affects work motivation. A third condition is that employees must have strong growth needs. People with strong growth needs have satisfied their relatedness or existence needs, and are looking for challenges from the work itself (see Chapter 3). In contrast, improving the core job characteristics will have little motivational effect on people who are primarily focused on existence or relatedness needs.[74]

INCREASING WORK MOTIVATION THROUGH JOB DESIGN

Three main strategies increase the motivational potential of jobs: job rotation, job enlargement, and job enrichment. As we will learn in this section, there are also several ways to implement job enrichment.

JOB ROTATION

Job rotation Moving employees from one job to another for short periods of time.

Job rotation is the practice of moving employees from one job to another. Consider a typical "one-hour" photofinishing retail outlet where one employee interacts with customers, another operates the photofinishing machine, and a third places the finished product into envelopes and files them for pickup. Job rotation would occur if employees moved around those three jobs every few hours or days.

Job rotation is widely practised in North America.[75] However, the main reason why many companies have introduced this form of job design isn't to reduce boredom. They want to develop a flexible workforce. Job rotation helps employees learn new tasks and thereby increase their ability to move to jobs where they are needed. A third reason for introducing job rotation is to reduce the incidence of repetitive strain injuries. Snap-On Tools of Canada relies on job rotation for this reason. The company experienced high injury rates at its Newmarket, Ontario, plant because employees were using the same muscles in their narrowly defined jobs. Job rotation, along with better workplace design, significantly reduced the rate of these soft-tissue injuries.[76]

JOB ENLARGEMENT

Job enlargement Increasing the number of tasks that employees perform within their job.

Rather than rotating employees through different jobs, **job enlargement** combines tasks into one job. We might combine two or more complete jobs into one, or just add one or two more tasks to an existing job. Either way, the job's skill variety has increased because there are more tasks to perform.

A dramatic example of job enlargement can be found in the newsroom of CBET, the Windsor, Ontario, affiliate of the Canadian Broadcasting Corporation (CBC). Traditionally, CBC requires up to four people to shoot a news clip: reporter, camera operator, sound operator, and lighting person. Now, one "video journalist" performs all four jobs. Due to the success of the CBET experiment, CBC now uses video journalists across the country for CBC Newsworld and on *Venture*. As a CBC technician in Windsor predicted: "[If] you can't do a couple of things, you're going to be a dinosaur."[77]

Exhibit 4.5 illustrates job enlargement at CBC and how this job design differs from job rotation. Under job rotation, the tasks for shooting a news clip are divided into four jobs, and

EXHIBIT 4.5 Comparing Job Rotation and Job Enlargement

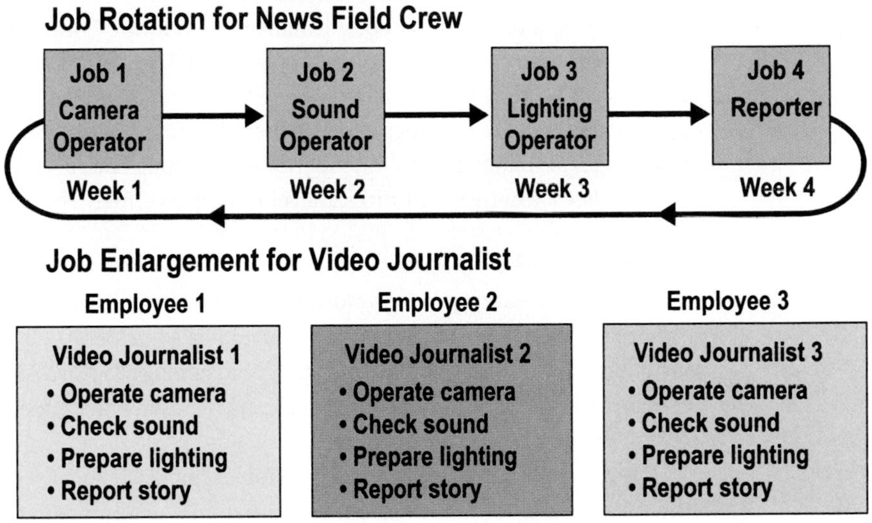
Job Rotation for News Field Crew
Job 1 Camera Operator
Job 2 Sound Operator
Job 3 Lighting Operator
Job 4 Reporter
Week 1
Week 2
Week 3
Week 4
Job Enlargement for Video Journalist
Employee 1
Employee 2
Employee 3
Video Journalist 1
• Operate camera
• Check sound
• Prepare lighting
• Report story
Video Journalist 2
• Operate camera
• Check sound
• Prepare lighting
• Report story
Video Journalist 3
• Operate camera
• Check sound
• Prepare lighting
• Report story

employees would move around these different jobs from time to time. Job enlargement, on the other hand, combines the tasks from all four jobs into one job so that one employee would be responsible for the entire work process. The exhibit shows that the company has created three of these video journalist jobs.

Job enlargement significantly improves work efficiency and flexibility. However, research suggests that simply giving employees more tasks won't affect motivation, performance, or job satisfaction. Instead, these benefits result only when skill variety is combined with more autonomy and job knowledge.[78] In other words, employees are motivated when they have a variety of tasks *and* have the freedom and knowledge to structure their work to achieve the highest satisfaction and performance. These job characteristics are at the heart of job enrichment, which we discuss next.

JOB ENRICHMENT

Job enrichment Assigning responsibility for scheduling, coordinating, and planning work to employees who actually make the product or provide the service.

Job enrichment occurs when employees are given more responsibility for scheduling, coordinating, and planning their own work. Although some writers suggest that job enrichment is any strategy that increases one or more of the core job characteristics, Herzberg's classic position was that jobs are enriched only through autonomy and the resulting feelings of responsibility.[79] Notice that this definition of job enrichment relates directly to *vertical job loading* because it reverses vertical job specialization that was described earlier. There are numerous ways to enrich jobs, but we will discuss three of the most popular methods: empowerment, forming natural work units, and establishing client relationships.

Empowering employees

Empowerment The feeling of control and self-efficacy that emerges when people are given power in a previously powerless situation.

Empowerment refers to a feeling of control and self-efficacy that emerges when people are given power in a previously powerless situation.[80] Empowered employees are given autonomy—freedom, independence, and discretion over their work activities. They are assigned work that has high levels of task significance—importance to themselves and others. Empowered employees also have control over performance feedback that guides their work.

Also notice from the definition that empowered employees have feelings of self-efficacy, that is, they believe that they are capable of successfully completing the task (see Chapter 2).

Empowerment may be an overused term in business, but it can have a noticeable effect on employee motivation and performance. The Liquor Control Board of Ontario empowered its employees by giving them the skills and knowledge for professional customer service rather than narrower roles. Bombardier empowered teams of employees to find defects in the production process and then correct them without management involvement. "[Y]ou don't have a team making recommendations to management; the team does it," explains a Bombardier executive. "It brings a level of empowerment."[81]

Forming natural work units

Another way to enrich jobs is to cluster tasks into a natural grouping, such as completing a whole task. Assembling an entire toaster rather than just some parts of it would be an example of forming a natural work unit. Or it might involve assigning employees to a specific client group, such as managing entire portfolios for specific clients rather than taking random client calls from a customer service pool.

By forming natural work units, jobholders have stronger feelings of responsibility for an identifiable body of work. They feel a sense of ownership and, therefore, tend to increase job

Bruno Schlumberger, Ottawa Citizen.

www.lcbo.com

Empowerment has made the Liquor Control Board of Ontario (LCBO) one of the hottest and most successful retailers in Canada. LCBO invested heavily in "That's the Spirit," a staff development program aimed at improving customer service skills and knowledge about distilled products. Now employees at the Ontario government's 600 retail outlets are able to serve customers better by helping them select the best product for their needs and tastes. "It's really about empowerment of the employee," explains an LCBO representative. "I think what this program has done is empower employees to be able to give customers more information and enable them to make better buying decisions."[82] What conditions are necessary to ensure that customer service training results in empowerment among employees at LCBO and elsewhere?

quality. Forming natural work units increases task identity and task significance because employees perform a complete product or service and can more readily see how their work affects others.

Establishing client relationships

As mentioned, some natural work units assign employees to a specific client group. However, establishing client relationships takes this one step further by putting employees in *direct contact* with their clients rather than using the supervisor as a go-between. The key factor is direct communication with clients. These clients submit work and provide feedback directly to the employee rather than through a supervisor.[83]

Nova Scotia Power applies this form of job enrichment in its rural districts. At one time, installing and disconnecting service, reading meters, and collecting overdue accounts were assigned to people in different jobs. Now, one employee completes all of these tasks for the same client and works directly with the client. By being directly responsible for specific clients, employees have more information and can make decisions affecting those clients.[84]

JOB DESIGN PROSPECTS AND PROBLEMS

Job design has become tremendously popular in recent years. Only 2 percent of Canadian firms had job design interventions before 1960, compared with somewhere between 30 to 50 percent today. These interventions also have a much higher survival rate than most work interventions.[85]

But to what extent does job enrichment improve employee and organizational effectiveness? A lot! Employees with high growth needs in enriched jobs have higher job satisfaction and work motivation, along with lower absenteeism and turnover. Productivity is also higher when task identity and job feedback are improved.[86] Error rates, the number of defects, and other quality indicators tend to improve because job enrichment increases the jobholder's felt responsibility and sense of ownership over the product or service. Quality improvements in production and service are particularly evident when the job enrichment intervention involves completing a natural work unit or establishing client relationships.[87]

OBSTACLES IN JOB DESIGN

In spite of its potential benefits, job design is not easy to implement. Most scholars and consultants rely on the employee's perceived job characteristics because more objective measurement is difficult and expensive. The problem is that these perceptions may be distorted by the employee's satisfaction with co-workers and other aspects of the job.[88] Another issue is that the job design literature has focused on individual jobs, and has overlooked task interdependence and other job design characteristics that apply to team settings.[89] Yet many job redesign projects occur in team-based settings, as we will explore in Chapters 9, 10, and 11.

Job design interventions also face resistance to change. Some supervisors don't like job redesign interventions because they change their roles and may threaten job security.[90] Labour union leaders have been bitter foes of job specialization and scientific management, yet they complain that job enrichment programs are management ploys to get more work out of employees for less money. Unskilled employees may lack the confidence or growth need strength to learn more challenging tasks. Skilled employees are known to resist job redesign because they believe that the intervention will undermine their power base and force them to perform lower-status work.[91]

Kellogg's, the U.S.-owned cereal company, experienced this problem at its production plant in Australia. The company wanted to enlarge and enrich jobs to gain a more flexible workforce, but maintenance employees refused to let production employees do simple maintenance tasks. "We had negotiated to lift the skill levels of operators through a comprehensive multiskilling program only to have the maintenance unions continually renege on that," says Kellogg's Australian human resource manager. To remove this barrier, the company contracted out all maintenance work.[92]

Lastly, an ongoing dilemma of job design is finding the ideal balance between job enrichment and job specialization. There are several competing factors to consider. Specialized jobs may improve work efficiency, but job performance may decline as employee motivation falls. Job enrichment may increase motivation, but performance may fall if employees lack the skills necessary to complete more challenging tasks. Job enrichment may increase recruiting and training costs, whereas job specialization may increase payroll costs if companies provide discontentment pay to entice people into boring jobs.[93] Job enrichment improves product quality, but error rates may increase when tasks become so challenging that employees lack the necessary skills or experience stress.[94] Of course, job specialization also increases stress if employees do not make effective use of their talents in narrowly defined jobs, as we will learn in Chapter 5.

MOTIVATING YOURSELF THROUGH SELF-LEADERSHIP

While most companies are busy finding new "carrots" to motivate employees, Canada Life Assurance Co. is teaching its employees how to motivate themselves.[95] The Toronto-based insurance company has put hundreds of employees through "Investing in Me," a special training program that teaches them to set their own goals and visualize achieving challenging objectives. The program is based on the philosophy that employees manage their own behaviour most of the time. Direct supervision is becoming too expensive and is increasingly incompatible with the values and expectations of today's workforce. The emerging view is that employees can take care of themselves.

Canada Life is encouraging employees to engage in **self-leadership**—the process of influencing oneself to establish the self-direction and self-motivation needed to perform a task.[96] This concept includes a toolkit of behavioural activities borrowed from social learning theory (Chapter 2) and goal setting (Chapter 3). It also includes constructive thought processes that have been extensively studied in sports psychology. Overall, self-leadership takes the view that individuals mostly regulate their own actions through these behavioural and cognitive (thought) activities.

Although we are in the early stages of understanding the dynamics of self-leadership, Exhibit 4.6 identifies the five main elements of this process. These elements, which generally follow each other in a sequence, include personal goal setting, constructive thought patterns, designing natural rewards, self-monitoring, and self-reinforcement.[97]

Self-leadership The process of influencing oneself to establish the self-direction and self-motivation needed to perform a task. This includes personal goal setting, constructive thought patterns, designing natural rewards, self-monitoring, and self-reinforcement.

PERSONAL GOAL SETTING

The first step in self-leadership is to set goals for your own work effort. This applies the ideas we learned in Chapter 3 on goal setting, such as identifying goals that are specific, results-oriented, and challenging. The only difference between personal goal setting and our previous discussion is that goals are set alone, rather than assigned by or jointly decided with a supervisor.[98] According to the self-leadership literature, effective organizations establish norms whereby employees have a natural tendency to set their own goals to motivate themselves.[99]

EXHIBIT 4.6 Elements of Self-Leadership

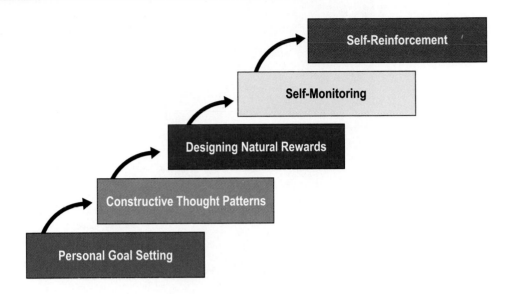

CONSTRUCTIVE THOUGHT PATTERNS

Before beginning a task and while performing it, employees should engage in positive (constructive) thoughts about that work and its accomplishment. In particular, employees are more motivated and better prepared to accomplish a task after they have engaged in positive self-talk and mental imagery.

Positive self-talk

Do you ever talk to yourself? Most of us do, according to a recent Canadian study of undergraduate students at the University of Waterloo.[100] **Self-talk** refers to any situation in which we talk to ourselves about our own thoughts or actions. Some of this internal communication assists the decision-making process, such as weighing the advantages and disadvantages of a particular choice. Self-leadership is mostly interested in evaluative self-talk, in which you evaluate your capabilities and accomplishments.

The problem with most evaluative self-talk is that it is negative; we criticize much more than encourage or congratulate ourselves. Negative self-talk undermines our self-efficacy, which, in turn, undermines our potential for performing a particular task.[101] In contrast, positive self-talk creates a "can-do" belief and thereby increases motivation by raising our E→P expectancy. We often hear that professional athletes "psych" themselves up before an important event. They tell themselves that they can achieve their goal and that they have practised enough to reach that goal. They are motivating themselves through self-talk.

Mental imagery

You've probably heard the phrase, "I'll cross that bridge when I come to it!" Self-leadership takes the opposite view. It suggests that we need to practise a task mentally and imagine successfully performing it beforehand. This process is known as **mental imagery**.[102]

As you can see from this definition, mental imagery has two parts. One part involves mentally practising the task, anticipating obstacles to goal accomplishment, and working out

Self-talk Talking to yourself about your own thoughts or actions, for the purpose of increasing self-efficacy and navigating through the decisions required to get the job done effectively.

Mental imagery Mentally practising a task and visualizing its successful completion.

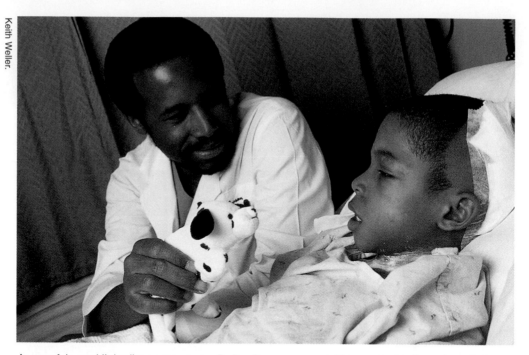

Keith Weller.

As one of the world's leading neurosurgeons, Dr. Ben Carson uses mental imagery to visualize each medical operation he performs—up to 500 of them each year. "I think through every procedure: how I expect it to go, how long each phase will last, when I can move on to the next one," explains the chief of pediatric neurosurgery at Baltimore's Johns Hopkins Hospital. Carson also imagines the worst thing that could happen, what he should do to make sure that doesn't happen, and what he would do if it does. "I always anticipate the worst-case scenario," says Carson.[103] How might Carson apply other elements of the self-leadership model in his work?

www.hopkinsmedicine.org
www.carolina.com/carson/
carson.htm

solutions to those obstacles before they occur. By mentally walking through the activities required to accomplish the task, we begin to see problems that may occur. We can then imagine what responses would be best for each contingency.[104]

While one part of mental imagery helps us to anticipate things that could go wrong, the other part involves visualizing successful completion of the task. We imagine the experience of completing the task and the positive results that follow. Everyone daydreams and fantasizes about being in a successful situation. You might imagine yourself being promoted to your boss's job, receiving a prestigious award, or taking time off work. This visualization increases goal commitment and motivates us to complete the task effectively.

DESIGNING NATURAL REWARDS

Self-leadership recognizes that employees can find ways to make the job itself more motivating.[105] Altering the way a task is accomplished is a common way to build natural rewards into a job. People often have enough discretion in their jobs to make slight changes to suit their needs and preferences. For instance, you might try out a new software program to design an idea, rather than sketch the image with pencil. By using the new software, you are adding challenge to a task that may have otherwise been mundane.

SELF-MONITORING

Self-monitoring is the process of keeping track of one's progress towards a goal. In the section on job design, we learned that feedback from the job itself communicates whether we are accomplishing the task successfully. Self-monitoring includes the notion of consciously looking at naturally occurring feedback at regular intervals. It also includes designing artificial feedback where natural feedback does not occur. Salespeople might arrange to receive monthly reports on sales levels in their territory. Production staff might have gauges or computer feedback systems installed so that they can see how many errors are made on the production line. Corporate leaders play a significant role in self-monitoring by supporting a culture that values performance measurement. According to one study, 42 percent of employees in measurement-oriented firms self-monitor their performance, compared to only 16 percent in firms that do not emphasize performance measurement.[106]

SELF-REINFORCEMENT

Self-leadership includes the social learning theory concept of self-reinforcement. Self-reinforcement occurs whenever an employee has control over a reinforcer but doesn't "take" the reinforcer until completing a self-set goal (see Chapter 2).[107] A common example is taking a break after reaching a predetermined stage of your work. The work break is a self-induced form of positive reinforcement. Self-reinforcement also occurs when you decide to do a more enjoyable task after completing a task that you dislike. For example, after slogging through a difficult report, you might decide to spend time doing a more pleasant task, such as scanning Web sites for information about competitors.

SELF-LEADERSHIP IN PRACTICE

It's too early to say that every component of self-leadership is useful, but evidence suggests that these practices generally improve self-efficacy, motivation, and performance. Studies in sports psychology indicate that self-set goals and constructive thought processes improve individual performance. For example, young Canadian skaters who received self-talk training had improved performance one year later. Self-talk and mental imagery have also improved the performance of tennis players and female college swimmers.[108]

One of the few studies conducted in organizational settings reported that new employees in a Canadian organization who practised self-set goals and self-reinforcement had higher internal motivation. Another study found that airline employees who received constructive thought training experienced better mental performance, enthusiasm, and job satisfaction than co-workers who did not receive this training.[109]

People with a high degree of conscientiousness have a more natural tendency to apply self-leadership strategies. People with a high degree of conscientiousness are meticulous, careful, organized, responsible, and self-disciplined (see Chapter 6). However, one of the benefits of self-leadership is that it can be learned. Training programs have helped employees to improve their self-leadership skills whether or not they have high conscientiousness. Organizations also need to develop reward systems and provide sufficient autonomy to encourage self-leadership.[110] Overall, self-leadership promises to be a valuable concept and practice for improving employee motivation and performance.

Self-leadership, job design, and rewards are valuable approaches to motivating people in organizational settings. However, they are not the only ways to motivate. Motivation is derived from a person's unique combination of natural and learned needs. Each of these needs can be fulfilled in many ways and from various sources. In some respects, many of the topics covered later in this book—such as team cohesiveness, work-related values, and corporate culture—also affect employee motivation.

CHAPTER SUMMARY

- Money and other financial rewards are a fundamental part of the employment relationship. They also potentially fulfil existence, relatedness, and growth needs. People experience various emotions and hold many attitudes towards financial rewards. They also tend to identify themselves in terms of how much money they have acquired and dispersed.

- Organizations reward employees for their membership and seniority, job status, competencies, and performance. Membership-based rewards may attract job applicants and seniority-based rewards reduce turnover. However, they are more likely to discourage turnover among those with the lowest performance. Rewards based on job status try to maintain internal equity and motivate employees to compete for promotions. However, job status–based rewards can lead to organizational politics and create a psychological distance between employees and management. Competency-based rewards are becoming increasingly popular because they improve workforce flexibility and are consistent with the emerging idea of employability. The problem with competency-based rewards is that competencies tend to be subjectively measured and, in the case of skill-based pay, employees eventually reach the highest pay rate.

- Although individual performance-based rewards are widely used, many companies are shifting to team-based and organizational rewards. The most popular among these are gainsharing, employee share ownership plans (ESOPs), share options, and profit sharing. ESOPs and share options create an ownership culture, but one problem with organizational rewards is that employees often perceive a weak connection between individual performance and the organizational reward.

- Financial rewards have been criticized for being used as quick fixes. There is also a risk that they distract employees from the motivational potential of the work, create a psychological distance between the persons giving and receiving the reward, and discourage creativity and risk-taking. To improve reward effectiveness, organizational leaders should ensure that rewards are linked to work performance, rewards are aligned with performance within the employee's control, team rewards are used where jobs are interdependent, rewards are valued by employees, and rewards do not have unintended consequences.

- Job design involves assigning tasks to a job and distributing work throughout the organization. Job specialization subdivides work into separate jobs for different people. This increases work efficiency because employees master the tasks quickly, spend less time changing tasks, require less training, and can be matched more closely with the jobs best suited to their skills. However, job specialization may reduce work motivation, create mental-health problems, lower product or service quality, and increase costs through discontentment pay, absenteeism, and turnover.

- Contemporary job design strategies reverse job specialization through job rotation, job enlargement, and job enrichment. Hackman's and Oldham's job characteristics model is the most popular foundation for recent job redesign interventions because it specifies core job dimensions, psychological states, and individual differences. Companies often enrich jobs by empowering employees, forming natural work units, and establishing client relationships.

- Self-leadership is the process of influencing oneself to establish the self-direction and self-motivation needed to perform a task. This includes personal goal setting, constructive thought patterns, designing natural rewards, self-monitoring, and self-reinforcement.

- Constructive thought patterns include self-talk and mental imagery. Self-talk refers to any situation in which a person talks to him- or herself about his or her own thoughts or actions. Mental imagery involves mentally practising a task and imagining performing it successfully beforehand.

KEY TERMS

Autonomy, p. 108

Competencies, p. 97

Employability, p. 98

Employee share ownership plan (ESOP), p. 99

Empowerment, p. 111

Gainsharing plan, p. 99

Job characteristics model, p. 107

Job design, p. 105

Job enlargement, p. 110

Job enrichment, p. 111

Job evaluation, p. 97

Job feedback, p. 109

Job rotation, p. 110

Job specialization, p. 105

Mental imagery, p. 115

Profit sharing, p. 100

Scientific management, p. 106

Self-leadership, p. 114

Self-talk, p. 115

Share options, p. 100

Skill variety, p. 108

Skill-based pay (SBP), p. 98

Task identity, p. 108

Task significance, p. 108

DISCUSSION QUESTIONS

1. As a consultant, you have been asked to recommend either a gainsharing plan or a profit-sharing plan for employees who work in the four regional distribution and warehousing facilities of a large retail organization. Which reward system would you recommend? Explain your answer.

2. A large technology company distributed 100 share options to each of its employees around the world. This was worth more than seven years' income to the company's production employees in Thailand. What effect do you think share options will have on these employees?

3. Inuvik Tire Corp. has redesigned its production facilities around a team-based system. However, the company president believes that employees will not be motivated unless they receive incentives based on their individual performance. Give three explanations why Inuvik Tire should introduce team-based rather than individual rewards in this setting.

4. Under what conditions would job specialization be most appropriate?

5. Most of us have watched pizzas being made while waiting in a pizzeria. What level of job specialization do you usually notice in these operations? Why does this high or low level of specialization exist? If some pizzerias have different levels of specialization than others, identify the contingencies that might explain these differences.

6. You have been asked by senior administration at your college or university to identify ways that instructors can "empower" students in the classroom. What specific recommendations would you provide? Your answer should identify specific things that instructors should do to generate empowerment.

7. Tomorrow, you present your first report to senior management to extend funding for your unit's special initiative. All of the materials are ready for the presentation. Following the five steps in self-leadership, describe how you can prepare for that meeting.

8. Several elements of self-leadership are derived from concepts presented earlier in this book. Identify those concepts and explain how they are applied in self-leadership.

 # Case Study

ACTIVITY 4.1

Keeping Suzanne Chalmers

Thomas Chan hung up the telephone and sighed. The vice-president of software engineering at Advanced Photonics Ltd. (APL) had just spoken to Suzanne Chalmers, who had called to arrange a meeting with Chan later that day. She didn't say what the meeting was about, but Chan almost instinctively knew that Chalmers was going to quit after having worked at APL for the past four years. Chalmers is a software engineer in Internet Protocol (IP), the software that directs fibre optic light through APL's routers. It was very specialized work, and Chalmers was one of APL's top talents in that area.

Thomas Chan had been through this before. A valued employee would arrange a private meeting. The meeting would begin with a few pleasantries, and then the employee would announce that he or she wanted to quit. Some employees say they are leaving because of the long hours and stressful deadlines. They say they need to need to decompress, get to know their kids again, etc. But that's not usually the real reason. Almost every organization in this industry is scrambling to keep up with technological advances and the competition. The employees would simply be leaving one stressful job for another one.

Many of the people who leave APL join a start-up company a few months later. These start-up firms can be pressure cookers where everyone works 16 hours each day and has to perform a variety of tasks. For example, engineers in these small firms might have to meet customers or work on venture capital pro-posals rather than focus on specialized tasks related to their knowledge. APL has over 1000 employees, so it is easier to assign people work that matches their technical competencies.

No, the problem isn't the stress or long hours, Chan thought. The problem is money—too much money. Most of the people who leave APL are millionaires. Suzanne Chalmers is one of them. Thanks to generous share options that have skyrocketed on the Toronto and NASDAQ stock markets, many employees at APL have more money than they can use. Most are under 40 years of age, so are too young to retire. But their financial independence gives them less incentive to remain with APL.

The meeting with Suzanne Chalmers took place a few hours after the telephone call. It began like the others, with the initial pleasantries and brief discussion about progress on the latest fibre optic router project. Then Suzanne made her well-rehearsed statement: "Thomas, I've really enjoyed working here, but I'm going to leave Advanced Photonics." Suzanne took a breath, then looked at Chan. When he didn't reply after a few seconds, she continued: "I need to take time off. You know, get away to recharge my batteries. The project's nearly done and the team can complete it without me. Well, anyway, I'm thinking of leaving."

Chan spoke in a calm voice. He suggested that Chalmers take an unpaid leave for two or three months, complete with paid benefits, then return refreshed. Chalmers politely rejected that offer, saying that she needed to get away from work for a while. Chan then asked Chalmers whether she was unhappy with her work environment—whether she

ACTIVITY 4.1 CONTINUED

had access to the latest computer technology to do her work, and whether there were problems with co-workers. The workplace was fine, Chalmers replied. The job was a bit routine at times, but she had a comfortable workplace with excellent co-workers.

Chan then apologized for the cramped workspace, due mainly to the rapid increase in the number of people hired over the past year. He suggested that if Chalmers took a couple of months off, APL would have a larger workspace with a better view of the park behind the campus-like building when she returned. Chalmers politely thanked Chan for that offer, but said it wasn't what she needed. Besides, it wouldn't be fair to have a large workspace when other team members work in smaller quarters.

Chan was running out of tactics, so he tried his last hope: money. He asked whether Chalmers had higher offers elsewhere. She replied that she regularly received calls from other companies, and that some of them offered more money. Most were start-up firms that offered a lower salary but higher potential gains in share options. Chan knew from market surveys that Chalmers was already paid well in the industry. He also knew that APL couldn't compete on share-option potential. Employees working in start-up firms some-

times saw their shares increase by five or ten times their initial value, whereas shares at APL and other large firms increased more slowly. However, Chan promised Chalmers that he would recommend that she receive a significant raise—maybe 25 percent—and more share options. Chan added that Chalmers was one of APL's most valuable employees and that the company would suffer if she left the firm.

The meeting ended with Chalmers promising to consider Chan's offer of higher pay and share options. Two days later, Chan received her resignation in writing. Five months later, Chan learned that after spending a few months travelling with her husband, Chalmers joined a start-up software firm in the area.

Discussion Questions

1. Do financial rewards have any value in situations such as this, where employees are relatively wealthy?

2. If you were Thomas Chan, what strategy, if any, would you use to motivate Suzanne Chalmers to stay at Advanced Photonics Ltd?

3. Of what importance is job design in this case?

© 2001 Steven L. McShane.

Video Case Study

ACTIVITY 4.2
Career Coach Program

Money can solve a lot of problems, but for high-tech companies desperate to hang on to their highly skilled employees, money alone doesn't cut it. Somebody else can always offer more. That's why the race is on to find new ways to keep staff happy.

Sixty-hour weeks. Unrealistic bosses. Demanding customers. Families not seen for days. These are common complaints heard around the water cooler at high-tech companies. And Dy4 is no exception. The Kanata, Ontario, designer of computers for harsh climates is stretching employees to the limit with rapid

growth and product backlogs. To recruit and retain the best employees, Dy4 has introduced a Career Coach Program that helps employees target those areas causing friction.

"The main issue is that they've lost a sense of control in their workplace," says Daniel O'Connor, the founder of Keepers Inc., which runs the program. "And what that leaves them feeling is very disempowered and subject to the whims of the industry, the whims of their managers, the whims of the company and that's a pretty discouraging feeling."

O'Connor is working with Grant, who manages one of Dy4's product lines. Grant suffers anxiety

ACTIVITY 4.2 CONTINUED

attacks when he thinks about the number of meetings that he must attend each day while trying to get his product out on time. But is Grant completely powerless? Maybe he's a pushover. Does he ever say no? O'Connor had Grant think about the things that led to all of these meetings. But it takes time to change. A few weeks later, O'Connor discovered that Grant had ten meetings and was backlogged with 600 e-mail messages.

Ernie is an engineer at Dy4 who is worried about work–life balance. O'Connor encouraged him to track his time for a week and then look at how his life is divided on a pie chart. Dy4 got a huge 61-hour slice of Ernie's pie last week. His family got the crumbs. To turn things around, O'Connor had Ernie set some goals, such as going out with his wife at least once every two weeks and eating dinner with the family at least five

nights a week. So far, Ernie only gets home by dinnertime one or two nights each week.

It's a slow start, but Dy4 employees are moving in the right direction. And as it takes hold, the Career Coach Program helps Dy4 keep its talent from looking for work elsewhere.

Discussion Questions

1. What effect does Dy4's Career Coach Program have on job design for Grant, Ernie, and other employees?

2. How does self-leadership play a role in the Career Coach Program?

3. This video program begins with the claim that money is not enough to recruit and retain employees. Do you believe this statement? What would be more important than money to you when looking for a job?

Source: Based on "Keepers Inc.," *Venture* 742 (March 7, 2000).

 **TEAM exercises**

ACTIVITY 4.3
IS STUDENT WORK ENRICHED?

Purpose: This exercise is designed to help students learn how to measure the motivational potential of jobs and to evaluate the extent to which jobs should be further enriched.

Instructions: Being a student is like having a job in several ways. You have tasks to perform and someone (such as your instructor) oversees your work. Although few people want to be students for most of their lives (the pay rate is too low!), it may be interesting to determine how enriched your job is as a student.

Step 1: Students are placed into teams (preferably of four or five people).

Step 2: Working alone, each student completes both sets of measures in this exercise. Then, using the guidelines below, each individual calculates the score for the five core job characteristics as well as the overall motivating potential score for the job.

Step 3: Members of each team compare their individual results. The group should identify differences of opinion for each core job characteristic. It should also note which core jobs characteristics have the lowest scores and recommend how these scores could be increased.

Step 4: The entire class will now meet to discuss the results of the exercise. The instructor may ask some teams to present their comparisons and recommendations for a particular core job characteristic.

JOB DIAGNOSTIC SURVEY

Circle the number on the right that best describes student work.	Very Little ▼		Moderately ▼			Very Much ▼
1. To what extent does student work permit you to decide on your own how to go about doing the work?	1	2	3	4	5	6	7
2. To what extent does student work involve doing a whole or an identifiable piece of work, rather than a small portion of the overall work process?	1	2	3	4	5	6	7
3. To what extent does student work require you to do many different things, using a variety of your skills and talents?	1	2	3	4	5	6	7
4. To what extent are the results of your work as a student likely to significantly affect the lives and well-being of other people (e.g., within your school, your family, society)?	1	2	3	4	5	6	7
5. To what extent does working on student activities provide information about your performance?	1	2	3	4	5	6	7

Circle the number on the right that best describes student work.	Very Inaccurate ▼		Uncertain ▼			Accurate ▼
6. Being a student requires me to use a number of complex and high-level skills.	1	2	3	4	5	6	7
7. Student work is arranged so that I do NOT have the chance to do an entire piece of work from beginning to end.	7	6	5	4	3	2	1
8. Doing the work required of students provides many chances for me to figure out how well I am doing.	1	2	3	4	5	6	7
9. The work students must do is quite simple and repetitive.	7	6	5	4	3	2	1
10. The work of a student is one where a lot of other people can be affected by how well the work gets done.	1	2	3	4	5	6	7
11. Student work denies me any chance to use my personal initiative or judgment in carrying out the work.	7	6	5	4	3	2	1
12. Student work provides me the chance to completely finish the pieces of work I begin.	1	2	3	4	5	6	7
13. Doing student work by itself provides very few clues about whether I am performing well.	7	6	5	4	3	2	1

14. As a student, I have considerable
    opportunity for independence and
    freedom in how I do the work.. 1   2   3   4   5   6   7

15. The work I perform as a student is
    NOT very significant or important in
    the broader scheme of things. 7   6   5   4   3   2   1

Adapted from the Job Diagnostic Survey, developed by J.R. Hackman and G.R. Oldham. The authors have released any copyright ownership of this scale (see J.R. Hackman and G. Oldham, *Work Redesign* (Reading, MA: Addison-Wesley, 1980), p. 275).

CALCULATING THE MOTIVATING POTENTIAL SCORE

Scoring Core Job Characteristics: Use the following set of calculations to estimate the motivating potential score for the job of being a student. Use your answers from the Job Diagnostic Survey above.

Skill Variety (SV) $\dfrac{\text{Questions } 3 + 6 + 9}{3}$ = _____

Task Identity (TI) $\dfrac{\text{Questions } 2 + 7 + 12}{3}$ = _____

Task Significance (TS) $\dfrac{\text{Questions } 4 + 10 + 15}{3}$ = _____

Autonomy $\dfrac{\text{Questions } 1 + 11 + 14}{3}$ = _____

Job Feedback $\dfrac{\text{Questions } 5 + 8 + 13}{3}$ = _____

Calculating Motivating Potential Score (MPS): Use the following formula and the results above to calculate the motivating potential score. Notice that skill variety, task identity, and task significance are averaged before being multiplied by the scores for autonomy and job feedback.

$$\left(\frac{\text{SV} + \text{TI} + \text{TS}}{3}\right) \times \textbf{Autonomy} \times \textbf{Job Feedback} = \left(\frac{\_\_\_ + \_\_\_ + \_\_\_}{3}\right) \times \_\_\_\_ \times \_\_\_\_ = \_\_\_\_\_$$

Self-Assessment exercise

ACTIVITY 4.4
ASSESSING YOUR SELF-LEADERSHIP

Purpose: This exercise is designed to help you understand self-leadership concepts and to assess your self-leadership tendencies.

Instructions: Read each of the statements below and circle the response that you believe best reflects your position regarding each statement. Then use the scoring key in Appendix B of this book to calculate your results. This exercise is completed alone so that students can assess themselves honestly without concerns of social comparison. However, class discussion will focus on the meaning of each self-leadership concept, how this scale might be applied in organizations, and the limitations of measuring self-leadership in work settings.

SELF-LEADERSHIP QUESTIONNAIRE

Circle the number that best reflects your position regarding each of these statements.	Describes Me Very Well ▼	Describes Me Well ▼	Describes Me Somewhat ▼	Does Not Describe Me Well ▼	Does Not Describe Me at All ▼
1. I try to keep track of how I am doing while I work.	5	4	3	2	1
2. I often use reminders to help me remember things I need to do.	5	4	3	2	1
3. I like to work towards specific goals I set for myself.	5	4	3	2	1
4. After I perform well on an activity, I feel good about myself.	5	4	3	2	1
5. I seek out activities in my work that I enjoy doing.	5	4	3	2	1
6. I often practise important tasks before I do them.	5	4	3	2	1
7. I usually am aware of how I am performing an activity.	5	4	3	2	1
8. I try to arrange my work area in a way that helps me positively focus my attention on my work.	5	4	3	2	1
9. I establish personal goals for myself.	5	4	3	2	1
10. When I have successfully completed a task, I often reward myself with something I like.	5	4	3	2	1
11. When I have a choice, I try to do my work in ways that I enjoy rather than just trying to get it over with.	5	4	3	2	1
12. I like to go over an important activity before I actually perform it.	5	4	3	2	1
13. I keep track of my progress on projects I am working on.	5	4	3	2	1
14. I try to surround myself with objects and people that bring out my desirable behaviours.	5	4	3	2	1
15. I like to set task goals for my performance.	5	4	3	2	1
16. When I do an assignment especially well, I like to treat myself to something or an activity I enjoy.	5	4	3	2	1
17. I try to build activities into my work that I like doing.	5	4	3	2	1
18. I often rehearse my plan for dealing with a challenge before I actually face that challenge.	5	4	3	2	1

Source: C.C. Manz, *Mastering Self-Leadership: Empower Yourself for Personal Excellence* (Englewood Cliffs, NJ: Prentice-Hall, 1992). Used with permission of the author. The scale presented here excludes the self-punishment dimension found in the SLQ1 instrument because it is not calculated in the SLQ1 total score. The designing natural rewards dimension presented here is measured by items in the third dimension of the SLQ2 instrument.

CHAPTER FIVE

Stress Management

LEARNING OBJECTIVES

After reading this chapter, you should be able to:

- Define stress and describe the stress experience.
- Outline the stress process from stressors to consequences.
- Identify the different types of stressors in the workplace.
- Explain why a stressor might produce different stress levels in two people.
- Discuss the physiological, psychological, and behavioural effects of stress.
- Identify five ways to manage workplace stress.

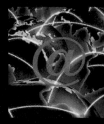

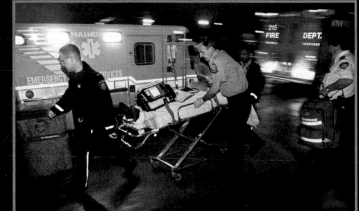

Winnipeg's paramedics experience stress as the city's ambulance service is stretched to the limit.

I t's Friday night, and Winnipeg's paramedics are racing from call to call without a break. The city's ambulance service is stretched to the limit. Twice tonight, the dispatcher has announced "no cars available," meaning that someone who needs assistance must wait half an hour or longer for an ambulance. This shortage is taking its toll on Winnipeg's paramedics, who feel unable to provide basic services in time.

"When you lose somebody, or you go through a bad streak, maybe a month without saving somebody's life, it accumulates," says Rick Boustead, a paramedic in Toronto, where resources are also limited. "That kind of stress breaks up marriages, it makes some people alcoholics."

Toronto's ambulance crews face an additional source of stress. Emergency rooms are sometimes packed to capacity, leaving paramedics with nowhere to take patients. On one day in December, 23 of Toronto's 25 hospitals were turning away ambulances. These delays add further pressure on paramedics.

"The stress level in here is incredible and increasing daily," says a Toronto ambulance dispatcher.[1]

www.city.winnipeg.mb.ca/
interhom/govern/
emergency/default.htm

www.city.toronto.on.ca/
ems/index.htm

Work-related stress is becoming an epidemic in the workplace. Recent studies report that nearly half of Canadian employees feel moderate or high levels of stress, compared with only one-quarter of employees a decade earlier. Another study, sponsored by the Canadian Heart and Stroke Foundation, reported that almost one-third of employees regularly has difficulty coping with the demands of their jobs. An international study reported that people born after 1955 are up to three times as likely to experience stress-related disorders as were their grandparents.[2]

According to the Conference Board of Canada, work-related stress costs Canadian businesses more than $12 billion each year in lower productivity and higher absenteeism, turnover, alcoholism, and medical costs. It can also cost employers in arbitration awards, court decisions, and occupational health and safety premiums. Insurance companies report a significant increase in stress-related disability claims. "A few years ago, stress-related claims made up 10 percent of total disability claims," says an executive at Sun Life of Canada. "Now it's as high as 30 percent." For example, almost half of long-term disability claims among teachers in Waterloo, Ontario, are related to stress.[3]

Chronic work-related stress is not just a Canadian affliction. Over three-quarters of U.S. employees describe their job as stressful; over half of them say that they experience high levels of stress at least once each week.[4] In the United Kingdom, 83 percent of human resource managers indicate that stress is a problem in their organizations. At the Escorts Heart Institute in Delhi, India, routine cardiac screenings indicate that most executives are in fairly advanced stages of stress. "Corporate India is finally waking up to the fact that a lot of human potential is being drained away because of stress and burnout," says Shekhar Bajaj, CEO of Bajaj Electricals, a consumer electronics manufacturer in India.[5]

In this chapter, we look at the dynamics of work-related stress and how to manage it. The chapter begins by describing the stress experience. Next, the causes and consequences of stress are examined, along with the factors that cause some people to experience stress when others do not. The final section of this chapter looks at ways to manage work-related stress from either an organizational or an individual perspective.

WHAT IS STRESS?

Stress An individual's adaptive response to a situation that is perceived to be challenging or threatening to the person's well-being.

Stress is an adaptive response to a situation that is perceived to be challenging or threatening to the person's well-being.[6] As we shall see, stress is the person's reaction to a situation, not the situation itself. Moreover, we experience stress when something is perceived to interfere with our well-being, that is, with our need fulfilment. Stress has both psychological and physiological dimensions. Psychologically, people perceive a situation and interpret it as challenging or threatening. This cognitive appraisal leads to a set of physiological responses, such as higher blood pressure, sweaty hands, and faster heartbeat.

We often hear about stress as a negative consequence of modern living. People are stressed from overwork, job insecurity, information overload,

"...now let's see how you react to scenes of your employees leaving early."

and the increasing pace of life. These events produce *distress*—the degree of physiological, psychological, and behavioural deviation from healthy functioning.[7] There is also a positive side of stress, called *eustress*, which refers to the healthy, positive, constructive outcome of stressful events and the stress response. Eustress is the stress experience in moderation, enough to activate and motivate people so that they can achieve goals, change their environments, and succeed in life's challenges. In other words, we need some stress to survive. However, most research focuses on distress, because it is a significant concern in organizational settings.[8] Employees frequently experience enough stress to hurt their job performance and increase their risk of mental and physical health problems. Consequently, our discussion will focus more on distress than on eustress.

GENERAL ADAPTATION SYNDROME

General adaptation syndrome A model of the stress experience, consisting of three stages: alarm reaction, resistance, and exhaustion.

The stress experience was first documented 50 years ago by Dr. Hans Selye, the Montreal-based pioneer in stress research.[9] Selye determined that people have a fairly consistent physiological response to stressful situations. This response, called the **general adaptation syndrome**, provides an automatic defence system to help us cope with environmental demands. Exhibit 5.1 illustrates the three stages of the general adaptation syndrome: alarm reaction, resistance, and exhaustion. The line in this exhibit shows the individual's energy and ability to cope with the stressful situation.

Alarm reaction

In the alarm reaction stage, the perception of a threatening or challenging situation causes the brain to send a biochemical message to various parts of the body, resulting in increased respiration rate, blood pressure, heartbeat, muscle tension, and other physiological responses. The individual's energy level and coping effectiveness initially decrease in response to the shock. Extreme shock, however, may result in incapacity or death because the body is unable to generate enough energy quickly enough. In most situations, the alarm reaction alerts the person to the environmental condition and prepares the body for the resistance stage.

EXHIBIT 5.1   Selye's General Adaptation Syndrome

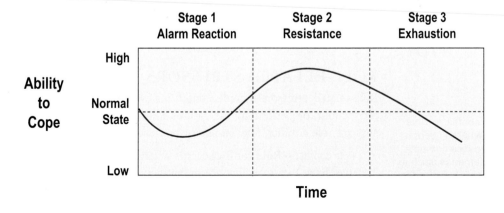

Source: Adapted from J.L. Gibson, J.M. Ivancevich, and J.H. Donnelly, *Organizations: Behavior, Structure, Processes,* 7th ed. (Burr Ridge, IL: Richard D. Irwin, 1994), p. 265.

Resistance

The person's ability to cope with the environmental demand rises above the normal state during the resistance stage because the body has activated various biochemical, psychological, and behavioural mechanisms. For example, the person has a higher than normal level of adrenalin during this stage, which gives him or her more energy to overcome or remove the source of stress. However, resistance is directed to only one or two environmental demands, so that the person is more vulnerable to other sources of stress. This explains why people are more likely to catch a cold or other illness when they have been working under pressure.

Exhaustion

People have a limited resistance capacity and, if the source of stress persists, they will eventually move into the exhaustion stage as this capacity diminishes. In most work situations, the general adaptation syndrome process ends long before total exhaustion. Employees resolve tense situations before the destructive consequences of stress become manifest, or they withdraw from the stressful situation, rebuild their survival capabilities, and return later to the stressful environment with renewed energy. However, people who frequently experience the general adaptation syndrome have increased risk of long-term physiological and psychological damage.[10]

The general adaptation syndrome describes the stress experience, but this is only part of the picture. To effectively manage work-related stress, we must understand its causes and consequences as well as individual differences in the stress experience.

STRESSORS: THE CAUSES OF STRESS

Stressor Any environmental condition that places a physical or emotional demand on a person.

Stressors, the causes of stress, include any environmental conditions that place a physical or emotional demand on a person.[11] There are numerous stressors in organizational settings and other life activities. Exhibit 5.2 lists the four main types of work-related stressors: physical environment, role-related, interpersonal, and organizational stressors.

PHYSICAL ENVIRONMENT STRESSORS

Some stressors are found in the physical work environment, such as excessive noise, poor lighting, and safety hazards. For example, a study of textile workers in a noisy plant found that their levels of stress measurably decreased when they were supplied with ear protectors.[12] Logging truck drivers in western Canada wear mouthguards because they would otherwise grind their teeth down from stress while driving their fully loaded rigs along treacherous mountain roads. Physical stressors—including poorly designed office space, lack of privacy, ineffective lighting, and poor air quality—are also becoming apparent in office settings.

ROLE-RELATED STRESSORS

Role conflict A situation whereby people experience competing demands, such as having job duties that are incompatible with personal values or receiving contradictory messages from different people.

Role-related stressors include conditions where employees have difficulty understanding, reconciling, or performing the various roles in their lives. The four main role-related stressors are role conflict, role ambiguity, workload, and task control:

- *Role conflict*—**Role conflict** occurs when people face competing demands.[13] An employee may have two roles that are in conflict with each other (called *interrole conflict*) or may receive contradictory messages from different people about how to perform a task (called *intrarole conflict*). Role conflict also occurs when organizational values and work obligations are incompatible with personal values (called *person-role conflict*). For example, we sometimes need to be nice to clients we don't like.[14]

EXHIBIT 5.2   Causes and Consequences of Stress

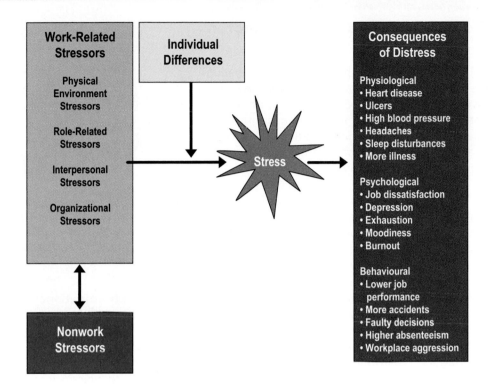

<table>
<tr><td>

Role ambiguity
Uncertainty about job duties, performance expectations, level of authority, and other job conditions.

</td></tr>
</table>

- *Role ambiguity*—**Role ambiguity** exists when employees are uncertain about their job duties, performance expectations, level of authority, and other job conditions. This tends to occur when people enter new situations, such as joining the organization or taking a foreign assignment, because they are uncertain about task and social expectations.[15]

- *Workload*—Work overload is a common stressor these days. Either Canadians have too much to do in too little time or they work too many hours on the job. Long work hours lead to unhealthy lifestyles, which, in turn, cause heart disease and strokes. Japanese employees, who have some of the longest working hours, are experiencing "karoshi"—sudden death from overwork. Karoshi is rare in Canada, but health experts are concerned that our average workweek has increased since the 1980s.[16] Work underload is less common, but can also cause stress. Work underload occurs when employees receive too little work or are given tasks that do not make sufficient use of their skills or knowledge.

- *Task control*—One of the most important findings to emerge from stress research is that employees are more stressed when they lack control over how and when they perform their tasks, as well as when they lack control over the pace of work activity.[17] Work is potentially more stressful when it is paced by a machine, involves monitoring equipment, or the work schedule is controlled by someone else. A recent Statistics Canada study of 12,000 Canadians reported that employees in production, sales, and service jobs have higher psychological stress because of their lack of work control.[18] As Connections 5.1 describes, cellular telephones and other information technologies are potential stressors because they tend to control our work lives.

CONNECTIONS 5.1

Technostress for Overconnected Canadians

Marilyn Cole once thought that her cellular telephone and other high-tech wizardry would produce a more laid-back lifestyle. It hasn't. Instead, this financial executive at a Canadian construction management company is putting in more time than ever and feeling less control over her work.

"I've been out for lunch and all of a sudden the accountant or lawyer would call," says Cole. "And I'm absolutely e-mailed to death by people who could just as easily say things to me when they see me."

Anger is an obvious sign of rising technostress at a time when "we're all running around just on edge," says Vancouver psychologist Janet Taylor.

Marilyn Cole is not alone. Over two-thirds of employees in large U.S. companies feel overwhelmed by the incessant demands of electronic communication. One-quarter of British managers experienced stress over the past year because they couldn't keep up with their e-mail. Little wonder that "technostress"—stress caused by information technology—has become one of the leading health hazards in the workplace. Information overload, an out-of-control work pace, and a crisis in communicating underlie the growing levels of stress and anger on the job, explains Vancouver psychologist Janet Taylor (shown in photo). Interpersonal relations often are trampled under this speed-crazed bias. "There's an intolerance, an impatience with what may be slower [than technology]," Taylor says.

Forty percent of Canadians blame technology for today's fast pace of life. Yet many of us are reluctant to disconnect, even when on vacation. "I know the stress my clients are under and how important an immediate response is," says Kim Coombs, owner of Easyguide Child Support Enforcement in Stoney Creek, Ontario. "So when I can't get to my messages, I get panicked." George Goulakos feels the same way: "My life is my work and vice versa," explains the sales and marketing vice-president of Montreal's CFCF-TV. "I feel I need to be in touch all the time."

Sources: P. Luke, "Rage: Download the Overload," *Vancouver Province*, April 9, 2000; C. Norton, "Stressed Managers Complain of E-mail Overload," *Independent* (London), February 24, 2000, p. 9; M. Habib, "Technology Rules at Close of the '90s," *Regina Leader-Post*, December 20, 1999, p. D3; S. Whittaker, "Vacation's Rarely a Getaway," *Montreal Gazette*, May 22, 1999, p. I1; K. Foss, "Stressed Out? Blame Technology," *Globe and Mail*, May 29, 1998, p. C8; Pitney Bowes, "Are Workers Overwhelmed by Communications?" News Release, May 1997.

INTERPERSONAL STRESSORS

Interpersonal stressors include ineffective supervision, office politics, and other conflicts we experience with people. Employees working at B.C. Ferries Corp. face irate passengers when there are sailing waits. Call centre employees in New Brunswick are stressed from uncooperative customers and high productivity quotas. "[Two hundred and sixty] calls a day from rude and angry people...it's hard to deal with at times," concludes one call centre employee.[19] The trend towards teamwork also seems to generate more interpersonal stressors because employees must interact more with co-workers. For instance, employees at Westrail, the government-owned rail transportation company in Western Australia, experienced higher stress when they were formed into work teams.[20]

Sexual harassment

Nicole Curling's job with Victoria Tea Company in Toronto was extremely stressful. The stress wasn't from long hours or difficult work; it was from her boss's persistent attempts to kiss and fondle her. The Ontario Human Rights Commission awarded Curling $40,000 in emotional distress damages, but the harassment and subsequent legal battle were overwhelming. "It's a gruelling, gruelling experience," she says.[21]

Nicole Curling has experienced the stress of **sexual harassment**—unwelcome conduct of a sexual nature that detrimentally affects the work environment or leads to adverse job-related consequences for its victims. Sexual harassment is not restricted to situations where a person's employment or job performance is conditional on unwanted sexual relations (called *quid pro quo*). The Supreme Court of Canada has concluded that sexual harassment may also occur when sexual conduct (such as posting pornographic material) unreasonably interferes with an individual's work performance or creates an intimidating, hostile, or offensive work environment.[22]

Nearly one-quarter of all Canadian women have been sexually harassed on the job, mostly by co-workers and supervisors. An internal Royal Canadian Mounted Police report revealed that 60 percent of female officers have experienced some form of sexual harassment at work.[23] Canadian corporate leaders increasingly recognize that sexual harassment (and other forms of harassment) is a serious concern. But harassment is more than a legal issue; it is a serious interpersonal stressor.[24] Victims of sexual harassment experience trauma (especially from rape or related exploitation) or must endure tense co-worker relations in a hostile work environment. Moreover, as Nicole Curling discovered, they are expected to endure more stress while these incidents are investigated.

Workplace violence

Another serious interpersonal stressor is the rising wave of physical violence in the workplace.[25] We immediately think about the United States, where 1000 employees are murdered on the job each year and 2 million others experience lesser forms of violence.[26] But the International Labour Organization reports that American employees face a lower incidence of workplace assaults and sexual harassment than do Canadian employees. In fact, Canada has the fourth-highest incidence of workplace assault and sexual harassment among the 32 countries studied. The report discovered that 1 percent of American women were assaulted in the workplace, compared to 4 percent of Canadian women. Canadian men had a slightly higher incidence of workplace assault than their U.S. counterparts.[27]

The Ontario Workplace Safety and Insurance Board receives more than 1400 claims for lost-time injuries due to violent acts each year. The highest number of claims are submitted by health-care workers as well as those in social and community services. One recent study reported that almost all emergency department staff at St. Paul's Hospital in Vancouver have experienced physical assault, 55 percent of them within the past year. Almost one-third of these employees said they experienced extreme stress as a result of the incident.[28]

Employees who experience violence usually have symptoms of severe distress after the traumatic event.[29] It is not uncommon for these primary victims to take long-term disability. Some never return to work. Workplace violence is also a stressor to those who observe the violence. After a serious workplace incident, counsellors work with many employees, not just

Sexual harassment Unwelcome conduct of a sexual nature that detrimentally affects the work environment or leads to adverse job-related consequences for its victims.

with the direct victims. Even employees who have not directly experienced or observed violence may show signs of stress if they work in high-risk jobs. For example, one study reported that the greatest cause of work-related stress among British bus drivers was their perceived risk of physical assault.[30]

ORGANIZATIONAL STRESSORS

Organizational stressors come in many forms. As we shall learn in Chapter 15, most forms of organizational change are stressful. Downsizing (reducing the number of employees) is a stressor not only for those who lose their jobs, but also for the survivors. Specifically, survivors experience higher workloads, increased job insecurity, and the loss of friends at work. Restructuring, privatization, mergers, and other forms of reorganization are stressful because employees face increased job insecurity, uncertain work demands, and new forms of interpersonal conflict.[31]

NONWORK STRESSORS

Work is usually the most stressful part of our lives, but it's not the only stressful part. We also experience numerous stressors outside of organizational settings. Employees do not park these stressors at the door when they enter the workplace. Instead, they carry over and ultimately affect work behaviour. Moreover, the stress model shown earlier in Exhibit 5.2 (see page 131) has a two-way arrow, indicating that stressors from work spill over into nonwork stressors and conflict with each other. For instance, almost half of the North American workforce experiences some type of work–family stressor. Increasingly, employees without families also express their need to balance work with personal life. There are three main work–nonwork stressors: time-based, strain-based, and role behaviour conflict.[32]

Time-based conflict

Rocco Marcantonio knows all about the stress of trying to balance time at work with family. The accountant carries the double duty of corporate reporting requirements for MDS Nordion's nuclear medicine operations in Kanata, Ontario, and Charleroi, Belgium. This means a lot of time at work and travelling. "I have a young boy, and both my wife and I work," explains Marcantonio. "So if I'm away for long, it's a source of stress for me and my family."[33]

Rocco Marcantonio has to contend with *time-based conflict*—the challenge of balancing the time demanded by work with family and other nonwork activities. Time-based conflict largely explains why stress increases with the number of hours of paid employment and the amount of business travel or commuting time. Inflexible work schedules and rotating shift schedules can also take a heavy toll because they prevent employees from effectively juggling work and nonwork.[34] Time-based conflict isn't restricted to people living in large cities. A task force in Saskatchewan recently concluded that it is a significant stressor among employees in that province. "Saskatchewan people are facing a time-crunch and are running hard to earn a living and care for children and elderly parents," said the task force report.[35]

Time-based conflict is more acute for women than it is for men. As Connections 5.2 describes, the problem is that housework and child care represent a "second shift" for many women in dual-career families. One estimate is that working mothers spend 31 hours per week on child care and household work, whereas their spouses spend only 15 hours each week.[36] Until men increase their contribution to homemaking and businesses learn to accommodate to the new social order, many of these "supermoms" will continue to experience superstress.

CONNECTIONS 5.2

Supermoms Face Superstress

Janet Vosman's workday would leave anyone feeling wrung out. The Nova Scotia government computer services officer wakes her two preschool kids at 6 a.m., prepares their breakfast, makes sure they have dressed and brushed their teeth, drops them off at daycare, catches the bus to work downtown, and is at her desk by 8:30 a.m. She works a full day, then rushes home for supper, chores, and getting the kids ready for bed. "There's too much to do," says Vosman about her daily 17.5-hour marathon. "I'm exhausted."

Janet Vosman and many other women in the Canadian workforce experience stress due to work–family conflict. Women perform an average of 75 hours of paid and unpaid work each week, so it isn't surprising that 38 percent of working moms say that they are severely time-stressed. Although Vosman's husband and other men are increasing their share of the housework, women still perform most of the chores—a "second shift" in addition to their paid employment tasks.

"It is very hard work where you are always balancing priorities," explains Claudine Simson, a vice-president at Nortel Networks in Toronto who has two children. "There are pressures everywhere—work, family, society. You must choose your objectives and then go after them. There is such personal satisfaction when you can balance both work and family."

Reprinted with permission from The Halifax Herald Ltd. (D. Pittman).

After finishing her full-time job with the Nova Scotia government, Janet Vosman begins her "second shift" at home.

Sources: S. LeBlanc, "A Woman's Work Is Never Done," *Halifax Chronicle-Herald*, March 9, 2000; L. Fattori, "Spotlight on Claudine Simson, VP, Global External Research and Intellectual Property, Nortel," *Silicon Valley North*, August 1999.

Strain-based conflict

Strain-based conflict occurs when stress from one domain spills over to the other. Relationship problems, financial difficulties, and loss of a loved one usually top the list of nonwork stressors. New responsibilities, such as marriage, the birth of a child, and a mortgage are also stressful to most of us. Stress at work also spills over into an employee's personal life and often becomes the foundation of stressful relations with family and friends.

Several Canadian studies have looked at this issue. One reported that the stresses of work spill over to home life more than vice versa. Another found that fathers who experience stress at work engage in dysfunctional parenting behaviours, which, in turn, explain their children's behaviour in school. A third Canadian study suggests that Canadian female managers mainly experience work–family stress due to strain-based conflict than to other work–family stressors.[37]

Role behaviour conflict

A third work–nonwork stressor, called *role behaviour conflict,* occurs when people are expected to enact different work and nonwork roles. People who act logically and impersonally at work have difficulty switching to a more compassionate role in their personal lives. For example, one study found that police officers were unable to shake off their professional role when they left the job. This was confirmed by their spouses, who reported that the officers would handle their children in the same manner as they would people in their job.[38]

STRESS AND OCCUPATIONS

Several studies have attempted to identify which jobs have more stressors than others.[39] These lists are not in complete agreement, but Exhibit 5.3 identifies a representative sample of jobs and their relative level of stressors. You should view this information with some caution, however. One problem with rating the stress of occupations is that task characteristics and job environments differ considerably for the same job in different organizations and societies. A police officer's job may be less stressful in a small town, for instance, than in a large city where crime rates are higher and the organizational hierarchy is more formal.

Another important point to remember when looking at Exhibit 5.3 is that what constitutes a major stressor to one person may be insignificant to another. In this respect, we must be careful not to conclude that people in high-stress occupations actually experience higher stress than do people in other occupations. They are exposed to more serious stressors, but careful selection and training can result in stress levels no different from those experienced by people in other jobs. The next section discusses individual differences in stress.

| **EXHIBIT 5.3** | Stressors in Occupations |

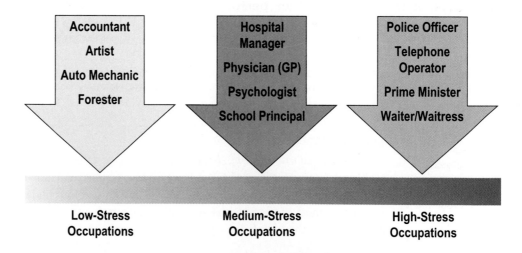

Low-Stress Occupations	Medium-Stress Occupations	High-Stress Occupations
Accountant	Hospital Manager	Police Officer
Artist	Physician (GP)	Telephone Operator
Auto Mechanic	Psychologist	Prime Minister
Forester	School Principal	Waiter/Waitress

INDIVIDUAL DIFFERENCES IN STRESS

Earlier, in Exhibit 5.2 (see page 131), we saw that individual characteristics moderate the extent to which different people experience stress or exhibit a specific stress outcome in a given situation. Two people may be exposed to the same stressor, such as having too many deadlines, yet they experience different stress levels or different stress symptoms.[40]

People exposed to the same stressors might have different stress symptoms for three reasons. First, each of us perceives the same situation differently. People with high self-efficacy, for instance, are less likely to experience stress consequences in that situation because the stressor is less threatening.[41] Self-efficacy refers to a person's belief that he or she has the ability, motivation, and situational contingencies to complete a task successfully (see Chapter 2). Similarly, some people have personalities that make them more optimistic, whereas others are more pessimistic. Those with pessimistic dispositions tend to develop more stress symptoms, probably because they interpret the situation in a negative light.[42]

A second reason why some people have more stress symptoms than others do in the same situation is that people have different threshold levels of resistance to a stressor. Younger employees generally experience fewer and less severe stress symptoms than older employees because they have a larger store of energy to cope with high stress levels. As we shall learn later, people who exercise regularly and have healthy lifestyles (e.g., good diet, adequate sleep) are also less likely to experience negative stress outcomes.

A third reason why people may experience the same level of stress and yet exhibit different stress outcomes is that they use different coping strategies.[43] Some employees tend to ignore the stressor, hoping that it will go away. This is usually an ineffective approach, which would explain why they experience higher stress levels. There is some evidence (although still inconclusive) that women cope with stress better than their male counterparts. Specifically, women are more likely to seek emotional support from others in stressful situations, whereas men try to change the stressor or use less effective coping mechanisms.[44] However, we must remember that this is not true for all women or men.

TYPE A/TYPE B BEHAVIOUR PATTERN

Type A behaviour pattern A behaviour pattern of people with high risk of premature coronary heart disease; Type As tend to be impatient, lose their temper, talk rapidly, and interrupt others.

A 52-year-old systems analyst recently collapsed on a downtown Calgary sidewalk. Paramedics discovered that he had blood flow problems to his heart, so they strapped him to an ambulance gurney and hooked him up to a heart monitor. Despite his confinement and health condition, the systems analyst tried to make business calls on his cellular telephone while the ambulance was racing him to the nearest hospital.[45]

This Calgary systems analyst probably has a **Type A behaviour pattern**. Type A people are hard-driving, competitive individuals with a strong sense of time urgency. They tend to be impatient, lose their temper, talk rapidly, and interrupt others during conversations (see Exhibit 5.4).[46] In contrast, those with a **Type B behaviour pattern** are less competitive and less concerned about time limitations. They tend to work steadily, take a relaxed approach to life, and be even-tempered. Type B people may be just as ambitious to achieve challenging tasks, but they generally approach life more casually and systematically than do Type A people.

Type B behaviour pattern A behaviour pattern of people with low risk of coronary heart disease; Type Bs tend to work steadily, take a relaxed approach to life, and be even-tempered.

The important distinction, however, is that Type B people are less likely than Type A people to experience distress and its physiological symptoms (such as blood flow problems to the heart) when exposed to a stressor. For example, a study of Montreal nurses reported that Type A nurses experienced significantly greater job stress and work overload than did Type B nurses.[47]

EXHIBIT 5.4 Characteristics of Type A and Type B Behaviour Patterns

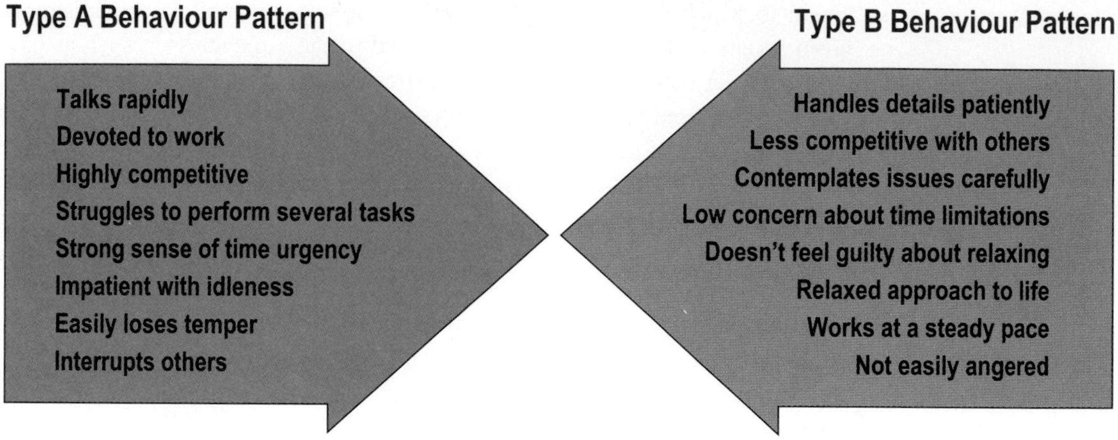

Type A Behaviour Pattern

Talks rapidly
Devoted to work
Highly competitive
Struggles to perform several tasks
Strong sense of time urgency
Impatient with idleness
Easily loses temper
Interrupts others

Type B Behaviour Pattern

Handles details patiently
Less competitive with others
Contemplates issues carefully
Low concern about time limitations
Doesn't feel guilty about relaxing
Relaxed approach to life
Works at a steady pace
Not easily angered

Regarding job performance, Type A people tend to work faster than Type B people, choose more challenging tasks, have higher self-motivation, and are more effective in jobs involving time pressure. On the other hand, Type A people are less effective than Type B people in jobs requiring patience, cooperation, and thoughtful judgment.[48] Type A people tend to be irritable and aggressive, so they generally have poorer interpersonal skills. Studies report that middle managers tend to exhibit Type A behaviours, whereas top-level executives tend to exhibit Type B behaviours.[49] One possible explanation is that Type B people receive more promotions due to their superior human relations skills.

CONSEQUENCES OF DISTRESS

As we learned from the discussion of the general adaptation syndrome at the beginning of this chapter, chronic stress diminishes the individual's resistance, resulting in adverse consequences for both the employee and the organization. Some of the more common outcomes or symptoms of work-related stress were listed earlier in Exhibit 5.2 (see page 131) and are discussed here.

PHYSIOLOGICAL CONSEQUENCES

Every day, Michael Dobler is bombarded with faxes, e-mail messages, computer printouts, and other sources of information. The resulting technostress gives the Hong Kong–based technical manager for a Swiss-based multinational firm frequent migraine headaches. "It really is painful and I have to stop working and go home and take medicine," Dobler explains. "My work is definitely a factor that causes it."[50]

Stress takes its toll on the human body.[51] For example, studies have found that medical students who are anxious about exams are more susceptible to colds and other illnesses.[52] Michael Dobler experiences tension headaches due to stress. Others get muscle pain and related back problems. These physiological ailments are attributed to muscle contractions that occur when people are exposed to stressors.

Cardiovascular diseases represent one of the most disturbing effects of stress in modern society. Approximately one-third of Canadians have hypertension (high blood pressure), much of which is the result of anxiety and worry. Coronary heart disease (including strokes and heart attacks) were virtually unknown a century ago but are now the leading causes of death among Canadian adults. Medical researchers believe that the long-term effect of stress on heart disease goes something like this: Whenever people are stressed, their blood pressure goes up and down. That frequent pressure causes injury to the blood vessel walls, which eventually makes them constrict and function abnormally. Over time, this leads to heart disease. The problem is that we often cannot tell when we are biologically stressed. For example, researchers have found that some people think their condition is normal when, in fact, their palms are sweating and their blood pressure has risen.[53]

PSYCHOLOGICAL CONSEQUENCES

Probably the most common psychological symptom of work-related stress is lower **job satisfaction**, which represents a person's evaluation of his or her job and work context.[54] Employees with a high level of stress also tend to be moody and depressed.[55] Emotional fatigue is another psychological consequence of stress and is related to job burnout.

Job burnout

Job burnout refers to the process of emotional exhaustion, depersonalization, and reduced personal accomplishment resulting from prolonged exposure to stress.[56] The phrase didn't exist 40 years ago; now it's heard regularly in everyday conversation. Job burnout is a complex process that includes the dynamics of stress, coping strategies, and stress consequences. Burnout is caused by excessive demands made on people who serve or frequently interact with others. In other words, burnout is mainly due to interpersonal and role-related stressors.[57] For this reason, it is most common in helping occupations (e.g., nurses, teachers, police officers).

Exhibit 5.5 diagrams the relationship among the three components of job burnout. *Emotional exhaustion* represents the first stage and plays a central role in the burnout process.[58] It is characterized by a lack of energy and a feeling that one's emotional resources are depleted. Emotional exhaustion is sometimes called compassion fatigue because the employee no longer feels able to give as much support and caring to clients.

Job satisfaction A person's attitude (beliefs, assessed feelings, and behavioural intentions) regarding the job and work context.

Job burnout The process of emotional exhaustion, depersonalization, and reduced personal accomplishment resulting from prolonged exposure to stress.

EXHIBIT 5.5   The Job Burnout Process

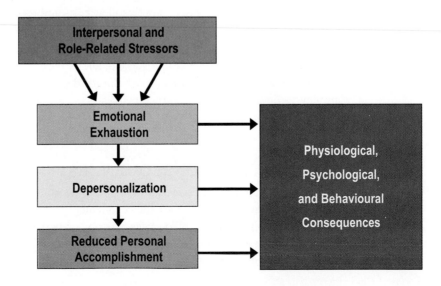

Marc Gallant, *Winnipeg Free Press*.

www.mbteach.org
www.otffeo.on.ca

Canadian teachers are experiencing job burnout as they try to absorb staff cuts and student behaviour problems. "Teachers look like they have been hit with a bucket of water," says Karen Minish, a grade 5 teacher in Winnipeg (shown in photo). Almost 5 percent of Manitoba's teachers are receiving stress counselling. In southern Ontario, Waterloo-area teachers are almost four times more likely than the general population to take long-term disability leave. Almost one-half of those claims are stress- or mental health–related. "There's just so much to do. It's almost like you don't have a life," says Sandra Johannson, a Riverton, Manitoba, teacher who suffered physical pain from her stress. "We're burning out fast."[59] Based on the job burnout model, what symptoms would suggest that Sandra Johannson and other teachers are experiencing job burnout?

Depersonalization follows emotional exhaustion and is identified by the treatment of others as objects rather than people. Burned-out employees become emotionally detached from clients and cynical about the organization. This detachment is to the point of callousness, far beyond the level of detachment normally required in helping occupations. For example, a burned-out nurse might coldly label a patient as "the kidney in room 307." Depersonalization is also apparent when employees strictly follow rules and regulations rather than try to understand the client's needs and search for a mutually acceptable solution.

Reduced personal accomplishment, the final component of job burnout, refers to the decline in one's feelings of competence and success, and is observed by feelings of diminished competency. In other words, the person's self-efficacy declines (see Chapter 2). In these situations, employees develop a sense of learned helplessness, as they no longer believe that their efforts make a difference.

BEHAVIOURAL CONSEQUENCES

When stress becomes distress, job performance falls and workplace accidents are more common. High stress levels impair our ability to remember information, make effective decisions, and take appropriate action.[60] You have probably experienced this in an exam or emergency work situation. You forget important information, make mistakes, and otherwise "draw a blank" under intense pressure.

Overstressed employees also tend to have higher levels of absenteeism. One reason is that stress makes people sick. The other reason is that absenteeism is a coping mechanism. At a basic level, we react to stress through fight or flight. Absenteeism is a form of flight—temporarily withdrawing from the stressful situation so that we have an opportunity to re-energize. Companies may try to minimize absenteeism, but it sometimes helps employees avoid the exhaustion stage of the stress experience (see Exhibit 5.1 earlier in this chapter—page 129).[61]

Workplace aggression

Workplace aggression is more than the serious interpersonal stressor described earlier. It is also an increasingly worrisome consequence of stress.[62] Aggression represents the "fight" (instead of flight) reaction to stress. In its mildest form, employees engage in verbal conflict. They "fly off the handle" and are less likely to empathize with co-workers. Occasionally, the combination of an individual's background and workplace stressors escalates this conflict into more dangerous levels of workplace hostility.

Co-worker aggression represents a relatively small proportion of workplace violence, but these behaviours are neither random nor inconsequential. Like most forms of organizational behaviour, both the person and the situation cause co-worker aggression.[63] While certain individuals are more likely to be aggressive, we must also remember that employee aggression is also a consequence of extreme stress.[64] In particular, employees are more likely to engage in aggressive behaviour if they believe that they have been treated unfairly, experience other forms of frustration beyond their personal control, and work in physical environments that are stressful (e.g., hot, noisy).

MANAGING WORK-RELATED STRESS

A few years ago, Mary Parniak was under a lot of pressure. The Baxter Corp. executive from Mississauga, Ontario, was involved in a messy corporate audit, faced a number of critical decisions involving ethical dilemmas, and was trying to adjust to a new boss. "I was on the brink of a stress-induced burnout," recalls Parniak. "I began to behave in ways that weren't normal for me, things like crying on the job or feeling that if one more person walked into my office I was going to scream." Fortunately, a colleague recognized the symptoms and urged Parniak to get some help before it was too late. Working with an industrial psychologist once a week for several months, Parniak learned to maintain a better balance in her life.[65]

Everyone needs to manage stress. Unfortunately, many of us deny the existence of our stress until it is too late. This avoidance strategy creates a vicious cycle because the failure to cope with stress becomes another stressor on top of the one that created the stress in the first place. The solution is to discover the tool kit of effective stress management strategies presented in this section, and to determine which ones are best for the situation.[66]

Several different stress-management strategies are described over the next few pages (see Exhibit 5.6). Each of these can be introduced as corporate initiatives, but they also represent ways that each of us can personally learn to cope with stress at work. As we look at each approach, also keep in mind that effective stress management often includes more than one of these strategies.

REMOVE THE STRESSOR

Exhibit 5.6 identifies several stress-management strategies, but some writers argue that the *only* way that companies can effectively manage stress is by removing the stressors that cause unnecessary tension and job burnout. Other stress-management strategies may keep employees "stress-fit," but they don't solve the fundamental causes of stress.[67]

EXHIBIT 5.6   Stress-Management Strategies

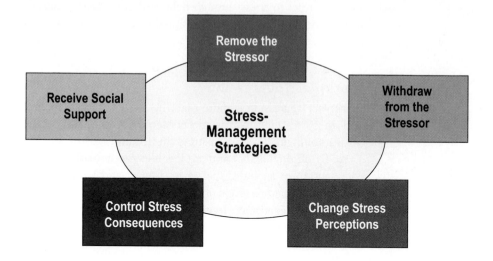

There are many ways to remove stressors in the workplace. One of the most powerful solutions is to empower employees so that they have more control over their work and work environment (see Chapter 4).[68] Role-related stressors can be minimized through more effective selection and placement of employees so that their competencies are compatible with job requirements. Noise and safety risks are stressful, so improving these conditions would also go a long way to minimize stress in the workplace. Companies can diffuse aggression by establishing procedures that minimize dysfunctional conflict and ensure that workplace decisions are perceived to be fair.

Of course, employees can also take an active role in removing stressors. If we experience stress due to ambiguous role expectations, for example, we might seek out more information from others to clarify these expectations. If a particular piece of work is too challenging, we might break it into smaller sets of tasks so that the overall project is less threatening or wearing. We can also minimize workplace violence by learning to identify early warning signs of aggression in customers and co-workers and by developing interpersonal skills that dissipate aggression.

Family-friendly and work–life initiatives

Not long ago, 42 percent of Baxter Healthcare employees were thinking of quitting because work conflicted with their personal lives. This was startling news because the health products company has one of the better "family-friendly" workplaces. But the complaints weren't so much from working mothers; they came from singles and dual earners without kids. So, Baxter morphed its work–family program into a "work–life" program and now evaluate managers on how well they help *all* employees maintain this balance.[69]

Recent surveys revealed that work–life balance is gaining acceptance by Baxter Healthcare and other Canadian employers as an important stress-management strategy. Several studies have also identified work–family or work–life balance as the most important concern among Canadian employees.[70] Family-friendly and work–life initiatives remove or reduce the stressors that cause time-based conflict. Five of the most common family-friendly and work–life initiatives are flextime, job sharing, telecommuting, personal leave, and child-care facilities.

Royal Bank of Canada successfully launched job sharing with its Work–Family Life program a decade ago and now has nearly 1000 job-sharing arrangements across Canada. Job sharing splits a career position between two people so that they experience less time-based stress between work and family.[71] What are the limitations of job sharing? Are there any jobs that might make job sharing difficult?

www.royalbank.com

Telecommuting (also called *teleworking*) Working from home or another location away from the office, usually with a computer connection to the office.

- *Flexible work time*—Many firms allow employees to decide when to begin and end their workday so that they can more easily balance personal life activities with their workday.

- *Job sharing*—Job sharing splits a career position between two people so that they experience less time-based stress between work and family. They typically work different parts of the week with some overlapping work time in the weekly schedule to coordinate activities.

- *Telecommuting*—Approximately 1.5 million Canadians have altered their employment relations through **telecommuting**—working from home, usually with a computer connection to the office (see Chapter 1). This reduces the time and stress of commuting to work and makes it easier to fulfil family obligations, such as temporarily leaving the home office to pick up children from school. Overall, telecommuters are more productive and experience a healthier balance between work and nonwork roles.[72]

- *Personal leave programs*—The Canadian and provincial governments require employers to provide paid maternity leave. Work–life employers typically offer extended maternity, paternity, and personal leaves to care for a new family or take advantage of a personal experience. Increasingly, employees are using personal leave to care for elderly parents and other relatives who need assistance.

- *Child-care facilities*—On-site child-care centres have existed since the Second World War, when women worked in war factories. In 1964, Toronto's Riverdale Hospital became one of the first organizations during the post-war era to have a child-care centre. Soon after opening the centre, the number of female applicants jumped 40 percent and absenteeism dropped significantly. Today, child-care facilities are found at National Bank of Canada, Husky Injection Molding Systems, and many other companies.[73]

WITHDRAW FROM THE STRESSOR

Removing the stressor may be the ideal solution, but it is often not feasible. One alternative strategy is to remove employees from the stressor permanently or temporarily. One permanent approach is to transfer employees to jobs for which they are better suited. A more drastic action is to have the employee leave the organization if a suitable position is not available.

Temporary withdrawal strategies

Vincent Tsang and Clinton Fox wanted their employees to relieve the constant stress of tight deadlines. So the partners in InfoCheck Ltd., a Toronto-based reference checking service, took everyone to a toy store and gave each person $20 to spend on the toys of their choice. Tsang got a basketball net and occasionally lobs a nerf ball into it to relieve stress. "We know stress is inevitable and we can't eliminate it," admits Tsang. "But we can provide our people with ways to release it."[74]

Whether it's a coffee break or a nerf ball break, temporarily withdrawing from stressors is the most frequent way that employees manage stress. Nortel Networks has a relaxation room complete with comfy chairs and comedy videos where employees can temporarily escape from the hassles of work.[75] Vacations represent another form of temporary withdrawal from workplace stressors. Eight of the *Globe and Mail's* 35 best firms to work for in Canada offer paid sabbaticals. This includes McDonald's of Canada, which offers salaried employees an eight-week paid sabbatical after ten years of service. "[The sabbatical] allows our employees to take the time to do things they wouldn't normally have an opportunity to do and to breathe, explore, enjoy their loved ones and do some special things," says a McDonald's of Canada spokesperson.[76]

Employees typically experience stress when living and working in another culture. Lacking common assumptions and expectations, expatriates must pay constant attention to how others react to their behaviours. For example, expatriates say that cultural differences—such as different lifestyles and interpersonal behaviours—make Vietnam the most

Courtesy of Pixar Animation Studios.

Andrew Stanton knows about impossible deadlines. The co-director of Pixar Animation Studios' film *A Bug's Life* had booked every working minute to complete the project. His wife and two kids were near-strangers to him. But was Stanton running on empty? Hardly. In fact, he acted almost carefree. Stanton's prescription for preventing burnout is to laugh hard, twice daily. "Something is horribly wrong," he says, "if I don't crack up at least a couple of times a day." Stanton doesn't force humour. It flows freely, such as during impromptu nerf battles and scooter races in the hallway.[77] How does humour help Stanton and his co-workers to manage stress?

www.pixar.com

stressful Asian nation in which to live and work. To manage this stress, some expatriates retreat into a stabilization zone—any place similar to the home country where they can rely on past routines to guide behaviour.[78] This may include attending a "Canadian night" at a club in the foreign country or having dinner with friends from the home country.

CHANGE STRESS PERCEPTIONS

Employees often experience different levels of stress in the same situation because they perceive it differently. Consequently, changing perceptions of the situation can minimize stress. This does not involve ignoring risks or other stressors. Rather, we can strengthen our self-efficacy and self-esteem so that job challenges are not perceived to be threatening. Humour can also improve perceptions by taking some psychological weight off of the situation. "Workplace pressures will keep increasing," says a clinical psychologist at Vancouver-based telecommunications company Telus Corp. "A lot of things aren't going to change, so we have to change people's perception."[79]

Several elements of self-leadership described in Chapter 4 can alter employee perceptions of job-related stressors. For example, mental imagery can reduce the uncertainty of future work activities. A study of newly hired Canadian accountants reported that personal goal setting and self-reinforcement can reduce the stress that people experience when they enter new work settings.[80] Positive self-talk can potentially change stress perceptions by increasing our self-efficacy and helping us to develop a more optimistic outlook, at least in that situation. As we noted earlier, a person's optimism can minimize the effects of stressors.

CONTROL THE CONSEQUENCES OF STRESS

Another way of coping with workplace stress is to control its consequences. Fifty-two percent of medium and large Canadian businesses have employee wellness plans, up from only 33 percent in 1993.[81] Research indicates that physical exercise reduces the physiological consequences of stress by helping employees lower their respiration, muscle tension, heartbeat, and stomach acidity.[82] Manitoba Telecom Services (MTS) has had on-site fitness centres for the past decade. The facilities include weight stations, multiple exercise machines, and a full slate of group exercise classes such as aerobics, yoga, and karate. "MTS has long recognized the benefits of in-office fitness in such areas as increased productivity, lower absenteeism and better staff morale," explains the company's fitness program coordinator.[83]

Along with physical fitness, wellness programs educate and support employees in better nutrition and fitness, regular sleep, and other good health habits. Canada Life Assurance Co. is a pioneer in wellness programs. Two decades ago, the insurance company discovered that its corporate wellness program paid back several times its cost in lower absenteeism and higher productivity. Canada Life's program includes healthy cafeteria menus, lifestyle seminars, early identification of illness among staff, stress management seminars, and an outreach program that includes the employees' families.[84]

Another way to control the physiological consequences of stress is through relaxation and meditation. Generally, these activities decrease the individual's heart rate, blood pressure, muscle tension, and breathing rate.[85] Steve Jones, who works for the City of London, England, uses meditation to avoid becoming stressed out at work. "I work in a very high-pressure environment," Jones explains. "If I know I'm going to have a really heavy day then I meditate before

G. Baglo, Vancouver Sun.

The new building for Pazmac Enterprises in Langley, B.C., includes a gym and a small lap pool. But Steve Scarlet, who owns the 21-employee machine shop, didn't stop there. To help employees keep fit, he hired personal trainer Ron Weeks (shown in photo with Scarlet) for two days each week to put employees through their paces before the workday begins. "I think working out leads to a better mindset, a healthier outlook on life," says Scarlet. "It certainly increases productivity and decreases the number of sick days."[89] In your opinion, how do personal trainers assist the stress-management process?

I go into work. It keeps me calm and clear-headed." Many Japanese companies have corporate meditation programs. Phatra Thanakit, one of Thailand's top finance and securities companies, sends stressed-out staffers to a one-week retreat in a Buddhist monastery.[86]

Nearly 80 percent of large Canadian employers offer **employee assistance programs (EAPs)**. EAPs are counselling services that help employees overcome personal or organizational stressors and adopt more effective coping mechanisms. Most EAPs in Canada started as alcoholism treatment programs, but most are now "broad-brush" programs that counsel employees on work or personal problems. Family problems often represent the largest percentage of EAP referrals, although this varies with industry and location. For instance, all of Canada's major banks provide post-trauma stress counselling for employees after a robbery, particularly when a weapon was visible.[87]

RECEIVE SOCIAL SUPPORT

Social support from co-workers, supervisors, family, friends, and others is one of the more effective stress-management practices.[88] Social support refers to the person's interpersonal transactions with others and involves providing either emotional or informational support to buffer the stress experience.

Social support reduces stress in at least three ways.[90] First, employees improve their perception that they are valued and worthy. This, in turn, increases their self-esteem and perceived ability to cope with the stressor (e.g., "I can handle this crisis because my colleagues have confidence in me"). Second, social support provides information to help employees interpret, comprehend, and possibly remove the stressor. For instance, social support might reduce a new employee's stress because co-workers describe ways to handle difficult customers. Finally, emotional support from others can directly help to buffer the stress experience. This last point reflects the idea that "misery loves company." People seek out and benefit from the emotional support of others when they face threatening situations.[91]

Social support is an important way to cope with stress that everyone can practise by maintaining friendships. This includes helping others when they need a little support from the

www.pazmac.com

Employee assistance programs (EAPs) Counselling services that help employees cope with personal or organizational stressors and adopt more effective coping mechanisms.

stressors of life. Organizations can facilitate social support by providing opportunities for social interaction among employees as well as their families. People in leadership roles also need to practise a supportive leadership style when employees work under stressful conditions and need this social support. Mentoring relationships with more senior employees may also help junior employees cope with organizational stressors.[92]

CHAPTER SUMMARY

- Stress is an adaptive response to a situation that is perceived to be challenging or threatening to the person's well-being. Distress represents high stress levels that have negative consequences, whereas eustress represents the moderately low stress levels needed to activate people. The stress experience, called the general adaptation syndrome, involves moving through three stages: alarm reaction, resistance, and exhaustion.

- The stress model shows that stressors cause stress. However, the effect of these stressors depends on individual characteristics. Stress affects a person's physiological and psychological well-being, and is associated with several work-related behaviours.

- Stressors are the causes of stress and include any environmental conditions that place a physical or emotional demand on the person. Stressors are found in the physical work environment, the employee's various life roles, interpersonal relations, and organizational activities and conditions. Conflicts between work and nonwork obligations represent a frequent source of employee stress.

- Two people exposed to the same stressor may experience different stress levels because they perceive the situation differently, they have different threshold stress levels, or they use different coping strategies. Employees with Type A behaviour patterns tend to experience more stress than do those who exhibit Type B behaviours.

- High levels of or prolonged stress can cause physiological symptoms, such as high blood pressure, ulcers, sexual dysfunction, headaches, and coronary heart disease. Behavioural symptoms of stress include lower job performance, poorer decisions, more workplace accidents, higher absenteeism, and more workplace aggression. Psychologically, stress reduces job satisfaction and increases moodiness, depression, and job burnout. Job burnout refers to the process of emotional exhaustion, depersonalization, and reduced personal accomplishment resulting from prolonged exposure to stress. It is mainly due to interpersonal and role-related stressors and is most common in helping occupations.

- Many interventions are available to manage work-related stress. Some directly remove unnecessary stressors or remove employees from the stressful environment. Others help employees alter their interpretation of the environment so that it is not viewed as a serious stressor. Wellness programs encourage employees to build better physical defences against stress experiences. Social support provides emotional, informational, and material resource support to buffer the stress experience.

KEY TERMS

Employee assistance programs (EAPs) p. 145

General adaptation syndrome, p. 129

Job burnout, p. 139

Job satisfaction, p. 139

Role ambiguity, p. 131

Role conflict, p. 130

Sexual harassment, p. 133

Stress, p. 128

Stressor, p. 130

Telecommuting, p. 143

Type A behaviour pattern, p. 137

Type B behaviour pattern, p. 137

DISCUSSION QUESTIONS

1. Several Web sites—including www.workdoctor.com and www.mybosssucks.com—describe problems that people experience at work. Scan through these and other Web sites and determine what type of work-related stressor is most commonly described.

2. Sally works as a lawyer for a leading Montreal law firm. She was married a few years ago and is currently pregnant with her first child. Sally expects to return to work full time a few months after the baby is born. Describe two types of work–nonwork conflict that Sally will likely experience during the first year after her return to work.

3. Police officer and waiter are often cited as high-stress jobs, whereas accountant and forester are low-stress jobs. Why should we be careful about describing these jobs as involving high or low stress?

4. Two recent graduates join the same major newspaper as journalists. Both work long hours and have tight deadlines to complete their stories. They are under constant pressure to scout out new leads and be the first to report new controversies. One journalist is increasingly fatigued and despondent, and has taken several days of sick leave. The other is getting the work done and seems to enjoy the challenges. Use your knowledge of stress to explain why these two journalists are reacting differently to their jobs.

5. Do people with Type A personalities make better managers? Why or why not?

6. A friend says that he is burned out by his job. What questions might you ask this friend to determine whether he is really experiencing job burnout?

7. How might fitness programs help employees working in stressful situations?

8. A senior official of a labour union stated: "All stress management does is help people cope with poor management. [Employers] should really be into stress reduction." Discuss the accuracy of this statement.

Case Study

ACTIVITY 5.1
Stress in the MBA Program

by Jack Duffy, Dalhousie University

The following is a day in the stressful life of first-year MBA student Iggy Potzereebi.

Iggy arrived at the School of Business Administration Building at 8:35 a.m. for his 8:30 class (parking problems again). As usual, he felt a little shaky from his two cups of coffee on an empty stomach, so he had stopped at Tim Horton's for a couple of doughnuts and a coffee with double cream, to go. He'd eaten the doughnuts in his car, but the coffee was too hot to sip, so he carried it to class. He knew this would be a bad day when he subsequently spilled the coffee on his homework assignment that was due at the end of class. He pondered asking the professor if he could have an extension so that he could print out a clean copy (assuming he hadn't deleted the file and could find it on his hard drive). He decided to wait until the break to make up his mind.

During the lecture, Iggy kept daydreaming about the female student seated two rows behind him. Probably because he frequently turned around to look at her, the instructor asked Iggy to explain the niceties of multiple regression forecasting for financial planning. This subject was, of course, quite a shift from Iggy's immediate train of thought and he did not answer the question admirably.

When the class break came, the professor immediately headed for the bathroom. Not able to follow her in there and not wanting to loiter outside the women's washroom, Iggy decided to chance finding the file, reprinting his paper, and handing it in tomorrow. And if he couldn't find it, it should only take a few hours to re-input.

After class Iggy was going to explain his decision to the professor, but the female student from two rows behind him appeared at his side and asked him to be her partner for the marketing case that was due the following week. Cogitating

for well over a nanosecond, Iggy said sure. They decided to go for lunch and discuss their approach.

While waiting to be seated at the Bistro, Iggy debated if he should have a glass of white wine with lunch. Since he was famished at this point, he feared that an alcoholic drink would quickly go to his head. When his date ordered a crantini, Iggy ordered a Bloody Mary figuring that he could chase his drink with coffee and thus balance his metabolism. When his date ordered dessert, he changed his coffee to an Irish coffee.

Back at class that afternoon, Iggy was surprised to hear that a mid-term exam was set for next week. Iggy had heard that there rarely were mid-terms in the MBA program, only finals. He had paced all of his reading on that assumption. He suddenly realized that within the next week five professors wanted him to read ten chapters each, he had to reprint his paper, he had three case assignments due, and he had to find time for an evening with Sissy Sassy (the woman two rows back who was now sitting next to him—much to his regret since she was snoring rather loudly).

Depressed at his workload he decided to cut class for the afternoon and go to the library to study. He found a padded seat next to a heat register and had a pleasant two-hour nap. When he awoke, he found a note from Sissy taped to his forehead. The note curtly told him that she had decided against getting an MBA degree. She was going to use her family inheritance to open a red tape factory. She believed she could sell enough red tape to the Canadian government to double her investment in the first year. She could foresee her company growing to international status, especially in developing countries, which are experiencing an almost completely inelastic demand for red tape among their bureaucrats. She concluded that this enterprise was better than studying. As a postscript she asked Iggy if he wanted to be her second-in-command in this new venture. Unfortunately she left no forwarding address.

ACTIVITY 5.1 CONTINUED

Since it was only 4:30 p.m., Iggy reasoned that he could go to the registrar's office and get Sissy's home address before the office closed. He was pretty sure he didn't want to leave the MBA program, but it never hurt to have options, particularly with mid-terms approaching. He decided that he'd get her address and then sleep on his decision. As he headed for the parking lot, he noticed that his car had a flat tire.

Discussion Questions

1. What can Iggy do to make his days less stressful?
2. What should Iggy do to get ready for his mid-terms?

 Video Case Study

ACTIVITY 5.2
The Speed Trap

E-mail, cell phones, and fax machines have put us on the fast track. But are we accelerating beyond our endurance? Are we speeding to a standstill? Rather than ease our burdens, these communication devices have increased our technostress. Tim Breen, a busy copy centre manager, points out that technology moves much faster than we do, and trying to keep up can wear us out, both mentally and physically.

The mad rush to squeeze more work activities into the day, with no time left for personal pursuits, led small-business owner Sandra Erickson to seek help. She turned to time management consultant Mark Ellwood, who teaches clients how to achieve balance in their lives.

"Eric," a patient at the Homewood Health Centre in Guelph, Ontario, wishes he had sought help earlier. A casualty of a 13- to 16-hour workday regime, the former construction executive found himself going into a tailspin. After climbing into the top income bracket, Eric was diagnosed as clinically depressed, and lost his job.

Psychiatrist Dr. Beth Reade says that even the most high-energy people have a limit to how much they can do. We all have to set priorities and learn how to say no, she says.

Japan has officially recognized overwork as a disease. It's called *karoshi* and 10,000 workers die of it each year. One victim, 23-year-old Yoshiko, was a graphic artist who died on the job suddenly due to a brain hemorrhage. According to her parents, who are suing their daughter's former employer, Yoshiko worked herself to death.

Although France has legislated a 35-hour workweek, four out of ten businesses have workers on the job for more than ten hours a day. Labour inspector Gerard Filoche says that a 13 percent unemployment rate means employers can coerce employees to work unreasonable hours.

This video looks not only at the sources of stress at work, but also at ways to overcome this stress. One example is SAS Institute, a profitable computer software company in North Carolina that doesn't believe in pushing its employees to the limit. SAS is renowned for its employee-friendly policies that have reduced stress levels and turnover.

Discussion Questions

1. While watching this video, identify the various incidents with the stressor categories described in this chapter. Which stressors seem to be more common?

2. What strategies are identified in this program that help employees minimize or avoid unnecessary stress at work and in their lives?

3. Are there any sources of work-related stress that this documentary overlooks? What are they?

Source: "The Speed Trap," 90th Parallel Productions.

TEAM exercise

ACTIVITY 5.3
STRESSED OUT OR "NO PROBLEM"?

Purpose: This exercise is designed to help students understand how people will have different stress reactions to the same stressors.

Instructions:

Step 1: Students individually indicate their responses to each of the incidents on the scoring sheet.

Step 2: The instructor places students into groups (typically of four or five people each) to compare their results. For each incident, group members should discuss why each person feels more or less stress. They should pay particular attention to the reasons why some students would feel little stress. Specifically, they should examine the extent to which each person (a) perceives the situation differently, (b) has more or less tolerance to stressors due to health or need to cope with other problems, and (c) would use different coping strategies to deal with any stress related to the incident.

Step 3: After group members have diagnosed these results, the instructor brings the class together to compare results and discuss why people react differently to stressors.

STRESSED OUT OR "NO PROBLEM"?

Circle the number on the right that best describes the extent to which you would feel stressed in this situation.	Very Stressed ▼		Moderately Stressed ▼			Little Stress ▼
1. Your final exam for an introductory economics course is in 48 hours. However, a bad flu and other assignments have prevented you from studying for it. You know that the instructor will not accept your illness and other assignments as an excuse to take the examination at another time.	7	6	5	4	3	2	1
2. You started work last month as a sales clerk in a small clothing store (men's or women's) and have been asked to mind the store while the other two clerks take their lunch break elsewhere in the shopping mall. During this usually slow time, four customers walk in, each one of them wanting your immediate attention.	7	6	5	4	3	2	1

3. You and two friends are driving in an older van with snow tires to a ski resort in the Canadian Rockies. You took over driving duty at 8 p.m., two hours ago. Your friends are asleep in the back seat while you approach a steep pass. It has been snowing so heavily that you must drive at a crawl to see where you're going and avoid sliding off the road. You passed the last community 50 kilometres back and the resort is 65 kilometres ahead (nearly two hours away at your current speed). 7   6   5   4   3   2   1

4. You work as an accountant in a large insurance company and, for the past month, have received unwanted attention several times each week from your supervisor, a married person of the opposite sex. The supervisor regularly touches your shoulder and comments on your looks. You are sure that they are advances rather than just friendly gestures. 7   6   5   4   3   2   1

5. You and your spouse purchased your first home one year ago, a detached house with mortgage payments that your spouse barely covers with his or her take-home pay. The economy has since entered a deep recession and the company informed you today that you will be laid off in two months. 7   6   5   4   3   2   1

Source: © Copyright 2000, Steven L. McShane.

Self-Assessment exercise

ACTIVITY 5.4
TIME-STRESS SCALE

Purpose: This self-assessment is designed to help you identify your level of time-related stress.

Instructions: Read each of the statements below and circle "yes" or "no." Then use the scoring key in Appendix B of this book to calculate your results for each scale. This exercise is completed alone so that students can assess themselves honestly without concerns of social comparison. However, class discussion will focus on the time-stress scale.

1. Yes   No   Do you plan to slow down in the coming year?

2. Yes   No   Do you consider yourself to be a workaholic?

3. Yes   No   When you need more time, do you tend to cut back on your sleep?

4. Yes   No   At the end of the day, do you often feel that you have not accomplished what you had set out to do?

5. Yes   No   Do you worry that you don't spend enough time with your family or friends?

6. Yes   No   Do you feel that you're constantly under stress trying to accomplish more than you can handle?

7. Yes   No   Do you feel trapped in a daily routine?

8. Yes   No   Do you feel that you just don't have time for fun any more?

9. Yes   No   Do you often feel under stress when you don't have enough time?

10. Yes   No   Would you like to spend more time alone?

Source: Statistics Canada's 1998 General Social Survey. Cited in P. DeMont, "Too Much Stress, Too Little Time," *Ottawa Citizen*, November 12, 1999.

CHAPTER SIX

Perception and Personality in Organizations

LEARNING OBJECTIVES

After reading this chapter, you should be able to:

- Outline the perceptual process.
- Explain how we perceive ourselves and others through social identity.
- Discuss the accuracy of stereotypes.
- Describe the attribution process and two attribution errors.
- Diagram the self-fulfilling prophecy process.
- Discuss the objectives and limitations of diversity management programs.
- Explain how the Johari Window can help improve our perceptions.
- Identify the "Big Five" personality dimensions.
- Discuss the psychological dimensions identified by Jung and measured in the Myers-Briggs Type Indicator.

Toronto's police service is trying to reduce racism and the perception of bias by encouraging more visible minorities to become police officers.

Toronto's police service is fighting to correct racial bias and the public perception of this bias. There have been several incidents where police have used derogatory language against people of different racial backgrounds. Some of these racial slurs even found their way into police reports. "There is a lot of racism within this force," says University of Toronto professor Peter Rosenthal.

One recent study found that blacks in Toronto were twice as likely to be stopped by police at least once in the previous two years and four times as likely to be stopped multiple times. "Sometimes when I'm out in the black community, the first thing said to me is that more young blacks are stopped," says Sylvia Hudson, a member of the Toronto Police Race Relations Committee.

Toronto's police service is taking steps to overcome racism and the perception of bias. Officers are required to attend diversity-training workshops that sensitize them to racial, gender, and other issues. The service is also recruiting more people from racial minorities. Less than 10 percent of police officers are nonwhite in a city where most citizens are nonwhite. However, its recruiting drive that targets nonwhite recruits is working. About 28 percent of new cadets to the service are considered to be racial minorities.[1]

Perception The process of selecting, organizing, and interpreting information in order to make sense of the world around us.

www.torontopolice.on.ca

The Greek philosopher Plato wrote long ago that we see reality only as shadows reflecting against the rough wall of a cave.[2] In other words, reality is filtered through an imperfect perceptual process. **Perception** is the process of receiving information about and making sense of the world around us. It involves deciding which information to notice, how to categorize this information, and how to interpret it within the framework of our existing knowledge. As we saw in the opening vignette, the perceptual process creates misunderstanding about how people think and behave. Some Toronto police officers may have preconceptions about the criminal intentions of black citizens, and the lack of nonwhite officers may be reinforcing the public's perception that police are biased.

This chapter begins by describing the perceptual process, that is, the dynamics of selecting, organizing, and interpreting external stimuli. Social identity theory is introduced, including how this process influences our self-perceptions and the perceptions of others. Social identity theory lays the foundation for our discussion of stereotyping, prejudice, and discrimination. The perceptual processes of attribution and self-fulfilling prophecy are described next, followed by an overview of strategies to minimize perceptual problems. Our perception of others, as well as most other organizational behaviour processes, are influenced by our personality. The final section of this chapter introduces this important concept and its relevance to organizational behaviour.

THE PERCEPTUAL PROCESS

As Exhibit 6.1 illustrates, the perceptual process begins when environmental stimuli are received through our senses. Most stimuli are screened out; the rest are organized and interpreted based on various information processing activities. The resulting perceptions influence our emotions and behaviour towards those objects, people, and events.[3]

SELECTIVE ATTENTION

Our five senses are constantly bombarded with stimuli. Some things are noticed, but most are screened out. A nurse working in post-operative care might ignore the smell of recently disinfected instruments or the sound of co-workers talking nearby. Yet, a small flashing red light on the nurse station console is immediately noticed because it signals that a patient's vital signs are failing. This process of filtering information received by our senses is called **selective attention**.

One influence on selective attention is the size, intensity, motion, repetition, and novelty of the target (including people). The red light on the nurse station console receives attention because it is bright (intensity), flashing (motion), and a rare event (novelty). As for people, we would notice two employees having a heated debate if co-workers normally don't raise their voices (novelty and intensity).

Notice that selective attention is also influenced by the context in which the target is perceived. You might be aware that a client has a German accent if the meeting takes place in Calgary, but not if the conversation takes place somewhere in Germany, particularly if you had been living there for some time. On the contrary, it would be your Canadian accent that others would notice!

Selective attention The process of filtering (selecting and screening out) information received by our senses.

Characteristics of the perceiver

Selective attention is partly influenced by the perceiver's emotions. We tend to remember information that is consistent with our attitudes and ignore information that is inconsistent.

EXHIBIT 6.1   Model of the Perceptual Process

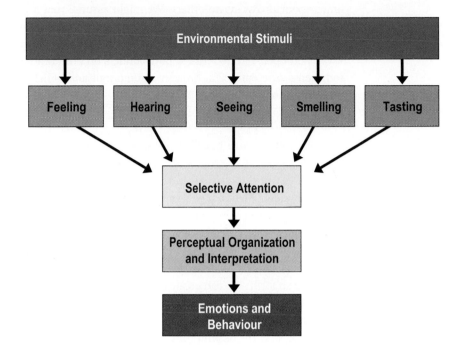

For example, interviewers who develop positive feelings towards a job applicant early in the interview subsequently tend to screen out negative information about that candidate.[4] In extreme cases, our emotions screen out large blocks of information that threaten our beliefs and values. This phenomenon, called **perceptual defence**, protects our self-esteem and may be a coping mechanism to minimize stress in the short run.[5]

Our expectations, which are shaped by preconceived ideas, also condition us to be "ready" for certain events and to ignore others.[6] Several professions are aware of this problem and try to counter its effect. Truck drivers learn to expect the unexpected, such as a child darting out onto the road. Police detectives try not to form expectations during the early stages of a criminal investigation. They engage in *splatter vision*—taking everything in as a whole, focusing on nothing. If crime investigators focus too early on one theory, they might screen out valuable information that is inconsistent with the erroneous theory. "We try to avoid theories in cases like this," said Ottawa-Carleton police detective Roch Lachance about a homicide where there were few leads or suspects. "When you get a theory, it can put blinders on to what really happened."[7] Corporate decision makers should apply the same principles to avoid missing unexpected threats and opportunities.

PERCEPTUAL ORGANIZATION AND INTERPRETATION

After selecting stimuli, we usually simplify and "make sense" of it. This involves organizing the information into general categories and interpreting it. Organizing information mainly occurs through the process of **perceptual grouping**. We rely on perceptual grouping principles to organize people and objects into recognizable and manageable patterns or categories. One grouping principle is closure, such as filling in missing information about what happened at a meeting that you missed (e.g., who was there, where it was held). Another perceptual

Perceptual defence A defensive psychological process that involves subconsciously screening out large blocks of information that threaten the person's beliefs and values.

Perceptual grouping The perceptual organization process of placing people and objects into recognizable and manageable patterns or categories.

grouping principle is identifying trends. Marketing analysts try to identify consumer trends from seemingly random information. A third grouping principle is based on a target person's similarity or proximity to others. We might assume that a particular employee is inefficient because he or she works in a department where employees tend to be inefficient.

Perceptual grouping helps us to make sense of the workplace, but it can also inhibit creativity and open-mindedness. It puts blinders on our ability to organize and interpret people and events differently. Our broader assumptions and beliefs, known as mental models, influence perceptual grouping.

Mental models

Communications guru Marshall McLuhan once wrote that people wear their own set of idiosyncratic goggles. In his colourful way, McLuhan was saying that each of us holds a unique view of what the world looks like and how it operates. These idiosyncratic goggles are known as **mental models**.[8] Mental models are the broad world views or "theories-in-use" that people rely on to guide their perceptions and behaviours. These theories are formed from past experience and become reinforced through their successful application. For example, most of us have a mental model about attending a college lecture or seminar. We have a set of assumptions and expectations about how people arrive, arrange themselves in the room, ask and answer questions, and so forth. We can create a mental image of what a class in progress would look like.

Mental models guide our perceptions and enable us to make decisions more quickly. They create the screens through which we select information, the boxes we use to contain that knowledge, and the assumptions we use to interpret events. Effective decision makers rely

Mental models The broad world views or "theories-in-use" that people rely on to guide their perceptions and behaviours.

CP PHOTO ARCHIVE (J. Rennison).

www.dofasco.ca

For years, steel company executives in Canada had a deeply entrenched mental model of their industry: a low-tech, low-skilled, cyclical business with a standardized commodity product that is only profitable if it operates at full capacity. But that's not the way that Dofasco executives perceive things. "We challenge every one of those assumptions every day, and it makes us a leader," says Dofasco president John Mayberry. Canada's second-largest steel producer is quickly becoming a purveyor of specialty steel products and high-tech solutions for its customers' problems. The new mental model has Dofasco embracing emerging technologies and hiring skilled people to apply that technology.[9] How can companies encourage employees to break out of their existing mental models?

on their mental models to quickly identify discrepancies and to find solutions to those discrepancies. In our classroom example, we would immediately notice if something is out of the ordinary (such as a student sitting on a desk rather than on a chair). In organizational settings, these discrepancies cue us to take appropriate action.

Mental models help us to make sense of our environment, but they may blind us to different ways of seeing the world.[10] For example, accounting professionals tend to see corporate problems in terms of accounting solutions, whereas marketing professionals see the same problems from a marketing perspective. Mental models also block our recognition of new opportunities. Consider the comment that Harry Warner of Warner Brothers Studios made when soundtracks for movies first appeared in 1927: "Who the hell wants to hear actors talk?" In the 1970s, General Motors continued to build big gas-guzzling cars even though oil prices had significantly altered what consumers looked for in a vehicle. And as recently as 1996, Microsoft's Bill Gates mocked the commercial viability of the Internet.[11] In each case, mental models blocked the ability to see emerging marketplace realities.

How do we change mental models? It's a tough challenge. After all, we developed models from several years of experience and reinforcement. The first step is to constantly question our existing mental models and their assumptions. The creative decision-making process that we will learn about in Chapter 11 helps in this regard. Working with people from diverse backgrounds is another way to break out of existing mental models. Some companies try to form new mental models by hiring outsiders—people who have not worked in the industry and are therefore free of the dominant perceptions that blind industry veterans. For example, Sony Corp's North American video game group successfully launched PlayStation by breaking away from long-established views of the market. They hired people with little or no experience in the industry so that the group could see opportunities differently.[12]

SOCIAL IDENTITY THEORY

• Social identity theory A model that explains self-perception and social perception in terms of our unique characteristics (personal identity) as well as membership in various social groups (social identity).

The perceptual process is more than just placing other people into groups. It is an interactive dynamic between our self-perceptions and perceptions of others. **Social identity theory** explains this process of self-perception and social perception.[13] According to social identity theory, people develop their self-perceptions through personal identity and social identity. *Personal identity* includes the individual's unique characteristics and experiences, such as physical appearance, personality traits, and special talents. An unusual achievement that distinguishes you from other people becomes a personal characteristic with which you partially identify yourself.

Social identity, on the other hand, refers to our self-perception as members in various social groups. For example, one person might have a self-identity as a Canadian, a graduate of the University of New Brunswick, and an employee at Acme Widget Company. This social categorization process helps us to locate ourselves within the social world (see Exhibit 6.2).

People adopt degrees of personal and social identity, depending on the situation. If your organizational behaviour class is well represented in terms of gender, race, and specialization (marketing, finance, etc.), you would tend to identify yourself in terms of personal identity characteristics in that context (e.g., "I'm probably the only one in this class who has trekked through Malaysia's Cameron Highlands!"). On the other hand, if you are one of the few computer science students in a class of primarily business students, your group membership— your social identity—would dominate your self-perception. In this situation, you would define yourself more by your field of specialization ("I'm from computer science.") than by any personal identity characteristics. As your distinguishing social identity becomes known to others, they, too, would likely identify you by that feature.

EXHIBIT 6.2   Self-Perception and Social Perception Through Social Identity

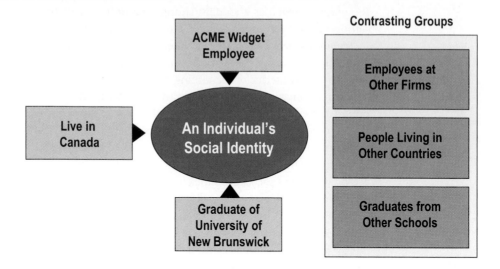

We tend to perceive ourselves as members of several groups, not just one or two. In this respect, social identity is a complex combination of many memberships determined by personal priorities. Also, we are motivated to create and present a positive self-image. According to social identity theory, this occurs by identifying ourselves with groups that have a positive public reputation. This explains why medical doctors usually define themselves in terms of their profession, whereas people in low-status jobs are less likely to do so. It also explains why some people like to mention their employer while others never mention where they work.[14] At one time, Continental Airlines had such a lousy reputation that some employees removed the company labels from their uniforms. Now that the airline is successful again, employees proudly wear Continental's logo on their uniforms and buy many labelled items for home use from the company store.[15]

PERCEIVING OTHERS THROUGH SOCIAL IDENTITY

Social identity theory doesn't just explain how we develop self-perceptions. It also explains the dynamics of social perception—how we perceive others. In particular, it describes how and why we categorize others into homogeneous and often less favourable groups. Social identity is a *comparative* process, meaning that we define ourselves in terms of our differences with people who belong to other groups. To simplify this comparison process, we tend to *homogenize* people within social categories. We think that people within our group share certain traits, and that people in comparison groups share a different set of traits. This may be partly true, but we further exaggerate these differences. For example, students from one college often describe students from a rival school (particularly before a football, basketball, or other sports competition) as though they come from a different planet!

Comparison and homogenization explain why we perceptually group other people and overgeneralize their traits. But we also tend to develop less positive (or sometimes downright negative) images of people outside of our social identity group. According to one source, some executives at Sony's Web site, The Station, perceive the young staff members as know-it-all kids who cannot run their own lives. Meanwhile, Sony's twentysomething employees think that the executives are utterly clueless about technology and dangerously out of touch with today's markets.[16]

Why do we tend to disparage people who are different from us? The answer is that our self-identity involves contrasting the groups we belong to with other groups. To maintain a positive self-image, we usually construct favourable images of our own social identity group and, as a result, less favourable images of people belonging to other social categories. This is particularly true when the groups are in competition and conflict with each other. The negative image of opponents preserves our self-image while the threat exists.[17]

To summarize, the social identity process explains how we perceive ourselves and others. We partly identify ourselves in terms of our membership in social groups. This comparison process includes creating a homogeneous image of our own social groups and different homogeneous images of people in other groups. We also tend to assign more favourable features to our own groups and less favourable features to other groups. This perceptual process makes our social world easier to understand. However, it also becomes the basis for stereotyping people in organizational settings, which is discussed next.

ERRORS IN THE PERCEPTUAL PROCESS

So far, we have outlined the main elements of social perception in organizations, including selective attention, perceptual organization and interpretation, and social identity processes. You probably noticed during this discussion that the perceptual process is less than perfect. People ignore and distort information, then try to make sense of it in ways that are often different from how other people perceive the same situation. Over the next several pages, we will more fully explore several phenomena that distort perceptions. Some topics—such as stereotyping and attribution—are natural perceptual processes. We stereotype and make attributions as part of the perceptual process. But these and other perceptual activities are better known for the perceptual errors they create.

Stereotyping The process of using a few observable characteristics to assign people to a preconceived social category, and then assigning less observable traits to those persons based on their membership in the group.

STEREOTYPING IN ORGANIZATIONAL SETTINGS

Stereotyping is an extension of social identity. It is the process of assigning traits to people based on their membership in a social category.[18] In other words, stereotypes define people by the demographic and organizational groups to which they belong. Exhibit 6.3 illustrates the three steps in the stereotyping process. First, we develop social categories and assign

EXHIBIT 6.3   The Stereotyping Process

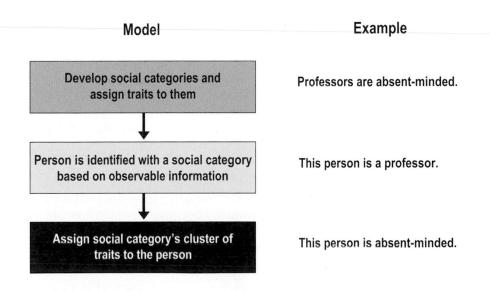

Model	**Example**
Develop social categories and assign traits to them	Professors are absent-minded.
Person is identified with a social category based on observable information	This person is a professor.
Assign social category's cluster of traits to the person	This person is absent-minded.

The *Edmonton Sun;* Photographer Christine Vanzella.

www.shell.ca

Most people are surprised to learn that Charlotte St. Germain is an oil refinery process operator. Their stereotype is of men crawling around the refinery's massive network of pipes and equipment with heavy overalls, steel-tipped boots, and a hard hat. "People often say, 'You don't look like the sort of person to be doing that,'" says the fiftysomething grandmother. St. Germain is one of 3 women among the 115 process operators at the Shell Scotford Refinery near Fort Saskatchewan, Alberta. Her retraining from an office job to process operator 20 years ago makes her a pioneer in this traditionally male job. "She has paved the way for women to take on such jobs," says another female process operator.[19] How can organizations break traditional stereotypes and encourage women to enter these types of jobs?

traits that are difficult to observe. For instance, students might form a stereotype that professors are both intelligent and absent-minded. These unobservable traits are, to some extent, formed from personal experiences, but they are anchored more in public images, such as movie characters and public figures.

Next, people are assigned to one or more social categories based on easily observable information about them, such as their gender, appearance, or physical location. Observable features allow us to assign people to a social group quickly and without much investigation. Lastly, the cluster of traits linked to the social category is assigned to people identified as members of that group. For example, we subconsciously assume that professors are absent-minded, at least until we know them better.

How accurate are stereotypes?

Early writers warned that stereotypes were almost completely false or, at best, that they exaggerated the traits of people in those groups. Scholars now take a more moderate view. They say that stereotypes generally have some inaccuracies, some overestimation or underestimation of real differences, and some degree of accuracy.[20] Still, we should remember that stereotypes are never as accurate as our personal knowledge of a person.

One problem with stereotyping is that stereotyped traits do not accurately describe every person in that social category. For instance, research has found that people with physical disabilities are stereotyped as being quiet, gentle-hearted, shy, insecure, dependent, and submissive.[21] While this may be true of some people, it is certainly not characteristic of everyone who has a physical disability. Another concern with stereotypes is that we often ignore or misinterpret information that is inconsistent with the stereotype.[22] Stereotypes are notoriously easy to confirm because they include abstract personality traits that are supported by ambiguous behaviours.

People also develop inaccurate stereotypes under *certain conditions*. One condition is the degree to which we interact with people in that group. If we don't communicate with and directly observe people, we tend to rely on distorted public images of them. Second, stereotypes are less accurate when we experience conflict with members of that group. Conflict creates an "us-versus-them" emotional state that subconsciously distorts the information we assign to the group.

The third problem is that we develop inaccurate stereotypes of groups that enhance our own social identity. Recall from social identity theory that identifying with certain social groups and contrasting them with other groups develops our self-perception. This creates less favourable images of other groups, which involves subconsciously assigning inaccurate traits to people in those different groups.[23]

Prejudice Negative emotions towards people belonging to a particular stereotyped group based on inaccurate perceptions about people in that group.

At this point, you might think that we should avoid stereotyping altogether. Unfortunately, it's not that simple. Stereotyping is a natural process to economize mental effort.[24] By remembering information about categories of people rather than every individual we meet, stereotyping saves a lot of investigative work. Moreover, this perceptual process fills in missing information when we lack the opportunity or motivation to directly know others. The good news is that the more we interact with someone, the less we rely on stereotypes to understand the individual. Stereotyping occurs when we lack personal information about the individual or when the information is ambiguous. As we get to know someone better, we remove our stereotypic perceptions of that individual.[25]

Ethical problems with stereotyping

Stereotypes may be part of the perceptual process, but inaccurate stereotypes raise serious ethical concerns. Perhaps the greatest concern is that stereotyping lays the foundation for **prejudice**—unfounded negative emotions towards people belonging to a particular stereotyped group.[26] For instance, a server at the Keg Restaurant in Kelowna, B.C., was fired when her pregnancy became known to management. In Quebec, a school bus driver was recently suspended, allegedly because of his race. One parent apparently complained that the driver is "big, black and scares the children." A supervisor apparently advised the driver that "blacks aren't welcome in the school-bus business because there are lots of parents who don't like their children being driven by blacks."[27]

Although these examples of overt prejudice still exist, it is probably fair to say that most people try to avoid discriminatory

Courtesy of Christine Cushing.

You won't find many female executive chefs in large Canadian hotels. Few women choose to apprentice in hotels because the regimented kitchen environment tends to uphold gender stereotypes. The locker room mentality and incidents of sexual harassment in some kitchens are also a problem. However, the situation is better than it was in the 1980s when Christine Cushing (shown in photo) became a chef. "It was very difficult," recalls the owner of Toronto's Chez Toi cooking school. "My confidence kept being attacked by people who didn't see me as being capable." Laura Prentice agrees that conditions have improved. "People don't treat me as a piece of fluff now," says the chef and business partner of Pan restaurant in Toronto and Lola restaurant in Port Dalhousie, Ontario.[28] How can corporate leaders minimize prejudice in the workplace?

behaviours. They support the notion of equality and try to act consistently with this equality value. People tend to monitor their own emotions and suppress prejudices arising from ingrained stereotypes.[29] Unfortunately, subtle discrimination occurs even when prejudices are minimized. The reason is that people rely on stereotypes to establish notions of the "ideal" person in specific roles.[30] When someone doesn't fit the ideal, they receive a less favourable evaluation. Connections 6.1 describes how this bias hurts the employment prospects of older workers. It's not that recruiters are overtly prejudiced against older people. Rather, their implicit image of an ideal job candidate is a young person.

Similarly, many women executives feel that negative preconceptions and stereotypes of their professional capabilities have limited their careers.[31] In support of this view, several studies (two of them Canadian) indicate that male business students continue to hold a masculine stereotype of successful middle managers. As long as they keep these images of the ideal manager, women will be less favourably evaluated in these positions.[32]

Before leaving this topic, we should note that stereotyping is also partly responsible for **sexual harassment**. As we learned in Chapter 5, sexual harassment refers to unwelcome conduct of a sexual nature that detrimentally affects the work environment or leads to adverse job-related consequences for its victims. Sexual harassment is mainly caused by the harasser's abuse of power, as we will discuss in Chapter 12. However, it is also more preva-

Sexual harassment
Unwelcome conduct of a sexual nature that detrimentally affects the work environment or leads to adverse job-related consequences for its victims.

CONNECTIONS 6.1

Age Bias and the Ideal Applicant

Craig Blair worked at several large Toronto investment banks, eventually working his way up to the level of senior money market specialist. Then he got pushed out, apparently because he was too old. Blair subsequently interviewed with the Toronto branch of a European brokerage and was confident that his previous performance would get him the job. A friend gave him the bad news. The friend had overheard a conversation in which the dealer who'd interviewed Blair told someone, "We're not going to hire him. He's too old."

At 46, Blair says he is over the hill in the securities industry. "In this business, you're looked upon in a sense as a sports figure," Blair explains. "And you have a very, very short lifespan."

Corporate leaders say that there is no age bias, just a few older employees whose skills don't fit current needs. But Sharon Adler will tell you otherwise. After the department store where she worked closed, the 55-year-old cosmetician has been unsuccessful at getting a job. Adler is attractive, looks professional, and has 20 years of experience in the business. Yet she believes that prospective employers are turned off by her age. "I've applied for about 10 jobs," explains Adler. "I think my age was a factor in all of these cases because I return to the stores and notice they've since hired a young woman in her 20s."

Walter Winsor had a similar experience. Winsor applied for work in Placentia Bay, Newfoundland, along with two other men in their twenties. The other men got work. Winsor, who is over 50, didn't. So Winsor has taken his case to the Newfoundland Human Rights Commission to receive compensation for lost wages. He also wants to warn other employers that they can't treat older workers the way he was treated.

Source: T. Cole, "Revenge of the Fortysomethings," *Report on Business Magazine,* June 2000, p. 34; "Placentia Man Charges Age Discrimination," *CBC Radio,* October 14, 1999; S. Whittaker, "Combatting Age Bias," *Montreal Gazette,* January 16, 1999, p. I1.

lent where the harasser (typically a man) holds sexist motives based on paternalism and gender stereotyping.[33] In other words, harassment is more likely to occur among people who stereotype the victim as subservient and powerless. For example, a study of female firefighters reported that sexual harassment is much more prevalent in fire departments where men hold strong sex stereotypes of women.[34] The implication here is that sexual harassment will continue as long as people maintain sexist perceptions.

ATTRIBUTION THEORY

Attribution process
A perceptual process whereby we interpret the causes of behaviour in terms of the person (internal attributions) or the situation (external attributions).

Our discussion so far has mainly looked at the dynamics of grouping, including social identity and stereotyping. A different perceptual activity, called the **attribution process**, helps us to interpret the world around us. The attribution process involves deciding whether an observed behaviour or event is largely caused by internal or external factors.[35] Internal factors originate from within a person, such as the individual's ability or motivation. We make an *internal attribution* by believing that an employee performs the job poorly because he or she lacks the necessary competencies or motivation. External factors originate from the environment, such as lack of resources, other people, or just luck. An *external attribution* would occur if we believe that the employee performs the job poorly because he or she doesn't receive sufficient resources to do the task.

How do people determine whether to make an internal or external attribution about a co-worker's excellent job performance or a supplier's late shipment? Basically, they rely on the three attribution rules shown in Exhibit 6.4. Internal attributions are made when the observed individual behaved this way in the past (high consistency), did not behave like this towards other people or in different situations (low distinctiveness), and other people do not behave

---

EXHIBIT 6.4   Rules of Attribution

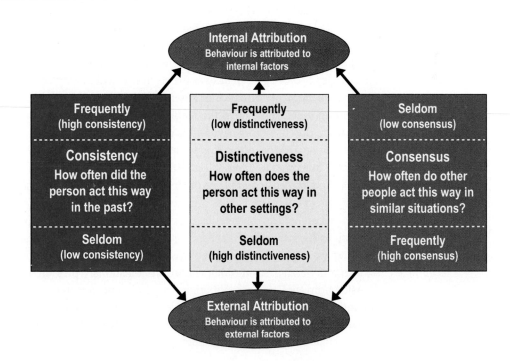

this way in similar situations (low consensus). On the other hand, an external attribution is made when there is low consistency, high distinctiveness, and high consensus.

The following example will help to clarify the three attribution rules. Suppose that an employee is making poor-quality products one day on a particular machine. We would probably conclude that there is something wrong with the machine (an external attribution) if the employee has made good-quality products on this machine in the past (low consistency), the employee makes good-quality products on other machines (high distinctiveness), and other employees have recently had quality problems on this machine (high consensus). We would make an internal attribution, on the other hand, if the employee usually makes poor-quality products on this machine (high consistency), other employees produce good-quality products on this machine (low consensus), and the employee also makes poor-quality products on other machines (low distinctiveness).[36]

Consequences of attribution

Attributing behaviour to internal versus external factors affects our subsequent reactions to that event.[37] One study of union grievances reported that arbitrators rely on the attribution process to decide whether employees are responsible for wrongdoing. In particular, arbitration decisions favour the employee when other employees have committed the same error and the employee has not been guilty of the wrongdoing before.[38]

Attribution decisions also affect the implications of performance feedback and reward allocation. Employees receive larger bonuses or pay increases when decision makers attribute good performance to the employee's ability or motivation.[39] Employees also develop a stronger self-efficacy and tend to have higher job satisfaction when they believe that positive feedback relates to events within their control rather than to external causes.[40]

Attribution errors

The attribution process is far from perfect. The most fundamental error we make in attribution is called (not surprisingly) **fundamental attribution error**. This refers to the tendency to attribute the behaviour of other people more to internal than external factors. If an employee is late for work, observers are more likely to conclude that the person is lazy than to think that external factors may have caused this behaviour. Fundamental attribution error occurs where there is limited information about the situational factors affecting other people. The person performing the behaviour is naturally more sensitive to situational influences. This can lead to disagreement over the degree to which employees should be held responsible for their poor performance or absenteeism.[41] The observer blames the employee's lack of motivation or ability, whereas the employee does not feel responsible because the behaviour seems to be due to factors beyond his or her control.

Another attribution error, known as **self-serving bias**, is the tendency to attribute our favourable outcomes to internal factors and our failures to external factors. Simply put, we take credit for our successes and blame others or the situation for our mistakes. The existence of self-serving bias in corporate life has been well documented. In a unique study of corporate annual reports, researchers discovered that organizational successes were typically explained by internal attributions such as management strategy, workforce qualities, and research/development efforts. But when explaining corporate problems, the annual reports relied more on external attributions such as bad weather, strong competition, and inflationary pressures.[42]

Aside from these errors, attributions vary from one person to another based on personal values and experiences. For instance, female managers are less likely than male managers to make internal attributions about their job performance.[43] Overall, we need to be careful about personal and systematic biases in the attribution process within organizations.

Fundamental attribution error The tendency to attribute the behaviour of other people more to internal than external factors.

Self-serving bias A perceptual error whereby people tend to attribute their own success to internal factors and their failures to external factors.

SELF-FULFILLING PROPHECY

For the past 35 years, Ottawa restaurant owner David Smith has known that employees will achieve remarkable performance levels when their boss believes that they can succeed. "When you show people you believe in them, it's amazing what can happen," advises Smith. As owner of Nate's Deli, Smith has seen his high expectations make some employees confident enough to take on more challenging assignments in the organization. "I've put busboys into tuxedos," he says.[44]

Self-fulfilling prophecy A phenomenon in which an observer's expectations of someone cause that person to act in a way consistent with the observer's expectation.

David Smith has been practising a powerful perceptual process called **self-fulfilling prophecy**. Self-fulfilling prophecy occurs when our expectations about another person cause that person to act in a way that is consistent with those expectations.[45] In other words, our perceptions can influence reality. If a supervisor believes that a new employee won't be able to perform the job, this expectation influences the supervisor's behaviour towards the employee and, without realizing it, may cause the recruit to perform the job poorly. Consequently, the supervisor's perception, even if originally incorrect, is confirmed. Exhibit 6.5 illustrates the four steps in the self-fulfilling prophecy process using the example of a supervisor and subordinate:[46]

1. *Expectations formed*—The supervisor forms expectations about the employee's future behaviour and performance. These expectations are sometimes inaccurate, because first impressions are usually formed from limited information.

2. *Behaviour towards the employee*—The supervisor's expectations influence his or her treatment of employees.[47] Specifically, high-expectancy employees (those expected to do well) receive more emotional support through nonverbal cues (e.g., more smiling and eye contact), more frequent and valuable feedback and reinforcement, more challenging goals, better training, and more opportunities to demonstrate their performance.

3. *Effects on the employee*—The supervisor's behaviours have two effects on the employee. First, through better training and more practice opportunities, a high-expectancy employee learns more skills and knowledge than a low-expectancy employee. Second, the employee develops a stronger **self-efficacy**.[48] Recall from Chapter 2 that high self-efficacy employees believe that they have the ability, motivation, and resources to complete a task successfully.[49] This results in higher motivation because employees develop stronger effort-to-performance expectancies and set more challenging goals for themselves.

Self-efficacy A person's belief that he or she has the ability, motivation, and resources to complete a task successfully.

EXHIBIT 6.5   The Self-Fulfilling Prophecy Cycle

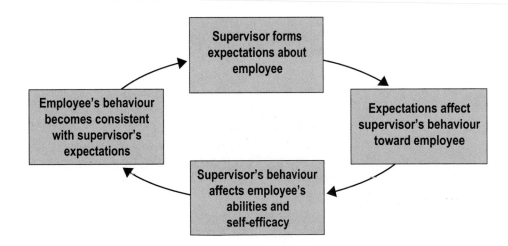

4. *Employee behaviour and performance*—With higher motivation and better skills, high-expectancy employees are more likely to demonstrate desired behaviours and better performance. This is observed by the supervisor and reinforces the original perception.

Self-fulfilling prophecies extend beyond supervisor-subordinate relationships. Some of the earliest research reported that teacher expectancies influenced the subsequent behaviour and performance of elementary school children. Courtroom research has found that judges influence jury decisions by nonverbally communicating their expectations. And while self-fulfilling prophecy is an interpersonal effect, it also operates at a macro level in the stability of financial institutions. The stability of a bank, for instance, depends on the public's expectation that it will be stable. As soon as people begin to doubt this belief, the financial institution has a "run on the bank" that threatens its survival.[50]

Self-fulfilling prophecies in organizations

In organizational settings, employees are more likely to be victims than benefactors of self-fulfilling prophecy.[51] This is unfortunate because, as David Smith knows, self-fulfilling prophecy is a potentially valuable strategy to maximize employee performance and satisfaction. Researchers have reported, for example, that hard-core unemployed trainees were more likely to find work and poor-performing sailors in the United States Navy were more likely to improve their performance when instructors or supervisors formed positive expectations about them.[52]

How can organizations harness the power of positive self-fulfilling prophecy? Like David Smith, corporate leaders must exhibit more contagious enthusiasm and, although providing accurate feedback, continue to express hope and optimism in each employee's potential.[53] In some situations, researchers have found that these positive expectations spread from one or two employees to the entire group. To block negative self-fulfilling prophecy, companies need to help employees fight negative stereotypes and avoid first impressions. They should also develop more objective performance measures and provide fair access to challenging assignments and training opportunities.

PRIMACY EFFECT

Primacy effect A perceptual error in which we quickly form an opinion of people based on the first information we receive about them.

Primacy effect relates to the saying that "first impressions are lasting impressions." It is our tendency to quickly form an opinion of people based on the first information we receive about them. This rapid perceptual organization fulfils our need to make sense of others and provides a convenient anchor to integrate subsequent information. For example, if we first meet someone who avoids eye contact and speaks softly, we quickly conclude that the person is bashful. It is easier to remember the person as bashful than to recall the specific behaviours exhibited during the first encounter. Unfortunately, once an inaccurate first impression is established, it is difficult to change. This is because people pay less attention to subsequent information after the impression has been formed and they tend to completely ignore information that contradicts the first impression.[54] Thus, the person we think is bashful will have difficulty shaking this first impression.

Under the right circumstances, primacy effect can be beneficial. Many organizations take extra care to ensure that customers have a positive first experience. They also make sure that employees have a good first impression when they join the firm. For instance, during one of its recruiting drives, the Royal Bank of Canada invited a group of students to spend the day rappelling with bank staffers in Ontario's Elora Gorge. As a Royal Bank recruiter explains: "What that says to prospective employees is, 'We're not necessarily just a bank of blue suits.'"[55] After people develop these first impressions, they are more likely to overlook minor exceptions.

RECENCY EFFECT

Recency effect A perceptual error in which the most recent information dominates our perception about a person.

The **recency effect** occurs when the most recent information dominates our perception of others.[56] This effect is stronger than the primacy effect when there is a long delay between the time when the first impression is formed and when the person is evaluated. In other words, the most recent information has the greater influence on our perception of someone when the first impression has worn off with the passage of time.

The recency effect is found in performance appraisals, for which supervisors must recall every employee's performance over the previous year. Recent performance information dominates the evaluation because it is the most easily recalled. Some employees are well aware of the recency effect and use it to their advantage by getting their best work on the manager's desk just before the performance appraisal is conducted.

HALO ERROR

Halo error A perceptual error whereby our general impression of a person, usually based on one prominent characteristic, biases our perception of other characteristics of that person.

Halo error occurs when our general impression of a person, usually based on one prominent characteristic, biases our perception of other characteristics of that person.[57] If we meet a client who speaks in a friendly manner, we tend to infer a host of other favourable qualities about that person. If a colleague doesn't complete tasks on time, we tend to view his or her other traits unfavourably. In each case, one trait important to the perceiver forms a general impression, and this impression becomes the basis for judgments about other traits. Halo error is most likely to occur when concrete information about the perceived target is missing or we are not sufficiently motivated to search for it.[58] Instead, we use our general impression of the person to fill in the missing information.

Halo error has received considerable attention in research on performance appraisal ratings.[59] Consider the situation in which two employees have the same level of work quality, quantity of work, and customer relations performance, but one tends to be late for work. Tardiness might not be an important factor in work performance, but the supervisor has a negative impression of employees who are late for work. Halo error would cause the supervisor to rate the tardy employee lower on *all* performance dimensions because the tardiness created a negative general impression of that employee. The punctual employee would tend to receive higher ratings on *all* performance dimensions even though his or her performance level is really the same as that of the tardy employee. Consequently, halo error distorts our judgments and can result in poor decision making.

PROJECTION

Projection bias A perceptual error in which we tend to believe that other people hold the same beliefs and attitudes that we do.

Projection bias occurs when we believe other people have the same beliefs and behaviours that we do.[60] If you are eager for a promotion, you might think that others in your position

DILBERT reprinted by permission of United Feature Syndicate, Inc.

are similarly motivated. If you are thinking of quitting your job, you start to believe that other people are also thinking of quitting.

Projection bias is usually a defence mechanism used to protect our self-esteem. If we break a work rule, projection justifies this infraction by claiming that "everyone does it." We feel more comfortable with the thought that our negative traits exist in others, so we are quick to believe that others also have these traits. Similarly, projection maintains the credibility of our goals and objectives. When we want an organizational policy changed, we tend to believe that others also have this goal.

IMPROVING PERCEPTIONS

We can't bypass the perceptual process, but we should make every attempt to minimize perceptual biases and distortions. This section introduces five strategies to improve our perceptions: introducing diversity management programs, learning to empathize with others, postponing our impression of others, comparing our perceptions with others, and becoming more aware of our values, beliefs, and prejudices.

DIVERSITY MANAGEMENT PROGRAMS

The National Hockey League has 600 players from 18 nationalities. It's also an aggressive game where players sometimes vent their emotions with racial slurs. "People are always picking on your heritage," says Philadelphia Flyers goalie John Vanbiesbrouck. "We're living in a stereotypical world, where nicknames come before names, and that sometimes leads to other things." To minimize fights and other things, the NHL has a zero tolerance policy regarding racial slurs. It also requires every player to attend a diversity management program each year.[61]

Diversity management programs focus on the awareness, understanding, and appreciation of differences in the workplace. They sensitize people to stereotypes and prejudices that may undermine the benefits of diversity. Diversity management programs usually try to dispel myths about people from different backgrounds. They might also include exercises that make participants aware of how their actions are biased. In addition to the NHL, CIBC, Bank of Montreal, Metropolitan Toronto Police (described at the beginning of this chapter), and many other Canadian organizations require employees to attend diversity management programs.[62]

Diversity management sessions are not intended to correct deep-rooted prejudice or intolerance. In fact, they could make matters worse because highly prejudiced employees are likely to view these sessions as a form of coercion if they are required to attend them. Diversity programs also tend to focus more on attitudes than on behaviours, which some critics argue results in little real change in the workplace.[63] To develop a deeper understanding of differences, executives at Hoechst Celanese joined two organizations in which they are an ethnic minority. "Joining these organizations has been more helpful to me than two weeks of diversity training," concludes a Hoechst Celanese executive.[64]

EMPATHIZE WITH OTHERS

Empathy A person's ability to understand and be sensitive to the feelings, thoughts, and situations of others.

Hoechst Celanese executives are taking diversity management to the next level by learning how to empathize with people from different backgrounds. **Empathy** refers to a person's ability to understand and be sensitive to the feelings, thoughts, and situations of others. This is particularly useful in reducing attribution errors because empathy makes us more sensitive to external causes of another person's performance and behaviour.[65]

Empathy comes naturally to some people. However, the rest of us can develop empathy skills by receiving feedback on how well we seem to empathize.[66] Another approach is to work closely with others and spend time participating in their environment. Connections 6.2 describes how some corporate leaders are spending time in the jobs performed by their employees. These activities increase the leaders' empathy with employees and customers by providing them with the opportunity to "walk in their shoes."

POSTPONE IMPRESSION FORMATION

It is very tempting to put people into boxes as soon as possible. After all, the sooner we label them, the sooner we can simplify the world and reduce the tension of uncertainty. Unfortunately, this practice of forming impressions with limited information forces us to rely on inaccurate and overgeneralized stereotypes. A much better perceptual strategy is to postpone impression formation until more information is collected about the individual or situation. By delaying closure, we rely less on stereotyped inferences to understand others.

When working with people from different cultural backgrounds, for instance, we should constantly challenge our stereotypic expectations and actively seek out contrary information. By blocking the effects of stereotypes, first impressions, and other perceptual blinders, we are better able to engage in a developmental learning process that forms a better understanding of others.[67]

www.mollymaid.com; www.homedepot.com
www.chateaufrontenac.com

 CONNECTIONS 6.2

Increasing Empathy by Being There

Linda Burzynski's first day of work at Molly Maid International included cleaning a home that looked like a disaster zone. But her shock soon changed to determination when a co-worker explained that the owner was going through a difficult divorce and a clean home gave some organization to her life.

Burzynski is not one of the regular cleaning crew at Molly Maid International. She is the new president of the company founded in Canada. To help her develop a better empathy for employees and customers, Burzynski spent a few weeks working in a front-line job. "I must admit, I prejudged people, and I ended up being a student," she says of her experience.

Annette Verschuren, president of Home Depot Canada, also keeps in touch with employees and customers by working in the retailer's stores and participating with employees in community events. Managers at Quebec City's Château Frontenac hotel switch roles with front-line employees for one

Annette Verschuren, president of Home Depot Canada, keeps her perceptions in focus by working in the stores and participating in this community service event in Cole Harbour, Nova Scotia.

(E. Wynne) Reprinted with permission from *The Halifax Herald* Ltd.

day each month. "I will certainly appreciate the amount of work [employees] are doing after this," says Château Frontenac's guest services manager after helping to serve some of the 500 breakfasts in the hotel's restaurant.

Sources: C. Tsai, "Executive Takes Uniform Approach," *Globe and Mail,* October 15, 1999, p. M2; F. Shalom, "Home Depot Attacks," *Montreal Gazette,* June 10, 1999, pp. C1, C2; M.H. Pounds, "Executives Should Get Out of the Office," *Hamilton Spectator,* April 24, 1999, p. F1; A. Gibbon, "The Onion-Busting Boss," *Globe and Mail,* June 13, 1995, p. B10.

COMPARE PERCEPTIONS WITH OTHERS

Another useful way to reduce perceptual bias is to compare our perceptions with the perceptions that other people have about the same target. By sharing perceptions, we learn different points of view and potentially gain a better understanding of the situation. If our colleagues have different backgrounds but similar perceptions of the situation, there is reason to be more confident in our interpretation. Of course, there is no way to know for sure that our perceptions are correct, but they are less likely to be wrong if people with different backgrounds have the same general interpretation of the situation.

KNOW YOURSELF: APPLYING THE JOHARI WINDOW

How do you get ahead in a corporation? According to Paul Houston, CEO of Scott's Restaurants, Inc. in Markham, Ontario, you start by knowing yourself and getting straight talk from a trusted source. "Be as brutally frank with yourself as you can be," says Houston. "[Get] somebody who will close the door to their office and say, 'Listen,...here's the reality.'"[68]

Knowing yourself—becoming more aware of your values, beliefs, and prejudices—is a powerful way to improve your perceptions.[69] For example, suppose that you dislike a particular client who treated you badly a few years ago. If the client meets with you to re-establish the relationship, you might be more open-minded about this business opportunity if you are conscious of these emotions. Moreover, if your colleagues are also aware of your unique values and past experiences, they are more likely to understand your actions and help you to improve in the future. If you act harshly towards the troublesome client, for example, your colleagues are likely to understand the reason for your behaviour and draw this to your attention.

The **Johari Window** is a popular model for understanding how co-workers can increase their mutual understanding.[70] Developed by Joseph Luft and Harry Ingram (hence the name *Johari*), this model divides information about yourself into four "windows"—open, blind, hidden, and unknown—based on whether your own values, beliefs, and experiences are known to you and to others.

As we see in Exhibit 6.6, the *open area* includes information about you that is known both to you and to others. For example, both you and your co-workers may be aware that you do not like to be near people who smoke cigarettes. The *blind area* refers to information that is known to others but not to you. For example, your colleagues might notice that you are embarrassed and awkward when meeting someone confined to a wheelchair, but you are unaware of this fact. Information known to you but unknown to others is found in the *hidden area*. We all have personal secrets about our likes, dislikes, and personal experiences. Finally, the *unknown area* includes your values, beliefs, and experiences that aren't known to you or to others.

The main objective of the Johari Window is to increase the size of the open area so that both you and your colleagues are aware of your perceptual limitations. This is partly accomplished by reducing the hidden area through *disclosure*—informing others of your beliefs, feelings, and experiences that may influence the work relationship. Disclosure must be reciprocal among team members; that is, team members should provide information about themselves as you reveal information about yourself. Fortunately, self-disclosure by one person tends to cause others to make a self-disclosure.[71] The open area also increases through *feedback* from others about your behaviours. This information helps you to reduce your blind area, because co-workers often see things in you that you do not see. Finally, the combination of disclosure and feedback occasionally produces revelations about information in the unknown area.

Johari Window A model of personal and interpersonal understanding that encourages disclosure and feedback to increase the open area and reduce the blind, hidden, and unknown areas of oneself.

EXHIBIT 6.6   Johari Window

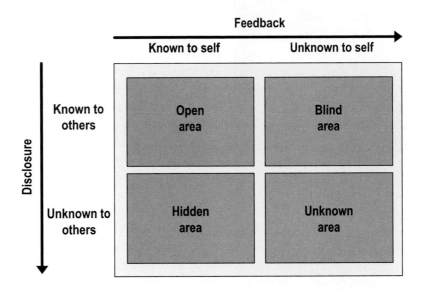

Source: Based on J. Luft, *Group Processes* (Palo Alto, CA: Mayfield, 1984).

Johari Window in practice

The Johari Window can be found in the diversity awareness programs that we described earlier. By learning about cultural differences and communicating more with co-workers from different backgrounds, we gain a better understanding of their behaviour patterns. Another strategy is to engage in open dialogue with co-workers. As we communicate with others, we naturally tend to disclose more information about ourselves and eventually feel comfortable providing candid feedback to them.

The 360-degree feedback process (Chapter 2) also applies the Johari Window because it represents a structured way to provide feedback to others. Jane Haberbusch, a manager at Toronto-based Consumers' Gas Co. describes such an incident. "Someone wrote [on the 360-degree feedback form] that I interrupted people when I spoke and that I was coming across as impatient. Actually, it was just enthusiasm, but it made me aware of how others perceived me and I was able to change."[72]

One limitation of the Johari Window model is that its assumptions of openness, egalitarianism, and face-saving are not embraced in many cultures. It is more difficult to implement in Asia, for example, where feedback and self-disclosure are less acceptable than in Canada. Similarly, some colleagues from Mexico may have difficulty with the Johari Window because of their stronger cultural norm of saving face. Lastly, in any country, we must remember that everyone needs to have a hidden self. Unfortunately, some individual development practices cross this ethical boundary by trying to invade that private space (see Chapter 15).

No matter which steps are taken to improve the perceptual process, we need to recognize that our perceptions of the world are partly structured by our personality. In fact, an individual's personality traits play a pervasive role in almost every aspect of organizational behaviour, from learning processes to one's willingness to adopt a company's cultural values. Let's now turn to the topic of personality in organizations.

Frank Stronach's personality is a driving force behind the success of Magna Corp. He built his humble machine shop into one of the world's largest automobile parts companies. Now, he is planning to transform the racetrack business. "Frank gets a bee in his bonnet," says a former Magna executive, "and off he goes."

www.magnaint.com

• **Personality** The relatively stable pattern of behaviours and consistent internal states that explain a person's behavioural tendencies.

PERSONALITY IN ORGANIZATIONS

Frank Stronach is a personality to reckon with in Canadian business. His tenaciousness, achievement orientation, and sociable style built Magna Corp. from a small machine shop into a $9 billion global empire. More recently, he has applied his passion for racehorses by purchasing several racetracks with the intent of reviving their former glory. "Frank gets a bee in his bonnet," says a former Magna executive, "and off he goes."[73]

It is difficult to describe Frank Stronach—or anyone else—without referring to the concept of **personality**. Personality refers to the relatively stable pattern of behaviours and consistent internal states that explain a person's behavioural tendencies.[74] Personality has both internal and external elements. The external traits are the observable behaviours that we rely on to identify someone's personality. For example, we can observe Frank Stronach's sociability in how often he interacts with other people and how comfortable he acts in those social settings. The internal states represent the thoughts, values, and genetic characteristics that we infer from the observable behaviours.

An individual's personality is relatively stable. If an individual's personality changes at all, it is only over a very long time or as the result of traumatic events. Personality explains behavioural tendencies, because a person's behaviour is influenced by the situation as well as by personality traits. Personality traits are less evident in situations where social norms, reward systems, and other conditions constrain our behaviour.[75] For example, talkative people remain relatively quiet in a library where "no talking" rules are explicit and strictly enforced.

An individual's personality is both inherited and shaped by the environment.[76] Our personalities are partly inherited genetically from our parents. However, these genetic personality characteristics are altered somewhat by life experiences. Frank Stronach's personality is partly handed down genetically from his parents, but it has also been shaped by a variety of life experiences, such as early friendships, interactions with his parents, and traumatic events.

PERSONALITY AND ORGANIZATIONAL BEHAVIOUR

At one time, scholars often explained employee behaviour in terms of personality traits and companies regularly administered personality tests to job applicants. This changed in the 1960s when researchers reported that there is a very weak relationship between personality and job performance.[77] They cited problems with measuring personality traits and explained that the connection between personality and performance exists only under very narrowly defined conditions. Companies stopped using personality tests due to concerns that these tests might unfairly discriminate against people of colour and other identifiable groups.

Over the past decade, personality has regained some of its credibility in organizational settings.[78] Recent studies have reported that certain personality traits predict certain work-related behaviours, stress reactions, and emotions fairly well under certain conditions. Scholars have reintroduced the idea that effective leaders have identifiable traits and that personality explains some of a person's positive attitudes and life happiness. Personality traits seem to help people find the jobs that best suit their needs.[79] Personality is still considered a relatively poor selection test, however. With these caveats in mind, let's look at the main personality traits and dimensions currently studied in organizational settings.

"BIG FIVE" PERSONALITY DIMENSIONS

Since the days of Plato, scholars have been trying to develop lists of personality traits. About 100 years ago, a few personality experts tried to catalogue and condense the many personality traits that had been described over the years. They found thousands of words in *Roget's Thesaurus* and *Webster's Dictionary* that represented personality traits. They aggregated these words into 171 clusters, then further reduced them to five abstract personality dimensions. Using more sophisticated techniques, a recent investigation identified the same five dimensions—known as the **"Big Five" personality dimensions**.[80] As Exhibit 6.7 shows, these five dimensions include:

- *Conscientiousness*—**Conscientiousness** refers to people who are careful, dependable, and self-disciplined. Some scholars argue that this dimension also includes the will to achieve, rather like the need for achievement described in Chapter 3. People with low conscientiousness tend to be careless, less thorough, more disorganized, and irresponsible.

- *Emotional stability*—People with high emotional stability are poised, secure, and calm. Those with emotional instability tend to be depressed, anxious, indecisive, and subject to mood swings.

- *Openness to experience*—This dimension is the most complex and has the least agreement among scholars. It generally refers to the extent that people are sensitive, flexible, creative, and curious. Those who score low on this dimension tend to be more resistant to change, less open to new ideas, and more fixed in their ways.

- *Agreeableness*—This includes the traits of being courteous, good-natured, empathic, and caring. Some scholars prefer the label of "friendly compliance" for this dimension, with its opposite being "hostile noncompliance." People with low agreeableness tend to be uncooperative, short-tempered, and irritable.

- *Extroversion*—**Extroversion** characterizes people who are outgoing, talkative, sociable, and assertive. The opposite is **introversion**, which refers to those who are quiet, shy, and cautious. This does not mean that introverts lack social skills. Rather, they are more inclined to direct their interests to ideas than to social events. Introverts feel quite comfortable being alone, whereas extroverts do not.

Several studies have found that these personality dimensions affect work-related behaviour and job performance.[81] Champions of organizational change (people who effectively gain support for new organizational systems and practices) seem to be placed along the positive end of the five personality dimensions described above.[82] People with high emotional stability tend to work better than others in high-stressor situations. Those with high agreeableness tend to handle customer relations and conflict-based situations more effectively.

Conscientiousness has taken centre stage as the most valuable personality trait for predicting job performance in almost every job group. Conscientious employees set higher personal

---

"Big Five" personality dimensions The five abstract personality dimensions under which most personality traits are represented. They are extroversion, agreeableness, conscientiousness, emotional stability, and openness to experience.

Conscientiousness A "Big Five" personality dimension that characterizes people who are careful, dependable, and self disciplined.

Extroversion A "Big Five" personality dimension that characterizes people who are outgoing, talkative, sociable, and assertive.

Introversion Refers to people who are quiet, shy, and cautious.

EXHIBIT 6.7 The "Big Five" Personality Traits

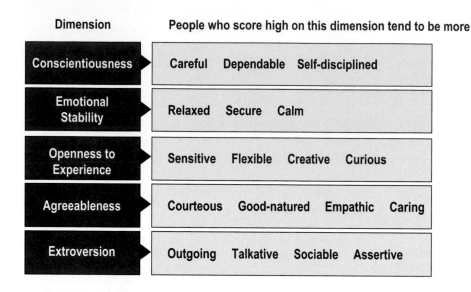

Dimension	People who score high on this dimension tend to be more
Conscientiousness	Careful Dependable Self-disciplined
Emotional Stability	Relaxed Secure Calm
Openness to Experience	Sensitive Flexible Creative Curious
Agreeableness	Courteous Good-natured Empathic Caring
Extroversion	Outgoing Talkative Sociable Assertive

goals for themselves and have higher performance expectations than do employees with low levels of conscientiousness. Moreover, as we learned in Chapter 2, high-conscientiousness employees tend to engage in more organizational citizenship behaviours. Conscientious employees are necessary for emerging organizational structures that rely on empowerment rather than on the traditional "command and control" system. This personality trait, along with agreeableness and emotional stability, also plays an important role in customer service.[83]

JUNG'S PSYCHOLOGICAL TYPES AND THE MYERS-BRIGGS TYPE INDICATOR

During the 1920s, Swiss psychiatrist Carl Jung proposed a personality theory that identifies the way that people prefer to perceive their environment as well as obtain and process information. Twenty years later, the mother and daughter team of Katherine Briggs and Isabel Briggs-Myers developed the **Myers-Briggs Type Indicator (MBTI)**, a personality test that measures each of the traits in Jung's model.[84]

The MBTI measures how people prefer to focus their attention (extroversion versus introversion), collect information (sensing versus intuition), process and evaluate information (thinking versus feeling), and orient themselves to the outer world (judging versus perceiving). Extroversion and introversion were discussed in the previous section, so let's examine the other dimensions:

- *Sensing/Intuition*—Sensing types like collecting information through their five senses. They use an organized structure to acquire factual and preferably quantitative details. In contrast, intuitive people collect information nonsystematically. They rely more on subjective evidence as well as on their intuition and sheer inspiration. Sensers are capable of synthesizing large amounts of seemingly random information to form quick conclusions.

- *Thinking/Feeling*—Thinking types rely on rational cause-effect logic and the scientific method (see Chapter 1) to make decisions. They weigh the evidence objectively and

Myers-Briggs Type Indicator (MBTI) A personality test that measures how people prefer to focus their attention (extroversion versus introversion), collect information (sensing versus intuition), process and evaluate information (thinking versus feeling), and orient themselves to the outer world (judging versus perceiving).

unemotionally. Feeling types, on the other hand, consider how their choices affect others. They weigh the options against their personal values more than rational logic.

- *Judging/Perceiving*—Some people prefer order and structure in their relationship with the outer world. These judging types enjoy the control of decision making and want to resolve problems quickly. In contrast, perceiving types are more flexible. They like to spontaneously adapt to events as they unfold and want to keep their options open.

The MBTI questionnaire combines the four pairs of traits into 16 distinct types. For example, corporate executives tend to be ESTJs, meaning that they are extroverted, sensing, thinking, and judging types. Each of the 16 types has its own strengths and weaknesses. ENTJs are considered to be natural leaders, ISFJs have a high sense of duty, and so on. Also, these types indicate a person's preferences, not the way they necessarily behave all of the time.

Effectiveness of the MBTI

Is the MBTI useful in organizations? Many business leaders think so. The MBTI is one of the most widely used personality tests. It is used by most counselling centres for career assessment. Many organizations also use this instrument to select people for particular positions. It is so popular in some companies that employees are encouraged to reveal their four-letter type so that co-workers can better understand their personalities.

Yet, in spite of its popularity, evidence regarding the effectiveness of the MBTI and Jung's psychological types is mixed.[85] The MBTI does a reasonably good job of measuring Jung's psychological types. There is also some indication that a person's type reveals his or her preferences for particular occupations. For example, people who score high on intuition tend to prefer careers in advertising, the arts, and teaching. Some popular press sources claim that the MBTI predicts business success. One indirect analysis of a dozen successful people who founded successful firms (e.g., Sony, Price Club, Microsoft, Honda) determined that all were intuitive thinkers.[86] However, other evidence is less supportive regarding the MBTI's ability to predict job performance.[87] Overall, the MBTI seems to be useful for career development and self-awareness, but probably should not be used in selecting job applicants.

OTHER PERSONALITY TRAITS

The "Big Five" personality dimensions and the MBTI don't capture every personality trait. A few others are frequently cited in the organizational behaviour literature, such as the Type A and Type B behaviour patterns (described in Chapter 5) and the learned needs (introduced in Chapter 3). Two other personality traits that you should know about are locus of control and self-monitoring.

Locus of control

Locus of control refers to a generalized belief about the amount of control people have over their own lives. Individuals who feel that they are very much in charge of their own destiny have an *internal locus of control*; those who think that events in their life are due mainly to fate or to luck have an *external locus of control*. Of course, externals believe that they control many specific events in their lives—such as opening a door or serving a customer—but they have a general belief that outside forces guide their fate. This is particularly apparent in new situations in which the person's control over events is uncertain.

People perform better in most employment situations when they have a moderately strong internal locus of control. They tend to be more successful in their careers and earn more

Locus of control A personality trait referring to the extent to which people believe what happens to them is within their control; those who feel in control of their destiny have an internal locus of control, whereas those who believe that life events are due mainly to fate or to luck have an external locus of control.

www.td-co.com

At a recent semi-annual retreat in Maine, employees at Thompson Doyle Hennessey & Everest did more than run rapids. Everyone at the Boston real estate company completed the Myers-Briggs Type Indicator and learned how their personalities can help them to relate to each other more effectively. For example, the assessments revealed that salespeople don't mind working in a crazed atmosphere, whereas support staff prefer a calmer environment. Both groups now understand each other better.[88] How is the MBTI being used here? Is this an effective use of this instrument?

money than their external counterparts. Internals are also more satisfied with their jobs, cope better in stressful situations, and are more motivated by performance-based reward systems. Internals are particularly well suited to leadership positions and other jobs requiring initiative, independent action, complex thinking, and high motivation.[89]

Self-monitoring

Self-monitoring A personality trait referring to the extent to which people are sensitive to situational cues and can readily adapt their own behaviour appropriately.

Self-monitoring refers to an individual's level of sensitivity and ability to adapt to situational cues. High self-monitors can adjust their behaviour quite easily and, therefore, show little stability in other underlying personality traits. In contrast, low self-monitors are more likely to reveal their moods and personal characteristics, so it is relatively easy to predict their behaviour from one situation to the next.[90]

The self-monitoring personality trait has been identified as a significant factor in many organizational activities. Employees who are high self-monitors tend to be better conversationalists, better organizational leaders, and better in boundary-spanning positions (in which incumbents work with people in different departments or organizations). They are also more likely than low self-monitors to be promoted within the organization and to receive better jobs elsewhere.[91]

Self-monitoring, locus of control, conscientiousness, and the many other personality traits help to explain the dynamics of organizational behaviour. At the same time, we must be careful about using personality traits to oversimplify a more complex world. Too often, we see problems as "personality clashes" rather than diagnose the situation to discover the underlying causes. These labels can become perceptual blinders that label people even after their personal dispositions have changed. As Nobel prize-winning scholar Herbert Simon warned many years ago, personality is often overused as "a magical slogan to charm away the problems that our intellectual tools don't handle."[92] Personality is only one of the many concepts that we need to understand in organizational behaviour.

CHAPTER SUMMARY

- Perception involves selecting, organizing, and interpreting information to make sense of the world. Selective attention is influenced by characteristics of the target, the target's setting, and the perceiver. Perceptual grouping principles organize incoming information. Our emotions and existing mental models also influence perception.

- According to social identity theory, people perceive themselves by their unique characteristics and membership in various groups. They also develop homogeneous, and usually positive, images of people in their own groups, and usually less positive, homogeneous images of people in other groups. This leads to overgeneralizations and stereotypes.

- Stereotyping is the process of assigning traits to people based on their membership in a social category. Stereotyping economizes mental effort and fills in missing information, but it often results in incorrect perceptions about others. These misperceptions may lead to prejudice, employment discrimination, and harassment.

- The attribution process involves deciding whether the behaviour or event is largely due to the situation (external attributions) or personal characteristics (internal attributions). Two attribution errors are fundamental attribution error and self-serving bias.

- Self-fulfilling prophecy occurs when our expectations about another person cause that person to act in a way that is consistent with those expectations.

- We can improve our perceptions in organizational settings through diversity awareness programs, empathizing with others, postponing our impression of others, comparing our perceptions with others, and becoming more aware of our values, beliefs, and prejudices.

- Personality refers to the relatively stable pattern of behaviours and consistent internal states that explain a person's behavioural tendencies. Both heredity and environmental factors shape personality. Personality traits are important for some job design activities, championing organizational change, and matching people to jobs. However, some concerns remain about relying too heavily on personality traits to understand and predict behaviour in organizations.

- Most personality traits are represented within the "Big Five" personality dimensions: extroversion, agreeableness, conscientiousness, emotional stability, and openness to experience.

- Based on Jung's theory of psychological types, the Myers-Brigg Type Indicator measures how people prefer to focus their attention, collect information, process and evaluate information, and orient themselves to the outer world. Locus of control and self-monitoring are two other traits that influence organizational behaviour.

KEY TERMS

Attribution process, p. 165

"Big Five" personality dimensions, p. 175

Conscientiousness, p. 175

Empathy, p. 170

Extroversion, p. 175

Fundamental attribution error, p. 166

Halo error, p. 169

Introversion, p. 175

Johari Window, p. 172

Locus of control, p. 177

Mental models, p. 158

Myers-Briggs Type Indicator (MBTI), p. 176

Perception, p. 156

Perceptual defence, p. 157

Perceptual grouping, p. 157

Personality, p. 174

Prejudice, p. 163

Primacy effect, p. 168

Projection bias, p. 169

Recency effect, p. 169

Selective attention, p. 156

Self-efficacy, p. 167

Self-fulfilling prophecy, p. 167

Self-monitoring, p. 178

Self-serving bias, p. 166

Sexual harassment, p. 164

Social identity theory, p. 159

Stereotyping, p. 161

DISCUSSION QUESTIONS

1. You are part of a task force to increase worker responsiveness to emergencies on the production floor. Identify four factors that should be considered when installing a device that will get every employee's attention when there is an emergency.

2. Western Technologies, Ltd. has just acquired a major competitor in the circuit board industry. Although senior executives expected a smooth transition, they soon discovered that employees at each company viewed each other with suspicion and had generally negative perceptions of each other's skills and motives. Use social identity theory to explain why this problem likely exists.

3. During a diversity management session, a manager suggests that stereotypes are a necessary part of working with others. "I have to make assumptions about what's in the other person's head, and stereotypes help me do that," she explains. "It's better to rely on stereotypes than to enter a working relationship with someone from another culture without any idea of what they believe in!" Discuss the merits of and problems with the manager's statement.

4. At the end of an NHL hockey game, the coach of the losing team was asked to explain his team's defeat. "I dunno," he begins, "we've done well in this rink over the past few years. Our busy schedule over the past two weeks has pushed the guys too hard, I guess. They're worn out. You probably noticed that we also got some bad breaks on penalties tonight. We should have done well here, but things just went against us." Use attribution theory to explain the coach's perceptions of the team's loss.

5. Self-fulfilling prophecies are common in organizations, but much of the research on this phenomenon originated in schools. Discuss how this perceptual process occurs in a college course. How might instructors use self-fulfilling prophecy beneficially?

6. You are the leader of a newly formed project team that will work closely together over the next three months. The seven team members are drawn from as many worldwide offices. They do not know each other and come from different professional specializations. Describe the activities at a one-day retreat that would minimize perceptual errors and potential communication problems among the team members.

7. NanoTech Enterprises wants to hire employees for its new production plant. Employees will need to have a high degree of autonomy, because the plant uses self-directed work teams. The work also requires employees who are careful, because the materials are sensitive to mishandling. Identify one personality trait from the "Big Five" that may be appropriate for selecting people in these jobs. Describe the trait and fully explain your answer.

8. Look over the four pairs of psychological types in the Myers-Briggs Type Indicator and identify the personality type (i.e., four letters) that would be best for a student taking this course. Would this type be appropriate for students in other fields of study (e.g., biology, fine arts)?

 Case Studies

ACTIVITY 6.1
Perceptions at Gull Products Incorporated
by James Buchowsky, Saskatchewan Institute of Applied Science & Technology

Gull Products Inc. is a small business in Moose Jaw, Saskatchewan, that supplies commercial products to other regional businesses. Recently there has been a movement of national and multinational corporations into that area. One of these corporations, Delnex, has just begun operations in the city and Gull's ownership is very excited about the potential to do business with it.

Gull's sales department has scheduled a meeting to discuss how best to approach this opportunity. Leading the discussion is Phil, the sales supervisor. While never having been a field representative himself, Phil does have strong management credentials and keeps the department running. Also present at the meeting are the four members of Gull's sales team.

Bob is the most experienced salesperson and handles many of the larger, long-time accounts. Bob keeps all of his current clients happy, but Phil is not pleased with his lack of new clients. John is a good,

hard-working employee, but Phil doesn't consider him to be a spectacular seller. Cindy recently transferred into sales from another position with Gull. Due to her inexperience, Cindy's only clients are the ones that Phil selects as being a "good fit" for her, such as a local clothing manufacturer. Most people at Gull don't know about Cindy's previous work experience in Quebec, where she had contacts with many big businesses, including Delnex. The fourth salesperson is Joe. Phil doesn't reveal the informal "salesman of the year award" until year-end but he already expects Joe to win due to his aggressive selling lately. Yet, Phil rarely discusses sales issues with Joe; instead, most of their conversations centre on their mutual passion: golf. Phil always coaxes Joe for the inside scoop about the private country club of which Joe is a member.

The conversation at the sales meeting progresses as follows:

Phil: Delnex has the potential to be our biggest account for a long time. They're a key for our future and we all should play a role in getting business from them. I'm looking for input on how to approach them and who will be the front man. Bob, what are your thoughts?

ACTIVITY 6.1 CONTINUED

Bob: Whoever pursues this one is going to have to devote a lot of time and I just don't have any to commit. Sorry, Phil.

Phil: Oh, all right, but we are going to need to draw on your experience somehow. John, we may need a team effort for Delnex, so expect to do some legwork and provide backup, okay?

John: Sure, I'll be glad to pitch in any way I can.

Joe: Looks like I'll be quarterbacking this one. Phil, what say you and I invite a couple of Delnex guys for a round at my club?

Phil: Now you're talking! I'd love to play that course.

Cindy: I don't think being too forward is a good idea. An informative soft sell worked best when I was...

Phil: I don't think a feminine approach is needed here. Joe, book a tee time while I give the Delnex manager a call. Meeting adjourned.

Discussion Questions

1. What perceptual errors is Phil making?

2. Use the four areas of the Johari Window to analyze Phil's behaviour.

3. How could Phil's perceptions be improved?

ACTIVITY 6.2
Nupath Foods Ltd.

James Ornath read the latest sales figures with a great deal of satisfaction. The vice-president of marketing at Nupath Foods Ltd. was pleased to see that the marketing campaign to improve sagging sales of Prowess cat food was working. Sales volume of the product had increased 20 percent in the past quarter compared with the previous year, and market share was up.

The improved sales of Prowess could be credited to Denise Roberge, the brand manager responsible for cat foods at Nupath. Roberge had joined Nupath less than two years ago as an assistant brand manager after leaving a similar job at a consumer products firm. She was one of the few women in marketing management at Nupath and had a promising career with the company. Ornath was pleased with Roberge's work and tried to let her know this in the annual performance review. He now had an excellent opportunity to reward her by offering the recently vacated position of market research coordinator. Although technically only a lateral transfer with a modest salary increase, the marketing research coordinator job would give Roberge broader experience in some high-profile work, which would enhance her career with Nupath. Few people were aware that Ornath's own career had been boosted by working as marketing research coordinator at Nupath several years before.

Denise Roberge had also seen the latest sales figures on Prowess cat food and was expecting Ornath's call to meet with her that morning. Ornath began the conversation by briefly mentioning the favourable sales figures, and then explained that he wanted Roberge to take the marketing research coordinator job. Roberge was shocked by the news. She enjoyed brand management, particularly the challenge involved with controlling a product that directly affected the company's profitability. Marketing research coordinator was a technical support position—a "backroom" job—far removed from the company's bottom-line activities. Marketing research was not the route to top management in most organizations, Roberge thought. She had been sidelined.

After a long silence, Roberge managed a weak "Thank you, Mr. Ornath." She was too bewildered to protest. She wanted to collect her thoughts and reflect on what she had done wrong. Also, she did not know her boss well enough to be openly critical. Ornath recognized Roberge's surprise, which he naturally assumed was a positive response to hearing of this wonderful career opportunity. He, too, had been delighted several years earlier about his temporary transfer to marketing research to round out his mar-

ACTIVITY 6.2 CONTINUED

keting experience. "This move will be good for both you and Nupath," said Ornath as he escorted Roberge from his office.

Roberge had several tasks to complete that afternoon, but was able to consider the day's events that evening. She was one of the top women in brand management at Nupath and feared that she was being sidelined because the company didn't want women in top management. Her previous employer had made it quite clear that women "couldn't take the heat" in marketing management and tended to place them in technical support positions after a brief term in lower brand management jobs. Obviously Nupath was following the same game plan. Ornath's comments that the coordinator job would be good for her was just a nice way of saying that Roberge couldn't go any further in brand management at Nupath. Roberge was now faced with the difficult decision of confronting Ornath and trying to change Nupath's sexist practices or submitting her resignation.

Discussion Questions

1. What symptom(s) exist in this case to suggest that something has gone wrong?

2. What are the root causes that have led to these symptoms?

3. What actions should the organization take to correct these problems?

ACTIVITY 6.3
THE ROYAL BANK OF CANADA VIGNETTES

Purpose: This exercise is designed to help you understand perceptual issues when working in a diverse workforce.

Instructions: The instructor will play a few vignettes portraying actual events at the Royal Bank of Canada. For each vignette, the class will follow these steps:

Step 1: Watch the vignette, keeping in mind the questions presented below.

Step 2: The instructor will stop the videotape at the appropriate place and the class will discuss the vignette, guided by the following questions (the instructor may ask additional questions):

a) What is your reaction to this incident?

b) What is the main issue in this vignette?

c) What perceptual problems might exist here?

d) What solutions, if any, would you recommend?

Step 3: After discussing the vignette, the instructor will play the video follow-up so that the class can hear what the Royal Bank of Canada recommends in this situation.

Video Source: Courtesy of Royal Bank.

Self-Assessment exercise

ACTIVITY 6.4
PERSONALITY ASSESSMENT OF JUNG'S PSYCHOLOGICAL TYPES

Purpose: This self-assessment is designed to help you estimate your psychological type within Jung's model.

Instructions: Circle the word in each pair that most appeals to you or that seems most characteristic of you. In some cases, both words may appeal to you or seem characteristic of you; in others, neither word may seem characteristic of you or be appealing. Nonetheless, please try to indicate which word in each pair you prefer. Work across the page (i.e., begin with the top row and move across) and answer as quickly as possible. As a rule of thumb, trust your first impression. After completing this exercise, your instructor will explain how to score it.

loud — quiet	realistic — intuitive	convincing — touching	systematic — flexible
active — reflective	blueprint — dream	objective — subjective	methodical — curious
gregarious — private	details — pattern	head — heart	organized — spontaneous
outgoing — reserved	sensible — imaginative	just — humane	deliberate — improvising
sociable — detached	practical — creative	principle — passion	exacting — impulsive
external — internal	present — future	fair — tender	definite — tolerant
do — think	factual — symbolic	clarity — harmony	decisive — open-minded
speak — write	specific — general	reason — emotion	plan — adapt
talk — read	formula — hunch	professional — warm	control — freedom

____ ____   ____ ____   ____ ____   ____ ____

Source: B.L. Dilla, G.J. Curphy, R.L. Hughes, R.C. Ginnett, and K.A. Ashley, *Instructor's Manual to Accompany Leadership: Enhancing the Lessons of Experience* (Homewood, IL: Irwin, 1993).

CHAPTER SEVEN

Workplace Emotions, Values, and Ethics

LEARNING OBJECTIVES

After reading this chapter, you should be able to:

- Discuss the linkages between emotions and behaviour.
- Outline the model of job satisfaction.
- Discuss the effect of job satisfaction on task performance and customer service.
- Describe five strategies to increase organizational commitment.
- Identify the conditions for and problems with emotional labour.
- Outline the dimensions of emotional intelligence.
- Define five main values that vary across cultures.
- Describe three ethical principles and other factors influencing ethical behaviour.
- Discuss why ethical conduct varies across cultures.

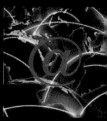

WestJet Airlines is soaring, thanks to enthusiastic employees who keep customers coming back to the Calgary-based discount airline.

Ian Lindsay, *Vancouver Sun*

The pilot reminded passengers to fasten their seat belts as the Boeing 737 from Vancouver began its descent into Calgary. Then he added, "I'd also like to remind you that this aircraft is equipped with special technology that allows us to determine if everyone is wearing his or her seat belt. So, if we find that anyone isn't buckled up, we'll have to return to Vancouver and try again, until we all get it right."

This isn't your typical in-flight announcement. But then WestJet Airlines Ltd. isn't your typical airline. The Calgary-based discount airline doesn't provide meals or reserved seating, but its fun and friendly employees certainly make customers happy. The company carefully selects people who have a customer-friendly attitude and a positive disposition. Then it gives them the freedom to charm customers with their friendly style.

WestJet pilots will tell jokes on the flight and pitch in with clean-up after passengers have departed. When flights are delayed, attendants entertain passengers with silly games. On one flight, for example, attendants announced an award to the first passenger who could find a hole in his or her sock!

"We have a group of employees who are pumped about coming to work, who are pumped working with WestJet, and are pumped working with each other," says a WestJet executive. "This is a pretty fun place to be these days," adds WestJet spokeswoman Siobhan Vinish.[1]

www.westjet.com

In four years, WestJet Airlines has grown from one aircraft and four employees to dozens of aircraft and over 1200 people. The discount airline's success isn't due to just low fares and conservative cost consciousness. WestJet executives claim that previous discount airlines have failed because they forgot the critical ingredients: hiring and keeping enthusiastic, energized, and loyal staff. In other words, WestJet and other organizations must pay attention to the emotions, attitudes, and values of their employees

This chapter explores the dynamics of these three concepts. The first part of this chapter looks at emotions in the workplace, the basic model of work attitudes, and key issues regarding two important work attitudes—job satisfaction and organizational commitment. Our attention then turns to managing emotions in the workplace, including the implications of emotional labour as well as the concept of emotional intelligence. The latter part of this chapter explores individual values at work, including how values differ across cultures. Then, we look at ethical values and behaviour, including specific ethical values, other factors that influence ethical conduct, why ethical behaviour varies across cultures, and specific strategies companies use to improve ethical behaviour at work.

EMOTIONS IN THE WORKPLACE

Emotions permeate organizational life.[2] A team leader is alarmed that critical supplies have not yet arrived. A new employee is proud to tell friends about being hired by ABC Corp. A nurse feels sympathy for a patient whose family has not visited the hospital. In each incident, someone has experienced one or more emotions. There are many different emotions, although scholars have organized them into the six categories shown in Exhibit 7.1.[3] These include anger, fear, joy, love, sadness, and surprise. All except one (surprise) of these general emotional categories include various specific emotional experiences. For example, researchers have found that alarm and anxiety cluster together to form the general emotional category called fear.

EXHIBIT 7.1   Types of Emotions in the Workplace

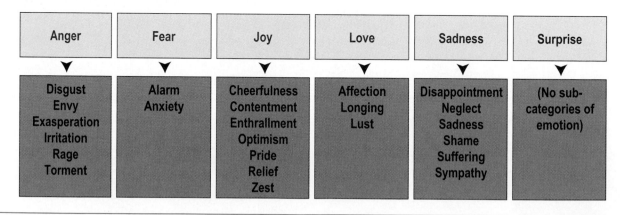

Anger	Fear	Joy	Love	Sadness	Surprise
Disgust Envy Exasperation Irritation Rage Torment	Alarm Anxiety	Cheerfulness Contentment Enthrallment Optimism Pride Relief Zest	Affection Longing Lust	Disappointment Neglect Sadness Shame Suffering Sympathy	(No sub-categories of emotion)

Sources: Based on H.M. Weiss and R. Cropanzano, "Affective Events Theory: A Theoretical Discussion of the Structure, Causes, and Consequences of Affective Experiences at Work," *Research in Organizational Behavior,* 18 (1996), pp. 1–74; P. Shaver, J. Schwartz, D. Kirson, and C. O'Connor, "Emotion Knowledge: Further Exploration of a Prototype Approach," *Journal of Personality and Social Psychology,* 52 (1987), pp. 1061–86.

"Biosensors. The whole company knows instantly when I'm displeased."

Emotions are feelings experienced towards an object, person, or event that create a state of readiness.[4] Emotional episodes are communications to ourselves. They make us aware of events that may affect important personal goals. In fact, strong emotions demand our attention and interrupt our train of thought. They also create a state of readiness to respond to those events. In other words, they generate the motivation to act towards the object of our attention.[5]

Emotions are experienced through our thoughts, behaviours, and physiological reactions. A person may experience fear in a stressful situation by mentally sensing it, showing it through facial expressions, and developing a higher heartbeat. Facial expressions and other behaviour play an interactive role in the emotional experience. For example, you tend to smile when feeling joyful, and this smiling reinforces your feeling of joyfulness. Similarly, your sense of fear is maintained when you notice your heart thumping.

Emotions are directed towards someone or something. We experience joy, fear, and other emotional episodes towards tasks, customers, public speeches we present, a software program we are using, and so on. This contrasts with *moods*, which are emotional states that are not directed towards anything in particular.[6] For example, you may be in a cheerful mood, but you don't know why you have this emotion. Your cheerfulness may be caused by something at work or elsewhere, but you aren't consciously aware of this.

EMOTIONS, ATTITUDES, AND BEHAVIOUR

Emotions are related to **attitudes**, but the two concepts are different. Attitudes represent the cluster of beliefs, assessed feelings, and behavioural intentions towards an object.[7] Emotions are *experiences*, whereas attitudes are *judgments*. We feel emotions, whereas we think about attitudes. We experience most emotions briefly, whereas our attitude towards someone or something is more stable over time.

Imagine hearing that the organization where you work will soon merge with a larger competitor. From this announcement, you might experience surprise, optimism, anger, excitement, or other emotions. These emotions might last a few minutes or hours at a time. Your attitude towards the merger is more complex and stable over time. As illustrated in Exhibit 7.2, attitudes consist of three components:

- *Beliefs*—These are your perceptions about the attitude object. For example, you might believe that mergers result in layoffs. Or you might believe that mergers ensure survival in an era of globalization. These beliefs develop from past experience and learning.[8]

- *Feelings*—These are the positive or negative evaluations of the attitude object. Some people think mergers are good; others think they are bad. Your like or dislike of mergers represents your assessed feelings towards the attitude object. These evaluations are partly determined by your beliefs regarding the attitude object. If you believe that mergers mainly result in layoffs, then you will likely develop negative feelings towards mergers. Your emotions also shape your feelings. You would likely develop positive feelings towards mergers if you experience the emotions of excitement and optimism when thinking about the merger.[9]

Emotions Feelings experienced towards an object, person, or event that create a state of readiness.

Attitudes The cluster of beliefs, assessed feelings, and behavioural intentions towards an object.

- *Behavioural intentions*—These represent your motivation to engage in a particular behaviour with respect to the attitude object. You might plan to quit rather than go through the merger. Alternatively, you might intend to e-mail senior executives that this merger was a good decision. These are examples of the behavioural intentions component of attitudes.

Linking emotions to behaviour

Exhibit 7.2 shows how emotions and attitudes affect behaviour.[10] First, beliefs influence our feelings towards something or someone. For example, you might think that mergers are good (a feeling) because you believe that they make companies more globally competitive and thereby improve your career opportunities (a belief).

Emotions also influence our feelings towards the attitude object. If you experience anxiety and irritation about the merger, you would likely develop negative feelings towards it. In the opening story to this chapter, we learned that WestJet employees are encouraged to tell jokes, play games, and generally have a good time at work. This produces positive emotions for employees and customers alike, which in turn creates positive feelings towards the airline. Connections 7.1 describes how other organizations encourage various "fun" activities to offset less pleasant emotions in the workplace. In each case, the idea is to create emotions that result in favourable judgments about the organization.

Exhibit 7.2 also shows that feelings have a direct influence on behavioural intentions. If you think that mergers are bad, you might intend to quit your job before the merger proceeds. People with the same feelings may form different behavioural intentions based on their unique past experience. For instance, some employees who think that the merger is

EXHIBIT 7.2   Model of Emotions, Attitudes, and Behaviour

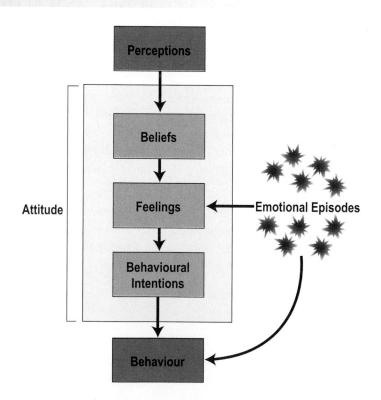

CONNECTIONS 7.1

Employees Just Want to Have Fun!

When Vancouver City Hall employees recently got too cranky, Nelson McLachlan brought in an improvisational comedy team to help them develop more positive emotions. "Cranky-itis is everywhere," explains McLachlan, who works in the city's human resources department. "There's road rage, air rage, it's on the seawall, it's everywhere. We all need to chill out and have some fun."

Fun at work? It sounds like an oxymoron. But in order to attract and keep valuable employees and to help relieve stress, Canadian organizations are encouraging employees to participate in—and even create—a little comedy relief. Employees at the Pacific National Exhibition in Vancouver fire off confetti cannons to celebrate birthdays and pass around a full-sized inflatable Bozo the Clown just to do something, well, different. At Entrust Technologies in Ottawa, CEO John Ryan challenges employees to foosball tournaments. Ryan is the defending champion.

At DY4 Systems Inc. in Ottawa, employees sit on plastic chairs that double as curling rocks for their human curling event. Project team members at Akanda Innovations in Thornhill, Ontario, dissolve their stress with a round of the popular software game, Quake. "Nothing beats a fun and relaxed environment that allows programmers to break from the frustrations of the project," says an Akanda team leader.

Entrust Technologies CEO John Ryan believes that fun should be part of the workplace experience.

Nathan Rudyk, president of DigIT Interactive Inc. (now part of Quebecor), sums up the theory this way: "If you want to make the most money, you must attract the best people. To get the best people you must be the most fun. It's pretty simple."

Sources: C. Kleiman, "'Fun' Activities Keep Staff Happy," *Chicago Tribune,* March 8, 2000; J. Elliott, "All Work and No Play Can Chase Workers Away," *Edmonton Journal,* February 28, 2000; A. Daniels, "Humour Specialists Bring Fun to Workplace," *Vancouver Sun,* January 29, 2000; J. Pappone, "Entrust Success Breeds Creative Paranoia," *Ottawa Citizen,* October 6, 1999; M. Kane, "Laugh Track Plays Well in Workplace," *Saskatoon Star-Phoenix,* June 12, 1999, p. E12; J.J. Mason, "The Development Phase: Riding Chaos," *ComputerWorld Canada,* April 23, 1999, pp. 18, 20.

bad may intend to quit whereas others might want to complain about the decision. People choose the behavioural intention that they think will work best for them (see expectancy theory in Chapter 3).

Behavioural intentions have the strongest influence on behaviour.[11] However, behavioural intentions don't perfectly predict behaviour. A co-worker who intends to leave the organization might stay because she can't find another suitable job. Generally, a person's behaviour depends not only on intentions (motivation), but also on ability, role perceptions, and situational factors (see the MARS model in Chapter 2).

Lastly, emotions sometimes have a direct effect on behaviour. This occurs when people react to their emotions rather than to their judgments (attitudes). When upset, an employee might stomp out of a meeting, bang a fist on the desk, or burst into tears. When overjoyed, an employee might embrace a co-worker or break into a little dance. These are not carefully thought-out behaviours. They are fairly automatic emotional responses that serve as coping mechanisms in that situation.[12]

Cognitive dissonance

The discussion so far implies that emotions and attitudes lead to behaviour. This is true much of the time, but behaviour sometimes influences our attitudes through the process of **cognitive dissonance**.[13] Cognitive dissonance occurs when we perceive an inconsistency between our beliefs, feelings, and behaviour. This inconsistency creates an uncomfortable tension (dissonance) that we are motivated to reduce by changing one or more of these elements. Behaviour is usually the most difficult element to change, particularly when it is known to everyone, was done voluntarily, and can't be undone. Thus, we usually change our beliefs and feelings to reduce the inconsistency.

Consider the following example. Imagine that you think that employment equity practices (hiring people from designated groups in proportion to their representation in the population) are probably a waste of money or an unrealistic demand on organizational hiring and promotions. Now, suppose that you are assigned to a committee to implement employment equity in your organization. As people eventually identify you as a committee member, it becomes difficult to maintain negative attitudes towards employment equity programs. You reduce the cognitive dissonance between your somewhat negative attitudes towards employment equity and your involvement in an employment equity implementation team by developing more favourable attitudes towards employment equity. Overall, your attitude towards employment equity changes to become more consistent with your behaviour.

EMOTIONS AND PERSONALITY

Before leaving this discussion of workplace emotions, we should mention that a person's emotions can result from their personality, not just from their workplace experiences. **Positive affectivity (PA)** is the tendency to experience positive emotional states. It is very similar to **extroversion**, described in Chapter 6 as a characteristic of people who are outgoing, talkative, sociable, and assertive. In contrast, some people are high on **negative affectivity (NA)**, which is the tendency to experience negative emotions.[14] Employees with high NA tend to be more distressed and unhappy because they focus on the negative aspects of life.

To what extent do these personality traits influence emotions. Some research indicates that our feelings about work can be predicted two years later from a person's PA. Studies of twins raised apart conclude that a person's heredity influences emotions and judgments about work. However, other evidence suggests that the effects of PA and NA are relatively weak.[15] Overall, it seems that PA and NA influence emotions and attitudes in the workplace, but their effects are not as strong as situational factors.

Now that we have introduced the conceptual dynamics of emotions and attitudes, let's look more closely at two of the most important work attitudes: job satisfaction and organizational commitment.

Cognitive dissonance A state of anxiety that occurs when an individual's beliefs, attitudes, intentions, and behaviours are inconsistent with one another.

Positive affectivity (PA) The tendency to experience positive emotional states.

Extroversion A "Big Five" personality dimension that characterizes people who are outgoing, talkative, sociable, and assertive.

Negative affectivity (NA) The tendency to experience negative emotional states.

JOB SATISFACTION

Job satisfaction A person's attitude (beliefs, assessed feelings, and behavioural intentions) regarding the job and work context.

One of the most important and widely studied work attitudes is **job satisfaction**. Job satisfaction represents a person's evaluation of his or her job and work context.[16] It is an *appraisal* of the perceived job characteristics and emotional experiences at work. Satisfied employees have a favourable evaluation of their job, based on their observations and emotional experiences.

Job satisfaction is really a collection of attitudes about specific facets of the job.[17] Employees can be satisfied with some elements of the job while simultaneously be dissatisfied with others. For example, you might like your co-workers, but are less satisfied with workload or other aspects of the job. Different types of satisfaction will lead to different intentions and behaviour. An employee might complain to the supervisor when dissatisfied with low pay but not when dissatisfied with co-workers. Overall job satisfaction is a combination of the person's feelings towards the different job satisfaction facets.

JOB SATISFACTION IN CANADA

Surveys indicate that between 82 and 86 percent of Canadians are moderately or very satisfied overall with their jobs.[18] Does this mean that we have high job satisfaction? Well, maybe, but it's probably not as high as these statistics suggest. The problem is that surveys often use a single direct question, such as "How satisfied are you with your job?" Many dissatisfied employees are reluctant to reveal their feelings in a direct question because this is tantamount to admitting that they made a poor job choice and are not enjoying life. "The employees who declare themselves satisfied with their jobs might do so only because they feel they should say they're satisfied," suggests an executive with one of the world's largest survey firms.[19]

How do we know that overall satisfaction ratings are inflated? One indication is that more than half of Canadians say they would leave if another organization offered a similar job with slightly higher pay. Also, less than half of Canadians would recommend the company as the best place to work in the community.[20] A third observation is that Canadians rate their satisfaction on most elements of the job lower than the overall rating. One survey reported that only 58 percent of Canadians are satisfied with pay, only 51 percent are satisfied with job security, and only 36 percent like the company's career advancement opportunities. Few aspects of the job are rated higher than the overall rating.[21]

Measuring job satisfaction across countries is even more challenging because of cultural differences. Exhibit 7.3 shows that Canadian employees have the fifth-highest job satisfaction ratings among the 22 countries surveyed. Mexicans and Brazilians are the most satisfied, whereas employees in Japan and Hong Kong are the least satisfied. Canadians might have high job satisfaction on a global scale, but these results also reflect cultural differences in how people reveal their attitudes. People in Japan and Hong Kong tend to subdue their opinions, whereas people in Brazil and Mexico are often more expressive.[22]

Discrepancy theory A theory that partly explains job satisfaction and dissatisfaction in terms of the gap between what a person expects to receive and what is actually received.

Equity theory A process motivation theory that explains how people develop perceptions of fairness in the distribution and exchange of resources.

A MODEL OF JOB SATISFACTION

What determines the level of job satisfaction? The best explanation is provided by the model in Exhibit 7.4 that combines **discrepancy theory** and **equity theory**.[23] Discrepancy theory states that the level of job satisfaction is determined by the discrepancy between what people expect to receive and what they experience. Job satisfaction or dissatisfaction results from a comparison of the amount the employee expects to receive and the perceived amount received. Job dissatisfaction occurs when the received condition is noticeably less than the expected condition. Job satisfaction improves as the person's expectations are met or exceeded (up to a point).[24]

EXHIBIT 7.3 Job Satisfaction Across Cultures

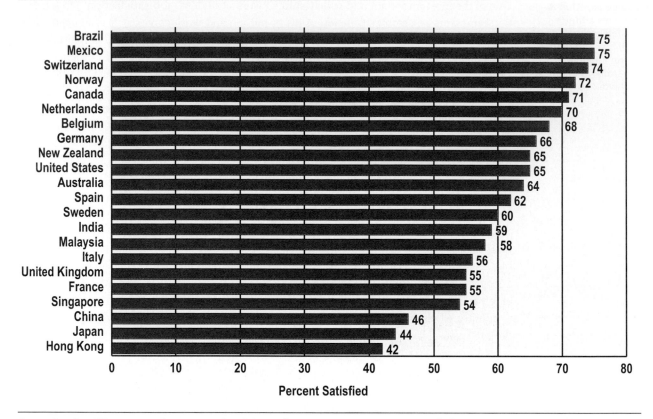

Source: Based on ISR survey results as reported in G. Law, "If You're Happy & You Know It, Tick the Box," *Management-Auckland,* 45 (March 1998), pp. 34–37.

Equity theory is also built into Exhibit 7.4. Equity occurs when the person and comparison other have similar outcome/input ratios (see Chapter 3). This is relevant to job satisfaction, because the amount we expect to receive is partly determined by our comparison with other people. For instance, the level of pay we expect to receive depends not only on how hard we work, but also on how hard other people work in this job compared to their level of pay. Thus, both discrepancy and equity theories predict that as reality meets and exceeds expectations, job satisfaction will increase.

JOB SATISFACTION AND WORK BEHAVIOURS

Nortel Networks, Telus, and Sears Canada are paying a lot more attention to employee satisfaction these days. In each of these firms, executive bonuses are partly determined by the level of job satisfaction indicated in annual employee surveys.[25] These companies pay attention to job satisfaction because this work attitude is related to many work behaviours.[26] Employees with higher levels of job satisfaction, particularly satisfaction with the work itself, are less likely to quit their jobs, be absent from work, and experience mental or physical health problems. Joining a labour union and going on strike often result from dissatisfaction with pay or working conditions. Dissatisfied employees are also more likely to steal, deliberately sabotage company products, and engage in acts of violence against their supervisor or co-workers.[27]

EXHIBIT 7.4   A Model of Job Satisfaction

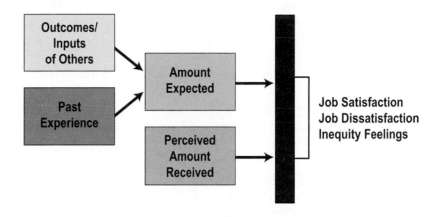

Source: Based on E.E. Lawler III, *Motivation in Work Organizations* (Monterey, CA: Brooks/Cole, 1973), p. 75.

Job satisfaction and task performance

Happy workers are productive workers, right? This is certainly a popular belief, but organizational behaviour research consistently reports an insignificant or modest association between job satisfaction and task performance.[28] Popular opinion may prove more accurate than research on this issue. As one scholar recently admitted: "I still suspect a consistent, significant job satisfaction–task performance relationship is out there to be found."[29]

One reason why organizational behaviour research reports a modest association between job satisfaction and task performance is because general attitudes don't predict specific behaviours very well. People have unique values and experiences, so they react differently to the same level of job satisfaction. One dissatisfied employee may decide to put in less work effort, whereas another maintains the same level of work effort while looking for employment elsewhere. Moreover, task performance depends on a person's ability and resources, not just on work effort. In jobs that operate automated processes, work effort might also have very little effect on task performance in the short run.

A second explanation is that job performance leads to job satisfaction (rather than vice versa), but only when performance is linked to valued rewards. Higher performers receive more rewards and, consequently, are more satisfied than low-performing employees who receive fewer rewards. The connection between job satisfaction and performance is weak because many organizations do not reward good performance.[30]

Third, the weak relationship between job satisfaction and performance may occur because satisfied employees engage in more **organizational citizenship** behaviours but not in higher levels of traditional job performance.[31] Organizational citizenship includes working beyond required job duties, such as assisting others with their tasks and promoting a positive work environment (Chapter 2). Satisfied employees—particularly those who are satisfied with co-workers—are more likely to help the company beyond their normal job duties.[32]

Job satisfaction and customer satisfaction

Job satisfaction has a much clearer effect on customer service. First, job satisfaction affects a person's general mood. Employees who are in a good mood are more likely to communicate

Organizational citizenship Employee behaviours that extend beyond the usual job duties. They include avoiding unnecessary conflicts, helping others without selfish intent, gracefully tolerating occasional impositions, being involved in organizational activities, and performing tasks that extend beyond normal role requirements.

friendliness and positive feelings, which customers appreciate. Second, satisfied employees are less likely to quit their jobs. With lower turnover, customers get the same employees to serve them, so there is more consistent service. Also, longer-service employees have more experience and better skills to serve clients.

Several organizations have discovered that employee morale improves customer service and have taken steps accordingly. CIBC helps employees balance work and lifestyles because "we see links between employee satisfaction and customer satisfaction," says a CIBC executive. Rod Eddington, the new chief of British Airways, puts the message more bluntly: "Management must treat staff the way it wants them to treat the customers; otherwise you're dead."[33] As Connections 7.2 describes, Sears Canada makes shareholders happier by making employees happier.

www.sears.ca

CONNECTIONS 7.2

Happy Employees = Happy Customers = Happy Shareholders

Few retail turnarounds are as impressive as Sears Canada's. Paul Walters, CEO of the Toronto-based department store chain, brought customers back by improving inventories, renovating stores, opening specialty store concepts, and transforming the catalogue operation into a Web-based retail juggernaut.

Another tactic in Sears' arsenal was to improve customer service by boosting staff morale. The idea originated at Sears Roebuck, & Co., Sears Canada's parent company in Chicago. After analyzing several years of data, Sears executives discovered that employee satisfaction affects customer satisfaction, and customer satisfaction affects sales revenue.

According to this "employee-customer-profit" model, a five-point improvement in job satisfaction (using the company's attitude survey) will increase customer satisfaction ratings by 1.3 points, which in turn will improve revenue growth by 0.5 percent. For example, if employee satisfaction in a particular Sears store is five points higher than last year, then

(E. Wynne). Reprinted with permission from The Halifax Herald Ltd.

Sears Canada CEO Paul Walters has applied the idea that customer satisfaction depends on the level of employee satisfaction.

this store will likely have about 0.5 percent higher sales revenue than if employee satisfaction had not changed.

To make employee morale a priority, one-quarter of Sears' annual bonus for managers is based on employee satisfaction ratings. Sears Canada awards bonuses and share options to its employees to further improve customer satisfaction.

Sources: D. Olive, "Walters Has Driven Sears with the Throttle Wide Open," *National Post*, September 21, 1999, p. C4; S. Chandler, "Sears' System of Rewards Has Ups and Downs," *Chicago Tribune*, February 15, 1998, p. C1; A.J. Rucci, S.P. Kirn, and R.T. Quinn, "The Employee-Customer-Profit Chain at Sears," *Harvard Business Review*, 76 (January–February 1998), pp. 83–97.

Now that we understand the dynamics of job satisfaction, how can companies ensure that they have happy workers? The job satisfaction concept is so broad—remember that there are many facets of job satisfaction—that the answer comes from every part of this textbook. Feedback, equity, rewards, leadership, corporate culture, change management, and other topics all implicitly or explicitly refer to job satisfaction as a possible outcome. We must also remember that individual differences, such as personality and personal beliefs, moderate the effects of the work environment on job satisfaction.

ORGANIZATIONAL COMMITMENT

During the mid-1800s, Samuel Cunard founded Cunard Lines, the greatest steamship line ever to cover the Atlantic Ocean. The energetic Nova Scotian was able to make ship transportation dependable and safe, long before it was thought possible, by having the best ships, officers, and crew. He insisted on safety before profits and, by listening to his technical experts, was able to introduce the latest innovations. Above all, Cunard had the quaint notion that if you picked employees well, paid them well, and treated them well, they would return the favour with loyalty and pride.[34]

- **Organizational commitment** A complex attitude pertaining to the strength of an individual's identification with and involvement in a particular organization; includes a strong belief in the organization's goals, as well as a motivation to work for and remain a member of the organization.

Nearly 150 years later, Samuel Cunard's assumptions about **organizational commitment** have found strong support in organizational behaviour research. Organizational commitment refers to the employee's emotional attachment to, identification with, and involvement in a particular organization.[35] Organizational behaviour scholars call this *affective commitment* because it refers to the individual's emotions towards the organization. Affective commitment is called organizational loyalty when the organization is the target of the individual's commitment. However, affective commitment can also refer to loyalty towards co-workers, customers, or a profession.[36] In this book, we will concentrate mainly on the employee's overall commitment to the organization.

Along with affective commitment, employees have varying levels of *continuance commitment*.[37] Continuance commitment occurs when employees believe it is in their own personal interest to remain with the organization. In other words, this form of commitment is a calculative bond with the organization, rather than an emotional attachment. For example, you may have met people who do not particularly identify with the organization for which they work but feel bound to remain there because it would be too costly to quit. Continuance commitment is this motivation to stay because of the high cost of leaving.[38]

IS ORGANIZATIONAL LOYALTY DECLINING?

Is organizational loyalty declining? According to several surveys, it is. One poll reported that 62 percent of Canadians were loyal to their employers a decade ago. This has fallen in the three subsequent surveys to the point where only 49 percent are loyal today. Loyalty seems to be highest among employees over 55 years old and lowest among younger employees.[39]

This does not mean that corporate loyalty is dead, just diminished. Several studies report that Canadian workers score the third-highest levels of loyalty, following only employees in Finland and Spain. People in the United Kingdom, several Asian countries, and Japan tend to have relatively low levels of organizational loyalty.[40] As we learned earlier in the chapter, these results may be distorted by the way people report their opinions in different cultures, but some of the surveys have tried to correct for this problem.

CONSEQUENCES OF ORGANIZATIONAL COMMITMENT

If organizational loyalty is declining, it would be bad news for employers. Research has found that employees with high levels of affective commitment are less likely to quit their jobs and be absent from work. This potentially improves customer service because long-tenure employees have better knowledge of work practices, and clients like to do business with the same employees because transactions are predictable.[41] Employees with high affective commitment also have higher work motivation and organizational citizenship.[42]

The value of organizational commitment is apparent at WestJet, the Calgary-based airline described in the opening story of this chapter. Canadian government officials shut down WestJet soon after it began operations a few years ago because the company's maintenance manuals were different from the ones required by the government. WestJet engineers worked 18-hour days to convert maintenance records, while pilots and flight attendants handled calls from perplexed customers. The unprecedented effort by everyone reduced the shutdown to 17 days and minimized a potentially disastrous situation. "I've never seen anything like it," exclaims WestJet founder Clive Beddoe. "Every single employee came through in an incredible display of company loyalty."[43]

Some firms try to build commitment by tying employees financially to the organization through low-cost loans and share options. These "golden handcuffs" reduce turnover, but they also increase continuance commitment, not affective commitment. Evidence suggests that employees with high levels of continuance commitment have *lower* performance ratings and are *less* likely to engage in organizational citizenship behaviours![44]

This doesn't suggest that organizations should avoid keeping people with rewards. In Canada's high-technology sector, acquiring firms typically offer share options that are "vested" (withheld) for two or more years. This motivates talented employees to stay because many high-tech firms have few assets beyond the people they employ. However, these incentives should not be a substitute for strategies to build and maintain employee loyalty. Employers still need to win employees' hearts (affective commitment) beyond tying them financially to the organization (continuance commitment).

BUILDING ORGANIZATIONAL COMMITMENT

When Eaton's went bankrupt, shoppers scooped up liquidation bargains while recruiters scooped up the retailer's most valuable assets: Eaton's employees. Business Depot, a nationwide office supply chain, purchased newspaper ads that promised Eaton's managers a mecca of opportunity. "We've had prior experience with people in the Eaton's organization," says a Business Depot executive. "The loyalty factor is very high."[45]

Business Depot might be able to build a more loyal workforce by hiring Eaton's employees and others who are known for their loyalty. However, companies mainly build organizational commitment by practising the recommendations in this and other organizational behaviour textbooks. While many workplace experiences influence organizational commitment, the following activities have been most prominent in the literature:[46]

- *Fairness and satisfaction*—The most important ingredients for a loyal workforce are positive and equitable work experiences. New employees must believe that the company is fulfilling its obligations.[47] Organizational commitment seems to suffer when people face increased workloads in companies with record profits and senior executives earning lucrative bonuses. Other companies have built commitment by sharing profits and distributing company shares to employees.

- *Job security*—Layoff threats are one of the greatest blows to employee loyalty, even among those whose jobs are not immediately at risk.[48] Building commitment doesn't require lifetime employment guarantees, although Federal Express Canada, Canada Post, and Cadet Uniforms have maintained such policies. Rather, there should be enough job security to nurture a relationship in which employees feel some permanence and mutuality in the employment relationship.[49]

- *Organizational comprehension*—Affective commitment is a person's identification with the company, so it makes sense that this attitude is strengthened when employees have a solid comprehension of the company. Employees feel disconnected when they don't know what's going on. This calls for improved communication processes (see Chapter 8) as well as opportunities to work in various parts of the organization. It also requires more social interaction, particularly where employees are often separated from each other.

- *Employee involvement*—Employees feel that they are part of the organization when they make decisions that guide the organization's future. Through participation, employees begin to see how the organization is a reflection of their decisions. Employee involvement also builds loyalty because giving this power is a demonstration of the company's trust in its employees.

Trust Positive expectations about another party's intentions and actions towards us in risky situations.

- *Trusting employees*—**Trust** occurs when we have positive expectations about another party's intentions and actions towards us in risky situations.[50] Trust means putting faith in the other person or group. It is also a reciprocal activity. In order to receive trust, you must demonstrate trust. Trust is important for organizational commitment because it touches the heart of the employment relationship (see Chapter 18). Employees identify with and feel obliged to work for an organization only when they trust its leaders.

MANAGING EMOTIONS

The Elbow Room Café is packed and noisy on this Saturday morning. A customer at the Vancouver eatery half shouts across the room for more coffee. A passing waiter scoffs: "You want more coffee, get it yourself!" The customer only laughs. Another diner complains loudly that he and his party are running late and they need their food. This time, restaurant manager Patrick Savoie speaks up: "If you're in a hurry, you should have gone to McDonald's." The diner and his companions chuckle.

To the uninitiated, the Elbow Room Café is an emotional basket case, full of irate guests and the rudest staff west of the Rockies. But it's all a performance—a place where guests can enjoy good food and play out their emotions about dreadful customer service. "It's almost like coming to a theatre," says Savoie, who spends much of his time inventing new ways to insult the clientele.[51]

Emotional labour The effort, planning, and control needed to express organizationally desired emotions during interpersonal transactions.

Whether deliberately being rude at the Elbow Room Café or giving passengers the friendliest service on a WestJet flight, employees are usually expected to manage their emotions in the workplace. **Emotional labour** refers to the effort, planning, and control needed to express organizationally desired emotions during interpersonal transactions.[52] When interacting with co-workers, customers, suppliers, and others, employees are expected to abide by *display rules*. These rules are norms requiring employees to display certain emotions and withhold others.

CONDITIONS REQUIRING EMOTIONAL LABOUR

Jobs require more emotional labour when employees have frequent and long durations of voice or face-to-face contact with clients and other people.[53] For instance, a tour guide must show patience and enthusiasm for several hours, requiring more effort to hide fatigue, anger, and other true emotions. Emotional labour is also more challenging where the job requires employees to display a variety of emotions (e.g., anger as well as joy) and intense emotions (e.g., showing delight rather than a weak smile). For instance, bill collectors have challenges with emotional labour because they must learn to show warmth to anxious first-time debtors and irritation (but not anger) to debtors who seem indifferent to their financial obligations.[54]

Jobs vary in the extent to which employees must abide by display rules. "Cast members" (employees) at Walt Disney World must constantly abide by display rules. Whether their role is a ticket seller or Mickey Mouse, they act out their role to satisfy the customer and fellow employees.[55] The extent to which someone must follow display rules also depends on the power

R. Leipscher, Cambridge Reporter.

Paula Skinner serves up plenty of good cheer at the Tim Hortons restaurant in Cambridge, Ontario. Skinner's positive attitude is so infectious that she brightens up almost anyone who stops by for a coffee and doughnut. "Customers are coming up to me all the time to comment on her," says Theresa Wakely, a co-owner of the Tim Hortons outlet. "She makes people happy." Skinner was recently awarded the Cambridge Tourism Front-line Staff of the Year Award because she displays emotions that make customers feel better.[56] How can Tim Hortons and other organizations select people with appropriate emotions for the job?

and personal relationship of the person receiving the service. You would closely follow display rules when meeting the owner of a client's organization, whereas more latitude might be possible when serving a friend.

There are also cross-cultural differences in emotional display norms and values. One survey reported that 83 percent of Japanese believe that it is inappropriate to become emotional in a business context, compared with 40 percent of Americans, 34 percent of French, and 29 percent of Italians. In other words, Italians are more likely to accept or tolerate people who display their true emotions at work, whereas this would be considered rude or embarrassing in Japan.[57]

Customer expectations must also be taken into account. In Canada and some other cultures, customers expect fairly consistent emotional displays in the service provided. In other cultures, customers give employees more latitude in their emotional displays. In fact, people who feign emotions may offend them. For instance, when McDonald's opened operations in Moscow, employees were taught to smile at customers. However, the company soon discovered that Russians do not expect this emotional display, and some customers thought that the employees were mocking them.[58]

EMOTIONAL DISSONANCE

Comedian George Burns once said: "The secret to being a good actor is honesty. If you can fake *that*, you've got it made." Burns' humour highlights the fact that some people are better

Emotional adaptability A person's ability to adjust emotions naturally to the situational context.

than others at **emotional adaptability**. Those with high emotional adaptability adjust their emotions naturally to the situational context. Most of us can do this to some extent. However, it is sometimes difficult to hide our true emotions. Instead, they "leak" out as voice intonations, posture, and in other subtle ways.[59] The problem is particularly true of anger, which is one of the most difficult emotions to control.

Emotional dissonance Conflict between required and true emotions.

Conflict between required and true emotions is called **emotional dissonance**, and it is a significant cause of stress and job burnout (see Chapter 5).[60] Emotional dissonance is most common where employees must display emotions that are quite different from their true feelings and where emotional display rules are highly regulated. This may explain why Safeway employees complained about its smile-and-make-eye-contact rule. The grocery store chain requires employees to constantly smile and say pleasantries ("Have a nice day!") to customers. "I believe in courteous service," says a former Safeway butcher, "but Safeway has taken it to such an extreme that it's torture for most of the employees."[61]

SUPPORTING EMOTIONAL LABOUR

Many organizations support emotional labour by teaching employees the subtle behaviours to express appropriate emotions. For instance, some Japanese companies are sending their employees to "smile school," where they learn the fine art of displaying pleasant facial expressions.[62] Other firms put employees through videotaped exercises where they receive feedback on their emotional labour.

Although training may help, some corporate leaders believe that employees must bring the right attitude with them to the job. "We hire people for attitude, not for experience," said Nejat Sarp, the Turkish-born Australian who opened the Pan Pacific Hotel in Yokohama, Japan. "You can teach somebody what to do but if the attitude is not there, it doesn't work. So we hire for attitude and the result is the young, energetic team."[63] Famous Players also hires for attitude. The Canadian theatre chain holds casting calls where "outgoing and bubbly" job applicants are identified as they sing and dance in front of the other candidates.[64]

EMOTIONAL INTELLIGENCE

Emotional intelligence (EQ) The ability to monitor your own and others' emotions, to discriminate among them, and to use the information to guide your thinking and actions.

Both Famous Players and the Pan Pacific Hotel want to hire people whose emotional tendencies match the job. They also want to find people with high levels of emotional intelligence. **Emotional intelligence (EQ)** is the ability to monitor your own and others' emotions, to discriminate among them, and to use the information to guide your thinking and actions.[65] EQ has its roots in the concept of social intelligence, which was introduced over 75 years ago, but scholars spent most of this time focused on cognitive intelligence (IQ). Now, many are realizing that EQ is just as important for an individual's success at work and in other social environments. Emotional intelligence includes the five dimensions illustrated in Exhibit 7.5 and described below:[66]

Self-monitoring A personality trait referring to the extent that people are sensitive to situational cues and can readily adapt their own behaviour appropriately.

- *Self-awareness*—People with high self-awareness recognize and understand their moods, emotions, and needs. They perceive and anticipate how their actions affect others. Self-aware people are also comfortable talking about and admitting their limitations, so they know when to ask for help. Notice that this (as well as some other EQ domains described here) is similar to the **self-monitoring** personality concept that was described in Chapter 6.

- *Self-regulation*—This is the ability to control or redirect emotional outbursts and other impulse behaviours. For example, rather than yelling at a client, you manage to remain calm and later "talk out" the emotion to a co-worker. Self-regulation includes the ability to suspend judgment—to think through the consequences of behaviour rather than acting on impulse.

EXHIBIT 7.5   Dimensions of Emotional Intelligence

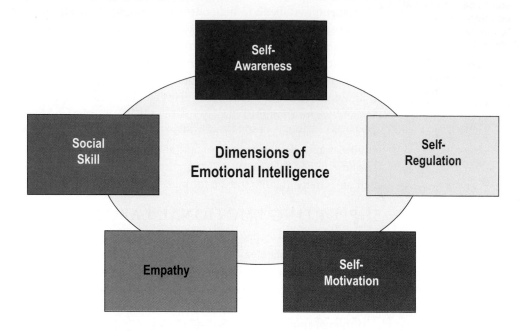

- *Self-motivation*—This includes stifling impulses, directing our emotions towards personal goals, and delaying gratification. Even when people do not achieve their goals, people with high motivation remain optimistic. Motivating yourself overlaps with the self-leadership concepts of self-reinforcement and constructive thought patterns (Chapter 4).

- *Empathy*—**Empathy** was defined in Chapter 6 as the ability to understand and be sensitive to the feelings, thoughts, and situations of others. This doesn't involve adopting other people's emotions; it means being sensitized to them.

- *Social skill*—This is the ability to manage the emotions of other people. It requires social competence and skills to guide the way other people act. Social skill includes the ability to build networks of relationships and to build rapport—finding common interests and understanding with others. Social skill requires other elements of emotional intelligence, particularly empathy and self-regulation.

Do Canadians have high emotional intelligence? Preliminary evidence indicates that we are on the low side—an average score of 95, where the global average is 100. Americans score slightly higher at 105. EQ tests are fairly new and their accuracy isn't known. However, that hasn't stopped Calgary-based Western Union Insurance from using the test to identify the social skills required for different jobs. American Express, the U.S. Air Force, and a few other organizations are also using these tests to select applicants with high EQ scores.[67]

Emotional intelligence can be learned to some extent, so Hongkong Telecom, the Hong Kong government, and other organizations offer training to help employees improve their emotional intelligence. "Many of us don't know that our emotions can be controlled and therefore just become victims of emotions," says the Hong Kong government's chief training officer.[68] However, people don't develop emotional intelligence just by learning about its dimensions. It requires personal coaching, plenty of practice, and frequent feedback. Emotional intelligence also increases with age; it is part of the process called maturity. Whether people are selected with high emo-

Empathy A person's ability to understand and be sensitive to the feelings, thoughts, and situations of others.

tional intelligence or they develop it through coaching, we still need to learn whether people with high emotional intelligence are better at coping with the emotional dissonance created by emotional labour requirements. Meanwhile, there is still much to learn about emotional intelligence, such as how robust these five dimensions are and how they relate to self-monitoring personality.

VALUES AT WORK

Values Stable, long-lasting beliefs about what is important to the individual.

Values represent stable, long-lasting beliefs about what is important. They are evaluative standards that help us define what is right or wrong, or good or bad, in the world.[69] Some people value practicality, whereas others value the aesthetic. Some people value frugality, whereas others value generosity. Values differ from attitudes. Values are general beliefs about life, whereas attitudes are directed towards specific objects, events, or people. Of course, values influence our attitudes towards those attitude objects.

There are two types of values: terminal and instrumental. *Terminal values* are desired states of existence that we consider to be worth striving for. A world of beauty, equality, wisdom, and a comfortable life are some of the terminal values that people might hold. *Instrumental values,* on the other hand, are desirable modes of behaviour that help us reach the objectives of terminal values. Some instrumental values include being polite, courageous, logical, self-controlled, and ambitious.[70] Organizational behaviour researchers tend to focus on instrumental values, possibly because they shape the person's behaviour and are more closely aligned with organizational values.

Values are gaining prominence in organizational behaviour.[71] Personal values influence our perceptions, decisions, and actions. They provide justification for our actions. Scholars have described over 100 personal values.[72] Organizational culture values, which we discuss in Chapter 17, shape the behaviours of employees aligned with those values. Cross-cultural values, which we discuss next, partially explain why people behave differently in other countries. Ethical values, which are discussed in the last section of this chapter, lay the foundation for the appropriateness of our actions.

CULTURAL DIFFERENCES IN VALUES

Not long ago, several Swedish and American employees at Swedish telecommunications giant Ericsson Telephone met to resolve a pressing issue. At the end of the discussion, the highest-ranking person in the room—an American—stated his position on the problem. The Americans understood that the senior executive was concluding debate by making the final decision. The Swedes, on the other hand, left the meeting feeling uneasy that no decision had been made. Scandinavians assume that decisions are made as a group, so they thought that the American executive's statements were merely his own opinions on the matter.[73]

Anyone who has worked long enough with people in other countries will know that values differ across cultures. As this true story illustrates, people in some cultures value group decisions, whereas others think that leaders should take charge. Meetings in Germany usually start on time, whereas people in Brazil usually don't worry if meetings start half an hour late. We need to understand cultural value differences to avoid unnecessary conflicts and subtle tensions between people from different countries. This is particularly important as companies develop global operations and information technology increases the frequency of cross-cultural communication.

Five cross-cultural values

Five values account for a large portion of the differences in orientations across cultures. They include individualism–collectivism, power distance, uncertainty avoidance, achievement–nurturing orientation, and long-term–short-term orientation.[74]

Individualism–collectivism The degree to which people value their individual versus group goals. Collectivists respect and value their membership in the group to which they belong, whereas individualists tend to give low priority to group interests.

Power distance The extent to which people accept unequal distribution of power in a society.

Uncertainty avoidance The degree to which people tolerate ambiguity (low uncertainty avoidance) or feel threatened by ambiguity and uncertainty (high uncertainty avoidance).

- *Individualism versus collectivism*—**Individualism–collectivism** refers to the degree to which people value their individual versus group goals. Collectivists define themselves by their group membership, give group goals priority over their personal goals, put more emphasis on harmonious relationships, and experience more socially based emotions (indebtedness, friendliness). Individualists, on the other hand, view themselves autonomously, give personal goals priority over group goals, put more emphasis on personal achievement, and experience more socially disengaged emotions (pride, anger).[75]

- *Power distance*—**Power distance** is the extent to which people accept unequal distribution of power in a society. Those with high power distance accept and value unequal power, whereas those with low power distance expect relatively equal power sharing. In high-power-distance cultures, employees expect to receive directives from their superiors, and conflicts are resolved through formal rules and authority. In contrast, participative management is preferred in low-power-distance cultures, and conflicts are resolved more through personal networks and coalitions.[76]

- *Uncertainty avoidance*—**Uncertainty avoidance** is the degree to which people tolerate ambiguity (low uncertainty avoidance) or feel threatened by ambiguity and uncertainty (high uncertainty avoidance). Employees with high uncertainty avoidance value structured situations where rules of conduct and decision making are clearly documented. They usually prefer direct rather than indirect or ambiguous communications.

- *Achievement versus nurturing orientation*—Achievement-oriented cultures value assertiveness, competitiveness, and materialism. As you might expect, this cultural value is strongly related to McClelland's need for achievement (see Chapter 3).[77] Recall that people with a high need for achievement desire reasonable challenges, personal responsibility, feedback, and recognition. These features would also generally describe people in achievement-oriented cultures. In contrast, people in nurturing-oriented cultures emphasize relationships and the well-being of others. They focus on human interaction and caring rather than on competition and personal success.

- *Long-term versus short-term orientation*—People in various cultures also differ in their long-term or short-term orientation. Those with a long-term orientation anchor their thoughts more in the future than in the past and present. They value thrift, savings, and persistence, whereas those with a short-term orientation place more emphasis on the past and present, such as respect for tradition and fulfilling social obligations.

Exhibit 7.6 shows how Canadians compare to other cultures on these five dimensions. In general, Canadians are individualistic with a somewhat short-term orientation and relatively low power distance. They have somewhat low uncertainty avoidance (i.e., they can tolerate ambiguity) and are neither strongly achievement-oriented nor nurturing-oriented. We should treat this information with some caution, however. The data for the first four scales were collected only from IBM employees in each country; data for the long-term–short-term orientation scale were collected from college students. Ideally, the information should come from a representative sample of people in the country.

A second concern is that the IBM data are now almost a generation old and some cultures have changed in that time. For instance, there is some evidence that Japan's culture, particularly its younger generation, has become more individualistic in recent years.[78] Another concern is that these data assume that everyone in a society has similar cultural values. This may be true in a few countries, but not in diverse societies such as Canada. Still, this information provides the best comparison available of these values across cultures.[79]

EXHIBIT 7.6 Cultural Differences in Values

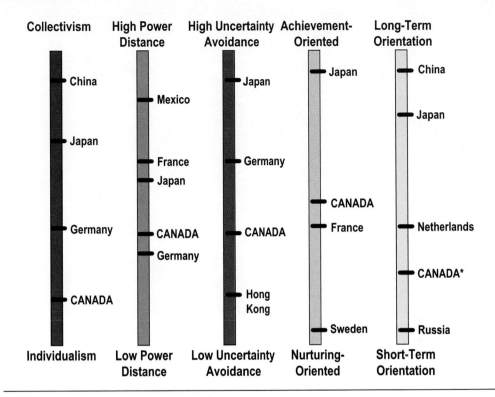

* Inferred from data on U.S., France, and Germany.

Note: Ratings on the first four scales are from IBM employees in these countries. Germany refers only to the former West Germany. Data for long-term–short-term orientation are from student samples.

Sources: Based on G. Hofstede, "Cultural Constraints in Management Theories," *Academy of Management Executive*, 7 (1993), pp. 81–94; G. Hofstede, "The Cultural Relativity of Organizational Practices and Theories," *Journal of International Business Studies*, 14 (Fall 1983), pp. 75–89.

ETHICAL VALUES AND BEHAVIOUR

Talisman Energy Inc. recently faced a tough dilemma. The U.S. government imposed sanctions against the Sudanese government because of evidence that profits from Sudan's state oil company are funding the brutal civil war in that country. But Calgary-based Talisman has extensive oil investments in Sudan, and abandoning those investments would be financial disaster. Under pressure from the Canadian government, Talisman's executives quickly signed a code of ethical conduct that the Canadian oil industry had developed a few years earlier. The code outlines standards of ethical conduct regarding community involvement, environmental protection, business conduct, and employee health and safety.[80]

Ethics refers to the study of moral principles or values that determine whether actions are right or wrong and outcomes are good or bad. We rely on our ethical values to determine "the right thing to do." Canadians value companies and leaders with ethical values. That's why Talisman Energy needed to demonstrate its ethical standards by signing the oil industry's code of conduct. A recent survey also reported that the employer's integrity is as important to most employees as their income. "Consumers are demanding ethical behaviour, and

Ethics The study of moral principles or values that determine whether actions are right or wrong and whether outcomes are good or bad.

L. Ball, *Ottawa Citizen.*

When Alan Kearns (left) and Doug Martin (centre) started TalentLab, they wanted to create an ethical organization that would give something back to the community. So, the founders of the Ottawa-based high-tech recruiting firm created "Give Back Day." On one workday each month, TalentLab's founders and staff contribute their services at a local organization of their choice. For example, Kearns works in the kitchen at the Ottawa Mission for Men. Other TalentLab staff members distribute books and read to sick kids at the Children's Hospital of Eastern Ontario. "[Give Back Day is] not about the branding of the company or image-boosting" says Kearns. "It's about doing, helping."[81] To what extent is an organization's ethical conduct and social responsibility a factor in your decision to work there?

www.talentlab.com

choosing to do business with those companies they perceive as ethical," says the president of Calgary-based Hughes Aircraft of Canada.[82] In this final section of the chapter, we explore the main concepts relating to ethical values and behaviour in the workplace.

THREE ETHICAL PRINCIPLES

Philosophers and other scholars have identified several general ethical principles, each of which has a few variations, that should guide our ethical conduct. We can condense most of these principles and variations into three basic values: utilitarianism, individual rights, and distributive justice.[83] You might prefer one over the others based on your personal values. However, all three principles should be applied to put important ethical issues to the test.

Utilitarianism A moral principle stating that decision makers should seek the greatest good for the greatest number of people when choosing among alternatives.

- *Utilitarianism*—**Utilitarianism** advises us to seek the greatest good for the greatest number of people. In other words, we should choose the option that provides the highest degree of satisfaction to those affected. This is sometimes known as a consequential principle because it focuses on the consequences of our actions, not on how we achieve those consequences. Unfortunately, utilitarianism can occasionally result in unethical choices because it judges morality by the results, not by the means used to attain those results. Moreover, it accepts situations in which a few people may be severely oppressed to benefit others.

- *Individual rights*—This ethical value is the belief that everyone has entitlements that let them act in a certain way. Some of the most widely cited rights are freedom of movement, physical security, freedom of speech, fair trial, and freedom from torture.[84] The individual rights principle is not restricted to legal rights. A person may have a right to privacy, but employers have a right to inspect everyone's e-mail messages. One problem with individual rights is that certain individual rights may conflict with others. The shareholders' right to be informed about corporate activities may ultimately conflict with an executive's right to privacy, for example.

- *Distributive justice*—This is the ethical value of fairness that was discussed in Chapter 3. It suggests that inequality is acceptable if (1) everyone has equal access to the more favoured positions in society, and (2) the inequalities are ultimately in the best interest of the least well off in society. The first part means that everyone should have equal access to higher-paying jobs and other valued positions in life. The second part says that some people can receive greater rewards than others if this benefits those who are less well off. Employees in risky jobs should be paid more if this benefits others who are less well off. The problem with this principle is that society can't seem to agree on what activities provide the greatest benefit to the least well off.

MORAL INTENSITY, ETHICAL SENSITIVITY, AND SITUATIONAL INFLUENCES

Ethical values play an important role in ethical behaviour, but we also need to consider other factors. Three central concepts in ethical behaviour are the moral intensity of the issue, the individual's ethical sensitivity, and situational factors.

Moral intensity is the degree to which an issue demands the application of ethical principles. The higher the moral intensity, the more that ethical principles should provide guidance to resolve the issue. Stealing from your employer is usually considered to be high on moral intensity, whereas taking a client to lunch is much lower on the scale. Several factors influence the moral intensity of an issue, such as the extent to which the issue clearly produces good or bad consequences, others in the society think it is good or evil, the issue quickly affects people, the decision maker feels close to the issue, and the person is able to influence the issue.[85]

Even if an issue has high moral intensity, some employees might not recognize its ethical importance because they have low ethical sensitivity. **Ethical sensitivity** is a personal characteristic that enables people to recognize the presence and determine the relative importance of an ethical issue.[86] Ethically sensitive people are not necessarily more ethical. Rather, they are more likely to recognize whether an issue requires ethical consideration, and can more accurately estimate the moral intensity of the issue. Ethically sensitive people tend to have higher empathy. They also have more information about the specific situation. For example, accountants would be more ethically sensitive regarding accounting procedures than would people who have not received training in this profession.

The situation is a third important reason why good people do bad things. For example, employees are more likely to make unethical choices when they face competitive pressure. According to one survey, 56 percent of American workers feel more pressure from employers and their personal situations to be unethical than they did five years ago. Another study reported that over 50 percent of sales managers claimed that their salespeople had lied to make a sale and over one-third claimed they had made unrealistic promises.[87] The point here is not to justify unethical conduct. Rather, we need to recognize the situational factors that influence wrongdoing so that organizations can correct these problems in the future.

Moral intensity The degree to which an issue demands the application of ethical principles.

Ethical sensitivity A personal characteristic that enables people to recognize the presence and determine the relative importance of an ethical issue.

CULTURAL DIFFERENCES IN BUSINESS ETHICS

When Harry Gould, Jr., visited Gould Paper's manufacturing plants in France, he asked his French counterpart to show him the books (financial statements). The French executive casually asked, "Which books do you want to see?" The executive kept three sets of records—one for his family, one for the revenue collector, and the real one. "[The French executive] didn't think anything about that," Gould recalls. "There's a cultural mindset that has no bearing on the reality we are used to here in the United States."[88]

As Harry Gould discovered, corporate decision makers face a larger set of ethical dilemmas when they enter the global marketplace. The French executive saw little wrong with having three sets of financial records, whereas most people in North America would consider this practice of falsifying information to be highly unethical. This isn't an isolated example. Kickbacks are illegal in Canada and the United States, whereas they still qualify as a tax deduction in a few European countries.[89] One research study found that Australian business students are more willing than American students to pad their résumé, sneak vacations on company time, and have lavish company-paid entertainment. Another study reported that Singaporeans seem to be less concerned than Americans about software piracy.[90]

These differences do not indicate that people in some cultures have fewer ethical values. Research suggests that people in most countries generally have similar beliefs about the ethics of stealing, physical abuse, misrepresentation, and so forth.[91] The main reason why ethical conduct varies across cultures is because people interpret the situation differently.[92] False financial reporting may be more common in France than in Canada because people believe it is widely practised and has little adverse effect on anyone. Canadians, on the other hand, are more likely to view false financial reporting as unethical because they believe it has adverse consequences.[93] Thus, financial reporting likely has higher moral intensity in Canada than in some other cultures.

SUPPORTING ETHICAL BEHAVIOUR

Most large and medium-sized organizations in Canada apply one or more strategies to improve ethical conduct. According to one survey, 85 percent of Canadian firms have a written ethical code of conduct. The code of ethics at McNeil Consumer Healthcare in Guelph, Ontario, is 50 pages long. Each year, the document is circulated and managers must sign it. Job applicants at UPS Canada receive a copy of the UPS Business Code of Conduct before they decide to join. "We want our employees to know from day one that we are expecting them to preserve our legacy of honesty, integrity, and ethical behaviour," says a UPS Canada executive.[94]

Ethical codes establish the organization's ethical standards, but critics say that this has little effect on ethical conduct. Companies must move beyond written codes to strategies that help employees alter their behaviour at work.[95] Nortel Networks holds a two-hour business ethics awareness presentation. It also has a 1-800 number for employees to report suspected ethics abuses or to seek advice on ethics issues. Along with these practices, a few Canadian organizations have ethics advisers or committees to provide guidance on specific ethical issues. Some companies also audit their ethics initiatives to ensure that they are working. However, Canadian companies generally have implemented relatively few ethics strategies.[96]

Ethical values, cultural values, and workplace emotions have a powerful effect on individual behaviour in the workplace. Throughout this chapter, it is apparent that the perceptual process (see Chapter 6) shapes values and emotions. Another vital factor in these processes is individual and organizational communication, which we discuss in the next chapter.

CHAPTER SUMMARY

- Emotions are feelings experienced towards an object, person, or event that create a state of readiness. They differ from attitudes, which represent the cluster of beliefs, feelings, and behavioural intentions towards an object. Beliefs are a person's perceptions about an attitude object. Feelings are judgments about our emotional experiences associated with the target. Behavioural intentions represent a motivation to engage in a particular behaviour with respect to the target. Emotions usually affect behaviour through beliefs, feelings, and behavioural intentions, respectively.

- Job satisfaction represents a person's evaluation of his or her job and work context. Satisfaction depends on the level of discrepancy between what people expect to receive and what they experience. Job satisfaction also increases with the perceived equity in the exchange relationship.

- Job satisfaction has a weak association with task performance because general attitudes do not predict specific behaviours very well, researchers measure specific performance rather than organizational citizenship, and performance isn't always linked to valued rewards. Job satisfaction has a stronger association with customer satisfaction because it affects moods and reduces employee turnover.

- Organizational commitment is a set of attitudes regarding the individual's relationship with the organization and his or her motivation to remain with the organization. Affective and continuance commitment have different effects on employee behaviour. Companies build loyalty through fairness and satisfaction, some level of job security, organizational comprehension, employee involvement, and trust.

- Emotional labour refers to the effort, planning, and control needed to express organizationally desired emotions during interpersonal transactions. This is more common in jobs with frequent and lengthy customer interaction, where the job requires a variety of emotions displayed, and where employees must abide by the display rules. Emotional labour creates problems because true emotions tend to leak out, and conflict between expected and true emotions (emotional dissonance) causes stress and burnout.

- Emotional intelligence is the ability to monitor your own and others' emotions, to discriminate among them, and to use the information to guide your thinking and actions. This includes self-awareness, self-regulation, self-motivation, empathy, and social skill.

- Values represent stable, long-lasting beliefs about what is important to us. They influence our decisions and interpretation of what is ethical. Five values that differ across cultures are individualism–collectivism, power distance, uncertainty avoidance, achievement–nurturing orientation, and long-term–short-term orientation.

- Three values that guide ethical conduct are utilitarianism, individual rights, and distributive justice. Three other factors that influence ethical conduct are the extent to which an issue demands ethical principles (moral intensity), the person's sensitivity to the presence and importance of an ethical dilemma, and situational factors that cause people to deviate from their moral values.

- People from different cultures tend to act differently when faced with an ethical issue. Although ethical values differ somewhat across cultures, most of this variation is explained by the fact that unique cultural experiences cause people to see different levels of moral intensity.

KEY TERMS

DISCUSSION QUESTIONS

1. After a few months on the job, Susan has experienced several emotional episodes ranging from frustration to joy towards the work she is assigned. Use the attitude model to explain how these emotions affect Susan's level of job satisfaction with the work itself.

2. The latest employee attitude survey in your organization indicates that employees are unhappy with some aspects of the organization. However, management tends to pay attention to the single-item question asking employees to indicate their overall satisfaction with the job. The results of this item indicate that 86 percent of staff members are very or somewhat satisfied, so management concludes that the other results refer to issues that are probably not important to employees. Explain why management's interpretation of these results may be inaccurate.

3. Universal Broadcasting Corp. is concerned about losing some of its best technical staff to competitors. Senior executives have decided that the best way to build a loyal workforce is to introduce a deferred profit-sharing plan. Employees would receive half of each year's profit share at the end of the year, but the other half would be paid out over the following two years as trailers. Anyone who leaves, other than due to retirement or layoffs, would forfeit some or all of the deferred payments. Explain what effect this plan may have on organizational commitment and employee behaviours.

4. A recent study reported that college instructors are frequently required to engage in emotional labour. Identify the situations in which emotional labour is required for this job. In your opinion, is emotional labour more troublesome for college instructors or for telephone operators working at a 911 emergency service?

5. If a co-worker told you that he or she had a high level of emotional intelligence, what would you look for to confirm that statement?

6. Your company is beginning to expand operations in Japan and wants you to form working relationships with Japanese suppliers. Considering only the values of individualism and uncertainty avoidance, what should you be aware of or sensitive to in your dealings with these suppliers? You may assume that your contacts hold typical Japanese values along these dimensions.

7. Microsoft recently set up a program whereby computer science professors would receive $200 for mentioning Microsoft's products at public presentations. The money is used to offset travel costs to attend these sessions. Discuss the ethical implications of this incentive.

8. Compare moral intensity and ethical sensitivity.

Case Study

ACTIVITY 7.1

Aline DeNeuve

by Alvin Turner, Brock University

Aline DeNeuve has just been promoted to director of training and development at Consolidated Inc. from her previous position as manager of special projects. This assignment took her from the Calgary regional office to the regional office in Montreal. DeNeuve had only been on the job for a few weeks when she was invited to a corporate retreat designed to cultivate harmonious working relationships with co-workers and to help the vice-president prepare a report on approaches to improving employees' attitudes.

Prior to assuming her new position, DeNeuve had designed and delivered a training program on employee diversity with a fairly high degree of success in the Calgary and Edmonton offices. There was little resistance and, based on the feedback received, employees felt satisfied with the outcome. The Calgary office was staffed by older workers and baby boomers. The demographics of employees in the central Canada offices were considerably different. In fact, it was once said that Consolidated's employees in central Canada looked like the United Nations. They also ranged from Generation Y (under 25) to people born before the Second World War.

DeNeuve has a no-nonsense managerial style. She does not believe that managers should socialize with employees because friendly relations with subordinates undermines managers' objectivity and compromises subordinates' respect for their bosses. She also does not believe in cultivating friendly relations with colleagues because she thinks that close friendships usually lead to undesirable, compromising outcomes. Before DeNeuve finalized the plans for the retreat, she decided to talk with a variety of employees chosen at random about their experiences at the first retreat and their views about attending another retreat. She spoke individually with Heather, Jack, June, Alison, and Richard, and encouraged each person to speak candidly and in confidence without any fear of retribution.

Heather, an administrative assistant, would prefer not to attend because she does not like retreats. She still resents Jack, her supervisor, for not promoting her six months ago. She believes she was overlooked because she is Chinese and Jack does not like foreigners. (Consequently, she has been taking an unusually large number of sick days.) She feels that interpersonal relations could be improved because most staff members do not socialize with one another and seem to tolerate each other only to complete job requirements. However, she believes that a three-day retreat held once a year will not solve the antisocial atmosphere that exists. She wonders whether it will be possible to change the situation considering the diverse background of employees and their different belief systems.

Jack, a certified management accountant, is manager of marketing. He does not want to attend the retreat. He is upset that he was not promoted to director (the position DeNeuve now occupies). He feels he was passed over because he is black. Jack

ACTIVITY 7.1 CONTINUED

suggests the organization use the money it plans to spend on the retreat to strengthen security because he is concerned that staff members have been taking home a lot of office supplies. He also believes that the organization should do a better job designing an orientation and socialization program for new employees to ensure a smoother transition into the existing workforce. He also feels that such a program would help promote and stimulate greater workplace harmony.

June, manager of customer services, is not keen on attending because she believes that the last retreat was a waste of time. She confides to Aline, off the record, that she does not enjoy her job any more because it has become too stressful. Senior management has been promising to hire more customer service representatives for more than two years, but has not yet hired anyone. June further indicates that she has grown tired of answering one customer question after another, and that many customers are overbearing, arrogant, and highly demanding and their inquiries are downright stupid. She feels that if half the customers who call simply use their common sense, they could easily solve their own silly problems. She says that the new computer system and headsets have increased substantially the number of calls and customer problems she has to resolve each day. June also confides that the increased workload and high traffic flow (volume of calls and complaints) have contributed to ruining her marriage. When she gets home in the evenings, she is very tired and feels very depressed. She also says that the job is ruining her nights and weekends, and that she is often terrified of going to work some days. "The last thing I want to do at this stage is to go on a retreat to listen to a bunch of boring, two-faced, pompous big shots who think that they're better than everyone

else," she complains. "I would prefer to spend my time visiting friends and family in Eastern Europe. At least over there I know who my friends and enemies are."

Alison, supervisor of employee benefits and services, also expresses reservation about attending the retreat. She believes that some employees view retreats as equal-opportunity sojourns to hit on one another. She feels that until the organization develops a policy regarding interoffice dating, it should not promote ventures of this type. Alison holds strong religious views and believes that certain behaviours should not take place in the workplace. She feels that management's silence on this matter condones the behaviour she considers inappropriate.

Richard, the last person selected for the retreat, says he would be pleased to attend because he has always felt that these events are very good for morale and interpersonal relationships and are good opportunities to socialize with senior management.

DeNeuve is astonished by the attitudes of the staff members with whom she spoke. On further reflection, she wonders how morale could have gotten so bad and why management has not moved more aggressively to improve it.

Discussion Questions

1. If you were Aline DeNeuve or a more senior executive at Consolidated Inc., what would you do to improve employee attitudes?

2. Is June realistic or unrealistic in expecting the organization to ensure that she has an interesting work life and an equally interesting life outside of work?

3. To what extent do individual values influence employee attitudes in this case?

Video Case Study

ACTIVITY 7.2
Truth or Consequences

These days, companies are using honesty tests to screen out people who misrepresent themselves or who might lie in the future. As a job applicant, you're asked to do nothing less than sit down with pencil and paper and lay your conscience bare. The problem, it seems, is that honesty tests reject more honest people than dishonest ones.

That's what happened to Trina Benedict. The married mother of two boys says that the biggest lie she's ever told is telling her sons that the needle wouldn't hurt at the doctor's office. "I try to live an honest life and I feel I have pretty good morals and beliefs," she says. Benedict left her job in the bakery at Sobey's to be with her kids. When she reapplied, the grocery store chain had a policy of requiring applicants to complete an honesty test.

One question asked whether she ever had been tempted to steal. Benedict answered yes, because she was often tempted to eat one of the warm cookies, cupcakes, and other goodies coming out of the oven. But she also answered that she had never stolen from the workplace. Despite a flawless work record, Benedict was never rehired. Her test results showed a tendency towards stealing. She was *too* honest when answering the questions!

Companies justify honesty testing by pointing to the huge problem of employee theft: Canadian retailers lose a staggering $1.4 million a day to the pockets of their own staff. Benedict sympathizes with the theft problem, but not with corporate Canada's use of honesty tests to catch people who steal. Benedict cried when she heard that her application had been rejected. "It's so unfair to just your average Joe that wants to go out and get a job and help support their family," she says.

Honesty test developers claim that their instruments are very successful at identifying people who steal. But the evidence also indicates that these tests have a lot of "false positives." For every thief that's identified, the tests falsely identify three to five honest people, like Trina Benedict. Another problem is that qualified professionals should evaluate these tests. Instead, employers typically evaluate the results, and they tend to look at individual items, such as whether you are tempted to steal. The problem is that the overall test might predict stealing, while the individual items do not.

Two American states have either banned or limited the use of honesty tests. Great Britain requires that all testers be qualified and that all tests be subject to independent review. But for the time being in Canada, they're totally unregulated. So what do you do if you face an honesty test? Industry insiders advise people not to be afraid to exaggerate a little: the tests are designed with the assumption that you'll paint a rosy picture of yourself.

Discussion Questions

1. Use the ethical principles described in this chapter to assess the ethical appropriateness of honesty tests. Should companies continue to use them, or are they unethical?

2. Trina Benedict has experienced emotions and has an attitude towards honesty tests. Use the model in Exhibit 7.2 to outline Benedict's attitude.

3. In your opinion, what effect, if any, would honesty testing have on the organizational commitment of new employees?

Source: Based on "Truth and Consequences," *The National Magazine* (August 24, 1999).

ACTIVITY 7.3
RANKING JOBS ON THEIR EMOTIONAL LABOUR

Purpose: This exercise is designed to help you understand the jobs in which people tend to experience higher or lower degrees of emotional labour.

Instructions:

Step 1: Individually rank the extent to which the jobs listed below require emotional labour. In other words, assign a "1" to the job you believe requires the most effort, planning, and control to express organizationally desired emotions during interpersonal transactions. Assign a "10" to the job you believe requires the least amount of emotional labour. Mark your rankings in column 1.

Step 2: The instructor will form teams of four or five members each. Each team will rank the items based on consensus (not simply by averaging the individual rankings). These results are placed in column 2.

Step 3: The instructor will provide expert ranking information. This information should be written in column 3. Then, students calculate the differences in columns 4 and 5.

Step 4: The class will compare the results and discuss the features of jobs with high emotional labour.

Occupation	(1) Individual Ranking	(2) Team Ranking	(3) Expert Ranking	(4) Absolute Difference of 1 and 3	(5) Absolute Difference of 2 and 3
Bartender					
Cashier					
Dental hygienist					
Insurance adjuster					
Lawyer					
Librarian					
Postal clerk					
Registered nurse					
Social worker					
Television announcer					
		TOTAL			
				Your score	Team score

(The lower the score, the better)

ACTIVITY 7.4
ETHICS CHECK

Purpose: This exercise is designed to help you assess your ethical response to various business and non-business situations.

Instructions: Read each of the scenarios below and indicate the likelihood that you would respond in the way indicated in the question in each scenario. There is no scoring key for this scale. Instead, the instructor will present the results of other students who have completed this instrument. This exercise is completed alone so students can assess themselves honestly without concerns of social comparison. However, class discussion will focus on business ethics and the issue of ethical sensitivity.

Please indicate the probability that you would do each of the following:	Yes ▼	Probably Yes ▼	Unsure ▼	Probably No ▼	No ▼
1. At work you use many different software packages. Several weeks ago your supervisor ordered a new package for you that several of your colleagues are currently using. The software is now late in arriving. The package would aid you tremendously in completing your current project, but it is not absolutely necessary. Earlier today your supervisor brought her copy of the software over to you and suggested that you copy it onto your computer for use until your copy arrives. You know that the software is licensed for installation on only one computer. Do you copy the software?	❑	❑	❑	❑	❑
2. While at lunch with several of your colleagues last week you overheard a discussion about a client company's financial situation. An accountant working closely with the company noticed significant decreases in sales and receivables. He wasn't sure exactly how bad it was until he heard a rumour at the company about the possibility of filing for bankruptcy. You're now worried because you own a significant block of shares in the company. Do you sell the shares based on this inside information?	❑	❑	❑	❑	❑

Please indicate the probability that you would do each of the following:	Yes ▼	Probably Yes ▼	Unsure ▼	Probably No ▼	No ▼
3. Yesterday you drove to the store with your neighbour and her young son. When you returned to the car, your neighbour noticed that her son had picked up a small item from the store worth about $5 that hadn't been paid for. Your neighbour reprimanded the child and then turned to you and said she was ready to go. You asked her if she was going to go back into the store to pay for the item. She said it wasn't worth the hassle. Did you refuse to drive her home unless she went back to the store and paid for the item?	❑	❑	❑	❑	❑
4. While on a trip out of town on business you had dinner with your sister. Your company has a policy of reimbursing dinner expenses up to $50 per meal. The total cost for this meal for both you and your sister was $35.70. The cost of your meal alone was $16.30. You know that others in your company routinely submit claims for dinner expenses for non-business parties. Do you claim the entire amount for reimbursement?	❑	❑	❑	❑	❑

Source: Adapted from R.R. Radtke, "The Effects of Gender and Setting on Accountants' Ethically Sensitive Decisions," *Journal of Business Ethics,* 24 (April 2000), pp. 299–312.

ACTIVITY 7.5
INDIVIDUALISM–COLLECTIVISM SCALE

Purpose: This self-assessment is designed to help you identify your level of individualism and collectivism.

Instructions: Read the statements below and circle the response that you believe best indicates how well each statement describes you. Then use the scoring key in Appendix B of this book to calculate your results for each scale. This exercise is completed alone so students can assess themselves honestly without concerns of social comparison. However, class discussion will focus on the individualism–collectivism values.

INDIVIDUALISM–COLLECTIVISM SCALE

Circle the number that best indicates how well these statements describe you.	Does Not Describe Me at All ▼	Does Not Describe Me Very Well ▼	Describes Me Somewhat ▼	Describes Me Well ▼	Describes Me Very Well ▼
1. I often do "my own thing."	1	2	3	4	5
2. The well-being of my co-workers is important to me.	1	2	3	4	5
3. One should live one's life independently of others.	1	2	3	4	5
4. If a co-worker gets a prize, I would feel proud.	1	2	3	4	5
5. I like my privacy.	1	2	3	4	5
6. If a relative were in financial difficulty, I would help within my means.	1	2	3	4	5
7. I prefer to be direct and forthright when discussing issues with people. ..	1	2	3	4	5
8. It is important to maintain harmony within my group.	1	2	3	4	5
9. I am a unique individual.	1	2	3	4	5
10. I like sharing little things with my neighbours.	1	2	3	4	5
11. What happens to me is my own doing.	1	2	3	4	5
12. I feel good when I cooperate with others.	1	2	3	4	5
13. When I succeed, it is usually because of my abilities.	1	2	3	4	5
14. My happiness depends very much on the happiness of those around me.	1	2	3	4	5
15. I enjoy being unique and different from others in many ways.	1	2	3	4	5
16. To me, pleasure is spending time with others.	1	2	3	4	5

Source: Theodore M. Singelis, Harry C. Triandis, Dharm P.S. Bhawuk, Michele J. Gelfand, "Horizontal and Vertical Dimensions of Individualism and Collectivism: A Theoretical and Measurement Refinement," *Cross-Cultural Research*, 29 (August 1995), pp. 240–75.

CHAPTER EIGHT

Communicating in Organizational Settings

LEARNING OBJECTIVES

After reading this chapter, you should be able to:

- Explain the importance of communication and diagram the communication process.
- Identify four common communication barriers.
- Describe problems with communicating through electronic mail.
- Discuss how the law of telecosm will affect organizational communication.
- Explain how nonverbal communication relates to emotional labour and emotional contagion.
- Identify two conditions requiring a channel with high media richness.
- Summarize four communication strategies in organizational hierarchies.
- Discuss the degree to which men and women communicate differently.
- Outline the key elements of active listening.
- Summarize the key features of persuasive communication.

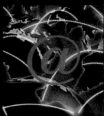

R. Stephenson, *Ottawa Citizen.*

Pearse Flynn tore down communication barriers at Ottawa-based Newbridge Networks (now part of Alcatel).

W hen Pearse Flynn joined Ottawa-based Newbridge Networks (now part of Alcatel) as vice-president of European operations, he noticed that employees were communicating in strange acronyms. Even the PowerPoint slides in briefing sessions looked like they were written in a foreign language.

"The only word I understood on the slide was 'Newbridge' down in the corner," jokes the Irish-born Flynn, who has university degrees in applied physics and digital systems. He quickly advised employees to communicate in plain language so that everyone could understand. "I said you need to make this so I can explain it to my mother."

Flynn further improved communication by changing the physical layout of Newbridge's European headquarters near London. Employees were spread across five buildings and discouraged from visiting co-workers by an internal security system. Flynn reorganized everyone into one building and moved security to the entrance so that people could visit each other more easily.

When Flynn became Newbridge's president in Ottawa, he finished meetings by handing out sticky notes and asked employees to write down what was on their minds after he left the room. "I guarantee you, you do five of those and you'll know what the issues are in the organization," he says. When Newbridge was acquired by Alcatel, Flynn and other executives broke the news to thousands of employees in a nearby hockey stadium (Corel Centre). "People have to know where they're going, so you have to have a plan and communicate that to people," Flynn explains.

Now as a senior Alcatel executive, Flynn oversees 40,000 employees and is constantly travelling around the world to visit Alcatel's far-flung businesses. But he still focuses on communication, particularly face-to-face dialogue. "I make so much of my decisions from the fact that I chat with people, and I pick up what's really going on in people's minds," he says.[1]

• **Communication** The process by which information is transmitted and understood between two or more people.

• **Communication competence** A person's ability to identify appropriate communication patterns in a given situation and to achieve goals by applying that knowledge.

• **Knowledge management** Any structured activity that improves an organization's capacity to acquire, share, and use knowledge in ways that improve its survival and success.

Communication refers to the process by which information is transmitted and *understood* between two or more people. We emphasize the word *understood* because transmitting the sender's intended meaning is the essence of good communication. Newbridge and other organizations require innovative strategies to keep communication pathways open. Smaller businesses may have fewer structural bottlenecks, but they, too, can suffer from subtle communication barriers.

In a knowledge-based economy, employees require a high level of communication competence. **Communication competence** refers to a person's ability to identify appropriate communication patterns in a given situation and to achieve goals by applying that knowledge.[2] Competent communicators quickly learn the meaning that listeners take from certain words and symbols, and they know which communication medium is best in a particular situation. Moreover, competent communicators use this knowledge to communicate in ways that achieve personal, team, and organizational objectives. Someone with high communication competence would quickly determine that an e-mail is the best way to convey a message to a co-worker rather than writing a memo or telephoning the person. Communication competence is particularly vital for executives. According to one recent study, Canadian CEOs spend most of their time and energy on communicating and meeting with employees, or spending time with customers. This is consistent with earlier research findings that corporate leaders spend almost 80 percent of their day communicating.[3]

Communication plays an important role in **knowledge management**.[4] Employees are the organization's brain cells, and communication represents the nervous system that carries this information and shared meaning to vital parts of the organizational body. Effective communication brings knowledge into the organization and disseminates it quickly to employees who require that information. Effective communication minimizes the "silos of knowledge" problem that undermines an organization's potential. This, in turn, allows employees to make more informed choices about corporate actions. For instance, British Telecom encourages employees to generate "knowledge moments"—occasions where shared knowledge results in better decisions.[5]

Along with decision making and knowledge management, effective communication coordinates work activities.[6] Through dialogue, co-workers develop common mental models—working models of the world (see Chapter 6)—so they can synchronize interdependent work activities through common expectations and assumptions.[7] Lastly, communication is the glue that bonds people together. It fulfils the need for affiliation and, as part of the dynamics of social support, eases work-related stress.[8]

This chapter begins by presenting a model of the communication process and discussing several communication barriers. Next, the different types of

Courtesy of Buckman Labs.

Buckman Laboratories is a pioneer in knowledge management. Yet, the chemical company sees internal communication as its main strength. "[W]e have designed a system and built a culture that facilitates the communication of whatever is needed across all of the organization's boundaries," explains CEO Robert Buckman. Employees work in 90 countries and spend much of their time with customers. Notebook computers, connected to Buckman Labs' worldwide information centre (called K'netix), allow them to share information quickly. For example, a representative in Indonesia won a $6 million proposal, partly because he requested vital information and received it within eight hours from colleagues in Canada, Sweden, Spain, and the United States.[9] In what additional ways might Buckman Labs and other companies improve communication across their global operations?

communication channels, including computer-mediated communication, are described, followed by factors to consider when choosing a communication medium. This chapter then presents some options for communicating in organizational hierarchies and describes the pervasive organizational grapevine. The latter part of the chapter examines cross-cultural and gender differences in communication, as well as strategies to improve interpersonal and persuasive communication.

A MODEL OF COMMUNICATION

The communication model presented in Exhibit 8.1 provides a useful "conduit" metaphor for thinking about the communication process.[10] According to this model, communication flows through channels between the sender and receiver. The sender forms a message and encodes it into words, gestures, voice intonations, and other symbols or signs. Next, the encoded message is transmitted to the intended receiver through one or more communication channels (media). The receiver senses the incoming message and decodes it into something meaningful. Ideally, the decoded meaning is what the sender had intended.

In most situations, the sender looks for evidence that the other person received and understood the transmitted message. This feedback may be a formal acknowledgement, such as "Yes, I know what you mean," or indirect evidence from the receiver's subsequent actions. Notice that feedback repeats the communication process. Intended feedback is encoded, transmitted, received, and decoded from the receiver to the sender of the original message.

This model recognizes that communication is not a free-flowing conduit.[11] Rather, the transmission of meaning from one person to another is hampered by noise—the psychological, social, and structural barriers that distort and obscure the sender's intended message. If any part of the communication process is distorted or broken, the sender and receiver will not have a common understanding of the message.

EXHIBIT 8.1 The Communication Process Model

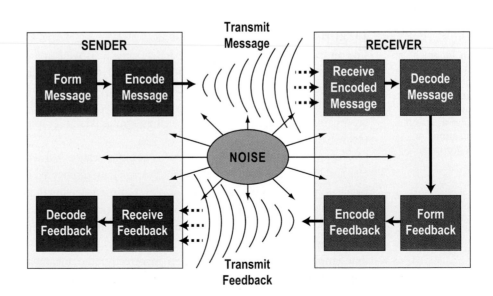

COMMUNICATION BARRIERS (NOISE)

In spite of the best intentions of sender and receiver to communicate, several barriers inhibit the effective exchange of information. As author George Bernard Shaw once wrote, "The greatest problem with communication is the illusion that it has been accomplished." Canadian executives estimate that 15 percent of their time is wasted due to poor communications with employees. This translates into approximately eight weeks per person each year![12] This chapter will identify several communication barriers (called "noise" in Exhibit 8.1), but we discuss four pervasive problems in this section: perceptions, filtering, language, and information overload.

PERCEPTIONS

As we learned in Chapter 6, the perceptual process determines what messages we select or screen out, as well as how the selected information is organized and interpreted. This can be a significant source of noise in the communication process if the sender's and receiver's perceptions are not aligned. For example, a plant superintendent in a Canadian concrete block plant picked up a piece of broken brick while talking with the supervisor. This action had no particular meaning to the superintendent—it was just something to toy with during the conversation. Yet as soon as the senior manager had left, the supervisor ordered a half-hour of overtime for the entire crew to clean up the plant. The supervisor mistakenly perceived the superintendent's action as a signal that the plant was messy.[13]

FILTERING

Some messages are filtered or stopped altogether on their way up or down the organizational hierarchy. Filtering may involve deleting or delaying negative information, or using less harsh words so that events sound more favourable. Employees and supervisors usually filter communication to create a good impression of themselves for superiors. Filtering is most common where the organization rewards employees who communicate mainly positive information and among employees with strong career mobility aspirations.[14]

LANGUAGE

Words and gestures carry no inherent meaning, so the sender must ensure that the receiver understands these symbols and signs. In reality, lack of mutual understanding is a common reason why messages are distorted. Two potential language barriers are jargon and ambiguity.

Jargon

Jargon Technical language of a particular occupational group or recognized words with specialized meaning in specific organizations or social groups.

Jargon includes technical language and acronyms as well as recognized words with specialized meaning in specific organizations or social groups. As discussed in Connections 8.1, "Microspeak" jargon at Microsoft can potentially improve communication efficiency when both sender and receiver understand this specialized language. It also shapes and maintains an organization's cultural values as well as symbolizes an employee's self-identity in a group (see Chapter 6).[15]

However, jargon can also be a serious communication barrier. In the opening story to this chapter, Newbridge Networks president Pearse Flynn discovered that jargon was a form of technical snobbery that prevented some employees from receiving important knowledge and undermined relations with customers. Jargon was also a problem at Wacker Siltronic Corp. Employees were breaking saw blades and causing a high rate of product defects after new machinery was introduced. Management eventually discovered that the manuals were written for engineers, and that employees were guessing (often incorrectly) the meaning of the jargon. Productivity improved and machine costs dropped after the manuals were rewritten without the jargon.[16]

www.microsoft.com
www.cinepad.com/mslex.htm

CONNECTIONS 8.1

Klugey Communication at Microspeak

"Hi Jack, I've worked out a klugey solution to the UI issue," an employee e-mails to a colleague in the next cubicle. "We need to get granular on this. Unfortunately, I'm OOF next week, so you'll have to burn up a few cycles on it. I'm worried that the blue-badges on this project will go totally nonlinear when they realize the RTM date is slipping."*

Welcome to the world of Microspeak—the unofficial language of Microsoft. Employees at the world's largest software company have acquired a lexicon that would baffle researchers at Webster's Dictionary. Microsoft staffers eat their own dog food, dislike weasel users, and avoid getting caught in reality distortion fields. This all makes sense to insiders, but not to people raised with the English language!

Most of this dialogue occurs in cybermedia rather than "fibre media" (paper) or "facemail" (face-to-face). That's not to say that Microsoft employees never meet. They do, in small groups around whiteboards in someone's office to share insights, resolve problems, and confirm deadlines. In fact, Microsoft makes sure that employees work at the same location so they can communicate and solve problems quickly in face-to-face meetings.

Sources: K. Barnes, "The Microsoft Lexicon" (www.cinepad.com/mslex.htm); S. Greenhouse, "Braindump on the Blue Badge: A Guide to Microspeak," *New York Times,* August 13, 1998, p. G1; M.A. Cusumano, "How Microsoft Makes Large Teams Work Like Small Teams," *Sloan Management Review,* 39 (Fall 1997), pp. 9–20.

*Translation: "Hi Jack, I've worked out a rough solution to the user interface problem. We need to examine the finer details. Unfortunately, I'm away next week, so you need to devote time and energy to this problem. I'm worried that the permanent Microsoft employees on this project will get really angry when they realize that we are getting behind on the released-to-manufacturing date."

Ambiguity

We usually think of ambiguous language as a communication problem because the sender and receiver interpret the same word or phrase differently. If a co-worker says, "Would you like to check the figures again?" the employee may be politely *telling* you to double-check the figures. But this message is sufficiently ambiguous that you may think that the co-worker is merely *asking* if you want to do this. The result is a failure to communicate.

Ambiguous language is sometimes used deliberately in work settings to avoid conveying undesirable emotions. Air Canada's CEO refers to the "integration process" with Canadian Airlines. This sounds better than the "m" words of merger and monopoly. Microsoft doesn't warn computer users about fatal software errors; they're "undocumented behaviours." And when millions of Microsoft Network customers suffered through significant e-mail delivery problems, the company described the incident as "a partial e-mail delay."[17] Why the obfuscation? Customers tend to respond more calmly to integration processes, undocumented behaviours, and partial e-mail delays than to monopolies, fatal software errors, and e-mail lost for weeks or forever.

Ambiguous language may be a barrier, but it is sometimes necessary where events or objects are ill defined or lack agreement.[18] Corporate leaders often use metaphors to describe complex organizational values so that they are interpreted broadly enough to apply to diverse situations. Scholars also rely on metaphors because they convey rich meaning about complex ideas. For example, some organizational behaviour scholars compare organizations to "jazz ensembles" or "machines" to reflect different variations of their complex nature.[19]

DILBERT reprinted by permission of United Feature Syndicate, Inc.

INFORMATION OVERLOAD

Every day, Dave MacDonald is flooded with up to 100 e-mail messages. The Xerox Canada executive is also bombarded with voice mail, faxes, memos, and other pieces of information. "Without some kind of system in place, I'd spend practically all my time trying to sort through it and not get much of anything else done," says MacDonald.[20]

Dave MacDonald is not alone. Canadian office workers send and receive an average of 169 e-mails, phone calls, voice mails, faxes, paper documents, and other messages each day![21] "One of the effects of living with electric information is that we live in a state of information overload," predicted Canadian communications guru Marshall McLuhan nearly 40 years ago. "There's always more than you can cope with."[22]

> **Information overload**
> A condition in which the volume of information received by an employee exceeds that person's ability to process it effectively.

Information overload occurs when the volume of information received exceeds the person's capacity to process it. Employees have a certain *information processing capacity*, that is, the amount of information that they are able to process in a fixed unit of time. At the same time, jobs have a varying *information load*, that is, the amount of information to be processed per unit of time.[23] As Exhibit 8.2 illustrates, information overload occurs whenever the job's information load exceeds the individual's information processing capacity.

Information overload creates noise in the communication system because information is overlooked or misinterpreted when people cannot process it fast enough. Moreover, as we learned in Chapter 5, it has become a common cause of workplace stress. One survey reports that two-thirds of managers blame information overload for interpersonal conflicts and dissatisfaction at work, and 43 percent say that they suffer from "paralysis of analysis" due to the volume of information they must process.[24]

Information overload is minimized in two ways: by increasing our information processing capacity and by reducing the job's information load.[25] We can increase information processing capacity by learning to read faster, scanning documents more efficiently, and removing distractions that slow information processing speed. Time management also increases information processing capacity. When information overload is temporary, information processing capacity can increase by working longer hours.

We can reduce information load by buffering, summarizing, or omitting information. Buffering occurs where assistants screen the person's messages and forward only those considered to be essential reading. Vancouver business leader Jimmy Pattison relies on Maureen Chant to be a buffer—a "mission control" person to screen people and messages each day.[26] Summarizing condenses information into fewer words, such as by reading abstracts and

| EXHIBIT 8.2 | Dynamics of Information Overload |

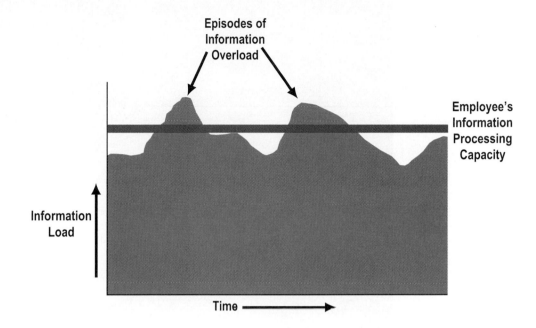

executive summaries rather than the entire document. Omitting is the practice of ignoring less important information. For example, some e-mail software programs have a filtering algorithm that screens out unwanted junk mail (called "spam").

Perceptions, filtering, language, and information overload are not the only sources of noise in the communication process, but they are probably the most common. Noise also occurs when we choose an inappropriate channel to send the message. The next section takes a closer look at communication channels.

COMMUNICATION CHANNELS

A critical part of the communication model is the channel through which information is transmitted. There are two main types of channels: verbal and nonverbal. *Verbal communication* includes any oral or written means of transmitting meaning through words. *Nonverbal communication,* which we discuss later, is any part of communication that does not use words.

VERBAL COMMUNICATION

Different forms of verbal communication should be used in different situations. Face-to-face interaction is usually better than written methods for transmitting emotions and persuading the receiver. This is because nonverbal cues, such as voice intonations and use of silence, accompany oral communications. Moreover, in face-to-face settings, the sender receives immediate feedback from the receiver and can adjust the emotional tone of the message accordingly.

Written communication is more appropriate for recording and presenting technical details. This is because ideas are easier to follow when written down than when communicated verbally. Traditionally, written communication has been slow to develop and transmit, but electronic mail and other computer-mediated communication channels have significantly improved written communication efficiency.[27]

www.angusreid.com

Angus Reid enjoys a good discussion about the latest trends in Canadian society. Indeed, the Vancouver-based pollster is well known for captivating audiences as he describes the policy implications of the latest survey results. But when it comes to technical details, Reid quickly grabs a writing instrument and scribbles down information on any available surface. One of the more unusual places he uses to provide written communication is his office window overlooking downtown Vancouver. How can you tell when to switch from oral to written communication or vice versa?

ELECTRONIC MAIL

Electronic mail (e-mail) is revolutionizing the way we communicate in organizational settings. According to one estimate, 110 trillion e-mail messages are sent every year. This is expected to increase to 452 trillion e-mails by 2003.[28] It's easy to understand the popularity of e-mail. Messages are quickly formed, edited, and stored. Information can be appended and transmitted to many people with a simple click of a mouse. E-mail is asynchronous (messages are sent and received at different times), so there is no need to coordinate a communication session. This technology also allows fairly random access of information; you can select any message in any order and skip to different parts of a message.

E-mail tends to be the preferred medium for coordinating work (e.g., confirming a co-worker's production schedule) and for sending well-defined information for decision making. It tends to increase the volume of communication and significantly alter the flow of that information throughout the organization.[29] Specifically, it reduces some face-to-face and telephone communication but increases the flow of information to higher levels in the organization. Some social and organizational status differences still exist with e-mail, but they are less apparent than in face-to-face or telephone communication. E-mail also reduces many selective attention biases because it hides our age, race, weight, and other features that are observable in face-to-face meetings.

Problems with e-mail

Anyone who has used e-mail knows that it has several problems and limitations.[30] Perhaps the most obvious of these is that e-mail contributes to information overload. Many e-mail users are overwhelmed by hundreds of messages each week, most of which are irrelevant to them. This is because it is so easy to transmit messages. E-mails can be written and copied quickly to thousands of people through group mailbox systems. Employees receive little e-mail training, which results in ineffective message quality and usage patterns.

A second concern is that e-mail seems to reduce our politeness and respect for others. This is mostly evident through the increased frequency of **flaming**. Flaming is the act of sending an emotionally charged message (called "flame-mail") to others. This occurs because people can post e-mail messages before their emotions subside, whereas the sender of a traditional memo or letter would have time for sober second thoughts. One recent survey found that over half of the people questioned receive abusive flame-mail and that men are both the most frequent victims and perpetrators. This is certainly true at Disney, where e-mail is the source of many conflicts. "Every fight that goes on [at Disney] seems to start with a misunderstanding over an e-mail," says Disney CEO Michael Eisner.[31]

A third problem is that it is difficult to interpret the emotional meaning behind e-mail messages. One scholar recently quipped that the result "of new information technologies within organizations has not been better communication, only faster misunderstandings."[32] For example, sarcasm is difficult to convey through e-mail because the verbal message requires contrasting nonverbal cues. E-mail aficionados try to clarify the emotional tone of their messages by combining ASCII characters to form graphic faces called emoticons or "smileys." An entire lexicon of emoticons has developed, including those shown in Exhibit 8.3. However, some experts warn that people should write what they mean rather than use smileys so often.[33]

Flaming Sending an emotionally charged electronic mail message.

EXHIBIT 8.3	Icons of Emotion (Emoticons) in E-Mail Messages

Icon	Meaning
:-)	Happy
:-}	Smirk
:-(	Unhappy
<:-)	Dumb question
0:-)	Angel (I'm being good)
:-p	Tongue sticking out
:-x	OOPS!
{ }	Hug
12x—<—@	A Dozen Roses

Source: Based on R. Peck, "Learning to Speak Computer Lingo," *The Times-Picayune*, June 5, 1997, p. E1; R. Weiland, "The Message Is the Medium," *Incentive*, September 1995, p. 37.

Presumably, flaming and other communication problems will become less common as employees learn the dynamics of e-mail. One Canadian court has already ruled on the meaning of *netiquette*—the largely unwritten and evolving code of conduct for communicating on the Internet.[34] Eventually, most of us will learn the many netiquette rules and courtesies that are forming for this new medium. Exhibit 8.4 displays a few netiquette rules for e-mail.

One last concern about e-mail is that it lacks the warmth of human interaction. As employees increasingly cocoon themselves through their computers and other forms of information technology, they lose the social support of human contact that potentially keeps their stress in check. As one computer consultant warns: "People are finding themselves spending a major portion of their day surrounded by machines and communicating through machines, and they feel hungry for human connection and warmth and perspective and wisdom."[35]

OTHER COMPUTER-MEDIATED COMMUNICATION

Internets, intranets, extanets, and other forms of computer-mediated communication have fuelled the hyperfast world of corporate information sharing. Canadian technology allows airline pilots in Norway to enter their flight plans and retrieve weather reports from their homes through a secure Web site. Geographically dispersed work teams can coordinate their work more efficiently through e-mail and intranets. Suppliers are networked together so tightly

---

EXHIBIT 8.4   Some Basic E-Mail Netiquette

- DO fill in the "subject" line of the e-mail header with an informative description of the message.
- DO keep e-mail messages to less than 25 lines—the length of a typical computer screen.
- DO quote the relevant parts (but not necessarily all) of the receiver's previous message when replying to ideas in that message. (The automatic ">" indicates the original message.)
- DO respond to someone's e-mail (where a reply is expected) within one day for most business correspondence.
- DO switch from e-mail to telephone or face-to-face communication when the discussion gets too heated (flaming), the parties experience ongoing misunderstanding, or the issue becomes too complex.
- DON'T forward private messages without the permission of the original sender.
- DON'T send mass e-mails (using group lists) unless authorized to do so and the message definitely calls for this action.
- DON'T send large attachments if the receiver likely has a narrow bandwidth (computer data are transmitted slowly).
- DON'T use e-mail to communicate sensitive issues, such as disciplining someone, or to convey urgent information, such as rescheduling a meeting within the next hour.
- DON'T write messages in ALL CAPITALS because this conveys anger or shouting. (This rule also applies to boldface text as e-mail software develops this feature.)
- DON'T use emoticons excessively, and avoid them in formal business e-mails and where there is some chance that the receiver won't know their meaning.

Sources: Based on M.M. Extejt, "Teaching Students to Correspond Effectively Electronically; Tips for Using Electronic Mail Properly," *Business Communication Quarterly,* 61 (June 1998), pp. 57+; K. Wasch, "Netiquette: Do's and Don'ts of E-mail Use," *Association Management,* 49 (May 1997), pp. 76, 115.

Nick Didlick, *Vancouver Sun.*

www.nunanet.com

Like most executives, Adamee Itorcheak carries a laptop computer and cellular telephone almost everywhere he goes. The difference is that Itorcheak lives in Iqaluit, the capital city of Nunavut Territory, and his travels include traditional Inuit hunting trips in the Arctic wilderness. As president of Nunavut's largest Internet service provider (Nunanet Communications) and a partner in a new high-speed wireless service (Inukshuk Communications), Itorcheak is probably the most wired person in the region. He is also connecting most people in Nunavut, from a fish plant in Pangnirtung to a fishing guide in Clyde River. Through online forums and chat rooms, the people of Nunavut are becoming a more closely knit community. "Here in this huge territory, 20,000 people live in scattered groups," explains Itorcheak. "The Internet is the only way to bring us all together."[36] What are the limitations of Internet-based communication for people who rarely communicate face-to-face?

through computer-mediated technology that customers see them as one organization (see Chapter 16). The U.S. Army's senior officers communicate around the world through a special online chat room. "The network allows me to be productive and to maintain a pulse on what is happening whether I'm in Washington or overseas," says the U.S. Army's chief of staff.[37]

The effectiveness of e-mail, intranet sites, chat rooms, and other forms of computer-mediated communication must be assessed on their own merits. However, they all have one clear benefit: they seem to reduce time and dissolve distances. This relates to the **law of telecosm**, which states that as the web of computer networks expands, distances will shrink and eventually become irrelevant.[38]

Law of telecosm
States that as the web of computer networks expands, distances will shrink and eventually become irrelevant.

You might think that emerging computer-mediated technologies further increase information overload. However, preliminary evidence suggests that they actually *reduce* overload because they offer greater control over the amount of information flowing from these sources. We decide how much information to receive from the Internet and intranet, whereas there is almost no control over the number of voice mails, e-mails, faxes, and paper-based memos we receive. This is supported by a recent survey of executives in 11 countries. Half of them indicated that the Internet is reducing information overload; only 19 percent claim that it is making matters worse.[39]

NONVERBAL COMMUNICATION

Computer-mediated communication is changing the face of organizations, but it hasn't yet replaced nonverbal communication. Nonverbal communication includes facial gestures, voice intonation, physical distance, and even silence. This communication channel is necessary where physical distance or noise prevents effective verbal exchanges and the need for immediate feedback precludes written communication. But even in close face-to-face meetings, most information is communicated nonverbally.[40] Nonverbal communication is also important in **emotional labour**. Recall from Chapter 7 that emotional labour refers to the effort, planning, and control needed to express organizationally desired emotions. Employees make extensive use of nonverbal cues to transmit prescribed feelings to customers, co-workers, and others.

Nonverbal communication differs from verbal communication in a couple of ways. First, verbal communication is typically conscious, whereas nonverbal communication is more automatic and unconscious. We normally plan the words we say or write, but rarely plan every blink, smile, or other gesture during a conversation. Second, nonverbal communication is less rule-bound than verbal communication. We receive a lot of formal training on how to understand spoken words, but very little on how to understand the nonverbal signals that accompany those words. Consequently, nonverbal cues are more ambiguous and more susceptible to misinterpretation.

Emotional contagion

What happens when you see a co-worker accidentally bang his or her head against a filing cabinet? Chances are, you wince and put your hand on your own head as if you had hit the cabinet. This automatic and unconscious tendency to mimic and synchronize our nonverbal behaviours with other people is called **emotional contagion**.[41] Emotional contagion is not a disease. It refers to the notion that we tend to "catch" other people's emotions by continuously mimicking the facial expressions and nonverbal cues of others. For instance, listeners smile more and exhibit other emotional displays of happiness while hearing someone describe a positive event. Similarly, listeners will wince when the speaker describes an event in which he or she was hurt.

Emotional contagion serves three purposes. First, mimicry provides continuous feedback, communicating that we understand and empathize with the sender. To consider the significance of this, imagine if employees remained expressionless after watching a co-worker bang his or her head! The lack of parallel behaviour conveys a lack of understanding or caring. Second, mimicking the nonverbal behaviours of other people seems to be a way of receiving emotional meaning from those people. If a co-worker is angry with a client, your tendency to frown and show anger while listening helps you share that emotion more fully. In other words, we receive meaning by expressing the sender's emotions as well as by listening to the sender's words.

Lastly, emotional contagion is a type of "social glue" that bonds people together. Social solidarity is built out of each member's awareness of a collective sentiment. Through nonverbal expressions of emotional contagion, people see others share the same emotions that we feel. This strengthens team cohesiveness by providing evidence of member similarity.

CHOOSING THE BEST COMMUNICATION CHANNELS

Employees perform better if they can quickly determine the best communication channels for the situation and are flexible enough to use different methods, as the occasion requires.[42] But which communication channels are most appropriate? We partly answered this question in our evaluation of the different communication channels. However, two additional contingencies worth noting are media richness and symbolic meaning.

Emotional labour
The effort, planning, and control needed to express organizationally desired emotions during interpersonal transactions.

Emotional contagion
The automatic and subconscious tendency to mimic and synchronize our nonverbal behaviours with other people.

MEDIA RICHNESS

Media richness The
data-carrying capac-
ity of a communica-
tion medium; the
volume and variety
of information that it
can transmit.

Communication channels can be organized into a hierarchy based on their **media richness**. This refers to their *data-carrying capacity*—the volume and variety of information that can be transmitted.[43] Face-to-face meetings have the highest data-carrying capacity because the sender simultaneously uses multiple communication channels (verbal and nonverbal), the receiver can provide immediate feedback, and the information exchange can be customized to suit the situation. In contrast, financial reports and other impersonal documents represent the leanest media because they allow only one form of data transmission (e.g., written), the sender does not receive timely feedback from the receiver, and the information exchange is standardized for everyone.

As Exhibit 8.5 shows, the most appropriate medium depends on whether the situation is nonroutine and ambiguous. Nonroutine situations require rich media because the sender and receiver have little common experience and, therefore, need to transmit a large volume of information with immediate feedback. During unexpected emergencies, for instance, you should use face-to-face meetings to coordinate work efforts quickly and minimize the risk of misunderstanding and confusion. Lean media may be used in routine situations because the sender and receiver have common expectations through shared mental models.

Ambiguous situations also require rich media because the parties must share large amounts of information with immediate feedback to resolve multiple and conflicting interpretations of

EXHIBIT 8.5   A Hierarchy of Media Richness

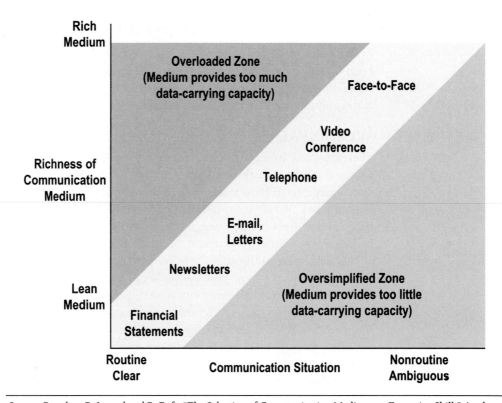

Source: Based on R. Lengel and R. Daft, "The Selection of Communication Media as an Executive Skill," *Academy of Management Executive,* 2(3) (August 1988), p. 226; R.L. Daft and R.H. Lengel, "Information Richness: A New Approach to Managerial Behavior and Organization Design," *Research in Organizational Behavior,* 1984, p. 199.

their observations and experiences.[44] Team members require rich media communication during the early stages of a project to resolve different interpretations of the project task, each member's role, and the parameters of acceptable behaviour. Similarly, research suggests that product development teams should work together in the same physical space because information technologies do not yet provide the level of media richness offered by face-to-face interaction.[45]

What happens when we choose the wrong level of media richness for the situation? When the situation is routine or clear, using a rich medium—such as holding a special meeting—would seem like a waste of time. On the other hand, if a unique and ambiguous issue is handled through lean media—such as memos—issues take longer to resolve and misunderstandings are more likely to occur.

SYMBOLIC MEANING OF THE MEDIUM

"The medium is the message."[46] This famous phrase by the late Canadian communication guru Marshall McLuhan means that the sender's choice of communication channel transmits meaning beyond the message content. For example, a personal meeting with an employee may indicate that the issue is important, whereas a brief handwritten note may suggest less importance.

The difficulty we face when choosing a communication medium is that its symbolic meaning may vary from one person to the next. Some people view e-mail as a symbol of professionalism, whereas others see it as evidence of the sender's efficiency. Still others might view an e-mail message as a low-status clerical activity because it involves typing.[47] Overall, we must be sensitive to the symbolic meaning of the selected communication medium to ensure that it amplifies rather than contradicts the meaning found in the message content.

COMMUNICATING IN ORGANIZATIONAL HIERARCHIES

In this era where knowledge is competitive advantage, corporate leaders need to maintain an open flow of communication up, down, and across the organization. In this section, we discuss four communication strategies: workspace design, employee surveys, newsletters and e-zines, and management by walking around.

WORKSPACE DESIGN

There's nothing like a wall to prevent employees from talking to each other. That's why the Montreal offices of marketing agency Ryan & Deslauriers consist of desks in a large, homey, open space. Nortel Networks turned its former manufacturing facility in Brampton, Ontario, into an open-plan cityscape headquarters. British Airways also moved to new headquarters near London with an open design that looks like a village square.[48] Most of these changes make more efficient use of space, but their main thrust is to provide direct line-of-sight among employees so that they share knowledge more easily.

Other companies have kept the walls up, but have rearranged the hallways to support spontaneous, horizontal communication.[49] Seagate Software's new offices in Vancouver include extra-wide hallways so that employees can chat without blocking others. Pearl Assurance redesigned its building for the same reason. The British insurance company installed "pit-stop" areas where people can spontaneously meet and share information.

The line-of-sight communication principle also works on the plant floor. Toyota Canada's production facilities in Cambridge, Ontario, consist of U-shaped subassembly cells so that everyone on the line can coordinate their work and solve problems more quickly through direct communication. This contrasts with the traditional I-shaped or L-shaped lines at General Motors, which make it difficult for employees to communicate with each other.[50]

Nortel Networks recently transformed its old manufacturing facility in Brampton, Ontario, into a global headquarters designed as an airy, indoor city for 3000 employees. The building has a main street (left photo), side streets, crossroads, and several treed parks (right photo). Departments are flag-decked neighbourhoods with their own distinctive décor (selected by employees). Dividers (not walls) temporarily separate the offices, but even the dividers will go when employees feel more comfortable with the open setting. The governing metaphor here is to break down the walls so that employees can communicate with each other more easily. "I've met hundreds of people I'd only talked to on the phone for years," says a Nortel employee.[51] How would the physical layout of Nortel's cityscape improve communication? What problems do you think might result from this design?

www.nortelnetworks.com

Hotelling An open workspace concept in which employees do not have permanent desks, offices, or workspace but rather are temporarily assigned a disk or cubicle when they visit the office.

Turning offices into hotels

Several organizations have taken the open workspace concept one step further by introducing **hotelling** (also called nonterritorial or free-address offices).[52] Employees do not have permanent desks, offices, or workspace. Instead, they are temporarily assigned a desk or cubicle when they visit the office. Hotelling conserves space and is most common when employees spend little time at the office. PricewaterhouseCoopers and Andersen Consulting, described in Connections 8.2, use hotelling mainly for this reason. Consultants spend most of their time with clients, so expensive office space would usually be vacant without hotelling. Hotelling also makes it easier to accommodate employees visiting from other offices.

By itself, hotelling just manages space more efficiently. However, most of these facilities also encourage dialogue by creating more open-space work areas. For example, employees at Danish hearing aid manufacturer Oticon A/S and U.S. financial services firm SEI Investments have their own desks, but no fixed location in which to put them. Instead, the desk, chair, and belongings are on wheels so that they can frequently move around the building. The result is that employees work together and share knowledge more freely than if they spent all of their time in an isolated space.[53]

One limitation of hotelling and open-space arrangements is that employees may feel stressed by the loss of privacy and personal space. Some people at TBWA Chiat/Day's Toronto office resorted to making telephone calls in bathroom stalls and under their desks. The advertising firm pioneered hotelling and open office design a decade ago. Now, it has moved to a "nesting" model of office design that encourages communication, yet gives employees some privacy at work.[54]

canada.ac.com/home.asp
www.pricewaterhousecoopers.com/ca   www.mckinsey.com

Canadian Consulting Firms Turn Their Offices into Hotels

Andersen Consulting has turned its Vancouver office into a hotel. Employees spent less than 25 percent of their time at the office, so the consulting firm took away everyone's permanent desks or cubicles. Now, local staff and out-of-town consultants reserve space with a concierge, who assigns them to one of six private cubicles or workstations in a communal area. When consultants need privacy for client calls, they can use one of four telephone booths equipped with a chair, desk, and plug-in for a laptop computer.

PricewaterhouseCoopers is also following this trend of hotelling. It recently moved its Toronto employees out of their private offices into open-concept workstations. To offset this lack of privacy, the consulting firm created quiet areas where employees can retreat from the open office. The new office design also has meeting rooms and breakout areas for noisy teamwork.

McKinsey & Co. didn't quite make the jump to hotelling, but its new offices in midtown Toronto have similar features. The main work areas are designed as clusters that try to strike a balance between open and private space. Junior staff share space, but they can use telephone booths for private conversations. Partners have small offices, which encourages them to get out and use meeting rooms.

"We want people to get up, to move around," says Mehrdad Baghai, a principal with McKinsey who helped develop the Toronto office. "We want people to bump into each other. We're trying to create a sense of community."

Sources: S. Elton, "Commercial Sites Undergo Major Shift," *Globe and Mail,* January 11, 2000, p. B19; N. Hulsman, "Farewell, Corner Office," *BC Business,* June 1999, p. 48; E. Church, "McKinsey Experiments with Its Workspace," *Globe and Mail,* June 21, 1999, p. M1.

EMPLOYEE SURVEYS

Twenty-nine of Canada's 35 "best" companies conduct regular employee opinion surveys. Most of these companies survey employees to monitor worker morale. However, many firms also use these surveys to involve employees in decisions on everything from dress codes to pension plans.[55] For example, Hong Kong's Kowloon-Canton Railway Corp. (KCRC) significantly improved service quality and performance by surveying employees about their thoughts on how the company can perform better. "A fundamental change has taken place at the KCRC because of the surveys," explains KCRC chairman and chief executive Kevin Hyde.[56]

Telus, Nortel Networks, and other firms also measure employee satisfaction as an indicator of executive and corporate performance (see Chapter 7). Federal Express relies on employee surveys as part of its "Survey-Feedback-Action" process of 360-degree feedback (see Chapter 2). "The first survey is always an experience for new managers," explains a Federal Express executive. "But they soon realize they need it. Good communication increases the morale—and the productivity—of the group."[57]

NEWSLETTERS AND E-ZINES

When First Leisure's 7000 employees were asked how they would like to receive corporate news, executives were surprised by the answer. Most people at the British health and fitness company didn't want regular e-mails or a fancy intranet site. "Staff wanted a publication—not delivered electronically, but something warm and cuddly which they could show family and friends," says the First Leisure executive who investigated this issue.[58]

In this networked world, First Leisure isn't the only firm where employees prefer a hard-copy magazine or tabloid. Mobil employees in more than 125 countries look forward to receiving their copy of *Mobil World* every two months. BASF, the German chemicals manufacturer, also distributes a regular news magazine to its 100,000 employees worldwide.[59] Employees generally appreciate hard-copy news because it personally connects them to the organization. As one American employee points out: "I can't share the company with my wife and family by showing them e-mails or asking them to visit our Web site."

This doesn't mean that e-mail news or Web-based magazines (called "e-zines," for electronic magazines) are ineffective. Electronic sources work well for timely news with brief snippets of information. For instance, Los Alamos National Laboratory in New Mexico supplements its monthly newsletter with a daily electronic newsletter through the Intranet. This e-zine is posted each evening so that employees have the news first thing each morning.[60] However, e-zines tend to supplement hard-copy news rather than replace it.

MANAGEMENT BY WALKING AROUND

> **Management by walking around (MBWA)** A method of communication in which executives get out their offices and learn from others in the organization through face-to-face dialogue.

Coined several years ago at Hewlett-Packard, **management by walking around (MBWA)** means that executives should get out their offices and learn from others in the organization through face-to-face dialogue.[61] MBWA minimizes filtering because executives listen to employees directly. It also helps executives acquire a deeper meaning and quicker understanding of internal organizational problems.

N. Betts, *Toronto Sun.*

www.sunmedia.ca

When Toronto Sun Publishing Corp. was put up for sale, former CEO Paul Godfrey (front) took the message directly to employees. Rather than send a memo or e-mail, Godfrey invited employees to meet in the foyer, where he directly communicated the news to them. The impending sale was an emotional event, so Godfrey had to get out of his office to convey the message and listen to feedback from employees. Through direct dialogue, executives communicate their emotional support and receive more accurate feedback.[62] What other forms of management by walking around should be used when communicating stressful news?

MBWA can take many forms. SaskTel president Donald Ching goes for regular "Ride Alongs" with installers or repair crews to hear what's on their minds. At Wescast Industries Inc. in Brantford, Ontario, executives hold monthly "report card" meetings during which employees communicate issues that concern them. Executives at PMC-Sierra in Burnaby, B.C., mingle with employees during Wednesday morning brunches, appropriately called "Connect Breaks."[63]

COMMUNICATING THROUGH THE GRAPEVINE

Grapevine The organization's informal communication network that is formed and maintained by social relationships rather than by the formal reporting relationships.

Whether or not executives get out of their offices, employees will always rely on the oldest communication channel: the corporate **grapevine**. The grapevine is an unstructured and informal network founded on social relationships rather than on organizational charts or job descriptions. Employees often receive news from the grapevine before they hear about it through formal channels. For example, 45 percent of Canadian employees say that they first hear about layoffs through the grapevine. It's not surprising that 75 percent of employees claim that the grapevine is their first source of important information in the organization.[64]

GRAPEVINE CHARACTERISTICS

The grapevine has several unique features.[65] It transmits information very rapidly in all directions throughout the organization. Grapevine news is relatively accurate, possibly because the parties tend to use media-rich communication channels (e.g., face to face) and are motivated to communicate effectively. Nevertheless, the grapevine distorts information by deleting fine details and exaggerating key points of the story. It transmits kernels of truth with several embellishments. Consequently, the grapevine should not be viewed as the definitive source of organizational news.

The grapevine typically transmits information through the *cluster chain* pattern illustrated in Exhibit 8.6. Senders transmit grapevine information only to people they know and believe are interested. Some employees rarely receive grapevine information because they are not integrated with the organization's social network.

The grapevine relies on social relations, so it is more active where employees have similar backgrounds and are able to communicate easily with each other. It is also more active when employees are anxious and information from formal channels does not satisfy their need to know.[66] For

---

EXHIBIT 8.6 Transmission Pattern of Grapevine Communication

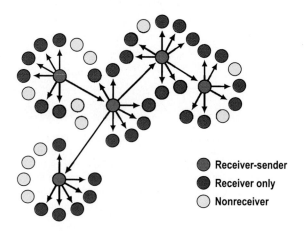

- ● Receiver-sender
- ● Receiver only
- ○ Nonreceiver

example, the rumour mill went into overdrive when Red Wing Shoe Company's acquisition of Kaufman Footwear in Kitchener, Ontario, was delayed (and later cancelled). "When people aren't hearing anything, they start making up rumours," says Kaufman's union president, who was receiving 15 to 20 calls per day.[67] Even when the formal network provides some information, employees will participate in the grapevine because social interaction relieves some of their anxiety.

GRAPEVINE ADVANTAGES AND DISADVANTAGES

Should the grapevine be encouraged, tolerated, or quashed? The difficulty in answering this question is that the grapevine has both advantages and disadvantages. One benefit is that the grapevine helps employees make sense of their workplace when the information is not available through formal channels.[68] It is also the main conduit through which organizational stories and other symbols of the organization's culture are communicated (see Chapter 16).

Along with its informational value, the grapevine is an important social process that bonds people together and fulfils their need for affiliation.[69] Finally, because it is most active when employees are worried, the grapevine is a valuable signal for corporate leaders to take appropriate action. This may include resolving the problems behind the rumours, or communicating more fully through formal networks.

The grapevine is not always beneficial. Morale tumbles when management is slower than the grapevine in communicating information, because it suggests a lack of sincerity and concern for employees. Moreover, grapevine information may become sufficiently distorted that it escalates rather than reduces employee anxieties. This is particularly true as the original information is transmitted through several people rather than by one or two people to several listeners.

What should companies do about the grapevine? Some executives try in vain to stop the grapevine, but it will always exist. A better strategy, as mentioned earlier, is to listen to the grapevine as a signal of employee anxiety, then correct the root cause of this anxiety. "In times of change, the company's rumour mill is working at a frenzied pitch," warns a CIBC executive in Toronto. "Being privy to rumours means you can clear up misinformation fast and replace speculation with fact."[70] Some organizations also treat the grapevine as a competitor against which their formal communication strategies are judged. However, with e-mail becoming the medium of choice for the rumour mill, it is very difficult to communicate faster than gossip!

CROSS-CULTURAL AND GENDER COMMUNICATION

In Chapter 1, we learned that organizations operate in a world of increasing globalization and cultural diversity. These dynamics bring new opportunities, as well as communication challenges. Employees must become more sensitive and competent in cross-cultural communication. They must also overcome their reluctance to communicate with co-workers from another cultural group. These communication competencies are also gaining importance as companies increasingly work with clients, suppliers, and joint venture partners from other countries.

Language is the most obvious cross-cultural barrier.[71] Words are easily misunderstood in verbal communication, either because the receiver has a limited vocabulary or because the sender's accent makes it difficult for the receiver to understand the sound. Some Canadian firms offer language skills training for people whose first language is not English or French. The issue is further complicated in global organizations where employees must share a common language. For example, it is increasingly common to find executives from several non-English countries discussing important matters in broken English.

Mastering the same language improves one dimension of cross-cultural communication, but problems may still occur when interpreting voice intonation.[72] A deep voice symbolizes masculinity in North America, but African men often express their emotions using a high-pitched voice. Middle Easterners sometimes speak loudly to show sincerity and interest in the discussion, whereas Japanese people tend to speak softly to communicate politeness or humility. These different cultural norms regarding voice loudness may cause one person to misinterpret the other.

NONVERBAL DIFFERENCES

Probably more serious than verbal communication is misunderstanding nonverbal communication across cultures. Nonverbal communication is more important in some cultures than in others. For example, people in Japan interpret more of a message's meaning from nonverbal cues. "A lot of Japanese is either unspoken or communicated through body language," explains Henry Wallace, the Scottish-born CEO of Mazda Corp. in Japan.[73]

To avoid offending or embarrassing the receiver (particularly outsiders), Japanese people will often say what the other person wants to hear (called *tatemae*) but send more subtle nonverbal cues indicating the sender's true feelings (called *honne*).[74] A Japanese colleague might politely reject your business proposal by saying, "I will think about that," while sending nonverbal signals that he or she is not really interested. This difference explains why Japanese employees may prefer direct conversation to e-mail and other media that lack nonverbal cues. "When you talk to someone in person, you can tell if there is real understanding," explains Chikako Lane, a Japanese-born manager at Calsonic North America, a subsidiary of the Nissan Group.[75]

Most nonverbal cues are specific to a particular culture and may have a completely different meaning to people raised in other cultures.[76] For example, Canadians shake their head from side to side to say "No," but this means "I understand" to some people from India. Filipinos raise their eyebrows to give an affirmative answer, yet Arabs interpret this expression (along with clicking one's tongue) as a negative response. Most Canadians are taught to maintain eye contact with the speaker to show interest and respect, yet some Native Canadians learn at an early age to show respect by looking down when an older or more senior person is talking to them.

Even the common handshake communicates different meaning across cultures. Canadians tend to appreciate a firm handshake as a sign of strength and warmth in a friendship or business relationship. In contrast, many Asians and Middle Easterners favour a loose grip and regard a firm clench as aggressive. Germans prefer one good handshake stroke, whereas anything less than five or six strokes may symbolize a lack of trust in Spain. If this isn't confusing enough, people from some cultures view any touching in public—including handshakes—as a sign of rudeness.

Silence and conversational overlaps

Communication includes the silence between our words and gestures. However, the meaning of silence varies from one culture to another. In Japan, people tend to remain silent for a few seconds after someone has spoken to contemplate what has just been said as a sign of respect.[77] To Japanese, silence is an important part of communication (called *haragei*) because it preserves harmony and is more reliable than talk. Silence is shared by everyone and belongs to no one, so it becomes the ultimate form of interdependence. Moreover, Japanese value empathy, which can only be demonstrated by understanding others without using words.

In contrast, most people in North America view silence as a *lack* of communication and often interpret long breaks as a sign of disagreement. For example, after presenting their proposal to a potential Japanese client, a group of North American consultants expected to be bombarded with questions. Instead, their proposal was greeted with a long silence. As the silence continued, most of the consultants concluded that the Japanese client disapproved, so they prepared to pack up and leave. But the lead consultant gestured them to stop, because the client's face and posture seemed to indicate interest rather than rejection. He was right: When the client finally spoke, it was to give the consulting firm the job.[78]

Conversational overlaps also send different messages in different cultures. Canadians usually stop talking when they are interrupted, whereas talking over the other person's speech is more common in Brazil and some other countries. The reason is that talking while someone is speaking to you is considered quite rude in Canada, whereas Brazilians are more likely to interpret this as the person's interest and involvement in the conversation. An American Coca-Cola executive discovered this at his first meeting in Puerto Rico. It seemed like everyone was talking at the same time, so the executive forced order to the meeting. However, it quickly became apparent that the Puerto Ricans were uncomfortable with the lack of conversational overlap when the executive's rules were applied.[79]

GENDER DIFFERENCES IN COMMUNICATION

Soon after Susan Herring joined her first Internet discussion group, she noticed that men were much more likely than women to engage in cantankerous debates with their own combative and condescending e-mail messages. To pique her curiosity, the linguistics professor asked list-group subscribers to tell her what they thought of these e-mail "flame wars." The anonymous and informal poll revealed that men generally accepted this communication style and usually found the barbs entertaining. Most women, on the other hand, were offended or cautious when these debates erupted.[80]

Herring and other scholars have observed that men and women often differ in their communication styles. Whether in a corporate meeting or a virtual chat room, men are more likely than women to view conversations as negotiations of relative status and power.[81] They assert their power by directly giving advice to others (e.g., "You should do the following") and using combative language. For instance, from a content analysis of e-mail messages in various discussion groups, Susan Herring found that 68 percent of messages written by men included criticisms, ridicule, or distancing of other participants, often while promoting the sender's own status. There is also evidence that men interrupt women far more often than vice versa and that they dominate the discussion time in conversations with women.

Men tend to engage in "report talk," in which the primary function of the conversation is impersonal and efficient information exchange. This may explain why men tend to quantify information (e.g., "It took us six weeks"). Women also engage in report talk, particularly when conversing with men. But conversations among women tend to have a higher incidence of relationship building through "rapport talk." Thus, women use more intensive adverbs ("I was *so happy* that he completed the report") and hedge their statements ("It seems to be…"). Rather than asserting status, women use indirect requests such as "Have you considered . . .?" Similarly, women apologize more often and seek advice from others more quickly than do men. Finally, research confirms that women are more sensitive than men to nonverbal cues in face-to-face meetings.[82]

After reading some popular books, you would think that men and women come from different planets (Mars and Venus) and require United Nations translators![83] This is not so. Although we have identified several differences, men and women mostly overlap in their verbal communication styles. Some men are very passive conversationalists, and some women are aggressive. Moreover, we know that women (and, to a less extent, men) vary their communication styles with the situation.

Both men and women usually understand each other, but there are irritants. For instance, Susan Herring and other women feel uncomfortable with aggressive male communication styles on the Internet. Female scientists in Canada have similarly complained that adversarial interaction among male scientists makes it difficult for women to participate in meaningful dialogue.[84]

Another irritant occurs when women seek empathy but receive male dominance in response. Specifically, women sometimes discuss their personal experiences and problems to develop closeness with the receiver. They look for expressions of understanding, such as "That's the way I felt when it happened to me." But when men hear problems, they quickly suggest solutions because this asserts their control over the situation. Not only does this frustrate a woman's need for common understanding, but also the advice actually says: "You and I are different; you have the problem and I have the answer." Meanwhile, men become frustrated because they can't understand why women don't appreciate their advice.

IMPROVING INTERPERSONAL COMMUNICATION

Effective interpersonal communication depends on the sender's ability to get the message across and the receiver's performance as an active listener. In this section, we outline these two essential features of effective interpersonal communication.

GETTING YOUR MESSAGE ACROSS

This chapter began with the statement that effective communication occurs when the other person receives and understands the message. To accomplish this difficult task, the sender must learn to empathize with the receiver, repeat the message, choose an appropriate time for the conversation, and be descriptive rather than evaluative.

> **Empathy** A person's ability to understand and be sensitive to the feelings, thoughts, and situations of others.

- *Empathize*—Recall from the previous two chapters that **empathy** is a person's ability to understand and be sensitive to the feelings, thoughts, and situations of others. In conversations, this involves putting yourself in the receiver's shoes when encoding the message. For instance, be sensitive to words that may be ambiguous or trigger the wrong emotional response.

- *Repeat the message*—Rephrase the key points a couple of times. The saying "Tell them what you're going to tell them; tell them; then tell them what you've told them" reflects this need for redundancy.

- *Use timing effectively*—Your message competes with other messages and noise, so find a time when the receiver is less likely to be distracted by these other matters.

- *Be descriptive*—Focus on the problem, not the person, if you have negative information to convey. People stop listening when the information attacks their self-esteem. Also, suggest things the listener can do to improve, rather than point to him or her as a problem.

ACTIVE LISTENING

Listening is at least as important as talking. As one sage wisely wrote: "Nature gave people two ears but only one tongue, which is a gentle hint that they should listen more than they talk."[85] But listening is more than just hearing the other person making sounds; it is a process of actively sensing the sender's signals, evaluating them accurately, and responding appropriately.

These three components of listening—sensing, evaluating, and responding—reflect the listener's side of the communication model described at the beginning of this chapter.[86]

Listeners receive the sender's signals, decode them as intended, and provide appropriate and timely feedback to the sender. Active listeners constantly cycle through sensing, evaluating, and responding during the conversation and engage in various activities to improve these processes (see Exhibit 8.7).

Sensing

Sensing is the process of receiving signals from the sender and paying attention to them. These signals include the words spoken, the nature of the sounds (speed of speech, tone of voice, etc.), and nonverbal cues. Active listeners improve sensing by postponing evaluation, avoiding interruptions, and maintaining interest.

- *Postpone evaluation*—Many listeners become victims of first impressions (see Chapter 6). They quickly form an opinion of the speaker's message and subsequently screen out important information. Active listeners try to stay as open-minded as possible and delay evaluation of the message until the speaker has finished.

- *Avoid interruptions*—Interrupting the speaker's conversation has two adverse effects on the sensing process. First, it disrupts the speaker's idea, so the listener does not receive the entire message. Second, interruptions tend to second-guess what the speaker is trying to say, so they support the problem of evaluating the speaker's ideas too early.

- *Maintain interest*—As with any behaviour, active listening requires motivation. Too often, we close our minds soon after a conversation begins because the subject is boring. Instead, active listeners maintain interest by taking the view—probably an accurate one—that there is always something of value in a conversation; it's just a matter of actively looking for it.

EXHIBIT 8.7   Components of Listening and Active Listening Strategies

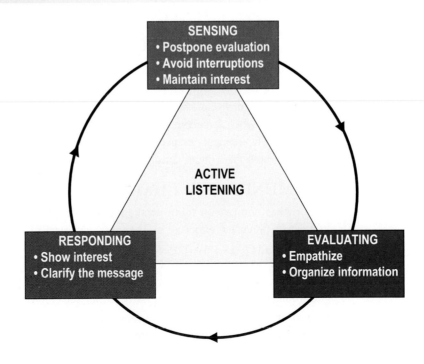

Evaluating

This component of listening includes understanding the message meaning, evaluating the message, and remembering the message. To improve their evaluation of the conversation, active listeners empathize with the speaker and organize information received during the conversation.

- *Empathize*—Active listeners try to understand and be sensitive to the speaker's feelings, thoughts, and situation. Empathy is a critical skill in active listening because the verbal and nonverbal cues from the conversation are accurately interpreted from the other person's point of view.

- *Organize information*—Listeners process information three times faster than the average rate of speech (450 words per minute versus 125 words per minute), so they are easily distracted. Active listeners use this spare time to organize the information into key points. In fact, it's a good idea to imagine that you must summarize what people have said after they have finished speaking.[87]

Responding

Responding, the third component of listening, refers to the listener's development and display of behaviours that support the communication process. Responsiveness is feedback to the sender, which motivates and directs the speaker's communication. Active listeners do this by showing interest and clarifying the message.

- *Show interest*—Active listeners show interest by maintaining sufficient eye contact and sending back channel signals such as "Oh, really!" and "I see" during appropriate breaks in the conversation.

- *Clarify the message*—Active listeners provide feedback by rephrasing the speaker's ideas at appropriate breaks ("So you're saying that...?"). This further demonstrates interest in the conversation and helps the speaker determine whether you understand the message.

PERSUASIVE COMMUNICATION: FROM UNDERSTANDING TO ACCEPTANCE

This chapter has focused mainly on how to get people to receive and understand messages. However, we usually want others to *accept* our information, not just *understand* it. People understand your message when they perceive the same meaning that you intended. They accept your message when it becomes part of their belief system and changes their opinions and behaviours. The elements of **persuasive communication** include characteristics of the communicator, message content, communication medium, and the audience being persuaded.[88]

Persuasive communication The process of having listeners accept rather than just understand the sender's message.

COMMUNICATOR CHARACTERISTICS

What makes one person more persuasive than another? One important factor is the communicator's perceived expertise on the topic. Listeners mainly consider the speaker's credentials and experience, but speech pattern also influences perceived expertise. Specifically, people seem to have expertise when they talk confidently and relatively quickly, use some technical language, and avoid pauses ("um," "uh") and hedges ("you know," "I guess").[89]

Communicators are more persuasive if they have credibility.[90] Thus, employees are more likely to accept a new policy if it is communicated and supported by a respected peer. Trustworthiness also exists when communicators do not seem to profit from the persuasion

www.compaq.ca

A recruiter at a computer company once asked David Booth why his résumé included work as a nightclub bouncer in Moncton, New Brunswick. "Hey, I'm not that big!" Booth replied. "If some great big guy is coming down on me, I'd rather talk him down than wrestle him." As CEO of Compaq Canada, Booth's persuasive communication skills have been used frequently since his days as a bouncer. One of the most memorable occasions occurred during his recent job at Compaq in the United States. Booth saw problems with the world's largest computer maker, so he wrote a letter to one of the company's board members. Booth had subverted the chain of command, but his letter was so convincing that he was given over $100 million to implement the changes he suggested.[91] In your opinion, what persuasive communication tactics are most effective for convincing aggressive customers to wait their turn in line?

attempt and state a few points against their position. For example, the effective persuader will acknowledge that an opposing position has one or two positive elements. Finally, people who are physically attractive or similar to us tend to be more persuasive because we tend to think that they have expertise and are trustworthy.[92]

MESSAGE CONTENT

We are persuaded more by the communicator's characteristics when we don't consider the issue to be extremely important. When the issue is important, however, the message content becomes the critical feature of persuasive communication. The best strategy is to present all sides of the argument. Begin by introducing facts sympathetic to the audience's viewpoint, then shift into the theme of your position. Discussing only one point of view reduces your perceived trustworthiness and gives listeners the feeling of being cornered. When this happens, they react by rejecting your information.[93]

Your message should be limited to a few strong arguments, because listeners are more likely to remember these points. These arguments should be repeated a couple of times, but not to the extent that you are battering listeners over the head with them.[94]

Is it better to be logical or emotional when communicating information? Generally, people should use both. Emotional appeals—such as graphically showing the unfortunate consequences of a bad decision—energize people, but they may also make them feel manipulated. Combining these emotional presentations with logical arguments tends to minimize this problem.[95] Also, emotional appeals should always be accompanied by specific recommendations to overcome the threat. In a safety campaign, for example, employees are more persuaded by graphic pictures of accident victims than by a lecture on recent accident statistics, but only if they are given explicit steps to avoid the danger.[96]

Finally, persuasive communicators use the **inoculation effect** to ensure that other points of view do not influence listeners. This involves warning listeners that others will try to influence them in the future and that they should be wary about the opponent's arguments. This inoculation effect causes listeners to generate counter-arguments to the anticipated attempts at persuasion. For instance, a coalition that wants the company to purchase new production equipment might warn senior management about arguments the finance department will use to try to convince them otherwise. This tends to make the finance department's subsequent persuasion attempts less effective.

> **Inoculation effect** A persuasive communication strategy of warning listeners that others will try to influence them in the future and that they should be wary about the opponent's arguments.

COMMUNICATION MEDIUM

Earlier in this chapter we recommended using two-way verbal communication to persuade or motivate the listener. The personal nature of this medium seems to increase the credibility of the information. Furthermore, it is easier for the sender to determine whether the persuasive message is having the desired effect. Two-way communication also increases the receiver's active participation in the process. As long as this participation does not involve presenting defensive statements, the receiver is more likely to be involved in the conversation and to internalize some of the information presented.

Persuasion may require written documentation, however, when dealing with technical issues. Whenever written communication is necessary for this purpose, it should be combined with direct discussions for the greatest persuasive effect. The verbal exchange could repeat highlights of the report and provide graphic images for the listener, thereby adding emotional appeal to an otherwise logical message.

AUDIENCE CHARACTERISTICS

Not everyone is equally persuaded by the strategies and conditions we have described. For example, it is more difficult to persuade people who have high self-esteem.[97] And, as mentioned above, it is very difficult to persuade those who have been inoculated against your persuasive intent.

One guiding piece of information that you should remember from this chapter is that communication is both essential and pervasive in organizational settings. Without communication, there would be no interaction and, consequently, no organizations. Communication affects how well people perform their jobs, how much stress they experience, how satisfied they are at work, and how well they work with others. As we will learn over the next few chapters, effective communication becomes even more important as companies increase their reliance on teams.

CHAPTER SUMMARY

- Communication supports knowledge management, decision making, work coordination, and the need for affiliation. The communication process involves forming, encoding, and transmitting the intended message to a receiver, who then decodes the message and provides feedback to the sender. Effective communication occurs when the sender's thoughts are transmitted to and understood by the intended receiver.

- Several barriers create noise in the communication process. People misinterpret messages because of misperceptions. Some information is filtered out as it gets passed up the hierarchy. Jargon and ambiguous language are barriers when the sender and receiver have different interpretations of the words and symbols used. People also screen out or misinterpret messages due to information overload.

- Electronic mail (e-mail) is a powerful way to communicate, and it has changed communication patterns in organizational settings. However, e-mail also contributes to information overload, tends to reduce politeness and respect in the communication process, is an ineffective channel for communicating emotions, and lacks the warmth of human interaction.

- Computer-mediated communication gives employees the freedom to communicate effectively from any location. This is part of the law of telecosm, which says that distances will shrink and eventually become irrelevant as electronic networks expand.

- Nonverbal communication includes facial gestures, voice intonation, physical distance, and even silence. Employees make extensive use of nonverbal cues when engaging in emotional labour because these cues help to transmit prescribed feelings to customers, co-workers, and others. Emotional contagion refers to the automatic and subconscious tendency to mimic and synchronize our nonverbal behaviours with other people.

- The most appropriate communication medium depends on its data-carrying capacity (media richness) and its symbolic meaning to the receiver. Nonroutine and ambiguous situations require rich media.

- Many organizations rely on workspace design, employee surveys, newsletters, and management by walking around to facilitate communication across the organization. In any organization, employees rely on the grapevine, particularly during times of uncertainty.

- Globalization and workforce diversity have brought new communication challenges. Words are easily misunderstood in verbal communication and employees are reluctant to communicate across cultures. Voice intonation, silence, and other nonverbal cues have different meaning and importance in other cultures. There are also some communication differences between men and women, such as the tendency for men to exert status and engage in report talk in conversations, whereas women use more rapport talk and are more sensitive than are men to nonverbal cues.

- To get a message across, the sender must learn to empathize with the receiver, repeat the message, choose an appropriate time for the conversation, and be descriptive rather than evaluative. Listening includes sensing, evaluating, and responding. Active listeners support these processes by postponing evaluation, avoiding interruptions, maintaining interest, empathizing, organizing information, showing interest, and clarifying the message.

- Persuasive communication tries to change behaviour by having listeners accept rather than just understand the message. Persuasive communicators have more perceived expertise and credibility. The message content should provide all sides of the argument, limit debate to a few strong points, repeat arguments a couple of times, combine emotional appeals with logical arguments, and inoculate the listener against opposing arguments. Two-way verbal communication is more persuasive than is written communication.

KEY TERMS

Communication, p. 220

Communication competence, p. 220

Emotional contagion, p. 230

Emotional labour, p. 230

Empathy, p. 240

Flaming, p. 227

Grapevine, p. 236

Hotelling, p. 233

Information overload, p. 224

Inoculation effect, p. 244

Jargon, p. 222

Knowledge management, p. 220

Law of telecosm, p. 229

Management by walking around (MBWA), p. 235

Media richness, p. 231

Persuasive communication, p. 242

DISCUSSION QUESTIONS

1. A Canadian city government intends to introduce electronic mail for office staff at its three buildings located throughout the city. Describe two benefits that the organization will likely experience from this medium as well as two potential problems that it may face.

2. Some cultures encourage people to be direct and precise when they communicate. Other cultures prefer more ambiguous language, even in business communication. Explain why ambiguous language may be desirable in the latter cultures and identify potential problems with ambiguity.

3. Marshall McLuhan coined the popular phrase "The medium is the message." What does this phrase mean, and why should we be aware of it when communicating in organizations?

4. Why is emotional contagion important in organizations and what effect does the increasing reliance on e-mail have on this phenomenon?

5. A Canadian executive recently admitted that she deliberately "leaks" information through the organizational grapevine before communicating the information through formal channels. The reason, she explains, is that this gives employees an opportunity to think about the information. "[B]y the time the message is formally announced, everybody has had a chance to think about it and feel like they're on the inside track." Discuss the advantages and limitations of this communication strategy.

6. The Bank of Western Ontario (BWO) has just moved into one of the tallest skyscrapers in the city. Senior management is proud of its decision, because each department is neatly located on its own floor with plenty of closed offices. BWO executives have a breathtaking view from their offices on the top floor. There is even a large BWO branch at street

level. Unfortunately, other tenants occupy some floors between those leased by BWO. Discuss the potential effects of this physical structure on communication at BWO.

7. Explain why men and women are sometimes frustrated with each other's communication behaviours.

8. This chapter makes several distinctions between communication in Japan and Canada. Discuss three distinctions between communication in these two cultures.

 Case Study

ACTIVITY 8.1
Sea Pines
By Terence P. Driscoll

The coastal town of Sea Pines, Nova Scotia, retained a Toronto consulting engineer to study the effect of greatly expanding the town's sewage system and discharging the treated waste into the harbour. At that time, fishermen in the town were experiencing massive lobster kills in the harbour and were concerned that the kills were caused by the effluent from the present Sea Pines sewage treatment plant. They were convinced that any expansion of the plant would further aggravate the problem. The fishermen invited Tom Stone, the engineer, to the monthly meeting of the local fishermen's organization to discuss their concerns. On the night of the meeting, the Legion Hall was filled with men in blue jeans and work jackets, many of whom were drinking beer. An account of the meeting follows, with Fred Mitchell, a local fisherman, speaking first.

Mitchell: Well, as you all know, Mr. Stone has been kind enough to meet with us tonight to explain his recommendations concerning the town's sewage disposal problem. We're all concerned about the lobster kills, like the one last summer, and I for one don't want to see any more sewage dumped into that harbour. [Murmurs of assent are heard throughout the hall.] So, Mr. Stone, we'd like to hear from you on what it is you want to do.

Stone: Thank you. I'm glad to have this opportunity to hear your concerns on the lobster situation. Let me say from the outset that we are still studying the problem closely and expect to make our formal recommenda-

tion to the town about a month from now. I am not prepared to discuss specific conclusions of our study, but I am prepared to incorporate any relevant comments into our study. As most of you are probably aware, we are attempting to model mathematically, or simulate, conditions in the harbour to help us predict the effects of sewage effluent in the harbour. We . . .

Mitchell: Now, wait a minute. I don't know anything about models except the kind I used to make as a kid. [Laughter.] I can tell you that we never had lobster kills like we have now until they started dumping that sewage into the harbour a few years back. I don't need any model to tell me that. It seems to me that common sense tells you that if we've got troubles now in the summer with the lobster, that increasing the amount of sewage by ten times the present amount is going to cause ten times the problem.

A fisherman: Yeah, you don't need to be an engineer to see that.

Stone: Although it's true that we're proposing to extend the sewage system in town, and that the resulting sewage flow will be about ten times the present flow, the location of the sewage discharge will be moved to a larger area of the harbour, where it will be diluted with much more sea water than is the present area. In addition, if the harbour is selected for the new discharge, we will design a special diffuser to mix the treated sewage effluent quickly with ocean water. As I indicated, we are attempting to use data on currents and water quality that we collected in the harbour and combine it with some mathematical equations in our computer to help us predict what the quality in the harbour will be.

ACTIVITY 8.1 CONTINUED

Mitchell: I don't understand why you need a computer to tell you that. I've been fishing in this area for over 35 years now, and I don't need any computer to tell me that my lobsters are going to die if that sewage goes into the harbour.

Stone: Let me say before this goes too far that we're not talking about discharging raw sewage into the harbour. The sewage is treated and disinfected before it is discharged.

Mitchell: Isn't the sewage that's being dumped into the harbour right now being treated and disinfected, Mr. Stone?

Stone: Yes, it is, but . . .

Mitchell: The lobsters still die, so it's clear to me that "treated and disinfected" doesn't solve the problem.

Stone: Our model will predict whether the treatment provided will be sufficient to maintain the water quality in the harbour at the province's standard for the harbour.

Mitchell: I don't give a damn about any provincial standard. I just care about my lobsters and how I'm going to put bread on the table for my kids! You engineers from Toronto can come out here spouting all kinds of things about models, data, standards, and your concern for lobsters, but what it really comes down to is that it's just another job. You can collect your fees for your study, go back to your office, and leave us holding the bag.

Stone: Now wait a minute, Mr. Mitchell. My firm is well established in Canada, and we didn't get that way by giving our clients that fast shuffle and making a quick exit out of town. We have no intention of leaving you with an unworkable solution to your sewage problems. We also will not solve your sewage problem and leave you with a lobster kill problem. Perhaps I have given you the wrong impression about this modelling. We regard this as one method of analysis that may be helpful in predicting future harbour conditions, but not the only method. We have over 40 years of experience in these harbour studies, and we fully intend to use this experience, *in addition to* whatever the model tells us, to come up with a reasonable solution.

Mitchell: Well, that's all well and good, but I can tell you, and I think I speak for all the lobstermen here, that if you recommend dumping that sewage into the harbour, we'll fight you all the way down the line! [Shouts of agreement.] Why can't you pipe the sewage out to the ocean if you're so concerned about dilution? I'm sure that your model will tell you there's enough dilution out there.

Stone: I agree that the ocean will certainly provide sufficient dilution, but the whole purpose of this study is to see if we can avoid a deep-ocean outfall.

Mitchell: Why?

Stone: Because the cost of constructing a deep-ocean outfall in this area is very expensive—say, about $500 per metre. Now, if the length of the outfall is 2000 metres, don't you think that it makes good sense to spend a few thousand dollars studying the harbour area if we can save you millions?

Mitchell: All that money that you're going to save the town doesn't do much for the lobstermen who'll be put out of business if that sewage goes into the harbour.

Stone: As I said, we wouldn't recommend that if we thought, based on our modelling and our experience in this area, that the quality of water in the harbour would kill the lobsters or any other aquatic life.

Mitchell: Well, I'm telling you again, if you try to put that stuff in our harbour, we'll fight you all the way. I think we've made our position clear on this thing, so if there are no further comments, I vote that we adjourn the meeting. [Seconded.]

When the meeting ended, the fishermen filed out, talking heatedly among themselves and leaving Mr. Stone standing on the platform.

Discussion Questions

1. What barriers to effective communication exist in this case? How would you overcome or minimize each of these barriers?

2. Use the model of persuasive communication to identify a more effective communication strategy that the engineering firm should consider.

Video Case Study

ACTIVITY 8.2
Cyberslacking

At work, do you spend just a little too much time looking at e-mail? Is it all work related? Or are you like the majority of e-mail users who receive the flood of junk mail, jokes, cartoons, animations, audio clips, and video clips?

Many companies across North America are finding that 75 percent of their employees' e-mail is non-work related. And not all the jokes are acceptable. Companies have been forced to set up workplace Internet policies, leading to some recent terminations. Recent surveys say that one-quarter of American businesses are monitoring e-mail.

This video program looks at the use and abuse of e-mail in the workplace. Video journalist Adam Little monitors his own e-mail for two months, and visits a few workplaces to find out what the fuss is all about.

Discussion Questions

1. Does nonwork-related e-mail offer any benefits to organizations?

2. In your opinion, should employee communication through e-mail be monitored by employers? If so, to what extent?

Source: Based on "Cyberslacking," *CBC Undercurrents* (July 2, 2000).

 **TEAM exercises**

ACTIVITY 8.3
TINKER TOY COMMUNICATION

Purpose: This exercise is designed to help you understand the importance of media richness and related issues that affect communicating effectively.

Materials: The instructor will provide each team with pieces from Tinker Toy, Lego, or Mega Blocks; straws; or other materials suitable for building. Each pair of teams must have identical pieces in shape, size, and colour. This activity works best with one room for each team in addition to the classroom. [Optional: One person on each team should have a working cellular telephone and be willing to use it during the exercise.]

Instructions:

Step 1: The instructor will divide the class into an even number of teams. Each team will have 4 to 5 students. The instructor might also choose some students to be observers. Each team is then paired with another team (e.g., Team 1A, Team 1B, Team 2A, Team 2B, etc.) and these paired teams receive an identical set of building materials. For example, Team 1A would have the same set of materials as Team 1B. Teams should check their materials to ensure that the paired team has identical pieces.

Step 2: The "A" team in each pair is moved to another room near the class while the "B" team remains in the classroom. Ideally, each team would be assigned to its own small tutorial room with paired teams located beside each other. In most classes, the instructor would have only two rooms, with one team from each pair in each room.

Step 3: Each "A" team builds a sculpture using all of the pieces in the material set. The instructor will provide a limited amount of time for this construction (about ten minutes). The "B" team is located in another room and must not observe this construction.

Step 4: This step involves one of two ways to communicate the sculpture to Team "B." The preferred method is for a representative from the "A" Team to telephone someone on the "B" Team and verbally describe the structure over the telephone. Only one person from each team may communicate, although the "B" Team communicator may convey the message to other "B" Team members, who are building the replicated structure. If cellular telephone communication is unavailable, one representative from each team will meet in a neutral location. The "B" Team representative cannot view the original structure and the "A" Team representative cannot view the replicated structure. However, the "B" Team representative may return to his or her group to collect more questions, and the "A" team representative may return to his or her group to recollect the sculpture's features. The instructor will limit the time for this communication activity (about 15 minutes).

Step 5: At the end of the exercise, each team may view the other team's sculpture. Better yet, if the structures are solid enough, they might be brought back to the classroom for comparison. The class will then discuss the factors that influence communication in this situation, including the importance of communication media, language, and perceptions.

Source: Based on a similar exercise described in C. Olofson, "Monster Board Has Fun," *Fast Company,* 16 (August 1998), p. 50.

ACTIVITY 8.4
A NOT-SO-TRIVIAL CROSS-CULTURAL COMMUNICATION GAME

Purpose: This exercise is designed to develop and test your knowledge of cross-cultural differences in communication and etiquette.

Instructions:

Step 1: The class is divided into an even number of teams. Ideally, each team would have three students. (Two or four student teams are possible if matched with an equal-sized team.) Each team is then matched with another team and the matched teams are assigned a private space away from other matched teams.

Step 2: The instructor will hand each pair of teams a stack of cards with the multiple choice questions face down. These cards have questions and answers about cross-cultural differences in communication and etiquette. No books or other aids are allowed.

Step 3: The exercise begins with a member of Team "A" picking up one card from the top of the pile and asking the question on that card to students on Team "B." The information given to Team "B" includes the question and all alternatives listed on the card. Team "B" has 30 seconds to give an answer and earns one point if the correct answer is given. If Team "B"'s answer is incorrect, however, Team "A" earns that point. Correct answers to each question are indicated on the card and, of course, should not be revealed until the question is correctly answered or the time is up. Whether Team "B" answers correctly or not, it picks up the next card on the pile and asks the question on it to members of Team "A". In other words, cards are read alternately to each team. This procedure is repeated until all of the cards have been read or the time has elapsed. The team that receives the most points wins.

Important note: The textbook provides very little information pertaining to the questions in this exercise. Rather, you must rely on past learning, logic, and luck to win.

© 2001 Steven L. McShane.

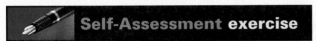

Self-Assessment **exercise**

ACTIVITY 8.5
ACTIVE LISTENING SKILLS INVENTORY

Purpose: This self-assessment is designed to help you estimate your strengths and weaknesses on various dimensions of active listening.

Instructions: Think back to face-to-face conversations you have had with a co-worker or client in the office, hallway, factory floor, or other setting. Indicate the extent to which each item below describes your behaviour during those conversations. Answer each item as truthfully as possible so that you can get an accurate estimate of where your active listening skills need improvement. Then use the scoring key in Appendix B of this book to calculate your results for each scale. This exercise is completed alone so students can assess themselves honestly without concerns of social comparison. However, class discussion will focus on the important elements of active listening.

ACTIVE LISTENING SKILLS INVENTORY

Circle the response that best indicates the extent to which each statement describes you when listening to others.					Score
1. I keep an open mind about the speaker's point of view until he or she has finished talking.	Not at all	A little	Somewhat	Very much	_____
2. While listening, I mentally sort out the speaker's ideas in a way that makes sense to me.	Not at all	A little	Somewhat	Very much	_____
3. I stop the speaker and give my opinion when I disagree with something he or she has said.	Not at all	A little	Somewhat	Very much	_____
4. People can often tell when I'm not concentrating on what they are saying.	Not at all	A little	Somewhat	Very much	_____

Circle the response that best indicates the extent to which each statement describes you when listening to others.

Score

5. I don't evaluate what a person is saying until he or she has finished talking. . . . .   Not at all   A little   Somewhat   Very much   ____

6. When someone takes a long time to present a simple idea, I let my mind wander to other things. . . . .   Not at all   A little   Somewhat   Very much   ____

7. I jump into conversations to present my views rather than wait and risk forgetting what I wanted to say. . . . .   Not at all   A little   Somewhat   Very much   ____

8. I nod my head and make other gestures to show that I'm interested in the conversation. . . . .   Not at all   A little   Somewhat   Very much   ____

9. I can usually stay focused on what people are saying to me even when they don't sound interesting. . . . .   Not at all   A little   Somewhat   Very much   ____

10. Rather than organizing the speaker's ideas, I usually expect the person to summarize them for me. . . . .   Not at all   A little   Somewhat   Very much   ____

11. I always say things like "I see" or "uh-huh" so people know that I'm really listening to them. . . . .   Not at all   A little   Somewhat   Very much   ____

12. While listening, I concentrate on what is being said and regularly organize the information. . . . .   Not at all   A little   Somewhat   Very much   ____

13. While the speaker is talking, I quickly determine whether I like or dislike his or her ideas. . . . .   Not at all   A little   Somewhat   Very much   ____

14. I pay close attention to what people are saying even when they are explaining something I already know. . . . .   Not at all   A little   Somewhat   Very much   ____

15. I don't give my opinion until I'm sure that the other person has finished talking. . . . .   Not at all   A little   Somewhat   Very much   ____

CHAPTER NINE

Team Dynamics

LEARNING OBJECTIVES

After reading this chapter, you should be able to:

- Define teams.
- Distinguish departmental teams from team-based organizations.
- Explain why virtual teams are becoming more common.
- Outline the model of team effectiveness.
- Identify six organizational and team environmental elements that influence team effectiveness.
- Explain the influence of the team's task, composition, and size on team effectiveness.
- Describe the five stages of team development.
- Identify four factors that shape team norms.
- List six factors that influence team cohesiveness.
- Discuss the limitations of teams.
- Explain how companies minimize social loafing.
- Summarize the four types of team building.

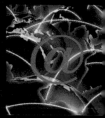

TRW Canada is one of Canada's most successful manufacturing plants, thanks to its reliance on teams to get the job done.

TRW Canada is a model of a team-based organization. Nestled in the quiet community of Tillsonburg, Ontario, the maker of automobile suspension components relies on self-directed work teams to almost completely operate its 20 cells (manufacturing processes). These teams are expected to think like a small business, and are given considerable autonomy to do so. TRW Canada still has supervisors, but they are removed from the traditional command-and-control jobs of the past. Instead, they serve as team advisers, operating as a link between team and management.

Each team is responsible for scheduling production, certifying skills, assigning daily jobs, hiring employees, managing materials, and training. Six coordinators on each team oversee these tasks as well as their normal production duties. For example, the team's training coordinator conducts an annual training needs analysis and works with the human resources group to enrol team members in training programs. A special plant-wide team evaluates the six coordinators on each team each year and rewards the team when all six coordinators pass an annual performance assessment.

TRW Canada's reliance on self-directed work teams is paying off. Over the past five years, the company has increased sales per employee by 179 percent and cut inventory and scrap costs by nearly 50 percent. *Industry Week* magazine recently recognized TRW Canada as one of North America's best manufacturing plants—the only Canadian plant to receive this distinction.

Employees also appreciate TRW Canada's team structure. "There's a certain excitement," explains Beth Penner, a member of the stabilizer link team. "We are much more involved in everyday decisions and feel much more part of a team."[1]

Teams are replacing individuals as the basic building blocks of organizations. TVA Group, Canada's largest producer and distributor of French-language television programs, has shifted to team-based projects and is giving more recognition to teams than to individuals. Bombardier relies on SWAT teams to solve quality problems, such as why the paint was peeling off its new Challenger jets. Dofasco is so focused on teams that it carefully selects applicants with team skills. "We're not just looking for technical ability," explains an executive at the Hamilton, Ontario, steel company. "We're [looking for people who can] work on teams and solve problems."[2]

Teams are groups of two or more people who interact and influence each other, are mutually accountable for achieving common objectives, and perceive themselves as a social entity within an organization.[3] All teams exist to fulfil some purpose, such as assembling a product, providing a service, playing a hockey game, or making an important decision. Team members are held together by their interdependence and need for collaboration to achieve common goals. All teams require some form of communication so members can coordinate and share common objectives. Team members also influence each other, although some members are more influential than others regarding the team's goals and activities.

All teams are **groups** because they consist of people with a unifying relationship. But not all groups are teams; some groups are just people assembled together.[4] For example, employees who meet for lunch are rarely called teams because they have no purpose beyond their

Team Groups of two or more people who interact and influence each other, are mutually accountable for achieving common objectives, and perceive themselves as a social entity within an organization.

Group Two or more people with a unifying relationship.

Credit: D. Chan, *Ottawa Citizen.*

Nortel Networks values teamwork. That's what Phuong Truong discovered when she joined Nortel's engineering group in Ottawa. Truong (shown here at Nortel's fitness centre) is part of a project team of 12 engineers who call themselves the Raptors. There's no particular reason for the name, except maybe that it sounds ferocious. Truong recruits new employees for the group and determines who would be an effective team member. She also volunteers as a member of the Employee Satisfaction team that communicates with senior management and employees about job concerns. "We have a big departmental discussion every month to tell us how the team is doing, find out where the team is going, what we are we doing next," explains Truong.[5] Why would Nortel Networks rely on teams rather than individuals to perform these tasks?

social interaction. Although the terms *group* and *team* are used interchangeably in this book, our main focus is on teams. This is partly because most of the discussion is about task-oriented teams rather than other types of groups, and partly because the term *team* has largely replaced *group* in the business language.[6]

This chapter looks at the dynamics and effectiveness of work teams as well as informal groups in organizations. After introducing the different types of teams in organizational settings, we present a model of team effectiveness. Most of the chapter examines each part of this model, including team and organizational environment, team design, and the team processes of development, norms, roles, and cohesiveness. The chapter concludes by surveying the strategies to build more effective work teams.

TYPES OF TEAMS AND OTHER GROUPS IN ORGANIZATIONS

There are many types of teams and other groups in organizations. Permanent work teams are responsible for a specific set of tasks in the organization. For instance, most departments are considered permanent teams because employees directly interact and coordinate work activities with each other (see Exhibit 9.1(a)).[7] Increasingly, employees with different skills work

---

EXHIBIT 9.1   Departments as Work Teams

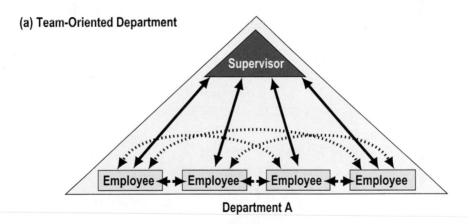

(a) Team-Oriented Department

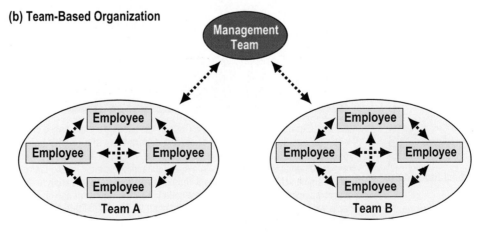

(b) Team-Based Organization

Team-based organization A type of departmentalization with a flat span of control and relatively little formalization, consisting of self-directed work teams responsible for various work processes.

Self-directed work team (SDWT) A work group that completes an entire piece of work requiring several interdependent tasks and that has substantial autonomy over the execution of these tasks.

together on work processes. Many Canadian hospitals have moved in this direction by forming surgical teams consisting of nurses, radiologists, anaesthetists, pharmacologists, and others. These people previously worked in departments based on their specialty. Now they work together on a specific work process.[8]

TRW Canada takes this team focus much further by forming a **team-based organization**. Team-based organizations rely extensively on **self-directed work teams (SDWTs)** organized around work processes rather than specialized departments as core work units.[9] These teams are fairly autonomous, as indicated by the dashed lines in Exhibit 9.1(b), so there is less need for direct supervision or someone to report continuously to the executive team. They are also *cross-functional*. This means that unlike traditional departments where employees have similar competencies (e.g., marketing, engineering), SDWTs rely on people with diverse and complementary skills, knowledge, and experience. SDWTs are described more fully in the next chapter because they represent the highest level of employee involvement.

Courtesy of Roberts Express.

Roberts Express (now Fedex Custom Critical) has become a team-based organization. Rather than divide employees into operations and customer service departments, the priority freight company organized them into 25 autonomous customer assistance teams (CATs). Each CAT has seven to nine people and is responsible for the entire customer service process in a specific geographic area. These teams arrange work hours, vacation days, and training schedules. The longest-running CATs also track and analyze their overhead costs. Supervisors have been replaced by facilitators who are called in by the teams for assistance. As the CATs become more comfortable with their roles, there has been less need for these facilitators.[10] What advantages would Roberts Express experience from this shift to a team-based organization?

customcritical.fedex.com

Employees often belong to secondary teams that parallel their more permanent positions in the organization. **Quality circles** fall into this category.[11] Quality circles are small teams of employees who meet for a few hours each week to identify quality and productivity problems, propose solutions to management, and monitor the implementation and consequences of these solutions in their work area. Quality circles are usually permanent, and typically include co-workers in the same work unit.

Along with permanent teams, organizations rely on temporary teams to make decisions or complete short-term projects. Companies bring together employees from various departments to design a product, solve a client's problem, or search for new opportunities.[12] *Task forces* (also called ad hoc teams) are temporary teams that investigate a particular problem and disband when the decision is made. For instance, Royal Dutch/Shell Group formed a cross-functional team to improve revenues for its service stations along major highways in Malaysia. This team, which included a service station dealer, a union truck driver, and four or five marketing executives, disbanded after it had reviewed the Malaysian service stations and submitted a business plan.[13]

SKUNKWORKS

Skunkworks are usually (but not always) temporary teams formed spontaneously to develop products or solve complex problems. They are initiated by an innovative employee (a *champion*) who borrows people and resources (called *bootlegging*) to help the organization.[14] Some skunkworks are isolated from the rest of the organization, and are able to ignore the more bureaucratic rules governing other organizational units. The earliest corporate intranets started as skunkworks, championed by employees with a UNIX computer and free software from universities used to create a Web server. Skunkworks are responsible for several innovations at 3M Corp. One example is a special micro-surface mouse pad that has become a commercial success. "Management had no idea the project was being worked on, until it was ready to be launched," explains a 3M executive. "Some lab, some manufacturing, and some marketing people got together as an informal team to do it."[15]

A skunkworks team helped make Vancouver-based Ballard Power Systems a global leader in fuel cell technology. Geoffrey Ballard, founder of Ballard Power Systems, wanted to develop a project to demonstrate the company's fuel cell technology in buses. Unfortunately, Ballard had stepped down as CEO of his company, and the current executives and board rejected his idea. Undaunted, Ballard proceeded with the project by borrowing people and resources throughout the company. The successful project proved crucial to Ballard Power's ability to attract DaimlerChrysler, Ford, and other partners.[16]

VIRTUAL TEAMS

Sitting in her Ottawa office, EDS Systemhouse executive Sue Ernst discusses a technical matter with Marvin Richardson in Minneapolis. Richardson replies right on cue, knowing almost instinctively when Ernst will finish. It's a skill that EDS Systemhouse employees have acquired through necessity. Few of Ernst's team members live in the same city, let alone the same office, so they communicate through e-mails and teleconferences. "We are a virtual team," says Ernst.[17]

Virtual teams are cross-functional groups that operate across space, time, and organizational boundaries with members who communicate mainly through electronic technologies.[18] Some groups become virtual teams when employees telecommute or communicate with team members while visiting clients. EDS Systemhouse and other firms also create virtual teams to leverage the best possible talent around the country or planet. Through communications technology, team members can participate in important decisions, yet remain on their home turf.

Quality circles Small teams of employees who meet for a few hours each week to identify quality and productivity problems, propose solutions to management, and monitor the implementation and consequences of these solutions in their work area.

Skunkwork A cross-functional team of employees borrowed from several functional areas of the organization to develop new products, services, or procedures, usually in isolation from the organization and without the normal restrictions.

Virtual teams Cross-functional teams that operate across space, time, and organizational boundaries with members who communicate mainly through electronic technologies.

Why are virtual teams becoming more common? Emerging communications technology has certainly facilitated their development. Recent evidence suggests that effective virtual teams creatively combine e-mail, videoconferencing, intranets, and other traditional electronic communication channels to suit their needs. They are not restricted to groupware.[19] Virtual teams leverage the law of telecosm; that is, they use technology to make distance less relevant by expanding the web of electronic networks (see Chapter 8).[20] The shift towards knowledge-based rather than production-based work has also made virtual teamwork feasible. Employees at EDS Systemhouse and other companies are able to complete knowledge-based tasks from a distance through information technology, whereas production-based work activities usually require co-location of team members.[21]

Technology and knowledge-based work make virtual teams *possible,* but globalization and the benefits of knowledge sharing and teamwork make them *necessary.* As we described in Chapter 1, globalization has become the new reality in many organizations. As companies open businesses overseas or form tight alliances with companies located elsewhere in the world, there is increasing pressure to form virtual teams that coordinate these operations. Virtual teams also leverage the benefits of team dynamics. They enable employees to collaborate and make potentially better decisions on complex issues.[22]

Lastly, virtual teams represent a natural extension of knowledge management because they minimize the "silos of knowledge" problem that tends to develop when employees are geographically scattered. In other words, virtual teams encourage employees to share and use knowledge where geography limits more direct forms of collaboration. Connections 9.1 provides two examples of the extent to which virtual teams can improve knowledge management.

www.waterford.com

CONNECTIONS 9.1

Virtual Teams Reshape the Corporate Landscape

Gordon Currie doesn't let a few kilometres get in the way of his business. Currie lives in Dawson Creek, British Columbia, but clients of his Web-design company are all based in the United States. What started out as a hobby 12 years ago is now a global business with clients that have included Virgin Records and Hitachi.

Currie's team members are even more geographically diverse than are his clients. "I currently have four [team members], and I have not met face to face with any of them," confides Currie. "I have one from Sweden, two from California, and one from Australia. I went out and hired them on the Net."

Gordon Currie is part of the cybersapce world of virtual teams. These people work together from a distance, often without meeting each other in person. Some never speak to each other, relying exclusively on e-mail or Web-based written communication. Yet corporate leaders are amazed at what can be accomplished.

Consider Waterford/Wedgwood, the fine crystal and china company that has offices in Ireland, England, and the United States. The company wanted to develop new china patterns by leveraging the expertise and creativity of employees at all three sites. It accomplished this by holding a series of virtual meetings via a videoconferencing system. "It's cut down on travel, we have better remote meetings, and it helps speed product development," says a Waterford/Wedgwood executive.

Sources: Adapted from A. Ford, "Web Ace Turns Hobby into Global Winner," *Vancouver Province,* February 15, 2000; J.C. McCune, "Working Together, but Apart," *Management Review,* 87 (September 1998), p. 45.

INFORMAL GROUPS

Informal group Two or more people who group together primarily to meet their personal (rather than organizational) needs.

Along with formal work teams, organizations consist of **informal groups** that exist primarily for the benefit of their members. Informal groups are not specifically formed by organizational decision makers, although their structure may be influenced by the existence of work teams. They shape communication patterns in the organization, particularly the grapevine described in Chapter 8. Informal groups can also interfere with the work team because members might resist team activities that conflict with the informal group's values. Some informal groups, such as the group you meet for lunch, might overlap with the work team. These groups form out of convenience and the need for affiliation. Other groups are bound together for reasons other than social needs. For instance, you might belong to an informal group that shares a car pool and another group that plays together on the company's sports team.

Coalition An informal group that attempts to influence people outside the group by pooling the resources and power of its members.

A **coalition** is an informal group that attempts to influence people outside the group by pooling the resources and power of its members. By banding together, coalition members have more power than if each person worked alone to influence others. They also reinforce each other and further mobilize support for their position.[23] The coalition's mere existence can be a source of power by symbolizing the importance or level of support for an issue.

Communities of practice Informal groups bound together by shared expertise and passion for a particular activity or interest.

Communities of practice are groups bound together by shared expertise and passion for a particular activity or interest.[24] Some communities are formally designed teams, but most are informal groups that congregate in person or cyberspace to share knowledge. People who have a common passion for environmental concerns, for example, might meet twice each month over lunch to share their knowledge. Other communities interact entirely through listservers and Web sites where participants exchange information on specific technical issues. Many communities of practice extend beyond organizational boundaries, so they represent a source of knowledge acquisition.

Why informal groups exist

One reason why people join informal groups is to fulfil their relatedness needs (see Chapter 3). We meet co-workers for lunch or stop by their work areas for brief chats because this activity satisfies our need for social interaction. Similarly, social identity theory (see Chapter 6) explains that we define ourselves by our group affiliations. If we belong to work teams or informal groups that are viewed favourably by others, we tend to view ourselves more favourably. We are motivated to become members of groups that are similar to ourselves because this reinforces our social identity.[25]

Some groups form because they accomplish tasks that cannot be achieved by individuals working alone. Coalitions and other task-oriented informal groups remain intact because members know they cannot achieve the same results alone. When groups are successful, it is easier to attract new members in the future. Lastly, informal groups tend to form in stressful situations because we are comforted by the physical presence of other people and are therefore motivated to be near them.[26] This explains why soldiers huddle together in battle, even though they are taught to disperse under fire. This also explains why employees tend to congregate when hearing the organization may be acquired or that some people may be laid off.

A MODEL OF TEAM EFFECTIVENESS

Team effectiveness
The extent to which the team achieves its objectives, achieves the needs and objectives of its members, and sustains itself over time.

Why are some teams more effective than others? This question has challenged organizational researchers for some time and, as you might expect, numerous models of team effectiveness have been proposed over the years.[27] **Team effectiveness** refers to how the team affects the organization, individual team members, and the team's existence.[28] First, most teams exist to serve some purpose relating to the organization or other system in which the group operates. As we read in the opening story of this chapter, production teams at TRW Canada in Tillsonberg, Ontario, take almost complete responsibility for the performance of their manufacturing cells. At Vancouver-based Great Little Box Company, teams are given the challenge of serving customers and improving quality. Some informal groups also have task-oriented goals, such as a coalition that wants to persuade senior management to change a corporate policy.

Second, team effectiveness considers the satisfaction and well-being of its members. People join groups to fulfil their personal needs, so it makes sense that effectiveness is partly measured by this need fulfilment. Finally, team effectiveness includes the team's viability—its ability to survive. It must be able to maintain the commitment of its members, particularly during the turbulence of the team's development. Without this commitment, people leave and the team will fall apart. It must also secure sufficient resources and find a benevolent environment in which to operate.

Exhibit 9.2 presents the model of team effectiveness that we will describe over the next several pages. We begin by looking at elements of the team's and organization's environment that influence team design, processes, and outcomes.

ORGANIZATIONAL AND TEAM ENVIRONMENT

Our discussion of team effectiveness logically begins with the contextual factors that influence the team's design, processes, and outcomes. Many elements in the organizational and team environment influence team effectiveness. Six of the most important elements are reward systems, communication systems, physical space, organizational environment, organizational structure, and organizational leadership.

*   *Reward systems*—Reward systems must be consistent with team dynamics.[29] Team members can still receive some pay based on individual performance, but team-based rewards

---

EXHIBIT 9.2   A Model of Team Effectiveness

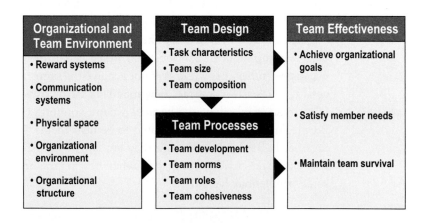

support the interdependence of effective teams. For instance, Coats Viyella Clothing Menswear, the Northern Ireland manufacturer of shirts, improved team dynamics by changing its reward system from individual incentive to fixed wage and team productivity bonus.[30]

- *Communications systems*—A poorly designed communication system can starve a team of valuable information and feedback, or it may swamp it with information overload.[31] Virtual teams particularly require the right combination of communication technologies. Communications are also important when team members are located together. Physical space might be arranged to encourage more face-to-face dialogue. In each of these cases, the team's communication systems are aligned with its task and structure.

- *Physical space*—The layout of an office or factory does more than improve communications among team members. It also influences the team's ability to accomplish tasks and shapes employee perceptions about being together as a team. That's why Trojan Technologies Inc. in London, Ontario, chose a building and furniture that allows teams to organize quickly and communicate effectively. "Nothing gets built without a team and office design needs to facilitate teamwork," explains Trojan president Hank Vander Laan.[32]

- *Organizational environment*—Team success depends on the company's external environment. If the organization cannot secure resources, for instance, the team cannot fulfil its performance targets. Similarly, high demand for the team's output creates feelings of success, which motivates team members to stay with the team. A competitive environment can motivate employees to work together more closely.

- *Organizational structure*—Many teams fail because the organizational structure does not support them. Teams work better when there are few layers of management and teams are given autonomy and responsibility for their work. This structure encourages interaction with team members rather than with supervisors. Teams also flourish when employees are organized around work processes rather than specialized skills. This structure increases interaction among team members.[33]

- *Organizational leadership*—Teams require ongoing support from senior executives to align rewards, organizational structure, communication systems, and other elements of team context.[34] Leaders also maintain a value system that supports team performance more than individual success.

TEAM DESIGN FEATURES

Putting together a team is rather like designing a mini-organization. There are several elements to consider, and the wrong combination will undermine team effectiveness. Three of the main structural elements to consider when designing teams are task characteristics, team size, and team composition. As we saw earlier in the team effectiveness model (Exhibit 9.2), these design features affect team effectiveness directly as well as indirectly through team processes. For example, the skills and diversity of team members affect team cohesiveness, but they also have a direct effect on how well the team performs its task. Similarly, the type of work performed by the team (task characteristics) may influence the types of roles that emerge, but it also has a direct effect on the satisfaction and well-being of team members.

TASK CHARACTERISTICS

Teams are generally more effective when tasks are clear and easy to implement, because team members can learn their roles more quickly.[35] In contrast, teams with ill-defined tasks require more time to agree on the best division of labour and the correct way to accomplish the goal. These are typically more complex tasks requiring diverse skills and backgrounds, which further strain the team's ability to develop and form a cohesive unit.

> • **Task interdependence**
> The degree to which a task requires collective action. High task interdependence exists when team members must share inputs or outcomes, or need to interact while executing their work.

Another important task characteristic is **task interdependence**. High task interdependence exists when team members must share common inputs to their individual tasks, need to interact in the process of executing their work, or receive outcomes (such as rewards) that are partly determined by the performance of others. Teams are well suited to highly interdependent tasks because people coordinate better when working together rather than separately. Moreover, recent evidence indicates that task interdependence creates an additional sense of responsibility among team members that motivates them to work together rather than alone.[36] This is why TRW Canada, described at the beginning of this chapter, organizes employees around work processes. Each cell includes highly interdependent tasks, so the multi-skilled team coordinates the work more efficiently than individuals working in specialized departments.

TEAM SIZE

Microsoft is a large organization with large development projects, yet it likes to think small about its teams. For example, most of the 450 people who worked on Microsoft's successful Windows NT operating system were assigned to small subteams with no more than ten peo-

Jonathan Player/NYT Pictures

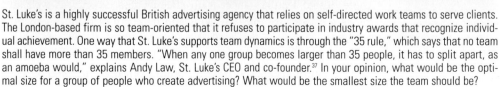

St. Luke's is a highly successful British advertising agency that relies on self-directed work teams to serve clients. The London-based firm is so team-oriented that it refuses to participate in industry awards that recognize individual achievement. One way that St. Luke's supports team dynamics is through the "35 rule," which says that no team shall have more than 35 members. "When any one group becomes larger than 35 people, it has to split apart, as an amoeba would," explains Andy Law, St. Luke's CEO and co-founder.[37] In your opinion, what would be the optimal size for a group of people who create advertising? What would be the smallest size the team should be?

www.stlukes.co.uk

ple responsible for a specific element. Through effective synchronization of these teams, Microsoft takes advantage of team dynamics without the coordination, cohesiveness, and communication problems that exist in large groups.[38]

Some writers claim that Microsoft is following the right strategy by limiting team size to ten people or less.[39] However, the optimal team size depends on several factors, such as the number of people required to complete the work and the amount of coordination needed to work together. The general rule is that teams should be large enough to provide the necessary competencies and perspectives to perform the work, yet small enough to maintain efficient coordination and meaningful involvement of each member.[40] Larger teams are typically less effective because members consume more time and effort coordinating their roles and resolving differences. Individuals have less opportunity to participate and, consequently, are less likely to feel that they are contributing to the team's success. Larger work units tend to break into informal subgroups around common interests and work activities, leading members to form stronger commitments to their subgroup than to the larger team.

TEAM COMPOSITION

Steve Currie vividly recalls his job interview at the Flight Centre travel agency in Toronto. After an initial telephone screening, Currie and about 30 other applicants attended a session where groups of four applicants were given several challenges. One task was to figure out how to survive on a desert island after a shipwreck. After lunch, candidates who performed well on these role-play exercises were given formal interviews.[41]

Flight Centre travel agency has a strong team orientation, so it carefully selects people with the necessary motivation *and* competencies to work together. With respect to motivation, every member must have sufficient drive to perform the task in a team environment. Specifically, team members must be motivated to agree on the goal, work together rather than alone, and abide by the team's rules of conduct. Employees with a collectivist orientation—those who value group goals more than their own personal goals (see Chapter 7)—tend to perform better in work teams, whereas those with a strong individualist orientation tend to perform better alone.[42]

Employees must possess the skills and knowledge necessary to accomplish the team's objectives.[43] Each person needs only some of the necessary skills, but the entire group must have the full set of competencies. Moreover, each team member's competencies need to be known to other team members. Along with these task competencies, team members must be able to work effectively with others. They must have sufficient emotional intelligence (see Chapter 7) to manage emotions, as well as conflict management skills to effectively resolve interpersonal differences.

How do companies ensure that employees have the ability and motivation to work in teams? Team-based reward systems can motivate employees to work with the team rather than focus on individual effort. However, it is often easiest to hire people at the outset who possess team-oriented competencies and values. Flight Centre travel agency conducts special group hiring sessions that identify people with team skills. Anchor Hocking, the glass and plastic kitchenware manufacturer, also has applicants complete a project in teams while evaluators identify those who work best in a team environment. Candidates also write an essay on what a team environment means to them.[44]

Team diversity

Another important dimension of team composition is the diversity of team members.[45] **Homogeneous teams** include members with common technical expertise, demographics

Homogeneous teams Formal or informal groups whose members have similar technical expertise, ethnicity, experiences, or values.

Heterogeneous teams Formal or informal groups whose members have diverse personal characteristics and backgrounds.

(age, gender), ethnicity, experiences, or values, whereas **heterogeneous teams** have members with diverse personal characteristics and backgrounds. Heterogeneous teams experience more conflict and take longer to develop. They are susceptible to "faultlines"—hypothetical dividing lines that may split a team into subgroups along gender, ethnic, professional, or other dimensions. In some situations, these faultlines may eventually split the team apart.[46] In contrast, members of homogeneous teams experience higher satisfaction, less conflict, and better interpersonal relations. Consequently, homogeneous teams tend to be more effective on tasks requiring a high degree of cooperation and coordination, such as emergency response teams or music groups.

Although heterogeneous teams are more difficult to develop, they are generally more effective than homogeneous teams on complex projects and problems requiring innovative solutions.[47] This is because people from different backgrounds see a problem or opportunity from different perspectives. Heterogeneous team members also solve complex problems more easily because they usually have a broader knowledge base. Finally, a team's diversity may give it more legitimacy or allow its members to obtain a wide network of cooperation and support in the organization.

Team composition, team size, and task characteristics affect team effectiveness directly as well as indirectly through team processes. The four team processes identified earlier in the team effectiveness model (Exhibit 9.2) include team development, team norms, team roles, and team cohesiveness.

TEAM DEVELOPMENT

Our discussion so far has presented two sets of elements in the team effectiveness model: (1) organizational and team environment and (2) team design. The next few pages introduce the third set of elements, collectively known as team processes. These processes—team development, norms, roles, and cohesiveness—are influenced by both team design and organizational and team environment factors.

Team members must resolve several issues and pass through several stages of development before emerging as an effective work unit. They must get to know each other, understand their respective roles, discover appropriate and inappropriate behaviours, and learn how to coordinate their work or social activities. This is an ongoing process because teams change as new members join and old members leave. The five-stage model of team development, shown in Exhibit 9.3, provides a general outline of how teams evolve by forming, storming, norming, performing, and eventually adjourning.[48] The model shows teams progressing from one stage to the next in an orderly fashion, but the dotted lines also illustrate that they might fall back to an earlier stage of development as new members join or other conditions disrupt the team's maturity.

1. *Forming*—The first stage of team development is a period of testing and orientation in which members learn about each other and evaluate the benefits and costs of continued membership. People tend to be polite during this stage and will defer to the existing authority of a formal or informal leader who must provide an initial set of rules and structures for interaction. Members experience a form of socialization (described in Chapter 18) as they try to find out what is expected of them and how they will fit into the team.

2. *Storming*—The storming stage is marked by interpersonal conflict as members become more proactive and compete for various team roles. Coalitions may form to influence

EXHIBIT 9.3   Stages of Team Development

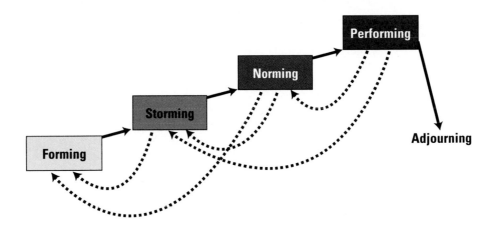

the team's goals and means of goal attainment. Members try to establish norms of appropriate behaviour and performance standards. This is a tenuous stage in the team's development, particularly when the leader is autocratic and lacks the necessary conflict-management skills.

3. *Norming*—During the norming stage, the team develops its first real sense of cohesion as roles are established and a consensus forms around group objectives. Members have developed relatively similar mental models, so they have common expectations and assumptions about how the team's goals should be accomplished.[49] This common knowledge structure allows them to interact more efficiently so they can move into the next stage, performing.

4. *Performing*—The team becomes more task-oriented in the performing stage. Team members have learned to coordinate and resolve conflicts more efficiently. Further coordination improvements must occasionally be addressed, but the greater emphasis is on task accomplishment. In high-performance teams, members are highly cooperative, have a high level of trust in each other, are committed to group objectives, and identify with the team. There is a climate of mutual support in which team members feel comfortable about taking risks, making errors, or asking for help.[50]

5. *Adjourning*—Most work teams and informal groups eventually end. Task forces disband when their project is completed. Informal work groups may reach this stage when several members leave the organization or are reassigned elsewhere. Some teams adjourn as a result of layoffs or plant shutdowns. Whatever the cause of team adjournment, members shift their attention away from task orientation to a socio-emotional focus as they realize that their relationship is ending.

The team development model is a useful framework for thinking about how teams develop. At the same time, we must keep in mind that it is not a perfect representation of the dynamics of team development.[51] The model does not explicitly show that some teams remain in a particular stage longer than others do, and that team development is a continuous process. As membership changes and new conditions emerge, teams cycle back to earlier stages in the developmental process to regain the equilibrium or balance lost by the change (as shown by the dotted lines in Exhibit 9.3).

TEAM NORMS

• **Norms** Informal rules and expectations that groups establish to regulate the behaviour of their members.

Have you ever noticed how employees in some departments almost run for the exit door the minute the workday ends, whereas people in the same jobs elsewhere almost seem to compete for who can stay at work the longest? These differences are partly due to **norms**—the informal rules and expectations that groups establish to regulate the behaviour of their members. Norms apply only to behaviour, not to private thoughts or feelings. Moreover, norms exist only for behaviours that are important to the team.[52]

Norms guide the way team members deal with clients, how they share resources, whether they are willing to work longer hours, and much other behaviour in organizational life. Some norms ensure that employees support organizational goals, whereas other norms might conflict with organizational objectives. For example, the level of employee absence from work is partly influenced by absence norms in the workplace. In other words, employees are more likely to take time off if they work in teams that support this behaviour.[53]

CONFORMITY TO TEAM NORMS

Everyone has experienced peer pressure at one time or another.[54] Co-workers grimace if we are late for a meeting or make sarcastic comments if we don't have our part of the project completed on time. In more extreme situations, team members may try to enforce their norms by temporarily ostracizing deviant co-workers or threatening to terminate their membership.

Norms are also directly reinforced through praise from high-status members, more access to valued resources, or other rewards available to the team.[55] But team members often conform to prevailing norms without direct reinforcement or punishment because they identify with the group and want to align their behaviour with the team's values. This effect is particularly strong in new members because they are uncertain of their status and want to demonstrate their membership in the team.

The power of conformity to team norms is revealed in the classic study of a pyjama factory employee assigned to work with a small group of pressers.[56] The group had informally established a norm that 50 units per hour was the upper limit of acceptable output. As Exhibit 9.4 illustrates, the newcomer quickly reached this level and soon began to exceed it. By Day 12, co-workers were making sarcastic remarks about her excessive performance, so the employee reduced her output to a level acceptable to the team. On Day 20, the work group was disbanded and everyone except the new employee was transferred to other jobs. With the others gone and the team norm no longer in effect, the employee's performance in the pressing room nearly doubled within a few days. For the next 20 days, she maintained a performance level of 92 units per hour compared with 45 units in the presence of co-workers.

HOW TEAM NORMS DEVELOP

Norms develop as team members learn that certain behaviours help them function more effectively.[57] Some norms develop when team members or outsiders make explicit statements that seem to aid the team's success or survival. For example, the team leader might frequently express the importance of treating customers with respect and courtesy. A second factor triggering the development of a new norm is a critical event in the team's history. A team might develop a strong norm to keep the work area clean after a co-worker slips on metal scraps and seriously injures herself.

Team norms are most strongly influenced by events soon after the team is formed.[58] Future behaviours are influenced by the way members of a newly formed team initially greet each

EXHIBIT 9.4   Influence of Team Norms on Individual Behaviour

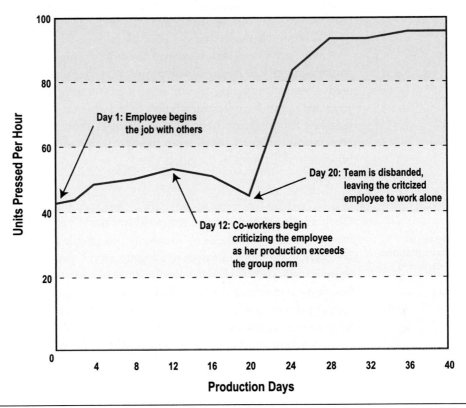

Source: Based on information in L. Coch and J.R.P. French, Jr., "Overcoming Resistance to Change," *Human Relations*, 1 (1948), pp. 512–32.

other, where they locate themselves in a meeting, and so on. A fourth influence on team norms is the beliefs and values that members bring to the team. For example, bargaining groups develop norms about appropriate bargaining behaviour based on each member's previous bargaining experience.[59]

TROUBLESHOOTING DYSFUNCTIONAL TEAM NORMS

Although many team norms are deeply anchored, there are ways to change or make them less influential on employee behaviour. One approach is to introduce performance-oriented norms as soon as the team is created. Another strategy is to select members who will bring desirable norms to the group. If the organization wants to emphasize safety, it should select team members who already value safety.

Selecting people with positive norms may be effective in new teams, but not when adding new members to existing teams with counterproductive norms. A better strategy for existing teams is to explicitly discuss the counterproductive norm with team members using persuasive communication tactics (see Chapter 8).[60] For example, the surgical team of a small Ontario hospital had developed a norm of arriving late for operations. Patients and other hospital staff often waited 30 minutes or more for the team to arrive. The hospital CEO eventually spoke to the surgical team about its lateness and, through moral suasion, convinced team members to arrive for operating room procedures no more than five minutes late.[61]

Team-based reward systems can sometimes weaken counterproductive norms. Unfortunately, the pressure to conform to the counterproductive norm is sometimes stronger than the financial incentive.[62] For instance, employees working in the pajama factory described earlier were paid under a piece rate system. Most individuals in the group were able to process more units and thereby earn more money, but they all chose to abide by the group norm of 50 units per hour.

Finally, a dysfunctional norm may be so deeply ingrained that the best strategy is to disband the group and replace it with people who have more favourable norms. This strategy is used at Sony's PlayStation division when a project team fails. "When you terminate a project, you have to break up the team," explains a Sony executive. "Failure usually means that the team dynamics weren't working."[63] Companies should seize the opportunity to introduce performance-oriented norms when the new team is formed, and select members who will bring desirable norms to the group.

TEAM ROLES

Role The set of behaviours that people are expected to perform because they hold certain positions in a team and organization.

Every work team and informal group has two sets of roles that help it to survive and be more productive. A **role** is the set of behaviours that people are expected to perform because they hold certain positions in a team and organization.[64] One set of roles helps focus the team on its objectives, such as giving and seeking information, elaborating ideas, coordinating activities, and summarizing the discussion or past events (see Exhibit 9.5). The other set of roles tries to maintain good working relations among team members. These relationship-oriented roles include resolving conflicts among team members, keeping communication channels open, reinforcing positive behaviours of other team members, and making team members aware of group process problems when they emerge.

Some team roles are formally assigned to specific people. For example, team leaders are usually expected to initiate discussion, ensure that everyone has an opportunity to present their views, and help the team reach agreement on the issues discussed. But team members often take on various roles informally. Some people like to encourage colleagues to participate more actively. Others prefer to mediate conflicts that may arise among team members. As noted earlier, these preferences are usually worked out during the storming stage of team development. The critical point is that team members need to ensure that these roles are fulfilled so that the team can function effectively.

TEAM COHESIVENESS

Team cohesiveness The degree of attraction people feel towards the team and their motivation to remain members.

Team cohesiveness—the degree of attraction people feel towards the team and their motivation to remain members—is usually an important factor in a team's success.[65] Employees feel cohesiveness when they believe that the team will help them achieve their personal goals, fulfil their need for affiliation or status, or provide social support during times of crisis or trouble. Cohesiveness is an emotional experience, not just a calculation of whether to stay or leave the team. It exists when team members make the team part of their social identity (see Chapter 6). Cohesiveness is the glue or *esprit de corps* that holds the group together and ensures that its members fulfil their obligations.[66]

CAUSES OF TEAM COHESIVENESS

The main factors influencing team cohesiveness are identified in Exhibit 9.6. For the most part, these factors reflect the individual's identity with the group and beliefs about how team membership will fulfil personal needs.[67] Several of these factors are related to our

EXHIBIT 9.5   Roles for Team Effectiveness

Role Activities	Description	Example
Task-Oriented Roles		
Initiator	Identifies goals for the meeting, including ways to work on goals.	"The main purpose of this meeting is to solve the problem our client is having with this product."
Information seeker	Asks for clarification of ideas or further information to support an opinion.	"Jang, why do you think the client is using the product incorrectly?"
Information giver	Shares information and opinions about the team's task and goals.	"Let me tell you what some of my clients did to overcome this problem…"
Coordinator	Coordinates subgroups and pulls together ideas.	"Susan, will you be meeting with Shaheem's group this week to review common issues with the client?"
Evaluator	Assesses the team's functioning against a standard.	"So far, we have resolved three of the client's concerns, but we still have a tough one to wrestle with."
Summarizer	Acts as the team's memory.	Person takes notes of meetings and summarizes the discussion when requested.
Orienter	Keeps the team focused on its goals.	"We seem to be going off on a tangent; let's focus on why the product isn't operating properly for our client."
Relationship-Oriented Roles		
Harmonizer	Mediates intragroup conflicts and reduces tension.	"Courtney, you and Brad may want to look at your positions on this; they aren't as different as they seem."
Gatekeeper	Encourages and facilitates participation of all team members.	"James, what do you think about this issue?"
Encourager	Praises and supports the ideas of other team members, thereby showing warmth and solidarity to the group.	"Tracy, that's a wonderful suggestion. I think we will solve the client's problem sooner than we expected."

Sources: Adapted from information in K.D. Benne and P. Sheats, "Functional Roles of Group Members," *Journal of Social Issues*, 4 (1948), pp. 41–49.

EXHIBIT 9.6   Factors Contributing to Team Cohesiveness

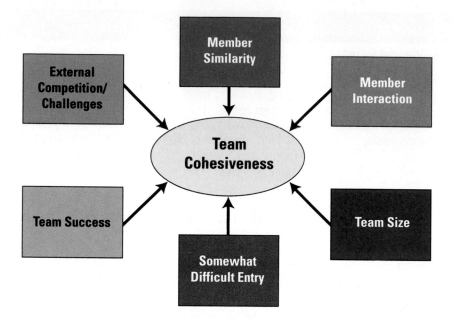

earlier discussion about why people join informal groups and how teams develop. Specifically, teams become more cohesive as they reach higher stages of development and are more attractive to potential members.

Member similarity

Homogeneous teams become cohesive more easily than heterogeneous teams. People in homogeneous teams have similar backgrounds and values, so they find it easier to agree on team objectives, the means to fulfil those objectives, and the rules applied to maintain group behaviour. This, in turn, leads to greater trust and less dysfunctional conflict within the group.[68] In contrast, diverse teams are susceptible to the previously described "faultlines" that psychologically impede cohesiveness, particularly during the early stages of development. The dilemma here is that heterogeneous teams are usually better than homogeneous teams at completing complex tasks or solving problems requiring creative solutions.

Team size

Smaller teams tend to be more cohesive than larger teams because it is easier for a few people to agree on goals and coordinate work activities. This does not mean that the smallest teams are the most cohesive, because not having enough members prevents the team from accomplishing its objectives. Continued failure may undermine the cohesiveness as members begin to question the team's ability to satisfy their needs. Thus, team cohesiveness is potentially greatest when teams are as small as possible, yet large enough to accomplish the required tasks.

Member interaction

Teams tend to be more cohesive when team members interact with each other fairly regularly. This occurs when team members perform highly interdependent tasks and work in the same

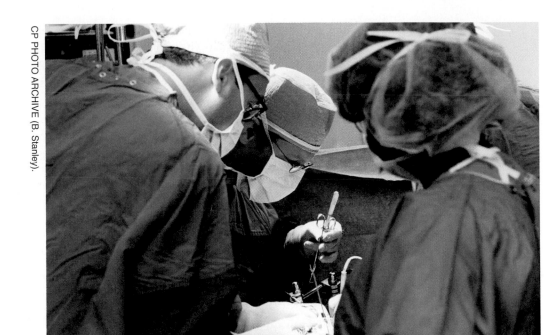

This surgical team performing a cancer operation at Vancouver General Hospital is probably a highly cohesive group. The team is small, separated from other teams, has members with similar backgrounds, and has a high level of interaction. Under the direction of Dr. Martin Gleave (centre), the team's relatively high success rate also motivates these people to remain members of the team. Would these factors also contribute to team cohesiveness in a financial investment team?

www.bccancer.bc.ca/research/
endo/People/gleave.htm
www.vanhosp.bc.ca

physical area.[69] As we noted earlier, Trojan Technologies in London, Ontario, has strengthened team cohesiveness by providing office space and furniture that allows employees to quickly form teams in the same physical area. Owens Corning has also designed new headquarters that supports team dynamics. "Today I'm not at the end of a row of offices," says an executive at the fibreglass and building materials manufacturer. "I'm in the middle of the team."[70]

The effect of physical proximity on team cohesiveness raises questions about how to maximize cohesiveness in virtual teams. The lack of face-to-face interaction makes it difficult for team members to feel a common bond, even when they work effectively over the Internet. One recent study reported that members of virtual teams establish a greater social connection when they have some opportunity to meet face to face. The ability to "put a face" to remote colleagues seems to strengthen the individual's emotional bond to the team. This problem may be worse for telecommuting employees who belong to a team that works in the same physical space. In the long run, these distant workers may feel left out of an otherwise cohesive team.[71]

Somewhat difficult entry

Teams tend to be more cohesive when it is *somewhat* difficult to become a member. Notice the emphasis on the word *somewhat*—severe initiations can do more damage than good with regards to bonding the individual to the group. Severe initiations, such as the cruel hazing rituals discovered in the Canadian Armed Forces' Airborne Regiment, can lead to humiliation and psychological distance from the group, even when a member successfully "passes" the initiation. Somewhat difficult entry, on the other hand, challenges recruits to the team without distancing them. For example, applicants tend to become more cohesive when they must pass through several interviews and selection tests before being accepted into the group. When entry to the team is somewhat difficult, teams are perceived as more prestigious to those within and outside of the team. Existing team members are also more willing to welcome and support new members after they have "passed the test," possibly because they have shared the same entry experience.[72]

Team success

Cohesiveness increases with the team's level of success.[73] Individuals are more likely to attach their social identity to successful teams than to those with a string of failures. Moreover, team members are more likely to believe that the group will continue to be successful, thereby fulfilling their personal goals (continued employment, pay bonus, etc.). Team leaders can increase cohesiveness by regularly communicating and celebrating the team's successes. Notice that this can create a spiral effect. Successful teams are more cohesive and, under certain conditions, increased cohesiveness increases the team's success.

External competition and challenges

Team cohesiveness increases when members face external competition or a valued objective that is challenging. This might include the threat from an external competitor or friendly competition from other teams. These conditions tend to increase cohesiveness because employees value the team's ability to overcome the threat or competition if they can't solve the problem individually. They also value their membership as a form of social support. We need to be careful about the degree of external threat, however. Evidence suggests that teams seem to be less effective when external threats are severe.[74] Although cohesiveness tends to increase, external threats are stressful and cause teams to make less effective decisions.

CONSEQUENCES OF TEAM COHESIVENESS

Every team must have some minimal level of cohesiveness to maintain its existence.[75] People who belong to high-cohesion teams are motivated to maintain their membership and to help the team work effectively. They are generally more sensitive to each other's needs and develop better interpersonal relationships, thereby reducing dysfunctional conflict. When conflict does arise, members of high-cohesion teams seem to resolve these differences swiftly and effectively. Compared to members of low-cohesion teams, high-cohesion team members spend more time together, share information more frequently, and are more satisfied with each other. They provide each other with better social support in stressful situations.[76] This is apparent in Connections 9.2, where co-workers play pranks on fellow team members as a way of showing support and empathy.

Cohesiveness and team performance

With better cooperation and more conformity to norms, high-cohesion teams usually perform better than low-cohesion teams.[77] However, the relationship is a little more complex. As we see in Exhibit 9.7, the extent to which cohesiveness results in higher team performance depends on the extent to which team norms are consistent with organizational goals. Cohesive teams will likely have lower task performance when norms conflict with organizational objectives, because cohesiveness motivates employees to perform at a level more consistent with group norms. In our earlier example of the pyjama factory, the new employee maintained low output because group norms discouraged high performance. If the group had low cohesiveness, she (and presumably others) would have performed at a higher level because group norms would be less influential.

CONNECTIONS 9.2

Team Cohesiveness Makes Life a Beach

Trevor Pound dreamt about spending his thirtieth birthday on a Mexican beach. But the Mitel software engineer's crucial role in a major project put those plans on hold. Pound mentioned his disappointment only twice, but fellow team members at the Ottawa-based high-technology firm wanted to make up for his loss.

Nearly a dozen co-workers spent a weekend transforming Pound's drab, grey cubicle into a colourful oasis. They brought in a five-foot-wide beach umbrella, a beach chair, a heat lamp, a ukulele, some beach toys, a dozen tropical plants, and 100 kilograms of sand. One software developer went so far as to design a screensaver featuring a sandy beach for Pound's computer. The culprits even supplied the requisite beach attire—colourful shorts and a Hawaiian-style shirt.

"We started on Thursday looking at logistics—we thought the team approach would work," said ringleader Claudio Gambetti, a Mitel software engineer. "It was fun to see the reaction of people as we were bringing in the supplies. They were a little puzzled by what we were doing."

But Pound was probably the most surprised of anyone at Mitel when he arrived at work on Monday morning. Pound celebrated his birthday in an almost tropical setting. More important, the practical joke expressed the team's support for his loss of personal time.

John Major, *Ottawa Citizen.*

Trevor Pound couldn't get away for a planned vacation, so other team members turned his work area into a mini-paradise.

Source: Adapted from J. Pappone, "Sometimes Life's Truly a Beach..." *Ottawa Citizen,* February 3, 2000.

THE TROUBLE WITH TEAMS

Scholars and business leaders have long recognized that teams can be a competitive advantage. Yet, it is easy to lose sight of the fact that teams aren't always needed.[78] Sometimes, a quick and decisive action by one person is more appropriate. Some tasks are also performed just as easily by one person as by a group. "Teams are overused," admits Philip Condit, president of Boeing, Inc. The aircraft manufacturer makes extensive use of teams, but knows that

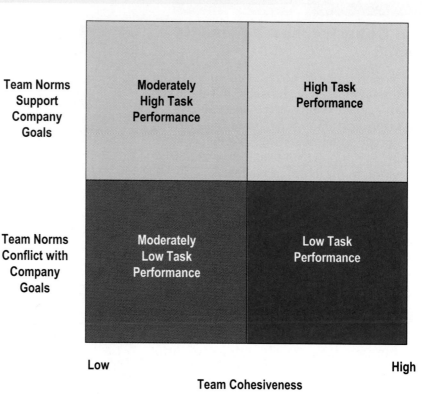

EXHIBIT 9.7   Effect of Team Cohesiveness on Task Performance

they aren't necessary for everything that goes on in organizations. Management guru Peter Drucker agrees. "The now-fashionable team in which everybody works with everybody on everything from the beginning rapidly is becoming a disappointment," he says.[79]

A second problem is that teams take time to develop and maintain. Scholars refer to these hidden costs as **process losses**—resources (including time and energy) expended towards team development and maintenance rather than towards the task.[80] It is much more efficient for an individual to work out an issue alone than to resolve differences of opinion with other people. The process loss problem becomes apparent when new people are added to the team. The group has to re-cycle through the team development process to bring everyone up to speed. The software industry even has a name for this: Brooks' Law says that adding more people to a late software project only makes it later. Researchers point out that the cost of process losses may be offset by the benefits of teams. Unfortunately, few companies conduct a cost-benefit analysis of their team activities.[81]

A third problem is that many companies don't create an environment that allows teams to flourish. As we learned earlier in the chapter, some organizational and team environments support team dynamics, whereas others do not. If companies simply put people in teams without considering the environmental factors, the effort will often be wasted.

SOCIAL LOAFING

Perhaps the best-known limitation of teams is the risk of productivity loss due to **social loafing**. Social loafing occurs when people exert less effort (and usually perform at a lower level) when working in groups than when working alone.[82] A few scholars question whether social

Process losses Resources (including time and energy) expended towards team development and maintenance rather than towards the task.

Social loafing The situation in which people perform at a lower level when working in groups than when working alone.

loafing is very common, but students can certainly report many instances of this problem in their team projects!

Social loafing is most likely to occur in large teams where individual output is difficult to identify. This particularly includes situations in which team members work alone towards a common output pool (i.e., they have low task interdependence). Under these conditions, employees aren't as worried that their performance will be noticed. Social loafing is less likely to occur when the task is interesting, because individuals have a higher intrinsic motivation to perform their duties. It is less common when the group's objective is important, possibly because individuals experience more pressure from other team members to perform well. Finally, social loafing is less common among members with a strong collectivist value, because they value group membership and believe in working towards group objectives (see Chapter 7).[83]

How to minimize social loafing

By understanding the causes of social loafing, we can identify ways to minimize this problem. Some of the strategies listed below reduce social loafing by making each member's performance more visible. Others increase each member's motivation to perform his or her tasks within the group.[84]

- *Form smaller teams*—Splitting the team into several smaller groups reduces social loafing because each person's performance becomes more noticeable and important for team performance. A smaller group also potentially increases cohesiveness, so would-be shirkers feel a greater obligation to perform fully for their team.

- *Specialize tasks*—It is easier to see everyone's contribution when each team member performs a different work activity. For example, rather than pooling their effort for all incoming customer inquiries, each customer service representative might be assigned a particular type of client.

- *Measure individual performance*—Social loafing is minimized when each member's contribution is measured. Of course, individual performance is difficult to measure in some team activities, such as problem-solving projects in which the team's performance depends on one person discovering the best answer.

- *Increase job enrichment*—Social loafing is minimized when team members are assigned more motivating jobs, such as requiring more skill variety or having direct contact with clients. However, this minimizes social loafing only if members have a strong growth need (see Chapter 4). More generally, however, social loafing is less common among employees with high job satisfaction.

- *Select motivated employees*—Social loafing can be minimized by carefully selecting job applicants who are motivated by the task and have a collectivist value orientation. Those with a collectivist value are motivated to work harder for the team because they value their membership in the group.

TEAM BUILDING

Team building Any formal intervention directed towards improving the development and functioning of a work team.

Team building is any formal activity intended to improve the development and functioning of a work team. Most team building accelerates the team development process, which, in turn, might reshape team norms or strengthen cohesiveness. Team building is sometimes applied to newly established teams, but it is more common among existing teams that have regressed to earlier stages of team development. Team building is therefore most appropriate when the team experiences high membership turnover or when members have lost track of their respective roles and team objectives.[85]

These Daewoo Motor Co. Ltd. employees are learning about teamwork and cooperation during this team-building exercise on Chebu Island, South Korea. In this exercise, employees at the Korean automobile company are divided into two teams and each tries to control the flag. Which types of team-building processes would this exercise include?

www.daewoo.com

TYPES OF TEAM BUILDING

There are four main types of team building: role definition, interpersonal process, goal setting, and problem solving. A typical team-building activity includes two or more of these.[86]

Role definition

The role-definition perspective examines role expectations among team members and clarifies their future role obligations to each other. Participants typically describe perceptions of their own role as well as the role expectations they have of other team members. After discussing these perceptions, team members revise their roles and present them for final acceptance.[87] This process determines whether individuals have the same role expectations that others assume of them.

Interpersonal process

Interpersonal-process activities try to build trust and open communications among team members by resolving hidden agendas and misperceptions. Wilderness adventures are popular interpersonal-process activities, in which teams face special challenges and threats in the woods.[88] For example, the Atlantic division of Canada Post hired a New Brunswick training firm to arrange a series of outdoor team-building challenges. By solving these types of problems in unfamiliar settings, team members learn more about each other's strengths and weaknesses, and discover how interpersonal relations at work can limit each person's potential. As one Canada Post employee concluded: "I discovered that showing someone what it means to be part of a team is a lot more effective than just telling them about it."[89]

There are many types of team building that emphasize interpersonal process. Wilderness team building, paintball wars, and obstacle course challenges can be fun while bringing home the message that trust and respect are important elements of effective teams. Notice that these exercises also help teams develop other abilities, such as improved decision making. However, some of these fun events were designed for personal growth, not team development. Consequently, they may provide personal development, but won't necessarily improve team dynamics.[90]

> **Dialogue** A process of conversation among team members in which they learn about each other's mental models and assumptions, and eventually form a common model for thinking within the team.

Another interpersonal process activity, called **dialogue**, helps team members learn about the different mental models and assumptions that each person applies when working together. Recall from Chapter 6 that mental models are working models of the world or "theories-in-use" that arise from our experiences and values. Dialogue is based on the idea that a team develops a "wholeness" or sense of unity when its members continually engage in conversations to understand each other. As they gain awareness of each other's models and assumptions, members eventually begin to form a common model for thinking within the team.[91]

Goal setting

As a team-building strategy, goal setting involves clarifying the team's performance goals, increasing the team's motivation to accomplish these goals, and establishing a mechanism for systematic feedback on the team's goal performance. This is very similar to individual goal setting (described in Chapter 3), except that the goals are applied to teams. Consequently, team dynamics must be addressed, such as reaching agreement on goals. Recent evidence suggests that goal setting is an important dimension of team building.[92]

Problem solving

This type of team building examines the team's task-related decision-making process and identifies ways to make it more effective.[93] Each stage of decision making is examined, such as how the team identifies problems and searches for alternatives (see Chapter 10). To improve their problem-solving skills, some teams participate in simulation games that require team decisions to be made in hypothetical situations.[94] As well as helping team members make better decisions, these team-building activities tend to improve interpersonal processes.

IS TEAM BUILDING EFFECTIVE?

Team-building activities have become more popular as companies increasingly rely on teams to get the work done. Some organizations are even experimenting with offbeat team-building activities in the hope that these sessions will improve team dynamics. For instance, employees at one of AT&T's Silicon Valley offices were sent to Corporate Space Camp, where they experienced the sensation of walking on the moon, building a structure in zero gravity, and other rudiments of astronaut training. Coca-Cola executives in China participated in a team-building program that included firewalking.[95] Are these and more traditional team-building programs effective? Is the organization's money well spent? So far, the answer is an equivocal "maybe." Some studies suggest that some team-building activities are successful, but that just

Gold of the Desert Kings is one of the most popular team-building games in North America. Developed and conducted by Eagle's Flight in Guelph, Ontario, this exercise places participants in a fictitious desert where they mine for gold and try to return before their water supply runs out. Each day is a few minutes in the game. What are the main team-building objectives of Gold of the Desert Kings and similar team-building games?

as many fail to improve team effectiveness.[96]

Too often, team building is ineffective because it is applied incorrectly.[97] One problem is that team building is introduced without anyone looking at the team's needs. As we just learned, team-building activities serve various purposes. Yet, many companies make the unfortunate assumption that "one size fits all" in team building. Another important consideration is the type of team that will receive the team building. Many work teams require a lot of coordination, so interpersonal process development may be most important. Cross-functional teams, on the other hand, often exist for a limited time to solve problems, so problem-solving training may be best for them.

A third problem is that companies tend to view team-building activities as medical inoculations that every team should receive when the team is formed. Corporate leaders forget that team building is an ongoing

www.eaglesflight.com

process, not a three-day jump-start. Some experts suggest, for example, that wilderness experiences often fail because they rarely include follow-up consultation to ensure that what team members learn during these events is transferred back to the workplace.[98] Effective team development requires members to frequently revisit the developmental issues and learning.

Lastly, we must remember that team building occurs on the job, not just in Algonquin Park. Organizations should encourage team members to reflect on their work experiences and to experiment with just-in-time learning for team development.

CHAPTER SUMMARY

- Teams are groups of two or more people who interact and influence each other, are mutually accountable for achieving common objectives, and perceive themselves as a social entity within an organization. All teams are groups because they consist of people with a unifying relationship, but not all groups are teams because some groups do not have purposive interaction.

- A team-based organization relies on self-directed work teams rather than on functional departments as the core work units. Traditional departments may be teams when employees are encouraged to interact directly and coordinate work activities. However, unlike traditional departments, team-based organizations tend to rely on cross-functional, autonomous teams with less need for supervisors in a communication or coordination role.

- Virtual teams operate across space, time, and organizational boundaries with members who communicate mainly through electronic technologies. They are becoming more common due to advanced computer-based technology, the shift from physical labour to knowledge-based work, corporate globalization, and the need for greater knowledge sharing.

- Team effectiveness includes the group's ability to survive, achieve its system-based objectives, and fulfil the needs of its members. The model of team effectiveness considers the team and organizational environment, team design, and team processes. The team or organizational environment influences team effectiveness directly, as well as through team design and team processes.

- Six elements in the organizational and team environment that influence team effectiveness are reward systems, communication systems, physical space, organizational environment, organizational structure, and organizational leadership.

- Three team design elements are task characteristics, team size, and team composition. Teams work best when tasks are clear, easy to implement, and require a high degree of interdependence. Teams should be large enough to perform the work, yet small enough for efficient coordination and meaningful involvement. Effective teams are composed of people with the competencies and motivation to perform tasks in a team environment. Heterogeneous teams operate best on complex projects and problems requiring innovative solutions.

- Teams develop through the stages of forming, storming, norming, performing, and eventually adjourning. However, some teams remain in a particular stage longer than do others, and team development is a continuous process.

- Teams develop norms to regulate and guide member behaviour. Critical events, explicit statements, initial experiences, and members' pre-group experiences may influence these norms.

- Cohesiveness is the degree of attraction people feel towards the team and their motivation to remain members. Cohesiveness increases with member similarity, degree of interaction, smaller team size, somewhat difficult entry, team success, and external challenges. Teams need some level of cohesiveness to survive, but high-cohesive units have higher task performance only when their norms do not conflict with organizational objectives.

- Teams are not necessary for all organizational activities. Moreover, they have hidden costs, known as process losses, and require particular environments in order to flourish. Teams often fail because they are not set up in supportive environments.

- Social loafing is another potential problem with teams. This is the tendency for individuals to perform at a lower level when working in groups than when alone. Social loafing can be minimized by making each member's performance more visible and increasing each member's motivation to perform his or her tasks within the group.

- Team building is any formal activity intended to improve the development and functioning of a work team. Four team-building strategies are role definition, interpersonal process, goal setting, and problem solving. Some team-building events succeed, but companies often fail to consider the contingencies of team building.

KEY TERMS

Coalition, p. 261

Communities of practice, p. 261

Dialogue, p. 279

Group, p. 256

Heterogeneous teams, p. 266

Homogeneous teams, p. 265

Informal group, p. 261

Norms, p. 268

Process losses, p. 276

Quality circles, p. 259

Role, p. 270

Skunkwork, p. 259

Self-directed work team (SDWT), p. 258

Social loafing, p. 276

Task interdependence, p. 264

Team, p. 256

Team building, p. 277

Team cohesiveness, p. 270

Team effectiveness, p. 262

Team-based organization, p. 258

Virtual teams, p. 259

DISCUSSION QUESTIONS

1. Suppose the instructor for this course assigned you to a project team consisting of three other students who are currently taking similar courses in Ireland, Singapore, and Brazil. All students speak English and have similar knowledge of the topic. Use your knowledge of virtual teams to discuss the problems that your team might face, compared with a team of local students who can meet face to face.

2. Informal groups exist in almost every form of social organization. What types of informal groups exist in your classroom? Why are students motivated to belong to these informal groups?

3. You have been put in charge of a cross-functional task force that will develop Internet banking services for retail customers. The team includes representatives from marketing, information services, customer service, and accounting, all of whom will move to the same location at headquarters for three months. Describe the evidence or behaviours that you might observe during each stage of the team's development.

4. You have just been transferred from the Regina office to the Saskatoon office of your company, a Canada-wide sales organization of electrical products for developers and contractors. In Regina, team members regularly called customers after a sale to ask whether the products arrived on time and whether they are satisfied. But when you moved to the Saskatoon office, no one seemed to make these follow-up calls. A recently hired co-worker explained that other co-workers discouraged her from making those calls. Later, another co-worker suggested that your follow-up calls were making everyone else look lazy. Give three possible reasons why the norms in Saskatoon might be different from those in the Regina office, even though the customers, products, sales commissions, and other characteristics of the workplace are almost identical.

5. You have been asked to lead a complex software project over the next year that requires the full-time involvement of approximately 100 people with diverse skills and backgrounds. Using your knowledge of team size, how can you develop an effective team under these conditions?

6. You have been assigned to a class project with five other students, none of whom you have met before. To what extent would team cohesiveness improve your team's performance on this project? What actions would you recommend to build team cohesiveness among student team members in this situation?

7. The CEO of Eastern Railway Corp. wants employees throughout the organization to perform their work in teams. According to the CEO, "Teams are our solution to increasing competition and customer demands." Discuss three problems with teams of which Eastern Railway's CEO may not be aware.

8. The Johari Window, described in Chapter 6, is sometimes used as the foundation of team building. What type of team building would occur through Johari Window activities?

Case Study

ACTIVITY 9.1
Treetop Forest Products Ltd.

Treetop Forest Products Ltd. is a sawmill operation in British Columbia that is owned by a major forest products company, but that operates independently of headquarters. It was built 30 years ago, and completely updated with new machinery five years ago. Treetop receives raw logs from the area for cutting and planing into building-grade lumber, mostly two-by-four and two-by-six pieces of standard lengths. Higher-grade logs leave Treetop's sawmill department in finished form and are sent directly to the packaging department. The remaining 40 percent of sawmill output are cuts from lower-grade logs, requiring further work by the planing department.

Treetop has 1 general manager, 16 supervisors and support staff, and 180 unionized employees. The unionized employees are paid an hourly rate specified in the collective agreement, whereas management and support staff are paid a monthly salary. The mill is divided into six operating departments: boom, sawmill, planer, packaging, shipping, and maintenance. The sawmill, boom, and packaging departments operate a morning shift starting at 6 a.m. and an afternoon shift starting at 2 p.m. Employees in these departments rotate shifts every two weeks. The planer and shipping departments operate only morning shifts. Maintenance employees work the night shift (starting at 10 p.m.).

Each department, except for packaging, has a supervisor on every work shift. The planer supervisor is responsible for the packaging department on the morning shift, and the sawmill supervisor is responsible for the packaging department on the afternoon shift. However, the packaging operation is housed in a separate building from the other departments, so supervisors seldom visit the packaging department. This is particularly true for the afternoon shift, because the sawmill supervisor is the furthest distance from the packaging building.

Packaging Quality

Ninety percent of Treetop's product is sold on the international market through Westboard Co., a large marketing agency. Westboard represents all forest products mills owned by Treetop's parent company, as well as several other clients in the region. The market for building-grade lumber is very price competitive, because there are numerous mills selling a relatively undifferentiated product. However, some differentiation does occur in product packaging and presentation. Buyers will look closely at the packaging when deciding whether to buy from Treetop or another mill.

To encourage its clients to package their products better, Westboard sponsors a monthly package quality award. The marketing agency samples and rates its clients' packages daily, and the sawmill with the highest score at the end of the month is awarded a

ACTIVITY 9.1 CONTINUED

plaque. Package quality is a combination of how the lumber is piled (e.g., defects turned in), where the bands and dunnage are placed, how neatly the stencil and seal are applied, the stencil's accuracy, and how neatly and tightly the plastic wrap is attached.

Treetop Forest Products won Westboard's packaging quality award several times over the past few years, and received high ratings in the months that it didn't win. However, the mill's ratings have started to decline over the past couple of years, and several clients have complained about the appearance of the finished product. A few large customers switched to competitors' lumber, saying that the decision was based on the substandard appearance of Treetop's packaging when it arrived in their lumberyard.

Bottleneck in Packaging

The planing and sawmilling departments have significantly increased productivity over the past few years. The sawmill operation recently set a new productivity record on a single day. The planer operation has increased productivity to the point where last year it reduced operations to just one (rather than two) shifts per day. These productivity improvements are due to better operator training, fewer machine breakdowns, and better selection of raw logs. (Sawmill cuts from high-quality logs usually do not require planing work.)

Productivity levels in the boom, shipping, and maintenance departments have remained constant. However, the packaging department has recorded decreasing productivity over the past couple of years, with the result that a large backlog of finished product is typically stockpiled outside of the packaging building. The morning shift of the packaging department is unable to keep up with the combined production of the sawmill and planer departments, so the unpackaged output is left for the afternoon shift. Unfortunately, the afternoon shift packages even less product than the morning shift, so the backlog continues to build. The backlog adds to Treetop's inventory costs and increases the risk of damaged stock.

Treetop has added Saturday overtime shifts as well as extra hours before and after the regular shifts for the packaging department employees to process this backlog. Last month, the packaging department employed 10 percent of the workforce but accounted for 85 percent of the overtime. This is frustrating to Treetop's management, because time and motion studies recently confirmed that the packaging department is capable of processing all of the daily sawmill and planer production without overtime. Moreover, with employees earning one-and-a-half or two times their regular pay on overtime, Treetop's cost competitiveness suffers.

Employees and supervisors at Treetop are aware that people in the packaging department tend to extend lunch by ten minutes and coffee breaks by five minutes. They also typically leave work a few minutes before the end of shift. This abuse has worsened recently, particularly on the afternoon shift. Employees who are temporarily assigned to the packaging department also seem to participate in this time-loss pattern after a few days. Although they are punctual and productive in other departments, these temporary employees soon adopt the packaging crew's informal schedule when assigned to that department.

Discussion Questions

1. Based on your knowledge of team dynamics, explain why the packaging department is less productive than are other teams at Treetop.

2. How should Treetop change the nonproductive norms that exist in the packaging group?

3. What structural and other changes would you recommend that may improve this situation in the long term?

Video Case Study

ACTIVITY 9.2
Management Training Outdoors

Increasingly, large companies are introducing management training programs that include outdoor wilderness activities. North American businesses have been training executives outdoors since the early 1970s. Outward Bound uses nature to encourage team building. Its clients range from Pepsi to General Electric to local hospital executives. Don Hanson of Porter Memorial Hospital said, "Some of them came with an awful lot of anxiety and oftentimes when you have a problem at the hospital you have a level of anxiety. But I think they just transfer that and say, 'Well look what we did when we were together as a team up there. Let's just figure out how to solve this problem together here.'"

Outward Bound includes briefings for clients who don't feel safe or fit to climb on the mountains. They counsel those who feel that their career could be damaged by their performance. While the Pecos River Learning Center also attracts Fortune 500 firms, their philosophy is more philosophical. The centre is the creation of Larry Wilson, author of the best-seller *Changing the Game: The New Way to Sell*. Wilson said, "We define winning as going as far as you can — using all that you've got." Wilson thinks that leaping off cliffs and poles helps clients transcend fears and nonproductive habits.

Wayne Townsend of General Motors of Canada, sends people to Wilson's training. He noted, "A lot of the old things that got us where we are today no longer work, and making that kind of a shift in our culture is a very significant task. And my goal is to involve the very senior people of our organization right into a conference centre like this and have that cultural change happen."

Critics have claimed that the Pecos River Learning Center doesn't tell the corporations how their employees' minds are being changed. Fundamentalists have even charged that what's really taught is theology. Wilson disputes this charge, stating, "In our case, our purpose is to help organizations change, to take advantage or be able to thrive in this global market. And in order to change they're going to have to do it quickly. It's not a one-seminar or one-event process. It's more like an 18-month to a 3-year process. And our goal is to help people tap into their courage and creativity to be able to see that they have other options, new ways of doing things. Because whatever got us where we are is not going to take us where we have to be."

Despite the constant stream of companies using this type of training, there are still many who don't believe in its effectiveness. Wilson noted, "The only way to really get you to believe it is to experience it. That is one of the advantages of this kind of learning. It's not an intellectual process; it's an intellectual, emotional, total process of new learning and breaking old patterns." Wilson pointed to an example of a woman who came to the Pecos River facility and went on to become a vice-president. "In her particular case, she went on to become a vice-president for her company after she realized that she had really been holding back her potential. She felt like if she could do this, she could do anything. And what it gave her was an experience of her own power, her own courage, and she realized that in all of her life that first step is what she's been holding back on. But on the other side of that step was joy and excitement and adventure, and those were the things that she was really looking for."

Wilson stated that his programs are based on a deep belief in human potential. He said, "We believe that people have a lot more potential than they are using and that our competitive advantage in the future from a business is going to be able to tap into people, more of their potential. We've been training people to play the game not to lose instead of playing the game to win."

Reflecting on his training programs, McCormick stated, "We think that Outward Bound is tied into

ACTIVITY 9.2 CONTINUED

very fundamental values that have always been a part of American industry. They have to do with being an effective leader, being an effective team player; they have to do with having the ability that when you sit down to solve a problem to use your best skills and the best skills of the people who are sitting around the table."

Discussion Questions

1. Do you think the type of training provided by organizations such as the Pecos River Learning Center or Outward Bound leads to developing effective workplace teams? Explain your answer.

2. The outdoor training facilities examined in the video claim to promote teamwork in the workplace. Do you think the training as currently offered also applies to virtual teams?

3. The outdoor training facilities are designed to teach people how to work together. What elements of effective teamwork are not covered in this type of training?

Source: NBC Archives.

 **TEAM exercises**

ACTIVITY 9.3
TEAM-TRUST EXERCISE

Purpose: This exercise is designed to help you understand the role of interpersonal trust in the development and maintenance of effective teams.

Materials: The instructor will provide the same 15 objects for each team as well as for the model.

Instructions:

Step 1: The instructor will divide the class into teams of approximately ten people each.

Step 2: Each team receives 15 objects from the instructor. The same 15 objects are arranged in a specific way on a table at the front of the room (or elsewhere, as designated by the instructor). The table is behind a screened area so participants cannot see the arrangements from their work areas. The goal of each team is to duplicate the exact arrangement (e.g., location, overlap, spacing) of the objects on the table, using its own matching set of objects, within 20 minutes (or other time limit given by the instructor). Participants are allowed one 30-second opportunity at the beginning of the exercise to view the screened table. They may not write, draw, or talk while viewing the screened table. However, each team has *up to two saboteurs*. These people have been selected by the instructor (either before the exercise or through notes distributed to all participants). Saboteurs will use any reasonable method to prevent the team from producing an accurate configuration of objects in its work area. The saboteurs are forbidden from revealing their identities.

Step 3: At the end of the time limit, the instructor will evaluate each team's configuration and decide which is the most accurate. The class members will then evaluate their experience in the exercise in terms of team development and other aspects of team dynamics.

Source: This exercise is based on ideas discussed in G. Thompson and P. Pearce, "The Team-Trust Game," *Training and Development,* May 1992, pp. 42–43.

ACTIVITY 9.4
TEAM TOWER POWER

Purpose: This exercise is designed to help you understand team roles, team development, and other issues in the development and maintenance of effective teams.

Materials: The instructor will provide enough Lego pieces or similar materials for each team to complete the assigned task. All teams should have an identical (or very similar) amount and types of pieces. The instructor will need a measuring tape and stopwatch. Students may use writing materials during the design stage (Step 2 below). The instructor will distribute a "Team Objectives Sheet" and "Tower Specifications Effectiveness Sheet" to all teams.

Instructions:

Step 1: The instructor will divide the class into teams. Depending on class size and space available, teams may have between four and seven members, but all should be of approximately equal size.

Step 2: Each team is given 20 minutes to design a tower that uses only the materials provided, is freestanding, and provides an optimal return on investment. Team members may wish to draw their tower on paper or a flip chart to assist the tower's design. Teams are free to practise building their towers during this stage. Preferably, teams are assigned to their own rooms so the design can be created privately. During this stage, each team will complete the Team Objectives Sheet distributed by the instructor. This sheet requires the Tower Specifications Effectiveness Sheet, also distributed by the instructor.

Step 3: Each team will show the instructor that it has completed its Team Objectives Sheet. Then, with all teams in the same room, the instructor will announce the start of the construction phase. The time will be closely monitored and the instructor will occasionally call out the amount of time elapsed (particularly if there is no clock in the room).

Step 4: Each team will advise the instructor as soon as it has completed its tower. Each team will write down the time elapsed that the instructor has determined. It may be asked to assist the instructor by counting the number of blocks used and the height of the tower. This information is also written on the Team Objectives Sheet. Then, the team calculates its profit.

Step 5: After presenting the results, the class will discuss the team dynamics that contribute to team effectiveness. Team members will discuss their strategy, division of labour (team roles), expertise within the team, and other elements of team dynamics.

Source: Several published and online sources describe variations of this exercise, but there is no known origin of this activity.

ACTIVITY 9.5

TEAM ROLES PREFERENCES SCALE

Purpose: This self-assessment is designed to help you identify your preferred roles in meetings and similar team activities.

Instructions: Read each of the statements below and circle the response that you believe best reflects your position regarding each statement. Then use the scoring key in Appendix B of this book to calculate your results for each team role. This exercise is completed alone so that students can assess themselves honestly without concerns of social comparison. However, class discussion will focus on the roles that people assume in team settings. This scale only assesses a few team roles.

TEAM ROLES PREFERENCES SCALE

Circle the number that best reflects your position regarding each of these statements.	Does Not Describe Me at All ▼	Does Not Describe Me Very Well ▼	Describes Me Somewhat ▼	Describes Me Well ▼	Describes Me Very Well ▼
1. I usually take responsibility for getting the team to agree on what the meeting should accomplish.	1	2	3	4	5
2. I tend to summarize to other team members what the team has accomplished so far.	1	2	3	4	5
3. I'm usually the person who helps other team members overcome their disagreements.	1	2	3	4	5
4. I try to ensure that everyone is heard on issues.	1	2	3	4	5
5. I'm usually the person who helps the team determine how to organize the discussion.	1	2	3	4	5
6. I praise other team members for their ideas more than do others in the meetings.	1	2	3	4	5
7. People tend to rely on me to keep track of what has been said in meetings.	1	2	3	4	5
8. The team typically counts on me to prevent debates from getting out of hand.	1	2	3	4	5

9. I tend to say things that make
   the group feel optimistic
   about its accomplishments.   1   2   3   4   5

10. Team members usually count
    on me to give everyone a
    chance to speak.   1   2   3   4   5

11. In most meetings, I am less
    likely than others to "put down"
    the ideas of teammates.   1   2   3   4   5

12. I actively help teammates
    resolve their differences in
    meetings.   1   2   3   4   5

13. I actively encourage quiet
    team members to describe
    their ideas on each issue.   1   2   3   4   5

14. People tend to rely on me
    to clarify the purpose of
    the meeting.   1   2   3   4   5

15. I like to be the person who
    takes notes or minutes of
    the meeting.   1   2   3   4   5

Decision Making and Employee Involvement

LEARNING OBJECTIVES

After reading this chapter, you should be able to:

- Diagram the general model of decision making.
- Explain why people have difficulty identifying problems and opportunities.
- Identify three factors that challenge our ability to choose the best alternative.
- Outline the causes of escalation of commitment to a poor decision.
- Outline the forms and levels of employee involvement.
- Describe sociotechnical systems theory recommendations for more successful self-directed work teams.
- Identify the four contingencies in the Vroom-Jago model that determine the optimal level of employee involvement.
- Discuss the challenges that prevent employee involvement.

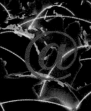

The B.C. government's ill-fated "PacifiCat" program illustrates the risks and problems with decision making.

In the mid-1990s, B.C. Ferries Corporation decided to design and build three catamaran-style ferries for the route between Vancouver and Nanaimo. The premier of British Columbia—the project's champion—promised that these "PacifiCats" would travel faster than conventional ferries. The entire project would cost no more than $210 million, "right down to the toilet paper."

Instead, costs ballooned to nearly $500 million as the project fell more than two years behind schedule. The first two PacifiCats were plagued by so many mechanical problems that each ferry was under repair half the time. A more devastating discovery was that the PacifiCats had a massive wake that caused ecological and property damage along the shoreline. This made them unsuitable for B.C. waters.

These problems were not unforeseen. During the project's first year, a marine engineer warned that the PacifiCats were not economically feasible and could endanger the public. Soon after, a British shipping journal reported that the ferries would cost much more to build than the original estimates. By the fifth year, the B.C. auditor-general slammed the project, saying that the B.C. Ferries' board of directors endorsed the project under government pressure. The board apparently raised concerns about the PacifiCats both before and many times after their decision.

Almost six years after the PacifiCat project was announced, a new premier of British Columbia cancelled the program and put the three ferries up for sale at less than one-quarter of their cost. The former premier, who had supported the PacifiCats until he stepped down for other reasons, was one of the few people who criticized the decision to end the project.[1]

The PacifiCat story is a dramatic example of the complexity and problems with decision making. **Decision making** is a conscious process of making choices among one or more alternatives with the intention of moving towards some desired state of affairs.[2] Some decisions are well planned with fairly clear consequences. But many organizational decisions are more complex. They have ill-defined goals, imperfect information, and biased decision makers who have difficulty evaluating the decision's success.

Decisions occur in response to problems or opportunities. A *problem* is a deviation between the current and the desired situation.[3] It is the gap between "what is" and "what ought to be." An *opportunity* is a deviation between current expectations and the recognition of a potentially better situation that is neither planned nor expected. In other words, decision makers realize that certain decisions may produce results beyond current goals or expectations.

This chapter, along with Chapter 11, explores the dynamics of decision making in organizations. We begin by looking at each step in the general decision-making model. The model is then examined more critically, by identifying the human conditions that impede effective decision making. The latter part of the chapter looks at employee involvement in the decision-making process. It begins with an overview of the forms and levels of employee involvement. Next, the chapter looks at the highest form of employee involvement: self-directed work teams. The final section of this chapter considers the potential benefits and limitations of employee involvement in the decision-making process.

A GENERAL MODEL OF DECISION MAKING

How do people make decisions? The best place to start to answer this question is the general model of decision making shown in Exhibit 10.1.[4] In this chapter, you will learn that people do not really make decisions that systematically. However, the model provides a useful template for our discussion of the topic and provides some guidance about how to make decisions under some conditions.[5]

EXHIBIT 10.1   General Model of Decision Making

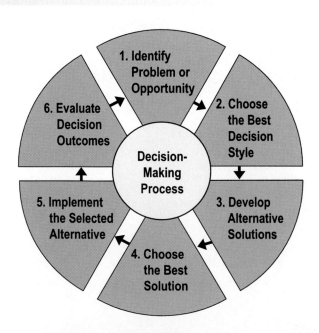

1. Identify Problem or Opportunity
2. Choose the Best Decision Style
3. Develop Alternative Solutions
4. Choose the Best Solution
5. Implement the Selected Alternative
6. Evaluate Decision Outcomes

Decision-Making Process

When Albert Einstein was asked how he would save the world in one hour, he replied that he would spend the first 55 minutes defining the problem and the last five minutes solving it. Problem identification is the first step in decision making and arguably the most important step. As mentioned above, a problem is a deviation between the current and the desired situation. This deviation is a *symptom* of more fundamental root causes in the organization. We need to correctly identify the problem in order to choose the best solution. This occurs by understanding the underlying causes of the symptom(s) that catch our attention. The decision process is then directed towards changing the root causes so that the symptoms are reduced or eliminated.[6]

• **Programmed decision** The process whereby decision makers follow standard operating procedures to select the preferred solution without the need to identify or evaluate alternative choices.

The second step is to determine the most appropriate decision style.[7] One important question is whether this is a **programmed decision** or **nonprogrammed decision**.[8] A programmed decision follows standard operating procedures. There is no need to explore alternative solutions because the optimal solution has already been identified and documented. For example, when customers call a General Electric Answer Centre, operators key in the problem and a computer database of 1.5 million issues provides the best solution for the client.[9] In contrast, new, complex, or ill-defined problems require nonprogrammed decisions. In these cases, decision makers must search for alternatives and possibly develop a unique solution. As problems reappear, however, programmed decision routines are formed. In this respect, programmed decisions drive out nonprogrammed decisions because we strive for predictable, routine situations.

• **Nonprogrammed decision** The process applied to unique, complex, or ill-defined situations whereby decision makers follow the full decision-making process, including a careful search for and/or development of unique solutions.

The third step in the general decision model is to develop a list of possible solutions.[10] This usually begins by searching for ready-made solutions, such as practices that have worked well on similar problems. If an acceptable solution cannot be found, decision makers try to design a custom-made solution or modify an existing one. B.C. Ferries followed the latter route by designing its own ferries, rather than choosing among existing designs. The fourth step involves choosing the best alternative. In a purely rational process, this would involve identifying all factors against which the alternatives are judged, assigning weights reflecting the importance of those factors, rating each alternative on those factors, and calculating each alternative's total value from the ratings and factor weights.[11]

In the fifth step, decision makers must rally employees and mobilize sufficient resources to translate their decisions into action. They must consider the motivation, ability, and role perceptions of employees implementing the solution, as well as resources to facilitate its implementation (see Chapter 2). The last step in the decision model involves evaluating whether the gap has narrowed between "what is" and "what ought to be." Ideally, this information should come from systematic benchmarks, so that relevant feedback is objective and easily observed.

The general model of decision making seems so logical, yet it is rarely observed in organizations. Decision makers experience a number of personal limitations that make it difficult to identify problems and opportunities, evaluate and choose solutions, and evaluate decision outcomes. Over the next few pages, we look at these challenges and ways to minimize them.

IDENTIFYING PROBLEMS AND OPPORTUNITIES

Problems and opportunities do not announce themselves. They are recognized and ultimately defined by the decision maker. However, people are not perfectly efficient or neutral thinking machines, so problems are often misdiagnosed and opportunities are overlooked. Two factors that interfere with identifying problems and opportunities are the decision maker's imperfect perceptions and diagnostic skills.

PERCEPTUAL BIASES

People define problems or opportunities based on their perceptions, values, and assumptions. Unfortunately, selective attention mechanisms cause relevant information to be unconsciously screened out. Moreover, employees, clients, and others with vested interests can influence the decision maker's perceptions so that information is more or less likely to be perceived as a problem or opportunity. Thus, politics and negotiation frequently mark decision making.[12]

A broader perceptual challenge is that people see problems or opportunities through their **mental models** (see Chapter 6).[13] These working models of the world help us to make sense of our environment, but they also perpetuate assumptions that blind us to new realities. Connections 10.1 describes how narrow mental models are the source of several famous missed opportunities.

> • **Mental models** The broad world views or "theories-in-use" that people rely on to guide their perceptions and behaviours.

POOR DIAGNOSTIC SKILLS

Perceptual problems block our ability to effectively diagnose problems and recognize opportunities.[14] People want to make sense of situations, so they quickly define problems based on stereotypes and other unsubstantiated information. They fail to see problems or opportunities due to insufficient time or information. Another concern is that organizations are complex systems (see Chapter 1), so decision makers may have trouble identifying where the main causes of problems occur.

Another common diagnostic error is defining problems in terms of their solutions. Someone who says, "The problem is that we need more control over our suppliers," has fallen into this trap. The problem might be that suppliers aren't delivering their product in time, but this statement focuses on a solution. The tendency to focus on solutions is based on a bias for action among business leaders as well as the need to reduce uncertainty. However, focusing on solutions can short-circuit the problem-identification stage of decision making.[15]

The solution-oriented problem also occurs because decision makers receive positive reinforcement from actions that worked in the past. Former Sunbeam CEO "Chainsaw" Al Dunlap saw the appliance manufacturer's problems in terms of the need to slash payroll, just as he had done at Scott Paper and other companies.[16] Other executives introduce a customer service program whenever they face a problem because this solution has worked for them in the past. The point here is that decision makers might look at problems from the perspective of their ready-made solutions. Sometimes, they *search* for problems so they can apply their existing solution.

© 1998 Randy Glasbergen.

"My team has created a very innovative solution, but we're still looking for a problem to go with it."

Randy Glasbergen. Used with permission.

IDENTIFYING PROBLEMS AND OPPORTUNITIES MORE EFFECTIVELY

Recognizing problems and opportunities will always be a challenge, but the process can be improved through awareness of these perceptual and diagnostic limitations. By recognizing how mental models restrict a person's understanding of the world, decision makers learn to openly consider other perspectives of reality. Discussing the situation with colleagues can also minimize perceptual

CONNECTIONS 10.1

www.SeikoUSA.com; www.parc.xerox.com

Famous Missed Opportunities

Mental models create road maps that guide our decisions. Unfortunately, these maps also potentially block our ability to recognize emerging problems and opportunities. Here are a few famous examples:

- *The Wealthy Barber* has sold more than 2 million copies, making it one of Canada's top-selling trade books ever. Yet author David Chilton marketed the book himself during its first year of publication after several publishers rejected the manuscript. The publishers didn't think that a story about three people visiting a local barber for financial advice would arouse much interest.

- A research institute in Switzerland introduced new electronic watch technology at the 1968 World Watch Conference. Swiss watchmakers had funded this research, but they didn't understand how a battery-powered watch could compete against their finely crafted wind-up watches. Meanwhile, executives at Seiko, the Japanese electronics company, immediately saw the potential of this new technology. Within a few years, Seiko watches were dominating the watch industry that the Swiss had led for centuries.

- Graphical user interfaces, mice, windows, pull-down menus, laser printing, distributed computing, and Ethernet technologies weren't invented by Apple, Microsoft, or IBM. These essential elements of contemporary personal computing originated in the 1970s with researchers at Xerox PARC. Unfortunately, Xerox executives were so focused on their photocopier business that they didn't even bother to patent these inventions. Today, the lost value of Xerox PARC's computing discoveries is much larger than the entire photocopier industry.

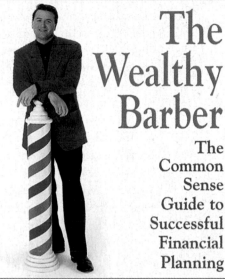

OVER ONE MILLION COPIES SOLD
The All-Time Canadian Bestseller

The Wealthy Barber

The Common Sense Guide to Successful Financial Planning

". . . 30 years from now Chilton could be best remembered not as a best-selling author, but as the man who inspired thousands to save their way to prosperity."
— *MACLEAN'S*

DAVID CHILTON

Published by Stoddart Publishing Co. Ltd. Cover design: Bill Douglas/The Bang. Cover photography: Kent Lacin Media Services.

Canadian publishers didn't recognize the potential of David Chilton's self-help book about financial advice from a local barber.

- When the World Wide Web burst onto the cyberspace scene in the early 1990s, Bill Gates wondered what all the fuss was about. Even as late as 1996, the founder and CEO of Microsoft lampooned investors for their love-in with companies that made Internet products. However, Gates eventually realized the error in his mental model of computing. Making up for lost time, Microsoft bought several Web-savvy companies and added Internet support to its Windows operating system.

Sources: B. Campbell and M. Conron, "Xerox Ready to Hit Another Home Run," *Ottawa Citizen,* June 28, 1999; M. Michalko, "Thinking Like a Genius: Eight Strategies Used by the Supercreative, from Aristotle and Leonardo to Einstein and Edison," *The Futurist,* 32 (May 1998), p. 21; O. Port, "Xerox Won't Duplicate Past Errors," *Business Week,* September 29, 1997, p. 98; T. Abate, "Meet Bill Gates, Stand-Up Comic," *San Francisco Examiner,* March 13, 1996, p. D1; L.E. Roseman, "How David Chilton Became a Wealthy Author," *Globe and Mail,* February 18, 1995, p. B20.

and diagnostic weaknesses. Decision makers discover blind spots in problem identification by hearing how others perceive certain information and diagnose them.[17] Opportunities also become apparent when outsiders explore this information from their different mental models.

Another strategy for problem identification is to create early-warning systems. If customer satisfaction ratings drop or costs increase beyond a fixed mark, executive procedures or computer programs can alert decision makers to these concerns. These cues may be determined from past practice or from preset goals for major stakeholders (customers, shareholders, employees, etc.). The effectiveness of these early-warning signs is only as good as the willingness of people to recognize them. Still, they may help people realize that problems exist before the situation deteriorates further.

Information technology also helps to identify opportunities and problems. Many firms now rely on *data mining*—computer programs that search through large databases and organize this information into meaningful trends. Data mining minimizes perceptual problems that occur when people manually look for trends and patterns in mountains of data. Other technology guides employees through the problem-finding process. For instance, line crews at Great Lakes Power Ltd. in Sault Ste. Marie, Ontario, use decision support software called Which & Why to help them identify functional and safety problems with the 25,000 or more electrical poles they need to inspect. Previously, crews used a paper-based survey of each pole, which left plenty of room for personal bias.[18]

EVALUATING AND CHOOSING SOLUTIONS

For many years, decision making was studied mainly by economists who made several assumptions about how people choose among alternatives. They assumed that decision makers have well-articulated and agreed-on organizational goals. They also assumed that decision makers are rational thinking machines who efficiently and simultaneously process facts about all alternatives and the consequences of those alternatives. Finally, these theorists assumed that decision makers always choose the alternative with the highest payoff. These were only hypothetical assumptions, but this rational perspective laid the foundation for popular misconceptions about how people make decisions.

Today, even the economists have cast off these unrealistic assumptions.[19] Instead, they are recognizing that decision making includes a variety of human limitations. Over the past 40 years, organizational behaviour researchers have debunked several economic assumptions about decision making, as Exhibit 10.2 highlights.

PROBLEMS WITH GOALS

We need clear goals to choose the best solution. Goals identify "what ought to be" and, therefore, provide a standard against which each alternative is evaluated. In reality, though, organizational goals are often ambiguous or in conflict with each other. The problem is compounded when organizational members disagree over the relative importance of these goals.[20] It is also doubtful that all decisions are based on organizational objectives; some decisions are made to satisfy the decision maker's personal goals even when they are incompatible with the organization's goals.

PROBLEMS WITH INFORMATION PROCESSING

People do not make perfectly rational decisions because they don't process information very well. One problem is that perceptual biases distort the selection and interpretation of information (see Chapter 6). Thus, decision makers are not aware of every piece of information

EXHIBIT 10.2 Traditional Economic Assumptions Versus Organizational Behaviour Findings About Choosing Decision Alternatives

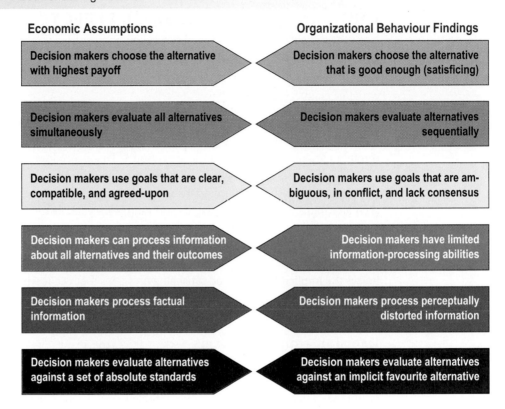

Economic Assumptions — **Organizational Behaviour Findings**

Economic Assumptions	Organizational Behaviour Findings
Decision makers choose the alternative with highest payoff	Decision makers choose the alternative that is good enough (satisficing)
Decision makers evaluate all alternatives simultaneously	Decision makers evaluate alternatives sequentially
Decision makers use goals that are clear, compatible, and agreed-upon	Decision makers use goals that are ambiguous, in conflict, and lack consensus
Decision makers can process information about all alternatives and their outcomes	Decision makers have limited information-processing abilities
Decision makers process factual information	Decision makers process perceptually distorted information
Decision makers evaluate alternatives against a set of absolute standards	Decision makers evaluate alternatives against an implicit favourite alternative

Selective attention The process of filtering (selecting and screening out) information received by our senses.

because the **selective attention** process screens much of it out. Second, decision makers can't possibly think through all of the possible alternatives and their outcomes, so they engage in a limited search for and evaluation of alternatives.[21] For example, there may be dozens of computer brands to choose from, but people typically evaluate only a few of these.

Third, decision makers typically look at alternatives sequentially rather than examine all alternatives at the same time. As a new alternative comes along, it is immediately compared to an implicit favourite. An *implicit favourite* is an alternative that the decision maker prefers over the others.[22] In some cases, this option is unconsciously chosen long before the formal decision process begins. The implicit favourite becomes a comparison against which all other alternatives are judged. This might be fine, except that people unconsciously distort information to make their implicit favourite come out the winner in most comparisons.[23]

PROBLEMS WITH MAXIMIZATION

Satisficing The tendency to select a solution that is satisfactory or "good enough" rather than optimal or "the best."

Decision makers tend to select the alternative that is acceptable or "good enough," rather than the best possible solution. In other words, they satisfice rather than maximize. **Satisficing** occurs because it isn't possible to identify all of the possible alternatives, and information about available alternatives is imperfect or ambiguous. Satisficing also occurs because decision makers tend to evaluate alternatives sequentially. They evaluate alternatives one at a time against the implicit favourite and eventually select an option that is good enough to satisfy their needs or preferences. What constitutes a good enough solution depends on the availability of acceptable alternatives. Standards rise when acceptable alternatives are easily found and fall when few are available.[24]

CHOOSING SOLUTIONS MORE EFFECTIVELY

It is very difficult to get around the human limitations of making choices, but four strategies worth considering are systematic evaluation, decision support systems, scenario planning, and possibly intuition.

Systematic evaluation

Biased choices due to implicit favourites and satisficing tend to occur with overall subjective judgments of alternatives. A preferred alternative is to systematically evaluate alternatives through careful measurement and calculation.[25] This procedure has four steps: (1) identify the relevant factors against which the alternatives are judged; (2) measure the alternatives on each factor; (3) weight the importance of each factor; and (4) compute an overall score for each alternative based on the weights and ratings for each factor.

For example, to choose the best job applicant, interviewers would rate each applicant on specific factors (communication skills, technical knowledge, etc.), then calculate a total score for each applicant using those factor ratings and the weights given to each factor. This minimizes the implicit favourite and satisficing problems that occur when relying on general subjective judgments. It also aids information processing because the calculations are made on paper rather than in our heads.

Decision support systems

Decision support systems are computer-based programs that guide people through the decision-making process.[26] For example, software developer Cerner Corp. uses a case-based reasoning process at its help desk. Callers' problems or questions are entered in simple English and the system replies with questions and eventually solutions to the problems presented. This decision support system cut in half Cerner's backlog of unresolved client issues and increased customer satisfaction ratings to record high levels.[27] Notice that this decision support software turns a seemingly nonprogrammed decision into a programmed decision. It helps employees to systematically identify the problem, which then points to a ready-made solution without the need to evaluate alternatives.

Scenario planning

Scenario planning is a disciplined method for imagining possible futures.[28] It typically involves thinking about what would happen if a significant environmental condition changed, and what the organization should do to anticipate and react to such an outcome. To some extent, scenario planning explores potential problems and opportunities. But it is also a vehicle for choosing the best solutions under possible scenarios long before they occur. The Canadian Passport Office used scenario planning to identify new directions for their organization so that their future was secure. Employees were asked to consider two divergent scenarios—one in which passports are issued by Canadian banks and the other in which citizens can go to a document supercentre to receive any government document they need.[29]

Should we rely on intuition?

Systematic evaluation, decision support systems, and scenario planning are highly rational ways to choose alternatives more effectively. But many corporate leaders will tell you that they also rely on their intuition.[30] "If I have to make a big decision, I listen to what others think,"

Scenario planning A disciplined method for imagining possible futures that typically involves thinking about what would happen if a significant environmental condition changed, and what the organization should do to anticipate and react to such an outcome.

explains Deborah Triant, CEO of Check Point Software Technologies. "But ultimately, I listen to my intuition. I postpone a decision until I wake up one morning and know where my gut is going."[31] **Intuition** is the ability to know when a problem or opportunity exists and to select the best course of action without conscious reasoning.[32] There is plenty of debate about the value of intuition. Deborah Triant and many other executives swear by their intuition, whereas some scholars warn against this practice.

Which of these views is correct? Both. It is true that we sometimes justify biased and non-systematic decision making as intuition. However, there is also increasing research evidence that intuition is the conduit through which people use their **tacit knowledge**. Recall from Chapter 2 that tacit knowledge is subtle information acquired through observation and experience that is not clearly understood and therefore cannot be explicitly communicated. This knowledge incorporates logical reasoning that has become habit over time. Thus, intuition allows us to draw on our vast storehouse of unconscious knowledge.[33]

Consider grand chess masters who play against several people at the same time. They look at the chessboard, make a move without time to systematically evaluate the situation, and proceed to the next chessboard. Chess masters make the right choice (most of the time) because they have learned patterns of chess arrangements and are able to quickly sense a pattern that threatens their position or presents an opportunity. Experienced decision makers in organizations have this same skill. They sense the best solution without consciously thinking through their preference. Certainly, we need to be careful that our "gut feelings" are not merely perceptual distortions and false assumptions, but we should also recognize the potential value of intuition in making sound choices.

EVALUATING DECISION OUTCOMES

Decision makers aren't completely honest with themselves when evaluating the effectiveness of their decisions. One concern is that after making a choice, decision makers tend to inflate the quality of the selected alternative and deflate the quality of the discarded alternatives. They ignore or suppress the importance of negative information about the selected alternative and emphasize positive information. This perceptual distortion, known as **postdecisional justification**, results from the need to maintain a positive self-identity.[34] Postdecisional justification gives people an excessively optimistic evaluation of their decisions, but only until they receive very clear and undeniable information to the contrary. Unfortunately, it also inflates the decision maker's initial evaluation of the decision, so reality often comes as a painful shock when objective feedback is finally received.

ESCALATION OF COMMITMENT

A second problem when evaluating decision outcomes is escalation of commitment. **Escalation of commitment** is the tendency to repeat an apparently bad decision or allocate more resources to a failing course of action.[35] The opening story to this chapter described how the PacifiCat ferry project escalated into a $500-million write-off. B.C. Ferries and the former premier of British Columbia evaluated the project favourably enough to let it continue in spite of clear warnings from several sources.

The PacifiCat incident is relatively minor against some of the world's great escalation-of-commitment fiascos. Planners at Tokyo's Metropolitan Transport Bureau promised to build a 29-kilometre high-speed subway loop under the city in record time and at enormous profit. Instead, the multibillion-dollar project is way over budget, more than three years overdue,

---

Intuition The ability to know when a problem or opportunity exists and to select the best course of action without conscious reasoning.

Tacit knowledge Subtle information, acquired through observation and experience, that is not clearly understood and therefore cannot be explicitly communicated.

Postdecisional justification A perceptual phenomenon whereby decision makers justify their choices by subconsciously inflating the quality of the selected option and deflating the quality of the discarded options.

Escalation of commitment Repeating an apparently bad decision or allocating more resources to a failing course of action.

Reuters/Matthew Grey/Archive Photos.

The London Stock Exchange started a project called Taurus to develop a new electronic system for processing stocks. Taurus was staffed by a powerful team of analysts, programmers, and strategy experts and was led by a highly respected director. The entire project was supposed to cost $75 million and take 18 months. Instead, complex issues and changing needs blew out these goals. Nearly $700 million were poured into the project before it was cancelled three years beyond its original deadline.[38] What factors likely contributed to escalation of commitment in the Taurus project? How might this problem be avoided in the future?

www.londonstock
exchange.com

and won't be profitable until 2040, if ever. The original cost of Ontario's Darlington nuclear power plant was $2 billion. It subsequently ballooned to more than $14 billion and will likely be sold off at far below cost. The U.S. Internal Revenue Service poured more than $3 billion into a document processing system that was supposed to cost $251 million. Escalation of commitment also occurred years ago when the British government continued to fund the Concorde supersonic jet long after its lack of commercial viability was apparent. To this day, some scholars refer to escalation of commitment as the "Concorde fallacy."[36]

Causes of escalating commitment

Why are people led deeper and deeper into failing projects? Organizational behaviour scholars have identified several reasons, including self-justification, gambler's fallacy, perceptual blinders, and closing costs.

- *Self-justification*—Escalation of commitment often occurs because people want to present themselves in a positive light (see Chapter 12).[37] Those who are personally identified with the decision tend to persist because this demonstrates confidence in their own decision-making ability. The B.C. Ferries PacifiCat project probably escalated because it was the former premier's pet project. It was difficult to cancel a symbol of his personal success as a government leader. This persistence is also a decision maker's way of saving face—looking good to avoid the embarrassment of admitting past errors. Some cultures have a stronger emphasis on saving face than do others, so escalation of commitment is probably more common in those societies.[39]

- *Gambler's fallacy*—Many projects result in escalation of commitment because decision makers underestimate the risk and overestimate the probability of success. They become victims of the so-called "gambler's fallacy" by having inflated expectations of their ability to control problems that may arise. In other words, decision makers falsely believe that luck is on their side, so they invest more in a losing course of action.

- *Perceptual blinders*—Escalation of commitment sometimes occurs because decision makers do not see problems soon enough. Through perceptual defence (see Chapter 6), they unconsciously screen out or explain away negative information. Serious problems initially look like random errors along the trend line to success. Even when they see that something is wrong, the information is sufficiently ambiguous that it can be misinterpreted or justified.

- *Closing costs*—Even when a project's success is in doubt, decision makers will persist because the costs of ending the project are high or unknown. Terminating a major project may involve large financial penalties, a bad public image, or personal political costs. This is probably the main reason why the Darlington nuclear plant project escalated. When a former Ontario premier was asked why the Ontario government didn't stop the Darlington project in the early 1980s, he explained: "I don't think anybody can look at a situation with . . . $7 billion in the ground and just cavalierly write it off."[40] In other words, terminating the Darlington project after this large expense may have been political suicide to the Ontario government.

EVALUATING DECISION OUTCOMES MORE EFFECTIVELY

One effective way to minimize escalation of commitment and postdecisional justification is to separate decision choosers from decision evaluators.[41] This tends to avoid the problem of self-justification because the person responsible for evaluating the decision would not be concerned with saving face if the project is cancelled. In support of this recommendation, a recent study found that banks were more likely to take action against bad loans after the executive responsible had left.[42] In other words, problem loans were effectively managed when someone else took over the portfolio. This occurred in the PacifiCat project, described at the beginning of this chapter. The project was cancelled only after the premier who started the project stepped down as leader.

A second strategy is to establish a preset level at which the decision is abandoned or re-evaluated.[43] This is similar to a stop-loss order in the stock market, whereby the stock is sold if it falls below a certain price. The problem with this solution is that conditions are often so complex that it is difficult to identify an appropriate point at which to abandon a project. A third strategy is to find a source of systematic and clear feedback. For example, companies might carefully survey customers during the early stages of a product launch rather than rely on less precise feedback. This reduces the problem that escalation occurs when feedback is ambiguous.[44]

Finally, projects might have less risk of escalation if several people are involved. Other participants continuously monitor key decision makers and might notice problems sooner than someone working alone on the project. Employee involvement offers these and many other benefits to the decision-making process, as we discuss next.

EMPLOYEE INVOLVEMENT

Employee involvement The degree to which employees share information, knowledge, rewards, and power throughout the organization.

Employee involvement (also called *participative management*) refers to the degree to which employees share information, knowledge, rewards, and power throughout the organization.[45] Employees have some level of activity in making decisions that were not previously within their mandate. Employee involvement extends beyond controlling resources for one's own job; it includes the power to influence decisions in the work unit and organization. The higher the level of involvement, the more power people have over the decision process and outcomes. Involved employees also receive information and possess the knowledge required to make a meaningful contribution to the decision process.

Employee involvement is not new to Canada. In 1942, Prime Minister William Lyon Mackenzie King called for the establishment of labour-management committees in every industry. By the end of the Second World War, more than 1000 committees had been created.[46] These committees were designed to advance cooperation between management and labour union leaders, as well as to boost productivity for the war effort.

After the war, the Canadian government continued to encourage employee involvement through these committees so that Canada would remain economically competitive. A few firms began to experiment with advanced forms of employee involvement. At the Lever

Brothers plant in Toronto, corporate leaders viewed employees as expert consultants whose ideas would improve productivity.[47] Another company, Kitchen Overall & Shirt Company in Brantford and Simcoe, Ontario, experimented with team-based structures and reward systems.

Today, most companies apply some form and level of employee involvement. Staff members at the Great Little Box Company actively participate in decisions affecting the Vancouver-based box manufacturer. "Every month, our employees meet to review our mission statement and discuss the company's goals and profits," says company founder Robert Meggy. Team members at Palliser Furniture Ltd. in Winnipeg are responsible for planning budgets and establishing production quotas with their co-workers. And at Enerfin, Inc. in Brossard, Quebec, employees came up with enough productivity and quality improvement ideas to save the cooling systems company from possible extinction.[48]

Why has employee participation become such an important part of corporate decision making? One reason is that employee involvement is an integral part of knowledge management. Corporate leaders are realizing that employee knowledge is a critical resource for competitive advantage, so they are encouraging employees to share this knowledge. Technology has also

www.mac.qc.ca

A. Pichette, Montreal Gazette.

You won't find any supervisors at MAC Closures' production plants in Quebec and Waterloo, Ontario. Instead, the 200 employees at Canada's largest plastic lid and cap manufacturer discuss issues directly with senior executives. Each year, a cross-section of staff—from top brass to plant-floor employees—participate in a two-day retreat to draft the company's strategic plan for the following year. Everyone reviews the company's monthly financial statements because they have a stake in the company's profits. "Only salaries are secret," says Gilles Decelles, CEO of MAC Closures (shown in photo).[49] What are the advantages of involving employees in strategic planning?

pushed employee involvement more than we would have imagined a decade ago. E-mail increases upward communication, most of which represents employee involvement (see Chapter 8). Other computer-mediated communication, such as the K'Netix knowledge database at Buckman Labs, also encourages employees to participate in corporate decision making.

FORMS OF EMPLOYEE INVOLVEMENT

Employee involvement exists in many forms, as shown in Exhibit 10.3.[50] *Formal participation* activities, such as the self-directed teams at TRW Canada (see the opening story in Chapter 9), are founded on codified policies and institutionalized practices. In other words, the company has established structures and formal expectations that support this form of participation. In contrast, *informal participation* includes casual events, such as approaching a supervisor about an idea or suggestion.

Employee involvement can also be *voluntary* or *statutory*. MAC Closures voluntarily involves employees in forming the manufacturer's strategic plan each year. In contrast, joint health and safety committees (JHSCs) at the company are statutory; they are required by law in most manufacturing facilities in Ontario and other jurisdictions. JHSCs have equal numbers of management and employee representatives and provide health and safety recommendations to management.[51] Statutory involvement is more widespread in Europe, where many countries have codetermination laws.

Codetermination law varies across Europe, but it generally requires employee involvement at both the work site and corporate levels. At the corporate level, employees hold up to

Codetermination A form of employee involvement required by some governments that typically operates at both the work site as work councils and the corporate level as supervisory boards.

EXHIBIT 10.3 Forms of Employee Involvement

Form of Involvement	Description	Example
Formality		
Formal	Participation is codified policy or institutionalized practice	Self-directed work teams at TRW Canada
Informal	Casual or undocumented activities at management's discretion	Employee on the shop floor makes a suggestion to the supervisor
Legal Mandate		
Statutory	Government-legislated activities	Joint health and safety committees at DuPont Canada
Voluntary	Any participation activity without any force of law	Employee involvement in strategic-planning sessions at MAC Closures
Directness		
Direct	Employees are personally involved in decisions	Employees at Pratt & Whitney Canada's Halifax plant have almost complete control over production decisions
Representative	Employees participate through representation of peers	Windsor Factory Supply employees vote for the company's board of directors

half of the supervisory board seats in Sweden, Norway, and some other European countries. These boards advise company executives on business issues and make decisions about their salaries. At the work site, codetermination occurs through employee representation committees called *works councils*. The employer must keep the works council informed of financial performance and employment decisions within the organization. It must consult with (not just inform) the council regarding matters of staffing, work processes, and individual dismissals. In Germany, legislation also requires mutual agreement between the employer and the works council on work hours, use of technology, wages, health and safety, and other "social matters."[52]

The third form of employee involvement is whether it is *direct* or *representative*. Direct participation occurs when employees personally influence the decision process. For example, employees at Palliser Furniture Ltd. in Winnipeg directly participate in decisions affecting their team's work objectives. Representative participation, on the other hand, occurs when employees are represented by peers. This occurs at Windsor Factory Supply in Windsor, Ontario. Everyone at the employee-owned company votes for nine people who will represent them on the board of directors.[53]

LEVELS OF EMPLOYEE INVOLVEMENT

There are different levels of employee involvement. These levels reflect both the degree of power over the decision and the number of decision steps over which they can apply that power.[54] The *lowest level* of involvement is selective consultation, in which employees are individually asked for specific information or opinions about one or two aspects of the decision. They do not necessarily recommend solutions and might not even know details of the problem for which the information will be used.

Moderate level of involvement

A *moderate level* of employee involvement occurs when employees are more fully consulted either individually or in a group. They are told about the problem and offer their diagnosis and recommendations, but the final decision is still beyond their control. Employee involvement at Enerfin, Inc. is such an example. As previously mentioned, employees at the Brossard, Quebec, cooling systems company identified several ideas that would reduce costs and improve quality. These ideas were submitted to senior executives for their approval.[55]

Communities of practice represent a moderate level of employee involvement. These were described in Chapters 1 and 9 as groups bound together by shared expertise and passion for a particular activity or interest.[56] Chevron, the California-based energy company, has nurtured dozens of these virtual communities. One group debates ways to more effectively measure customer satisfaction; another considers options for improving workplace safety; several others look at strategies to improve the quality of specific production processes.[57]

Employee participation is an essential ingredient in **gainsharing plans** (see Chapter 4) because cost savings result from the ideas that employees recommend.[58] For example, Wescast Industries Inc. in Wingham, Ontario, has a gainsharing program that emphasizes competence, participation, identity, and equity. The process tries to ensure that employees have the necessary skills (competencies), are continuously involved in ways to reduce costs (participation), think of themselves as partners in the enterprise (identity), and receive financial returns from their work and ideas (equity).[59]

MAC Closures, the Great Little Box Company, and several other Canadian firms practise variations of **open book management**.[60] Open book management involves sharing financial information with employees and encouraging them to recommend ideas that improve those

Communities of practice Informal groups bound together by shared expertise and passion for a particular activity or interest.

Gainsharing plan A reward system usually applied to work teams that distributes bonuses to team members based on the amount of cost reductions and increased labour efficiency in the production process.

Open book management Involves sharing financial information with employees and encouraging them to recommend ideas that improve those financial results.

financial results. The process encourages employees to think of financial performance as a game they can play and win. Employees become active participants by learning how to read financial statements (the rules of the game). Regina-based Wascana Energy Inc. does this by taking employees through an oil company's first three years of operation. Through this process, employees learn about financial statements, royalties, depletion expenses, and the like.[61] With their financial training and game-oriented perspective, employees are more likely to make meaningful recommendations that will improve the company's financial performance.

High involvement

The highest level of involvement occurs when employees have complete power over the decision process. They discover and define problems, identify solutions, choose the best option, and monitor the results of their decision. These *high-involvement* conditions are characteristic of the team-based organizations introduced in Chapter 9.[62] Team-based organizational structures rely on self-directed work teams, which we discuss next.

SELF-DIRECTED WORK TEAMS (SDWTS)

When Bayer Inc. consolidated five companies in four years, the health care and chemical company decided it was time to restructure its Canadian warehouse operations into self-directed work teams. All warehouse employees now work in a team-based environment and have the same job title—warehouse operator. They are expected to share work activities by learning the four skill levels representing the previous job categories (e.g., picker, forklift operator). "It took nearly two years to develop and institute this transformation, but it has been worth it," says a Bayer executive. "From the outset, employees took ownership of their respective jobs [and] supported the warehouse team concept."[63]

> **Self-directed work team (SDWT)** A work group that completes an entire piece of work requiring several interdependent tasks and that has substantial autonomy over the execution of these tasks.

The Canadian warehouse operations of Bayer, Inc. are following the trend towards **self-directed work teams (SDWTs)**. These formal groups complete an entire piece of work requiring several interdependent tasks and have substantial autonomy over the execution of these tasks. By most estimates, almost half of the medium-sized and large organizations in North America use SDWT structures for part of their operations.[64]

SDWTs vary somewhat from one firm to the next, but they generally have the features listed in Exhibit 10.4.[65] First, SDWTs complete an entire piece of work, whether it's a product, a service, or part of a larger product or service. For example, self-directed teams at Pratt & Whitney Canada's plant near Halifax are responsible for producing specific engine casing components. Second, the team—not supervisors—assigns tasks that individual team members perform. In other words, the team plans, organizes, and controls work activities with little or no direct involvement of a higher-status supervisor.

Third, SDWTs control most work inputs, flow, and output. Pratt & Whitney Canada's teams do this by hiring new team members, redesigning their work process layout, and buying new equipment. Electrical power company AES Corp. also relies on teams to run the business. "Everything in the company is divided up into teams, small groups of people that are multi-disciplinary in nature," explains Dennis W. Bakke, AES Corp. CEO and co-founder. "They have total authority to make all decisions: I mean total, complete authority on every aspect of business."[66]

Fourth, SDWTs are responsible for correcting work flow problems as they occur. In other words, the teams maintain their own quality and logistical control. Lastly, SDWTs receive team-level feedback and rewards. This recognizes and reinforces the fact that the team—not individuals—is responsible for the work, although team members may also receive individual feedback and rewards.

EXHIBIT 10.4 Attributes of Self-Directed Work Teams

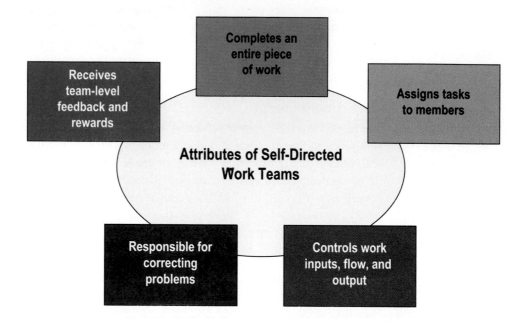

You may have noticed from this description that members of SDWTs have enriched and enlarged jobs (see Chapter 4). The team's work is horizontally loaded because it includes all the tasks required to make an entire product or provide the service. It is also vertically loaded because the team is mostly responsible for scheduling, coordinating, and planning these tasks.[67] Self-directed work teams were initially designed around production processes, but they are also found in administrative and service activities. For example, Roberts Express has 26 customer assistance teams that are completely responsible for serving clients and arranging package deliveries for a specific geographic area.[68] This situation is well suited to self-directed teams because members have interdependent tasks and decisions are frequently made that require the employee's knowledge and experience.[69]

SOCIOTECHNICAL SYSTEMS AND SDWTs

How do you create successful self-directed work teams? To answer this question, we need to look at **sociotechnical systems (STS)** theory, which is the main source of current SDWT practices. STS theory was introduced during the 1940s at the Tavistock Institute, where Eric Trist and his colleagues had been studying the effects of technology on coal mining in the United Kingdom.[70]

The Tavistock researchers observed that the new coal mining technology (called the "long wall" method) led to lower, not higher, job performance. They analyzed the causes of this problem and established the idea that organizations need "joint optimization" between the social and technical systems of the work unit. In other words, they need to introduce technology in a way that creates the best structure for semi-autonomous work teams. Moreover, the Tavistock group concluded that teams should be sufficiently independent so that they can control the main "variances" in the system. This means that the team must control the factors with the greatest impact on quality, quantity, and the cost

Sociotechnical systems (STS) A theory stating that effective work sites have joint optimization of their social and technological systems, and that teams should have sufficient autonomy to control key variances in the work process.

of the product or service. From this overview of STS, we can identify several conditions for successful SDWTs:[71]

- *Primary work unit*—STS suggests that SDWTs work best in a primary work unit, which is any work team that makes a product, provides a service, or otherwise completes an entire work process. By making an entire product or service together, the team is sufficiently independent from other work units that it can make adjustments without affecting or being affected by others too much. At the same time, employees within a primary work unit perform interdependent subtasks so they have a sense of performing a common task.[72]

- *Semi-autonomous work groups*—STS advocates a team-based structure in which employees in the primary work unit have sufficient autonomy to manage the work process. STS writers call it *collective self-regulation*, which means that the team can decide how to divide work among its members as well as how to coordinate that work. Collective self-regulation is a central feature in self-directed work teams and represents a team-based version of autonomy in job enrichment (see Chapter 4).

www.celestica.com

- *Controlling key variances*—STS says that productivity improves when the work team has control over "key variances." These variances represent the disturbances or interruptions that occur in a work process, such as the mixture of ingredients in soup manufacturing or the courteousness of service at an airline reservations call centre. By controlling these factors, work teams control the quantity and quality of output in the work process. In contrast, STS has little advantage when the main causes of good or poor performance are mainly due to technology, supplies, or other factors beyond the team's control.

- *Joint optimization*—Perhaps the most crucial feature of STS is that a balance must be struck between the social and technical systems to maximize the operation's effectiveness.[74] Production demands and social dynamics must be compatible with each other. In particular, the technological system should be implemented in a way that encourages or facilitates team dynamics, job enrichment, and meaningful feedback. This idea of joint optimization was quite radical in the 1940s, a time when many thought there was only one best way to install technology in the workplace and that jobs must be designed around this necessary structure. STS, on the other hand, says that companies have considerable latitude in how technology is introduced. In particular, it assumes that technology is flexible enough to support a semi-autonomous, team-based structure.

Courtesy of Celestica Inc.

Celestica Inc., Canada's largest high-technology company, operates in a competitive environment where technology and employees need careful alignment. To achieve this alignment, the computer and Internet gear manufacturer adopted sociotechnical systems (STS) as its template for corporate renewal. Employee study teams mapped work process flows and identified key variances—disturbances or interruptions that occur in a work process. Several changes were introduced that addressed each of the key variances. Permanent self-directed work teams of 15 to 40 people were established to complete each work process. As a result of STS, productivity and quality doubled and job satisfaction increased significantly. As one employee wrote: "What I like about the STS process is that the change has been driven by the employees—those responsible for execution—as opposed to management dictating how it's going to be."[73] To what extent has Celestica applied the four STS conditions necessary for successful self-directed work teams?

Sociotechnical systems theory in practice

Shell Canada, Pratt & Whitney Canada, Nortel Networks, and several other Canadian organizations have applied sociotechnical systems since the early 1970s. In each case, they found that team-based structures will not succeed simply by calling several employees a team and giving them some team-building exercises. Instead, corporate leaders need to diagnose and redesign the technological structure to ensure that it supports a team-based work environment.

In spite of these successes, some firms have trouble finding the optimal alignment of the social and technical systems. Volvo's Kalmar and Uddevalla plants in Sweden may have demonstrated this point.[75] These plants replaced the traditional assembly line with fixed workstations at which teams of approximately 20 employees assemble and install components in an unfinished automobile chassis. This technological structure creates a strong team orientation, but productivity at the two Volvo plants is among the lowest in the automobile industry because the technological design is not sufficiently flexible. In other words, in its attempt to accommodate the social system, Volvo's production system may have become technologically too inefficient.

BENEFITS OF EMPLOYEE INVOLVEMENT

For the past half-century, organizational behaviour scholars have advised that self-directed work teams and other forms of employee involvement offer potential benefits for both employees and their organizations.[76] These benefits include improved decision quality and commitment, as well as employee satisfaction, empowerment, and development.

DECISION QUALITY

Probably the number-one reason why corporate leaders embrace employee involvement is that it can potentially improve decision-making quality. This is particularly true for complex decisions where employees possess relevant information.[77] Employees are closer to customers and production activities, so they often know where the company can save money, improve product or service quality, and realize unused opportunities.

Employee involvement may improve the quality of decisions in three ways, as Exhibit 10.5 illustrates. First, it may lead to a more accurate definition of the problem. Employees are, in many respects, the sensors of the organization's environment. When the organization's activities misalign with customer expectations, employees are usually the first to know. Employee involvement ensures that everyone in the organization is quickly alerted to these problems.

Second, employee involvement can potentially improve the number and quality of solutions generated. In a well-managed meeting, team members create **synergy** by pooling their knowledge to form new alternatives that no one would have designed alone. In other words, several people working together and building on each other's strengths can potentially generate more and better solutions than if these people worked alone. For example, as we noted in the previous chapter, heterogeneous teams—those whose members have diverse backgrounds—tend to develop more innovative solutions to complex problems compared to homogeneous teams.[78]

Third, involving employees in decisions increases the likelihood that the best option will be selected. This occurs because the decision is reviewed by people with diverse perspectives

Synergy A condition in which the interaction of two or more people produces higher quality and quantity of solutions than if these people worked alone on the problem.

EXHIBIT 10.5 How Employee Involvement Improves Decision Quality

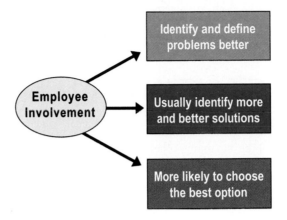

and a broader representation of values than if one executive made the choice alone. In other words, there is less chance that a grossly inaccurate solution will be selected when knowledgeable people are involved.

DECISION COMMITMENT

An old maxim says that the best person to put in charge of a problem is the one most directly affected by its outcome. In other words, employees who are expected to implement organizational decisions should be involved in choosing the course of action. This participation creates psychological ownership of the decision. Rather than viewing themselves as agents of someone else's decision, staff members feel personally responsible for its success. Consequently, they tend to exhibit less resistance to change and are more motivated to implement these decisions.[79]

Employee involvement can also increase the sense of fairness that people feel about organizational decisions. If a company begins a gainsharing plan or some other reward system (see Chapter 4), individuals are more likely to believe that the reward distribution is fair if they had the opportunity to influence the rules for distributing those rewards.[80] This may occur even when the reward distribution does not favour the employee.

EMPLOYEE SATISFACTION, EMPOWERMENT, AND DEVELOPMENT

Empowerment The feeling of control and self-efficacy that emerges when people are given power in a previously powerless situation.

Employee involvement often (although not always) improves job satisfaction and feelings of **empowerment**.[81] Recall from Chapter 4 that empowerment refers to a feeling of control and self-efficacy that emerges when people are given power in a previously powerless situation.[82] Empowerment increases job satisfaction because employees feel less stress when they have some control over life's events. It also includes feelings of self-efficacy— the "can-do" attitude that people have towards a specific task and, more generally, towards other challenges in life.[83] Employee involvement is a form of job enrichment, so the situational factors described in the job characteristics model must also be considered (see Chapter 4). Specifically, employee involvement is more likely to increase satisfaction when employees receive adequate training, are sufficiently happy with their work context, and have a high growth need.

Lastly, we should note that many forms of involvement give employees the opportunity to improve their decision-making skills and prepare for higher levels of responsibility. High involvement may offer the additional benefits of fostering teamwork and collegiality as co-workers learn more about each other and come to appreciate each other's talents.[84]

CHOOSING THE OPTIMAL LEVEL OF EMPLOYEE INVOLVEMENT

If employee involvement is so wonderful, why isn't everyone in self-directed work teams? The answer is that the optimal level of employee involvement depends on the situation. Like so many other organizational behaviour topics, we need to take a contingency approach to determine the optimal level of employee involvement. Organizational behaviour scholars Victor Vroom and Alfred Jago have developed four decision trees to direct us towards the best level of employee involvement under different conditions.[85] Each of these decision trees considers five levels of employee participation ranging from purely autocratic to team consensus:

AI   You make the decision alone with no employee involvement.

AII Subordinates provide information that you request, but they don't offer recommendations and they might not be aware of the problem.

CI   You describe the problem to relevant subordinates individually, getting their information and recommendations. You make the final decision, which does not necessarily reflect the advice that subordinates have provided.

CII You describe the problem to subordinates in a meeting, in which they discuss information and recommendations. You make the final decision, which does not necessarily reflect the advice that subordinates have provided.

GII You describe the problem to subordinates in a meeting. They discuss the problem and make a decision that you are willing to accept and implement if it has the entire team's support. You might chair this session, but you do not influence the team's decision.

Exhibit 10.6 presents the most common decision tree in which the leader faces a problem relevant to employees and has a limited amount of time to make the decision. Working from the left to the right side of the decision tree, the decision maker answers eight questions that relate to four important contingencies of employee involvement: decision quality, decision commitment, decision conflict, and programmed decision.

Three questions among these problem attributes consider the effect of employee involvement on decision quality. The first question in the decision tree asks whether the problem has a high- or low-quality dimension (QR). In other words, is it possible to make a "good" or "bad" decision, or are all of the options of equal quality? Most decisions have a quality requirement because some alternatives are more likely than others to achieve organizational objectives. Two other questions ask whether the leader has enough information to make the decision alone (LI) and whether subordinates have enough information to make a high-quality decision (SI). Generally, employee involvement is higher where the leader does not have enough information and subordinates do have enough information to make the decision alone.

EXHIBIT 10.6 Vroom-Jago Time-Driven Decision Tree for Employee Involvement

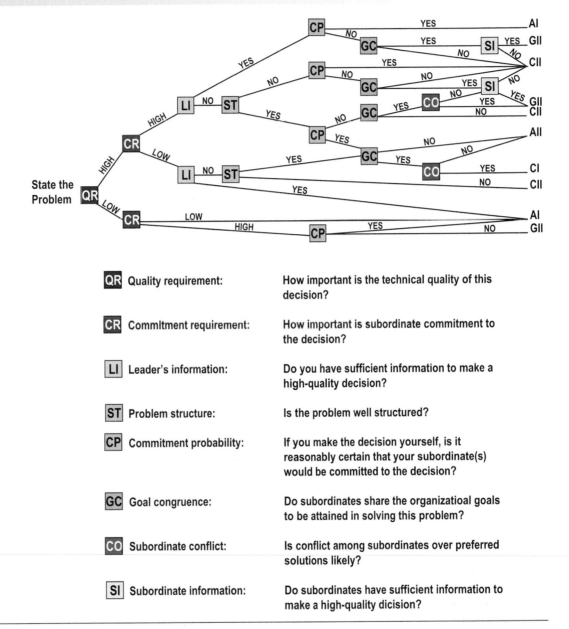

QR	Quality requirement:	How important is the technical quality of this decision?
CR	Commitment requirement:	How important is subordinate commitment to the decision?
LI	Leader's information:	Do you have sufficient information to make a high-quality decision?
ST	Problem structure:	Is the problem well structured?
CP	Commitment probability:	If you make the decision yourself, is it reasonably certain that your subordinate(s) would be committed to the decision?
GC	Goal congruence:	Do subordinates share the organizatioal goals to be attained in solving this problem?
CO	Subordinate conflict:	Is conflict among subordinates over preferred solutions likely?
SI	Subordinate information:	Do subordinates have sufficient information to make a high-quality dicision?

Source: V.H. Vroom and A.G. Jago, *The New Leadership: Managing Particiaption in Organizations* (Englewood Cliffs, NJ: Prentice Hall, 1988), p. 184. © 1987 V.H. Vroom and A.G. Jago. Used with permisison of the authors.

Two questions in the Vroom-Jago model address the issue of decision commitment. One question asks whether decision commitment is important (CR); another asks whether employees will be committed to a decision made exclusively by the leader (CP). If employee commitment is important and employees are unlikely to accept the leader's decision, a higher level of employee involvement is usually necessary.

Two questions refer to another important contingency: conflict. One question asks whether employee goals are congruent or in conflict with organizational goals (GC). If employees are likely to make a decision contrary to organizational goals, lower involvement is preferred. Another question asks whether employees will be in conflict with each other when choosing the preferred solution (CO). If so, the leader should limit the level of involvement.

The remaining question in the Vroom-Jago decision tree asks whether the problem is structured (ST). This refers to the idea presented at the beginning of this chapter that some decisions are programmed whereas others are nonprogrammed. Programmed decisions are less likely to need employee involvement because the solutions are already worked out from past experience.

Overall, the Vroom-Jago decision tree may look like a confusing array of issues, but it really breaks down into four important contingencies of employee involvement: decision quality, decision commitment, decision conflict, and programmed decision. Unfortunately, as the next section describes, there are also several challenges to overcome when implementing employee involvement.

OVERCOMING CHALLENGES TO EMPLOYEE INVOLVEMENT

Employee involvement is not a panacea for all organizational problems. In some situations, participation may be useful but resistance to it could threaten the company's effectiveness in other ways. In other situations, involvement practices are incompatible with the needs and values of the people affected. However, where employee involvement is desirable, corporate leaders need to recognize and overcome at least three potential barriers: cultural differences, management resistance, and employee and labour-union resistance.

CULTURAL DIFFERENCES

Various forms and levels of employee involvement have been implemented in many countries. For instance, self-directed work teams and other forms of employee participation have been successfully introduced in Malaysia, Germany, Japan, India, and Scandinavian countries.[86] Still, employee involvement is more compatible with some cultural values than with others.[87] Employee involvement is typically an interpersonal or team-based activity, so it is adopted most readily in cultures with high collectivism. Recall from Chapter 7 that people with a collectivist value appreciate and support their membership in the group to which they belong. Consequently, they are usually comfortable discussing their ideas with co-workers. In contrast, individualistic people may be less comfortable with employee involvement because of their preference to work alone.

> **Power distance** The extent to which people accept unequal distribution of power in a society.

Employee involvement also works better in low **power-distance** cultures because employees are expected to engage in self-leadership rather than receive direction from superiors. Power distance refers to the extent to which people accept unequal distribution of power in a society (see Chapter 7). Employees with low power distance usually want to be involved in corporate decisions, whereas those in high power-distance cultures prefer having supervisors give them directions and answers. One recent Canadian study reported that high power distance probably explains why Mexican firms have difficulty implementing self-directed work teams. Employees expect managers to make decisions that affect their work, whereas SDWTs emphasizes self-initiative and individual responsibility within teams.[88]

How do organizations overcome these cultural challenges? First, we should remember that few cultures are so extreme in either collectivism or power distance to prohibit employee involvement. Moreover, some forms of employee involvement are more problematic than are others. For instance, people with high power distance may feel comfortable providing anonymous ideas (such as through a suggestion system) or ideas through a spokesperson. A third consideration is that people with fairly high power distance and high individualism may adjust over time to a workplace that espouses collectivist and low power-distance values.

MANAGEMENT RESISTANCE

Supervisors have difficulty making the transition to self-directed work teams.[89] Their main worry is losing power when employees gain power through participation. Some are concerned that their jobs will lose value, whereas others believe that they will not have any jobs at all. Another problem is that supervisors do not know how to become "hands-off" facilitators of several work teams rather than "hands-on" supervisors of several employees.[90] For example, one of the biggest stumbling blocks to self-directed work teams at TRW Canada (described in Chapter 9) is that many supervisors slipped back into their command-and-control supervisory styles. As one TRW Canada explains: "One of the toughest things for some of them was to shift from being a boss to a coach, moving from saying, 'I know what's good for you' to 'How can I help you?'"[91]

Education and training are the first steps in minimizing management resistance to employee involvement. The company needs to assure these people that their careers are not threatened. They also need to receive considerable training to adjust from the old "command-and-control" style to the more ambiguous facilitator style of leadership. However, even with education and training, many companies that introduce employee involvement practices eventually have to transfer or replace supervisors and managers who cannot adjust to the new style.

EMPLOYEE AND LABOUR-UNION RESISTANCE

Employees resist employee involvement for several reasons. Most have been bombarded with previous management fads and do not want to develop false hopes for the latest initiative. Employee involvement also requires new—and usually more ambiguous—role patterns and possibly new skills (e.g., working in teams). Thus, many employees feel uncomfortable as they explore their new roles, and they may be worried that they lack the skills to adapt to the new work requirements. As Connections 10.2 describes, BP Norge experienced these problems when BP's Norwegian business introduced self-directed work teams on its remote North Sea oil platforms. This story also illustrates that employee concerns can be overcome through education, training, and plenty of on-the-job feedback.

Labour unions have been strong advocates of joint health and safety committees and supported the early sociotechnical changes in Europe and India. Some labour unions in North America have also supported high-involvement practices, but many have publicly resisted them for three reasons.[92] First, they believe that employee involvement programs improve productivity at the price of higher stress levels among employees. This is sometimes true. SDWTs and other practices tend to give employees more tasks and responsibilities, which may lead to greater work pressure. Second, high-involvement practices require more flexibility by reversing work rules and removing job categories that unions have negotiated over the years. Labour-union leaders are therefore concerned that it will be a difficult battle to regain these hard-fought union member rights. Finally, a few union leaders believe that companies use employee involvement programs as a subtle strategy to bypass the union and thereby weaken its power in the workplace.

These union fears are troublesome because employee involvement programs require union support and partnership.[93] Fortunately, there are many examples of successful labour-management initiatives that give employees more control in the workplace. In most cases, labour union resistance was minimized through the slow development of trust between the corporate and labour leader as well as evidence that the company is sincere in its willingness to distribute more power to employees in their work. At the same time, labour union involvement requires labour leaders who perceive long-term value of the employee involvement activity for their membership and the labour union's survival.

CONNECTIONS 10.2

BP Norge Tests the Seaworthiness of SDWTs

An oil platform is one of the most complex workplaces in the world. It is a chemical plant, mining operation, airport, harbour, power station, hotel, and leisure centre. It is also the setting in which BP Norge, the Norwegian arm of British Petroleum, overcame the challenges of introducing self-directed work teams (SDWTs).

Senior executives at BP Norge wanted to dismantle the company's hierarchy and replace it with a high-involvement business model. A significant part of this process was to help BP Norge employees operate North Sea oil platforms through SDWTs. John Vemmestad, director of BP Norge, explains: "[Self-directed work teams] fit perfectly with the corporate direction, which involves pushing responsibility down to the lowest levels possible."

The transition did not occur easily, however. Some employees were skeptical that management would really give them more power. Others wanted higher status and payoffs for the additional responsibilities. Consequently, BP Norge held a workshop where employee and supervisor representatives discussed these issues with senior management. The company also gave employees the option of not being involved in the SDWT process.

It also took a bit of nudging to get employees to think autonomously. For example, an instrument team and electrical team at BP Norge wanted to remove the wall between their adjacent workshops. When they asked the project leader for permission, the leader

AP Worldwide.

BP Norge encouraged employees on its North Sea oil platforms to form self-directed work teams.

told them to do what they thought was right. The two teams realized that they use the same setup lathes, so they went back to the leader for permission to move the lathes beside each other. The project leader's reply was "I'm not sure why you're asking me that." Two weeks later, the team representatives reported to the project leader, "We decided that two lathes were too many, so we only have one now." With the leader's guidance, the teams had assumed a higher level of autonomy and self-accountability.

Sources: Adapted from M. Moravec, O.J. Johannessen, and T.A. Hjelmas, "The Well-Managed SMT," *Management Review,* 87 (June 1998), pp. 56–58; M. Moravec, O.J. Johannessen, and T.A. Hjelmas, "Thumbs Up for Self-Managed Teams," *Management Review,* July 17, 1997, p. 42.

Employee involvement is becoming a pervasive part of organizational life. Indeed, it is difficult to think of many organizations in North America where employees are not allowed to provide their ideas or be involved in some corporate level decisions. Increasingly, an organization's competitive advantage is the knowledge and ideas of its employees. In the next chapter, we will learn how companies leverage this competitive advantage by supporting creativity.

CHAPTER SUMMARY

- Decision making is a conscious process of making choices among one or more alternatives with the intention of moving towards some desired state of affairs. This involves identifying problems and opportunities, choosing the best decision style, developing alternative solutions, choosing the best solution, implementing the selected alternative, and evaluating decision outcomes.

- Perceptual biases and poor diagnostic skills make it difficult to identify problems and opportunities. These challenges are minimized by being aware of these human limitations, discussing the situation with colleagues, creating early warning systems, and using data mining to systematically identify trends.

- Choosing the best alternative is often challenging because organizational goals are ambiguous or in conflict, human information processing is incomplete and subjective, and people tend to satisfice rather than maximize. Solutions can be chosen more effectively by systematically identifying and weighting the factors used to evaluate alternatives, using decision support systems to guide the decision process, conducting scenario planning, and using intuition where we possess enough tacit knowledge on the issue.

- Postdecisional justification and escalation of commitment make it difficult to accurately evaluate decision outcomes. Escalation of commitment is caused mainly by self-justification, the gambler's fallacy, perceptual blinders, and closing costs. These concerns are minimized by separating decision choosers from decision evaluators, establishing a preset level at which the decision is abandoned or re-evaluated, relying on more systematic and clear feedback about the project's success, and involving several people in decision making.

- Employee involvement (or participation) refers to the degree to which employees share information, knowledge, rewards, and power throughout the organization. It may be formal or informal, direct or indirect, and voluntary or statutory. The level of participation may range from an employee providing specific information to management without knowing the problem or issue, to complete involvement in all phases of the decision process. A few companies have representative participation, in which employee representatives are on the board of directors. Several moderate levels of employee involvement include communities of practice, gainsharing programs, and open book management. Open book management involves sharing financial information with employees and encouraging them to recommend ideas that improve those financial results. It includes training employees to read financial statements and getting them to think of financial performance as a game that they can play and win.

- Self-directed work teams (SDWTs) are work groups that complete an entire piece of work requiring several interdependent tasks and have substantial autonomy over the execution of these tasks. They assign tasks to team members; control most work inputs, flow, and output; are responsible for correcting problems; and receive team-level feedback and rewards. SDWTs are more effective when they following the guidance of sociotechnical systems (STS) theory. According to STS, teams should be primary work units that involve completion of an entire product or service. They must be sufficiently independent to control the main "variances" in the system. STS calls for a balance between the social and technological systems in the work process, but it can be difficult to find this optimum balance.

- Employee involvement may lead to higher decision quality, decision commitment, employee satisfaction and empowerment, and employee development in decision-making skills. The Vroom-Jago decision tree guides decision makers through a series of questions to determine the optimal level of involvement. The model mainly considers four contingencies: decision quality, decision commitment, decision conflict, and programmed decision.

- Management, employees, and labour unions often resist employee involvement, although this can be resolved through education, training, and trust building. Employees with high individualism and power distance are also less comfortable with some forms of employee involvement.

KEY TERMS

Codetermination, p. 303

Communities of practice, p. 304

Decision making, p. 292

Employee involvement, p. 301

Empowerment, p. 309

Escalation of commitment, p. 299

Gainsharing plan, p. 304

Intuition, p. 299

Mental models, p. 294

Nonprogrammed decision, p. 293

Open book management, p. 304

Postdecisional justification, p. 299

Power distance, p. 312

Programmed decision, p. 293

Satisficing, p. 297

Scenario planning, p. 298

Selective attention, p. 297

Self-directed work team (SDWT), p. 305

Sociotechnical systems (STS), p. 306

Synergy, p. 308

Tacit knowledge, p. 299

DISCUSSION QUESTIONS

1. A major software developer in Vancouver is experiencing an increasing number of customer complaints and a general trend towards lower sales. Describe three reasons why executives in this organization might be slow to realize that a problem exists or to identify the root cause(s) of these symptoms.

2. A management consultant is hired by a manufacturing firm to determine the best site for its next production facility. The consultant has had several meetings with the company's

senior executives regarding the factors to consider when making its recommendation. Discuss three decision-making problems that might prevent the consultant from choosing the best site location.

3. A Canadian developer received financial backing for a new business financial centre along a derelict section of the waterfront, a few kilometres from the current downtown area of a large European city. The idea was to build several high-rise structures, attract large tenants to those sites, and have the city extend transportation systems out to the new centre. Over the next decade, the developer believed that others would build in the area, thereby attracting the regional or national offices of many financial institutions. Interest from potential tenants was much lower than initially predicted and the city did not build transportation systems as quickly as expected. Still, the builder proceeded with the original plans. Only after financial support was curtailed did the developer reconsider the project. Using your knowledge of escalation of commitment, discuss three possible reasons why the developer was motivated to continue with the project.

4. Ancient Book Company has a problem with new book projects. Even when it is apparent to others that a book is far behind schedule or may not have much public interest, sponsoring editors are reluctant to terminate contracts with authors whom they have signed. The result is that developmental editors invest more time on these projects rather than on more fruitful projects. As a form of escalation of commitment, describe two methods that Ancient Book Company can use to minimize this problem.

5. When Great West Life Assurance Co. decided to build new headquarters in Winnipeg, it formed a task force of employees representing different areas of the organization. The group's mandate was to identify features of the new building that would help employees do their jobs more effectively and work more comfortably. Describe the forms and level of employee involvement in this task force.

6. A chicken processing company wants to build a processing plant designed around sociotechnical systems principles. In a traditional chicken processing plant, employees work in separate departments—cleaning and cutting, cooking, packaging, and warehousing. The cooking and packaging processes are controlled by separate workstations in the traditional plant. How would the company change this operation according to sociotechnical systems design?

7. Employee involvement applies just as well to the classroom as it does to the office or factory floor. Explain how student involvement in classroom decisions typically made by the instructor alone might improve decision quality. What potential problems may occur in this process?

8. Advanced Telecom Ltd. has successfully introduced self-directed work teams (SDWTs) at its operations throughout Canada. The company now wants to introduce SDWTs at its plants in Singapore and Mexico. What potential cross-cultural challenges might Advanced Telecom experience as it introduces SDWTs in these countries?

Case Study

ACTIVITY 10.1
Employee Involvement Cases

Case 1: The Sugar Substitute Research Decision

You are the head of research and development (R&D) for a major Canadian beer company. While working on a new beer product, one of the scientists in your unit seems to have tentatively identified a new chemical compound that has few calories but tastes closer to sugar than current sugar substitutes. The company has no foreseeable need for this product, but it could be patented and licensed to manufacturers in the food industry.

The sugar substitute discovery is in its preliminary stages and would require considerable time and resources before it would be commercially viable. This means that it would necessarily take some resources away from other projects in the lab. The sugar substitute project is beyond your technical expertise, but some of the R&D lab researchers are familiar with that field of chemistry. As with most forms of research, it is difficult to determine the amount of work required to identify and further perfect the sugar substitute. You do not know how much demand is expected for this product. Your department has a decision process for funding projects that fall behind schedule. However, there are no rules or precedents about funding projects that would be licensed but not used by the organization.

The company's R&D budget is limited and other scientists in your work group have recently complained that they require more resources and financial support to complete their projects. Some of these other R&D projects hold promise for future beer sales. You believe that most researchers in the R&D unit are committed to ensuring that the company's interests are achieved.

Case 2: Coast Guard Cutter Decision

You are the captain of a 72-metre Coast Guard cutter, with a crew of 16, including officers. Your mission is general at-sea search and rescue. At 2 a.m. this morning, while en route to your home port after a routine 28-day patrol, you received word from the nearest Coast Guard station that a small plane had crashed 100 kilometres offshore. You obtained all the available information concerning the location of the crash, informed your crew of the mission, and set a new course at maximum speed for the scene to commence a search for survivors and wreckage.

You have now been searching for 20 hours. Your search operation has been increasingly impaired by rough seas, and there is evidence of a severe storm building. The atmospherics associated with the deteriorating weather have made communications with the Coast Guard station impossible. A decision must be made shortly about whether to abandon the search and place your vessel on a course that would ride out the storm (thereby protecting the vessel and your crew but relegating any possible survivors to almost certain death from exposure) or to continue a potentially futile search with the risks that would entail.

Before losing communications, you received an updated weather advisory concerning the severity and duration of the storm. Although your crew members are extremely conscientious about their responsibility, you believe that they would be divided about whether to leave or to stay.

Discussion Questions

1. To what extent should your subordinates be involved in these decisions? (Note: You may assume that both cases have time constraints, so the lowest level of involvement is preferred.) Choose one of the following:

   AI. You make the decision alone with no employee involvement.

   AII. Subordinates provide information that you request, but they don't offer recommendations and they might not be aware of the problem.

   CI. You describe the problem to relevant subordinates individually, getting their information and recommendations. You make the final decision, which does not necessarily reflect the advice that subordinates have provided.

   CII. You describe the problem to subordinates in a meeting, at which they discuss information and recommendations. You make the final decision, which does not necessarily reflect the advice that subordinates have provided.

ACTIVITY 10.1 CONTINUED

GII. You describe the problem to subordinates in a meeting. They discuss the problem and make a decision that you are willing to accept and implement if it has the entire team's support. You might chair this session, but you do not influence the team's decision.

2. What factors led you to choose these alternatives rather than the others?

3. What problems might occur if less or more involvement occurred in these cases (where possible)?

Source: The Coast Guard case is adapted from V.H. Vroom and A.G. Jago, *The New Leadership: Managing Participation in Organizations* (Englewood Cliffs, NJ: Prentice Hall, 1988). © 1987 V.H. Vroom and A.G. Jago. Used with permission of the authors.

Video Case Study

ACTIVITY 10.2
Baron of Beer

A lot of things can go wrong when you're creating a business from scratch, especially if you're also building a new brand in a fiercely competitive market. But Gary Depape didn't think so. He's the guy building the Agassiz Brewing Company, a $1.3-million project that requires a million decisions.

Depape is trying to introduce a new brand of beer in Winnipeg, but he has to do it fast. Molson and Labatt recently shut down their local plants, which alienated some of the local beer drinkers from the big brands, providing an opportunity for Depape. But Winnipeg already has one microbrewery—Depape used to work there—and a third one is just weeks away from start-up. Agassiz Brewing Company may have an edge, however. Depape played pro hockey in Germany, where he learned about good-quality beer.

Depape's goal is to have beer on the shelves by March. He's got the logos, the kegs, the custom-made brew house, and the glass. Unfortunately, the used bottling line he bought from Germany is missing parts, and the directions on how to put it together are baffling. An expert bottler from Victoria, B.C., had to be flown to Winnipeg to piece it together. Adding to these costs, Depape realized that he hired his two brewers and sales rep two months too early.

When the brewery started up, Depape and his crew experienced problems with the brewing system. Then the bottling machine broke down, which

required another expensive house call from the expert in Victoria. This delayed beer sales for three weeks. Fortunately, the competition also had problems, which delayed their sales as well. By the time the beer finally started to flow, Depape had signed up 200 accounts.

The weather doesn't cooperate, so sales are initially slow. When it warms up, Agassiz's production is on track and sales are steady. But Depape doesn't hit the numbers forecasted in his business plan. At the annual shareholders' meeting, Depape wants to explain the effects of bad weather. The investors convince Depape that his projections were too optimistic. Rather than launching another brew for Christmas, his mandate is to cut costs.

"We'll find a way to get this company to make some money quicker, if that's the issue here," says Depape.

Discussion Questions

1. What decision-making problems did Gary Depape experience during the start-up of his microbrewery?

2. The bottling machine caused considerable trouble for Agassiz Brewing Company. Describe Gary Depape's search for alternative solutions to solve these problems. Were these programmed or nonprogrammed decisions?

3. Identify the situations in which Gary Depape would have benefited from more involvement of other people in his decision making.

Source: Based on "Baron of Beer," *Venture* 729 (November 16, 1999).

TEAM exercises

ACTIVITY 10.3
WHERE IN THE WORLD ARE WE?

Purpose: This exercise is designed to help you understand the potential advantages of involving others in decisions rather than making decisions alone.

Materials: Students require an unmarked copy of the map of Canada with grid marks (Exhibit 2). The instructor will provide copies of the answer sheet after students have estimated the locations of communities individually and in teams.

Instructions:

Step 1: Working alone, students will identify the location of the communities listed in Exhibit 1, all of which are found on this map. For example, mark a small "1" in Exhibit 2 on the spot where you believe Hanover is located. Mark a small "2" where you think Bella Coola is located, and so on. Be sure to number each location clearly and with numbers small enough to fit within one grid space. You are not allowed to look at any maps or use any other materials.

Step 2: The instructor will organize students into teams of approximately equal size (five to six people). Working with your team members, reach a consensus on the location of each community listed in Exhibit 1. The instructor might provide teams with a separate copy of this map, or each member can identify the team's numbers using a different-coloured pen on their individual maps. The team's decision for each location should occur by consensus, not by voting or averaging.

Step 3: The instructor will provide or display an answer sheet, showing the correct locations of the Canadian communities. Using this answer sheet, count the minimum number of grid squares between the location individually marked and the true location of each community. Write the number of grid squares in the second column of Exhibit 1, then calculate the total. Next, count the minimum number of grid squares between the location the team marked and the true location of each community. Write the number of grid squares in the third column of Exhibit 1, then calculate the total.

Step 4: The instructor will ask for information about the totals and the class will discuss the implication of these results for employee involvement and decision making.

EXHIBIT 1   List of Selected Communities in Canada

Number	City	Individual distance in grid units from the true location	Team distance in grid units from the true location
1	Hanover		
2	Bella Coola		
3	Glace Bay		
4	Granby		
5	Estevan		
6	Inuvik		
7	Marathon		
8	Churchill		
		Total:	Total:

© 2001 Steven L. McShane

EXHIBIT 2   Map of Canada

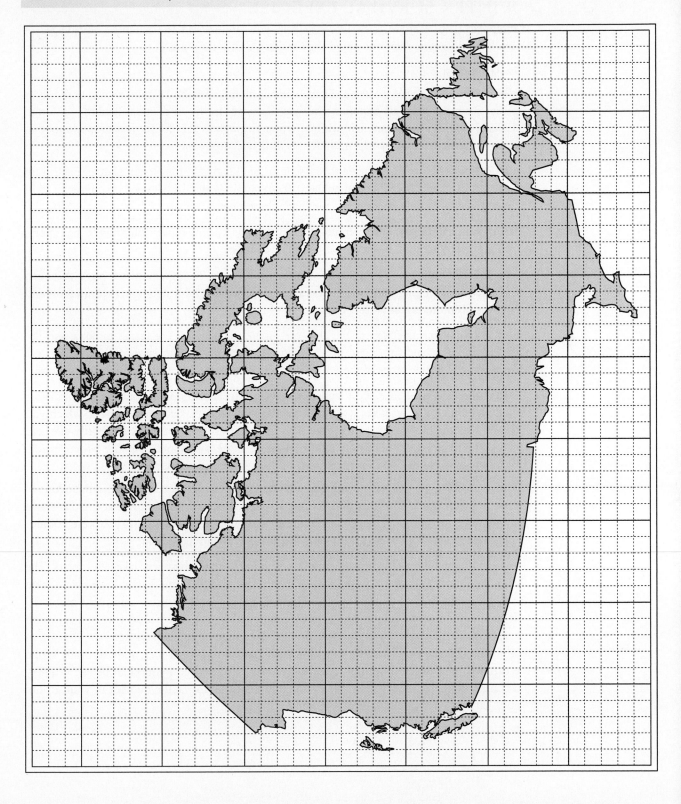

ACTIVITY 10.4
WINTER SURVIVAL EXERCISE

Purpose: This exercise is designed to help you understand the potential advantages of involving others in decisions rather than making decisions alone.

Instructions:

Step 1: Read the "Situation" below. Then, working alone, rank the 12 items shown in the chart below according to their importance to your survival. In the "Individual Ranking" column, indicate the most important item with "1," going through to "12" for the least important item. Keep in mind the reasons why each item is or is not important.

Step 2: The instructor will divide the class into small teams of four to six people. Each team will rank the items in the second column. Team rankings should be based on consensus, not determined by simply averaging the individual rankings.

Step 3: When the teams have completed their rankings, the instructor will provide the expert's ranking, which should be entered in the third column.

Step 4: Each student will compute the absolute difference (i.e., ignore minus signs) between the individual ranking and the expert's ranking, record this information in column four, and sum the absolute values at the bottom of column four.

Step 5: In column five, record the absolute difference between the team's ranking and the expert's ranking, and sum these absolute scores at the bottom. A class discussion will follow regarding the implications of these results for employee involvement and decision making.

Situation: You have just crash-landed somewhere in the woods of southern Manitoba or possibly northern Minnesota. It is 11:32 a.m. in mid-January. The small plane in which you were travelling crashed on a small lake. The pilot and co-pilot were killed. Shortly after the crash, the plane sank completely into the lake with the pilot's and co-pilot's bodies inside. Everyone else on the flight escaped to land dry and without serious injury.

The crash occurred suddenly before the pilot had time to radio for help or inform anyone of your position. Since your pilot was trying to avoid the storm, you know that the plane was considerably off course. The pilot announced shortly before the crash that you were 70 kilometres northwest of a small town that is the nearest known habitation.

You are in a wilderness area made up of thick woods broken by many lakes and rivers. The snow depth varies from above the ankles in windswept areas to more than knee-deep where it has drifted. The last weather report indicated that the temperature would reach minus 10 degrees Celsius in the daytime and minus 25 degrees at night. There are plenty of dead wood and twigs in the area around the lake. You and the other surviving passengers are dressed in winter clothing appropriate for city wear—suits, pantsuits, street shoes, and overcoats. While escaping from the plane, your group salvaged the 12 items listed in the chart below. You may assume that the number of persons in the group is the same as the number in your group, and that you have agreed to stay together.

WINTER SURVIVAL TALLY SHEET

Items	Step 1 Your individual ranking	Step 2 Your team's ranking	Step 3 Survival expert's ranking	Step 4 Difference between steps 1 and 3	Step 5 Difference between steps 2 and 3
Ball of steel wool					
Newspapers					
Compass					
Hand axe					
Cigarette lighter					
45-caliber pistol					
Section air map					
Canvas					
Shirt and pants					
Can of shortening					
Whisky					
Chocolate bars					
Total					
				Your score	Team score

(The lower the score, the better)

Source: Adapted from "Winter Survival" in D. Johnson and F. Johnson, *Joining Together,* 3rd ed. (Englewood Cliffs, NJ: Prentice Hall, 1984).

Self-Assessment exercise

ACTIVITY 10.5
DECISION-MAKING STYLE INVENTORY

Purpose: This self-assessment exercise is designed to help you estimate your preferred style of decision making.

Instructions: Listed below are statements describing how individuals go about making important decisions. Please indicate whether you agree or disagree with each statement. Answer each item as truthfully as possible so that you get an accurate estimate of your decision-making style. Then use the scoring key in Appendix B of this book to calculate your results. This exercise is completed alone so that students can assess themselves honestly without concerns of social comparison. However, class discussion will focus on the decision-making style that people prefer in organizational settings.

Please indicate the extent to which you agree or disagree with the following statements about your decision-making style.	Strongly Agree	Agree	Neutral	Disagree	Strongly Disagree
1. I make decisions based more on facts than on my gut instincts.	5	4	3	2	1
2. I feel more comfortable making decisions in a logical and systematic way.	5	4	3	2	1
3. When making decisions, I rely on my intuition more than anything else.	5	4	3	2	1
4. When I make a decision, it is more important for me to feel the decision is right than to have a rational reason for it.	5	4	3	2	1
5. I won't make a choice that doesn't feel right, even when the facts indicate it is the right choice.	5	4	3	2	1
6. My decision making tends to involve careful analysis of facts and weighting of decision criteria.	5	4	3	2	1
7. When I make a decision, I trust my inner feelings and reactions.	5	4	3	2	1
8. The best decisions I make are based on detailed analysis of factual information. . . .	5	4	3	2	1

Sources: Inspired from ideas in C.W. Allinson and J. Hayes, "The Cognitive Style Index: A Measure of Intuition-Analysis for Organizational Research," *Journal of Management Studies,* 33 (1996), pp. 119–35; S.G. Scott and R.A. Bruce, "Decision-Making Style: The Development and Assessment of a New Measure," *Educational & Psychological Measurement,* 55 (October 1995), pp. 818–31.

CHAPTER ELEVEN

Creativity and Team Decision Making

LEARNING OBJECTIVES

After reading this chapter, you should be able to:

- Define creativity.
- Outline the four steps in the creative process.
- Describe the characteristics of creative employees.
- Discuss the workplace conditions that support creativity.
- Identify five problems facing teams when making decisions.
- Compare the five structures for team decision making.

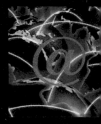

Executives at Ottawa marketing agency Hewson Bridge and Smith Ltd. demonstrate their creative capabilities at a client presentation.

A gang of sword-wielding Zorros recently stormed the boardroom of Prior Data Sciences in Kanata, Ontario. The event wasn't part of a Hollywood movie or a hostile takeover. Behind the masks were employees at Hewson Bridge and Smith Ltd. (HBS), one of three marketing agencies vying for Prior's business. HBS wanted the meeting to stand out from other presentations, and it did. The Ottawa-based marketing agency got the contract.

HBS president Don Hewson admits that there's "an element of risk" to using creative theatrics. "You can offend, sometimes, as much as you can stimulate . . . you have to really look at the situation." But HBS is willing to take those risks to help its high-tech clients develop corporate images that stand out from the crowd.

HBS also takes creative risks when bidding on new contracts. To become the marketing agency for JetForm Corp., HBS put up a bus shelter ad outside the Ottawa high-tech company's offices. The ad read: "JetForm: We did this because we made your short list. Imagine what we'll do as your agency." HBS also sent a series of cakes to JetForm executives with messages proclaiming HBS's commitment to the company. Toothbrushes were delivered after the cakes.

"That was incredibly creative of them to target me so directly," says Robert Lendvai, the JetForm marketing executive whose window overlooks the bus shelter ad. "I think even the (executives) on the fifth floor of this building appreciate people that go the distance or think outside the box."[1]

www.hbs.ca
www.prior.ca
www.jetform.com

Creativity The capability to develop an original product, service, or idea that makes a socially recognized contribution.

H̲ewson Bridge and Smith Ltd. is in the creativity business. Its employees must continually develop new ideas for shaping and promoting the images of corporate clients. But creativity is not restricted to marketing and advertising firms. In this increasingly knowledge-based economy, creativity is the competitive advantage of every organization.[2] Creativity is part of experimentation in knowledge management (see Chapter 1). It also helps to draw in knowledge from the external environment and to break down silos of knowledge across work units.

Creativity refers to developing an original product, service, or idea that makes a socially recognized contribution.[3] Although there are unique conditions for creativity that we discuss in this chapter, it is really part of the decision-making process described in the previous chapter. We rely on creativity to find problems, identify alternatives, and implement solutions. Creativity is not something saved for special occasions. It is an integral part of decision making.

After describing the creative process, this chapter looks at the characteristics of creative people and organizational conditions that support creativity. This is followed by a discussion of specific practices that encourage creative thought. The latter part of this chapter extends the discussion of creativity in team settings. Specifically, we look at various factors that restrict effective team decision making and creativity, then examine team structures that help to overcome these constraints.

Sheila Robertson.

Jacqueline Gautier likes to remind people that an organization's competitive advantage is the knowledge created by its employees. "Companies know creativity is intellectual capital," says the Saskatoon-based creativity specialist. "If they want to stay innovative, they have to have creative employees." The problem, says Gautier, is that many organizations squeeze the creative spirit out of their organizations. She cites her own past as an executive in Saskatchewan's potash industry: "There was a hole in my soul. I hadn't had a creative thought in probably ten years." Today, Gautier's seminars encourage others to rediscover their creative potential through painting, sculpting, and other forms of artistic expression.[6] What elements of knowledge management are affected by creativity?

THE CREATIVE PROCESS MODEL

Henry Yuen wanted to record a baseball game on TV while out of town, but the scientist had problems setting his VCR properly. While venting his anger, Yuen had an idea. "I thought that taping a program should be as easy as dialling a telephone," he says. So he and co-inventor Daniel Kwoh set out to develop a system that makes VCR recording just that simple. Today, most VCR owners enjoy the fruit of Yuen's creative inspiration through VCR Plus (also known as G-code). Users simply punch in the appropriate number from the TV guide listing and the system does the rest.[4]

Henry Yeun's inspiration for VCR Plus illustrates the quirky nature of the creative process. Several scholars have attempted over the past century to document the creative process. One of the earliest and most influential models is shown in Exhibit 11.1.[5] This model does not perfectly describe the creative process in every situation. For instance, it ignores team dynamics and the social context in which much creativity occurs (as we learn later in this chapter). Nevertheless, this model has some support and lays a useful foundation for our discussion of creativity.

PREPARATION

If there is one thing that scholars agree on, it is that preparation is an important condition for creativity. Preparation is the person's or group's effort to acquire knowledge and skills regarding the problem or opportunity.[7] Creativity is not a passive activity. It requires detailed study of information surrounding the issue. For example,

EXHIBIT 11.1 The Creative Process Model

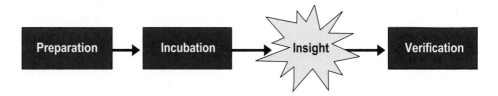

people usually have more creative insight when they take a problem apart and closely analyze each component.

Preparation also involves developing a clear understanding of what you are trying to achieve through a novel solution. It is directed by wishing for something, just as Henry Yuen wished for an easy way to program his VCR. "The key to creativity is clarity," explains the "Creativity and Innovation" manager at Bank of Montreal's learning institute in Toronto. "Never work on a creative challenge without first writing down a problem statement in the form of a question."[8]

INCUBATION

Incubation is the stage of reflective thought. We put the problem aside (sometimes out of frustration), but our mind is still working on it in the background. Some scholars question the importance of incubation for creative insight, while others suggest that it plays a powerful role in dissolving previously fixed perspectives about the problem.[9] The important condition here is to maintain a low-level awareness by frequently revisiting the problem. Incubation does not mean that you forget about the problem or issue. Metaphorically speaking, it involves putting the problem on the back burner. The problem is still simmering in your mind, but is not at the forefront of your attention. This may explain why some creative people seem to be absent-minded. They are tossing a problem around in the back of their mind, rather than fully concentrating on the current activity (having lunch, working on another project, etc.).

Along with dissolving fixed perspectives of the problem, incubation assists **divergent thinking**. Divergent thinking involves reframing the problem in a unique way and generating different approaches to the issue. This contrasts with *convergent thinking*, which refers to calculating the conventionally accepted "right answer" to a logical problem.[10] Henry Yuen's inspiration for VCR Plus and G-coding is an example of divergent thinking because we don't normally think of VCRs in terms of dialling a telephone. Divergent thinking is also responsible for the threaded caps on light fixtures. The experimental bulbs in Thomas Edison's lab kept falling out of their fixtures until a technician wondered whether the threaded caps that screwed down tightly on kerosene bottles would work on light bulbs. They did, and the design remains in use to this day.[11] Divergent thinkers are able to break away from known uses or perspectives and apply concepts or processes from completely different areas of life.

Incubation assists divergent thinking when people spend time doing something different. You can see this at Rueff, the Austrian fabric printer, where the head designer spends most of his time playing nocturnes on a grand piano. Similarly, employees at Nintendo have free rein of their time to achieve their creative goals. "We have kept quiet even when [designers] go to see a movie or play during work," explains Hiroshi Yamauchi, president of the Japanese game maker.[12]

> **Divergent thinking** The ability to reframe problems in a unique way and generate different approaches to the issue.

INSIGHT

People receive insight at some point during the incubation stage.[13] Insight refers to the experience of suddenly becoming aware of a unique idea. These flashes of inspiration don't keep a particular schedule; they might come to you at any time of day or night. They are also fleeting and can be quickly lost if not documented. For this reason, many creative people keep a journal or notebook nearby at all times, so that they can jot down these ideas before they disappear.[14] Ronalda Maillet is one of those note-takers. "[I] keep a note pad and pencil beside my bed so when I wake up in the middle of the night, I can jot down ideas or things I need to do," says the owner of an antique store in Moncton, New Brunswick.[15]

VERIFICATION

Insights are merely rough ideas. Their usefulness still requires verification through conscious evaluation and experimentation. Henry Yuen's insight about programming a VCR like making a telephone call was not a complete solution. Yuen still had to determine whether the idea was feasible as well as design a workable solution. In other words, verification is the beginning—not the ending—of creativity.

CONDITIONS FOR CREATIVITY

Minnesota Mining & Manufacturing Co. (3M) introduces an average of ten new products every week and generates 30 percent of its annual revenue from products developed within the previous four years.[16] The company achieves these impressive goals by finding creative people and putting them in an environment that encourages creative ideas. 3M executives have learned that creativity is a function of both the person and the situation. Exhibit 11.2 highlights the main conditions of people and the workplace that affect creativity.

CHARACTERISTICS OF CREATIVE PEOPLE

Everyone is creative, but some people seem to be more creative than others. This doesn't mean that organizations should follow the popular notion that creative people are "right-brained." The scientific evidence that creativity is a special function of the brain's right hemisphere is

---

EXHIBIT 11.2   Conditions for Creativity

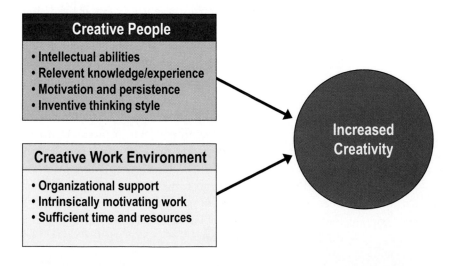

quite weak.[17] More important, few organizations have the resources to test the brain-activity patterns of job applicants. Rather than looking for right-brained people, we should consider the four general characteristics that researchers have identified in creative people: intellectual abilities, relevant knowledge and experience, a strong motivation and persistence, and an inventive thinking style.

Intellectual abilities

Creative people have the intellectual abilities to synthesize and analyze ideas, as well as to apply their ideas.[18] First, they are able to synthesize information by connecting seemingly diverse facts into a coherent idea. Like the fictional sleuth Sherlock Holmes, people with synthetic intelligence recognize the significance of small bits of information and are able to connect them in ways that no one else could imagine. Second, creative people use their analytic intelligence—their IQ—to evaluate the potential usefulness of their ideas. Third, creative people have practical ability. They can see how their ideas can be applied in the real world. Equally important, they are able to communicate these abstract ideas so that others understand and support them.

Relevant knowledge and experience

Employees are more creative when they possess a good foundation of knowledge and experience on a subject.[19] Some experts suggest that people are most creative after an average of ten years in a field of inquiry, because discovering new ideas requires knowledge of the fundamentals. For example, the Beatles produced most of their songs only after they had played together for several years. They developed extensive experience singing and adapting the music of other artists before their creative talents soared.[20]

But lengthy experience isn't always an asset in creativity. Some experts suggest that the more experience we gain, the more mental models we form.[21] Recall from Chapter 6 that these mental models eventually become so ingrained that we cease to question them. This may explain why creative output tends to decline as people move beyond mid-life.[22] Although there are exceptions, we tend to become set in our ways and have difficulty breaking out of the mental models we have learned over the years.

To minimize the problem of mental stagnation, Sony brought in people from outside the music industry to launch its highly successful Sony Music record company. These people had technical knowledge and experience, but not in the music industry, so they didn't have a fixed mental model of what would work. "We didn't want people from the record business," explains a Sony executive. "They would just bring their old ways with them. We wanted people who would have to figure things out all over again, who would question everything, people who 'didn't know any better.'"[23]

Motivation and persistence

Thomas Edison once remarked that genius is 1 percent inspiration and 99 percent perspiration. He learned this from experience; Edison and his staff discovered 1800 ways *not* to build a light bulb before they got it right! Like Edison, creative people are persistent because of their high need for achievement and at least moderate degree of self-confidence.[24] In Chapter 3, we learned that people with a **need for achievement** want to accomplish reasonably challenging goals. They also have a strong need to assume personal responsibility for their work.[25] This need to achieve, along with at least a moderate level of self-confidence, gives creative people the energy to persist in the face of skeptics and setbacks that litter the path to success.

Need for achievement A learning need that causes people to want to accomplish reasonably challenging goals through their own efforts.

Rick Ernst, Vancouver Province.

Illich Cheng and his employees at Millennium Technology Inc. are a persistent group. For nearly five years, people doubted that a small company from Vancouver could design a better magnetic resonance imaging (MRI) system, the technology used by medical professionals to view internal body structures. "[J]ust a few years ago people were laughing at us, feeling that it was impossible for a small company to achieve what we set out to do," Cheng acknowledges. Now, Cheng's persistence has paid off. His company has government approval and buyers across North America for their sophisticated MRI system that takes less space and costs half the price of traditional MRIs.[26] Along with persistence, what are other characteristic of creative people?

www.millennium.ca

Inventive thinking style

Creative people think in novel ways rather than follow set patterns. In other words, they engage in divergent thinking more easily than the rest of us. Creative people would rather think about creating things than improving on them. They take a broad view of problems, don't like to abide by rules or status, and are less concerned about social approval of their actions.[27] Creative people are risk-takers. They are not bothered about working with ambiguous information or issues and are willing to take the chance of making mistakes. This risk-taking orientation partly explains the creative output at Hewson Bridge and Smith Ltd., the Ottawa-based marketing agency described in the opening story of this chapter.

CREATIVE WORK ENVIRONMENT

Hiring creative people will not have the desired results unless these people are put in a work environment that supports the creative process.[28] These environmental conditions also improve creativity for the rest of us. Researchers have identified several workplace conditions that support creativity, including organizational support, intrinsically motivating tasks, and sufficient resources and time.

Organizational support

Creativity flourishes in organizations with free-flowing communication. These companies also support risk-taking and the inevitable failures that result from those risks. Corporate leaders not only allow employees to make mistakes; they encourage them to try out ideas where failure is more than a remote possibility. "Our beliefs are embedded in our philosophy: failure is not fatal," explains a 3M executive. "Innovations are simply chance breakthroughs. And when you take a chance, there is always the possibility of a failure."[29] Connections 11.1 describes two successful Vancouver-based companies that encourage creativity through open communication and a supportive attitude toward failure.

Organizations further support creativity by maintaining a reasonable level of job security. In contrast, evidence suggests that creative output drops significantly when organizations engage in downsizing, restructuring, and other activities that threaten the individual's employment relationship. This occurs because employees who fear job loss tend to take fewer risks and, instead, rely on more predictable and routine behaviour patterns.[30]

www.silent-witness.com
www.seppsfoods.com

 CONNECTIONS 11.1

Supporting Creativity Through Communication and Fearless Failure

Creativity and innovation have made Silent Witness Enterprises a North American leader in video-surveillance equipment. "Everyone comes to the office with a mind to be creative," explains Rob Bakshi, CEO of the 125-employee firm in Surrey, a Vancouver suburb.

"We have a culture that says, 'Nothing is a dumb idea,'" Bakshi explains. "It's always healthy to ask why or why not. And on top of that, when someone does have an idea, we listen. It may be a totally dumb idea, but we look at it."

Sepp's Gourmet Foods also thrives on the creativity of offbeat ideas. "We sometimes talk about having a Department of Wacky Ideas because sometimes the best ideas are the ones that are completely off the wall," says Jim Pratt, CEO of the pâté and meat pie manufacturer. The Burnaby, B.C., company is working hard to create an organizational environment in which employees feel free to try out new product development ideas.

A. Redekop, *Vancouver Province.*

Vancouver-based Silent Witness and Sepp's Gourmet Foods support creativity through a culture that views failure as part of the learning process.

"In our new product development department, the most damaging thing to creativity is if someone has a fear of failure," warns Pratt. "So you have to remove that from your culture. We try to create a culture that says, 'It's okay to fail.'"

Source: Adapted from "It's OK to Fail," *Profit,* 18 (November 1999), pp. 25–32.

Organizational support extends to the roles of project leaders and co-workers.[31] Project leaders have a difficult balancing act in their quest for creativity. They must provide support and encouragement, yet give individuals and teams enough freedom to work independently. They must apply enough pressure to complete the project, yet avoid so much pressure that it undermines creativity. Team members and other co-workers improve creativity when they trust each other, communicate well, and are committed to the assigned project. In contrast, creativity is undermined when co-workers criticize new ideas, are competitive against each other, and engage in political tactics to achieve personal goals.

Intrinsically motivating work

One of the most important influences on creativity is the job's intrinsic motivation.[32] This relates back to most of the job characteristics described in Chapter 4. First, employees tend to be more creative when they believe that their work has a substantial impact on the organization and/or larger society (i.e., task significance). Second, creativity increases with autonomy—the freedom to pursue novel ideas without bureaucratic delays. Creativity is about changing things, and change is only possible when employees have the authority to experiment. Third, creativity is an ongoing learning process, so employees need access to fairly continuous feedback from the job and other sources.

Creative productivity is also higher when people engage in self-set creativity goals, feedback, and other elements of self-leadership (see Chapter 4).[33] This worked for Thomas Edison. By setting goals of one minor invention every ten days and one major invention every six months, the inventor and others in his lab produced over 1000 patents during his lifetime.

More generally, jobs encourage creativity when they are challenging and aligned with the employee's competencies.[34] Challenging work pushes employees to draw on their fullest potential. Employees must also have the necessary skills and knowledge, as was noted in the previous section. This alignment of job challenge and employee competencies creates an enjoyable psychological condition called "flow." In a state of flow, our concentration and mental acuity surge and we experience the highest possible sense of involvement in the task.[35]

Sufficient time and resources

According to the MARS model, employee performance depends on more than motivation and ability (see Chapter 2). The model indicates that performance also requires sufficient time and resources. The same is true of creativity. People are usually more likely to produce innovative ideas when they have sufficient funds, materials, facilities, information, and time. This doesn't mean that creativity flourishes in the most lavish work settings. Rather, people need enough resources to explore alternatives and test their ideas.

Time is one of the more important resources for creativity.[36] Extreme time pressures, unrealistic goals, and ongoing distractions are well-known inhibitors of creativity. While we need some pressure to produce, companies also need to minimize pressure when it strangles creative output. Marcel LeBrun handles this pressure by going fishing with his son. "I've never caught anything," admits the CEO of ImagicTV in Saint John, New Brunswick. "Catching the fish is not the point. It's about catching a good idea, or simply trying to get myself out of one context into another and allow myself to think things that aren't tactical."[37]

CREATIVE PRACTICES

Along with hiring creative people and giving them a supportive work environment, organizations apply specific practices that crank up the creative potential. Entire books have been written on these practices. Some of them work; many lack any empirical validation. The team structures described later in this chapter try to improve creativity and decision making. In this section, we look at three other sets of activities: redefining the problem, associative play, and cross-pollination.

REDEFINING THE PROBLEM

Creativity isn't just a matter of finding a creative solution. It also includes understanding the problem in different ways.[38] By redefining the problem, we discover unique solutions from a different perspective. Consider the following true example: An automobile executive in Detroit loved his job, but was fed up with his boss. To get away from the tyrant, the executive contacted an executive search firm about finding a job with another company. That evening, the executive told his wife about calling the headhunter; she, in turn, described her day as a college instructor. By coincidence, her lesson that day was about how to redefine a problem. The executive thought carefully about this and, the next day, called the headhunter to discuss a different strategy. Soon after, the executive's surprised boss received and accepted a job offer from the executive search firm. By redefining the problem, the executive managed to get away from the troublesome boss without having to leave the job he loved.[39]

Creativity experts have suggested various ways to help people redefine problems. One writer introduced the concept of creative "jamming."[40] Based on the metaphor of an improvising jazz group, jamming involves having a group of people give a problem or idea a thorough workout—passing it around, tearing it apart, putting it back together, turning it over, and so forth. Another suggestion is to schedule some time to look through the notes and files of past projects. After a few months of neglect, these projects might be seen in new ways.[41]

A third strategy, called "tell me, stranger," involves asking people unfamiliar with the issue (preferably with different expertise) to explore the problem. You state the objectives and give some facts, then let the "stranger" ask questions to further understand the situation. All of this occurs without mentioning your current thoughts on the topic. By verbalizing the problem, listening to questions, and hearing what others think, you are more likely to form new perspectives on the issue.[42]

"Thank you for calling Creative Business Seminars. If you'd like to become a more creative problem solver, press 1 without touching any part of your telephone."

Randy Glasbergen. Used with permission.

ASSOCIATIVE PLAY

Earlier in this chapter, we learned that divergent thinking involves reframing the problem in a unique way and generating different approaches to the issue. Some people are naturally better at divergent thinking, but associative playful activities can help the rest of us think more divergently.

Monster Board, the online career Web site, sparks creativity on Monday mornings with a meeting that features Tinker Toys, storytelling, and various games. One activity is the object-oriented chain story. Someone brings in several unrelated items—perhaps a fishing pole, a book, a toy, etc.—

and the group develops a story around them. One person starts by picking an item and telling a story about it. The next person picks another item and adds that item to the first person's story, and so on. The activity gets everyone thinking differently while they have fun.[43]

Another form of associative play involves engaging in art or some other creative nonwork activity. Lion Apparel took its employees to an art school where they transformed wire mesh into alligators and empty paper-towel rolls into robots. The designer and manufacturer of firefighter clothing hoped that this creative expression would give staff members more divergent thinking back on the job. "This was a way to help them learn to think 'outside the box,'" explains Lion Apparel manager Leise Ling. "To solve the kinds of problems they encounter every hour, they have to be able to think creatively."[44]

A third associative-play strategy is to use metaphors to compare a situation with something else.[45] A telephone company used this approach to find ways to reduce damage to its pay phones. Participants were asked to think of a telephone booth as some other object that protects—such as a bank vault or a medicine capsule. Then they looked at features of these other objects that might protect telephone booths.

Another structured associative-play activity is called *morphological analysis*. Morphology involves listing different dimensions of a system and the elements of each dimension, then looking at each combination. This encourages people to carefully examine combinations that initially seem nonsensical. Tyson Foods, the world's largest poultry producer, recently applied this activity to identify new ways to serve chicken for lunch. The marketing and research team assigned to this task focused on three categories: occasion, packaging, and taste. Next, the team worked through numerous combinations of items in the three categories. This created unusual ideas, such as cheese and chicken pasta (taste) in pizza boxes (packaging) for concessions at baseball games (occasion). Later, the team looked more closely at the feasibility of these combinations and sent them to customer focus groups for further testing.[46]

CROSS-POLLINATION

Another way to spark creativity is to deliberately cross-pollinate ideas and knowledge across the organization.[47] One approach is to ensure that employees work with different people on each project. This diversity of experience improves information sharing and increases the number of perspectives that team members bring to new projects. IDEO, a highly successful industrial design firm, does this by encouraging employees to consider how features of one product they've worked on might be relevant to another. For instance, while designing a quieter fan for a computer system, designers might recall how they designed a quieter vacuum cleaner a few months earlier.[48]

Cross-pollination also occurs through formal information sessions where people from different parts of the organization share their knowledge. Mitel, the Ottawa-based high-technology company, holds Demo Days—internal trade shows where Mitel teams exhibit their projects and are encouraged to steal ideas from other groups within the organization.[49] Walt Disney Corp. encourages employees to engage in "displayed thinking" by leaving their work out in the open for others to view and comment on. Colleagues are encouraged to write anonymous Post-it notes providing suggestions and feedback.

CONSTRAINTS ON TEAM DECISION MAKING AND CREATIVITY

Cross-pollination highlights the fact that creativity rarely occurs alone. Some creative people may be individualistic, but most creative ideas are generated in formal teams and through other types of social interaction. Under certain conditions, teams can more effectively identify problems, choose alternatives, and evaluate their decisions. Individual biases are partly or completely offset by the divergent views and experiences of other team members. In spite of these potential advantages, team dynamics can also interfere with creativity and effective decision making. In this section, we look at the main factors that restrict effective creativity and decision making in team settings. In the final section of this chapter, we look at specific team structures that try to overcome these constraints.

TIME CONSTRAINTS

When Fred Tomczyk became CEO of London Life Insurance Co., one of his first actions was to cut the size of the executive committee from 35 to just 12 people. External consultants concluded that the larger committee had become "an ineffective decision-making group." With so many team members, London Life's executive meetings were taking too long and those attending had difficulty reaching agreement.[50]

London Life experienced the age-old saying that "committees keep minutes and waste hours." Unlike individuals, teams require extra time to organize, coordinate, and socialize. The larger the group, the more time is required to make a decision. Team members need time to learn about each other and build rapport. They need to manage an imperfect communication process so that there is sufficient understanding of each other's ideas. They also need to coordinate roles and rules of order within the decision process.

Another time constraint found in most team structures is that only one person can speak at a time.[51] This problem, known as **production blocking**, causes participants to forget potentially creative ideas by the time it is their turn to speak. Team members who concentrate on remembering their fleeting thoughts end up ignoring what others are saying, even though their statements could trigger more creative ideas.

Production blocking A time constraint in meetings due to the procedural requirement that only one person may speak at a time.

EVALUATION APPREHENSION

Individuals are reluctant to mention ideas that seem silly because they believe (often correctly) that other team members are silently evaluating them. This **evaluation apprehension** is based on the individual's desire to create a favourable self-presentation and his or her need for social esteem. It is most common in meetings attended by people with different levels of status or expertise, or where members formally evaluate each other's performance throughout the year (as in 360-degree feedback). Evaluation apprehension is a problem when the group wants to generate creative ideas, because these thoughts often sound bizarre or lack logic when presented. Unfortunately, many potentially valuable ideas are never presented to the group because these creative thoughts initially seem ridiculous and a waste of time.

Evaluation apprehension The reluctance to mention ideas to others that seem silly or peripheral in order to create a favourable self-presentation and maintain social esteem.

CONFORMITY TO PEER PRESSURE

Chapter 9 described how cohesiveness leads individual members to conform to the team's norms. This control keeps the group organized around common goals, but it may also cause team members to suppress their dissenting opinions when the issue potentially conflicts with a strong team norm. When someone does state a point of view that violates the majority opinion, other members might punish the violator or try to persuade him or her that the opinion is incorrect. It's not surprising, then, that nearly half of the managers surveyed in one study say that they give up in team decisions because of pressure from others to conform to the team's decision.[52] Conformity can also be subtle. To some extent, we depend on the opinions that others hold to validate our own views. If co-workers don't agree with us, we begin to question our own opinions even without overt peer pressure.[53]

GROUPTHINK

Groupthink is the tendency of highly cohesive groups to value consensus at the price of decision quality.[54] Groupthink goes beyond the problem of conformity. There are strong social pressures on individual members to maintain harmony by avoiding conflict and disagreement. They suppress doubts about decision alternatives preferred by the majority or group leader. Team members want to maintain this harmony because their self-identity is enhanced by membership in a powerful decision-making body that speaks with one voice.[55] Team harmony also helps members cope with the stress of making crucial top-level decisions.

High cohesiveness isn't the only cause of groupthink. It is also more likely to occur when a team is isolated from outsiders, the team leader is opinionated (rather than impartial), the team is under stress due to an external threat, the team has experienced recent failures or other decision-making problems, and the team lacks clear guidance from corporate policies or procedures. Several symptoms of groupthink have been identified and are summarized in Exhibit 11.3. In general, teams overestimate their invulnerability and morality, become closed-minded to outside and dissenting information, and experience several pressures towards consensus.[56]

Most research on groupthink has analyzed policy decisions that turned into fiascos. The best-known example of groupthink is NASA's space shuttle *Challenger* explosion in 1986.[57]

EXHIBIT 11.3   Symptoms of Groupthink

Groupthink Symptom	Description
Illusion of Invulnerability	The team feels comfortable with risky decisions because possible weaknesses are suppressed or glossed over.
Assumption of Morality	There is such an unquestioned belief in the inherent morality of the team's objectives that members do not feel the need to debate whether their actions are ethical.
Rationalization	Underlying assumptions, new information, and previous actions that seem inconsistent with the team's decision are discounted or explained away.
Stereotyping Outgroups	The team stereotypes or oversimplifies the external threats on which the decision is based; "enemies" are viewed as purely evil or moronic.
Self-censorship	Team members suppress their doubts to maintain harmony.
Illusion of Unanimity	Self-censorship results in harmonious behaviour, so individual members believe that they alone have doubts; silence is automatically perceived as evidence of consensus.
Mindguarding	Some members become self-appointed guardians to prevent negative or inconsistent information from reaching the team.
Pressuring Dissenters	Members who happen to raise their concerns about the decision are pressured to fall into line and be more loyal to the team.

Source: Based on I.L. Janis, *Groupthink: Psychological Studies of Policy Decisions and Fiascoes,* 2nd ed. (Boston: Houghton Mifflin, 1982), p. 244.

The technical cause of the explosion that killed all seven crew members was a faulty O-ring seal that did not withstand the freezing temperatures the night before the launch. However, a government commission pointed to a faulty decision-making process as the primary cause of the disaster. Key decision makers at NASA experienced many groupthink symptoms. They were under intense pressure to launch due to previous delays and promises of the space shuttle program's success. Information about O-ring problems was withheld to avoid conflict. Engineers raised concerns about the O-rings before the launch, but they were criticized for this.

GROUP POLARIZATION

Group polarization
The tendency for teams to make more extreme decisions (either more risky or more risk-averse) than the average team member would if making the decision alone.

Group polarization refers to the tendency of teams to make more *extreme* decisions than individuals working alone.[58] Exhibit 11.4 shows how the group-polarization process operates. Individuals form initial preferences when given several alternatives. Some of these choices are riskier than others, and the average member's opinion leans one way or the other. Through open discussion, team members become comfortable with more extreme positions when they realize that co-workers hold similar opinions. Persuasive arguments favouring the dominant position convince doubtful members and help form a consensus around the extreme option. Finally, individuals feel less personally responsible for the decision consequences because the decision is made by the team.

Social support, persuasion, and shifting responsibility explain why teams make more *extreme* decisions, but why do they usually make riskier decisions? The answer is that decision makers often have an illusion of control. They become victims of the "gambler's fallacy" that they can beat the odds. For example, team members tend to think, "This strategy might be unsuccessful 80 percent of the time, but it will work for us!" Thus, team members are more likely to favour the risky option.[59] The result of group polarization is that decision-making groups sometimes avoid solid opportunities, and bet the company on risky investments.

EXHIBIT 11.4   The Group-Polarization Process

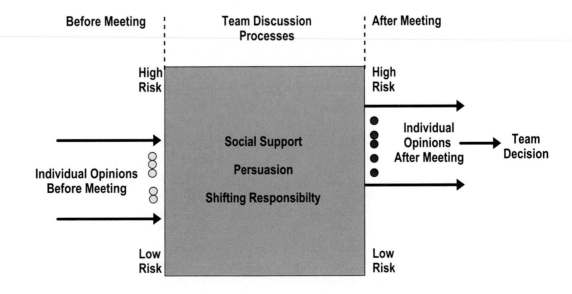

TEAM STRUCTURES FOR CREATIVITY AND DECISION MAKING

These problems with team dynamics in decision making may be reduced in a number of ways. One approach is to ensure that neither the team leader nor any other participant dominates the process. This limits the adverse effects of conformity and lets other team members generate more creative and controversial ideas.[60] Another practice is to maintain an optimal team size. The group should be large enough that members possess the collective knowledge to resolve the problem, yet small enough that the team doesn't consume too much time or restrict individual input.[61] Team norms are also important to ensure that individuals engage in critical thinking rather than follow the group's implicit preferences.

Evaluation apprehension, groupthink, production blocking, and other team-dynamics problems are most common in traditional team meetings where members meet face to face to suggest solutions and debate alternatives. Discussion is usually unstructured, ideas are generated and evaluated simultaneously, and solutions are often suggested long before the problem is sufficiently understood. Five alternative team structures have been proposed over the years to improve creativity and decision making in team settings: constructive controversy, brainstorming, electronic brainstorming, the Delphi technique, and the nominal group technique.

CONSTRUCTIVE CONTROVERSY

Constructive controversy Any situation in which team members debate their different opinions regarding a problem or issue in a way that minimizes socioemotional conflict.

Constructive controversy occurs when team members debate their different perceptions about an issue in a way that keeps the conflict focused on the task rather than on people. Through dialogue, participants learn about other points of view, which encourages them to re-examine their basic assumptions about a problem and its possible solution. Constructive controversy is *constructive* because the discussion minimizes negative conflict while discussing differences. This can occur if participants focus on facts rather than on people and avoid statements that threaten the esteem and well-being of other team members.[62]

How do we generate constructive controversy? First, decision-making groups should be heterogeneous.[63] As we learned in previous chapters, heterogeneous teams are better than homogeneous teams at perceiving issues and potential solutions from different perspectives. "Every time I have put together a diverse group of people, that team has always come up with a more breakthrough solution than any homogeneous group working on the same problem," says Arnold Donald, senior vice-president at chemical giant Monsanto.[64]

Second, these heterogeneous team members need to meet often enough to allow for meaningful discussion of contentious issues. The team's diversity won't generate constructive controversy if the team leader makes most of the decisions alone. Only through dialogue can team members better understand different perspectives, generate more creative ideas, and improve decision quality.

Third, effective teams generate constructive controversy when individual members take on different discussion roles. Some participants are action-oriented, others insist on reviewing details, one or two might try to minimize dysfunctional conflict, and so on. Where team members have too much agreement, some people should act as *devil's advocates* by challenging the others to explain the logic of their preferences.[65]

Lastly, constructive controversy is more likely to occur when team members think through the consequences of the preferred choice in several scenarios.[66] Before buying another company, for instance, an executive team should consider the wisdom of this decision if the economy stumbles, the government changes, a supply shortage occurs, and so on. Considering different angles also means comparing the preferred alternative against many choices, not just one or two limited options. To identify these varied alternatives, effective teams engage in some form of brainstorming.

BRAINSTORMING

Brainstorming A freewheeling, face-to-face meeting in which team members generate as many alternative solutions to the problem as possible, piggyback on the ideas of others, and avoid evaluating anyone's ideas during the idea-generation stage.

In the 1950s, advertising executive Alex Osborn wanted to find a better way for teams to generate creative ideas.[67] Osborn's solution, called **brainstorming**, requires team members to abide by the four rules displayed in Exhibit 11.5. Osborn believed that these rules encourage divergent thinking while minimizing evaluation apprehension and other team-dynamics problems:

- *No criticism*—The most important rule in brainstorming is that no one should criticize any ideas that are presented. Without criticism, team members might be more willing to suggest crazy solutions to the problem, which results in a larger number of and potentially better ideas.

- *Provide as many ideas as possible*—Brainstorming is based on the idea that quantity breeds quality. In other words, quality increases with the number of ideas presented. This relates to the belief that divergent thinking occurs after traditional ideas have been exhausted. Therefore, the group should think of as many solutions as possible and go well beyond the traditional answers to a problem.

- *Speak freely*—Brainstorming welcomes wild and wacky ideas; these become the seeds of divergent thinking in the creative process. Crazy suggestions are sometimes crazy only because they break out of the mould set by existing mental models.

- *Build on the ideas of others*—Team members are encouraged to "piggyback" or "hitchhike," that is, combine and improve on the ideas already presented. Building on existing ideas encourages the synergy of team processes (see Chapter 10).

Brainstorming is the most popular team structure for encouraging creative ideas. For example, brainstorming helped project teams at pharmaceuticals firm SmithKline Beecham to think of innovative alternatives to existing action plans.[68] Yet, for several years, organizational behaviour researchers have identified several limitations of this practice. One problem

---

EXHIBIT 11.5   Rules of Brainstorming

Rules of Brainstorming

1. **Don't criticize ideas**

2. **Provide as many ideas as possible**

3. **Say all ideas that come to mind, no matter how wild**

4. **Combine and improve ideas suggested by others**

Source: Based on information in A.F. Osborn, *Applied Imagination*, 3rd ed. (New York: Scribner's, 1963).

is that brainstorming rules do not completely remove evaluation apprehension; employees still know that others are silently evaluating the quality of their ideas. Production blocking and related time constraints prevent all ideas from being presented. And some research reports that individuals working alone produce more potential solutions to a problem than if they work together using brainstorming.[69]

These problems shouldn't deter companies from using brainstorming much of the time. As discussed in Connections 11.2, IDEO thrives on brainstorming sessions, largely because the industrial design firm knows how to make them work more effectively than the literature suggests. Recent studies have reported that brainstorming rules seem to minimize socioemotional

www.ideo.com

CONNECTIONS 11.2

IDEO Catches a Brainstorm

No one does brainstorming as well—or as often—as the folks at IDEO. Engineers at the California-based industrial design firm that created 3Com's Palm V and the stand-up toothpaste tube attend an average of 24 brainstorming sessions each year. A few participate in as many as 80 brainstorming sessions annually.

IDEO's brainstorms are scheduled, face-to-face meetings that generate ideas, usually about designing products. A typical session lasts between one and two hours and is attended by the design team as well as other IDEO engineers with relevant skills. For instance, one brainstorming session aimed at designing better ski goggles invited engineers who knew about foam, clear plastics, and manufacturing processes. Clients are also included in some sessions.

Since its founding in 1978, IDEO has developed a clear set of brainstorming rules: defer judgment, build on the ideas of others, conduct one conversation at a time, stay focused on the topic, and encourage wild ideas. These rules are prominently displayed throughout the meeting room and violators are given friendly reminders. IDEO's brainstorming par-

Brainstorming is one of the first steps in creativity at IDEO.

E. Luse, San Francisco Chronicle.

ticipants might shoot for 150 ideas in less than an hour. Their creative sparks are aided by studying similar products as well as unrelated items brought to the session.

Newcomers at IDEO quickly discover that brainstorming requires special interpersonal skills, not just rules and props. "The skills for successful brainstorming develop in an individual over time," explains an IDEO engineer. "I consider myself a good brainstormer but only a fair facilitator. A year ago, I was a good brainstormer and a poor facilitator."

Sources: A. Hargadon and R.I. Sutton, "Building an Innovation Factory," *Harvard Business Review*, 78 (May–June 2000), pp. 157–66; R. Garner, "Innovation for Fun and Profit," *Upside Magazine*, March 2000; P. Sinton, "Teamwork the Name of the Game for IDEO," *San Francisco Chronicle*, February 23, 2000; E. Brown, "A Day at Innovation U.," *Fortune,* April 12, 1999, pp. 163–65; R.I. Sutton and A. Hargadon, "Brainstorming Groups in Context: Effectiveness in a Product Design Firm," *Administrative Science Quarterly*, 41 (December 1996), pp. 685–718.

conflict among members and improve the team's focus on the required task. Brainstorming participants interact and participate directly, thereby increasing decision acceptance and team cohesiveness. Evaluation apprehension is less of a problem in high-performing teams that have high degrees of trust. There is some evidence that effective brainstorming sessions create emotional contagion (see Chapter 8). Specifically, team members share feelings of optimism and excitement that may encourage a more creative climate. Clients are often involved in brainstorming sessions, so this emotional contagion may produce higher customer satisfaction than if people are working alone on the product.[70]

ELECTRONIC BRAINSTORMING

• Electronic brainstorming
A structured team decision-making process whereby several people individually generate ideas or make decisions through computer software that posts each participant's ideas or opinions anonymously.

When DuPont Canada wants to get innovative, it sends employees to "focused creativity" sessions at Queen's University's **electronic brainstorming** facility. CIBC, IBM Canada, and other Canadian firms have built their own specially designed electronic brainstorming meeting rooms. With the aid of groupware (special computer software for groups), electronic brainstorming lets participants share ideas while minimizing the team-dynamics problems inherent in traditional brainstorming sessions.[71] Individuals can enter ideas at any time on their computer terminal. These ideas are posted anonymously and randomly on the screens of all participants. A central convenor monitors the input to ensure that participants remain focused on the issue.

Courtesy of McGraw-Hill Ryerson. Photo by Rodney Daw.

www.mcgrawhill.ca

When John Dill (centre, arms crossed) noticed a sudden sales surge in one division, the McGraw-Hill Ryerson CEO decided to investigate. Dill soon discovered that the group had been attending electronic brainstorming sessions to develop more creative solutions. So Dill decided to use the technology for the book publisher's strategic planning sessions. The results were impressive. "They came up with a better, more soundly developed strategy, with more commitment on the part of the people," says Dill. "People feel very committed to the outcomes of the process because they don't feel like they've been strong-armed into the outcomes. They've had a voice in it."[72] Considering the advantages of electronic brainstorming, why would this technology increase commitment to decisions?

Effectiveness of electronic brainstorming

The greatest benefit of electronic brainstorming is that it significantly reduces production blocking. Participants are able to document their ideas as soon as they pop into their heads, rather than wait their turn to communicate.[73] This process also supports creative synergy because participants can easily develop new ideas from those generated by other people. Electronic brainstorming also minimizes the problem of evaluation apprehension because ideas are posted anonymously. "The equipment allows them to throw some crazy ideas out without people knowing they are the author of it," explains David Lindsay, the civil servant who organized a brainstorming session among Ontario government Cabinet ministers.[74]

Electronic brainstorming is far more efficient than traditional team decision making because there is little socializing. A study of 64 electronic brainstorming groups at aircraft manufacturer Boeing Co. found that total meeting time was reduced by 71 percent.[75] Research has found that electronic brainstorming generates more ideas than traditional brainstorming and that participants seem to be more satisfied, motivated, and confident in the decision-making exercise than they are in other team structures.[76]

Despite its advantages, electronic brainstorming is perhaps too structured and technology-bound for most people. Some critics have noted that the additional number of ideas generated through electronic brainstorming is not enough to justify its cost. Another concern is that organizational participants are generally less enthusiastic about electronic brainstorming sessions than are students who participate in research samples.[77] It would seem odd, for example, to advise clients to conduct an electronic brainstorm rather than talk to each other. This reflects the notion that electronic brainstorming removes face-to-face conversation and the hidden benefits (such as emotional contagion and social bonding) that may exist in that communication medium. Lastly, we must consider the political dynamics of electronic brainstorming. Some people may feel threatened by the honesty of some statements and by their inability to control the discussion.

DELPHI TECHNIQUE

The **Delphi technique** systematically pools the collective knowledge of experts on a particular subject to make decisions, predict the future, or identify opposing views (called *dissensus*).[78] Delphi groups do not meet face to face; in fact, participants are often located in different parts of the world and may not know each other's identity. Moreover, like electronic brainstorming, participants do not know who "owns" the ideas submitted. Typically, Delphi group members submit possible solutions or comments regarding an issue to a central convenor. The compiled results are returned to the panel for a second round of comments. This process may be repeated a few more times until consensus or dissensus emerges. The Delphi technique recently helped a British electricity supply company understand how to respond to customers who don't pay their bills. It was also used by rehabilitation counsellors to reach consensus on rehabilitation credentialling.[79]

NOMINAL GROUP TECHNIQUE

Nominal group technique is a variation of traditional brainstorming and the Delphi technique that tries to combine individual efficiencies with team dynamics.[80] The method is called *nominal* because participants form a group *in name only* during two stages of decision making. This process, shown in Exhibit 11.6, first involves the individual, then the group, and finally the individual again.

EXHIBIT 11.6   Nominal Group Technique

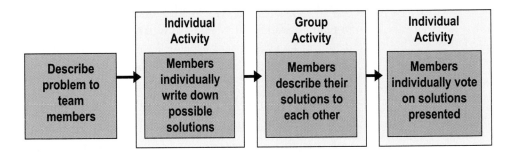

After the problem is described, team members silently and independently write down as many solutions as they can. During the group stage, participants describe their solutions to the other team members, usually in a round-robin format. As with brainstorming, there is no criticism or debate, although members are encouraged to ask for clarification of the ideas presented. In the final stage, participants silently and independently rank or vote on each proposed solution. Ranking is preferred because this forces each person to carefully review all of the alternatives presented.[81] Nominal group technique prefers voting or ranking over reaching consensus to avoid dysfunctional conflict that accompanies debate.

Nominal group technique tends to produce more and better-quality ideas than do traditional interacting groups.[82] Due to its high degree of structure, nominal group technique usually maintains a high task orientation and relatively low potential for conflict within the team. However, team cohesiveness is generally lower in nominal decisions because the structure minimizes social interaction. Production blocking and evaluation apprehension still occur to some extent.

Throughout this chapter, we have learned various ways to improve creativity in the workplace. We also learned about team dynamics that potentially undermine creativity and decision making, as well as team structures that minimize these problems. However, decisions are also political events because implementing decisions requires change and potential risk. In the next chapter we will look at the dynamics of power and politics in organizational settings.

CHAPTER SUMMARY

- Creativity refers to developing an original product, service, or idea that makes a socially recognized contribution. It is an integral part of decision making and an important practice in knowledge management.

- The four creativity stages are preparation, incubation, insight, and verification. Preparation is the person's or group's effort to acquire knowledge and skills regarding the problem or opportunity. Incubation is the stage of reflective thought, where an individual puts the problem aside but continues to work on it in the back of his or her mind. Incubation assists divergent thinking, which involves reframing the problem in a unique way and generating different approaches to the issue. Insight is the experience of suddenly becoming aware of a unique idea. These creative thoughts are quickly documented and tested in the verification stage.

- Some people are more creative than others. Creative people have the intellectual abilities to synthesize and analyze ideas, as well as to apply their ideas. They possess a good foundation of knowledge and experience on the subject, but not so much that they have formed rigid mental models. Creative people have a high need for achievement and at least a moderate level of self-confidence. Lastly, creative people have an innovative thinking style. They avoid set patterns and are willing to risk failure.

- Organizational support—including supporting risk-taking, job security, reasonable work pressure, and trustworthy co-workers—increases the level of creativity. One of the most important influences on creativity is the job's intrinsic motivation, including its task significance, autonomy, and job feedback. Challenging work aligned with a person's competencies can generate a state of flow that enhances creative output. A creative work environment also provides sufficient resources and time to accomplish a task. Corporate leaders can further enhance creativity by encouraging employees to redefine the problem, engage in associative play, and experience cross-pollination. Redefining the problem can occur through jamming sessions where people tear the problem apart, by revisiting old projects, and by having other people look at the problem. Associative-play activities include object-oriented chain storytelling, painting, using metaphors, and morphological analysis. Cross-pollination occurs when people work with different people on each project and where employees publicly display their projects to others in the organization.

- Team decisions are impeded by time constraints, evaluation apprehension, conformity to peer pressure, groupthink, and group polarization. Production blocking—where only one person typically speaks at a time—is a form of time constraint on teams. Evaluation apprehension occurs when employees believe that others are silently evaluating them, so they avoid stating seemingly silly ideas. Conformity keeps team members aligned with team goals, but it also tends to suppress dissenting opinions. Groupthink is the tendency of highly cohesive groups to value consensus at the price of decision quality. Group polarization refers to the tendency of teams to make more extreme decisions compared with individuals working alone. Team decision-making problems can be minimized by ensuring that the team leader does not dominate, maintaining an optimal team size, ensuring that team norms support critical thinking, and introducing team structures that support more creative decision making.

- Five team structures that potentially improve creativity and team decision making are constructive controversy, brainstorming, electronic brainstorming, Delphi technique, and nominal group technique. Brainstorming requires team members to avoid criticizing, provide as many ideas as possible, speak freely, and build on the ideas of others. Electronic brainstorming uses computer software to share ideas while minimizing team dynamics problems. The Delphi technique systematically pools the collective knowledge of experts on a particular subject without face-to-face meetings. In nominal group technique, participants write down ideas alone, describe these ideas in a group, then silently vote on these ideas.

KEY TERMS

Brainstorming, p. 341

Constructive controversy, p. 340

Creativity, p. 328

Delphi technique, p. 344

Divergent thinking, p. 329

Electronic brainstorming, p. 343

Evaluation apprehension, p. 337

Group polarization, p. 339

Groupthink, p. 338

Need for achievement, p. 331

Nominal group technique, p. 344

Production blocking, p. 337

DISCUSSION QUESTIONS

1. The Chinese word for business is "Sheng-yi," which literally means "to give birth to ideas." Explain how creativity is an inherent part of business decision making.

2. Think of a time when you experienced the creative process. Maybe you woke up with a brilliant (but usually sketchy and incomplete) idea, or you solved a baffling problem while doing something else. Describe this incident to your class and explain how the experience followed the creative process.

3. Two characteristics of creative people are that they have relevant experience and are persistent in their quest. Does this mean that people with the most experience and the highest need for achievement are the most creative? Explain your answer.

4. One feature of companies that support creativity is that they minimize their employees' fear of failure. Why does this affect creativity and how can organizations minimize this fear of failure? What are the limitations of this creative strategy?

5. Mitel and other companies host internal trade shows, where employees display their knowledge and "trade" information with other employees. Explain how these internal trade shows improve creativity.

6. Production blocking is often identified as a problem in creativity and team decision making. Describe production blocking and identify a team structure that minimizes this problem.

7. A senior executive committee wants to make better decisions by practising constructive controversy. Identify four things that the group must do to increase constructive controversy.

8. Cornerbrook Technologies Ltd. wants to use brainstorming with its employees and customers to identify new uses for its technology. Advise Cornerbrook's president about the rules to follow for this session, as well as its potential limitations.

Case Study

ACTIVITY 11.1
Eastern Province Light and Power

I work as a systems and procedures analyst for the Eastern Province Light and Power Company. The systems and procedures department analyzes corporate policies, procedures, forms, equipment, and methods to simplify and standardize operations. We apply "organized common sense" to develop new practices and to improve old ones.

Requests for analysis of organizational problems are submitted to the systems and procedures department by department heads or people with even higher status. Our manager assigns them to an analyst on the basis of availability; projects are accepted and assigned on the first-in, first-out (FIFO) method. Projects must undergo analysis, design, and implementation before a change in procedure is realized. What follows is a description of a problem assigned to me. I am in the midst of investigating it right now.

The Problem

For some time, management had been concerned with the inventory-carrying charges that accrue when material is stored in company warehouses. Not only is a cost attached to carrying inventory for future use, but there are additional related costs such as labour to handle the inventory, warehouse usage in terms of square feet taken up in storage, and clerical time used to account for materials flowing into and out of inventory. One type of material stored is office supplies—pens, writing pads, forms, stationery, envelopes, and dozens of similar items. A desire to reduce the costs of storing these items prompted the head of the department of purchasing and material control to submit a request for study by systems and procedures.

The request was made in the required written form. It described the current procedures, estimated their costs, and invited us to explore ways of changing the procedures to reduce costs. In brief, at the time the study request was submitted, purchases of office supplies were made through 11 vendors. The items were stored in a common warehouse area and disbursed to departments as requested. As is customary, I convened a meeting of the requesting manager and others who seemed to be most directly involved with the problem.

The First Meeting

I opened the meeting by summarizing the present procedures for purchasing and storing office supplies and the estimated costs associated with these problems. I explained that we were meeting to explore ways to reduce these costs. I suggested that we try to generate as many ideas as we could without being too critical of them, then narrow the list by criticizing and eliminating the ideas with obvious weaknesses.

As soon as I finished my opening remarks, the head of purchasing and material control suggested that we conduct a pilot study in which we would contract with one of the company's regular vendors to supply each department directly, eliminating the need for storage of inventory. The vendor would continue to sell us whatever we purchased, but would sell and deliver the items to various departments instead of to our central purchasing group. A pilot study with one vendor would indicate how such a system would work with all vendors of office supplies. If it worked well, we could handle all office supplies in this way.

She went on to explain that she had already spoken to the vice-president to whom she (and, through intermediate levels, the rest of us) reported and that he recognized the potential savings that would result. She also said that she had gone over the idea with the supervisor of stores (who reported to her) and that he had agreed. She wanted to know how long it would take to carry out the pilot study. I looked at a few faces around the table to see if anybody would say anything, but nobody did. I said I didn't know. She said, "Let's meet in a week when you've come up with a proposal." The meeting ended without anything else of any real substance being said.

ACTIVITY 11.1 CONTINUED

I felt completely frustrated. She was the highest-ranking person in the meeting. She had said what she wanted and, if her stature alone wasn't enough, she had invoked the image of the vice-president being in agreement with her. Nobody, including me, had said anything. No idea other than hers was even mentioned, and no comments were made about her idea.

I decided that I would work as hard as I could to study the problem and her proposed pilot study before the next meeting and prepare to give the whole issue a critical review.

Between Meetings

I talked to my boss about my feelings that I was expected to rubber-stamp the pilot study. I said that I wished he would come to the next meeting. I also said that I wanted to talk to some people close to the problem, some clerks, some vendors, and some buyers in purchasing to see if I could come up with any good ideas or find any problems with the pilot study. He told me to learn all that I could and promised to come to the next meeting.

My experience with other studies has taught me that sometimes the people closest to the work have expertise to contribute, so I located one clerk, two buyers, and two vendor sales representatives. Nobody had spoken to any of them about the pilot study or the general plan it was meant to test. This surprised me. Each of these people had some interesting things to say about the proposed way of handling office supplies. One buyer, for example, thought it would be chaotic to have 17 different departments ordering the same items. She thought we might also lose out on some quantity discounts, and predicted it would mean 17 times the paperwork. One sales rep said that he didn't think any vendor would like the idea because it would increase the number of contacts necessary to sell the same amount of product that could be sold now through one contact—the buyer in the purchasing department. The clerk said it might be risky to depend on a vendor to maintain inventories at adequate levels. He said, "What if a vendor failed to supply us with, say, enough mark-sensing tools for our meter readers one month, thereby causing them to be unable to complete their task and our company to be unable to get its monthly billings out on time?"

The Second Meeting

Armed with thorough notes, I arrived at the next meeting prepared to discuss these and other criticisms. One of the clerks had even agreed to attend so that I could call on him for comments. But when I looked around the conference room, everyone was there except the clerk. The head of purchasing and material control said that she had talked to the clerk, could convey any of his ideas, and had told him it wasn't necessary to attend the meeting.

I pointed out that the clerk had raised a question about the company's ability to control inventory. He had said that we now have physical control of inventory, but that the proposal involved making ourselves dependent on the vendors maintaining adequate inventory. The head of purchasing and material control said, "Not to worry. It will be in the vendor's own interest to keep us well supplied." No one, including my boss, said anything.

I brought up the subject of selecting a vendor to participate in the pilot study. My boss mentioned that I had told him that some vendors might object to the scheme because the additional contacts would increase their costs of sales. The head of purchasing and material control said, "Any vendor would be interested in doing business with a company as big as Eastern Province Light and Power." No further comments were made.

I mentioned that it was the practice of the systems and procedures staff to estimate independently the costs and benefits of any project before undertaking it, and also to have the internal auditing department review the proposal. I said that we would need to go ahead with those steps. I asked the head of purchasing and material control to give me the name of somebody in her area I should contact to get the costs of the present system. She said that it really didn't

ACTIVITY 11.1 CONTINUED

seem necessary to go through all of the usual steps in this case since she had already submitted an estimate. Besides, it was only going to be a pilot study. She said, "I think we can all agree on that and just move ahead now with the designation of a vendor." She looked around the table and nobody said anything. She said, "Fine. Let's use Moore Business Forms." Nobody said anything. She then said to me, "Okay, let's get back together after you've lined things up."

Discussion Questions

1. Did this group at Eastern Province Light and Power make its decision effectively? Why or why not?

2. Identify any decision-making problems that seem to exist in this case.

3. What team structure would you recommend to make this type of decision in the future?

Source: D.R. Hampton, *Contemporary Management* (New York: McGraw-Hill, 1981). Used with permission.

Video Case Study

ACTIVITY 11.2
I-Power—The Power Within

The sales staff and management at Kacey's Fine Furniture have come up with an idea to attract new customers. It's called I-Power, short for ideas power. Companies using the technique ask their employees to come up with at least two ideas per week.

At Kacey's, employees suggested that the trucks feature pictures of the products they sell, and that leather products be packed in foam and shrink-wrapped before shipping. The employees and their bosses gather at meetings where problems are posed and solutions are offered. Rewards for good ideas range from toys and candy to cash.

I-Power also works for Board Room, Inc., a Connecticut-based publishing firm. In fact, it's used by some 1500 companies worldwide, including Federal Express, Rubbermaid, and McCormick's, the world's largest spice company. It was even used by an army intelligence unit involved in the Persian Gulf war.

The I-Power system is a brainchild of Kacey's president, Martin Edelstein. He said, "I-Power makes people think and it makes them cooperate. It changes their spirit." One Kasey's employee remarked, "In this era of economic uncertainty, job insecurity and management mistrust, it's given us very good bond and relationship."

I-Power is a hit for major league baseball. After two depressing strike-shortened seasons, the Los Angeles Dodgers are using I-Power. Labour and management have teamed up. One Dodgers employee said, "If they can take time to think about what they do and ways to improve themselves, ways for the ball club to improve themselves, ways to improve customer service, then that's the real benefit of I-Power." Another said, "Today's I-Power theme is what we can do to help other departments. I've got $200 in our Dodger dollars to give away today and we're going to play our I-Power monopoly."

The history of modern business is packed with ideas—some good, some bad—that were supposed to boost employee morale, productivity, and company profits. The bottom line in most of them, including I-Power, is this: Managers, listen to your employees; they are smarter than you think.

Discussion Questions

1. I-Power is a technique for generating new ideas for workplace improvement. What creativity conditions and practices does it use?

2. I-Power requires that employees come up with two ideas per week. Besides the number of ideas required, what other parameters or guidelines do you think would make the ideas generated more useful?

3. What are some potential pitfalls of using I-Power in the workplace?

Source: NBC Archives.

TEAM exercises

ACTIVITY 11.3
THE HOPPING ORANGE

Purpose: To help students understand the dynamics of creativity and team problem solving.

Instructions: You will be placed in teams of six students. One student serves as the official timer for the team and must have a watch, preferably with a stopwatch timer. The instructor will give each team an orange (or a similar object) with a specific task involving the use of the orange. The objective is easily understood and nonthreatening, and will be described by the instructor at the beginning of the exercise. Each team will have a few opportunities to achieve the objective more efficiently.

ACTIVITY 11.4
CREATIVITY BRAINBUSTERS

Purpose: To help students understand the dynamics of creativity and team problem solving.

Instructions: This exercise may be completed alone or in teams of three to four people. If teams are formed, students who already know the solutions to one or more of these problems should identify themselves and serve as silent observers. When finished (or, more likely, when the time is up), the instructor will review the solutions and discuss the implications of this exercise. In particular, be prepared to discuss what you needed to solve these puzzles and what may have prevented you from solving them more quickly (or at all).

Double Circle Problem: Draw two circles, one inside the other, with a single line and with neither circle touching the other (as shown below). In other words, you must draw both of these circles without lifting your pen (or other writing instrument).

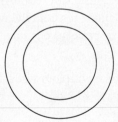

Nine Dot Problem: Below are nine dots. Without lifting your pencil, draw no more than four straight lines that pass through all nine dots.

Nine Dot Problem Revisited: Referring to the nine dots above, describe how, without lifting your pencil, you could pass a pencil line through all of the dots by using three or fewer straight lines.

Word Search: In the following line of letters, cross out five letters so that the remaining letters, without altering their sequence, spell a familiar English word.

FCIRVEEALTETITVEERS

Burning Ropes: You have two pieces of rope of unequal lengths and a box of matches. In spite of their different lengths, each piece of rope takes one hour to burn; however, parts of each rope burn at unequal speeds. For example, the first half of one piece might burn in ten minutes. Use these materials to accurately determine when 45 minutes have elapsed.

 Self-Assessment **exercises**

ACTIVITY 11.5
TESTING YOUR CREATIVE BENCH STRENGTH

Purpose: This self-assessment is designed to help you determine how well you engage in divergent thinking, problem identification, and other creativity practices.

 Instructions: This self-assessment exercise consists of 12 questions. Answer each question, and provide an explanation, on a separate piece of paper. When finished, the instructor will provide the correct answer for each question, along with an explanation. (Note: This activity may be done as a self-assessment exercise or as a team activity.)

1. There is one word in the English language that is always pronounced incorrectly. What is it?

2. A man gave one son 10 cents and another son 15 cents. What time is it?

3. A boat has a ladder with six rungs. Each rung is 30 centimetres apart. The bottom rung is 30 centimetres from the water. The tide rises at 30 centimetres every 15 minutes. High tide peaks in one hour. When the tide is at it's highest, how many rungs are under water?

4. There is a house with four walls. Each wall faces south. There is a window in each wall. A bear walks by one of the windows. What colour is the bear?

5. Is half of two plus two equal to two or three?

6. There is a room. The shutters are blowing in. There is broken glass on the floor. There is water on the floor. You find Sloppy dead on the floor. How did Sloppy die?

7. How much dirt would be in a hole two metres deep and two metres wide that has been dug with a square-edged shovel?

8. If I were in Hawaii and simultaneously dropped one bowling ball in a bucket of 45-degrees-Fahrenheit water and dropped another ball of the same weight, mass, and size in a bucket of 30-degrees-Fahrenheit water, which ball would hit the bottom of the bucket first? Same question, but the location is in Canada?

9. What is the significance of the following: The year is 1978, 34 minutes past noon on May 6.

10. What can go up a chimney down, but can't go down a chimney up?

11. If a farmer has five haystacks in one field and four haystacks in another field, how many haystacks would he have if he combined them all in the centre field?

12. What is it that goes up and goes down but does not move?

Source: The origin of these brainteasers is unknown. They were distributed by J. Gushue in *St. John's Telegram Online*, April 11, 2000.

ACTIVITY 11.6
ASSESSING YOUR CREATIVE DISPOSITION

Purpose: This self-assessment exercise is designed to help you estimate the extent to which you have a creative personality.

Instructions: Listed below is a checklist with 30 adjectives that may or may not describe you. Put a mark in the boxes beside the words that you think accurately describe you. *Do not* mark the boxes beside words that do not describe you. When finished, you can score the test using the scoring key in Appendix B of this book. This exercise is completed alone so that students can assess themselves without concerns of social comparison. However, class discussion will focus on how this scale might be applied in organizations, and the limitations of measuring creativity in work settings.

ADJECTIVE CHECKLIST

Affected ☐	Honest ☐	Reflective ☐
Capable ☐	Humorous ☐	Resourceful ☐
Cautious ☐	Individualistic ☐	Self-confident ☐
Clever ☐	Informal ☐	Sexy ☐
Commonplace ☐	Insightful ☐	Sincere ☐
Confident ☐	Intelligent ☐	Snobbish ☐
Conservative ☐	Inventive ☐	Submissive ☐
Conventional ☐	Mannerly ☐	Suspicious ☐
Dissatisfied ☐	Narrow interests ☐	Unconventional ☐
Egotistical ☐	Original ☐	Wide interests ☐

Source: Based on information in H.G. Gough, "A Creative Personality Scale for the Adjective Check List," *Journal of Personality and Social Psychology*, 37(8) (August 1979), pp. 1398–1405.

CHAPTER TWELVE

Organizational Power and Politics

LEARNING OBJECTIVES

After reading this chapter, you should be able to:

- Define the meaning of power and counterpower.
- Describe the five bases of power in organizations.
- Explain how information relates to power in organizations.
- Discuss the four contingencies of power.
- Discuss the role of power in sexual harassment.
- Explain how organizational power creates problems in romantic relationships at work.
- Summarize the advantages and disadvantages of organizational politics.
- List six types of political activity found in organizations.
- Describe the conditions that encourage organizational politics.
- Identify ways to control dysfunctional organizational politics.

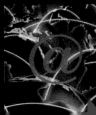

Gary Withers, general manager of Drake International New Zealand, says that telecommuting allows him to escape office politics.

The headquarters of Drake International New Zealand is located in Auckland, but you won't find its general manager there. Gary Withers leads the New Zealand operations of the Canadian-founded consulting firm from his home in Queenstown, hundreds of kilometres away on the south island. Withers claims that the telecommute keeps him closer to favourite fishing spots and further away from organizational politics. "I don't get involved in the office politics, which probably took up most of my time [before moving to Queenstown]," explains Withers.

On the other side of the planet, Rosemary Bruus also believes that telecommuting helps her avoid the political infighting of the workplace. "I've been [telecommuting] for seven years," said Bruus, who runs a Calgary consulting business. "I get a lot more done at home. . .You can avoid office politics."

Employees may think that telecommuting allows them to avoid office politics, but experts warn that out-of-sight employees might be out of mind when corporate leaders hand out bonuses and promotions. "Being removed from your company carries both risks and advantages," warns Val Arnold, senior vice-president of Personnel Decisions International, a management and human resources consulting firm. "You need to maintain visibility and develop yourself professionally in order to succeed as a telecommuter."

A few years ago, telecommuters at Nortel Networks expressed their concern about lack of visibility and loss of networking opportunities. Their worries have subsided as more Nortel staffers telecommute. Still, Nortel encourages employees to visit the office regularly so they can minimize the negative political consequences. "We don't recommend anyone stay at home five days a week, 52 weeks a year," says the executive who oversees Nortel's telecommuting program.[1]

www.drakeintl.com/nz/
www.nortelnetworks.com

Telecommuters in Canada and elsewhere face a dilemma: In their quest to escape from organizational politics, they unwittingly become its victims. The solution, ironically, is to become an expert in visibility and other political tactics. No one escapes from organizational power and politics. They exist in every organization and, according to some writers, in every decision and action.[2] Consequently, we need to be aware of the dynamics of power and politics. This knowledge will become even more important as companies redistribute power by flattening hierarchies and empowering employees.[3]

We begin this chapter by defining power and presenting a basic model depicting the dynamics of power in organizational settings. We then discuss the five bases of power, as well as information as a power base. Next, we look at the contingencies necessary to translate those sources into meaningful power. Our discussion of power finishes with a look at sexual harassment as an abuse of power, as well as how organizational power complicates office romances. The latter part of this chapter examines the dynamics of organizational politics, including the various types of political activity, the conditions that encourage organizational politics, and the ways it can be controlled.

THE MEANING OF POWER

Power The capacity of a person, team, or organization to influence others.

Power is the capacity of a person, team, or organization to influence others.[4] Power is not the act of changing others' attitudes or behaviour; it is only the *potential* to do so. People frequently have power they do not use; in fact, they might not even know they have power.

The most basic prerequisite of power is that one party believes that he or she is dependent on the other for something of value.[5] This relationship is shown in Exhibit 12.1, where Person A has power over Person B by controlling something that Person B needs to achieve his or her goals. You might have power over others by controlling a desired job assignment, useful information, important resources, or even the privilege of being associated with you! To make matters more complex, power is ultimately a perception, so people might gain power simply by convincing others that they have something of value. Thus, power exists when others believe that you control resources that they want.[6]

Although power requires dependence, it is really more accurate to say that the parties are *interdependent*. One party may be more dependent than the other, but the relationship exists only when both parties have something of value to the other. Exhibit 12.1 shows a dotted line

EXHIBIT 12.1 Dependence in the Power Relationship

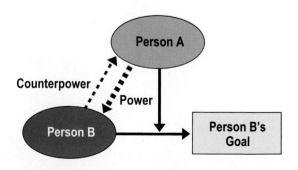

Courtesy of the Rapid Phase Group, www.madameve.co.za

Counterpower The capacity of a person, team, or organization to keep a more powerful person or group in the exchange relationship.

to illustrate the weaker party's (Person B's) power over the dominant participant (Person A). This **counterpower**, as it is known, is strong enough to maintain Person A's participation in the exchange relationship. For example, executives have power over subordinates by controlling their job security and promotional opportunities. At the same time, employees have counterpower by controlling the ability to work productively and thereby creating a positive impression of the supervisor to his or her boss. Counterpower usually motivates executives to apply their power judiciously, so that the relationship is not broken.

A MODEL OF POWER IN ORGANIZATIONS

Power involves more than just dependence. As we see in Exhibit 12.2, the model of power includes both power sources and contingencies. It indicates that power is derived from five sources: legitimate, reward, coercive, expert, and referent. The model also indicates that these power bases yield power only under certain conditions. These contingencies of power include the employee's or department's substitutability, centrality, discretion, and visibility. Finally, as we will discuss later, the type of power applied affects the type of influence the powerholder has over the other person or work unit.

EXHIBIT 12.2 A Model of Power within Organizations

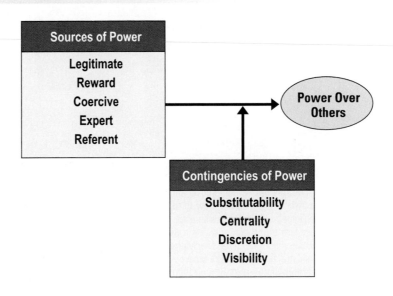

SOURCES OF POWER IN ORGANIZATIONS

Legitimate power
The capacity to influence others through formal authority; that is, the perceived right to direct certain behaviours of people in other positions.

Over 40 years ago, French and Raven listed five sources of power within organizations: legitimate, reward, coercive, expert, and referent.[7] Many researchers have studied these five power bases and searched for others. For the most part, French and Raven's list remains intact.[8] The first three power bases are derived from the powerholder's position; that is, the person receives these power bases because of the specific authority or roles they are assigned in the organization. The latter two sources of power originate from the powerholder's own characteristics. In other words, people bring these power bases to the organization.[9]

LEGITIMATE POWER

www.filmsite.org/cain.html

Legitimate power is an *agreement* among organizational members that people in certain roles can request certain behaviours of others. This perceived right partly comes from formal job descriptions as well as from informal rules of conduct. Executives have considerable legitimate power, but all employees also have this power based on company rules and government laws.[10] For example, an organization might give employees the right to request customer files if this information is required for their job.

Reuters Archive Photos.

The Caine Mutiny is a classic Pulitzer Prize–winning novel and film about the limits of legitimate power. Captain Queeg (Humphrey Bogart, seated centre) is a hard disciplinarian who shapes up the crew of the *Caine*, a battered minesweeper during the Second World War. However, Queeg's judgment and focus have been impaired by too much combat. After Queeg makes several critical mistakes and forces the crew to search for missing strawberries, some officers fear that their captain is a danger to himself and the crew. Sure enough, a beleaguered Queeg panics during a storm at sea, so two key officers—Lt. Keefer (Fred MacMurray, standing centre) and Lt. Maryk (Van Johnson, seated right)—stage a mutiny and assume command. The story illustrates how Queeg's orders and competence tested the limits of his legitimate power over crew members. What "mutinies" have you heard about in more recent organizational settings? What commands triggered employees to refuse to obey their boss?

Legitimate power depends on more than job descriptions. It also depends on mutual agreement from those expected to abide by this authority. Your boss's power to make you work overtime partly depends on your agreement to this power. Classic stories of shipboard mutinies, such as *The Caine Mutiny* and *Mutiny on the Bounty,* illustrate this point. Today, employees question their boss's right to make them stay late, perform unsafe tasks, and other activities. Thus, legitimate power is the person's authority to make discretionary decisions as long as followers accept this discretion.[11]

People in high **power distance** cultures (i.e., those who accept an unequal distribution of power—see Chapter 7) are more likely to comply with legitimate power than are people in low power distance cultures. Thus, an employee in Mexico (a high power distance culture) is more likely than someone in Canada (a low power distance culture) to accept an order, particularly when the person's right to give that order is uncertain. Legitimate power is also stronger in some organizations than in others. A 3M scientist might continue to work on a project after being told by superiors to stop working on it. This is because the 3M culture supports an entrepreneurial spirit, which includes ignoring formal authority from time to time.[12]

More generally, employees are becoming less tolerant of legitimate power. They increasingly expect to be involved in decisions rather than be told what to do. "People won't tolerate the command-and-control mode," says Bank of Montreal CEO Tony Comper.[13] Thus, the command style of leadership that often guided employee behaviour in the past must be replaced by other forms, particularly expert and referent power, which are described below.

> **Power distance** The extent to which people accept unequal distribution of power in a society.

REWARD POWER

> **Reward power** The capacity to influence others by controlling the allocation of rewards valued by them and the removal of negative sanctions.

Reward power is derived from the person's ability to control the allocation of rewards valued by others and to remove negative sanctions (i.e., negative reinforcement). Managers have formal authority that gives them power over the distribution of organizational rewards such as pay, promotions, time off, vacation schedules, and work assignments. Employees also have reward power over their bosses through the use of 360-degree feedback systems (see Chapter 2). Employee feedback affects the supervisor's promotions and other rewards, so bosses tend to behave differently towards employees after 360-degree feedback is introduced.

COERCIVE POWER

> **Coercive power** The capacity to influence others through the ability to apply punishment and remove rewards affecting these people.

Coercive power is the ability to apply punishment. Managers have coercive power through their authority to reprimand, demote, and fire employees. Labour unions might use coercive power tactics, such as withholding services, to influence management in collective agreement negotiations. Team members sometimes apply sanctions, ranging from sarcasm to ostracism, to ensure that co-workers conform to team norms.[14]

Many firms rely on the coercive power of team members to control co-worker behaviour.[15] For example, 44 percent of production employees at the CAMI automobile plant in Ingersoll, Ontario, believe that team members use coercive power to improve co worker performance.[16] The coercive power of team members is also apparent at Eaton Corp.'s forge plant in South Bend, Indiana. "They say there are no bosses here," says an Eaton Corp. employee, "but if you screw up, you find one pretty fast."[17]

EXPERT POWER

Expert power The capacity to influence others by possessing knowledge or skills that they want.

For the most part, legitimate, reward, and coercive power originate from the position. In contrast, **expert power** originates from within the person. It is an individual's or work unit's capacity to influence others by possessing knowledge or skills that they want. For instance, civilians working at Canada's Department of National Defence have acquired a lot of power because they know how to operate the bureaucracy. Military personnel are rotated around various Canadian Forces bases, so they depend on the civilians for their expertise as the corporate memory.[18]

Employees are gaining expert power as our society moves from an industrial to a knowledge-based economy. The reason is that employee knowledge becomes the means of production, not some machine that the owner controls.[19] And without this control over production, owners are more dependent on employees to achieve their corporate objectives. This is quite apparent in Canada's high-technology sector, where the skill shortage is so acute that companies have been forced to limit growth. Job applicants can demand generous salaries and preferential working conditions because of their expert power. "Employers are kind of over a barrel," admits a Vancouver recruiting consultant who specializes in hiring high-tech engineers. "Candidates have control, for perhaps the first time in history, over employers."[20]

REFERENT POWER

Referent power The capacity to influence others by virtue of the admiration of and identification with the powerholder.

People have **referent power** when others identify with them, like them, or otherwise respect them. Like expert power, referent power comes from within the person. It is largely a function of the person's interpersonal skills and usually develops slowly. Referent power is usually associated with charismatic leadership. *Charisma* is often defined as a form of interpersonal attraction whereby followers develop a respect for and trust in the charismatic individual.[21]

INFORMATION AND POWER

Information is power.[22] This phrase is increasingly relevant in a knowledge-based economy. Information power derives from either the legitimate or the expert sources of power described above and exists in two forms: (a) control over the flow and interpretation of information given to others, and (b) the perceived ability to cope with organizational uncertainties

EXHIBIT 12.3 Power Through the Control of Information

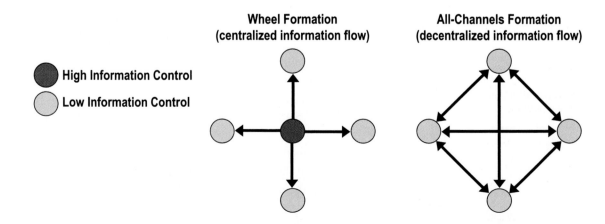

Wheel Formation
(centralized information flow)

All-Channels Formation
(decentralized information flow)

High Information Control

Low Information Control

Control over information flow

Some people are communication "traffic cops." Their job is to distribute, regulate, and filter out information throughout the organizational hierarchy.[23] This right to control information flow is a form of legitimate power and is most common in highly bureaucratic firms. The wheel formation in Exhibit 12.3 depicts this highly centralized control over information flow. The information gatekeeper in the middle of this configuration can influence others through the amount, type, and quality of information he or she receives.

The centralized information control structure is incompatible with knowledge management and team-based organizations. Instead, knowledge sharing requires the all-channels communication structure in which all employees have relatively equal access to information. This allows employees and self-directed work teams to make better decisions. However, the all-channels network may seem rather chaotic in larger, more structured organizations, so there is a tendency to slip back into the wheel pattern.[24]

www.kelloggs.com

Coping with uncertainty

Organizations operate in changing environments, so they require information to reduce the uncertainty of future events. The more the organization can cope with the uncertainty of future events, the more easily it can achieve its goals.[25] Individuals and work units acquire power by helping the organization cope with uncertainty. Coping includes any activity that effectively deals with environmental uncertainties affecting the organization. A groundbreaking study of Canadian breweries and container companies identified three general strategies to help organizations cope with uncertainty. These coping strategies are arranged in a hierarchy of importance, with the first being the most powerful:[26]

John Sobczak/SKB Productions

Not many people have the job of "coolhunter." But that's what Keith Whitham does at Bozell Worldwide Canada Inc. Whitham is a strategic planner in the Toronto ad agency's future-planning department. His job is to spot "cool" consumer trends among people in various age groups. To do this, he spends most of his time absorbing magazines and newspapers, keeping an eye on the Internet, and talking to people. "You have to be an information junkie," Whitham explains, "but there is no substitute for getting out there among the people who make the buying decisions." Whitham's knowledge helps clients cope with the uncertainty of fads and longer-term shifts in buying behaviour. The danger of this work is the cost of a wrong prediction. "This is my calling, but heaven help me if I make the wrong call," says Whitham.[27] What other occupational groups have power in organizational settings through their perceived ability to forecast the environment?

- *Prevention*—The most effective strategy is to prevent environmental changes from occurring. For example, financial experts acquire power by preventing the organization from experiencing a cash shortage or defaulting on loans.

- *Forecasting*—The next best strategy is to predict environmental changes or variations. In this respect, marketing specialists gain power by predicting changes in consumer preferences.

- *Absorption*—People and work units also gain power by absorbing or neutralizing the impact of environmental shifts as they occur. An example is the ability of maintenance crews to come to the rescue when machines break down and the production process stops.

CONTINGENCIES OF POWER

Let's say that you have expert power by virtue of your ability to forecast and possibly even prevent dramatic changes in the organization's environment. Does this incredible expertise mean that you can apply this power? Not necessarily. As we saw earlier in Exhibit 12.2, power bases generate power only under certain conditions. These conditions—called the contingencies of power—include substitutability, centrality, discretion, and visibility.[28] These are not sources of power; rather, they determine the extent to which people can leverage their power bases. You may have lots of expert power, but you won't be able to influence others with this power base if the contingency factors are not in place.

SUBSTITUTABILITY

Substitutability The extent to which those dependent on a resource have alternative sources of supply of the resource or can use other resources that would provide a reasonable substitute.

Substitutability refers to the availability of alternatives. Power is strongest when someone has a monopoly over a valued resource. Conversely, power decreases as the number of alternative sources of the critical resource increases. Substitutability refers not only to other sources that offer the resource, but also to substitutions of the resource itself. For instance, labour unions are weakened when companies introduce technologies that replace the need for their union members. At one time, a strike by telephone employees would have shut down operations, but computerized systems and other technological innovations now ensure that telephone operations continue during labour strikes and reduce the need for telephone operators during normal operations. Technology is a substitute for employees and, consequently, reduces union power.

How do people and work units increase their power through nonsubstitutability? There are several ways, although not all of them are ethical. We describe some of them here for your information—not necessarily for you to practice.

- *Controlling tasks*—Professions have legislation preventing outsiders from performing certain tasks within their domain. Lawyers keep paralegals out of certain activities, and doctors keep nurses, midwives, and others away from certain interventions. Certified public accountants require public corporations to use their services in audits.

- *Controlling knowledge*—Professions control access to the knowledge of their work domain, such as through restricted enrolment in educational programs. Knowledge is also restricted on the job. Several years ago, maintenance workers in a French tobacco processing plant had become very powerful because they controlled the knowledge required to repair the tobacco machines.[29] The maintenance manuals had mysteriously disappeared and the machines had been redesigned enough that only the maintenance staff knew how to fix them if they broke down (which they often did). Knowing the power of nonsubstitutability, maintenance staff carefully avoided documenting the repair procedures and didn't talk to production employees about their trade knowledge.

- *Controlling labour*—Aside from their knowledge resource, people gain power by controlling the availability of their labour. Labour unions attempt to organize as many people as possible within a particular trade or industry so that employers have no other source of labour supply.[30] When unionized workers produce almost all of a particular product or service in a society, the union has an easier time increasing wages. The current fight against outsourcing—having outside companies perform some of the work—is more than union concerns about losing jobs; it is also a fight against losing union power through substitutability. The union's power during a strike is significantly weakened when the employer can continue production through these outside contractors.

- *Differentiation*—Differentiation occurs when an individual or work unit claims to have a unique resource—such as raw materials or knowledge—that the organization would want. By definition, the uniqueness of this resource means that no one else has it. The tactic here isn't so much the nonsubstitutability of the resource, but making organizational leaders believe that the resource is unique. Some people claim that consultants use this tactic. They take skills and knowledge that many consulting firms can provide and wrap them into a package (with the latest buzz words, of course) so that it looks like a service no one else can offer.

CENTRALITY

Centrality The degree and nature of interdependence between the power-holder and others.

Employees and departments have more power as their centrality increases. **Centrality** refers to the degree and nature of interdependence between the powerholder and others.[31] Specifically, centrality increases with (a) the number of people affected by your actions, and (b) the speed with which other people are affected by your actions. Think about your own centrality for a moment: If you decided not to show up for work or school tomorrow, how many people would be affected, and how much time would pass before they are affected? If you have high centrality, most people in the organization would be adversely affected by your absence, and they would be affected quickly.

The importance of centrality was recently demonstrated when a strike by a few hundred employees at a parts plant in Flint, Michigan, shut down most of General Motors' (GM's) North American manufacturing. GM has a just-in-time inventory system, so parts are delivered from the Flint plant to most GM assembly plants just before those parts are needed. Less than one week after the Flint employees went on strike, GM plants in Canada and the United States started shutting down as they ran out of the doors, hoods, and fenders supplied by the Flint plant. Within a month, the Flint strike had stopped most of GM's North American production. Soon after, dealers were running out of vehicles to sell.[32] The small group of employees in Flint, Michigan, had very high centrality because they quickly disrupted most of GM's North American production.

DISCRETION

The freedom to exercise judgment—to make decisions without referring to a specific rule or receiving permission from someone else—is another important contingency of power in organizations. Consider the plight of first-line supervisors. It may seem that they have legitimate power over employees, but this power is often curtailed by specific rules. They must administer programs developed from above and follow specific procedures in their implementation. They administer rewards and punishments, but must abide by precise rules regarding their distribution. Indeed, supervisors are often judged not on their discretionary skills, but on their ability to follow prescribed rules and regulations. This lack of discretion makes supervisors largely powerless even though they may have access to some of the power bases described earlier in this chapter.[33]

VISIBILITY

Power does not flow to unknown people in the organization. Someone with valuable knowledge will yield power only when others are aware of it. Someone with higher authority will yield power only when others are aware of their position in the organization. Only when a person's or work unit's source of power is visible—when it is known to others—will that source of power be meaningful.[34]

Employees use many strategies to maintain their visibility. One strategy is to take people-oriented jobs and work on projects that require frequent interaction with senior decision makers. Another strategy is to work on tasks that are important to key decision makers. One study revealed that software engineers developing a new colour laser printer gained power by working on the most critical components of the project. Corporate leaders paid more attention to engineers working on parts of the project that they believed were most important and faced more crises.[35]

Employees also gain visibility by being, quite literally, visible. They play the game of "face time"—spending more time at work and showing that they are working productively. One female engineer on the colour laser printer project made a habit of going to the office once a week at 2 a.m., after her boss once saw her working at that hour. "[A]fter the reaction I got from my manager I decided it was important to do that early morning work in the office," explains the engineer. "It is better to be seen here if you are going to work in the middle of the night."[36]

People often use public symbols as subtle (and not-so-subtle) cues to make their power sources known to others.[37] Professionals display their educational diplomas and awards on office walls to remind visitors of their expertise. Some executives still rely on the size of their office and related status symbols to show their legitimate power in the organization. Even the clothing we wear communicates power. Medical professionals wear white coats with a stethoscope around their neck to symbolize their legitimate and expert power in hospital settings. One Canadian study reported that women who wear jackets are initially perceived as having more legitimate and expert power than women without jackets.[38]

Mentoring The process of learning the ropes of organizational life from a senior person within the company.

Another way to increase visibility is through **mentoring**—the process of learning the ropes of organizational life from a senior person within the company. Mentors give proteges more visible and meaningful work opportunities, and open doors for them to meet more senior people in the organization. Mentors also teach these newcomers political skills and tactics supported by the organization's senior decision makers.[39]

CONSEQUENCES OF POWER

We use power to influence others, but the type of influence depends on the power source used.[40] Coercive power is generally the least desirable source because it generates resistance by the person or department being influenced. In other words, the targeted person tends to oppose the influence attempt and actively tries to avoid carrying it out. Applying coercive power also reduces trust between the parties and increases employee dissatisfaction. Resistance and distrust also occur when other power bases are used arrogantly or in a manipulative way.

Reward and legitimate power tend to produce compliance, whereby people are motivated to implement the powerholder's request for purely instrumental reasons. You will consciously agree to perform an extra task if your boss gives you a bonus for performing that task, but you aren't enthusiastic about it and will certainly do no more than is necessary to receive the reward. Commitment is the strongest form of influence, whereby people identify with the powerholder's request and are motivated to implement it even when there are no extrinsic benefits for doing so. Commitment is the most common consequence of expert and referent power. For instance, employees will follow a charismatic leader and do more than is asked because this power base evokes commitment rather than compliance or resistance.

Power also affects the powerholder. Chapter 3 described how some people have a strong need for power and are motivated to acquire it for personal or organizational purposes. These individuals are more satisfied and committed to their jobs when they have increased responsibility, authority, and discretion. However, people who acquire too much power often abuse their position to better their personal interests and to gain more power.[41] Powerful employees tend to use their influence more often than is necessary, devalue their less powerful co-workers, and reduce their interpersonal associations with them. They also use their power to acquire more power. If unchecked, powerful employees eventually become even more powerful. In short, there appears to be some truth in Lord Acton's well-known statement that "power tends to corrupt; absolute power corrupts absolutely."[42]

SEXUAL HARASSMENT: AN ABUSE OF POWER

Six weeks after joining Posicom Inc., a Montreal telemarketing firm, Susan (not her real name) was called into her boss's office. The manager began by asking about her sexual habits, then demanded a neck massage and more intimate attention. When Susan protested, the manager turned out the lights and tried to kiss her. She fought him off and fled when a co-worker unexpectedly walked into the room. Susan was afraid to return to work. When she did return, the manager gave her more difficult work to perform. Six weeks later, he fired Susan for incompetence.[43]

Susan's experience at the Montreal telemarketing firm illustrates that sexual harassment is not only stressful (see Chapter 5), but also an abuse of power. **Sexual harassment** includes any unwelcome conduct of a sexual nature that detrimentally affects the work environment or leads to adverse job-related consequences for its victims.[44] It partly occurs because people stereotype the victim as subservient and powerless (see Chapter 6). Sexual harassment also occurs because the harasser is willing to use his or her power over the victim.[45]

Statistics Canada reports that nearly one in four women has been sexually harassed on the job.[46] Abuse of power is most obvious where the harasser threatens the employee's job security or personal safety through coercive or legitimate power (known as *quid pro quo* harassment). Susan experienced this form of harassment, and she is not alone. The Statistics Canada study revealed that nearly one out of five sexually harassed women were threatened with job loss if they did not engage in a sexual relationship. Abuse of power also occurs where sexual harassment takes the form of a hostile work environment. This includes unwelcome conduct, such as sexual jokes, leering, and showing pornographic material. A hostile work environment persists because the victim does not have sufficient power to stop the behaviour.

Minimizing sexual harassment

Organizations accused of sexual harassment pay a tremendous price in public moral embarrassment, loss of talented employees, and financial penalties.[47] Some corporate leaders believe that the best solution is to introduce confidential complaint procedures for people who have been sexually harassed. While these are certainly necessary, they are reactive procedures. Much more important are preventive strategies that reduce the likelihood of sexual harassment incidents.

One way to prevent sexual harassment is to ensure that powerful employees realize how their actions are interpreted by others. Incidents of sexual harassment may seem obvious after the fact, but many harassers really don't realize this at the time, or that they have abused their power in the organization.[48] For example, men often think that a comment about an employee's figure is a compliment, whereas female co-workers often feel threatened by these statements because of the harasser's potential use of power if they react defensively. Moreover, executives sometimes forget that they are role models for the entire organization. Their actions signal whether sexual harassment is prohibited or condoned.

Sexual harassment
Unwelcome conduct of a sexual nature that detrimentally affects the work environment or leads to adverse job-related consequences for its victims.

OFFICE ROMANCE AND ORGANIZATIONAL POWER

Most contemporary workplaces employ almost as many women as men. They work long hours together, often on collaborative projects requiring frequent interaction. The long days also make it more difficult to meet people outside the workplace. It's little wonder that so many romantic relationships today begin in the workplace.[49] The problem with this trend is that office romances don't mix very well with organizational power. As Connections 12.1 describes, they may cause co-workers to perceive bias and abuse of power, particularly where one person in the relationship has higher status.[50] If the relationship fails, power imbalances can escalate the fallout into a case of sexual harassment.

Several companies have tried to minimize the adverse effects of organizational power by prohibiting office romances altogether. For example, Staples, the office supply company, fired the company president when an internal investigation revealed that he had had an affair with his secretary.[51] The difficulty with prohibiting amorous relationships is that employees still

CONNECTIONS 12.1

Power and Romance in the Workplace

Romance is blooming, and much of it originates in the workplace. A recent survey reported that 40 percent of employees in Canada and other countries have dated a co-worker and 72 percent know of others who have dated co-workers. According to another recent poll, 26 percent of Canadian employees say that they have had intimate relations with a co-worker.

But office romances and organizational power don't mix very well. Half of the Canadian employees recently surveyed say that intimate relations among co-workers "probably" harm the work atmosphere; another 27 percent say intimate relations "definitely" worsen it.

One problem is that co-workers tend to think that one or both employees in the relationship abuse their power by favouring each other. A senior correspondent at a Toronto newspaper discovered this after he broke up

a year-long relationship with a younger reporter. "[T]he talk in the office was that I helped her write all of her stories."

A more serious concern is that some consensual relationships can lead to sexual harassment when the relationship falls apart.[52] "A lot of sexual harassment complaints result from consensual relationships that went bad," advises a lawyer who specializes in sexual harassment cases. "One of them decides to break it off. The other continues to pursue and it becomes something other than consensual, and the person claims he or she is being sexually harassed."

The risk of sexual harassment is potentially greater in a supervisor–subordinate relationship. If the subordinate ends the relationship, the supervisor might create a hostile work environment through subtle day-to-day decisions. Even where the jilted supervisor acts appropriately, the subordinate may still feel intimidated by the former lover's power over work and career decisions.

Sources: N. Nejat-Bina, "Employers as Vigilant Chaperones Armed with Dating Waivers: The Intersection of Unwelcomeness and Employer Liability in Hostile Work Environment Sexual Harassment Law," *Berkeley Journal of Employment and Labor Law,* December 22, 1999, p. 325; R. Dhooma, "Taking Care of Business and Pleasure," *Toronto Sun*, September 20, 1999, p. 38; A. Kingston, "Working It," *Flare*, 21 (April 1999), pp 104, 106; E. Edmonds, "Love and Work," *Ottawa Sun*, February 14, 1999, p. S10.

fall in love with each other; they just keep the relationship quiet. Moreover, at least one Canadian court has ruled that companies can't prevent employees from having consensual relationships with co-workers, even when one of them supervises the other.[53]

Experts suggest that a better solution than banning relationships is to ensure that employees make them known. In some cases, employees must sign a document indicating that the relationship is consensual. These "love forms" reduce the risk that one party will later claim that the relationship occurred through an abuse of power.[54]

Even with disclosure, an office romance can have damaging consequences unless the power dynamics are sorted out. That's why some firms advise employees to remove themselves from a position of power over their partner. For example, when Heather and Mike McClure starting dating at Arthur Andersen Inc., they approached the managing partner for a satisfactory arrangement. "The partner in charge simply said we couldn't work on accounts together and that I couldn't sit in on any meetings where Heather's name came up for promotion or salary increase," explains Mike McClure, who holds a more senior position at the accounting firm. "For that, I believe, Arthur Andersen is a little ahead of the curve."[55]

Power permeates organizations and has both desirable and adverse effects on employees. But our interest isn't just in who has power. It is also about how that power is gained and used to influence others in organizational settings. This involves the dynamics of organizational politics, which we discuss next.

ORGANIZATIONAL POLITICS

Charlene Pedrolie was ready for trouble when she replaced an old assembly line with a new team-based work structure. As head of manufacturing at Rowe Furniture Company, Pedrolie knew there would be glitches and plenty of resistance. Naysayers in the corporate office shook their heads and distanced themselves from Pedrolie's experiment. The computer people wouldn't even respond to her urgent requests for more information. Using her sharpest political skills, Petrolie convinced corporate leaders to fire the firm's computer chief and hire one of her friends from General Electric, where she previously had worked. Eventually, Petrolie's persistence and political savvy paid off as production employees worked out the kinks in the team-based work processes.[56]

As this true story reveals, organizational politics can work either for or against the organization. **Organizational politics** represents attempts to influence others using discretionary behaviours to promote personal objectives.[57] It is the exercise of power to get one's own way, including the acquisition of more power, often at the expense of others. Behaviours are discretionary if they are neither formally prescribed nor prohibited by the organization. For example, the naysayers at Rowe Furniture Company who distanced themselves from Pedrolie probably didn't do anything that was against company policy. They just kept quiet and avoided any image that aligned them with the project.

> • **Organizational politics** Attempts to influence others using discretionary behaviours for the purpose of promoting personal objectives; discretionary behaviours are neither explicitly prescribed nor prohibited by the organization and are linked to one or more power bases.

ORGANIZATIONAL POLITICS: GOOD OR BAD?

Tenneco Packaging has an unusual credo that states: "Management with no fear, egos, or politics."[58] This theme supports the packaging company's quest for a team-based organization with high levels of trust among employees. But should companies try to prevent anyone from engaging in organizational politics? Dysfunctional politics should be discouraged, of course. But we need to recognize that many of our day-to-day actions—the way we dress, how we act towards other people, and so on—are political tactics that help the organization achieve its objectives. In fact, experts suggest that people need to be good politicians, particularly as they reach higher levels in the corporation.[59]

Consider the events described in Connections 12.2. It appears that Steven Jobs used organizational politics to regain Apple's top post. Were these tactics good or bad? Many people

www.apple.com

CONNECTIONS 12.2

Organizational Politics Saves Apple Computer

Gil Amelio thought that purchasing NeXT Software, Inc. would be a masterstroke that would save Apple Computer. Instead, it began a series of political events that would soon see Steven Jobs—who founded both NeXT and Apple—replace Amelio as Apple's CEO. Steven Jobs started NeXT after he was ousted from Apple in the 1980s. NeXT wasn't very successful, but it had a respectable operating system. Apple was looking for a new operating system, so Jobs convinced Amelio to buy NeXT.

Following the buyout, Amelio invited Jobs to serve as a special adviser, mainly to raise morale among Apple employees and customers. But Jobs quickly became more than a cheerleader. He visited or phoned Amelio several times each week, advising him on how to integrate NeXT people and products, cut costs, and redraw the organization chart. He convinced Amelio to put former NeXT people in the top positions. Within a few months, Jobs and his NeXT colleagues held key positions for evaluating and weeding out teams of Apple employees. "NeXT is taking over from inside," said one Apple employee. "It's a Jobs–NeXT regime," said another.

Publicly, Jobs supported Amelio's leadership at Apple. Privately, he ridiculed Amelio's lethargic decision making. Eventually, Jobs demonstrated his nonconfidence in Amelio

Steven Jobs (right) used several political tactics to replace Gil Amelio (left) as Apple's CEO.

Reuters/Lou Dematteis/Archive photos.

more publicly by selling the 1.5 million Apple shares he had received as part of the NeXT purchase. This action got the attention of Apple's board of directors. The board removed Amelio and invited Jobs to become Apple's "interim" CEO. Jobs then convinced Apple's current board to resign and picked a new board consisting of friends and allies.

Some writers believe that Amelio's days were numbered and that Jobs was the long-awaited saviour for Apple. But in his biography, Gil Amelio portrayed Jobs as a conniving backstabber "obsessed with power" who cunningly manoeuvred him out of Apple. "I was . . . trapped in a web of plotting as intricate as the War of the Roses," he said.

Sources: J. Reingold, "What Gil Amelio Thinks of Steve Jobs and Apple Now," *Business Week*, January 21, 2000; D. Kirkpatrick, "The Second Coming of Apple," *Fortune*, November 9, 1998; D. Takahash, "An Exponential Life & Death," *Electronic Business*, 24 (June 1998), pp. 82–88; J. Carlton, "Thinking Different," *Wall Street Journal*, April 14, 1998; J. Mardesich, "Office Gossip Points at Jobs as Mastermind of a Coup," *San Jose Mercury*, July 10, 1997; Brent Schlender, "Something's Rotten in Cupertino," *Fortune*, March 3, 1997, pp. 100–08; J. Pearlstein, "Rumors Fly as Staffers Brace for Apple Cuts," *MacWeek*, February 28, 1997.

would argue that Jobs took these steps guided by the belief that Apple's future was in jeopardy with Gil Amelio in charge. In other words, Steven Jobs used political tactics to gain power for the organization's benefit. Apple's sales and profitability soared after Jobs became CEO, so his political activities possibly saved the company. The point here is that some political tactics can help organizations achieve their objectives where traditional methods of influence may fail.

Problems with organizational politics

Of course, organizational politics are often more of a problem than a benefit. One concern is that they consume time and disrupt work activities. They are part of the process loss that occurs in team discussions and work dynamics. Many political tactics reduce trust and the motivation to collaborate. This is why the Tenneco Packaging credo implies that politics is a problem. When people operate in a tense political environment, they have difficulty relating to other employees. This undermines the conditions for active knowledge sharing. Employees who experience more organizational politics also report higher stress, psychological withdrawal, and turnover. However, people tend to feel less stress and dissatisfaction as they become familiar with the work environment in which they experience the political tactics.[60]

The ethics of organizational politics

How can we tell whether our political actions are good or bad? The answer may be to assess the action against the three ethical standards that we learned about in Chapter 7. Generally, a political behaviour is ethical only if it satisfies all three moral principles.[61]

1. *Utilitarian rule*—Does the political tactic provide the greatest good for the greatest number of people? If it mainly benefits the individual and possibly harms the welfare of others, the political behaviour is inappropriate.

2. *Individual rights rule*—Does the political tactic violate anyone's legal or moral rights? If the political activity threatens another person's privacy, free speech, due process, or other rights, it should not be used even if the results might be beneficial to a larger audience.

3. *Distributive justice rule*—Does the political activity treat all parties fairly? If the political behaviour benefits those who are better off at the expense of those who are already worse off, the activity is unethical.

© Ted Goff. www.tedgoff.com

TYPES OF POLITICAL ACTIVITY

So far, we have alluded to the fact that there are various types of political games or tactics found in organizational settings. Organizational behaviour scholars have conveniently grouped most of them into the six categories illustrated in Exhibit 12.4.[62]

ATTACKING OR BLAMING OTHERS

Probably the most direct and nastiest form of organizational politics is attacking and blaming others. This includes giving rivals a bad image in the eyes of decision makers. Not all blaming is overt. A subtle tactic occurs when people dissociate themselves from undesirable situations or use excuses to

EXHIBIT 12.4 Types of Political Behaviour in Organizations

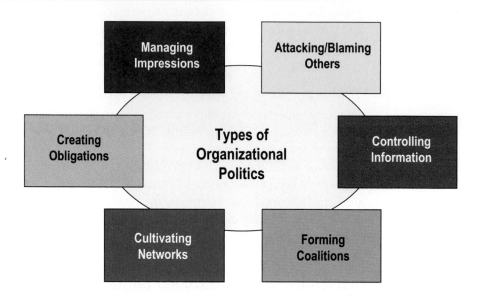

form an external attribution of the cause of the problem.[63] You might explain to your boss that a report is late because of lack of support from another work unit or other conditions beyond your control. In other words, people try to frame their failures in terms of external attributions (see Chapter 6).

CONTROLLING INFORMATION

Information is a political tool as well as a source of power.[64] People influence perceptions, limit the opportunities of rival employees, and further increase their power by strategically controlling how information is shared. For instance, a former CEO at Canadian Imperial Bank of Commerce (CIBC) routinely locked up the files of important clients while he was away so that no other executive would gain power. A few years later, a CIBC president removed the chairman's name from certain circulation lists so that the chairman no longer received information vital to his position. The chairman had lost power, so he retired early.[65]

Some people engage in information politics by organizing meeting agendas to suit their personal interests. For example, they might place a particular issue near the bottom of the agenda so that the committee either doesn't get to it or is too fatigued to make a final judgment. Others arrange meetings in a way that controls who attends. "I know where meetings have been [intentionally] called when someone is away on vacation," says Patsy Marshall, who operates a training firm in Guelph, Ontario.[66]

FORMING COALITIONS

Cindy Casselman felt that Xerox needed a complete intranet system to allow employees to share knowledge, but the communications manager lacked the formal authority to put this "WebBoard" together. Her solution was to quietly assemble a coalition of people who would benefit from WebBoard. The informal group included an executive who wanted the site to test his unit's work on virtual document delivery systems. Another executive joined the coalition because WebBoard would showcase Xerox's new structure of networked personal computers. These and other people gave Casselman enough power to convince her boss to support the project.[67]

Cindy Casselman relied on a **coalition** to get what she wanted. A coalition attempts to influence people outside the group by pooling the resources and power of its members (see Chapter 9). Creating this informal group is a political tactic because it pools the power of several people towards a common objective that each member is unable to influence alone. By demonstrating their strength in numbers, coalitions also create a sense that an issue has broad appeal and therefore deserves legitimate support.[68] Although coalitions are usually formed with good intentions, one possible problem is that they put pressure on others to change, thereby creating compliance rather than commitment to the change.[69]

> **Coalition** An informal group that attempts to influence people outside the group by pooling the resources and power of its members.

CULTIVATING NETWORKS

"It's not what you know, but who you know that counts!" This often-heard statement reflects the philosophy behind another political tactic known as **networking**. Networking refers to cultivating social relationships with others to accomplish one's goals. By forming a trust network, people receive valuable information that increases their expert power in the organization.[70] Networking also nurtures allies and sponsors, thereby making it easier to get approval for projects and other initiatives. Finally, networking helps employees increase their referent power, and this may lead to more favourable decisions by others in the network.

> **Networking** Cultivating social relationships with others for the purpose of accomplishing one's goals.

Networking is a natural part of the informal organization, yet it can create a formidable barrier to those who are not actively connected to it. Women have difficulty getting into senior management because they are usually excluded from male networks.[71] This occurs partly because men (still the dominant powerholders in most organizations) don't feel as comfortable networking with women as they do with other men. Moreover, many men don't realize that their informal networks exclude women from information and decision making.

Calgary Herald. Used with permission.

While researching a book on women in the high-tech industry, Nattalie Lea (far left) became convinced that women needed a network to share resources, knowledge, and support. "Women have made significant contributions to computers and computing, but women who are working in high tech are sometimes feeling isolated," says the Calgary-based engineer, author, and cartoonist. So Lea and four other high-tech women sprouted the concept of a high-tech women's group, called High Tech Women for the 21st Century (HTW21C). The group is modelled after a similar women's network in the energy industry, another sector dominated by men. "You can get a lot of your support from this group and a lot of your resources from this group," says Rita Phillips (second from left), who works for a Calgary-based capital markets software developer.[72] How would networks like HTW21C help women gain power in male-dominated industries?

www.htw21c.calgary.ab.ca

One survey reported that nearly one-third of female senior executives in Canada say that exclusion from informal networks of communication is a barrier to women's advancement in the organization. In contrast, only 12 percent of Canadian chief executives thought that exclusion from informal networks was a problem for women.[73] An executive at Avon Products Inc. sums up the issue: "It's there all the time," she says. "How many business conversations [and] business decisions are made in the men's room or on golf day?"[74]

CREATING OBLIGATIONS

The obligation to help someone who has once helped you—called the norm of reciprocity—is deeply embedded in many societies. It is also a political tactic.[75] An employee who has helped someone might later ask that person to put in a good word for them or support them on a promotion. The indebted co-worker is more likely to agree to this than if there is no debt to repay. Some organizational politicians are able to leverage these debts for a greater return than what was given initially.

MANAGING IMPRESSIONS

Impression management | **Impression management** is the practice of actively shaping our public images.[76] Many impression-management activities are done routinely to satisfy the basic norms of social behaviour. Others are political tactics because they are used deliberately to get one's way. For example, some job applicants lie on their résumés to get a job.[77] Some political tactics described earlier—including blaming others, filtering information, and increasing the visibility of one's power base—are forms of impression management. Another well-known impression-management tactic is to manage your appearance and behaviour so that others develop a desired image of you.[78] For example, the way we dress is part of the impression-management process.

Impression management The practice of actively shaping our public images.

Employees use a variety of impression-management tactics, often without realizing it. For example, we make a point of attending meetings where senior executives are present, even though our time might be better spent elsewhere. We keep in mind that many bosses still value "face time," the physical presence suggesting that we are hard at work. As we read in the opening story to this chapter, the trend towards telecommuting may remove employees from office politics, but it also may increase their career risks as it provides less face time and other impression-management tactics.

CONDITIONS FOR ORGANIZATIONAL POLITICS

Organizational politics flourish under the right conditions.[79] One of those conditions is scarce resources. When budgets are slashed, people rely on political tactics to safeguard their resources and maintain the status quo. This happened at Exponential Technology, which was working on a superfast chip for the Apple Macintosh. When Apple's future became uncertain, the company hired a second group of engineers to develop a similar chip for the Intel-compatible market. But with budget restrictions, the Mac-compatible engineers did their best to run the new group out of town. "It got really ugly," recalls Exponential CEO Rick Shriner. "It came down to a battle for limited resources." To reduce the political infighting, Shriner moved the Intel group to another city.[80]

Along with resource scarcity, office politics flourish when resource allocation decisions are ambiguous, complex, or lack formal rules. This occurs because decision makers are given more discretion over resource allocation, so potential recipients of those resources use political tactics to influence the factors that should be considered in the decision. Organizational change encourages political behaviours for this reason. Change creates uncertainty and ambiguity as the company moves from an old set of rules and practices to a new set. During these times, employees apply political strategies to protect their valued resources, positions, and self-image.

Organizational politics also becomes commonplace when it is tolerated and transparently supported by the organization.[81] Companies sometimes promote people who are the best politicians, not necessarily the best talent to run the company. If left unchecked, organizational politics can paralyze an organization as people focus more on protecting themselves than on fulfilling their roles. Political activity becomes self-reinforcing unless the conditions supporting political behaviour are altered.

PERSONAL CHARACTERISTICS

Several personal characteristics affect a person's motivation to engage in organizational politics.[82] Some people have a strong need for personal power as opposed to socialized power (see Chapter 3). They seek power for its own sake, and use political tactics to acquire more power. People with an internal locus of control are more likely than those with an external locus of control to engage in political behaviours. This does not mean that internals are naturally political; rather, they are more likely to use influence tactics when political conditions are present because, unlike externals, they feel very much in charge of their own destiny.

Some people have strong **Machiavellian values**. Machiavellianism is named after Niccolo Machiavelli, the sixteenth-century Italian philosopher who wrote *The Prince*, a famous treatise about political behaviour. People with high Machiavellian values believe that deceit is a natural and acceptable way to influence others. They seldom trust co-workers and frequently use power to manipulate others towards their own personal goals, even when these goals are unfavourable to the organization. In particular, these people tend to use cruder influence tactics, such as bypassing one's boss or being assertive.[83]

> **Machiavellian values** The belief that deceit is a natural and acceptable way to influence others.

Gender differences in organizational politics

Some experts on gender issues suggest that men and women differ in their use of political tactics. Men apparently use more impression-management strategies. They are more comfortable advertising their achievements and taking personal credit for successes of others reporting to them. Women are more reluctant to force the spotlight on themselves, preferring instead to share the credit with others.[84]

Men and women also seem to differ in assigning blame.[85] Research suggests that women are more likely to apologize—that is, personally take blame—even for problems not caused by them. Men are more likely to assign blame and less likely to assume it. In fact, some men try to turn their errors into achievements by appearing as the white knight to save the day. This difference is consistent with our discussion of gender communication (Chapter 8), namely, that men tend to communicate and behave in ways that support their status and power.

If they don't rely on blaming or impression management, which political tactics do women tend to use? Some writers claim that women don't use any political tactics very well in organizations, and that this has limited their opportunities for promotion.[86] More likely, women use indirect impression management as well as forms of networking and coalition building. Of course, we must be careful not to generalize gender differences too much. Some women are very agile corporate politicians, and some men are politically inept in organizations.

CONTROLLING POLITICAL BEHAVIOUR

The conditions that fuel organizational politics also provide some clues about how to control dysfunctional political activities.[87] Here are several strategies that should keep dysfunctional politics in check:

- Ensure that there is a sufficient supply of critical resources. This is not easy, but it is possible to ensure that sufficient inventory and cash flow exist in many cases.

- Where resources are necessarily scarce, introduce clear rules and regulations to specify the use of these resources.

- Establish a free flow of information so that the organization is less dependent on a few people at the centre of a communications wheel.

- Use effective organizational change management practices—particularly education and involvement—to minimize uncertainty during the change process (see Chapter 15).

- Restructure team and organizational norms (as described in Chapter 9) to reject political tactics that appear to interfere with the organization's goals.

- Select people who have a moderately strong socialized need for power and a relatively low level of Machiavellianism.

- Provide opportunities for open and candid dialogue to resolve conflicts between employees and work units.

- Have employees monitor the workplace and actively discourage co-workers who engage in political tactics.

CHAPTER SUMMARY

- Power is the capacity to influence others. It exists when one party perceives that he or she is dependent on the other for something of value. However, the dependent person must also have counterpower—some power over the dominant party—to maintain the relationship.

- There are five power bases. Legitimate power is an agreement among organizational members that people in certain roles can request certain behaviours of others. Reward power is derived from the ability to control the allocation of rewards valued by others and to remove negative sanctions. Coercive power is the ability to apply punishment. Expert power is the capacity to influence others by possessing knowledge or skills that they want. People have referent power when others identify with them, like them, or otherwise respect them.

- Information plays an important role in organizational power. Employees gain power by controlling the flow of information that others need, and by being able to cope with uncertainties related to important organizational goals.

- Four contingencies determine whether these power bases translate into real power. Individuals and work units are more powerful when they are nonsubstitutable, that is, when there is a lack of alternatives. Employees, work units, and organizations reduce substitutability by controlling tasks, knowledge, and labour, and by differentiating themselves from competitors. A second contingency is centrality. People have more power when they have high centrality, that is, the number of people affected and how quickly others are affected by their actions. Discretion, the third contingency of power, refers to the freedom to exercise judgment. Power increases when people have freedom to use their power. The fourth contingency, visibility, refers to the idea that power increases to the extent that a person's or work unit's competencies are known to others. People gain visibility by taking people-oriented jobs, working on important tasks, engaging in face time, using public symbols of their power, and relying on mentors. Power is applied to influence others, but the type of influence depends on the power source. Coercive power tends to produce resistance; reward and legitimate power result in compliance; expert and referent power produce commitment. People with a high need for power feel more satisfied and committed to their jobs when they have power, but many people tend to abuse their power when given too much of it.

- Sexual harassment is a serious abuse of power. It is most obvious where the harasser threatens the employee's job security or personal safety through coercive or legitimate power. Sexual harassment may be minimized by making people aware of their actions, establishing clear rules regarding intimate relationships among co-workers, and ensuring that existing relationships are voluntary.

- Organizational power also complicates workplace romances. Co-workers tend to believe that employees in a sexual relationship will abuse their power. If the relationship ends, power imbalances between the two employees may lead to sexual harassment. Some organizations try to prohibit romantic relationships at work, but experts recommend that employees disclose their relationship and remove themselves from a position of power over their partner.

- Organizational politics attempts to influence others using discretionary behaviours that promote personal objectives. People tend to have an unfavourable view of organizational politics, but some political activities benefit the organization. Still, we must always consider the ethical implications of political behaviours, including whether the action provides the greatest good for the greatest number of people, violates anyone's legal or moral rights, and treats all parties fairly.

- There are many types of organizational politics. The most common tactics include attacking or blaming others, controlling information, forming coalitions, cultivating networks, creating obligations, and managing impressions.

- Organizational politics is more prevalent when scarce resources are allocated using complex and ambiguous decisions, and when the organization tolerates or rewards political behaviour. Individuals with a high need for personal power, an internal locus of control, and strong Machiavellian values have a higher propensity to use political tactics. Men tend to engage in explicit impression management (taking credit for successes) and blaming tactics. Women tend to use fewer political strategies.

- Dysfunctional organizational politics may be controlled by providing sufficient resources, providing clear rules for resource allocation, establishing a free flow of information, using education and involvement during organizational change, designing norms that discourage dysfunctional politics, selecting people who are less likely to use dysfunctional politics, trying to resolve conflicts before people use political tactics against the other party, and having employees actively discourage co-workers from using dysfunctional politics.

KEY TERMS

Centrality, p. 363

Coalition, p. 371

Coercive power, p. 359

Counterpower, p. 357

Expert power, p. 360

Impression management, p. 372

Legitimate power, p. 358

Machiavellian values, p. 373

Mentoring, p. 364

Networking, p. 371

Organizational politics, p. 367

Power, p. 356

Power distance, p. 359

Referent power, p. 360

Reward power, p. 359

Sexual harassment, p. 365

Substitutability, p. 362

DISCUSSION QUESTIONS

1. What role does counterpower play in the power relationship? Give an example where you have counterpower at school or work.

2. You have just been hired as a brand manager of toothpaste for a large Canadian consumer products company. Your job mainly involves encouraging the advertising and production groups to promote and manufacture your product more effectively. These departments aren't under your direct authority, although company procedures indicate that they must complete certain tasks requested by brand managers. Describe the sources of power you can use to ensure that the advertising and production departments will help you make and sell toothpaste more effectively.

3. Suppose you have formal authority to allocate performance bonuses to your employees. What contingencies must exist before this source of power will translate into actual power?

4. Three managers in the regional office of a national energy company were found guilty of demanding sexual relations with female support staff. Some women who refused were fired. The energy company has hired your consulting firm to minimize the probability of future sexual harassment in this regional office. What would you do? You may assume that the three guilty managers have been replaced, but other managers are still there and will not be fired.

5. Visibility exists in many forms in almost any setting. Without offending any individuals in your class, identify strategies that people use in the classroom to strengthen their power through visibility.

6. The author of a popular business book wrote, "Office politics is a demotivator that must be eliminated." He argues that when companies allow politics to determine who gets ahead, employees put their energy into political behaviour rather than job performance. Discuss the author's comments about organizational politics.

7. This book frequently emphasizes that successful companies engage in knowledge management. What political tactics were described in this chapter that directly interfere with knowledge management objectives?

8. Not long ago, senior executives at a medium-sized company were deciding whether to replace the company's mainframe with a client/server system of microcomputers. During this tense time, the mainframe and microcomputer experts in the information systems department engaged in a heated battle of political infighting by openly bad-mouthing each other. Meanwhile, people who controlled the mainframe information actively resisted the change to client/server system, which would effectively allow users to bypass these people. What strategies would you recommend to minimize these incidents of organizational politics?

Case Study

ACTIVITY 12.1
Foreign Exchange Confrontation

I worked in the foreign exchange (FX) back office, where deals made by our 150 dealers were checked, payment instructions were added, and queries were addressed. My job was to resolve problems arising from deals. Much of the time, this involved going upstairs and talking to the dealers.

Now, you never told a dealer that he or she was wrong, even when handling those dealers who, throughout the whole of my placement, were never correct. You just briefly stated what the problem was and asked them to kindly look into it.

This particular incident involves Nick, one of the men who always made mistakes. This time he had mixed up the currencies on a deal. The payment was due in half an hour, so it was important to get him to amend the deal. I went up to see him, but Lee, also from the back office, was already talking to him about something else. Because my problem was urgent, I waited for Lee to finish. When Lee left, Nick glanced at me and then, to my surprise, left his desk and went over to another dealer, John, from whom we had heard juicy comments for quite a while. A group of dealers assembled and I could see from their behaviour that they were not discussing business.

I went over and discovered that they were looking at two pages from *The Sun* newspaper filled with pictures of naked women. Something inside me snapped. I told Nick that my job was actually meant as a service to the dealers, to help make them aware of errors before it costs them money. I explained how much work I had to do and how much other dealers appreciated my corrections, and made it clear that by ignoring me he was not only wasting my time but his own colleagues' right to the service the back office offers. I added that considering his error statistics, I would imagine he had better things to do than to stare at pictures of naked women.

I turned around, left my sheet of paper on his desk, and departed.

My main emotion both then and now is anger. I felt I had been patient and endured much more rude behaviour than was acceptable. The way Nick ignored me to go and look at pictures of naked women was the straw that broke the camel's back. I also felt helpless and vulnerable. They were discussing naked women in detail in a room filled almost entirely with men, and I knew my views were in the minority. I was afraid that any reaction from me would be ridiculed. Writing about it now, I also feel proud for having had the courage to tell him off.

The FX dealers, nearly all men, were the most arrogant group of people I have ever come across in my life. If it had not been for me gradually understanding some of the reasons for their behaviour, an outburst like the one I have just described would have come much earlier. You need to appreciate the fact that the FX department, at the moment, produces some of the best results in this firm, and that this creates a feeling of invulnerability and extreme self-importance among those working there. I did not feel that this was a valid excuse for their behaviour; still, I learned to accept it.

The back-office policy was to accept any amount of attitude from the dealers, and then let it all out afterwards when you were safely back at your desk. This policy was no good, as it only helped increase the hostility between dealers and back-office staff. My telling Nick off meant that I had broken the main taboo in the office. Over several weeks, I realized that this had earned me much respect. I had done something many of my colleagues had wanted to do for years, but dared not do. The risk was smaller for me, as I was only there for a short while. As a result of my actions, I achieved respect both from the back office and from some of the dealers. And perhaps, even more importantly, I respected myself more for having done what I felt was right.

Discussion Questions

1. Describe the power bases and contingencies of power held by Nick and this back-office staff member during this incident.

2. How did the back-office staff member's power change after this incident? Why did it change?

Source: Adapted from Y. Gabriel, "An Introduction to the Social Psychology of Insults in Organizations," *Human Relations*, 51 (November 1998), pp. 1329–54.

Video Case Study

ACTIVITY 12.2
Behind the Boardrooms

Bob Verdun is owner of the Elmira Independent newspaper and a crusader against the high-priced directors of Canada's most powerful corporations. He claims that it's still an old boy's club. Company CEOs are playing politics by appointing big names to the boards of directors in the hopes that shareholders will be impressed. However, these big names often do not have the time or inclination to interfere in somebody else's business.

"That's just the way it's done," says Verdun. "You scratch my back, I'll scratch yours. You sit on my board and I won't ask any questions. And I'll sit on your board and not ask any questions."

Examine the list of Canada's corporate directors and you'll find the same people on several boards. Conrad Black, Paul Desmarais, and several others sit on more than a dozen boards. Even Peter Lougheed, who sits on 14 boards, agrees that the country's corporate directors are too clubby.

"They went to school together, they play golf at the same places, they socialize in the same circles," complains Donald Thain, professor emeritus at Ivey School of Business. Thain says that this clubby culture supports conformance, mutual support, and a don't-rock-the-boat attitude. He also points out that many of these directors are either incompetent or cannot possibly know what's going on in the company. "[As] a result, they don't have the power to really step in and do something," Thain warns.

One exception to the clubby boardroom is the Alberta Power Pool, where chairman Maury Parsons established new rules: no insiders. Board members cannot have a stake in the business and cannot have any connections to management. Anne Fawcett, the Caldwell Partners executive who searches for board members, would like to see new faces at the board tables. The problem is that board chairmen don't want to take chances. Moreover, the only way a director can be removed is by resigning or being asked to leave by fellow directors.

To help board members perform better, 68 percent of Canadian companies now have an annual board evaluation. That's good. But in almost all these cases, a committee of board members performs the evaluation. That hardly provides for a neutral assessment. "[B]ecause it's a social club, you never move in," explains Donald Thain. "Very, very seldom do you see directors fired. And that's the problem in evaluation."

Discussion Questions

1. What political tactics do board chairpersons seem to use to maintain their control and power over directors?

2. What power base(s) primarily influences who becomes a board member?

3. What team dynamics and decision-making issues probably affect corporate boards of directors? What are the consequences for the board's effectiveness? How can these team dynamics and decision-making issues be improved?

Source: Based on "Boardrooms," *Venture* 714 (July 13, 1999).

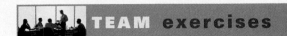
TEAM exercises

ACTIVITY 12.3
GENERAL SOFTWARE PRODUCTS: AN IN-BASKET EXERCISE

by Daphne Eylon, University of Richmond, and Susan Herman, Keene State College

Purpose: This exercise is designed to help you understand the dynamics and feelings of power in an organizational setting.

Materials: The instructor will distribute in-basket materials and, later, an attitude questionnaire. Teams should have a private area where they can make their decisions.

Instructions:

Step 1: The instructor will briefly describe what an in-basket is, including the time constraints. Students are then put into groups (typically of four to five people) and each group receives a package with copies of e-mails and memos. (Note: Instead of working in teams, your instructor may decide to assign the in-basket exercise to individuals working alone. If so, the following steps still apply, but Step 2 would refer to individuals.)

Step 2: Teams have 25 minutes to go through the in-basket, regardless of how many items they actually complete. Please respond to each item in the package.

Step 3: Immediately after completing the in-basket exercise, each student will individually complete the attitude scale provided by the instructor.

Step 4: The instructor will debrief students on the exercise.

In-Basket Setting: Students take the role of J. Carter, a personal computer (PC) software department manager in General Software Products, one of the companies owned by General Holding Corp. You are requested to respond to several e-mails, letters, and memos that have been left in your in-basket. General Holding Corp. is a large company that competes in the computer industry.

General Software develops a wide variety of software products. You, J. Carter, have just been promoted from the position of computer games group manager. This new promotion represents a natural progression for someone fast-tracking through management levels at General Software Products. Your new position as PC software department manager also carries with it membership in the firm's Software Steering Committee. This committee meets with the firm's CEO, David Brown, to discuss key strategic policy decisions. The previous department manager for PC software, Sam White, died suddenly of a heart attack three weeks ago and, as many predicted (including yourself), you were appointed to the position.

Source: D. Eylon and S. Herman, "Exploring Empowerment: One Method for the Classroom," *Journal of Management Education*, 23 (February 1999), pp. 80–94. Used with permission of the authors.

ACTIVITY 12.4
BUDGET DELIBERATIONS

by Sharon Card, Saskatchewan Institute of Applied Science & Technology

Purpose: This exercise is designed to help you understand some of the power dynamics that occur across hierarchical levels in organizations.

Materials: This activity works best where one small room leads to a larger room, which then leads to a larger area. The instructor will distribute a budget sheet showing a list of budget requests and their costs.

Instructions: These instructions are based on a class size of about 30 students. The instructor may adjust the size of the first two groups slightly for larger classes. The instructor will organize students as follows: A few (three to four) students are assigned the position of executives. They are preferably located in a secluded office or corner of a large classroom. Another six to eight students are assigned positions as middle managers. These people will ideally be located in an adjoining room or space, allowing privacy for the executives. The remaining students represent the nonmanagement employees in the organization. They are located in an open area outside the executive and management rooms.

Rules: Members of the executive group are free to enter the space of either the middle management or nonmanagement groups and to communicate whatever they wish, whenever they wish. Members of the middle management group may enter the space of the nonmanagement group whenever they wish, but must request permission to enter the executive group's space. The executive group can refuse the middle management group's request. Members of the nonmanagement group are not allowed to disturb the top group in any way unless specifically invited by members of the executive group. The nonmanagement group does have the right to request permission to communicate with the middle management group. The middle management group can refuse the lower group's request.

Task: Your organization is in the process of preparing a budget. The challenge is to balance needs with financial resources. Of course, the needs are greater than the resources. Each group has control over a portion of the budget and must decide how to spend the money over which they have control. Nonmanagement has discretion over a relatively small portion and the executive group has discretion over the greatest portion. The exercise is finished when the organization has negotiated a satisfactory budget, or when the instructor calls time out. The class will then debrief with the following questions and others the instructor might ask.

Discussion Questions

1. What can we learn from this exercise about power in organizational hierarchies?

2. How is this exercise similar to relations in real organizations?

3. How did students in each group feel about the amount of power they held?

4. How did they exercise their power in relations with the other groups?

Self-Assessment exercise

ACTIVITY 12.5
PERCEPTIONS OF POLITICS SCALE (POPS)

Purpose: This self-assessment is designed to help you assess the degree to which you view your school environment as politically charged.

Instructions: Listed below are statements that may or may not describe the school where you are attending classes. These statements refer to the administration of the school, not to the classroom. Please indicate whether you agree or disagree with each statement. Then, calculate your score using the scoring key in Appendix B of this book.

Indicate the extent to which you agree or disagree with the following statements about the administration of the school you attend.	Strongly Agree	Agree	Neutral	Disagree	Strongly Disagree
1. Administrators at this school tend to build themselves up by tearing others down.	5	4	3	2	1
2. Employees at this school are encouraged to speak out frankly even when they are critical of well-established ideas.	5	4	3	2	1
3. There is no place for "yes-men" here; good ideas are desired even if it means disagreeing with superiors.	5	4	3	2	1
4. Agreeing with powerful administrators is the best alternative in this organization.	5	4	3	2	1
5. There has always been an influential group of administrators at this school that no one ever crosses.	5	4	3	2	1
6. Sometimes it is easier to remain quiet than to fight the system at this school.	5	4	3	2	1
7. It is best not to rock the boat in this organization.	5	4	3	2	1
8. At this school, telling others what they want to hear is sometimes better than telling the truth.	5	4	3	2	1
9. At this school, employees have to follow what they are told rather than make up their own minds.	5	4	3	2	1

Source: Adapted from K.M. Kacmar, "Further Validation of the Perceptions of Politics Scale (POPS): A Multiple Sample Investigation," *Journal of Management,* 23 (1997), pp. 627 58.

CHAPTER THIRTEEN

Organizational Conflict and Negotiation

LEARNING OBJECTIVES

After reading this chapter, you should be able to:

- Distinguish task-related conflict from socioemotional conflict.
- Discuss the advantages and disadvantages of conflict in organizations.
- Identify six sources of organizational conflict.
- Outline the five interpersonal styles of conflict management.
- Summarize six structural approaches to managing conflict.
- Outline four situational influences on negotiations.
- Compare the three types of third-party dispute resolution.

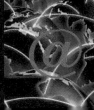

P. Doyle, *Ottawa Citizen*.

Captain Eddie Albert and other Ottawa fire department staff were angry that the city spent money on diversity training that could have been put to better use.

You know things aren't working right when sensitivity training sessions turn into shouting matches. That's what happened at the City of Ottawa fire department's first-ever diversity training seminars. "There have been shouting matches, there has been a lot of anger in the room directed at the instructor," says deputy fire chief Dave Smith.

The conflict started when firefighters disputed Ottawa city council's decision to hire three female firefighters by bypassing the usual selection process. The diversity training instructor fuelled the conflict by defending city council's decision. "The instructor is an ex-prison guard who got hired because of affirmative action and she started her sessions by praising the benefits of affirmative action," explains Smith. "That didn't go over well."

Ottawa firefighters are also angry that Ottawa city council spent money on diversity training rather than on higher priorities. Crews have been "screaming" for new medical and water rescue training, are driving trucks that badly need repair, and haven't had a pay raise in seven years. "I just don't think we should be spending money on sensitivity training," says Captain Eddie Albert, adding that several female dispatchers and inspectors already work in the department.

The diversity training instructor agrees that the first few sessions were "stormy." The conflict subsided after she stopped defending city council's affirmative action decisions. "Now, if anyone complains," the instructor says, "I tell them I just won't talk about it, and we stick with the materials for the session. It's been much better since then."[1]

Conflict The process in which one party perceives that its interests are being opposed or negatively affected by another party.

www.fire.ottawa.on.ca

Conflict is a process in which one party perceives that its interests are being opposed or negatively affected by another party.[2] The City of Ottawa firefighters experienced conflict because they believed their personal and professional interests were opposed when city council bypassed the selection process for female applicants and used scarce financial resources for diversity training. The firefighters felt that the money was more desperately needed to repair trucks and provide other training. They probably felt that bypassing the selection process increased the risk of hiring unqualified people.

This chapter looks at the dynamics of conflict in organizational settings. We begin by describing the conflict process and discussing the consequences and sources of conflict in organizational settings. Five conflict management styles are then described, followed by a discussion of the structural approaches to conflict management. The last two sections of this chapter introduce two procedures for resolving conflict: negotiation and third-party resolution.

THE CONFLICT PROCESS

When describing an incident involving conflict, we are usually referring to the observable part of conflict—the angry words, shouting matches, and actions that symbolize opposition. But this *manifest conflict* is only a small part of the conflict process. As Exhibit 13.1 illustrates, the conflict process begins with the sources of conflict.[3] Incompatible goals, different values, and other conditions lead one or both parties to perceive that conflict exists. We will look closely at these sources of conflict later in this chapter because understanding and changing the root causes is the key to effective conflict management.

CONFLICT PERCEPTIONS AND EMOTIONS

At some point, the sources of conflict lead one or both parties to perceive that conflict exists. They also experience various conflict-laden emotions towards the other party. For example, the Ottawa firefighters felt anger towards city council because they believed council's training and selection decisions interfered with their job and personal needs (e.g., higher pay, better working conditions). The firefighters also felt anger towards the diversity management instructor because she repeatedly supported Ottawa city council's decisions.

Task-related versus socioemotional conflict

When asked what Toyota Motor Company does to make great cars, one engineer replied, "Lots of conflict."[4] Toyota employees know that conflict is not always bad. Successful organizations

EXHIBIT 13.1 The Conflict Process

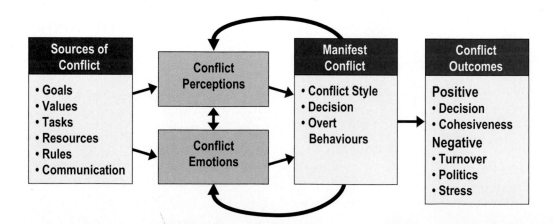

encourage mild forms of conflict without having it escalate into an emotional battle among employees or work units. The key is to create *task-related conflict*, and to prevent it from escalating into *socioemotional conflict*.[5] Task-related conflict occurs when people disagree about task issues, such as goals, key decision areas, procedures, and the appropriate choice for action. The conflict is separate from them, an object "out there" that must be addressed. This conflict is potentially healthy and valuable because it makes people rethink their perspectives of reality. As long as the conflict remains focused on the issue, new ideas may emerge and the conflict remains controlled.

Unfortunately, conflict often becomes personal. Rather than focusing on the issue, each party perceives the other party to be the problem. This socioemotional conflict is apparent in the opening story of this chapter. The Ottawa firefighters believed that city council and the diversity training instructor were deliberately trying to undermine their personal and professional goals. With socioemotional conflict, differences are viewed as personal attacks rather than as attempts to resolve an issue. The discussion becomes emotionally charged, which introduces perceptual biases and distorts information processing.

MANIFEST CONFLICT

Conflict perceptions and emotions usually manifest themselves in the decisions and overt behaviours of one party towards the other. These conflict episodes may range from subtle nonverbal behaviours to warlike aggression. Conflict is also manifested by the style each side uses to resolve the conflict, such as whether one side tries to defeat the other or find a mutually beneficial solution. Conflict management styles will be described later in this chapter. At this point, you should know that these styles influence each side's decisions and behaviours. Consequently, they play a critical role in determining whether the conflict will escalate or be quickly resolved.

Conflict escalation cycle

The conflict process in Exhibit 13.1 shows arrows looping back from manifest conflict to conflict perceptions and emotions. These loops represent the fact that the conflict process is really a series of episodes that potentially link together into an escalation cycle or spiral.[6] It doesn't take much to start this conflict cycle—just an inappropriate comment, a misunderstanding, or an undiplomatic action. These behaviours communicate to the other party in a way that creates a perception of conflict. If the first party did not intend to demonstrate conflict, the second party's response may create that perception.

If the conflict remains task-related, both parties may resolve the conflict through logical analysis. However, the communication process has enough ambiguity that a wrong look or word may trigger an emotional response by the other side and set the stage for socioemotional conflict. These distorted beliefs and emotions reduce each side's motivation to communicate, making it more difficult for them to discover common ground and ultimately resolve the conflict.[7] The parties then rely more on stereotypes and emotions to reinforce their perceptions of the other party. Some structural conditions increase the likelihood of conflict escalation. Employees who are more confrontational and less diplomatic also tend to escalate conflict.[8]

CONFLICT OUTCOMES

There is a natural tendency to suppress conflict. While suppression may be appropriate for socioemotional conflict, task-related conflict should be encouraged under some conditions.[9] Thus, **conflict management** refers to interventions that alter the level and form of conflict in ways that maximize its benefits and minimize its dysfunctional consequences.

Conflict management Interventions that alter the level and form of conflict in ways that maximize its benefits and minimize its dysfunctional consequences.

CONNECTIONS 13.1

Mavericks Like Randy Powell Create Constructive Controversy

Randy Powell doesn't like to follow the crowd. Instead, the former Campbell Soup marketer (now president of coffee retailer Second Cup Ltd.) believes that differences of opinion should be heard and appreciated. "Groupthink can happen," warns Powell. "What the senior person says tends to rule. I have always believed I should speak for what I believe to be true."

Powell demonstrated his penchant for constructive controversy early in his career—in fact, just one month after being hired as a brand manager at the Canadian operations of Campbell Soup Ltd. in Toronto. He had been assigned to Prego spaghetti sauce products and, during the brand review, Campbell's CEO concluded that Prego was losing out to price-cutting competitors. Powell mustered his courage and said that he disagreed with the veteran marketer. He explained that Prego's line needed more variety and advertising budget. The CEO accepted Powell's reasoning.

Later, Powell's supervisor approached him and confided: "I wanted to say that, but I just didn't have the courage to step in front of [the CEO]." By the end of the day, more than a dozen colleagues had congratulated Powell for speaking up.

Some time later, Campbell's CEO sent Powell and 40 other executives to a week-long New Age management session. Powell soon concluded that the consultants were off base with their "planning back from the future" stuff. Between sessions, most of the other Campbell's executives confided that they felt the same way. The consultants heard about

Randy Powell demonstrated a penchant for constructive controversy early in his career.

the dissent on the fourth day and dramatically asked participants whether they were in or out. Those who said "out" had to leave immediately.

As the consultants went around the room, every executive who privately grumbled about the session said "in." Powell was third from last. "I believed it could be political suicide to go against [the CEO] on an issue he believed to be true," Powell recalls. Every executive before him had agreed to stay in. Still, when it was his turn, Powell said "out" and left the room.

The next day, the CEO called Powell into his office and told him that he respected his decision, even if he disagreed with it. Two months later, at 31 years of age, Powell was promoted to vice-president of sales.

Source: Adapted from S. Silcoff, "The Sky's Your Limit," *Canadian Business*, April 1997, pp. 58–66.

It has been said that if two people agree, one of them is unnecessary. This means that conflict is good (potentially) and that agreement is redundant. Conflict is a catalyst for change and improved decision making. It occurs when people offer new perspectives and these emerging views are debated.[10] **Constructive controversy** is a positive application of conflict. As explained in Chapter 11, constructive controversy helps people to learn about other points of view, which encourages them to re-examine their basic assumptions about a problem and its possible solution. Connections 13.1 describes how Randy Powell used constructive controversy to improve decision making at Campbell Soup Ltd. Notice that Powell (now the CEO of Second Cup Ltd.) and his colleagues maintained task-related conflict and avoided personal attacks. Task-related conflict helps people to recognize problems, to identify a variety of solutions, and to understand the issues involved better.[11]

> **Constructive contro-
> versy** Any situation
> in which team mem-
> bers debate their dif-
> ferent opinions
> regarding a problem
> or issue in a way that
> minimizes socioemo-
> tional conflict.

Conflict is also beneficial where intergroup conflict improves team dynamics within those units. Teams increase their cohesiveness and task orientation when they face an external threat. Conditions of moderate conflict motivate team members to work more efficiently towards goals, thereby increasing the team's productivity.

There is, of course, a darker side to conflict in organizations. When intergroup conflict becomes emotionally charged, teams become so cohesive that they are no longer motivated to seek outside information. In other words, a high level of socioemotional conflict may lead to groupthink, the tendency of highly cohesive groups to value consensus at the price of decision quality.[12]

At an individual level, socioemotional conflict increases frustration, job dissatisfaction, and stress. In the longer term, this leads to increased turnover and absenteeism.[13] These symptoms are showing up among executives at Walt Disney Corp. Disney CEO Michael Eisner apparently supports an environment in which executives battle each other over scarce resources. The idea is to bring out constructive controversy, but some insiders claim that several executives have left the animation and entertainment firm because the constant conflict wears them down.[14]

SOURCES OF CONFLICT IN ORGANIZATIONS

Personality clashes come to mind when thinking about the sources of conflict. Although personality differences certainly influence conflict, this phrase often masks the underlying causes of conflict behaviour and perceptions. Instead, organizational research has identified six conditions, shown in Exhibit 13.2 and described over the next few pages, under which conflict tends to germinate and flourish. If you see incidents of manifest conflict, one or more of these sources is probably the root cause.

INCOMPATIBLE GOALS

A common source of conflict is goal incompatibility. This is the situation in which people or work units have goals that interfere with each other. Financial rewards for goal accomplishment further entrench the perceived conflict because employees are more motivated to pursue their own goals.[15]

Goal incompatibility explains the conflict that has occurred between "hot-end" and "cold-end" production employees at the Consumers Packaging plant in Bramalea, Ontario.[16] The hot-end employees form the glass containers and receive a bonus for the number of bottles formed. These bottles work their way to the cold end, where they are packed for shipment. The cold-end employees receive bonuses for minimizing customer complaints and bottle returns, so they weed out jars that don't meet high standards. But the more jars discarded by

EXHIBIT 13.2 Sources of Conflict in Organizations

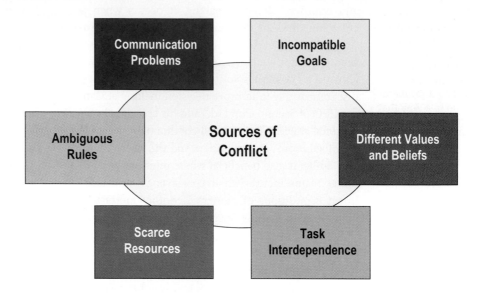

the cold-end employees, the lower the bonus for the hot-end employees. Conflicts occur when the hot-end employees complain that their cold-end co-workers are too fussy about product quality. Cold-end employees don't like the hot-end employees questioning their quality control decisions.

DIFFERENT VALUES AND BELIEFS

Conflict is more likely to occur when employees have different values and beliefs due to their unique backgrounds, experiences, or training. These differences partly explain why some conflict occurs between people from different cultures. Cultural diversity makes it difficult to understand or accept the beliefs and values that other people hold towards organizational decisions and events.

Mergers often produce conflict because they bring together people with divergent corporate cultures. Employees fight over the "right way" to do things because of their unique experiences in the separate companies. This often results in the loss of valuable talent as people quit to escape the conflict. For example, after National Bank of Canada acquired investment firm Lévesque Beaubien Geoffrion Inc., 10 of Lévesque's 25 investment bankers—including all senior people—left the company. Most of these people apparently quit because they disagreed with National's executives about Lévesque's future direction.[17]

Differing values and beliefs also account for the increasing number of disputes between Generation Xers and baby boomers in the workplace. Each generation was raised with different experiences, different skills, and, consequently, a different set of values. Consider the conflict over work hours at Techneglas Inc. Older employees want to keep eight-hour shifts because this gives them the opportunity for more overtime. But few of the younger employees want overtime. Instead, they would prefer a 12-hour shift that gives them more time off. The Generation Xers say it's not a matter of work ethic; they just have different values about work-life balance. "The old people don't have a life," snaps one young production worker. "Their jobs are their lives."[18]

TASK INTERDEPENDENCE

> **Task interdependence** The degree to which a task requires collective action. High task interdependence exists when team members must share inputs or outcomes, or need to interact while executing their work.

Conflict tends to increase with the level of task interdependence. **Task interdependence** exists when team members must share common inputs to their individual tasks, need to interact in the process of executing their work, or receive outcomes (such as rewards) that are partly determined by the performance of others (see Chapter 9).[19] The higher the level of task interdependence, the greater the risk of conflict, because there is a greater chance that each side will disrupt or interfere with the other side's goals.[20] Exhibit 13.3 illustrates the three levels of task interdependence:[21]

- *Pooled interdependence*—This is the weakest form of interdependence (other than independence), in which work units operate independently except for reliance on a common resource or authority. Students experience this level of interdependence when they are lined up at the laser printers trying to get their assignments done just before a class deadline. The same thing happens in organizations. Corporate divisions must share scarce resources provided by headquarters, thereby increasing potential conflict.

- *Sequential interdependence*—This occurs where the output of one person or unit becomes the direct input for another person or unit. This interdependent linkage is found in fish processing plants. Fish are handled by the slitters, then passed to the gutters, who then pass their work to the slimers, who then send their work to the graders.[22]

- *Reciprocal interdependence*—This is the highest level of interdependence, in which work output is exchanged back and forth among individuals or work units. This relationship exists between bus drivers and maintenance crews in almost every Canadian transit authority. Drivers are dependent on the maintenance crews to keep the buses in good repair, while the maintenance crews are dependent on the drivers to operate the vehicles wisely so that their work is minimized.

SCARCE RESOURCES

Scarce resources generate conflict because scarcity motivates people to compete with others who also need those resources to achieve their objectives.[23] This occurs at Sony's video game

---

EXHIBIT 13.3 Levels of Task Interdependence

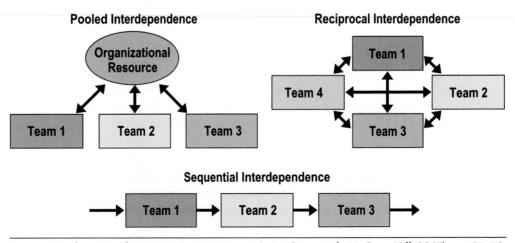

Source: Based on J.D. Thompson, *Organizations in Action* (New York: McGraw-Hill, 1967), pp. 54–56.

group, where the artists who develop Spawn and other sci-fi games must compete for resources with the artists who develop sports-related games like NFL GameDay. Differentiation partly explains this conflict. "We call them the 'Ghouls and Goblins' and they call us the 'Dumb Jocks,'" laughs the head of the sports group. But the conflict is aggravated by the fact that both groups share a limited budget. "Teams are competing for internal resources for marketing dollars, support for their products," explains a Sony executive. "And they know how much that matters."[24]

AMBIGUOUS RULES

Ambiguous rules—or the complete lack of rules—breed conflict. This occurs because the uncertainty increases the risk that one party intends to interfere with the other party's goals. Ambiguity also encourages political tactics and, in some cases, employees enter a free-for-all battle to win decisions in their favour. When rules exist, on the other hand, everyone knows what to expect from each other and has agreed to abide by those rules.

COMMUNICATION PROBLEMS

Conflict often occurs due to the lack of opportunity, ability, or motivation to communicate effectively. Let's look at each of these causes. First, when two parties lack the opportunity to communicate, they tend to use stereotypes to explain past behaviours and anticipate future actions. Unfortunately, stereotypes are sufficiently subjective that emotions can negatively distort the meaning of an opponent's actions, thereby escalating perceptions of conflict. Moreover, without direct interaction, the two sides have less psychological empathy for each other.

Second, some people lack the necessary skills to communicate in a diplomatic, nonconfrontational manner. When one party communicates its disagreement in an arrogant way, opponents are more likely to heighten their perception of the conflict. Arrogant behaviour also sends a message that one side intends to be competitive rather than cooperative. This may lead the other party to reciprocate with a similar conflict management style.[25] Consequently, as we explained earlier, ineffective communication often leads to an escalation in the conflict cycle.

Ineffective communication can also lead to a third problem: less motivation to communicate in the future. For example, an accountant was verbally abused by an information services manager soon after he was hired. Since then, he has avoided the manager, leaving some problems undetected and unresolved. Another employee reported that the relationship with his manager deteriorated to such an extent that for five months they communicated only by e-mail.[26] These reactions aren't surprising. Socioemotional conflict is uncomfortable, so people are less motivated to interact with others in a conflicting relationship. Unfortunately, less communication can escalate the conflict because there is less opportunity to empathize with the opponent's situation and opponents are more likely to rely on distorted stereotypes of the other party. In fact, conflict tends to further distort these stereotypes through the process of social identity (see Chapter 6).[27] We begin to see competitors less favourably so that our self-identity remains strong during these uncertain times.

The lack of motivation to communicate also explains (along with differentiation, described earlier) why conflict is more common in cross-cultural relationships. People tend to feel uncomfortable or awkward interacting with co-workers from different cultures, so they are less motivated to engage in dialogue with them.[28] With limited communication, people rely more on stereotypes to fill in missing information. They also tend to misunderstand each other's verbal and nonverbal signals, further escalating the conflict.

INTERPERSONAL CONFLICT MANAGEMENT STYLES

Win-win orientation
A person's belief that the parties will find a mutually beneficial solution to their conflict.

Win-lose orientation
A person's belief that the conflicting parties are drawing from a fixed pie, so that his or her gain is the other person's loss.

vw.weyerhaeuser.com/canada/

The six structural factors described above set the stage for conflict. As the conflict process identified earlier (see Exhibit 13.1), these sources of conflict lead to perceptions and emotions. Some people enter a conflict with a **win-win orientation**. This is the perception that the parties will find a mutually beneficial solution to their disagreement. They believe that the resources at stake are expandable rather than fixed if the parties work together to find a creative solution. Other people enter a conflict with a **win-lose orientation**. They adopt the belief that the parties are drawing from a fixed pie, so that the more one party receives, the less the other party will receive.

Conflict tends to escalate when the parties develop a win-lose orientation because they rely on power and politics to gain advantage. A win-lose orientation may occasionally be appropriate when the conflict really is over a fixed resource, but few organizational conflicts are due to perfectly opposing interests with fixed resources. To varying degrees, the opposing groups can gain by believing that their positions aren't perfectly opposing and that creative solutions are possible. For instance, a supplier and customer may initially think they have opposing interests—the supplier wants to receive more money for the product, whereas the customer wants to pay less money for it. Yet, further discussion may reveal that the customer would be willing to pay more if the product could be provided earlier than originally arranged. The vendor may actually value that earlier delivery because it saves inventory costs. By looking at the bigger picture, both parties can often discover common ground.

Adopting a win-win or win-lose orientation influences our conflict management style, that is, our actions towards the other person. Researchers have categorized five interpersonal styles of approaching the other party in a conflict situation. As we see in Exhibit 13.4, each approach can be placed in a two-dimensional grid reflecting the person's motivation to satisfy his or her own interests (called *assertiveness*) and to satisfy the other party's interests (called *cooperativeness*).[29] Collaboration is the only style that represents a purely win-win orientation. The other four styles represent variations of the win-lose approach. For effective conflict management, we should learn to apply different conflict management styles to different situations:[30]

Ian Lindsay, *Vancouver Sun*.

Weyerhaeuser Canada is trying to develop a win-win relationship with environmentalists. "We've got a basic philosophy that in most situations, there don't need to be losers," says Tom Stephens, CEO of the Vancouver-based forest products company. Weyerhaeuser executives scoured the world for forestry practices that would replace the contentious clear-cut logging practices of the past. "We've been asking ourselves questions like ... 'Is clearcutting the only way to manage forests?'" says Stephens. The company settled on variable retention harvesting, a method that preserves sections of forest in the interests of biodiversity. The results have environmentalists as well as employees and shareholders cheering.[32] What conditions are necessary for this win-win orientation to work?

- *Collaborating*—Collaboration tries to find a mutually beneficial solution for both parties through problem solving. An important feature of collaboration is information sharing so that both parties can identify common ground and potential solutions that satisfy both (or all) of them.

- *Avoiding*—Avoiding tries to smooth over or avoid conflict situations altogether. For example, some employees will rearrange their work area or tasks to minimize interaction with certain co-workers.[31]

- *Competing*—Competing involves trying to win the conflict at the other's expense. This style has the strongest win-lose orientation because it has the highest level of assertiveness and the lowest level of cooperativeness.

EXHIBIT 13.4   Interpersonal Conflict Management Styles

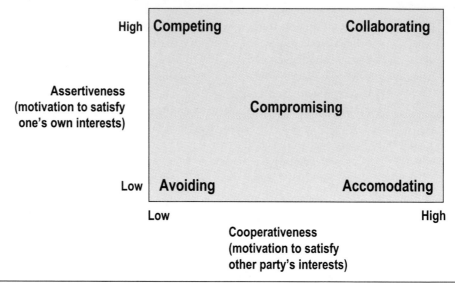

Source: Adapted from T.L. Ruble and K. Thomas, "Support for a Two-Dimensional Model of Conflict Behavior," *Organizational Behavior and Human Performance,* 16 (1976), p. 145.

- *Accommodating*—Accommodating involves giving in completely to the other side's wishes, or at least cooperating with little or no attention to your own interests.

- *Compromising*—Compromising tries to reach a middle ground with the other party. You look for a position in which your losses are offset by equally valued gains.

CHOOSING THE BEST CONFLICT MANAGEMENT STYLE

Most people have a preferred conflict management style, but they will use different styles under different conditions. The skill of conflict management is to apply the right style for the situation. In other words, we need to recognize the contingency approach to conflict management.

The collaborative style is usually recognized as the preferred approach to conflict resolution, but it really only works under certain conditions. Specifically, it is best when the parties do not have perfectly opposing interests and when they have enough trust and openness to share information. Collaborating is usually desirable because organizational conflicts are rarely win-lose situations. There is usually some opportunity for mutual gain if the parties search for creative solutions.[33]

You might think that avoiding is an ineffective conflict management strategy, but it may be the best approach under certain conditions. It is quite appropriate where the issue is trivial or as a temporary tactic to cool down heated disputes. However, conflict avoidance should not be a long-term solution because it increases the other party's frustration.

The competing style to conflict resolution is usually inappropriate because organizational relationships rarely involve complete opposition. However, competing may be necessary where you know you are correct and the dispute requires a quick solution. For example, a competing style may be necessary when the other party engages in unethical conduct because you don't want to be associated with that unacceptable behaviour. The competing style may also be necessary where the other party would take advantage of more cooperative strategies.

The accommodating style may be appropriate when the other party has substantially more power or the issue is not as important to you as to the other party. On the other hand, accommodating behaviours may give the other side unrealistically high expectations, thereby motivating them to seek more from you in the future. In the long run, accommodating may produce more conflict rather than resolve it.

The compromising style may be best when there is little hope for mutual gain through problem solving, both parties have equal power, and both are under time pressure to settle their differences. However, compromise is rarely a final solution and may cause the parties to overlook options for mutual gain.

CULTURAL AND GENDER DIFFERENCES IN CONFLICT MANAGEMENT STYLES

Although the conflict style we choose is partly influenced by the type of dispute, it is also affected by personal characteristics, including cultural background. Culture determines the values and interests on which conflict is defined. Cultural values cause some people to perceive a conflict where others do not. Moreover, even where two people from different cultures perceive the same conflict, their conflict management style may differ. This is because conflict styles must be consistent with the person's personal and cultural value system.[34]

People from collectivist cultures—where group goals are valued more than individual goals—tend to collaborate or avoid conflict with other team members. People from individualistic cultures more frequently compromise or compete with co-workers. Collectivists tend to collaborate more than individualists within the group because they identify themselves with the team's common goals and are therefore motivated to maintain harmonious relations. Notice that this collaboration is limited to the person's own social group. People from collectivist cultures can be just as competitive as individualists with people outside their group.[35]

Cultural similarity also seems to influence the conflict management style used. Research on international joint ventures has found that a collaborative style to conflict resolution is more commonly used where the partners view themselves as being culturally alike.[36] They discuss concerns more quickly and openly, seek their partner's opinions, and explain their course of action more fully than when dealing with culturally divergent partners. As you might expect, the collaborative conflict management style results in better joint venture performance.

Some writers suggest that men and women tend to rely on different conflict management styles.[37] Generally speaking, women pay more attention than do men to the relationship between the parties. Consequently, they tend to adopt a collaborative style in business settings, and are more willing to compromise to protect the relationship. Men tend to be more competitive and take a short-term orientation to the relationship. Of course, we must be cautious about these observations because gender has a weak influence on conflict management style.

STRUCTURAL APPROACHES TO CONFLICT MANAGEMENT

The conflict management styles described above focus on how to approach the other party in a conflict situation, but conflict management also involves altering the underlying structural causes of potential conflict. The main structural approaches are identified in Exhibit 13.5. Although this section discusses ways to reduce conflict, we should keep in mind that conflict management sometimes calls for increasing conflict. This occurs mainly by reversing the strategies described over the next few pages.[38]

EXHIBIT 13.5   Structural Approaches to Conflict Management

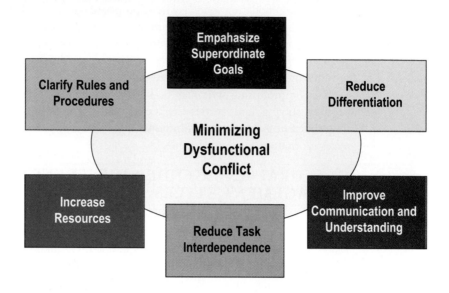

EMPHASIZING SUPERORDINATE GOALS

Superordinate goal
A common objective held by conflicting parties that is more important than their conflicting departmental or individual goals.

One way to minimize conflict is by focusing everyone on **superordinate goals**. Superordinate goals are common objectives held by conflicting parties that are more important than the departmental or individual goals on which the conflict is based. For instance, corporate leaders might focus everyone on customer needs so that the goals of individual work units are viewed from a common overall objective. The organization's overarching values also serve as superordinate goals. If a company values employee well-being, for example, then departmental goals are assessed against this common objective.

Focusing attention on superordinate goals is particularly useful where conflict is caused by goal incompatibility and differentiation. By increasing commitment to corporate-wide goals, employees place less emphasis on departmental goals and, consequently, feel less conflict toward co-workers elsewhere in the firm.[39] Superordinate goals offset the problem of differentiation because they establish a common frame of reference. Heterogeneous team members still perceive different ways to achieve corporate objectives, but the superordinate goal strategy ensures that they mutually understand and agree on the objectives themselves.

Superordinate goals have a powerful effect on conflict management. For instance, a recent study reported that marketing managers in Hong Kong, China, Japan, and the United States were more likely to develop a collaborative conflict management style when executives aligned departmental goals with corporate objectives. A study of a large Canadian utility found that relationships were more productive during budget deliberations when the executive in charge focused on cooperative rather than competitive goals. A third study found that the most effective executive teams consistently apply a superordinate goal strategy. They frame their decisions as collaborations, thereby drawing attention and commitment away from sublevel goals. Moreover, the study found that superordinate goals minimize socioemotional conflict. Team members are more likely to support common objectives even though they might disagree on the means to achieving those objectives.[40]

REDUCING DIFFERENTIATION

Superordinate goals offset differentiation by establishing a common frame of reference, but they don't actually remove any of the underlying diversity that people bring to the relationship. Hibernia Management and Development Co. in Newfoundland removed the "destructive differences" between hourly and salaried personnel by putting employees on salary rather than hourly wages. DaimlerChrysler reduced differentiation at its plant in Windsor, Ontario, by getting managers to dress more like the employees. "Although this may seem insignificant, it did make a difference," says an executive at the Windsor plant. "Our supervisors and managers were viewed by the workers as less 'different' without suits and ties!"[41]

To fundamentally reduce differentiation, some firms encourage and reinforce a generalist rather than specialist career orientation. For example, many Japanese companies move people around to different jobs, departments, and regions so that they eventually develop common experiences with other senior decision makers in the organization.[42] Similarly, W.L. Gore and Associates reduces differentiation by moving employees around to different teams. The manufacturer of GoreTex and other products introduced this team rotation system after it became apparent that employees were becoming too committed to co-workers on their own team. "You can get a little too focused on your own team and forget the good of the whole company," admits one of Gore's team members.[43]

IMPROVING COMMUNICATION AND UNDERSTANDING

Communication is critical to effective conflict management. This can range from casual gatherings among employees who rarely meet otherwise, to formal processes where differences are identified and discussed. Military organizations learned long ago that multinational forces work together more effectively when troops eat and socialize together.[44] By improving the opportunity, ability, and motivation to share information, employees develop less extreme perceptions of each other than if they rely on stereotypes and emotions. Direct communication provides a better understanding of the other person's or department's work environment and resource limitations. Ongoing communication is particularly important where the need for functional specialization makes it difficult to reduce differentiation.[45]

Oticon Holdings A/S, the Danish hearing aid company, keeps dysfunctional conflict to a minimum because its open office design naturally improves communication and understanding. "When people move around and sit next to different people, they learn something about what others are doing," explains an Oticon executive. "It's hard to maintain 'enemy pictures' in this company—they're not 'those bloody fools in marketing.' You know too much about what people do."[47]

Some companies introduce **dialogue** meetings, in which the disputing parties discuss their differences. Dialogue helps participants understand each other's mental models and fundamental assumptions so that they can create a common thinking process and mental models for the team (see Chapter 9).[48] Several companies, including Xerox Canada, Microsoft, Dell Computer, and Hewlett-Packard are taking this dialogue process in new directions through drum circles. As Connections 13.2 describes, participants in this unique team-building activity use drums and other percussive instruments to learn the process of working together. It teaches harmony, not only in music, but in how employees communicate and understand each other.

Dialogue A process of conversation among team members in which they learn about each other's mental models and assumptions, and eventually form a common model for thinking within the team.

Arlen Redekop, Vancouver Province.

The 100 or so employees at Vancouver-based Stratford Internet Technologies can receive a free lunch—up to $20 per person per day—at any of the trendy restaurants in the area. There's just one catch: Employees must eat with a co-worker they don't know. Stratford CEO Robert Craig (second from left) says it's worth the $6000 per month in lunch money to reduce conflict and improve collaboration. "No cliques, no cronyism," says Craig, co-founder of the e-commerce and Web design firm. To further improve dialogue among employees, everyone on the payroll is invited to dinner once each month, adding another $10,000 to the food bill. "This is about collaboration, cultivation, sharing information, people talking to people and getting to know each other," explains Craig.[46] How does sharing lunch with strangers in the organization reduce dysfunctional conflict?

www.stratfordinternet.com

Relationship restructuring

> **Relationship restructuring program** A formal process of diagnosing the underlying causes of workplace conflict and implementing a long-term solution that will address the sources of these conflicts.

When relations between two or more work teams or departments are openly hostile, it may be advisable to introduce a **relationship restructuring program** with the assistance of a consultant. This is a formal process of diagnosing the underlying causes of workplace conflict and implementing a long-term solution that will address the sources of these conflicts.[49] With full agreement from the parties, the process begins with a relationship audit in which consultants meet with individuals and groups of employees to identify the employment-connected relationships that have caused the current disruption and disagreement. For example, one audit of the Toronto sorting centre for a national mail delivery organization included over 200 individual and group interviews in which employees vented their anger and explained what they wanted.

Information collected from the relationship audit is used to evaluate the relationships, such as communication deficiencies, misaligned expectations, corporate culture shifts, and so on. The report also recommends a relationship management plan that helps the parties avoid unnecessary conflict in the future. It includes systems to anticipate and resolve issues before they ripen into full-blown disputes. At the Toronto sorting centre, the relationship management plan included formation of a union-management task force that met monthly to discuss important issues. The final stage involves implementation of the plan, including a process for evaluating its effectiveness. For example, the organization might monitor employee attitudes and grievances following implementation of the plan.

Drumming Out Their Differences

Dozens of business people pour into an auditorium at Georgian College near Barrie, Ontario. Drums of all types—Latin American congas, African doumbeks, and Brazilian surdos—line the room, while participants anxiously take their seats. Few have played drums before, but they will all play in harmony tonight. They will learn to cooperate and coordinate through the beating of their drums.

Leading the two-hour drumming session is Doug Sole, co-owner of Toronto's Soul Drums. He starts by pointing randomly to individuals, asking them to play a beat that others will imitate. The rhythm intensifies as others join in, then falls apart into cacophony. "We're having a communication problem here," Sole interrupts. "If we all start banging our own thing, it's going to be chaos." Sole begins again, and repeats the process until the auditorium is filled with the hypnotic beat of strangers working together.

Drum circles represent a metaphor for cooperation, coordination, communication, and teamwork in nontraditional corporate structures. They focus participants on the process of working together, not just on the outcome of achieving a goal. "Drum circles thrive on collaborative creativity, and that is so important in the Internet world," explains Christine Stevens, founder of Upbeat Drum Circles in Fort Collins, Colorado.

Drum circle leader Doug Sole builds cooperation and mutual understanding with drumsticks and boomwhackers.

Photo: Gary Diggens; Author: Doug Sole, The Soul of Hand Drumming.

Onye Onyemaechi, a Nigerian master drummer in California, had learned from his drum circles with corporate clients that employees often work side by side for years without really getting to know one another. He warns that this lack of unity and understanding hinders the organization's potential, whereas drum circles begin the process of creating harmony among these strangers. "Drum circles bring people together to realize their common base," explains Onyemaechi. "The rhythm of the drum creates expansive conscious."

Sources: M.K. Pratt, "A Pound of Cure," *Fast Company*, April 2000; A. Georgiades, "Business Heeds the Beat," *Toronto Star*, August 4, 1999.

REDUCING TASK INTERDEPENDENCE

Another way to minimize dysfunctional conflict is by reducing the level of interdependence between the parties. If cost effective, this might occur by dividing the shared resource so that each party has exclusive use of part of it. Sequentially or reciprocally interdependent jobs might be combined so that they form a pooled interdependence. For example, rather than having one employee serve customers and another operate the cash register, each employee could handle both customer activities alone. Another way to reduce task interdependence is to introduce buffers between people. Buffers might take the form of resources, such as adding more inventory between people who perform sequential tasks. We also find human buffers in organizations—people who intervene between highly interdependent people or work units.[50]

INCREASING RESOURCES

An obvious way to reduce conflict due to resource scarcity is to increase the amount of resources available. Corporate decision makers might quickly dismiss this solution because of the costs involved. However, they need to carefully compare these costs with the costs of dysfunctional conflict arising out of resource scarcity.

CLARIFYING RULES AND PROCEDURES

Some conflicts arise from ambiguous decision rules regarding the allocation of scarce resources. Consequently, these conflicts can be minimized by establishing rules and procedures. Rules clarify the distribution of resources, such as when students can use the laser printer or for how long they can borrow library books. Consider the following situation that occurred when Armstrong World Industries, Inc., brought in consultants to implement a client/server network. Information systems employees at the flooring and building materials company experienced conflict with the consultants because it wasn't clear who was in charge. Another conflict occurred when the consultants wanted to work long hours and take Fridays off to fly home whereas Armstrong employees preferred a traditional work week. Armstrong minimized these conflicts by spelling out as much as possible in the contract about each party's responsibilities and roles. Issues that were unclear or overlooked in the contract were clarified by joint discussion between two senior executives at the companies.[51]

Rules establish changes to the terms of interdependence, such as an employee's hours of work or a supplier's fulfilment of an order. In most cases, the parties affected by these rules are involved in the process of deciding these terms of interdependence. By redefining the terms of interdependence, the strategy of clarifying rules is part of the larger process of negotiation.

RESOLVING CONFLICT THROUGH NEGOTIATION

• **Negotiation** Any attempt by two or more conflicting parties to resolve their divergent goals by redefining the terms of their interdependence.

Think back through yesterday's events. Maybe you had to work out an agreement with other students about what tasks to complete for a team project. Chances are that you shared transportation with someone, so you had to clarify the timing of the ride. Then perhaps there was the question of who made dinner. Each of these daily events created potential conflict, and they were resolved through negotiation. **Negotiation** occurs whenever two or more conflicting parties attempt to resolve their divergent goals by redefining the terms of their interdependence.[52] In other words, people negotiate when they think that discussion can produce a more satisfactory arrangement (at least for them) in their exchange of goods or services.

As you can see, negotiation is not an obscure practice reserved for labour and management bosses during collective bargaining. Everyone negotiates—every day. Most of the time, you often don't even realize that you are in negotiations. "Life is a negotiation," says a Wall Street columnist.[53] Negotiation is particularly evident in the workplace because employees work interdependently with others. They negotiate with their supervisors over next month's work assignments, with customers over the sale and delivery schedules of their product, and with co-workers over when to have lunch. And yes, they occasionally negotiate with each other in labour disputes and collective bargaining.

Some writers suggest that negotiations are more successful when the parties adopt a collaborative style, whereas others caution that this conflict management style is sometimes costly.[54] We know that any win-lose style (competing, accommodating, etc.) is unlikely to produce the optimal solution, because the parties have not shared information necessary to discover a mutually satisfactory solution. On the other hand, we must be careful about

Negotiation occurs all around us in organizational settings. At this *Globe and Mail* meeting, editors negotiate with each other for line space and the priority of items that should appear in the next day's newspaper. These people negotiate to resolve their divergent goals by redefining the terms of their interdependence.

www.globeandmail.com

adopting an openly collaborative style until mutual trust has been established.

The concern with collaboration is that information is power, so information sharing gives the other party more power to leverage a better deal if the opportunity occurs. Skilled negotiators often adopt a *cautiously* collaborative style at the outset by sharing information slowly and determining whether the other side will reciprocate. In this respect, they try to establish trust with the other party.[55] They switch to one of the win-lose styles only when it becomes apparent that a win-win solution is not possible or that the other party is unwilling to share information with a cooperative orientation.

BARGAINING ZONE MODEL OF NEGOTIATIONS

The negotiation process moves each party along a continuum with an area of potential overlap called the *bargaining zone*.[56] Exhibit 13.6 displays one possible bargaining zone situation. This linear diagram illustrates a purely win-lose situation—one side's gain will be the other's loss. However, the bargaining zone model can also be applied to situations in which both sides potentially gain from the negotiations. As this model illustrates, the parties typically establish three main negotiating points. The *initial offer point* is the team's opening offer to the other party. This may be its best expectation or a pie-in-the-sky starting point. The *target point* is the team's realistic goal or expectation for a final agreement. The *resistance point* is the point beyond which the team will not make further concessions.

The parties begin negotiations by describing their initial offer point for each item on the agenda. In most cases, the participants know that this is only a starting point that will change as both sides offer concessions. In win-lose situations, neither the targets nor the resistance points are revealed to the other party. However, people try to discover the other side's resistance point because this knowledge helps them determine how much they can gain without breaking off negotiations.

EXHIBIT 13.6   Bargaining Zone Model of Negotiations

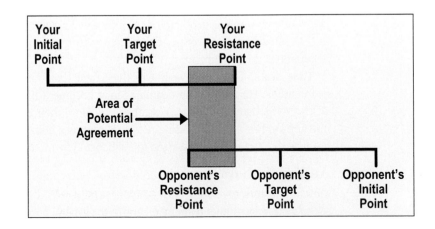

When the parties have a win-win orientation, on the other hand, the objective is to find a creative solution that keeps everyone close to their initial offer points. The parties can hopefully find an arrangement by which each side loses relatively little value on some issues and gains significantly more on other issues. For example, a supplier might want to delay delivery dates, whereas delivery times are not important to the business customer. If the parties share this information, they can quickly agree to a delayed delivery schedule, thereby costing the customer very little and gaining the supplier a great deal. On other items (financing, order size, etc.), the supplier might give something with minimal loss even though it is a significant benefit to the business customer.

SITUATIONAL INFLUENCES ON NEGOTIATIONS

The effectiveness of negotiating depends on both the situation and the behaviours of the negotiators. Four of the most important situational factors are location, physical setting, time, and audience.

Location

It is easier to negotiate on your own turf because you are familiar with the negotiating environment and are able to maintain comfortable routines.[57] Also, there is no need to cope with travel-related stress or depend on others for resources during the negotiation. Of course, you can't walk out of negotiations as easily when on your own turf, but this is usually a minor issue. Considering these strategic benefits of home turf, many negotiators agree to neutral territory. Information technology and videoconferencing is a possible solution. However, electronic messages are subject to misinterpretation and negotiators often feel that videoconference technology does not sufficiently display nonverbal cues.[58]

Physical setting

The physical distance between the parties and formality of the setting can influence the parties' orientation towards each other and the disputed issues.[59] So can the seating arrangements. People who sit face to face are more likely to develop a win-lose orientation towards the conflict situation. In contrast, some negotiation groups deliberately intersperse participants around the table to convey a win-win orientation. Others arrange the seating so that both parties face a whiteboard, reflecting the notion that both parties face the same problem or issue.

Time passage and deadlines

The more time people invest in negotiations, the stronger is their commitment to reaching an agreement. This increases the motivation to resolve the conflict, but it also fuels the escalation of commitment problems described in Chapter 11. For example, the more time put into negotiations, the stronger the tendency to make unwarranted concessions so that the negotiations do not fail.

Time deadlines may be useful to the extent that they motivate the parties to complete negotiations. However, time deadlines may become a liability when exceeding deadlines is costly.[60] Negotiators make concessions and soften their demands more rapidly as the deadline approaches. Moreover, time pressure inhibits a collaborative conflict management style, because the parties have less time to exchange information or present flexible offers.

Audience characteristics

Most negotiators have audiences—anyone with a vested interest in the negotiation outcomes, such as executives, other team members, or the general public. Negotiators tend to act differently when their audience observes the negotiation or has detailed information about the process, compared to situations in which the audience only sees the end results.[61] When the audience has direct surveillance over the proceedings, negotiators tend to be more competitive, less willing to make concessions, and more likely to engage in political tactics against the other party.[62] This "hard-line" behaviour shows the audience that the negotiator is working for their interests. With their audience watching, negotiators also have more interest in saving face. Sometimes, audiences are drawn into the negotiations by acting as a source of indirect appeals. The general public often takes on this role when groups negotiate with governments.[63]

NEGOTIATOR BEHAVIOURS

Negotiator behaviours play an important role in resolving conflict. Four of the most important behaviours are setting goals, gathering information, communicating effectively, and making concessions.

- *Planning and goal setting*—Research has consistently reported that people have more favourable negotiation results when they plan and set goals.[64] In particular, negotiators should carefully think through their initial offer, target, and resistance points. They need to check their underlying assumptions, as well as stated and unstated goals and values. This typically involves some level of internal negotiations—working out differences among team members before proceeding to negotiate with the other party.[65]

- *Gathering information*—"Seek to understand before you seek to be understood." This popular philosophy from management guru Stephen Covey applies to effective negotiations. It means that we should spend more time listening than talking during negotiations. In particular, we should listen closely to the other party and ask them for details of their position.[66] One way to improve the information gathering process is to have a team of people participate in negotiations. Asian companies tend to have large negotiation teams for this purpose, whereas North American negotiators have small teams or work alone.[67] With more information about the opponent's interests and needs, negotiators are better able to discover low-cost concessions or proposals that will satisfy the other side.

- *Communicating effectively*—Effective negotiators communicate in a way that maintains effective relationships between the parties.[68] Specifically, they minimize socioemotional conflict by focusing on issues rather than people. Effective negotiators also avoid irritating statements such as "I think you'll agree that this is a generous offer." Third, effective negotiators are masters of persuasive communication. This does not involve misleading the other party. Rather, as discussed in Chapter 8, negotiators structure the content of their message so that it is accepted by others, not merely understood.[69]

- *Making concessions*—Concessions are important because they (1) enable the parties to move towards the area of potential agreement, (2) symbolize each party's motivation to bargain in good faith, and (3) tell the other party of the relative importance of the negotiating items.[70] How many concessions should you make? This varies with the other party's expectations and the level of trust between you. For instance, many Chinese negotiators are wary of people who change their position during the early stages of negotiations. Similarly, some writers warn that Russian negotiators tend to view concessions as a sign of weakness, rather than a sign of trust.[71] Generally, the best strategy is to be moderately tough and give just enough concessions to communicate sincerity and motivation to resolve the conflict.[72] Being too tough can undermine relations between the parties; giving too many concessions implies weakness and encourages the other party to use power and resistance.

THIRD-PARTY CONFLICT RESOLUTION

Third-party conflict resolution Any attempt by a relatively neutral person to help the parties resolve their differences.

Most of this chapter has focused on people directly involved in a conflict, yet many disputes in organizational settings are resolved with the assistance of a third party. **Third-party conflict resolution** is any attempt by a relatively neutral person to help the parties resolve their differences. This may range from formal labour arbitration to informal managerial interventions to resolve disagreements among employees.

There are four main objectives in third-party conflict resolution.[73] One objective is *efficiency*. Those who take the third-party role try to resolve the dispute quickly and with minimum expenditure of organizational resources. Second, the conflict resolution should be *effective*, meaning that the process should find the best long-term solution that will correct the underlying causes of the conflict. Third, this process should have outcome fairness. This ensures that the parties feel the solution provided by the third-party intervention is fair. Although outcome fairness is similar to effectiveness, they are not the same because people sometimes think that a solution is fair even though it does not work well in the long term.

Procedural fairness Perceptions of fairness regarding the dispute resolution process, whether or not the outcome is favourable to the person.

Finally, third-party conflict resolution should ensure that the parties feel the dispute resolution process is fair, whether or not the outcome is favourable to them. This objective, known as **procedural fairness**, is particularly important when the third party makes a binding decision to resolve the dispute. In these situations, procedural fairness increases when the third party isn't biased (e.g., doesn't have a vested interest towards one party), is well informed about the facts of the situation, and has listened to all sides of the dispute. It also increases when the decision can be appealed to a higher authority and the third party applies existing policies consistently.[74]

TYPES OF THIRD-PARTY INTERVENTION

There are generally three types of third-party dispute resolution activities: arbitration, inquisition, and mediation. These activities can be classified by their level of control over the process and control over the decision (see Exhibit 13.7):[75]

- *Arbitration*—Arbitrators have high control over the final decision, but low control over the process.[76] Executives engage in this strategy by following previously agreed rules of due process, listening to arguments from the disputing employees, and making a binding decision. Arbitration is also applied as the final stage of grievances by unionized employees.

EXHIBIT 13.7 Types of Third-Party Intervention

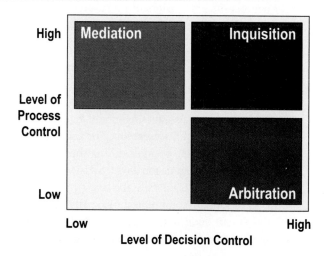

- *Inquisition*—Inquisitors control all discussion about the conflict. Like arbitrators, they have high decision control because they choose the form of conflict resolution. However, they also have high process control because they choose which information to examine, how to examine it, and generally decide how the conflict resolution process will be handled.

- *Mediation*—Mediators have high control over the intervention process. In fact, their main purpose is to manage the process and context of interaction between the disputing parties. However, the parties make the final decision about how to resolve their differences. Thus, mediators have little or no control over the conflict resolution decision. Some organizations, including MacMillan Bloedel (now Weyerhauser Canada) and DuPont Canada have an ombuds officer to mediate conflicts between management and employees, such as allegations of employment discrimination.[77]

CHOOSING THE BEST THIRD-PARTY INTERVENTION STRATEGY

Team leaders, executives, and co-workers regularly intervene in disputes between employees and departments. Sometimes they adopt a mediator role; other times they serve as arbitrators. However, research suggests that people in positions of authority (e.g., managers) usually adopt an inquisitional approach whereby they dominate the intervention process as well as make a binding decision.[78] Managers like the inquisition approach because it is consistent with the decision-oriented nature of managerial jobs, gives them control over the conflict process and outcome, and tends to resolve disputes efficiently.

However, the inquisitional approach to third-party conflict resolution is usually the least effective in organizational settings.[79] One problem is that leaders who take an inquisitional role tend to collect limited information about the problem, so their imposed decision may produce an ineffective solution to the conflict. Moreover, employees tend to think that the procedures and outcomes of inquisitions are unfair because they have little control over this approach.

Which third-party intervention is most appropriate in organizations? The answer partly depends on the situation.[80] For example, arbitration is much less popular among Hong Kong than Canadian employees. But generally speaking, for everyday disputes between two employees, the mediation approach is usually best because this gives employees more responsibility for resolving their own disputes. The third-party representative merely establishes an appropriate context for conflict resolution. Although not as efficient as other strategies, mediation potentially offers the highest level of employee satisfaction with the conflict process and outcomes.[81] When employees cannot resolve their differences, arbitration seems to work best because the predetermined rules of evidence and other processes create a higher sense of procedural fairness. Moreover, arbitration is preferred where the organization's goals should take priority over individual goals.

Alternative dispute resolution

Alternative dispute resolution (ADR) A third-party dispute resolution process that includes mediation, typically followed by arbitration.

One way to combine third-party dispute resolution in an orderly sequence is through **alternative dispute resolution (ADR)**. A typical ADR process begins with a grievance process in which the employer and employee try to negotiate their differences. If this fails, an external mediator is brought in to help the parties reach a mutually agreeable solution. If mediation fails, the parties submit their case to an arbitrator whose decision may be either binding or voluntarily accepted by the employer.[82]

ADR is useful in nonunion settings where a formal grievance process does not already exist. Although still rare in Canada, ADR is increasingly found in employee–employer disputes involving potentially legalistic processes. For instance, Workers Compensation agencies in

HR Professional/Ryerson Clark.

The Nova Scotia Workers' Compensation Appeals Tribunal, Worker's Compensation Board, and the Workers Advisers' Program turned to alternative dispute resolution (ADR) to ease its huge backlog of appeals cases. Through ADR, the employer and injured employee mediate their differences rather than wait for a legalistic arbitration decision. ADR is an informal and nonthreatening process that gives both parties the opportunity to discuss the conflict and find a mutually acceptable solution. "In the traditional process [injured workers] feel helpless," says Anne S. Clark (seated, second from left), who assists employees in Nova Scotia's ADR process. "In mediation, even without settlement, they feel good about being able to participate."[83] What other employment conflicts might be resolved more effectively through ADR?

www.gov.ns.ca/wcat/

some Canadian provinces encourage employees and employers to participate in an ADR process rather than proceed directly to a quasi-judicial arbitration. ADR is more conciliatory and helps the parties solve their own problems.

Whether resolving conflict through third-party dispute resolution or direct negotiation, we need to recognize that many solutions come from the sources of conflict that were identified earlier in this chapter. This may seem obvious, but in the heat of conflict, people often focus on each other rather than on the underlying causes. Recognizing these conflict sources is the role of effective leadership, which is discussed in the next chapter.

CHAPTER SUMMARY

- Conflict is the process in which one party perceives that its interests are being opposed or negatively affected by another party. The conflict process begins with the sources of conflict. These sources lead one or both sides to perceive a conflict and to experience conflict emotions. This, in turn, produces manifest conflict, such as behaviours towards the other side. When conflict is task-related, the parties view the conflict experience as something separate from them. Disputes are much more difficult to resolve when they produce socioemotional conflict, where the parties perceive each other to be the problem. The conflict process often escalates through a series of episodes and shifts from task-related to socioemotional conflict.

- Conflict management maximizes the benefits and minimizes the dysfunctional consequences of conflict. Conflict is beneficial in the form of constructive controversy because it makes people think more fully about issues. Positive conflict also increases team cohesiveness when conflict is with another group. The main problems with conflict are that it may lead to job stress, dissatisfaction, and turnover. Dysfunctional intergroup conflict may undermine decision making.

- Conflict tends to increase when people have incompatible goals, different values and beliefs, interdependent tasks, scarce resources, ambiguous rules, and problems communicating with each other. Conflict is more common in a multicultural workforce because of greater differentiation and communication problems among employees.

- People with a win-win orientation believe the parties will find a mutually beneficial solution to their disagreement. Those with a win-lose orientation adopt the belief that the parties are drawing from a fixed pie. The latter orientation tends to escalate conflict. Among the five interpersonal conflict management styles, only collaborating represents a purely win-win orientation. The four other styles—avoiding, competing, accommodating, and compromising—adopt some variation of a win-lose orientation. Women and people with high collectivism tend to use a collaborative or avoidance style more than do men and people with high individualism.

- Structural approaches to conflict management include emphasizing superordinate goals, reducing differentiation, improving communication and understanding, reducing task interdependence, increasing resources, and clarifying rules and procedures. These elements can also be altered to stimulate conflict.

- Negotiation occurs whenever two or more conflicting parties attempt to resolve their divergent goals by redefining the terms of their interdependence. Negotiations are influenced by several situational factors, including location, physical setting, time passage and deadlines, and audience. Important negotiator behaviours include planning and goal setting, gathering information, communicating effectively, and making concessions.

- Third-party conflict resolution is any attempt by a relatively neutral person to help the parties resolve their differences. The main objectives are to resolve the dispute efficiently and effectively, and to ensure that the parties feel that the process and outcome are fair. The three main forms of third-party dispute resolution are mediation, arbitration, and inquisition. Managers tend to use an inquisition approach, although mediation and arbitration are more appropriate, depending on the situation. Alternative dispute resolution (ADR) applies mediation, but may also involve arbitration.

KEY TERMS

Alternative dispute resolution (ADR), p. 403

Conflict, p. 384

Conflict management, p. 385

Constructive controversy, p. 387

Dialogue, p. 395

Negotiation, p. 398

Procedural fairness, p. 402

Relationship restructuring program, p. 396

Superordinate goal, p. 394

Task interdependence, p. 389

Third-party conflict resolution, p. 402

Win-lose orientation, p. 391

Win-win orientation, p. 391

DISCUSSION QUESTIONS

1. Distinguish task-related conflict from socioemotional conflict and explain where these two forms fit into the conflict-escalation cycle.

2. The president of Creative Toys Ltd. read about cooperation in Japanese companies and has vowed to bring this same philosophy to the company. The goal is to avoid all conflict, so that employees would work cooperatively and be happier at Creative Toys. Discuss the merits and limitations of the president's policy.

3. Conflict among managers emerged soon after a Swedish company was bought by a French company. The Swedes perceived the French management to be hierarchical and arrogant, whereas the French thought the Swedes were naive, cautious, and lacking an achievement orientation. Describe a relationship restructuring intervention that would reduce dysfunctional conflict in this situation. What conditions might make the relationship restructuring process difficult here?

4. This chapter describes three levels of task interdependence that exist in interpersonal and intergroup relationships. Identify examples of these three levels in your work or school activities. How do these three levels affect potential conflict for you?

5. Jane has just been appointed purchasing manager of Canadian Technologies Ltd. The previous purchasing manager, who recently retired, was known for his "winner-take-all" approach to suppliers. He continually fought for more discounts and was skeptical about any special deals that suppliers would propose. A few suppliers refused to do business with Canadian Technologies, but senior management was confident that the former purchasing manager's approach minimized the company's costs. Jane wants to try a more collaborative approach to working with suppliers. Will her approach work? How should she adopt a more collaborative approach in future negotiations with suppliers?

6. You are a special assistant to the commander-in-chief of a peacekeeping mission to a wartorn part of the world. The unit consists of several hundred peacekeeping troops from Canada and four other countries. The troops will work together for approximately one year. What strategies would you recommend to improve mutual understanding and minimize conflict among these troops?

7. Suppose that you head one of five divisions in a multinational organization and are about to begin this year's budget deliberations at headquarters. What are the characteristics of your audience in these negotiations and what effect might they have on your negotiation behaviour?

8. Managers tend to use an inquisitional approach to resolving disputes between employees and departments. Describe the inquisitional approach and discuss its appropriateness in organizational settings.

Case Study

ACTIVITY 13.1

Conflict in Close Quarters*

A team of psychologists at Moscow's Institute for Biomedical Problems (IBMP) wanted to learn more about the dynamics of long-term isolation in space. This knowledge would be applied to the International Space Station, a joint project of several countries, including Canada, that would send people into space for more than six months. It would eventually include a trip to Mars taking up to three years.

IBMP set up a replica of the Mir space station in Moscow. It then arranged for three international researchers from Canada, Japan, and Austria to spend 110 days isolated in a chamber the size of a train car. This chamber joined a smaller chamber where four Russian cosmonauts had already completed half of their 240 days of isolation. This was the first time an international crew was involved in the studies. None of the participants spoke English as their first language, yet they communicated throughout their stay in English at varying levels of proficiency.

Judith Lapierre was the only Canadian and the only female in the experiment. Along with a PhD in public health and social medicine, Lapierre studied space sociology at the International Space University in France and conducted isolation research in the Antarctic. This was her fourth trip to Russia, where she had learned the language. The mission was supposed to have a second female participant from the Japanese space program, but she was not selected by IBMP.

The Japanese and Austrian participants viewed the participation of a woman as a favourable factor, says Lapierre. For example, to make the surroundings more comfortable, they rearranged the furniture, hung posters on the wall, and put a tablecloth on the kitchen table. "We adapted our environment, whereas the Russians just viewed it as something to be endured," she explains. "We decorated for Christmas, because I'm the kind of person who likes to host people."

New Year's Eve Turmoil

Ironically, it was at a social event, the New Year's Eve party, that events took a turn for the worse. After drinking vodka (allowed by the Russian space agency), two of the Russian cosmonauts got into a fistfight that left blood splattered on the chamber walls. At one point, a colleague hid the knives in the station's kitchen because of fears that the two Russians were about to stab each other. The two cosmonauts, who generally did not get along, had to be restrained by other men. Soon after the brawl, the Russian commander grabbed Lapierre, dragged her out of view of the television monitoring cameras, and kissed her aggressively—twice. Lapierre fought him off, but the message didn't register. He tried to kiss her again the following morning.

The next day, the international crew complained to IBMP about the behaviour of the Russian cosmonauts. The Russian institute apparently took no action against any of the aggressors. Instead, the institute's psychologists replied that the incidents were part of the experiment. They wanted crew members to solve their personal problems with mature discussion, without asking for outside help. "You have to understand that Mir is an autonomous object, far away from anything," Vadim Gushin, the IBMP psychologist in charge of the project, explained after the experiment had ended in March. "If the crew can't solve problems among themselves, they can't work together."

Following IBMP's response, the international crew wrote a scathing letter to the Russian institute and the space agencies involved in the experiment. "We had never expected such events to take place in a highly controlled scientific experiment where individuals go through a multistep selection process," they wrote. "If we had known . . . we would not have joined it as subjects." The letter also complained about IBMP's response to their concerns.

Informed of the New Year's Eve incident, the Japanese space program convened an emergency meeting on January 2 to address the incidents. Soon after, the Japanese team member quit, apparently shocked by IBMP's inaction. He was replaced with a Russian researcher on the international team. Ten days after the fight—a little over a month after the international team began the mission—the doors between the Russian and international crews' chambers were barred at the request of the international research team. Lapierre later emphasized that this action was taken because of concerns about violence, not the incident involving her.

ACTIVITY 13.1 CONTINUED

A Stolen Kiss or Sexual Harassment?

By the end of the experiment in March, news of the fistfight between the cosmonauts and the commander's attempts to kiss Lapierre had reached the public. Russian scientists attempted to downplay the kissing incident by saying that it was one fleeting kiss, a clash of cultures, and a female participant who was too emotional.

"In the West, some kinds of kissing are regarded as sexual harassment. In our culture it's nothing," said Russian scientist Vadim Gushin in one interview. In another interview, he explained: "The problem of sexual harassment is given a lot of attention in North America but less in Europe. In Russia it is even less of an issue, not because we are more or less moral than the rest of the world; we just have different priorities."

Judith Lapierre says that the kissing incident was tolerable compared to this reaction from the Russian scientists who conducted the experiment. "They don't get it at all," she complains. "They don't think anything is wrong. I'm more frustrated than ever. The worst thing is that they don't realize it was wrong."

Norbert Kraft, the Austrian scientist on the international team, also disagreed with the Russian interpretation of events. "They're trying to protect themselves," he says. "They're trying to put the fault on others. But this is not a cultural issue. If a woman doesn't want to be kissed, it is not acceptable."

Leena Tomi, the Canadian Space Agency representative sent to Moscow to help resolve the conflict soon after the incident occurred, said, "We'll be digesting all this. The purpose is to help future space crews avoid these problems. We're learning all the time."

Discussion Questions

1. Identify the different conflict episodes that exist in this case. Who was in conflict with whom? What are the structural sources of conflict for each of them?

2. What conflict management style(s) did Lapierre, the international team, and Gushin use to resolve these conflicts? What style(s) would have worked best in these situations?

3. What structural conflict management interventions were applied here? Did they work? What alternative strategies would work best in this situation and in the future?

*The facts of this case are pieced together from the following sources: G. Sinclair, Jr., "If You Scream in Space, Does Anyone Hear?" *Winnipeg Free Press*, May 5, 2000, p. A4; S. Martin, "Reining in the Space Cowboys," *Globe and Mail*, April 19, 2000, p. R1; M. Gray, "A Space Dream Sours," *Maclean's*, April 17, 2000, p. 26; E. Niiler, "In Search of the Perfect Astronaut," *Boston Globe*, April 4, 2000, p. E4; J. Tracy, "110-Day Isolation Ends in Sullen . . . Isolation," *Moscow Times*, March 30, 2000, p. 1; M. Warren, "A Mir Kiss?" *Daily Telegraph* (London), March 30, 2000, p. 22; G. York, "Canadian's Harassment Complaint Scorned," *Globe and Mail*, March 25, 2000, p. A2; S. Nolen, "Lust in Space," *Globe and Mail*, March 24, 2000, p. A3.

Video Case Study

ACTIVITY 13.2

A War of Words

Around the world, more and more media outlets and fierce competition are putting intense pressure on owners, managers, and journalists. A strike involving a few hundred journalists, editors, and graphics workers at the *Calgary Herald* reverberates nationally. What happens in this dispute at the chain-owned newspaper could set the tone and the agenda in other newsrooms. How it's resolved may tell us something about the kind of journalism we'll see in Canada.

After 116 years, *Calgary Herald* employees have formed a union. Now they're on strike and looking for their first contract. This has become a battleground for a war of words. For management, it's a fight over the right to control the content of the paper and the right to choose its staff. The strikers say they're fighting to defend the principles of journalism—to protect the truth.

ACTIVITY 13.2 CONTINUED

Calgary Herald journalist Lise Dempster sums up the issue: "It's not about money," she says. "We would like to have the ability to speak up about issues of journalistic integrity without the fear or worry that if what we say is unpopular or does not coincide with our current manager's wishes, that we wouldn't be vulnerable to being fired or laid off."

Ken King, *Calgary Herald's* publisher when the dispute began, sees the conflict differently. The newspaper "really wasn't doing a job for the shareholders. And to some degree, I'm not sure it was doing the job it should have for the city either." For example, King notes that the Reform Party represents most areas of Calgary, yet receives little mention in the *Calgary Herald*. He tried to move the paper more to the political right, more in line with its conservative business-savvy readers. This also was more consistent with the personal politics of Conrad Black, who owned the *Herald* at the time.

King also had a mandate to make the *Calgary Herald* more profitable. He did that not by increasing readership, but by signing lucrative deals with local commercial productions and events. Critics say that these *Herald*-sponsored events received excessive attention in the newspaper. For example, singer Shania Twain was sponsored by the *Herald* and was featured in almost 30 articles over a ten-day period.

As profits at the paper increased, so did tensions in the *Herald* newsroom. Many journalists say that they felt uncomfortable with their assignments. And it wasn't just the pro-business shift that bothered them. They questioned story ideas handed down from the desk of Ken King. They also complained that senior editors were changing articles, spicing them up to sell more papers, sometimes even with factual errors. One journalist called it "drive-by editing."

Dan Gaynor, *Calgary Herald's* current publisher, is trying to resolve the conflict. "There are some angry, bitter people," Gaynor admits. "And you know we have to take steps to put in place again constructive participation in the future of this newspaper, both at a staff level and in a management level."

But Gaynor also riled some journalists by trying to remove the seniority clause that protects longer-service employees. He wants to be able to remove employees who are working at a minimum level of effort, even if they have long seniority. Gaynor also supports newspaper partnerships, as long as they are managed carefully. "What is very important is that we have a separation between what we do as journalists and what we do as a promotional department, or in that other arm of the newspaper."

Kevin Peterson, another former *Herald* publisher, believes that this separation is difficult in practice. "What happens when you become involved in a partnership is that, in effect, you're agreeing to become an advocate for the goals of that partnership," Peterson explains. "And where that begins to affect coverage is not so much in the stories that are done, as the ones that aren't. So that if you're a partner, you do treat your partner kindly."

Lisa Dempster and other journalists are willing to stay on strike to change the way newspapers are run. But the strike may have a limited effect. About a quarter of the newsroom staff never went on strike; a handful have since crossed the picket line to return to work. Replacement workers from other Conrad Black newspapers have been flown in from across the country. And all of this takes place in a province with low regard for labour unions.

Discussion Questions

1. Discuss the sources of conflict in the dispute between the *Calgary Herald* and its newsroom staff.

2. In your opinion, what conflict resolution styles seem to be emphasized by former publisher Ken King and current publisher Dan Gaynor? Which style would be most appropriate under these circumstances?

3. This video provides some information about the relative power of the striking employees. Identify the sources and contingencies of power that they possess.

Source: Based on "A War of Words," *National Magazine* (January 24, 2000).

ACTIVITY 13.3
UGLI ORANGE ROLE PLAY

Purpose: This exercise is designed to help you understand the dynamics of interpersonal and intergroup conflict as well as the effectiveness of negotiation strategies under specific conditions.

Materials: The instructor will distribute roles for Dr. Roland, Dr. Jones, and a few observers. Ideally, each negotiation should occur in a private area away from other negotiations.

Instructions:

Step 1: The instructor will divide the class into an even number of teams of three people each, with one participant left over for each team formed (e.g., six observers if there are six teams). One-half of the teams will take the role of Dr. Roland and the other half will be Dr. Jones. The instructor will distribute roles after the teams have been formed.

Step 2: Members within each team are given ten minutes (or other time limit stated by the instructor) to learn their roles and decide on a negotiating strategy.

Step 3: After reading their roles and discussing strategy, each Dr. Jones team is matched with a Dr. Roland team to conduct negotiations. Two observers will be assigned to watch the paired teams during pre-negotiations and subsequent negotiations.

Step 4: At the end of the negotiations, the class will congregate for a discussion. The observers will describe the process and outcomes in their negotiating session. The instructor will then invite the negotiators to describe their experiences and the implications for conflict management.

Source: This exercise was developed by Dr. Robert J. House, Wharton Business School, University of Pennsylvania.

ACTIVITY 13.4
CONFLICT MANAGEMENT STYLE ORIENTATION SCALE

Purpose: This self-assessment exercise is designed to help you identify your preferred conflict management style.

Instructions: Read each of the statements below and circle the responses that you believe best reflect your position regarding each statement. Then use the scoring key in Appendix B of this book to calculate your results for each conflict management style. This exercise is completed alone so that students can assess themselves honestly without concerns of social comparison. However, class discussion will focus on the different conflict management styles and the situations in which each is most appropriate.

Circle the number that best indicates how well each statement describes you.	Rarely ▼				Always ▼
1. If someone disagrees with me, I vigorously defend my side of the issue.	1	2	3	4	5
2. I go along with suggestions from co-workers, even if I don't agree with them.	1	2	3	4	5
3. I give and take so that a compromise can be reached.	1	2	3	4	5
4. I keep my opinions to myself rather than openly disagree with people.	1	2	3	4	5
5. In disagreements or negotiations, I try to find the best possible solution for both sides by sharing information.	1	2	3	4	5
6. I try to reach a middle ground in disputes with other people.	1	2	3	4	5
7. I accommodate the wishes of people who have different points of view than my own.	1	2	3	4	5
8. I avoid openly debating issues where there is disagreement.	1	2	3	4	5
9. In negotiations, I hold on to my position rather than give in.	1	2	3	4	5
10. I try to solve conflicts by finding solutions that benefit both me and the other person.	1	2	3	4	5
11. I let co-workers have their way rather than jeopardize our relationship.	1	2	3	4	5
12. I try to win my position in a discussion.	1	2	3	4	5
13. I like to investigate conflicts with co-workers so that we can discover solutions that benefit both of us.	1	2	3	4	5
14. I believe that it is not worth the time and trouble to discuss my differences of opinion with other people.	1	2	3	4	5
15. To reach an agreement, I give up some things in exchange for others.	1	2	3	4	5

Sources: Adapted from items in M.A. Rahim, "A Measure of Styles of Handling Interpersonal Conflict," *Academy of Management Journal*, 26 (June 1983), pp. 368–76; K.W. Thomas and R.H. Kilmann, *Thomas-Kilmann Conflict Mode Instrument* (Sterling Forst, NY: Xicom, 1977).

CHAPTER FOURTEEN

Organizational Leadership

LEARNING OBJECTIVES

After reading this chapter, you should be able to:

- Define leadership.
- List seven traits identified with effective leaders.
- Describe the people-oriented and task-oriented leadership styles.
- Outline the path-goal theory of leadership.
- Discuss the importance of Fiedler's contingency model of leadership.
- Contrast transactional and transformational leadership.
- Describe the four elements of transformational leadership.
- Identify three reasons why people inflate the importance of leadership.
- Discuss similarities and differences in the leadership styles of women and men.

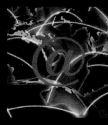

Rick George's leadership has transformed Suncor Energy Inc. from the "unluckiest oil company in Canada" to one of the top performers in the country.

Courtesy of Suncor Energy Inc.

A decade ago, Suncor Energy Inc. was "the unluckiest oil company in Canada." It experienced a devastating fire and crippling labour dispute at a time when it was one of the world's highest-cost oil producers. That's when Rick George became Suncor's CEO. Through George's leadership, the Calgary-based oil company has achieved several years of record profits and is rated as one of best employers in the country.

George believes that effective leaders help shape the organization's vision and then act consistently with that vision. "Setting clear goals and leading by example are exceedingly important," says George. "The example you set at the top is probably the most important thing a CEO does in terms of what you ask people to do. You have got to walk that same line yourself." Communication is another critical skill in George's leadership tool kit. "You can't over-communicate, whether it's your vision, your values and beliefs, or your goals and objectives," he says.

George also relies on participative leadership to make Suncor a much more efficient and effective organization. He involves a lot of people in decision making and then gives them freedom to implement their ideas. Through this participative leadership, Suncor's oil sands operations have cut the cost of oil production from $19 a few years ago to less than $11 today. "[Y]ou've got to treat [employees] as part owners," George advises. "They've got to have a direct interest in the business, and you have to communicate very clearly."[1]

www.suncor.com

• **Leadership** The process of influencing people and providing an environment for them to achieve team or organizational objectives.

By most accounts, Rick George is an effective organizational leader. He inspires Suncor's employees and creates an environment for them to work more effectively towards organizational objectives. George continually communicates his vision of Suncor's future and builds employee commitment to that future through a participative leadership style.

What is **leadership**? Some people say that leadership is difficult to define, but we know it when we see it. Others argue that a leader can only be defined as someone who has followers. Leaders are not people in specific positions. Rather, leaders are defined by the people they serve. Recent reviews of the leadership literature note that scholars do not sufficiently agree on the definition of leadership.[2] As one respected scholar acknowledged, "leadership is one of the most observed and least understood phenomena on earth."[3]

With these caveats in mind, we will cautiously define leadership as the process of influencing people and providing an environment for them to achieve team or organizational objectives. Effective leaders help groups of people define their goals and find ways to achieve them.[4] They use power and persuasion to ensure that followers have the motivation and role clarity to achieve specified goals. Leaders also arrange the work environment—such as allocating resources and altering communication patterns—so that employees can achieve corporate objectives more easily.

However leadership is defined, only 8 percent of executives in large firms think that their organizations have enough of it.[5] Most are concerned about a lack of leadership talent. But leadership isn't restricted to the executive suite. Anyone in the organization may be a leader. Effective self-directed work teams, for example, consist of members who share leadership responsibilities or otherwise allocate this role to a responsible coordinator. Successful technology champions—employees who overcome technical and organizational obstacles to introduce technological change in their area of the organization—are effective leaders because they influence co-workers and transform the environmental conditions that have prevented the innovation from being introduced. In fact, Canadian studies report that one of the most common reasons why technology champions fail is that they lack the traits or behaviours we associate with effective leadership.[6] Overall, we should avoid the idea that leaders are people in certain positions. Anyone may be a leader at an appropriate time and place.

PERSPECTIVES OF LEADERSHIP

Leadership has been contemplated since the days of Greek philosophers, and it is one of the most popular research topics among organizational behaviour scholars. As we describe the leadership of Rick George—or any other leader in the private or public sector—it becomes apparent that there are many ways to understand leadership in organizational settings. Although some leadership perspectives are currently more popular than others, each helps us to understand this complex issue more fully.

This chapter looks at the different leadership perspectives outlined in Exhibit 14.1. Some scholars have studied the traits or competencies of great leaders, whereas others have looked at their behaviours. More recent studies have looked at leadership from a contingency approach by considering the appropriate leader behaviours in different settings. Currently, the most popular perspective is that leaders transform organizations through their vision, communication, and ability to build commitment. Finally, an emerging perspective suggests that leadership is mainly a perceptual bias. We distort reality and attribute events to leaders because we feel more comfortable believing that a competent individual is at the organization's helm.[7]

Exhibit 14.1 Perspectives of Leadership

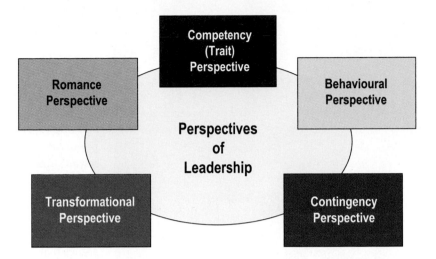

Literally dozens of theories have developed within these five leadership perspectives. Don't worry. We won't present every theory because this would undermine your capacity and willingness to understand the critical issues in leadership. Although the field of organizational behaviour tends to retain leadership theories long after their validity has been put into doubt, this chapter will focus on the handful of theories that seem to have the strongest research support.

COMPETENCY (TRAIT) PERSPECTIVE OF LEADERSHIP

As chief operating officer of Halifax-based Air Nova, Lynn Loewen is considered an intelligent leader who employees respect for her integrity and drive. Born in Grand Falls, Newfoundland, Loewen made her way into the airline's executive offices by working hard and developing a deep knowledge of the industry. "She is a remarkable lady in terms of her leadership qualities, her ability to focus on the business and the decisions that need to be made," says Joe Randell, CEO of Air Canada's three regional airlines (of which Air Nova is one).[8]

Competencies The abilities, individual values, personality traits, and other characteristics of people that lead to superior performance.

From these accounts, it seems that Lynn Loewen is an effective leader because she possesses certain leadership competencies. Recall from Chapter 2 that **competencies** are the underlying characteristics of people that lead to superior performance.[9] These include the person's knowledge, natural and learned abilities, values, and personality traits. Since the beginning of recorded civilization, people have been interested in personal characteristics that distinguish great leaders from the rest of us. Very early interest focused on personality traits and physical appearance. The ancient Egyptians demanded authority, discrimination, and justice from their leaders. The Greek philosopher Plato called for prudence, courage, temperance, and justice.[10]

For the first half of the twentieth century, organizational behaviour scholars used scientific methods to determine whether certain personality traits and physical characteristics (particularly, a person's height and weight) actually distinguish leaders from lesser souls. A major review in the late 1940s concluded that no consistent list of traits could

Lynn Loewen is well known for her leadership competencies. The chief operating officer of Halifax-based Air Nova has unwavering drive, a keen intelligence, and a detailed knowledge of the airline industry. Are these personal characteristics sufficient for effective leadership? Moreover, do you think that people like Lynn Loewen are born as great leaders, or can companies develop leaders?

www.airnova.ca

be distilled from the hundreds of studies conducted up to that time. A subsequent review suggested that a few traits are consistently associated with effective leaders, but that most are unrelated to effective leadership.[11] These conclusions caused many scholars to give up their search for personal characteristics that distinguish effective leaders.

Over the past decade, management consultants and organizational behaviour scholars have popularized competency-based selection and reward practices. Competencies encompass a broader range of personal characteristics—such as knowledge, abilities, and values—that were not considered by earlier studies on leadership traits. This new generation of leadership experts argues that the earlier studies focused too much on abstract personality traits and the physical appearance of leaders. The recent leadership literature identifies seven competencies that are characteristic of effective leaders.[12] These competencies are listed in Exhibit 14.2 and are briefly described below.

- *Drive*—This refers to the inner motivation that leaders possess to pursue their goals. Leaders have a high need for achievement (see Chapter 3). This inspires an unbridled inquisitiveness and a need for constant learning. You can see this in Lynn Loewen through her unwavering tenacity and energy at Air Nova.

- *Leadership motivation*—As we learned in Chapter 3, leaders have a strong need for power because they want to influence others. However, they tend to have a need for "socialized power" because their motivation is constrained by a strong sense of altruism and social responsibility.[13] In other words, effective leaders try to gain power so that they can influence others to accomplish goals that benefit the team or organization.

- *Integrity*—This refers to the leader's truthfulness and tendency to translate words into deeds. Several large-scale studies have reported that followers consistently identify integrity as the most important leadership characteristic. Similarly, a recent survey reports that Canadian CEOs consider honesty to be an important leadership attribute. Lynn Loewen and other leaders will only have followers when trust is maintained through integrity.[14]

- *Self-confidence*—Leaders believe in their leadership skills and their ability to achieve objectives. They also use impression management tactics (see Chapter 12) to convince followers of their confidence.

EXHIBIT 14.2 Seven Competencies of Effective Leaders

Leadership Trait	Description
Drive	The leader's inner motivation to pursue goals.
Leadership motivation	The leader's need for socialized power to accomplish team or organizational goals.
Integrity	The leader's truthfulness and tendency to translate words into deeds.
Self-confidence	The leader's belief in his/her own leadership skills and ability to achieve objectives.
Intelligence	The leader's above-average cognitive ability to process enormous amounts of information.
Knowledge of the business	The leader's understanding of the company's environment that allows him/her to make more intuitive decisions.
Emotional intelligence	The leader's ability to monitor his/her own and others' emotions, discriminate among them, and use the information to guide his/her thoughts and actions.

Sources: Most elements of this list were derived from S.A. Kirkpatrick and E.A. Locke, "Leadership: Do Traits Matter?" *Academy of Management Executive,* 5 (May 1991), pp. 48–60. Several of these ideas are also discussed in H.B. Gregersen, A.J. Morrison, and J.S. Black, "Developing Leaders for the Global Frontier," *Sloan Management Review,* 40 (Fall 1998), pp. 21–32; R.J. House and R.N. Aditya, "The Social Scientific Study of Leadership: Quo Vadis?" *Journal of Management,* 23 (1997), pp. 409–73.

- *Intelligence*—Leaders have above-average cognitive ability to process enormous amounts of information. Leaders aren't necessarily geniuses; rather, they have superior ability to analyze alternate scenarios and identify potential opportunities.

- *Knowledge of the business*—Lynn Loewen and other leaders know the business environment in which they operate. This develops an intuitive ability to recognize opportunities and understand their organization's capacity to capture those opportunities.

Emotional intelligence (EQ) The ability to monitor your own and others' emotions, to discriminate among them, and to use the information to guide your thinking and actions.

- *Emotional intelligence*—Effective leaders have a high level of **emotional intelligence (EQ)**. They monitor their own and others' emotions, discriminate among them, and use the information to guide their thoughts and actions (see Chapter 7).[15] Emotional intelligence requires a strong **self-monitoring** personality (see Chapter 6) because leaders must be sensitive to situational cues and readily adapt their own behaviour appropriately.[16] It also requires the ability to empathize with others and possess the social skills necessary to build rapport as well as network with others. Moreover, the contingency leadership perspective described later in this chapter assumes that effective leaders are high self-monitors so they can adjust their behaviour to match the situation.

Self-monitoring A personality trait referring to the extent that people are sensitive to situational cues and can readily adapt their own behaviour appropriately.

COMPETENCY (TRAIT) PERSPECTIVE LIMITATIONS AND PRACTICAL IMPLICATIONS

One concern with the competency perspective is that it assumes great leaders have the same personal characteristics and all of these characteristics are equally important in all situations. This is probably a false assumption; leadership is far too complex to have a universal list of traits that apply to every condition. Some competencies might not be important all the time, although researchers have not yet explored this aspect of traits.

Don't look for Kim Jung Tae in his office. The CEO of South Korea's Housing and Commercial Bank (HCB) is busy travelling throughout the company's nearly 500 branches and offices, instilling a new way of thinking about banking. "Our bank has to survive doing retail business," explains Kim. "That means customer satisfaction." Kim's marketing savvy and years of experience in the financial services industry make him well suited to lead HCB. Kim also has a strong drive and enough self-confidence to be paid in stock options rather than with a salary.[19] What competencies seem to make Kim Jung Tae an effective leader?

A few scholars have also warned that some personal characteristics might only influence our perception that someone is a leader, not whether the individual really makes a difference to the organization's success.[17] People who exhibit integrity, self-confidence, and other traits are called leaders because they fit our stereotype of an effective leader. Or we might see a successful person, call that person a leader, and then attribute self-confidence and other unobservable traits that we consider essential for great leaders. We will discuss this perceptual distortion more fully towards the end of the chapter. At this point, you should be aware that our knowledge of leadership competencies may be partly due to perceptual distortions.

Aside from these limitations, the competency perspective recognizes that some people possess personal characteristics that offer them a higher potential to be great leaders. The most obvious implication of this is that organizations are relying increasingly on competency-based methods to hire people for future leadership positions.[18] Leadership talents are important throughout the organization, so this recommendation should extend to all levels of hiring, not just senior executives. Companies also need to determine which behaviours represent these competencies so that employees with leadership talents are identified early for promotion.

The competency perspective of leadership does not necessarily imply that people are born as great leaders. On the contrary, competencies only indicate leadership potential, not leadership performance. People with these characteristics become effective leaders only after they have developed and mastered the necessary leadership behaviours. People with somewhat lower leadership competencies may become very effective leaders because they have leveraged their potential more fully. This means that companies must do more than hire people with certain competencies. They must also develop their potential through leadership development programs and practical experience in the field.

BEHAVIOURAL PERSPECTIVE OF LEADERSHIP

In the 1940s and 1950s, scholars from Ohio State University launched an intensive research investigation to answer the question: What behaviours make leaders effective? Questionnaires were administered to subordinates, asking them to rate their supervisors on a large number of behaviours. These studies, along with similar research at the University of Michigan and Harvard University, distilled two clusters of leadership behaviours from more than 1800 items.[20]

One cluster represented people-oriented behaviours. This included showing mutual trust and respect for subordinates, demonstrating a genuine concern for their needs, and having a desire to look out for their welfare. Leaders with a strong people-oriented style listen to employee suggestions, do personal favours for employees, support their interests when required, and treat employees as equals. The other cluster represented a task-oriented leadership style and included behaviours that define and structure work roles. Task-oriented leaders assign employees to specific tasks, clarify their work duties and procedures, ensure that they follow company rules, and push them to reach their performance capacity. They establish stretch goals and challenge employees to push beyond those high standards. The problem with task-oriented leadership is knowing how much to challenge employees. As Connections 14.1 describes, some bosses are friendly tyrants while others cross the line as bullies.

After identifying the two clusters of leader behaviour, researchers associated them with specific measures of leadership effectiveness. The early studies concluded that people-oriented leadership is associated with higher job satisfaction among subordinates, as well as lower absenteeism, grievances, and turnover. However, job performance was lower than for employees with task-oriented leaders.[21] Task-oriented leadership, on the other hand, was associated with lower job satisfaction as well as higher absenteeism and turnover among subordinates. But this leadership style also seems to increase productivity and team unity. College students apparently value task-oriented instructors because they want clear course objectives and well-prepared lectures that abide by the course objectives.[22]

THE "HI-HI" LEADERSHIP HYPOTHESIS

Behavioural leadership scholars initially thought that people-oriented leadership and task-oriented leadership were at opposite ends of a behaviour spectrum. In other words, they believed that a strong task-oriented leader was necessarily a weak people-oriented leader. But researchers later concluded that these styles are independent of each other. Some people are high or low on both styles, others are high on one style and low on the other, and most are somewhere in between.

www.confederationbridge.com

 CONNECTIONS 14.1

Friendly Tyrants and Abusive Bosses

Paul Giannelia admits that he was tough on employees during construction of the Confederation Bridge linking Prince Edward Island and the mainland. "[T]he tough schedule made it hard to keep everyone focused," explains the project director. But Giannelia believes that he balanced his task-oriented leadership with a supportive style to offset the stress. "I had to be the benevolent dictator while being the head cheerleader."

Unfortunately, not everyone has a friendly tyrant for a boss. According to a former executive at Livent Inc., senior managers at the Toronto-based theatre company bullied and verbally abused employees. The executive contends that the mistreatment started with Livent's founder, Garth Drabinsky. "I had never before experienced anyone with Drabinsky's abusive and profane management style," says the executive.

Livent's employees are not alone. According to a recent U.S. survey, 39 percent of employees think that employers are more abusive today than they were 20 years ago, compared with 31 percent who think that they are less abusive. The most popular explanation by far is the constant pressure on managers to produce. Most employees recommended better leadership training as well as surveying employees more often for incidents of abuse by their bosses.

Sources: D. Armstrong, "Got an Abusive Boss?" *Foxmarketwire.com* (online), February 16, 2000; A. Clark, "An Epic from Livent," *Maclean's*, March 1, 1999, pp. 40–41; "A Conversation with Paul Giannelia," *Initiative Media Special Feature Supplement*, April 1997.

With the revised assumption that leaders could be both people-oriented and task-oriented, behavioural leadership scholars hypothesized that the most effective leaders exhibit high levels of both types of behaviour. This became known as the **"hi-hi" leadership hypothesis**.[23] Effective leaders, it was thought, should have a high people-oriented style and a high task-oriented style.

A popular leadership program that grew out of the "hi-hi" leadership hypothesis is the **Leadership Grid®** (formerly known as the *Managerial Grid*).[24] Participants begin by assessing their own leadership style on the Grid, then develop skills to move towards the best leadership style. According to the model, the best leadership style is team management (9,9). This equates to "hi-hi" leadership in which leaders have high levels of concern for people and production. People with 9,9 scores tend to rely on commitment, participation, and conflict resolution to get results. The Leadership Grid also labels people with less than perfect scores, such as "country club" managers (high concern for people, low concern for production) and "impoverished" managers (low concern for both people and production).

LIMITATIONS OF THE BEHAVIOURAL LEADERSHIP PERSPECTIVE

Organizational behaviour scholars have mostly abandoned the behavioural perspective of leadership because it takes a universal approach to leadership. It ignores the possibility that the best leadership style may depend on the situation.[25] On a positive note, the behavioural perspective laid the foundation for two of the main leadership styles—people-oriented and task-oriented—found in many contemporary leadership theories. These contemporary theories adopt a contingency perspective, which we describe next.

CONTINGENCY PERSPECTIVE OF LEADERSHIP

The contingency perspective of leadership is based on the idea that the most appropriate leadership style depends on the situation. Most (although not all) contingency leadership theories assume that effective leaders must be both insightful and flexible.[26] They must be able to adapt their behaviours and styles to the immediate situation. This isn't easy to do, however. Leaders typically have a preferred style. It takes considerable effort for leaders to learn when and how to alter their styles to match the situation. As we noted earlier, leaders must have a high emotional intelligence, particularly a self-monitoring personality, so they can diagnose the circumstances and match their behaviours accordingly.[27]

PATH-GOAL THEORY OF LEADERSHIP

Several contingency theories have been proposed over the years, but **path-goal leadership theory** has withstood scientific critique better than the others. It has its roots in the expectancy theory of motivation (see Chapter 3). Early research by Martin Evans incorporated expectancy theory into the study of how leader behaviours influence employee perceptions of expectancies (paths) between employee effort and performance (goals). Based on this perspective, Robert House and other scholars developed and refined path-goal theory as a contingency leadership model.[28]

Path-goal theory states that effective leaders influence employee satisfaction and performance by making their need satisfaction contingent on effective job performance. Leaders strengthen the performance-to-outcome expectancy and valences of those outcomes by ensuring that employees who perform their jobs well have a higher degree of need fulfilment than employees who perform poorly.

"Hi-hi" leadership hypothesis A proposition stating that effective leaders exhibit high levels of both people-oriented and task-oriented behaviours.

Leadership Grid® A leadership model that assesses an individual's leadership effectiveness in terms of his or her concern for people and concern for production.

Path-goal leadership theory A contingency theory of leadership based on expectancy theory of motivation that includes four leadership styles as well as several employee and situational contingencies.

Effective leaders strengthen the effort-to-performance expectancy by providing the information, support, and other resources necessary to help employees complete their tasks.[29] For instance, the best-performing self-directed work teams at Xerox had leaders who gave first priority to arranging organizational support for the team.[30] In other words, path-goal theory advocates **servant leadership**.[31] Servant leaders do not view leadership as a position of power; rather, they are coaches, stewards, and facilitators. Leadership is an obligation to understand employee needs and to facilitate employee work performance. Servant leaders ask, "How can I help you?" rather than expect employees to serve them. As Connections 14.2 describes, Wal-Mart Canada, Royal Dutch/Shell, and other organizations increasingly expect people to think like servant leaders.

Servant leadership
The belief that leaders serve followers by understanding their needs and helping to achieve their work performance.

Leadership styles

Exhibit 14.3 illustrates the path-goal theory of leadership. This model specifically highlights four leadership styles and several contingency factors leading to three indicators of leader effectiveness. The four leadership styles are:[32]

CONNECTIONS 14.2

www.benfold.navy.mil

Turning Leaders into Servants

Wal-Mart Canada fired a store manager in Nova Scotia after he deleted unauthorized overtime from payroll sheets. The retailer has a policy of no overtime, but it has a stronger policy called servant leadership. Wal-Mart expects all of its managers to exhibit exemplary behaviour, including serving employees and ensuring they are treated fairly.

D. Michael Abrashoff is a role model for servant leadership. The former commander of the *USS Benfold* (Abrashoff now works in the Pentagon) takes the view that leaders support employees, not the other way around. He argues that the highest boss isn't the person with the most stripes; it's the sailors who do the work. Abrashoff meets face to face with all crew members to understand their background and goals, then finds ways to add meaning to their work.

Executives at Royal Dutch/Shell have also embraced the servant leadership philosophy.

Wal-Mart Canada's strong ethical standards include the idea that leaders must serve their employees.

The Dutch and British-based energy company's leadership development program (called LEAP) emphasizes that effective leaders create conditions that enable others to realize their potential in the workplace. Servant leaders involve and empower employees, which develops greater trust in the leader.

Sources: S. Hughes, "Wal-Mart's Overtime Edict Under Fire in N.S. Court," *Halifax Chronicle-Herald*, December 3, 1999, p. C4; P. LaBarre, "The Agenda—Grassroots Leadership," *Fast Company*, 23 (April 1999); W.B. Brenneman, J.B. Keys, and R.M. Fulmer, "Learning Across a Living Company: The Shell Companies' Experiences," *Organizational Dynamics*, 27 (Autumn 1998), pp. 61–69.

EXHIBIT 14.3 Path-Goal Leadership Theory

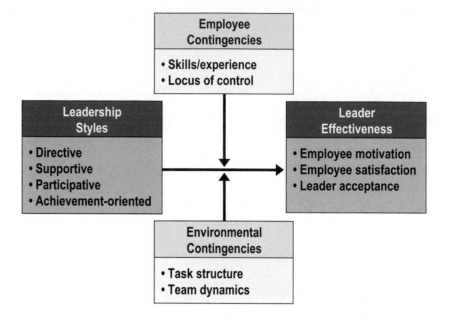

- *Directive*—These are clarifying behaviours that provide a psychological structure for subordinates. The leader clarifies performance goals, the means to reach those goals, and the standards against which performance will be judged. It also includes judicious use of rewards and disciplinary actions. Directive leadership is the same as task-oriented leadership described earlier and echoes our discussion in Chapter 2 on the importance of clear role perceptions in employee performance.

- *Supportive*—These behaviours provide psychological support for subordinates. The leader is friendly and approachable; makes the work more pleasant; treats employees with equal respect; and shows concern for the status, needs, and well-being of employees. Supportive leadership is the same as people-oriented leadership described earlier and reflects the benefits of social support to help employees cope with stressful situations (see Chapter 5).

- *Participative*—These behaviours encourage and facilitate subordinate involvement in decisions beyond their normal work activities. The leader consults with employees, asks for their suggestions, and takes these ideas into serious consideration before making a decision. Participative leadership relates to the employee involvement concepts and issues described in Chapter 10.

- *Achievement-oriented*—These behaviours encourage employees to reach their peak performance. The leader sets challenging goals, expects employees to perform at their highest level, continuously seeks improvement in employee performance, and shows a high degree of confidence that employees will assume responsibility and accomplish challenging goals. Achievement-oriented leadership applies goal-setting theory (Chapter 3) as well as positive expectations in self-fulfilling prophecy (Chapter 6).

The path-goal model contends that effective leaders are capable of selecting the most appropriate behavioural style (or styles) for that situation. Leaders might simultaneously use more than one style. For example, they might be both supportive and participative in a specific situation.

CONTINGENCIES OF PATH-GOAL THEORY

As a contingency theory, path-goal theory states that each of the four leadership styles will be effective in some situations but not in others. The path-goal leadership model specifies two sets of situational variables that moderate the relationship between a leader's style and effectiveness: (1) employee characteristics and (2) characteristics of the employee's work environment. Several contingencies have already been studied within the path-goal framework, and the model is open for more variables in the future.[33] However, we will examine only four contingencies here (see Exhibit 14.4).

Skill and experience

A combination of directive and supportive leadership is best for employees who are (or perceive themselves to be) inexperienced and unskilled. Directive leadership gives subordinates information about how to accomplish the task, whereas supportive leadership helps them cope with the uncertainties of unfamiliar work situations. Directive leadership is detrimental when employees are skilled and experienced because it introduces too much supervisory control.

Locus of control

Locus of control
A personality trait referring to the extent to which people believe what happens to them is within their control; those who feel in control of their destiny have an internal locus of control, whereas those who believe that life events are due mainly to fate or to luck have an external locus of control.

Recall from Chapter 6 that people with an internal **locus of control** believe they have control over their work environment. Consequently, these employees prefer participative and achievement-oriented leadership styles and may become frustrated with a directive style. In contrast, people with an external locus of control believe that their performance is due more to luck and fate, so they tend to be more satisfied with directive and supportive leadership.

Task structure

Directive leadership should be adopted when the task is nonroutine, because this style minimizes role ambiguity that tends to occur in these complex work situations (particularly for inexperienced employees).[34] This style is ineffective when employees have routine and simple tasks because the manager's guidance serves no purpose and may be viewed as unnecessarily close control. Employees in highly routine and simple jobs may require supportive leadership to help them cope with the tedious nature of the work and lack of control over the pace of work. Participative leadership is preferred for employees performing nonroutine tasks because the lack

EXHIBIT 14.4   Selected Contingencies of Path-Goal Theory

	Directive	Supportive	Participative	Achievement-oriented
Employee Contingencies				
Skill and Experience	Low	Low	High	High
Locus of Control	External	External	Internal	Internal
Environmental Contingencies				
Task Structure	Nonroutine	Routine	Nonroutine	???
Team Dynamics	Negative norms	Low cohesion	Positive norms	???

of rules and procedures gives them more discretion to achieve challenging goals. This style is ineffective for employees in routine tasks because they lack discretion over their work.

Team dynamics

Cohesive teams with performance-oriented norms act as a substitute for most leader interventions. High team cohesiveness substitutes for supportive leadership, whereas performance-oriented team norms substitute for directive and possibly achievement-oriented leadership. Thus, when team cohesiveness is low, leaders should use the supportive style. Leaders should apply a directive style to counteract team norms that oppose the team's formal objectives. For example, the team leader may need to use legitimate power if team members have developed a norm to "take it easy" rather than complete a project on time.

RECENT EXTENSIONS OF PATH-GOAL THEORY

The original path-goal theory primarily relates to dyadic relations between a supervisor and employee.[35] Yet leadership also applies to the work unit and organization. Recognizing this gap, Robert House (who we mentioned was an early developer of the original path-goal theory) recently extended the model by adding leader styles that apply more to work units and organizations than to individual relations.[36] One of these is *networking*, which recognizes that leaders play an important political role. They represent the work unit and engage in political networking activities (see Chapter 12) to legitimize the work unit and maintain positive influences on other areas of the organization. Another is *value-based leadership*, which includes articulating a vision of the future, displaying passion for this vision, demonstrating self-confidence in the attainment of the vision, communicating the vision, and acting in ways consistent with the vision. This is the same as the transformational leadership perspective that we describe later in this chapter.

PRACTICAL IMPLICATIONS AND LIMITATIONS OF PATH-GOAL THEORY

Path-goal theory reinforces the idea that effective leaders vary their style with the situation. There are times to give directions, times to empathize, times to use stretch goals, and times to involve subordinates in decision making. Path-goal theory also offers a fairly precise set of contingency factors that provide practical advice on when to use various leadership styles.

Path-goal theory has received considerable research support, certainly more than other contingency leadership models.[37] However, one or two contingencies (i.e., task structure) have found limited research support. Other contingencies and leadership styles in the path-goal leadership model haven't received scholarly investigation at all.[38] For example, some cells in Exhibit 14.4 have question marks because we do not yet know how those leadership styles apply to those contingencies. The recently expanded model adds new leadership styles and contingencies, but they have not yet been tested. Until further study comes along, it is unclear whether certain contingencies should be considered when choosing the best leadership style.

Another concern is that as path-goal theory expands, the model may become too complex for practical use. Although the expanded model provides a closer representation of the complexity of leadership, it may become too cumbersome for training people in leadership styles. Few people would be able to remember all the contingencies and appropriate leadership styles for those contingencies. In spite of these limitations, path-goal theory remains a relatively complete and robust contingency leadership theory.

OTHER CONTINGENCY THEORIES

At the beginning of this chapter we noted that numerous leadership theories have developed over the years. Most of them are found in the contingency perspective of leadership. Some overlap with the path-goal model in terms of leadership styles, but most use simpler and more abstract contingencies. We will very briefly mention only two here because of their popularity and historical significance to the field.

Situational leadership model

One of the most popular contingency theories among trainers is the **situational leadership** model, developed by Paul Hersey and Ken Blanchard.[39] The model suggests that effective leaders vary their style with the "readiness" of followers. (An earlier version of the model called this "maturity.") Readiness refers to the employee's or work team's ability and willingness to accomplish a specific task. Ability refers to the extent that the follower has the skills and knowledge to perform the task without the leader's guidance. Willingness refers to the follower's self-motivation and commitment to perform the assigned task. The model compresses these distinct concepts into a single situational condition.

The situational leadership model also identifies four leadership styles—telling, selling, participating, and delegating—that Hersey and Blanchard distinguish in terms of the amount of directive and supportive behaviour provided. For example, "telling" has high task behaviour and low supportive behaviour. The situational leadership model is similar to the Leadership Grid described earlier, except that the four quadrants represent a leadership style that may be appropriate under different circumstances.

In spite of its popularity, at least three reviews have concluded that the situational leadership model lacks empirical support.[40] Only one part of the model apparently works; namely, that leaders should use "telling" (i.e., directive style) when employees lack motivation and ability. (Recall that is also documented in path-goal theory.) The model's elegant simplicity is attractive and entertaining, but other parts don't represent reality very well. The most recent review also concluded that the theory has logical and internal inconsistencies.

Fiedler's contingency model

Fred Fiedler and his associates developed the earliest contingency theory of leadership, called **Fiedler's contingency model**.[41] According to this model, leader effectiveness depends on whether the person's natural leadership style is appropriately matched to the situation. The theory examines two leadership styles that essentially correspond to the previously described people-oriented and task-oriented styles. Unfortunately, Fiedler's model relies on a questionnaire that does not measure either leadership style very well.

Fiedler's model suggests that the best leadership style depends on the level of *situational control*, that is, the degree of power and influence that the leader possesses in a particular situation. Situational control is affected by three factors in the following order of importance: leader–member relations, task structure, and position power.[42] Leader–member relations is the degree to which employees trust and respect the leader and are willing to follow his or her guidance. Task structure refers to the clarity or ambiguity of operating procedures. Position power is the extent to which the leader possesses legitimate, reward, and coercive power over subordinates. These three contingencies form the eight possible combinations of *situation favourableness* from the leader's viewpoint. Good leader–member relations, high task structure, and strong position power create the most favourable situation for the leader because he or she has the most power and influence under these conditions.

Fiedler has gained considerable respect for pioneering the first contingency theory of leadership. However, his theory has faired less well. As mentioned, the leadership style scale used

---

Situational leadership model Suggests that effective leaders vary their style with the "readiness" of followers.

Fiedler's contingency model States that leader effectiveness depends on whether the person's natural leadership style is appropriately matched to the situation.

by Fiedler has been widely criticized. There is also no scientific justification for placing the three situational control factors in a hierarchy. Moreover, it seems that leader–member relations is actually an indicator of leader effectiveness (as in path-goal theory) rather than a situational factor. Finally, the theory considers only two leadership styles whereas other models present a more complex and realistic array of behaviour options. These concerns explain why the theory has limited empirical support.[43]

Changing the situation to match the leader's natural style

Fiedler's contingency model may become a historical footnote, but it does make an important and lasting contribution by suggesting that leadership style is related to the individual's personality and, consequently, is relatively stable over time. Leaders might be able to alter their style temporarily, but they tend to use a preferred style in the long term. This contrasts with most other contingency leadership theories that assume leaders can comfortably change their style to match a given situation.

If leadership style is influenced by a person's personality, organizations should engineer the situation to fit the leader's dominant style rather than expect leaders to change their style with the situation. A directive leader might be assigned inexperienced employees who need direction rather than seasoned people who work less effectively under a directive style. Alternatively, companies might transfer supervisors to workplaces where their dominant style fits best. For instance, directive leaders might be parachuted into work teams with counterproductive norms, whereas leaders who prefer a supportive style should be sent to departments in which employees face work pressures and other stressors.

Leadership substitutes

So far, we have looked at theories that recommend using different leadership styles in various situations. But one theory, called **leadership substitutes,** identifies contingencies that either limit the leader's ability to influence subordinates or make that particular leadership style unnecessary. When substitute conditions are present, employees are effective without a formal leader who applies a particular style. Although the leadership substitute model requires further refinement, there is general support for the overall notion that some conditions neutralize or substitute for leadership styles.[44]

Several conditions have been identified in the literature that possibly substitute for task-oriented or people-oriented leadership. For example, performance-based reward systems keep employees directed towards organizational goals, so they probably replace or reduce the need for task-oriented leadership. Task-oriented leadership is also less important when employees are skilled and experienced. Notice how these propositions are similar to path-goal leadership theory, namely that directive leadership is unnecessary—and may be detrimental—when employees are skilled or experienced.[45]

Leadership substitutes have become more important as organizations remove supervisors and shift towards team-based structures. In fact, an emerging concept is that effective leaders help team members learn to lead themselves through leadership substitutes.[46] Some writers suggest that co-workers are powerful leader substitutes in these organizational structures. Co-workers instruct new employees, thereby providing directive leadership. They also provide social support, which reduces stress among fellow employees (see Chapter 5). Teams with norms that support organizational goals may substitute for achievement-oriented leadership, because employees encourage (or pressure) co-workers to stretch their performance levels.

Self-leadership has also been discussed as a potentially valuable leadership substitute in self-directed work teams.[47] Recall from Chapter 4 that self-leadership is the process of influ-

---

Leadership substitutes Characteristics of the employee, task, or organization that either limit the leader's influence or make it unnecessary.

Self-leadership The process of influencing oneself to establish the self-direction and self-motivation needed to perform a task. This includes personal goal setting, constructive thought patterns, designing natural rewards, self-monitoring, and self-reinforcement.

Fortunato Restagno (front) and his three colleagues at Pursue Associates rely on leadership substitutes more than on traditional supervision to get their work done. Everyone at the Kitchener, Ontario, graphics start-up firm stays focused on organizational objectives through common values, a performance-based reward system, formal training, and guidance from co-workers. The result is an efficient team that creates the motion signage showing airline logos with moving text in Toronto's Pearson International Airport.[50] What other leadership substitutes might help teams to lead themselves without direct supervision?

www.pursueassociates.com

Transformational leadership A leadership perspective that explains how leaders change teams or organizations by creating, communicating, and modelling a vision for the organization or work unit, and inspiring employees to strive for that vision.

encing oneself to establish the self-direction and self-motivation needed to perform a task.[48] It includes self-set goals, self-reinforcement, constructive thought processes, and other activities that influence the person's own motivation and behaviour. As employees become more proficient in self-leadership, they presumably require less supervision to keep them focused and energized towards organizational objectives.

TRANSFORMATIONAL PERSPECTIVE OF LEADERSHIP

When Ted Pattenden became president of National Rubber, the air in the plant was so bad that employees couldn't see across it. The Toronto-based manufacturer of recycled rubber products also had a narrow product focus, broken equipment, and a terrible work accident record. Pattenden soon articulated a new vision for the company, one that would expand the firm's product lines and bring new hope to employees for a better workplace. Pattenden demonstrated his sincerity and integrity towards that vision by introducing ventilation systems and training programs that improved worker health and safety. He held regular all-employee meetings to communicate the importance of a safe and healthy work environment, as well as the need for employee involvement to turn the company around. It was a slow process, but Pattenden's persuasiveness and consistency paid off. "Leadership is an emotional thing," says Pattenden. "If you are going to lead people, you have to have some sort of emotional link to them.[49]

Ted Pattenden is a **transformational leader.** Through his vision and actions, he turned National Rubber from a money-losing company with a dismal safety record into a profitable firm with high safety standards and employees who are proudly involved in the company's success. Transformational leaders are agents of change. They develop a vision for the organization or work unit, inspire and collectively bond employees to that vision, and give them a "can-do" attitude that makes the vision achievable.[51]

Transformational leaders such as Timothy Eaton, William Cornelius Van Horne, H.R. MacMillan, Elizabeth Arden, and Samuel Cunard dot the landscape of Canadian history. Most Canadian CEOs today see their role primarily as setting the strategic vision for the organization and then working with colleagues to guide and mentor them for success.[52] You can see this transformational leadership in all types of organizations, and at all levels of the enterprise. At the beginning of this chapter, we described how Rick George revived Suncor Energy. John Roth has transformed Nortel Networks into a leading developer of Internet gear. Moses Znaimer formed CITY-TV and led the expansion of emerging television programming. Jack Welch (GE), Richard Branson (Virgin), Anita Rodderick (The Body Shop), and other transformational leaders around the world have defined a vision for the organization, communicated that vision, and built employee commitment to it.

Dennis W. Bakke, CEO and co-founder of the global power company AES Corp., is continually looking for leaders who are both transformational and transactional. "We need people who can both lead and manage," says Bakke. "The traditional idea is that a manager takes what is there and makes certain it works well, while a leader takes a visionary look at what is already known to discover something new. But the world changes so much that you can no longer just manage 'what is there.' Leadership that doesn't consider practical execution is ridiculous. It's not either/or. It is much better to think about those two abilities together."[56] How can AES and other organizations ensure that people maintain a balance between transformational and transactional leadership? Or do you think that these roles should occur in different people?

TRANSFORMATIONAL VERSUS TRANSACTIONAL LEADERSHIP

Transformational leadership is different from **transactional leadership**. Transactional leadership is "managing"—helping organizations achieve their current objectives more efficiently, such as by linking job performance to valued rewards and ensuring that employees have the resources needed to get the job done.[53] The contingency and behavioural theories described earlier adopt the transactional perspective because they focus on leader behaviours that improve employee performance and satisfaction.

In contrast, transformational leadership is about "leading"—changing the organization's strategies and culture so that they have a better fit with the surrounding environment.[54] Transformational leaders are change agents who energize and direct employees to a new set of corporate values and behaviours. Rick George is like that. The opening story to this chapter described how George has transformed Suncor Energy into a more efficient company focused on niche markets, innovative production, and environmental sensitivity.

Should organizations have transactional or transformational leaders? The answer is that they need both. Transactional leadership improves organizational efficiency, whereas transformational leadership steers organizations onto a better course of action. Unfortunately, too many leaders get trapped in the daily managerial activities that represent transactional leadership.[55] They lose touch with the transformational aspect of effective leadership. Without transformational leaders, organizations stagnate and eventually become seriously misaligned with their environments.

www.aesc.com

Transactional leadership Leadership that helps organizations achieve their current objectives more efficiently by linking job performance to valued rewards and ensuring that employees have the resources needed to get the job done.

TRANSFORMATIONAL VERSUS CHARISMATIC LEADERSHIP

Another important distinction is between transformational and charismatic leadership. These concepts have generated some controversy and confusion among leadership experts.[57] A few writers use the words charismatic and transformational leadership interchangeably, as if they have the same meaning.[58] However, charismatic leadership differs from transformational leadership. As we learned in Chapter 12, *charisma* is a form of interpersonal attraction whereby followers develop a respect for and trust in the charismatic individual. Charismatic leadership therefore extends beyond behaviours to personal traits that provide referent power over followers.[59] Transformational leadership, on the other hand, is mainly about behaviours that people use to lead the change process. The remainder of this section will focus on transformational leadership because it offers more specific behavioural implications.

ELEMENTS OF TRANSFORMATIONAL LEADERSHIP

There are several descriptions of transformational leadership, but most include the four elements illustrated in Exhibit 14.5. These elements include creating a strategic vision, communicating the vision, modelling the vision, and building commitment towards the vision.

Creating a strategic vision

Transformational leaders are the brokers of dreams.[60] They shape a strategic vision of a realistic and attractive future that bonds employees together and focuses their energy towards a superordinate organizational goal.[61] Visions represent the substance of transformational leadership. They reflect a future for the company or work unit that is ultimately accepted and valued by organizational members. Notice that leadership vision is not a mission statement plastered on someone's wall. Rather it is part of the corporate meaning—the organization's goals and reason why it exists. Strategic visions might originate with the leader, but they are just as likely to emerge from employees, clients, suppliers, or other constituents. They typically begin as abstract ideas that become progressively clearer through critical events and discussions with staff about strategic and operational plans.[62]

There is some evidence that visions are the most important part of transformational leadership.[63] Visions offer the motivational benefits of goal setting, but they are more than mundane goals. Visions are compelling future states that bond employees and motivate them to strive for those objectives. Visions are typically described in a way that distinguishes them from the current situation, yet makes the goal both appealing and achievable.

Communicating the vision

If vision is the substance of transformational leadership, then communicating that vision is the process. Canadian CEOs say that the most important leadership qualities are being able to build and share their vision for the organization.[64] They communicate meaning and elevate the importance of the visionary goal to employees. They frame messages around a grand purpose with emotional appeal that captivates employees and other corporate stakeholders. Framing helps transformational leaders establish a common mental model so that the group or organization will act collectively towards the desirable goal.[65] For example, Home Depot co-founder Arthur Blank likes to remind employees that they are "in the business of making people's

EXHIBIT 14.5   Elements of Transformational Leadership

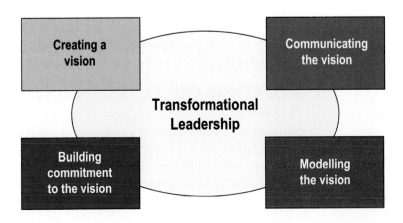

dreams come true."[66] Blank helps employees see their role towards customers in a different light, one that is much more meaningful and motivating than "selling hammers and nails."

Transformational leaders also bring their visions to life through symbols, metaphors, stories, and other vehicles that transcend plain language.[67] Metaphors borrow images of other experiences, thereby creating richer meaning of the vision that has not yet been experienced. When George Cohen, the ebullient CEO of McDonald's Canada, faced the difficult challenge of opening restaurants in Moscow, he frequently reminded his team members that they were establishing "hamburger diplomacy." And in the mid-1800s, when ocean transportation was treacherous, Samuel Cunard emphasized that he was creating an "ocean railway." At the time, railroads provided one of the safest forms of transportation, and Cunard's metaphor reinforced the notion to employees and passengers alike that Halifax-based Cunard Steamship Lines would provide equally safe transportation across the Atlantic Ocean.[68]

Modelling the vision

Transformational leaders not only talk about a vision; they enact it. They "walk the talk" by stepping outside the executive suite and doing things that symbolize the vision.[69] Moreover, transformational leaders are reliable and persistent in their actions. They stay on course, thereby legitimizing the vision and providing further evidence that they can be trusted. Leaders walk the talk through significant events, but they also alter mundane activities—meeting agendas, office locations, executive schedules—so they are consistent with the vision and its underlying values. "If you talk about speed in action, yet procrastinate on difficult decisions, you are not believable," warns Percy Barnevik, chairman of the Swiss/Swedish electrical conglomerate ABB. "I and the members of my executive committee must 'walk the talk' and live up to what we say."[70]

According to one survey, Canadian employees give executives low ratings in their ability to walk the talk.[71] This is unfortunate because employees and other stakeholders are executive watchers who look for behaviours to symbolize values and expectations. The greater the consistency between the leader's words and actions, the more employees will believe and follow the leader. Walking the talk also builds employee trust because trust is partly determined by the consistency of the person's actions.[72]

Building commitment towards the vision

Transforming a vision into reality requires employee commitment. Transformational leaders build this commitment in several ways. Their words, symbols, and stories build a contagious enthusiasm that energizes people to adopt the vision as their own. Leaders demonstrate a "can-do" attitude by enacting their vision and staying on course. Their persistence and consistency reflect an image of honesty, trust, and integrity. Finally, leaders build commitment by involving employees in the process of shaping the organization's vision. A ten-year study of Australian employees found that the organization's leadership and vision runs a close second to a staff member's own perception of his or her job role as the source of employee motivation.[73]

EVALUATING THE TRANSFORMATIONAL LEADERSHIP PERSPECTIVE

Transformational leaders do make a difference, according to organizational behaviour studies.[74] Subordinates are more satisfied and have higher affective organizational commitment under transformational leaders. They also perform their jobs better, engage in more organizational citizenship behaviours, and make better or more creative decisions. One study also reported that organizational commitment and financial performance seem to increase in branches of a Canadian bank where the branch manager completed a transformational leadership training program.[75]

Transformational leadership is currently the most popular leadership perspective, but it faces a number of challenges. One problem is that some transformational leadership writers define this concept in terms of the leader's success.[76] They suggest that leaders are transformational when they successfully bring about change, rather than when they engage in certain behaviours we call transformational. Another concern is that the transformational leadership model seems to be universal rather than contingency-oriented. Only very recently have writers begun to explore the idea that transformational leadership is more appropriate in some situations than others.[77] For instance, transformational leadership is probably more appropriate when organizations need to adapt than when environmental conditions are stable. Preliminary evidence suggests that the transformational leadership perspective is relevant across cultures. However, there may be specific elements of transformational leadership, such as the way visions are formed and communicated, that are more appropriate in North America than in other cultures.[78]

ROMANCE PERSPECTIVE OF LEADERSHIP

The trait, behaviour, contingency, and transformational leadership perspectives make the basic assumption that leaders "make a difference." Certainly, there is evidence that senior executives do influence organizational performance.[79] However, leaders might have less influence than most of us would like to believe. Some leadership experts suggest that three perceptual processes cause people to inflate the importance of leadership in explaining organizational events. These processes, collectively called the "romance of leadership," include attribution errors, stereotyping, and the need for situational control.[80]

ATTRIBUTING LEADERSHIP

Fundamental attribution error The tendency to attribute the behaviour of other people more to internal than external factors.

People have a strong need to attribute the causes of events around them so they can feel more confident about how to control them in the future. As we described in Chapter 6, the fundamental attribution error is a common perceptual bias in this attribution process. **Fundamental attribution error** is the tendency to attribute the behaviour of other people to their own motivation and ability rather than to situational contingencies. In the context of leadership, it causes employees to believe that organizational events are due more to the motivation and ability of their leaders than to environmental conditions. Leaders are given credit or blame for the company's success or failure because employees do not readily see the external forces that also influence these events. Leaders reinforce this belief by taking credit for organizational successes.[81]

STEREOTYPING LEADERSHIP

There is some evidence that people rely on leadership stereotypes to make sense of organizational events. Almost everyone has a set of shared expectations regarding what an effective leader should look and act like.[82] These preconceived ideas influence perceptions about whether someone is an effective leader. By relying on these stereotypes, employees and other stakeholders evaluate a leader's effectiveness more on his or her appearance and actions than on actual outcomes. This occurs partly because the outcome of a leader's actions may not be known for months or years. Consequently, employees depend on immediate information to decide whether the leader is effective. If the leader fits the mould, employees are more confident that the leader is effective.

NEED FOR SITUATIONAL CONTROL

A third perceptual distortion of leadership suggests that people want to believe that leaders make a difference. There are two basic reasons for this belief.[83] First, leadership is a useful way for us to simplify life events. It is easier to explain organizational successes and failures in terms of the leader's ability than to analyze a complex array of other forces. For example, there are usually many reasons why a company fails to change quickly enough in the marketplace, yet we tend to simplify this explanation to the notion that the company president or some other corporate leader was ineffective.

Second, there is a strong tendency in Canada and similar cultures to believe that life events are generated more from people than from uncontrollable natural forces.[84] Believing that events result from the rational actions of leaders satisfies this illusion of control. In short, employees feel better believing that leaders make a difference, so they actively look for evidence that this is so.

The romance of leadership perspective questions the importance of leadership, but it also provides valuable advice to improve leadership effectiveness. This approach highlights the fact that leadership is a perception of followers as much as the actual behaviours and characteristics of people calling themselves leaders. Potential leaders must be sensitive to this fact, understand what followers expect, and act accordingly. Individuals who do not make an effort to fit leadership prototypes will have more difficulty bringing about necessary organizational change.[85]

GENDER ISSUES IN LEADERSHIP

Do women lead differently than men? Most Canadian CEOs think so. A recent survey revealed that 76 percent of male and female chief executives believe that the leadership and management skills of women differ markedly from those of their male counterparts, with women generally seen as consensus builders better able to "nurture strong interpersonal relationships."[86]

Several writers also argue that women have an interactive style that includes more people-oriented and participative leadership.[87] They suggest that women are more relationship-oriented, cooperative, nurturing, and emotional in their leadership roles. They further assert that these qualities make women particularly well suited to leadership roles at a time when companies are adopting a stronger emphasis on teams and employee involvement. These arguments are consistent with sex role stereotypes; namely, that men tend to be more task-oriented whereas women are more people-oriented.

Are these stereotypes true? Do women adopt more people-oriented and participative leadership styles? The answer is no and yes, respectively. Leadership studies in field settings have generally found that male and female leaders do not differ in their levels of task-oriented or people-oriented leadership. The main explanation as to why men and women do not differ on these styles is that real-world jobs require similar behaviour from male and female job incumbents.[88]

However, women do adopt a participative leadership style more readily than their male counterparts. Scholars suggest that women are possibly more participative because their upbringing has made them more egalitarian and less status-oriented. There is also some evidence that women have somewhat better interpersonal skills than men, and that this translates into their relatively greater use of the participative leadership style. A third explanation is that subordinates expect female leaders to be more participative, based on their own sex stereotypes. If a female manager tries to be more autocratic, subordinates are more likely to complain (or use some other power base) because they expect the female executive or team leader to be participative.[89]

G. Domenico, *Ottawa Citizen.*

www.msdw.com

Kirsten Feldman has glowing words for everyone on her team who launched Martha Stewart's new company on the New York Stock Exchange. Everyone, that is, except herself. "We had a large team, all of whom are specialists in different aspects of an (initial stock) offering," says the Ottawa-born and -raised Feldman, who is a managing director at Morgan Stanley Dean Witter in Manhattan. "It's never one person and I wouldn't want to leave that impression." Feldman is known for her participative and people-oriented leadership style. Some people would say that Feldman and other female executives differ from male leaders in the traditionally macho investment industry. Others suggest that men and women adapt similar leadership styles in various situations.[90] In your opinion, do women generally prefer the same or different leadership styles than men?

A disturbing finding is that people evaluate female leaders slightly less favourably than equivalent male leaders, and that this difference is almost completely due to sex stereotype bias. Specifically, women are evaluated negatively when they adopt a stereotypically male leadership style (i.e., autocratic) and occupy traditionally male-dominated positions. Men tend to give female leaders lower ratings than do other women, and male subordinates have lower acceptance of female supervisors as role models.[91] These negative evaluations suggest that women "pay the price" for entering traditionally male leadership jobs and for adopting a male-stereotypic leadership style.[92] It also lends further support to our earlier point as to why women adopt a more participative style.

The debate regarding leadership differences between men and women isn't over yet. Meanwhile, we should be careful about perpetuating the apparently false assumptions that women leaders are less task-oriented or more people-oriented. By holding these assumptions, many corporate decision makers have shifted women into staff roles—such as human resources, public relations, and customer service—and out of line management jobs that most frequently lead to senior management positions.

Remember, too, that our implicit assumptions about how female leaders should act may lead to unfair negative evaluations of them under conditions in which the leader must adopt a stereotypically male style. This is consistent with our discussion in the previous section on the romance of leadership. Leaders must be sensitive to the fact that followers have expectations about how leaders should act, and that leaders who deviate from those expectations may receive negative evaluations.

CHAPTER SUMMARY

- Although leadership is difficult to define, it is often described as the process of influencing people and providing an environment for them to achieve team or organizational objectives. Leaders use power and persuasion to motivate followers, and arrange the work environment so that they do the job more effectively.

- The competency perspective tries to identify the characteristics of effective leaders. Recent writing suggests that leaders have drive, leadership motivation, integrity, self-confidence, above-average intelligence, knowledge of the business, and high emotional intelligence.

- The behavioural perspective of leadership identified two clusters of leader behaviour: people-oriented and task-oriented. People-oriented behaviours include showing mutual trust and respect for subordinates, demonstrating a genuine concern for their needs, and having a desire to look out for their welfare. Task-oriented behaviours include assigning employees to specific tasks, clarifying their work duties and procedures, ensuring that they follow company rules, and pushing them to reach their performance capacity. The "hi-hi" leadership hypothesis states that the most effective leaders exhibit high levels of both types of behaviours, but this hypothesis has since been cast into doubt.

- The contingency perspective of leadership takes the view that effective leaders diagnose the situation and adapt their style to fit that situation. The path-goal model is the prominent contingency theory that identifies four leadership styles—directive, supportive, participative, and achievement-oriented—and several contingencies relating to the characteristics of the employee and of the situation. A recent extension of path-goal theory adds more leader styles and moves the model from a dyadic to a team and organizational level.

- Two other contingency leadership theories include the situational leadership model and Fiedler's contingency theory. Research support is quite weak for both theories. However, a lasting element of Fiedler's theory is the idea that leaders have natural styles and, consequently, companies need to change the leaders' environment to suit their style. Leadership substitutes identify contingencies that either limit the leader's ability to influence subordinates or make that particular leadership style unnecessary. This idea will become more important as organizations remove supervisors and shift towards team-based structures.

- Transformational leaders create a strategic vision, communicate that vision through framing and use of metaphors, model the vision by "walking the talk" and acting consistently, and build commitment towards the vision. This contrasts with transactional leadership, which involves linking job performance to valued rewards and ensuring that employees have the resources needed to get the job done. The contingency and behavioural perspectives adopt the transactional view of leadership.

- According to the romance perspective, people inflate the importance of leadership through attribution, stereotyping, and fundamental needs for human control.

- Women generally do not differ from men in the degree of people-oriented or task-oriented leadership. However, female leaders more often adopt a participative style. Research also suggests that people evaluate female leaders slightly less favourably than equivalent male leaders, but this is mainly due to sex stereotype biases.

KEY TERMS

Competencies, p. 415

Emotional intelligence (EQ), p. 417

Fiedler's contingency model, p. 425

Fundamental attribution error, p. 431

"Hi-hi" leadership hypothesis, p. 420

Leadership, p. 414

Leadership Grid®, p. 420

Leadership substitutes, p. 426

Locus of control, p. 423

Path-goal leadership theory, p. 420

Self-leadership, p. 426

Self-monitoring, p. 417

Servant leadership, p. 421

Situational leadership model, p. 425

Transactional leadership, p. 428

Transformational leadership, p. 427

DISCUSSION QUESTIONS

1. Northern Lights Industrials Ltd. wants to select executives based on their leadership potential. Which leadership perspective mainly applies to this practice? Also, based on leadership research, identify four selection factors that Northern Lights will probably identify in effective executives.

2. Consider your favourite teacher. What people-oriented and task-oriented leadership behaviours did he or she use effectively? In general, do you think that students prefer an instructor who is more people-oriented or task-oriented? Explain your answer.

3. Your employees are skilled and experienced customer service representatives who perform nonroutine tasks, such as solving unique customer problems or special needs with the company's equipment. Use path-goal theory to identify the most appropriate leadership style(s) you should use in this situation. Be sure to fully explain your answer and discuss why other styles are inappropriate.

4. Discuss the accuracy of the following statement: "Contingency theories don't work because they assume leaders can adjust their style to the situation. In reality, people have a preferred leadership style that they can't easily change."

5. Is it possible to be a transformational leader and have poor communication skills? Why or why not?

6. Transformational leadership is currently the most popular perspective of leadership. However, it is far from perfect. Discuss three concerns with transformational leadership.

7. Identify a current political leader (e.g., prime minister, mayor of your city) and his or her recent accomplishments. Now, using the romance of leadership perspective, think of ways that the leader's accomplishments may be overstated. In other words, explain why they may be due to factors other than the leader.

8. You hear two people debating the merits of women as leaders. One person claims that women make better leaders than men because women are more sensitive to their employees' needs and involve them in organizational decisions. The other person counters that although these leadership styles may be increasingly important, most women have trouble gaining acceptance as leaders when they face tough situations in which a more autocratic style is required. Discuss the accuracy of these comments.

Case Study

ACTIVITY 14.1
Jeremiah Bigatallio's Leadership Challenge
by Alvin Turner, Brock University

Jeremiah Bigatallio was very eager to start his new job at InterContinental Communication, a high-tech company located near Toronto's Pearson International Airport. Bigatallio, a civil engineer, joined the organization because it was a relatively young, growing, and dynamic organization that claimed in a brochure five years ago that its work environment was modelled on Microsoft's. Bigatallio was hired as director of engineering services to supervise a staff of 25. The staff includes ten engineers, seven technicians, and eight lab assistants.

Bigatallio's predecessor was John Angle, who was fired for just cause. The official reason for his dismissal was not made public, but it is well known that he was having trouble managing his staff and interacting with other departments. First, most of the engineers did not get along with each other; some have not spoken for more than two years. Second, the technicians disliked the engineers because they were perceived to be arrogant prima donnas only concerned about themselves. The engineers did not have any respect for or confidence in the technicians. They felt that the technicians were a group of bungling incompetents who should all be sent back to trade school. Third, both of these teams were in almost complete harmony in their contempt for the lab assistants, all of whom they felt were lacking in initiative, vastly overpaid, vastly underqualified, and more concerned with abusing overtime privileges and being promoted than achieving and maintaining minimum productivity standards.

Other line and staff department heads were very upset with John Angle. The head of corporate financial control was dissatisfied with him because Angle's department was constantly over budget allocations, particularly because of the excessive amount of overtime worked by his staff. He did not keep good records and did not submit accounting information on time. A recent audit revealed major financial irregularities of more than $300,000 in salaries. And there are also concerns about potential misappropriation of $250,000 of a Human Resources Development Canada jobs grant program. People in other departments (research and development, manufacturing, quality assurance) were very displeased with Angle because the internecine warfare ongoing in his department made it difficult to work with anyone in engineering. This lack of communication and the frequent substandard lathes, dies, and design surveys resulted in backlogged work and unnecessary overtime expenses. And when communication did occur, the engineering unit's performance was generally unreliable.

John Angle believed in self-directing and autonomous work teams. Consequently, he believed in empowering his subordinates to make decisions and feel responsible for the successes of the department as well as their own successes. Angle provided little or no direction or support for his subordinates. He did not articulate his vision, leadership style, or expectations. He felt that his subordinates are highly trained professionals who should know what is expected of them and should be "willing to do the right thing." He also felt that by self-regulating and solving their own problems as they arise, employees would learn from their mistakes. Angle saw this as the best way for employees to grow and develop on the job and for the organization to realize maximum output from workers.

John Angle viewed himself as a progressive, liberal thinker whose new-age leadership style would transform and motivate employees to achieve great things. He believed that sharing power would enhance employees' self-worth and energize them. He also believed in maintaining a convivial work atmosphere. Thus, absenteeism and lateness were overlooked. Angle was also fairly lax in enforcing work rules and work productivity standards. As a result, employees took advantage of the situation and worked at their leisure; in addition, they were frequently late or absent and mismanaged other aspects of their work schedules. They also took frequent cof-

ACTIVITY 14.1 CONTINUED

fee breaks and tended to work substantially higher amounts of overtime relative to other employees in the organization.

When Bigatallio was hired, he was told that he had the full confidence of the CEO and the vice-presidents to clean up the mess in the engineering department. He was given four months to fix all existing problems in the department.

On his first day on the job, Bigatallio typed on his laptop: "What type of leadership style should I use on this diverse team of individuals?" Then he stopped to retrieve a note from his pocket that he had found under his door that morning. It said: "Try

changing our overtime around here and we will cut you down to size!"

Discussion Questions

1. In what way was John Angle's leadership style ineffective?

2. Use the path-goal leadership model to identify the best leadership style(s) for Jeremiah Bigatallio.

3. What other type of leadership style could Jeremiah use to lead his staff? Explain why you believe the style you have selected will be effective in resolving the inter- and intra-department conflicts.

 Video Case Study

ACTIVITY 14.2

Lou Gerstner's Leadership at IBM

Effective leadership is a key ingredient for the success of any organization. Leading involves creating a vision and guiding employees to achieve goals. As competition accelerates, one of these goals inevitably involves a belief in the culture of service. Corporate leaders must inspire employees to make customer satisfaction a priority.

Effective leadership can raise a company from a state of decline to one of vitality. And few companies have had a more dramatic corporate resurrection than has computer giant IBM. When Lou Gerstner was called in to heal IBM, the patient was failing fast. Now IBM—also known as Big Blue—is healthy again.

Turning around a corporation the size of IBM meant Gerstner had to create a new vision for the computer giant's future. But he also knew that more than vision was needed to get the job done. Walter Scott, professor at the J.L. Kellogg Graduate School of Management, Northwestern University, said "When Gerstner came in, he disclaimed the need for

vision in the company, but clearly he had to be generating a strong sense of purpose within the organization. And that purpose had to be something that they would execute. He had to change the whole atmosphere in the organization to have people executing against customer needs, which they certainly had forgotten how to do over a period of time."

Gerstner's approach was based on his attention to the four management functions. When Gerstner first arrived he assessed his existing staff and made a number of changes. He knew the key to success was in forming the right management team. Hiring bright, talented people became his first priority. Several key positions once held by insiders now went to persons from outside the computer industry, bringing new perspectives to a corporation, which had become bogged down by outdated ways of doing business. In many cases, these new executives had worked with Gerstner at other companies. The IBM chief was able to rely on them to take control of their own areas.

Gerstner came to IBM with a history of guiding and motivating employees to work effectively.

ACTIVITY 14.2 CONTINUED

Hiring outside the company carries risk. Employee morale can be weakened if insiders believe that only outsiders will get decision-making positions. As a leader, Gerstner understood this. He also knew that outsiders would bring fresh perspectives to a company that had become stagnant. He was able to overcome the morale issue by creating an open atmosphere of communication among all his employees. Opinions were requested and responded to—often over the IBM corporate Intranet system.

Gerstner also needed to create a new culture of service at IBM. This meant that he had to set up new goals for the company that were responsive to the needs of consumers. IBM had lost touch with its customers. To get back their business, the company had to devise better lines of communication with them. Among Gerstner's first moves was to push IBM feet first into the fledgling Intranet industry. The Intranet is an in-house information system designed to move information and communication rapidly throughout the workplace. Before Gerstner's arrival, IBM would have created the hardware for this system, but would not have provided support. Now, by installing the hardware along with the customized business solutions, IBM is improving relations with its customers. And IBM service and consulting contracts keep the company involved with the customer long after the system is in place.

Throughout his tenure Gerstner has always provided sound fiscal supervision, something that was desperately needed. When he arrived at IBM, Gerstner was faced with a difficult financial question. How could a company with $60 billion in annual revenues be operating in the red? The answer was painfully simple—IBM was bloated. The company was top heavy with management and its expenses were out of control. Gerstner, working with chief financial officer Jerry York, set out on an ambitious cost-cutting program. By tightening expenses, dropping unprofitable lines, and cutting back on employees, the two were able to trim the annual budget by nearly $6 billion within 3 years. By 1996 Big Blue was reporting a profit for the first time in three years.

Many people credit Lou Gerstner as the person who led IBM's dramatic turnaround. The once arrogant Big Blue is now a leader in customer service as well as hardware manufacturing.

Discussion Questions

1. To what extent is Lou Gerstner a transformational leader? Provide evidence that he applies the four elements of transformational leadership.

2. What competencies of effective leaders does Lou Gerstner seem to possess? What evidence do you see of these competencies?

Source: McGraw-Hill/Irwin Management Video Series.

ACTIVITY 14.3
LEADERSHIP DIAGNOSTIC ANALYSIS

Purpose: To help students learn about the different path-goal leadership styles and when to apply each style.

Instructions:

Step 1: Students individually write down two incidents in which someone had been an effective manager or leader for them. The leader and situation might be from a work experience, a sports team, a student work group, or any other setting where leadership might emerge. For example, students might describe how their supervisor in a summer job pushed them to reach higher performance goals than they would have done otherwise. Each incident should state the actual behaviours that the leader used, not just general statements (e.g., "My boss sat down with me and we agreed on specific targets and deadlines, then he said several times over the next few weeks that I was capable of reaching those goals.") Each incident only requires two or three sentences.

Step 2: After everyone has written down their two incidents, the instructor will form small groups (typically between four and five students). Each team will address the following for each incident presented to that team:

1. Identify which path-goal theory leadership style(s)—directive, supportive, participative, or achievement-oriented—the leader applied in the incident.

2. Ask the person who wrote the incident about the conditions that made this leadership style (or these styles, if more than one was used) appropriate in this situation. The team should list these contingency factors clearly and, where possible, connect them to the contingencies described in the path-goal theory. (Note: the team might identify path-goal leadership contingencies that are not described in the book. These, too, should be noted and discussed.)

Step 3: After the teams have diagnosed the incidents, each team will describe to the entire class the most interesting incident as well as its diagnosis of that incident. Other teams will critique the diagnosis. Any leadership contingencies not mentioned in the textbook should also be presented and discussed.

ACTIVITY 14.4
SELECTING THE BEST LEADER

by Robert Cunningham, University of Tennessee

Purpose: To help students understand the competency (trait) and romance perspectives in leadership.

Instructions: You are on a task force responsible for selecting a new chief executive officer for your organization. The instructor may provide more details about the type of organization (e.g., large private-sector firm, manager of a suburban city).

Step 1: The instructor will place students in teams, preferably of between five and eight people. Each team will have an opportunity to meet one of the candidates, identify the candidate's observable characteristics, and evaluate the candidate's leadership qualities (both positive and negative) based on these characteristics. Each team member should have an opportunity to personally touch and inspect the candidate. The team will document the characteristics and leadership qualities identified for other teams to view later (e.g., overhead transparency, flip chart).

Step 2: Each team will report to the class on the characteristics and leadership qualities as well as the appropriateness of the candidate it evaluated for the position.

Step 3: Students will discuss the assessments of each candidate and try to reach agreement on the best candidate. If time does not permit this extended discussion, or if the class cannot reach consensus, the instructor may call for a vote on the best candidate.

Source: Adapted from R. Cunningham, "Meet Dr. Clay and Dr. Glass: A Leadership Exercise," *Journal of Management Education*, 21 (May 1997), pp. 262–64.

ACTIVITY 14.5
LEADERSHIP DIMENSIONS INSTRUMENT

Purpose: This self-assessment exercise is designed to help you understand two important dimensions of leadership and to identify which of these dimensions is more prominent in your supervisor, team leader, coach, or other person to whom you are accountable.

Instructions: Read each of the statements below and circle the response that you believe best describes your supervisor. You may substitute "supervisor" with anyone else to whom you are accountable, such as a team leader, CEO, course instructor, or sports coach. Then use the scoring key in Appendix B of this book to calculate the results for each leadership dimensions. After completing this assessment, be prepared to discuss in class the distinctions between these leadership dimensions.

My supervisor...	Strongly Agree	Agree	Neutral	Disagree	Strongly Disagree
1. Focuses attention on irregularities, mistakes, exceptions, and deviations from what is expected of me.	5	4	3	2	1
2. Engages in words and deeds that enhance his/her image of competence.	5	4	3	2	1
3. Monitors performance for errors needing correction.	5	4	3	2	1
4. Serves as a role model for me.	5	4	3	2	1
5. Points out what I will receive if I do what is required.	5	4	3	2	1
6. Instills pride in being associated with him/her.	5	4	3	2	1
7. Keeps careful track of mistakes.	5	4	3	2	1
8. Can be trusted to help me overcome any obstacle.	5	4	3	2	1
9. Tells me what to do to be rewarded for my efforts.	5	4	3	2	1
10. Makes me aware of strongly held values, ideals, and aspirations that are shared.	5	4	3	2	1
11. Is alert to failure to meet standards.	5	4	3	2	1
12. Mobilizes a collective sense of mission.	5	4	3	2	1
13. Works out agreements with me on what I will receive if I do what needs to be done.	5	4	3	2	1
14. Articulates a vision of future opportunities. . . .	5	4	3	2	1
15. Talks about special rewards for good work. . . .	5	4	3	2	1
16. Talks optimistically about the future.	5	4	3	2	1

Source: Items and dimensions are adapted from D.N. Den Hartog, J.J. Van Muijen, and P.L. Koopman, "Transactional Versus Transformational Leadership: An Analysis of the MLQ," *Journal of Occupational & Organizational Psychology,* 70 (March 1997), pp. 19–34. Den Hartog et al. label transactional leadership as "rational-objective leadership" and label transformational leadership as "inspirational leadership." Many of their items may have originated from B.M. Bass and B.J. Avolio, *Manual for the Multifactor Leadership Questionnaire* (Palo Alto, CA: Consulting Psychologists Press, 1989).

CHAPTER FIFTEEN

Organizational Change and Development

LEARNING OBJECTIVES

After reading this chapter, you should be able to:

- Identify four forces for change in the business environment.
- Describe the elements of Lewin's force field analysis model.
- Outline six reasons why people resist organizational change.
- Discuss six strategies to minimize resistance to change.
- Outline the role of change agents.
- Define organization development.
- Discuss three things consultants need to determine in a client relationship.
- Explain how appreciative inquiry differs from the more traditional approach to organization development.
- Discuss four ethical issues in organization development.

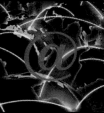

Celestica Inc. relied on a strategic vision and high-involvement change management processes to become one of Canada's largest high-technology manufacturers.

E mployees at Celestica Inc. have experienced a lifetime of change over the past five years. The Toronto-based company has been transformed from an IBM subsidiary with 2500 employees into a leading high-technology manufacturer with approximately 23,000 employees at 34 sites around the world.

Celestica was acquired by an investor group led by Onex Corporation and Celestica management from IBM in October 1996. Since that time, Celestica has undergone a dramatic transformation. It has significantly expanded its global presence, broadened its manufacturing and service capabilities, and become more customer focused.

Celestica's profitability and past reliance on IBM made it more difficult to create urgency for change. To overcome this, Celestica's executives and employees created a values statement that highlighted people, partnerships, customer service, and quality. These core values became the springboard for the company's transformation.

Next, Celestica's leaders applied a high-involvement change process to build commitment to the transformation. A steering team with senior management representation from all functions guided the change process; a central design team maintained consistency and dissemination across the sites; and members of a resources team served as facilitators and internal consultants.

Nearly two dozen design teams represented the heart of the change initiative. These teams targeted specific change initiatives by diagnosing Celestica's work processes against the company's critical success factors. Numerous study teams then developed recommendations and implementation strategies in the areas that required change.

Celestica's change strategy produced dramatic results. The company quickly introduced self-directed work teams in the process, significantly improved efficiency in various support services, and developed a corporate culture focused more clearly around customer needs.[1]

Change is difficult enough in small firms. At Celestica and other large organizations, it requires monumental effort and persistence. Organizational change is also very messy. Celestica's change process looks like a well-executed strategy, but all organizational transformations are buffeted by uncertain consequences, organizational politics, and various forms of employee resistance. It's little wonder that only 20 percent of Canadian employees believe that their organizations are very good at managing organizational change. Moreover, only 5 percent of executives at large Canadian companies claim they have an excellent ability to manage large change projects.[2]

This chapter examines ways to bring about meaningful change in organizations. After considering some of the more significant forces for organizational change, we introduce Lewin's model of change and its component parts. This includes sources of resistance to change, ways to minimize this resistance, and stabilizing desired behaviours. The latter part of this chapter introduces the field of organization development (OD). In particular, we review the OD process, emerging OD processes, and issues relating to OD effectiveness.

EXTERNAL FORCES FOR CHANGE

Today's business environment is changing so rapidly that it leaves anyone breathless. "The velocity of change is so rapid, so quick, that if you don't accept the change and move with the change, you're going to be left behind," says Ford CEO Jacques Nasser.[3] The speed of change is so dramatic that many of Canada's highest-valued companies today—such as JDS Uniphase, Celestica, and PMC-Sierra—didn't exist 20 years ago. Others, such as Nortel Networks, 360networks, and Chapters, have dramatically transformed their businesses over

Courtesy of the National Board of Antiquities, Finland.

www.nokia.com

Nokia is a classic example of how companies survive and remain competitive by adapting to environmental changes. The Finnish conglomerate started in 1865 as a pulp and paper company in a mill town near Helsinki (see photo, taken around 1890). The company bought into the rubber business 30 years later and into cable wiring in the 1920s. Many Finns still associate Nokia with the rubber snow boots they wore as children. In the 1960s, Nokia invested in electronics and was soon making televisions and computer monitors. In the 1980s, Nokia executives sensed an emerging market for mobile telecommunications and took enormous risks by investing in that environmental shift. Today, people around the world know of Nokia because of its sleek cellular telephones.[4] What factors do you think helped Nokia executives anticipate new opportunities and change the organization to realize those opportunities?

the past few years. And unless these firms anticipate and adapt to continual change, few of them will be around 20 years from now. As open systems (see Chapter 1), successful organizations monitor their environments and take appropriate steps to maintain a compatible fit with the new external conditions. This adaptability requires continual change. It is an ongoing process because environmental change does not end.

There are many forces for change in the external environment, but the prominent forces are information technology, globalization, competition, and demographics. Not surprisingly, most of these are emerging organizational behaviour issues that we discussed in the opening chapter of this book.

INFORMATION TECHNOLOGY

The system of networks that connect computers throughout the planet has become a major driver of rapid environmental change.[5] Chapters Online, TD Waterhouse, and other Canadian firms are leveraging the power of the Internet to offer a variety of electronic commerce experiences. Intranets have also made it easy and inexpensive to transfer information throughout an organization.[6] Suppliers are hooked up to computer-based networks (called *extranets*) to accelerate just-in-time management deliveries. Major clients are also hooked up to the organization's product database for direct ordering and delivery.[7]

Information technology does more than open up business opportunities. It forces corporate leaders to rethink how their organizations are configured, as well as what competencies and expectations employees must have in these emerging organizational forms.[8] Information technology creates new structures that allow companies to compete globally through network alliances (see Chapter 16). It facilitates telecommuting and opens up new employment relationships with employees. It places more emphasis on knowledge management rather than on physical presence and manufacturing capacity as a driver of competitive advantage.

GLOBAL AND LOCAL COMPETITION

Increasing global and local competition are also powerful forces for organizational change.[9] Competitors are just as likely to be located in a distant part of the world than within a company's own country. Emerging trading blocs in North America, Europe, Asia-Pacific, and other areas add another dimension to these competitive forces. Technology has played a role in increasing global and local competition. A few years ago, no one would have guessed that Telus Corp. would be competing with Bell Canada in Ontario, or that Chapters would be competing with an online book store from Seattle called Amazon.com.

Energy companies in some Canadian provinces now compete where they previously held monopolies. Post offices in Australia and the United Kingdom have also been forced to reinvent themselves as their governments open up some mail services to the private sector. Government-owned telephone companies in Singapore, Canada, and other countries have been transformed into private (or semi-private) enterprises.[10]

Global and domestic competition often leads to corporate restructuring. To increase their competitiveness, companies reduce layers of management, sell entire divisions of employees, and reduce payroll through downsizing. Chapters laid off staff and closed down unprofitable stores when it took over Coles and SmithBooks. Corel Corp., Canada's major banks, *Toronto Sun*, and many other firms have laid off thousands of employees due to increased competition and other pressures to increase efficiency. A recent survey found that fully one-third of Canadians worked for companies that had restructured over the previous year.[11]

In less than a decade, CEO Larry Stevenson has built Chapters into Canada's largest bricks-and-mortar book retailer. He began by acquiring Coles and SmithBooks, then closed unprofitable stores and opened dozens of big-box outlets across the country. These competitive tactics catapulted Chapters to one-third market share and raised complaints from small independent book stores. But a new level of competition emerged when Seattle-based Amazon.com started selling books to Canadians through its Web site. Chapters responded by introducing Chapters Online in 1999 and, within one year, became Canada's preferred online bookseller. "If you don't change, you're in trouble," warns Stevenson.[13] What changes do you think Chapters employees have experienced from this local and global competition?

www.chapters.ca

Global competition has also fuelled an unprecedented number of mergers and acquisitions in recent years. Seagram Co., Canada's venerable liquor company, acquired Universal Studios and other entertainment companies, then was acquired by French-based Vivendi. Daimler-Benz merged with Chrysler, which then bought Western Star, a large Canadian truck manufacturer. Quebecor has become the world's largest printing firm by acquiring dozens of companies over the past decade.[12] These and other mergers potentially improve a company's competitive advantage through greater efficiency and global reach, but they also result in significant disruptions and changes in employment relationships and the way people work.

DEMOGRAPHY

While firms adjust to global competition, they are also adapting to changes in the workforce. Employees are more educated and, consequently, expect more involvement and interesting work. Generation-X employees are less intimidated by management directives and they work to live more than they live to work. In Japan, corporate leaders must adjust to a younger workforce that is more individualistic. In Singapore, which traditionally has a high power distance (respect for authority), young employees are increasingly willing to question and debate executive decisions. Meanwhile, in many parts of the world, companies employ a far more diverse workforce than they did a few decades ago (see Chapter 1). These changes have put pressure on organizational leaders to alter work practices, develop more compatible structures and rewards, and discover new ways to lead.

LEWIN'S FORCE FIELD ANALYSIS MODEL

It is easy to see that these environmental forces push companies to change the way they operate. What is more difficult to see is the complex interplay of these forces against other organizational dynamics. Psychologist Kurt Lewin developed the force field analysis model to help us understand how the change process works (see Exhibit 15.1).[14] Although developed more than 50 years ago, Lewin's **force field analysis** model remains the prominent way to view this process.

> **Force field analysis** A model that helps change agents diagnose the forces that drive and restrain proposed organizational change.

One side of the force field model represents the *driving forces* that push organizations towards a new state of affairs. We began this chapter by describing four driving forces in the external environment: computer technology, globalization, competition, and demographics. Along with these external forces are driving forces that seem to originate from within the organization, such as competition across divisions of the company and the leader's need to make his or her mark on the organization.

The other side of Lewin's model represents the *restraining forces* that maintain the status quo. These restraining forces are commonly called "resistance to change" because they appear

EXHIBIT 15.1   Lewin's Force Field Analysis Model

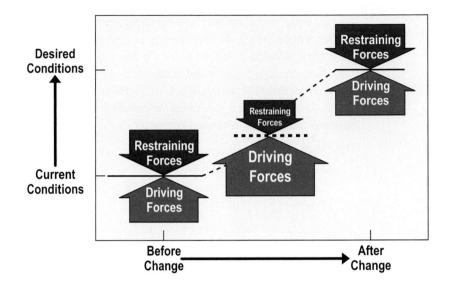

as employee behaviours that block the change process. Stability occurs when the driving and restraining forces are roughly in equilibrium, that is, when they are of approximately equal strength in opposite directions.

Lewin's force field model emphasizes that effective change occurs by **unfreezing** the current situation, moving to a desired condition, and then **refreezing** the system so that it remains in this desired state. Unfreezing involves producing a disequilibrium between the driving and restraining forces. As we will describe later, this may occur by increasing the driving forces, reducing the restraining forces, or a combination of both. Refreezing occurs when the organization's systems and structures are aligned with the desired behaviours. They must support and reinforce the new role patterns and prevent the organization from slipping back into the old way of doing things. This stabilization does not occur automatically; rather, organizational leaders must continuously restabilize the desired behaviours. Over the next few pages, we use Lewin's model to understand why change is blocked and how the process can evolve more smoothly.

Unfreezing The first part of the change process whereby the change agent produces a disequilibrium between the driving and restraining forces.

Refreezing The latter part of the change process in which systems and conditions are introduced that reinforce and maintain the desired behaviours.

RESTRAINING FORCES

When BP Norge introduced self-directed work teams (SDWTs) on its North Sea drilling rigs, the Norwegian subsidiary of British Petroleum faced more resistance from employees than from the infamous North Sea weather. Many skeptical employees claimed that previous attempts to create SDWTs didn't work. Others were convinced that they already had SDWTs, so why change anything? Several people complained that SDWTs required more responsibility, so they wanted more status and pay. Still others were worried that they lacked the skills to operate in SDWTs. Some BP Norge supervisors were slow to embrace SDWTs because they didn't want to give away their cherished power.[15]

BP Norge employees aren't the only people to block the organizational change process.[16] According to one recent survey, 43 percent of U.S. executives identify employee resistance as the main reason why their organization is not more productive.[17] This resistance takes many forms, including passive noncompliance, complaints, absenteeism, turnover, and collective action (e.g., strikes, walkouts).

However, some organizational behaviour scholars suggest that employee "resistance" represents symptoms of underlying restraining forces that need to be removed.[18] Some employees are worried about the *consequences* of change, such as that the new conditions will take away their power and status. Others are concerned about the *process* of change itself, such as the effort required to break old habits and learn new skills. The main reasons why people create obstacles to change are shown in Exhibit 15.2 and described below. They include direct costs, saving face, fear of the unknown, breaking routines, incongruent organizational systems, and incongruent team dynamics:[19]

- *Direct costs*—People tend to block actions that result in higher direct costs or lower benefits than the existing situation provides. For instance, supervisors at BP Norge resisted self-directed work teams because they believed they would lose power as the change process empowered employees.

- *Saving face*—Some people resist change as a political strategy to "prove" that the decision is wrong or that the person encouraging change is incompetent. For example, senior executives in a manufacturing firm bought a computer other than the system recommended by the information systems department. Soon after the system was in place, several information systems employees let minor implementation problems escalate to demonstrate that senior management had made a poor decision.

- *Fear of the unknown*—People resist change because they are worried that they cannot adopt the new behaviours. This fear of the unknown increases the *risk* of personal loss. This happened at a company where the owner wanted sales staff to telephone rather than personally visit prospective customers. These employees had little experience in telephone sales, so they argued against telephone calls. Some didn't even show up for the training program that taught them how to make telephone sales. "The salespeople were

EXHIBIT 15.2 Forces Resisting Organizational Change

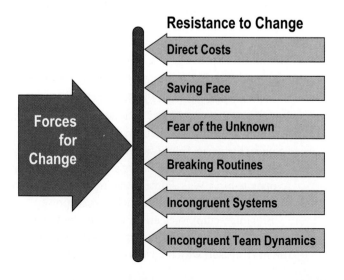

afraid of failing," explained the owner. "Each of them was very successful in the field, but they had never been exposed to a formalized telephone lead development program."[20]

- *Breaking routines*—Chapter 1 described how organizations need to unlearn, not just learn.[21] This means that employees need to abandon the behavioural routines that are no longer appropriate. Unfortunately, people are creatures of habit. They like to stay within their comfort zones by continuing routine role patterns that make life predictable.[22] Consequently, many people resist organizational changes that force employees out of their comfort zones and require time and energy to learn new role patterns.

- *Incongruent organizational systems*—Rewards, selection, training, and other control systems ensure that employees maintain desired role patterns. Yet the organizational systems that maintain stability also discourage employees from adopting new ways.[23] The implication, of course, is that organizational systems must be altered to fit the desired change. Unfortunately, control systems can be difficult to change, particularly when they have supported role patterns that worked well in the past.[24]

- *Incongruent team dynamics*—Teams develop and enforce conformity to a set of norms that guide behaviour (see Chapter 9). However, conformity to existing team norms may discourage employees from accepting organizational change. Team norms that conflict with the desired changes need to be altered.

UNFREEZING, CHANGING, AND REFREEZING

According to Lewin's force field analysis model, effective change occurs by unfreezing the current situation, moving to a desired condition, and then refreezing the system so that it remains in this desired state. Unfreezing occurs when the driving forces are stronger than the restraining forces. This involves making the driving forces stronger, weakening or removing the restraining forces, or a combination of both. With respect to the first option, driving forces must certainly increase enough to motivate change. However, change rarely occurs by increasing driving forces alone because the restraining forces often adjust to counterbalance the driving forces. It is rather like the coils of a mattress. The harder corporate leaders push for change, the stronger the restraining forces push back. This antagonism threatens the change effort by producing tension and conflict within the organization.

The preferred option is to both increase the driving forces and reduce or remove the restraining forces. Increasing the driving forces creates an urgency for change, whereas reducing the restraining forces minimizes resistance to change.

CREATING AN URGENCY FOR CHANGE

Driving forces represent the booster rockets that push employees out of their comfort zones. They energize people to face the risks that change presents to them. Driving forces must be real, not contrived; otherwise, employees will doubt the change agent's integrity. Some threats are well known to employees. For example, employees at Nortel Networks are always aware of the competitive pressures from Cisco Systems. Celestica employees are motivated to continually improve efficiency and customer service because clients can switch to Solectron Corp. and other manufacturers.

However, many driving forces are unknown to employees below the top ranks of the organization. Thus, the change process must begin by informing employees about competitors, changing consumer trends, impending government regulations, and other driving forces.[25] As described in the opening story to this chapter, Celestica employees developed a stronger urgency to change through a high-involvement strategy of developing a set of critical success factors and then discovering how many parts of the organization fell short of those ideals.

Customer driven change

Another powerful driver of change is customer expectations.[26] Dissatisfied customers represent a compelling force for change because of the adverse consequences for the organization's survival and success. Customers also provide a human element that further energizes employees to change current behaviour patterns. Executives at Continental Airlines took on the painful task of listening to customer complaints, then communicated these concerns to employees. Al Galdi, CEO of architectural design firm ARCNET, relied on customer-driven change by having employees listen to a voice mail message from an angry customer. "I played it to the entire staff. It's not something for me to fix, it's something for all of us to fix," he says.[27]

Joel Kocher, CEO of Micron Electronics, also engaged in customer-driven change in his previous job as an executive with Power Computing. At a large employee meeting, Kocher read an angry customer letter. Then, to everyone's surprise, he brought the customer who wrote the letter into the meeting. "We actually brought the customer to the meeting, to personalize it for every single person in the room," says Kocher. "And it was very, very interesting to see the metamorphosis that occurred within the context of these several hundred people when you actually had a customer talking about how their foul-up had hurt this person and hurt their business."[28]

REDUCING THE RESTRAINING FORCES

Effective change involves more than making employees aware of the driving forces. It also involves reducing or removing the restraining forces. Exhibit 15.3 identifies six ways to overcome employee resistance. Communication, training, employee involvement, and stress management try to reduce the restraining forces and, if feasible, should be attempted first.[29] However, negotiation and coercion are necessary for people who will clearly lose something from the change and when the speed of change is critical.

Communication

Hydro-Québec restructured from 40 different geographical units to just 3 operations with 20 percent fewer employees. No one was forced out or fired, but employees were understandably concerned about how and where they would fit into the restructured organization. "One of the biggest challenges was making sure that all our employees would understand the new organization in which they were to function," says Roger Lanoue, Hydro-Québec's director of strategic planning. "It took a lot of communication."[30]

Communication is the highest priority and first strategy required for any organizational change. It reduces the restraining forces by keeping employees informed about what to expect from the change effort. Although time-consuming and costly, communication can potentially reduce fear of the unknown and develop team norms that are more consistent with the change effort. "Change takes time and we need to do hearing and some listening so people understand why it is so important," says Gay Mitchell, an executive vice-president at Royal Bank of Canada.[31]

Training

Training is an important process in most change initiatives because employees need to learn new knowledge and skills. When a company introduces a new sales database, for instance,

EXHIBIT 15.3 Methods for Dealing with Resistance to Change

Strategy	Example	When Used	Problems
Communication	Customer complaint letters shown to employees.	When employees don't feel urgency for change, or don't know how the change will affect them.	Time-consuming and potentially costly.
Training	Employees learn how to work in teams as company adopts a team-based structure.	When employees need to break old routines and adopt new role patterns.	Time-consuming and potentially costly.
Employee Involvement	Company forms task force to recommend new customer service practices.	When the change effort needs more employee commitment, some employees need to save face, and/or employee ideas would improve decisions about the change strategy.	Very time-consuming. Might also lead to conflict and poor decisions if employees' interests are incompatible with organizational needs.
Stress Management	Employees attend sessions to discuss their worries about the change.	When communication, training, and involvement do not sufficiently ease employee worries.	Time-consuming and potentially expensive. Some methods may not reduce stress for all employees.
Negotiation	Employees agree to replace strict job categories with multi-skilling in return for increased job security.	When employees will clearly lose something of value from the change and would not otherwise support the new conditions. Also necessary when the company must change quickly.	May be expensive, particularly if other employees want to negotiate their support. Also tends to produce compliance but not commitment to the change.
Coercion	Company president tells managers to "get on board" with the change or leave.	When other strategies are ineffective and the company needs to change quickly.	Can lead to more subtle forms of resistance, as well as long-term antagonism with the change agent.

Sources: Adapted from J.P. Kotter and L.A. Schlesinger, "Choosing Strategies for Change," *Harvard Business Review,* 57 (1979), pp. 106–14; P.R. Lawrence, "How to Deal with Resistance to Change," *Harvard Business Review* (May–June 1954), pp. 49–57.

representatives need to learn how to adapt their previous behaviour patterns to benefit from the new system. Training is time-consuming, but it helps employees break routines by learning new role patterns. Some training programs, such as action learning projects (see Chapter 2), can also minimize employee resistance caused by saving face. This occurs because employees are actively involved in the change process as they learn about the organization's opportunities. Connections 15.1 describes how Ford CEO Jacques Nasser is applying training as a central feature of his transformation of the auto manufacturer. Notice how Nasser's "teachable point of view" also creates an urgency to change.

CONNECTIONS 15.1

www.ford.com

Teaching Change at Ford Motor Company

Jacques Nasser is transforming Ford Motor Company into a more nimble organization focused on shareholder value. "I am an agent of change," says the Lebanese-born Australian, who recently became Ford's CEO in Detroit. "I don't believe in stagnation."

Nasser believes that lasting change comes through the "teachable point of view." This means that employees change their perceptions and behaviours through active learning. Nasser began this process by personally teaching Ford's 55,000 salaried employees in offices and factories around the world. At each session, he explained about cutting costs, adding shareholder value, and becoming a more entrepreneurial organization.

Ford's middle managers experience the teachable point of view through an action learning program called Capstone. Global teams of six mid-level Ford executives are formed and given six months to tackle a strategic challenge, such as how to change Ford's distribution system in the Internet era. The projects take about 30 percent of each participant's time and each team is assigned a mentor from Nasser's senior executive group.

CEO Jacques Nasser takes a "teachable point of view" to transforming Ford Motor Company into a more nimble organization.

R. Cook. Used with permission of Reuters.

Capstone begins with an intensive five-day workshop in which Nasser and his senior executive group share their teachable point of view with the action learning teams. The teams also experience team-building exercises, 360-degree feedback sessions, and plenty of coaching and debate regarding their project. At the end of six months, team members present their findings and receive feedback from Nasser, his senior executive group, and fellow participants.

"We have to change our DNA," say Nasser. "And teaching does that better than any other way I know."

Sources: K.H. Hammonds, "Grassroots Leadership—Ford Motor Company," *Fast Company*, April 2000, p. 138; S. Wetlaufer, "Driving Change: An Interview with Ford Motor Company's Jacques Nasser," *Harvard Business Review*, 77 (March–April 1999), pp. 76–88.

Employee involvement

The opening story to this chapter described how Celestica executives brought about meaningful change by involving employees in the process of determining the company's values and then using those objectives to improve its effectiveness. Employee involvement can be an effective way to reduce the restraining forces because it creates a psychological ownership of the decision (see Chapter 10). Rather than viewing themselves as agents of someone else's decision, staff members feel personally responsible for its success. Employee involvement also minimizes resistance to change by reducing problems of saving face and fear of the unknown.[32]

Bell Canada improved customer satisfaction and sales performance at its Consumer Answer Centre by involving employees in the change process. An investigative team of employees surveyed customers and visited call centres in several industries to find out how to change Bell Canada's centre. "One of the most important lessons we learned was about involvement," concludes Bell Canada's regional manager who oversaw the change. "Gaining the commitment of an employee's hands and head can be ineffective unless the heart is also involved."[33]

It's fairly easy to involve everyone where the change process occurs in small work units. But how do you apply employee involvement when there are thousands of employees? The answer is to involve as many people as possible through **search conferences**. Search conferences are large group sessions, usually lasting a few days, in which participants identify environmental trends and establish strategic solutions for those conditions.[34] Search conferences are often known as "putting the entire system in the room" because they attempt to congregate representatives throughout the organization's entire system. This means involving as

• Search conferences Large group sessions, usually lasting a few days, in which participants identify environmental trends and establish strategic solutions for those conditions.

Courtesy of Richmond Savings Credit Union.

Richmond Savings, Canada's third-largest credit union, was able to involve all 400 employees in a six-day search conference to create a new vision for the Vancouver-based financial institution. Half of the employees attended sessions on Tuesday and Wednesday, and the other half attended on Thursday and Friday. During these sessions, outside speakers talked about Richmond Savings' customers and reputation, as well as changes in the financial services industry. Employee teams then identified corporate objectives and discussed action plans for each objective. Richmond Savings' executives met on Saturday to review these objectives and action plans. On Sunday, the executives met with all 400 employees to explain what they had decided to change.[35] What forms of employee resistance to change are minimized through search conferences?

www.richmondsavings.com

many employees as possible, along with others associated with the organization. For instance, Eicher Motors, a large manufacturer of light commercial vehicles in central India, holds an annual three-day search conference that includes a representation of suppliers, buyers, and shareholders as well as all employees.[36]

Various types of organizations, including Richmond Savings Credit Union, Peco Energy, the U.S. Forest Service, Microsoft, and a high school have used search conferences to assist the change process.[37] Of course, search conferences and other forms of employee involvement require follow-up action by decision makers. If employees do not see meaningful decisions and actions resulting from these meetings, they begin to question the credibility of the process and are more cynical about similar change strategies in the future.

Stress management

For most of us, organizational change is a stressful experience.[38] It threatens our self-esteem and creates uncertainty about our future. Communication, training, and employee involvement can reduce some of these stressors, but companies also need to introduce stress-management practices to help employees cope with the changes. Labatt Breweries recognized the need for stress management during a corporate restructuring. "[Labatt] had systems in place from day one to help people cope with the stress of the change," recalls the general manager of Labatt's Newfoundland operations. These systems included "rap sessions" in which employees shared their thoughts and concerns with Labatt's senior managers.[39]

Negotiation

Organizational change is, in large measure, a political activity.[40] People have vested interests and apply their power to ensure that the emerging conditions are consistent with their personal values and needs. Consequently, negotiation may be necessary for employees who will clearly lose out from the change activity. This negotiation offers certain benefits to offset some of the cost of the change.

Consider the experience of GE Capital Fleet Services in Richmond Hill, Ontario. When the company removed two levels of management, it faced serious resistance from supervisors who worried that they would lose their status. After several months, senior management negotiated with the supervisors and eventually created an intermediate manager position to overcome this resistance. "In our case, the decision to delay was non-negotiable," recalls a GE Capital manager. "As time was subsequently to show, however, we should have been prepared to negotiate on the number of layers to be eliminated."[41]

Coercion

When Ted Pattenden became CEO of National Rubber, he replaced the entire management team at the Toronto-based company because they were not in tune with the changes he wanted to make. Similarly, Gordon Bethune and Greg Brenneman orchestrated the turnaround of Continental Airlines, partly by replacing 50 of the company's 61 executive officers.[42] These are not isolated examples. One survey reported that two-thirds of senior management in large U.S. firms were replaced by the time the businesses were revived.[43]

Firing people is the least desirable way to change organizations. However, dismissals and other forms of coercion are sometimes necessary when speed is essential and other tactics are ineffective. For example, it may be necessary to remove several members of an executive team who are unwilling or unable to change their existing mental models of the ideal organization. This is also a radical form of organizational "unlearning" (see Chapter 1) because when executives leave, they remove knowledge of the organization's past routines. This potentially opens up opportunities for new practices to take hold.[44] At the same time, we should keep in mind that coercion is a risky strategy because survivors (employees who are not fired) may have less trust in corporate leaders and engage in more political tactics to protect their own job security. More generally, various forms of coercion may change behaviour through compliance, but it won't develop commitment to the change effort (see Chapter 12).

CHANGING TO THE DESIRED FUTURE STATE

Organizational change takes many forms. When Ford CEO Jacques Nasser began teaching employees about shareholder value, the actual changes were quite subtle at first. Employees still performed their same jobs, but their attitudes and mental model of the ideal company shifted. Eventually, Nasser's change initiative encouraged everyone to engage in new behaviours more consistent with shareholder value. Change was more dramatic at Celestica, described at the beginning of this chapter. Task forces identified specific changes, which resulted in new tasks and roles in the organization. Overall, change results in new behaviours that employees must learn and internalize.

REFREEZING THE DESIRED CONDITIONS

After unfreezing and changing behaviour patterns, we need to refreeze desired behaviours so people do not slip back into their old work practices.[45] Refreezing occurs when organizational systems and team dynamics are realigned with the desired changes. The desired patterns of behaviour can be "nailed down" by changing the physical structure and situational conditions. For instance, Bell Canada successfully reduced environmental waste by removing trash bins and replacing Styrofoam cups with reusable ceramic mugs.

Organizational rewards are also powerful systems that refreeze behaviours.[46] If the change process is supposed to encourage efficiency, rewards should be realigned to motivate and reinforce efficient behaviour. Information systems play a complementary role in the change process, particularly as conduits for feedback.[47] Feedback mechanisms help employees learn how well they are moving towards the desired objectives, and they provide a permanent architecture to support the new behaviour patterns in the long term. The adage "What gets measured, gets done" applies here. Employees concentrate on the new priorities when they receive a continuous flow of feedback about how well they are achieving those goals.

STRATEGIC VISIONS, CHANGE AGENTS, AND DIFFUSING CHANGE

Kurt Lewin's force field analysis model provides a rich understanding of the dynamics of organizational change. But it overlooks three other ingredients in effective change processes: strategic visions, change agents, and diffusing change. Every successful change requires a clear, well-articulated vision of the desired future state. In the opening story, Celestica's strategic vision began the process of change. Celestica's vision provided a sense of direction and established the critical success factors against which the real changes were evaluated. A vision of the ideal organization also minimizes employee fear of the unknown and provides a better understanding about what behaviours employees must learn for the future state.[48] Not surprisingly, then, one survey reported that executives in large U.S. organizations believe that a clear vision of the proposed change is the most important feature of successful change initiatives.[49]

Courtesy of CHC Helicopter Corp.

From its headquarters in St. John's, Newfoundland, CHC Helicopter Corp. has become the world's largest helicopter services company with 350 aircraft in 60 bases around the world. CHC employees have experienced considerable change throughout the company's recent growth spurt, but the turbulence has been eased by the company's well-established strategic vision. CHC clearly lays out its four principles: (1) safety is first and foremost, (2) customers must receive value through quality service, (3) the workplace must promote teamwork, and (4) CHC must build on its strengths to sustain profitable growth.[50] Why are strategic visions and guiding principles an important part of managing change?

www.chc.ca

CHANGE AGENTS

Change agent A person who possesses enough knowledge and power to guide and facilitate the change effort.

Transformational leaders Individuals who form a vision of the desired future state, communicate that vision in ways that are meaningful to others, behave in ways that are consistent with the vision, and build commitment to the vision.

Organizational change also requires change agents to help form, communicate, and build commitment towards the desired future state. A **change agent** is anyone who possesses enough knowledge and power to guide and facilitate the change effort. Some organizations rely on external consultants to serve as change agents. However, change agents are typically people within the organization who possess the leadership competencies necessary to bring about meaningful change. Corporate executives certainly need to be change agents. However, as companies rely increasingly on self-directed work teams, change agents will be found in any employee.

Effective change agents are **transformational leaders** (see Chapter 14).[51] They form a vision of the desired future state, communicate that vision in ways that are meaningful to others, behave in ways that are consistent with the vision, and build commitment to the vision. Jacques Nasser, CEO of Ford Motor Company, has a reputation as a transformational leader. He effectively changed Ford Australia a few years ago and is now engaging employees throughout the organization to become more proactive and entrepreneurial.[52]

DIFFUSION OF CHANGE

Change agents are discovering that it is often better to test the transformation process with a pilot project, then diffuse what has been learned from this experience to other parts of the organization. The reason is that pilot projects are more flexible and less risky than centralized, organization-wide programs.[53] Roberts Express, the expedited delivery service firm (now part of Federal Express), started its team-based organizational structure in this way. Seven employees from operations, customer service, and safety/recruiting agreed to form a pilot team, representing the first cross-functional customer service unit. As problems were ironed out, the company expanded this process to form other teams. Today, the entire work process is operated by self-directed teams.[54]

How are the results of pilot projects successfully diffused to other parts of the organization? Richard Walton, who has studied the diffusion of work restructuring programs at Alcan Aluminum and other companies, offers several recommendations for the effective diffusion of change.[55] Generally, diffusion is more likely to occur when the pilot project is successful within one or two years and receives visibility (e.g., favourable news media coverage). These conditions tend to increase top management support for the change program and persuade other managers to introduce the change effort in their operations. Successful diffusion also depends on labour union support and active involvement in the diffusion process.

Another important condition is that the diffusion strategy should not be described too abstractly, because this makes the instructions too vague to introduce the change elsewhere. Neither should the strategy be stated too precisely, because it might not seem relevant to other areas of the organization. Finally, without producing excessive turnover in the pilot group, people who have worked under the new system should be moved to other areas of the organization. These employees transfer their knowledge and commitment of the change effort to work units that have not yet experienced it.

ORGANIZATION DEVELOPMENT

Organization development (OD) A planned system-wide effort, managed from the top with the assistance of a change agent, that uses behavioural science knowledge to improve organizational effectiveness.

So far, we have discussed the dynamics of change that occur every day in organizations. However, an entire field of study, called **organization development (OD)**, tries to understand how to manage planned change in organizations. OD is a planned system-wide effort, managed from the top with the assistance of a change agent, that uses behavioural science knowledge to improve organizational effectiveness.[56]

OD relies on many of the organizational behaviour concepts described in this book, such as team dynamics, perceptions, job design, and conflict management. OD also takes an open systems perspective, because it recognizes that organizations have many interdependent parts and must adapt to their environments. Thus, OD experts try to ensure that all parts of the organization are compatible with the change effort, and that the change activities help the company fit its environment.[57]

Action research A data-based, problem-oriented process that diagnoses the need for change, introduces the OD intervention, and then evaluates and stabilizes the desired changes.

Most OD activities rely on **action research** as the primary blueprint for planned change. As depicted in Exhibit 15.4, action research is a data-based, problem-oriented process that diagnoses the need for change, introduces the OD activity, and then evaluates and stabilizes the desired changes.[58]

Action research is a highly participative process, involving the client throughout the various stages.[59] It typically includes an action research team consisting of people both affected by the organizational change and having the power to facilitate it. This participation is a fundamental

EXHIBIT 15.4 The Action Research Approach to OD

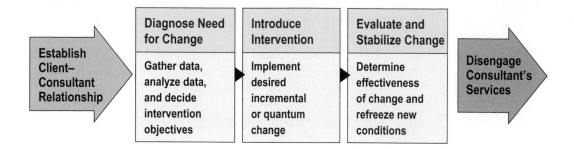

philosophy of OD, but it also increases commitment to the change process and provides valuable information to conduct organizational diagnosis and evaluation. Let's look at the main elements of the action research process.

THE CLIENT–CONSULTANT RELATIONSHIP

The organization development process begins by forming a relationship between the client and consultant. External consultants might become change agents, but they are usually retained as facilitators to assist an internal change agent (usually a senior executive or team leader). Consultants need to determine three things when forming a client relationship in organization development: the client's readiness for change, the consultant's power base, and the consultant's role in the relationship.

First, consultants need to determine the client's readiness for change, including whether people are motivated to participate in the process, are open to meaningful change, and possess the abilities to complete the process. Consultants watch out for people who enter the process with preconceived answers before the situation is fully diagnosed, or who intend to use the change effort to their personal advantage (e.g., closing down a department or firing a particular employee).

Second, consultants need to establish their power base in the client relationship.[60] Effective consultants rely on expertise and perhaps referent power to have any influence on the participants (see Chapter 12). However, they *should not* use reward, legitimate, or coercive power, because these bases may weaken trust and neutrality in the client–consultant relationship.

Lastly, consultants need to agree with their clients on the most appropriate role in the relationship.[61] This might range from providing technical expertise on a specific change activity to facilitating the change process. Many OD experts prefer the latter role, commonly known as **process consultation**.[62] Process consultation involves helping the organization solve its own problems by making it aware of organizational processes, the consequences of those processes, and the means by which they can be changed. Rather than providing expertise about the content of the change—such as how to introduce continuous improvement teams—process consultants help participants learn how to solve their own problems by guiding them through the change process.[63]

DIAGNOSE THE NEED FOR CHANGE

Action research is a problem-oriented activity that carefully diagnoses the problem (or opportunity) through systematic analysis of the situation. *Organizational diagnosis* involves gathering and analyzing data about an ongoing system. Organizational diagnosis is important

Process consultation A method of helping the organization solve its own problems by making it aware of organizational processes, the consequences of those processes, and the means by which they can be changed.

because it establishes the appropriate direction for the change effort.[64] Data collection may occur through interviews, survey questionnaires, direct observation, analysis of documents, or any combination of these.

Dominion Life Assurance of Canada has taken organizational diagnosis into the information technology age with its "control self-assessment workshops." A dozen or more employees from different departments begin the workshop by using an electronic voting system to anonymously identify the highest-priority issues for change. A structured online questionnaire guides this process. When the key issues have been identified, Dominion Life participants type in their anonymous comments and recommendations on each issue.[65]

Along with gathering and analyzing data, the diagnostic process involves agreeing on specific prescriptions for action, including the appropriate change method and the schedule for these actions. This process, known as *joint action planning*, ensures that everyone knows what is expected of them and that standards are established to properly evaluate the process after the transition.[66]

INTRODUCE CHANGE

An important issue in any change process is whether to implement incremental or quantum change.[67] **Incremental change** is an evolutionary strategy whereby the organization fine-tunes the existing organization and takes small steps towards the change effort's objectives.[68] Incremental change is generally less threatening and less stressful to employees because they have time to adapt to the new conditions. Moreover, any problems in the process can be corrected while the change process is occurring, rather than afterwards.[69]

However, incremental change may be inadequate where companies face extreme environmental turbulence. Instead, they may require **quantum change** (also called *episodic change*) in which the organization breaks out of its existing ways and moves towards a totally different configuration of systems and structures.[70] Organizational restructuring and re-engineering are common forms of quantum change. At the same time, many companies have suffered the adverse consequences of quantum change. Quantum change can be costly as organizational systems and structures are torn apart and replaced. Employees typically need to learn completely new roles, which are not known until the change process has begun. Quantum change is usually traumatic and rapid, so change agents rely more on coercion and negotiation than on employee involvement to build support for the change effort.[71]

EVALUATE AND STABILIZE CHANGE

OD activities can be very expensive, so it makes sense that we should measure their effectiveness. To evaluate an OD process, we need to recall its objectives that were developed during the organizational diagnosis and action planning stages. But even when these goals are clearly stated, the effectiveness of an OD activity might not be apparent for several years. It is also difficult to separate the effects of the activity from external factors (e.g., improving economy, introduction of new technology).

If the activity has the desired effect, the change agent and participants need to stabilize the new conditions. This refers to the refreezing process that we described earlier. Rewards, information systems, team norms, and other conditions are redesigned so that they support the new values and behaviours. Even with stabilizing systems and structures in place, the desired conditions may erode without the ongoing support of a change champion. For example, one ALCOA magnesium plant was a model of efficiency until the company prematurely transferred its plant manager and human resource manager. This unintentionally had the effect of

---

• **Incremental change**
An evolutionary approach to change in which existing organizational conditions are fine-tuned and small steps are taken towards the change effort's objectives.

• **Quantum change**
A revolutionary approach to change in which the organization breaks out of its existing ways and moves towards a totally different configuration of systems and structures.

removing the change champions and undermining the previous four years of change effort. "[ALCOA] stripped away the leadership that could have supported the change efforts afterwards," says one of the original change agents.[72]

EMERGING TRENDS IN ORGANIZATION DEVELOPMENT

Organization development includes any planned change intended to make a firm more effective. In theory, this means that OD covers almost every area of organizational behaviour, as well as many aspects of strategic and human resource management. In practice, OD consultants have favoured one perspective and level of process more than others at various periods in OD's history.

When the field of OD emerged in the 1940s and 1950s, few OD activities were involved with macro-level organization-wide changes. Instead, OD practitioners focused almost exclusively on interpersonal and small-group dynamics. The field was equated with T-groups, encounter groups, and other forms of sensitivity training. **Sensitivity training** is an unstructured and agendaless session in which a small group of people meet face to face, often for a few days, to learn more about themselves and their relations with others.[73] Learning occurs as participants disclose information about themselves and receive feedback from others during the session.

Today, the reverse is true.[74] OD processes now are mostly aimed at improving service quality, corporate restructuring, and knowledge management. They are typically organization-wide, affecting organizational systems and structures with less emphasis on individual emotions and values. OD practitioners are paying more attention to productivity, customer service, product or service quality, and related business outcomes.[75] And although surveys suggest that OD consultants still value their humanistic roots, there is also increasing awareness that the field's values have shifted to focus more on the bottom line.

There are numerous OD activities. Some are discussed elsewhere in this book, such as job design (Chapter 4), team building and dialogue (Chapter 9), and changing organizational culture (Chapter 17). In this section, we briefly discuss two emerging OD activities: parallel learning structures and appreciative inquiry.

PARALLEL LEARNING STRUCTURES

Parallel learning structures are highly participative arrangements, composed of people from most levels of the organization who follow the action research model to produce meaningful organizational change. They are social structures developed alongside the formal hierarchy with the purpose of increasing the organization's learning.[76] Ideally, parallel learning structure participants are sufficiently free from the constraints of the larger organization so that they can more effectively solve organizational issues.

Celestica's change process, described at the beginning of this chapter, relied on a parallel learning structure because the task forces operated alongside the existing organization. Connections 15.2 describes how Royal Dutch/Shell's retail boot camp teams also represent a form of parallel structure because they work outside the normal structure. These teams represent various countries and establish a more entrepreneurial approach to getting things done at Shell. The retail teams are separated from the traditional hierarchy so that it is easier to instill new attitudes, role patterns, and work behaviours.

Sensitivity training An unstructured and agendaless session in which participants become more aware through their interactions of how they affect others and how others affect them.

Parallel learning structures Highly participative social structures constructed alongside (i.e., parallel to) the formal organization with the purpose of increasing the organization's learning.

CONNECTIONS 15.2

Royal Dutch/Shell Changes Through Parallel Learning Structures

A few years ago, competitors were threatening Royal Dutch/Shell's market share. The oil company's executives in London and The Hague spent two years reorganizing, downsizing, and educating several layers of management, but this top-down approach had minimal effect. Managers in charge of Shell's operations for a particular country resisted changes that threatened their autonomy, and headquarters managers couldn't break out of the routines that worked for them in the past.

So Steve Miller, head of Shell's worldwide oil products business, decided to apply a parallel learning structure and change the company from the bottom up. He and his executive team held several five-day workshops, each attended by six country teams of front-line people (e.g., gas station managers, truck drivers, marketing professionals). Participants at these "retailing boot camps" learned about worrisome competitive trends in their regions and were taught powerful marketing tools to identify new opportunities. The teams then returned home to study their markets and develop proposals for improvement. For example, a team in South Africa proposed ways to increase liquid gas market share. The Malaysian team developed plans to increase gasoline sales in that country.

Four months later, the teams returned for a second workshop where each proposal was critiqued by Miller's executive team in "fishbowl" sessions that the other teams watched. Videotapes from these sessions became socialization tools for other employees back

John Thoeming.

Royal Dutch/Shell relied on a parallel learning structure to change the company from the bottom up.

in the home country. Each team had 60 days to put its ideas into action, then return for a third workshop to analyze what had and had not worked.

These workshops, along with field tours and several other grassroots activities, had a tremendous effect. Front-line employees developed an infectious enthusiasm and a stronger business approach to challenging the competition. "I can't overstate how infectious the optimism and energy of these committed employees was on the many managers above them," says Miller. The change process also resulted in solid improvements in profitability and market share in most regions where employees had attended the sessions.

Sources: R.T. Pascale, "Leading from a Different Place," in J.A. Conger, G.M. Spreitzer, and E.E. Lawler III (eds.), *The Leader's Change Handbook* (San Francisco: Jossey-Bass, 1999), pp. 301–20; D.J. Knight, "Strategy in Practice: Making It Happen," *Strategy & Leadership*, 26 (July–August 1998), pp. 29–33; R.T. Pascale, "Grassroots Leadership—Royal Dutch/Shell," *Fast Company*, 14 (April–May 1998), pp. 110–20; J. Guyon, "Why Is the World's Most Profitable Company Turning Itself Inside Out?" *Fortune*, August 4, 1997, pp. 120–25.

APPRECIATIVE INQUIRY

The action research process described earlier in this chapter is based on the traditional problem-solving model. OD participants focus on problems with the existing organizational system and identify ways to correct those problems. Unfortunately, this deficiency model of the world—in which something is wrong and must be fixed—focuses on the negative dynamics of the group or system rather than on its positive opportunities.

● **Appreciative inquiry**
An organization development intervention that directs the group's attention away from its own problems and focuses participants on the group's potential and positive elements.

Appreciative inquiry tries to break out of the problem-solving mentality by reframing relationships around the positive and the possible.[77] It takes the view that organizations are creative entities in which people are capable of building synergy beyond their individual capabilities. To avoid dwelling on the group's own shortcomings, the process usually directs its inquiry towards successful events and successful organizations. This external focus becomes a form of behavioural modelling, but it also increases open dialogue by redirecting the group's attention away from its own problems. Appreciative inquiry is especially useful when participants are aware of their "problems" or already suffer from enough negativity in their relationships. The positive orientation of appreciative inquiry enables groups to overcome these negative tensions and build a more hopeful perspective of their future by focusing on what is possible.

Exhibit 15.5 outlines the four main stages of appreciative inquiry.[78] The process begins with *discovery*—identifying the positive elements of the observed events or organization. This might involve documenting positive customer experiences elsewhere in the organization. Or it might include interviewing members of another organization to discover its fundamental strengths. As participants discuss their findings, they shift into the *dreaming* stage by envisioning what might be possible in an ideal organization. By directing their attention to a theoretically ideal organization or situation, participants feel safer revealing their hopes and aspirations than if they were discussing their own organization or predicament.

● **Dialogue** A process of conversation among team members in which they learn about each other's mental models and assumptions, and eventually form a common model for thinking within the team.

As participants make their private thoughts public to the group, the process shifts into the third stage, called *designing*. Designing involves the process of **dialogue** (see Chapter 9), in which participants listen with selfless receptivity to each others' models and assumptions and eventually form a collective model for thinking within the team.[79] In effect, they create a common image of what should be. As this model takes shape, group members shift the focus back to their own situation. In the final stage of appreciative inquiry, called *delivering*, participants establish specific objectives and direction for their own organization based on their model of what will be.

EXHIBIT 15.5   The Appreciative Inquiry Process

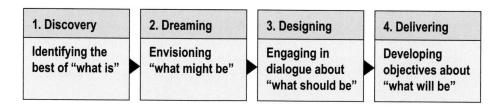

1. Discovery	2. Dreaming	3. Designing	4. Delivering
Identifying the best of "what is"	Envisioning "what might be"	Engaging in dialogue about "what should be"	Developing objectives about "what will be"

Source: Based on D. Whitney and C. Schau, "Appreciative Inquiry: An Innovative Process for Organization Change," *Employment Relations Today,* 25 (Spring 1998), pp. 11–21; F.J. Barrett and D.L. Cooperrider, "Generative Metaphor Intervention: A New Approach for Working with Systems Divided by Conflict and Caught in Defensive Perception," *Journal of Applied Behavioral Science,* 26 (1990), p. 229.

Chrysler Canada practised a form of appreciative inquiry by beginning each meeting with a success story. "We had found that too often we would dwell on our mistakes and failures, subsequently spiralling around them," says a Chrysler Canada executive. Writing success stories helped Chrysler's managers see themselves and their colleagues in a more positive and optimistic light. At first, people were hard pressed to think of successes, but they eventually realized that these gems of experience existed every day in their part of the operation.[80]

EFFECTIVENESS OF ORGANIZATION DEVELOPMENT

Is organization development effective? Considering the incredible range of organization development activities, answering this question is not easy. Nevertheless, a few studies have generally reported that some OD processes have a moderately positive effect on employee productivity and attitudes. According to some reviews, team building produces the most favourable results when a single activity is applied.[81] Others report that self-directed work teams are very effective.[82] One of the most consistent findings is that OD is most effective when it includes two or more change processes.

CROSS-CULTURAL CONCERNS WITH OD

One significant concern with OD techniques originating in North America is that they conflict with cultural values in other countries.[83] Some scholars argue that OD practices in North America assume a linear model of change, as shown earlier in the force field analysis, that is punctuated by tension and overt conflict. Indeed, sensitivity training and other OD practices encourage open display of conflict. But these assumptions are incompatible with cultures that view change as a natural cyclical process with harmony and equilibrium as the objectives.[84] For instance, people in many Asian countries try to minimize conflict in order to respect others and save face.[85] These concerns do not mean that OD is ineffective elsewhere. Rather, it suggests that the field needs to develop a more contingency-oriented perspective with respect to the cultural values of its participants.

ETHICAL CONCERNS WITH OD

The field of organization development also faces ethical concerns with respect to some processes.[86] One ethical concern is that OD activities may threaten the individual's privacy rights. The action research model is built on the idea of collecting information from organizational members, yet this requires employees to provide personal information and emotions that they may not want to divulge. The scientific nature of the data collection exercise may mislead employees into believing that their information is confidential when, in reality, executives can sometimes identify opinions of individual employees.[87]

A second ethical concern is that OD activities potentially increase management's power by inducing compliance and conformity in organizational members. This power shift occurs because OD initiatives create uncertainty and re-establish management's position in directing the organization. Moreover, because OD is a system-wide activity, it requires employee participation rather than allowing individuals to become involved voluntarily. Indeed, one of the challenges of OD consultants is to "bring onside" those who are reluctant to engage in the process.

A third concern is that some OD activities undermine the individual's self-esteem. The unfreezing process requires participants to disconfirm their existing beliefs, sometimes including their own competence at certain tasks or interpersonal relations. Sensitivity training and intergroup mirroring may involve direct exposure to personal critique by co-workers as well as public disclosure of one's personal limitations and faults.

The ethical concerns of violating self-esteem apparently occurred at SaskTel a few years ago. The Regina-based telecommunications company brought in consultants to improve team dynamics. Instead, the 20 SaskTel employees involved in the project claim that the consultants isolated them in an office suite with paper taped over its glass walls so that no one could see inside. They were also quarantined in small cubicles and prevented from talking to each other. The employees eventually united and forced SaskTel to get rid of the consultants. "Team members regularly received insults in front of the group," recalls Kathryn Markus, a seven-year SaskTel manager. "The isolation, long hours, and purposeless activity left me feeling abandoned, betrayed, and frightened." Markus and several other SaskTel employees took sick leave when they abandoned the project.[88]

A fourth ethical dilemma facing OD consultants is their role in the client relationship. Generally, they should occupy "marginal" positions with the clients they are serving. This means that they must be sufficiently detached from the organization to maintain objectivity and avoid having the client become too dependent on them.[89] However, this can be a difficult objective to satisfy due to the politics of organizational change. OD consultants and clients have their own agendas, and these are not easily resolved without moving beyond the marginal positions that change agents should ideally attain.

The OD practices described in this section facilitate the change process, and Lewin's force field analysis model provides a valuable template for understanding how the change process works. Still, you can see from reading this chapter that organizational change is easier said than done. Many corporate leaders have promised more change than they were able to deliver because they underestimated the time and challenges involved with this process. This is certainly true of corporate restructuring, where leaders typically have difficulty redesigning the organization's departments, reporting relationships, and distribution of formal power. The next chapter investigates these and other elements of organizational structure and design.

CHAPTER SUMMARY

- Organizations face numerous forces for change because they are open systems that need to adapt to changing environments. Some current environmental dynamics include information technology, globalization, competition, and demographics.

- Lewin's force field analysis model states that all systems have driving and restraining forces. Change occurs through the process of unfreezing, changing, and refreezing. Unfreezing involves producing a disequilibrium between the driving and restraining forces. Refreezing occurs when the organization's systems and structures are aligned with the desired behaviours.

- Almost all organization change efforts face one or more forms of employee resistance. The main reasons why people resist change are direct costs, saving face, fear of the unknown, breaking routines, incongruent organizational systems, and incongruent team dynamics.

- Resistance to change may be minimized by keeping employees informed about what to expect from the change effort (communicating); teaching employees valuable skills for the desired future (training); involving employees in the change process; helping employees cope with the stress of change; negotiating trade-offs with those who will clearly lose from the change effort; and using coercion (sparingly and as a last resort).

- A change agent is anyone who possesses enough knowledge and power to guide and facilitate the change effort. Change agents rely on transformational leadership to develop a vision, communicate that vision, behave consistently with the vision, and build commitment to the vision of a desirable future state.

- Organization development (OD) is a planned system-wide effort, managed from the top with the assistance of a change agent, that uses behavioural science knowledge to improve organizational effectiveness.

- When forming a client relationship, OD consultants need to determine the client's readiness for change, establish their power base in the client–consultant relationship, and understand their appropriate role in the change process. An important issue is whether change should be evolutionary (incremental change) or revolutionary (quantum change).

- Appreciative inquiry focuses participants on the positive and possible. It tries to break out of the problem-solving mentality that dominates OD through the action research model. The four stages of appreciative inquiry include discovery, dreaming, designing, and delivering.

- OD activities, particularly those with multiple activities, have a moderately positive effect on employee productivity and attitudes. However, there are some cross-cultural concerns with OD processes. Moreover, there are ethical concerns with some OD activities, including increasing management's power over employees, threatening individual privacy rights, undermining individual self-esteem, and making clients dependent on the OD consultant.

KEY TERMS

Action research, p. 457

Appreciative inquiry, p. 462

Change agent, p. 456

Dialogue, p. 462

Force field analysis, p.446

Incremental change, p. 459

Organization development (OD), p. 457

Parallel learning structures, p. 460

Process consultation, p. 458

Quantum change, p. 459

Refreezing, p. 447

Search conferences, p. 453

Sensitivity training, p. 460

Transformational leaders, p. 456

Unfreezing, p. 447

DISCUSSION QUESTIONS

1. Chances are that the school you are attending is currently undergoing some sort of change to adapt more closely to its environment. Discuss the external forces that are driving these changes. What internal drivers for change also exist?

2. Use Lewin's force field analysis to describe the dynamics of organizational change at Royal Dutch/Shell, as described in Connections 15.2 (see page 461).

3. Senior management of a large multinational corporation is planning to restructure the organization. Currently, the organization is decentralized around geographical areas so that the executive responsible for each area has considerable autonomy over manufacturing and sales. The new structure will transfer power to the executives responsible for different product groups; the executives responsible for each geographic area will no longer be responsible for manufacturing in their area but will retain control over sales activities. Describe two types of resistance that senior management might encounter from this organizational change.

4. Read about the organizational change process at Richmond Savings Credit Union (page 453), then explain how this process reduced resistance to change.

5. Web Circuits, Inc. is a Montreal-based manufacturer of computer circuit boards for high-technology companies. Senior management wants to introduce value-added management practices to reduce production costs and remain competitive. A consultant has recommended that the company start with a pilot project in one department and, when successful, diffuse these practices to other areas of the organization. Discuss the merits of this recommendation and identify three conditions (other than the pilot project's success) that would make diffusion of the change effort more successful.

6. You are an organization development consultant who has been asked by the president of Atlantic Textiles Ltd. to explore "issues" that may account for poor sales in the company's prairie provinces region. Before accepting this role, what three things should you consider when forming the client–consultant relationship? How would you determine whether the client–consultant relationship is well suited to organizational development?

7. Suppose that you are vice-president of branch services at Bank of Toronto. You notice that several branches have consistently low customer service ratings even though there are no apparent differences in resources or staff characteristics. Describe an appreciative inquiry process in one of these branches that might help to overcome these problems.

8. This chapter suggests that some organization development activities face ethical concerns. Yet, several OD consultants actively use these processes because they believe that they benefit the organization and do less damage to employees than it may seem on the surface. For example, some OD activities try to open up the employee's hidden area (see Johari Window in Chapter 6) so that there is better mutual understanding with co-workers. Discuss the merits of this argument and identify how and when you think OD should limit this process.

Case Study

ACTIVITY 15.1

TransAct Insurance Corporation

TransAct Insurance Corporation (TIC) provides automobile insurance in parts of Canada that allow private insurers. Last year, a new president was brought in by TIC's board of directors to improve the company's competitiveness and customer service. After spending several months assessing the situation, the new president introduced a strategic plan to improve TIC's competitive position. He also replaced three vice-presidents. Jim Leon was hired as vice-president of claims, TIC's largest division with 1500 employees, 50 claims centre managers, and 5 regional directors.

Leon immediately met with all claims managers and directors, and visited employees at TIC's 50 claims centres. As an outsider, this was a formidable task, but his strong interpersonal skills and uncanny ability to remember names and ideas helped him through the process. Through these visits and discussions, Leon discovered that the claims division had been managed in a relatively authoritarian, top-down manner. He could also see that morale was very low and employee–management relations were guarded. High workloads and isolation (adjusters work in tiny cubicles) were two other common complaints. Several managers acknowledged that the high turnover among claims adjusters was partly due to these conditions.

Following discussions with TIC's president, Leon decided to make morale and supervisory leadership his top priority. He initiated a divisional newsletter with a tear-off feedback form on which employees could register their comments. He announced an open-door policy in which any claims division employee could speak to him directly and confidentially without going first to his or her immediate supervisor. Leon also fought organizational barriers to initiate a flex-time program so that employees could design work schedules around their needs. This program later became a model for other areas of TIC.

One of Leon's most pronounced symbols of change was the "Claims Management Credo," which outlined the philosophy that every claims manager would follow. At his first meeting with the complete claims management team, Leon presented a list of what he thought were important philosophies and actions of effective managers. The management group was asked to select and prioritize items from this list. They were told that the resulting list would be the division's management philosophy and that all managers would be held accountable for abiding by its principles. Most claims managers were uneasy about this process, but they also understood that the organization was under competitive pressure and that Leon was using this exercise to demonstrate his leadership.

The claims managers developed a list of ten items, such as encouraging teamwork, fostering a trusting work environment, setting clear and reasonable goals, and so on. The list was circulated to senior management in the organization for their comment and approval, and sent back to all claims managers for their endorsement. Once this was done, a copy of the final document was sent to every claims division employee. Leon also announced plans to follow up with an annual survey to evaluate each claims manager's performance. This concerned the managers, but most of them believed that the credo exercise was a result of Leon's initial enthusiasm and that he would be too busy to introduce a survey after settling into the job.

One year after the credo had been distributed, Leon announced that the first annual survey would be conducted. All claims employees would complete the survey and return it confidentially to the human resources department, where the survey results would be compiled for each claims centre manager. The survey asked the extent to which the manager had lived up to each of the ten items in the credo. Each form also provided space for comments.

Claims centre managers were surprised that a survey would be conducted, but they were even more

ACTIVITY 15.1 CONTINUED

worried about Leon's statement that the results would be shared with employees. What "results" would employees see? Who would distribute these results? What would happen if a manager received poor ratings from his or her subordinates? "We'll work out the details later," said Leon in response. "Even if the survey results aren't great, the information will give us a good baseline for next year's survey."

The claims division survey had a high response rate. In some centres, every employee completed and returned a form. Each report showed the claim centre manager's average score for each of the ten items, as well as how many employees rated the manager at each level of the five-point scale. The reports also included every comment made by employees at that centre.

No one was prepared for the results of the first survey. Most managers received moderate or poor ratings on the ten items. Very few managers averaged above 3.0 (out of 5.0) on more than a couple of items. This suggested that, at best, employees were ambivalent about whether their claims centre managers had abided by the ten management philosophy items. The comments were even more devastating than the ratings; they ranged from being mildly disappointed in to extremely critical of the claims managers. Employees also described their long-standing frustration with TIC, high workloads, and isolated working conditions. Several people bluntly stated that they were skeptical about the changes that Leon had promised. "We've heard the promises before, but now we've lost faith," wrote one claims adjuster.

The survey results were sent to each claims manager, the regional director, and each employee at the claims centre. Leon instructed managers to discuss the survey data and comments with their regional manager and directly with employees. The claims centre managers, who thought that employees were only provided

with average scores, went into shock when they realized that the reports included individual comments. Some managers went to their regional director and complained that revealing the personal comments would ruin their careers. Many directors sympathized, but the results were already available to employees.

When Leon heard about these concerns, he agreed that the results were lower than expected and that the comments should not have been shown to employees. After discussing the situation with his directors, he decided that the discussion meetings between claims managers and their employees should proceed as planned. To delay or withdraw the reports would undermine the credibility and trust that Leon was trying to develop with employees. However, the regional director attended the meeting in each claims centre to minimize direct conflict between the claims centre manager and employees.

Although many of these meetings went smoothly, a few created harsh feelings between managers and their employees. The authors of some comments were easily identified by their content, and this created a few delicate moments in several sessions. A few months after these meetings, two claims centre managers quit and three others requested transfers to nonmanagement positions in TIC. Meanwhile, Leon wondered how to manage this process more effectively, particularly since employees expected another survey in the following year.

Discussion Questions

1. Identify the forces pushing for change and the forces restraining the change effort in this case.

2. Was Jim Leon successful at bringing about change? Why or why not?

3. What should Jim Leon do now?

© Copyright 2000. Steven L. McShane and Terrance J. Bogyo. This case is based on actual events, but names, industry, and some characteristics have been changed to maintain anonymity.

Video Case Study

ACTIVITY 15.2
Wendy's Restaurants of Canada

Employees working at Wendy's Restaurants of Canada are about to be swept up in a tide of extraordinary change. To boost profits, Wendy's needed a fundamental makeover from the top down. It wanted to break down the military style of management and, in its place, create a culture of vulnerability and trust. Wendy's vice-president, Chris Park, says that he wants managers to realize that they don't have to be in control all the time, that they can let go and take support from their team members.

Wendy's brought together 160 restaurant managers from across Canada to an Ontario resort where New Mexico–based Pecos River guided them to a new way of working with their employees. The course included trust falls, tightrope walking with a partner, sessions where they "revealed their inner selves," and discussions about the new culture at Wendy's. As the program unfolded, the lessons from Pecos River began to sink in. Managers felt the mutual support and increased their willingness to depend on others.

Craig Stapon is responsible for leading change in Wendy's six Winnipeg restaurants. Stapon joined Wendy's as district manager just before the course began, and he wants to make his mark. During the Pecos River course, Stapon and his restaurant managers shared their inner thoughts and discussed their vision of the new Wendy's. But Stapon's vision wasn't quite what some of the other managers saw. When Stapon suggested that everyone should be "normalized" by working Monday to Friday, Edie Helfrick shot back that Stapon was seeing every-thing his way. "There's going to be big changes, I know that," she said, "but it's his changes—it's what he wants."

A few weeks after the retreat, Stapon tried to get his Winnipeg managers "on board" with the change. He introduced a magic wand so that managers could be honest during the weekly meetings. He also used these meetings to openly evaluate managers on their commitment to the change process. But some managers suggested that Stapon wasn't promoting the change in a positive way.

Craig Stapon and other Wendy's managers are discovering that it's a struggle to change the old corporate culture with a new philosophy. It's a long, difficult journey to create a company that's truly trusting and supportive. But Chris Parks believes that at least they've taken the first step: "Pecos River is really a working model of ... getting a commitment from everybody who is working together to support each other."

Discussion Questions

1. What changes did executives at Wendy's Restaurants of Canada expect to result from the Pecos River program? Did these changes occur in the Winnipeg restaurants?

2. Was there any resistance to change among the Winnipeg restaurant managers? If so, what form of resistance did it take?

3. What change management strategies did Craig Stapon use among the Winnipeg managers? Were these strategies effective? Why or why not?

Source: Based on "Wendy's Restaurants," *Venture* (September 1992).

TEAM exercises

ACTIVITY 15.3
STRATEGIC CHANGE MANAGEMENT

Purpose: This exercise is designed to help you identify strategies to facilitate organizational change in various situations.

Instructions:

Step 1: The instructor will place students in teams, and each team will be assigned one of the scenarios presented below.

Step 2: Each team will diagnose its assigned scenario to determine the most appropriate set of change management practices. Where appropriate, these practices should (a) create an urgency to change, (b) minimize resistance to change, and (c) refreeze the situation to support the change initiative. Each of these scenarios is based on real events that occurred in Canada and elsewhere.

Step 3: Each team will present and defend its change management strategy. Class discussion regarding the appropriateness and feasibility of each strategy will occur after all teams assigned the same scenario have presented. The instructor will then describe what the organizations actually did in these situations.

Scenario 1: Greener Telco

The board of directors of a large telephone company wants its executives to make the organization more environmentally friendly by encouraging employees to reduce waste in the workplace. There are also expectations by government and other stakeholders for the company to take this action and be publicly successful. Consequently, the managing director wants to significantly reduce the use of paper, refuse, and other waste throughout the company's many widespread offices. Unfortunately, a survey indicates that employees do not value environmental objectives and do not know how to "reduce, reuse, recycle." As vice-president of administration, you have been asked to develop a strategy that might bring about meaningful behavioural change towards these environmental goals. What would you do?

Scenario 2: Go Forward Airline

A major airline had experienced a decade of rough turbulence, including two bouts of bankruptcy protection, ten CEOs, and morale so low that employees had ripped company logos from their uniforms out of embarrassment. Service was terrible and the airplanes rarely arrived or left the terminal on time. This was costing the airline significant amounts of money in passenger layovers. Managers were paralyzed by anxiety and many had been with the firm so long that they didn't know how to set strategic goals that worked. One-fifth of all flights were losing money and the company overall was near financial collapse (just three months from defaulting on payroll obligations). The newly hired CEO and you must get employees to quickly improve operational efficiency and customer service. What actions would you take to bring about these changes in time?

ACTIVITY 15.4
APPLYING LEWIN'S FORCE FIELD ANALYSIS

Purpose: This exercise is designed to help you understand how to diagnose situations using force field analysis, and to identify strategies to facilitate organizational change.

Instructions: This exercise involves diagnosing the situation described below, identifying the forces for and against change, and recommending strategies to reduce resistance to change. The exercise is described as a team activity, although the instructor may choose to have it completed individually. Also, the instructor may choose a situation other than the one presented here.

Step 1: Students will form teams of four or five people and everyone will read the following situation. (Note: The following applies to most colleges and universities in Canada. If your school currently has a full-trimester system, imagine the situation below as though your school currently has a two-semester system.)

> Like most post-secondary institutions in Canada, your college/university has two semesters (beginning in September and January) as well as a six-week "intersession" from early May to mid-June. Instructors typically teach their regular load of courses during the two semesters. Intersession courses are taught primarily by part-time faculty, although some full-time faculty teach during intersession for extra pay. After carefully reviewing costs, student demand, and competition from other institutions, senior administration has decided that your college/university should switch to a trimester curriculum. In a trimester system, courses are taught in three equal semesters: September to December, January to April, and May to early August. Faculty must teach during any two semesters in which their courses are offered (for universities) or during all three semesters (for colleges). Senior administration has determined that this change will allow the institution to admit more students without building additional classrooms or other facilities. Moreover, market surveys indicate that over 50 percent of current students would continue their studies in the new summer semester and that the institution would attract more full-fee students from other countries. The provincial government looks very favourably on the trimester plan because it increases the efficiency of college/university resources and eases the significant shortage of spaces available. (There are many more applicants to your college/university than people admitted for the foreseeable future.) The Faculty Association has not yet had time to state its position on this proposed change.

Step 2: Using Lewin's force field analysis model (diagrammed on the following page), identify the forces that seem to support the change and the forces that likely oppose the change to a trimester system. Team members should consider all possible sources of support and resistance, not just those stated in the situation above.

Step 3: For each source of resistance, identify one or more strategies that would most effectively manage change. Recall from the textbook that change management strategies include communication, training, employee involvement, stress management, negotiation, and coercion.

Step 4: The class will discuss each team's results.

FORCE FIELD ANALYSIS MODEL

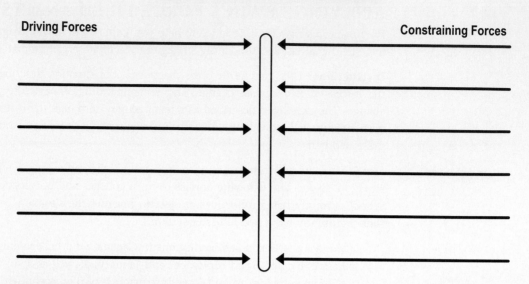

Driving Forces   Constraining Forces

ACTIVITY 15.5
TOLERANCE OF CHANGE SCALE

Purpose: This exercise is designed to help you understand how people differ in their tolerance of change.

Instructions: Read each of the statements below and circle the response that best matches your personal belief. Then use the scoring key in Appendix B of this book to calculate your results. This self-assessment is completed alone so students can rate themselves honestly without concerns of social comparison. However, class discussion will focus on the meaning of the concept measured by this scale and its implications for managing change in organizational settings.

TOLERANCE OF CHANGE SCALE

To what extent does each statement describe you? Indicate your level of agreement by marking the appropriate responses on the right.	Strongly Agree	Moderately Agree	Slightly Agree	Neutral	Slightly Disagree	Moderately Disagree	Strongly Disagree
1. An expert who doesn't come up with a definite answer probably doesn't know too much.	☐	☐	☐	☐	☐	☐	☐
2. I would like to live in a foreign country for a while.	☐	☐	☐	☐	☐	☐	☐

3. There is really no such thing as a problem that can't be solved. ...... ❑ ❑ ❑ ❑ ❑ ❑ ❑

4. People who fit their lives into a schedule probably miss most of the job of living. .... ❑ ❑ ❑ ❑ ❑ ❑ ❑

5. A good job is one where it is always clear what is to be done and how it is to be done. .... ❑ ❑ ❑ ❑ ❑ ❑ ❑

6. It is more fun to tackle a complicated problem than to solve a simple one. ... ❑ ❑ ❑ ❑ ❑ ❑ ❑

7. In the long run it is possible to get more done by tackling small, simple problems rather than large, complicated ones. .... ❑ ❑ ❑ ❑ ❑ ❑ ❑

8. Often the most interesting and stimulating people are those who don't mind being different and original. .... ❑ ❑ ❑ ❑ ❑ ❑ ❑

9. What we are used to is always preferable to what is unfamiliar. ... ❑ ❑ ❑ ❑ ❑ ❑ ❑

10. People who insist on a yes or no answer just don't know how complicated things really are. ..... ❑ ❑ ❑ ❑ ❑ ❑ ❑

11. A person who leads an even, regular life in which few surprises or unexpected happenings arise really has a lot to be grateful for. .... ❑ ❑ ❑ ❑ ❑ ❑ ❑

12. Many of our most important decisions are based on insufficient information. .... ❑ ❑ ❑ ❑ ❑ ❑ ❑

13. I like parties where I know most of the people more than ones where all or most of the people are complete strangers. .... ❑ ❑ ❑ ❑ ❑ ❑ ❑

14. Teachers or supervisors who hand out vague assignments give me a chance to show initiative and originality. .... ❑ ❑ ❑ ❑ ❑ ❑ ❑

15. The sooner everyone acquires similar values and ideals, the better. .... ❑ ❑ ❑ ❑ ❑ ❑ ❑

16. A good teacher is one who makes you wonder about your way of looking at things. .... ❑ ❑ ❑ ❑ ❑ ❑ ❑

Source: Adapted from S. Budner, "Intolerance of Ambiguity as a Personality Variable," *Journal of Personality*, 30 (1962), pp. 29–50.

CHAPTER SIXTEEN

Organizational Structure and Design

LEARNING OBJECTIVES

After reading this chapter, you should be able to:

- Describe the two fundamental requirements of organizational structures.
- Explain why firms can have flatter structures than previously believed.
- Discuss the dynamics of centralization and formalization as organizations get larger and older.
- Contrast functional structures and divisional structures.
- Outline the features and advantages of the matrix structure.
- Describe four features of team-based organizational structures.
- Discuss the merits of the network structure.
- Summarize three contingencies of organizational design.
- Explain how organizational strategy relates to organizational structure.

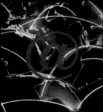

Jonathan Player/NYT Pictures.

The writing was on the wall for Chiat/Day's 35 employees in London, England. The American advertising company had been acquired by a larger firm, which planned to lay off most people at Chiat/Day's London office. But the entire London office had other plans. They held a retreat to design their concept of the ideal organization, then negotiated a deal that would let them apply that ideal model to their newly formed advertising agency, called St. Luke's.

Named after the patron saint of creativity, St. Luke's is fashioned after a medieval guild. All of the original employees (and most of the 100 people now employed there) are company owners and receive equal shares each year. A five-member board elected by employees governs the agency. Other committees monitor finances, resources (including salaries), and quality control.

St. Luke's has a very flat, team-based organizational structure. There aren't any bosses or corporate layers—just apprentices and practitioners. "We wanted to do something radical," explains David Abraham, one of St. Luke's founders. "Many ad agencies have a very hierarchical structure and exist only to benefit shareholders that you never meet or owners with little direct involvement, so we created a corporate structure to match our ideals."

The converted toffee factory in London where St. Luke's makes its headquarters doesn't have any offices. The only work spaces, other than the front reception and cafeteria, are client rooms with visual themes to support creative thinking. For example, employees responsible for the Clarks shoe account meet in the Clarks room, which looks and smells like a shoe store.

It hasn't been easy for some employees to adjust to St. Luke's unique organizational structure. "Working without a formal structure presents pressures—ambiguity is stressful," explains Abraham. Still, Britain's most unusual ad agency has become its most successful. In its first three years of operation, St. Luke's attracted Coca-Cola, IKEA, Clarks Shoes, and other major clients, and was recently named ad agency of the year in the United Kingdom.[1]

Organizational structure The division of labour as well as the patterns of coordination, communication, work flow, and formal power that direct organizational activities.

Organizational design The creation and modification of organizational structures.

There is something of a revolution occurring in how organizations are structured. Driven by global competition and facilitated by computer-based information technology, St. Luke's and many other companies are throwing out the old organizational charts and experimenting with new designs that will hopefully improve coordination, sharing knowledge, and employee focus on critical objectives. **Organizational structure** refers to the division of labour as well as to the patterns of coordination, communication, work flow, and formal power that direct organizational activities.[2] An organizational structure reflects its culture and power relationships.[3] Our knowledge of this subject provides the tools to engage in **organizational design**, that is, to create and modify organizational structures.

In the previous chapter, we learned that organizational structures are tools for change. They establish new communication patterns and refreeze the change initiatives. For example, CEO Jac Nasser recently restructured Ford Motor Company's many business units so that employees are closer to specific types of customers, such as luxury car buyers (Jaguar, Volvo), services (Hertz, e-commerce), and Ford's mainstream car buyers. "I've said that it's our aspiration for all Ford employees to develop a 'consumer headset,'" Nasser explains. "Strategic business units organized around brands and regions will help move the company forward by creating a culture that focuses on every point of contact with the consumer."[4]

We begin this chapter by considering the two fundamental processes in organizational structure: division of labour and coordination. This is followed by a detailed investigation of the four main elements of organizational structure: span of control, centralization, formalization, and departmentalization. The latter part of this chapter examines the contingencies of organizational design, including organizational size, technology, external environment, and strategy.

DIVISION OF LABOUR AND COORDINATION

All organizational structures include two fundamental requirements: the division of labour into distinct tasks and the coordination of that labour so that employees are able to accomplish common goals.[5] Organizations are groups of people who work interdependently towards some purpose (see Chapter 1). To efficiently accomplish their goals, these groups typically divide the work into manageable chunks, particularly when there are many different tasks to perform. They also introduce various coordinating mechanisms to ensure that everyone is working effectively towards the same objectives.

DIVISION OF LABOUR

Job specialization The result of division of labour in which each job now includes a narrow subset of the tasks required to complete the product or service.

Division of labour refers to the subdivision of work into separate jobs assigned to different people. Subdivided work leads to **job specialization**, because each job now includes a narrow subset of the tasks necessary to complete the product or service (see Chapter 4). Launching a space shuttle at NASA, for example, requires tens of thousands of specific tasks that are divided among thousands of people. Tasks are also divided vertically, such as having supervisors coordinate work while employees perform the work.

Work is divided into specialized jobs because it potentially increases work efficiency.[6] Job incumbents can master their tasks quickly because work cycles are very short. Less time is wasted changing from one task to another. Training costs are reduced because employees require fewer physical and mental skills to accomplish the assigned work. Finally, job specialization makes it easier to match people with specific aptitudes or skills to the jobs for which they are best suited.

COORDINATING WORK ACTIVITIES

As soon as people divide work among themselves, coordinating mechanisms are needed to ensure that everyone works in concert.[7] Every organization—from the two-person corner convenience store to the largest corporate entity—uses one or more of the following coordinating mechanisms: informal communication, formal hierarchy, and standardization (see Exhibit 16.1).

Coordination through informal communication

Informal communication is a coordinating mechanism in all organizations.[8] This includes sharing information on mutual tasks as well as forming common mental models so that employees synchronize work activities using the same mental road map.[9] Informal communication permits considerable flexibility because employees transmit a large volume of information through face-to-face communication and other media-rich channels (see Chapter 8). Consequently, informal communication is a vital coordinating mechanism in nonroutine and ambiguous situations.

Coordination through informal communication is easiest in small firms and work units where employees face few communication barriers. Emerging information technologies have further leveraged this coordinating mechanism in large organizations, even where employees are scattered around the globe. Larger organizations can also support informal communication by forming temporary cross-functional teams and moving team members into a common physical area (called *co-locating*). For example, **concurrent engineering** (also called *platform teams*) involves assigning product development to a cross-functional project team consisting of people from marketing, design, manufacturing, customer service, and other areas.[10] These employees are typically co-located to improve coordination through informal communication, whereas more formal and less flexible coordinating mechanisms exist where product development occurs through several departments.

Concurrent engineering The integration and concurrent development of a product or service and its associated processes, usually guided by a cross-functional team.

EXHIBIT 16.1   Coordinating Mechanisms in Organizations

Form of Coordination	Description	Subtypes
Informal communication	Sharing information on mutual tasks; forming common mental models to synchronize work activities	• Direct communication • Liaison roles • Integrator roles
Formal hierarchy	Assigning legitimate power to individuals, who then use this power to direct work processes and allocate resources	• Direct supervision • Reporting structure
Standardization	Creating routine patterns of behaviour or output	• Standardized skills • Standardized processes • Standardized output

Source: Based on information in D.A. Nadler and M.L. Tushman, *Competing by Design: The Power of Organizational Architecture* (New York: Oxford University Press, 1997), Chapter 6; H. Mintzberg, *The Structuring of Organizations* (Englewood Cliffs, NJ: Prentice Hall, 1979), Chapter 1; J. Galbraith, *Designing Complex Organizations* (Reading, MA: Addison-Wesley, 1973), pp. 8–19.

W.L. Gore & Associates Inc. avoids hierarchies and formal supervision. Instead, the maker of Gore-Tex fabric and other high-tech products encourages informal communication to coordinate most work activities among its nearly 6000 employees in 45 locations. It does this by limiting the size of each facility to about 200 people and ensuring that each unit is self-sufficient. "People sometimes get concerned and worried that there is no structure and no organization, and I don't think that is true at all," says a senior Gore associate. Project leaders serve as integrators by coordinating the work of various individuals and work units.[11] If Gore coordinates mainly through informal communications, can this coordinating mechanism work at a General Motors of Canada assembly plant?

www.gore.com

Larger organizations also encourage coordination through informal communication by creating *integrator roles*. These people are responsible for coordinating a work process by encouraging employees in each work unit to share information and informally coordinate work activities. Integrators do not have authority over the people involved in that process, so they must rely on persuasion and commitment. Brand managers at Procter & Gamble coordinate work among marketing, production, and design groups. Project leaders at W.L. Gore & Associates and other companies also serve as integrators by encouraging people from various work units to work together on the project.

Coordination through formal hierarchy

Informal communication is the most flexible form of coordination, but it can be time-consuming. Consequently, as organizations grow, they develop a second coordinating mechanism in the shape of a formal hierarchy. Hierarchy assigns legitimate power to individuals, who then use this power to direct work processes and allocate resources (see Chapter 12). In other words, work is co-ordinated through direct supervision.

Any organization with a formal structure coordinates work to some extent through the formal hierarchy. For instance, team leaders at Nortel Networks coordinate work by ensuring that employees in their group remain on schedule and that their respective tasks are compatible with tasks completed by others in the group. The team leader has direct authority to reassign people to different work activities and to resolve conflicts by dictating solutions. The formal hierarchy also coordinates work among executives through the division of organizational activities. If the organization is divided into geographic areas, the structure gives the heads of those regional groups legitimate power over executives responsible for production, customer service, and other activities in those areas. If the organization is divided into product groups, the heads of those groups have the right to coordinate work across regions.

The formal hierarchy has traditionally been applauded as the optimal coordinating mechanism for large organizations. Henri Fayol, an early scholar on the subject, argued that organizations are most effective where managers exercise their authority and employees receive orders from only one supervisor. Coordination should occur through the chain of command, that is, up the hierarchy and across to the other work unit.[12] This approach to coordination is practised at the British conglomerate Rentokil Initial. Rentokil operates like a military organization with eight levels of management and a strict chain of command. "I don't encourage people to pick up the phone directly to me because that is attempting to bypass their boss," warns Rentokil CEO Sir Clive Thompson.[13]

Coordination through formal hierarchy may have been popular with classic organizational theorists, but it is often a very inefficient coordinating mechanism. Later in this chapter, we will learn that there are limits to how many employees a supervisor can coordinate. Furthermore, the chain of command is rarely as fast or accurate as direct communication between employees. And, as recent scholars have warned, today's educated and individualistic workforce is less tolerant of rigid structures and legitimate power.[14]

Coordination through standardization

Standardization—creating routine patterns of behaviour or output—is the third means of coordination. Many organizations standardize work activities through job descriptions and procedures. This coordinates work requiring routine and simple tasks, but not in complex and ambiguous situations. In these situations, companies might coordinate work by standardizing the individual's or team's goals and product or service output (e.g., customer satisfaction, production efficiency). For instance, to coordinate the work of salespeople, companies assign sales targets rather than specific behaviours.

When work activities are too complex to standardize through procedures or goals, companies often coordinate work effort by extensively training employees or hiring people who have learned precise role behaviours from educational programs. This form of coordination is used in hospital operating rooms. Surgeons, nurses, and other operating room professionals coordinate their work more through training than through goals or company rules.

ELEMENTS OF ORGANIZATIONAL STRUCTURE

The division of labour and coordination of work represent the fundamental requirements of organizations. These requirements relate to four basic elements of organizational structure. This section introduces three of them: span of control, centralization, and formalization. The fourth element—departmentalization—is presented in the next section.

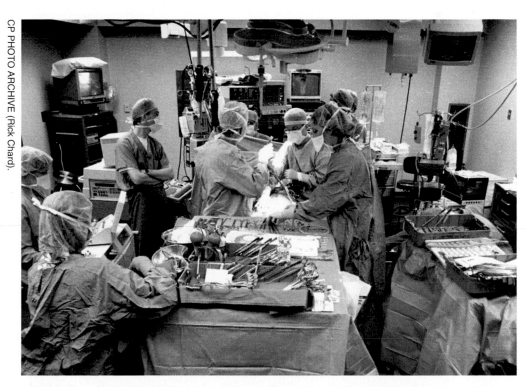

CP PHOTO ARCHIVE (Rick Chard).

www.uhealthnet.on.ca

Led by Dr. Tirone David, this open-heart surgery team at Toronto General Hospital is divided into specialized jobs so that each person has the required competencies for each position. To some extent, surgical work is coordinated through informal communication. However, much of the work activity can occur without discussion because team members also coordinate through standardization of skills. Through extensive training, each medical professional has learned precise role behaviours so that his or her task activities are coordinated with others on the surgical team. What other types of organizations make extensive use of standardization of skills to coordinate work?

SPAN OF CONTROL

Span of control The number of people directly reporting to a supervisor.

Span of control refers to the number of people directly reporting to the next level in the hierarchy. As we mentioned earlier, Henri Fayol strongly recommended the formal hierarchy as the primary coordinating mechanism. Consequently, he and other theorists at the time prescribed a relatively narrow span of control, typically no more than 20 employees per supervisor and 6 supervisors per manager. These prescriptions were based on the assumption that managers simply cannot monitor and control any more subordinates closely enough.

Today, we know better. The best-performing manufacturing facilities currently have an average of 31 employees per supervisor. This is a much wider span of control than past scholars had recommended. Yet these operations plan to stretch this span to an average of 75 employees per supervisor over the next few years.[15]

What's the secret here? Did Fayol and others miscalculate the optimal span of control? The answer is that early scholars thought in terms of Frederick Taylor's scientific management model (see Chapter 4). They believed that employees should "do" the work, whereas supervisors and other management personnel should monitor employee behaviour and make most of the decisions. This division of labour limited the span of control. It is very difficult to supervise 75 people directly. It is much easier to *oversee* 75 subordinates who are grouped into several self-directed work teams. Employees manage themselves, thereby releasing supervisors from the time-consuming tasks of monitoring behaviour and making everyone else's decisions.

Vancom Zuid-Limburg, a joint venture that operates a public bus company in the Netherlands, illustrates this point. Vancom has about 40 bus drivers for each manager, whereas other bus companies have 8 drivers per manager. Vancom is able to operate with a much wider span of control because bus drivers are organized into self-directed work teams that manage their own schedules and budgets.[16]

The underlying principle here is that the span of control depends on the presence of other coordinating mechanisms.[17] Self-directed work teams supplement direct supervision with informal communication and specialized knowledge. This also explains why dozens of surgeons and other medical professionals may report to the head surgeon in a major hospital. The head surgeon doesn't engage in much direct supervision because the standardized skills of medical staff coordinate the unit's work. A wider span of control is possible when employees perform similar tasks or have routine jobs. In these situations, the organization relies more on standardization of work processes to coordinate work, thereby reducing the need for hands-on supervision.

Tall and flat structures

The Development Bank of South Africa recently increased employee productivity by restructuring and flattening the organization. In particular, the government-owned financial institution slashed the number of managers from 74 to 27 and cut out one of its four management layers. "[T]he essence of transformation was not to shift the chairs, but to ensure that some of the chairs came out of the room," says a bank executive.[18]

The Development Bank of South Africa joins a long list of companies that are moving towards flatter organizational structures. Canadian National slashed its bureaucratic hierarchy from ten levels down to just five. Royal Mail, which delivers mail throughout Great Britain, went from 16 layers of management to 6 layers. St. Luke's, the British advertising agency described in the opening story of this chapter, has only two layers.[19] This trend towards delayering—moving from a tall structure to a flat structure—is partly in response

www.ducks.ca

Ducks Unlimited Canada recently flattened its organizational structure by removing layers of management. The Winnipeg-based environmental conservation group wanted to help empower employees, making it easier for the professionals in the field to make decisions quickly without having to go up and down the proverbial power ladder. "I think by having that flattened structure there is more job enrichment," says Cheryl Barber, Ducks Unlimited Canada's human resources administrator. "People feel that they are in control of what they are doing and that also helps to retain the employees."[22] What conditions should corporate leaders consider when determining the optimal number of management layers?

to the recommendations of management gurus. For example, Tom Peters challenged corporate leaders to cut the number of layers to three within a facility and to five within an entire organization.[20]

The main arguments in favour of delayering are that it potentially cuts overhead costs and puts decision makers closer to front-line staff and information about customer needs. However, some organizational experts warn that corporate leaders may be cutting out too much hierarchy. They argue that the much-maligned "middle managers" serve a valuable function by controlling work activities and managing corporate growth. Moreover, companies will always need hierarchy because someone has to make quick decisions and represent a source of appeal over conflicts.[21]

One last point before leaving this topic: The size of an organization's hierarchy depends on both the average span of control and the number of people employed by the organization. As shown in Exhibit 16.2, a tall structure has many hierarchical levels, each with a relatively narrow span of control, whereas a flat structure has few levels, each with a wide span of control.[23] Larger organizations that depend on hierarchy for coordination necessarily develop taller structures. For instance, Microsoft is considered to be a high-involvement organization, yet it has at least seven levels of corporate hierarchy to coordinate its 25,000 or more employees.[24]

EXHIBIT 16.2 Span of Control and Tall/Flat Structures

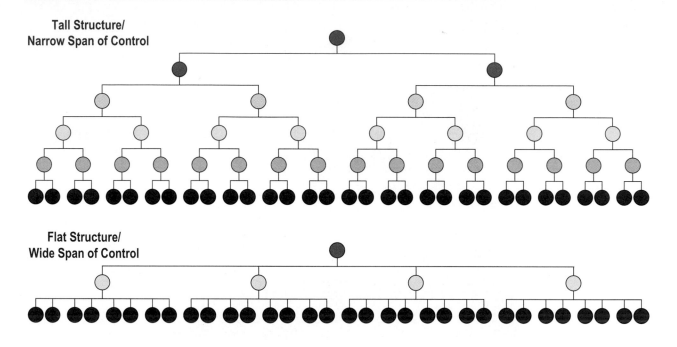

**Tall Structure/
Narrow Span of Control**

**Flat Structure/
Wide Span of Control**

CENTRALIZATION AND DECENTRALIZATION

Centralization and decentralization represents a second element of organizational design. **Centralization** means that formal decision authority is held by a small group of people, typically those at the top of the organizational hierarchy. Most organizations begin with centralized structures, as the founder makes most of the decisions and tries to direct the business towards his or her vision. But as organizations grow, they become more complex. Work activities are divided into more specialized functions, a broader range of products or services is introduced, and operations expand into different regions or countries. Under these conditions, the founder and senior executives lack the necessary time and expertise to process all the decisions that significantly influence the business. Consequently, growing organizations become *decentralized*; that is, they disperse decision authority and power throughout the organization.

Organizational and environmental complexity push organizations towards decentralization, but some corporate leaders further encourage this process. They have learned that decentralized organizations are potentially more entrepreneurial and responsive to the local environments in which they operate. Connections 16.1 describes how Douglas Daft is decentralizing Coca-Cola for this reason. The Australian-born CEO believes that people have different preferences in different parts of the world, and that *decentralizing* will make Coca-Cola's decision makers more responsive to those local needs.

Organizational complexity may encourage decentralization, but other forces push for centralization. Senior executives centralize to increase their power over organizational events. They particularly try to gain decision control during times of turbulence and organizational crisis. Yet, when the problems are over, these leaders are reluctant to decentralize decision making to lower levels.

> **Centralization** The degree to which formal decision authority is held by a small group of people, typically those at the top of the organizational hierarchy.

www.coke.com

Decentralization Helps Coca-Cola Executives Experience the "Real Thing"

One of Douglas Daft's first tasks as Coca-Cola's new CEO was to cut one-fifth of the workforce. The goal wasn't just to slash costs, but to decentralize the world's largest soft drink maker. Almost half of the layoffs occurred at Coke's Atlanta headquarters, where centralized decision making has hampered Coke's ability to respond quickly and precisely to local needs.

Daft has plenty of experience with Coke's centralized structure. The Australian-born executive spent most of his career working at Coke's far-flung operations. He has plenty of stories about how the company's centralized structure undermined its competitiveness. One example is Coke's recent launch of a new carbonated tea in northeast China, several months behind its rivals: "We had the formula, we had the flavour, we had done all the taste-testing," complains Daft, "but Atlanta kept saying 'are you sure?'"

Coca-Cola's centralized structure is mainly based on the assumption that Coke has global appeal. But Daft argues that Coke isn't "it" in all cultures. He cites Japan—the company's most profitable market—where two-thirds of Coke's sales are in non-carbonated drinks. "People don't buy drinks globally," Daft explains. "You can't pander to similarities between people: you have to find the differences."

To find those differences, Daft is moving the regional chieftains out of the company's headquarters in Atlanta and closer to their local markets. These local managers, he claims, will have the authority to make decisions, as well as be accountable for any mistakes.

Sources: P. O'Kane, "Coca Cola's Canny Man," *The Herald* (Glasgow), June 18, 2000, p. 3; "Debunking Coke," *The Economist*, February 12, 2000; "World Has Changed at Coca-Cola as 6,000 Lose Jobs," *National Post*, January 27, 2000, p. C10.

Centralization may improve consistency and reduce costs if, as just mentioned, it doesn't reduce local flexibility. This is why Procter and Gamble has centralized marketing activities that were previously scattered to various geographic divisions. Brand managers and other marketing people are still employed in each region, but most decisions are made at corporate headquarters so that the product or service is delivered consistently and at a lower marketing cost.[25]

FORMALIZATION

Have you ever wondered why a McDonald's hamburger in Saanich, B.C., looks and tastes the same as one in Singapore? The reason is that the fast-food company has engineered out all variation through formalization. **Formalization** is the degree to which organizations standardize behaviour through rules, procedures, formal training, and related mechanisms.[26] In other words, formalization represents the establishment of standardization as a coordinating mechanism.

> **Formalization** The degree to which organizations standardize behaviour through rules, procedures, formal training, and related mechanisms.

McDonald's Restaurants has a formalized structure because it prescribes every activity in explicit detail. Each McDonald's franchise must dole out five perfect drops of mustard, a quarter-ounce of onions, and two pickles—three if they're small—on each hamburger. Drink cups are filled with ice up to a point just below the arches on their sides. The procedure for cooking and bagging fries is explained in 19 steps. Employees who work on the grill must put the hamburger patties in six rows of six patties each. A Big Mac is supposed to be assembled in 25 seconds from the time it appears on the order screen.[27]

Older companies tend to become more formalized because work activities become routinized, making them easier to document into standardized practices. Larger companies formalize as a coordinating mechanism, because direct supervision and informal communication among employees do not operate as easily. External influences, such as government safety legislation and strict accounting rules, also encourage formalization.

Problems with formalization

Formalization may increase efficiency, but it can also create problems. Rules and procedures reduce organizational flexibility, so employees follow prescribed behaviours even when the situation clearly calls for a customized response. Some work rules become so convoluted that organizational efficiency would decline if they were actually followed as prescribed. Labour unions sometimes call work-to-rule strikes, in which their members closely follow the formalized rules and procedures established by an organization. This tactic increases union power, because the company's productivity falls significantly when employees follow the rules that are supposed to guide their behaviour.

Another concern is that although employees with very strong security needs and a low tolerance for ambiguity like working in highly formalized organizations, others become alienated and feel powerless in these structures. Finally, rules and procedures have been known to take on a life of their own in some organizations. They become the focus of attention rather than the organization's ultimate objectives of producing a product or service and serving its dominant stakeholders.

MECHANISTIC VERSUS ORGANIC STRUCTURES

You may have noticed that organizations seem to cluster around their span of control, centralization, and formalization. Some companies, such as McDonald's, have a **mechanistic structure**.[28] Mechanistic structures are characterized by a narrow span of control and a high degree of formalization and centralization. They have many rules and procedures, limited decision making at lower levels, tall hierarchies of people in specialized roles, and vertical rather than horizontal communication flows. Tasks are rigidly defined, and are altered only when sanctioned by higher authorities.

Companies with an **organic structure** have the opposite characteristics. They have a wide span of control, little formalization, and decentralized decision making. Tasks are fluid, adjusting to new situations and organizational needs. The organic structure values knowledge and takes the view that information may be located anywhere in the organization rather than among senior executives. Thus, communication flows in all directions with little concern for the formal hierarchy.

Mechanistic structures operate best in stable environments because they rely on efficiency and routine behaviours. However, as we have emphasized throughout this book, most organizations operate in a world of dramatic change. New technology, globalization, a changing workforce, and other factors have strengthened the need for a more organic structure that is flexible and responsive to these changes. Moreover, organic structures are more consistent with knowledge management because they emphasize information sharing rather than hierarchy and status.

Mechanistic structure An organizational structure with a narrow span of control and high degrees of formalization and centralization.

Organic structure An organizational structure with a wide span of control, very little formalization, and highly decentralized decision making.

TRADITIONAL FORMS OF DEPARTMENTALIZATION

Span of control, centralization, and formalization are important elements of organizational structure, but most people think about organizational charts when discussing organizational structure. The organizational chart represents the fourth element in the structuring of organizations, called departmentalization. Departmentalization specifies how employees and their activities are grouped together. It is a fundamental strategy for coordinating organizational activities because it influences organizational behaviour in the following ways:[29]

- Departmentalization establishes a system of common supervision among positions and units within the organization. It establishes formal work teams, as we learned in Chapter 9. Departmentalization typically determines which positions and units must share resources. Thus, it establishes interdependencies among employees and subunits (see Chapter 13).

- Departmentalization usually creates common measures of performance. Members of the same work team, for example, share common goals and budgets, giving the company standards against which to compare subunit performance.

- Departmentalization encourages coordination through informal communication among people and subunits. With common supervision and resources, members within each configuration typically work near each other, so they can use frequent and informal interaction to get the work done.

There are almost as many organizational charts as there are businesses, but we can identify five pure types of departmentalization: simple, functional, divisional, matrix, and team-based. Few companies fit exactly into any of these categories, but they represent a useful framework for discussing more complex hybrid forms of departmentalization. The next section introduces emerging variations of network structures, also known as virtual corporations.

www.levysleathers.com

Photo by Shelly Cameron-McCarron.

When Levy's Leathers started business 30 years ago, it was the ultimate simple structure. Dennis Levy and Jerome MacPherson (shown, left, with employee Chris DeCoste) made the leather accessories themselves, then peddled their wares out of the back of a truck. The owners of the Antigonish, Nova Scotia, firm and a few employees performed several diverse jobs and relied mainly on informal communication to coordinate their work. As the company grew, the work was divided into more specialized tasks and a functional structure emerged. Today, Levy's Leathers employs about 200 people in Antigonish and Winnipeg and is the world's largest manufacturer of guitar straps.[31] Why would Levy's Leathers and most other firms move away from the simple structure as they become larger?

SIMPLE STRUCTURE

Most companies begin with a *simple structure*.[30] They employ only a few people and typically offer only one distinct product or service. There is minimal hierarchy— usually just employees reporting to the owners. Employees are grouped into broadly defined roles because there are insufficient economies of scale to assign them to specialized roles. Simple structures are flexible, yet they usually depend on the owner's direct supervision to coordinate work activities. Consequently, this structure is very difficult to operate under complex conditions. For instance, Levy's Leathers, the Antigonish, N.S., leather products manufacturer, replaced its simple structure with a functional structure as its sales increased, markets expanded, and products became more diverse.

FUNCTIONAL STRUCTURE

A **functional structure** organizes employees around specific knowledge or other resources. Employees with marketing expertise are grouped into a marketing unit, those with production skills are located in manufacturing, engineers are found in product development, and so on. Organizations with functional structures are typically centralized to coordinate their activities effectively. Standardization of work processes is the most common form of coordination used in a functional structure. Most organizations use functional structures at some level or at some time in their development.

Advantages and disadvantages

An important advantage of functional structures is that they foster professional identity and clarify career paths. They permit greater specialization so that the organization has expertise in each area. Direct supervision is easier, because managers have backgrounds in that functional area and employees approach them with common problems and issues. Finally, functional structures create common pools of talent that typically serve everyone in the organization. This creates an economy of scale that would not exist if functional specialists were spread over different parts of the organization.[32]

Functional structures also have limitations. Because people are grouped together with common interests and backgrounds, these designs tend to emphasize subunit goals over superordinate goals. For this reason, functional structures tend to have higher dysfunctional conflict and poorer coordination with other work units. Employees in purchasing, accounting, engineering, and other functional units are less likely to give priority to the company's product or service than to the goals of their specific department. Unless people are transferred from one function to the next, they fail to develop a broader understanding of the business. A related concern is that functional structures emphasize differences across work units. Together, these problems require substantial formal controls and coordination when functional structures are used.

DIVISIONAL STRUCTURE

A **divisional structure** groups employees around geographic areas, clients, or outputs (products/services). Divisional structures are sometimes called *strategic business units* (SBUs), because they are normally more autonomous than functional structures and may operate as subsidiaries rather than as departments of the enterprise.

Exhibit 16.3 illustrates the three pure forms of divisional structure.[33] *Geographic divisionalized structures* organize employees around distinct areas of the country or globe. For example, Exhibit 16.3(a) displays the geographic divisional structure at Toronto-based Bata Ltd., the world's largest footwear company. *Product/service structures* organize work around distinct outputs. Exhibit 16.3(b) illustrates this type of structure at Bombardier. The Montreal-based transportation leader divides its workforce mainly into product divisions, ranging from recreational to aerospace products. *Client structures* organize work activities around specific customers. For example, Exhibit 16.3(c) highlights some of the industry segments around which Andersen Consulting staff are organized.

Advantages and disadvantages

The divisional form is a building block structure, because it accommodates growth relatively easily. Related products or clients can be added to existing divisions with little need for additional learning, whereas sprouting a new division may accommodate increasing diversity.

EXHIBIT 16.3 Three Types of Divisional Structure

(a) Geographic Structure

(b) Product/Service Structure

(c) Client Structure

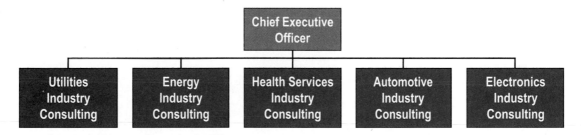

Note: (a) is similar to the geographic divisional structure of Bata Corp; (b) shows the product/service divisions at Bombardier; and (c) shows five of the industry customer groups at Andersen Consulting.

Organizations typically reorganize around divisional structures as they expand into distinct products, services, and domains of operation, because coordinating functional units becomes too unwieldy with increasing diversity.[34]

Organizations tend to adopt divisional structures as they grow and become more complex, but this structural configuration is not perfect. The most common complaint is that divisional structures duplicate and underuse resources. This structure creates "silos of knowledge" because functional specialists are spread throughout the various business units. Consequently, new knowledge and practices in one part of the organization are not shared elsewhere. Divisional structures also tend to reduce cooperation across groups. For instance, Nortel Networks developed a special communication program, called "Come Together," to remind employees in each division of their responsibility to work more closely and cooperatively with each other.[35]

MATRIX STRUCTURE

While most advertising and public relations agencies keep employees in their functional silos, Cossette Communication Inc. integrates employees across departments into specific client groups. For example, the Quebec City–based firm has client teams for Saturn, Bombardier, Bell Mobility, McDonald's, and several other accounts. Each cross-functional team includes employees from public relations, advertising, market research, and graphic design departments, depending on the client's needs.[36]

Cossette Communication Inc. relies on a **matrix structure** to serve its clients. A matrix structure overlays two organizational structures in order to leverage the benefits of both types of structure. There are mainly two forms of matrix structure. Cossette relies on one of these—a matrix structure that overlaps a functional structure with project teams.[37] As Exhibit 16.4 illustrates, employees are assigned to a cross-functional project team, yet also belong to a permanent functional unit to which they return when a project is completed.

The second form of matrix structure is found in multinational corporations that want to balance power between two divisional groups. ABB Asea Brown Boveri's matrix structure combines a product and geographical structure. The product-based structure lets the Swiss/Swedish manufacturer of industrial electrical systems exploit global economies of scale, whereas the geographic structure keeps knowledge close to the needs of individual countries. Tenneco, a leading automobile parts company, also has a matrix structure that overlays product and regional divisions.[38]

> • **Matrix structure**
> A type of departmentalization that overlays a divisionalized structure (typically a project team) with a functional structure.

EXHIBIT 16.4   A Simplified Matrix Structure

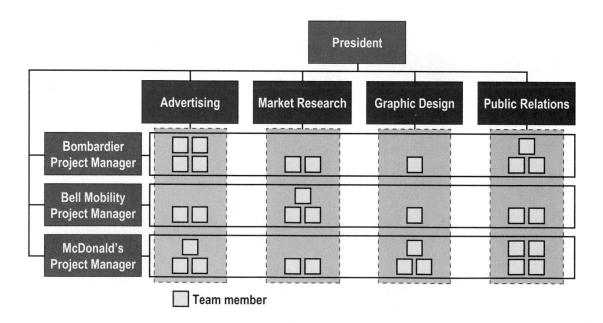

Notice that some employees have two bosses within a matrix structure. For example, the head of ABB's transformer group in Guelph, Ontario, would report to both the Canadian country manager and the global manager of ABB's transformer business. Some companies give these managers equal power; more often, each has authority over different elements of the employee's or work unit's tasks.[39] However, only a small percentage of people report to two bosses in these multinational matrix structures. At ABB, for example, only about 500 plant managers and group leaders have matrix roles. The other 200,000 ABB employees work in direct authority structures below the matrix structure.

Advantages and disadvantages

Matrix structures usually optimize the use of resources and expertise, making them ideal for project-based organizations with fluctuating workloads.[40] Compared to purely functional designs, properly managed matrix structures improve communication efficiency, project flexibility, and innovation. Matrix structures focus technical specialists on the goals of serving clients and creating marketable products. Yet, by maintaining a link to their functional unit, employees are able to interact and coordinate with others in their technical specialty.

In spite of these advantages, matrix structures require more coordination than functional or pure divisional structures. The existence of two bosses can also dilute accountability. Royal Dutch/Shell is moving away from a matrix design for these reasons.[41] Matrix structures also tend to generate conflict, organizational politics, and stress.[42] In project-based firms, for example, project leaders must have a general management orientation and conflict-resolution skills to coordinate people with diverse functional backgrounds. They also need good negotiation skills and persuasive communication skills to gain support from functional leaders. Employees who feel comfortable in structured bureaucracies tend to have difficulty adjusting to the relatively fluid nature of matrix structures. Stress is a common symptom of poorly managed matrix structures, because employees must cope with two managers with potentially divergent needs and expectations.

www.nortelnetworks.com

Courtesy of Nortel Networks.

Nortel Networks keeps changing its organizational structure. In the 1980s, Nortel was mainly a telecommunications equipment provider organized into three geographic businesses—Canada, United States, and World Trade—each with its own marketing and manufacturing to serve the telephone monopolies. As Nortel globalized and telephone monopolies deregulated, the company reorganized around three product groups and four geographically based subsidiaries. Unfortunately, this structure was confusing and increased conflict between geographical and product heads. Today, Nortel is mainly structured around two client groups—enterprises and service providers/carriers—as well as three geographical groups. "Nortel's new structure reinforces the tie-in with the market and with our customers," explains a Nortel executive.[44] Why wasn't Nortel's new structure applied in the 1980s?

HYBRID STRUCTURE

Very few organizations adopt a purely functional, divisional, or matrix structure. Instead, they combine some parts of various designs into a hybrid structure. Research suggests that multinational corporations need to develop structures and systems that maintain some balance of power and effectiveness across functional, product, geographic, and client-focused units.[43] In other words, they must ensure that functional executives do not dominate product executives, product executives do not dominate regional executives, and so forth.

TEAM-BASED (LATERAL) STRUCTURE

Flight Centre is an icon of success in the travel agency business. The Australian-based company has had eight straight years of profitability and at least 20 percent annual growth. In spite of its size, Flight Centre has only three layers of hierarchy and yet provides incredibly consistent service at each of its 565 offices around the world. What's the secret? According to Flight Centre CEO and Managing Director Graham Turner, the company's success is due mainly to its team-based structure. Turner explains that a team-based structure facilitates easy replication, which in turn fuels organic growth.[45]

Some writers call Flight Centre's **team-based organization** structure a *lateral structure* because, with few organizational levels, it is very flat (like a pizza) and relies on extensive lateral communication. Others refer to it as a *cluster structure*, because it is composed of a cluster of teams. The team-based organization is also known as a *circle structure* because the organization has several circles of activity with free-floating teams operating within each domain.[46] Exhibit 16.5 illustrates two of these views of team-based organizations.

No matter what name is used or how it is drawn, the team-based structure has a few distinguishing features from other organizational forms. First, it uses self-directed work teams rather than individuals as the basic building block of organizations. Second, teams are typically organized around work processes, such as making a specific product or serving a specific client group. At St. Luke's, described at the beginning of this chapter, client accounts are assigned to teams rather than to individual employees in different departments. Contrast this with a typical advertising agency where the client works with an

• Team-based organization A type of departmentalization with a flat span of control and relatively little formalization, consisting of self-directed work teams responsible for various work processes.

EXHIBIT 16.5 Two Perspectives of a Team-Based (Lateral) Structure

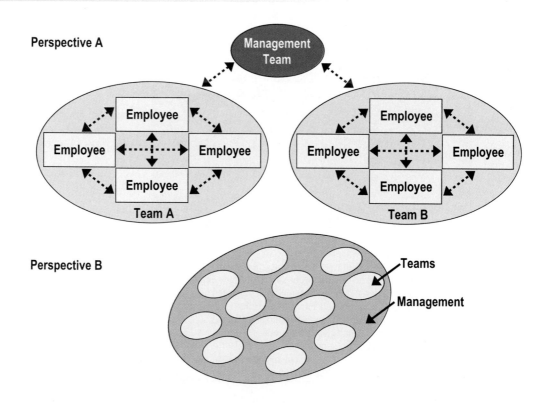

Courtesy of Pratt & Whitney Canada.

Pratt & Whitney Canada's Halifax plant has no middle managers, no supervisors, no executive washrooms, no executive parking spaces, and no fancy job titles. Instead, a team of six executives sets overall plant objectives for manufacturing turbine blades and related aircraft engine parts. The operation's 450 employees belong to self-directed work teams that are almost completely responsible for meeting those objectives. Employees also belong to special task forces to review plant rules and evaluate job applicants. Together with extensive use of robotics technology, these team practices have dramatically improved operating efficiency, job satisfaction, and admiration from others in the industry.[48] What are the main features of team-based organizational structures?

account manager, who then coordinates with people located in several functional departments—art, copy writing, design, and so on.[47]

A third distinguishing feature of team-based organizational structures is that they have a very flat hierarchy, usually with no more than two or three management levels. Most supervisory activities are delegated to the team by having members take turns as the coordinator. Finally, this type of structure has very little formalization. Almost all day-to-day decisions are made by team members rather than someone further up the organizational hierarchy. Teams are given relatively few rules about how to organize their work. Instead, the executive team typically assigns output goals to the team, such as the volume and quality of product or service, or productivity improvement targets for the work process. Teams are then encouraged to use available resources and their own initiative to achieve those objectives.

Team-based structures are usually found within larger divisionalized forms. For example, Pratt & Whitney's manufacturing facilities are organized around a team-based structure, but each unit is part of a larger divisionalized structure. However, St. Luke's (described at the beginning of this chapter) and a few other innovative companies are experimenting with a team-based structure from the top to the bottom of the organization.

www.pwc.ca

Advantages and disadvantages

The team-based organization represents an increasingly popular structure because it is usually more responsive and flexible.[49] Teams empower employees and reduce reliance on a managerial hierarchy, thereby reducing costs. A cross-functional team structure improves communication and cooperation across traditional boundaries. With greater autonomy, this structure also allows quicker and more informed decision making.[50] Some hospitals in Ontario and elsewhere have shifted from functional departments to cross-functional teams for this reason. Teams composed of nurses, radiologists, anaesthetists, a pharmacology representative, possibly social workers, a rehabilitation therapist, and other specialists communicate and coordinate more efficiently, therefore reducing delays and errors.[51]

One concern with team-based structures is that they can be costly to maintain due to the need for ongoing interpersonal skills training. Teamwork potentially takes more time to coordinate than formal hierarchy during the early stages of team development (see Chapter 9). Employees may experience more stress due to increased ambiguity in their roles. Team leaders also experience more stress due to increased conflict, loss of functional power, and unclear career progression ladders.[52]

NETWORK STRUCTURES

To the outside world, Cisco Systems is one company. But the world's leading provider of business-to-business computer networks is mostly a constellation of suppliers, contract manufacturers, assemblers, and other partners connected through an intricate web of computer technology.

Cisco's network springs into action as soon as a customer places an order (usually through the Internet). Suppliers send the required materials to assemblers who ship the product directly to the client, usually the same day. Seventy percent of Cisco's product is outsourced in this way. In many cases, Cisco employees never touch the product. "Partnerships are key to the new world strategies of the 21st century," says a Cisco senior vice-president. "Partners collapse time because they allow you to take on more things and bring them together quicker."[53]

Network structure
An alliance of several organizations for the purpose of creating a product or serving a client.

Cisco is a living example of the **network structure**. A network structure (also known as a *virtual corporation* or *modular structure*) is an alliance of several organizations for the purpose of creating a product or serving a client.[54] As Exhibit 16.6 illustrates, this collaborative structure typically consists of several satellite organizations beehived around a "hub" or "core" firm. The core firm coordinates the network process and provides one or two other core competencies, such as marketing or product development. For instance, Cisco mainly designs and markets new products. Nike, another network organization, mainly provides marketing expertise for its sports footwear and apparel.

The core firm might be the main contact with customers, but most of the product or service delivery and support activities are farmed out to satellite organizations located anywhere in the world. Extranets (Web-based networks with partners) and other technologies ensure that information flows easily and openly between the core firm and its array of satellites. For instance, Nokia, the Finnish company, entered the U.S. video display market with only five employees. All of the major tasks—marketing, sales, logistics, and technical support—were contracted out to specialists around the country. This diverse network was then connected through information technology to a common database.[55]

One of the main forces pushing towards a network structure is the recognition that an organization has only a few *core competencies*. A core competency is a knowledge base that

---

EXHIBIT 16.6 A Network Structure

resides throughout the organization and provides a strategic advantage. Imperial Oil's core competency is its ability to distribute and market oil products. Most people think of Yahoo! as a search engine, but the Internet company's core competency is really Internet-based marketing. Yahoo! relies on Inktomi, a Web-based search engine founded by Paul Gauthier, a computer science graduate of Dalhousie University in Halifax.[56]

As companies discover their core competency, they outsource noncritical tasks to other organizations that have a core competency at performing those tasks. Many firms have outsourced information systems for this reason. Many also rely on independent sales agencies to provide sales support in certain territories. Several have their manufacturing done by outside firms, such as Toronto-based Celestica Inc. Each of these relations represents part of a network organization structure. "The traditional idea of the unit of business has always been the company," explains Jayson Myers, chief economist at the Alliance of Manufacturers and Exporters Canada. "Now, it's the network, going beyond one company and encompassing all its suppliers and many of its customers."[57]

AFFILIATE NETWORKS

Affiliate networks Network organizations where the satellite companies have a special affiliation with the core firm. The satellites may have been spun-off departments from the core firm, or the core firm may be a major investor in the satellite.

Some network organizations are called **affiliate networks** because they have a special historical or financial affiliation with the core company. Affiliates may be former departments or divisions of the core firm that have been spun off to form independent businesses. Other affiliates are recent start-ups that receive financial support from the core firm. For example, Nortel Networks has an in-house incubator called the Business Ventures Group where employees develop their ideas to the point of being spun off into a separate company. In either case, affiliate networks have a special relationship with the core firm that distinguishes them from arm's-length network structures.[58]

Microsoft Corp. also provides start-up funding for several affiliate companies, such as Teledesic, a satellite-based telecommunications company. However, many affiliates were launched by former Microsoft employees with generous stock options earned at the software giant. These "Baby Bills" (named after Microsoft founder Bill Gates) became affiliates by working with—rather than competing against—Microsoft on emerging technology.[59]

CELLULAR ORGANIZATIONS

The network structures that exist at Nortel Networks, Cisco Systems, Nike, Dell Computer, and other firms generally perform a patterned set of tasks for all clients. When you order a computer from Dell, the network partners follow the same set of transactions as they do for the next person who orders a computer. The specific computer configuration may change, but the relationships among the partners and the production process are fairly standardized until the partnership is reconfigured every few years.

Cellular organizations A type of network structure in which unique partnership teams are formed to provide customized products or services, usually to specific clients, for a limited time.

In contrast, some network structures—called **cellular organizations**—form unique partnership teams that provide customized products or services, usually to specific clients, for a limited time.[60] When an opportunity emerges, a unique combination of partners in the network structure form a special team that works on the assignment until it is completed. These network structures are called cellular organizations because they reshape themselves quickly to fit immediate needs. They are also self-organizing, meaning that they rearrange their own communication patterns and roles to fit the situation. The relationship among the partners is mutually determined rather than imposed by a core firm. In this respect, cellular firms are the ultimate virtual corporation. Connections 16.2 describes a recently developed alliance in Atlantic Canada that will form cellular structures for global competitiveness.

www.newsouthalliance.com

CONNECTIONS 16.2

NewSouth Alliance Adopts the Cellular Structure

Representatives from several United Kingdom and Canadian companies recently met in St. John's, Newfoundland, to form an alliance that brokers commercial business opportunities for the marine technology industry. NewSouth Alliance selects partners from the alliance to form a consortium. In effect, it creates cellular organizations—unique partnerships of organizations that provide customized products or services to specific clients for a limited time.

"NewSouth Alliance has the ability to put high-quality teams together very quickly, allowing us to bid on projects we would otherwise not be capable of responding to," explains a managing director of a British company in the alliance. BAE-NewPlan, a division of SNC-Lavalin, is an active participant in NewSouth Alliance because it also hopes to form virtual organizations for some global projects.

"By networking, smaller firms can act like a large firm, reduce costs, spread risk and compete more effectively," explains Clayton Burry, broker for NewSouth Alliance.

Source: Adapted from P. Doyle, "Getting Their Act Together," *St. John's Telegram*, October 29, 1999.

ADVANTAGES AND DISADVANTAGES OF NETWORK STRUCTURES

For several years, scholars have argued that organizational leaders must develop a metaphor of organizations as plasma-like organisms rather than rigid machines.[61] Network structures come close to the organism metaphor because they offer the flexibility to realign their structure with changing environmental requirements. If customers demand a new product or service, the core firm forms new alliances with other firms that offer the appropriate resources. For example, by finding partners with available plant facilities, Cisco Systems expanded its business much more rapidly than it would have had it built its own production facilities. When Cisco changes its product line, it isn't saddled with nonessential facilities and resources.

These virtual organizations also offer efficiencies because the core firm becomes globally competitive as it shops worldwide for subcontractors with the best people and the best technology at the best price. Indeed, the pressures of global competition have made network structures more vital, and computer-based information technology has made them possible.[62]

A potential disadvantage of network structures is that they expose the core firm to market forces. Other companies may bid up the price for subcontractors, whereas the short-term cost would be lower if the company hired its own employees to provide this function. Another problem is that although information technology makes worldwide communication much easier, it will never replace the degree of control that organizations have when manufacturing, marketing, and other functions are in house. The core firm can use arm's-length incentives and contract provisions to maintain the subcontractor's quality, but these actions are relatively crude compared to those used to maintain performance of in-house employees.

CONTINGENCIES OF ORGANIZATIONAL DESIGN

Organizational theorists and practitioners are interested not only in the elements of organizational structure, but also in the contingencies that determine or influence the optimal design. In this section, we introduce four contingencies of organizational design: size, technology, environment, and strategy.

ORGANIZATIONAL SIZE

Larger organizations have considerably different structures than do smaller organizations.[63] As the number of employees increases, job specialization increases due to a greater division of labour. Larger firms also have more elaborate coordinating mechanisms to manage the greater division of labour. They are more likely to use standardization of work processes and outputs to coordinate work activities. These coordinating mechanisms create an administrative hierarchy and greater formalization. Informal communication has traditionally decreased as a coordinating mechanism as organizations get larger. However, emerging computer technologies and increased emphasis on empowerment have caused informal communication to regain its importance in large firms.[64]

Larger organizations also tend to be more decentralized. As we noted earlier in this chapter, neither founders nor senior managers have sufficient time or expertise to process all of the decisions that significantly influence the business as it grows. Therefore, decision-making authority is pushed down to lower levels, where incumbents are able to cope with the more narrow range of issues under their control.[65]

TECHNOLOGY

Based on the open systems model (see Chapter 1), we know that an organization's structure needs to be aligned with its dominant technology. Two important technological contingencies that influence the best type of organizational structure are the variety and analyzability of work activities.[66] *Variety* refers to the number of exceptions to standard procedure that can occur in the team or work unit. *Analyzability* refers to the extent to which the transformation of input resources to outputs can be reduced to a series of standardized steps.

Some jobs are routine: employees perform the same tasks all the time and rely on set rules (standard operating procedures) when exceptions do occur. Almost everything is predictable. These situations, such as automobile assembly lines, have high formalization and centralization as well as standardization of work processes.

When employees perform tasks with high variety and low analyzability, they apply their skills to unique situations with little opportunity for repetition. Research project teams operate under these conditions. These situations call for an organic structure, one with low formalization, highly decentralized decision-making authority, and coordination mainly through informal communication among team members.

High-variety and high-analyzability tasks have many exceptions to routines, but these exceptions can usually be resolved through standard procedures. Maintenance groups and engineering design teams experience these conditions. Work units that fall into this category should use an organic structure, but it is possible to have somewhat greater formalization and centralization due to the analyzability of problems.

Skilled tradespeople tend to work in situations with low variety and low analyzability. Their tasks involve few exceptions but the problems that arise are difficult to resolve. This situation allows more centralization and formalization than in a purely organic structure, but coordination must include informal communication among the skilled employees so that unique problems can be resolved.

EXTERNAL ENVIRONMENT

The best structure for an organization depends on its external environment. The external environment includes anything outside the organization, including most stakeholders (e.g., clients, suppliers, government), resources (e.g., raw materials, human resources, information, finances), and competitors. Four relatively distinct characteristics of external environments influence the type of organizational structure best suited to a particular situation: dynamism, complexity, diversity, and hostility.[67]

- *Dynamic versus stable environments*—Dynamic environments have a high rate of change, leading to novel situations and a lack of identifiable patterns. Organic structures are better suited to this type of environment so that the organization can adapt more quickly to changes.[68] Network and team-based structures seem to be most effective in dynamic environments, because they usually have these features. In contrast, stable environments are characterized by regular cycles of activity and steady changes in supply and demand for inputs and outputs. Events are more predictable, enabling the firm to apply rules and procedures. Thus, more mechanistic structures tend to work best under these conditions.

- *Complex versus simple environments*—Complex environments have many elements, whereas simple environments have few things to monitor. For instance, a multinational corporation has a complex environment because it has many stakeholders. Decentralized structures seem to be better suited to complex environments, because these subunits are close to their local environment and are able to make more informed choices.

- *Diverse versus integrated environments*—Organizations located in diverse environments have a greater variety of products or services, clients, and regions. In contrast, an integrated environment has only one client, product, and geographic area. The more diversified the environment, the more the firm needs to use a divisionalized form aligned with that diversity. If it sells a single product around the world, a geographic divisionalized form would align best with the firm's geographic diversity. As we noted earlier with Nortel, global firms with several products and client groups have a continuous dilemma as to which form of diversity is most important.

- *Hostile versus munificent environments*—Firms located in a hostile environment face resource scarcity and more competition in the marketplace. Hostile environments are typically dynamic ones because they reduce the predictability of access to resources and demand for outputs. Organic structures tend to be best in hostile environments. However, when the environment is extremely hostile—such as during a severe shortage of supplies or lower market share—organizations tend to temporarily centralize so that decisions can be made more quickly and executives feel more comfortable being in control.[69] Ironically, centralization may result in lower-quality decisions during organizational crises, because top management has less information, particularly when the environment is complex.

ORGANIZATIONAL STRATEGY

Organizational strategy The way the organization positions itself in its setting in relation to its stakeholders given the organization's resources, capabilities, and mission.

Strategic choice The idea that an organization interacts with its environment rather than being totally determined by it.

Although size, technology, and environment influence the optimal organizational structure, these contingencies do not necessarily determine structure. Instead, there is increasing evidence that corporate leaders formulate and implement strategies that shape both the characteristics of these contingencies as well as the organization's resulting structure. **Organizational strategy** refers to the way the organization positions itself in its setting in relation to its stakeholders, given the organization's resources, capabilities, and mission.[70] The idea that an organization interacts with its environment rather than being totally determined by it is known as **strategic choice**.[71] In other words, organizational leaders take steps to define and manipulate their environments, rather than let the organization's fate be entirely determined by external influences.

The notion of strategic choice can be traced back to the work of Alfred Chandler in the early 1960s.[72] Chandler's proposal was that structure follows strategy. He observed that organizational structures follow the growth strategy developed by the organization's decision makers. Moreover, he noted that organizational structures change only after decision makers decide to do so. This recognizes that the link between structure and the contingency factors described earlier is mediated by organizational strategy.

Chandler's thesis that structure follows strategy has become the dominant perspective of business policy and strategic management. An important aspect of this view is that organizations can choose the environments in which they want to operate. Some businesses adopt a *differentiation strategy* by bringing unique products to the market or attracting clients who want customized goods and services. They try to distinguish their outputs from those provided by other firms through marketing, special services, and innovation. Others adopt a *cost leadership strategy*, in which they maximize productivity and are, thereby, able to offer popular products or services at a competitive price.[73]

The type of organizational strategy selected leads to the best organizational structure to adopt.[74] Organizations with a cost leadership strategy should adopt a mechanistic, functional structure with high levels of job specialization and standardized work processes. This is similar to the routine technology category described earlier because organizations maximize production and service efficiency. A differentiation strategy, on the other hand, requires more customized relations with clients. A matrix or team-based structure with less centralization and formalization is most appropriate here so that technical specialists are able to coordinate their work activities more closely with the client's needs. Overall, it is now apparent that organizational structure is influenced by size, technology, and environment, but the organization's strategy may reshape these elements and loosen their connection to organizational structure.

CHAPTER SUMMARY

- Organizational structure refers to the division of labour as well as to the patterns of coordination, communication, work flow, and formal power that direct organizational activities. All organizational structures divide labour into distinct tasks and coordinate that labour to accomplish common goals. The primary means of coordination are informal communication, formal hierarchy, and standardization.

- The four basic elements of organizational structure include span of control, centralization, formalization, and departmentalization. At one time, scholars suggested that firms should have a tall hierarchy with a narrow span of control. Today, most organizations have the opposite because they rely on informal communication and standardization, rather than just on direct supervision, to coordinate work processes.

- Centralization means that formal decision authority is held by a small group of people, typically senior executives. Many companies decentralize as they become larger and more complex because senior executives lack the necessary time and expertise to process all the decisions that significantly influence the business. Companies also tend to become more formalized over time because work activities become routinized. Formalization increases in larger firms because standardization works more efficiently than informal communication and direct supervision.

- A functional structure organizes employees around specific knowledge or other resources. This fosters greater specialization and improves direct supervision, but makes it more difficult for people to see the organization's larger picture or to coordinate across departments. A divisional structure groups employees around geographic areas, clients, or outputs. This structure accommodates growth and focuses employee attention on products or customers rather than tasks. However, this structure creates silos of knowledge and duplication of resources.

- The matrix structure combines two structures to leverage the benefits of both types of structure. However, this approach requires more coordination than functional or pure divisional structures, may dilute accountability, and increases conflict.

- One emerging form of departmentalization is the team-based structure. This structure is very flat with low formalization that organizes self-directed teams around work processes rather than functional specialties.

- A network structure is an alliance of several organizations for the purpose of creating a product or serving a client. Cellular organizations are network structures that can quickly reorganize themselves to suit the client's requirements.

- The best organizational structure depends on the firm's size, technology, and environment. Generally, larger organizations are decentralized and more formalized, with greater job specialization and elaborate coordinating mechanisms. The work unit's technology—including variety of work and analyzability of problems—influences whether to adopt an organic or mechanistic structure. We need to consider whether the external environment is dynamic, complex, diverse, and hostile.

- Although size, technology, and environment influence the optimal organizational structure, these contingencies do not necessarily determine structure. Rather, organizational leaders formulate and implement strategies to define and manipulate their environments. These strategies, rather than the other contingencies, directly shape the organization's structure.

KEY TERMS

Affiliate networks, p. 493

Cellular organizations, p. 493

Centralization, p. 482

Concurrent engineering, p. 477

Divisional structure, p. 486

Formalization, p. 483

Functional structure, p. 486

Job specialization, p. 476

Matrix structure, p. 488

Mechanistic structure, p. 484

Network structure, p. 492

Organic structure, p. 484

Organizational design, p. 476

Organizational strategy, p. 496

Organizational structure, p. 476

Span of control, p. 480

Strategic choice, p. 496

Team-based organization, p. 490

DISCUSSION QUESTIONS

1. Why are organizations moving towards flatter structures?

2. Canuck Technologies makes four types of products, each sold to different types of clients. For example, one product is sold exclusively to automobile repair shops, whereas another is used mainly in hospitals. Customer expectations within each product are surprisingly similar throughout the world. However, the company has separate marketing, product design, and manufacturing facilities in North America, Europe, Asia, and South America because, until recently, each jurisdiction had unique regulations governing the production and sales of these products. Several governments are now deregulating the products that Canuck

designs and manufactures, and trade agreements have opened several markets to foreign-made products. Which form of departmentalization might be best for Canuck Technologies if deregulation and trade agreements occur?

3. Why don't all organizations group people around product-based divisions?

4. Several global organizations have tried implementing a matrix structure to balance the power of its functional and divisional groups. However, many of these firms experienced problems and eventually switched to a hybrid form of divisionalized structure. Identify some of the problems these companies may have experienced with a matrix structure.

5. St. Luke's has a team-based structure from top to bottom. Is this typical? Could such a structure exist at Canadian National or Canada Post?

6. Some writers believe that a network structure is an effective design for global competition. Is this true, or are there situations for which this organizational structure may be inappropriate?

7. Suppose that you have been hired as a consultant to diagnose the environmental characteristics of your college or university. How would you describe the school's external environment? Is the school's existing structure appropriate for this environment?

8. What do we mean by "structure follows strategy"?

 Case Study

ACTIVITY 16.1
The Rise and Fall of PMC AG

Founded in 1930, PMC AG is a German manufacturer of high-priced sports cars. During its early years, PMC was a small consulting engineering firm that specialized in solving difficult automotive design problems for clients. At the end of the Second World War, however, the son of PMC's founder decided to expand the business beyond consulting engineering. He was determined that PMC would build its own precision automobiles.

In 1948, the first PMC prototypes rolled out of the small manufacturing facility. Each copy was handmade by highly skilled craftspeople. For several years, parts and engines were designed and built by other companies and assembled at the PMC plant. By the 1960s, however, PMC had begun to design and build its own parts.

PMC grew rapidly from the 1960s to mid-1980s. The company designed a completely new car in the early 1960s, launched a lower-priced model in 1970, and added a mid-priced model in 1977. By the mid-1980s, PMC had become very profitable and its name had become an icon for wealthy entrepreneurs and jetsetters. In 1986, the year of highest production, PMC sold 54,000 cars. Nearly two-thirds of these were sold in North America.

PMC's Structure

PMC's organizational structure expanded with its success. During its early years, the company consisted only of an engineering department and a production department. By the 1980s, employees were divided into more than ten functional departments representing different stages of the production process as well as upstream (e.g., design, purchasing) and downstream (e.g., quality control, marketing) activities. Employees worked exclusively in one department. It was almost considered mutiny for an employee to voluntarily move to another department.

PMC's production staff members were organized into a traditional hierarchy. Front-line employees reported to work group leaders, who reported to supervisors, who reported to group supervisors in

ACTIVITY 16.1 CONTINUED

each area. Group supervisors reported to production managers, who reported to production directors, who reported to PMC's executive vice-president of manufacturing. At one point in time, nearly 20 percent of production staff members were involved in supervisory tasks. In the early 1990s, for example, there were 48 group supervisors, 96 supervisors, and 162 work group leaders supervising about 2500 front-line production employees.

PMC's Craft Tradition

PMC had a long tradition and culture that supported craft expertise. This appealed to Germany's skilled workforce because it gave employees an opportunity to test and further develop their skills. PMC workers were encouraged to master long work cycles, often as long as 15 minutes per unit. Their ideal was to build as much of the automobile as possible alone. For example, a few masters were able to assemble an entire engine. Their reward was to personally sign their name on the completed component.

Design engineers worked independently of the production department, with the result that production employees had to adjust designs to fit the available parts. Rather than being a nuisance, the production employees viewed this as a challenge that would further test their well-developed craft skills. Similarly, manufacturing engineers occasionally redesigned the product to fit manufacturing capabilities.

To improve efficiency, a moving track assembly system was introduced in 1977. Even then, the emphasis on craft skills was apparent. Employees were encouraged to quickly put all the parts on the car, knowing that highly skilled troubleshooting craftspeople would discover and repair defects after the car came off the line. This was much more costly and time-consuming than assembling the vehicle correctly the first time, but it provided yet another challenging set of tasks for skilled craftspeople. And to support the company's position, PMC vehicles were known for their few defects by the time they were sold to customers.

The End of Success?

PMC sports cars filled a small niche in the automobile market for those who wanted a true sports car just tame enough for everyday use. PMC cars were known for their superlative performance based on excellent engineering technology, but they were also becoming very expensive. Japanese sports cars were not quite in the same league as PMC cars, but the cost of manufacturing the Japanese vehicles was a small fraction of the cost of manufacturing a vehicle at PMC.

This cost inefficiency hit PMC's sales during the late 1980s and early 1990s. First, the German currency appreciated against the U.S. and Canadian dollar, which made PMC sports cars even more expensive in the North American market. By 1990, PMC was selling only half of the cars it had sold just four years earlier. Then, the North American recession hit, driving PMC sales down further. In 1993, PMC sold just 14,000 vehicles, compared to 54,000 in 1987. And although sales rebounded to 20,000 by 1995, the high price tag put PMC cars out of reach of many potential customers. It was clear to PMC's founding family that changes were needed, but they weren't sure where to begin.

Discussion Questions

1. Describe PMC's organizational structure in terms of the four organizational design features (i.e., span of control, centralization, formalization, and departmentalization).

2. Discuss the problems with PMC's current structure.

3. Identify and justify an organizational structure that, in your opinion, would be more appropriate for PMC.

Source: Written by Steven L. McShane based on information from several sources about "PMC." The company name and some details of actual events have been altered to provide a fuller case discussion.

Video Case Study

ACTIVITY 16.2
Colgate-Palmolive's Team-based Organization

A few years ago, Colgate-Palmolive set out to build a factory of the future from the ground up. This facility, located in Cambridge, Ohio, would combine the best people with the best technology in a team environment. It would be a focused factory that incorporated the latest quality management practices, computer-aided manufacturing, and customer-focused culture.

Hiring the best people was a critical issue at the Cambridge plant. Colgate wanted employees who would actively participate in corporate decisions, have self-leadership, and feel ownership in the entire work process. Ten thousand people applied for the 170 positions. Aptitude tests, interviews, and other activities were used to narrow the applicant list down.

With the right people selected, Colgate had to create a work environment that supported a team structure. First, it established an all-salary workforce. Then, on the production floor, employees belong to one of only two job classifications: operator technician and maintenance technician. And all employees are expected to learn other jobs. Finally, every employee belongs to a team. These teams have managers, but their task is to work themselves out of the job as employees learn to manage themselves. These teams hold meetings to discuss issues ranging from productivity improvement to social events and plant policies.

At the plant, training is an ongoing process. With manuals for all equipment available to every employee and team members encouraged to take on other jobs within their team, everyone can spot problems and take corrective action. The plant has a skill-based pay system to encourage and reward multiskilling.

Discussion Questions

1. To what extent is this Colgate-Palmolive plant a team-based organizational structure?

2. What organizational systems support the team-based structure at the Cambridge plant?

3. Discuss the division of labour and methods of coordination used in this facility.

Source: "Colgate-Palmolive," McGraw-Hill/Irwin Management Video Series.

 **TEAM** exercise

ACTIVITY 16.3
THE CLUB ED EXERCISE

by Cheryl Harvey and Kim Morouney, Wilfrid Laurier University

Purpose: This exercise is designed to help you understand the issues to consider when designing organizations at various stages of growth.

Instructions: Each team discusses the scenario presented. The first scenario is presented below. The instructor will facilitate discussion and advise teams when to begin the next step. This exercise may be continued in a second class session.

Step 1: Students are placed in teams (typically of four or five people).

Step 2: After reading Scenario 1 presented below, each team will design an organizational chart (departmentalization) that is most appropriate for this situation. Students should be able to describe the type of structure drawn and explain why it is appropriate. The structure should be drawn on an overhead transparency or flip chart for others to see during later class discussion. The instructor will set a fixed time (e.g., 15 minutes) to complete this task.

> *Scenario 1:* Determined never to shovel snow again, you are establishing a new resort business on a small Caribbean island. The resort is under construction and is scheduled to open one year from now. You decide that it is time to draw up an organizational chart for this new venture, called Club Ed.

Step 3: At the end of the time allowed, the instructor will present Scenario 2 and each team will be asked to draw another organizational chart to suit that situation. Again, students should be able to describe the type of structure drawn and explain why it is appropriate.

Step 4: At the end of the time allowed, the instructor will present Scenario 3 and each team will be asked to draw another organizational chart to suit that situation.

Step 5: Depending on the time available, the instructor might present a fourth scenario. The class will gather to present their designs for each scenario. During each presentation, teams should describe the type of structure drawn and explain why it is appropriate.

Source: Adapted from C. Harvey and K. Morouney, *Journal of Management Education*, 22 (June 1998), pp. 425–29. Used with permission of the authors.

Self-Assessment **exercise**

ACTIVITY 16.4
IDENTIFYING YOUR PREFERRED ORGANIZATIONAL STRUCTURE

Purpose: This exercise is designed to help you understand how an organization's structure influences the personal needs and values of people working in that structure.

Instructions: Personal values influence how comfortable you are working in different organizational structures. You might prefer an organization with clearly defined rules or no rules at all. You might prefer a firm in which almost any employee can make important decisions, or in which senior executives screen important decisions. Read the statements below and indicate the extent to which you would like to work in an organization with that characteristic. When finished, use the scoring key in Appendix B of this book to calculate your results. This self-assessment is completed alone so students can answer honestly without concerns of social comparison. However, class discussion will focus on the elements of organizational design and their relationship to personal needs and values.

ORGANIZATIONAL STRUCTURE PREFERENCE SCALE

I would like to work in an organization where...   **Score**

1. A person's career ladder has several steps towards higher status and responsibility. . . . . . .   Not at all   A little   Somewhat   Very much   _____

2. Employees perform their work with few rules to limit their discretion. . . . .   Not at all   A little   Somewhat   Very much   _____

3. Responsibility is pushed down to employees who perform the work. . . . .   Not at all   A little   Somewhat   Very much   _____

4. Supervisors have few employees, so they work closely with each person. . . . .   Not at all   A little   Somewhat   Very much   _____

5. Senior executives make most decisions to ensure that the company is consistent in its actions. . . . .   Not at all   A little   Somewhat   Very much   _____

6. Jobs are clearly defined so there is no confusion over who is responsible for various tasks. . . . .   Not at all   A little   Somewhat   Very much   _____

7. Employees have their say on issues, but senior executives make most of the decisions. . . . .   Not at all   A little   Somewhat   Very much   _____

8. Job descriptions are broadly stated or nonexistent. . . . .   Not at all   A little   Somewhat   Very much   _____

9. Everyone's work is tightly synchronized around top management's operating plans. . . . .   Not at all   A little   Somewhat   Very much   _____

10. Most work is performed in teams without close supervision. . . . .   Not at all   A little   Somewhat   Very much   _____

11. Work gets done through informal discussion with co-workers rather than through formal rules. . . . .   Not at all   A little   Somewhat   Very much   _____

12. Supervisors have so many employees that they can't watch anyone very closely. . . . .   Not at all   A little   Somewhat   Very much   _____

13. Everyone has clearly understood goals, expectations, and job duties. . . . .   Not at all   A little   Somewhat   Very much   _____

14. Senior executives assign overall goals, but leave daily decisions to front-line teams. . . . . . .   Not at all   A little   Somewhat   Very much   _____

15. Even in a large company, the CEO is only three or four levels above the person in the lowest position. . . . .   Not at all   A little   Somewhat   Very much   _____

CHAPTER SEVENTEEN

Organizational Culture

LEARNING OBJECTIVES

After reading this chapter, you should be able to:

- Describe the elements of organizational culture.
- Discuss the importance of organizational subcultures.
- List four categories of artifacts through which corporate culture is communicated.
- Identify three functions of organizational culture.
- Discuss the conditions under which cultural strength improves corporate performance.
- Discuss the effect of organizational culture on business ethics.
- Compare four strategies for merging organizational cultures.
- Identify five strategies to strengthen an organization's culture.

With casual clothes and a canine companion, ExtendMedia founder and CEO Keith Kocho represents the digital media company's unique corporate culture.

Edward Gajdel Photography.

ExtendMedia has one of the most "casual cool" corporate cultures in Canada. The digital media company's 150 employees work out of a funky, brick-and-wood, former carpet factory. A gigantic slide will soon connect the two floors; stairs are optional. ExtendMedia employees have free access to cappuccino machines and draught beer. A hammock hangs high above the open reception area. There's even a lot of couch space for naps.

Creativity is another cultural value that becomes apparent when you enter the Toronto-based company's headquarters. ExtendMedia has an art space where employees can express their artistic flair. A display of employee artwork further reflects the company's desire for employees to break out of square thinking.

Look a bit closer and you'll see that ExtendMedia is a status-free zone. Everyone wears casual clothes and no one has a private office. It's difficult—if not impossible—to tell the executives from the entry-level staff. Founder and CEO Keith Kocho sits amid a sea of desks, usually with his dog Scoutie by his side. All employees can bring their dogs to work.

ExtendMedia also has a team-based culture. Employee desks have wheels that can be moved quickly to form new project groups. "You're in control of the work you do and you're working on a team—there's no hierarchy," explains Deborah Middleton, who designed ExtendMedia's workspace. "[Y]our value is based upon how you're contributing to the team."[1]

www.extendmedia.com

• **Organizational culture** The basic pattern of shared assumptions, values, and beliefs governing the way employees within an organization think about and act on problems and opportunities.

E xtendMedia has a distinctive organizational culture. Moreover, it is a culture that seems to work well for the digital media company's competitiveness. **Organizational culture** is the basic pattern of shared assumptions, values, and beliefs considered to be the correct way of thinking about and acting on problems and opportunities facing the organization. It defines what is important and unimportant in the company. You might think of it as the organization's DNA—invisible to the naked eye, yet a powerful template that shapes what happens in the workplace.[2]

This chapter begins by examining the elements of organizational culture and how culture is deciphered through artifacts. This is followed by a discussion of the relationship between organizational culture and corporate performance, including the effects of cultural strength, fit, and adaptability. Then we turn to the issue of mergers and corporate culture. The final section of this chapter looks at specific strategies for maintaining a strong organizational culture.

ELEMENTS OF ORGANIZATIONAL CULTURE

• **Mental models** The broad world views or "theories-in-use" that people rely on to guide their perceptions and behaviours.

As we see in Exhibit 17.1, the assumptions, values, and beliefs that represent organizational behaviour operate beneath the surface. They are not directly observed, yet their effects are everywhere. Assumptions represent the deepest part of organizational culture because they are unconscious and taken for granted. Assumptions are the shared **mental models**, the broad world views or theories-in-use that people rely on to guide their perceptions and behaviours (see Chapter 6). At ExtendMedia, for example, employees practise "constructive eavesdropping" because they assume that speaking up when overhearing someone else's conversation is good for the business. It is an assumption that's ingrained and taken for granted. In other companies, employees might assume it is rude or unnecessary to become involved in someone else's work.

An organization's cultural beliefs and values are somewhat easier than assumptions to decipher because people are aware of them. *Beliefs* represent the individual's perceptions of reality.

EXHIBIT 17.1 Elements of Organizational Culture

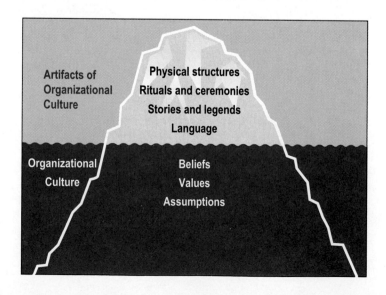

Artifacts of Organizational Culture

Physical structures
Rituals and ceremonies
Stories and legends
Language

Organizational Culture

Beliefs
Values
Assumptions

Values Stable, long-lasting beliefs about what is important to the individual.

Values are more stable, long-lasting beliefs about what is important. They help us define what is right or wrong, or good or bad, in the world (see Chapter 7).[3] In some organizations, wearing T-shirts and drinking beer on the job is considered to be inappropriate and evidence of poor performance. But ExtendMedia's culture values the "casual cool" culture of work.

We cannot determine an organization's cultural values just by asking employees and other people about them. Values are socially desirable, so what people say they value (called *espoused values*) may differ from what they truly value (*enacted values*).[4] Espoused values do not represent an organization's culture. Rather, they establish the public image that corporate leaders want to display. Enacted values, on the other hand, are values in use. They are the values that guide individual decisions and behaviour in the workplace.

CONTENT OF ORGANIZATIONAL CULTURE

www.rim.net

Organizations differ in their cultural content, that is, in their relative ordering of beliefs, values, and assumptions. Consider the following companies and their apparent dominant cultures:

Fast is too mild a word to describe the corporate culture at Research in Motion (RIM). The Kitchener, Ontario, pioneer in wireless digital assistants (think Blackberry) is doubling its number of employees and producing five times more of its popular devices over the next year. Fortunately, RIM's intense culture is also supportive and oriented towards fun. For example, the company recently threw a surprise party and hired Barenaked Ladies as the musical entertainment. All of RIM's employees were invited, along with hundreds of computer science, engineering, and business students from the area. "This is a fun, creative, intense and inclusive corporate culture," explains RIM co-CEO Jim Balsillie (right). "It's a collegial culture," adds Mike Lazaridis, RIM's other co-CEO (left).[8] How would you try to determine whether Research in Motion really has these cultural values?

- *Q-Media*—A thrifty culture has kept this Vancouver-based software packaging and distribution company in business. Q-Media relies on higher-cost small manufacturing runs, whereas its U.S. competitors have more lucrative large contracts. To survive, Q-Media employees are focused on reducing costs. Profit and loss are calculated daily, and full-time staff receive a share of cost savings. "We had to be thrifty," explains Q-Media CEO Robert Lawrie. "I would argue it is our core asset, although it never shows up in our balance sheet."[5]

- *Nokia Corp.*—Nokia Corp. is a leader in cellular telephones. But unlike the "me-first" cultures found in other high-technology firms, Nokia employees avoid taking personal credit for their successes. Instead, the Helsinki, Finland, conglomerate emphasizes understated collegiality. "We don't snap our suspenders," says Nokia CEO Jorma Ollila.[6]

- *MDS Nordion*—Employees at MDS Nordion always have health on their minds. It's not just because the Kanata, Ontario, firm is a world leader in radioisotopes and other high-tech hospital equipment. It's because the company's culture places employee health as a top priority. The company teaches employees how to eat well and encourages regular exercise. "Our approach to employee health is results-oriented, emphasizing a supportive culture," says MDS Nordion CEO John Morrison.[7]

Thrifty. Collegial. Health-conscious. How many corporate cultural values are there? No one knows for certain. There are dozens of individual and cross-cultural values, so there are likely as many organizational values. Some writers and consultants have attempted to classify organizational cultures into a few categories with catchy labels such as "clubs" and

© Kitchener-Waterloo Record.

"fortresses." Although these typologies might reflect the values of a few organizations, they oversimplify the diversity of cultural values in organizations. Worse, they tend to distort rather than clarify our attempts to diagnose corporate culture.

ORGANIZATIONAL SUBCULTURES

When discussing organizational culture, we are actually referring to the *dominant culture,* that is, the themes shared most widely by the organization's members. However, organizations are also composed of subcultures located throughout its various divisions, geographic regions, and occupational groups.[9] Some *subcultures* enhance the dominant culture by espousing parallel assumptions, values, and beliefs; others are called *countercultures* because they directly oppose the organization's core values.

Subcultures, particularly countercultures, potentially create conflict and dissension among employees, but they also serve two important functions. First, they maintain the organization's standards of performance and ethical behaviour. Employees who hold countercultural values are an important source of surveillance and critique over the dominant order.[10] They encourage constructive controversy and more creative thinking about how the organization should interact with its environment. Subcultures prevent employees from blindly following one set of values and thereby help the organization to abide by society's ethical values.

Second, subcultures are the spawning grounds for emerging values that keep the firm aligned with the needs of customers, suppliers, communities, and other stakeholders. Companies eventually need to replace their dominant values with ones that are more appropriate for the changing environment. If subcultures are suppressed, the organization may take longer to discover and adopt values aligned with the emerging environment.

DECIPHERING ORGANIZATIONAL CULTURE THROUGH ARTIFACTS

Artifacts The observable symbols and signs of an organization's culture, including its physical structures, ceremonies, language, and stories.

We can't directly see an organization's cultural assumptions, values, and beliefs. Instead, as Exhibit 17.1 illustrated, organizational culture is deciphered indirectly through artifacts. **Artifacts** are the observable symbols and signs of an organization's culture, such as the way visitors are greeted, the physical layout, and how employees are rewarded.[11] "You show your corporate culture in everything—the way the building looks, the way people act, the names of the conference rooms," says Joe Kraus, a co-founder of Excite, an Internet gateway and search engine company.[12]

Understanding an organization's culture requires painstaking assessment of many artifacts because they are subtle and often ambiguous.[13] The process is very much like an anthropological investigation of a new society. Some scholars extract organizational values from the narratives of everyday corporate life.[14] Others survey employees, observe workplace behaviour, and study written documents. We probably need to do all of these things to accurately assess an organization's culture. Although this book tries to present accurate examples, we should remain cautious about public statements regarding a company's culture. Most often, these statements are based on no more than a journalist's quick scan or the company's own public relations pronouncements of its espoused values. With this in mind, let's consider four broad categories of artifacts: organizational stories and legends, rituals and ceremonies, language, and physical structures and symbols.

ORGANIZATIONAL STORIES AND LEGENDS

In the late 1980s, so the story goes, executives at Maritime Life Assurance Co. were pouring over the plans for a new head office in Halifax. The crowning glory of the architectural design was a spectacular ocean view from the ninth-floor offices. Naturally, the architects designed the space for the executive suite. But Maritime's CEO believed that this would be inconsistent with the company's culture. Instead, the plum location went to the employees in the form of an elegant, wood-panelled cafeteria. The executives had to put their offices elsewhere.[15]

This story illustrates one of Maritime Life Assurance's core values—that employee well-being and satisfaction come before executive status. Stories and legends about past corporate incidents serve as powerful social prescriptions of the way things should (or should not) be done. They provide human realism to corporate expectations, individual performance standards, and assumptions about the way things should work around the organization.

Not all stories and legends are positive. Some are repeated to demonstrate what is wrong with the corporate culture. For instance, General Motors employees who rejected the auto maker's dominant culture liked to tell stories about how dozens of GM people would arrive at the airport to meet a senior executive. An executive's status was symbolized by the number of vehicles leaving the airport with that person.[16] This story didn't just symbolize respect for authority; it was repeated because it highlighted the decadence and waste that characterized GM's dominant culture.

Courtesy of Four Seasons Hotels and Resorts.

www.fourseasons.com

Toronto-based Four Seasons Hotels and Resorts hires, trains, and rewards employees for superior customer service. Yet founder Isadore Sharp will tell you that the company's legendary service is also ingrained in Four Seasons' corporate culture. There is certainly evidence of the customer service value in corporate stories and legends. One story recounts an incident in which rock star Rod Stewart asked Four Seasons staff to find someone to play the bagpipes in his suite. The employees were able to find a bagpipe player, even though Stewart phoned in the request at *midnight!*[17] In what ways do these stories and legends support organizational culture?

Organizational stories and legends are most effective at communicating cultural values when they describe real people, are assumed to be true, and are known by employees throughout the organization. Stories are also prescriptive—they advise people what or what not to do.[18] Research on organizational stories reveals that they tend to answer one or more of the following questions: How does the boss react to mistakes? What events are so important that people get fired? Who, if anyone, can break the rules? How do people rise to the top of this organization? How much help can employees expect from the organization for transfers and other events? How will the organization deal with crises?[19]

RITUALS AND CEREMONIES

Soon after moving from IBM to Digital Equipment Corporation (now part of Compaq Computers) several years ago, Peter DeLisi noticed that Digital employees seemed to fight a lot with each other. "Shouting matches were a frequent occurrence, and I came to conclude that Digital people didn't like one another," he recalls. Eventually, DeLisi learned that Digital employees didn't dislike each other; they were engaging in the ritual of "pushing back"— defending ideas until truth ultimately prevailed.[20]

"Pushing back" at Digital was a ritual that reflected the firm's belief that constructive conflict is useful. **Rituals** are the programmed routines of daily organizational life that dramatize the organization's culture. Along with shouting matches at Digital, rituals include how visitors are greeted, how often senior executives visit subordinates, how people communicate with each other, how much time employees take for lunch, and so on. Ceremonies are more formal than rituals. **Ceremonies** are planned activities conducted specifically for the benefit of an audience. This would include publicly rewarding (or punishing) employees, or celebrating the launch of a new product or newly won contract.[21]

> **Rituals** The programmed routines of daily organizational life that dramatize the organization's culture.

> **Ceremonies** Deliberate and usually dramatic displays of organizational culture, such as celebrations and special social gatherings.

ORGANIZATIONAL LANGUAGE

The language of the workplace speaks volumes about the company's culture. How employees address co-workers, describe customers, express anger, and greet stakeholders are all verbal symbols of cultural values. Organizational leaders also use phrases, metaphors, and other special vocabularies to symbolize the company's culture.[22] Consider the "grocery store" metaphor that General Electric CEO Jack Welch often uses. He wants everyone to think of GE not as a electrical manufacturing colossus, but as a small business where customer service and the constant search for new opportunities keeps the "shop" in business.[23] We need to keep in mind, however, that the language of leaders often represents *espoused values*—the values that leaders want people to believe exist—rather than the company's true values (called *enacted values*).

Language also highlights values held by organizational subcultures. This was recently apparent to consultants working at Whirlpool. They kept hearing employees talk about the appliance company's "PowerPoint culture." This phrase, which names Microsoft's presentation software, is a critique of Whirlpool's hierarchical culture in which communication is one way (from executives to employees) and employees have limited opportunity to voice opinions or concerns to company executives.[24]

PHYSICAL STRUCTURES AND SYMBOLS

British Airways (BA) is changing its corporate culture by changing its headquarters building. The old multi-story headquarters near London's Heathrow Airport reinforced hierarchical and bureaucratic values that the airline was trying to cast off. The new headquarters is designed with a central village square and work units spreading out from it. Executives are located with their units, not cloistered on a separate executive floor. In the words of one British Airways executive, "move the office, change the culture."

Creative Options, a 60-employee advertising firm in Waterloo, Ontario, also designed its new building around cultural values. With extensive employee input, the new design has 14-foot windows, exposed wiring and support beams, two cafés, and quirky pink walls. "The building really speaks to the culture of Creative Options," says company president Pat Scott.[25]

Creative Options and British Airways are part of the recent wave in which corporate leaders are redesigning the workplace to fit the organization's culture (or create a new one). The size, shape, location, and age of buildings might suggest the organization's emphasis on teamwork, risk aversion, flexibility, or another set of values. These structures may be deliberately designed to shape the culture, or they may be merely artifacts of the existing culture.[26]

Even if an organization's building doesn't make much of a statement, there is a treasure trove of physical artifacts inside. Desks, chairs, cafeteria food, and wall hangings are just a few of the items that might convey cultural meaning. Walk into Amazon.com's headquarters and you will soon notice evidence of a frugal culture. Desks are made from wooden doors and computers are propped up on telephone books to avoid having to buy monitor stands. Extra chairs are considered to be an extravagance.

Stroll around the Bolton, Ontario, headquarters of Husky Injection Molding Systems and you will find artifacts of a healthy culture. Books on wildlife greet visitors in the front foyer. The gardens around the four campus-like buildings are free of pesticides. The company is years ahead of government standards on recycling. The manufacturing area is almost spotless. In the cafeteria, employees pay for coffee, but herbal tea is available for free. The closest thing to a hamburger is made from baked turkey.[27] Each artifact alone might not say much, but put enough of them together and the company's cultural values become easier to decipher.

ORGANIZATIONAL CULTURE AND PERFORMANCE

www.oakley.com

Does organizational culture affect corporate performance? Zero-Knowledge thinks so. The Montreal-based software company even has its own Director of Culture and Learning. Several writers on this subject also conclude that a strong corporate culture is good for business.[28]

Oakley, Inc. is at war. At least, that's the impression you get when visiting its recently built headquarters in Foothill Ranch, California. The maker of ultrahip eyewear and footwear has a front lobby (right) that looks like a bomb shelter. Sleek pipes, watertight doors, and towering metallic walls studded with oversized bolts suggest a place that is routinely subjected to laser fire and floods. Ejection seats from B-52 bombers furnish the waiting area. A full-size torpedo lies in a rack behind the receptionist's armoured desk. "We've always had a fortress mentality," says an Oakley executive. "What we make is gold, and people will do anything to get it, so we protect it."[29] Visit Oakley's Web site (www.oakley.com). In what ways does the information at this site reflect Oakley's warlike and protective culture?

Generally, they argue that culture serves three important functions. First, corporate culture is a deeply embedded form of social control that influences employee decisions and behaviour.[30] Culture is pervasive and operates unconsciously. You might think of it as an automatic pilot, directing employees in ways that are consistent with organizational expectations.

Second, corporate culture is the "social glue" that bonds people and makes them feel part of the organizational experience.[31] Employees are motivated to internalize the organization's dominant culture because it fulfils their need for social identity. This social glue is increasingly important as a way to attract new staff and retain top performers. "If the company can sell the culture to the employee, that makes it a little harder for them to walk away and a little more attractive to other prospective employees," says Scott Moses, a hardware designer at Ottawa-based computer maker DY4.[32]

Finally, corporate culture assists the sense-making process.[33] It helps employees understand organizational events. They can get on with the task at hand rather than spend time trying to figure out what is expected of them. Employees can also communicate more efficiently and reach higher levels of cooperation because they share common mental models of reality.

ORGANIZATIONAL CULTURE STRENGTH AND FIT

Each of these functions of organizational culture assumes that a strong culture is better than a weak one. A *strong organizational* culture exists when most employees across all subunits hold the dominant values. The values are also institutionalized through well-established artifacts, thereby making it difficult for those values to change. Lastly, strong cultures are long lasting. In many cases, they can be traced back to the beliefs and values established by the company's founder.[34] In contrast, companies have weak cultures when the dominant values are short lived and held mainly by a few people at the top of the organization.

The discussion so far suggests that companies with strong cultures should have higher performance, but studies have found only a modestly positive relationship.[35] One reason for the weak relationship is that a strong culture increases organizational performance only when the cultural content is appropriate for the organization's environment (see Exhibit 17.2). Companies that operate in a highly competitive environment might be better served by a culture that engenders efficiency. Companies in environments that require dedicated employees

---

EXHIBIT 17.2 Organizational Culture and Performance

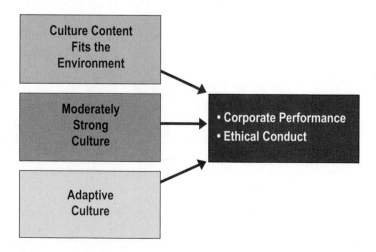

will be more successful with an employee-oriented culture. When a firm's culture does not fit its environment, on the other hand, employees have difficulty anticipating and responding to the needs of customers or other dominant stakeholders.

A second concern is that a company's culture might be so strong that employees blindly focus on the mental model shaped by that culture. When an organization's culture intensely emphasizes customer service, for example, employees tend to see problems as customer service problems, even though some are really problems related to efficiency or technology. Thus, strong cultures might cause decision makers to overlook or incorrectly define subtle misalignments between the organization's activities and the changing environment.[36]

Finally, very strong cultures tend to suppress dissenting subcultural values. In the long term, this prevents organizations from nurturing new cultural values that should become dominant values as the environment changes. In the short term, a strong culture might undermine constructive controversy (see Chapter 13). Procter & Gamble CEO Durk I. Jager thinks this is a problem at his organization. He complains that recruits are quickly "Procterized"—they eventually sound alike, think alike, and look alike. With common values, the company lacks conflict. "Great ideas generally come from conflict—a dissatisfaction with the status quo," explains Jager. "I'd like to have an organization where there are rebels."[37] Thus, corporate leaders need to recognize that healthy organizations have subcultures with dissenting values that may produce dominant values in the future.

ADAPTIVE CULTURES

So far, we have learned that strong cultures are more effective when the cultural values are aligned with the organization's environment. Also, no corporate culture should be so strong that it blinds employees to alternative viewpoints or completely suppresses dissenting subcultures. One last point to add to this discussion is that organizations are more likely to succeed when they have an adaptive culture.[38] An **adaptive culture** exists when employees focus on the changing needs of customers and other stakeholders, and support initiatives to keep pace with these changes.

Organizational culture experts are starting to piece together the elements of adaptive cultures.[39] First and foremost, adaptive cultures have an external focus. Employees hold a common mental model that the organization's success depends on continuous change to support stakeholders. Nortel Networks has shifted from telephones to Internet gear. Nokia has moved from toilet paper and rubber boots to cellular telephones. Both of these firms have maintained an adaptive culture because employees believe that change is both necessary and inevitable to keep pace with a changing external environment.

Second, employees in adaptive cultures pay attention to corporate goals, but they pay more attention to organizational processes to achieve those goals. They engage in continuous improvement of internal processes (production, customer service, etc.) to serve external stakeholders. Third, employees in adaptive cultures have a strong sense of ownership. They assume responsibility for the organization's performance. In other words, they believe in "it's our job" rather than "it's not my job." Fourth, adaptive cultures are proactive and quick. Employees seek out opportunities, rather than wait for them to arrive. They act quickly to learn through discovery rather than engage in "paralysis by analysis."

ORGANIZATIONAL CULTURE AND BUSINESS ETHICS

Along with other forms of performance, an organization's culture can potentially influence ethical conduct. In fact, a recent survey by consulting firm KPMG found that Canadian executives

• Adaptive culture An organization culture in which employees focus on the changing needs of customers and other stakeholders, and support initiatives to keep pace with these changes.

John Thoeming.

For more than 100 years, Shiseido's corporate culture has valued beauty and knowledge. "For us, beauty is art and knowledge is science," explains Akira Gemma, president of Japan's largest cosmetics company. "It is who we are. It is our corporate culture." But after complaints in the mid-1990s about its sales methods, Shiseido is also trying to make business ethics part of its corporate culture. A new set of corporate values called The Shiseido Code was developed, and several hundred employees have become standard-bearers of this code in Shiseido's 250 Japanese offices. When the ethics code was distributed, the company designated two months as "a period of reflection" during which employees were asked to consider their past activities in light of business ethics. Shiseido hopes that these practices, along with training and communication, will embed the ethics code in the company's culture.[42] What factors suggest that Shiseido might eventually be successful at creating a more ethical culture?

www.shiseido.co.jp

identified organizational culture as one of the three main influences on ethical conduct at work. (The other two were executive leadership and personal commitment to ethical principles.)[40] This makes sense because, as we learned in Chapter 7, good behaviour is driven by ethical values. An organization can guide the conduct of its employees by embedding ethical values in its dominant culture.

Lockheed Martin provides a good example of this. The aerospace giant was created in the mid-1990s from the merger of 16 companies. Some of these firms had previously been accused of unethical conduct in government procurement contracts. When these diverse cultures were integrated, senior executives wanted to be sure that the emerging culture emphasized ethical conduct. So they adopted six core values that represented both the company's culture and its ethical standards: honesty, integrity, respect, trust, responsibility, and citizenship.[41]

Although organizational culture can support ethical values, it can also become the source of ethical problems. As was mentioned earlier, corporate culture is a form of control because it guides employee decisions and behaviour. All organizations require some control to ensure that employee actions are aligned with organizational objectives. But as Connections 17.1 describes, a few organizations imprint their cultural values so strongly on employees that they risk becoming corporate cults. They take over employees' lives and rob their individualism. Thus, an organization's culture should be consistent with society's ethical values and should not be so strong that it undermines individual freedom.

MERGING ORGANIZATIONAL CULTURES

Employees at Russell & DuMoulin in Vancouver and Fasken Martineau in Toronto, Montreal, and Quebec City spent a lot of time together before their recent merger into Canada's second-largest law firm, Fasken Martineau DuMoulin. The meetings didn't just work out the contractual details of their proposed marriage. The cross-country trips were mainly reconnaissance missions to determine whether they had compatible corporate cultures. The merger process turned due diligence on its head by looking at whether the two firms had compatible corporate values *before* determining whether the computer systems and financial procedures were similar. "If the people don't fit, it doesn't matter how good the computers are," says the managing partner at Fasken Martineau DuMoulin's Vancouver office.[43]

Fasken Martineau DuMoulin's recent merger is a stellar example of how to decide on and implement a merger or acquisition from a corporate cultural perspective. Unfortunately, it is also the exception. Companies typically look at financial or marketing issues when deciding to merge with or acquire another firm, but few of them conduct due-diligence audits on their respective

CONNECTIONS 17.1

When Corporate Culture Becomes a Corporate Cult

When Andrew Brenner interviewed for a legal job at Microsoft a couple of years ago, he was troubled by the experience. "All the lawyers seemed to think it was a forgone conclusion Microsoft would take over the world," says Brenner. Ultimately, Brenner decided not to pursue the job. "It's a very strong culture. Too strong for me."

While many writers seem to celebrate organizations with strong cultures, a few are worried that some firms are becoming corporate cults. A recent book on the subject suggests that employees are victims of corporate cults when they work crushingly long hours, have few friends outside the workplace, develop emotional attitudes about their job, and have difficulty distinguishing "who I am" from "what I do."

Microsoft has been accused of being a corporate cult. Some employees practically live at the software giant's campus in Redmond, Washington. "There's people working here 24 hours a day," says a Microsoft manager. "It's set up so you never have to go home." Microsoft employees also develop a strong belief system that is difficult to distinguish from their life outside of work. "The Microsoft corporate culture can be broken down into four key parts," explains Michael Gartenberg, an analyst at Gartner Group Inc: "A tremendous work ethic; Bill Gates is always right; an us-versus-them mentality; and Bill Gates is always right."

Razorfish, an Internet professional services organization, also has characteristics of a corporate cult. "We've been accused of creating a cult-like atmosphere here, but to us there's Razorfish and not-Razorfish," says Len Sellers, managing director of Razorfish's San Francisco office.

Sellers defends the strong culture at Razorfish, but he also describes how it has taken over his life. "I used to be an avid sailor, but haven't been on a boat in a year," he admits. "I used to have girlfriends, but they left out of boredom and frustration. I used to have a cat, but it moved in with a neighbour. It's one thing when a girlfriend leaves, but it's another when a cat goes."

Sources: T.C. Doyle, "New Economy, New Culture," *VarBusiness,* July 10, 2000, p. 26; J. Useem, "Welcome to the New Company Town," *Fortune,* January 10, 2000, pp. 62–70; D. Arnott, *Corporate Cults* (New York: AMACOM, 1999).

corporate cultures. Yet attempting to merge two organizations with distinct values and beliefs could result in a cultural collision that threatens the success of an otherwise strategically compatible merger.[44] One survey recently reported that over two-thirds of executives in major U.S. companies identified integrating organizational cultures as the top challenge in a merger.[45]

The corporate world is littered with mergers that failed or had a difficult gestation because of clashing organizational cultures. For example, Quebecor is feeling the side effects of imposing its "tight ship" culture on SunMedia. Morale has apparently plummeted and turnover has increased because staff at *Toronto Sun* and other SunMedia newspapers have difficulty adjusting to Quebecor's harsh values.[46]

Organizational leaders can minimize these cultural collisions and fulfil their duty of due diligence by conducting a bicultural audit. A **bicultural audit** diagnoses cultural relations of the companies and determines the extent to which cultural clashes will likely occur.[47] Connections 17.2 describes how Abitibi-Consolidated has completed successful mergers using this important process.

Bicultural audit
Diagnoses cultural relations of merging companies and determines the extent to which cultural clashes will likely occur.

CONNECTIONS 17.2

Abitibi-Consolidated Minimizes Culture Clashes

Ron Oberlander predicted that there would be unprecedented consolidation of the pulp-and-paper industry. The CEO of Abitibi-Price (now Abitibi-Consolidated) also knew that no matter how good mergers look in financial terms, most produce disappointing results because corporate culture is often left out of the calculations.

So, with several potential partners at hand, Oberlander wanted to know how much culture clash would occur if Abitibi merged with each of them. To answer this question, executives at the Toronto-based pulp-and-paper company developed the Merging Cultures Evaluation Index (MCEI), an evaluation system that would help Abitibi compare its culture with other companies in the industry. The MCEI analyzes several dimensions of corporate culture, such as concentration of power versus diffusion of power, innovation versus tradition, wide versus narrow flow of information, and consensus versus authoritative decision making.

Abitibi executives completed the questionnaire to assess their own culture. Then they sent the questionnaire to the executives of potential suitors. Individual scores were aggregated into company scores. These results were then presented in a summary report showing each firm's overall compatibility with Abitibi, as well as the degree to which executives within each firm had similar scores on each dimension.

The MCEI results, along with financial and infrastructural information, served as the basis for Abitibi-Price to merge with Stone Consolidated to become Abitibi-Consolidated, the world's largest pulp-and-paper firm. The CEO of Stone-Consolidated was impressed with this process. "I think you should have to do due diligence on culture," he agreed.

Sources: M.L. Marks, "Mixed Signals," *Across the Board,* May 2000, pp. 21–26; M.L. Marks, "Adding Cultural Fit to Your Diligence Checklist," *Mergers & Acquisitions,* December 1999; S. Greengard, "Due Diligence: The Devil in the Details," *Workforce,* October 1999, p. 68; J. MacFarland, "An Unusual Team, on Paper," *Globe and Mail,* February 19, 1997, pp. B1, B11; G. MacDonald, "What Happens After the Deal Is Done," *Globe and Mail,* February 20, 1997, p. B14.

The bicultural audit process begins with interviews, questionnaires, focus groups, and observation of cultural artifacts to identify cultural differences between the merging companies. This includes carefully examining artifacts of each organization—the office layout, how they bill customers, how decisions are made, how information is shared, and so on. Next, the audit data are analyzed to determine which differences between the two firms will result in conflict and which cultural values provide common ground on which to build a cultural foundation in the merged organization. The final stage of the bicultural audit involves identifying strategies and preparing action plans to bridge the two organizations' cultures.

STRATEGIES TO MERGE DIFFERENT ORGANIZATIONAL CULTURES

In some cases, the bicultural audit results in a decision to end merger talks because the two cultures are too different to merge effectively. For instance, GE Capital has rejected potential acquisitions when it became apparent that the other firm's cultural values were incompatible. Nortel Networks walked away from a joint venture with Cisco Systems because it wasn't comfortable with Cisco's cultural values.[48] However, even with substantially different cultures, two

EXHIBIT 17.3   Strategies for Merging Different Organizational Cultures

Merger Strategy	Description	Works Best When
Assimilation	Acquired company embraces acquiring firm's culture.	Acquired firm has a weak culture.
Deculturation	Acquiring firm imposes its culture on unwilling acquired firm.	Rarely works—may be necessary only when acquired firm's culture doesn't work but employees don't realize it.
Integration	Combining two or more cultures into a new composite culture.	Existing cultures can be improved.
Separation	Merging companies remain distinct entities with minimal exchange of culture or organizational practices.	Firms operate successfully in different businesses requiring different cultures.

Source: Based on ideas in K.W. Smith, "A Brand-New Culture for the Merged Firm," *Mergers and Acquisitions,* 35 (June 2000), pp. 45–50; A.R. Malekazedeh and A. Nahavandi, "Making Mergers Work by Managing Cultures," *Journal of Business Strategy,* May–June 1990, pp. 55–57.

companies may form a workable union if they apply the appropriate merger strategy. The four main strategies for merging different corporate cultures are assimilation, deculturation, integration, and separation (see Exhibit 17.3).[49]

Assimilation

Assimilation occurs when employees at the acquired company willingly embrace the cultural values of the acquiring organization. This tends to occur when the acquired company has a weak culture that is dysfunctional, whereas the acquiring company has a strong culture that is focused on clearly defined values. Sun Microsystems has acquired many smaller organizations using this strategy. It refuses to digest larger firms because it is much more difficult to apply Sun's aggressive culture.[50] Culture clash is rare with assimilation because the acquired firm's culture is weak and employees are looking for better cultural alternatives.

Deculturation

Assimilation is rare. Employees usually resist organizational change, particularly when it includes throwing away personal and cultural values. Under these conditions, some acquiring companies apply a *deculturation* strategy by imposing their culture and business practices on the acquired organization. The acquiring firm strips away artifacts and reward systems that support the old culture. People who cannot adopt the acquiring company's culture are often terminated.

This happened when Anderson Exploration Ltd. acquired Home Oil Co. Ltd. Both oil firms have headquarters in Calgary, but they are different in every other way. Home Oil valued status and splendour, with a bit of extravagance thrown in. The firm had an executive dining room, two floors of executive offices, a small fleet of planes, and expensive art. Not any more. Anderson's founder, J.C. Anderson, replaced Home Oil's belief system with the efficient and lean cultural values that dominate Anderson Exploration. "They had a culture, we had a culture," says Anderson with characteristic bluntness. "Ours worked, theirs didn't. At the end of the day, we've got to have this combined organization being a lot closer to our culture."[51]

Deculturation may be necessary when the acquired firm's culture doesn't work but employees aren't convinced of this. However, this strategy rarely works because it increases the risk of socioemotional conflict (see Chapter 13). Employees from the acquired firm resist the cultural intrusions of the buying firm, thereby delaying or undermining the merger process.

Integration

A third strategy is to integrate the corporate cultures of the merging organizations. This involves combining two or more cultures into a new composite culture that preserves the best features of the previous cultures. Integration is slow and potentially risky, because many forces preserve the existing cultures. However, this strategy should be considered when the companies have relatively weak cultures, or when their cultures include several overlapping values. Integration also works best when people realize that their existing cultures are ineffective and are, therefore, motivated to adopt a new set of dominant values.

Nortel Networks' acquisition of Bay Networks in California is a case in point. The Brampton, Ontario, telecommunications manufacturer bought Bay Networks partly because Nortel wanted a bigger piece of the Internet hardware business. But CEO John Roth also candidly says that he wanted to shake off Nortel's slower, more bureaucratic ways by acquiring some of Bay Networks' culture that was moving at "Web speed."[52]

Separation

A separation strategy occurs where the merging companies agree to remain distinct entities with minimal exchange of culture or organizational practices. This strategy is most appropriate when the two merging companies are in unrelated industries because the most appropriate cultural values tend to differ by industry. Unfortunately, few acquired firms have independent cultures for very long because executives in the acquiring firm want to control corporate decisions. It's not surprising, therefore, that only 15 percent of acquisitions leave the purchased organization as a stand-alone unit.[53]

CHANGING AND STRENGTHENING ORGANIZATIONAL CULTURE

Whether merging two cultures or reshaping the firm's existing values, corporate leaders need to understand how to change and strengthen the organization's dominant culture. Indeed, some organizational scholars conclude that the only way to ensure any lasting change is to realign cultural values with those changes. In other words, changes "stick" when they become "the way we do things around here."[54]

Changing organizational culture requires the change management tool kit that we learned about in Chapter 15. Corporate leaders need to make employees aware of the urgency for change. Then they need to "unfreeze" the existing culture by removing artifacts that represent that culture and "refreeze" the new culture by introducing artifacts that communicate and reinforce the new values.

Executives at Hitachi are changing their bureaucratic and inflexible corporate culture by altering artifacts that communicate and reinforce those values. The Japanese electronics manufacturer has abolished daily morning exercises because executives believe that this reinforced a group

AP Wide World.

Different national and corporate cultures have created problems in the merger of Chrysler and Daimler-Benz. North American auto maker Chrysler values lean efficiency, empowerment, and fairly egalitarian relations among staff. In contrast, German auto maker Daimler-Benz seems to value respect for authority, bureaucratic precision, and centralized decision making. For example, Chrysler executives quickly became frustrated with the attention Daimler executives gave to trivial matters, such as the shape of a pamphlet sent to employees. Daimler executives were equally perplexed when Chrysler chairman Robert Eaton showed his emotions with tears in a speech to other executives. To minimize this cultural clash, DaimlerChrysler CEO Juergen Schrempp decided to adopt a separation strategy that would allow both groups to maintain their existing cultures. The former Chrysler group was given autonomy to crank out lucrative mass-market cars and trucks, while the Germans continued to build luxury Mercedes.[55] In your opinion, is a separation strategy a long-term solution to the corporate culture clash at DaimlerChrysler?

www.daimlerchrysler.com

mentality at the expense of individual initiative. To encourage a more open and communicative culture, Hitachi's employees are encouraged to dress in polo shirts and other casual wear rather than in formal attire. The company is also breaking the long tradition of calling each other by title. Instead, employees are now asked to call each other by name. "Even when employees talk to the chairman or the president, they should use their names," says a Hitachi representative.[56]

STRENGTHENING ORGANIZATIONAL CULTURE

Artifacts communicate and reinforce the new corporate culture, but we also need to consider ways to further strengthen that culture. Five approaches that are commonly cited in the literature are the actions of founders and leaders, introducing culturally consistent rewards, maintaining a stable workforce, managing the cultural network, and selecting and socializing new employees (see Exhibit 17.4).

Actions of founders and leaders

Founders establish an organization's culture.[57] In the opening story to this chapter, we saw how Keith Kocho's casual and egalitarian style has become embedded in the culture of ExtendMedia, the company he founded. Founders develop the systems and structures that support their personal values. Founders are often visionaries whose energetic style provides a powerful role model for others to follow.

In spite of the founder's effect, subsequent leaders can break the organization away from the founder's values if they apply the transformational leadership concepts that were described in Chapter 14. Transformational leaders strengthen organizational culture by communicating and

EXHIBIT 17.4 Strategies for Strengthening Organizational Culture

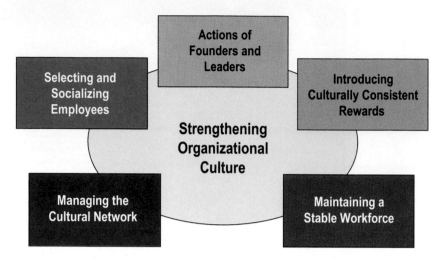

enacting their vision of the future.[58] Cultural values are particularly reinforced when leaders behave in ways that are consistent with the vision ("walking the talk"). Four Seasons Hotels founder Isadore Sharp maintains a strong quality service culture by ensuring that managers are consistent with this cultural standard. "Employees watch their managers and take their cues from them, so our managers have to act as role models," says Sharp. "We made changes at the very top—head-office senior executives, hotel general managers—until those whom others would imitate were setting the proper standard. The message got through and superior service became our competitive edge."[59]

Introducing culturally consistent rewards

Reward systems strengthen corporate culture when they are consistent with cultural values.[60] For example, paternalistic cultures would emphasize employee assistance programs, medical insurance, and other benefits that support employee well-being. Nortel Networks offers these, but CEO John Roth also introduced share options for almost every employee so the company would adopt a more aggressive culture. Home Depot also has share options to maintain an ownership culture. "We've always wanted this to be part of our culture," explains Home Depot CEO and co-founder Arthur Blank, "that associates feel that they own the stores, that they own the merchandise, that they have total responsibility for the customers in their aisles, and that they create the value."[61]

Maintaining a stable workforce

An organization's culture is embedded in the minds of its employees. Organizational stories are rarely written down; rituals and ceremonies do not usually exist in procedure manuals; organizational metaphors are not found in corporate directories. Thus, organizations depend on a stable workforce to communicate and reinforce the dominant beliefs and values. The organization's culture can literally disintegrate during periods of high turnover and precipitous downsizing because the corporate memory leaves with these employees.[62]

Conversely, corporate leaders who want to change the corporate culture have accelerated the turnover of senior executives and older employees who held the cultural values in place. For instance, the two executives who revived Continental Airlines claim that they introduced a more customer-focused culture partly by replacing most of the 60 executives with people who had more compatible cultural values. Hoechst, the German chemical company, also seems to be applying this tactic through early retirement of its older employees. "The company is trying to lower the average age of the workforce," says a Hoechst spokesperson. "Perhaps the main reason for replacing older workers is that it makes it easier to 'defrost' the corporate culture."[63]

Managing the cultural network

Organizational culture is learned, so an effective network of cultural transmission is necessary to strengthen the company's underlying assumptions, values, and beliefs. According to Max De Pree, CEO of furniture manufacturer Herman Miller Inc., every organization needs "tribal storytellers" to keep the organization's history and culture alive.[64] The cultural network exists through the organizational grapevine. It is also supported through frequent opportunities for interaction so employees can share stories and re-enact rituals. Senior executives must tap into the cultural network, sharing their own stories and creating new ceremonies and other opportunities to demonstrate shared meaning. Company magazines and other media can also strengthen organizational culture by communicating cultural values and beliefs more efficiently.

Selecting and socializing employees

Akanda Innovations wants to hire people with solid technical skills. But there is one thing that's more important: Recruits' values must be compatible with the firm's cultural values. The Thornhill, Ontario, software company wants to avoid conflicts and turnover that occur when a new hire's values are incompatible with the company's culture. "I will often hire for office-cultural match over someone with technical superiority who may cause ripples with my existing staff," says Akanda's Rob Lavigne.[65]

Akanda Innovations and a flock of other organizations strengthen their corporate cultures by hiring people with beliefs, values, and assumptions similar to those cultures. They realize that a good fit of personal and organizational values makes it easier for employees to adopt the corporate culture. A good person–organization fit also improves job satisfaction and organizational loyalty because new hires with values compatible to the corporate culture adjust more quickly to the organization.[66]

Job applicants are also paying more attention to corporate culture during the hiring process. According to one recent survey, job applicants ask about corporate culture more than any other topic, aside from pay and benefits.[67] Applicants realize that they must feel comfortable with the company's values, not just the job duties and hours of work.

Kathy Wheeler learned this important point the hard way. A few years ago, the Hewlett-Packard engineer accepted a career opportunity at Apple Computer. Apple's headquarters is just

three kilometres away from HP, but its corporate culture is on another planet. HP's culture emphasizes collaboration, consensus, and advanced engineering technology, whereas Apple's culture applauds marketers rather than engineers and slick user interfaces rather than advanced technology. Fourteen months later, Wheeler was back at HP. "I admire Apple to a large extent," says Wheeler. "But I wouldn't work there again because of the cultural issues."[68] The point here is that we need to look at corporate culture artifacts when deciding whether to join a particular organization. By diagnosing the company's dominant culture, we are more likely to determine whether its values are compatible with our own.

Along with selecting people with compatible values, companies maintain strong cultures through the effective socialization of new employees. **Organizational socialization** refers to the process by which individuals learn the values, expected behaviours, and social knowledge necessary to assume their roles in the organization.[69] By communicating the company's dominant values, job candidates and new hires are more likely to internalize these values quickly and deeply.

We will learn more about the organizational socialization process in the following chapter on employment relations and career dynamics. At this point, you should know that socialization partially includes the process of learning about the company's culture and adopting its set of values. For example, Carolyn Arnott has lived and breathed the IKEA culture almost all her working life. She started as a cashier in Ottawa and soon got her first lessons about the Scandinavian home furnishing company's values through its mandatory "Culture Days." Today, as manager of IKEA's store in Ottawa's west end, Arnott easily recites the cultural values that make the company unique: thrift, hard work, fair play, and inventiveness.[70]

Throughout this chapter, we have learned that organizational culture is pervasive and powerful. For corporate leaders, it is either a force for change or an insurmountable barrier to change. For employees, it is either the glue that bonds people together or drives them away from the organization. So many artifacts communicate and reinforce the existing culture that it requires monumental effort to replace the current values. Transformational leadership and effective management of change can assist this process, but it is a challenge that no leader should take lightly.

Organizational socialization The process by which individuals learn the values, expected behaviours, and social knowledge necessary to assume their roles in the organization.

CHAPTER SUMMARY

- Organizational culture is the basic pattern of shared assumptions, values, and beliefs that govern behaviour within a particular organization. Assumptions are the shared mental models or theories in use that people rely on to guide their perceptions and behaviours. Beliefs represent the individual's perceptions of reality. Values are more stable, long-lasting beliefs about what is important. They help us define what is right or wrong, or good or bad, in the world. Cultural content refers to the relative ordering of beliefs, values, and assumptions.

- Organizations have subcultures as well as the dominant culture. Some subcultures enhance the dominant culture, whereas countercultures have values that oppose the organization's core values. Subcultures maintain the organization's standards of performance and ethical behaviour. They are also the source of emerging values that replace aging core values.

- Artifacts are the observable symbols and signs of an organization's culture. Four broad categories of artifacts include organizational stories and legends, rituals and ceremonies, language, and physical structures and symbols. Understanding an organization's culture requires painstaking assessment of many artifacts because they are subtle and often ambiguous.

- Organizational culture has three main functions. First, it is a deeply embedded form of social control. Second, it is the "social glue" that bonds people together and makes them feel part of the organizational experience. Third, corporate culture helps employees make sense of the workplace.

- Companies with strong cultures generally perform better than those with weak cultures, but only when the cultural content is appropriate for the organization's environment. Also, the culture should not be so strong that it drives out dissenting values that may form emerging values for the future. Organizations should have adaptive cultures so that employees focus on the need for change and support initiatives and leadership that keep pace with these changes.

- Organizational culture relates to business ethics in two ways. First, corporate cultures can support ethical values of society, thereby reinforcing ethical conduct. Second, some cultures are so strong that they rob a person's individualism and discourage constructive controversy.

- Mergers should include a bicultural audit to diagnose the compatibility of the organizational cultures. The four main strategies for merging different corporate cultures are assimilation, deculturation, integration, and separation.

- Organizational culture is very difficult to change. However, this may be possible by creating urgency for change and replacing artifacts that support the old culture with artifacts aligned more with the desired future culture. Organizational culture may be strengthened through the actions of founders and leaders, introducing culturally consistent rewards, maintaining a stable workforce, managing the cultural network, and selecting and socializing employees.

KEY TERMS

Adaptive culture, p. 513

Artifacts, p. 508

Bicultural audit, p. 515

Ceremonies, p. 510

Mental models, p. 506

Organizational culture, p. 506

Organizational socialization, p. 522

Rituals, p. 510

Values, p. 507

DISCUSSION QUESTIONS

1. Superb Consultants Inc. have submitted a proposal to analyze the cultural values of your organization. The proposal states that Superb has developed a revolutionary new survey to tap the company's true culture. The survey takes just ten minutes to complete and accurate results can be based on a small sample of employees. Discuss the merits and limitations of this proposal.

2. Some people suggest that the most effective organizations have the strongest cultures. What do we mean by the "strength" of organizational culture, and what possible problems are there with a strong organizational culture?

3. The CEO of a Canadian fibre optics firm wants everyone to support the organization's dominant culture of lean efficiency and hard work. The CEO has introduced a new reward system to reinforce this culture and personally interviews all professional and managerial

applicants to ensure that they bring similar values to the organization. Some employees who criticized these values had their careers sidelined until they left. Two mid-level managers were fired for supporting contrary values, such as work–life balance. Based on your knowledge of organizational subcultures, what potential problems is the CEO creating?

4. Identify four types of artifacts used to communicate organizational culture. Why are artifacts used for this purpose?

5. Acme Corp. is planning to acquire Beta Corp., which operates in a different industry. Acme's culture is entrepreneurial and fast paced, whereas Beta employees value slow, deliberate decision making by consensus. Which merger strategy would you recommend to minimize culture shock when Acme acquires Beta? Explain your answer.

6. Under what conditions is assimilation likely to occur when two companies merge? Your answer should clearly describe the assimilation strategy.

7. Explain how transformational leadership strengthens corporate culture.

8. Suppose that you are asked by senior officers of a Canadian city to identify ways to reinforce a new culture of teamwork and collaboration. The senior executive group clearly supports these values, but it wants everyone in the organization to embrace them. Identify four types of activities that would strengthen these cultural values.

Case Study

ACTIVITY 17.1
Hillton's Transformation

Twenty years ago, Hillton was a small city of 30,000 residents that served as an outer suburb to one of Canada's largest metropolitan areas. The City of Hillton treated its employees like family and gave them a great deal of autonomy in their work. Everyone in the organization (including two labour unions representing employees) implicitly agreed that the leaders and supervisors should rise through the ranks based on their experience. Few people were ever hired from the outside into middle or senior positions. The rule of employment was to learn the job skills, maintain a reasonably good work record, and wait your turn for promotion.

Hillton has grown rapidly since the mid-1960s. As the population grew, so did the municipality's workforce. This meant that employees were promoted fairly quickly and were almost assured guaranteed employment. In fact, until recently, Hillton had never laid off

any employee. The organization's culture could be described as one of entitlement and comfort. Neither elected city councillors nor the city manager bothered the departmental managers about their work. There were few cost controls because the rapid growth placed more emphasis on keeping up with the population expansion. The public became somewhat more critical of the city's poor service, including road construction at inconvenient times and the apparent lack of respect some employees showed towards taxpayers.

During these expansion years, Hillton placed most of its money with "outside" (also called "hard") municipal services. These included road building, utility construction and maintenance, fire and police protection, recreational facilities, and land use control. This emphasis occurred because an expanding population demanded more of these services and most of Hillton's senior people came from the outside services group. For example, Hillton's city manager for many years was a road development engineer. The "inside" workers (taxation, community services,

ACTIVITY 17.1 CONTINUED

etc.) tended to have less seniority and their departments were given lower priority.

As commuter and road systems developed, more upwardly mobile professionals began to live in Hillton. Some infrastructure demands continued, but now these suburban dwellers wanted more of the "soft" services, such as libraries, social activities, and community services. They also began complaining about the way the municipality was being run. The city's population had more than tripled by the early 1990s, and it was increasingly apparent that the organization needed more corporate planning, information systems, organization development, and cost control systems. In various ways, residents voiced their concerns that the municipality was not providing the quality of management that they would expect from a city of its size.

In 1996, a new mayor and council replaced most of the previous incumbents, mainly on the platform of improving the municipality's management structure. The new council gave the city manager, along with two other senior managers, an early retirement buyout package. Rather than promoting from the lower ranks, council decided to fill all three positions with qualified candidates from large municipal corporations elsewhere in Canada. The following year, several long-term managers left Hillton and people from outside the organization filled at least half of the vacant positions.

In less than two years, Hillton had hired eight senior or departmental managers from other municipalities. These eight managers played a key role in changing the organization's value system, and were called the "professionals" by employees, usually with negative connotations. The managers worked closely to change the way middle and lower-level managers had operated for many years. They brought in a new computer system and emphasized cost controls where managers previously had complete autonomy. Promotions were increasingly based on merit rather than seniority.

These managers frequently announced in meetings and newsletters that municipal employees must provide superlative customer service, and that Hillton will become one of the most customer-friendly places for citizens and those who do business with the municipality. To this end, these managers were quick to support the public's increasing demand for more "soft" services, including expanded library services and recreational activities. And when population growth recently flattened out for a few years, the city manager and other professionals gained council support to lay off a few of the outside workers due to lack of demand for hard services.

One of the most significant changes was that the "outside" departments no longer held dominant positions in city management. Most of the "professional" managers had worked exclusively in administrative and related inside jobs. Two had MBA degrees. This led to some tension between the professional managers and the older outside managers.

Even before the layoffs, managers of outside departments resisted the changes more than others. They complained that their employees with the highest seniority were turned down for promotions. They argued for increased budgets and warned that infrastructure problems would cause liability problems. Informally, these outside managers were supported by the labour union representing outside workers. The union leaders tried to bargain for more job guarantees, whereas the union representing inside workers focused more on improving wages and benefits. Leaders of the outside union made several statements in the local media that the city had "lost its heart" and that the public would suffer from the actions of the new professionals.

Discussion Questions

1. Contrast Hillton's earlier corporate culture and the emerging set of cultural values.

2. Considering the difficulty in changing organizational culture, why does Hillton's management seem to be successful at this transformation?

3. Identify two other strategies that the city might consider to reinforce the new set of corporate values.

ACTIVITY 17.2
SAP Software

SAP has millions of followers, a visionary leader, and demands total allegiance. SAP is not a religion; it's a software company. From all over the globe, pilgrims have flocked to Philadelphia for a high-tech revival called Sapphire '99. They've come to hear the prophecy of the German software Goliath—SAP.

Few people outside this industry know about SAP, but in the world of business management software, SAP has become the gospel. The majority of Fortune 500 companies, thousands of medium-sized businesses, and many public institutions around the world rely on SAP to run their operations. All departments of a company become one with SAP. Chances are that your bank, your food, and your electricity depend on SAP. And so does the Canadian Broadcasting Corporation.

Management consultant and former MIT professor Michael Hammer says that if Microsoft went down somehow, it would cause massive headaches. But if SAP applications were wiped out, the worldwide industrial complex would come to a halt. "SAP controls the jugular of the world industrial complex," explains Hammer.

The good shepherd of the SAP flock is Hastnel Platner. He's one of the world's richest men—worth about US$7 billion—and he's on a mission at Sapphire '99 to increase SAP's supremacy in the business software market.

"As a CEO of a company... I have to deliver the vision," explains Platner. "I have to drive the company in the direction our customers want us to see. And the customers all came. And the reason: You have to tell us the way we're to go."

SAP has over 12,000 clients and 10 million users. Its bread-and-butter software package, called R-3, is incredibly complex and has to be installed by certified programmers and consultants. Becoming an SAP consultant is like being initiated into a very lucrative high-tech priesthood. But being an SAP consultant isn't all that easy. Employees often resent SAP disciples coming onto their turf, shaking up their world, and changing the way they've done their job for ten years.

Sony Canada is one of the many companies that turned to SAP. It wasn't cheap, costing about $13 million, including changes to infrastructure, computers, and networks. "We had a pitch from their marketing people who came in and talked about it, solving all of our problems," recalls Barry Hasler, a Sony Canada executive who helped implement SAP. "And [they] showed us a very nice video that when they turned it on live, we would have people in the warehouse dancing. So it was supposed to solve everything."

SAP is more than software, says Platner. It's "a powerful catalyst for change. Once you bring in a system like SAP, nothing stays the same. Jobs change, ways you work change, organizations change. And if you're not ready for that, it's going to take you by surprise."

But SAP demands loyalty. "It does make you a slave to data accuracy and jobs change a lot," says Sony's Barry Hasler. "You're devoting your time to make sure the information in the system is totally accurate."

Michael Hammer has written that "fanatical belief" is one of the keys to successful implementation of SAP and related software. And the Sapphire conference certainly looks like a cult of believers. Platner disagrees: "No, no, definitely we are not religious. But being successful and doing something you can start to believe that it has to be done that way."

The Sapphire extravaganza is just another way to communicate SAP's vision of the future. "If the vision gets blurred, the whole company slows down," says Platner. "I think this is true for all companies, especially companies which have to constantly renovate the product."

ACTIVITY 17.2 CONTINUED

But some of SAP's followers believe that the software company does have a cult following. "SAP is a cult," says computer consultant Rob Colemen. "It is; it's a fun cult. We're not walking around in orange robes and selling pencils. But if you're an SAP consultant with an SAP consultant company, there is a bond with everybody else. And cult is probably a strong term. Call it a bond."

Discussion Questions

1. Based on this video, what do you think are the dominant values in SAP's corporate culture?

2. How does SAP strengthen its culture?

3. This video program connects SAP's culture with organizational change. How are the two topics related here?

Source: Based on "In Tech We Trust," *Undercurrents 61-2-2160-90133* (October 31, 1999).

 **TEAM exercise**

ACTIVITY 17.3
ORGANIZATIONAL CULTURE METAPHORS

by David L. Luechauer, Butler University, and Gary M. Shulman, Miami University

Purpose: Both parts of this exercise are designed to help you understand, assess, and interpret organizational culture using metaphors.

Part A: Assessing Your School's Culture

Instructions: A metaphor is a figure of speech that contains an implied comparison between a word or phrase that is ordinarily used for one thing but can be applied to another. Metaphors also carry a great deal of hidden meaning—they say a lot about what we think and feel about an object. Therefore, this activity asks you to use several metaphors to define the organizational culture of your university or college. (Alternatively, the instructor might ask students to assess another organization that most students know about.)

Step 1: The class will be divided into teams of four to six members.

Step 2: Each team will reach consensus on which words or phrases should be inserted in the blanks of the statements presented below. This information should be recorded on a flip chart or overhead acetate for class presentation. The instructor will provide 15 to 20 minutes for teams to determine which words best describe the organization's culture.

If our school were an animal, it would be a _____ because _____ .

If our school were a food, it would be _____ because _____ .

If our school were a place, it would be _____ because _____ .

If our school were a season, it would be _____ because _____ .

If our school were a TV show or movie, it would be _____ because _____ .

Step 3: The class will listen to each team present the metaphors that it believes symbolize the school's culture. For example, a team that picks winter as its season might feel cold or distant about the school and its people.

Step 4: The class will discuss the questions listed below.

Discussion Questions for Part A:

1. How easy was it for your group to reach consensus regarding these metaphors? What does that imply about the culture of your school?

2. How do you see these metaphors in action? In other words, what are some critical school behaviours or other artifacts that reveal the presence of your culture?

3. Think of another organization to which you belong (e.g., work, religious congregation). What are its dominant cultural values, how do you see them in action, and how do they affect the effectiveness of that organization?

Part B: Analyzing and Interpreting Cultural Metaphors

Instructions: Previously, you completed a metaphor exercise to describe the culture of your school. That exercise gave you a taste of how to administer such a diagnostic tool and draw inferences from the results generated. This activity builds on that experience and is designed to help refine your ability to analyze such data and make suggestions for improvement. Five work teams (of four to seven members, mixed gender in all groups) of an organization located in Cincinnati completed a metaphor exercise similar to the one in which you participated. Their responses are shown in the table below. Working in teams, analyze the information in this table and answer the following questions.

Discussion Questions for Part B:

1. In your opinion, what are the dominant cultural values in this organization? Explain your answer.

2. What are the positive aspects of this type of culture?

3. What are the negative aspects of this type of culture?

4. What is this organization's main business, in your opinion? Explain your answer.

5. These groups all reported to one manager. What advice would you give to her about this unit?

METAPHOR RESULTS OF FIVE TEAMS IN A CINCINNATI ORGANIZATION

Team	Animal	Food	Place	TV Show	Season
1	Rabbit	Big Mac	Casino	*48 Hrs.* (movie)	Spring
2	Horse	Taco	Racetrack	*Miami Vice*	Spring
3	Elephant	Ribs	Circus	*Roseanne*	Summer
4	Eagle	Big Mac	Las Vegas	CNN	Spring
5	Panther	Chinese	New York	*L.A. Law*	Racing

Source: Adapted from D.L. Luechauer and G.M. Shulman, "Using a Metaphor Exercise to Explore the Principles of Organizational Culture," *Journal of Management Education,* 22 (December 1998), pp. 736–44. Used with permission of the authors.

ACTIVITY 17.4
CORPORATE CULTURE PREFERENCE SCALE

Purpose: This self-assessment exercise is designed to help you identify a corporate culture that fits most closely with your personal values and assumptions.

Instructions: Read each pair of statements in the Corporate Culture Preference Scale and circle the ones that describe the organization for which you would prefer to work. Then use the scoring key in Appendix B of this book to calculate your results for each subscale. This exercise is completed alone so students can assess themselves honestly without concerns of social comparison. However, class discussion will focus on the importance of matching job applicants to the organization's dominant values.

CORPORATE CULTURE PREFERENCE SCALE

I would prefer to work in an organization:

1a. Where employees work well together in teams.	**OR**	1b. That produces highly respected products or services.
2a. Where top management maintains a sense of order in the workplace.	**OR**	2b. Where the organization listens to customers and responds quickly to their needs.
3a. Where employees are treated fairly.	**OR**	3b. Where employees continuously search for ways to work more efficiently.
4a. Where employees adapt quickly to new work requirements.	**OR**	4b. Where corporate leaders work hard to keep employees happy.
5a. Where senior executives receive special benefits not available to other employees.	**OR**	5b. Where employees are proud when the organization achieves its performance goals.
6a. Where employees who perform the best get paid the most.	**OR**	6b. Where senior executives are respected.
7a. Where everyone gets their jobs done like clockwork.	**OR**	7b. That is on top of new innovations in the industry.
8a. Where employees receive assistance to overcome any personal problems.	**OR**	8b. Where employees abide by company rules.
9a. That is always experimenting with new ideas in the marketplace.	**OR**	9b. That expects everyone to put in 110 percent for peak performance.
10a. That quickly benefits from market opportunities.	**OR**	10b. Where employees are always kept informed of what is happening in the organization.
11a. That can quickly respond to competitive threats.	**OR**	11b. Where most decisions are made by the top executives.
12a. Where management keeps everything under control.	**OR**	12b. Where employees care for each other.

CHAPTER EIGHTEEN

Employment Relationship and Career Dynamics

LEARNING OBJECTIVES

After reading this chapter, you should be able to:

- Discuss the different types of psychological contract.
- Identify three types of trust in organizational settings.
- Discuss the employment trends of employability and contingent work.
- Discuss the two primary functions of organizational socialization.
- Describe the stages of organizational socialization.
- Explain how realistic job previews and socialization agents assist the socialization process.
- Describe the main features of Holland's theory of occupational choice.
- Identify three conditions that would encourage lateral career development.
- Explain why boundaryless careers have become more common.
- List five strategies that assist personal career development.

Adina Trowhill Smith enjoys more career satisfaction as a "virtual assistant" in the contingent workforce than in her former job as an employee in a large computer company

Adina Trowhill Smith describes herself as a "virtual assistant." Her Vancouver-based company, North American Exec-Works, provides administrative support to people who are starting their own businesses or need extra help on quick notice. "A lot of people just starting out their own business want someone on call, but they can't afford, or don't need, a full-time administrative assistant, so they come to me," explains Smith.

Smith almost fell into the job by accident. "I quit my old job and started looking around, but I couldn't find anything I was interested in, so I started thinking about what I could do," she says. That's when Smith discovered a large demand for virtual assistants. "I had no idea I would do so well," Smith admits. She also appreciates the fact that her new job offers more scheduling flexibility and the opportunity to work at home.

Cathie Walker also left the comforts of traditional employment for a career that more closely fulfils her personal needs. While working as a secretary at the University of Victoria, Walker became interested in the Internet and developed a Web site (www.amused.com) devoted to humour. The site became so popular that a New York company bought it from Walker and offered her the job of running it.

Walker agonized over leaving her secure secretarial job at the university, but the decision paid off. She was recently promoted to executive producer and now earns in the low six figures. But her biggest gain is doing something that fuses her creativity, technical curiosity, and organizational skills. "I have such an incredible life," Walker says.[1]

www.amused.com

Adina Trowhill Smith and Cathie Walker have made career transitions that reflect the trend away from traditional employment.[2] Smith became a "free agent" by contracting her time and competencies to different organizations. Walker works for a larger organization, but her new career as a Web site coordinator represents the shift towards more entrepreneurial work in a virtual organization. These anecdotes paint a glowing picture of emerging career trends, but they also carry risks and hardships. Both Smith and Walker gave up job security to pursue new career opportunities, but many people would rather have more permanent employment with greater job security.

This chapter begins by looking at the most fundamental element of the employment relationship: the psychological contract. We consider the type of contracts, how contracts change, the importance of trust in employment relationships, and the dynamics of contingent work. Next, this chapter examines the process of employee socialization, including the stages of socialization and specific socialization strategies. We then turn to the topic of career development, including models of occupational choice and career patterns, as well as the emerging trends towards lateral and boundaryless career development. This chapter closes with an overview of specific strategies to guide your career development.

THE PSYCHOLOGICAL CONTRACT

Psychological contract The individual's beliefs about the terms and conditions of a reciprocal exchange agreement between that person and another party.

Employees at AOC Brown and Root Canada Ltd. (ABC) were recently shocked when two dozen of them got layoff notices. ABC hires pipefitters and welders to carry out modifications to the Hibernia oil platform, so employees thought they had a few decades of job security, not a couple of years. The layoffs were even more surprising because Hibernia had just announced its intentions to increase oil production. "It's unfortunate they may have had the impression that they'd be there for the life of the project ... 20 or 25 years or so," admits a spokesperson for the St. John's, Newfoundland, company.[3]

ABC's employees have experienced the shock of having their **psychological contract** violated. This isn't unusual. According to one university study, 24 percent of employees are "chronically" angry at work, mostly because they feel their employers violate basic promises and don't fulfil the psychological contract.[4] The psychological contract refers to the individual's beliefs about the terms and conditions of a reciprocal exchange agreement between that person and another party.[5] This is inherently perceptual, so one person's understanding of the psychological contract may differ from the other party's understanding. In employment relationships, psychological contracts consist of beliefs about what the employee is entitled to receive and is obliged to offer the employer in return. For example, ABC's employees believed they would have job security for 20 years or more, not layoffs a couple of years after being hired.[6]

Organizational citizenship Employee behaviours that extend beyond the usual job duties. They include avoiding unnecessary conflicts, helping others without selfish intent, gracefully tolerating occasional impositions, being involved in organizational activities, and performing tasks that extend beyond normal role requirements.

Everyone has a unique psychological contract, but one British study has found some common elements. Specifically, employers expect employees to work contracted hours, perform quality work, deal honestly with clients, guard the organization's reputation, treat property carefully, dress and behave correctly, and engage in some **organizational citizenship**. The psychological contract for most British employees emphasizes fairness in decisions (e.g., selection, promotion, and layoffs), the application of rules, and allocation of pay and benefits. Employees also expect enough personal time off, consultation on matters affecting them, minimal interference in how they do their job, supportive leadership, reward for long service and good performance, a safe work environment, and as much job security as the organization can reasonably provide.[7]

TYPES OF PSYCHOLOGICAL CONTRACTS

Psychological contracts vary in many ways. One of the most fundamental differences is the extent to which they are transactional or relational.[8] As Exhibit 18.1 describes, *transactional contracts* are primarily short-term economic exchanges. Responsibilities are well defined around a fairly narrow set of obligations that do not change over the life of the contract. People hired in temporary positions and as consultants tend to have transactional contracts. To some extent, new employees also form transactional contracts until they develop a sense of continuity with the organization.

Relational contracts, on the other hand, are rather like marriages; they are long-term attachments that encompass a broad array of subjective mutual obligations. Employees with a relational psychological contract are more willing to contribute their time and effort without expecting the organization to repay this debt in the short term. Relational contracts are also dynamic, meaning that the parties tolerate and expect that mutual obligations will not necessarily be balanced in the short term. Not surprisingly, organizational citizenship behaviours are more likely to prevail under relational than transactional contracts. Permanent employees are more likely to believe they have a relational contract.

Brent MacIntosh, a Web designer at Ottawa-based Jetform Corp., has a relational psychological contract because he doesn't keep track of his hours. Like most skilled technology workers, MacIntosh isn't paid overtime for the extra hours he works. Instead, he has enough freedom with Jetform to take days off during slower periods.[9] This contrasts with transactional contracts where employees keep close watch over their hours and other inputs, and expect appropriate payment in return.

PSYCHOLOGICAL CONTRACTS ACROSS CULTURES

Psychological contracts are influenced by the social contexts in which the contracting process occurs.[10] Organizations maintain their status as good "corporate citizens" by recognizing and applying the prevailing social norms. In other words, psychological contracts vary across cultures, and employers must align their employment expectations with those societal norms.

EXHIBIT 18.1 Types of Psychological Contracts in Employment

Contract Characteristics	Transactional Contracts	Relational Contracts
Focus	Economic	Economic and socioeconomic
Time Frame	Closed-ended and short-term	Open-ended and indefinite
Stability	Static	Dynamic
Scope	Narrow	Pervasive
Tangibility	Well defined	More subjective

Source: Based on information in D.M. Rousseau and J.M. Parks, "The Contracts of Individuals and Organizations," *Research in Organizational Behavior,* 15 (1993), pp. 1–43.

CP PHOTO ARCHIVE (Y. Berg)

Scott Mayor knows all about relational psychological contracts. Twelve years ago, Mayor joined Nortel Networks as a production employee, building telephone switching equipment at the company's Brampton, Ontario, manufacturing plant. The job paid well, but Nortel was changing and Mayor was willing to adapt his expectations to those changes. As a result, he took night classes to complete degrees in business and marketing, which gave him valuable customer service skills. Today, Nortel doesn't make anything at its Brampton facility, but Mayor's willingness to change landed him a job as a Nortel project manager. "Change has always been a big part of the environment," says Mayor, shown here contrasting the latest cellphone technology with an old Nortel switchboard.[11] How can organizations encourage employees to develop a relational psychological contract?

www.nortelnetworks.com

For instance, employees in low power-distance cultures (such as Canada) are less likely than employees in high power-distance cultures (such as Singapore or Mexico) to accept arbitrary commands from their supervisors. Taking an afternoon siesta is a cultural norm (although quickly disappearing) in Spain, so this is embedded in most psychological contracts in that country.[12] Mexicans generally assume that organizations in their society have a strong obligation to provide "life, health, dignity and liberty." These expectations, which can be traced to the Mexican Revolution, form part of the psychological contract. Overall, we must be sensitive to cultural differences in the psychological contracting process as well as interpretations and assumptions about the content of those contracts.

TRUST AND THE PSYCHOLOGICAL CONTRACT

Trust Positive expectations about another party's intentions and actions towards us in risky situations.

Any relationship—including an employment relationship—depends on a certain degree of trust between the parties.[13] **Trust** occurs when we have positive expectations about another party's intentions and actions towards us in risky situations (see Chapter 7). A high level of trust occurs when the other party's actions affect you in situations where you are vulnerable, but you believe they will not adversely affect your needs.

There are many trust relationships in organizations.[14] Employees learn to trust their co-workers, team leaders, subordinates, and representatives from suppliers and customers.

Organizational behaviour scholars also refer to *institutional trust*, which is the employee's trust of the organization's CEO and top management. Along with whom to trust, there are three types of trust, each representing a different level and form of relationship:[15]

- *Calculus-based trust*—This minimal level of trust refers to an expected consistency of behaviour based on deterrence. Each party believes that the other will deliver on its promises because punishments will be administered if they fail. For example, most of us trust our employer enough to expect a paycheque at the end of the work period because we believe the company will face government sanctions if payment isn't received.

- *Knowledge-based trust*—Knowledge-based trust is grounded on the other party's predictability. This predictability develops from meaningful communication and experience with the other party. The better you know senior management's past actions, the more accurately you can predict what they will do in the future. Similarly, the more consistent the leader's behaviour—the more he or she "walks the talk"—the more employees are willing to trust that person.[16]

- *Identification-based trust*—This third type of trust is based on mutual understanding and emotional bond between the parties. Identification occurs when one party thinks like, feels like, and responds like the other party. High-performance teams exhibit this level of

Photo by K. Wade. Used with permission of the *San Francisco Chronicle*.

www.att.com

Terry Akre (right) put in 37 years as a technician at AT&T, waking up at 5:30 a.m. each day to be on the job by 7:30. Then he was laid off without any warning. Terry's son Daniel (left), who was 18 at the time, vowed never to let that happen to him. "I said then and there, I'm going to 'employ' my employers," Daniel recalls. So Daniel, a top-performing salesman, has worked for seven employers since graduating from college a dozen years ago. Each job change resulted in higher pay or more challenging work.[17] How does Daniel Akre's psychological contract differ from his father's? What level of trust do you think he has with his employer compared to the trust his father had in AT&T?

trust. To some extent, employees can have a high level of identification-based trust in organizations with strong cultures. By identifying with the company's dominant values, employees understand what to expect and what is expected of them.

Calculus-based trust is the weakest of the three types because a violation of expectations and the subsequent application of sanctions against the violating party easily break it. It is difficult to develop a strong level of trust based on the threat of punishment if one party fails to deliver its promises. Generally, calculus-based trust alone cannot sustain a relational type of psychological contract.

Knowledge-based trust is more stable than calculus-based trust because it is developed over time. Suppose that an employer hires someone from outside the company rather than promotes from within, as it almost always did in the past. A trusting employee "knows" that this is probably an exception because it deviates from the employer's past actions. Identification-based trust is the most robust of all three types. Because the individual identifies with the organization (or any other party), he or she is more likely to forgive transgressions. Moreover, employees are reluctant to acknowledge a violation of this high-level trust because it strikes at the heart of their self-image.

Trust is important in the employment relationship because it affects the type of psychological contract. When employees experience psychological contract violations, they lose trust in the employer and are less likely to engage in organizational citizenship behaviours.[18] If violations continue, the loss of trust shifts the employee's psychological contract from being open and dynamic to precise and static. In other words, loss of trust moves the psychological contract from relational to transactional. That explains why the Canadian Federation of Independent Business identified "the trust factor" as one of the more important issues in its recent survey of Canadian employees. They proudly reported that 60 percent of small business employees say they have complete trust in their employer. This is almost double the proportion of employees in medium and large firms and three times the proportion of public sector employees who express this level of trust.[19]

TRENDS IN EMPLOYMENT RELATIONSHIPS

Employment relationships evolve over time, particularly for people in relational psychological contracts. These changes are typically mutual accommodations to the existing contract. The parties believe the original contract is still in place and has minor additions or modifications. How much change can occur to the original contract, yet still maintain this sense of continuity? The answer depends on the flexibility of the employer and employee, which is largely determined by the degree of trust between them.[20]

Along with these minor adjustments over time, some people experience radical transformations of their employment relationship. These transformations occur when one party—usually the employer—wants to significantly change the employee's expectations regarding rewards, career development, corporate culture, or other important elements of the employment relationship. Some parts of the original relationship usually remain, but other features are sufficiently different that the parties believe they are entering into a new relationship. Over the next few pages, we look at two trends in employment relationships: employability and contingent work.

FROM SECURITY TO EMPLOYABILITY

The most dramatic transition in recent years is the shift away from a psychological contract that emphasizes job security in return for loyalty. The old contract established the expectation that if you are loyal to the company, the company will be loyal to you by providing job security and managing your career development.[21] Many employees could expect lifelong career progression through the ranks with ever-increasing salaries. Although this paternalistic contract didn't exist for everyone (e.g., construction, forestry), it was considered the norm in banking and other office-related businesses.

Employability The "new deal" employment relationship in which the job is viewed as a temporary event, so employees are expected to keep pace with changing competency requirements and shift to new projects as demand requires.

The emerging psychological contract, called **employability**, says that employees must take responsibility for their own careers by continually developing new competencies for future work opportunities within and beyond the organization. In this "new deal," jobs are temporary events and organizations are no longer perceived as paternalistic institutions that take care of their employees. Rather, organizations are customers, and employees keep their jobs by continuing to offer valuable skills and knowledge to their clients. From this perspective, individuals must anticipate future organizational needs and develop new competencies accordingly. In other words, new challenges and learning opportunities are the currency of employability.[22]

"Today's career emphasizes self-reliance," says Toronto-based career consultant Barbara Moses. She suggests that career security (not job security) originates with an individual's self-confidence and proactive effort to keep pace with changing organizational needs. Brian Haier, a vice-president at Toronto Dominion Bank, agrees. "The environment is switching from job security to skill security," he advises. "If you're an individual who is willing to learn and change and grow with the demands of our customer base, then I think you can be very well positioned for a long period of time."[23]

Permanence of employability

Some people might argue that the pendulum will swing from employability back to job security as low unemployment gives employees enough power to push for more job guarantees. After all, the concept of employability began in the early 1990s when unemployment rates were high and companies could demand more favourable employment relationships. With low unemployment, won't employees demand job guarantees again?

So far, the evidence suggests that job security might increase somewhat with low unemployment, but other factors will tend to preserve the psychological contracts of employability. One important factor is increasing turbulence in the business environment (see Chapter 15). Global competition, deregulation, and information technologies have made it difficult for employers to provide the job security that was possible in more stable conditions. Organizations need employability to remain flexible and adaptive.

Another factor is changing employee expectations. Some scholars suggest that job security has less value to Generation-X employees than to baby boomers. Generation Xers have mainly experienced a psychological contract based on employability and are comfortable with minimal employment guarantees.[24] In fact, younger employees say that the old psychological contract would be stifling—rather like serving time—because there is less opportunity to steer one's career through personal achievement. "The lifetime employment contract is dead," declares Robert Barnard, a Toronto-based consultant who specializes in Generation-X Canadians. Barnard argues that baby-boom executives are bewildered when they offer long-term employment and Generation Xers aren't interested.[25]

Of course, we can't say that every Generation Xer wants the new-deal psychological contract, but it seems that they are more comfortable with the career risks and opportunities that employability offers. This trend is also apparent in Japan, which is traditionally a stalwart of job security. Connections 18.1 describes how some recent Japanese university graduates prefer challenging work and performance-based pay than lifelong employment.

CONNECTIONS 18.1

Japan's New Psychological Contract

Ogura Junpei is looking for a job after graduating from Japan's Keio University. But he isn't interested in a career with one of the traditional job-for-life Japanese companies. Instead, Ogura-san has found more challenging work and better pay at a consulting firm and a foreign investment bank. "I'm not just looking for a job," explains Ogura-san, "but a place where I find it worthwhile to work."

Japan's well-known psychological contract—lifetime employment, steady advancement, and seniority-based pay increases—is starting to fall apart. One reason is that Japan's recent recession forced Honda, Sony, NEC, and other major corporations to introduce performance-based relationships that weakened job-security guarantees. The other reason is that many younger Japanese employees want challenging work and better pay now, not after waiting a decade or more. "I'm suffocating from the rigid seniority system in my office," complains a young electronics engineer with a major Japanese company.

Not every young Japanese employee is abandoning the lifetime employment relationship. "Lifelong employment is suitable to the Japanese character," explains Kentaro Takahashi, a 23-year-old engineering graduate. "From long ago, people donated their whole lives to the company. So we should give our full support to our new firm."

Still, restructuring in traditional Japanese firms and performance-based rewards in start-up and foreign businesses are changing the psychological contract. For example, hundreds of job seekers recently attended one of Japan's first international job fairs where more than 50 foreign firms were recruiting. "The young urban Japan is already voting for change with their careers," says Kenneth Courtis, strategist and chief economist at Deutsche Bank Group in Tokyo.

Sources: M. Zielenziger, "The Fading Salary Man," *National Post*, April 5, 2000, p. C15; M. Mutsuko, "Who Needs Life Employment?" *AsiaWeek*, March 17, 2000; B. McKenna, "Restructuring Fever Sweeps Japan," *Globe and Mail*, May 29, 1999; M. Millett, "Jobs-for-Life Mentality Severely Restructured," *The Age* (Melbourne), May 15, 1999.

CONTINGENT WORK

The world's largest employer isn't General Motors or IBM. It's Manpower Inc., a temporary services agency that provides contingent workers in almost any occupation a company could want. Manpower annually provides 2 million temps to over 250,000 employers around the globe.[26] It is riding the trend towards a contingent workforce. **Contingent work** is any job in which the individual does not have an explicit or implicit contract for long-term employment, or one in which the minimum hours of work can vary in a nonsystematic way.[27]

Contingent work includes employees with a fixed-term contract, or who work for a client organization through an employment agency. It includes self-employed individuals who contract their services directly to organizations. Contingent work excludes permanent part-time employees because their employment is stable and long term. However, it would include "on-call" part-timers because their work hours can vary considerably from one month to the next. Statistics Canada estimates that 12 percent of the workforce has "nonpermanent" employment. Over 90 percent of U.S. companies use some form of temporary help and contingent

Contingent work
Any job in which the individual does not have an explicit or implicit contract for long-term employment, or one in which the minimum hours of work can vary in a nonsystematic way.

workers represent up to one-quarter of the U.S. workforce. Contingent work has become common in many parts of Europe because labour laws make it difficult to lay off or terminate permanent employees [28]

Types of contingent workers

Exhibit 18.2 illustrates the three main types of contingent workers based on their motivation and ability to find permanent employment. The largest group, representing approximately two-thirds of all contingent workers, are those who have a high motivation but low ability to secure permanent employment.[29] These "temporary temporaries" have been laid off or contracted out and cannot easily find a permanent job. Some have outdated skills; others are young people who lack work experience. These people accept contract work to meet basic economic needs, gain work experience, and find leads to more permanent employment.

Adina Trowhill Smith, described in the opening story of this chapter, represents the smaller but growing cadre of professional contingent workers known as "free agents." Free agents possess valued competencies that make them confident in their independence, and they are less interested in permanent employment. They recognize that their career success depends on maintaining up-to-date knowledge and skills rather than on a paternalistic employment relationship.[30] Free agents are typically found in technical fields, such as accounting and information systems management. Many contingent professionals eventually return to permanent employment to avoid the nuisance of continuously marketing themselves. However, they have sufficient expert power in the labour market to make this choice regarding permanent employment, whereas most contingent workers lack the necessary skills and expertise.

Lastly, some people in the contingent workforce lack both the motivation and the ability to obtain permanent employment. These "transients" lack the skills or experience to command

EXHIBIT 18.2   Types of Contingent Workers

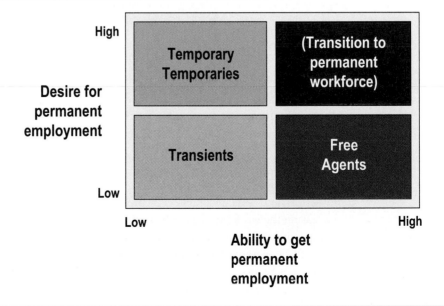

Note: Those who want permanent employment and have high demand skills tend to leave the contingent workforce quickly, so are defined in brackets.

Workers Temporary Help Ltd. in North York is one of the places where Mattel, Humpty Dumpty, and other companies hire contingent workers. These jobs may last a few days or a few months, but they usually pay minimum wage with no benefits beyond the mandatory vacation pay. "It's a terrible way to make a living," says Workers Temporary manager Dan McGarry about the low wages and long hours.[31] What are the main reasons that Canadian firms hire these contingent workers? What problems might occur when relying on this type of labour force?

much power over work opportunities, but they are also unwilling or unable to abide by the confined work schedules and organizational control systems of permanent employment. Work opportunities beyond basic needs are not important to them because they reject the idea that long-term employment is a sign of career success.[32]

Reasons for contingent work

Contingent work has become more common because it provides companies with greater numerical and skill flexibility.[33] It provides numerical flexibility by easily increasing or decreasing the workforce through contingent work contracts rather than by hiring and firing permanent employees. With respect to skill flexibility, organizations respond faster to market demands by temporarily contracting skilled people than by retraining current staff in the new skills. Consultants and other skilled contractors bring valuable knowledge to the organization that is immediately applied and shared with others. This knowledge can also have a catalytic effect on the knowledge creation process because permanent employees learn the foundations for further knowledge acquisition.[34]

A second reason for the increasing reliance on contingent workers is because many organizations offer fewer employer-paid benefits and lower wages to contingent workers than to permanent staff. Some employers also reduce administrative costs by outsourcing and leasing back non-core employees from a large professional company specializing in that field (e.g., information technology services).[35] A third reason for the increase in contingent work is that information technology makes it easier for people in some professions to contract out their services without worrying about commuting or travel. Some writers speculate that telecommuting will produce a new regime of electronically connected freelancers—called e-lancers—who join together into temporary organizations.[36]

Contingent workforce issues

The literature tends to either glamorize or vilify contingent work, but this emerging employment relationship is much more complex than that. Free agents tend to cherish their freedom, yet many also appreciate the social connectedness of more permanent employment. They dislike the rigid boundaries of organizational careers, yet complain about the lack of career boundaries in contingent work.[37]

It is also difficult to say that contingent workers are more or less satisfied with their work. It depends on the individual's personal needs and the type of contingent work. One study of Canadian part-time employees found that those with regular employment were more satisfied with security, benefits, and job growth than were part-time employees with casual (unpredictable) employment. Some writers argue that both contingent and permanent employees feel inequity when they work side by side because they receive different compensation, benefits, and job security for performing the same work.[38] However, other studies report that contingent workers are equally satisfied as people in more permanent employment.[39]

Another concern is that contingent workers may have less ability or motivation to perform their jobs. Some writers argue that contingent workers are less motivated because their tenuous employment creates transactional psychological contracts.[40] Others suggest that contingent workers have less training and work experience, which leads to lower-quality products or services and higher accident rates.[41] With less psychological connection to the organization, some contingent workers may also pose a higher security risk. For instance, Simon Fraser University replaced its security department with a contracted security firm, but fired the firm just three months later. The institution discovered that several employees at the contracted firm were stealing from the offices they were supposed to protect![42]

Against these criticisms are arguments that contingent workers may be more productive than permanent employees under certain conditions. Many professionals are contracted precisely because they have better skills and experience than permanent employees with specific equipment or situations. To increase the probability of future contract or permanent employment, some contingent workers may also be highly motivated to perform the job well. This particularly applies to professionals because their "reputational capital" affects future contract opportunities. And although professionals may have low commitment to the contracting organization, they typically have a strong sense of loyalty and obligation to the standards of their profession.

Farcus   by David Waisglass / Gordon Coulthart

Minimizing contingent workforce problems

One way to minimize the organizational problems with contingent workers is to give contingent workers the same respect and treatment as permanent staff.[43] Where possible, they should receive similar pay and prorated benefits. If this isn't possible, it may be better to staff an entire work activity with either temps or core staff, not both. This reduces feelings of inequity because contingent workers are less likely to compare themselves with permanent employees and vice versa.

Careful selection of temporary employees is another way to minimize problems, particularly with high turnover and risk of theft. For example, one study of temporary service workers at a Canadian theme park reported that those with high work ethic had higher organizational commitment and were less likely to quit before their contract ended.[44] Lastly, contingent workers can develop a stronger relational contract and make a better contribution to the organization when they learn the values, expected behaviours, and social knowledge necessary to assume their roles in the organization. In other words, they should receive effective organizational socialization, which is discussed next.

ORGANIZATIONAL SOCIALIZATION

Markham Stouffville Hospital has won some of the highest awards in Canada for quality and service in a health care facility. Located north of Toronto, the community hospital relies heavily on formal socialization of employees to ensure that quality standards and values are maintained. "You don't just rely on training," advises Markham Stouffville Hospital president Marilyn Bruner. "You need a whole socialization process."[45]

Markham Stouffville Hospital and other organizations pay attention to the **organizational socialization** process so that employees adjust quickly and appropriately to their new situation. Organizational socialization refers to the process by which individuals learn the values, expected behaviours, and social knowledge necessary to assume their roles in the organization.[46] The effectiveness of this socialization process may increase or hinder job performance and job satisfaction, whether the recruits are unskilled and new to the workforce or are highly skilled and have many years of work experience.[47]

> **Organizational socialization** The process by which individuals learn the values, expected behaviours, and social knowledge necessary to assume their roles in the organization.

SOCIALIZATION AS A LEARNING PROCESS

Organizational socialization is a process of both learning and change. It is a learning process because newcomers try to make sense of the company's physical workplace, social dynamics, and strategic/cultural environment. Organizational behaviour research has identified six content dimensions of organizational socialization (see Exhibit 18.3).[48] Newcomers need to learn what is required to perform the assigned work (performance proficiency) as well as who holds power and how they gain power in the organization (politics). They need to form successful and satisfying relationships with other people from whom they can learn the ropes (people).[49] Newcomers need to learn technical jargon so that information is acquired from co-workers and communicated to them more easily (language). They also need to understand the company's espoused goals as well as its underlying cultural values and beliefs (organizational goals and values). Finally, newcomers need to learn about the organization's past as well as its stories, legends, and rituals (history).

Intel includes many of these content elements in its employee socialization process. The world's largest computer chip manufacturer sends new employees a complete package of materials about the company before they begin their first day. On day one, recruits learn

EXHIBIT 18.3 Content Dimensions of Organizational Socialization

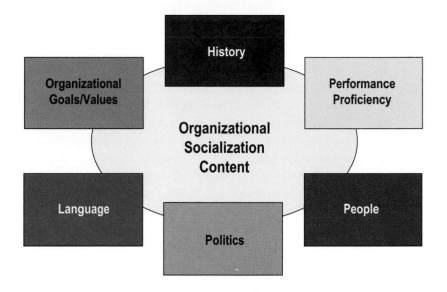

Source: Based on information in G.T. Chao, A. O'Leary-Kelly, S. Wolf, H.J. Klein, and P.D. Gardner, "Organizational Socialization: Its Content and Consequences," *Journal of Applied Psychology*, 79 (1994), pp. 450–63.

about Intel's corporate strategy and get a clear message about performance expectations. A month later, they spend an entire day learning about Intel's corporate culture. At the six-month mark, employees experience a two-hour review of how much they have learned about Intel.[50] The idea is to transmit knowledge in a way that enables new recruits to form a cognitive map of the physical, social, and strategic/cultural dynamics of the organization without information overload.

SOCIALIZATION AS A CHANGE PROCESS

Organizational socialization is also a process of change, because individuals need to adapt to their new work environment.[51] They develop new work roles, adopt new team norms, and practise new behaviours. To varying degrees, newcomers also acquire the values and assumptions of the organization's dominant culture as well as the local subculture. Some people quickly internalize the company's culture; a few others rebel against these attempts to change their mental models and values. Ideally, newcomers adopt a level of creative individualism in which they accept the essential elements of the organization's culture and team norms, yet maintain a healthy individualism that challenges the allegedly dysfunctional elements of organizational life.

Socialization is a continuous process, beginning long before the first day of employment and continuing throughout one's career within the company. However, it is most intense when people cross organizational boundaries, such as when they first join a company, move to a new department or regional branch office, are transferred to (or return from) an international assignment, or are promoted to a higher level in the firm. For each of these transitions, employees need to learn about and adjust to an entirely new work context as well as learn role-specific behaviours.[52]

STAGES OF SOCIALIZATION

The organizational socialization process can be divided into three stages: pre-employment socialization, encounter, and role management (see Exhibit 18.4). These stages parallel the individual's transition from outsider to newcomer and then to insider.[53]

STAGE 1: PRE-EMPLOYMENT SOCIALIZATION

Think back to the months and weeks before you began working in a new job (or attending a new school). You actively searched for information about the company, formed expectations about working there, and felt some anticipation about fitting into that environment. The pre-employment socialization stage encompasses all of the learning and adjustment that occurs prior to the first day of work in a new position.

Much of the socialization adjustment process occurs prior to the first day of work.[54] This is not an easy process, however. Individuals are outsiders, so they must rely on friends, employment interviews, recruiting literature, and other indirect information to form expectations about what it will be like to work in the organization. The employer also forms a set of expectations about the job applicant, such as the unique skills and vitality that he or she will bring to the organization.

Conflicts when exchanging information

Job applicants and employers need an open exchange of accurate information during pre-employment socialization to ensure that they form the same psychological contract. Unfortunately, as Exhibit 18.5 illustrates, four conflicts make it difficult for both parties to send or receive accurate information.[55]

Conflict A occurs between the employer's need to attract qualified applicants and the applicant's need for complete information to make accurate employment decisions. Many firms use a "flypaper" approach by describing only positive aspects of the job and company, causing applicants to accept job offers on the basis of incomplete or false expectations.

Conflict B occurs between the applicant's need to look attractive to employers and the organization's need for complete information to make accurate selection decisions. The problem is that applicants sometimes emphasize favourable employment experiences and leave out less favourable events in their careers. This provides employers with inaccurate data, thereby distorting their expectations of the job candidate and weakening the quality of organizational selection decisions.

EXHIBIT 18.4 Stages of Organizational Socialization

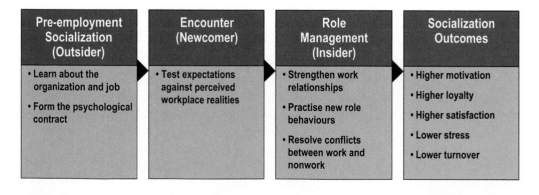

Pre-employment Socialization (Outsider)	Encounter (Newcomer)	Role Management (Insider)	Socialization Outcomes
• Learn about the organization and job • Form the psychological contract	• Test expectations against perceived workplace realities	• Strengthen work relationships • Practise new role behaviours • Resolve conflicts between work and nonwork	• Higher motivation • Higher loyalty • Higher satisfaction • Lower stress • Lower turnover

EXHIBIT 18.5   Information Exchange Conflicts During Pre-Employment Socialization

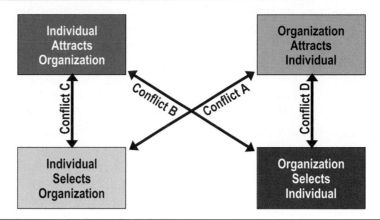

Source: L.W. Porter, E.E. Lawler III, and J.R. Hackman, *Behavior in Organizations* (New York: McGraw-Hill, 1975), p. 134. Reprinted by permission.

Conflict C occurs when applicants avoid asking important career decision questions because they convey an unfavourable image. For instance, applicants usually don't like to ask about salaries and promotion opportunities because it makes them sound greedy or overaggressive. Yet, unless the employer presents this information, applicants might fill in the missing information with false assumptions that produce an inaccurate psychological contract.

Finally, conflict D occurs when employers avoid asking certain questions or using potentially valuable selection devices because they might put the organization in a bad light. For instance, some employers refuse to use aptitude or ability tests, because they don't want to give the impression that they treat employees like mice running through a maze. Unfortunately, without the additional information, employers may form a less accurate opinion of the job candidate's potential.

In spite of these conflicts, job applicants do manage to discover some information about the organization. They learn from casual acquaintances with current and former employees. They receive some information from brochures, advertisements, public news about the company, and initial recruitment visits to the organization's offices.

Postdecisional justification

Postdecisional justification A perceptual phenomenon whereby decision makers justify their choices by subconsciously inflating the quality of the selected option and deflating the quality of the discarded options.

Both employers and job applicants further distort their perceptions of the psychological contract through the process of **postdecisional justification** (see Chapter 10). To maintain a positive self-identity, new hires tend to subconsciously increase the importance of favourable elements of the job and justify or completely forget about some negative elements. At the same time, they reduce the quality of job offers that they turned down. Employers often distort their expectations of new hires in the same way. The result is that both parties develop higher expectations of each other than they will actually experience during the encounter stage.

STAGE 2: ENCOUNTER

The first day on the job typically marks the beginning of the encounter stage of organizational socialization. This is the stage in which newcomers test their prior expectations with the perceived realities. Many employers fail the test. For example, Maple Leaf Foods recently hired 1000 employees for its huge pork processing plant in Brandon, Manitoba. Within six months, over 250 of them had quit or been fired. Plant manager Dave Wood wasn't surprised. He says that many workers join Maple Leaf without understanding what packing work is like.[56]

At Maple Leaf Foods and other organizations, the encounter stage of socialization is marked by varying degrees of **reality shock**. Reality shock occurs for one of two reasons. First, newcomers are often overwhelmed by the experience of sudden entry into a new work environment. They experience the stress of information overload and have difficulty adjusting quickly to their new role. Second, reality shock occurs when newcomers perceive discrepancies between their pre-employment expectations and on-the-job reality.[57] This is a specific application of discrepancy theory (described in Chapter 7) in which the perceived reality falls significantly short of the newcomer's pre-employment expectations. The larger the gap, the greater the shock and sense of psychological contract violation.

> **Reality shock** The gap between pre-employment expectations and the perceived organizational reality that employees experience as they enter a new work situation.

Perhaps it's difficult to imagine working at a Maple Leaf Foods pork plant, but reality shock is common in many organizations. For example, human resource executives in Australia indicate that the most common reason why recently hired employees quit is that their expectations had not been met.[58] Reality shock sometimes occurs because the employer is unable to live up to its promises. It also occurs because new hires develop a distorted psychological contract through the previously described information exchange conflicts and postdecisional justification. Whatever the cause, reality shock impedes the socialization process because the newcomer's energy is directed towards managing the stress rather than learning and accepting organizational knowledge and roles.[59]

STAGE 3: ROLE MANAGEMENT

During the role management stage in the socialization process, employees settle in as they make the transition from newcomers to insiders. They strengthen relationships with co-workers and supervisors, practise new role behaviours, and adopt attitudes and values consistent with their new position and organization.

Role management also involves resolving the conflicts between work and nonwork activities. In particular, employees must redistribute their time and energy between work and family, reschedule recreational activities, and deal with changing perceptions and values in the context of other life roles. They must address any discrepancies between their existing values and those emphasized by the organizational culture. New self-identities are formed that are more compatible with the work environment.

MANAGING THE SOCIALIZATION PROCESS

Organizational socialization has a profound effect on individual performance, organizational commitment, and turnover, so companies should consider various ways to guide this process. Two important strategies are realistic job previews and effectively engaging socialization agents.

REALISTIC JOB PREVIEWS

> **Realistic job preview (RJP)** Giving job applicants a realistic balance of positive and negative information about the job and work context.

Many companies use a flypaper approach to recruiting: They exaggerate positive features of the job and neglect to mention the undesirable elements in the hope that the best applicants will get "stuck" on the organization. In reality, as was described earlier, this strategy tends to produce a distorted psychological contract that eventually leads to lower trust and higher turnover.[60] A better approach is to give job applicants a **realistic job preview (RJP)**, that is, a balance of positive and negative information about the job and work context.[61]

Wayne Cuddington, Ottawa Citizen.

www.sears.ca

Sears Canada Inc. searched the country for people like Linda Nguien (shown in photo) to work at its renovated Eaton's store chain. But low unemployment and competition made it a tough challenge to find 4000 new employees with above-average customer service skills. "There is pressure because there are lots of jobs out there," admits a Sears executive. Eager to attract the best talent, Sears lured job applicants by marketing itself as "a great place to work" and portraying the Eaton's reopening as a unique career opportunity. "We're offering an opportunity to take part in a new venture, an exciting new venture. That doesn't come along very often," another Sears executive announced.[65] Does it sound like Sears is providing realistic job previews in its recruiting process? What are the consequences of providing RJPs under these conditions?

Consider the RJP for people applying for bus driver positions at the British Columbia Transit Authority (B.C. Transit). Job applicants are shown a video depicting angry riders, knife attacks, and other abuses that drivers must endure on their routes. Next, applicants meet with a union representative who explains, among other things, that new drivers are typically assigned night shifts and the poorest routes. Finally, applicants are given the opportunity to actually drive a bus. For many, it is their first experience manoeuvring a large vehicle.

Although RJPs scare away some applicants, they tend to reduce turnover and increase job performance.[62] This is because RJPs help applicants develop more accurate pre-employment expectations, thereby minimizing reality shock. RJPs represent a type of vaccination by preparing employees for the more challenging and troublesome aspects of work life. Moreover, applicants self-select themselves when given realistic information. For example, B.C. Transit applicants who don't like working with people tend to withdraw their job application when they realize that bus drivers frequently interact with customers. There is also some evidence that RJPs increase organizational loyalty. A possible explanation for this is that companies that provide candid information are easier to trust. RJPs also show respect for the psychological contract and concern for employee welfare.[63]

SOCIALIZATION AGENTS

Organizations also improve the socialization process by effectively involving supervisors, co-workers, and other socialization agents.[64] Newcomers tend to ask supervisors for technical information as well as performance feedback and information about job duties. Supervisors also improve the socialization process by giving newcomers reasonably challenging first assignments, buffering them from excessive demands, and helping them form social ties with co-workers.[66] Co-workers are also important socialization agents because they are easily accessible, can answer questions when problems arise, and serve as role models for appropriate behaviour. New employees tend to receive this information and support when co-workers integrate them into the work team. Co-workers also aid the socialization process by being flexible and tolerant in their interactions with these new hires.

Several Canadian firms rely on a "buddy system" whereby newcomers are assigned to co-workers for sources of information and social support. For example, Sega Software (Canada) Inc. assigns a buddy to every new employee. The buddy provides need-to-know information and ensures the newcomer has adequate resources. ExtendMedia also has a formal buddy system, but equally valuable is the box of Timbits that newcomers put on their desk on the first day of work. "The Timbits are there to break the ice so that other people come and talk to them. We are introducing people through their stomachs," explains an executive at ExtendMedia's Toronto headquarters. New employees at Cargill Foods in High River, Alberta, wear light-blue safety helmets so that they are easily identified. "We can focus on them because we know they are new employees and we can nurture them along," says Cargill's regulations superintendent.[67]

Newcomers who quickly form social relations with co-workers tend to have a less traumatic socialization experience and are less likely to quit their jobs within the first year of employment.[68] However, co-workers sometimes engage in hazing—the practice of fooling or intimidating newcomers as a practical joke or initiation ritual. Connections 18.2 describes how employees at a McDonald's restaurant haze new employees by asking them to look for "steam mix." This initiation seems innocent enough and certainly provides entertainment for other staff members, but it can further stress new hires and interfere with their need to form social bonds with co-workers.

Organizational socialization is a continuous process as employees make adjustments through different jobs and organizations. As we learn in the next section, we must also view careers as dynamic and multi-organizational processes in today's rapidly changing environment.

ORGANIZATIONAL CAREERS

If changing jobs is one of life's greatest stresses, then someone forgot to tell Steve Koskie. This 30-year-old has worked for ten employers over the past dozen years. With each job change, he gained experience and new career challenges that the previous employer couldn't offer. Today, Koskie is founder of OceanLake Commerce Inc., a Vancouver-based company that makes Internet transaction verification software for the banking industry. His career challenge now is to retain his own employees. "[Employees] are looking out for themselves and making sure they're in the best position they can be in," says Koskie.[69]

Career A sequence of work-related experiences that people participate in over the span of their working lives.

Steve Koskie may be your above-average job hopper, but his career pattern is becoming more the norm than the exception. A **career** entails not just moving up a ladder within one organization. It is a sequence of work-related experiences that people participate in over the span of their working lives.[70] A person's career might include moving across the organization (i.e., laterally) or temporarily moving down the hierarchy to acquire new skills. Increasingly, Steve Koskie and other people are extending their careers across organizational boundaries.[71]

Effective career development improves employee satisfaction and self-esteem, minimizes stress, and strengthens the employee's psychological and physical health. Effective career development benefits organizations because employees adapt more quickly to changing organizational needs.[72] In this section, we explore the prominent career development concepts, starting with Holland's model of occupational choice and following through to the emerging trends in lateral and boundaryless career paths.

Separating the Steam from the Haze

"We need more steam mix for our hamburger buns," a veteran employee calls out to the new hire at a McDonald's restaurant in suburban Vancouver. "Get another package of mix, please."

For the newly hired employee, this is just another task to learn in the confusing world of fast-food restaurants. For seasoned employees, it is a ritual for newcomers that usually brings hilarity to the otherwise serious work-oriented setting.

Some new employees get the joke immediately, but most scurry to the food storage area in search of the elusive package of steam mix. They check among the stacks of hamburger buns and in the freezer around the boxes of french fries for a package that says "steam mix." After five or ten minutes, the discouraged recruits return empty handed and ask for further directions.

Sometimes, if it isn't too busy, co-workers might say: "It's the big bag clearly marked `Steam Mix'—the one with a picture of a kettle on it." Occasionally, the hazing might go one step further. With a straight face, an employee might reply, "Oh, that's right. We're out of steam mix. Here, take this bucket and go next door to Wendy's. We often borrow some of their mix."

Eager to please their fellow employees, newcomers jaunt across the parking lot with a

Hazing new employees at McDonald's poses a challenge in the socialization process.

McDonald's bucket in hand and politely ask a Wendy's employee for some of their steam mix. A few Wendy's staff members have learned to play along with the game by telling the visitor that their steam mix is different than McDonald's. More often, the new worker is politely reminded that steam comes from boiled water and doesn't require any other ingredients.

Across the parking lot, co-workers watch the embarrassed (and occasionally angry) newcomer return with the empty bucket. Somehow, the hazing ritual never loses its appeal, maybe because it provides a welcome break from work. No one has quit over the experience, although most newcomers are cautious whenever co-workers ask them to retrieve anything from the storage area.

Source: Based on information provided to Steven L. McShane by a student who survived this hazing ritual and watched many others experience it.

HOLLAND'S THEORY OF OCCUPATIONAL CHOICE

At one time, Miriam Goldberger produced sound effects for movies, then ran a prenatal and postpartum women's fitness program, and later edited books for a publisher. She performed each job well, but was frustrated with the work environment (e.g., dark, cramped sound rooms), lack of job autonomy, or people. That's when Goldberger took stock of what she liked and didn't like. "I can't behave in meetings," Goldberger admits. "I can't use diplomatic doublespeak. I'm movement-oriented; I enjoy physical hard work, and I like to do something different every day."

With that self-assessment, Miriam Goldberger decided to turn her favourite hobby—gardening—into a full-time career. Today, she is president of Wildflower Farm in the rolling hills of Schomberg, Ontario, north of Toronto. She and her husband (a former advertising executive) landscape gardens, design meadows, and sell low-maintenance wildflowers. The couple gave up stable paycheques and scaled back their lifestyle, but now earn more than ever before.[73]

Miriam Goldberger and many other people have discovered that a career is not just about matching your skills with job requirements. It is a complex alignment of personality, values, and competencies with the requirements of work and conditions of the work environment. Goldberger may have been talented in these other jobs, but her personality and values were more aligned with physical work that produces tangible results.

John Holland, a career development scholar, was an early proponent of the notion that career success depends on the degree of fit between the person and his or her work environment.[74] Specifically, Holland's theory of occupational choice states that the degree of congruence between an individual's personality traits and the work environment has a significant effect on the person's performance, satisfaction, and length of time in that career. Moreover, a person's occupational choice is an expression of his or her personality.[75] Thus, we would expect that medical doctors have similar traits and interests, which differ from the traits and interests of, say, marketing analysts. With similar personality characteristics, people in a particular occupational group will respond in similar ways to problems and situations.

Holland's six types

Holland's theory contends that there are six types or "themes" that represent characteristics of both the work environment and the personality traits and interests of people working in those environments. These six categories include realistic, investigative, artistic, social, enterprising, and conventional. Exhibit 18.6 defines these types of people and work environments, along with sample occupations representing those environments.

Before trying to categorize your occupational preference, you should be aware that few people fall squarely into only one type. Instead, Holland refers to a person's degree of *differentiation*, that is, the extent to which the individual fits into one or several types. A highly differentiated person is aligned with a single category, whereas most people relate to two or more categories.

Since most people have more than one career type, Holland developed a hexagonal model that helps people determine the consistency of their personality in the career model (see Exhibit 18.7). *Consistency* refers to the extent to which a person is aligned with similar rather than dissimilar types. Similar types are adjacent to each other in the hexagon, whereas dissimilar types are opposite. For instance, individuals with enterprising personalities are more similar to social people than to investigative people. Those who mainly fit into the enterprising category but also relate to the social type are considered consistent, whereas enterprising people who also relate to the investigative type are inconsistent.

"Big Five" personality dimensions The five abstract personality dimensions under which most personality traits are represented. They are extroversion, agreeableness, conscientiousness, emotional stability, and openness to experience.

Practical implications of Holland's theory

There is ongoing debate regarding how well Holland's categories represent personality traits and whether his model should be hexagonal.[76] Holland's personality types represent only the **"Big Five" personality dimensions** of openness and extroversion (see Chapter 6). This begs

EXHIBIT 18.6 Holland's Six Types of Personality and Work Environment

Holland Type	Personality Traits	Work Environment Characteristics	Sample Occupations
Realistic	Practical, shy, materialistic, stable	Work with hands, machines, or tools; focus on tangible results	Assembly worker, dry cleaner, mechanical engineer
Investigative	Analytic, introverted, reserved, curious, precise, independent	Work involves discovering, collecting, and analyzing; solving problems.	Biologist, dentist, systems analyst
Artistic	Creative, impulsive, idealistic, intuitive, emotional	Work involves creation of new products or ideas, typically in an unstructured setting	Journalist, architect, advertising executive
Social	Sociable, outgoing, conscientious, need for affiliation	Work involves serving or helping others; working in teams	Social worker, nurse, teacher, counsellor
Enterprising	Confident, assertive, energetic, need for power	Work involves leading others; achieving goals through others in a results-oriented setting	Salesperson, stockbroker, politician
Conventional	Dependable, disciplined, orderly, practical, efficient	Work involves systematic manipulation of data or information	Accountant, banker, administrator

Sources: Based on information in D.H. Montross, Z.B. Leibowitz, and C.J. Shinkman, *Real People, Real Jobs* (Palo Alto, CA: Davies-Black, 1995); J.H. Greenhaus, *Career Management* (Chicago, IL: Dryden, 1987).

the question of whether Holland's types are incomplete because the other three personality dimensions are not represented. Also, research has reported that Holland's model should look more like a skewed polygon than a hexagon. In other words, some opposing categories are less opposite than others. Aside from these concerns, research using Holland's concepts has found that job stress is related to a lack of congruence between personality and work environment.[77]

Holland's model of occupational choice has laid the foundation for many career development activities in use today. If you take a vocational interest test, there is a good chance that the results are presented around Holland's six dimensions.[78] The idea that an individual's personality should be congruent with the work environment is now well established in research and practice. Holland's hexagonal model (Exhibit 18.7) helps to identify the degree of congruence between an individual's dominant personality type and his or her work environment. Someone who fits mostly in the realistic category would, of course, be most congruent with a realistic environment. The adjacent environments (conventional and investigative) would

EXHIBIT 18.7 Holland's Hexagon Model

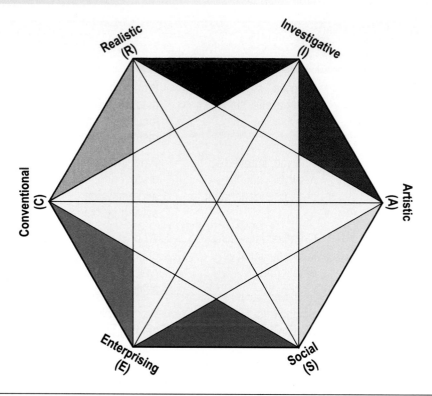

Source: J.L. Holland, *Making Vocational Choices: A Theory of Vocational Personalities and Work Environments,* 2nd ed. (Englewood Cliffs, NJ: Prentice-Hall, 1985).

offer the next best degree of congruence. The lowest congruence occurs for realistic people working in a social environment. Overall, Holland's theory emphasizes the point that effective career development involves finding a good "fit" between the individual's personality and the work environment.

LATERAL CAREER DEVELOPMENT

The traditional career path up the corporate ladder is not as common as it once was. Instead, many firms now define career success in terms of **lateral career development**, rather than how many steps employees have taken up the corporate hierarchy.[79] The idea behind lateral career development is that people can fulfil their personal needs in different jobs across the organization. Employees must think about their careers as a "lattice" rather than a ladder. They must also redefine career success in terms of the variety of challenging work assignments a person completes across the few organizational levels that still remain.

One reason why organizations encourage lateral career development is because much of the existing career ladder is still filled with baby boomers who aren't going anywhere.[80] Lateral career development helps employees to fulfil their personal needs in different jobs across the organization when promotional opportunities are limited. A second reason for lateral career development is that many organizations have transformed their tall hierarchies into flattened team-based structures. In these structures, employees tend to move to different projects across the organization than to higher management levels.

• Lateral career development The view that career success occurs when employees fulfil their personal needs in different jobs across the organization rather than by moving through the organizational hierarchy.

Consider Debbie McNamara's first five years at Lend Lease Corp., the Australian conglomerate with global businesses in real estate development and financial services. The 26-year-old's first job was working with financial advisers who sell Lend Lease products. A year later, she became project manager to simplify business processes in the fund management division's call-centre group. When that was near completion, McNamara was transferred to the United Kingdom where she helped retailers open their businesses at Lend Lease's Bluewater development. McNamara's career path across the organization is typical at Lend Lease because the company wants "careening careers" where employees continuously acquire new competencies.[81]

A third reason for the increasing emphasis on lateral career development is that it is consistent with the shifting emphasis from job status to competencies. Promotions through the traditional corporate ladder tend to reinforce job status, whereas lateral career development helps people learn new competencies and remain competitive in the labour market. This is also aligned with the trend towards employability rather than job security. Employees must anticipate future demand for skills and knowledge and manage their careers accordingly by seeking out work opportunities that develop those competencies.

Consider Glaxo Wellcome in the UK, Volkswagen in Germany, IBM in the U.S., and Michelin Tires in France. Each of these firms has developed fewer and wider pay grades to reflect the fewer promotional opportunities in the organization (see Chapter 4).[82] Instead, these companies advise employees to broaden their knowledge and experience through lateral career paths. The result is a more flexible workforce with multiple skills.

Encouraging lateral career development

Many people have difficulty adjusting to lateral career development. Baby boomers, in particular, were raised with the belief that career success is defined in terms of how high you climb up the corporate hierarchy. Employees are also reluctant to engage in lateral career development because it involves the risk of leaving their long-time jobs and departments. Moreover, they may face interference from supervisors who don't want to see their prized staff move elsewhere.

Statistics Canada minimizes resistance to lateral career development by allowing employees who transfer to another job the right to move back if the new position doesn't work out. The federal government agency also makes it clear that supervisors cannot prevent employees who have held their current job for four or more years from participating in lateral career development opportunities. As a result, over 600 Statistics Canada employees have been involved in the lateral career development initiative.[83]

To encourage lateral career development, companies also need to regularly communicate new job openings and help employees with career self-assessments. For example, Starbucks Coffee Company posts all job openings every week. Both the TD Bank and Bank of Montreal have virtual career centres where employees can assess their skills, see how those skills fit in the organization, and learn how they can gain the skills needed to meet their career goals. Raychem offers career seminars that encourage employees to think of themselves as self-employed and to explore many career options. The electronics firm also has a career centre where employees explore their potential through self-assessments, career workshops, and referrals to career resources. Employees compare their current competencies with current and future market demands.[84]

BOUNDARYLESS CAREERS

Forty years ago in his best-selling book *Organization Man*, William H. Whyte painted a satirical picture of American white-collar career success in terms of secure employment with slow, steady promotion through several professional and management layers. These people devoted their entire lives to the same company, slowly working their way up the corporate ladder.[85]

Some people still follow this structured model of career development, but most do not. Instead, there is a growing trend towards the **boundaryless career**—the idea that careers operate across company and industry boundaries rather than just within a single organizational hierarchy.[86] This is the view that careers unfold throughout one's life, not necessarily throughout one company.

Steve Koskie, described at the beginning of this section, advanced his career by switching jobs rather than waiting for the next great challenge within one organization. In Silicon Valley's hyperpaced high-tech firms, one-quarter of the workforce switches jobs each year. Some observers note that many high-tech workers have embraced the boundaryless career to such an extent that they think they work for one large organization called "Silicon Valley."[87]

Boundaryless career
The idea that careers operate across company and industry boundaries rather than just within a single organizational hierarchy.

Reasons why people adopt boundaryless careers

Boundaryless careers are more common today than they were ten years ago, but this does not imply that employees enjoy changing jobs. On the contrary, by a two-to-one margin, high-tech job hoppers would rather stay with one employer for 20 years than hold five jobs for four years each.[88] This suggests that the boundaryless career is more a function of necessity than motivation. The trend towards boundaryless careers accelerated with massive corporate downsizing over the past decade.[89] These layoffs and early retirements forced people to realign their careers with other organizations. From this painful experience, many people developed the attitude that it is better to accept career opportunities as they come along rather than remain loyal to one employer.

A related explanation for the rise in boundaryless careers is that many psychological contracts have shifted from job security to employability. As was mentioned earlier in this chapter, the "new deal" rewards people who take control of their own career development.[90] But moving away from a loyalty-based contract also weakens the internal labour market. Thus, employees are more likely to seek career development opportunities outside the organization. And while job hopping was once a liability, recruiters are now developing a more favourable attitude towards this type of career path. "There was a point when jumping around was viewed more negatively than it is today," says an American Express recruiter. "It's not uncommon today to see lots of job changes. Instead of dismissing an applicant as being unreliable because of frequent changes, we try to look at what was the motivation for the changes."[91]

What can organizations do about boundaryless careers and the trend towards job hopping? One obvious solution is to provide enough career opportunities within the organization to make external job hopping unnecessary. While this may seem impossible in smaller firms, we must remember that career opportunities can be created through new projects and challenges, not just through existing positions elsewhere in the company.

More generally, corporate leaders need to re-examine the drivers of organizational loyalty that were identified in Chapter 7. Employees are more likely to take their careers elsewhere when they lack sufficient commitment to and identity with the organization. Thus, people are more likely to keep their careers in-house when they have positive and equitable work experiences, a reasonable level of job security, continuous understanding of organizational activities, involvement in organizational decisions, and a high level of trust in corporate leaders and co-workers.

Finally, we need to recognize that it is natural and desirable for some employees to leave for better career opportunities elsewhere. In some cases, employees return to their previous

Personal needs have driven Randy VanDerStarren's career decisions and contributed to his career success. VanDerStarren planned on a career in architecture, but eventually realized that he wasn't excited about designing suburban homes for the next ten years. Instead, he studied graphic arts in college and soon discovered his passion for advertising—the creativity, strategic thinking, and never-ending churn of ideas. Armed with a college and university education, VanDerStarren joined a major Toronto ad agency. His love of advertising and a knack at strategy led to jobs at other ad agencies over the next decade. VanDerStarren is now senior vice-president of marketing with Canadian mutual fund firm AGF Management Ltd., a position that continues to fulfil his personal needs. "AGF has allowed me...to do what I love," says VanDerStarren. "It's a pretty amazing ride for me right now."[95] How can you tell when a particular career path fulfils your personal needs?

employer after developing new competencies elsewhere. In this wired world, employees quickly gain information about career opportunities through workopolis.com and other job vacancy Web sites. It is unlikely that the boundaryless career will disappear any time soon.

CAREER DEVELOPMENT: RULES FOR THE ROAD AHEAD

Whether you are just starting your career or already well along the road, the following ideas should help you improve both your prospects and your long-term career satisfaction. These points do not cover everything you need to remember about developing your career. Instead, they highlight some of the key strategies that will help you along your journey.

UNDERSTAND YOUR NEEDS AND VALUES

Whether you are part of the contingent workforce or are a permanent employee with one organization for most of your life, you should keep in mind that career development begins by understanding your personal needs and values.[92] "Find something you love, that you would do for free and then try to make a living at it," advises Toronto comedian and talk show host Mike Bullard.[93]

How do you know what type of career is most fulfilling for you? This involves doing self-assessments of your vocational interests and recounting experiences that you enjoyed. Holland's occupational choice model presented earlier in this chapter helps to align your personality and interests with the work environment. It may also be useful to get feedback from others regarding activities that they notice you like or dislike. This applies the Johari Window model described in Chapter 6, whereby you learn more about yourself through information presented by close associates.

UNDERSTAND YOUR COMPETENCIES

Knowing yourself also involves knowing what you are capable of doing.[94] In Chapter 2, we learned that each of us has a set of aptitudes—natural talents that help us learn specific tasks more quickly and perform them better. Although we might visualize our future as an engineering wizard or Canada's prime minister, we need to take our potential abilities into account. The more careers are aligned with personal competencies, the more we develop a strong sense of self-efficacy—the "can-do" attitude that further empowers our career. Self-assessments, performance results, and constructive feedback from friends can help us identify our capabilities. Also, keep in mind that employers look beyond technical skills to generic competencies, such as communication, problem solving, and interpersonal relations. Indeed, some recruiters say they pay more attention to these foundations and assume that employees will develop job-specific skills at work.

SET CAREER GOALS

When Dave Clark joined the fire department in Hamilton, Ontario, he didn't plan on rising to the level of deputy platoon chief. "I didn't really have a goal in mind," Clark admits. Fortunately, one of Clark's senior officers urged him to develop his career. "I guess somebody saw the potential that I had, and they gave me that extra push," says Clark.[96]

Dave Clark was lucky. He had someone to help him move his career forward. But we usually can't count on others to guide our career development. We need to set our own goals to realize our potential and ultimately fulfil our needs. Goal setting is a powerful way to motivate and achieve results, and this applies as much to careers as to any other activity. Career goals are benchmarks against which we evaluate our progress and identify strategies to develop our competencies.

Toronto-based career consultant Barbara Moses emphasizes that career goal setting is a fundamental element in becoming a "career activist." It involves writing your own script rather than waiting for someone to write it for you, being vigilant by identifying and preparing for opportunities, and becoming an independent agent by separating your self-identity from your job title, your organization, or what other people think you should be.[97]

MAINTAIN NETWORKS

As people develop boundaryless careers, their career opportunities depend more on trusting relationships than on documented information about their performance. As one successful Canadian job hunter advises: "Be prepared, know your story, and network, network, network."[98] Several research studies have confirmed that networking is an increasingly important feature of career development. In particular, people with large, nonredundant networks tend to be more successful job seekers and receive greater organizational rewards. One important piece of advice is to network in areas beyond your current sphere of work. The reason is that careers change much more than in the past, so you need to establish connections to other fields where you may someday find yourself.[99]

GET A MENTOR

So far, our discussion has emphasized self-leadership in career development (see Chapter 4). We need to set our own goals, motivate ourselves for career advancement, and visualize where we want to go. But career development also benefits from the help of others. **Mentoring** is the process of learning the ropes of organizational life from a senior person within the company (see Chapter 12). Mentors give proteges more visible and meaningful work opportunities, but they also provide ongoing career guidance. You might think of them as a career coach because they provide ongoing advice and feedback.[100]

Mentoring is so important at McKinsey & Company that several offices of the management consulting firm ask all associates at regular intervals which partners they view as mentors. Surprisingly, no partner was initially identified by any more than four associates as a mentor. In other words, McKinsey partners provided less mentoring than they had assumed. This discovery has resulted in significantly more mentoring at McKinsey.[101]

Mentoring The process of learning the ropes of organizational life from a senior person within the company.

CAREERS AND ORGANIZATIONAL BEHAVIOUR

Wherever your career leads, you will invariably remain inside or close to those abstract constructs called "organizations." As such, the topics discussed through this book will continuously relate to your career success and personal fulfilment. You will discover how organizational behaviour topics are interrelated. It is difficult to discuss motivation without referring to personality. We can't understand communication without noting power and politics. Leadership embraces change. Change embraces knowledge management. And as you apply organizational behaviour throughout your career, remember that organizations are the people in them. They are human entities—full of life, sometimes fragile, always exciting.

CHAPTER SUMMARY

- The psychological contract is a set of perceived mutual obligations about the employer's and employee's exchange relationship. Some contracts are transactional while others are more relational.

- Trust is an important factor in the employment relationship. There are three levels of trust: calculus-based, knowledge-based, and identification-based. Knowledge-based and identification-based trust are stronger and more flexible than calculus-based trust.

- One trend in employment relationships is the shift from job security to employability. This "new deal" psychological contract says that employees must take responsibility for their own careers by continually developing new competencies for future work opportunities within and beyond the organization. The other trend is the increase in contingent work. This refers to any job in which the individual does not have an explicit or implicit contract for long-term employment or one in which the minimum hours of work can vary in a nonsystematic way. Contingent work is growing because companies want more flexibility and lower payroll costs, and many are outsourcing non-core work activities.

- Organizational socialization is the process by which individuals learn the values, expected behaviours, and social knowledge necessary to assume their roles in the organization. It is a learning process because newcomers need to acquire information about performance proficiency, people, politics, language, organizational goals and values, and history. Socialization is also a process of change as newcomers develop new work roles, adopt new team norms, and practise new behaviours.

- Employees typically pass through three socialization stages. Pre-employment socialization occurs before the first day and includes conflicts between the organization's and applicant's need to collect information and attract the other party. Encounter begins on the first day and typically involves adjusting to reality shock. Role management involves resolving work–nonwork conflicts and settling in to the workplace.

- To manage the socialization process, organizations should introduce realistic job previews (RJPs) and recognize the value of socialization agents in the process. RJPs give job applicants a realistic balance of positive and negative information about the job and work context. Socialization agents provide information and social support during the socialization process.

- A career is a sequence of work-related experiences in which people participate over the span of their working lives. Holland's theory of occupational choice states that the degree of congruence between an individual's personality traits and the work environment affects career performance, satisfaction, and longevity. The theory includes six personality types and work environments: realistic, investigative, artistic, social, enterprising, and conventional. Individuals are differentiated if they fit mainly in one of these categories, and they are consistent if they relate to adjacent rather than opposite types.

- Companies are encouraging lateral career development, rather than climbing the traditional corporate ladder, because there are fewer steps on the corporate ladder, baby boomers block upward mobility of employees further down the hierarchy, and lateral career development is consistent with the shifting emphasis from job status to competencies.

- Boundaryless careers are careers that operate across company and industry boundaries. They are becoming more common due to corporate downsizing and the shift from job security to employability contracts.

- Five strategies that assist personal career development are to understand your needs and values, understand your competencies, set career goals, maintain networks, and get a mentor.

KEY TERMS

"Big Five" personality dimensions, p. 550

Boundaryless career, p. 554

Career, p. 548

Contingent work, p. 538

Employability, p. 537

Lateral career development, p. 552

Mentoring, p. 556

Organizational citizenship, p. 532

Organizational socialization, p. 542

Postdecisional justification, p. 545

Psychological contract, p. 532

Realistic job preview (RJP), p. 546

Reality shock, p. 546

Trust, p. 534

DISCUSSION QUESTIONS

1. Jack Santoni works on the field production crew at Gusher Drilling Co. When he joined the company five years ago, the supervisor who hired him said Jack could use the company's old pickup truck on weekends. Now, the company plans to sell the truck and won't replace it, leaving Jack without a vehicle. Discuss the implications of this action on Jack's psychological contract with Gusher Drilling Co.

2. Many organizations are moving towards a psychological contract based on employability. What does this mean, and how does it differ from the psychological contract that most employees believed in a few decades ago? Do you think this employability contract will continue or revert to a security-based contract in the future?

3. WestCrude, a major oil company, has just decided that its core competency is exploring and drilling for oil deposits, and will outsource most of its support services (human resources, information systems). This will result in a large contingent workforce in these functions. What issues should WestCrude consider before moving to a contingent workforce?

4. The textbook states that organizational socialization is a process of learning and change. What does this mean, and how do organizations facilitate both for new employees?

5. After three months on the job, you feel that the company has violated the psychological contract. The job is not as exciting as you originally expected, and your current boss is no better than the supervisor in your previous job. The people who interviewed you are concerned about your feelings, but say that they didn't misrepresent either the job or the fact that some supervisors are not as good as others. Explain how your perceived psychological contract may have been distorted during pre-employment socialization.

6. ExtendMedia, Sega Software, and many other Canadian organizations rely on a "buddy" system to socialize new employees. What are the advantages of relying on this type of socialization agent? What problems can you foresee (or have you personally experienced) with co-worker socialization practices?

7. You have just completed a vocational test that concludes that you have an enterprising personality, along with fairly high levels of the artistic and investigative type in Holland's model. Assuming that this vocational test is accurate, what are its implications for your career?

8. Although companies encourage lateral career development, many baby-boom generation employees still prefer the opportunity to climb the corporate ladder. Do you think that these employees are correct in thinking that "real" career development occurs only when you are promoted? Will Generation-X employees develop a similar attachment to promotions later in their career?

Case Study

ACTIVITY 18.1
Quantor Corp.'s Contingent Workforce

Three years ago, Quantor Corp., a large manufacturer of computer printers and other peripherals, established a task force to determine the most appropriate use of contingent workers throughout the company. The company had started to rely on contract, part-time, and temporary help agency people to fill temporary jobs. At the time, this represented less than 1 percent of Quantor's workforce, but the company wanted to review these practices to ensure consistency and effectiveness.

After reviewing current ad hoc practices, the task force concluded that Quantor needed contingent workers when demand for the company's products expanded rapidly or a new product was launched.

Quantor needed this workforce flexibility because of uncertain production demand beyond the short term. At the same time, the task force warned that treating contingent workers the same as permanent employees would undermine the benefits of flexibility, create false hopes of permanent employment among contingent workers, and possibly create feelings of inequity between the two groups. Thus, policies were introduced that treated contingent workers differently than permanent employees.

Quantor's task force established two contingent worker categories: on-call and on-contract. On-call workers are employed by Quantor as part-time staff. They work a full day, but only up to two-thirds of the hours of a full-time permanent employee. Their managers can alter their work schedules at will to suit production demands. On-contract workers are employed full time by Quantor for a fixed period,

ACTIVITY 18.1 CONTINUED

usually six months. Their contract may be renewed up to three times for a maximum employment of two years.

On-call and on-contract employees received no employee benefits other than the government-mandated minimum vacation and holiday pay. Benefits therefore represented approximately 10 percent of their total pay, compared to nearly 40 percent for permanent employees. However, contingent workers earned the midpoint of the pay grade for their job group, which represented 15 percent above the entry rate. This rate was paid even when the contingent worker lacked experience in the job.

Quantor's Contingent Workforce Problems

Three years after Quantor's task force recommendations, the contingent workforce policy was in trouble. Current practices succeeded in creating a more flexible workforce, and there was some evidence that using contingent workers increased profitability. However, these practices created unanticipated problems that became apparent as the percentage of contingent workers increased.

One problem was that few people wanted only contract employment. Most were seeking full-time permanent work and were using their contingent position as a stepping stone to those jobs at Quantor. The result was that many contract workers remained for the entire two-year maximum period and beyond. The company was reluctant to apply the task force's recommendation of not renewing contracts beyond two years because of the perceived arbitrariness of this action as well as loss of knowledge to the organization. Several contract staff members asked the company for an employee-paid benefit package (benefits are mainly employer-paid for permanent employees). Quantor rejected this because it would add further permanence to their employment relationship.

Quantor's managers also began to complain about the company policy that contingent workers could not be offered permanent employment. They appreciated the opportunity to select permanent employees based on observations of their performance in on-contract or on-call positions. Quantor's task force had warned against this practice because it might create inequities and raise false expectations about the likelihood of permanent employment. Managers acknowledged this risk, but the inability to permanently hire good contract staff was frustrating to them.

The third problem was that Quantor's treatment of contingent workers was incompatible with its organizational culture. Quantor had a strong culture based on the philosophy of employee well-being. The company had a generous benefits package, supportive leadership, and a belief system that made employees a top priority in corporate decisions. The company did not treat contingent workers in a way that was consistent with this philosophy. Yet if Quantor treated contingent workers the same as permanent staff members, flexibility would be lost. For example, managers would continue renewing contract workers even when their employment was not essential, and would be reluctant to schedule on-call people at awkward times.

Quantor's team orientation was also incompatible with its use of contingent workers. Permanent staff members frequently gathered to discuss organizational and group decisions. Contingent workers were not invited to these team activities because they might be working at Quantor for only a few more months. This barrier created some awkward moments for managers as contingent workers continued working while permanent employees went to meetings and team sessions.

As these problems intensified, senior management formed another task force to re-examine Quantor's contingent workforce policy. The company needed contingent workers, but it was increasingly apparent that the current practices were not working.

Discussion Questions

1. Identify the problems that Quantor experienced with its contingent workforce practices. Also identify other possible contingent workforce problems that have not been explicitly mentioned in this case.

2. Discuss the problems with contingent workers at Quantor in terms of the psychological contract and organizational commitment.

3. What alternative strategies might allow Quantor to include a contingent workforce with fewer problems?

Video Case Study

ACTIVITY 18.2
How a B.C. Union Saved Jobs by Giving Up Overtime

In Powell River, British Columbia, pulp mill workers and managers are in the midst of a controversial struggle. The employees' labour union, Communications Energy and Paperworkers Union (CEP), has asked its members to refuse overtime so that more people can recover from the hardship of unemployment.

Gary Jackson knows just how hard unemployment can be. Jackson had worked for nine years at the pulp mill, the town's main employer, until he was laid off two years ago. At one time, working at the mill was a job for life. The company was productive and demand was high, but not any more. The Powell River mill has cut more than 1000 positions in the last 15 years. "Security is so important to myself," says Jackson.

To bring jobs back, CEP hatched a plan whereby its members would stop working most overtime. Workers cut their regular hours from 42 to 40 and overtime dropped from 7 to 1 percent, the lowest rate of any mill in the province. The company had to rescind its layoff notices and hire 22 people. Gary Jackson went back to work.

CEP claims that reducing overtime reduces costs, but employers don't accept that argument. They say that overtime is necessary for flexibility during times of peak demands. Moreover, hiring more people adds fixed costs. The bottom line is that companies want employees to accept overtime as a normal part of their psychological contract.

There's another problem: Reducing overtime costs employees real money. Tony Leach gave up his overtime, which cost him $5000 per year. Leach doesn't mind, but some mill employees want to keep clocking overtime even if it means that colleagues are laid off. "I don't get to teach other people what I think," says Ben Speckling, a Powell River employee who continues to work overtime. Speckling believes it is his right to work overtime, even if the union puts pressure on him to stop.

In some places around the world, employees are expected to work overtime if they are asked to do so. Overtime is voluntary in British Columbia, but executives at Pacifica Papers, which owns the Powell River mill, think that some mandatory overtime would be a good idea. In contrast, most Powell River employees are willing to change their expectations and the amount of time they give their employer. Eighty-nine percent of workers surveyed at the mill say they support the union's action taken on overtime.

Discussion Questions

1. How does this action by Communications Energy and Paperworkers Union affect the psychological contract between employees and the employer at the Powell River mill?

2. Discuss the level of trust between employees and employer at the Powell River mill. Why is trust at this level, in your opinion?

3. Suppose that you represented either Pacifica Papers or CEP and could be involved in the socialization of new employees. What strategies would you use to shape their expectations regarding overtime?

Source: Based on "Over Time," *The National Magazine* (November 8, 1999).

TEAM exercises

ACTIVITY 18.3
ORGANIZATIONAL SOCIALIZATION DIAGNOSTIC EXERCISE

Purpose: To help students understand the socialization strategies that organizations should use for new employees, and learn about the impediments to forming an accurate psychological contract.

Instructions: The instructor will form teams (typically of four or five people). Each team will follow these steps:

Step 1: Each team member will describe one particularly memorable positive or negative experience encountered when entering an organization. (Students with limited organizational experience may describe entry to school.) Entry to the organization would include any interaction with the company before, on, and a short while after the first day of work. The incident might describe how the individual was greeted on the first day of work, how the company kept him or her informed before the first day of work, how the company did (or did not) inform the person about negative aspects of the work or job context, and so forth. The team will consider all of these experiences, but will pick the most interesting one for description in class.

Step 2: Based on these experiences, the team will develop a list of strategies that companies should use to improve the organizational entry process. Some experiences will reflect effective management of this process. Other experiences will indicate what companies have done ineffectively, so the team must identify strategies to avoid those problems.

Step 3: In class, one person from each team will describe his or her organizational entry experience. (This person is chosen in Step 1.) The team will explain what the company did well or poorly with respect to that incident. After each team has presented one incident, the class will discuss other ideas from the team discussion.

ACTIVITY 18.4
TRUTH IN ADVERTISING

Purpose: This team activity is designed to help you diagnose the degree to which recruitment advertisements and brochures provide realistic previews of the job and/or organization.

Materials: The instructor will bring to class either recruiting brochures or newspaper advertisements.

Instructions: The instructor will place students in teams and give them copies of recruiting brochures and/or advertisements. The instructor might assign one lengthy brochure or several newspaper advertisements. All teams should receive the same materials so that everyone is familiar with the items and results can be compared. Teams will evaluate the recruiting material(s) and answer the following questions for each item:

1. What information in the text of this brochure/advertisement identifies conditions or activities in this organization or job that some applicants may not like?

2. If there are photographs or images of people at work, do they show only positive conditions, or do any show conditions or events that some applicants may not like?

3. After reading this item, would you say that it provides a realistic preview of the job and/or organization?

Self-Assessment exercise

ACTIVITY 18.5
MATCHING HOLLAND'S CAREER TYPES

Purpose: This self-assessment is designed to help you understand Holland's career types.

Instructions: Holland's theory identifies six different types of work environments and occupations in which people work. Few jobs fit purely in one category, but all have a dominant type. Your task is to circle the letter representing the Holland type that you believe best fits each of the occupations listed. A brief description of each work environment is included below. When finished, the instructor will provide the correct answers. Add up the number of occupations that you matched correctly to determine your score.

Descriptions of Holland's Six Work Environments:

R Realistic—Work with hands, machines, or tools; focus on tangible results

I Investigative—Work involves discovering, collecting, and analyzing; solving problems

A Artistic—Work involves creation of new products or ideas, typically in an unstructured setting

S Social—Work involves serving or helping others; working in teams

E Enterprising—Work involves leading others; achieving goals through others in a results-oriented setting

C Conventional—Work involves systematic manipulation of data or information

OCCUPATION	HOLLAND CATEGORY					
Actuary	R	I	A	S	E	C
Archaeologist	R	I	A	S	E	C
Buyer	R	I	A	S	E	C
Computer operator	R	I	A	S	E	C
Corporate executive	R	I	A	S	E	C
Corporate trainer	R	I	A	S	E	C
Dietitian	R	I	A	S	E	C
Economist	R	I	A	S	E	C
Elementary school teacher	R	I	A	S	E	C
Fashion model	R	I	A	S	E	C
Firefighter	R	I	A	S	E	C
Foreign exchange trader	R	I	A	S	E	C
Jeweller	R	I	A	S	E	C
Life insurance agent	R	I	A	S	E	C
Lobbyist	R	I	A	S	E	C
Mathematics teacher	R	I	A	S	E	C
Medical illustrator	R	I	A	S	E	C
Minister/priest/rabbi	R	I	A	S	E	C
Pediatrician	R	I	A	S	E	C
Pharmacist	R	I	A	S	E	C
Pilot	R	I	A	S	E	C
Production manager	R	I	A	S	E	C
Professional athlete	R	I	A	S	E	C
Public relations director	R	I	A	S	E	C
Recreation leader	R	I	A	S	E	C
School administrator	R	I	A	S	E	C
Sculptor	R	I	A	S	E	C
Tax auditor	R	I	A	S	E	C
Veterinarian	R	I	A	S	E	C
Winemaker	R	I	A	S	E	C

Interpreting Your Score:

Number Correct	Interpretation
26–30	Excellent understanding of Holland's career types
21–25	Good understanding of Holland's career types
16–20	Fair understanding of Holland's career types
11–15	Need to look more closely at Holland's descriptions
0–10	Career counselling might not be your calling!

Additional Cases

CASE 1
An Untimely Incident at Ancol

Paul Simard was delighted when Ancol Ltd. offered him the job of manager at its Jonquière, Quebec, plant. Simard was happy enough managing a small metal stamping plant with another company, but the headhunter's invitation to apply for the plant manager job at one of Canada's leading metal fabrication companies was irresistible. Although the Jonquière plant was the smallest of Ancol's 15 operations across Canada, the plant manager position was a valuable first step in a promising career.

One of Simard's first observations at Ancol's Jonquière plant was that relations between employees and management were strained. Taking a page from a recent executive seminar he had attended on building trust in the workplace, Simard ordered the removal of all time clocks from the plant. Instead, the plant would assume that employees had worked their full shift. This symbolic gesture, he believed, would establish a new level of credibility and strengthen relations between management and employees at the site.

Initially, the 250 production employees at the Jonquière plant appreciated their new freedom. They felt respected and saw this gesture as a sign of positive change from the new plant manager. Two months later, however, problems started to appear. A few people began showing up late, leaving early, or taking extended lunch breaks. Although these people represented only about 5 percent of the employees, others perceived the situation to be unfair. Moreover, the increased absenteeism levels were beginning to have a noticeable effect on plant productivity. The problem had to be managed.

Simard asked supervisors to observe and record when the employees came and went and to discuss attendance problems with those abusing their privileges. But the supervisors had no previous experience with keeping attendance and many lacked the necessary interpersonal skills to discuss the matter with subordinates. Employees resented the reprimands, so relations with supervisors deteriorated. The additional responsibility of keeping track of attendance also made it difficult for supervisors to complete their other responsibilities. After just a few months, Ancol found it necessary to add another supervisor position and reduce the number of employees assigned to each supervisor.

But the problems did not end there. Without time clocks, the payroll department could not deduct pay when employees were late. Instead, a letter of reprimand was placed in the employee's personnel file. However, this required yet more time and additional skills from the supervisors. Employees did not want these letters to become part of their permanent records, so they filed grievances with their labour union. The number of grievances doubled over six months, which required even more time from both union officials and supervisors to handle these disputes.

Nine months after removing the time clocks, Simard met with union officials, who agreed that it would be better to reinstall the time clocks. Employee–management relations had deteriorated below the level they were at when Simard had started at Ancol. Supervisors were burnt out from overwork. Productivity had dropped due to poor attendance records and increased administrative workloads.

A couple of months after the time clocks were reinstalled, Simard attended an operations meeting at

Ancol's headquarters in Toronto. During lunch, Simard described the time clock incident to Liam Jackson, Ancol's plant manager in northern British Columbia. Jackson looked surprised, then chuckled. Jackson explained that the previous B.C. plant manager had done something like that with similar consequences six or seven years ago. The previous manager had since retired, but Jackson heard about the B.C. time clock incident from a supervisor who went through the experience.

"I guess it's not quite like lightning striking the same place twice," said Simard to Jackson. "But it sure feels like it."

Discussion Questions

1. What symptom(s) exist in this case to suggest that something has gone wrong?

2. What are the root causes that have led to these symptoms?

3. What actions should Ancol or Paul Simard take to correct these problems?

© Copyright 1998 Steven L. McShane. This case is based on actual events, but names and some facts have been changed to provide a fuller case discussion.

CASE 2
Arctic Mining Consultants

Tom Parker enjoyed working outdoors. At various times, he had worked as a ranch hand, high steel rigger, headstone installer, prospector, and geological field technician. Now 43, Parker is a geological field technician and field coordinator with Arctic Mining Consultants. He has specialized knowledge and experience in all non-technical aspects of mineral exploration, including claim staking, line cutting and grid installation, soil sampling, prospecting, and trenching. He is responsible for hiring, training, and supervising field assistants for all Arctic Mining Consultants' programs. Field assistants are paid a fairly low daily wage (no matter how long they work, which may be up to 12 hours or more) and are provided meals and accommodation. Many of the programs are operated by a project manager who reports to Parker.

Parker sometimes acts as a project manager, as he did on a job that involved staking 15 claims near Eagle Lake, British Columbia. He selected John Talbot, Greg Boyce, and Brian Millar, all of whom had worked with him as the field assistants. To stake a claim, the project team marks a line with flagging tape and blazes along the perimeter of the claim, cutting a claim post every 500 metres (called a "length"). The 15 claims would require almost 100 kilometres of line in total. Parker had budgeted seven days (plus mobilization and demobilization) to complete the job. This meant that each of the four stakers (Parker, Talbot, Boyce, and Millar) would have to complete a little over seven "lengths" each day. The following is a chronology of the project.

Day 1

The crew assembled in the morning and drove to Eagle Lake, from where they were flown by helicopter to the claim site. On arrival, they set up tents at the edge of the area to be staked and agreed on a schedule for cooking duties. After supper, they pulled out maps and discussed the job—how long it would take, the order in which the areas were to be staked, possible helicopter landing spots, and areas that might be more difficult to stake.

Parker pointed out that with only a week to complete the job, everyone would have to average 7.5 lengths per day. "I know that is a lot," he said, "but you've all staked claims before and I'm confident that each of you is capable of it. And it's only for a week. If we get the job done in time, there's a $300 bonus for each of us." Two hours later, the crew had developed what seemed to be a workable plan.

Day 2

Millar completed six lengths, Boyce six, Talbot eight, and Parker eight. Parker was not pleased with Millar's or Boyce's production. However, he didn't make an issue of it, thinking that they would develop their "rhythm" quickly.

Day 3

Millar completed five and a half lengths, Boyce four, and Talbot seven. Parker, who was nearly twice as old as the other three, completed eight lengths. He also had enough time to check the quality of Millar's and

Boyce's stakes, then walk back to his own area for helicopter pickup back to the tent site.

That night Parker exploded with anger. "I thought I told you that I wanted seven and a half lengths a day!" he shouted at Boyce and Millar. Boyce said that he was slowed down by unusually thick underbrush in his assigned area. Millar said that he had done his best and would try to pick up the pace. Parker did not mention that he had inspected their work. He explained that, as far as he was concerned, they were supposed to finish their assigned areas for the day, no matter what.

Talbot, who was sharing a tent with Parker, talked to him later. "I think that you're being a bit hard on them, you know. I know it has been more by luck than anything else that I've been able to complete my quota. Yesterday I only had five lengths done after the first seven hours and there was only an hour until I was supposed to be picked up. Then I hit a patch of really open bush and was able to do three lengths in 70 minutes. Why don't I take Millar's area tomorrow and he can have mine? Maybe that will help."

"Conditions are the same in all of the areas," replied Parker, rejecting Talbot's suggestion. "Millar just has to try harder."

Day 4

Millar completed seven lengths and Boyce completed six and a half. When they reported their production that evening, Parker grunted uncommunicatively. Parker and Talbot completed eight lengths each.

Day 5

Millar completed six lengths, Boyce six, Talbot seven and a half, and Parker eight. Once again Parker blew up, but he concentrated his diatribe on Millar: "Why don't you do what you say you are going to do? You know that you have to do seven and a half lengths a day. We went over that when we first got here, so why don't you do it? If you aren't willing to do the job, you never should have taken it in the first place!"

Millar replied that he was doing his best, he hadn't even stopped for lunch, and he didn't know how he could possibly do any better. Parker launched into him again: "You have got to work harder! If you put enough effort into it, you will get the area done!"

Later Millar commented to Boyce, "I hate getting dumped on all the time! I'd quit if it didn't mean that

I'd have to walk 80 kilometres to the highway. And besides, I need the bonus money. Why doesn't he pick on you? You don't get any more work done than I do; in fact, you usually get less done. Maybe if you did a bit more he wouldn't be so bothered about me."

"I only work as hard as I have to," Boyce replied.

Day 6

Millar raced through breakfast, was the first one to be dropped off by the helicopter, and arranged to be the last one picked up. That evening the production figures were Millar eight and a quarter lengths, Boyce seven, and Talbot and Parker eight each. Parker remained silent when the field assistants reported their performance for the day.

Day 7

Millar was again the first out and last in. That night, he collapsed in an exhausted heap at the table, too tired to eat. After a few moments, he announced in an abject tone, "Six lengths. I worked like a dog all day and I only got a lousy six lengths!" Boyce completed five lengths, Talbot seven, and Parker seven and a quarter.

Parker was furious. "That means we have to do a total of 34 lengths tomorrow if we are to finish this job on time!" With his eyes directed at Millar, he added, "Why is it that you never finish the job? Don't you realize that you are part of a team, and that you are letting the rest of the team down? I've been checking your lines and you're doing too much blazing and wasting too much time making picture-perfect claim posts! If you worked smarter, you'd get a lot more done!"

Day 8

Parker cooked breakfast in the dark. The helicopter drop-offs began as soon as light appeared on the horizon. Parker instructed each assistant to complete eight lengths and, if they finished early, to help the others. He promised to finish the other ten lengths. Helicopter pickups were arranged for one hour before dark.

By noon, after working as hard as he could, Millar had only completed three lengths. "Why bother?" he thought to himself. "I'll never be able to do another five lengths before the helicopter comes, and I'll get the same amount of abuse from Parker for doing six lengths as for seven and a half." So he sat down and had lunch and a rest. "Boyce won't finish his eight lengths either, so even if I did finish mine, I still wouldn't get the bonus. At least I'll get one more day's pay this way."

That night, Parker was livid when Millar reported that he had completed five and a half lengths. Parker had done ten and a quarter lengths, and Talbot had completed eight. Boyce proudly announced that he had finished seven and a half lengths, but sheepishly added that Talbot had helped him with some of it. All that remained were the two and a half lengths that Millar had not completed.

The job was finished the next morning and the crew demobilized. Millar has never worked for Arctic Mining Consultants again, despite being offered work several times by Parker. Boyce sometimes does staking for Arctic, and Talbot works full time with the company.

Discussion Questions

1. What symptom(s) exist in this case to suggest that something has gone wrong?

2. What are the root causes that have led to these symptoms?

3. What should Arctic Mining Consultants and/or Tom Parker do to minimize these problems in the future?

© Copyright Steven L. McShane and Tim Neale. This case is based on actual events, but names and some characteristics have been changed to maintain anonymity.

CASE 3
A Window on Life

To Gilles LaCroix, nothing is quite as beautiful as a handcrafted wood-framed window. LaCroix's passion for windows goes back to his youth in St. Jean, Quebec, where an elderly carpenter taught him everything he knows. He learned about the characteristics of good wood, the best tools to use, and how to choose the best glass from local suppliers. LaCroix apprenticed with the carpenter in his small workshop and was given the opportunity to operate the business himself when the carpenter retired.

LaCroix hired his own apprentice as he built up business in the local area. His small operation expanded as the quality of windows built by LaCroix

Industries Ltd. became better known. Within eight years, the company employed nearly 25 people and had moved to larger facilities to accommodate the increased demand from southern Quebec. In these early years, LaCroix spent most of his time in the production shop, teaching new apprentices the unique skills he had mastered and applauding the journeymen for their accomplishments. He would constantly state that LaCroix products had to be of the highest quality because they gave families a "window on life."

After 15 years, LaCroix Industries employed more than 200 people. A profit-sharing program was introduced to give employees a financial reward for their contribution to the organization's success. Due to expansion, headquarters had to be moved to another area of town, but LaCroix never lost touch with the workforce. Although new apprentices were now taught entirely by the master carpenters and other craftspeople, LaCroix still chatted with plant and office employees several times each week.

When a second work shift was added, LaCroix showed up during the evening break with coffee and doughnuts to discuss how the business was doing and how it became so successful through quality workmanship. Production employees enjoyed the times when he would gather them together to announce new contracts with developers from Montreal and Toronto. After each announcement, LaCroix would thank everyone for making the business a success. Employees knew that LaCroix quality had become a standard of excellence in window manufacturing across Canada.

It seemed that almost every time he visited LaCroix would repeat the well-known phrase that LaCroix products had to be of the highest quality because they provided a window on life for so many families. Employees never grew tired of hearing this from the company founder. However, it gained extra meaning when LaCroix began posting photos of families looking through LaCroix windows. At first, LaCroix would personally visit developers and homeowners with a camera in hand. Later, as developers and customers became aware of the "window on life" photos, people would send in photos of their families looking through elegant front windows made by LaCroix Industries. The company's marketing staff began using this idea, as well as LaCroix's famous phrase, in their advertising. After one such marketing campaign, satisfied customers sent in hundreds of photos. Production and office employees took time after work to write personal letters of thanks to those who had submitted photos.

As the company reached the quarter-century mark, LaCroix, now in his mid-fifties, realized that the organization's success and survival depended on expansion into the United States. After consulting with employees, LaCroix made the difficult decision to sell a majority share to Build-All Products, Inc., a conglomerate with international marketing expertise in building products. As part of the agreement, Build-All brought in a vice-president, Jan Vlodoski, to oversee production operations while LaCroix spent more time meeting with developers around North America. LaCroix returned to the plant and office at every opportunity, but often this would be only once a month.

Rather than visiting the production plant, Vlodoski rarely left his office at the company's downtown headquarters. Instead, production orders were sent to supervisors by memoranda. Although product quality had been a priority throughout the company's history, less attention had been paid to inventory controls. Vlodoski introduced strict inventory guidelines and outlined procedures on using supplies for each shift. Goals were established for supervisors to meet specific inventory targets. Whereas employees previously could have tossed out several pieces of warped wood, they would now have to justify this action, usually in writing.

Vlodoski also announced new procedures for purchasing production supplies. LaCroix Industries had highly trained purchasing staff who worked closely with senior craftspeople when selecting suppliers, but Vlodoski wanted to institute Build-All's procedures. The new purchasing methods removed production leaders from the decision process and, in some cases, resulted in trade-offs that LaCroix's employees would not have made previously. A few employees quit during this time, saying that they did not feel comfortable producing a window that would not stand the test of time. However, unemployment was high in St. Jean, so most staff members remained with the company.

After one year, inventory expenses had decreased by approximately 10 percent, but the number of defective windows returned by developers and wholesalers had increased markedly. Plant employees knew that the number of defective windows would increase as they used somewhat lower-quality materials to reduce inventory costs. However, they heard almost no news about the seriousness of the problem until Vlodoski sent a memo to all production staff saying that quality must be maintained. During the latter part of the first year under Vlodoski's management, a few employees had the opportunity to ask LaCroix about the changes and express their concerns. LaCroix apologized, saying that due to his travels he had not heard about the problems, and that he would look into the matter.

Exactly 18 months after Build-All had become the majority shareholder of LaCroix Industries, LaCroix called together five of the original staff members in the plant. The company founder looked pale and shaken as he said that Build-All's actions were inconsistent with his vision of the company and, for the first time in his career, he did not know what to do. Build-All was not pleased with the arrangement either. Although LaCroix windows still enjoyed a healthy market share and were competitive for their value, the company did not quite provide the minimum 18 percent return on equity that the conglomerate expected. LaCroix asked his long-time companions for advice.

Discussion Questions

1. What symptom(s) exist in this case to suggest that something has gone wrong?

2. What are the root causes that have led to these symptoms?

3. What should LaCroix do to minimize these problems in the future?

© Copyright Steven L. McShane.

CASE 4
Jim Black: Sales Representative

Jim Black impatiently drummed the steering wheel and puffed a cigarette as his car moved slowly northbound along the Don Valley Parkway in Toronto. Traffic congestion was normal in the late afternoon, but it seemed much heavier today. In any event, it was another irritation that was going to make him late for his next appointment.

As a sales representative at Noram Canada Ltd., Jim could not afford to keep clients waiting. Sales of compressed oxygen and other gases were slower during this prolonged recession. Other compressed gas suppliers were eager to grab new accounts and it was becoming more common for clients to switch from one supplier to another. Jim pressed his half-finished cigarette into the ashtray and accelerated into another lane.

Buyers of compressed gas knew that the market was in their favour, and many were demanding price discounts and shorter delivery times. Earlier in the week, for example, one of Jim's more-demanding customers ordered another shipment of liquid oxygen to be delivered the next morning. To meet the deadline, Jim had to complete an expedited delivery form and then personally convince the shipping group to make the delivery in the morning rather than later in the day. Jim disliked making expedited delivery requests, even though they were becoming increasingly common, because they often delayed shipment of Noram's products to other clients. Discounts were even more troublesome because they reduced Jim's commission and, except for very large orders, were frowned upon by Noram management.

Meanwhile, at Noram's headquarters in nearby Brampton, senior managers were putting more pressure on sales reps to produce. They complained that the reps weren't aggressive enough, and area supervisors were told to monitor each sales rep's monthly numbers more closely. Jim fumbled for another cigarette as the traffic stopped momentarily.

Two months ago, the area sales supervisor had "a little chat" (as he called it) with Jim about stagnant sales in his district and the loss of a client to the competition. There wasn't exactly a threat of being fired—other reps also received these chats—but Jim felt nervous about his work and began having sleepless nights. He began making more calls to potential clients, but was only able to find time to do this by completing paperwork in the evenings. This evening work wasn't helping relations with his family.

To make matters worse, Noram's parent company in New York announced that it planned to sell the Canadian operations. Jim had heard rumours that a competitor was going to purchase the firm, primarily to expand its operations through Noram's western Canadian sales force and production facilities. The competitor was well established in Ontario and probably wouldn't need a larger sales force there, so Jim's job would be in jeopardy if the acquisition took place. Jim felt another headache coming on as he stared at the endless line of red tail lights slithering along the highway ahead of him.

Even if Jim kept his job, any promotion into management would be a long way off if the competitor acquired Noram Canada. Jim had no particular desire to become a manager, but his wife was eager for him to receive a promotion because a management job would involve less travel and provide a more stable salary (i.e., one less dependent on monthly sales). Business travel was a nuisance, particularly for out-of-town appointments, but Jim felt less comfortable with the idea of sitting behind a desk all day.

The loud honk of another car startled Jim as he swerved into the exit lane at Eglinton Avenue. A few minutes later, he arrived at the client's parking lot. Jim rummaged through his briefcase for some aspirin to relieve the headache. He heaved a deep sigh as he glanced at his watch: He was 15 minutes late for the appointment.

Discussion Questions

1. What stress symptoms is Jim experiencing?

2. What stressors can you identify in this case?

3. What should Jim do to minimize his stress?

© Copyright Steven L. McShane.

CASE 5

Sandra Lee: Principal of South Heights Public School (A)

by Robert Ellis and Raymond Adamson, Wilfrid Laurier University

Sandra Lee hit bottom in February 1998. She was physically and emotionally drained by her experiences as the new principal of an inner-city school. Stunning success had marked her previous teaching career. In fact, she had gained a wide reputation as a leading educational innovator. All of this had meant nothing when she encountered the brick walls of South Heights Public School. After six months during which she attempted to infuse the school with new vitality, she could see few changes that had made a difference in the lives of her students. Indeed, the only significant change was a campaign to get rid of her launched by a group of disaffected teachers. Should she resign and go back to the classroom she so loved or should she forge ahead?

The South Side

South Heights Public School of the Sherwood School Board is located in a small city in southern Ontario. The city is a short commute from Toronto, and is widely known as an automobile manufacturing centre in Canada. Most of the inhabitants work either at the auto plants or at the other manufacturing and service enterprises that support them. There is also a significant commuting population that leaves the city on a daily basis.

The school is located on the South Side, in an area that was once a commercial centre. Over the years the focus of commerce has shifted to suburban shopping centres. The only recent commercial developments have been some fast food restaurants and a few service businesses, but they come and go and do little to create any sense of prosperity or revival in the area.

The residences around the school have been largely neglected. Most of them were originally constructed as row housing for the immigrants who came to work at the auto plants after the Second World War. As the families of these workers prospered and moved on to other areas of the city and province, their homes were converted to low-rent and subsidized housing. Most of the current residents are attracted to the area because it is one of the cheapest places to live in Ontario. The South Side is known locally as the "welfare zone" since most of its residents are dependent on some form of government support.

There is chronic unemployment of about 70 percent in the South Heights school area. Many of the families in this area are headed by a single parent, mostly women, and some of these families are third- and fourth-generation welfare recipients. The South Side is only a step from the North Side, but it is a world away in terms of economic and social status. People on the North Side generally own their homes, have new cars, send their children to college, and, most importantly, are employed. This level of stability and material well-being is almost non-existent on the South Side because the residents are largely transients who appear unable to find or keep jobs for any sustained period of time.

This transience in their working lives is also reflected in their family structures. Many of the single mothers are young and became mothers in their mid-to-late teens. They were forced into major family responsibilities quite abruptly and were ill prepared for their new role as parents. They often have no network of family and friends to advise and support them. The fathers often stayed only a short time. The combination of these factors create severe stress. This stress is frequently expressed in violent confrontations among family members, often involving the children directly. Violence or threats of violence by parents and open defiance by children are commonplace methods of dealing with problems, and this violent and defiant behaviour is frequently transferred to the school setting. Equally disturbing, many of the children come to school hungry, without having eaten breakfast, and sometimes with only a bag of chips for lunch.

Another feature of the South Side culture is its association with drugs, violence, and petty crime. Although this activity is less frequent than in the worst areas of large cities, it further undermines the residents' sense of security.

South Heights Public School

Just as the South Side is neglected and run down, so is South Heights Public School. Built in 1916 to serve children from kindergarten to grade eight, it is typical of the stolid and enduring institutional style of the times. With its brick walls and vaulted ceilings and windows, it is functional but grey, drab, and uninviting. Virtually nothing has been done to renew the building, spruce it up, or even keep it very clean. The school serves as a metaphor for the whole South Side. It is a challenge for the educational system, much as the area is for the municipality, but there seems to be no collective will to change either one.

The school's location and reputation frightens off most experienced teachers. South Heights is often a first posting for new teachers and administrators, a place where they would "pay their dues." But this hasn't always been so; indeed, the school has a rich and proud history. Past students and teachers have fond memories of their days at South Heights and have witnessed the continual neglect and decay of recent times with considerable regret.

One particular difficulty for the school is that a significant number of parents had negative experiences when they were part of the school system. Many of them are dropouts and others were just turned off by formal schooling. In spite of this, most parents view education as important for their children. The problem is that they don't know how to help their children be successful in school. Apart from this, given the conditions in which they live, many parents are primarily concerned with survival. As a result, parents do not get involved in the education process and do not encourage school activities.

The school has such a poor reputation that it is continually rumoured to be closing. In fact, this is a topic of debate within the school board: Should South Heights remain open or be closed? The school board sees an aging school with a multitude of problems, and little else. As a result, very little is invested in the school to either improve or maintain it. The result is a school with little future or hope.

In 1997, an opportunity arose to change this dismal picture. The principal of South Heights was moving to another school and some senior officials of the school board saw this as a chance to intervene. The chair of the publicly elected school trustees commented, "South Heights had become a dumping ground for bad teachers. I was determined to veto the appointment of anyone who wasn't going to change this place." In the end the school board chose Sandra Lee, a young vice-principal who had gained a strong reputation for innovative programs for children with disabilities, but who had relatively little administrative experience for the type of situation she would encounter at South Heights.

The New Principal: Sandra Lee

Sandra Lee became the principal of South Heights Public School in 1997. She was not happy about being placed there. Friends and peers advised her that South Heights would be a difficult situation to endure even for a short period of time. However, one did not turn down an administrative appointment. To do so would have effectively ended her career in administration. Since, in her own words, she was "very ambitious" about her career progress, she accepted the job. She came directly from a vice-principal position at a new model public school and the change to South Heights was far greater and more traumatic than she could ever have imagined.

Lee's background in education was somewhat unusual in that her decision to become a teacher was made later in life than most, after she had emigrated to Canada from Trinidad. She had two children and waited until her youngest was two years old before beginning her educational career. Lee graduated from teachers college as a special education teacher and embraced this as an anchor for her whole career. She began her practice teaching with mentally handicapped children and this early experience served to confirm her choice—this was what she wanted to do.

Lee spent the next three years working for the school board on special education programs. Her specific focus during that time was children with developmental disabilities, which included children who functioned at the lowest level within the educational system. Her goal was to discover ways that would make a difference in their ability to learn and consequently in their quality of life. She also wanted to improve their status in the educational system and attract many more competent educators to that part of the system. It was around this time that she developed what was to become an enduring foundation of her philosophy of education: "There is always a way, you just have to find it."

Lee's time at the school board was followed by another three-year stint developing diagnostic and training classes for the learning disabled. Her proudest accomplishment was a writing program for children with learning disabilities. This was a singularly successful activity that provided her with a high profile at the school board as well as among other educators from all over the continent who came to observe the program. This program reflected her belief that "...every child could bring out their ideas in writing."

From this foundation arose the idea of a Writing Guild, where children in the regular school program would write and present their own work during Education Week. She envisioned children in each city presenting their work to parents and members of the community, with panels of authors and illustrators to provide guidance. To make this happen, she enlisted a socially and politically skilful principal to co-chair the Writing Guild. This support enabled the program to be successfully implemented in schools across the board.

Lee's final three-year period prior to her appointment as vice-principal involved a combination of expanding and developing her educational programs and positioning herself for promotion in the system. First, she enrolled in and completed a Masters of Education program. She also completed a leadership course through the school board during this time, a course that emphasized the importance of both vision and a team approach to leadership. Participants in these courses and, more importantly, her mentors at the school board began to persuade her that she could have a wider impact on the school system as a principal or executive administrator than as a classroom teacher. Lee finally applied to be a vice-principal. She felt she was getting valuable support from senior board administrators both for her programs and for her career advancement. Whatever happened, Lee was steadfast in her view that she would make career moves only if they helped to promote programs she had developed for writing and for children with learning disabilities. Her application for vice-principal was successful and she was placed at Academy Hill Public School.

During her first year there, Academy Hill was selected by the school board as a pilot project for developing a cooperative learning program at the public-school level. In this program children learned to work together in positive ways to build social and team skills. This provided a friendly environment for innovative programming. Quite conveniently, the principal at Academy Hill was not very familiar with new program development, thus giving Lee fairly free rein. Once again her efforts were very successful and boosted her strong reputation for implementing new educational concepts. Indeed, she was gaining the attention and support of educators at the forefront of educational innovation and change.

Following her two-year stay at Academy Hill, Lee accepted an internal board transfer to Don Valley Public School. Her placement at Don Valley had been carefully planned to cultivate her administrative skills. Her new principal worked with and managed people very well. She was advised by her mentors to observe and emulate those skills, with this note of caution: "...sometimes you go too fast. You think so far ahead and move so quickly, you leave people behind in the dust. We want you to learn that change takes time. You won't always have us around..."

Welcome to South Heights Public School

Lee's first visit to South Heights Public School was a horrifying experience. She arrived fresh from Don Valley, a new model suburban public school, and the contrast was shocking. The schools she had experience with were bright, happy places that welcomed students and teachers alike. To Lee, South Heights seemed dark and depressing. It exuded an institutional atmosphere from its box-like shape to its brick exterior. There was some grass, but no flowers were to be seen anywhere. The school may have once been appealing but now it seemed to be part of a world that years of modern education had passed by completely.

While the school's exterior was forbidding enough, its interior was even worse. The paint on some walls appeared to be original and on others was peeling in patches. The dominant colours were green, yellow, and burgundy, which created a drab and sombre effect. The classrooms were very spartan. Classroom displays were neither colourful nor appealing to the eye. Lee found out later that decorations and other classroom embellishments were repeatedly stolen and attempts to create a more appealing atmosphere had long been abandoned. The staff room was located in a former coal bin in the basement, isolated from the rest of the school. It was even more squalid than other areas of the school.

Lee was not only shocked but also felt hurt and angry that a school would be allowed to deteriorate to such a state. Her first trip to South Heights was in early spring and she immediately decided that the first order of the day would be to clean and paint the school. The board arranged to have this done. Lee enlisted family and friends and spent most of the summer improving and decorating the staff room. She also had murals painted in the school. The notion was to create "bright and happy" scenes to relieve some of the interior gloom. Lee admits that she did not have a clear strategy for improving conditions at the school beyond these initial steps. She essentially had no idea of what she should do next.

The first days of school held further surprises. Arriving early one morning, Lee observed some parents waiting with their children in the schoolyard. She approached them, introduced herself, and engaged in a few pleasantries. She could feel that they were rather reticent and uncomfortable but she very shortly invited them inside for coffee. There was a brief hesitation and then one father blurted, "Lady, I don't want to have coffee with you. Just go to hell." Lee had arrived at South Heights.

The confrontation with the parents foreshadowed what would happen inside the school. In the halls, in the playground, and in the classroom, students shouted incessantly at each other. If shouting didn't resolve an issue, they slugged it out. Cathy, a first-year teacher who arrived at the same time as Lee, described what she encountered: "I grew up in a big family, a protected world. My initial reaction in coming here was utter shock. When I was a kid, I wouldn't have looked at a teacher sideways. These children have grown up where they are not respected, they think it is normal, they don't know any different."

The staff knew that most of these children's home lives reinforced this aggressive behaviour and that the only responses they seemed to understand were shouting even louder in return and using physical restraint to keep them in line. Some staff members shouted almost as much as the children! Lee was appalled, but the staff seemed hardly aware of their conduct. There

were certainly many other school problems, but these highly vocal confrontations seemed symbolic of a basic mistrust and resentment between the school and the families it was meant to serve.

Equally disturbing was how low standards had fallen in the school. Some staff members were continually late for their classes; others did not appear to have lesson plans prepared. The books in the school library seemed to be shelved on a random basis, and the library itself was closed as often as it was open. The school was not kept clean; dust and dirt accumulated in the hallways and classrooms. Lee felt she had to act quickly and soon called a staff meeting. The purpose was to devise a plan, at least for that year, to give the staff a mission.

The planning meetings were conducted as a series so that the task was not perceived as too formidable. The format used the cooperative group techniques that Lee had learned at Academy Hill and Don Valley. These techniques involved assigning roles to group members so that each person had to interact with others to fulfil their roles. This was intended to build team spirit as the plan was being developed.

The simple objective of the sessions was to identify what staff should continue doing or expand and what should be eliminated. A formal planning document that identified both positive and negative practices evolved from these meetings. Many of the items seemed to have Lee's stamp on them, but she insisted that the plan arose through consensus.

The central features of the plan were grouped around the motto, "Together we light the way." This concept focused on teacher, student, and parent relationships and implied a partnership in the learning process. In keeping with this theme, other objectives were developed. These included an agreement that the learning process would be student-centred, that is, focused on student needs rather than teacher needs. It was also decided that teachers would make every effort to model appropriate behaviours for the students. This was obviously directed at eliminating aggressive verbal and physical confrontations among students, and between staff and students. However, the plan also included many other things, such as being on time, having lesson plans prepared for each class, standing at the door with a smile and welcoming the students as they entered class, giving parents clear and detailed information on their child's progress on report cards, and generally taking personal responsibility for creating a good learning environment.

According to the plan, teachers were also expected to work together to develop lesson plans so that both the content and the consistency of instruction would improve. Teachers were responsible for the students' learning development, particularly for their reading and writing skills. This presumably meant that teachers were accountable if a student's performance fell below some reasonable level of expectation.

Two months later, Lee asked herself what had changed as a result of the plan. In short, the answer was very little. The staff members who had previously arrived late and been unprepared, continued in their behaviour. Those who engaged in verbal and physical confrontations with students continued this practice. Lee took some comfort in the efforts of several new and enthusiastic teachers to implement the plan. She was also pleased that one of her initiatives to get parents more involved in the school was having some success. A group called Parent Rap had been formed to bring parents and teachers together to discuss issues affecting the children. Unfortunately, only three parents were attending the meetings on a regular basis.

Most senior teachers were not cooperating with Lee's attempts to improve the school. Many of these teachers had not been to a professional development workshop in years, and were not simply skeptical of her new approach to education but openly hostile and confrontational. Their opposition rested on the conviction that an authoritarian manner was the only thing that worked with these children. Further, their skepticism towards new approaches had been strengthened by the failure of past efforts to make meaningful changes at South Heights.

Some of the confrontations with senior staff were quite unpleasant. For example, Lee refused to sign the report cards of one senior teacher because he wrote only one or two words on each report card, rather than the detailed feedback the staff had agreed to provide to parents. To the teacher this activity seemed pointless: "Would any of the parents bother reading this?" This teacher confronted Lee in the hallway and yelled at her in front of students and other teachers. Lee told him quietly but firmly to go into her office. Once in her office he continued to yell and swept everything off Lee's desk onto the floor. Lee received a visit the next day from an official of the teachers' union, who said that the problems she was having with this teacher could best be explained as, "...a new female principal trying to intimidate the males in the system." Lee had similar hostile confrontations with the librarian and a few other senior teachers. She had only a vague knowledge of her rights as principal to enforce standards, as standards had never been an issue in her previous jobs.

Some of the senior staff members have recently begun a campaign to have Lee dismissed, and have tried to enlist other teachers and parents to their cause "to save the children." A senior teacher who was sympathetic to Lee's attempts to improve the school told her that the campaign was gaining momentum. She also confided that she was not fully convinced of the ideas underlying the school plan.

Two events around this time brought Lee to an emotional low point in her life. Her father died suddenly and unexpectedly at the beginning of December. No one close to her had ever died and the pain she felt was "absolutely unendurable." She did not look forward to returning to South Heights after the Christmas break. A second event shortly thereafter brought her to the point of resignation. One day in early February she asked a female custodian to clean something up. The custodian screamed that Lee had "...ridiculous expectations...the school was fine before you came here...why don't you go back to where you came from!" Lee was crushed. It was the "first time in my career I had experienced racism." Equally bad, she realized that "...even the custodian felt she could lace into me."

Lee drove home in tears. She thought, "This is it: I can't take this any more." Should she resign now as principal of South Heights? She could quickly return to developing programs for children with learning disabilities; indeed, the school board would welcome her back. On the other hand, the children of South Heights desperately needed her help. The pain of her failure to make a meaningful change in their lives was acute. But if she stayed, what could she do to transform South Heights?

Discussion Questions

1. What are the problems here?

2. What were the important aspects of the situation confronting Sandra Lee on her arrival at South Heights?

3. Why has the plan failed?

4. What theories and concepts help to explain the events in this case?

5. Should Sandra Lee resign and return to the classroom? What are the implications for her career if she chooses to return to the classroom? If she chooses to stay on as principal?

6. If she chooses to stay and attempt to transform South Heights, what should she do? What are the reasonable alternatives? What course of action should she pursue? How should she implement these actions?

APPENDIX A

Theory Building and the Scientific Method

Theory A general set of propositions that describes interrelationships among several concepts.

People need to make sense of their world, so they form theories about the way the world operates. A **theory** is a general set of propositions that describes interrelationships among several concepts. We form theories to predict and explain the world around us.[1] What does a good theory look like? First, it should be stated clearly and as simply as possible so that the concepts can be measured and there is no ambiguity regarding its propositions. Second, the theory's elements must be logically consistent with each other, because we cannot test anything that doesn't make sense. Finally, a good theory provides value to society; it helps people understand their world better than without the theory.[2]

Theory building is a continuous process that typically includes the inductive and deductive stages shown in Exhibit A.1.[3] The inductive stage draws on personal experience to form a preliminary theory, whereas the deductive stage uses the scientific method to test the theory.

The inductive stage of theory building involves observing the world around us, identifying a pattern of relationships, and then forming a theory from these personal observations. For example, you might casually notice that new employees want their supervisor to give direction, whereas this leadership style irritates long-service employees. From these observations, you form a theory about the effectiveness of directive leadership. (See Chapter 14 for a discussion of this leadership style.)

EXHIBIT A.1   The Theory Building Process

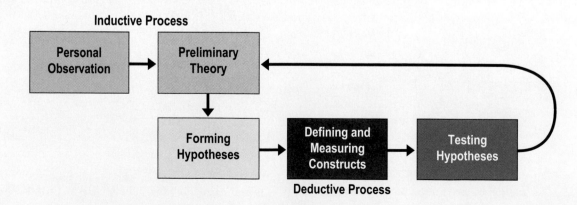

POSITIVISM VERSUS INTERPRETIVISM

Research requires an interpretation of reality, and researchers tend to perceive reality in one of two ways. A common view, called **positivism**, is that reality exists independent of people. It is "out there" to be discovered and tested. Positivism is the foundation for most quantitative research (statistical analysis). It assumes that we can measure variables and that those variables have fixed relationships with other variables. For example, the positivist perspective says that we could study whether a supportive style of leadership reduces stress. If we find evidence of this, then someone else studying leadership and stress would "discover" the same relationship.

Interpretivism takes a different view of reality. It suggests that reality comes from shared meaning among people in that environment. For example, supportive leadership is a personal interpretation of reality, not something that can be measured across time and people. Interpretivists rely mainly on qualitative data, such as observation and nondirective interviews. They particularly listen to the language people use to understand the common meaning that people have towards various events or phenomena. For example, they might argue that you need to experience and observe supportive leadership to effectively study it. Moreover, you can't really predict relationships because the specific situation shapes reality.[4]

Most OB scholars identify themselves somewhere between the extreme views of positivism and interpretivism. Many believe that inductive research should begin with an interpretivist angle. We should enter a new topic with an open mind and search for shared meaning of people in that situation. In other words, researchers should let participants define reality rather than have the researcher's preconceived notions shape that reality. This process involves gathering qualitative information and letting this information shape their theory.[5] After the theory emerges, researchers shift to a positivist perspective by quantitatively testing relationships in that theory.

THEORY TESTING: THE DEDUCTIVE PROCESS

Once a theory has been formed, we shift to the deductive stage of theory building. This process includes forming hypotheses, defining and measuring constructs, and testing hypotheses (see Exhibit A.1). **Hypotheses** make empirically testable declarations that certain variables and their corresponding measures are related in a specific way proposed by the theory. For instance, to find support for the directive leadership theory described earlier, we need to form and then test a specific hypothesis from that theory. One such hypothesis might be: "New employees are more satisfied with supervisors who exhibit a directive rather than nondirective leadership style." Hypotheses are indispensable tools of scientific research, because they provide the vital link between the theory and empirical verification.

Defining and measuring constructs

Hypotheses are testable only if we can define and then form measurable indicators of the concepts stated in those hypotheses. Consider the hypothesis in the previous paragraph about new employees and directive leadership. To test this hypothesis, we first need to define the concepts, such as "new employees," "directive leadership," and "supervisor." These are known as **constructs**, because they are abstract ideas constructed by the researcher that can be linked to observable information. Organizational behaviour scholars developed the construct called directive leadership to help them understand the different effects that leaders have over followers. We can't directly see, taste, or smell *directive leadership*; instead, we rely on indirect indicators that it exists, such as observing someone giving directions, maintaining clear performance standards, and ensuring that procedures and practices are followed.

As you can see, defining constructs well is very important, because these definitions become the foundation for finding or developing acceptable measures of those constructs.

Positivism The view held in quantitative research that reality exists independent of people.

Interpretivism A view that suggests that reality comes from shared meaning among people in that environment.

Hypotheses Statements making empirically testable declarations that certain variables and their corresponding measures are related in a specific way proposed by a particular theory.

Constructs Abstract ideas constructed by researchers that can be linked to observable information.

We can't measure directive leadership if we only have a vague idea about what this concept means. The better the definition is, the better our chances are of applying a measure that adequately represents that construct. However, even with a good definition, constructs can be difficult to measure, because the empirical representation must capture several elements in the definition. A measure of directive leadership must be able to identify not only people who give directions, but also those who maintain performance standards and ensure that procedures are followed.

Testing hypotheses

The third step in the deductive process is to collect data for the empirical measures of the variables. Following our directive leadership example, we might conduct a formal survey in which new employees indicate the behaviour of their supervisors and their attitudes towards their supervisor. Alternatively, we might design an experiment in which people work with someone who applies either a directive or nondirective leadership style. When the data have been collected, we can use various procedures to statistically test our hypotheses.

A major concern in theory building is that some researchers might inadvertently find support for their theory simply because they use the same information used to form the theory during the inductive stage. Consequently, the deductive stage must collect new data that are completely independent of the data used during the inductive stage. For instance, you might decide to test your theory of directive leadership by studying employees in another organization. Moreover, the inductive process may have relied mainly on personal observation, whereas the deductive process might use survey questionnaires. By studying different samples and using different measurement tools, we minimize the risk of conducting circular research.

USING THE SCIENTIFIC METHOD

Earlier, we said that the deductive stage of theory building follows the scientific method. The **scientific method** is a systematic, controlled, empirical, and critical investigation of hypothetical propositions about the presumed relationships among natural phenomena.[6] There are several elements to this definition, so let's look at each one. First, scientific research is systematic and controlled because researchers want to rule out all but one explanation for a set of interrelated events. To rule out alternative explanations, we need to control them in some way, such as by keeping them constant or removing them entirely from the environment.

Second, scientific research is empirical because researchers need to use objective reality—or as close as they can get to it—to test a theory. They measure observable elements of the environment, such as what a person says or does, rather than rely on their own subjective opinion to draw conclusions. Moreover, scientific research analyzes these data using acceptable principles of mathematics and logic.

Finally, scientific research involves critical investigation. This means that the study's hypotheses, data, methods, and results are openly described so that other experts in the field can properly evaluate the research. It also means that scholars are encouraged to critique and build on previous research. Eventually, the scientific method encourages the refinement and replacement of a particular theory with one that better suits our understanding of the world.

SELECTED ISSUES IN ORGANIZATIONAL BEHAVIOUR RESEARCH

There are many issues to consider in theory building, particularly when we use the deductive process to test hypotheses. Some of the more important issues are sampling, causation, and ethical practices in organizational research.

Scientific method A set of principles and procedures that help researchers to systematically understand previously unexplained events and conditions.

SAMPLING IN ORGANIZATIONAL RESEARCH

When finding out why things happen in organizations, we typically gather information from a few sources and then draw conclusions about the larger population. If we survey several employees and determine that older employees are more loyal to their company, we would like to generalize this statement to all older employees in our population, not just those whom we surveyed. Scientific inquiry generally requires researchers to engage in **representative sampling**—that is, sampling a population in such a way that we can extrapolate the results of that sample to the larger population.

One factor that influences representativeness is whether the sample is selected in an unbiased way from the larger population. Let's suppose that you want to study organizational commitment among employees in your organization. A casual procedure might result in sampling too few employees from the head office and too many located elsewhere in the country. If head office employees actually have higher loyalty than employees located elsewhere, the biased sampling would cause the results to underestimate the true level of loyalty among employees in the company. If you repeat the process again next year but somehow overweight employees from the head office, the results might wrongly suggest that employees have increased their organizational commitment over the past year. In reality, the only change may be the direction of sampling bias.

How do we minimize sampling bias? The answer is to randomly select the sample. A randomly drawn sample gives each member of the population an equal probability of being chosen, so there is less likelihood that a subgroup within that population dominates the study's results.

The same principle applies to random assignment of subjects to groups in experimental designs. If we want to test the effects of a team development training program, we need to randomly place some employees in the training group and randomly place others in a group that does not receive training. Without this random selection, each group might have different types of employees, so we wouldn't know whether the training explains the differences between the two groups. Moreover, if employees respond differently to the training program, we couldn't be sure that the training program results are representative of the larger population. Of course, random sampling does not necessarily produce a perfectly representative sample, but we do know that this is the best approach to ensure unbiased selection.

The other factor that influences representativeness is sample size. Whenever we select a portion of the population, there will be some error in our estimate of the population values. The larger the sample, the less error will occur in our estimate. Let's suppose that you want to find out how employees in a 500-person firm feel about smoking in the workplace. If you asked 400 of those employees, the information would provide a very good estimate of how the entire workforce feels. If you survey only 100 employees, the estimate might deviate more from the true population. If you ask only 10 people, the estimate could be quite different from what all 500 employees feel.

Notice that sample size goes hand in hand with random selection. You must have a sufficiently large sample size for the principle of randomization to work effectively. In our example of attitudes towards smoking, we would do a poor job of random selection if our sample consisted of only 10 of 500 employees, because those 10 people probably wouldn't capture the diversity of employees throughout the organization. In fact, the more diverse the population, the larger the sample size should be, to provide adequate representation through random selection.

CAUSATION IN ORGANIZATIONAL RESEARCH

Theories present notions about relationships among constructs. Often, these propositions suggest a causal relationship, namely, that one variable has an effect on another variable. When discussing causation, we refer to variables as being independent or dependent.

• **Representative sampling** Sampling a population in such a way that we can extrapolate the results of that sample to the larger population.

Independent variables are the presumed causes of dependent variables, which are the presumed effects. In our earlier example of directive leadership, the main independent variable (there might be others) would be the supervisor's directive or nondirective leadership style, because we presume that it causes the dependent variable (satisfaction with supervision).

In laboratory experiments (described later), the experimenter always manipulates the independent variable. In our research on directive leadership, we might have subjects (new employees) work with supervisors who exhibit directive or nondirective leadership behaviours. If subjects are more satisfied under the directive leaders, we would be able to infer an association between the independent and dependent variables.

Researchers must satisfy three conditions to provide sufficient evidence of causality between two variables.[7] The first condition of causality is that the variables are empirically associated with each other. An association exists whenever one measure of a variable changes systematically with a measure of another variable. This condition of causality is the easiest to satisfy, because there are several well-known statistical measures of association. A research study might find, for instance, that heterogeneous groups (in which members come from diverse backgrounds) produce more creative solutions to problems. This might be apparent because the measure of creativity (such as the number of creative solutions produced within a fixed time) is higher for teams that have a high score on the measure of group heterogeneity. They are statistically associated or correlated with each other.

The second condition of causality is that the independent variable precedes the dependent variable in time. Sometimes, this condition is satisfied through simple logic. In our group heterogeneity example, it doesn't make sense to say that the number of creative solutions caused the group's heterogeneity, because the group's heterogeneity existed before it produced the creative solutions. In other situations, however, the temporal relationship among variables is less clear. One example is the ongoing debate about job satisfaction and organizational commitment. Do companies develop more loyal employees by increasing their job satisfaction, or do changes in organizational loyalty cause changes in job satisfaction? Simple logic does not answer these questions; instead, researchers must use sophisticated longitudinal studies to build up evidence of a temporal relationship between these two variables.

The third requirement for evidence of a causal relationship is that the statistical association between two variables cannot be explained by a third variable. There are many associations that we quickly dismiss as being causally related. For example, there is a statistical association between the number of storks in an area and the birth rate in that area. We know that storks don't bring babies, so something else must cause the association between these two variables. The real explanation is that both storks and birth rates have a higher incidence in rural areas.

In other studies, the third variable effect is less apparent. Many years ago, before polio vaccines were available, a study in the United States reported a surprisingly strong association between consumption of a certain soft drink and the incidence of polio. Did drinking this pop cause polio, or did people with polio have an unusual craving for this beverage? Neither. Both polio and consumption of the drink were caused by a third variable: climate. There was a higher incidence of polio in the summer months and in warmer climates, and people drink more liquids in these climates.[8] As you can see from this example, researchers have a difficult time supporting causal inferences, because third-variable effects are sometimes difficult to detect.

ETHICS IN ORGANIZATIONAL RESEARCH

Organizational behaviour researchers need to abide by the ethical standards of the society in which the research is conducted. One of the most important ethical considerations is the individual subject's freedom to participate in the study. For example, it is inappropriate to force employees to fill out a questionnaire or attend an experimental intervention for research purposes only. Moreover, researchers have an obligation to tell potential subjects about any potential risks inherent in the study so that participants can make an informed choice about whether to be involved.

Finally, researchers must be careful to protect the privacy of those who participate in the study. This usually includes letting people know when they are being studied as well as guaranteeing that their individual information will remain confidential (unless publication of identities is otherwise granted). Researchers maintain anonymity through careful security of data. The research results usually aggregate data in numbers large enough that they do not reveal the opinions or characteristics of any specific individual. For example, we would report the average absenteeism of employees in a department rather than state the absence rates of each person. When sharing data with other researchers, it is usually necessary to code each case so that individual identities are not revealed.

RESEARCH DESIGN STRATEGIES

So far, we have described how to build a theory, including the specific elements of empirically testing that theory within the standards of scientific inquiry. But what are the different ways to design a research study so that we get the data necessary to achieve our research objectives? There are many strategies, but they mainly fall under three headings: laboratory experiments, field surveys, and observational research.

LABORATORY EXPERIMENTS

Laboratory experiment Any research study in which independent variables and variables outside the researcher's main focus of inquiry can be controlled to some extent.

A **laboratory experiment** is any research study in which independent variables and variables outside the researcher's main focus of inquiry can be controlled to some extent. Laboratory experiments are usually located outside the everyday work environment, such as a classroom, simulation lab, or other artificial setting in which the researcher can manipulate the environment. Organizational behaviour researchers sometimes conduct experiments in the workplace (called *field experiments*) in which the independent variable is manipulated. However, the researcher has less control over the effects of extraneous factors in field experiments than in laboratory situations.

Advantages of laboratory experiments

Laboratory experiments have many advantages. By definition, this research method offers a high degree of control over extraneous variables that would otherwise confound the relationships being studied. Suppose we wanted to test the effects of directive leadership on the satisfaction of new employees. One concern might be that employees are influenced by how much leadership is provided, not just the leadership style. An experimental design would allow us to control how often the supervisor exhibited this style so that this extraneous variable does not confound the results.

A second advantage of laboratory studies is that the independent and dependent variables can be developed more precisely than in a field setting. For example, the researcher can ensure that supervisors in a lab study apply specific directive or nondirective behaviours, whereas real-life supervisors would use a more complex mixture of leadership behaviours. By using more precise measures, we are more certain that we are measuring the intended construct. Thus, if new employees are more satisfied with supervisors in the directive leadership condition, we are more confident that the independent variable was directive leadership rather than some other leadership style.

A third benefit of laboratory experiments is that the independent variable can be distributed more evenly among participants. In our directive leadership study, we can ensure that approximately half of the subjects have a directive supervisor, while the other half have a nondirective supervisor. In natural settings, it might be difficult to find people who have worked with a nondirective leader and, consequently, we couldn't determine the effects of this condition.

Disadvantages of laboratory experiments

With these powerful advantages, you might wonder why laboratory experiments are the least appreciated form of organizational behaviour research.[9] One obvious limitation of this method is that it lacks realism and, consequently, the results might be different in the real world. One argument is that laboratory experiment subjects are less involved than their counterparts in an actual work situation. This is sometimes true, although many lab studies have highly motivated participants. Another criticism is that the extraneous variables controlled in the lab setting might produce a different effect of the independent variable on the dependent variables. This might also be true, but remember that the experimental design controls variables in accordance with the theory and its hypotheses. Consequently, this concern is really a critique of the theory, not the laboratory study.

Finally, there is the well-known problem that participants are aware they are being studied and this causes them to act differently than they normally would. Some participants try to figure out how the researcher wants them to behave and then deliberately try to act that way. Other participants try to upset the experiment by doing just the opposite of what they believe the researcher expects. Still others might act unnaturally simply because they know they are being observed. Fortunately, experimenters are well aware of these potential problems and are usually (although not always) successful at disguising the study's true intent.

FIELD SURVEYS

> **Field survey** Any research design in which information is collected in a natural environment.

Field surveys collect and analyze information in a natural environment—an office, factory, or other existing location. The researcher takes a snapshot of reality and tries to determine whether elements of that situation (including the attitudes and behaviours of people in that situation) are associated with each other as hypothesized. Everyone does some sort of field research. You might think that people from some provinces are better drivers than others, so you "test" your theory by looking at the way people with out-of-province licence plates drive. Although your methods of data collection might not satisfy scientific standards, this is a form of field research because it takes information from a naturally occurring situation.

Advantages and disadvantages of field surveys

One advantage of field surveys is that the variables often have a more powerful effect than they would in a laboratory experiment. Consider the effect of peer pressure on the behaviour of members within the team. In a natural environment, team members would form very strong cohesive bonds over time, whereas a researcher would have difficulty replicating this level of cohesiveness and corresponding peer pressure in a lab setting.

Another advantage of field surveys is that the researcher can study many variables simultaneously, thereby permitting a fuller test of more complex theories. Ironically, this is also a disadvantage of field surveys, because it is difficult for the researcher to contain his or her scientific inquiry. There is a tendency to shift from deductive hypothesis testing to more inductive exploratory browsing through the data. If these two activities become mixed together, the researcher can lose sight of the strict covenants of scientific inquiry.

The main weakness of field surveys is that it is very difficult to satisfy the conditions for causal conclusions. One reason is that the data are usually collected at one point in time, so the researcher must rely on logic to decide whether the independent variable really preceded the dependent variable. Contrast this with the laboratory study in which the researcher can usually be confident that the independent variable was applied before the dependent variable occurred. Increasingly, organizational behaviour studies use longitudinal research to provide a better indicator of temporal relations among variables, but this is still not as precise as the laboratory setting. Another reason why causal analysis is difficult in field surveys is that extraneous variables are not controlled as they are in laboratory studies. Without this control, there is a higher chance that a third variable might explain the relationship between the hypothesized independent and dependent variables.

OBSERVATIONAL RESEARCH

In their study of brainstorming and creativity, Robert Sutton and Andrew Hargadon observed 24 brainstorming sessions at IDEO, a product design firm in Palo Alto, California. They also attended a dozen "Monday morning meetings," conducted 60 semi-structured interviews with IDEO executives and designers, held hundreds of informal discussions with these people, and read through several dozen magazine articles about the company.[10]

Sutton's and Hargadon's use of observational research and other qualitative methods was quite appropriate for their research objectives, which were to re-examine the effectiveness of brainstorming beyond the number of ideas generated. Observational research generates a wealth of descriptive accounts about the drama of human existence in organizations. It is a useful vehicle for learning about the complex dynamics of people and their activities, such as brainstorming. (The results of Sutton and Hargadon's study are discussed in Chapter 11.)

Participant observation takes the observation method one step further by having the observer take part in the organization's activities. This experience gives the researcher a fuller understanding of the activities compared to just watching others participate in those activities.

In spite of its intuitive appeal, observational research has a number of weaknesses. The main problem is that the observer is subject to the perceptual screening and organizing biases that we discuss in Chapter 6 of this textbook. There is a tendency to overlook the routine aspects of organizational life, even though they may prove to be the most important data for research purposes. Instead, observers tend to focus on unusual information, such as activities that deviate from what the observer expects. Because observational research usually records only what the observer notices, valuable information is often lost.

Another concern with the observation method is that the researcher's presence and involvement may influence the people whom he or she is studying. This can be a problem in short-term observations, but in the long term people tend to return to their usual behaviour patterns. With ongoing observations, such as Sutton's and Hargadon's study of brainstorming sessions at IDEO, employees eventually forget that they are being studied.

Finally, observation is usually a qualitative process, so it is more difficult to empirically test hypotheses with the data. Instead, observational research provides rich information for the inductive stages of theory building. It helps us form ideas about the way things work in organizations. We begin to see relationships that lay the foundation for new perspectives and theory. We must not confuse this inductive process of theory building with the deductive process of theory testing.

APPENDIX B

Scoring Keys for Self-Assessments

Chapter 2
SCORING KEY FOR ASSESSING YOUR SELF-EFFICACY

To calculate your score on the general self-efficacy scale, assign the appropriate number to each question from the scoring key below. Then add up the numbers. Higher scores indicate that you have a higher level of self-efficacy. This means that you have a stronger "can-do" attitude towards new tasks and other challenges in life.

FOR STATEMENT ITEMS 1, 3, 8, 9, 13, 15:	FOR STATEMENT ITEMS 2, 4, 5, 6, 7, 10, 11, 12, 14, 16, 17:
Strongly Agree = 5	Strongly Agree = 1
Agree = 4	Agree = 2
Neutral = 3	Neutral = 3
Disagree = 2	Disagree = 4
Strongly Disagree = 1	Strongly Disagree = 5

Chapter 3
SCORING KEY FOR MEASURING YOUR GROWTH NEED STRENGTH

Step 1: The Growth Need Strength Scale yields a number from 1 (Strongly Prefer A) to 5 (Strongly Prefer B). Write your circled numbers for the items indicated below and total them:

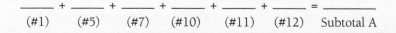

$$\underline{\hspace{1cm}} + \underline{\hspace{1cm}} + \underline{\hspace{1cm}} + \underline{\hspace{1cm}} + \underline{\hspace{1cm}} + \underline{\hspace{1cm}} = \underline{\hspace{2cm}}$$
(#1)   (#5)   (#7)   (#10)   (#11)   (#12)   Subtotal A

Step 2: The remaining items in the Growth Need Strength Scale need to be reverse-scored. To calculate a reverse score, subtract the direct score from 6. For example, if you circled 4 in one of these items, the reverse score would be 2 (i.e., $6 - 4 = 2$). If you circled 1, the reverse score would be 5 (i.e., $6 - 1 = 5$). Calculate the *reverse score* for each of the items indicated below and write them in the space provided. Then calculate Subtotal B by totalling these reverse scores.

$$\underline{\hspace{1cm}} + \underline{\hspace{1cm}} + \underline{\hspace{1cm}} + \underline{\hspace{1cm}} + \underline{\hspace{1cm}} + \underline{\hspace{1cm}} = \underline{\hspace{2cm}}$$
(#2)   (#3)   (#4)   (#6)   (#8)   (#9)   Subtotal B

Step 3: Calculate the total score by summing Subtotal A and Subtotal B.

$$\underline{\hspace{2cm}} + \underline{\hspace{2cm}} = \underline{\hspace{2cm}}$$
(Subtotal A)   (Subtotal B)   TOTAL

Chapter 4
SCORING KEY FOR ASSESSING YOUR SELF-LEADERSHIP

To calculate your score on the Self-Leadership Questionnaire, assign the appropriate number to each question from the scoring key below. Then total the numbers for that dimension. The self-leadership total score is calculated by adding up all scores on all dimensions.

SELF-LEADERSHIP DIMENSION	CALCULATION	YOUR SCORE
Personal Goal Setting	Item 3 + Item 9 + Item 15 =	_____
Mental Practice*	Item 6 + Item 12 + Item 18 =	_____
Designing Natural Rewards	Item 5 + Item 11 + Item 17 =	_____
Self-Monitoring**	Item 1 + Item 7 + Item 13 =	_____
Self-Reinforcement	Item 4 + Item 10 + Item 16 =	_____
Cueing Strategies***	Item 2 + Item 8 + Item 14 =	_____
SELF-LEADERSHIP TOTAL	Add up all dimension scores =	_____

* Mental practice is similar to constructive thought patterns, but does not represent self-talk and mental imagery quite as clearly.

** Self-monitoring is called "self-observation" in the SLQ1.

** Cueing strategies represent activities that help us behave in certain ways. Although not explicitly described in Chapter 4, it is similar to "antecedents" in the A-B-C model of organizational behaviour modification described in Chapter 2. The only difference is that these antecedents are self-developed or self-controlled rather than introduced and controlled by others.

Chapter 5
SCORING KEY FOR TIME-STRESS SCALE

Add up the number of "Yes" items. You are considered "time-stressed" if you answer yes to seven or more of these items. Low time-stress is less than four points.

Chapter 7
SCORING KEY FOR INDIVIDUALISM–COLLECTIVISM SCALE

Individualism: Add up the results for the odd-numbered items (i.e., 1, 3, 5, 7, 9, 11, 13, 15). Maximum score is 40. Higher scores indicate more individualism.

Collectivism: Add up the results for the even-numbered items (i.e., 2, 4, 6, 8, 10, 12, 14, 16). Maximum score is 40. Higher scores indicate more collectivism.

Chapter 8

SCORING KEY FOR ACTIVE LISTENING SKILLS INVENTORY

Step 1: Using the table below, assign the number corresponding to the answer you indicated for each statement. For example, if you indicated "Very much" for statement 1, assign a "3" to the space provided to the right of the statement.

FOR STATEMENT ITEMS 3, 4, 6, 7, 10, 13:	**FOR STATEMENT ITEMS 1, 2, 5, 8, 9, 11, 12, 14, 15:**
Not at all = 3	Not at all = 0
A little = 2	A little = 1
Somewhat = 1	Somewhat = 2
Very much = 0	Very much = 3

Step 2: Write the scores for each item on the appropriate line below (statement numbers are in brackets), and total each scale. Then calculate the overall score by summing all scales.

Avoiding Interruption (AI)   _____ + _____ + _____ = _____
                                   (3)   (7)   (15)

Maintaining Interest (MI)   _____ + _____ + _____ = _____
                                   (6)   (9)   (14)

Postponing Evaluation (PE)   _____ + _____ + _____ = _____
                                   (1)   (5)   (13)

Organizing Information (OI)   _____ + _____ + _____ = _____
                                   (2)   (10)   (12)

Showing Interest (SI)   _____ + _____ + _____ = _____
                                   (4)   (8)   (11)

Active Listening (total score):   _____

(Note: This scale does not explicitly measure two other dimensions of active listening, namely, empathizing and providing feedback. Empathizing is difficult to measure and providing feedback involves similar behaviours as showing interest.)

Chapter 9

SCORING KEY FOR TEAM ROLES PREFERENCES SCALE

Write the scores circled for each item on the appropriate line below (statement numbers are in brackets) and total each scale. These roles are described in Chapter 9.

Encourager   _____ + _____ + _____ = _____
                    (6)   (9)   (11)

Gatekeeper   _____ + _____ + _____ = _____
                    (4)   (10)   (13)

Harmonizer   _____ + _____ + _____ = _____
                    (3)   (8)   (12)

Initiator   _____ + _____ + _____ = _____
                    (1)   (5)   (14)

Summarizer   _____ + _____ + _____ = _____
                    (2)   (7)   (15)

Chapter 10

SCORING KEY FOR DECISION-MAKING STYLE INVENTORY

Write the scores for each item on the appropriate line below (statement numbers are in brackets), and total each scale.

Rational Decision Style   _____ + _____ + _____ + _____ = _____
                               (1)   (2)   (6)   (8)

Intuitive Decision Style   _____ + _____ + _____ + _____ = _____
                               (3)   (4)   (5)   (7)

Chapter 11

SCORING KEY FOR ASSESSING YOUR CREATIVE DISPOSITION

Assign plus one (+1) point beside the following words if you marked them: Capable, Clever, Confident, Egotistical, Humorous, Individualistic, Informal, Insightful, Intelligent, Inventive, Original, Reflective, Resourceful, Self-confident, Sexy, Snobbish, Unconventional, Wide interests

Assign negative one (−1) point beside the following words if you marked them: Affected, Cautious, Commonplace, Conservative, Conventional, Dissatisfied, Honest, Mannerly, Narrow interests, Sincere, Submissive, Suspicious

Add up the total score, which will range from −12 to +18.

Chapter 12

SCORING KEY FOR PERCEPTIONS OF POLITICS SCALE (POPS)

To calculate your score on the POPS, assign the appropriate number to each question from the scoring key below. Then total the numbers.

FOR STATEMENT ITEMS 1, 4, 5, 6, 7, 8, 9	**FOR STATEMENT ITEMS 2, 3**
Strongly Agree = 5	Strongly Agree = 1
Agree = 4	Agree = 2
Neutral = 3	Neutral = 3
Disagree = 2	Disagree = 4
Strongly Disagree = 1	Strongly Disagree = 5

Write the scores for each item on the appropriate line below (statement numbers are in brackets), and total each scale.

General Political   ____ + ____ = _____
Behaviour   (1)   (5)   (Subtotal A)

Go Along to Get Ahead   ____ + ____ + ____ + ____ + ____ + ____ + ____ = _____
                        (2)   (3)   (4)   (6)   (7)   (8)   (9)   (Subtotal B)

TOTAL SCORE: _____ + _____ = _____
                    (Subtotal A)   (Subtotal B)   (Total)

Chapter 13

SCORING KEY FOR CONFLICT MANAGEMENT STYLE ORIENTATION SCALE

Write the scores circled for each item on the appropriate line below (statement numbers are in brackets), and total each scale. Higher scores indicate that you are stronger on that particular conflict management style.

Competing   ____ + ____ + ____ = ____
               (1)   (9)   (12)

Accommodating ____ + ____ + ____ = ____
               (2)   (7)   (11)

Compromising   ____ + ____ + ____ = ____
               (3)   (6)   (15)

Avoiding   ____ + ____ + ____ = ____
               (4)   (8)   (14)

Collaboration ____ + ____ + ____ = ____
               (5)   (10)   (13)

Chapter 14

SCORING KEY FOR LEADERSHIP DIMENSIONS INSTRUMENT

Write the scores circled for each item on the appropriate line below (statement numbers are in brackets), and total each scale. Higher scores indicate that your supervisor is stronger on that particular leadership dimension.

Transactional Leadership: Total scores for the odd-numbered items (i.e., 1, 3, 5, 7, 9, 11, 13, 15). Maximum score is 40. Higher scores indicate that your supervisor has a strong inclination towards transactional leadership.

Transformational Leadership: Total scores for the even-numbered items (i.e., 2, 4, 6, 8, 10, 12, 14, 16). Maximum score is 40. Higher scores indicate that your supervisor has a strong inclination towards transformational leadership.

Chapter 15

SCORING KEY FOR TOLERANCE OF CHANGE SCALE

This measurement instrument is formally known as the "tolerance of ambiguity" scale. Although it was developed 40 years ago, the instrument is still used today in research. People with a high tolerance of ambiguity are comfortable with uncertainty, sudden change, and new situations—characteristics of the hyperfast changes occurring in many organizations today.

To calculate your tolerance of change score, assign the appropriate number to each question from the scoring key below. Then total the numbers. Higher scores indicate that you have a higher tolerance of ambiguity.

FOR STATEMENT ITEMS 2, 4, 6, 8, 10, 12, 14, 16:	FOR STATEMENT ITEMS 1, 3, 5, 7, 9, 11, 13, 15:
Strongly Agree = 7	Strongly Agree = 1
Moderately Agree = 6	Moderately Agree = 2
Slightly Agree = 5	Slightly Agree = 3
Neutral = 4	Neutral = 4
Slightly Disagree = 3	Slightly Disagree = 5
Moderately Disagree = 2	Moderately Disagree = 6
Strongly Disagree = 1	Strongly Disagree = 7

Chapter 16

SCORING KEY FOR IDENTIFYING YOUR PREFERRED ORGANIZATIONAL STRUCTURE

Step 1: Using the table below, assign the number corresponding to the answer you indicated for each statement. For example, if you indicated "Very much" for statement 1, write "3" in the space provided to the right of the statement.

FOR STATEMENT ITEMS 2, 3, 8, 10, 11, 12, 14, 15:	**FOR STATEMENT ITEMS 1, 4, 5, 6, 7, 9, 13:**
Not at all = 3	Not at all = 0
A little = 2	A little = 1
Somewhat = 1	Somewhat = 2
Very much = 0	Very much = 3

Step 2: Write the scores for each item on the appropriate line below (statement numbers are in brackets), and total each scale. Then calculate the overall score by summing all scales.

Tall Hierarchy (H)   _____ + _____ + _____ + _____ + _____ = _____
                      (1)   (4)   (10)   (12)   (15)   (H)

Formalization (F)   _____ + _____ + _____ + _____ + _____ = _____
                      (2)   (6)   (8)   (11)   (13)   (F)

Centralization (C)   _____ + _____ + _____ + _____ + _____ = _____
                      (3)   (5)   (7)   (9)   (14)   (C)

Total Score*   _____ + _____ + _____ = _____
                      (H)   (F)   (C)   Total

*A higher total score indicates preference for mechanistic organizations, whereas a lower score indicates preference for more organic organizations.

Chapter 17

SCORING KEY FOR CORPORATE CULTURE PREFERENCE SCALE

In each space below, write in a "1" if you circled the item and "0" if you did not. Then add up the scores for each subscale. The maximum score for each subscale is 6 and the minimum is 0. The higher the score, the more you would likely feel comfortable in that type of culture.

Control Culture   _____ + _____ + _____ + _____ + _____ + _____ = _____
                          (2a)   (5a)   (6b)   (8b)   (11b)   (12a)

Performance Culture   _____ + _____ + _____ + _____ + _____ + _____ = _____
                          (1b)   (3b)   (5b)   (6a)   (7a)   (9b)

Relationship Culture   _____ + _____ + _____ + _____ + _____ + _____ = _____
                          (1a)   (3a)   (4b)   (8a)   (10b)   (12b)

Responsive Culture   _____ + _____ + _____ + _____ + _____ + _____ = _____
                          (2b)   (4a)   (7b)   (9a)   (10a)   (11a)

EXPLANATION OF SUBSCALES

These subscales may be found in many organizations, but they represent only four of the many possible organizational culture values. Also, keep in mind that none of these subscales is inherently good or bad. Each is effective in different situations.

Control Culture: This culture values the role of senior executives to lead the organization. Its goal is to keep everyone aligned and under control.

Performance Culture: This culture values individual and organizational performance and strives for effectiveness and efficiency.

Relationship Culture: This culture values nurturing and well-being. It considers open communication, fairness, teamwork, and sharing to be a vital part of organizational life.

Responsive Culture: This culture values its ability to keep in tune with the external environment, including being competitive and realizing new opportunities.

Glossary

The number(s) after each definition indicates the chapter in which the term is defined.

Ability The natural aptitudes and learned capabilities required to successfully complete a task. (2)

Absorptive capacity Employees must have a sufficient level of related knowledge to be aware of and make sense of information outside the organization. (2)

Action learning A form of on-site, experiential-based learning in which participants investigate an organizational problem or opportunity and possibly implement their solution. (2)

Action research A data-based, problem-oriented process that diagnoses the need for change, introduces the OD intervention, and then evaluates and stabilizes the desired changes. (15)

Actor-observer error An attribution error whereby people tend to attribute their own actions more to external factors, and the behaviour of others more to internal factors. (6) (14)

Adaptive culture An organization culture in which employees focus on the changing needs of customers and other stakeholders, and support initiatives to keep pace with these changes. (17)

Affiliate networks Network organizations where the satellite companies have a special affiliation with the core firm. The satellites may have been spun-off departments from the core firm, or the core firm may be a major investor in the satellite. (16)

Agency theory An economic theory that assumes company owners (principals) and employees (agents) have different goals and interests, so rewards and other control systems are required to align the agent's goals with those of the principals. (4)

Alternative dispute resolution (ADR) A third-party dispute resolution process that includes mediation, typically followed by arbitration. (13)

Appreciative inquiry An organization development intervention that directs the group's attention away from its own problems and focuses participants on the group's potential and positive elements. (15)

Artifacts The observable symbols and signs of an organization's culture, including its physical structures, ceremonies, language, and stories. (17)

Attitudes The cluster of beliefs, assessed feelings, and behavioural intentions towards an object. (7)

Attribution process A perceptual process whereby we interpret the causes of behaviour in terms of the person (internal attributions) or the situation (external attributions). (6)

Autonomy The degree to which a job gives employees the freedom, independence, and discretion to schedule their work and determine the procedures to be used to complete the work. (4)

Behaviour modification (also known as *operant conditioning* and *reinforcement theory*) A theory that explains learning in terms of antecedents and consequences of behaviour.

Behaviourism A perspective that focuses entirely on behaviour and observable events, rather than on a person's thoughts. (2)

Benchmarking A systematic and ongoing process of improving performance by measuring a product, service, or process against a partner that has mastered it. (10)

Bicultural audit Diagnoses cultural relations of merging companies and determines the extent to which cultural clashes will likely occur. (17)

"Big Five" personality dimensions The five abstract personality dimensions under which most personality traits are represented. They are extroversion, agreeableness, conscientiousness, emotional stability, and openness to experience. (6) (18)

Boundaryless career The idea that careers operate across company and industry boundaries rather than just within a single organizational hierarchy. (18)

Brainstorming A freewheeling, face-to-face meeting in which team members generate as many alternative solutions to the problem as possible, piggyback on the ideas of others, and avoid evaluating anyone's ideas during the idea-generation stage. (11)

Career A sequence of work-related experiences that people participate in over the span of their working lives. (18)

Career anchor A person's self-image of his or her abilities, motivations, and interests relating to a particular career orientation. (17)

Cellular organizations A type of network structure in which unique partnership teams are formed to provide customized products or services, usually to specific clients, for a limited time. (16)

Centrality The degree and nature of interdependence between the powerholder and others. (12)

Centralization The degree to which formal decision authority is held by a small group of people, typically those at the top of the organizational hierarchy. (16)

Ceremonies Deliberate and usually dramatic displays of organizational culture, such as celebrations and special social gatherings. (17)

Change agent A person who possesses enough knowledge and power to guide and facilitate the change effort. (15)

Coalition An informal group that attempts to influence people outside the group by pooling the resources and power of its members. (9) (12)

Codetermination A form of employee involvement required by some governments that typically operates at both the work site as work councils and the corporate level as supervisory boards. (10)

Coercive power The capacity to influence others through the ability to apply punishment and remove rewards affecting these people. (12)

Cognitive dissonance A state of anxiety that occurs when an individual's beliefs, attitudes, intentions, and behaviours are inconsistent with one another. (7)

Cohesiveness The degree of attraction that members feel towards their team and their motivation to remain members. (9)

Communication The process by which information is transmitted and understood between two or more people. (8)

Communication competence A person's ability to identify appropriate communication patterns in a given situation and to achieve goals by applying that knowledge. (8)

Communities of practice Informal groups bound together by shared expertise and passion for a particular activity or interest. (1) (9) (10)

Competencies The abilities, individual values, personality traits, and other characteristics of people that lead to superior performance. (2) (4) (14)

Concurrent engineering The integration and concurrent development of a product or service and its associated processes, usually guided by a cross-functional team. (10) (16)

Conflict The process in which one party perceives that its interests are being opposed or negatively affected by another party. (13)

Conflict management Interventions that alter the level and form of conflict in ways that maximize its benefits and minimize its dysfunctional consequences. (13)

Conscientiousness A "Big Five" personality dimension that characterizes people who are careful, dependable, and self-disciplined. (6)

Constructive controversy Any situation in which team members debate their different opinions regarding a problem or issue in a way that minimizes socioemotional conflict. (11) (13)

Constructs Abstract ideas constructed by researchers that can be linked to observable information. (Appendix A)

Content theories of motivation Theories that explain the dynamics of employee needs, such as why people have different needs at different times. (3)

Contingency approach The idea that a particular action may have different consequences in different situations; that no single solution is best in all circumstances. (1)

Contingent work Any job in which the individual does not have an explicit or implicit contract for long-term employment, or one in which the minimum hours of work can vary in a nonsystematic way. (1) (18)

Continuous reinforcement A schedule that reinforces behaviour every time it occurs. (2)

Counterpower The capacity of a person, team, or organization to keep a more powerful person or group in the exchange relationship. (12)

Creativity The capability to develop an original product, service, or idea that makes a socially recognized contribution. (11)

Cross-functional teams Groups that overlay a more permanent structure, usually functional departments. (9)

Decision making A conscious process of making choices among one or more alternatives with the intention of moving towards some desired state of affairs. (10) (11)

Delphi technique Systematically pools the collective knowledge of experts on a particular subject to make decisions, predict the future, or identify opposing views (called *dissensus*). (11)

Departmentation An element of organizational structure specifying how employees and their activities are grouped together, such as by function, product, geographic location, or some combination. (18)

Devil's advocates People who challenge others to explain the logic of their preferences and who identify problems with that logic. (11)

Dialogue A process of conversation among team members in which they learn about each other's mental models and assumptions, and eventually form a common model for thinking within the team. (9) (13) (15)

Discrepancy theory A theory that partly explains job satisfaction and dissatisfaction in terms of the gap between what a person expects to receive and what is actually received. (7)

Divergent thinking The ability to reframe problems in a unique way and generate different approaches to the issue. (11)

Divisional structure A type of departmentation that groups employees around outputs, clients, or geographic areas. (16)

Effort-to-performance (E→P) expectancy An individual's perceived probability that a particular level of effort will result in a particular level of performance. (3)

Electronic brainstorming A structured team decision-making process whereby several people individually generate ideas or make decisions through computer software that posts each participant's ideas or opinions anonymously. (11)

Emotional adaptability A person's ability to adjust emotions naturally to the situational context. (7)

Emotional contagion The automatic and subconscious tendency to mimic and synchronize our nonverbal behaviours with other people. (8)

Emotional dissonance Conflict between required and true emotions. (7)

Emotional intelligence (EQ) The ability to monitor your own and others' emotions, to discriminate among them, and to use the information to guide your thinking and actions. (7) (14)

Emotional labour The effort, planning, and control needed to express organizationally desired emotions during interpersonal transactions. (7) (8)

Emotions Feelings experienced towards an object, person, or event that create a state of readiness. (7)

Empathy A person's ability to understand and be sensitive to the feelings, thoughts, and situations of others. (6) (7) (8)

Employability The "new deal" employment relationship in which the job is viewed as a temporary event, so employees are expected to keep pace with changing competency requirements and shift to new projects as demand requires. (1) (4) (18)

Employee assistance programs (EAPs) Counselling services that help employees cope with personal or organizational stressors and adopt more effective coping mechanisms. (5)

Employee involvement The degree to which employees share information, knowledge, rewards, and power throughout the organization. (10)

Employee share ownership plan (ESOP) A reward system that encourages employees to buy shares of the company. (4)

Empowerment The feeling of control and self-efficacy that emerges when people are given power in a previously powerless situation. (4) (10)

Environmental scanning Receiving information from the external and internal environments so that more effective strategic decisions can be made. (1)

Equity theory A process motivation theory that explains how people develop perceptions of fairness in the distribution and exchange of resources. (3) (7)

ERG theory Alderfer's content motivation theory of three instinctive needs arranged in a hierarchy, in which people progress to the next higher need when a lower one is fulfilled, and regress to a lower need if unable to fulfil a higher need. (3)

Escalation of commitment Repeating an apparently bad decision or allocating more resources to a failing course of action. (10) (11)

Ethical sensitivity A personal characteristic that enables people to recognize the presence and determine the relative importance of an ethical issue. (7)

Ethical values Beliefs about whether certain actions are good or bad, directing them to what is virtuous and right. (7)

Ethics The study of moral principles or values that determine whether actions are right or wrong and whether outcomes are good or bad. (1) (7)

Evaluation apprehension The reluctance to mention ideas to others that seem silly or peripheral in order to create a favourable self-presentation and maintain social esteem. (11)

Existence needs A person's physiological and physically related safety needs, such as the need for food, shelter, and safe working conditions. (3)

Expectancy theory A process motivation theory stating that work effort is directed towards behaviours that people believe will lead to desired outcomes. (3)

Expert power The capacity to influence others by possessing knowledge or skills that they want. (12)

Extinction Occurs when the removal or withholding of a consequence decreases the frequency or future probability of the behaviour preceding that event. (2)

Extroversion A "Big Five" personality dimension that characterizes people who are outgoing, talkative, sociable, and assertive. (6) (7)

Family-friendly workplaces Organizations that try to minimize work-family time conflict by offering flexible work arrangements, job sharing, telework, family leave, and childcare facilities. (5)

Feedback Any information that people receive about the consequences of their behaviour. (2)

Fiedler's contingency model States that leader effectiveness depends on whether the person's natural leadership style is appropriately matched to the situation. (14)

Field survey Any research design in which information is collected in a natural environment. (Appendix A)

Fixed interval schedule A schedule that reinforces behaviour after it has occurred for a fixed period of time. (2)

Fixed ratio schedule A schedule that reinforces behaviour after it has occurred a fixed number of times. (2)

Flaming Sending an emotionally charged electronic mail message. (8)

Force field analysis A model that helps change agents diagnose the forces that drive and restrain proposed organizational change. (15)

Formalization The degree to which organizations standardize behaviour through rules, procedures, formal training, and related mechanisms. (16)

Frustration-regression process Process whereby people who are unable to satisfy a higher need become frustrated and regress to the next lower need level. (3)

Functional structure A type of departmentation that organizes employees around specific skills or other resources. (16)

Fundamental attribution error The tendency to attribute the behaviour of other people more to internal than external factors. (6) (14)

Gainsharing plan A reward system usually applied to work teams that distributes bonuses to team members based on the amount of cost reductions and increased labour efficiency in the production process. (4) (10)

General adaptation syndrome A model of the stress experience, consisting of three stages: alarm reaction, resistance, and exhaustion. (5)

Globalization Occurs when an organization extends its activities to other parts of the world, actively participates in other markets, and competes against organizations located in other countries. (1)

Goal setting The process of motivating employees and clarifying their role perceptions by establishing performance objectives. (3)

Goals The immediate or ultimate objectives that employees are trying to accomplish from their work effort. (3)

Grafting The process of acquiring knowledge by hiring individuals or buying entire companies. (1)

Grapevine The organization's informal communication network that is formed and maintained by social relationships rather than by the formal reporting relationships. (8)

Group Two or more people with a unifying relationship. (9)

Group polarization The tendency for teams to make more extreme decisions (either more risky or more risk-averse) than the average team member would if making the decision alone. (11)

Groupthink The tendency of highly cohesive groups to value consensus at the price of decision quality by avoiding conflict and withholding their dissenting opinions. (11)

Growth needs A person's self-esteem through personal achievement as well as self-actualization. (3)

Halo error A perceptual error whereby our general impression of a person, usually based on one prominent characteristic, biases our perception of other characteristics of that person. (6)

Harassment Unwelcome conduct that detrimentally affects the work environment or leads to adverse job-related consequences for the victims of harassment. (6) (12)

Heterogeneous teams Formal or informal groups whose members have diverse personal characteristics and backgrounds. (9)

"Hi-hi" leadership hypothesis A proposition stating that effective leaders exhibit high levels of both people-oriented and task-oriented behaviours. (14)

Homogeneous teams Formal or informal groups whose members have similar technical expertise, ethnicity, experiences, or values. (9)

Hotelling An open workspace concept in which employees do not have permanent desks, offices, or workspaces but rather are temporarily assigned a disk or cubicle when they visit the office. (8)

Hypotheses Statements making empirically testable declarations that certain variables and their corresponding measures are related in a specific way proposed by a particular theory. (Appendix A)

Implicit learning The experiential phenomenon of acquiring information about relationships in the environment without any conscious attempt to do so. (2) (3)

Impression management The practice of actively shaping our public images. (12)

Incremental change An evolutionary approach to change in which existing organizational conditions are fine-tuned and small steps are taken towards the change effort's objectives. (15)

Individualism-collectivism The degree to which people value their individual versus group goals. Collectivists respect and value their membership in the group to which they belong, whereas individualists tend to give low priority to group interests. (7) (10)

Informal group Two or more people who group together primarily to meet their personal (rather than organizational) needs. (9)

Information overload A condition in which the volume of information received by an employee exceeds that person's ability to process it effectively. (8)

Inoculation effect A persuasive communication strategy of warning listeners that others will try to influence them in the future and that they should be wary about the opponent's arguments. (8)

Intellectual capital The knowledge that resides in an organization, including its human, structural, and relationship capital. (1) (2)

Intergroup mirroring A structured conflict management intervention in which the parties discuss their perceptions of each other and look for ways to improve their relationship by correcting misperceptions. (13)

Interpretivism A view that suggests that reality comes from shared meaning among people in that environment. (Appendix A)

Introversion Refers to people who are quiet, shy, and cautious. (6)

Intuition The ability to know when a problem or opportunity exists and to select the best course of action without conscious reasoning. (10)

Jargon Technical language of a particular occupational group or recognized words with specialized meaning in specific organizations or social groups. (8)

Job burnout The process of emotional exhaustion, depersonalization, and reduced personal accomplishment resulting from prolonged exposure to stress. (5)

Job characteristics model A job design model that relates five core job dimensions to three psychological states and several personal and organizational consequences. (4)

Job design The process of assigning tasks to a job and distributing work throughout the organization. (4)

Job enlargement Increasing the number of tasks that employees perform within their job. (4)

Job enrichment Assigning responsibility for scheduling, coordinating, and planning work to employees who actually make the product or provide the service. (4)

Job evaluation Systematically evaluating the worth of jobs within the organization by measuring their required skill, effort, responsibility, and working conditions. Job evaluation results create a hierarchy of job worth. (4)

Job feedback The degree to which employees can tell how well they are doing based on direct sensory information from the job itself. (4)

Job rotation Moving employees from one job to another for short periods of time. (4)

Job satisfaction A person's attitude (beliefs, assessed feelings, and behavioural intentions) regarding the job and work context. (2) (3) (5) (7)

Job specialization The result of division of labour in which each job now includes a narrow subset of the tasks required to complete the product or service. (4) (16)

Johari Window A model of personal and interpersonal understanding that encourages disclosure and feedback to increase the open area and reduce the blind, hidden, and unknown areas of oneself. (6)

Knowledge management Any structured activity that improves an organization's capacity to acquire, share, and use knowledge in ways that improve its survival and success. (1) (2) (8)

Laboratory experiment Any research study in which independent variables and variables outside the researcher's main focus of inquiry can be controlled to some extent. (Appendix A)

Lateral career development The view that career success occurs when employees fulfil their personal needs in different jobs across the organization rather than by moving through the organizational hierarchy. (18)

Law of effect States that the likelihood that an operant behaviour will be repeated depends on its consequences. (2)

Law of telecosm States that as the web of computer networks expands, distances will shrink and eventually become irrelevant. (8)

Leadership The process of influencing people and providing an environment for them to achieve team or organizational objectives. (14)

Leadership Grid® A leadership model that assesses an individual's leadership effectiveness in terms of his or her concern for people and concern for production. (14)

Leadership substitutes Characteristics of the employee, task, or organization that either limit the leader's influence or make it unnecessary. (14)

Lean production The practice of continuously pushing for more output with less human effort, less equipment, less time, and less space. (5)

Learning A relatively permanent change in behaviour (or behaviour tendency) that occurs as a result of a person's interaction with the environment. (2)

Legitimate power The capacity to influence others through formal authority; that is, the perceived right to direct certain behaviours of people in other positions. (12)

Locus of control A personality trait referring to the extent to which people believe what happens to them is within their control; those who feel in control of their destiny have an internal locus of control, whereas those who believe that life events are due mainly to fate or to luck have an external locus of control. (6) (14)

Machiavellian values The belief that deceit is a natural and acceptable way to influence others. (12)

Management-by-objectives (MBO) A formal, participative goal-setting process in which organizational objectives are cascaded down to work units and individual employees. (3)

Management by walking around (MBWA) A method of communication in which executives get out of their offices and learn from others in the organization through face-to-face dialogue. (8)

Masculinity-femininity The degree to which people value assertiveness, competitiveness, and materialism (masculinity) versus relationships and the well-being of others (femininity). (7)

Matrix structure A type of departmentalization that overlays a divisionalized structure (typically a project team) with a functional structure. (16)

Mechanistic structure An organizational structure with a narrow span of control and high degrees of formalization and centralization. (16)

Media richness The data-carrying capacity of a communication medium; the volume and variety of information that it can transmit. (8)

Mental imagery Mentally practising a task and visualizing its successful completion. (4)

Mental models The broad world views or "theories-in-use" that people rely on to guide their perceptions and behaviours. (6) (10) (11) (17)

Mentoring The process of learning the ropes of organizational life from a senior person within the company. (12) (18)

Methods-time measurement The process of systematically observing, measuring, and timing the smallest physical movements to identify more efficient work behaviours. (4)

Moods Emotional states that are not directed towards anything in particular. (7)

Moral intensity The degree to which an issue demands the application of ethical principles. (7)

Motivation The internal forces that affect the direction, intensity, and persistence of a person's voluntary choice of behaviour. (2) (3)

Motivator-hygiene theory Herzberg's theory proposes that employees are primarily motivated by growth and esteem needs such as recognition, responsibility, advancement, achievement, and personal growth. (3)

Myers-Briggs Type Indicator (MBTI) A personality test that measures how people prefer to focus their attention (extroversion versus introversion), collect information (sensing versus intuition), process and evaluate information (thinking versus feeling), and orient themselves to the outer world (judging versus perceiving). (6)

Need for achievement (nAch) A learning need that causes people to want to accomplish reasonably challenging goals through their own efforts. (3) (11)

Need for affiliation (nAff) A desire to seek approval from others, conform to their wishes and expectations, and avoid conflict and confrontation. (3)

Need for power (nPow) A desire to control one's environment, including people and material resources. (3)

Needs Deficiencies that energize or trigger behaviours to satisfy those needs. (3)

Needs hierarchy theory Maslow's content motivation theory of five instinctive needs arranged in a hierarchy, whereby people are motivated to fulfil a higher need as a lower one becomes gratified. (3)

Negative affectivity (NA) The tendency to experience negative emotional states. (7)

Negative reinforcement Occurs when the removal or termination of a consequence increases or maintains the frequency or future probability of the behaviour preceding that event. (2)

Negotiation Any attempt by two or more conflicting parties to resolve their divergent goals by redefining the terms of their interdependence. (13)

Network organization An alliance of several organizations for the purpose of creating a product or serving a client. (1)

Network structure An alliance of several organizations for the purpose of creating a product or serving a client. (16)

Networking Cultivating social relationships with others for the purpose of accomplishing one's goals. (12)

Nominal group technique A structured team decision-making technique whereby members independently write down ideas, describe and clarify them to the group, and then independently rank or vote on them. (11)

Nonprogrammed decision The process applied to unique, complex, or ill-defined situations whereby decision makers follow the full decision-making process, including a careful search for and/or development of unique solutions. (10) (11)

Nonterritorial offices Office arrangements in which employees work at any available workstation and are not assigned to specific desks, offices, or workspaces. (8)

Norms Informal rules and expectations that groups establish to regulate the behaviour of their members. (9)

Open book management Involves sharing financial information with employees and

encouraging them to recommend ideas that improve those financial results. (10)

Open systems Organizations and other entities with interdependent parts that work together to continually monitor and transact with the external environment. (1)

Organic structure An organizational structure with a wide span of control, very little formalization, and highly decentralized decision making. (16)

Organization A group of people who work interdependently towards some purpose. (1)

Organization development (OD) A planned system-wide effort, managed from the top with the assistance of a change agent, that uses behavioural science knowledge to improve organizational effectiveness. (15)

Organizational behaviour (OB) The study of what people think, feel, and do in and around organizations. (1)

Organizational behaviour modification A theory that explains learning in terms of the antecedents and consequences of behaviour. (2)

Organizational citizenship Employee behaviours that extend beyond the usual job duties. They include avoiding unnecessary conflicts, helping others without selfish intent, gracefully tolerating occasional impositions, being involved in organizational activities, and performing tasks that extend beyond normal role requirements. (2) (7) (18)

Organizational commitment A complex attitude pertaining to the strength of an individual's identification with and involvement in a particular organization; includes a strong belief in the organization's goals, as well as a motivation to work for and remain a member of the organization. (7)

Organizational culture The basic pattern of shared assumptions, values, and beliefs governing the way employees within an organization think about and act on problems and opportunities. (17)

Organizational design The creation and modification of organizational structures. (16)

Organizational learning An organization's capacity to acquire, disseminate, and apply knowledge for its survival and success. (1) (2)

Organizational memory The storage and preservation of the organization's knowledge (i.e., its intellectual capital). (1)

Organizational politics Attempts to influence others using discretionary behaviours for the purpose of promoting personal objectives;

discretionary behaviours are neither explicitly prescribed nor prohibited by the organization and are linked to one or more power bases. (12)

Organizational socialization The process by which individuals learn the values, expected behaviours, and social knowledge necessary to assume their roles in the organization. (16) (18)

Organizational strategy The way the organization positions itself in its setting in relation to its stakeholders given the organization's resources, capabilities, and mission. (16)

Organizational structure The division of labour as well as the patterns of coordination, communication, work flow, and formal power that direct organizational activities. (16)

Organizations Groups of people who work interdependently towards some purpose. (1)

Parallel learning structures Highly participative social structures constructed alongside (i.e., parallel to) the formal organization with the purpose of increasing the organization's learning. (15)

Path-goal leadership theory A contingency theory of leadership based on expectancy theory of motivation that includes four leadership styles as well as several employee and situational contingencies. (14)

Perception The process of selecting, organizing, and interpreting information in order to make sense of the world around us. (6)

Perceptual defence A defensive psychological process that involves subconsciously screening out large blocks of information that threaten the person's beliefs and values. (6)

Perceptual grouping The perceptual organization process of placing people and objects into recognizable and manageable patterns or categories. (6)

Performance-to-outcome (P→O) expectancy An individual's perceived probability that a specific behaviour or performance level will lead to specific outcomes. (3)

Personality The relatively stable pattern of behaviours and consistent internal states that explain a person's behavioural tendencies. (6)

Persuasive communication The process of having listeners accept rather than just understand the sender's message. (8)

Positive affectivity (PA) The tendency to experience positive emotional states. (7)

Positive reinforcement Occurs when the introduction of a consequence increases or maintains the frequency or future probability of the behaviour preceding that event. (2)

Positivism The common view that reality exists independent of people. (Appendix A)

Postdecisional justification A perceptual phenomenon whereby decision makers justify their choices by subconsciously inflating the quality of the selected option and deflating the quality of the discarded options. (10) (11) (18)

Power The capacity of a person, team, or organization to influence others. (12)

Power distance The extent to which people accept unequal distribution of power in a society. (7) (10) (12)

Prejudice Negative emotions towards people belonging to a particular stereotyped group based on inaccurate perceptions about people in that group. (6)

Primacy effect A perceptual error in which we quickly form an opinion of people based on the first information we receive about them. (6)

Procedural fairness Perceptions of fairness regarding the dispute resolution process, whether or not the outcome is favourable to the person. (13)

Process consultation A method of helping the organization solve its own problems by making it aware of organizational processes, the consequences of those processes, and the means by which they can be changed. (15)

Process losses Resources (including time and energy) expended towards team development and maintenance rather than towards the task. (9)

Process theories of motivation Theories that describe the processes through which need deficiencies are translated into behaviour. (3)

Production blocking A time constraint in meetings due to the procedural requirement that only one person may speak at a time. (11)

Profit sharing A reward system in which a designated group of employees receives a share of corporate profits. (4)

Programmed decision The process whereby decision makers follow standard operating procedures to select the preferred solution without the need to identify or evaluate alternative choices. (10) (11)

Projection bias A perceptual error in which we tend to believe that other people hold the same beliefs and attitudes that we do. (6)

Psychological contract The individual's beliefs about the terms and conditions of a reciprocal exchange agreement between that person and another party. (18)

Punishment Occurs when the introduction of a consequence decreases the frequency or future probability of the behaviour preceding that event. (2)

Quality The value that the end user perceives from the product or service, including satisfying customer needs or expectations and conforming to a standard. (10)

Quality circles Small teams of employees who meet for a few hours each week to identify quality and productivity problems, propose solutions to management, and monitor the implementation and consequences of these solutions in their work area. (9) (10)

Quantum change A revolutionary approach to change in which the organization breaks out of its existing ways and moves towards a totally different configuration of systems and structures. (15)

Realistic job preview (RJP) Giving job applicants a realistic balance of positive and negative information about the job and work context. (18)

Reality shock The gap between pre-employment expectations and the perceived organizational reality that employees experience as they enter a new work situation. (18)

Recency effect A perceptual error in which the most recent information dominates our perception about a person. (6)

Referent power The capacity to influence others by virtue of the admiration of and identification with the powerholder. (12)

Refreezing The latter part of the change process in which systems and conditions are introduced that reinforce and maintain the desired behaviours. (15)

Relatedness needs A person's need to interact with other people, receive public recognition, and feel secure around people (i.e., interpersonal safety). (3)

Relationship restructuring program A formal process of diagnosing the underlying causes of workplace conflict and implementing a long-term solution that will address the sources of these conflicts. (13)

Representative sampling Sampling a population in such a way that we can extrapolate the results of that sample to the larger population. (Appendix A)

Reward power The capacity to influence others by controlling the allocation of rewards valued by them and the removal of negative sanctions. (12)

Rituals The programmed routines of daily organizational life that dramatize the organization's culture. (17)

Role The set of behaviours that people are expected to perform because they hold certain positions in a team and organization. (9)

Role ambiguity Uncertainty about job duties, performance expectations, level of authority, and other job conditions. (5)

Role conflict A situation whereby people experience competing demands, such as having job duties that are incompatible with personal values or receiving contradictory messages from different people. (5)

Role perceptions A person's beliefs about what behaviours are appropriate or necessary in a particular situation, including the specific tasks that make up the job, their relative importance, and the preferred behaviours to accomplish those tasks. (2)

Satisfaction-progression process A process whereby people become increasingly motivated to fulfil a higher need as a lower need is gratified. (3)

Satisficing The tendency to select a solution that is satisfactory or "good enough" rather than optimal or "the best." (10) (11)

Scenario planning A disciplined method for imagining possible futures that typically involves thinking about what would happen if a significant environmental condition changed, and what the organization should do to anticipate and react to such an outcome. (10)

Scientific management The process of systematically determining how work should be partitioned into its smallest possible elements and how the process of completing each task should be standardized to achieve maximum efficiency. (4)

Scientific method A set of principles and procedures that help researchers to systematically understand previously unexplained events and conditions. (1) (Appendix A)

Search conferences Large group sessions, usually lasting a few days, in which participants identify environmental trends and establish strategic solutions for those conditions. (15)

Selective attention The process of filtering (selecting and screening out) information received by our senses. (6) (10)

Self-directed work team (SDWT) A work group that completes an entire piece of work requiring several interdependent tasks and that has substantial autonomy over the execution of these tasks. (9) (10)

Self-efficacy A person's belief that he or she has the ability, motivation, and resources to complete a task successfully. (2) (3) (6) (18)

Self-fulfilling prophecy A phenomenon in which an observer's expectations of someone cause that person to act in a way consistent with the observer's expectation. (6)

Self-leadership The process of influencing oneself to establish the self-direction and self-motivation needed to perform a task. This includes personal goal setting, constructive thought patterns, designing natural rewards, self-monitoring, and self-reinforcement. (4) (14)

Self-monitoring A personality trait referring to the extent to which people are sensitive to situational cues and can readily adapt their own behaviour appropriately. (6) (7) (14)

Self-serving bias A perceptual error whereby people tend to attribute their own success to internal factors and their failures to external factors. (6)

Self-talk Talking to yourself about your own thoughts or actions, for the purpose of increasing self-efficacy and navigating through the decisions required to get the job done effectively. (4)

Sensitivity training An unstructured and agenda-less session in which participants become more aware through their interactions of how they affect others and how others affect them. (15)

Servant leadership The belief that leaders serve followers by understanding their needs to achieve their work performance. (14)

Sexual harassment Unwelcome conduct of a sexual nature that detrimentally affects the work environment or leads to adverse job-related consequences for its victims. (5) (6) (12)

Shaping The strategy of initially reinforcing crude approximations of the ideal behaviour, then increasing reinforcement standards until only the ideal behaviour is rewarded. (2)

Share options A reward system that gives employees the right to purchase shares from the company at a future date at a predetermined price. (4)

Situational contingencies Environmental conditions beyond the employee's immediate control that constrain or facilitate employee behaviour and performance. (2)

Situational leadership model Suggests that effective leaders vary their style with the "readiness" of followers. (14)

Skill variety The extent to which a job requires employees to use different skills and talents to complete a variety of work activities. (4)

Skill-based pay (SBP) Pay structures in which employees earn higher pay rates with the number of skill modules they have mastered, even though they perform only some of the mastered tasks in a particular job. (4)

Skunkwork A cross-functional team of employees borrowed from several functional areas of the organization to develop new products, services, or procedures, usually in isolation from the organization and without the normal restrictions. (9)

Social identity theory A model that explains self-perception and social perception in terms of our unique characteristics (personal identity) as well as membership in various social groups (social identity). (6)

Social learning theory A theory stating that learning mainly occurs by observing others and then modelling the behaviours that lead to favourable outcomes and avoiding behaviours that lead to punishing consequences. (2)

Social loafing The situation in which people perform at a lower level when working in groups than when working alone. (9)

Social responsibility A person's or an organization's moral obligation towards others who are affected by its actions. (2)

Sociotechnical systems (STS) A theory stating that effective work sites have joint optimization of their social and technological systems, and that teams should have sufficient autonomy to control key variances in the work process. (10)

Span of control The number of people directly reporting to a supervisor. (16)

Stakeholders Shareholders, customers, suppliers, governments, and any other groups with a vested interest in the organization. (1)

Stereotyping The process of using a few observable characteristics to assign people to a preconceived social category, and then assigning less observable traits to those persons based on their membership in the group. (6)

Strategic choice The idea that an organization interacts with its environment rather than being totally determined by it. (16)

Stress An individual's adaptive response to a situation that is perceived to be challenging or threatening to the person's well-being. (5)

Stressor Any environmental condition that places a physical or emotional demand on a person. (5)

Substitutability The extent to which those dependent on a resource have alternative sources of supply of the resource or can use other resources that would provide a reasonable substitute. (12)

Superordinate goal A common objective held by conflicting parties that is more important than their conflicting departmental or individual goals. (13)

Synergy A condition in which the interaction of two or more people produces higher quality and quantity of solutions than if these people worked alone on the problem. (10)

Tacit knowledge Subtle information, acquired through observation and experience, that is not clearly understood and therefore cannot be explicitly communicated. (2) (10)

Task identity The degree to which a job requires completion of a whole or identifiable piece of work. (4)

Task interdependence The degree to which a task requires collective action. High task interdependence exists when team members must share inputs or outcomes, or need to interact while executing their work. (9) (13)

Task performance Goal-directed activities that are under the individual's control. (2)

Task significance The degree to which the job has a substantial impact on the organization and/or larger society. (4)

Team Groups of two or more people who interact and influence each other, are mutually accountable for achieving common objectives, and perceive themselves as a social entity within an organization. (9)

Team-based organization A type of departmentalization with a flat span of control and relatively little formalization, consisting of self-directed work teams responsible for various work processes. (9) (16)

Team building Any formal intervention directed towards improving the development and functioning of a work team. (9)

Team cohesiveness The degree of attraction people feel towards the team and their motivation to remain members. (9)

Team effectiveness The extent to which the team achieves its objectives, achieves the needs and objectives of its members, and sustains itself over time. (9)

Telecommuting (also called *teleworking*) Working from home or another location away from the office, usually with a computer connection to the office. (1) (5)

Theory A general set of propositions that describes interrelationships among several concepts. (Appendix A)

Third-party conflict resolution Any attempt by a relatively neutral person to help the parties resolve their differences. (13)

360-degree feedback Performance feedback is received from a full circle of people around the employee. (2)

Transactional leadership Leadership that helps organizations achieve their current objectives more efficiently by linking job performance to valued rewards and ensuring that employees have the resources needed to get the job done. (14)

Transformational leaders Individuals who form a vision of the desired future state, communicate that vision in ways that are meaningful to others, behave in ways that are consistent with the vision, and build commitment to the vision. (15)

Transformational leadership A leadership perspective that explains how leaders change teams or organizations by creating, communicating, and modelling a vision for the organization or work unit, and inspiring employees to strive for that vision. (14)

Trust Positive expectations about another party's intentions and actions towards us in risky situations. (7) (18)

Type A behaviour pattern A behaviour pattern of people with high risk of premature coronary heart disease; Type As tend to be impatient, lose their temper, talk rapidly, and interrupt others. (5)

Type B behaviour pattern A behaviour pattern of people with low risk of coronary heart disease; Type Bs tend to work steadily, take a relaxed approach to life, and be even-tempered. (5)

Uncertainty avoidance The degree to which people tolerate ambiguity (low uncertainty avoidance) or feel threatened by ambiguity and uncertainty (high uncertainty avoidance). (7)

Unfreezing The first part of the change process whereby the change agent produces a disequilibrium between the driving and restraining forces. (15)

Utilitarianism A moral principle stating that decision makers should seek the greatest good for the greatest number of people when choosing among alternatives. (7)

Valence The anticipated satisfaction or dissatisfaction that an individual feels towards an outcome. (3)

Values Stable, long-lasting beliefs about what is important to the individual. (7) (17)

Variable interval schedule A schedule that reinforces behaviour after it has occurred for a variable period of time around some average. (2)

Variable ratio schedule A schedule that reinforces behaviour after it has occurred a varying number of times around some average. (2)

Virtual corporation An extreme form of network structure in which almost every activity is distributed to satellite organizations in the network. (18)

Virtual teams Cross-functional teams that operate across space, time, and organizational boundaries with members who communicate mainly through electronic technologies. (1) (9)

Visible leadership A management practice of having frequent face-to-face communication with employees so that managers are better informed about employee concerns and organizational activities. (8)

Win-lose orientation A person's belief that the conflicting parties are drawing from a fixed pie, so that his or her gain is the other person's loss. (13)

Win-win orientation A person's belief that the parties will find a mutually beneficial solution to their conflict. (13)

Notes

Chapter One

1 G. James, "Canadian Underdog Shows Its Teeth," *Upside*, May 2000; A. Rivera, "On Today's Show...," *Successful Meetings*, 49 (January 2000), pp. 43–52; J .Bagnall, "Nortel Rides Optic Wave Past Lucent," *Ottawa Citizen*, January 26, 2000; J. Weber and A. Reinhardt, "Racing Ahead at Nortel," *Business Week*, November 8, 1999, pp. 93–99; "Nortel Workers Enjoy Virtual Headspace," *Silicon Valley North* (Toronto edition), July 1999; M. McClearn, "Roth Turning Nortel 'Ship'," *Calgary Herald*, June 9, 1999; J. Greenwood, "All the Right Moves: Make Radical Moves," *Financial Post 500 Magazine*, June 3, 1999, p. 48; Marlene Orton, "The Best and Brightest," *Ottawa Citizen*, March 15, 1999.

2 M.C. Brandon, "The Making of a Merger," *Communication World*, 16 (June–July 1999), pp. 23–25.

3 M. Warner, "Organizational Behavior Revisited," *Human Relations*, 47 (October 1994), pp. 1151–66. The various historical sources are described in T. Takala, "Plato on Leadership," *Journal of Business Ethics*, 17 (May 1998), pp. 785–98; R. Kanigel, *The One Best Way: Frederick Winslow Taylor and the Enigma of Efficiency* (New York: Viking, 1997); M. Weber, *The Theory of Social and Economic Organization*, A.M. Henderson and T. Parsons (trans.) (New York: Oxford University Press, 1947); N. Machiavelli, *The Prince and the Discourses* (New York: Modern Library, 1940); F.J. Roethlisberger and W.J. Dickson, *Management and the Worker* (Cambridge, MA: Harvard University Press, 1939); A. Smith, *The Wealth of Nations* (London: Dent, 1910).

4 L.E. Greiner, "A Recent History of Organizational Behavior," in *Organizational Behavior*, ed. S. Kerr (Columbus, OH: Grid, 1979), pp. 3–14.

5 B. Schlender, "The Three Faces of Steve," *Fortune*, November 9, 1998.

6 R.N. Stern and S.R. Barley, "Organizations as Social Systems: Organization Theory's Neglected Mandate," *Administrative Science Quarterly*, 41 (1996), pp. 146–62; D. Katz and R.L. Kahn, *The Social Psychology of Organizations* (New York: Wiley, 1966), Chapter 2.

7 J. Pfeffer, *New Directions for Organization Theory* (New York: Oxford University Press, 1997), pp. 7–9.

8 "Top Canadian Engineering Achievements of the 20th Century Unveiled," *Canada NewsWire*, March 1, 1999; "Schreyer Award: Confederation Bridge, PEI," *Canadian Consulting Engineer*, 39 (August–September, 1998), pp. 38–42; B. Bergman, "An Engineering Marvel," *Maclean's*, June 2, 1997, p. 34.

9 Etzioni, *Modern Organizations* (Englewood Cliffs, NJ: Prentice-Hall, 1964), p. 1.

10 P.R. Lawrence, "Historical Development of Organizational Behavior," in L.W. Lorsch (ed.), *Handbook of Organizational Behavior* (Englewood Cliffs, NJ: Prentice Hall, 1987), pp. 1–9; D.S. Pugh, "Modern Organizational Theory: A Psychological and Sociological Study," *Psychological Bulletin*, 66 (1966), pp. 235–51. For a contrary view, see A.P. Brief and J.M. Dukerich, "Theory in Organizational Behavior: Can It Be Useful?" *Research in Organizational Behavior*, 13 (1991), pp. 327–52.

11 M.S. Myers, *Every Employee a Manager* (New York: McGraw Hill, 1970).

12 R. Barner, "The New Millennium Workplace: Seven Changes that Will Challenge Managers—and Workers," *The Futurist*, 30 (March 1996), pp. 14–18.

13 Cited in P. Verburg, "New Kid on the Beach," *Canadian Business*, 72 (February 12, 1999), pp. 52–56.

14 H. Schachter, "The 21st Century CEO," *Profit*, 18 (April 1999), pp. 25–35; M.A. Hitt, B.W. Keats, and S.M. DeMarie, "Navigating in the New Competitive Landscape: Building Strategic Flexibility and Competitive Advantage in the 21st Century," *Academy of Management Executive*, 12 (November 1998), pp. 22–42.

15 J. Spears, "How Canadian Will Nortel Be?" *Ottawa Citizen*, January 28, 2000.

16 D.L. Nelson and R.J. Burke, "Lessons Learned," *Canadian Journal of Administrative Sciences*, 15 (December 1998), pp. 372–81; J. Vahtera, M. Kivimaki, and J. Pentti, "Effect of Organizational Downsizing on Health of Employees," *Lancet*, 350 (1997), pp. 1124–28.

17 K.L. Newman and S.D. Nollen, "Culture and Congruence: The Fit Between Management Practices and National Culture," *Journal of International Business Studies*, 27 (1996), pp. 753–78. Early warnings came from A.R. Negandhi and B.D. Estafen, "A Research Model to Determine the Applicability of American Management Knowhow in Different Cultures and/or Environment," *Academy of Management Journal*, 8 (1965), pp. 309–18.

18 P.R. Sparrow, "Reappraising Psychological Contracting: Lessons for the Field of Human-Resource Development from Cross-Cultural and Occupational Psychology Research," *International Studies of Management & Organization*, 28 (March 1998), pp. 30–63; R. Schuler and N. Rogovsky, "Understanding Compensation Practice Variations Across Firms: The Impact of National Culture," *Journal of International Business Studies*, 29 (1998), pp. 159–77.

19 P. Diekmeyer, "From Cellar-Dwellers to Top Sellers," *Montreal Gazette*, June 1, 1999, p. D2.

20 P. Haapaniemi and W.R. Hill, "Not Just for the Big Guys!" *Chief Executive*, September 1998, pp. 62–73.

21 J. Duncanson, "Mostly White, Mostly Male: Why Police Are Reaching Out Again," *Toronto Star*, March 6, 1999, p. 1; R.A. Wanner, "Prejudice, Profit or Productivity: Explaining Returns to Human Capital among Male Immigrants to Canada," *Canadian Ethnic Studies*, 30 (September 1998), pp. 24–55; "Canada's Changing Face," *Maclean's*, December 30, 1996, pp. 38–39; V.M. Esses and R.C. Gardner, "Multiculturalism in Canada: Context and Current Status," *Canadian Journal of Behavioural Science*, 28 (July 1996), pp. 145–52; C.L. Taylor, *Dimensions of Diversity in Canadian Business* (Ottawa: Conference Board of Canada, 1995).

22 P. Rich, "Doctors, Women, Mothers, Wives," *Medical Post*, 34 (December 1, 1998), pp. Suppl. 48–51; D. Mangan, "Remember When...A Women Doctor Was a Rarity?" *Medical Economics*, 75 (May 11, 1998), pp. 225–26.

23 Most writers define Generation X as people born immediately after the baby-boom generation ended (1964) through to around 1977. The exception is University of Toronto professor David Foot, who describes Generation Xers as people born from 1960 to 1964 (i.e., the end of the baby boom). See B. Losyk, "Generation X: What They Think and What They Plan to Do," *The Futurist*, Vol. 31 (March–April 1997), pp. 29–44. For a discussion of Generation X at work and as a consumer in Canada, see R. Barnard , D. Cosgrave , J. Welsh, *Chips and Pop* (Toronto: Malcolm Lester Books, 1998).

24 R. Zemke and B. Filipczak, *Generations at Work: Managing the Clash of Veterans, Boomers, Xers, and Nexters in Your Workplace* (New York: Amacom, 1999); B. Losyk, "Generation X: What They Think and What They Plan to Do," pp. 29–44.

25 D.C. Lau and J.K. Murnighan, "Demographic Diversity and Faultlines: The Compositional Dynamics of Organizational Groups," *Academy of Management Review*, 23 (April 1998), pp. 325–40; G. Robinson and K. Dechant, "Building a Business Case for Diversity," *Academy of Management Executive*, 11 (August 1997), pp. 21–31; J.R.W. Joplin and C.S. Daus, "Challenges of Leading a Diverse Workforce," *Academy of Management Executive*, 11 (August 1997), pp. 32–47.

26 "Mixing Nationalities in the Workplace," *Guardian* (London), November 11, 1999, p. 23.

27 D.L. Nelson and R.J. Burke, "Women Executives: Health, Stress, and Success," *Academy of Management Executive*, May 2000, pp. 107–21.

28 B.H. Peters and J. Peters, "Leadership Redefined," *Across the Board*, June 2000, pp. 48–52.

29 S.D. Friedman, P. Christensen, J. DeGroot, "Work and Life: The End of the Zero-Sum Game," *Harvard Business Review*, 76 (November–December 1998), pp. 119–29.

30 M. Gibb-Clark, "Canadian Workers Satisfied but Anxious," *Globe and Mail*, October 8, 1996, p. B13.

31 A. Clark and T. Davies, "Young, Impatient and Empowered," *Maclean's*, May 17, 1999, p. A3.

32 M. Armstrong-Stassen, "Alternative Work Arrangements: Meeting the Challenges," *Canadian Psychology*, 39 (1998), pp. 108–23; J. Dionne-Proulx, J-C. Bernatchez, and R. Boulard, "Attitudes and Satisfaction Levels Associated with Precarious Employment," *International Journal of Employment Studies*, 6 (1998), pp. 91–114; P. Cappelli et al., *Change at Work* (New York: Oxford

University Press, 1997); M.G. Evans, H.P. Gunz, and R.M. Jalland, "The Aftermath of Downsizing: A Cautionary Tale of Restructuring and Careers," *Business Horizons*, 39 (March 1996), pp. 62–66.

33 P. Kulig, "Temporary Employment Changing the Character of Canada's Labour Force," *Canadian HR Reporter*, November 16, 1998, pp. 1, 15. For a definition of contingent work, see A.E. Polivka, "Contingent and Alternative Work Arrangements, Defined," *Monthly Labour Review*, 119 (October 1996), pp. 3–10; S. Nollen and H. Axel, *Managing Contingent Workers* (New York: AMACOM, 1996), pp. 4–9.

34 M. Saville, "The Future Is e-Me," *Sydney Morning Herald*, February 26, 2000.

35 S.B. Gould, K.J. Weiner, and B.R. Levin, *Free Agents: People and Organizations Creating a New Working Community* (San Francisco: Jossey-Bass, 1997).

36 A 1997 Statistics Canada study revealed that there are over 1 million telecommuters in Canada. From this information, various sources have estimated there will be 1.5 million telecommuters by 2001. See D. Quigley, "Plugged In! Computers Let Millions of Canadians Punch a Clock at Home," *Edmonton Sun*, December 12, 1999, p. SE4; T. Shephard, "Former Sprinters Specialize in Teleworking with Xworx," *Silicon Valley North*, May 1998.

37 D. Finlayson, "The Home Office Blues," *Edmonton Journal*, March 20, 2000; N.B. Kurland and D.E. Bailey, "Telework: The Advantages and Challenges of Working Here, There, Anywhere, and Anytime," *Organizational Dynamics*, 28 (Autumn 1999), pp. 53–68; A. Dunkin, "Saying Adios to the Office," *Business Week*, October 12, 1998; M. Armstrong-Stassen, "Alternative Work Arrangements: Meeting the Challenges," *Canadian Psychology*, 39 (1998), pp. 108–23; J.A. Challenger, "There Is No Future for the Workplace," *Futurist*, 32 (October 1998), pp. 16–20; A. Mahlon, "The Alternative Workplace: Changing Where and How People Work," *Harvard Business Review*, 76 (May–June 1998), pp. 121–30; M. Armstrong-Stassen, N. Solomon, and A. Templer, "Telework and Job Security: A Case Study," 33rd Annual Conference of the Canadian Industrial Relations Association, St. Catharines, Ontario, May 1996.

38 J. Lipnack and J. Stamps, *Virtual Teams: Reaching Across Space, Time, and Organizations with Technology* (New York: John Wiley & Sons, 1997), pp. 5–8; D.J. Armstrong and P. Cole, "Managing Distances and Differences in Geographically Distributed Work Groups," in S.E. Jackson and M.N. Ruderman (eds.), *Diversity in Work Teams: Research Paradigms for a Changing Workplace* (Washington, DC: American Psychological Association, 1995), pp. 187–215.

39 P. Chisholm, "What the Boss Needs to Know," *Maclean's*, May 29, 2000, p. 18; A. Tergesen, "Making Stay-at-Homes Feel Welcome," *Business Week*, October 12, 1998, pp. 155–57.

40 D. Parker, "Web Savvy Captures Bermuda Design Job," *Calgary Herald*, February 28, 2000.

41 J.A. Byrne "The Corporation of the Future," *Business Week*, August 31, 1998, pp. 102–104.

42 W.J. Mitchell, "Do We Still Need Skyscrapers?" *Scientific American*, 277 (December 1997), pp. 112–13.

43 "Teamwork Grows ROOTS in China," *Industry Week*, October 19, 1998, pp. 26–27.

44 T. Stevens, "TRW Canada, Ltd.," *Industry Week*, October 19, 1998, pp. 76–78; P. Kulig, "Reconciling Employer Needs with Employee Wants Is the HR Challenge," *Canadian HR Reporter*, November 2, 1998, p. 2.

45 M. Acharya, "OSC Hearings Promise Dirt on Mining Scandals," *Toronto Star*, February 28, 2000; P. DeMont, "Drug Giants Admit Price Fixing," *Ottawa Citizen*, September 23, 1999; B. Bouw, "Livent Employees Fight Back: Gottlieb to Blame," *National Post*, April 1, 1999, p. C3.

46 M.N. Zald, "More Fragmentation? Unfinished Business in Linking the Social Sciences and the Humanities," *Administrative Science Quarterly*, 41 (1996), pp. 251–61.

47 T.S. Kuhn, *The Structure of Scientific Revolutions* (Chicago: University of Chicago Press, 1970).

48 For an excellent critique of the "one best way" approach of past scholars, see P.F. Drucker, "Management's New Paradigms," *Forbes*, October 5, 1998, pp. 152–77.

49 H.L. Tosi and J.W. Slocum, Jr., "Contingency Theory: Some Suggested Directions," *Journal of Management*, 10 (1984), pp. 9–26.

50 D.M. Rousseau and R.J. House, "Meso Organizational Behavior: Avoiding Three Fundamental Biases," in C.J. Cooper and D.M. Rousseau (eds.), *Trends in Organizational Behavior*, Vol. 1 (Chichester, UK: John Wiley & Sons, 1994), pp. 13–30.

51 P.M. Senge, "Leading Learning Organizations: The Bold, the Powerful, and the Invisible," in F. Hesselbein, M. Goldsmith, and R. Beckhard (eds.), *The Leader of the Future* (San Francisco: Jossey-Bass, 1996), pp. 41–57.

52 P. Senge et al., *The Dance of Change* (New York: Currency Doubleday, 1999), pp. 137–48; A. Waring, *Practical Systems Thinking* (Boston: International Thomson Business Press, 1997); K. Ellis et al. (eds.), *Critical Issues in Systems Theory and Practice* (New York: Plenum, 1995); P.M. Senge, *The Fifth Discipline: The Art and Practice of the Learning Organization* (New York: Doubleday Currency, 1990), Chapter 4; F.E. Kast and J.E. Rosenweig, "General Systems Theory: Applications for Organization and Management," *Academy of Management Journal*, 1972, pp. 447–65.

53 A.A. Atkinson, J.H. Waterhouse, and R.B. Wells, "A Stakeholder Approach to Strategic Performance Measurement," *Sloan Management Review*, 38 (Spring 1997), pp. 25–37; G.T. Savage, T.W. Nix, C.J. Whitehead, and J.D. Blair, "Strategies for Assessing and Managing Organizational Stakeholders," *Academy of Management Executive*, 5 (May 1991), pp. 61–75; R.E. Freeman, *Strategic Management: A Stakeholder Approach* (Marshfield, MA: Pitman Publishing, 1984).

54 C. Cattaneo, "The Man who Saved Suncor," *National Post*, September 11, 1999, p. D1.

55 H. Mintzberg, *The Rise and Fall of Strategic Planning* (New York: Free Press, 1994).

56 M.L. Tushman, M.B. Nadler, and D.A. Nadler, *Competing by Design: The Power of Organizational Architecture* (New York: Oxford University Press, 1997).

57 D. Fenn, "Breakthrough Leadership: Higher Ground," *Inc.*, October 1996, pp. 92–97.

58 E.P. Lima, "Pioneering in People," *Air Transport World*, April 1995, pp. 51–54; "British Airways Encourages Employees to Be Conceited," *Travel Weekly*, October 8, 1992, pp. 41, 42; K. Macher, "Creating Commitment," *Training and Development Journal*, April 1991, pp. 45–52; J. Aspery, "British Companies Meet the Challenge of Change," *IABC Communication World*, 7 (December 1990), pp. 39–41.

59 G.F.B. Probst, "Practical Knowledge Management: A Model That Works," *Prism* (Second Quarter 1998), pp. 17–23; G. Miles, R.E. Miles, V. Perrone, and L. Edvinsson, "Some Conceptual and Research Barriers to the Utilization of Knowledge," *California Management Review*, 40 (Spring 1998), pp. 281–88; E.C. Nevis, A.J. DiBella, and J.M. Gould, "Understanding Organizations as Learning Systems," *Sloan Management Review*, 36 (Winter 1995), pp. 73–85; G. Huber, "Organizational Learning: The Contributing Processes and Literature," *Organizational Science*, 2 (1991), pp. 88–115.

60 F. Belaire, "IC: The Ultimate Renewable Resource," *Silicon Valley North*, 2 (December 1998), p. 16; T.A. Stewart, *Intellectual Capital: The New Wealth of Organizations* (New York: Currency/Doubleday, 1997); H. Saint-Onge, "Tacit Knowledge: The Key to the Strategic Alignment of Intellectual Capital," *Strategy & Leadership*, 24 (March/April 1996), pp. 10–14; G. Petrash, "Dow's Journey to a Knowledge Value Management Culture," *European Management Journal*, 14 (August 1996), pp. 365–73.

61 Relationship capital was initially called customer capital in the knowledge management literature. However, its concept is evolving to relationships among external stakeholders. For example, see D. Halloran, "Putting Knowledge Management Initiatives into Action at Motorola," Presentation by Motorola Vice-President and Director of Human Resources Dan Halloran at The Future of Business in the New Knowledge Economy Conference, March 22–23, 2000, Pan Pacific Hotel, Singapore.

62 B. Hill, "PMC-Sierra Heats Up Talent Hunt," *Ottawa Citizen*, April 14, 2000; J. Bagnall, "Kanata's Instant High-Tech Millionaires," *Ottawa Citizen*, March 4, 2000.

63 Huber, "Organizational Learning," *Organizational Science*.

64 L. Wah, "Behind the Buzz," *Management Review*, 88 (April 1999), pp. 16–19; C.W. Wick and L.S. Leon, "From Ideas to Actions: Creating a Learning Organization," *Human Resource Management*, 34 (Summer 1995), pp. 299–311; D. Ulrich, T. Jick, and M. Von Glinow, "High Impact Learning: Building and Diffusing Learning Capability," *Organizational Dynamics*, 22 (Autumn 1993), pp. 52–66. This is similar to "synthetic learning" described in D. Miller, "A Preliminary Typology of Organizational Learning: Synthesizing the Literature," *Journal of Management*, 22 (1996), pp. 485–505.

65 D. Webb, "Corporate Culture Blocks Better Use of Knowledge," *Computing Canada*, September 1, 1998, p. 77. Also see G.S. Richards and S.C. Goh, "Implementing Organizational Learning: Toward a Systematic Approach," *The Journal of Public Sector Management* (Autumn 1995), pp. 25–31.

66 D.N. Gage, "Knowledge Is King," *ComputerWorld Canada*, 14 (September 11, 1998), pp. 34, 36.

67 Etienne C. Wenger and William M. Snyder, "Communities of Practice: The Organizational Frontier," *Harvard Business Review*, 78 (January–February 2000), pp. 139–45; C. O'Dell and C.J. Grayson, "If Only We Knew What We Know: Identification and Transfer of Internal Best Practices," *California Management Review*, 40 (Spring 1998), pp. 154–74.

68 S. Greengard, "Will Your Culture Support KM?" *Workforce*, 77 (October 1998), pp. 93–94; M. Groves, "Asset Values Shifting as Firms Begin to Account for Employee Brainpower," *Los Angeles Times*, January 18, 1998, p. D5.

69 D.N. Gage, "Knowledge Is King," pp. 34, 36.

70 J. Schmitt, "High-Tech Job Hopping," *USA Today*, August 21, 1998, p. B1.

71 A. Purvis et al., "A New Generation Gap," *Time Canada*, May 31, 1999, pp. 56–57.

72 Stewart, *Intellectual Capital*, Chapter 7.

73 B. Riggs and M.E. Thyfault, "The Modern Call Center—Customer Relationships and Loyalty Take Center Stage," *InformationWeek*, October 4, 1999.

74 D. Lei, J.W. Slocum, and R.A. Pitts, "Designing Organizations for Competitive Advantage: The Power of Unlearning and Learning," *Organizational Dynamics*, 27 (Winter 1999), pp. 24–38; M.E. McGill and J.W. Slocum, Jr., "Unlearn the Organization," *Organizational Dynamics*, 22(2) (1993), pp. 67–79.

75 R. Eade, "Errors Traced to Staff Cuts, Audit Revealed," *Ottawa Citizen*, August 2, 1996, p. B6.

Chapter Two

1 G. Crone, "Home Schooling," *National Post*, January 31, 2000, p. C1; D. Parkes, "Wanted: Skilled Workers," *Montreal Gazette*, November 14, 1999.

2 C.C. Pinder, *Work Motivation in Organizational Behavior* (Upper Saddle River, NJ: Prentice-Hall, 1998); E.E. Lawler III, *Motivation in Work Organizations* (Monterey, CA: Brooks/Cole, 1973), pp. 2–5.

3 J. Kochanski, "Competency-Based Management," *Training & Development*, October 1997, pp. 40–44; Hay Group et al., *Raising the Bar: Using Competencies to Enhance Employee Performance* (Scottsdale, AZ: American Compensation Association, 1996); L.M. Spencer and S.M. Spencer, *Competence at Work: Models for Superior Performance* (New York: Wiley, 1993).

4 Royal Bank of Canada's competencies were described at their Web site on February 14, 2000: www.royalbank.com/careers/workressurv/ron2.html.

5 J.R. Edwards, "Person-Job Fit: A Conceptual Integration, Literature Review, and Methodological Critique," *International Review of Industrial and Organizational Psychology*, 6 (1991), pp. 283–357; J.E. Hunter and R.F. Hunter, "Validity and Utility of Alternative Predictors of Job Performance," *Psychological Bulletin*, 96 (1984), pp. 72–98.

6 S. Pearlstein, "Canadian Stores Take on U.S. Rivals," *Plain Dealer* (Cleveland), January 24, 1999, p. H1; J.W. Johnson, "Linking Employee Perceptions of Service Climate to Customer Satisfaction," *Personnel Psychology*, 19 (1996), pp. 831–51, A. Sharma and D. Sarel, "The Impact of Customer Satisfaction Based Incentive Systems on Salespeople's Customer Service Response: An Empirical Study," *Journal of Personal Selling & Sales Management*, 15 (Summer 1995), pp. 17–29; R.A. Guzzo, R.D. Jette, and R.A. Katzell, "The Effects of Psychologically Based Intervention Programs on Worker Productivity: A Meta-Analysis," *Personnel Psychology*, 38 (1985), pp. 275–91.

7 B. Riggs and M.E. Thyfault, "The Modern Call Center—Customer Relationships and Loyalty Take Center Stage," *InformationWeek*, October 4, 1999.

8 "Crew's Disasterous Response Mars Report on Ferry Safety," *Vancouver Sun*, January 9, 1997, p. B3.

9 L. Ramsay, "Time to Examine the Exam," *National Post*, October 18, 1999, p. C15. The effects of poor role perceptions are studied in S.P. Brown and R.A. Peterson, "The Effect of Effort on Sales Performance and Job Satisfaction," *Journal of Marketing*, 58 (April 1994), pp. 70–80.

10 S.B. Bacharach and P. Bamberger, "Beyond Situational Constraints: Job Resources Inadequacy and Individual Performance at Work," *Human Resource Management Review*, 5 (1995), pp. 79–102; K.F. Kane (ed.), "Special Issue: Situational Constraints and Work Performance," *Human Resource Management Review*, 3 (Summer 1993), pp. 83–175.

11 J.H. Sheridan, "Lockheed Martin Corp.," *Industry Week*, 247 (October 19, 1998), pp. 54–56.

12 D. Yankelovich, "Got to Give to Get," *Mother Jones*, 22 (July 1997), pp. 60–63.

13 A. Derfel, "Nurse Deficit Grows Worse at Children's," *Montreal Gazette*, March 1, 2000.

14 S.M. Jacoby, "Most Workers Find a Sense of Security in Corporate Life," *Los Angeles Times*, September 7, 1998, p. B5.

15 R.W. Griffeth and P.W. Hom, "The Employee Turnover Process," *Research in Personnel and Human Resource Management*, 13 (1995), pp. 245–93.

16 E. Beauchesne, "Employee Sick Days Soar to 72 Million," *Saskatoon Star-Phoenix*, September 2, 1999, p. A1; V. Lu, "Rising Sick Days Cost Billions," *Toronto Star*, August 15, 1999.

17 D.F. Colemen and N.V. Schaefer, "Weather and Absenteeism," *Canadian Journal of Administrative Sciences*, 7(4) (1990), pp. 35–42; S.R. Rhodes and R.M. Steers, *Managing Employee Absenteeism* (Reading, MA: Addison-Wesley, 1990).

18 D. Sefton, "Healthy Workers Tap Sick Days for Family Time," *Times Union* (Albany, NY), November 30, 1998, p. C1.

19 D.A. Harrison and J.J. Martocchio, "Time for Absenteeism: A 20-Year Review of Origins, Offshoots, and Outcomes," *Journal of Management*, 24 (Spring 1998), pp. 305–50; R.D. Hackett and P. Bycio, "An Evaluation of Employee Absenteeism as a Coping Mechanism Among Hospital Nurses," *Journal of Occupational & Organizational Psychology*, 69 (December 1996) pp. 327–38; R.G. Ehrenberg, R.A. Ehrenberg, D.I. Rees, and E.L. Ehrenberg, "School District Leave Policies, Teacher Absenteeism, and Student Achievement," *Journal of Human Resources*, 26 (Winter 1991), pp. 72–105; I. Ng, "The Effect of Vacation and Sick Leave Policies on Absenteeism," *Canadian Journal of Administrative Sciences*, 6 (December 1989), pp. 18–27; V.V. Baba and M.J. Harris, "Stress and Absence: A Cross-Cultural Perspective," *Research in Personnel and Human Resources Management, Supplement 1* (1989), pp. 317–37.

20 J.P. Campbell, R.A. McCloy, S.H. Oppler, and C.E. Sager, "A Theory of Performance," in N. Schmitt, W.C. Borman, and Associates (eds.), *Personnel Selection in Organizations* (San Francisco: Jossey-Bass, 1993), pp. 35–70.

21 S.T. Hunt, "Generic Work Behavior: An Investigation into the Dimensions of Entry-Level, Hourly Job Performance," *Personnel Psychology*, 49 (1996), pp. 51–83.

22 A. Czarnecki, "Customer Service Training: More Than an 'Event'," *Learning for the Workplace* (*Canadian HR Reporter* Supplement), May 20, 1996, pp. L4–L7.

23 C.I. Barnard, *The Functions of the Executive* (Cambridge, MA: Harvard University Press, 1938), pp. 83–84; D. Katz and R.L. Kahn, *The Social Psychology of Organizations* (New York: Wiley, 1966), pp. 337–40.

24 P.M. Podsakoff, M. Ahearne, and S.B. MacKenzie, "Organizational Citizenship Behavior and the Quantity and Quality of Work Group Performance," *Journal of Applied Psychology*, 82 (1997), pp. 262–70; D.W. Organ, "The Motivational Basis of Organizational Citizenship Behavior," *Research in Organizational Behavior*, 12 (1990), pp. 43–72. The discussion of altruism is also based on R.N. Kanungo and J.A. Conger, "Promoting Altruism as a Corporate Goal," *Academy of Management Executive*, 7(3) (1993), pp. 37–48.

25 P. Cappelli and N. Rogovsky, "Employee Involvement and Organizational Citizenship: Implications for Labor Law Reform and 'Lean Production'," *Industrial and Labor Relations Review*, 51 (July 1998), pp. 633–53; R.H. Moorman, G.L. Blakely, and B.P. Niehoff, "Does Perceived Organizational Support Mediate the Relationship Between Procedural Justice and Organizational Citizenship Behavior?" *Academy of Management Journal*, 41 (1998), pp. 351–57; Organ, "The Motivational Basis of Organizational Citizenship Behavior," pp. 60–63.

26 Kanungo and Conger, "Promoting Altruism as a Corporate Goal," p. 42.

27 T.A. Stewart, "Gray Flannel Suit? *Moi?*" *Fortune*, March 16, 1998, pp. 76–82.

28 D.M. Harris and R.L. DeSimone, *Human Resource Development* (Fort Worth, TX: Harcourt Brace, 1994), p. 54; B. Bass and J. Vaughn, *Training in Industry: The Management of Learning* (Belmont, CA: Wadsworth, 1966), p. 8; W. McGehee and P.W. Thayer, *Training in Business and Industry* (New York: Wiley, 1961), pp. 131–34.

29 P. Kulig, "Reconciling Employer Needs with Employee Wants Is the HR Challenge," *Canadian HR Reporter*, November 2, 1998, p. 2.

30 G.F.B. Probst, "Practical Knowledge Management: A Model That Works," *Prism* (Second Quarter 1998), pp. 17–23; G. Miles, R.E. Miles, V. Perrone, and L. Edvinsson, "Some Conceptual and Research Barriers to the Utilization of Knowledge," *California Management Review*, 40 (Spring 1998), pp. 281–88; E.C. Nevis, A.J. DiBella, and J.M. Gould, "Understanding Organizations as Learning Systems," *Sloan Management Review*, 36 (Winter 1995), pp. 73–85; G. Huber, "Organizational Learning: The Contributing Processes and Literature," *Organizational Science*, 2 (1991), pp. 88–115.

31 D. Ulrich, T. Jick, and M. Von Glinow, "High Impact Learning: Building and Diffusing Learning Capability," *Organizational Dynamics*, 22 (Autumn 1993), pp. 52–66.

32 E. Sivadas and F.R. Dwyer, "An Examination of Organizational Factors Influencing New Product Success in Internal and Alliance-Based Processes," *Journal of Marketing*, 64 (January 2000), pp. 31–49; R. Madhavan and R. Grover, "From Embedded Knowledge to Embodied Knowledge: New Product Development as Knowledge Management," *Journal of Marketing*, 62 (October 1998), pp. 1–12; M.G. Evans, "Basic Research, Development and Absorptive Capacity," *Policy Options*, 15(10) (1994), pp. 40–44; W. Cohen and D. Levinthal, "Absorptive Capacity: A New Perspective on Learning and Innovation," *Administrative Science Quarterly*, 35 (1990), pp. 128–52.

33 L. D'Amato, "Learning to Learn," *Kitchener-Waterloo Record*, July 17, 1999, p. D4.

34 R. Madhavan and R. Grover, "From Embedded Knowledge to Embodied Knowledge: New Product Development as Knowledge Management," *Journal of Marketing*, 62 (October 1998), pp. 1–12; D. Leonard and S. Sensiper, "The Role of Tacit Knowledge in Group Innovation," *California Management Review*, 40 (Spring 1998), pp. 112–32; I. Nonaka and H. Takeuchi, *The Knowledge-Creating Company* (New York: Oxford University Press, 1995); R.K. Wagner and R.J. Sternberg, "Practical Intelligence in Real-World Pursuits: The Role of Tacit Knowledge," *Journal of Personality and Social Psychology*, 49 (1985), pp. 436–58.

35 M.J. Kerr, "Tacit Knowledge as a Predictor of Managerial Success: A Field Study," *Canadian Journal of Behavioural Science*, 27 (1995), pp. 36–51.

36 W.F. Dowling, "Conversation with B.F. Skinner," *Organizational Dynamics*, Winter 1973, pp. 31–40.

37 R.G. Miltenberger, *Behavior Modification: Principles and Procedures* (Pacific Grove, CA: Brooks/Cole, 1997); J. Komaki, T. Coombs, and S. Schepman, "Motivational Implications of Reinforcement Theory," in R.M. Steers, L.W. Porter, and G.A. Bigley (eds.), *Motivation and Leadership at Work* (New York: McGraw-Hill, 1996), pp. 34–52; H.P. Sims and P. Lorenzi, *The New Leadership Paradigm: Social Learning and Cognition in Organizations* (Newbury Park, CA: Sage, 1992), Part II.

38 B.F. Skinner, *The Behavior of Organisms* (New York: Appleton-Century-Crofts, 1938).

39 F. Luthans and R. Kreitner, *Organizational Behavior Modification and Beyond* (Glenview, IL: Scott, Foresman, 1985); pp. 85–88; and T.K. Connellan, *How to Improve Human Performance* (New York: Harper & Row, 1978), pp. 48–57.

40 Miltenberger, *Behavior Modification*, Chapters 4–6.

41 T.C. Mawhinney and R.R. Mawhinney, "Operant Terms and Concepts Applied to Industry," in *Industrial Behavior Modification: A Management Handbook*, ed. R.M. O'Brien, A.M. Dickinson, and M.P. Rosow (New York: Pergamon Press, 1982), p. 117; R. Kreitner, "Controversy in OBM: History, Misconceptions, and Ethics," in *Handbook of Organizational Behavior Management*, ed. L.W. Frederiksen (New York: Wiley, 1982), pp. 76–79.

42 Luthans and Kreitner, *Organizational Behavior Modification and Beyond*, pp. 53–54.

43 K.D. Butterfield, L.K. Trevino, and G.A. Ball, "Punishment from the Manager's Perspective: A Grounded Investigation and Inductive Model," *Academy of Management Journal*, 39 (1996), pp. 1479–1512; L.K. Trevino, "The Social Effects of Punishment in Organizations: A Justice Perspective," *Academy of Management Review*, 17 (1992), pp. 647–76.

44 B.S. Klaas and H.N. Wheeler, "Managerial Decision Making about Employee Discipline: A Policy-Capturing Approach," *Personnel Psychology*, 43 (1990), pp. 117–34.

45 Butterfield et al., "Punishment from the Manager's Perspective"; G. Eden, "Progressive Discipline: An Oxymoron?" *Relations Industrielles*, 47 (1992), pp. 511–27; Luthans and Kreitner, *Organizational Behavior Modification and Beyond*, pp. 139–44; J.M. Beyer and H.M. Trice, "A Field Study of the Use and Perceived Effects of Discipline in Controlling Work Performance," *Academy of Management Journal*, 27 (1984), pp. 743–64.

46 G.P. Latham and V.L. Huber, "Schedules of Reinforcement: Lessons from the Past and Issues for the Future," *Journal of Organizational Behavior Management*, 13 (1992), pp. 125–49.

47 F. Luthans and A.D. Stajkovic, "Reinforce for Performance: The Need to Go Beyond Pay and Even Rewards," *Academy of Management Executive*, 13 (May 1999), pp. 49–57; Alexander D. Stajkovic and F. Luthans, "A Meta-Analysis of the Effects of Organizational Behavior Modification on Task Performance, 1975–95," *Academy of Management Journal*, 40 (1997), pp. 1122–49.

48 G. Masek, "Dana Corp.," *Industry Week*, October 19, 1998, p. 48; J. Schilder, "White Water, Safe Passage," *Human Resource Professional*, June 1993, pp. 13–16; K. Cox, "A Drifting Crew Finds an Anchor," *Globe and Mail*, March 23, 1993, p. B22.

49 G.A. Merwin, J.A. Thomason, and E.E. Sanford, "A Methodological and Content Review of Organizational Behavior Management in the Private Sector: 1978–1986," *Journal of Organizational Behavior Management*, 10 (1989), pp. 39–57.

50 P. Drucker, *Management: Tasks, Responsibilities, Practices* (New York: Harper & Row, 1974).

51 Latham and Huber, "Schedules of Reinforcement," pp. 132–33.

52 T.C. Mawhinney, "Philosophical and Ethical Aspects of Organizational Behavior Management: Some Evaluative Feedback," *Journal of Organizational Behavior Management*, 6 (Spring 1984), pp. 5–31; F.L. Fry, "Operant Conditioning in Organizational Settings: Of Mice or Men?" *Personnel*, 51 (July–August 1974), pp. 17–24.

53 D. Brown, "Corp. Culture Change Combats Absenteeism," *Canadian HR Reporter*, November 29, 1999, pp. 1, 16; R. Curren, "Lottery Helps Solve Absenteeism," *Winnipeg Free Press*, November 6, 1999.

54 L. Csoka, *Closing the Human Performance Gap: A Research Report* (New York: Conference Board, 1994).

55 A.N. Kluger and A. DeNisi, "The Effects of Feedback Interventions on Performance: A Historical Review, a Meta-Analysis, and a Preliminary Feedback Intervention Theory," *Psychological Bulletin*, 119 (March 1996), pp. 254–84; A.A. Shikdar and B. Das, "A Field Study of Worker Productivity Improvements," *Applied Ergonomics*, 26 (1995), pp. 21–27; L.M. Sama and R.E. Kopelman, "In Search of a Ceiling Effect on Work Motivation: Can Kaizen Keep Performance 'Risin'?" *Journal of Social Behavior & Personality*, 9 (1994), pp. 231–37.

56 R. Waldersee and F. Luthans, "The Impact of Positive and Corrective Feedback on Customer Service Performance," *Journal of Organizational Behavior*, 15 (1994), pp. 83–95; P.K. Duncan and L.R. Bruwelheide, "Feedback: Use and Possible Behavioral Functions," *Journal of Organizational Behavior Management*, 7 (Fall 1985), pp. 91–114; J. Annett, *Feedback and Human Behavior* (Baltimore: Penguin, 1969).

57 R. Brillinger, "The Many Faces of 360-Degree Feedback," *Canadian HR Reporter*, December 16, 1996, pp. 20–21; P. Jay, "What Goes Around, Comes Around," *Workplace News*, 2 (October 1996), p. 3; M. Marchetti, "Pepsi's New Generation of Employee Feedback," *Sales & Marketing Management*, August 1996, pp. 38–39; C. Kapel, "Performing with Abandon," *Human Resource Professional*, June 1996, pp. 16–18; K. Kein, "Searching 360 Degrees for Employee Evaluation," *Incentive*, October 1996, pp. 40–42.

58 For a discussion of multi-source feedback, see W.W. Tornow and M. London, *Maximizing the Value of 360-degree Feedback: A Process for Successful Individual and Organizational Development* (San Francisco: Jossey-Bass, 1998); D.A. Waldman and L.E. Atwater, *The Power of 360 Feedback: How to Leverage Performance Evaluations for Top Productivity* (Houston, TX: Gulf, 1998); M. Edwards and A. Ewan, *360 Feedback: The Powerful New Model for Employee Assessment & Performance Improvement* (New York: AMACOM, 1996).

59 P.G. Dominick, R.R. Reilly, and J.W. McGourty, "The Effects of Peer Feedback on Team Member Behavior," *Group & Organization Management*, 22 (December 1997), pp. 508–20. Employee concerns with 360-degree feedback are reported in B. Usher and J. Morley, "Overcoming the Obstacles to a Successful 360-Degree Feedback Program," *Canadian HR Reporter*, February 8, 1999, p. 17.

60 A.S. DeNisi and A.N. Kluger, "Feedback Effectiveness: Can 360-Degree Appraisals Be Improved?" *Academy of Management Executive*, 14 (February 2000), pp. 129–39; J. Ghorpade, "Managing Five Paradoxes of 360-Degree Feedback," *Academy of Management Executive*, 14 (February 2000), pp. 140–50.

61 D.M. Herold, R.C. Linden, and M.L. Leatherwood, "Using Multiple Attributes to Assess Sources of Performance Feedback," *Academy of Management Journal*, 1987, pp. 826–35.

62 M. London, "Giving Feedback: Source-Centered Antecedents and Consequences of Constructive and Destructive Feedback," *Human Resource Management Review*, 5 (1995), pp. 159–88; D. Antonioni, "The Effects of Feedback Accountability on 360-Degree Appraisal Ratings," *Personnel Psychology*, 47 (1994), pp. 375–90; S.J. Ashford and G.B. Northcraft, "Conveying More (or Less) Than We Realize: The Role of Impression Management in Feedback Seeking," *Organizational Behavior and Human Decision Processes*, 53 (1992), pp. 310–34; E.W. Morrison and R.J. Bies, "Impression Management in the Feedback-Seeking Process: A Literature Review and Research Agenda," *Academy of Management Review*, 16 (1991), pp. 522–41.

63 J.R. Williams, C.E. Miller, L.A. Steelman, and P.E. Levy, "Increasing Feedback Seeking in Public Contexts: It Takes Two (or More) to Tango," *Journal of Applied Psychology*, 84 (December 1999), pp. 969–76; G.B. Northcraft and S.J. Ashford, "The Preservation of Self in Everyday Life: The Effects of Performance Expectations and Feedback Context on Feedback Inquiry," *Organizational Behavior and Human Decision Processes*, 47 (1990), pp. 42–64.

64 C. Travell, "Nissan Switches Focus to Owner Loyalty as Measure of Success," *Toronto Star*, September 11, 1999, p. 1 (Wheels section); R.D. Pritchard, P.L. Roth, S.D. Jones, and P.G. Roth, "Implementing Feedback Systems to Enhance Productivity: A Practical Guide," *National Productivity Review*, 10 (Winter 1990–1991), pp. 57–67.

65 P.M. Posakoff and J. Fahr, "Effects of Feedback Sign and Credibility on Goal Setting and Task Performance," *Organizational Behavior and Human Decision Processes*, 44 (1989), pp. 45–67.

66 R.D. Guzzo and B.A. Gannett, "The Nature of Facilitators and Inhibitors of Effective Task Performance," in F.D. Schoorman and B. Schneider (eds.), *Facilitating Work Effectiveness* (Lexington, MA: Lexington Books, 1988), p. 23; R.C. Linden and T.R. Mitchell, "Reactions to Feedback: The Role of Attributions," *Academy of Management Journal*, 1985, pp. 291–308.

67 S. Robinson and E. Weldon, "Feedback Seeking in Groups: A Theoretical Perspective," *British Journal of Social Psychology*, 32 (1993), pp. 71–86; S.J. Ashford and L.L. Cummings, "Feedback as an Individual Resource: Personal Strategies of Creating Information," *Organizational Behavior and Human Performance*, 32 (1983), pp. 370–98; S.J. Ashford, "Feedback Seeking in Individual Adaptation: A Resource Perspective," *Academy of Management Journal*, 29 (1986), pp. 465–87.

68 J.M. Mishra and S.M. Crampton, "Employee Monitoring: Privacy in the Workplace?" *SAM Advanced Management Journal*, 63 (June 1998), p. 4; W.S. Brown, "The Rising Rate of Snooping," *Journal of Commerce*, August 7, 1997, p. 8a. The opening sentence paraphrases a quotation from the Office of the Privacy Commissioner of Canada, cited in M. McClearn, "Canadians Begin to Share Author George Orwell's Concern," *Calgary Herald*, September 4, 1999.

69 G. Teel, "Alberta Firms Keep Covert Tabs on Workers," *Calgary Herald*, May 22, 2000; T. Blackwell, "High-Tech Device Keeps Track of Workers," *Ottawa Citizen*, March 30, 2000; D. DeCloet, "The Best and the Worst Discount Brokers: The Good, the Bad, and the Ho-Hum," *Canadian Business*, September 24, 1999, pp. 74–78; E. Church, "Employers Read E-mail as Fair Game," *Globe and Mail*, April 14, 1998, p. B16; M. Drummond, "Are You Watched at Work? Right to Privacy Stops at the Door," *Dayton Daily News*, March 8, 1998, p. 1A.

70 N.B. Fairweather, "Surveillance in Employment: The Case of Teleworking," *Journal of Business Ethics*, 22 (October 1999), pp. 39–49; L.L. McMurchie, "E-mail Opens 'Pandora's Box' of Vulnerabilities," *Computing Canada*, January 15, 1999, p. 14; P. Boniferro, "Workplace Privacy and Surveillance Issues," *Human Resources Professional*, February–March 1999, pp. 49–51; B.E. Bohling, "Workplace Video Surveillance," *Monthly Labor Review*, 120 (July 1997), p. 41.

71 D. Lyon, *The Electronic Eye: The Rise of the Surveillance Society* (Minneapolis, MN: University of Minnesota Press, 1994); B.P. Niehoff and R.H. Moorman, "Justice as a Mediator of the Relationship Between Methods of Monitoring and Organizational Citizenship Behavior," *Academy of Management Journal*, 36 (1993), pp. 527–56; J. Chalykoff and T.A. Kochan, "Computer-Aided Monitoring: Its Influence on Employee Job Satisfaction and Turnover," *Personnel Psychology*, 42 (1989), pp. 807–34.

72 A. Bandura, *Social Foundations of Thought and Action: A Social Cognitive Theory* (Englewood Cliffs, NJ: Prentice Hall, 1986).

73 A. Pescuric and W.C. Byham, "The New Look of Behavior Modeling," *Training & Development*, 50 (July 1996), pp. 24–30; H.P. Sims, Jr., and C.C. Manz, "Modeling Influences on Employee Behavior," *Personnel Journal*, January 1982, pp. 58–65.

74 A.D. Stajkovic and F. Luthans, "Social Cognitive Theory and Self-Efficacy: Going Beyond Traditional Motivational and Behavioral Approaches," *Organizational Dynamics*, 26 (Spring 1998), pp. 62–74; A. Bandura, *Self-Efficacy: The Exercise of Control* (W.H. Freeman & Co., 1996); M.E. Gist and T.R. Mitchell, "Self-Efficacy: A Theoretical Analysis of Its Determinants and Malleability," *Academy of Management Review*, 17 (1992), pp. 183–211; R.F. Mager, "No Self-Efficacy, No Performance," *Training*, 29 (April 1992), pp. 32–36.

75 L.K. Trevino, "The Social Effects of Punishment in Organizations: A Justice Perspective," *Academy of Management Review*, 17 (1992), pp. 647–76; M.E. Schnake, "Vicarious Punishment in a Work Setting," *Journal of Applied Psychology*, 71 (1986), pp. 343–45.

76 M. Foucault, *Discipline and Punish: The Birth of the Prison* (Harmondsworth: Penguin, 1977).

77 L.K. Trevino, "The Social Effects of Punishment in Organizations: A Justice Perspective," *Academy of Management Review*, 17 (1992), pp. 647–76; M.E. Schnake, "Vicarious Punishment in a Work Setting," *Journal of Applied Psychology*, 71 (1986), pp. 343–45.

78 A.W. Logue, *Self-Control: Waiting Until Tomorrow for What You Want Today* (Englewood Cliffs, NJ: Prentice-Hall, 1995); A. Bandura, "Self-Reinforcement: Theoretical and Methodological Considerations," *Behaviorism*, 4 (1976), pp. 135–55.

79 C.A. Frayne, "Improving Employee Performance Through Self-Management Training," *Business Quarterly*, 54 (Summer 1989), pp. 46–50.

80 M. Gibb-Clark, "First Shots That Shook Up Their Lives," *Globe and Mail,* May 15, 1998, p. B23.

81 S. Gherardi, D. Nicolini, and F. Odella, "Toward a Social Understanding of How People Learn in Organizations," *Management Learning*, 29 (September 1998), pp. 273–97; Ulrich, Jick, and Von Glinow, "High Impact Learning."

82 R.P. DeShon and R.A. Alexander, "Goal Setting Effects on Implicit and Explicit Learning of Complex Tasks," *Organizational Behavior and Human Decision Processes*, 65 (1996), pp. 18–36; C.A. Seger, "Implicit Learning," *Psychological Bulletin*, 115 (1994), pp. 163–96.

83 *1995 Environmental Report* (Vancouver: International Forest Products Limited, 1996), p. 7.

84 J. Jusko, "Always Lessons to Learn," *Industry Week*, February 15, 1999, p. 23; A.C. Edmondson, "Learning from Mistakes Is Easier Said Than Done: Group and Organizational Influences on the Detection and Correction of Human Error," *Journal of Applied Behavioral Science*, 32 (1996), pp. 5–28.

85 R.M. Fulmer, P. Gibbs, and J.B. Keys, "The Second Generation Learning Organizations: New Tools for Sustaining Competitive Advantage," *Organizational Dynamics*, 27 (Autumn 1998), pp. 6–20; A.L. Stern "Where the Action Is," *Across the Board*, 34 (September 1997), pp. 43–47; R.W. Revans, "What Is Action Learning?" *Journal of Management Development*, 15 (1982), pp. 64–75.

86 J.A. Conger and K. Xin, "Executive Education in the 21st Century," *Journal of Management Education*, February 2000, p. 73.

87 T.T. Baldwin, C. Danielson, and W. Wiggenhorn, "The Evolution of Learning Strategies in Organizations: From Employee Development to Business Redefinition," *Academy of Management Executive*, 11 (November 1997), pp. 47–58.

Chapter Three

1 B. Sedo, "CEO@30.com," *Hamilton Spectator*, December 16, 1999, p. B4; S. Hays, "Generation X and the Art of the Reward," *Workforce,* 78 (November 1999), pp. 44–48; W. Stephenson, "What Animates These Creators?" *Winnipeg Sun*, November 1, 1999, p.54; M. Walker, "Frantic Success Animation," *Winnipeg Free Press*, September 10, 1998, p. D1; B. Tiernan, "Generations Xers, Employers Adapt to Changes," *Tulsa World*, November 30, 1997, p. E1.

2 C.C. Pinder, *Work Motivation in Organizational Behavior* (Upper Saddle River, NJ: Prentice-Hall, 1998); E.E. Lawler III, *Motivation in Work Organizations* (Monterey, CA: Brooks/Cole, 1973), pp. 2–5.

3 B. Losyk, "Generation X: What They Think and What They Plan to Do," *The Futurist*, 31 (March–April 1997), pp. 29–44; B. Tulgan, *Managing Generation X: How to Bring Out the Best in Young Talent* (Oxford: Capstone, 1996).

4 D.J. McNerney, "Creating a Motivated Workforce," *HR Focus,* August 1996, pp. 1, 4–6. For a Canadian discussion on motivating Generation X (also called the Nexus generation), see R. Barnard, D. Cosgrave, and J. Welsh, *Chips and Pop* (Toronto: Malcolm Lester Books, 1998).

5 An effective critique of "command-and-control" leadership is presented in J.A. Conger, *Winning 'em Over* (New York: Simon & Shuster, 1998), Appendix A.

6 C.C. Pinder, *Work Motivation in Organizational Behavior*, Chapter 3.

7 A.H. Maslow, "A Theory of Human Motivation," *Psychological Review*, 50 (1943), pp. 370–96; A.H. Maslow, *Motivation and Personality* (New York: Harper & Row, 1954).

8 M.A. Wahba and L.G. Bridwell, "Maslow Reconsidered: A Review of Research on the Need Hierarchy Theory," *Organizational Behavior and Human Performance*, 15 (1976), pp. 212–40.

9 C.P. Alderfer, *Existence, Relatedness, and Growth* (New York: The Free Press, 1972).

10 J.P. Wanous and A.A. Zwany, "A Cross-Sectional Test of Need Hierarchy Theory," *Organizational Behavior and Human Performance*, 18 (1977), pp. 78–97.

11 H.M. Weiss and R. Cropanzano, "Affective Events Theory: A Theoretical Discussion of the Structure, Causes, and Consequences of Affective Experiences at Work," *Research in Organizational Behavior*, 18 (1996), pp. 1–74.

12 F. Herzberg, B. Mausner, and B.B. Snyderman, *The Motivation to Work* (New York: Wiley, 1959).

13 A.K. Korman, *Industrial and Organizational Psychology* (Englewood Cliffs, NJ: Prentice-Hall, 1971), p. 149; N. King, "Clarification and Evaluation of the Two Factor Theory of Job Satisfaction," *Psychological Bulletin*, 74 (1970), pp. 18–31.

14 P. Maasland, "How to Build an Employee-Centric Culture," *Computing Canada*, 25 (July 9, 1999), p. 33; D. Leidl, "Little Sweeteners," *BC Business*, 26 (September 1998), pp. 5–60; S. Caudron, "Be Cool!" *Workforce*, 77 (April 1998), pp. 50–61. The motivational value of money is effectively argued in T. Kinni, "Why We Work," *Training*, 35 (August 1998), pp. 34–39.

15 R.M. Steers and L.W. Porter, *Motivation and Work Behavior,* 5th ed. (New York: McGraw-Hill, 1991), p. 413.

16 D.C. McClelland, *The Achieving Society* (New York: Van Nostrand Reinhold, 1961); M. Patchen, *Participation, Achievement, and Involvement on the Job* (Englewood Cliffs, NJ: Prentice-Hall, 1970).

17 G. Scotton, "Pamela Grof's InterVisual on the Fast Lane to Success," *Calgary Herald*, January 10, 2000.

18 For example, see J. Langan-Fox and S. Roth, "Achievement Motivation and Female Entrepreneurs," *Journal of Occupational and Organizational Psychology*, 68 (1995), pp. 209–18; H.A. Wainer and I.M. Rubin, "Motivation of Research and Development Entrepreneurs: Determinants of Company Success, Part I," *Journal of Applied Psychology*, 53 (June 1969), pp. 178–84.

19 D.C. McClelland, "Retrospective Commentary," *Harvard Business Review*, 73 (January–February 1995), pp. 138–39; D. McClelland and R. Boyatzis, "Leadership Motive Pattern and Long-Term Success in Management," *Journal of Applied Psychology,* 67 (1982), pp. 737–43.

20 D.C. McClelland, *The Achieving Society*; R. deCharms and G.H. Moeller, "Values Expressed in American Children's Readers: 1800–1950," *Journal of Abnormal and Social Psychology*, 64 (1962), pp. 136–42.

21 R.J. House and R.N. Aditya, "The Social Scientific Study of Leadership: Quo Vadis?" *Journal of Management*, 23 (1997), pp. 409–73; D.C. McClelland and D.H. Burnham, "Power Is the Great Motivator," *Harvard Business Review*, 73 (January–February 1995), pp. 126–39 (reprinted from 1976).

22 McClelland and Burnham, "Power Is the Great Motivator."

23 D. Vredenburgh and Y. Brender, "The Hierarchical Abuse of Power in Work Organizations," *Journal of Business Ethics*, 17 (September 1998), pp. 1337–47.

24 N. Nejat-Bina, "Employers as Vigilant Chaperones Armed with Dating Waivers: The Interesection of Unwelcomeness and Employer Liability in Hostile Work Environment Sexual Harassment Law," *Berkeley Journal of Employment and Labor Law*, December 22, 1999, p. 325; C. Argyris, "Empowerment: The Emperor's New Clothes," *Harvard Business Review*, May–June 1998, pp. 98–105; C. Hardy and S. Leiba-O'Sullivan, "The Power Behind Empowerment: Implications for Research and Practice," *Human Relations*, 51 (April 1998), pp. 451–83.

25 D.G. Winter, "A Motivational Model of Leadership: Predicting Long-Term Management Success from TAT Measures of Power Motivation and Responsibility," *Leadership Quarterly*, 2 (1991), pp. 67–80.

26 House and Aditya, "The Social Scientific Study of Leadership: Quo Vadis?"

27 D.C. McClelland and D.G. Winter, *Motivating Economic Achievement* (New York: The Free Press, 1969); and D. Miron and D. McClelland, "The Impact of Achievement Motivation Training on Small Business," *California Management Review*, 21 (1979), pp. 13–28.

28 D. Hawaleshka "The Power in the Perks," *Maclean's*, May 31, 1999, p. 24.

29 J. Mills, "Employee Preferences: Choosing the Right Recognition Award," *Canadian HR Reporter*, November 2, 1998, pp. 18, 23.

30 A, Kohn, *Punished by Rewards* (New York: Houghton Mifflin, 1993).

31 Expectancy theory of motivation in work settings originated in V.H. Vroom, *Work and Motivation* (New York: Wiley, 1964). The version of expectancy theory presented here was developed by Edward Lawler. Lawler's model provides a cleaner presentation of the model's three components. P-to-O expectancy is similar to "instrumentality" in Vroom's original expectancy theory model. The difference is that instrumentality is a correlation whereas P-to-O expectancy is a probability. See D.A. Nadler and E.E. Lawler, "Motivation: A Diagnostic Approach," in J.R. Hackman, E.E. Lawler III, and L.W. Porter (eds.), *Perspectives on Behavior in Organizations*, 2nd ed. (New York: McGraw-Hill, 1983), pp. 67–78; J.P. Campbell, M.D. Dunnette, E.E. Lawler, and K.E. Weick, *Managerial Behavior, Performance, and Effectiveness* (New York: McGraw-Hill, 1970), pp. 343–48; E.E. Lawler, *Motivation in Work Organizations* (Monterey, CA: Brooks/Cole, 1973), Chapter 3.

32 Nadler and Lawler, "Motivation: A Diagnostic Approach," pp. 70–73.

33 Lawler, *Motivation in Work Organizations*, pp. 53–55.

34 K.A. Karl, A.M. O'Leary-Kelly, and J.J. Martoccio, "The Impact of Feedback and Self-Efficacy on Performance in Training," *Journal of Organizational Behavior*, 14 (1993), pp. 379–94; T. Janz, "Manipulating Subjective Expectancy Through Feedback: A Labouratory Study of the Expectancy-Performance Relationship," *Journal of Applied Psychology*, 67 (1982), pp. 480–85.

35 K. May, "Managers Rewarded for Presiding over $1B Bungle," *Ottawa Citizen*, January 27, 2000.

36 J.B. Fox, K.D. Scott, and J.M. Donohoe, "An Investigation into Pay Valence and Performance in a Pay-for-Performance Field Setting," *Journal of Organizational Behavior*, 14 (1993), pp. 687–93.

37 Y. Ghahremani, "In the Company of Millionaires," *Asia Week*, March 17, 2000; B. McKenna, "Restructuring Fever Sweeps Japan," *Globe and Mail*, May 29, 1999; M. Tanikawa, "The Corporate Samurai Are Getting Less Loyal," *Business Week*, March 16, 1998; R.M. Hodgetts, "Discussing Incentive Compensation with Donald Hastings of Lincoln Electric," *Compensation and Benefits Review*, 29 (September 1997), pp. 60–66.

38 W. Van Eerde and H. Thierry, "Vroom's Expectancy Models and Work-Related Criteria: A Meta-Analysis," *Journal of Applied Psychology*, 81 (1996), pp. 575–86; T.R. Mitchell, "Expectancy Models of Job Satisfaction, Occupational Preference and Effort: A Theoretical, Methodological, and Empirical Appraisal," *Psychological Bulletin*, 81 (1974), pp. 1053–77.

39 D.D. Baker, R. Ravichandran, and D.M. Randall, "Exploring Contrasting Formulations of Expectancy Theory," *Decision Sciences*, 20 (1989), pp. 1–13; Vroom, *Work and Motivation*, pp. 14–19.

40 M.L. Ambrose and C.T. Kulik, "Old Friends, New Faces: Motivation Research in the 1990s," *Journal of Management*, 25 (May 1999), pp. 231–92; K.C. Snead and A.M. Harrell, "An Application of Expectancy Theory to Explain a Manager's Intention to Use a Decision Support System," *Decision Sciences*, 25 (1994), pp. 499–513.

41 "Commission Withdraws Complaint in Light of Pay Equity Agreement," *M2 Presswire*, September 24, 1999; C. Silverthorn, "Rights Commission Launches Investigation into Safeway Pay Practices," *Canadian Press Newswire*, January 9, 1998.

42 J.S. Adams, "Toward an Understanding of Inequity," *Journal of Abnormal and Social Psychology*, 67 (1963), pp. 422–36; R.T. Mowday, "Equity Theory Predictions of Behavior in Organizations," in *Motivation and Work Behavior*, 5th ed., ed. R.M. Steers and L.W. Porter (New York: McGraw-Hill, 1991), pp. 111–31.

43 G. Blau, "Testing the Effect of Level and Importance of Pay Referents on Pay Level Satisfaction," *Human Relations*, 47 (1994), pp. 1251–68; C.T. Kulik and M.L. Ambrose, "Personal and Situational Determinants of Referent Choice," *Academy of Management Review*, 17 (1992), pp. 212–37; J. Pfeffer, "Incentives in Organizations: The Importance of Social Relations," in *Organization Theory: From Chester Barnard to the Present and Beyond*, ed. O.E. Williamson (New York: Oxford University Press, 1990), pp. 72–97.

44 P.P. Shah, "Who Are Employees' Social Referents? Using a Network Perspective to Determine Referent Others," *Academy of Management Journal*, 41 (June 1998), pp. 249–68; K.S. Law and C.S. Wong, "Relative Importance of Referents on Pay Satisfaction: A Review and Test of a New Policy-Capturing Approach," *Journal of Occupational and Organizational Psychology*, 71 (March 1998), pp. 47–60.

45 "Canadian CEOs Give Themselves Top Marks for Leadership!" *Canada NewsWire*, September 9, 1999.

46 T.P. Summers and A.S. DeNisi, "In Search of Adams' Other: Reexamination of Referents Used in the Evaluation of Pay," *Human Relations*, 43 (1990), pp. 497–511.

47 J.S. Adams, "Inequity in Social Exchange," in *Advances in Experimental Psychology*, ed. L. Berkowitz (New York: Academic Press, 1965), pp. 157–89.

48 J. Barling, C. Fullagar, and E.K. Kelloway, *The Union and Its Members: A Psychological Approach* (New York: Oxford University Press, 1992).

49 L. Greenberg and J. Barling, "Employee Theft," in C.L. Cooper and D.M. Rousseau (eds.), *Trends in Organizational Behavior*, 3 (1996), pp. 49–64.

50 J. Greenberg, "Cognitive Reevaluation of Outcomes in Response to Underpayment Inequity," *Academy of Management Journal*, 32 (1989), pp. 174–84; E. Hatfield and S. Sprecher, "Equity Theory and Behavior in Organizations," *Research in the Sociology of Organizations*, 3 (1984), pp. 94–124.

51 Cited in *Canadian Business*, February 1997, p. 39.

52 J. Rawls, *A Theory of Justice* (Cambridge, MA: Harvard University Press, 1971). For recent discussion of justice and ethics, see M. Schminke, M.L. Ambrose, and T.W. Noel, "The Effect of Ethical Frameworks on Perceptions of Organizational Justice," *Academy of Management Journal*, 40 (October 1997), pp. 1190–1207.

53 R. Folger and R.A. Baron, "Violence and Hostility at Work: A Model of Reactions to Perceived Injustice," in G.R. VandenBos and E.Q. Bulatao (eds.), *Violence on the Job: Identifying Risks and Developing Solutions* (Washington: American Psychological Association, 1996); J. Greenberg, "Stealing in the Name of Justice: Informational and Interpersonal Moderators of Theft Reactions to Underpayment Inequity," *Organizational Behavior and Human Decision Processes*, 54 (1993), pp. 81–103; R.D. Bretz, Jr. and S.L. Thomas, "Perceived Equity, Motivation, and Final-Offer Arbitration in Major League Baseball," *Journal of Applied Psychology*, 77 (1993), pp. 280–87.

54 R.P. Vecchio and J.R. Terborg, "Salary Increment Allocation and Individual Differences," *Journal of Organizational Behavior*, 8 (1987), pp. 37–43.

55 David Beardsley, "This Company Doesn't Brake for (Sacred) Cows," *Fast Company*, 16 (August 1998), pp. 66.

56 For recent research on the effectiveness of goal setting, see L.A. Wilk and W.K. Redmon, "The Effects of Feedback and Goal Setting on the Productivity and Satisfaction of University Admissions

Staff," *Journal of Organizational Behavior Management*, 18 (1998), pp. 45–68; K.H. Doerr and T.R. Mitchell, "Impact of Material Flow Policies and Goals on Job Outcomes," *Journal of Applied Psychology*, 81 (1996), pp. 142–52; A.A. Shikdar and B. Das, "A Field Study of Worker Productivity Improvements," *Applied Ergonomics*, 26 (February 1995), pp. 21–27; M.D. Cooper and R.A. Phillips, "Reducing Accidents Using Goal Setting and Feedback: A Field Study," *Journal of Occupational & Organizational Psychology*, 67 (1994), pp. 219–40.

57 T.H. Poister and G. Streib, "MBO in Municipal Government: Variations on a Traditional Management Tool," *Public Administration Review*, 55 (1995), pp. 48–56.

58 E.A. Locke and G.P. Latham, *A Theory of Goal Setting and Task Performance* (Englewood Cliffs, NJ: Prentice Hall, 1990); A.J. Mento, R.P. Steel, and R.J. Karren, "A Meta-analytic Study of the Effects of Goal Setting on Task Performance: 1966–1984," *Organizational Behavior and Human Decision Processes,* 39 (1987), pp. 52–83; M.E. Tubbs, "Goal-setting: A Meta-analytic Examination of the Empirical Evidence," *Journal of Applied Psychology,* 71 (1986), pp. 474–83.

59 I.R. Gellatly and J.P. Meyer, "The Effects of Goal Difficulty on Physiological Arousal, Cognition, and Task Performance," *Journal of Applied Psychology*, 77 (1992), pp. 694–704; A. Mento, E.A. Locke, and H. Klein, "Relationship of Goal Level to Valence and Instrumentality," *Journal of Applied Psychology*, 77 (1992), pp. 395–405.

60 J.T. Chambers, "The Future of Business," *Executive Excellence*, 17 (February 2000), pp. 3–4; K.R. Thompson, W.A. Hochwarter, and N.J. Mathys, "Stretch Targets: What Makes Them Effective?" *Academy of Management Executive*, 11 (August 1997), pp. 48–60; S. Sherman, "Stretch Goals: The Dark Side of Asking for Miracles," *Fortune*, 132 (November 13, 1995), pp. 231–32.

61 R. Williamson, "Motivation on the Menu," *Globe and Mail*, November 24, 1995, p. B7.

62 H.J. Klein, "Further Evidence of the Relationship Between Goal Setting and Expectancy Theory," *Organizational Behavior and Human Decision Processes*, 49 (1991), pp. 230–57.

63 M.E. Tubbs, "Commitment as a Moderator of the Goal-Performance Relation: A Case for Clearer Construct Definition," *Journal of Applied Psychology,* 78 (1993), pp. 86–97.

64 "Goal-Driven Incentives," *Inc.*, August 1996, p. 91.

65 G.P. Latham, D.C. Winters, and E.A. Locke, "Cognitive and Motivational Effects of Participation: A Mediator Study," *Journal of Organizational Behavior*, 15 (1994), pp. 49–63.

66 J. Chowdhury, "The Motivational Impact of Sales Quotas on Effort," *Journal of Marketing Research,* 30 (1993), pp. 28–41; Locke and Latham, *A Theory of Goal Setting and Task Performance*, Chapters 6 and 7; E.A. Locke, G.P. Latham, and M. Erez, "The Determinants of Goal Commitment," *Academy of Management Review,* 13 (1988), pp. 23–39.

67 P.M. Wright, "Goal Setting and Monetary Incentives: Motivational Tools That Can Work Too Well," *Compensation and Benefits Review* (May–June 1994), pp. 41–49.

68 Adapted from L. Struebing, "Measuring for Excellence," *Quality Progress*, 29 (December 1996), pp. 25–28.

69 F.M. Moussa, "Determinants and Process of the Choice of Goal Difficulty," *Group & Organization Management*, 21 (1996), pp. 414–38.

70 R.P. DeShon and R.A. Alexander, "Goal Setting Effects on Implicit and Explicit Learning of Complex Tasks," *Organizational Behavior and Human Decision Processes*, 65 (1996), pp. 18–36.

71 G. Audia, K.G. Brown, A. Kristof-Brown, and E.A. Locke, "Relationship of Goals and Microlevel Work Processes to Performance on a Multipath Manual Task," *Journal of Applied Psychology*, 81 (1996), pp. 483–97.

72 D.S. Elenkov, "Can American Management Concepts Work in Russia? A Cross-Cultural Comparative Study," *California Management Review*, 40 (Summer 1998), pp. 133–56; N.J. Adler, *International Dimensions of Organizational Behavior*, 3rd ed. (Cincinnati: South-Western, 1997),

Chapter 6; G. Hofstede, "Motivation, Leadership, and Organization: Do American Theories Apply Abroad?" *Organizational Dynamics*, Summer 1980, pp. 42–63.

73 A. Sagie, D. Elizur, and H. Yamauchi, "The Structure and Strength of Achievement Motivation: A Cross-Cultural Comparison," *Journal of Organizational Behavior*, 17 (September 1996), pp. 431–44; D. Elizur, I. Borg, R. Hunt, and I.M. Beck, "The Structure of Work Values: A Cross Cultural Comparison," *Journal of Organizational Behavior*, 12 (1991), pp. 21–38.

74 Elenkov, "Can American Management Concepts Work in Russia?"; N.A. Boyacigiller and N.J. Adler, "The Parochial Dinosaur: Organizational Science in a Global Context," *Academy of Management Review*, 16 (1991), pp. 262–90; Adler, *International Dimensions of Organizational Behavior*, 3rd ed., Chapter 6.

75 D.H.B. Welsh, F. Luthans, and S.M. Sommer, "Managing Russian Factory Workers: The Impact of U.S.-Based Behavioral and Participative Techniques," *Academy of Management Journal*, 36 (1993), pp. 58–79; T. Matsui and I. Terai, "A Cross-Cultural Study of the Validity of the Expectancy Theory of Motivation," *Journal of Applied Psychology*, 60 (1979), pp. 263–65.

76 K.I. Kim, H.-J. Park, and N. Suzuki, "Reward Allocations in the United States, Japan, and Korea: A Comparison of Individualistic and Collectivistic Cultures," *Academy of Management Journal*, 33 (1990), pp. 188–98.

Chapter Four

1 A. Crawford, "Unique IKEA Promotion Rewards Front-Line Workers," *Calgary Herald*, October 25, 1999; "IKEA Workers Likely to Receive $2,500 Bonus," *Kitchener-Waterloo Record*, October 14, 1999, p. F6; J. Pritchett, "IKEA Staff Gets Fat Thank You," *Ottawa Citizen*, October 12, 1999; "IKEA Puts $118m into Workers' Pay," *Edmonton Sun*, October 12, 1999, p. 51.

2 IKEA's salary information comes from one of its two unionized stores in Montreal as stated in P. Tam, "Frugal Founder Rewards Employees," *Ottawa Citizen*, November 21, 1999.

3 S.L. McShane and B. Redekop, "Compensation Management and Canadian Wrongful Dismissal: Lessons from Litigation," *Relations Industrielles*, 45 (1990), pp. 357–80.

4 M.C. Bloom and G.T. Milkovich, "Issues in Managerial Compensation Research," in C.L. Cooper and D.M. Rousseau (eds.), *Trends in Organizational Behavior*, Vol. 3 (Chicester, UK: John Wiley & Sons, 1996), pp. 23–47.

5 M. Leder, "Better Perks Resonate in Boom Times," *New York Times*, November 21, 1999, p. 24; J. Juergens, "Corporate Spotlight: ARCNET," *Incentive*, 173 (September 1999), pp. 68–69.

6 T. Kinni, "Why We Work," *Training*, 35 (August 1998), pp. 34–39; A. Furnham and M. Argyle, *The Psychology of Money* (London: Routledge, 1998); T.L-P. Tang, "The Meaning of Money Revisited," *Journal of Organizational Behavior*, 13 (March 1992), pp. 197–202.

7 Cited in T.R. Mitchell and A.E. Mickel, "The Meaning of Money: An Individual-Difference Perspective," *Academy of Management Review* (July 1999), pp. 568–78.

8 A. Furnham and R. Okamura, "Your Money or Your Life: Behavioral and Emotional Predictors of Money Pathology," *Human Relations*, 52 (September 1999), pp. 1157–77; O. Mellan, "Men, Women & Money," *Psychology Today*, 32 (February 1999), pp. 46–50.

9 T.L-P. Tang, J.K. Kim, and D.S-H. Tang, "Does Attitude Toward Money Moderate the Relationship between Intrinsic Job Satisfaction and Voluntary Turnover?" *Human Relations*, 53 (February 2000), pp. 213–45.

10 "Quarter Century Banquet at Stelco," *Canadian HR Reporter*, December 1998, p. 24; H.Y. Park, "A Comparative Analysis of Work Incentives in U.S. and Japanese Firms," *Multinational Business Review*, 4 (Fall 1996), pp. 59–70.

11 J.M. Newman and F.J. Krzystofiak, "Value-Chain Compensation," *Compensation and Benefits Review*, 30 (May 1998), pp. 60–66.

12 "High-Performing Companies More Successful Using Wide Range of Reward," *Canada NewsWire*, November 8, 1999.

13 R. Thériault, *Mercer Compensation Manual: Theory and Practice* (Boucherville, QC: G. Morin Publisher, 1992), pp. 75–78; R.N. Kanungo and M. Mendonca, *Compensation: Effective Reward Management* (Toronto: Butterworths, 1992), p. 247.

14 M. Gunderson and R.E. Robb, "Equal Pay for Work of Equal Value: Canada's Experience," *Advances in Industrial and Labor Relations*, 5 (1991), pp. 151–68.

15 F.F. Reichheld, *The Loyalty Effect* (Boston, MA: Harvard Business School Press, 1996), p. 137; M. Quaid, *Job Evaluation: The Myth of Equitable Assessment* (Toronto: University of Toronto Press, 1993); S.L. McShane, "Two Tests of Direct Gender Bias in Job Evaluation Ratings," *Journal of Occupational Psychology*, 63 (1990), pp. 129–40.

16 L.M. Spencer and S.M. Spencer, *Competence at Work: Models for Superior Performance* (New York: Wiley, 1993).

17 N. Winter, "Competencies Help Create New Culture," *Canadian HR Reporter*, April 22, 1996, p. 6.

18 N.C. Agarwal, "Reward Systems: Emerging Trends and Issues," *Canadian Psychology*, 39 (February–May 1998), pp. 60–70; D. Hofrichter, "Broadbanding: A 'Second Generation' Approach," *Compensation & Benefits Review*, 25 (September–October 1993), pp. 53–58.

19 D-O. Kim and K. Mericle, "From Job-Based Pay to Skill-Based Pay in Unionized Establishments: A Three-Plant Comparative Analysis," *Relations Industrielles*, 54 (Summer 1999), pp. 549–80; Agarwal, "Reward Systems: Emerging Trends and Issues;" E.E. Lawler III, "From Job-Based to Competency-Based Organizations," *Journal of Organizational Behavior*, 15 (1994), pp. 3–15.

20 E.E. Lawler III, G.E. Ledford, Jr., and L. Chang, "Who Uses Skill-Based Pay, and Why," *Compensation and Benefits Review*, 25 (March–April 1993), pp. 22–26.

21 E.E. Lawler III, "Competencies: A Poor Foundation for the New Pay," *Compensation & Benefits Review*, November–December 1996, pp. 20, 22–26.

22 E. Cowing, "Get Richer by Keeping Your Staff Happy," *Sunday Times* (London), November 28, 1999, p. 20.

23 S. Desker-Shaw "Revving Up Asia's Workers," *Asian Business*, 32 (February 1996), pp. 41–44.

24 E.B. Peach and D.A. Wren, "Pay for Performance from Antiquity to the 1950s," *Journal of Organizational Behavior Management*, 1992, pp. 5–26.

25 A. Swift, "Bombardier and Noranda Profit from Costly Six Sigma Management Technique," *Vancouver Sun*, March 5, 2000.

26 J.S. DeMatteo, L.T. Eby, and E. Sundstrom, "Team-Based Rewards: Current Empirical Evidence and Directions for Future Research," in B.M. Staw and L.L. Cummings (eds.), *Research in Organizational Behavior*, 20 (1998), pp. 141–83; P. Pascarella, "Compensating Teams," *Across the Board*, 34 (February 1997), pp. 16–23; D.G. Shaw and C.E. Schneier, "Team Measurement and Rewards: How Some Companies Are Getting It Right," *Human Resource Planning*, 1995, pp. 34–49.

27 E. Robb, "Call Centre in the Home," *Moncton Times and Transcript*, December 21, 1999, p. C2.

28 T. Pender, "Public Hearings Urged on Winshare," *Kitchener-Waterloo Record*, July 7, 2000; J. Size, "City Staff Enjoy Another Cut of Surplus," *Kitchener-Waterloo Record*, May 4, 1999, p. B1; G. Pearson, "Looking for More Discretionary Effort? A Little Recognition Can Go a Long Way," *Canadian HR Reporter*, July 15, 1996, pp. 19–20.

29 D.P. O'Bannon and C.L. Pearce, "An Exploratory Examination of Gainsharing in Service Organizations: Implications for Organizational Citizenship Behavior and Pay Satisfaction," *Journal*

of Managerial Issues, 11 (Fall 1999), p. 363; C. Cooper and B. Dyck, "Improving the Effectiveness of Gainsharing: The Role of Fairness and Participation," *Administrative Science Quarterly*, 37 (1992), pp. 471–90.

30 M. Gunderson, J. Sack, J. McCartney, D. Wakely, and J. Eaton, "Employee Buyouts in Canada," *British Journal of Industrial Relations*, 33 (September 1995), pp. 417–42; R.J. Long, "The Incidence and Nature of Employee Profit Sharing and Share Ownership in Canada," *Relations Industrielles*, 47 (1992), pp. 463–86.

31 P. Gorham, "Adventures in Compensation," *Benefits Canada*, 23 (May 1999), pp. 20–22.

32 J.M. Newman and M. Waite, "Do Broad-Based Stock Options Create Value?" *Compensation and Benefits Review*, 30 (July 1998), pp. 78–86.

33 T.H. Wagar, and R.J. Long, "Profit Sharing in Canada: Incidence and Predictors," *1995 ASAC Conference, Human Resources Division*, 16(9) (1995), pp. 97–105.

34 K. Kilpatrick and D. Walton, "What a Joy to Work for Dofasco," *Globe and Mail*, February 23, 2000, p. B1.

35 "A Fair Day's Pay," *Economist*, May 8, 1999, p. 12; D. Bencivenga, "Employee-Owners Help Bolster the Bottom Line," *HRMagazine*, 42 (February 1997), pp. 78–83; D. Tyson, *Profit Sharing in Canada* (Toronto: John Wiley & Sons, 1996); J. Chelius and R.S. Smith, "Profit Sharing and Employment Stability," *Industrial and Labor Relations Review*, 43 (1990), pp. 256s–273s.

36 A. Kohn, "Challenging Behaviorist Dogma: Myths About Money and Motivation," *Compensation and Benefits Review*, 30 (March 1998), pp. 27–33; A. Kohn, *Punished by Rewards* (Boston: Houghton Mifflin, 1993); W.C. Hamner, "How to Ruin Motivation with Pay," *Compensation Review*, 7(3) (1975), pp. 17–27.

37 B. Nelson, *1001 Ways to Reward Employees* (New York: Workman Publishing, 1994), p. 148.

38 "Global Survey Finds Common Trends in Ways Top Companies Reward High Performers," *Business Wire*, May 22, 2000; "High-Performing Companies More Successful Using Wide Range of Reward," *Canada NewsWire*, November 8, 1999; J. Pfeffer, *The Human Equation* (Boston: Harvard Business School Press, 1998). For an early summary of research supporting the motivational value of performance-based rewards, see E.E. Lawler III, *Pay and Organizational Effectiveness: A Psychological View* (New York: McGraw-Hill, 1971).

39 S. Kerr, "Organization Rewards: Practical, Cost-Neutral Alternatives That You May Know, but Don't Practice," *Organizational Dynamics,* 28 (Summer 1999), pp. 61–70

40 K. May, "Managers Rewarded for Presiding Over $1B Bungle," *Ottawa Citizen*, January 27, 2000.

41 "New Survey Finds Variable Pay Has Yet to Deliver on Its Promise," *Pay for Performance Report*, March 2000, p. 1; Towers Perrin Inc., *Towers Perrin Workplace Index: How Canadian Employees Really Feel About Their Work* (Toronto: Towers Perrin, 1996).

42 D. Collins, *Gainsharing and Power? Lessons from Six Scanlon Plans* (Ithaca: Cornell University Press, 1998); K.M. Bartol and D.C. Martin, "When Politics Pays: Factors Influencing Managerial Compensation Decisions," *Personnel Psychology,* 43 (1990), pp. 599–614.

43 L. Ramsay, "Time to Examine the Exam," *National Post*, October 18, 1999, p. C15.

44 Kerr, "Organization Rewards."

45 "New Survey Finds Variable Pay Has Yet to Deliver on Its Promise," *Pay for Performance Report*, March 2000, p. 1.

46 S. Chandler, "Sears' System of Rewards Has Ups and Downs," *Chicago Tribune*, February 15, 1998, p. C1.

47 DeMatteo et al., "Team-Based Rewards."

48 R. Wageman, "Interdependence and Group Effectiveness," *Administrative Science Quarterly*, 40 (1995), pp. 145–80.

49 H. Syedain, "The Rewards of Recognition," *Management Today*, May 1995, pp. 72–74.

50 "Dream Teams," *Human Resources Professional*, November 1994, pp. 17–19.

51 S.D. Shaw, "Revving Up Asia's Workers," *Asian Business*, February 1996. The issue of creative rewards is discussed in B. Nelson, "The Ironies of Motivation," *Strategy & Leadership*, 27 (January–February 1999), pp. 26–31.

52 S. Kerr, "On the Folly of Rewarding A, While Hoping for B," *Academy of Management Journal*, 18 (1975), pp. 769–83.

53 D.R. Spitzer, "Power Rewards: Rewards That Really Motivate," *Management Review*, May 1996, pp. 45–50.

54 S. McKay, "Hiring Line Blues," *National Post*, October 1, 1999, p. 52.

55 J. Bagnall, "Kanata's Instant High-Tech Millionaires," *Ottawa Citizen*, March 4, 2000.

56 This definition is more consistent with popular use of the word "job" and with *Webster's Collegiate Dictionary*. However, some scholars have used this definition for a "position" and have defined a "job" as a group of similar positions. See K. Pearlman, "Job Families: A Review and Discussion of Their Implications for Personnel Selection," *Psychological Bulletin*, 87 (January 1980), pp. 1–28.

57 M. Bensaou and M. Earl, "The Right Mind-Set for Managing Information Technology," *Harvard Business Review*, September–October, 1998, pp. 118–28; B.B. Arnetz "Technological Stress: Psychophysiological Aspects of Working with Modern Information Technology," *Scandinavian Journal of Work and Environmental Health*, 23, Suppl. 3 (1997), pp. 97–103; J.W. Medcof, "The Effect of Extent of Use and Job of the User Upon Task Characteristics," *Human Relations*, 42 (1989), pp. 23–41, R.J. Long, *New Office Information Technology: Human and Managerial Implications* (London: Crom Helm, 1987).

58 G.L. Dalton, "The Collective Stretch: Workforce Flexibility" *Management Review*, 87 (December 1998), pp. 54–59; C. Hendry and R. Jenkins, "Psychological Contracts and New Deals," *Human Resource Management Journal*, 7 (1997), pp. 38–44.

59 M. Hequet, "Worker Involvement Lights Up Neon," *Training*, June 1994, pp. 23–29.

60 A. Smith, *The Wealth of Nations* (London: Dent, 1910).

61 M.A. Campion, "Ability Requirement Implications of Job Design: An Interdisciplinary Perspective," *Personnel Psychology*, 42 (1989), pp. 1–24; H. Fayol, *General and Industrial Management*, trans. C. Storrs (London: Pitman, 1949); E.E. Lawler III, *Motivation in Work Organizations* (Monterey, CA: Brooks/Cole, 1973), Chapter 7.

62 For a review of Taylor's work and life, see R. Kanigel, *The One Best Way: Frederick Winslow Taylor and the Enigma of Efficiency* (New York: Viking, 1997). Also see C.R. Littler, "Taylorism, Fordism, and Job Design," in *Job Design: Critical Perspectives on the Labor Process*, ed. D. Knights, H. Willmott, and D. Collinson (Aldershot, UK: Gower Publishing, 1985), pp. 10–29; F.W. Taylor, *The Principles of Scientific Management* (New York: Harper & Row, 1911).

63 E.E. Lawler III, *High-Involvement Management* (San Francisco: Jossey-Bass, 1986), Chapter 6; C.R. Walker and R.H. Guest, *The Man on the Assembly Line* (Cambridge, MA: Harvard University Press, 1952).

64 A. Markels, "Power to the People," *Fast Company*, 13 (February–March 1998), p. 161. For a Canadian discussion of the adverse effects of job specialization, see D.F. Coleman, "Job Characteristics and Work Alienation at Multiple Levels of Analysis," *1996 ASAC Proceedings, Organizational Behaviour Division*, 17(5) (1996), pp. 1–10; J.W. Rhinehart, *The Tyranny of Work*, 2nd ed. (Don Mills, ON: HBJ Canada, 1987).

65 W.F. Dowling, "Job Redesign on the Assembly Line: Farewell to Blue-Collar Blues?" *Organizational Dynamics*, Autumn 1973, pp. 51–67; Lawler, *Motivation in Work Organizations*, p. 150.

66 M. Keller, *Rude Awakening* (New York: HarperPerennial, 1989), p. 128.

67 C.S. Wong and M.A. Campion, "Development and Test of a Task Level Model of Motivational Job Design," *Journal of Applied Psychology*, 76 (1991), pp. 825–37; R.W. Griffin, "Toward an Integrated Theory of Task Design," *Research in Organizational Behavior*, 9 (1987), pp. 79–120.

68 F. Herzberg, B. Mausner, and B.B. Snyderman, *The Motivation to Work* (New York: Wiley, 1959).

69 R.M. Steers and L.W. Porter, *Motivation and Work Behavior*, 5th ed. (New York: McGraw-Hill, 1991), p. 413.

70 J.R. Hackman and G. Oldham, *Work Redesign* (Reading, MA: Addison-Wesley, 1980).

71 "Public Servants Love Their Jobs," *Ottawa Business Journal*, November 11, 1999.

72 A. Daniels, "Independent Brewer Plagued with Success," *Vancouver Sun*, November 29, 1999.

73 G. Johns, J.L. Xie, and Y. Fang, "Mediating and Moderating Effects in Job Design," *Journal of Management*, 18 (1992), pp. 657–76.

74 P.E. Spector, "Higher-Order Need Strength as a Moderator of the Job Scope—Employee Outcome Relationship: A Meta Analysis," *Journal of Occupational Psychology*, 58 (1985), pp. 119–27.

75 P. Osterman, "How Common Is Workplace Transformation and Who Adopts It?" *Industrial and Labor Relations Review*, 47 (1994), pp. 173–88.

76 W. List, "Under the Gun About Safety," *Globe and Mail*, January 4, 1994, p. B14. Also see C. Gannage "Union Women in the Garment Industry Respond to New Managerial Strategies," *Canadian Journal of Sociology*, 20 (1995), pp. 469–95.

77 S. Yaffe and L. Rice-Barker, "CBC: Regs Don't Make Sense," *Playback*, January 24, 2000, p. 1; "Windsor's Enterprise Going Where No TV News Station Has Gone Before," *Broadcaster*, 54 (April 1995), pp. 12–14; H. Enchin, "Video Players," *Globe and Mail*, December 6, 1994, p. B22.

78 N.G. Dodd and D.C. Ganster, "The Interactive Effects of Variety, Autonomy, and Feedback on Attitudes and Performance," *Journal of Organizational Behavior*, 17 (1996), pp. 329–47; M.A. Campion and C.L. McClelland, "Follow-up and Extension of the Interdisciplinary Costs and Benefits of Enlarged Jobs," *Journal of Applied Psychology*, 78 (1993), pp. 339–51.

79 This point is emphasized in C. Pinder, *Work Motivation* (Glenview, IL: Scott, Foresman, 1984), p. 244; and F. Herzberg, "One More Time: How Do You Motivate Employees?" *Harvard Business Review*, 46 (January–February 1968), pp. 53–62. For a full discussion of job enrichment, also see R.W. Griffin, *Task Design: An Integrative Approach* (Glenview, IL: Scott Foresman, 1982); J.R. Hackman, G. Oldham, R. Janson, and K. Purdy, "A New Strategy for Job Enrichment," *California Management Review*, 17(4) (1975), pp. 57 71.

80 C.S. Koberg, R.W. Boss, J.C. Senjem, and E.A. Goodman, "Antecedents and Outcomes of Empowerment," *Group and Organization Management*, 24 (1999), pp. 71–91; R.C. Liden and S. Arad, "A Power Perspective of Empowerment and Work Groups: Implications for Human Resource Management Research," *Research in Personnel and Human Resource Management*, 14 (1996), pp. 205–51; G.M. Spreitzer, "Psychological Empowerment in the Workplace: Dimensions, Measurement, and Validation," *Academy of Management Journal*, 38 (1995), pp. 1442–65; J.A. Conger and R.N. Kanungo, "The Empowerment Process: Integrating Theory and Practice," *Academy of Management Review*, 13 (1988), pp. 471–82.

81 A. Swift, "Bombardier and Noranda Profit from Costly Six Sigma Management Technique," *Vancouver Sun*, March 5, 2000.

82 P. Kulig, "LCBO Has Taste for Training," *Canadian HR Reporter*, August 10, 1998, pp. 1, 10; D. Olive, "Toasting the LCBO's Success," *Financial Post*, June 6, 1998, p. 14.

83 Hackman and Oldham, *Work Redesign*, pp. 137–38.

84 L.R. Comeau, "Re-engineering for a More Competitive Tomorrow," *Canadian Business Review*, Winter 1994, pp. 51–52.

85 P. Osterman, "How Common Is Workplace Transformation and Who Adopts It?"; R.J. Long, "Patterns of Workplace Innovation," *Relations Industrielles*, 44 (1989), pp. 805–26.

86 Y. Fried and G.R. Ferris, "The Validity of the Job Characteristics Model: A Review and Meta-analysis," *Personnel Psychology*, 40 (1987), pp. 287–322; B.T. Loher, R.A. Noe, N.L. Moeller, and M.P. Fitzgerald, "A Meta-Analysis of the Relation of Job Characteristics to Job Satisfaction," *Journal of Applied Psychology*, 70 (1985), pp. 280–89.

87 D.E. Bowen and E.E. Lawler III, "The Empowerment of Service Workers: What, Why, How, and When," *Sloan Management Review*, Spring 1992, pp. 31–39.

88 C-S. Wong, C. Hui, and K.S. Law, "A Longitudinal Study of the Job Perception–Job Satisfaction Relationship: A Test of the Three Alternative Specifications," *Journal of Occupational and Organizational Psychology*, 71 (June 1998), pp. 127–46.

89 G. van der Vegt, B. Emans, and E. van de Vliert, "Motivating Effects of Task and Outcome Interdependence in Work Teams," *Group & Organization Management*, 23 (June 1998), pp. 124–43; J.B. Cunningham, "A Look at Four Approaches to Work Design," *Optimum*, 20(1) (1989/90), pp. 39–55.

90 D.I. Levine, *Reinventing the Workplace* (Washington, DC: Brookings, 1995), pp. 63–66, 86.

91 R. Hodson, "Dignity in the Workplace Under Participative Management: Alienation and Freedom Revisited," *American Sociological Review*, 61 (1996), pp. 719–38; A.C. Frost, "Labour-Management Collaboration Over the Redesign of Work: The Impact of Alternative Approaches," Paper presented at the Organizational Practices and the Changing Employment Relationship Conference, University of British Columbia, October 18–19, 1996; J. Rinehart, "Improving the Quality of Working Life Through Job Redesign: Work Humanization or Work Rationalization?" *Canadian Review of Sociology and Anthropology*, 23 (1986), pp. 507–30.

92 "Bodies for Hire—The Contracting Out Debate," *Workplace Change* (Australia), April 1996, pp. 1–3.

93 Campion, "Ability Requirement Implications of Job Design: An Interdisciplinary Perspective," p. 20; R.B. Dunham, "Relationships of Perceived Job Design Characteristics to Job Ability Requirements and Job Value," *Journal of Applied Psychology*, 62 (1977), pp. 760–63.

94 R. Martin and T.D. Wall, "Attentional Demand and Cost Responsibility as Stressors in Shopfloor Jobs," *Academy of Management Journal*, 32 (1989), pp. 69–86; and D.P. Schwab and L.L. Cummings, "Impact of Task Scope on Employee Productivity: An Evaluation Using Expectancy Theory," *Academy of Management Review*, 1 (1976), pp. 23–35.

95 M. Commanducci, "Training Employees to Be High Performers," *Canadian HR Reporter*, September 7, 1998, pp. 6–7.

96 C.P. Neck and C.C. Manz, "Thought Self-Leadership: The Impact of Mental Strategies Training on Employee Cognition, Behavior, and Affect," *Journal of Organizational Behavior*, 17 (1996), pp. 445–67.

97 C.C. Manz and H.P. Sims, Jr., *Superleadership: Leading Others to Lead Themselves* (Englewood Cliffs, NJ: Prentice-Hall, 1989); C.C. Manz, "Self-Leadership: Toward an Expanded Theory of Self-Influence Processes in Organizations," *Academy of Management Review*, 11 (1986), pp. 585–600.

98 A.M. Saks, R.R. Haccoun, and D. Laxer, "Transfer Training: A Comparison of Self-Management and Relapse Prevention Interventions," *ASAC 1996 Conference Proceedings, Human Resources Division*, 17(9) (1996), pp. 81–91; M.E. Gist, A.G. Bavetta, and C.K. Stevens, "Transfer Training Method: Its Influence on Skill Generalization, Skill Repetition, and Performance Level," *Personnel Psychology*, 43 (1990), pp. 501–23.

99 H.P. Sims, Jr. and C.C. Manz, *Company of Heroes: Unleashing the Power of Self-Leadership* (New York: Wiley, 1996).

100 R.M. Duncan and J.A. Cheyne, "Incidence and Functions of Self-reported Private Speech in Young Adults: A Self-verbalization Questionnaire," *Canadian Journal of Behavioural Science*, 31 (April 1999), pp. 133–36. For an organizational behaviour discussion of constructive thought patterns, see C.P. Neck and C.C. Manz, "Thought Self-Leadership: The Influence of Self-Talk and Mental Imagery on Performance," *Journal of Organizational Behavior*, 13 (1992), pp. 681–99.

101 G.E. Prussia, J.S. Anderson, and C.C. Manz, "Self-leadership and Performance Outcomes: The Mediating Influence of Self-efficacy," *Journal of Organizational Behavior*, September 1998, pp. 523–38; Neck and Manz, "Thought Self-Leadership: The Impact of Mental Strategies Training on Employee Cognition, Behavior, and Affect."

102 Early scholars seem to distinguish mental practice from mental imagery, whereas recent literature combines mental practice with visualizing positive task outcomes within the meaning of mental imagery. For recent discussion of this concept, see C.P. Neck, G.L. Stewart, and C.C. Manz, "Thought Self-Leadership as a Framework for Enhancing the Performance of Performance Appraisers," *Journal of Applied Behavioral Science*, 31 (September 1995), pp. 278–302; W.P. Anthony, R.H. Bennett III, E.N. Maddox, and W.J. Wheatley, "Picturing the Future: Using Mental Imagery to Enrich Strategic Environmental Assessment," *Academy of Management Executive*, 7(2) (1993), pp. 43–56.

103 C. Salter, "This Is Brain Surgery," *Fast Company*, 13 (February–March 1998), pp. 147–50.

104 J.E. Driscoll, C. Cooper, and A. Moran, "Does Mental Practice Enhance Performance?" *Journal of Applied Psychology*, 79 (1994), pp. 481–92.

105 Manz, "Self-Leadership: Toward an Expanded Theory of Self-Influence Processes in Organizations."

106 S. Ross, "Corporate Measurements Shift from Punishment to Rewards," *Reuters*, February 28, 2000.

107 A.W. Logue, *Self-Control: Waiting Until Tomorrow for What You Want Today* (Englewood Cliffs, NJ: Prentice-Hall, 1995).

108 K.E. Thiese and S. Huddleston, "The Use of Psychological Skills by Female Collegiate Swimmers," *Journal of Sport Behavior,* December 1999, pp. 602–10; D. Landin and E.P. Hebert, "The Influence of Self-talk on the Performance of Skilled Female Tennis Players," *Journal of Applied Sport Psychology*, 11 (September 1999), pp. 263–82; C. Defrancesco and K.L. Burke, "Performance Enhancement Strategies Used in a Professional Tennis Tournament," *International Journal of Sport Psychology*, 28 (1997), pp. 185–95; S. Ming and G.L. Martin, "Single-Subject Evaluation of a Self-Talk Package for Improving Figure Skating Performance," *Sport Psychologist*, 10 (1996), pp. 227–38.

109 A.M. Saks and B.E. Ashforth, "Proactive Socialization and Behavioral Self-Management," *Journal of Vocational Behavior*, 48 (1996), pp. 301–23; Neck and Manz, "Thought Self-Leadership: The Impact of Mental Strategies Training on Employee Cognition, Behavior, and Affect."

110 M. Castaneda, T.A. Kolenko, and R.J. Aldag, "Self-Management Perceptions and Practices: A Structural Equations Analysis," *Journal of Organizational Behavior*, 20 (1999), pp. 101–20; G.L. Stewart, K.P. Carson, and R.L. Cardy, "The Joint Effects of Conscientiousness and Self-Leadership Training on Employee Self-Directed Behavior in a Service Setting," *Personnel Psychology*, 49 (1996), pp. 143–64.

Chapter Five

1 K. Guttormson, "Need an Ambulance? Take a Number," *Winnipeg Free Press*, March 26, 2000; L. Nguyen and J. Quinn, "ER Crisis Rivals Worst Ever in GTA," *Toronto Star,* January 4, 2000; M. Potter, "The Prognosis on a Movie," *Toronto Star,* October 26, 1999.

2 G. Kirbyson, "Stressed Out? You're Not Alone," *Winnipeg Free Press,* May 17, 2000; S. Lem, "Snowed Under by Stress," *London Free Press,* February 3, 2000, p. C4; Cross-National Collaborative Group, "The Changing Rate of Major Depression: Cross-National Comparisons," *JAMA: The Journal of the American Medical Association*, 268 (December 2, 1992), pp. 3098–3105.

3 T. Pender, "Region Teachers 'Burning Out,'" *Kitchener-Waterloo Record,* June 9, 2000; J. Corville and L.M. Bernardi, "Helping Employees Manage Stress," *Canadian Manager,* 24 (Fall 1999), pp. 11–13; N. Williams, "Stress Cost Rising, Study Finds," *Toronto Star,* September 8, 1999; S. Felix, "Taking the Sting Out of Stress," *Benefits Canada,* 22 (November 1998), pp. 21–24.

4 From the American Institute of Stress Web site: www.stress.org.

5 N. Chowdhury and S. Menon, "Beating Burnout," *India Today,* June 9, 1997, p. 86; R. Rees, "This Is the Age of the Strain," *Sunday Times,* May 18, 1997.

6 R.S. DeFrank and J.M. Ivancevich, "Stress on the Job: An Executive Update," *Academy of Management Executive,* 12 (August 1998), pp. 55–66; J.C. Quick and J.D. Quick, *Organizational Stress and Prevention Management* (New York: McGraw-Hill, 1984).

7 J.C. Quick, J.D. Quick, D.L. Nelson, and J.J. Hurrell, Jr., *Preventive Stress Management in Organizations* (Washington, DC: American Psychological Association, 1997).

8 S. Sauter and L.R. Murphy (eds.), *Organizational Risk Factors for Job Stress* (Washington, DC: American Psychological Association, 1995).

9 H. Selye, *Stress without Distress* (Philadelphia: J.B. Lippincott, 1974).

10 S.E. Taylor, R.L. Repetti, and T. Seeman, "Health Psychology: What Is an Unhealthy Environment and How Does It Get Under the Skin?" *Annual Review of Psychology,* 48 (1997), pp. 411–47.

11 K. Danna and R.W. Griffin, "Health and Well-Being in the Workplace: A Review and Synthesis of the Literature," *Journal of Management,* Spring 1999, p. 357; Quick and Quick, *Organizational Stress and Prevention Management,* p. 3.

12 S. Melamed and S. Bruhis, "The Effects of Chronic Industrial Noise Exposure on Urinary Cortisol, Fatigue, and Irritability: A Controlled Field Experiment," *Journal of Occupational and Environmental Medicine,* 38 (1996), pp. 252-56.

13 M. Siegall and L.L. Cummings, "Stress and Organizational Role Conflict," *Genetic, Social, and General Psychology Monographs,* 12 (1995), pp. 65–95; E.K. Kelloway and J. Barling, "Job Characteristics, Role Stress and Mental Health," *Journal of Occupational Psychology,* 64 (1991), pp. 291–304; R.L. Kahn, D.M. Wolfe, R.P. Quinn, J.D. Snoek, and R.A. Rosenthal, *Organizational Stress: Studies in Role Conflict and Ambiguity* (New York: Wiley, 1964).

14 G.R. Cluskey and A. Vaux, "Vocational Misfit: Source of Occupational Stress Among Accountants," *Journal of Applied Business Research,* 13 (Summer 1997), pp. 43–54; A. Kristof, "Person-Organization Fit: An Integrative Review of Its Conceptualizations, Measurement, and Implications," *Personnel Psychology,* 49 (1996) pp. 1–50; J.R. Edwards, "An Examination of Competing Versions of the Person-Environment Fit Approach to Stress," *Academy of Management Journal,* 39 (1996), pp. 292–339; B.E. Ashforth and R.H. Humphrey, "Emotional Labor in Service Roles: The Influence of Identity," *Academy of Management Review,* 18 (1993), pp. 88–115.

15 A.M. Saks and B.E. Ashforth, "Proactive Socialization and Behavioural Self-Management." *Journal of Vocational Behaviour,* 48 (1996), pp. 301–23; D.L. Nelson and C. Sutton, "Chronic Work Stress and Coping: A Longitudinal Study and Suggested New Directions," *Academy of Management Journal,* 33 (1990), pp. 859–69.

16 M. Shields, "Long Working Hours and Health [1994-1997 Data]," *Health Reports,* 11 (Fall 1999), pp. 3–48; K. Nishiyama and J.V. Johnson, "Karoshi-Death from Overwork: Occupational Health Consequences of Japanese Production Management," *International Journal of Health Services,* 27 (1997), pp. 625–41.

17 L.D Sargent and D.J. Terry, "The Effects of Work Control and Job Demands on Employee Adjustment and Work Performance," *Journal of Occupational and Organizational Psychology,* 71 (September 1998), pp. 219–36; M.G. Marmot, H. Bosma, H. Hemingway, E. Brunner, and S. Stansfeld, "Contribution of Job Control and Other Risk Factors to Social Variations in Coronary

Heart Disease Incidence," *Lancet,* 350 (July 26, 1997), pp. 235–39; P.M. Elsass and J.F. Veiga, "Job Control and Job Strain: A Test of Three Models," *Journal of Occupational Health Psychology,* 2 (July 1997), pp. 195–211; B.B. Arnetz, "Technological Stress: Psychophysiological Aspects of Working with Modern Information Technology," *Scandinavian Journal of Work and Environment Health,* 23 (1997, Supplement 3), pp. 97–103; R. Karasek and T. Theorell, *Healthy Work: Stress, Productivity, and the Reconstruction of Working Life* (New York: Basic Books, 1990).

18 P. Fayerman, "Job Stress Linked to Control, Says Statistics Canada," *Vancouver Sun,* January 18, 1999, pp. B1, B3.

19 J. MacFarland, "Many Are Called, but What Are the Choices: Working in New Brunswick's 1-800 Call Centres," *New Maritimes,* 14 (July–August 1996), pp. 10–19.

20 D.F. Elloy and A. Randolph, "The Effect of Superleader Behaviour on Autonomous Work Groups in a Government Operated Railway Service," *Public Personnel Management,* 26 (June 1997), pp. 257–72.

21 "Commission Powerless to Enforce Judgment," *London Free Press,* February 21, 2000, p. A7.

22 S.I. Paish and A.A. Alibhai, *Act, Don't React: Dealing with Sexual Harassment in Your Organization* (Vancouver: Western Legal Publications, 1996). For a discussion of these two forms of sexual harassment from the U.S. perspective, see V. Schultz, "Reconceptualizing Sexual Harassment," *Yale Law Journal,* 107 (April 1998), pp. 1683–1805.

23 "Female Mounties Sexually Harassed," *Globe and Mail,* September 27, 1996, p. A6; J. Carlisle, "Sexual Harassment Is Now a Health and Safety Issue," *Financial Post,* July 9, 1996; H. Johnson, "Work-Related Sexual Harassment," *Perspectives on Labour and Income,* Winter 1994, pp. 9–12; A. Picard, "Plagued by Racist Taunts, Teacher Awarded $10,000," *Globe and Mail,* April 14, 1993, p. A4.

24 L.J. Munson, C. Hulin, and F. Drasgow, "Longitudinal Analysis of Dispositional Influences and Sexual Harassement: Effects on Job and Psychological Outcomes," *Personnel Psychology* (Spring 2000), pp. 21–46; L.F. Fitzgerald, F. Drasgow, C.L. Hulin, M.J. Gelfand, and V. Magley, "The Antecedents and Consequences of Sexual Harassment in Organizations: A Test of an Integrated Model," *Journal of Applied Psychology,* 82 (1997), pp. 578–89; C.S. Piotrkowski, "Gender Harassment, Job Satisfaction, and Distress Among Employed White and Minority Women," *Journal of Occupational Health Psychology,* 3 (January 1998), pp. 33–43; J. Barling, I. Dekker, C.A. Loughlin, E.K. Kelloway, C. Fullagar, and D. Johnson, "Prediction and Replication of the Organizational and Personal Consequences of Workplace Sexual Harassment," *Journal of Managerial Psychology,* 11(5) (1996), pp. 4–25.

25 J.H. Neuman and R.A. Baron, "Workplace Violence and Workplace Aggression: Evidence Concerning Specific Forms, Potential Causes, and Preferred Targets," *Journal of Management,* 24 (May 1998), pp. 391–419.

26 G. Lardner, Jr., "Violence at Work Is Largely Unreported," *Washington Post,* July 27, 1998, p. A2.

27 "Bosses Blamed for Work Rage," *London Free Press,* March 15, 2000, p. C4; T. Cole, "All the Rage," *Report on Business Magazine,* January 29, 1999, p. 50; "ILO Survey Reveals Extent of Violence at Work," *Agence France Presse,* July 19, 1998.

28 J.M. Christenson et al., "Violence in the Emergency Department: A Survey of Health Care Workers," *Canadian Medical Association Journal,* 161 (November 16, 1999), pp. 1245–48; L. Fowlie, "Protecting Staff from Violence," *National Post,* May 31, 1999, p. C15.

29 J. Barling, "The Prediction, Experience, and Consequences of Workplace Violence," in G.R. VandenBos and E.Q. Bulatao (eds.), *Violence on the Job: Identifying Risks and Developing Solutions* (Washington, DC: American Psychological Association, 1996), pp. 29–49.

30 C.A. Duffy and A.E. McGoldrick, "Stress and the Bus Driver in the UK Transport Industry," *Stress and Work,* 4 (1990), pp. 17–27.

31 B.L. Galperin, "Impact of Privatization on Stress in Different Cultures," *Proceedings of the Annual ASAC Conference, International Business Division,* 17(8) (1996), pp. 8–16; P.H. Mirvis and M.L. Marks, *Managing the Merger: Making It Work* (Englewood Cliffs, NJ: Prentice-Hall, 1992), Chapter 5.

32 G.A. Adams, L.A. King, and D.W. King, "Relationships of Job and Family Involvement, Family Social Support, and Work-Family Conflict with Job and Life Satisfaction," *Journal of Applied Psychology,* 81 (August 1996), pp. 411–20; S. Lewis and C.L. Cooper, "Balancing the Work/Home Interface: A European Perspective," *Human Resource Management Review,* 5 (1995), pp. 289–305; L. Duxbury, C. Higgins, and C. Lee, "The Impact of Job Type and Family Type on Work–Family Conflict and Perceived Stress: A Comparative Analysis," *Proceedings of the Annual ASAC Conference, Human Resources Division,* 14(9) (1993), pp. 21–30; K.J. Williams and G.M. Alliger, "Role Stressors, Mood Spillover, and Perceptions of Work-Family Conflict in Employed Parents," *Academy of Management Journal,* 37 (1994), pp. 837–68.

33 R. Andrew, "Years of Living Dangerously," *CA Magazine,* March 1999, p. 26.

34 M. Jamal and V.V. Baba, "Shiftwork and Department-Type Related to Job Stress, Work Attitudes and Behavioural Intentions: A Study of Nurses," *Journal of Organizational Behaviour,* 13 (1992), pp. 449–64; C. Higgins, L. Duxbury, and R. Irving, "Determinants and Consequences of Work–Family Conflict," *Organizational Behaviour and Human Decision Processes,* 51 (February 1992), pp. 51–75.

35 "Earning a Life," *London Free Press,* September 6, 1999, p. A8; A. Kyle, "Feeling the Heat," *Regina Leader-Post,* July 15, 1999, p. A1.

36 C.S. Rogers, "The Flexible Workplace: What Have We Learned?" *Human Resource Management,* 31 (Fall 1992), pp. 183–99; L.E. Duxbury and C.A. Higgins, "Gender Differences in Work–Family Conflict," *Journal of Applied Psychology,* 76 (1991), pp. 60–74; and A. Hochschild, *The Second Shift* (New York: Avon, 1989).

37 M.P. Leiter and M.J. Durup, "Work, Home, and In-Between: A Longitudinal Study of Spillover," *Journal of Applied Behavioural Science,* 32 (1996), pp. 29–47; W. Stewart and J. Barling, "Fathers' Work Experiences Effect on Children's Behaviours via Job-Related Affect and Parenting Behaviours," *Journal of Organizational Behaviour,* 17 (1996), pp. 221–32; C.A. Beatty, "The Stress of Managerial and Professional Women: Is the Price Too High?" *Journal of Organizational Behaviour,* 17 (1996), pp. 233–51. Also see D.L. Morrison and R. Clements, "The Effect of One Partner's Job Characteristics on the Other Partner's Distress: A Serendipitous, but Naturalistic, Experiment," *Journal of Occupational and Organizational Psychology,* 70 (December 1997), pp. 307–24; C. Higgins, L. Duxbury, and R. Irving, "Determinants and Consequences of Work–Family Conflict," *Organizational Behaviour and Human Decision Processes,* 51 (February 1992), pp. 51–75.

38 A.S. Wharton and R.J. Erickson, "Managing Emotions on the Job and at Home: Understanding the Consequences of Multiple Emotional Roles," *Academy of Management Review,* 18 (1993), pp. 457–86; S.E. Jackson and C. Maslach, "After-Effects of Job-Related Stress: Families as Victims," *Journal of Occupational Behaviour,* 3 (1982), pp. 63–77.

39 International Labor Office, *World Labor Report* (Geneva: ILO, 1993), Chapter 5; Karasek and Theorell, *Healthy Work.*

40 Quick et al., *Preventive Stress Management in Organizations,* Chapter 3.

41 J.A. Roberts, R.S. Lapidus, and L.B. Chonko, "Salespeople and Stress: The Moderating Role of Locus of Control on Work Stressors and Felt Stress," *Journal of Marketing Theory & Practice,* 5 (Summer 1997), pp. 93–108; J. Schaubroeck and D.E. Merritt, "Divergent Effects of Job Control on Coping with Work Stressors: The Key Role of Self-Efficacy," *Academy of Management Journal,* 40 (June 1997), pp. 738–54; A. O'Leary and S. Brown, "Self-Efficacy and the Physiological Stress Response," in J.E. Maddux (ed.), *Self-Efficacy, Adaptation, and Adjustment: Theory, Research, and Application* (New York: Plenum Press, 1995).

42 S.C. Segerstrom, S.E. Taylor, M.E. Kemeny, and J.L. Fahey, "Optimism Is Associated with Mood, Coping, and Immune Change in Response to Stress," *Journal of Personality & Social Psychology,* 74 (June 1998), pp. 1646–55.

43 K.R. Parkes, "Personality and Coping as Moderators of Work Stress Processes: Models, Methods and Measures," *Work & Stress,* 8 (April 1994), pp. 110–29; S.J. Havlovic and J.P. Keenen, "Coping

with Work Stress: The Influence of Individual Differences," in P.L. Perrewé (ed.), Handbook on Job Stress [Special Issue], *Journal of Social Behaviour and Personality,* 6 (1991), pp. 199–212.

44 B.C. Long and S.E. Kahn (eds.), *Women, Work, and Coping: A Multidisciplinary Approach to Workplace Stress* (Montreal: McGill-Queen's University Press, 1993); E.R. Greenglass, R.J. Burke, and M. Ondrack, "A Gender-Role Perspective of Coping and Burnout," *Applied Psychology: An International Review,* 39 (1990), pp. 5–27; T.D. Jick and L.F. Mitz, "Sex Differences in Work Stress," *Academy of Management Review,* 10 (1985), pp. 408–20.

45 B. Bergman, R. Sheppard, and J. DeMont, "Pressure Point," *Maclean's,* February 7, 2000, p. 48.

46 M. Friedman and R. Rosenman, *Type A Behaviour and Your Heart* (New York: Knopf, 1974). For more recent discussion, see P.E. Spector and B.J. O'Connell, "The Contribution of Personality Traits, Negative Affectivity, Locus of Control and Type A to the Subsequent Reports of Job Stressors and Job Strains," *Journal of Occupational and Organizational Psychology,* 67 (1994), pp. 1–11; K.R. Parkes, "Personality and Coping as Moderators of Work Stress Processes: Models, Methods and Measures," *Work & Stress,* 8 (April 1994), pp. 110–29.

47 M. Jamal and V.V. Baba, "Type A Behaviour, Its Prevalence and Consequences Among Women Nurses: An Empirical Examination," *Human Relations,* 44 (1991), pp. 1213–28; and T. Kushnir and S. Melamed, "Work-Load, Perceived Control and Psychological Distress in Type A/B Industrial Workers," *Journal of Organizational Behaviour,* 12 (1991), pp. 155–68.

48 M. Jamal, "Type A Behaviour and Job Performance: Some Suggestive Findings," *Journal of Human Stress,* 11 (Summer 1985), pp. 60–68; C. Lee, P.C. Earley, and L.A. Hanson, "Are Type As Better Performers?" *Journal of Organizational Behaviour,* 9 (1988), pp. 263–69.

49 E. Greenglass, "Type A Behaviour and Occupational Demands in Managerial Women," *Canadian Journal of Administrative Sciences,* 4 (1987), pp. 157–68.

50 K. Kwong, "Saturday Review," *South China Morning Post,* May 10, 1997, p. 1.

51 R.J. Benschop et al., "Cardiovascular and Immune Responses to Acute Psychological Stress in Young and Old Women: A Meta-Analysis," *Psychosomatic Medicine,* 60 (May–June 1998), pp. 290–96; H. Bosma, R. Peter, J. Siegrist, and M. Marmot, "Two Alternative Job Stress Models and the Risk of Coronary Heart Disease," *American Journal of Public Health,* 88 (January 1998), pp. 68–74; Taylor et al., "Health Psychology" *Annual Review of Psychology;* S. Cohen and T.B. Herbert, "Health Psychology," *Annual Review of Psychology,* 47 (1996), pp. 113–42.

52 S. Cohen, D.A. Tyrrell, and A.P. Smith, "Psychological Stress and Susceptibility to the Common Cold," *New England Journal of Medicine,* 325 (August 29, 1991), pp. 654–56.

53 D.K. Sugg, "Study Shows Link Between Minor Stress, Early Signs of Coronary Artery Disease," *Baltimore Sun,* December 16, 1997, p. A3; C. Nair, F. Colburn, D. McLean, and A. Petrasovits, "Cardiovascular Disease in Canada," *Statistics Canada Health Reports,* 1(1) (1989), pp. 1–22.

54 H.M. Weiss and R. Cropanzano, "Affective Events Theory: A Theoretical Discussion of the Structure, Causes, and Consequences of Affective Experiences at Work," *Research in Organizational Behaviour,* 18 (1996), pp. 1–74.

55 R.C. Kessler, "The Effects of Stressful Life Events on Depression," *Annual Review of Psychology,* 48 (1997), pp. 191–214.

56 R.T. Lee and B.E. Ashforth, "A Meta-analytic Examination of the Correlates of the Three Dimensions of Job Burnout," *Journal of Applied Psychology,* 81 (1996), pp. 123–33; R.J. Burke, "Toward a Phase Model of Burnout: Some Conceptual and Methodological Concerns," *Group and Organization Studies,* 14 (1989), pp. 23–32; C. Maslach, *Burnout: The Cost of Caring* (Englewood Cliffs, NJ: Prentice Hall, 1982).

57 C.L. Cordes and T.W. Dougherty, "A Review and Integration of Research on Job Burnout," *Academy of Management Review,* 18 (1993), pp. 621–56.

58 R.T. Lee and B.E. Ashforth, "A Further Examination of Managerial *Burnout: Toward an Integrated Model,*" *Journal of Organizational Behaviour,* 14 (1993), pp. 3–20.

59 T. Pender, "Region Teachers 'Burning Out,'" *Kitchener-Waterloo Record,* June 9, 2000; R. Turner, "Stressed-Out Teachers Can't Make the Grade," *Winnipeg Free Press,* September 20, 1996, pp. A1, A2; R. Turner, "Teachers Pushed to the Edge," *Winnipeg Free Press,* September 20, 1996, p. A6; C. Dawson, "Study Shows Teachers Stressed," *Calgary Herald,* May 30, 1996, p. B2.

60 Jamal, "Job Stress and Job Performance Controversy: An Empirical Assessment"; G. Keinan, "Decision Making Under Stress: Scanning of Alternatives Under Controllable and Uncontrollable Threats," *Journal of Personality and Social Psychology,* 52 (1987), pp. 638–44; S.J. Motowidlo, J.S. Packard, and M.R. Manning, "Occupational Stress: Its Causes and Consequences for Job Performance," *Journal of Applied Psychology,* 71 (1986), pp. 618–29.

61 R.D. Hackett and P. Bycio, "An Evaluation of Employee Absenteeism as a Coping Mechanism Among Hospital Nurses," *Journal of Occupational & Organizational Psychology,* 69 (December 1996), pp. 327–38; V.V. Baba and M.J. Harris, "Stress and Absence: A Cross-Cultural Perspective," *Research in Personnel and Human Resources Management,* Supplement 1 (1989), pp. 317–37.

62 DeFrank and Ivancevich, "Stress on the Job: An Executive Update"; Neuman and Baron, "Workplace Violence and Workplace Aggression."

63 L. Greenberg and J. Barling, "Predicting Employee Aggression Against Coworkers, Subordinates and Supervisors: The Roles of Person Behaviors and Perceived Workplace Factors," *Journal of Organizational Behavior,* 20 (1999), pp. 897–913; M.A. Diamond, "Administrative Assault: A Contemporary Psychoanalytic View of Violence and Aggression in the Workplace," *American Review of Public Administration,* 27 (September 1997), pp. 228–47.

64 Neuman and Baron, "Workplace Violence and Workplace Aggression"; L. Berkowitz, *Aggression: Its Causes, Consequences, and Control* (New York: McGraw-Hill, 1993).

65 Andrew, "Years of Living Dangerously."

66 Siegall and Cummings, "Stress and Organizational Role Conflict," *Genetic, Social, & General Psychology Monographs;* Havlovic and Keenen, "Coping with Work Stress: the Influence of Individual Differences."

67 T. Newton, J. Handy, and S. Fineman, *Managing Stress: Emotion and Power at Work* (Newbury Park, CA: Sage, 1995).

68 N. Terra, "The Prevention of Job Stress by Redesigning Jobs and Implementing Self-Regulating Teams," in L.R. Murphy (ed.), *Job Stress Interventions* (Washington, DC: American Psychological Association, 1995); T.D. Wall and K. Davids, "Shopfloor Work Organization and Advanced Manufacturing Technology," *International Review of Industrial and Organizational Psychology,* 7 (1992), pp. 363–98; Karasek and Theorell, *Healthy Work.*

69 S. Shellenbarger, "Concern Rises Over Work-Life Conflict," *Orange County Register,* September 29, 1997, p. D18.

70 At least three Canadian surveys have recently indicated that work–life or work–family is a top priority. See Royal Bank of Canada, "Balancing Work, Family and Life," June 18, 1999, at Web site: www.royalbank.com/careers/workressurv/rbaon.html; J. Hampton, "Balancing Between Work and Life," *Canadian HR Reporter,* June 14, 1999, pp. G1–G2; P. Kulig, "Reconciling Employer Needs with Employee Wants Is the HR Challenge," *Canadian HR Reporter,* November 2, 1998, p. 2. For employer views on work–life stress management, see E. Church, "Firms Still Struggling with How to Help Workers Who Care for Others," *Globe and Mail,* June 28, 2000, p. B8.

71 D.J. McNerney, "Contingent Workers: Companies Refine Strategies," *HRFocus,* October 1996, pp. 4–6; B.S. Watson, "Share and Share Alike," *Management Review,* October 1995; T. McCallum, "The Old 'Seven to Three,'" *Human Resources Professional,* June 1995, pp. 12–14.

72 E.J. Hill, B.C. Miller, S.P. Weiner, J. Colihan, "Influences of the Virtual Office on Aspects of Work and Work/Life Balance," *Personnel Psychology,* 51 (Autumn 1998), pp. 667–83; A. Mahlon, "The Alternative Workplace: Changing Where and How People Work," *Harvard Business Review* (May–June 1998), pp. 121–30; M. Armstrong-Stassen, "Alternative Work Arrangements: Meeting the Challenges," *Canadian Psychology,* 39 (1998), pp. 108–23

73 B. Livesey, "Provide and Conquer," *Report on Business Magazine,* March 1997, pp. 34–44; K. Mark, "Balancing Work and Family," *Canadian Banker,* January–February 1993, pp. 22–24; Bureau of Municipal Research, *Work-Related Day Care—Helping to Close the Gap* (Toronto: BMR, 1981).

74 S. Whittaker, "Workplace Stress Wearing," *Montreal Gazette,* March 27, 1999, p. 11.

75 P. DeMont, "Too Much Stress, Too Little Time," *Ottawa Citizen,* November 12, 1999.

76 A. Gordon, "Perks and Stock Options Are Great, but It's Attitude That Makes the Difference," *Globe and Mail,* January 28, 2000; A. Vincola, "Working Sabbaticals Offer Employees More Than Rejuvenation," *Canadian HR Reporter,* November 15, 1999, pp. 11, 13; L. Ramsay, "Good for the Employee, Good for the Employer," *National Post,* July 30, 1999, p. C15.

77 "Asian Nations Graded for Stress," *Daily Commercial News,* April 25, 1996, pp. B1; J.M. Brett, L.K. Stroh, and A.H. Reilly, "Job Transfer," *International Review of Industrial and Organizational Psychology,* 7 (1992), pp. 323–62.

78 T. Balf, "Out of Juice? Recharge!" *Fast Company,* 16 (August 1998), p. 168.

79 S. Felix, "Taking the Sting Out of Stress," *Benefits Canada,* 22 (November 1998), pp. 21–24.

80 A.M. Saks and B.E. Ashforth, "Proactive Socialization and Behavioural Self-Management," *Journal of Vocational Behaviour,* 48 (1996), pp. 301–23; M. Waung, "The Effects of Self-Regulatory Coping Orientation on Newcomer Adjustment and Job Survival," *Personnel Psychology,* 48 (1995), pp. 633–50; J.E. Maddux (ed.), *Self-Efficacy, Adaptation, and Adjustment: Theory, Research, and Application* (New York: Plenum Press, c1995).

81 S. Cordon, "Employers Try to Help Stressed Workers," *Halifax Chronicle-Herald,* September 8, 1999, p. A9.

82 K. Press, J. White, and A. Davis, "The State of Wellness," *Benefits Canada,* 23 (March 1999), pp. 28–39; H. Kohl, "From Stress to Strength," *Financial Post Magazine,* November 1, 1998, p. 165; A.J. Daley and G. Parfitt, "Good Health—Is It Worth It? Mood States, Physical Well-Being, Job Satisfaction and Absenteeism in Members and Non-Members of British Corporate Health and Fitness Clubs," *Journal of Occupational and Organizational Psychology,* 69 (1996), pp. 121–34; L.E. Falkenberg, "Employee Fitness Programs: Their Impact on the Employee and the Organization," *Academy of Management Review,* 12 (1987), pp. 511–22; and R.J. Shephard, M. Cox, and P. Corey, "Fitness Program Participation: Its Effect on Workers' Performance," *Journal of Occupational Medicine,* 23 (1981), pp. 359–63.

83 N. Boomer, "Fitness Boom," *Business Matters Manitoba,* 2 (October 1999).

84 P. Dalby, "Corporate World Has Poor Track Record on Wellness Programs," *Toronto Star,* May 27, 1999.

85 A.S. Sethi, "Meditation for Coping with Organizational Stress," in *Handbook of Organizational Stress Coping Strategies,* A.S. Sethi and R.S. Schuler (Cambridge, MA: Ballinger, 1984), pp. 145–65; M.T. Matteson and J.M. Ivancevich, *Managing Job Stress and Health* (New York: The Free Press, 1982), pp. 160–66.

86 H. Jones, "Walk This Way to a Better Business," *The Independent* (London), March 18, 1998, p. C2; P. Janssen "Refresher Course at Temple," *Asian Business,* August 1995.

87 J. Mackie, "Workplace Workouts," *Vancouver Sun,* December 14, 1998, p. B11.

88 J. McCoy, "Company Stress Programs 'a Sham,'" *Ottawa Citizen,* November 15, 1999; S. MacDonald and S. Wells, "The Prevalence and Characteristics of Employee Assistance, Health

Promotion and Drug Testing Programs in Ontario," *Employee Assistance Quarterly,* 10 (1994), pp. 25–60; R. Loo and T. Watts, "A Survey of Employee Assistance Programs in Medium and Large Canadian Organizations," *Employee Assistance Quarterly,* 8 (1993), pp. 65–71.

89 B.N. Uchino, J.T. Cacioppo, and J.K. Kiecolt-Glaser, "The Relationship Between Social Support and Physiological Processes: A Review with Emphasis on Underlying Mechanisms and Implications for Health," *Psychological Bulletin,* 119 (May 1996), pp. 488–531; M.R. Manning, C.N. Jackson, and M.R. Fusilier, "Occupational Stress, Social Support, and the Costs of Health Care," *Academy of Management Journal,* 39 (June 1996), p. 738; J.M. George, T.F. Reed, K.A. Ballard, J. Colin, and J. Fielding, "Contact with AIDS Patients as a Source of Work-Related Distress: Effects of Organizational and Social Support," *Academy of Management Journal,* 36 (1993), pp. 157–71.

90 J.S. House, *Work Stress and Social Support* (Reading, MA: Addison-Wesley, 1981); S. Cohen and T.A. Wills, "Stress, Social Support, and the Buffering Hypothesis," *Psychological Bulletin,* 98 (1985), pp. 310–57.

91 S. Schachter, *The Psychology of Affiliation* (Stanford, CA: Stanford University Press, 1959).

92 S.L. Dolan and P. Zeilig, "Occupational Stress, Emotional Exhaustion, and Propensity to Quit Amongst Female Accountants: The Moderating Role of Mentoring," *Proceedings of the Annual ASAC Conference, Human Resources Division,* 15(9) (1994), pp. 124–33.

Chapter Six

1 E. Carey, "Police 'Bias' Hits Blacks, Study Says," *Toronto Star,* March 23, 2000, p. GT1; J. Duncanson, "Mostly White, Mostly Male: Why Police Are Reaching Out Again," *Toronto Star,* March 6, 1999, p. 1; W. Immen, "Police Apologize for Second 'Yellow' Slur," *Globe and Mail,* February 16, 1999, p. A1.

2 Plato, *The Republic,* trans. D. Lee (Harmondsworth, UK: Penguin, 1955), Part VII, Section 7.

3 S.F. Cronshaw and R.G. Lord, "Effects of Categorization, Attribution, and Encoding Processes on Leadership Perceptions," *Journal of Applied Psychology,* 72 (1987), pp. 97–106.

4 R.H. Fazio, D.R. Roskos-Ewoldsen, and M.C. Powell, "Attitudes, Perception, and Attention," in P.M. Niedenthal and S. Kitayama (eds.), *The Heart's Eye: Emotional Influences in Perception and Attention* (San Diego, CA: Academic Press, 1994), pp. 197–216.

5 D. Goleman, *Vital Lies, Simple Truths: The Psychology of Deception* (New York: Touchstone, 1985); M. Haire and W.F. Grunes, "Perceptual Defenses: Processes Protecting an Organized Perception of Another Personality," *Human Relations,* 3 (1950), pp. 403–12.

6 J.M. Beyer et al., "The Selective Perception of Managers Revisited," *Academy of Management Journal,* 40 (June 1997), pp. 716–37; C.N. Macrae and G.V. Bodenhausen, "The Dissection of Selection in Person Perception: Inhibitory Processes in Social Stereotyping," *Journal of Personality & Social Psychology,* 69 (1995), pp. 397–407; J.P. Walsh, "Selectivity and Selective Perception: An Investigation of Managers' Belief Structures and Information Processing," *Academy of Management Journal,* 31 (1988), pp. 873–96; D.C. Dearborn and H.A. Simon, "Selective Perception: A Note on the Departmental Identification of Executives," *Sociometry,* 21 (1958), pp. 140–44.

7 J. Rupert, "We Haven't Forgotten About Her," *Ottawa Citizen,* December 6, 1999; W. Burkan, "Developing Your Wide-Angle Vision; Skills for Anticipating the Future," *Futurist,* 32 (March 1998), pp. 35–38. For splatter vision applied to professional birdwatchers, see E. Nickens, "Window on the Wild," *Backpacker,* 25 (April 1997), pp. 28–32.

8 D. Gurteen, "Knowledge, Creativity and Innovation," *Journal of Knowledge Management,* 2 (September 1998), p. 5; C. Argyris and D.A. Schön, *Organizational Learning II* (Reading, MA: Addison-Wesley, 1996); P.M. Senge, *The Fifth Discipline: The Art and Practice of the Learning Organization* (New York: Doubleday Currency, 1990), Chapter 10; P.N. Johnson-Laird, *Mental Models* (Cambridge, UK: Cambridge University Press, 1984). Mental models are widely discussed in the philosophy of logic. For example, see J.L. Aronson, "Mental Models and Deduction," *American Behavioral Scientist,* 40 (May 1997), pp. 782–97.

9   J. Deverell, "Big Steel Strives to Survive," *Toronto Star,* May 31, 1999.

10 "What Are Mental Models?" *Sloan Management Review,* 38 (Spring 1997), p. 13; P. Nystrom and W. Starbuck, "To Avoid Organizational Crises, Unlearn," *Organizational Dynamics,* 12 (Winter 1984), pp. 53–65.

11 T. Abate, "Meet Bill Gates, Stand-Up Comic," *San Francisco Examiner,* March 13, 1996, p. D1; P.J.H. Schoemaker "Scenario Planning: A Tool for Strategic Thinking," *Sloan Management Review,* 36 (Winter 1995), pp. 25–40.

12 P. Roberts, "Sony Changes the Game," *Fast Company,* 10 (1997), p. 116.

13 M.A. Hogg and D.J. Terry, "Social Identity and Self-categorization Processes in Organizational Contexts," *Academy of Management Review,* 25 (January 2000), pp. 121–40; B.E. Ashforth and F. Mael, "Social Identity Theory and the Organization," *Academy of Management Review,* 14 (1989), pp. 20–39; H. Tajfel, *Social Identity and Intergroup Relations* (Cambridge, UK: Cambridge University Press, 1982).

14 J.E. Dutton, J.M. Dukerich, and C.V. Harquail, "Organizational Images and Member Identification," *Administrative Science Quarterly,* 39 (June 1994), pp. 239–63.

15 G. Brenneman, "Right Away and All at Once: How We Saved Continental," *Harvard Business Review,* September–October 1998, pp. 162–79.

16 P. Kruger, "Stop the Fight," *Fast Company,* 17 (September 1998), p. 93.

17 J.W. Jackson and E.R. Smith, "Conceptualizing Social Identity: A New Framework and Evidence for the Impact of Different Dimensions," *Personality & Social Psychology Bulletin,* 25 (January 1999), pp. 120–35.

18 W.G. Stephan and C.W. Stephan, *Intergroup Relations* (Boulder, CO: Westview, 1996), Chapter 1; L. Falkenberg, "Improving the Accuracy of Stereotypes within the Workplace," *Journal of Management,* 16 (1990), pp. 107–18; D.L. Hamilton, S.J. Sherman, and C.M. Ruvolo, "Stereotype-Based Expectancies: Effects on Information Processing and Social Behaviour," *Journal of Social Issues,* 46 (1990), pp. 35–60.

19 S. Johnston, "Oil's Well for Gutsy Women," *Edmonton Sun,* March 7, 1999, p. SE8.

20 S. Madon et al., "The Accuracy and Power of Sex, Social Class, and Ethnic Stereotypes: A Naturalistic Study in Person Perception," *Personality & Social Psychology Bulletin,* 24 (December 1998), pp. 1304–18; L. Jussim, C. McCauley, and Y.T. Lee, "Why Study Stereotype Accuracy and Inaccuracy?" in Y.T. Lee, L. Jussim, and C. McCauley (eds.), *Stereotype Accuracy: Toward an Appreciation of Group Differences* (Washington, DC: American Psychological Association, 1995), pp. 1–23. For early discussion of stereotypes, see W. Lippmann, *Public Opinion* (New York: Macmillan, 1922).

21 D.L. Stone and A. Colella, "A Model of Factors Affecting the Treatment of Disabled Individuals in Organizations," *Academy of Management Review,* 21 (1996), pp. 352–401.

22 C. Stangor and L. Lynch, "Memory for Expectancy-Congruent and Expectancy-Incongruent Information: A Review of the Social and Social Development Literatures," *Psychological Bulletin,* 111 (1992), pp. 42–61; C. Stangor, L. Lynch, C. Duan, and B. Glass, "Categorization of Individuals on the Basis of Multiple Social Features," *Journal of Personality and Social Psychology,* 62 (1992), pp. 207–18.

23 P.J. Oaks, S.A. Haslam, and J.C. Turner, *Stereotyping and Social Reality* (Cambridge, MA: Blackwell, 1994).

24 C.N. Macrae, A.B. Milne, and G.V. Bodenhausen, "Stereotypes as Energy-Saving Devices: A Peek Inside the Cognitive Toolbox," *Journal of Personality and Social Psychology,* 66 (1994), pp. 37–47; S.T. Fiske, "Social Cognition and Social Perception," *Annual Review of Psychology,* 44 (1993), pp. 155–94.

25 Z. Kunda and P. Thagard, "Forming Impressions from Stereotypes, Traits, and Behaviours: A Parallel-Constraint Satisfaction Theory," *Psychological Review,* 103 (1996), pp. 284–308.

26 S.O. Gaines and E.S. Reed, "Prejudice: From Allport to DuBois," *American Psychologist, 50* (February 1995), pp. 96–103; L. Jussim and T.E. Nelson, "Prejudice, Stereotypes, and Labeling Effects: Sources of Bias in Person Perception," *Journal of Personality & Social Psychology,* 68 (February 1995), pp. 228–46.

27 M. King, "'Scary' Driver Alleges Racism," *Montreal Gazette,* March 16, 2000; H. Horwood, "Keg Wrongly Fired Two Moms-to-Be," *Vancouver Province,* March 12, 2000.

28 D. McCauley, "Women Chefs: Shattering the Glass Ceiling," *Foodservice and Hospitality,"* January 1996, pp. 25–30.

29 A.P. Brief et al., "Beyond Good Intentions: The Next Steps Toward Racial Equality in the American Workplace," *Academy of Management Executive, 11* (November 1997), pp. 59–72; M.J. Monteith, "Self-Regulation of Prejudiced Responses: Implications for Progress in Prejudice-Reduction Efforts," *Journal of Personality and Social Psychology,* 65 (1993), pp. 469–85.

30 P.M. Buzzanell, "Reframing the Glass Ceiling as a Socially Constructed Process: Implications for Understanding and Change," *Communication Monographs,* 62 (December 1995), pp. 327–54; M.E. Heilman, "Sex Stereotypes and Their Effects in the Workplace: What We Know and What We Don't Know," *Journal of Social Behaviour & Personality,* 10 (1995), pp. 3–26.

31 D.L. Nelson and R.J. Burke, "Women Executives: Health, Stress, and Success," *Academy of Management Executive,* May 2000, pp. 107–21; R.F. Maruca, "Says Who?" *Harvard Business Review,* 75 (November–December 1997), pp. 15–17.

32 L. Everett, D. Thorne, and C. Danehower, "Cognitive Moral Development and Attitudes Toward Women Executives," *Journal of Business Ethics,* 15 (November 1996), pp. 1227–35; J.M. Norris and A.M. Wylie, "Gender Stereotyping of the Managerial Role Among Students in Canada and the United States," *Group & Organization Management,* 20 (1995), pp. 167–82; R.J. Burke, "Canadian Business Students' Attitudes Towards Women as Managers," *Psychological Reports,* 75 (1994), pp. 1123–29; S. Coate and G.C. Loury, "Will Affirmative-Action Policies Eliminate Negative Stereotypes?" *American Economic Review,* 83 (1993), pp. 1220–40; C.L. Owen and W.D. Todor, "Attitudes Toward Women as Managers: Still the Same," *Business Horizons,* 36 (March–April 1993), pp. 12–16; V.E. Schein and R. Mueller, "Sex Role Stereotyping and Requisite Management Characteristics: A Cross Cultural Look," *Journal of Organizational Behaviour,* 13 (1992), pp. 439–47; O.C. Bremmer, J. Tomkiewicz, and V.E. Schein, "The Relationship Between Sex Role Stereotypes and Requisite Management Characteristics Revisited," *Academy of Management Journal,* 32 (1989), pp. 662–69.

33 S.T. Fiske and P. Glick, "Ambivalence and Stereotypes Cause Sexual Harassment: A Theory with Implications for Organizational Change," *Journal of Social Issues,* 51 (1995), pp. 97–115; K. Deaux, "How Basic Can You Be? The Evolution of Research on Gender Stereotypes," *Journal of Social Issues,* 51 (1995), pp. 11–20.

34 E. Rosell and K. Miller, "Firefighting Women and Sexual Harassment," *Public Personnel Management,* 24 (Fall 1995), pp. 339–50.

35 H.H. Kelley, *Attribution in Social Interaction* (Morristown, NJ: General Learning Press, 1971).

36 H.H. Kelley, "The Processes of Causal Attribution," *American Psychologist,* 28 (1973), pp. 107–28; J.M. Feldman, "Beyond Attribution Theory: Cognitive Processes in Performance Appraisal," *Journal of Applied Psychology,* 66 (1981), pp. 127–48.

37 J.D. Ford, "The Effects of Causal Attributions on Decision Makers' Responses to Performance Downturns," *Academy of Management Review,* 10 (1985), pp. 770–86; M.J. Martinko and W.L. Gardner, "The Leader/Member Attribution Process," *Academy of Management Review,* 12 (1987), pp. 235–49.

38 B. Bemmels, "Attribution Theory and Discipline Arbitration," *Industrial and Labor Relations Review,* 44 (April 1991), pp. 548–62.

39 J.M. Crant and T.S. Bateman, "Assignment of Credit and Blame for Performance Outcomes," *Academy of Management Journal,* 36 (1993), pp. 7–27.

40 J. Martocchio and J. Dulebohn, "Performance Feedback Effects in Training: The Role of Perceived Controllability," *Personnel Psychology,* 47 (1994), pp. 357–73; D.R. Norris and R.E. Niebuhr, "Attributional Influences on the Job Performance-Job Satisfaction Relationship," *Academy of Management Journal,* 27 (1984), pp. 424–31.

41 H.J. Bernardin and P. Villanova, "Performance Appraisal," in *Generalizing from Laboratory to Field Settings,* ed. E.A. Locke (Lexington, MA: Lexington Books, 1986), pp. 43–62; S.G. Green and T.R. Mitchell, "Attributional Processes of Leader-Member Interactions," *Organizational Behaviour and Human Performance,* 23 (1979), pp. 429–58.

42 J.R. Bettman and B.A. Weitz, "Attributions in the Board Room: Causal Reasoning in Corporate Annual Reports," *Administrative Science Quarterly,* 28 (1983), pp. 165–83.

43 P. Rosenthal and D. Guest, "Gender Difference in Managers' Causal Explanations for Their Work Performance: A Study in Two Organizations," *Journal of Occupational & Organizational Psychology,* 69 (1996), pp. 145–51.

44 "The Motive Isn't Money," *Profit,* 14 (Spring 1995), pp. 20–29.

45 J.M. Darley and K.C. Oleson, "Introduction to Research on Interpersonal Expectations," in *Interpersonal Expectations: Theory, Research, and Applications* (Cambridge, UK: Cambridge University Press, 1993), pp. 45–63; D. Eden, *Pygmalion in Management* (Lexington, MA: Lexington, 1990); L. Jussim, "Self-Fulfilling Prophecies: A Theoretical and Integrative Review," *Psychological Review,* 93 (1986), pp. 429–45.

46 Similar models are presented in R.H.G. Field and D.A. Van Seters, "Management by Expectations (MBE): The Power of Positive Prophecy," *Journal of General Management,* 14 (Winter 1988), pp. 19–33; D. Eden, "Self-Fulfilling Prophecy as a Management Tool: Harnessing Pygmalion," *Academy of Management Review,* 9 (1984), pp. 64–73.

47 M.J. Harris and R. Rosenthal, "Mediation of Interpersonal Expectancy Effects: 31 Meta-Analyses," *Psychological Bulletin,* 97 (1985), pp. 363–86.

48 D. Eden, "Interpersonal Expectations in Organizations," in *Interpersonal Expectations: Theory, Research, and Applications* (Cambridge, UK: Cambridge University Press, 1993), pp. 154–78.

49 A. Bandura, *Self-Efficacy: The Exercise of Control* (W.H. Freeman & Co., 1996); M.E. Gist and T.R. Mitchell, "Self-Efficacy: A Theoretical Analysis of Its Determinants and Malleability," *Academy of Management Review,* 17 (1992), pp. 183–211.

50 P.D. Blanck, "Interpersonal Expectations in the Courtroom: Studying Judges' and Juries' Behaviour," in *Interpersonal Expectations: Theory, Research, and Applications* (Cambridge, UK: Cambridge University Press, 1993), pp. 64–87; J.B. Rosser, Jr., "Belief: Its Role in Economic Thought and Action," *American Journal of Economics & Sociology,* 52 (1993), pp. 355–68; R. Rosenthal and L. Jacobson, *Pygmalion in the Classroom: Teacher Expectation and Student Intellectual Development* (New York: Holt, Rinehart, & Winston, 1968).

51 J-F. Manzoni, "The Set-Up-to-Fail Syndrome," *Harvard Business Review,* 76 (March–April 1998), pp. 101–13; J.S. Livingston, "Retrospective Commentary," *Harvard Business Review,* 66 (September–October 1988), p. 125.

52 For a review of organizational studies of self-fulfilling prophecy, see Eden, "Interpersonal Expectations in Organizations," in *Interpersonal Expectations: Theory, Research, and Applications.*

53 S. Oz and D. Eden, "Restraining the Golem: Boosting Performance by Changing the Interpretation of Low Scores," *Journal of Applied Psychology,* 79 (1994), pp. 744–54; D. Eden, "OD and Self-Fulfilling Prophecy: Boosting Productivity by Raising Expectations," *Journal of Applied Behavioural Science,* 22 (1986), pp. 1–13.

54 T. Hill, P. Lewicki, M. Czyzewska, and A. Boss, "Self-Perpetuating Development of Encoding Biases in Person Perception," *Journal of Personality and Social Psychology,* 57 (1989), pp. 373–87; C.L. Kleinke, *First Impressions: The Psychology of Encountering Others* (Englewood Cliffs, NJ: Prentice Hall, 1975).

55 R. Wright, "Great X-pectations," *Canadian Banker,* 106 (January–February 1999), pp. 11–15.

56 D.D. Steiner and J.S. Rain, "Immediate and Delayed Primacy and Recency Effects in Performance Evaluation," *Journal of Applied Psychology,* 74 (1989), pp. 136–42; R.L. Heneman and K.N. Wexley, "The Effects of Time Delay in Rating and Amount of Information Observed in Performance Rating Accuracy," *Academy of Management Journal,* 26 (1983), pp. 677–86.

57 W.H. Cooper, "Ubiquitous Halo," *Psychological Bulletin,* 90 (1981), pp. 218–44; K.R. Murphy, R.A. Jako, and R.L. Anhalt, "Nature and Consequences of Halo Error: A Critical Analysis," *Journal of Applied Psychology,* 78 (1993), pp. 218–25.

58 S. Kozlowski, M. Kirsch, and G. Chao, "Job Knowledge, Rate Familiarity, Conceptual Similarity, and Halo Error: An Exploration," *Journal of Applied Psychology,* 71 (1986), pp. 45–49; H.C. Min, "Country Image: Halo or Summary Construct?" *Journal of Marketing Research,* 26 (1989), pp. 222–29.

59 W.K. Balzer and L.M. Sulsky, "Halo and Performance Appraisal Research: A Critical Examination," *Journal of Applied Psychology,* 77 (1992), pp. 975–85; H.J. Bernardin and R.W. Beatty, *Performance Appraisal: Assessing Human Behaviour at Work* (Boston: Kent, 1984).

60 G.G. Sherwood, "Self-Serving Biases in Person Perception: A Re-examination of Projection as a Mechanism of Defense," *Psychological Bulletin,* 90 (1981), pp. 445–59.

61 B. Parks, "Club Swinging a Sticky Situation in NHL," *Star-Ledger* (Newark, NJ), March 28, 2000, p. 61; L. Hornby, "Racism Meeting Hits Home With Leafs Players," *Toronto Sun,* September 27, 1999, p. 81; K.C. Johnson, "When Words Collide," *Chicago Tribune,* May 2, 1999, p. 7.

62 M.J. Reid, "Profit Motivates Corporate Diversity," *San Francisco Examiner,* March 15, 1998, p. W42; G. Flynn, "Bank of Montreal Satisfies Customers by Satisfying Employees," *Workforce,* 76 (February 1997), pp. 46–47; H. Kluge, "Reflections on Diversity: Cultural Assumptions," *Vital Speeches of the Day,* 63 (January 1, 1997), pp. 171–75.

63 H. Hemphill and R. Haines, *Discrimination, Harassment, and the Failure of Diversity Training: What to Do Now* (Westport, CT: Quorum Books, 1997); J.R.W. Joplin and C.S. Daus, "Challenges of Leading a Diverse Workforce," *Academy of Management Executive,* August 1997, pp. 32–47.

64 M.J. Reid, "Profit Motivates Corporate Diversity," *San Francisco Examiner,* March 15, 1998, p. W42.

65 G. Egan, *The Skilled Helper: A Model for Systematic Helping and Interpersonal Relating* (Belmont, CA: Brooks/Cole, 1975); D.B. Fedor and K.M. Rowland, "Investigating Supervisor Attributions of Subordinate Performance," *Journal of Management,* 15 (1989), pp. 405–16.

66 D. Goleman, "What Makes a Leader?" *Harvard Business Review,* 76 (November–December 1998), pp. 92–102.

67 L. Beamer, "Learning Intercultural Communication Competence," *Journal of Business Communication,* 29 (1992), pp. 285–303; D. Landis and R.W. Brislin (eds.), *Handbook of Intercultural Training* (New York: Pergamon, 1983).

68 S. Silcoff, "The Sky's Your Limit," *Canadian Business,* April 1997, p. 62.

69 T.W. Costello and S.S. Zalkind, *Psychology in Administration: A Research Orientation* (Englewood Cliffs, NJ: Prentice Hall, 1963), pp. 45–46.

70 J. Luft, *Group Processes* (Palo Alto, CA: Mayfield Publishing, 1984). For a variation of this model, see J. Hall, "Communication Revisited," *California Management Review,* 15 (Spring 1973), pp. 56–67.

71 L.C. Miller and D.A. Kenny, "Reciprocity of Self-Disclosure at the Individual and Dyadic Levels: A Social Relations Analysis," *Journal of Personality and Social Psychology,* 50 (1986), pp. 713–19.

72 R. Laver, "A Jury System for Jobs," *Maclean's*, August 5, 1996, p. 45.

73 K. Noble, "Frank Stronach: Empire Builder," *Maclean's*, March 29, 1999, p. 13.

74 R.T. Hogan, "Personality and Personality Measurement," in M.D. Dunnette and L.M. Hough (eds.), *Handbook of Industrial and Organizational Psychology*, 2nd ed, Vol. 2 (Palo Alto, CA: Consulting Psychologists Press, 1991), pp. 873–919. Also see W. Mischel, *Introduction to Personality* (New York: Holt, Rinehart, & Winston, 1986).

75 H.M. Weiss and S. Adler, "Personality and Organizational Behaviour," *Research in Organizational Behaviour*, 6 (1984), pp. 1–50.

76 W. Revelle, "Personality Processes," *Annual Review of Psychology*, 46 (1995), pp. 295–328.

77 R.M. Guion and R.F. Gottier, "Validity of Personality Measures in Personnel Selection," *Personnel Psychology*, 18 (1965), pp. 135–64. Also see N. Schmitt, R.Z. Gooding, R.D. Noe, and M. Kirsch, "Meta-Analyses of Validity Studies Published Between 1964 and 1982 and the Investigation of Study Characteristics," *Personnel Psychology*, 37 (1984), pp. 407–22.

78 P.G. Irving, "On the Use of Personality Measures in Personnel Selection," *Canadian Psychology*, 34 (April 1993), pp. 208–14.

79 K.M. DeNeve and H. Cooper, "The Happy Personality: A Meta-Analysis of 137 Personality Traits and Subjective Well-Being," *Psychological Bulletin*, 124 (September 1998), pp. 197–229; M.K. Mount and M.R. Barrick, "The Big Five Personality Dimensions: Implications for Research and Practice in Human Resources Management," *Research in Personnel and Human Resources Management*, 13 (1995), pp. 153–200; B.M. Bass, *Stogdill's Handbook of Leadership: A Survey of Theory and Research*, 3rd ed. (New York: Free Press, 1990); J.L. Holland, *Making Vocation Choices: A Theory of Careers* (Englewood Cliffs, NJ: Prentice Hall, 1973).

80 This historical review and the trait descriptions in this section are discussed in R.J. Schneider and L.M. Hough, "Personality and Industrial/Organizational Psychology," *International Review of Industrial and Organizational Psychology*, 10 (1995), pp. 75–129; M.K. Mount and M.R. Barrick, "The Big Five Personality Dimensions: Implications for Research and Practice in Human Resources Management," *Research in Personnel and Human Resources Management*, 13 (1995), pp. 153–200; J.M. Digman, "Personality Structure: Emergence of the Five-Factor Model," *Annual Review of Psychology*, 41 (1990), pp. 417–40.

81 I.R. Gellatly, "Dispositional Determinants of Task Performance: Focus on the Big Five Factor of Conscientiousness," *Proceedings of the Annual ASAC Conference*, Human Resources Division, 17(9) (1996), pp. 43–52; M.K. Mount, M.R. Barrick, and J.P. Strauss, "Validity of Observer Ratings of the Big Five Personality Factors," *Journal of Applied Psychology*, 79 (1994), pp. 272–80; R.P. Tett, D.N. Jackson, and M. Rothstein, "Personality Measures as Predictors of Job Performance: A Meta-Analytic Review," *Personnel Psychology*, 44 (1991), pp. 703–42.

82 J.M. Howell and C.A. Higgins, "Champions of Change: Identifying, Understanding, and Supporting Champions of Technological Innovations," *Organizational Dynamics*, Summer 1990, pp. 40–55.

83 K.P. Carson and G.L. Stewart, "Job Analysis and the Sociotechnical Approach to Quality: A Critical Examination," *Journal of Quality Management*, 1 (1996), pp. 49–64; Mount and Barrick, "The Big Five Personality Dimensions," pp. 177–78.

84 I.B. Myers, *The Myers-Briggs Type Indicator* (Palo Alto, CA: Consulting Psychologists Press, 1987); C.G. Jung, *Psychological Types* (translated by H.G. Baynes, revised by R.F.C. Hull) (Princeton, NJ: Princeton University Press, 1971). (Original work published in 1921.)

85 D.W. Salter and N.J. Evans, "Test-Retest of the Myers-Briggs Type Indicator: An Examination of Dominant Functioning," *Educational & Psychological Measurement*, 57 (August 1997), pp. 590–97; W.L. Gardner and M.J. Martinko, "Using the Myers-Briggs Type Indicator to Study Managers: A Literature Review and Research Agenda," *Journal of Management*, 22 (1996), pp. 45–83; R. Zemke,

"Second Thoughts About the MBTI," *Training,* April 1992, pp. 42–47; M.H. McCaulley, "The Myers-Briggs Type Indicator a Measure for Individuals and Groups," *Measurement and Evaluation in Counseling and Development,* 22 (1990), pp. 181–95.

86 G.N. Landrum, *Profiles of Genius* (New York: Prometheus, 1993).

87 Gardner and Martinko, "Using the Myers-Briggs Type Indicator to Study Managers."

88 C. Caggiano, "Psycho Path," *Inc.,* 20 (July 1998), pp. 76–85.

89 S.S.K. Lam and J. Schaubroeck, "The Role of Locus of Control in Reactions to Being Promoted and to Being Passed Over: A Quasi Experiment," *Academy of Management Journal,* 43 (February 2000), pp. 66–78; J.M. Howell and B.J. Avolio, "Transformational Leadership, Transactional Leadership, Locus of Control, and Support for Innovation: Key Predictors of Consolidated-Business-Unit Performance," *Journal of Applied Psychology,* 78 (1993), pp. 891–902; D. Miller and J.-M. Toulouse, "Chief Executive Personality and Corporate Strategy and Structure in Small Firms," *Management Science,* 32 (1986), pp. 1389–1409; P.E. Spector, "Behavior in Organizations as a Function of Employee's Locus of Control," *Psychological Bulletin,* 91 (1982), pp. 482–97.

90 M. Snyder, *Public Appearances/Private Realities: The Psychology of Self-Monitoring* (New York: W.H. Freeman, 1987).

91 M.A. Warech, J.W. Smither, R.R. Reilly, R.E. Millsap, and S.P. Reilly "Self-Monitoring and 360-Degree Ratings," *Leadership Quarterly,* 9 (Winter 1998), pp. 449–73; M. Kilduff and D.V. Day, "Do Chameleons Get Ahead? The Effects of Self-Monitoring on Managerial Careers," *Academy of Management Journal,* 37 (1994), pp. 1047–60; R.J. Ellis and S.E. Cronshaw, "Self-Monitoring and Leader Emergence: A Test of Moderator Effects," *Small Group Research,* 23 (1992), pp. 113–29; S.J. Zaccaro, R.J. Foti, and D.A. Kenny, "Self-Monitoring and Trait-Based Variance in Leadership: An Investigation of Leader Flexibility Across Multiple Group Situations," *Journal of Applied Psychology,* 76 (1991), pp. 308–15.

92 H.A. Simon, *Administrative Behaviour* (New York: The Free Press, 1957), p. xv.

Chapter Seven

1 D. Mabell, "Staff Praised for WestJet Success," *Lethbridge Herald,* March 14, 2000; M. Cash, "WestJet Throttles Up Flight Plan," *Winnipeg Free Press,* March 1, 2000; T. Johnson, "High Jinks and Low Fares," *Report on Business Magazine,* November 26, 1999, p. 70; P. Flint, "WestJet Defies the Odds," *Air Transport World,* 36 (June 1999), pp. 82–83.

2 B.E. Ashforth and R.H. Humphrey, "Emotion in the Workplace: A Reappraisal," *Human Relations,* 48 (1995), pp. 97–125.

3 For a more complete discussion of specific emotions, see R. Pekrun and M. Frese, "Emotions in Work and Achievement," *International Review of Industrial and Organizational Psychology,* 7 (1992), pp. 153–200.

4 This definition is based on material in H.M. Weiss and R. Cropanzano, "Affective Events Theory: A Theoretical Discussion of the Structure, Causes, and Consequences of Affective Experiences at Work," *Research in Organizational Behavior,* 18 (1996), pp. 1-74; S. Kitayama and P.M. Niedenthal, "Introduction," in P.M. Niedenthal and S. Kitayama, *The Heart's Eye: Emotional Influences in Perception and Attention* (San Diego, CA: Academic Press, 1994), pp. 6–7.

5 R.B. Zajonc, "Emotions," in D.T. Gilbert, S.T. Fiske, and L. Gardner (eds.), *Handbook of Social Psychology* (New York: Oxford University Press, 1998), pp. 591–634; K. Oatley and J.M. Jenkins, "Human Emotions: Function and Dysfunction," *Annual Review of Psychology,* 43 (1992), pp. 55–85.

6 J.M. George and A.P. Brief, "Motivational Agendas in the Workplace: The Effects of Feelings on Focus of Attention and Work Motivation," *Research in Organizational Behavior,* 18 (1996), pp. 75–109; J.M. George, "Mood and Absence," *Journal of Applied Psychology,* 74 (1989), pp. 317–24.

7 J.M. George and G.R. Jones, "Experiencing Work: Values, Attitudes, and Moods," *Human Relations,* 50 (April 1997), pp. 393–416; J.M. Olson and M.P. Zama, "Attitudes and Attitude Change,"

Annual Review of Psychology, 44 (1993), pp. 117–54; M. Fishbein and I. Ajzen, *Belief, Attitude, Intention, and Behavior* (Reading, MA: Addison-Wesley, 1975).

8 M.D. Zalesny and J.K. Ford, "Extending the Social Information Processing Perspective: New Links to Attitudes, Behaviors, and Perceptions," *Organizational Behavior and Human Decision Processes*, 52 (1992), pp. 205–46; G. Salancik and J. Pfeffer, "A Social Information Processing Approach to Job Attitudes and Task Design," *Administrative Science Quarterly*, 23 (1978), pp. 224–53.

9 Weiss and Cropanzano, "Affective Events Theory."

10 For a full discussion of several theories on this topic, see K.T. Strongman, *The Psychology of Emotion: Theories of Emotion in Perspective*, 4th ed. (Chichester, UK: John Wiley & Sons, 1996), Chapter 6.

11 D.M. Irvine and M.G. Evans, "Job Satisfaction and Turnover Among Nurses: Integrating Research Findings Across Studies," *Nursing Research*, 44 (1995), pp. 246–53.

12 Weiss and Cropanzano, "Affective Events Theory," pp. 52–57.

13 L. Festinger, *A Theory of Cognitive Dissonance* (Evanston, IL: Row, Peterson, 1957); G.R. Salancik, "Commitment and the Control of Organizational Behavior and Belief," in B.M. Staw and G.R. Salancik (eds.), *New Directions in Organizational Behavior* (Chicago: St. Clair, 1977), pp. 1–54.

14 T.A. Judge, E.A. Locke, and C.C. Durham, "The Dispositional Causes of Job Satisfaction: A Core Evaluations Approach," *Research in Organizational Behavior*, 19 (1997), pp. 151–88; A.P Brief, A.H. Butcher, and L. Roberson, "Cookies, Disposition, and Job Attitudes: The Effects of Positive Mood-Inducing Events and Negative Affectivity on Job Satisfaction in a Field Experiment," *Organizational Behavior and Human Decision Processes*, 62 (1995), pp. 55–62.

15 J. Schaubroeck, D.C. Ganster, and B. Kemmerer, "Does Trait Affect Promote Job Attitude Stability?" *Journal of Organizational Behavior*, 17 (1996), pp. 191–96; R.D. Arvey, B.P. McCall, T.L. Bouchard, and P. Taubman, "Genetic Differences on Job Satisfaction and Work Values," *Personality and Individual Differences*, 17 (1994), pp. 21–33; B.M. Staw and J. Ross, "Stability in the Midst of Change: A Dispositional Approach to Job Attitudes," *Journal of Applied Psychology*, 70 (1985), pp. 469–80.

16 Weiss and Cropanzano, "Affective Events Theory." The definition of job satisfaction is still being debated. This definition captures the most popular view that job satisfaction is an evaluation and represents both beliefs and feelings. For details, see A.P. Brief, *Attitudes In and Around Organizations* (Thousand Oaks, CA: Sage, 1998), Chapters 2 and 4.

17 E.A. Locke, "The Nature and Causes of Job Satisfaction," in *Handbook of Industrial and Organizational Psychology*, ed. M. Dunnette (Chicago: Rand McNally, 1976), pp. 1297–1350.

18 "Workplace Satisfaction Hits 82 Percent," *Vancouver Sun*, November 1, 1999; S. Lambert, "Annual Poll Finds We're a Happy Lot," *Toronto Star*, October 10, 1998, p. B2.

19 S. MacDonald, "Do You Really Enjoy Your Work?" *Times of London*, January 15, 1998.

20 R. Laver, "The Best & Worst Jobs," *Maclean's*," May 31, 1999, pp. 18–23.

21 M. Gibb-Clark, "Workers Pinpoint Bosses' Flaws," *Globe and Mail*, October 18, 1996, p. B12.

22 See G. Law, "If You're Happy & You Know It, Tick the Box," *Management-Auckland*, 45 (March 1998), pp. 34–37. The problems with measuring work attitudes across cultures is also discussed in K. Bae and C. Chung, "Cultural Values and Work Attitudes of Korean Industrial Workers in Comparison with Those of the United States and Japan," *Work and Occupations*, 24 (February 1997), pp. 80–96.

23 E.E. Lawler III, *Motivation in Work Organizations* (Belmont, CA: Wadsworth, 1973), pp. 66–69, 74–77.

24 A. Bussing, T. Bissels, V. Fuchs, K.-M. Perrar, "A Dynamic Model of Work Satisfaction: Qualitative Approaches," *Human Relations*, 52 (August 1999), pp. 999–1028; D.B. McFarlin and R.W. Rice,

"The Role of Facet Importance as a Moderator in Job Satisfaction Processes," *Journal of Organizational Behavior*, 13 (1992), pp. 41–54.

25 A.J. Rucci, S.P. Kirn, and R.T. Quinn, "The Employee-Customer-Profit Chain at Sears," *Harvard Business Review*, 76 (January–February 1998), pp. 83–97; M. Kerr, "Developing a Corporate Culture for the Maximum Balance Between the Utilization of Human Resources and Employee Fulfillment in Canada," *Canada-United States Law Journal*, 22 (1996), pp. 169–76.

26 For a review, see P.E. Spector, *Job Satisfaction: Application, Assessment, Causes, and Consequences* (Thousand Oaks, CA: Sage Publications, 1997); Brief, *Attitudes in and Around Organizations*, Chapter 2.

27 R.D. Hackett and P. Bycio, "An Evaluation of Employee Absenteeism as a Coping Mechanism Among Hospital Nurses," *Journal of Occupational & Organizational Psychology*, 69 (December 1996), pp. 327–38; J. Barling, "The Prediction, Psychological Experience, and Consequences of Workplace Violence," in G.R. VandenBos and E.Q. Bulatao (eds.), *Violence on the Job* (Washington, DC: American Psychological Association, 1996), pp. 29–49. S.D. Bluen, "The Psychology of Strikes," *International Review of Industrial and Organizational Psychology*, 9 (1994), pp. 113–45; P.Y. Chen and P.E. Spector, "Relationships of Work Stressors with Aggression, Withdrawal, Theft and Substance Use: An Exploratory Study," *Journal of Occupational & Organizational Psychology*, 65 (1992), pp. 177–84.

28 B.M. Staw and S.G. Barsade, "Affect and Managerial Performance: A Test of the Sadder-but-Wiser vs. Happier-and-Smarter Hypotheses," *Administrative Science Quarterly*, 38 (1993), pp. 304–31; M.T. Iaffaldano and P.M. Muchinsky, "Job Satisfaction and Job Performance: A Meta-Analysis," *Psychological Bulletin*, 97 (1985), pp. 251–73; D.P. Schwab and L.L. Cummings, "Theories of Performance and Satisfaction: A Review," *Industrial Relations*, 9 (1970), pp. 408–30.

29 Brief, *Attitudes in and Around Organizations*, p. 43.

30 E.E. Lawler III and L.W. Porter, "The Effect of Performance on Job Satisfaction," *Industrial Relations*, 7 (1967), pp. 20–28.

31 C.D. Fisher and E.A. Locke, "The New Look in Job Satisfaction Research and Theory," in Cranny et al. (eds.), *Job Satisfaction*, pp. 165–94; P.M. Podsakoff, S.B. MacKenzie, and C. Hui, "Organizational Citizenship Behaviors and Managerial Evaluations of Employee Performance: A Review and Suggestions for Future Research," *Research in Personnel and Human Resources Management*, 11 (1993), pp. 1–40; D.W. Organ, "The Motivational Basis of Organizational Citizenship Behavior," *Research in Organizational Behavior*, 12 (1990), pp. 43–72.

32 D.S. Bolon, "Organizational Citizenship Behavior Among Hospital Employees: A Multidimensional Analysis Involving Job Satisfaction and Organizational Commitment," *Hospital & Health Services Administration*, 42 (Summer 1997), pp. 221–41.

33 G. Thomas, "New Leader Wants BA Staff to Be Smiles Ahead," *West Australian*, April 29, 2000, p. 61; J. Lee, "Dealing with Stress Now an Investment," *Vancouver Sun*, April 5, 1999, pp. C1, C3; P. Kulig, "LCBO Has Taste for Training," *Canadian HR Reporter*, August 10, 1998, pp. 1, 10; R. Hallowell, L.A. Schlesinger, and J. Zornitsky, "Internal Service Quality, Customer and Job Satisfaction: Linkages and Implications for Management," *Human Resource Planning*, 19(2) (1996), pp. 20–31.

34 S. Franklin, *The Heroes: A Saga of Canadian Inspiration* (Toronto: McClelland & Stewart, 1967), pp. 53–59.

35 R.T. Mowday, L.W. Porter, and R.M. Steers, *Employee Organization Linkages: The Psychology of Commitment, Absenteeism, and Turnover* (New York: Academic Press, 1982).

36 C.W. Mueller and E.J. Lawler, "Commitment to Nested Organizational Units: Some Basic Principles and Preliminary Findings," *Social Psychology Quarterly* (December 1999), pp. 325–46; T.E. Becker, R.S. Billings, D.M. Eveleth, and N.L. Gilbert, "Foci and Bases of Employee Commitment: Implications for Job Performance," *Academy of Management Journal*, 39 (1996), pp. 464–82.

37 J.P. Meyer, "Organizational Commitment," *International Review of Industrial and Organizational Psychology*, 12 (1997), pp. 175–228. Along with affective and continuance commitment, Meyer identifies "normative commitment," which refers to employee feelings of obligation to remain with the organization. This commitment has been excluded so that students focus on the two most common perspectives of commitment.

38 R.D. Hackett, P. Bycio, and P.A. Hausdorf, "Further Assessments of Meyer and Allen's (1991) Three-Component Model of Organizational Commitment," *Journal of Applied Psychology*, 79 (1994), pp. 15–23.

39 Watson Wyatt, "Survey Says Employee Commitment Declining," News release, March 14, 2000.

40 M. Stepanek, "Poll Finds Workers Secure, Loyal," *News and Observer* (Raleigh, NC), August 30, 1997, p. A8; Walker Information, *The International Employee Commitment Project* (Walker Information, 1997) from www.walkernet.com; Bae and Chung, "Cultural Values and Work Attitudes of Korean Industrial Workers in Comparison with Those of the United States and Japan"; "Japanese Worker Loyalty Overrated, Survey Says," *Japan Weekly Monitor*, September 9, 1996.

41 F.F. Reichheld, *The Loyalty Effect* (Boston: Harvard Business School Press, 1996), Chapter 4.

42 D.S. Bolon, "Organizational Citizenship Behavior Among Hospital Employees: A Multidimensional Analysis Involving Job Satisfaction and Organizational Commitment," *Hospital & Health Services Administration*, 42 (Summer 1997), pp. 221–41; Meyer, "Organizational Commitment," pp. 203–15; J.P. Meyer, S.V. Paunonen, I.R. Gellatly, R.D. Goffin, and D.N. Jackson, "Organizational Commitment and Job Performance: It's the Nature of the Commitment That Counts," *Journal of Applied Psychology*, 74 (1989), pp. 152–56.

43 P. Verburg, "The Little Airline That Could," *Canadian Business*, April 1997, pp. 34–40; A. Daniels, "The Jokes Are Free," *Vancouver Sun*, May 17, 1996, pp. A1, A8.

44 A.A. Luchak and I.R. Gellatly, "Employer-Sponsored Pensions and Employee Commitment," *Proceedings of the Annual ASAC Conference, Human Resource Management Division*, 17(9) (1996), pp. 64–71; H.L. Angle and M.B. Lawson, "Organizational Commitment and Employees' Performance Ratings: Both Type of Commitment and Type of Performance Count," *Psychological Reports*, 75 (1994), pp. 1539–51; L.M. Shore and S.J. Wayne, "Commitment and Employee Behavior: Comparison of Affective Commitment and Continuance Commitment with Perceived Organizational Support," *Journal of Applied Psychology*, 78 (1993), pp. 774–80; Meyer et al., "Organizational Commitment and Job Performance: It's the Nature of the Commitment That Counts."

45 A. Baillie, "Eaton's Employees in Demand," *Saint John's Telegram*, August 28, 1999.

46 J.P. Meyer and N.J. Allen, *Commitment in the Workplace: Theory, Research, and Application* (Thousand Oaks, CA: Sage, 1997), Chapter 4.

47 E.W. Morrison and S.L. Robinson, "When Employees Feel Betrayed: A Model of How Psychological Contract Violation Develops," *Academy of Management Review*, 22 (1997), pp. 226–56.

48 C. Hendry and R. Jenkins, "Psychological Contracts and New Deals," *Human Resource Management Journal*, 7 (1997), pp. 38–44; D.M. Noer, *Healing the Wounds* (San Francisco: Jossey-Bass, 1993); S. Ashford, C. Lee, and P. Bobko, "Content, Causes, and Consequences of Job Insecurity: A Theory-Based Measure and Substantive Test," *Academy of Management Journal*, 32 (1989), pp. 803–29.

49 K. Mark, "No More Pink Slips," *Human Resources Professional*, November 1996, pp. 21–23; Shore and Wayne, "Commitment and Employee Behavior;" D.M. Rousseau and J.M. Parks, "The Contracts of Individuals and Organizations," *Research in Organizational Behavior*, 15 (1993), pp. 1–43.

50 R.J. Lewicki and B.B. Bunker, "Developing and Maintaining Trust in Work Relationships," in R.M. Kramer and T.R. Tyler (eds.), *Trust in Organizations: Frontiers of Theory and Research* (Thousand Oaks, CA: Sage, 1996), pp. 114–39; S.L. Robinson, "Trust and Breach of the Psychological Contract," *Administrative Science Quarterly*, 41 (1996), pp. 574–99; J.M. Kouzes and B.Z. Posner, *The Leadership Challenge* (San Francisco: Jossey-Bass, 1987), pp. 146–52.

51 R. Corelli, "Dishing Out Rudeness," *Maclean's*, January 11, 1999, p. 44.

52 J.A. Morris and D.C. Feldman, "The Dimensions, Antecedents, and Consequences of Emotional Labor," *Academy of Management Review*, 21 (1996), pp. 986–1010; B.E. Ashforth and R.H. Humphrey, "Emotional Labor in Service Roles: The Influence of Identity," *Academy of Management Review*, 18 (1993), pp. 88–115.

53 J.A. Morris and D.C. Feldman, "Managing Emotions in the Workplace," *Journal of Managerial Issues*, 9 (Fall 1997), pp. 257–74.

54 R.I. Sutton, "Maintaining Norms About Expressed Emotions: The Case of Bill Collectors," *Administrative Science Quarterly*, 36 (1991), pp. 245–68.

55 S. Fish and F. Jamerson (eds.), *Inside the Mouse: Work and Play at Disney World*, (Durham, NC: Duke University Press, 1995).

56 C. Bellissimo, "Hostess with the Mostess," *Cambridge Reporter*, May 9, 2000.

57 E. Forman, "'Diversity Concerns Grow as Companies Head Overseas,' Consultant Says," *Fort Lauderdale Sun-Sentinel*, June 26, 1995.

58 Ashforth and Humphrey, "Emotional Labor in Service Roles: The Influence of Identity," *Academy of Management Review*, p. 91.

59 J. Schaubroeck and J.R. Jones, "Antecedents of Workplace Emotional Labor Dimensions and Moderators of Their Effects on Physical Symptoms," *Journal of Organizational Behavior*, 21 (2000), 163–83; R. Buck, "The Spontaneous Communication of Interpersonal Expectations," in *Interpersonal Expectations: Theory, Research, and Applications* (Cambridge, UK: Cambridge University Press, 1993), pp. 227–41. The quotation from George Burns comes from the Buck source. However, this line has also been attributed to Groucho Marx.

60 K. Pugliesi, "The Consequences of Emotional Labor: Effects on Work Stress, Job Satisfaction, and Well-Being," *Motivation & Emotion*, 23 (June 1999), pp. 125–54; A.S. Wharton, "The Psychosocial Consequences of Emotional Labor," *Annals of the American Academy of Political & Social Science*, 561 (January 1999), pp. 158–76; J.A. Morris and D.C. Feldman, "Managing Emotions in the Workplace," *Journal of Managerial Issues*, 9 (Fall 1997), pp. 257–74; P.K. Adelmann "Emotional Labor as a Potential Source of Job Stress," in S. Sauter and L.R. Murphy (eds.), *Organizational Risk Factors for Job Stress* (Washington, DC: American Psychological Association, 1995), Chapter 24.

61 "Safeway Employees Announce the Filing of a Charge with the Equal Employment Opportunity Commission," *Business Wire*, November 16, 1998; K.D. Grimsley, "Service with a Forced Smile," *Washington Post*, October 18, 1998, p. A1; "Safeway Smiles Flirt with Trouble, Workers Charge," *Toronto Star*, September 3, 1998.

62 V. Reitman, "Learning To Grin—And Bear It," *Los Angeles Times*, February 22, 1999, p. A1.

63 I. Anai, "Here to Stay," *Daily Yomiuri* (Japan), November 21, 1997, p. 17.

64 D. Flavelle, "Firms Try to Rope Winners by Hiring Out of the Herd," *Toronto Star*, January 30, 2000.

65 J.D. Mayer and P. Salovey, "The Intelligence of Emotional Intelligence," *Intelligence*, 17 (1993), pp. 433–42.

66 D. Goleman, "What Makes a Leader?" *Harvard Business Review*, 76 (November–December 1998), pp. 92–102.

67 B. Evenson, "Americans Are More Emotionally Mature: Test," *National Post*, July 15, 1999, pp. A1, A11; K. Vermond, "Emotional Intelligence," *HR Professional* (Ontario), April–May 1999, pp. 38–39; "Unconventional Smarts," *Across the Board*, 35 (January 1998), pp. 22–23; M.N. Martinez, "The Smarts That Count," *HRMagazine*, 42 (November 1997), pp. 72–78.

68 L. Yeung, "Stress-Busters Strive for Balance," *South China Morning Post*, October 18, 1998, p. 2; J. Cheung, " 'Emotions' Class for Civil Servants," *South China Morning Post*, September 14, 1998, p. 3.

69 A. Sagie and D. Elizur, "Work Values: A Theoretical Overview and a Model of Their Effects," *Journal of Organizational Behavior*, 17 (1996), pp. 503–14; W.H. Schmidt and B.Z. Posner, *Managerial Values in Perspective* (New York: American Management Association, 1983).

70 M. Rokeach, *Understanding Human Values* (New York: Free Press, 1979).

71 B.R. Agle and C.B. Caldwell, "Understanding Research on Values in Business," *Business and Society*, 38 (September 1999), pp. 326–87; B.M. Meglino and E.C. Ravlin, "Individual Values in Organizations: Concepts, Controversies, and Research," *Journal of Management*, 24 (May 1998), pp. 351–89; P. McDonald and J. Gandz, "Getting Value from Values," *Organizational Dynamics*, Winter 1992, pp. 64–77.

72 M. Rokeach, The Nature of Human Values (New York: The Free Press, 1973); F. Kluckhorn and F.L. Strodtbeck, *Variations in Value Orientations* (Evanston, IL: Row, Peterson, 1961).

73 A. Gove, "Culture Club," *Red Herring*, November 1998.

74 K.L. Newman and S.D. Nolan, "Culture and Congruence: The Fit Between Management Practices and National Culture," *Journal of International Business Studies*, 27 (1996), pp. 753–79; G. Hofstede, "Cultural Constraints in Management Theories," *Academy of Management Executive*, 7 (1993), pp. 81–94; G. Hofstede, *Culture's Consequences: International Differences in Work-Related Values* (Beverly Hills, CA: Sage, 1980).

75 F.S. Niles, "Individualism-Collectivism Revisited," *Cross-Cultural Research*, 32 (November 1998), pp. 315–41; C.P. Earley and C.B. Gibson, "Taking Stock in Our Progress on Individualism-Collectivism: 100 Years of Solidarity and Community," *Journal of Management*, 24 (May 1998), pp. 265–304; W.G. Stephan and C.W. Stephan, *Intergroup Relations* (Boulder, CO: Westview, 1996), pp. 119–21; J.A. Wagner III, "Studies of Individualism-Collectivism: Effects of Cooperation in Groups," *Academy of Management Journal*, 38 (1995), pp. 152–72; H.C. Triandis, *Individualism and Collectivism* (Boulder, CO: Westview, 1995).

76 M. Erez and P. Christopher Earley, *Culture, Self-Identity, and Work* (New York: Oxford University Press, 1993), pp. 126–27.

77 G. Hofstede, *Cultures and Organizations: Software of the Mind* (New York: McGraw-Hill, 1991), p. 124. Hofstede used the terms "masculinity" and "femininity" for achievement and nurturing orientation, respectively. We have adopted the latter terms to minimize the sexist perspective of these concepts. The achievement and nurturing orientation labels are also used in G.R. Jones, J.M. George, and C.W.L. Hill, *Contemporary Management* (Burr Ridge, IL: Irwin/Mcgraw-Hill, 1998), pp. 112–13.

78 C.W. Stephan, W.G. Stephan, I. Saito, and S.M. Barnett, "Emotional Expression in Japan and the United States: The Nonmonolithic Nature of Individualism and Collectivism," *Journal of Cross-Cultural Psychology*, 29 (November 1998), pp. 728–48; D. Matsumoto, T. Kudoh, and S. Takeuchi, "Changing Patterns of Individualism and Collectivism in the United States and Japan," *Culture and Psychology*, 2 (1996), pp. 77–107.

79 For counter-arguments to these criticisms, see G. Hofstede, "Attitudes, Values and Organizational Culture: Disentangling the Concepts," *Organization Studies*, 19 (June 1998), pp. 477–92.

80 M. Drohan, "Corporations Add Values," *Globe and Mail*, February 24, 2000; C. Harrington, "Talisman Says Peacemaking Is the Business of Governments, Not Business," *Vancouver Sun*, February 18, 2000.

81 H. McLaughlin, "A Social Passion," *Ottawa Citizen*, July 19, 1999.

82 Leslie Goodson, "Doing the Right Thing," *Human Resources Professional*, March 1996, pp. 21–22. The recent survey is reported in C. Savoye, "Workers Say Honesty Is Best Company Policy," *Christian Science Monitor*, June 15, 2000.

83 W.H. Shaw and V. Barry, *Moral Issues in Business*, 5th ed. (Belmont, CA: Wadsworth, 1992), Chapters 1 to 3; and M.G. Velasquez, *Business Ethics*, 2nd ed. (Englewood Cliffs, NJ: Prentice Hall, 1988), Chapter 2.

84 R. Berenbeim, "The Search for Global Ethics," *Vital Speeches of the Day*, 65 (January 1999), pp. 177–78.

85 J.M. Dukerich, M.J. Waller, E. George, and G.P. Huber "Moral Intensity and Managerial Problem Solving," *Journal of Business Ethics*, 24 (March 2000), pp. 29–38; S.A. Morris and R.A. McDonald, "The Role of Moral Intensity in Moral Judgments: An Empirical Investigation," *Journal of Business Ethics*, 14 (1995), pp. 715–26; T.J. Jones, "Ethical Decision Making by Individuals in Organizations: An Issue Contingent Model," *Academy of Management Review*, 16 (1991), pp. 366–95.

86 J.R. Sparks and S.D. Hunt, "Marketing Researcher Ethical Sensitivity: Conceptualization, Measurement, and Exploratory Investigation," *Journal of Marketing*, 62 (April 1998), pp. 92–109.

87 K. Blotnicky, "Is Business in Moral Decay?" *Halifax Chronicle-Herald*, June 11, 2000; D. McDougall and B. Orsini, "Fraudbusting Ethics," *CMA Management*, 73 (June 1999), pp. 18–21. For a discussion of the situational effects on ethical conduct, see C.J. Thompson, "A Contextualist Proposal for the Conceptualization and Study of Marketing Ethics," *Journal of Public Policy and Marketing*, 14 (1995), pp. 177–91.

88 P. Haapaniemi and W.R. Hill, "Not Just for the Big Guys!" *Chief Executive*, September 1998, pp. 62–73.

89 Canada passed laws against foreign bribery very recently. See N. Nankivell, "New Legislation Forces Companies to Take Foreign Bribery Seriously," *National Post*, February 11, 1999, p. C7.

90 T.H. Stevenson and C.D. Bodkin, "A Cross-National Comparison of University Students' Perceptions Regarding the Ethics and Acceptability of Sales Practices," *Journal of Business Ethics*, 17 (January 1998), pp. 45–55; T. Jackson and M.C. Artola, "Ethical Beliefs and Management Behavior: A Cross-Cultural Comparison," *Journal of Business Ethics*, 16 (August 1997), pp. 1163–73; M.-K. Nyaw and I. Ignace, "A Comparative Analysis of Ethical Beliefs: A Four Country Study," Journal of Business Ethics, 13 (1994), pp. 543–55; W.R. Swinyard, H. Rinne, and A.K. Kau, "The Morality of Software Piracy: A Cross-Cultural Analysis," *Journal of Business Ethics*, 9 (1990), pp. 655–64.

91 S.J. Vitell, S.L. Nwachukwu, and J.H. Barnes, "The Effects of Culture on Ethical Decision-Making: An Application of Hofstede's Typology." *Journal of Business Ethics*, 12 (1993), pp. 753–60; R. Abratt, D. Nel, and N.S. Higgs, "An Examination of the Ethical Beliefs of Managers Using Selected Scenarios in a Cross-Cultural Environment," *Journal of Business Ethics*, 11 (1992), pp. 29–35; S. Lysonski and W. Gaidis, "A Cross-Cultural Comparison of the Ethics of Business Students," *Journal of Business Ethics*, 10 (1991), pp. 141–50.

92 P.F. Buller, J.J. Kohls, and K.S. Anderson, "A Model for Addressing Cross-Cultural Ethical Conflicts," *Business and Society*, 36 (June 1997), pp. 169–93.

93 This point relates to the attitude-behavior model described earlier in the chapter. See J. Weber and J. Gillespie, "Differences in Ethical Beliefs, Intentions, and Behaviors," *Business and Society*, 37 (December 1998), pp. 447–67.

94 V. Kirsch, "Sometimes the Lines Between Right and Wrong Can Become a Little Blurred," *Guelph Mercury*, October 18, 1999, p. B1; L. Young, "Ethics Training Is the Key," *Canadian HR Reporter*, June 14, 1999, p. 2; M. Acharya, "A Matter of Business Ethics," *Kitchener-Waterloo Record*, March 23, 1999, p. C2.

95 M.A. Clark and S.L. Leonard, "Can Corporate Codes of Ethics Influence Behavior?" *Journal of Business Ethics,* 17 (April 1998), pp. 619–30.

96 L. Young, "Employer Ethics Codes Lack Supports Needed for Success," *Canadian HR Reporter*, April 19, 1999, pp. 1, 11; K. Sibley, "Technology Complicates Workplace Ethics," *Computer Dealer News*, June 15, 1998, pp. 14–15.

Chapter Eight

1 P. Tam, "The Bulldog Unchained," *Ottawa Citizen*, July 24, 2000; K. Goff, "Workers Ponder Their Futures," *Ottawa Citizen*, February 24, 2000; K. Standen, "Just What the Doctor Ordered," *Ottawa Citizen*, November 3, 1999; E. Mulqueen, "The Director's Chair—Pearse Flynn, Vice-President, Newbridge," *Irish Times*, August 27, 1999, p. 64; J. Bagnall, "Shaking Newbridge to the Core," *Ottawa Citizen*, March 17, 1999.

2 N. Sriussadaporn-Charoenngam and F.M. Jablin, "An Exploratory Study of Communication Competence in Thai Organizations," *Journal of Business Communication*, 36 (October 1999), pp. 382–418; F.M. Jablin et al., "Communication Competence in Organizations: Conceptualization and Comparison Across Multiple Levels of Analysis," in L. Thayer and G. Barnett (eds.), *Organization Communication: Emerging Perspectives*, Vol. 4 (Norwood, NJ: Ablex, 1994), pp. 114–40.

3 "Canadian CEOs Love Their 'Coaching' Jobs," *London Free Press*, September 10, 1999, p. D7; H. Mintzberg, *The Nature of Managerial Work* (New York: Harper & Row, 1973); E.T. Klemmer and F.W. Snyder, "Measurement of Time Spent Communicating," *Journal of Communication*, 22 (June 1972), pp. 142–58.

4 R.T. Barker and M.R. Camarata, "The Role of Communication in Creating and Maintaining a Learning Organization: Preconditions, Indicators, and Disciplines," *Journal of Business Communication*, 35 (October 1998), pp. 443–67.

5 R. Grenier and G. Metes, "Wake Up and Smell the Syzygy," *Business Communications Review*, 28 (August 1998), pp. 57–60; "We Are the World," *CIO,* 9 (August 1996), p. 24.

6 G. Calabrese, "Communication and Co-operation in Product Development: A Case Study of a European Car Producer," *R & D Management*, 27 (July 1997), pp. 239–52; C. Downs, P. Clampitt, and A.L. Pfeiffer, "Communication and Organizational Outcomes," in *Handbook of Organizational Communication*, ed. G. Goldhaber and G. Barnett (Norwood, NJ: Ablex, 1988), pp. 171–211.

7 V.L. Shalin, and G.V. Prabhu, "A Cognitive Perspective on Manual Assembly," *Ergonomics*, 39 (1996), pp. 108–27; I. Nonaka and H. Takeuchi, *The Knowledge-Creating Company* (New York: Oxford University Press, 1995).

8 L.K. Lewis and D.R. Seibold, "Communication During Intraorganizational Innovation Adoption: Predicting User's Behavioral Coping Responses to Innovations in Organizations," *Communication Monographs*, 63(2), (1996), pp. 131–57; R.J. Burke and D.S. Wilcox, "Effects of Different Patterns and Degrees of Openness in Superior–Subordinate Communication on Subordinate Satisfaction," *Academy of Management Journal*, 12 (1969), pp. 319–26.

9 S.L. Pan and H. Scarbrough, "Knowledge Management in Practice: An Exploratory Case Study," *Technology Analysis & Strategic Management*, 11 (September 1999), pp. 359–74; S. Greengard, "Will Your Culture Support KM?" *Workforce*, 77 (October 1998), pp. 93–94; M.N. Martinez, "The Collective Power of Employee Knowledge," *HRMagazine*, 43 (February 1998), pp. 88–94; R.K. Buckman, "Knowledge Sharing at Buckman Labs," *Journal of Business Strategy*, January–February 1998, pp. 11–15.

10 C.E. Shannon and W. Weaver, *The Mathematical Theory of Communication* (Urbana, IL: University of Illinois Press, 1949). For a more recent discussion, see K.J. Krone, F.M. Jablin, and L.L. Putnam, "Communication Theory and Organizational Communication: Multiple Perspectives," in F.M. Jablin, L.L. Putnam, K.H. Roberts, and L.W. Porter (eds.), *Handbook of Organizational Communication: An Interdisciplinary Perspective* (Newbury Park, CA: Sage, 1987), pp. 18–40.

11 S. Axley, "Managerial and Organizational Communication in Terms of the Conduit Metaphor," *Academy of Management Review*, 9 (1984), pp. 428–37.

12 N. Larin, "Ignore Communication Problems at Your Peril," *Canadian HR Reporter,* November 16, 1998, p. 12. The George Bernard Shaw quotation is cited at Web site: http://www.synco.com/communct.html.

13 M. Meissner, "The Language of Work," in R. Dubin (ed.), *Handbook of Work, Organization, and Society* (Chicago: Rand McNally, 1976), pp. 205–79.

14 M.J. Glauser, "Upward Information Flow in Organizations: Review and Conceptual Analysis," *Human Relations*, 37 (1984), pp. 613–43.

15 L. Larwood, "Don't Struggle to Scope Those Metaphors Yet," *Group and Organization Management*, 17 (1992), pp. 249–54; L.R. Pondy, P.J. Frost, G. Morgan, and T.C. Dandridge (eds.), *Organizational Symbolism* (Greenwich, CT: JAI Press, 1983).

16 M. Kaeter, "Quality Through Clarity," *Quality*, May 1993, pp. 19–22.

17 P. Robertson, "Fear of Flying," *Business in Calgary*, May 2000; J. Gleick, "A Bug by Any Other Name," *New York Times Magazine*, June 17, 1997.

18 A. Markham, "Designing Discourse: A Critical Analysis of Strategic Ambiguity and Workplace Control," *Management Communication Quarterly*, 9 (1996), pp. 389–421; Larwood, "Don't Struggle to Scope Those Metaphors Yet"; R. Mead, *Cross-Cultural Management Communication* (Chichester, UK: Wiley, 1990), pp. 130–37; E.M. Eisenberg, "Ambiguity as a Strategy in Organizational Communication," *Communication Monographs*, 51 (1984), pp. 227–42; R. Daft and J. Wiginton, "Language and Organization," *Academy of Management Review*, 4 (1979), pp. 179–91.

19 M.J. Hatch, "Exploring the Empty Spaces of Organizing: How Improvisational Jazz Helps Redescribe Organisational Structure," *Organization Studies*, 20 (1999), pp. 75–100; G. Morgan, *Images of Organization*, 2nd ed. (Thousand Oaks, CA: Sage, 1997); L.L. Putnam, N. Phillips, and P. Chapman, "Metaphors of Communication and Organization," in S.R. Clegg, C. Hardy, and W.R. Nord (eds.), *Handbook of Organization Studies* (London: Sage, 1996), pp. 373–408.

20 "Information Technology in the 21st Century," *Globe and Mail*, September 17, 1999.

21 S. Bury, "Does E-mail Make You More Productive?" *Silicon Valley North*, September 1999.

22 From "The Best of Ideas," CBC Radio, 1967. Cited at Web site: www.mcluhan4managers.com.

23 K. Alesandrini, *Survive Information Overload* (Homewood, IL: Business One-Irwin, 1993); A.G. Schick, L.A. Gordon, and S. Haka, "Information Overload: A Temporal Approach," *Accounting, Organizations & Society*, 15 (1990), pp. 199–220.

24 J. Kaye, "The Devil You Know," *Computer Weekly*, March 19, 1998, p. 46; D. Shenk, "Data Smog: Surviving the Info Glut," *Technology Review*, May 15, 1997, pp. 18–26.

25 Schick et al., "Information Overload," pp. 209–14; C. Stohl and W.C. Redding, "Messages and Message Exchange Processes," in Jablin et al. (eds.), *Handbook of Organizational Communication*, pp. 451–502.

26 M. McCullough, "The Gatekeeper," *BC Business*, 27 (September 1999), pp. 34–41.

27 J.H.E. Andriessen, "Mediated Communication and New Organizational Forms," *International Review of Industrial and Organizational Psychology*, 6 (1991), pp. 17–70; L. Porter and K. Roberts, "Communication in Organizations," in *Handbook of Industrial and Organizational Psychology*, ed. M. Dunnette (Chicago: Rand McNally, 1976), pp. 1553–89.

28 "Information Technology in the 21st Century," *Globe and Mail*, September 17, 1999. For discussion of the merits of e-mail, see J. Hunter and M. Allen, "Adaptation to Electronic Mail," *Journal of Applied Communication Research*, August 1992, pp. 254–74; M. Culnan and M.L. Markus, "Information Technologies," in Jablin et al., (eds.), *Handbook of Organizational Communication: An Interdisciplinary Perspective*, pp. 420–43.

29 C.S. Saunders, D. Robey, and K.A. Vaverek, "The Persistence of Status Differentials in Computer Conferencing," *Human Communications Research*, 20 (1994), pp. 443–72; D.A. Adams, P.A. Todd, and R.R. Nelson, "A Comparative Evaluation of the Impact of Electronic and Voice Mail on Organizational Communication," *Information & Management*, 24 (1993), pp. 9–21.

30 K. Foss, "Stressed Out? Blame Technology," *Globe and Mail*, May 29, 1998, p. C8; M.M. Extejt, "Teaching Students to Correspond Effectively Electronically: Tips for Using Electronic Mail Properly," *Business Communication Quarterly*, 61 (June 1998), pp. 57–67; V. Frazee, "Is E-mail Doing More Harm Than Good?" *Personnel Journal*, 75 (May 1996), p. 23.

31 "Eisner: E-mail Is Biggest Threat," *Associated Press*, May 12, 2000 (reported on www.excite.com); A. Gumbel, "How E-mail Puts Us in a Flaming Bad Temper," *The Independent* (London), January 3, 1999, p. 14; J. Kaye, "The Devil You Know," *Computer Weekly*, March 19, 1998, p. 46; S. Kennedy, "The Burning Issue of Electronic Hate Mail," *Computer Weekly*, June 5, 1997, p. 22.

32 A.D. Shulman, "Putting Group Information Technology in Its Place: Communication and Good Work Group Performance," in Clegg et al. (eds.), *Handbook of Organization Studies*, pp. 373–408.

33 M. Gibbs, "Don't Say It with Smileys," *Network World*, August 9, 1999, p. 62.

34 "Don't E-Mail with Your Mouth Full," *Computing Canada*, November 19, 1999, p. 30.

35 "Technology a Source of Stress," *Canadian Press Newswire*, January 30, 1997. For further discussion of emotions and computer-based communication, see J.L. Locke, "Q: Is E-Mail Degrading Public and Private Discourse? Yes: Electronic Mail Is Making Us Rude, Lonely, Insensitive and Dishonest," *Insight on the News*, October 19, 1998, p. 24.

36 W. Boei, "The Most Wired Person in Nunavut," *Ottawa Citizen*, November 13, 1999; S. De Santis, "Across Tundra and Cultures, Entrepreneur Wires Arctic," *Wall Street Journal*, October 19, 1998, p. B1; T. Saito, "Internet Helps Keep Scattered Inuit in Touch," *Daily Yomiuri*, June 7, 1997.

37 W. Boei, "Pilots Latest to Fly with MDA Net Technology," *Vancouver Sun*, February 24, 2000; A. Mahlon, "The Alternative Workplace: Changing Where and How People Work," *Harvard Business Review* (May–June 1998), pp. 121–30; C. Meyer and S. Davis, *Blur: The Speed of Change in the Connected Economy* (Reading, MA: Addison-Wesley, 1998); P. Bordia, "Face-to-Face Versus Computer-Mediated Communication: A Synthesis of the Experimental Literature," *Journal of Business Communication*, 34 (January 1997), pp. 99–120.

38 J.S. Brown, "Seeing Differently: A Role for Pioneering Research," *Research Technology Management*, 41 (May–June 1998), pp. 24–33; in particular, see comments by George Gilder, who is credited with developing the law of telecosm, in "Is Bigger Better?" *Fast Company*, 17 (September 1998).

39 "New Age Heralds End of Information Overload," *Financial News*, December 8, 1998.

40 T.E. Harris, *Applied Organizational Communication: Perspectives, Principles, and Pragmatics* (Hillsdale, NJ: Lawrence Erlbaum Associates, 1993), Chapter 5; R.E. Rice and D.E. Shook, "Relationships of Job Categories and Organizational Levels to Use of Communication Channels, Including Electronic Mail: A Meta-Analysis and Extension," *Journal of Management Studies*, 27 (1990), pp. 195–229; Sitkin et al., "A Dual-Capacity Model of Communication Media Choice in Organizations," p. 584.

41 B. Parkinson, *Ideas and Realities of Emotion* (London: Routledge, 1995), pp. 182–83; E. Hatfield, J.T. Cacioppo, and R.L. Rapson, *Emotional Contagion* (Cambridge, UK: Cambridge University Press, 1993).

42 R.L. Daft, R.H. Lengel, and L.K. Tevino, "Message Equivocality, Media Selection, and Manager Performance: Implications for Information Systems," *MIS Quarterly*, 11 (1987), pp. 355–66.

43 R. Lengel and R. Daft, "The Selection of Communication Media as an Executive Skill," *Academy of Management Executive*, 2 (1988), pp. 225–32; G. Huber and R. Daft, "The Information Environments of Organizations," in Jablin et al. (eds.), *Handbook of Organizational Communication: An Interdisciplinary Perspective*, pp. 130–64; R. Daft and R. Lengel, "Information Richness: A New Approach to Managerial Behavior and Organization Design," *Research in Organizational Behavior*, 6 (1984), pp. 191–233.

44 R.E. Rice, "Task Analyzability, Use of New Media, and Effectiveness: A Multi-Site Exploration of Media Richness," *Organization Science*, 3 (1992), pp. 475–500; J. Fulk, C.W. Steinfield, J. Schmitz,

and J.G. Power, "A Social Information Processing Model of Media Use in Organizations," *Communication Research*, 14 (1987), pp. 529–52.

45 R. Madhavan and R. Grover, "From Embedded Knowledge to Embodied Knowledge: New Product Development as Knowledge Management," *Journal of Marketing*, 62 (October 1998), pp. 1–12; D. Stork and A. Sapienza, "Task and Human Messages over the Project Life Cycle: Matching Media to Messages," *Project Management Journal*, 22 (December 1992), pp. 44–49.

46 M. McLuhan, *Understanding Media: The Extensions of Man* (New York: McGraw-Hill, 1964).

47 S.B. Sitkin, K.M. Sutcliffe, and J.R. Barrios-Choplin, "A Dual-Capacity Model of Communication Media Choice in Organizations," *Human Communication Research*, 18 (June 1992), pp. 563–98; J. Schmitz and J. Fulk, "Organizational Colleagues, Media Richness, and Electronic Mail: A Test of the Social Influence Model of Technology Use," *Communication Research*, 18 (1991), pp. 487–523.

48 P. Diekmeyer, "From Cellar-Dwellers to Top Sellers," *Montreal Gazette*, June 1, 1999, p. D2; J. Myerson, "Britain's Most Creative Offices," *Management Today*, April 1999, pp. 62–67; "Places to Linger," *Economist*, August 1, 1998, pp. 55–56; G. Levitch, "Pizzas and Piazzas: Workplace of the Future," *Globe and Mail*, October 12, 1996, p. C7.

49 N. Hulsman, "Farewell, Corner Office," *BC Business*, June 1999, p. 48; L. Stuart, "Why Space Is the New Frontier," *The Guardian* (London), October 31, 1998, p. 24; T.H. Walker, "Designing Work Environments That Promote Corporate Productivity," *Site Selection and Industrial Development*, April 1992, pp. 8–10.

50 A. Goldman, "Implications of Japanese Total Quality Control for Western Organizations: Dimensions of an Intercultural Hybrid," *Journal of Business Communication*, 30 (1993), pp. 29–47; J.P. Womack, D.T. Jones, and D. Roos, *The Machine That Changed the World* (New York: Rawson, 1990), p. 79.

51 J. Dobrian, "Amenities Gain Ground as Recruiting/Retention Tools," *HR Focus*, 76 (November 1999), pp. 11–12; M. McDonald, "The Latte Connections," *U.S. News & World Report*, March 29, 1999, p. 63; L. Chadderdon, "Nortel Switches Cities," *Fast Company*, 16 (August 1998), p. 112.

52 T. Petzinger, Jr., "Elimination of Permanent Desks Has Some Office Workers Fuming," *Chicago Tribune*, April 13, 1997, p. H5; J. Macht, "When the Walls Come Tumbling Down," *Inc. Technology*, 17 (September 1995), pp. 70–72; F. Becker, "A Workplace by Any Other Name: The Unassigned Office," *Facilities Design & Management*, 12 (July 1993), pp. 50–53.

53 S. Kirsner, "Every Day, It's a New Place," *Fast Company*, April–May, 1998, pp. 130–34; J.S. Russell, "A Company Headquarters Planned for Flexibility," *New York Times*, September 7, 1997, p. 7; P. LaBarre, "The Dis-Organization of Oticon," *Industry Week*, July 18, 1994, pp. 23–28.

54 Hulsman, "Farewell, Corner Office"; "Why Chiat/Day Is Putting Down Its Binoculars," *Creative Review*, April 1998, p. 67; C. Knight, "Gone Virtual," *Canadian HR Reporter*, December 16, 1996, pp. 24, 26.

55 A. Gordon, "Perks and Stock Options Are Great, But It's Attitude That Makes the Difference," *Globe and Mail*, January 28, 2000; B. Schneider, S.D. Ashworth, A.C. Higgs, and L. Carr, "Design, Validity, and Use of Strategically Focused Employee Attitude Surveys," *Personnel Psychology*, 49 (1996), pp. 695–705; T. Geddie, "Surveys Are a Waste of Time...Until You Use Them," *Communication World*, April 1996, pp. 24–26; D.M. Saunders and J.D. Leck, "Formal Upward Communication Procedures: Organizational and Employee Perspectives," *Canadian Journal of Administrative Sciences*, 10 (1993), pp. 255–68.

56 M. Allix, "Surveys Plumb Corporate Depths," *Asian Business*, November 1996.

57 K. Mark, "No More Pink Slips," *Human Resources Professional* (Ontario), November 1996, pp. 21–23; R.V. Lindahl, "Automation Breaks the Language Barrier," *HRMagazine*, 41 (March 1996), pp. 79–83.

58 A. Kimber, "Exploring What Staff Truly Think," *Marketing*, June 10, 1999, p. 27.

59 G. Grates, "Is the Employee Publication Extinct?" *Communication World*, 17 (Decemeber 1999/January 2000), pp. 27–30.

60 "Modernize Your Agency's Internal Communications," *Federal Human Resources Week*, April 13, 1998; M. Goldberg, "Cisco's Most Important Meal of the Day," *Fast Company*, 13 (February 1998), p. 56.

61 The original term is "management by *wandering* around," but this has been replaced with "walking" over the years. T. Peters and R. Waterman, *In Search of Excellence* (New York: Harper and Row, 1982), p. 122; W. Ouchi, *Theory Z* (New York: Avon Books, 1981), pp. 176–77.

62 J. Wells, "Rogers in Retreat," *Maclean's*, May 20, 1996, pp. 36–37.

63 A. Gordon, "Perks and Stock Options Are Great, But It's Attitude That Makes the Difference," *Globe and Mail*, January 28, 2000; G. Flynn, "Stop Toxic Managers Before They Stop You!" *Workforce*, 78 (August 1999), pp. 40–46; R. Laver, "The Best & Worst Jobs," *Maclean's*, May 31, 1999, pp. 18–23. Thanks to a reviewer of this book for describing PMC-Sierra's Connect Breaks.

64 "Survey Finds Good and Bad Points on Worker Attitudes," *Eastern Pennsylvania Business Journal*, May 5, 1997, p. 13; M. Gibb-Clark, "Most Job Losers Find Out Second-Hand," *Globe and Mail*, April 14, 1993, pp. B1, B4.

65 G. Kreps, *Organizational Communication* (White Plains, NY: Longman, 1986), pp. 202–06; W.L. Davis and J.R. O'Connor, "Serial Transmission of Information: A Study of the Grapevine," *Journal of Applied Communication Research*, 5 (1977), pp. 61–72; K. Davis, "Management Communication and the Grapevine," *Harvard Business Review*, 31 (September–October 1953), pp. 43–49.

66 R.L. Rosnow, "Inside Rumor: A Personal Journey," *American Psychologist*, 46 (May 1991), pp. 484–96; C.J. Walker and C.A. Beckerle, "The Effect of State Anxiety on Rumor Transmission," *Journal of Social Behavior & Personality*, 2 (August 1987), pp. 353–60.

67 R. DeRuyter, "Red Wing Shoe Purchase Delayed," *Kitchener-Waterloo Record*, May 12, 2000.

68 D. Krackhardt and J.R. Hanson, "Informal Networks: The Company Behind the Chart," *Harvard Business Review*, 71 (July–August 1993), pp. 104–11; H. Mintzberg, *The Structuring of Organizations* (Englewood Cliffs, NJ: Prentice Hall, 1979), pp. 46–53.

69 M. Noon and R. Delbridge, "News from Behind My Hand: Gossip in Organizations," *Organization Studies*, 14 (1993), pp. 23–36.

70 J. Beaurivage, "Yentas and Shamans: The Many Roles of Corporate Communicators," *Canadian Speeches*, 12 (July–August 1998), pp. 42–47.

71 G. Dutton, "One Workforce, Many Languages," *Management Review*, 87 (December 1998), pp. 42–47.

72 Mead, *Cross-Cultural Management Communication*, pp. 161–62; and J.V. Hill and C.L. Bovée, *Excellence in Business Communication* (New York: McGraw-Hill, 1993), Chapter 17.

73 F. Cunningham, "A Touch of the Tartan Treatment for Mazda," *The Scotsman*, October 14, 1997, p. 27.

74 R.M. March, *Reading the Japanese Mind* (Tokyo: Kodansha International, 1996), Chapter 1; H. Yamada, *American and Japanese Business Discourse: A Comparison of Interaction Styles* (Norwood, NJ: Ablex, 1992), p. 34.

75 "E-mail, Bloody E-mail," *Training*, January 1996, p. 12.

76 R. Axtell, *Gestures: The Do's and Taboos of Body Language around the World* (New York: Wiley, 1991); P. Harris and R. Moran, *Managing Cultural Differences* (Houston: Gulf, 1987); P. Ekman, W.V. Friesen, and J. Bear, "The International Language of Gestures," *Psychology Today*, May 1984, pp. 64–69.

77 H. Yamada, *Different Games, Different Rules* (New York: Oxford University Press, 1997), pp. 76–79; H. Yamada, *American and Japanese Business Discourse*, Chapter 2; D. Tannen, *Talking from 9 to 5* (New York: Avon, 1994), pp. 96–97; D.C. Barnlund, *Communication Styles of Japanese and Americans: Images and Realities* (Belmont, CA: Wadsworth, 1988).

78 D. Goleman, What Makes a Leader?" *Harvard Business Review*, 76 (November–December 1998), pp. 92–102.

79 G. Gourlay, "Quality's Cultural Foundation," in F. Caropreso (ed.), *Making Total Quality Happen* (New York: Conference Board, 1990), pp. 71–74.

80 S. Herring, "Gender Differences in Computer-Mediated Communication: Bringing Familiar Baggage to the New Frontier," paper presented at the American Library Association Annual Conference, Miami, June 27, 1994.

81 M. Crawford, *Talking Difference: On Gender and Language* (Thousand Oaks, CA: Sage, 1995), pp. 41–44; Tannen, *Talking from 9 to 5*; D. Tannen, *You Just Don't Understand: Men and Women in Conversation* (New York: Ballentine Books, 1990); S. Helgesen, *The Female Advantage: Women's Ways of Leadership* (New York: Doubleday, 1990).

82 A. Mulac et al., " 'Uh-Huh. What's That All About?' Differing Interpretations of Conversational Backchannels and Questions as Sources of Miscommunication Across Gender Boundaries," *Communication Research*, 25 (December 1998), pp. 641–68; G.H. Graham, J. Unruh, and P. Jennings, "The Impact of Nonverbal Communication in Organizations: A Survey of Perceptions," *Journal of Business Communication*, 28 (1991), pp. 45–61; J. Hall, "Gender Effects in Decoding Nonverbal Cues," *Psychological Bulletin*, 68 (1978), pp. 845–57.

83 This stereotypic notion is prevalent throughout J. Gray, *Men Are From Mars, Women Are From Venus* (New York: HarperCollins, 1992). For a critique of this view see Crawford, *Talking Difference*, Chapter 4; D.J. Canary, T.M. Emmers-Sommer, *Sex and Gender Differences in Personal Relationships* (New York: Guilford Press, 1997), Chapter 1.

84 P. Tripp-Knowles "A Review of the Literature on Barriers Encountered by Women in Science Academia," *Resources for Feminist Research*, 24 (Spring/Summer 1995) pp. 28–34.

85 Cited in K. Davis and J.W. Newstrom, *Human Behavior at Work: Organizational Behavior*, 7th ed. (New York: McGraw-Hill, 1985), p. 438.

86 The three components of listening discussed here are based on several recent studies, including K. de Ruyter and M.G.M. Wetzels, "The Impact of Perceived Listening Behavior in Voice-to-Voice Service Encounters," *Journal of Service Research*, 2 (February 2000), pp. 276–84; S.B. Castleberry, C.D. Shepherd, and R. Ridnour, "Effective Interpersonal Listening in the Personal Selling Environment: Conceptualization, Measurement, and Nomological Validity," *Journal of Marketing Theory and Practice*, 7 (Winter 1999), pp. 30–38; L.B. Comer and T. Drollinger, "Active Empathetic Listening and Selling Success: A Conceptual Framework," *Journal of Personal Selling & Sales Management*, 19 (Winter 1999), pp. 15–29.

87 S. Silverstein, "On the Job but Do They Listen?," *Los Angeles Times*, July 19, 1998.

88 A.P. Brief, *Attitudes in and Around Organizations* (Thousand Oaks, CA: Sage, 1998), pp. 69–84; K.K. Reardon, *Persuasion in Practice* (Newbury Park, CA: Sage, 1991); P. Zimbardo and E.B. Ebbeson, *Influencing Attitudes and Changing Behavior* (Reading, MA: Addison-Wesley, 1969).

89 J. Cooper and R.T. Coyle, "Attitudes and Attitude Change," *Annual Review of Psychology*, 35 (1984), pp. 395–426; and N. MacLachlan, "What People Really Think About Fast Talkers," *Psychology Today*, 113 (November 1979), pp. 112–17.

90 J.A. Conger, *Winning 'Em Over: A New Model for Managing in the Age of Persuasion* (New York: Simon & Schuster, 1998).

91 A. Cochrane, "Ex-bouncer Heads Compaq Canada," *Moncton Times and Transcript*, June 19, 2000.

92 D.B. Freeland, "Turning Communication into Influence," *HR Magazine*, 38 (September 1993), pp. 93–96; M. Snyder and M. Rothbart, "Communicator Attractiveness and Opinion Change," *Canadian Journal of Behavioural Science*, 3 (1971), pp. 377–87.

93 E. Aronson, *The Social Animal* (San Francisco: W.H. Freeman, 1976), pp. 67–68; R.A. Jones and J.W. Brehm, "Persuasiveness of One- and Two-Sided Communications as a Function of Awareness That There Are Two Sides," *Journal of Experimental Social Psychology*, 6 (1970), pp. 47–56.

94 D.G. Linz and S. Penrod, "Increasing Attorney Persuasiveness in the Courtroom," *Law and Psychology Review*, 8 (1984), pp. 1–47; R.B. Zajonc, "Attitudinal Effects of Mere Exposure," *Journal of Personality and Social Psychology Monograph*, 9 (1968), pp. 1–27; R. Petty and J. Cacioppo, *Attitudes and Persuasion: Classic and Contemporary Approaches* (Dubuque, IA: W.C. Brown, 1981).

95 Conger, *Winning 'Em Over*.

96 Zimbardo and Ebbeson, *Influencing Attitudes and Changing Behavior*.

97 M. Zellner, "Self-Esteem, Reception, and Influenceability," *Journal of Personality and Social Psychology*, 15 (1970), pp. 87–93.

Chapter Nine

1 J. Jusko, "Always Lessons to Learn," *Industry Week*, February 15, 1999, p. 23; T. Stevens, "TRW Canada, Ltd.," *Industry Week*, October 19, 1998, p. 76.

2 A. Swift, "Management Method Catching On," *London Free Press*, March 8, 2000; I. Bloomstone, "Everyone Wins When Workers Participate," *Montreal Gazette*, June 21, 1999, p. F3; M. Greissel, "Dofasco Supports Research at the University of British Columbia," *Iron Age New Steel*, 14 (May 1998), pp. 64–68.

3 S.G. Cohen and D.E. Bailey, "What Makes Teams Work: Group Effectiveness Research from the Shop Floor to the Executive Suite," *Journal of Management*, 23 (May 1997), pp. 239–90; M.A. West, "Preface: Introducing Work Group Psychology," in M.A. West (ed.), *Handbook of Work Group Psychology* (Chichester, UK: Wiley, 1996), p. xxvi; S.A. Mohrman, S.G. Cohen, and A.M. Mohrman, Jr., *Designing Team-Based Organizations: New Forms for Knowledge Work* (San Francisco: Jossey-Bass, 1995), pp. 39–40; J.R. Katzenbach and K.D. Smith, "The Discipline of Teams," *Harvard Business Review*, 71 (March–April 1993), pp. 111–20;); M.E. Shaw, *Group Dynamics*, 3rd ed. (New York: McGraw-Hill, 1981), p. 8.

4 *Webster's Ninth New Collegiate Dictionary* (Springfield, MA: Merriam-Webster, 1986), p. 539. David Nadler similarly distinguishes *crowds* from *groups* and *teams*. See D.A. Nadler, "From Ritual to Real Work: The Board as a Team," *Directors and Boards*, 22 (Summer 1998), pp. 28–31.

5 M. Orton, "Enamoured with Creativity," *Ottawa Citizen* (High Tech Supplement), May 30, 1999.

6 The preference for using the term *team* rather than *group* is also discussed in Cohen and Bailey, "What Makes Teams Work"; R.A. Guzzo and M.W. Dickson, "Teams in Organizations: Recent Research on Performance and Effectiveness," *Annual Review of Psychology*, 47 (1996), pp. 307–38.

7 G.E. Huszczo, *Tools for Team Excellence* (Palo Alto, CA: Davies-Black, 1996), pp. 9–15; R. Likert, *New Patterns of Management* (New York: McGraw-Hill, 1961), pp. 106–108.

8 L.Y. Chan and B.E. Lynn, "Operating in Turbulent Times: How Ontario's Hospitals Are Meeting the Current Funding Crisis," *Health Care Management Review*, 23 (June 1998), p. 7.

9 Mohrman, Cohen, and Mohrman, Jr., *Designing Team-Based Organizations*, p. 6; J.H. Shonk, *Team-Based Organizations: Developing a Successful Team Environment* (Homewood, IL: Business Irwin One, 1992).

10 C. Salter, "Roberts Rules the Road," *Fast Company*, 17 (September 1998); J. Childs, "Five Years and Counting: The Path to Self-Directed Work Teams," *Hospital Materiel Management Quarterly*, May 1997, pp. 34–43.

11 N.S. Bruning and P.R. Liverpool, "Membership in Quality Circles and Participation in Decision Making," *Journal of Applied Behavioral Science*, 29 (March 1993), pp. 76–95; S.D. Saleh, Z. Guo, and T. Hull, "The Use of Quality Circles in the Automobile Parts Industry," *Proceedings of the Annual ASAC Conference, Organizational Behaviour Division*, 9, pt. 5 (1988), pp. 95–104.

12 Mohrman, Cohen, and Mohrman, Jr., *Designing Team-Based Organizations*, Chapter 2; R.S. Wellins, W.C. Byham, and G.R. Dixon, Inside Teams (San Francisco: Jossey-Bass, 1994), pp. 9–10.

13 R. Pascale, "Change How You Define Leadership, and You Change How You Run a Company," *Fast Company*, April–May 1998, pp. 110–20.

14 T. Peters, *Thriving on Chaos* (New York: Knopf, 1987), pp. 211–18; T. Kidder, *Soul of a New Machine* (Boston: Little, Brown, 1981); T. Peters and N. Austin, *A Passion for Excellence* (New York: Random House, 1985), Chapters 9 and 10.

15 S. Zesiger, "Dial 'M' For Mystique," *Fortune*, January 12, 1998, p. 175; R. Hertzberg, "No Longer a Skunkworks," *Internet World*, November 3, 1997; R. Lim, "Innovation, Innovation, Innovation," *Business Times* (Singapore), October 27, 1997, p. 18.

16 T. Koppel, *Powering the Future* (Toronto: John Wiley & Sons, 1999).

17 A. Anderson, "Virtual Office at SHL," *Silicon Valley North*, May 1997, p. 32.

18 J. Lipnack and J. Stamps, *Virtual Teams: Reaching Across Space, Time, and Organizations with Technology* (New York: John Wiley & Sons, 1997), pp. 5–8; D.J. Armstrong and P. Cole, "Managing Distances and Differences in Geographically Distributed Work Groups," in S.E. Jackson and M.N. Ruderman (eds.), *Diversity in Work Teams: Research Paradigms for a Changing Workplace* (Washington, DC: American Psychological Association, 1995), pp. 187–215.

19 D. Robey, H.M. Khoo, and C. Powers, "Situated Learning in Cross-functional Virtual Teams," *Technical Communication* (February 2000), pp. 51–66.

20 J.S. Brown, "Seeing Differently: A Role for Pioneering Research," *Research Technology Management*, 41 (May–June 1998), pp. 24–33; in particular, see comments by George Gilder, who is credited with developing the law of telecosm, in "Is Bigger Better?" *Fast Company*, 17 (September 1998).

21 A.M. Townsend, S.M. DeMarie, and A.R. Hendrickson, "Virtual Teams: Technology and the Workplace of the Future," *Academy of Management Executive*, 12 (August 1998), pp. 17–29.

22 J.A. Wagner III, C.R. Leana, E.A. Locke, and D.M. Schweiger, "Cognitive and Motivational Frameworks in U.S. Research on Participation: A Meta-Analysis of Primary Effects," *Journal of Organizational Behavior*, 18 (1997), pp. 49–65.

23 W.B. Stevenson, J.L. Pearce, and L.W. Porter, "The Concept of 'Coalition' in Organization Theory and Research," *Academy of Management Review*, 10 (1985), pp. 256–68; Shaw, *Group Dynamics*, pp. 105–10.

24 E.C. Wenger and W.M. Snyder, "Communities of Practice: The Organizational Frontier," *Harvard Business Review*, 78 (January–February 2000), pp. 139–45; J.W. Botkin, *Smart Business: How Knowledge Communities Can Revolutionize Your Company* (New York: Free Press, 1999).

25 M.A. Hogg and D.J. Terry, "Social Identity and Self-categorization Processes in Organizational Contexts," *Academy of Management Review*, 25 (January 2000), pp. 121–40; B.E. Ashforth and F. Mael, "Social Identity Theory and the Organization," *Academy of Management Review*, 14 (1989), pp. 20–39.

26 A.S. Tannenbaum, *Social Psychology of the Work Organization* (Belmont, CA: Wadsworth, 1966), p. 62; S. Schacter, *The Psychology of Affiliation* (Stanford, CA: Stanford University Press, 1959), pp. 12–19.

27 R. Forrester and A.B. Drexler, "A Model for Team-based Organization Performance," *Academy of Management Executive*, 13 (August 1999), pp. 36–49; M.A. West, C.S. Borrill, and K.L. Unsworth, "Team Effectiveness in Organizations," *International Review of Industrial and Organizational Psychology*, 13 (1998), pp. 1–48; R.A. Guzzo and M.W. Dickson, "Teams in Organizations: Recent Research on Performance and Effectiveness," *Annual Review of Psychology*, 47 (1996), pp. 307–38.

28 West et al., "Team Effectiveness in Organizations;" Mohrman, Cohen, and Mohrman, Jr., *Designing Team-Based Organizations*, pp. 58–65; J.E. McGrath, "Time, Interaction, and Performance (TIP): A Theory of Groups," *Small Group Research*, 22 (1991), pp. 147–74; G.P. Shea and R.A. Guzzo, "Group Effectiveness: What Really Matters?" *Sloan Management Review*, 27 (1987), pp. 33–46.

29 "Team Incentives Prominent Among 'Best-Practice' Companies," *Quality*, 35 (April 1996), p. 20. For discussion of the role of rewards in team dynamics, see J.S. DeMatteo, L.T. Eby, and E. Sundstrom, "Team-Based Rewards: Current Empirical Evidence and Directions for Future Research," in B.M. Staw and L.L. Cummings (eds.), *Research in Organizational Behavior*, 20 (1998), pp. 141–83; A. Barua, C.H.S. Lee, and A.B. Whinston, "Incentives and Computing Systems for Team-Based Organizations," *Organization Science*, 6 (1995), pp. 487–504; R.L. Heneman and C. von Hippel, "Balancing Group and Individual Rewards: Rewarding Individual Contributions to the Team," *Compensation & Benefits Review*, 27 (July–August 1995), pp. 63–68.

30 F. Burlage, "Master the Art of Kaizen," *The European*, February 20, 1997, p. 12.

31 P. Bordia "Face-to-Face Versus Computer-Mediated Communication: A Synthesis of the Experimental Literature," *Journal of Business Communication*, 34 (January 1997), pp. 99–120; A.D. Shulman, "Putting Group Information Technology in Its Place: Communication and Good Work Group Performance," in S.R. Clegg, C. Hardy, and W.R. Nord (eds.), *Handbook of Organization Studies* (London: Sage, 1996), pp. 357–74; J.E. McGrath and A.B. Hollingshead, *Groups Interacting with Technology* (Thousand Oaks, CA: Sage, 1994).

32 A. Smith, "Perfect Fits Vander Laan," *London Free Press*, May 3, 1999, p. 11. Workspace design and team dynamics are discussed in J. Wineman and M. Serrato, "Facility Design for High-Performance Teams," in E. Sundstrom and Associates (eds.), *Supporting Work Team Effectiveness* (San Francisco: Jossey-Bass, 1998), pp. 271–98.

33 R. Wageman, "Case Study: Critical Success Factors for Creating Superb Self-Managing Teams at Xerox," *Compensation and Benefits Review*, 29 (September–October 1997), pp. 31–41; D. Dimancescu and K. Dwenger, "Smoothing the Product Development Path," *Management Review*, 85 (January 1996), pp. 36–41.

34 D. G. Ancona and D. E. Caldwell, "Demography and Design: Predictors of New Product Team Performance," *Organization Science* 3 (August 1992), pp. 331–41.

35 M.A. Campion, E.M. Papper, and G.J. Medsker, "Relations Between Work Team Characteristics and Effectiveness: A Replication and Extension," *Personnel Psychology*, 49 (1996), pp. 429–52; S. Worchel and S.L. Shackelford, "Groups Under Stress: The Influence of Group Structure and Environment on Process and Performance," *Personality & Social Psychology Bulletin*, 17 (1991), pp. 640–47; E. Sundstrom, K.P. De Meuse, and D. Futrell, "Work Teams: Applications and Effectiveness," *American Psychologist*, 45 (1990), pp. 120–33.

36 G. van der Vegt, B. Emans, and E. van de Vliert, "Motivating Effects of Task and Outcome Interdependence in Work Teams," *Group & Organization Management*, 23 (June 1998), pp. 124–43; R.C. Liden, S.J. Wayne, and L.K. Bradway, "Task Interdependence as a Moderator of the Relation Between Group Control and Performance," *Human Relations*, 50 (1997), pp. 169–81; R. Wageman, "Interdependence and Group Effectiveness," *Administrative Science Quarterly*, 40 (1995), pp.145–80; M.A. Campion, G.J. Medsker, and A.C. Higgs, "Relations Between Work Group Characteristics and Effectiveness: Implications for Designing Effective Work Groups," *Personnel Psychology*, 46 (1993), pp. 823–50; M.N. Kiggundu, "Task Interdependence and the Theory of Job Design," *Academy of Management Review*, 6 (1981), pp. 499–508.

37 A. Muoio, "Growing Smart," *Fast Company*, 16 (August 1998); A.R. Sorkin, "Gospel According to St. Luke's," *New York Times*, February 12, 1998, p. D1.

38 M.A. Cusumano, "How Microsoft Makes Large Teams Work Like Small Teams," *Sloan Management Review*, 39 (Fall 1997), pp. 9–20.

39 G.R. Hickman and A. Creighton-Zollar, "Diverse Self-Directed Work Teams: Developing Strategic Initiatives for 21st Century Organizations," *Public Personnel Management*, 27 (Spring 1998), pp. 187–200.

40 J.R. Katzenbach and D.K. Smith, *The Wisdom of Teams: Creating the High-Performance Organization* (Boston: Harvard University Press, 1993), pp. 45–47; G. Stasser, "Pooling of Unshared Information During Group Discussion," in S. Worchel, W. Wood, and J.A. Simpson (eds.), *Group Process and Productivity* (Newbury Park, CA: Sage, 1992), pp. 48–67.

41 D. Flavelle, "Firms Try to Rope Winners by Hiring Out of the Herd," *Toronto Star*, January 30, 2000.

42 L.T. Eby and G.H. Dobbins, "Collectivist Orientation in Teams: An Individual and Group-Level Analysis," *Journal of Organizational Behavior*, 18 (1997), pp. 275–95; P.C. Earley, "East Meets West Meets Mideast: Further Explorations of Collectivistic and Individualistic Work Groups," *Academy of Management Journal*, 36 (1993), pp. 319–48.

43 Mohrman, Cohen, and Mohrman, Jr., *Designing Team-Based Organizations*, pp. 248–54; M.J. Stevens and M.A. Campion, "The Knowledge, Skill and Ability Requirements for Teamwork: Implications for Human Resources Management," *Journal of Management*, 20 (1994), pp. 503–30; A.P. Hare, *Handbook of Small Group Research*, 2nd ed. (New York: The Free Press, 1976), pp. 12–15.

44 "New Anchor Hocking Plant Incorporates 'Socio-Tech' Work Environment Philosophy," *Business Wire*, October 19, 1995. For a comprehensive discussion of selecting people for team-based work, see R.J. Klimoski and L.B. Zukin, "Selection and Staffing for Team Effectiveness," in E. Sundstrom and Associates (eds.), *Supporting Work Team Effectiveness* (San Francisco: Jossey-Bass, 1998), pp. 63–91.

45 D.C. Hambrick, S.C. Davison, S.A. Snell, and C.C. Snow, "When Groups Consist of Multiple Nationalities: Towards a New Understanding of the Implications," *Organization Studies*, 19 (1998), pp. 181–205; F.J. Milliken and L.L. Martins, "Searching for Common Threads: Understanding the Multiple Effects of Diversity in Organizational Groups," *Academy of Management Review*, 21 (1996), pp. 402–33; J.K. Murnighan and D. Conlon, "The Dynamics of Intense Work Groups: A Study of British String Quartets," *Administrative Science Quarterly*, 36 (1991), pp. 165–86.

46 P.C. Earley and E. Mosakowski, "Creating Hybrid Team Cultures: An Empirical Test of Transnational Team Functioning," *Academy of Management Journal*, 43 (February 2000), pp. 26–49; D.C. Lau and J.K. Murnighan, "Demographic Diversity and Faultlines: The Compositional Dynamics of Organizational Groups," *Academy of Management Review*, 23 (April 1998), pp. 325–40.

47 L.H. Pelled, K.M. Eisenhardt, and K.R. Xin, "Exploring the Black Box: An Analysis of Work Group Diversity, Conflict, and Performance," *Administrative Science Quarterly*, 44 (March 1999), pp. 1–28; K.Y. Williams and C.A. O'Reilly, III, "Demography and Diversity in Organizations: A Review of 40 Years of Research," *Research in Organizational Behavior*, 20 (1998); B. Daily, A. Wheatley, S.R. Ash, and R.L. Steiner, "The Effects of a Group Decision Support System on Culturally Diverse and Culturally Homogeneous Group Decision Making," *Information & Management*, 30 (1996), pp. 281–89; W.E. Watson, K. Kumar, and L.K. Michaelson, "Cultural Diversity's Impact on Interaction Process and Performance: Comparing Homogeneous and Diverse Task Groups," *Academy of Management Journal,* 36 (1993), pp. 590–602.

48 B.W. Tuckman and M.A.C. Jensen, "Stages of Small-Group Development Revisited," *Group and Organization Studies*, 2 (1977), pp. 419–42. For a humorous and somewhat cynical discussion of team dynamics through these stages, see H. Robbins and M. Finley, *Why Teams Don't Work* (Princeton, NJ: Peterson's/Pacesetters, 1995), Chapter 21.

49 J.A. Cannon-Bowers, S.I. Tannenbaum, E. Salas, and C.E. Volpe, "Defining Competencies and Establishing Team Training Requirements," in Guzzo, Salas, and Associates (eds.), *Team Effectiveness and Decision Making in Organizations* (San Francisco: Jossey-Bass, 1995), pp. 333–80.

50 A. Edmondson, "Psychological Safety and Learning Behavior in Work Teams," *Administrative Science Quarterly*, 44 (1999), pp. 350–83.

51 D.L. Miller, "Synergy in Group Development: A Perspective on Group Performance," *Proceedings of the Annual ASAC Conference, Organizational Behaviour Division*, 17, pt. 5 (1996), pp. 119–28; Worchel, D. Coutant-Sassic, and M. Grossman, "A Developmental Approach to Group Dynamics: A Model and Illustrative Research," in *Group Process and Productivity*, ed. Worchel et al., pp. 181–202; C.J.G. Gersick, "Time and Transition in Work Teams: Toward a New Model of Group Development," *Academy of Management Journal*, 31 (1988), pp. 9–41.

52 D.C. Feldman, "The Development and Enforcement of Group Norms," *Academy of Management Review*, 9 (1984), pp. 47–53; L.W. Porter, E.E. Lawler, and J.R. Hackman, *Behavior in Organizations* (New York: McGraw-Hill, 1975), pp. 391–94.

53 I.R. Gellatly, "Individual and Group Determinants of Employee Absenteeism: Test of a Causal Model," *Journal of Organizational Behavior*, 16 (1995), pp. 469–85; G. Johns, "Absenteeism Estimates by Employees and Managers: Divergent Perspectives and Self-Serving Perceptions," *Journal of Applied Psychology*, 79 (1994), pp. 229–39.

54 B. Latané, "The Psychology of Social Impact," *American Psychologist*, 36 (1981), pp. 343–56; C.A. Kiesler and S.B. Kiesler, *Conformity* (Reading, MA: Addison-Wesley, 1970).

55 Porter, Lawler, and Hackman, *Behavior in Organizations*, pp. 399–401.

56 L. Coch and J.R.P. French, Jr., "Overcoming Resistance to Change," *Human Relations*, 1 (1948), pp. 512–32.

57 Feldman, "The Development and Enforcement of Group Norms," pp. 50–52.

58 Katzenbach and Smith, *The Wisdom of Teams*, pp. 121–23.

59 K.L. Bettenhausen and J.K. Murnighan, "The Development of an Intragroup Norm and the Effects of Interpersonal and Structural Challenges," *Administrative Science Quarterly*, 36 (1991), pp. 20–35.

60 R.S. Spich and K. Keleman, "Explicit Norm Structuring Process: A Strategy for Increasing Task-Group Effectiveness," *Group & Organization Studies*, 10 (March 1985), pp. 37–59.

61 Chan and Lynn, "Operating in Turbulent Times: How Ontario's Hospitals Are Meeting the Current Funding Crisis."

62 D.I. Levine, "Piece Rates, Output Restriction, and Conformism," *Journal of Economic Psychology*, 13 (1992), pp. 473–89.

63 P. Roberts, "Sony Changes the Game," *Fast Company*, 10 (1997), p. 116.

64 D. Katz and R.L. Kahn, *The Social Psychology of Organizations* (New York: John Wiley & Sons, 1966), Chapter 7; J.W. Thibault and H.H. Kelley, *The Social Psychology of Groups* (New York: John Wiley & Sons, 1959), Chapter 8.

65 D. Vinokur-Kaplan, "Treatment Teams That Work (and Those That Don't): An Application of Hackman's Group Effectiveness Model to Interdisciplinary Teams in Psychiatric Hospitals," *Journal of Applied Behavioral Science*, 31 (1995), pp. 303–27; Shaw, *Group Dynamics*, pp. 213–26; Goodman et al., "Understanding Groups in Organizations," pp. 144–46.

66 S. Lembke and M.G. Wilson, "Putting the 'Team' into Teamwork: Alternative Theoretical Contributions for Contemporary Management Practice," *Human Relations*, 51 (July 1998), pp. 927–44; B.E. Ashforth and R.H. Humphrey, "Emotion in the Workplace: A Reappraisal," *Human Relations*, 48 (1995), pp. 97–125; P.R. Bernthal and C.A. Insko, "Cohesiveness without Groupthink: The Interactive Effects of Social and Task Cohesiveness," *Group and Organization Management*, 18 (1993), pp. 66–87.

67 A. Lott and B. Lott, "Group Cohesiveness as Interpersonal Attraction: A Review of Relationships with Antecedent and Consequent Variables," *Psychological Bulletin*, 64 (1965), pp. 259–309.

68 S.E. Jackson, "Team Composition in Organizational Settings: Issues in Managing an Increasingly Diverse Work Force," in Worchel et al. (eds.), *Group Process and Productivity*, pp. 138–73; J. Virk, P. Aggarwal, and R.N. Bhan, "Similarity versus Complementarity in Clique Formation," *Journal of Social Psychology*, 120 (1983), pp. 27–34.

69 M.B. Pinto, J.K. Pinto, and J.E. Prescott, "Antecedents and Consequences of Project Team Cross-Functional Cooperation," *Management Science*, 39 (1993), pp. 1281–96; W. Piper, M. Marrache, R. Lacroix, A. Richardson, and B. Jones, "Cohesion as a Basic Bond in Groups," *Human Relations*, 36 (1983), pp. 93–108.

70 A. Smith, "Perfect Fits Vander Laan," *London Free Press*, May 3, 1999, p. 11; D. Bencivenga, "A Humanistic Approach to Space," *HRMagazine*, 43 (March 1998), pp. 68–76; M. Jackson, "Walls Come Tumbling Down," *Akron Beacon Journal*, May 21, 1998.

71 Robey et al, "Situated Learning in Cross-functional Virtual Teams;" E.J. Hill, B.C. Miller, S.P. Weiner and J. Colihan, "Influences of the Virtual Office on Aspects of Work and Work/Life Balance," *Personnel Psychology*, 51 (Autumn 1998), pp. 667–83; S.B. Gould, K.J. Weiner, and B.R. Levin, *Free Agents: People and Organizations Creating a New Working Community* (San Francisco: Jossey-Bass, 1997), pp. 158–60.

72 J.E. Hautaluoma and R.S. Enge, "Early Socialization into a Work Group: Severity of Initiations Revisited," *Journal of Social Behavior & Personality*, 6 (1991) pp. 725–48; E. Aronson and J. Mills, "The Effects of Severity of Initiation on Liking for a Group," *Journal of Abnormal and Social Psychology*, 59 (1959), pp. 177–81.

73 B. Mullen and C. Copper, "The Relation Between Group Cohesiveness and Performance: An Integration," *Psychological Bulletin*, 115 (1994), pp. 210–27; Shaw, *Group Dynamics*, p. 215.

74 M. Rempel and R.J. Fisher, "Perceived Threat, Cohesion, and Group Problem Solving in Intergroup Conflict," *International Journal of Conflict Management*, 8 (1997), pp. 216–34.

75 J.M. McPherson and P.A. Popielarz, "Social Networks and Organizational Dynamics," *American Sociological Review*, 57 (1992), pp. 153–70; Piper et al., "Cohesion as a Basic Bond in Groups," pp. 93–108.

76 C.A. O'Reilly III, D.F. Caldwell, and W.P. Barnett, "Work Group Demography, Social Integration, and Turnover," *Administrative Science Quarterly*, 34 (1989), pp. 21–37.

77 R.D. Banker, J.M. Field, R.G. Schroeder, and K.K. Sinha, "Impact of Work Teams on Manufacturing Performance: A Longitudinal Study," *Academy of Management Journal,* 39 (1996), pp. 867–90; D. Vinokur-Kaplan, "Treatment Teams That Work (and Those That Don't): An Application of Hackman's Group Effectiveness Model to Interdisciplinary Teams in Psychiatric Hospitals," *Journal of Applied Behavioral Science*, 31 (September 1995), pp. 303–27; Mullen and Copper, "The Relation Between Group Cohesiveness and Performance," *Psychological Bulletin*; C.R. Evans and K.L. Dion, "Group Cohesion and Performance: A Meta-Analysis," *Small Group Research*, 22 (1991), pp. 175–86.

78 Robbins and Finley, *Why Teams Don't Work*, Chapter 20; "The Trouble with Teams," *Economist*, January 14, 1995, p. 61; A. Sinclair, "The Tyranny of Team Ideology," *Organization Studies*, 13 (1992), pp. 611–26. For discussion of the benefits of teams, see J. Pfeffer, "Seven Practices of Successful Organizations," *California Management Review*, 40 (1998), pp. 96–124.

79 P. Panchak, "The Future Manufacturing," *Industry Week*, 247 (September 21, 1998), pp. 96–105; B. Dumaine, "The Trouble with Teams," *Fortune*, September 5, 1994, pp. 86–92.

80 I.D. Steiner, *Group Process and Productivity* (New York: Academic Press, 1972).

81 D. Dunphy and B. Bryant, "Teams: Panaceas or Prescriptions for Improved Performance?" *Human Relations*, 49 (1996), pp. 677–99. For discussion of Brooke's Law, see Cusumano, "How Microsoft Makes Large Teams Work Like Small Teams."

82 M. Erez and A. Somech "Is Group Productivity Loss the Rule or the Exception? Effects of Culture and Group-Based Motivation," *Academy of Management Journal*, 39 (1996), pp. 1513–37; S.J. Karau and K.D. Williams, "Social Loafing: A Meta-Analytic Review and Theoretical Integration," *Journal of Personality and Social Psychology*, 65 (1993), pp. 681–706; J.M. George, "Extrinsic and Intrinsic Origins of Perceived Social Loafing in Organizations," *Academy of Management Journal*, 35 (1992), pp. 191–202; R. Albanese and D.D. Van Fleet, "Rational Behavior in Groups: The Free-Riding Tendency," *Academy of Management Review*, 10 (1985), pp. 244–55.

83 M. Erez and A. Somech "Is Group Productivity Loss the Rule or the Exception? Effects of Culture and Group-Based Motivation," *Academy of Management Journal*, 39 (1996), pp. 1513–37; P.C. Earley, "Social Loafing and Collectivism: A Comparison of the U.S. and the People's Republic of China," *Administrative Science Quarterly*, 34 (1989), pp. 565–81.

84 T.A. Judge and T.D. Chandler, "Individual-level Determinants of Employee Shirking," *Relations Industrielles*, 51 (1996), pp. 468–86; J.M. George, "Asymmetrical Effects of Rewards and Punishments: The Case of Social Loafing," *Journal of Occupational and Organizational Psychology*, 68 (1995), pp. 327–38; R.E. Kidwell and N. Bennett, "Employee Propensity to Withhold Effort: A Conceptual Model to Intersect Three Avenues of Research," *Academy of Management Review*, 19 (1993), pp. 429–56; J.A. Shepperd, "Productivity Loss in Performance Groups: A Motivation Analysis," *Psychological Bulletin*, 113 (1993), pp. 67–81.

85 W.G. Dyer, *Team Building: Issues and Alternatives*, 2nd ed. (Reading, MA: Addison-Wesley, 1987); and S.J. Liebowitz and K.P. De Meuse, "The Application of Team Building," *Human Relations*, 35 (1982), pp. 1–18.

86 Sundstrom et al., "Work Teams: Applications and Effectiveness," *American Psychologist*, p. 128; M. Beer, *Organizational Change and Development: A Systems View* (Santa Monica, CA: Goodyear, 1980), pp. 143–46.

87 Beer, *Organizational Change and Development*, p. 145.

88 J.J. Laabs, "Team Training Goes Outdoors," *Personnel Journal*, June 1991, pp. 56–63.

89 D. Menzies, "The Adrenalin Agenda," *Meetings & Incentive Travel*, 25 (November 1996), pp. 24–27.

90 Robbins and Finley, *Why Teams Don't Work*, Chapter 17.

91 M.J. Brown, "Let's Talk About It, Really Talk About It," *Journal for Quality & Participation*, 19(6) (1996) pp. 26–33; F.H. Schein, "On Dialogue, Culture, and Organizational Learning," *Organizational Dynamics*, Autumn 1993, pp. 40–51; and P.M. Senge, *The Fifth Discipline* (New York: Doubleday Currency, 1990), pp. 238–49.

92 G. Coetzer, *A Study of the Impact of Different Team Building Techniques on Work Team Effectiveness*. Unpublished MBA research project (Burnaby, BC: Simon Fraser University, 1993).

93 T.G. Cummings and C.G. Worley, *Organization Development & Change*, 6th ed. (Cincinnati: South-Western, 1997), pp. 218–19; P.F. Buller and C.H. Bell, Jr., "Effects of Team Building and Goal Setting on Productivity: A Field Experiment," *Academy of Management Journal*, 29 (1986), pp. 305–28.

94 C.J. Solomon, "Simulation Training Builds Teams Through Experience," *Personnel Journal*, 72 (June 1993), pp. 100–106.

95 "AT&T Has 'The Right Stuff' at Corporate Space Academy," *Business Wire*, December 17, 1997; C. Prystay, "Executive Rearmament: Tempering Asia's Executive Mettle," *Asian Business*, October 1996.

96 R.W. Woodman and J.J. Sherwood, "The Role of Team Development in Organizational Effectiveness: A Critical Review," *Psychological Bulletin*, 88 (1980), pp. 166–86; Sundstrom et al., "Work Teams: Applications and Effectiveness," p. 128.

97 Huszczo, *Tools for Team Excellence*, pp. 50–58.

98 P. McGraw, "Back from the Mountain: Outdoor Management Development Programs and How to Ensure the Transfer of Skills to the Workplace," *Asia Pacific Journal of Human Resources*, 31 (Spring 1993), pp. 52–61; G.E. Huszczo, "Training for Team Building," *Training and Development Journal*, 44 (February 1990), pp. 37–43.

Chapter Ten

1 K. Fraser, "Ferry-Tale Alarms," *Vancouver Province*, June 14, 2000; P. Willcocks, "Fast Ferries May Sell for Under $40 Million Each," *Vancouver Sun*, May 31, 2000; K. Lunman, "B.C. Admits Failure, Puts Fast Ferries Up for Sale," *Globe and Mail*, March 14, 2000, p. A1; C. McInnes, "Victoria Sinks Fast Ferries," *Vancouver Sun*, March 14, 2000; K. Lunman, "B.C. NDP Blasted in Report on Ferries," *Globe and Mail*, October 29, 1999, p. A7.

2 F.A. Shull, Jr., A.L. Delbecq, and L.L. Cummings, *Organizational Decision Making* (New York: McGraw-Hill, 1970), p. 31. Also see J.G. March, "Understanding How Decisions Happen in Organizations," in Z. Shapira (ed.), *Organizational Decision Making* (New York: Cambridge University Press, 1997), pp. 9–32.

3 B.M. Bass, Organizational Decision Making (Homewood, IL: Irwin, 1983), Chapter 3; W.F. Pounds, "The Process of Problem Finding," *Industrial Management Review*, 11 (Fall 1969), pp. 1–19; C. Kepner and B. Tregoe, *The Rational Manager* (New York: McGraw-Hill, 1965).

4 This model is adapted from several sources: H. Mintzberg, D. Raisinghani, and A. Théorét, "The Structure of 'Unstructured' Decision Processes," *Administrative Science Quarterly*, 21 (1976), pp. 246–75; H.A. Simon, *The New Science of Management Decision* (New York: Harper & Row, 1960); C. Kepner and B. Tregoe, *The Rational Manager* (New York: McGraw-Hill, 1965); W.C. Wedley and R.H.G. Field, "A Predecision Support System," *Academy of Management Review*, 9 (1984), pp. 696–703.

5 J.W. Dean, Jr., and M.P. Sharfman, "Does Decision Process Matter? A Study of Strategic Decision-Making Effectiveness," *Academy of Management Journal*, 39 (1996), pp. 368–96.

6 P.F. Drucker, *The Practice of Management* (New York: Harper & Brothers, 1954), pp. 353–57.

7 Wedley and Field, "A Predecision Support System," p. 696; Drucker, *The Practice of Management*, p. 357; L.R. Beach and T.R. Mitchell, "A Contingency Model for the Selection of Decision Strategies," *Academy of Management Review*, 3 (1978), pp. 439–49.

8 I.L. Janis, *Crucial Decisions* (New York: The Free Press, 1989), pp. 35–37; Simon, *The New Science of Management Decision*, pp. 5–6.

9 I. Nonaka and H. Takeuchi, *The Knowledge-Creating Company* (New York: Oxford University Press, 1995), p. 69.

10 Mintzberg, Raisinghani, and Théorét, "The Structure of 'Unstructured' Decision Processes," pp. 255–56.

11 B. Fischhoff and S. Johnson, "The Possibility of Distributed Decision Making," in Shapira, *Organizational Decision Making*, pp. 216–37.

12 J.E. Dutton, "Strategic Agenda Building in Organizations," in Shapira, *Organizational Decision Making*, pp. 81–107; M. Lyles and H. Thomas, "Strategic Problem Formulation: Biases and Assumptions Embedded in Alternative Decision-Making Models," *Journal of Management Studies*, 25 (1988), pp. 131–45; I.I. Mitroff, "On Systematic Problem Solving and the Error of the Third Kind," *Behavioral Science*, 9 (1974), pp. 383–93.

13 D. Gurteen, "Knowledge, Creativity and Innovation," *Journal of Knowledge Management*, 2 (September 1998), p. 5; P.M. Senge, *The Fifth Discipline: The Art and Practice of the Learning Organization* (New York: Doubleday Currency, 1990), Chapter 10.

14 D. Domer, *The Logic of Failure* (Reading, MA: Addison-Wesley, 1996); M. Basadur, "Managing the Creative Process in Organizations," in M.A. Runco (ed.), *Problem Finding, Problem Solving, and Creativity* (Norwood, NJ: Ablex Publishing, 1994), pp. 237–68.

15 P.C. Nutt, "Preventing Decision Debacles," *Technological Forecasting and Social Change*, 38 (1990), pp. 159–74.

16 J.A. Byrne, *Chainsaw* (New York: HarperCollins, 1999).

17 P.C. Nutt, *Making Tough Decisions* (San Francisco: Jossey-Bass, 1989).

18 S. Wintrob, "Utility Empower Line Crews," *Computing Canada*, March 28, 1996, p. 36.

19 J. Conlisk, "Why Bounded Rationality?" *Journal of Economic Literature*, 34 (1996), pp. 669–700; B.L. Lipman, "Information Processing and Bounded Rationality: A Survey," *Canadian Journal of Economics*, 28 (1995), pp. 42–67.

20 L.T. Pinfield, "A Field Evaluation of Perspectives on Organizational Decision Making," *Administrative Science Quarterly*, 31 (1986), pp. 365–88.

21 H.A. Simon, *Administrative Behavior*, 2nd ed. (New York: The Free Press, 1957), pp. xxv, 80–84; J.G. March and H.A. Simon, *Organizations* (New York: Wiley, 1958), pp. 140–41.

22 P.O. Soelberg, "Unprogrammed Decision Making," *Industrial Management Review,* 8 (1967), pp. 19–29; H.A. Simon, "A Behavioral Model of Rational Choice," *Quarterly Journal of Economics,* 69 (1955), pp. 99–118.

23 J.E. Russo, V.H. Medvec, and M.G. Meloy, "The Distortion of Information During Decisions," *Organizational Behavior & Human Decision Processes,* 66 (1996), pp. 102–10.

24 H.A. Simon, *Models of Man: Social and Rational* (New York: Wiley, 1957), p. 253.

25 Y. Ganzach, A.H. Kluger, and N. Klayman, "Making Decisions from an Interview: Expert Measurement and Mechanical Combination," *Personnel Psychology,* 53 (Spring 2000), pp. 1–20.

26 A. Rangaswamy and G.L. Lilien, "Software Tools for New Product Development," *Journal of Marketing Research,* 34 (1997), pp. 177–84.

27 G.H. Anthes, "Learning How to Share," *Computerworld,* 32 (February 23, 1998), pp. 75–77.

28 P.J.H. Schoemaker, "Disciplined Imagination: From Scenarios to Strategic Options," *International Studies of Management & Organization,* 27 (Summer 1997), pp. 43–70.

29 B. Withrow, "How to Generate Employee Buy-In the Easy Way," *Canadian HR Reporter,* February 8, 1999, pp. 16–17.

30 L.A. Burke and M.K. Miller, "Taking the Mystery Out of Intuitive Decision Making," *Academy of Management Executive,* 13 (November 1999), pp. 91–99.

31 A. Muoio, "Decisions, Decisions—Unit of One," *Fast Company,* 18 (October 1998), pp. 93–106.

32 O. Behling and N.L. Eckel, "Making Sense Out of Intuition," *Academy of Management Executive,* 5 (February 1991), pp. 46–54; Nutt, *Making Tough Decisions,* p. 54; H.A. Simon, "Making Management Decisions: The Role of Intuition and Emotion," *Academy of Management Executive* (February 1987), pp. 57–64; W.H. Agor, "The Logic of Intuition," *Organizational Dynamics* (Winter 1986), pp. 5–18.

33 E.N. Brockmann and W.P. Anthony, "The Influence of Tacit Knowledge and Collective Mind on Strategic Planning," *Journal of Managerial Issues,* 10 (Summer 1998), pp. 204–22; D. Leonard and S. Sensiper, "The Role of Tacit Knowledge in Group Innovation," *California Management Review,* 40 (Spring 1998), pp. 112–32.

34 R.N. Taylor, *Behavioral Decision Making* (Glenview, IL: Scott, Foresman, 1984), pp. 163–66.

35 D.R. Bobocel and J.P. Meyer, "Escalating Commitment to a Failing Course of Action: Separating the Role of Choice and Justification," *Journal of Applied Psychology,* 79 (1994), pp. 360–63; G. Whyte, "Escalating Commitment in Individual and Group Decision Making: A Prospect Theory Approach," *Organizational Behavior and Human Decision Processes,* 54 (1993), pp. 430–55; G. Whyte, "Escalating Commitment to a Course of Action: A Reinterpretation," *Academy of Management Review,* 11 (1986), pp. 311–21.

36 "Tokyo's Newest Subway Line Derailed by Costly Errors," *Toronto Star,* July 19, 1999; S. Paige and A. Howd, "If at First They Don't Succeed, Cry, Cry, Again," *Insight on the News,* July 27, 1998, p. 44; P. Ayton and H. Arkes, "Call It Quits," *New Scientist,* June 20, 1998; "When Government Buys Computers," *Washington Post,* March 20, 1997, p. A26; J. Lorinc, "The Politics of Power," *Canadian Business,* March 1993, pp. 41–42; J. Lorinc, "Power Failure," *Canadian Business,* November 1992, pp. 50–58.

37 F.D. Schoorman and P.J. Holahan, "Psychological Antecedents of Escalation Behavior: Effects of Choice, Responsibility, and Decision Consequences," *Journal of Applied Psychology,* 81 (1996), pp. 786–93.

38 H. Drummond, *Escalation in Decision Making* (New York: Oxford University Press, 1997).

39 S.W. Geiger, C.J. Robertson, and J.G. Irwin, "The Impact of Cultural Values on Escalation of Commitment," *International Journal of Organizational Analysis,* 6 (April 1998), pp. 165–76; D.K.

Tse, K. Lee, I. Vertinsky, and D.A. Wehrung, "Does Culture Matter? A Cross-Cultural Study of Executives' Choice, Decisiveness, and Risk Adjustment in International Marketing," *Journal of Marketing,* 52 (1988), pp. 81–95.

40   S. McKay, "When Good People Make Bad Choices," *Canadian Business,* February 1994, pp. 52–55.

41   M. Keil and D. Robey, "Turning Around Troubled Software Projects: An Exploratory Study of the Deescalation of Commitment to Failing Courses of Action," *Journal of Management Information Systems,* 15 (Spring 1999), pp. 63–87.

42   B.M. Staw, K.W. Koput, and S.G. Barsade, "Escalation at the Credit Window: A Longitudinal Study of Bank Executives' Recognition and Write-Off of Problem Loans," *Journal of Applied Psychology,* 82 (1997), pp. 130–42.

43   W. Boulding, R. Morgan, and R. Staelin, "Pulling the Plug to Stop the New Product Drain," *Journal of Marketing Research,* 34 (1997), pp. 164–76; I. Simonson and B.M. Staw, "De-escalation Strategies: A Comparison of Techniques for Reducing Commitment to Losing Courses of Action," *Journal of Applied Psychology,* 77 (1992), pp. 419–26.

44   D. Ghosh, "De-Escalation Strategies: Some Experimental Evidence," *Behavioral Research in Accounting,* 9 (1997), pp. 88–112.

45   G.C. McMahon and E.E. Lawler, III, "Effects of Union Status on Employee Involvement: Diffusion and Effectiveness," *Research in Organizational Change and Development,* 8 (1995), pp. 47–76; V.H. Vroom and A.G. Jago, *The New Leadership: Managing Participation in Organizations* (Englewood Cliffs, NJ: Prentice Hall, 1988), p. 15.

46   P.S. McInnis, "Teamwork for Harmony: Labour-Management Production Committees and the Postwar Settlement in Canada," *Canadian Historical Review,* 77 (September 1996), pp. 317–52.

47   R. Dubin, "Union–Management Co-operation and Productivity," *Industrial and Labor Relations Review,* 2 (1949), pp. 195–209; W.R. Dymond, "Union–Management Cooperation at the Toronto Factory of Lever Brothers Limited," *Canadian Journal of Economics and Political Science,* 10 (February 1947), pp. 26–67.

48   R. Kang, "Turnarounds of the Year: Power from the People," *Profit,* November 1999, p. 36; R. Mang, "Great Little Box Company," *B.C. Business,* 27 (September 1999), pp. 51–54; D. Roberts, "A Long Way from Cambodia," *Globe and Mail,* July 5, 1994, p. B18.

49   P. Delean, "These Caps Are Tops," *Montreal Gazette,* September 27, 1999.

50   A.M. Berg, "Participatory Strategies in Quality Improvement Programs," *Public Productivity & Management Review,* 21 (September 1997), pp. 30–43; D.I. Levine, *Reinventing the Workplace* (Washington, DC: Brookings, 1995), Chapter 3; E.A. Locke and D.M. Schweiger, "Participation in Decision-Making: One More Look," *Research in Organizational Behavior,* 1 (1979), pp. 265–339.

51   B.R. Gordon, "Employee Involvement in the Enforcement of the Occupational Safety and Health Laws of Canada and the United States," *Comparative Labor Law Journal,* 15 (1994), pp. 527–60.

52   J.T. Addison, "Nonunion Representation in Germany," *Journal of Labor Research,* 20 (Winter 1999), pp. 73–92; G. Strauss, "Collective Bargaining, Unions, and Participation," in F. Heller, E. Pusic, G. Strauss, and B. Wilpert (eds.), *Organizational Participation: Myth and Reality* (New York: Oxford University Press, 1998), pp. 97–143; Levine, *Reinventing the Workplace,* pp. 47–48.

53   "Employee Share Ownership Can Pay Big Dividends," *Globe and Mail,* March 14, 1997, p. C7.

54   R.C. Liden and S. Arad, "A Power Perspective of Empowerment and Work Groups: Implications for Human Resources Management Research," *Research in Personnel and Human Resources Management,* 14 (1996), pp. 205–51; R.C. Ford and M.D. Fottler, "Empowerment: A Matter of Degree," *Academy of Management Executive,* 9 (August 1995), pp. 21–31; R.W. Coye and J.A. Belohlav, "An Exploratory Analysis of Employee Participation," *Group & Organization Management,* 20 (1995), pp. 4–17; Vroom and Jago, *The New Leadership.*

55 Kang, "Turnarounds of the Year: Power from the People."

56 E.C. Wenger and W.M. Snyder, "Communities of Practice: The Organizational Frontier," *Harvard Business Review,* 78 (January–February 2000), pp. 139–45; J.W. Botkin, *Smart Business: How Knowledge Communities Can Revolutionize Your Company* (New York: Free Press, 1999).

57 C. O'Dell and C.J. Grayson, "If Only We Knew What We Know: Identification and Transfer of Internal Best Practices," *California Management Review,* 40 (Spring 1998), pp. 154–74; C.J. Grayson and C. O'Dell, "Mining Your Hidden Resources," *Across the Board,* 35 (April 1998), pp. 23–28; B. Manville and N. Foote, "Harvest Your Workers' Knowledge," *Datamation,* 42 (July 1996), pp. 78–80.

58 P.E. Rossler and C.P. Koelling, "The Effect of Gainsharing on Business Performance at a Papermill," *National Productivity Review,* 12 (Summer 1993), pp. 365–82; C.R. Gowen, III, "Gainsharing Programs: An Overview of History and Research," *Journal of Organizational Behavior Management,* 11(2) (1990), pp. 77–99; F.G. Lesieur (ed.), *The Scanlon Plan: A Frontier in Labor-Management Cooperation* (Cambridge, MA: MIT Press, 1958).

59 M. Pettapiece, "Staffing the e-Revolution," *Hamilton Spectator,* May 1, 2000.

60 J. Case, "Opening the Books," *Harvard Business Review,* 75 (March–April 1997), pp. 118–27; T.R.V. Davis, "Open-Book Management: Its Promise and Pitfalls," *Organizational Dynamics,* Winter 1997, pp. 7–20; J. Case, *Open Book Management: The Coming Business Revolution* (New York: HarperBusiness, 1995).

61 P. Robertson and S. Matthews, "Like an Open Book," *CA Magazine,* May 1997, pp. 33–35.

62 D.E. Yeatts and C. Hyten, *High-Performing Self-Managed Work Teams: A Comparison of Theory and Practice* (Thousand Oaks, CA: Sage, 1998); S.A. Mohrman, S.G. Cohen, and A.M. Mohrman, Jr., *Designing Team-Based Organizations: New Forms for Knowledge Work* (San Francisco: Jossey-Bass, 1995); Lawler, *High-Involvement Management,* Chapters 11 and 12; L.C. Plunkett and R. Fournier, *Participative Management: Implementing Empowerment* (New York: Wiley, 1991).

63 R. Robertson, "Pain Relief," *Materials Management and Distribution,* April 1997.

64 S.G. Cohen, G.E. Ledford, Jr., and G.M. Spreitzer, "A Predictive Model of Self-Managing Work Team Effectiveness," *Human Relations,* 49 (1996), pp. 643–76.

65 The SDWT attributes discussed here are discussed in Yeatts and Hyten, *High-Performing Self-Managed Work Teams;* B.L. Kirkman and D.L. Shapiro, "The Impact of Cultural Values on Employee Resistance to Teams: Toward a Model of Globalized Self-Managing Work Team Effectiveness," *Academy of Management Review,* 22 (July 1997), pp. 730–57; Mohrman et al., *Designing Team-Based Organizations.*

66 L. Rittenhouse, "Dennis W. Bakke—Empowering a Workforce with Principles," *Electricity Journal,* January 1998, pp. 48–59.

67 P.S. Goodman, R. Devadas, and T.L.G. Hughson, "Groups and Productivity: Analyzing the Effectiveness of Self-Managing Teams," in J.P. Campbell, R.J. Campbell, and Associates (eds.), *Productivity in Organizations* (San Francisco: Jossey-Bass, 1988), pp. 295–327.

68 J. Childs, "Five Years and Counting: The Path to Self-Directed Work Teams," *Hospital Materiel Management Quarterly,* 18 (May 1997), pp. 34–43.

69 D. Tjosvold, *Teamwork for Customers* (San Francisco: Jossey-Bass, 1993); D.E. Bowen and E.E. Lawler III, "The Empowerment of Service Workers: What, Why, How, and When," *Sloan Management Review,* Spring 1992, pp. 31–39.

70 E.L. Trist, G.W. Higgin, H. Murray, and A.B. Pollock, *Organizational Choice* (London: Tavistock, 1963). The origins of SDWTs from sociotechnical systems research is also noted in R. Beckham, "Self-Directed Work Teams: The Wave of the Future?" *Hospital Materiel Management Quarterly,* 20 (August 1998), pp. 48–60.

71 The main components of sociotechnical systems are discussed in M. Moldaschl and W.G. Weber, "The 'Three Waves' of Industrial Group Work: Historical Reflections on Current Research on Group Work," *Human Relations,* 51 (March 1998), pp. 347–88; W. Niepce and E. Molleman, "Work Design Issues in Lean Production from a Sociotechnical Systems Perspective: Neo-Taylorism or the Next Step in Sociotechnical Design?" *Human Relations,* 51 (March 1998), pp. 259–87.

72 E. Ulich and W.G. Weber, "Dimensions, Criteria, and Evaluation of Work Group Autonomy," in M.A. West (ed.), *Handbook of Work Group Psychology* (Chichester, UK: John Wiley & Sons, 1996), pp. 247–82.

73 M. Evans, T. Hamilton, L. Surtees and S. Tuck, "The Road to a Billion," *Globe and Mail,* January 6, 2000; R. Dyck and N. Halpern, "Team-based Organizations Redesign at Celestica," *Journal for Quality & Participation,* 22 (September–October 1999), pp. 36–40.

74 C.C. Manz and G.L. Stewart, "Attaining Flexible Stability by Integrating Total Quality Management and Socio-technical Systems Theory," *Organization Science,* 8 (1997), pp. 59–70; K.P. Carson and G.L. Stewart, "Job Analysis and the Sociotechnical Approach to Quality: A Critical Examination," *Journal of Quality Management,* 1 (1996), pp. 49–65.

75 P.S. Adler and R.E. Cole, "Designed for Learning: A Tale of Two Auto Plants," *Sloan Management Review,* 34 (Spring 1993), pp. 85–94; O. Hammarström and R. Lansbury, "The Art of Building a Car: The Swedish Experience Re-examined," *New Technology, Work and Employment,* 2 (Autumn 1991), pp. 85–90; J.P. Womack, D.T. Jones, and D. Roos, *The Machine That Changed the World* (New York: MacMillan, 1990). For more favorable evaluations of Volvo's plants, see I. Magaziner and M. Patinkin, *The Silent War* (New York: Random House, 1988); P.G. Gyllenhammar, *People at Work* (Reading, MA: Addison-Wesley, 1977).

76 R. Likert, *New Patterns of Management* (New York: McGraw-Hill, 1961); D. McGregor, *The Human Side of Enterprise* (New York: McGraw-Hill, 1960); C. Argyris, *Personality and Organization* (New York: Harper & Row, 1957).

77 J.A. Wagner, III, C.R. Leana, E.A. Locke, and D.M. Schweiger, "Cognitive and Motivational Frameworks in U.S. Research on Participation: A Meta-Analysis of Primary Effects," *Journal of Organizational Behavior,* 18 (1997), pp. 49–65; G.P. Latham, D.C. Winters, and E.A. Locke, "Cognitive and Motivational Effects of Participation: A Mediator Study," *Journal of Organizational Behavior,* 15 (1994), pp. 49–63; Cotton, *Employee Involvement,* Chapter 8; S.J. Havlovic, "Quality of Work Life and Human Resource Outcomes," *Industrial Relations,* 1991, pp. 469–79; K.I. Miller and P.R. Monje, "Participation, Satisfaction, and Productivity: A Meta-Analytic Review," *Academy of Management Journal,* 29 (1986), pp. 727–53.

78 K.Y. Williams and C.A. O'Reilly, III, "Demography and Diversity in Organizations: A Review of 40 Years of Research," *Research in Organizational Behavior,* 20 (1998).

79 J.P. Walsh and S.-F. Tseng, "The Effects of Job Characteristics on Active Effort at Work," *Work & Occupations,* 25 (February 1998), pp. 74–96; K.T. Dirks, L.L. Cummings, and J.L. Pierce, "Psychological Ownership in Organizations: Conditions Under Which Individuals Promote and Resist Change," *Research in Organizational Change and Development,* 9 (1996), pp. 1–23.

80 C.L. Cooper, B. Dyck, and N. Frohlich, "Improving the Effectiveness of Gainsharing: The Role of Fairness and Participation," *Administrative Science Quarterly,* 37 (1992), pp. 471–90.

81 The limits of employee involvement for improving employee satisfaction are discussed in J.A. Wagner, III, C.R. Leana, E.A. Locke, and D. Schweiger, "Cognitive and Motivational Frameworks in U.S. Research on Participation: A Meta-Analysis of Primary Effects," *Journal of Organizational Behavior,* (1997), pp. 49–65; V. Smith, "Employee Involvement, Involved Employees: Participative Work Arrangements in a White-Collar Service Occupation," *Social Problems,* 43 (May 1996), pp. 166–79; D.J. Glew, A.M. O'Leary-Kelly, R.W. Griffin, and D.D. Van Fleet, "Participation in Organizations: A Preview of the Issues and Proposed Framework for Future Analysis," *Journal of Management,* 21 (1995), pp. 395–421.

82 J.A. Conger and R.N. Kanungo, "The Empowerment Process: Integrating Theory and Practice," *Academy of Management Review,* 13 (1988), pp. 471–82.

83 A. Bandura, *Self-Efficacy: The Exercise of Control* (W.H. Freeman & Co., 1996); M.E. Gist and T.R. Mitchell, "Self-Efficacy: A Theoretical Analysis of Its Determinants and Malleability," *Academy of Management Review*, 17 (1992), pp. 183–211; R.F. Mager, "No Self-Efficacy, No Performance," *Training*, 29 (April 1992), pp. 32–36.

84 Vroom and Jago, *The New Leadership*, pp. 151–52.

85 Vroom and Jago, *The New Leadership*.

86 Berg, "Participatory Strategies in Quality Improvement Programs;" A.A. Aziz, "A Grip on Employee Absenteeism," *New Straits Times* (Malaysia), June 20, 1996, p. 3; A. Haasen, "Opel Eisenach GMBH—Creating a High-Productivity Workplace," *Organizational Dynamics*, 24 (January 1996), pp. 80–85; T. Murakami, "Introducing Team Working—A Motor Industry Case Study from Germany," *Industrial Relations Journal*, 26 (1995), pp. 293–305; R.S. Wellins, W.C. Byham, and G.R. Dixon, *Inside Teams* (San Francisco: Jossey-Bass, 1994), pp. 262–71.

87 B.L. Kirkman and D.L. Shapiro, "The Impact of Cultural Values on Employee Resistance to Teams: Toward a Model of Globalized Self-Managing Work Team Effectiveness," *Academy of Management Review*, 22 (July 1997), pp. 730–57; C. Pavett and T. Morris, "Management Styles within a Multinational Corporation: A Five Country Comparative Study." *Human Relations*, 48 (1995), pp. 1171–91; M. Erez and P.C. Earley, *Culture, Self-Identity, and Work* (New York: Oxford University Press, 1993), pp. 104–12.

88 C.E. Nicholls, H.W. Lane, and M.B. Brechu, "Taking Self-Managed Teams to Mexico," *Academy of Management Executive*, 13 (August 1999), p. 15.

89 D.I. Levine, *Reinventing the Workplace* (Washington, DC: Brookings, 1995), pp. 63–66, 86; C.C. Manz, D.E. Keating, and A. Donnellon, "Preparing for an Organizational Change to Employee Self-Management: The Managerial Transition," *Organizational Dynamics*, 19 (Autumn 1990), pp. 15–26.

90 G.T. Fairhurst, S. Green, and J. Courtright, "Inertial Forces and the Implementation of a Socio-Technical Systems Approach: A Communication Study," *Organization Science*, 6 (1995), pp. 168–85; Manz et al., "Preparing for an Organizational Change to Employee Self-Management," pp. 23–25.

91 J. Jusko, "Always Lessons to Learn," *Industry Week*, February 15, 1999, p. 23.

92 R. Yonatan and H. Lam, "Union Responses to Quality Improvement Initiatives: Factors Shaping Support and Resistance," *Journal of Labor Research*, 20 (Winter 1999), p. 20; Levine, *Reinventing the Workplace*, pp. 66–69; I. Goll and N.B. Johnson, "The Influence of Environmental Pressures, Diversification Strategy, and Union/Nonunion Setting on Employee Participation," *Employee Responsibilities and Rights Journal*, 10 (1997), pp. 141–54; R. Hodson, "Dignity in the Workplace Under Participative Management: Alienation and Freedom Revisited," *American Sociological Review*, 61 (1996), pp. 719–38.

93 E.C. Rosenthal, "Sociotechnical Systems and Unions: Nicety or Necessity," *Human Relations*, 50 (May 1997), pp. 585–604; R.E. Allen and K.L. Van Norman, "Employee Involvement Programs: The Noninvolvement of Unions Revisited," *Journal of Labor Research*, 17 (Summer 1996), pp. 479–95; B. Gilbert, "The Impact of Union Involvement on the Design and Introduction of Quality of Working Life," *Human Relations*, 42 (1989), pp. 1057–78; T.A. Kochan, H.C. Katz, and R.B. McKersie, *The Transformation of American Industrial Relations* (New York: Basic Books, 1986), pp. 238–45.

Chapter Eleven

1 S. Taylor, "Hi-Tech Gets Hip Edge," *Ottawa Sun*, January 10, 1999, p. 26.

2 D. Gurteen, "Knowledge, Creativity and Innovation," *Journal of Knowledge Management*, 2 (September 1998), p. 5.

3 A. Cummings and G.R. Oldham, "Enhancing Creativity: Managing Work Contexts for the High Potential Employee," *California Management Review*, 40 (Fall 1997), pp. 22–38; T.M. Amabile, *The Social Psychology of Creativity* (New York: Springer-Verlag, 1983), pp. 32–35.

4 A. MacKensie "Innovate or Be Damned," *Asian Business,* January 1995, pp. 30–34.

5 B. Kabanoff and J.R. Rossiter, "Recent Developments in Applied Creativity," *International Review of Industrial and Organizational Psychology,* 9 (1994), pp. 283–324.

6 S. Robertson, "Flinging Open Doors to Creativity," *Saskatoon Star-Phoenix,* June 12, 1999, p. E16.

7 J.R. Hayes, "Cognitive Processes in Creativity," in J.A. Glover, R.R. Ronning, and C.R. Reynolds (eds.), *Handbook of Creativity* (New York: Plenum, 1989), pp. 135–45.

8 A. Muoio, "David Hardy," *Fast Company,* 10 (August 1997).

9 R.S. Nickerson, "Enhancing Creativity," in R.J. Sternberg (ed.), *Handbook of Creativity* (New York: Cambridge University Press, 1999), pp. 392–430; A. Hiam, "Obstacles to Creativity—and How You Can Remove Them," *Futurist,* 32 (October 1998), p. 30.

10 R.T. Brown, "Creativity: What Are We to Measure," in J.A. Glover, R.R. Ronning, and C.R. Reynolds (eds.), *Handbook of Creativity* (New York: Plenum, 1989), pp. 3–32.

11 A. Hargadon and R.I. Sutton, "Building an Innovation Factory," *Harvard Business Review,* 78 (May–June 2000), pp. 157–66.

12 A. van de Vliet, "Perish Not the Thought," *Management Today,* April 1997, pp. 70–73; C.M. Farkus and P. DeBacker, *Maximum Leadership* (New York: Henry Holt and Company, 1996), pp. 154–55.

13 For a thorough discussion of insight, see R.J. Sternberg and J.E. Davidson (eds.), *The Nature of Insight* (Cambridge, MA: MIT Press, 1995).

14 V. Parv, "The Idea Toolbox: Techniques for Being a More Creative Writer," *Writer's Digest,* 78 (July 1998), p. 18; J. Ayan, *Aha! 10 Ways to Free Your Creative Spirit and Find Your Great Ideas* (New York: Crown Trade, 1997), pp. 50–56.

15 E. Robb, "Following Her Path of Passion," *Moncton Times and Transcript,* December 10, 1999, p. D2.

16 K. Cottrill, "Reinventing Innovation," *Journal of Business Strategy,* March–April 1998, pp. 47–51; M.J. Kiernan, "Get Innovative or Get Dead," *Business Quarterly,* 61 (Autumn 1996), pp. 51–58; T.A. Stewart, "3M Fights Back," *Fortune,* February 5, 1996, pp. 94–99.

17 C. Martindale, "Biological Bases of Creativity," in R.J. Sternberg (ed.), *Handbook of Creativity* (New York: Cambridge University Press, 1999), pp. 137–52. For a critical view of "right-brained thinking," see T. Hines, "Left Brain/Right Brain Mythology and Implications for Management and Training," *Academy of Management Review,* 12 (1987), pp. 600–606.

18 R.J. Sternberg and L.A. O'Hara, "Creativity and Intelligence," in R.J. Sternberg (ed.), *Handbook of Creativity* (New York: Cambridge University Press, 1999), pp. 251–72.

19 R.J. Sternberg, L.A. O'Hara, and T.I. Lubart, "Creativity as Investment," *California Management Review,* 40 (Fall 1997), pp. 8–21.

20 R.W. Weisberg, "Creativity and Knowledge: A Challenge to Theories," in Sternberg (ed.), *Handbook of Creativity,* pp. 226–50.

21 R.J. Sternberg, *Thinking Styles* (New York: Cambridge University Press, 1997).

22 M. Michalko, "Thinking Like a Genius: Eight Strategies Used by the Supercreative, from Aristotle and Leonardo to Einstein and Edison," *The Futurist,* 32 (May 1998), pp. 21–25; J.S. Dacey, "Peak Periods of Creative Growth Across the Lifespan," *Journal of Creative Behavior,* 23 (1989), pp. 224–47; F. Barron and D.M. Harrington, "Creativity, Intelligence, and Personality," *Annual Review of Psychology,* 32 (1981), pp. 439–76.

23 P. Roberts, "Sony Changes the Game," *Fast Company,* 10 (1997), p. 116.

24 G.J. Feist, "The Influence of Personality on Artistic and Scientific Creativity," in R.J. Sternberg (ed.), *Handbook of Creativity* (New York: Cambridge University Press, 1999), pp. 273–96; M.A. West, *Developing Creativity in Organizations* (Leicester, UK: BPS Books, 1997), pp. 10–19.

25 D.C. McClelland, *The Achieving Society* (New York: Van Nostrand Reinhold, 1961); M. Patchen, *Participation, Achievement, and Involvement on the Job* (Englewood Cliffs, NJ: Prentice-Hall, 1970).

26 J. Jamieson, "Success Is Sweet for Small Firm," *Vancouver Province,* March 7, 2000.

27 A. Cummings and G.R. Oldham, "Enhancing Creativity: Managing Work Contexts for the High Potential Employee," *California Management Review,* 40 (Fall 1997), pp. 22–38.

28 T.M. Amabile, R. Conti, H. Coon, J. Lazenby, and M. Herron, "Assessing the Work Environment for Creativity," *Academy of Management Journal,* 39 (1996), pp. 1154–84; G.R. Oldham and A. Cummings, "Employee Creativity: Personal and Contextual Factors at Work," *Academy of Management Journal,* 39 (1996), pp. 607–34; R.M. Burnside, "Improving Corporate Climates for Creativity," in ed. M. A. West and J. L. Farr, *Innovation and Creativity at Work* (Chichester, UK: Wiley, 1990), pp. 265–84.

29 D. Maitra, "Livio D. Desimone: We Do Not See Failures as Failure," *Business Today* (India), June 22, 1998, p. 66.

30 T.M. Amabile, "Changes in the Work Environment for Creativity During Downsizing," *Academy of Management Journal,* 42 (December 1999), pp. 630–40.

31 Cummings and Oldham, "Enhancing Creativity."

32 R. Tierney, S.M. Farmer, and G.B. Graen, "An Examination of Leadership and Employee Creativity: The Relevance of Traits and Relationships," *Personnel Psychology,* 52 (Autumn 1999), pp. 591–620; Cummings and Oldham, "Enhancing Creativity."

33 Michalko, "Thinking Like a Genius."

34 T.M. Amabile, "Motivating Creativity in Organizations: On Doing What You Love and Loving What You Do," *California Management Review,* 40 (Fall 1997), pp. 39–58.

35 M. Csikszentmihalyi, *Creativity—Flow and the Psychology of Discovery and Invention* (New York: HarperCollins, 1996).

36 T.M. Amabile, "A Model of Creativity and Innovation in Organizations," *Research in Organizational Behavior,* 10 (1988), pp. 123–67.

37 C. Comeau-Kirschner and L. Wah, "Who Has Time to Think?" *Management Review,* 89 (January 2000), pp. 16–23.

38 S.Z. Dudek and R. Côté, "Problem Finding Revisited," in Runco (ed.), *Problem Finding, Problem Solving, and Creativity,* pp. 130–50.

39 Sternberg, "Creativity as Investment."

40 J. Kao, *Jamming* (New York: HarperBusiness, 1996).

41 Hiam, "Obstacles to Creativity—and How You Can Remove Them."

42 West, *Developing Creativity in Organizations,* pp. 33–35.

43 Cathy Olofson, "Monster Board Has Fun," *Fast Company,* 16 (August 1998), p. 50.

44 K.W. Jesse, "A Creative Approach to Doing Business," *Dayton Daily News,* June 19, 1998, p. C1.

45 W.J.J. Gordon, *Synectics: The Development of Creative Capacity* (New York: Harper & Row, 1961).

46 J. Neff, "At Eureka Ranch, Execs Doff Wing Tips, Fire Up Ideas," *Advertising Age,* 69 (March 9, 1998), pp. 28–29.

47 A.G. Robinson and S. Stern, Corporate Creativity, *How Innovation and Improvement Actually Happen* (San Francisco: Berrett-Koehler Publishers, 1997).

48 Hargadon and Sutton, "Building an Innovation Factory"; R.I. Sutton and A. Hargadon, "Brainstorming Groups in Context: Effectiveness in a Product Design Firm," *Administrative Science Quarterly,* 41 (1996), pp. 685–718.

49 D. Beardsley, "This Company Doesn't Brake for (Sacred) Cows," *Fast Company,* 16 (August 1998).

50 J. Partridge, "London Life Overhauling Management," *Globe and Mail,* February 15, 1997, p. B3.

51 R.B. Gallupe, W.H. Cooper, M.L. Grisé, and L.M. Bastianutti, "Blocking Electronic Brainstorms," *Journal of Applied Psychology,* 79 (1994), pp. 77–86; M. Diehl and W. Stroebe, "Productivity Loss in Idea-Generating Groups: Tracking Down the Blocking Effects," *Journal of Personality and Social Psychology,* 61 (1991), pp. 392–403.

52 P.W. Mulvey, J.F. Veiga, P.M. Elsass, "When Teammates Raise a White Flag," *Academy of Management Executive,* 10 (February 1996), pp. 40–49.

53 S. Plous, *The Psychology of Judgment and Decision Making* (Philadelphia: Temple University Press, 1993), pp. 200–202.

54 I.L. Janis, *Crucial Decisions* (New York: Free Press, 1989), pp. 56–63; I.L. Janis, *Groupthink: Psychological Studies of Policy Decisions and Fiascoes,* 2nd ed. (Boston: Houghton Mifflin, 1982).

55 M.E. Turner and A.R. Pratkanis, "Threat, Cohesion, and Group Effectiveness: Testing a Social Identity Maintenance Perspective on Groupthink," *Journal of Personality and Social Psychology,* 63 (1992), pp. 781–96.

56 M. Rempel and R.J. Fisher, "Perceived Threat, Cohesion, and Group Problem Solving in Intergroup Conflict," *International Journal of Conflict Management,* 8 (1997), pp. 216–34.

57 G. Moorhead, R. Ference, and C.P. Neck, "Group Decision Fiascoes Continue: Space Shuttle *Challenger* and a Revised Groupthink Framework," *Human Relations,* 44 (1991), pp. 539–50; Janis, *Crucial Decisions,* pp. 76–77.

58 C. McGarty, J.C. Turner, M.A. Hogg, B. David, and M.S. Wetherell, "Group Polarization as Conformity to the Prototypical Group Member," *British Journal of Social Psychology,* 31 (1992), pp. 1–20; D. Isenberg, "Group Polarization: A Critical Review and Meta-analysis," *Journal of Personality and Social Psychology,* 50 (1986), pp. 1141–51; D.G. Myers and H. Lamm, "The Group Polarization Phenomenon," *Psychological Bulletin,* 83 (1976), pp. 602–27.

59 D. Friedman, "Monty Hall's Three Doors: Construction and Deconstruction of a Choice Anomaly," *American Economic Review,* 88 (September 1998), pp. 933–46; D. Kahneman and A. Tversky, "Prospect Theory: An Analysis of Decision Under Risk," *Econometrica,* 47 (1979), pp. 263–91.

60 Janis, *Crucial Decisions,* pp. 244–49.

61 F.A. Schull, A.L. Delbecq, and L.L. Cummings, *Organizational Decision Making* (New York: McGraw-Hill, 1970), pp. 144–49.

62 A.C. Amason, "Distinguishing the Effects of Functional and Dysfunctional Conflict on Strategic Decision Making: Resolving a Paradox for Top Management Teams," *Academy of Management Journal,* 39 (1996), pp. 123–48; G. Katzenstein, "The Debate on Structured Debate: Toward a Unified Theory," *Organizational Behavior and Human Decision Processes,* 66 (1996), pp. 316–32; D. Tjosvold, *Team Organization: An Enduring Competitive Edge* (Chichester, UK: Wiley, 1991).

63 K.M. Eisenhardt, J.L. Kahwajy, and L.J. Bourgeois III, "Conflict and Strategic Choice: How Top Management Teams Disagree," *California Management Review,* 39 (Winter 1997), pp. 42–62.

64 L. Tucci, "Owens Drake Consulting Fosters Systematic Change," *St. Louis Business Journal,* May 25, 1998.

65 J.S. Valacich and C. Schwenk, "Structuring Conflict in Individual, Face-to-Face, and Computer-Mediated Group Decision Making: Carping Versus Objective Devil's Advocacy," *Decision Sciences,* 26 (1995), pp. 369–93; D.M. Schweiger, W.R. Sandberg, and P.L. Rechner, "Experiential Effects of Dialectical Inquiry, Devil's Advocacy, and Consensus Approaches to Strategic Decision Making," *Academy of Management Journal,* 32 (1989), pp. 745–72.

66 P.J.H. Schoemaker, "Disciplined Imagination: From Scenarios to Strategic Options," *International Studies of Management & Organization,* 27 (Summer 1997), pp. 43–70.

67 A.F. Osborn, *Applied Imagination* (New York: Scribner, 1957).

68 T. Keelin, "How SmithKline Beecham Makes Better Resource-Allocation Decisions," *Harvard Business Review,* 76 (March–April 1998), pp. 45–57.

69 B. Mullen, C. Johnson, and E. Salas, "Productivity Loss in Brainstorming Groups: A Meta-analytic Integration," *Basic and Applied Psychology,* 12 (1991), pp. 2–23.

70 Sutton and Hargadon, "Brainstorming Groups in Context," *Administrative Science Quarterly;* P.B. Paulus and M.T. Dzindolet "Social Influence Processes in Group Brainstorming," *Journal of Personality and Social Psychology,* 64 (1993), pp. 575–86; B. Mullen, C. Johnson, and E. Salas, "Productivity Loss in Brainstorming Groups: A Meta-Analytic Integration." *Basic and Applied Psychology,* 12 (1991), pp. 2–23.

71 Gallupe et al., "Blocking Electronic Brainstorms."

72 Crone, "Electrifying Brainstorms."

73 P. Bordia, "Face-to-Face versus Computer-Mediated Communication: A Synthesis of the Experimental Literature," *Journal of Business Communication,* 34 (1997), pp. 99–120; J.S. Valacich, A.R. Dennis, and T. Connolly "Idea Generation in Computer-Based Groups: A New Ending to an Old Story," *Organizational Behavior and Human Decision Processes,* 57 (1994), pp. 448–67; R.B. Gallupe, W.H. Cooper, M.L. Grisé, and L.M. Bastianutti, "Blocking Electronic Brainstorms," *Journal of Applied Psychology,* 79 (1994), pp. 77–86.

74 G. Crone, "Electrifying Brainstorms," *National Post,* July 3, 1999, p. D11.

75 W.M. Bulkeley, " 'Computerizing' Dull Meetings Is Touted as an Antidote to the Mouth That Bored," *Wall Street Journal,* January 28, 1992, pp. B1, B2.

76 B. Daily, A. Wheatley, S.R. Ash, and R.L. Steiner, "The Effects of a Group Decision Support System on Culturally Diverse and Culturally Homogeneous Group Decision Making," *Information & Management,* 30 (1996), pp. 281–89; R.B. Gallupe, A.R. Dennis, W.H. Cooper, J.S. Valacich, L.M. Bastianutti, and J.F. Nunamaker, Jr., "Electronic Brainstorming and Group Size," *Academy of Management Journal,* 35 (June 1992), pp. 350–69; R.B. Gallupe, L.M. Bastianutti, and W.H. Cooper, "Unblocking Brainstorms," *Journal of Applied Psychology,* 76 (1991), pp. 137–42.

77 B. Kabanoff and J.R. Rossiter, "Recent Developments in Applied Creativity," *International Review of Industrial and Organizational Psychology,* 9 (1994), pp. 283–324.

78 H.A. Linstone and M. Turoff (eds.), *The Delphi Method: Techniques and Applications* (Reading, MA: Addison-Wesley, 1975).

79 C. Critcher and B. Gladstone, "Utilizing the Delphi Technique in Policy Discussion: A Case Study of a Privatized Utility in Britain," *Public Administration,* 76 (Autumn 1998), pp. 431–49; S.R. Rubin et al., "Research Directions Related to Rehabilitation Practice: A Delphi Study," *Journal of Rehabilitation,* 64 (Winter 1998), p. 19.

80 A.L. Delbecq, A.H. Van de Ven, and D.H. Gustafson, *Group Techniques for Program Planning: A Guide to Nominal Group and Delphi Processes* (Middleton, WI: Green Briar Press, 1986).

81 A.B. Hollingshead, "The Rank-Order Effect in Group Decision Making," *Organizational Behavior and Human Decision Processes,* 68 (1996), pp. 181–93.

82 S. Frankel, "NGT + MDS: An Adaptation of the Nominal Group Technique for Ill-Structured Problems," *Journal of Applied Behavioral Science,* 23 (1987), pp. 543–51; D.M. Hegedus and R. Rasmussen, "Task Effectiveness and Interaction Process of a Modified Nominal Group Technique in Solving an Evaluation Problem," *Journal of Management,* 12 (1986), pp. 545–60.

Chapter Twelve

1 "Work at Home Saves Time and Money," *Moncton Times and Transcript,* November 6, 1999, p. E2; H. Scoffield, "Nortel Leaves Employees at Home," *Globe and Mail,* May 27, 1998, p. B27; J.K. Stewart, "Out-of-Sight Telecommuters Might Be Out of Mind," *Chicago Tribune,* April 5, 1998, p. 7; S. Fea, "Boss Moves Office to Lakeside," *Southland Times* (New Zealand), February 26, 1998, p. 1.

2 C. Hardy and S. Leiba-O'Sullivan, "The Power Behind Empowerment: Implications for Research and Practice," *Human Relations,* 51 (April 1998), pp. 451–83; R. Farson, *Management of the Absurd* (New York: Simon & Schuster, 1996), Chapter 13; R.M. Cyert and J.G. March, *A Behavioral Theory of the Firm* (Englewood Cliffs, NJ: Prentice Hall, 1963).

3 R.C. Liden and S. Arad, "A Power Perspective of Empowerment and Work Groups: Implications for Human Resources Management Research," *Research in Personnel and Human Resource Management,* 14 (1996), pp. 205–51.

4 For a discussion of the definition of power, see J. Pfeffer, *New Directions in Organizational Theory* (New York: Oxford University Press, 1997), Chapter 6; J. Pfeffer, *Managing with Power* (Boston: Harvard Business University Press, 1992), pp. 17, 30; H. Mintzberg, *Power in and Around Organizations* (Englewood Cliffs, NJ: Prentice Hall, 1983), Chapter 1.

5 A.M. Pettigrew, *The Politics of Organizational Decision-Making* (London: Tavistock, 1973); R.M. Emerson, "Power-Dependence Relations," *American Sociological Review,* 27 (1962), pp. 31–41; R.A. Dahl, "The Concept of Power," *Behavioral Science,* 2 (1957), pp. 201–18.

6 D.J. Brass and M.E. Burkhardt, "Potential Power and Power Use: An Investigation of Structure and Behaviour," *Academy of Management Journal,* 36 (1993), pp. 441–70; K.M. Bartol and D.C. Martin, "When Politics Pays: Factors Influencing Managerial Compensation Decisions," *Personnel Psychology,* 43 (1990), pp. 599–614.

7 P.P. Carson and K.D. Carson, "Social Power Bases: A Meta-Analytic Examination of Interrelationships and Outcomes," *Journal of Applied Social Psychology,* 23 (1993), pp. 1150–69; P. Podsakoff and C. Schreisheim, "Field Studies of French and Raven's Bases of Power: Critique, Analysis, and Suggestions for Future Research," *Psychological Bulletin,* 97 (1985), pp. 387–411; J.R.P. French and B. Raven, "The Bases of Social Power," in D. Cartwright (ed.), *Studies in Social Power* (Ann Arbor, MI: University of Michigan Press, 1959), pp. 150–67.

8 For example, see S. Finkelstein, "Power in Top Management Teams: Dimensions, Measurement, and Validation," *Academy of Management Journal,* 35 (1992), pp. 505–38.

9 G. Yukl and C.M. Falbe, "Importance of Different Power Sources in Downward and Lateral Relations," *Journal of Applied Psychology,* 76 (1991), pp. 416–23.

10 G.A. Yukl, *Leadership in Organizations,* 3rd ed. (Englewood Cliffs, NJ: Prentice Hall, 1994), p. 13; B.H. Raven, "The Bases of Power: Origins and Recent Developments," *Journal of Social Issues,* 49 (1993), pp. 227–51.

11 C. Hardy and S.R. Clegg, "Some Dare Call It Power," in S.R. Clegg, C. Hardy, and W.R. Nord (eds.), *Handbook of Organization Studies* (London: Sage, 1996), pp. 622–41; C. Barnard, *The Function of the Executive* (Cambridge, MA: Harvard University Press, 1938).

12 I. Nonaka and H. Takeuchi, *The Knowledge-Creating Company* (New York: Oxford University Press, 1995), pp. 138–39.

13 H. Schachter, "The 21st Century CEO," *Profit,* April 1999, p. 25; J.A. Conger, *Winning 'em Over* (New York: Simon & Schuster, 1998), Appendix A.

14 R. Hodson, "Group Relations at Work: Solidarity, Conflict, and Relations with Management," *Work & Occupations,* 24 (November 1997), pp. 426–52.

15 G. Sewell, "The Discipline of Teams: The Control of Team-Based Industrial Work Through Electronic and Peer Surveillance," *Administrative Science Quarterly,* 43 (June 1998), p. 397.

16 D. Robertson, J. Rinehart, C. Huxley, and the CAW Research Group at CAMI, "Team Concept and Kaizen: Japanese Production Management in a Unionized Canadian Auto Plant," *Studies in Political Economy,* 39 (Autumn 1992), pp. 77–107.

17 "Empowerment Torture to Some," *Tampa Tribune,* October 5, 1997, p. 6.

18 J. Sallot, "New Chief of Forces Must Rebuild Their Morale," *Globe and Mail,* October 12, 1996, pp. A1, A6.

19 P. Panchak, "The Future Manufacturing," *Industry Week,* 247 (September 21, 1998), pp. 96–105.

20 P. Luke, "Hustling for Talent," *Vancouver Province,* March 26, 2000.

21 J.D. Kudisch and M.L. Poteet, "Expert Power, Referent Power, and Charisma: Toward the Resolution of a Theoretical Debate," *Journal of Business & Psychology,* 10 (Winter 1995), pp. 177–95.

22 Yukl and Falbe, "Importance of Different Power Sources in Downward and Lateral Relations."

23 Pitney Bowes, "Study Finds Growth of Communication Options Is Fundamentally Changing Work," News Release, April 8, 1997. (www.pitneybowes.com)

24 D.J. Brass, "Being in the Right Place: A Structural Analysis of Individual Influence in an Organization," *Administrative Science Quarterly,* 29 (1984), pp. 518–39; N.M. Tichy, M.L. Tuchman, and C. Frombrun, "Social Network Analysis in Organizations," *Academy of Management Review,* 4 (1979), pp. 507–19; H. Guetzkow and H. Simon, "The Impact of Certain Communication Nets upon Organization and Performance in Task-Oriented Groups," *Management Science,* 1 (1955), pp. 233–50.

25 C.S. Saunders, "The Strategic Contingency Theory of Power: Multiple Perspectives," *The Journal of Management Studies,* 27 (1990), pp. 1–21; D.J. Hickson, C.R. Hinings, C.A. Lee, R.E. Schneck, and J.M. Pennings, "A Strategic Contingencies' Theory of Intraorganizational Power," *Administrative Science Quarterly,* 16 (1971), pp. 216–27; J.D. Thompson, *Organizations in Action* (New York: McGraw-Hill, 1967).

26 C.R. Hinings, D.J. Hickson, J.M. Pennings, and R.E. Schneck, "Structural Conditions of Intraorganizational Power," *Administrative Science Quarterly,* 19 (1974), pp. 22–44.

27 R. Colapinto, "Nine-to-Five Nirvana," *Canadian Business,* 72 (April 30, 1999), pp. 34–38.

28 Hickson et al., "A Strategic Contingencies' Theory of Intraorganizational Power"; Hinings et al., "Structural Conditions of Intraorganizational Power"; R.M. Kanter, "Power Failure in Management Circuits," *Harvard Business Review,* July–August 1979, pp. 65–75.

29 M. Crozier, *The Bureaucratic Phenomenon* (London: Tavistock, 1964).

30 M.F. Masters, *Unions at the Crossroads: Strategic Membership, Financial, and Political Perspectives* (Westport, CT: Quorum Books, 1997).

31 Brass and Burkhardt, "Potential Power and Power Use," pp. 441–70; Hickson et al., "A Strategic Contingencies' Theory of Intraorganizational Power," pp. 219–21; J.D. Hackman, "Power and Centrality in the Allocation of Resources in Colleges and Universities," *Administrative Science Quarterly,* 30 (1985), pp. 61–77.

32 B. Koenig, "GM to Shut Most of Its U.S. Plants," *Indianapolis News,* June 26, 1998, p. D10; P. Kaplan, "GM Dealers Fear Strike May Cause Car Shortage," *Washington Times,* June 19, 1998, p. B9; D.W. Nauss, "Strike at GM Facility Forces 5 Plants to Shut," *Los Angeles Times,* June 9, 1998, p. 1.

33 Kanter, "Power Failure in Management Circuits," p. 68; B.E. Ashforth, "The Experience of Powerlessness in Organizations," *Organizational Behaviour and Human Decision Processes,* 43 (1989), pp. 207–42.

34 M.L.A. Hayward and W. Boeker, "Power and Conflicts of Interest in Professional Firms: Evidence from Investment Banking," *Administrative Science Quarterly,* 43 (March 1998), p. 1.

35 L.A. Perlow, "The Time Famine: Toward a Sociology of Work Time," *Administrative Science Quarterly,* 44 (March 1999), pp. 5–31.

36 Perlow, "The Time Famine."

37 Raven, "The Bases of Power," pp. 237–39.

38 L.E. Temple and K.R. Loewen, "Perceptions of Power: First Impressions of a Woman Wearing a Jacket," *Perceptual and Motor Skills,* 76 (1993), pp. 339–48.

39 B.R. Ragins, "Diversified Mentoring Relationships in Organizations: A Power Perspective," *Academy of Management Review,* 22 (1997), pp. 482–521; G.R. Ferris, D.D. Frink, D.P.S. Bhawuk, J. Zhou, and D.C. Gilmore, "Reactions of Diverse Groups to Politics in the Workplace," *Journal of Management,* 22 (1996), pp. 23–44.

40 C.M. Falbe and G. Yukl, "Consequences for Managers of Using Single Influence Tactics and Combinations of Tactics," *Academy of Management Journal,* 35 (1992), pp. 638–52.

41 D. Kipnis, *The Powerholders* (Chicago: University of Chicago Press, 1976); G.R. Salancik and J. Pfeffer, "The Bases and Use of Power in Organizational Decision Making: The Case of a University," *Administrative Science Quarterly*, 19 (1974), pp. 453–73.

42 G.E.G. Catlin, *Systematic Politics* (Toronto: University of Toronto Press, 1962), p. 71.

43 G. Kalogerakis, "Fired Manager Fined Over Office Pass," *National Post*, May 9, 2000, p. A5.

44 S.I. Paish and A.A. Alibhai, *Act, Don't React: Dealing with Sexual Harassment in Your Organization* (Vancouver: Western Legal Publications, 1996).

45 D.E. Terpstra, "The Effects of Diversity on Sexual Harassment: Some Recommendations on Research," *Employee Responsibilities and Rights Journal*, 9 (1996), pp. 303–13; J.A. Bargh and P. Raymond, "The Naive Misuse of Power: Nonconscious Sources of Sexual Harassment," *Journal of Social Issues*, 51 (1995), pp. 85–96; R.A. Thacker and G.R. Ferris, "Understanding Sexual Harassment in the Workplace: The Influence of Power and Politics with the Dyadic Interaction of Harasser and Target," *Human Resource Management Review*, 1 (1991), pp. 23–37.

46 H. Johnson, "Work-Related Sexual Harassment," *Perspectives on Labour and Income*, Winter 1994, pp. 9–12.

47 For a discussion of the ethical implications of sexual harassment, see T.I. White, "Sexual Harassment: Trust and the Ethic of Care," *Business and Society Review* (January 1998), pp. 9–20; J. Keyton and S.C. Rhodes, "Sexual Harassment: A Matter of Individual Ethics, Legal Definitions, or Organizational Policy?" *Journal of Business Ethics*, 16 (February 1997), pp. 129–46.

48 T.L. Tang and S.L. McCollum, "Sexual Harassment in the Workplace," *Public Personnel Management*, 25 (1996), pp. 53–58; J.A. Bargh and P. Raymond, "The Naive Misuse of Power: Nonconscious Sources of Sexual Harassment," *Journal of Social Issues*, 51 (1995), pp. 85–96.

49 G.N. Powell and S. Foley, "Something to Talk About: Romantic Relationships in Organizational Settings," *Journal of Management*, 24 (1998), p. 421.

50 For a discussion of perceived justice and office romance, see S. Foley and G.N. Powell, "Not All Is Fair in Love and Work: Coworkers' Preferences for and Responses to Managerial Interventions Regarding Workplace Romances," *Journal of Organizational Behavior*, 20 (1999), pp. 1043–56.

51 M. Kasindorf, S. Armour, and A. Stone, "In Work World, Affairs Can Drag Down People at the Top," *USA Today*, August 24, 1998, p. A8.

52 C.M. Solomon, "The Secret's Out: How to Handle the Truth of Workplace Romance," *Workforce*, 7 (July 1998), p. 42.

53 M. MacKillop, "When the Thrill Is Gone from Office Flings," *Globe and Mail*, October 11, 1999, p. B9. See also *John Dooley v. C.N. Weber Limited* (1994), 3 C.C.E.L. (2d) 95 (Ont. C.J.), appeal dismissed (1995), 80 O.A.C. 234 (O.C.A.), leave to appeal dismissed without reasons, [1995] 197 N.R. 160 (S.C.C.).

54 N. Nejat-Bina, "Employers as Vigilant Chaperones Armed with Dating Waivers: The Interesection of Unwelcomeness and Employer Liability in Hostile Work Environment Sexual Harassment Law," *Berkeley Journal of Employment and Labor Law*, December 22, 1999, p. 325; H. Pauly, "Sex and the Workplace: Companies Revisit the Rules," *Chicago Sun-Times*, August 26, 1998 (online).

55 M. Jameson, "Partners in Work and Play," *Los Angeles Times*, August 16, 1999, p. E1.

56 T. Petzinger, Jr., *The New Pioneers: The Men and Women Who Are Transforming the Workplace and Marketplace* (New York: Simon & Schuster, 1999), Chapter 1.

57 K.M. Kacmar and G.R. Ferris, "Politics at Work: Sharpening the Focus of Political Behaviour in Organizations," *Business Horizons*, 36 (July–August 1993), pp. 70–74; A. Drory and T. Romm, "The Definition of Organizational Politics: A Review," *Human Relations*, 43 (1990), pp. 1133–54; P.J. Frost and D.C. Hayes, "An Exploration in Two Cultures of a Model of Political Behaviour in Organizations," in *Organizational Influence Processes*, ed. R.W. Allen and L.W. Porter (Glenview, IL: Scott, Foresman, 1983), pp. 369–92.

58 K. Ohlson, "Leadership in an Age of Mistrust," *Industry Week,* 247 (February 2, 1998), pp. 37–46.

59 T.H. Davenport, R.G. Eccles, and L. Prusak, "Information Politics," *Sloan Management Review,* Fall 1992, pp. 53–65; Pfeffer, *Managing with Power,* Chapter 17.

60 J.C. Howes, A.A. Grandey, and P. Toth, "The Relationship of Organizational Politics and Support to Work Behaviours, Attitudes, and Stress," *Journal of Organizational Behaviour*, 18 (March 1997), pp. 159–80; G.R. Ferris and D.D. Frink, "Reactions of Diverse Groups to Politics in the Workplace," *Journal of Management*, 22 (Spring 1996), pp. 23–44; P. Kumar and R. Ghadially, "Organizational Politics and Its Effects on Members of Organizations," *Human Relations,* 42 (1989), pp. 305–14.

61 M. Velasquez, D.J. Moberg, and G.F. Cavanaugh, "Organizational Statesmanship and Dirty Politics: Ethical Guidelines for the Organizational Politician," *Organizational Dynamics,* 11 (1983), pp. 65–79.

62 R.W. Allen, D.L. Madison, L.W. Porter, P.A. Renwick, and B.T. Mayes, "Organizational Politics: Tactics and Characteristics of Its Actors," *California Management Review,* 22 (Fall 1979), pp. 77–83; V. Murray and J. Gandz, "Games Executives Play: Politics at Work," *Business Horizons,* December 1980, pp. 11–23.

63 B.E. Ashforth and R.T. Lee, "Defensive Behaviour in Organizations: A Preliminary Model," *Human Relations,* 43 (1990), pp. 621–48.

64 For examples and discussion of these information "turf wars," see A. Simmons, *Territorial Games: Understanding & Ending Turf Wars* (New York: AMACOM, 1998).

65 S. Gittins, "Retirement No Life of Leisure for Ex-CEOs," *Financial Post,* February 13, 1989, p. 17. Also see R. McQueen, *The Money Spinners* (Toronto: Macmillan, 1983), Chapter 4.

66 V. Kirsch, "Sometimes the Lines Between Right and Wrong Can Become a Little Blurred," *Guelph Mercury*, October 18, 1999, p. B1. For an example of exclusion from meetings as a political tactic, see Y. Gabriel, "An Introduction to the Social Psychology of Insults in Organizations," *Human Relations,* 51 (November 1998), pp. 1329–54.

67 M. Warshaw, "The Good Guy's Guide to Office Politics," *Fast Company*, 14 (April–May 1998), pp. 157–78.

68 E.A. Mannix, "Organizations as Resource Dilemmas: The Effects of Power Balance on Coalition Formation in Small Groups," *Organizational Behaviour and Human Decision Processes,* 55 (1993), pp. 1–22; A.T. Cobb, "Toward the Study of Organizational Coalitions: Participant Concerns and Activities in a Simulated Organizational Setting," *Human Relations,* 44 (1991), pp. 1057–79; W.B. Stevenson, J.L. Pearce, and L.W. Porter, "The Concept of 'Coalition' in Organization Theory and Research," *Academy of Management Review,* 10 (1985), pp. 256–68.

69 Falbe and Yukl, "Consequences for Managers of Using Single Influence Tactics and Combinations of Tactics," pp. 638–52.

70 D. Krackhardt and J.R. Hanson, "Informal Networks: The Company Behind the Chart," *Harvard Business Review,* 71 (July–August 1993), pp. 104–11; R.E. Kaplan, "Trade Routes: The Manager's Network of Relationships," *Organizational Dynamics,* Spring 1984, pp. 37–52.

71 R.J. Burke and C.A. McKeen, "Women in Management," *International Review of Industrial and Organizational Psychology,* 7 (1992), pp. 245–83; B.R. Ragins and E. Sundstrom, "Gender and Power in Organizations: A Longitudinal Perspective," *Psychological Bulletin,* 105 (1989), pp. 51–88.

72 G. Scotton, "These Women Just Wanna Have High-Tech Fun," *Calgary Herald*, January 3, 2000.

73 V. Smith, "A Delicate Balance for Women," *Globe and Mail*, February 7, 1998, pp. D1, D3.

74 "Balancing Briefcase and Baby," *Daily Commercial News*, March 4, 1996, p. B1.

75 A.R. Cohen and D.L. Bradford, "Influence without Authority: The Use of Alliances, Reciprocity, and Exchange to Accomplish Work," *Organizational Dynamics,* 17(3) (1989), pp. 5–17.

76 A. Rao and S.M. Schmidt, "Upward Impression Management: Goals, Influence Strategies, and Consequences," *Human Relations*, 48 (1995), pp. 147–67; R.A. Giacalone and P. Rosenfeld (eds.), *Applied Impression Management* (Newbury Park, CA: Sage, 1991); J.T. Tedeschi (ed.), *Impression Management Theory and Social Psychological Research* (New York: Academic Press, 1981).

77 S.L. McShane, "Applicant Misrepresentation in Résumés and Interviews," *Labor Law Journal*, 45 (January 1994), pp. 15–24.

78 W.L. Gardner III, "Lessons in Organizational Dramaturgy: The Art of Impression Management," *Organizational Dynamics,* Summer 1992, pp. 33–46; R.C. Liden and T.R. Mitchell, "Ingratiatory Behaviours in Organizational Settings," *Academy of Management Review,* 13 (1988), pp. 572–87; A. MacGillivary, S. Ascroft, and M. Stebbins, "Meritless Ingratiation," *Proceedings of the Annual ASAC Conference, Organizational Behaviour Division,* 7, pt. 7 (1986), pp. 127–35.

79 C. Hardy, *Strategies for Retrenchment and Turnaround: The Politics of Survival* (Berlin: Walter de Gruyter, 1990), Chapter 14; J. Gandz and V.V. Murray, "The Experience of Workplace Politics," *Academy of Management Journal,* 23 (1980), pp. 237–51.

80 P. Dillon, "Failure IS an Option," *Fast Company*, 22 (February–March, 1999), pp. 154–71.

81 G.R. Ferris, G.S. Russ, and P.M. Fandt, "Politics in Organizations," in R.A. Giacalone and P. Rosenfeld (eds.), *Impression Management in the Organization* (Hillsdale, NJ: Erlbaum, 1989), pp. 143–70; H. Mintzberg, "The Organization as Political Arena," *Journal of Management Studies,* 22 (1985), pp. 133–54.

82 R.J. House, "Power and Personality in Complex Organizations," *Research in Organizational Behaviour,* 10 (1988), pp. 305–57; L.W. Porter, R.W. Allen, and H.L. Angle, "The Politics of Upward Influence in Organizations," *Research in Organizational Behaviour,* 3 (1981), pp. 120–22.

83 S.M. Farmer, J.M. Maslyn, D.B. Fedor, and J.S. Goodman, "Putting Upward Influence Strategies in Context," *Journal of Organizational Behaviour*, 18 (1997), pp. 17–42; P.E. Mudrack, "An Investigation into the Acceptability of Workplace Behaviours of a Dubious Ethical Nature," *Journal of Business Ethics,* 12 (1993), pp. 517–24; R. Christie and F. Geis, *Studies in Machiavellianism* (New York: Academic Press, 1970).

84 D. Tannen, *Talking from 9 to 5* (New York: Avon, 1995), pp. 137–41, 151–52.

85 Tannen, *Talking from 9 to 5*, Chapter 2; M. Crawford, *Talking Difference: On Gender and Language* (Thousand Oaks, CA: Sage, 1995), pp. 41–44; D. Tannen, *You Just Don't Understand: Men and Women in Conversation* (New York: Ballantine Books, 1990); S. Helgesen, *The Female Advantage: Women's Ways of Leadership* (New York: Doubleday, 1990).

86 S. Mann, "Politics and Power in Organizations: Why Women Lose Out," *Leadership & Organization Development Journal*, 16 (1995), pp. 9–15; L. Larwood and M.M. Wood, "Training Women for Management: Changing Priorities," *Journal of Management Development*, 14 (1995), pp. 54–65. A recent popular press book even serves as a guide for women to learn organizational politics. See H. Rubin, *The Princessa: Machiavelli for Women* (New York: Doubleday/Currency, 1996).

87 G.R. Ferris et al., "Perceptions of Organizational Politics: Prediction, Stress-Related Implications, and Outcomes," *Human Relations*, 49 (1996), p. 233–63.

Chapter Thirteen

1 R. Corbett, "Fights Break Out at Sensitivity Course," *Ottawa Citizen*, July 17, 1999, p. C1.

2 J.A. Wall and R.R. Callister, "Conflict and Its Management," *Journal of Management*, 21 (1995), pp. 515–58; D. Tjosvold, *Working Together to Get Things Done* (Lexington, MA: Lexington, 1986), pp. 114–15.

3 The conflict process is described in K.W. Thomas, "Conflict and Negotiation Processes in Organizations," in M.D. Dunnette and L.M. Hough (eds.), *Handbook of Industrial and Organizational Psychology*, 2nd ed., Vol. 3 (Palo Alto, CA: Consulting Psychologists Press, 1992),

pp. 651–718; L. Pondy, "Organizational Conflict: Concepts and Models," *Administrative Science Quarterly*, 2 (1967), pp. 296–320.

4   A.C. Ward, "Another Look at How Toyota Integrates Product Development," *Harvard Business Review* (July–August 1998), pp. 36–49.

5   L.H. Pelled, K.M. Eisenhardt, and K.R. Xin, "Exploring the Black Box: An Analysis of Work Group Diversity, Conflict, and Performance," *Administrative Science Quarterly*, 44 (March 1999), pp. 1–28; A.C. Amason, "Distinguishing the Effects of Functional and Dysfunctional Conflict on Strategic Decision Making: Resolving a Paradox for Top Management Teams," *Academy of Management Journal*, 39 (1996), pp. 123–48; K.A. Jehn, "A Multimethod Examination of the Benefits and Detriments of Intragroup Conflict," *Administrative Science Quarterly*, 40 (1995), pp. 256–82.

6   J.M. Brett, D.L. Shapiro, and A.L. Lytle, "Breaking the Bonds of Reciprocity in Negotiations," *Academy of Management Journal*, 41 (August 1998), pp. 410–24; G.E. Martin and T.J. Bergman, "The Dynamics of Behavioural Response to Conflict in the Workplace," *Journal of Occupational & Organizational Psychology*, 69 (December 1996), pp. 377–87; G. Wolf, "Conflict Episodes," in *Negotiating in Organizations*, ed. M.H. Bazerman and R.J. Lewicki (Beverly Hills, CA: Sage, 1983), pp. 135–40; L.R. Pondy, "Organizational Conflict: Concepts and Models," *Administrative Science Quarterly*, 12 (1967), pp. 296–320.

7   H. Witteman, "Analyzing Interpersonal Conflict: Nature of Awareness, Type of Initiating Event, Situational Perceptions, and Management Styles," *Western Journal of Communications*, 56 (1992), pp. 248–80; F.J. Barrett and D.L. Cooperrider, "Generative Metaphor Intervention: A New Approach for Working with Systems Divided by Conflict and Caught in Defensive Perception," *Journal of Applied Behavioural Science*, 26 (1990), pp. 219–39.

8   Wall and Callister, "Conflict and Its Management," pp. 526–33.

9   Amason, "Distinguishing the Effects of Functional and Dysfunctional Conflict on Strategic Decision Making."

10 K.M. Eisenhardt, J.L. Kahwajy, and L.J. Bourgeois III, "Conflict and Strategic Choice: How Top Management Teams Disagree," *California Management Review*, 39 (Winter 1997), pp. 42–62; J.K. Bouwen and R. Fry, "Organizational Innovation and Learning: Four Patterns of Dialog Between the Dominant Logic and the New Logic," *International Studies of Management and Organizations*, 21 (1991), pp. 37–51.

11 L.L. Putnam, "Productive Conflict: Negotiation as Implicit Coordination," *International Journal of Conflict Management*, 5 (1994), pp. 285–99; D. Tjosvold, *The Conflict-Positive Organization* (Reading, MA: Addison-Wesley, 1991); R.A. Baron, "Positive Effects of Conflict: A Cognitive Perspective," *Employee Responsibilities and Rights Journal*, 4 (1991), pp. 25–36.

12 M. Rempel and R.J. Fisher, "Perceived Threat, Cohesion, and Group Problem Solving in Intergroup Conflict," *International Journal of Conflict Management*, 8 (1997), pp. 216–34.

13 R.R. Blake and J.S. Mouton, *Solving Costly Organizational Conflicts* (San Francisco: Jossey-Bass, 1984).

14 F. Rose, "The Eisner School of Business," *Fortune*, July 6, 1998, pp. 29–30. For a more favourable view of these conflicts, see S. Wetlaufer, "Common Sense and Conflict: An Interview with Disney's Michael Eisner," *Harvard Business Review*, 78 (January–February 2000), pp. 114–24.

15 R.E. Walton and J.M. Dutton, "The Management of Conflict: A Model and Review," *Administrative Science Quarterly*, 14 (1969), pp. 73–84.

16 D. Evans, "Team Players," *Canadian Business*, August 1991, pp. 28–31.

17 B. Critchley, "Lévesque Beaubien's Brain Drain," *Financial Post*, October 17, 1996, p. 5.

18 T. Aeppel, "Technology Sparks Friction Between Young and Old on the Shop Floor," *Wall Street Journal*, April 7, 2000. For a fuller discussion of conflict across the generations, see R. Zemke and B. Filipczak, *Generations at Work: Managing the Clash of Veterans, Boomers, Xers, and Nexters in Your Workplace* (New York: Amacom, 1999).

19 R.C. Liden, S.J. Wayne, and L.K. Bradway, "Task Interdependence as a Moderator of the Relation Between Group Control and Performance," *Human Relations*, 50 (1997), pp. 169–81; R. Wageman, "Interdependence and Group Effectiveness," *Administrative Science Quarterly*, 40 (1995), pp.145–80; M.A. Campion, G.J. Medsker, and A.C. Higgs, "Relations Between Work Group Characteristics and Effectiveness: Implications for Designing Effective Work Groups," *Personnel Psychology*, 46 (1993), pp. 823–50; M.N. Kiggundu, "Task Interdependence and the Theory of Job Design," *Academy of Management Review*, 6 (1981), pp. 499–508.

20 K. Jelin, "A Multimethod Examination of the Benefits and Detriments of Intragroup Conflict," *Administrative Science Quarterly*, 40 (1995), pp. 245–82; P.C. Earley and G.B. Northcraft, "Goal Setting, Resource Interdependence, and Conflict Management," in M.A. Rahim (ed.), *Managing Conflict: An Interdisciplinary Approach* (New York: Praeger, 1989), pp. 161–70.

21 J.D. Thompson, *Organizations in Action* (New York: McGraw-Hill, 1967), pp. 54–56.

22 K.H. Doerr, T.R. Mitchell, and T.D. Klastorin, "Impact of Material Flow Policies and Goals on Job Outcomes," *Journal of Applied Psychology*, 81 (1996), pp. 142–52.

23 W.W. Notz, F.A. Starke, and J. Atwell, "The Manager as Arbitrator: Conflicts Over Scarce Resources," in Bazerman and Lewicki (eds.), *Negotiating in Organizations*, pp. 143–64.

24 P. Roberts, "Sony Changes the Game," *Fast Company*, 10 (1997), p. 116.

25 Brett et al., "Breaking the Bonds of Reciprocity in Negotiations"; R.A. Baron, "Reducing Organizational Conflict: An Incompatible Response Approach," *Journal of Applied Psychology*, 69 (1984), pp. 272–79.

26 K.D. Grimsley "Slings and Arrows on the Job," *Washington Post*, July 12, 1998, p. H1; "Flame Throwers," *Director*, 50 (July 1997), p. 36.

27 J.W. Jackson and E.R. Smith, "Conceptualizing Social Identity: A New Framework and Evidence for the Impact of Different Dimensions," *Personality & Social Psychology Bulletin*, 25 (January 1999), pp. 120–35.

28 D.C. Dryer and L.M. Horowitz, "When Do Opposites Attract? Interpersonal Complementarity versus Similarity," *Journal of Personality and Social Psychology*, 72 (1997), pp. 592–603.

29 K.W. Thomas, "Conflict and Conflict Management," in M.D. Dunnette (ed.), *Handbook of Industrial and Organizational Psychology* (Chicago: Rand McNally, 1976), pp. 889–935. For similar models see R.R. Blake and J.S. Mouton, *The Managerial Grid* (Houston: Gulf Publications, 1964); M.A. Rahim, "A Measure of Styles of Handling Interpersonal Conflict," *Academy of Management Journal*, 26 (1983), pp. 368–76.

30 R.J. Lewicki and J.A. Litterer, *Negotiation* (Homewood, IL: Irwin, 1985), pp. 102–106; K.W. Thomas, "Toward Multi-Dimensional Values in Teaching: The Example of Conflict Behaviours," *Academy of Management Review*, 2 (1977), pp. 484–90.

31 Jehn, "A Multimethod Examination of the Benefits and Detriments of Intragroup Conflict," p. 276.

32 G. Hamilton, "High-Tech Hits Forest," *Vancouver Sun*, May 8, 2000; C. Taylor, "The Innovators: A (Very) Short List of BC's Best and Brightest," *B.C. Business Magazine*, 27 (June 1999), pp. 22–38; A. Gibbon, "MacBlo Boss Helps Giant Gain Footing," *Globe and Mail*, October 12, 1998.

33 Tjosvold, *Working Together to Get Things Done*, Chapter 2; D.W. Johnson, G. Maruyama, R.T. Johnson, D. Nelson, and S. Skon, "Effects of Cooperative, Competitive, and Individualistic Goal Structures on Achievement: A Meta-Analysis," *Psychological Bulletin*, 89 (1981), pp. 47–62; R.J. Burke, "Methods of Resolving Superior-Subordinate Conflict: The Constructive Use of Subordinate Differences and Disagreements," *Organizational Behaviour and Human Performance*, 5 (1970), pp. 393–441.

34 K. Leung and D. Tjosvold (eds.), *Conflict Management in the Asia Pacific* (Singapore: John Wiley & Sons, 1998); M.A. Rahim and A.A. Blum (eds.), *Global Perspectives on Organizational Conflict* (Westport, CT: Praeger, 1995); M. Rabie, *Conflict Resolution and Ethnicity* (Westport, CT: Praeger, 1994).

35   C.C. Chen, X.P. Chen, and J.R. Meindl, "How Can Cooperation Be Fostered? The Cultural Effects of Individualism-Collectivism," *Academy of Management Review*, 23 (1998), pp. 285–304; S.M. Elsayed-Ekhouly and R. Buda, "Organizational Conflict: A Comparative Analysis of Conflict Styles Across Cultures," *International Journal of Conflict Management*, 7 (1996), pp. 71–81; D.K. Tse, J. Francis, and J. Walls, "Cultural Differences in Conducting Intra- and Inter-Cultural Negotiations: A Sino-Canadian Comparison," *Journal of International Business Studies*, 25 (1994), pp. 537–55; S. Ting-Toomey et al., "Culture, Face Management, and Conflict Styles of Handling Interpersonal Conflict: A Study in Five Cultures," *International Journal of Conflict Management*, 2 (1991), pp. 275–96.

36   L. Xiaohua and R. Germain, "Sustaining Satisfactory Joint Venture Relationships: The Role of Conflict Resolution Strategy," *Journal of International Business Studies*, 29 (March 1998), pp. 179–96.

37   L. Karakowsky, "Toward an Understanding of Women and Men at the Bargaining Table: Factors Affecting Negotiator Style and Influence in Multi-Party Negotiations," *Proceedings of the Annual ASAC Conference, Women in Management Division,* (1996), pp. 21–30; W.C. King, Jr., and T.D. Hinson, "The Influence of Sex and Equity Sensitivity on Relationship Preferences, Assessment of Opponent, and Outcomes in a Negotiation Experiment," *Journal of Management*, 20 (1994), pp. 605–24; R. Lewicki, J. Litterer, D. Saunders, and J. Minton (eds.), *Negotiation: Readings, Exercises, and Cases* (Homewood, IL: Irwin, 1993).

38   E. Van de Vliert, "Escalative Intervention in Small Group Conflicts," *Journal of Applied Behavioural Science*, 21 (Winter 1985), pp. 19–36.

39   M.B. Pinto, J.K. Pinto, and J.E. Prescott, "Antecedents and Consequences of Project Team Cross-Functional Cooperation," *Management Science*, 39 (1993), pp. 1281–97; M. Sherif, "Superordinate Goals in the Reduction of Intergroup Conflict," *American Journal of Sociology*, 68 (1958), pp. 349–58.

40   X.M. Song, J. Xile, B. Dyer, "Antecedents and Consequences of Marketing Managers' Conflict-Handling Behaviors," *Journal of Marketing*, January 2000, p. 50; L. Etherington and D. Tjosvold, "Managing Budget Conflicts: Contribution of Goal Interdependence and Interaction," *Canadian Journal of Administrative Sciences*, 15 (June 1998), pp. 142–51; K.M. Eisenhardt, J.L. Kahwajy, and L.J. Bourgeois III, "How Management Teams Can Have a Good Fight," *Harvard Business Review*, July–August 1997, pp. 77–85.

41   "How Hibernia Helped Its Hourly Employees Make a Leap to PFP," *Pay for Performance Report*, January 2000, p. 2; A. Vido, "Chrysler and Minivans: Are We There Yet?" *CMA Magazine*, November 1993, pp. 11–16.

42   M. Zimmerman, *How to Do Business with the Japanese* (New York: Random House, 1985), pp. 170, 200; W.G. Ouchi, *Theory Z* (New York: Avon, 1982), pp. 25–32.

43   "American Factories Halt Their Assembly Lines," *Globe and Mail*, January 7, 1995, p. D4.

44   This strategy and other conflict management practices in joint military operations are fully discussed in E. Elron, B. Shamir, and E. Ben-Ari, "Why Don't They Fight Each Other? Cultural Diversity and Operational Unity in Multinational Forces," *Armed Forces & Society*, October 1999, p. 73.

45   R.J. Fisher, E. Maltz, and B.J. Jaworski, "Enhancing Communication Between Marketing and Engineering: The Moderating Role of Relative Functional Identification," *Journal of Marketing*, 61 (1997), pp. 54–70.

46   A. Daniels, "Internet Firm Treats Employees Royally," *Vancouver Sun*, January 31, 2000.

47   P. Labarre "This Organization Is Dis-Organization," *Fast Company* (online), 3 (1997).

48   W.N. Isaacs, "Taking Flight: Dialog, Collective Thinking, and Organizational Learning," *Organizational Dynamics*, Autumn 1993, pp. 24–39; E.H. Schein, "On Dialog, Culture, and Organizational Learning," *Organizational Dynamics*, Autumn 1993, pp. 40–51; P.M. Senge, *The Fifth Discipline* (New York: Doubleday Currency, 1990), pp. 238–49.

49   J. Sanderson and C. Taylor, "Using a Relationship-Restructuring Program to Allay Poisonous Disputes," *Canadian HR Reporter*, April 5, 1999, pp. 18–19.

50 P.R. Lawrence and J.W. Lorsch, *Organization and Environment* (Homewood, IL: Irwin, 1969).

51 E. Horwitt, "Knowledge, Knowledge, Who's Got the Knowledge." *Computerworld*, April 8, 1996, pp. 80, 81, 84.

52 D.G. Pruitt and P.J. Carnevale, *Negotiation in Social Conflict* (Buckingham, UK: Open University Press, 1993), p. 2; and J.A. Wall, Jr., *Negotiation: Theory and Practice* (Glenview, IL: Scott, Foresman, 1985), p. 4.

53 L. Edson, "The Negotiation Industry," *Across the Board*, April 2000, pp. 14–20.

54 For a critical view of collaboration in negotiation, see J.M. Brett, "Managing Organizational Conflict," *Professional Psychology: Research and Practice*, 15 (1984), pp. 664–78.

55 R.E. Fells, "Overcoming the Dilemmas in Walton and Mckersie's Mixed Bargaining Strategy," *Industrial Relations* (Laval), 53 (March 1998), pp. 300–25; R.E. Fells, "Developing Trust in Negotiation," *Employee Relations*, 15 (1993), pp. 33–45.

56 R. Stagner and H. Rosen, *Psychology of Union–Management Relations* (Belmont, CA: Wadsworth, 1965), pp. 95–96, 108–10; R.E. Walton and R.B. McKersie, *A Behavioural Theory of Labour Negotiations: An Analysis of a Social Interaction System* (New York: McGraw-Hill, 1965), pp. 41–46.

57 J. Mayfield, M. Mayfield, D. Martin, and P. Herbig, "How Location Impacts International Business Negotiations," *Review of Business*, 19 (December 1998), p. 21; J.W. Salacuse and J.Z. Rubin, "Your Place or Mine? Site Location and Negotiation," *Negotiation Journal*, 6 (January 1990), pp. 5–10; Lewicki and Litterer, *Negotiation*, pp. 144–46.

58 B.C. Herniter, E. Carmel, and J.F. Nunamaker, Jr., "Computers Improve Efficiency of the Negotiation Process," *Personnel Journal*, April 1993, pp. 93–99.

59 Lewicki and Litterer, *Negotiation*, pp. 146–51; B. Kniveton, *The Psychology of Bargaining* (Aldershot, UK: Avebury, 1989), pp. 76–79.

60 Pruitt and Carnevale, *Negotiation in Social Conflict*, pp. 59–61; Lewicki and Litterer, *Negotiation*, pp. 151–54.

61 B.M. Downie, "When Negotiations Fail: Causes of Breakdown and Tactics for Breaking the Stalemate," *Negotiation Journal*, April 1991, pp. 175–86.

62 Pruitt and Carnevale, *Negotiation in Social Conflict*, pp. 56–58; Lewicki and Litterer, *Negotiation*, pp. 215–22.

63 V.V. Murray, T.D. Jick, and P. Bradshaw, "To Bargain or Not to Bargain? The Case of Hospital Budget Cuts," in *Negotiating in Organizations*, ed. Bazerman & Lewicki, pp. 272–95.

64 R.L. Lewicki, A. Hiam, and K. Olander, *Think Before You Speak: The Complete Guide to Strategic Negotiation* (New York: John Wiley & Sons, 1996); G.B. Northcraft and M.A. Neale, "Joint Effects of Assigned Goals and Training on Negotiator Performance," *Human Performance*, 7 (1994), pp. 257–72.

65 S. Doctoroff, "Reengineering Negotiations," *Sloan Management Review*, 39 (March 1998), pp. 63–71.

66 M.A. Neale and M.H. Bazerman, *Cognition and Rationality in Negotiation* (New York: Free Press, 1991), pp. 29–31; L.L. Thompson, "Information Exchange in Negotiation," *Journal of Experimental Social Psychology*, 27 (1991), pp. 161–79.

67 Y. Paik, and R.L. Tung "Negotiating with East Asians: How to Attain 'Win-Win' Outcomes," *Management International Review*, 39 (1999), pp. 103–22; L. Thompson, E. Peterson, and S.E. Brodt, "Team Negotiation: An Examinaton of Integrative and Distributive Bargaining," *Journal of Personality and Social Psychology*, 70 (1996), pp. 66–78.

68 L.L. Putnam and M.E. Roloff (eds.), *Communication and Negotiation* (Newbury Park, CA: Sage, 1992).

69 L. Hall (ed.), *Negotiation: Strategies for Mutual Gain* (Newbury Park, CA: Sage, 1993); D. Ertel, "How to Design a Conflict Management Procedure That Fits Your Dispute," *Sloan Management Review*, 32 (Summer 1991), pp. 29–42.

70 Lewicki and Litterer, *Negotiation*, pp. 89–93.

71 Paik and Tung "Negotiating with East Asians;" P. Brethour, "Toronto Firm Takes to Heart Cultural Lessons," *Globe and Mail*, August 30, 1996, p. B6; N.J. Adler, *International Dimensions of Organizational Behavior*, 2nd ed. (Belmont, CA: Wadsworth, 1991), pp. 180–81.

72 Kniveton, *The Psychology of Bargaining*, pp. 100–101; J.Z. Rubin and B.R. Brown, *The Social Psychology of Bargaining and Negotiation* (New York: Academic Press, 1976), Chapter 9; and Brett, "Managing Organizational Conflict," pp. 670–71.

73 B.H. Sheppard, R.J. Lewicki, and J.W. Monton, *Organizational Justice: The Search for Fairness in the Workplace* (New York: Lexington, 1992).

74 L.B. Bingham, "Mediating Employment Disputes: Perceptions of Redress at the United States Postal Service," *Review of Public Personnel Administration*, 17 (Spring 1997), pp. 20–30; R. Folger and J. Greenberg, "Procedural Justice: An Interpretive Analysis of Personnel Systems," *Research in Personnel and Human Resources Management*, 3 (1985), pp. 141–83.

75 A.R. Elangovan, "The Manager as the Third Party: Deciding How to Intervene in Employee Disputes," in R. Lewicki, J. Litterer, and D. Saunders (eds.), *Negotiation: Readings, Exercises, and Cases*, 3rd ed. (New York: McGraw-Hill, 1999), pp. 458–69; L.L. Putnam, "Beyond Third Party Role: Disputes and Managerial Intervention," *Employee Responsibilities and Rights Journal*, 7 (1994), pp. 23–36; Sheppard et al., *Organizational Justice*.

76 M.A. Neale and M.H. Bazerman, *Cognition and Rationality in Negotiation* (New York: The Free Press, 1991), pp. 140–42.

77 "An Ombudsperson Can Improve Management–Labour Relations," *Personnel Journal*, August 1993, p. 62; M. Crawford, "The New Office Etiquette," *Canadian Business*, May 1993, pp. 22–31.

78 B.H. Sheppard, "Managers as Inquisitors: Lessons from the Law," in M. Bazerman and R.J. Lewicki (eds.), *Bargaining Inside Organizations* (Beverly Hills, CA: Sage, 1983), pp. 193–213.

79 R. Cropanzano, H. Aguinis, M. Schminke, and D.L. Denham, "Disputant Reactions to Managerial Conflict Resolution Tactics," *Group & Organization Management*, 24 (June 1999), pp. 124–53; R. Karambayya and J.M. Brett, "Managers Handling Disputes: Third Party Roles and Perceptions of Fairness," *Academy of Management Journal*, 32 (1989), pp. 687–704.

80 A.R. Elangovan, "Managerial Intervention in Organizational Disputes: Testing a Prescriptive Model of Strategy Selection," *International Journal of Conflict Management*, 4 (1998), pp. 301–35.

81 J.P. Meyer, J.M. Gemmell, and P.G. Irving, "Evaluating the Management of Interpersonal Conflict in Organizations: A Factor-Analytic Study of Outcome Criteria," *Canadian Journal of Administrative Sciences*, 14 (1997), pp. 1–13.

82 M. Barrier, "A Working Alternative for Settling Disputes," *Nation's Business*, 86 (July 1998), pp. 43–46.

83 J. MacPherson, "Workers' Compensation Appeal Tribunals & Mediation: Alternative Approaches to Resolving Appeals," *HRProfessional* (Ontario), August–September 1999, pp. 21–27.

Chapter Fourteen

1 M. Proulx, "Suncor Boss One Cool CEO," *Edmonton Sun*, March 13, 2000, p. 42; S. Ewart, "Unique Suncor Boasts Unique CEO," *Calgary Herald*, September 11, 1999, p. 1; C. Cattaneo, "The Man Who Saved Suncor," *National Post*, September 11, 1999, p. D1; G. Gordon, "An Interview with This Year's EXCEL Honoree Rick George," *Communication World*, 15 (August 1998), p. 36.

2 R.A. Barker, "How Can We Train Leaders If We Do Not Know What Leadership Is?" *Human Relations*, 50 (1997), pp. 343–62; P.C. Drucker, "Forward," in F. Hesselbein et al., *The Leader of the Future* (San Francisco: Jossey-Bass, 1997).

3 J.M. Burns, *Leadership* (New York: Harper & Row, 1978), p. 2.

4 D. Miller, M.F.R. Ket de Vries, and J.M. Toulouse, "Top Executive Locus of Control and Its Relationship to Strategy-Making, Structure, and Environment," *Academy of Management Journal,* 25 (1982), pp. 237–53; P. Selznick, *Leadership in Administration* (Evanston, IL: Row, Peterson, 1957), p. 37.

5 M. Groves, "Cream Rises to the Top, but From a Small Crop," *Los Angeles Times*, June 8, 1998. A recent study also reported that only 3 percent of executives in large firms agreed that their company develops leadership talent quickly and effectively. See H. Handfield-Jones, "How Executives Grow," *McKinsey Quarterly*, January 2000, p. 117.

6 C.A. Beatty, "Implementing Advanced Manufacturing Technologies: Rules of the Road," *Sloan Management Review,* Summer 1992, pp. 49–60; J.M. Howell and C.A. Higgins, "Champions of Technological Innovation," *Administrative Science Quarterly,* 35 (1990), pp. 317–41.

7 Many of these perspectives are summarized in R.N. Kanungo, "Leadership in Organizations: Looking Ahead to the 21st Century," *Canadian Psychology*, 39 (Spring 1998), pp. 71–82.

8 T. Peters, "Air Nova Chief Attracts National Attention," *Halifax Chronicle-Herald*, June 6, 2000; M. Daly, S. McKay, and V. Smith, "Top 40 Under 40," *Report on Business Magazine*, April 28, 2000, p. 110.

9 J. Kochanski, "Competency-Based Management," *Training & Development*, October 1997, pp. 40–44; Hay Group et al., *Raising the Bar: Using Competencies to Enhance Employee Performance* (Scottsdale, AZ: American Compensation Association, 1996); L.M. Spencer and S.M. Spencer, *Competence at Work: Models for Superior Performance* (New York: Wiley, 1993).

10 T. Takala, "Plato on Leadership," *Journal of Business Ethics,* 17 (May 1998), pp. 785–98.

11 R.M. Stogdill, *Handbook of Leadership* (New York: The Free Press, 1974), Chapter 5.

12 Most elements of this list were derived from S.A. Kirkpatrick and E.A. Locke, "Leadership: Do Traits Matter?" *Academy of Management Executive*, 5 (May 1991), pp. 48–60. Several of these ideas are also discussed in H.B. Gregersen, A.J. Morrison, and J.S. Black, "Developing Leaders for the Global Frontier," *Sloan Management Review*, 40 (Fall 1998), pp. 21–32; R.J. House and R.N. Aditya, "The Social Scientific Study of Leadership: Quo Vadis?" *Journal of Management*, 23 (1997), pp. 409–73; R.J. House and M.L. Baetz, "Leadership: Some Empirical Generalizations and New Research Directions," *Research in Organizational Behavior,* 1 (1979), pp. 341–423.

13 House and Aditya, "The Social Scientific Study of Leadership."

14 "Canadian CEOs Give Themselves Top Marks for Leadership!" *Canada NewsWire*, September 9, 1999; J.M. Kouzes, and B.Z. Posner, *Credibility: How Leaders Gain and Lose It, Why People Demand It* (San Francisco: Jossey-Bass, 1993).

15 D. Goleman, "What Makes a Leader?" *Harvard Business Review*, 76 (November–December 1998), pp. 92–102; J.D. Mayer and P. Salovey, "The Intelligence of Emotional Intelligence," *Intelligence*, 17 (1993), pp. 433–42.

16 J.A. Kolb, "The Relationship Between Self-Monitoring and Leadership in Student Project Groups," *Journal of Business Communication*, 35 (April 1998), pp. 264–82; S.J. Zaccaro, R.J. Foti, and D.A. Kenny, "Self-Monitoring and Trait-Based Variance in Leadership: An Investigation of Leader Flexibility Across Multiple Group Situations," *Journal of Applied Psychology,* 76 (1991), pp. 308–15; S.E. Cronshaw and R.J. Ellis, "A Process Investigation of Self-Monitoring and Leader Emergence," *Small Group Research*, 22 (1991), pp. 403–20; S.J. Zaccaro, R.J. Foti, and D.A. Kenny, "Self-Monitoring and Trait-Based Variance Is Leadership: An Investigation of Leader Flexibility Across Multiple Group Situations," *Journal of Applied Psychology*, 76 (1991), pp. 308–15; G.H. Dobbins, W.S. Long, E.J. Dedrick, and T.C. Clemons, "The Role of Self-Monitoring and Gender on Leader Emergence: A Labouratory and Field Study," *Journal of Management,* 16 (1990), pp. 609–18.

17 L. Nakarmi, "Here Come the Mavericks," *Asiaweek*, April 9, 1999; "Korea's Kim Jung Tae," *Business Week*, June 29, 1998.

18 R.G. Lord and K.J. Maher, *Leadership and Information Processing: Linking Perceptions and Performance* (Cambridge, MA: Unwin Hyman, 1991).

19 W.C. Byham, "Grooming Next-Millennium Leaders," *HRMagazine,* 44 (February 1999), pp. 46–50; R. Zemke and S. Zemke, "Putting Competencies to Work," *Training,* 36 (January 1999), pp. 70–76.

20 G.A. Yukl, *Leadership in Organizations,* 3rd ed. (Englewood Cliffs, NJ: Prentice Hall, 1994), pp. 53–75; R. Likert, *New Patterns of Management* (New York: McGraw-Hill, 1961).

21 A.K. Korman, "Consideration, Initiating Structure, and Organizational Criteria—A Review," *Personnel Psychology,* 19 (1966), pp 349–62; E.A. Fleishman, "Twenty Years of Consideration and Structure," in E.A. Fleishman and J.C. Hunt (eds.), *Current Developments in the Study of Leadership* (Carbondale, IL: Southern Illinois University Press, 1973), pp. 1–40.

22 V.V. Baba, "Serendipity in Leadership: Initiating Structure and Consideration in the Classroom," *Human Relations,* 42 (1989), pp. 509–25.

23 R.L. Kahn, "The Prediction of Productivity," *Journal of Social Issues,* 12(2) (1956), pp. 41–49; P. Weissenberg and M.H. Kavanagh, "The Independence of Initiating Structure and Consideration: A Review of the Evidence," *Personnel Psychology,* 25 (1972), pp. 119–30; Stogdill, *Handbook of Leadership,* Chapter 11.

24 R.R. Blake and A.A. McCanse, *Leadership Dilemmas—Grid Solutions* (Houston: Gulf Publishing Company, 1991); R.R. Blake and J.S. Mouton, "Management by Grid Principles or Situationalism: Which?" *Group and Organization Studies,* 7 (1982), pp. 207–10.

25 L.L. Larson, J.G. Hunt, and R.N. Osborn, "The Great Hi–Hi Leader Behavior Myth: A Lesson from Occam's Razor," *Academy of Management Journal,* 19 (1976), pp. 628–41; S. Kerr, C.A. Schriesheim, C.J. Murphy, and R.M. Stogdill, "Towards a Contingency Theory of Leadership Based upon the Consideration and Initiating Structure Literature," *Organizational Behavior and Human Performance,* 12 (1974), pp. 62–82; A.K. Korman, "Consideration, Initiating Structure, and Organizational Criteria—A Review," *Personnel Psychology,* 19 (1966), pp. 349–62.

26 R. Tannenbaum and W.H. Schmidt, "How to Choose a Leadership Pattern," *Harvard Business Review,* May–June 1973, pp. 162–80.

27 For a recent discussion of the contingency perspective of leadership and emotional intelligence, see D. Goleman, "Leadership That Gets Results," *Harvard Business Review,* 78 (March–April 2000), pp. 78–90.

28 M.G. Evans, "The Effects of Supervisory Behavior on the Path-Goal Relationship," *Organizational Behavior and Human Performance,* 5 (1970), pp. 277–98; M.G. Evans, "Extensions of a Path-Goal Theory of Motivation," *Journal of Applied Psychology,* 59 (1974), pp. 172–78; R.J. House, "A Path-Goal Theory of Leader Effectiveness," *Administrative Science Quarterly,* 16 (1971), pp. 321–38.

29 R.J. House and T.R. Mitchell, "Path-Goal Theory of Leadership," *Journal of Contemporary Business,* Autumn 1974, pp. 81–97.

30 R. Wageman, "Case Study: Critical Success Factors for Creating Superb Self-Managing Teams at Xerox," *Compensation and Benefits Review,* 29 (September–October 1997), pp. 31–41.

31 M.E. McGill and J.W. Slocum, Jr., "A Little Leadership, Please?" *Organizational Dynamics,* 39 (Winter 1998), pp. 39–49; R.J. Doyle, "The Case of a Servant Leader: John F. Donnelly, Sr.," in R.P. Vecchio (ed.), *Leadership: Understanding the Dynamics of Power and Influence in Organizations* (Notre Dame, IN: University of Notre Dame Press, 1997), pp. 439–57.

32 R.J. House, "Path-Goal Theory of Leadership: Lessons, Legacy, and a Reformulated Theory," *Leadership Quarterly,* 7 (1996), pp. 323–52.

33 J.C. Wofford and L.Z. Liska, "Path-Goal Theories of Leadership: A Meta-Analysis," *Journal of Management,* 19 (1993), pp. 857–76; J. Indvik, "Path-Goal Theory of Leadership: A Meta-Analysis," *Academy of Management Proceedings,* 1986, pp. 189–92.

34 R.T. Keller, "A Test of the Path-Goal Theory of Leadership with Need for Clarity as a Moderator in Research and Development Organizations," *Journal of Applied Psychology,* 74 (1989), pp. 208–12.

35 J.M. Jermier, "The Path-Goal Theory of Leadership: A Subtextural Analysis," *Leadership Quarterly,* 7 (1996), pp. 311–16.

36 House, "Path-Goal Theory of Leadership: Lessons, Legacy, and a Reformulated Theory."

37 Wofford and Liska, "Path-Goal Theories of Leadership: A Meta-Analysis"; Yukl, *Leadership in Organizations,* pp. 102–104; Indvik, "Path-Goal Theory of Leadership: A Meta-Analysis."

38 C.A. Schriesheim and L.L. Neider, "Path-Goal Leadership Theory: The Long and Winding Road," *Leadership Quarterly,* 7 (1996), pp. 317–21. One of the more prominent studies that found evidence against path-goal theory is H.K. Downey, J.E. Sheridan, and J.W. Slocum, "Analysis of Relationships Among Leader Behavior, Subordinate Job Performance and Satisfaction: A Path-Goal Approach," *Academy of Management Journal,* 18 (1975), pp. 253–62.

39 P. Hersey and K.H. Blanchard, *Management of Organizational Behavior: Utilizing Human Resources,* 5th ed. (Englewood Cliffs, NJ: Prentice Hall, 1988).

40 C.L. Graeff, "Evolution of Situational Leadership Theory: A Critical Review," *Leadership Quarterly,* 8 (1997), pp. 153–70; W. Blank, J.R. Weitzel, and S.G. Green, "A Test of the Situational Leadership Theory," *Personnel Psychology,* 43 (1990), pp. 579–97; R.P. Vecchio, "Situational Leadership Theory: An Examination of a Prescriptive Theory," *Journal of Applied Psychology,* 72 (1987), pp. 444–51.

41 F.E. Fiedler, *A Theory of Leadership Effectiveness* (New York: McGraw-Hill, 1967); F.E. Fiedler and M.M. Chemers, *Leadership and Effective Management* (Glenview, IL: Scott, Foresman, 1974).

42 F.E. Fiedler, "Engineer the Job to Fit the Manager," *Harvard Business Review,* 43(5) (1965), pp. 115–22.

43 For a summary of criticisms, see Yukl, *Leadership in Organizations,* pp. 197–98.

44 P.M. Podsakoff and S.B. MacKenzie, "Kerr and Jermier's Substitutes for Leadership Model: Background, Empirical Assessment, and Suggestions for Future Research," *Leadership Quarterly,* 8 (1997), pp. 117–32; P.M. Podsakoff, B.P. Niehoff, S.B. MacKenzie, and M.L. Williams, "Do Substitutes Really Substitute for Leadership? An Empirical Examination of Kerr and Jermier's Situational Leadership Model," *Organizational Behavior and Human Decision Processes,* 54 (1993), pp. 1–44.

45 This observation has also been made by C.A. Schriesheim "Substitutes-for-Leadership Theory: Development and Basic Concepts," *Leadership Quarterly,* 8 (1997), pp. 103–108.

46 D.F. Elloy and A. Randolph, "The Effect of Superleader Behavior on Autonomous Work Groups in a Government Operated Railway Service," *Public Personnel Management,* 26 (Summer 1997), pp. 257–72.

47 "Air Travellers See K-W Firm's Handiwork," *Kitchener-Waterloo Record,* May 3, 2000.

48 C. Manz and H. Sims, *Superleadership; Getting to the Top by Motivating Others* (San Francisco: Berkley Publishing, 1990).

49 C.P. Neck and C.C. Manz, "Thought Self-Leadership: The Impact of Mental Strategies Training on Employee Cognition, Behavior, and Affect," *Journal of Organizational Behavior,* 17 (1996), pp. 445–67.

50 D. Kramer, "How National Rubber Bounced Back from the Edge of Disaster," *Canadian Occupational Safety,* November–December 1996, pp. 15–16.

51 J.M. Howell and B.J. Avolio, "Transformational Leadership, Transactional Leadership, Locus of Control, and Support for Innovation: Key Predictors of Consolidated-Business-Unit Performance," *Journal of Applied Psychology,* 78 (1993), pp. 891–902; J.A. Conger and R.N. Kanungo, "Perceived Behavioural Attributes of Charismatic Leadership," *Canadian Journal of Behavioural Science,* 24 (1992), pp. 86–102; J. Seltzer and B.M. Bass, "Transformational Leadership: Beyond Initiation and Consideration," *Journal of Management,* 16 (1990), pp. 693–703.

52 "Canadian CEOs Give Themselves Top Marks for Leadership!" *Canada NewsWire,* September 9, 1999.

53 B.J. Avolio and B.M. Bass, "Transformational Leadership, Charisma, and Beyond," in J.G. Hunt, H.P. Dachler, B.R. Baliga, and C.A. Schriesheim (eds.), *Emerging Leadership Vistas* (Lexington, MA: Lexington Books, 1988), pp. 29–49.

54 J. Kotter, *A Force for Change* (Cambridge, MA: Harvard Business School Press, 1990); W. Bennis and B. Nanus, *Leaders: The Strategies for Taking Charge* (New York: Harper & Row, 1985), p. 21; A. Zaleznik, "Managers and Leaders: Are They Different?" *Harvard Business Review,* 55(5) (1977), pp. 67–78.

55 W. Bennis, *An Invented Life: Reflections on Leadership and Change* (Reading, MA: Addison-Wesley, 1993); D. Tjosvold and M.M. Tjosvold, *The Emerging Leader* (New York: Lexington, 1993), p. 25.

56 B.S. Pawar and K.K. Eastman, "The Nature and Implications of Contextual Influences on Transformational Leadership: A Conceptual Examination," *Academy of Management Review*, 22 (1997), pp. 80–109.

57 L. Rittenhouse, "Dennis W. Bakke—Empowering a Workforce with Principles," *Electricity Journal*, January 1998, pp. 48–59.

58 J.A. Conger and R.N. Kanungo, "Toward a Behavioral Theory of Charismatic Leadership in Organizational Settings," *Academy of Management Review*, 12 (1987), pp. 637–47; R.J. House, "A 1976 Theory of Charismatic Leadership," in J.G. Hunt and L.L. Larson (eds.), *Leadership: The Cutting Edge* (Carbondale, IL: Southern Illinois University Press, 1977), pp. 189–207.

59 Y.A. Nur, "Charisma and Managerial Leadership: The Gift That Never Was," *Business Horizons*, 41 (July 1998), pp. 19–26; J.E. Barbuto, Jr., "Taking the Charisma Out of Transformational Leadership," *Journal of Social Behavior & Personality*, 12 (September 1997), pp. 689–97.

60 L. Sooklal, "The Leader as a Broker of Dreams," *Organizational Studies*, 1989, pp. 833–55.

61 I.M. Levin, "Vision Revisited," *Journal of Applied Behavioral Science*, 36 (March 2000), pp. 91–107; J.M. Stewart, "Future State Visioning—A Powerful Leadership Process," *Long Range Planning*, 26 (December 1993), pp. 89–98; Bennis and Nanus, *Leaders*, pp. 27–33, 89.

62 T.J. Peters, "Symbols, Patterns, and Settings: An Optimistic Case for Getting Things Done," *Organizational Dynamics*, 7 (Autumn 1978), pp. 2–23.

63 I.R. Baum, E.A. Locke, and S.A. Kirkpatrick, "A Longitudinal Study of the Relation of Vision and Vision Communication to Venture Growth in Entrepreneurial Firms," *Journal of Applied Psychology*, 83 (1998), pp. 43–54; S.A. Kirkpatrick and E.A. Locke, "Direct and Indirect Effects of Three Core Charismatic Leadership Components on Performance and Attitudes," *Journal of Applied Psychology*, 81 (1996), pp. 36–51.

64 "Canadian CEOs Give Themselves Top Marks for Leadership!" *Canada NewsWire*, September 9, 1999.

65 G.T. Fairhurst and R.A. Sarr, *The Art of Framing: Managing the Language of Leadership* (San Francisco, CA: Jossey-Bass, 1996); J.A. Conger, "Inspiring Others: The Language of Leadership," *Academy of Management Executive*, 5 (February 1991), pp. 31–45.

66 R.S. Johnson, "Home Depot Renovates," *Fortune*, November 23, 1998, pp. 200–206.

67 Fairhurst and Sarr, *The Art of Framing*, Chapter 5; J. Pfeffer, "Management as Symbolic Action: The Creation and Maintenance of Organizational Paradigms," *Research in Organizational Behavior*, 3 (1981), pp. 1–52.

68 L. Black, "Hamburger Diplomacy," *Report on Business Magazine*, 5 (August 1988), pp. 30–36; S. Franklin. *The Heroes: A Saga of Canadian Inspiration* (Toronto: McClelland and Stewart, 1967), p. 53.

69 McGill and Slocum, Jr., "A Little Leadership, Please?"; N.H. Snyder and M. Graves, "Leadership and Vision," *Business Horizons*, 37 (January 1994), pp. 1–7; D.E. Berlew, "Leadership and Organizational Excitement," in D.A. Kolb, I.M. Rubin, and J.M. McIntyre (eds.), *Organizational Psychology: A Book of Readings* (Englewood Cliffs, NJ: Prentice Hall, 1974).

70 M.F.R. Kets de Vries "Charisma in Action: The Transformational Abilities of Virgin's Richard Branson and ABB's Percy Barnevik," *Organizational Dynamics*, 26 (Winter 1998), pp. 6–21; M.F.R. Kets de Vries, "Creative Leadership: Jazzing Up Business," *Chief Executive*, March 1997, pp. 64–66; F. Basile, "Hotshots in Business Impart Their Wisdom," *Indianapolis Business Journal*, July 21, 1997, p. A40.

71 C. Knight, "Canada, U.S. Share Similar Leadership Concerns," *Canadian HR Reporter*, May 5, 1997 pp. 1, 3.

72 E.M. Whitener, S.E. Brodt, M.A. Korsgaard, and J.M. Werner, "Managers as Initiators of Trust: An Exchange Relationship Framework for Understanding Managerial Trustworthy Behavior," *Academy of Management Review*, 23 (July 1998), pp. 513–30; Bennis and Nanus, *Leaders*, pp. 43–55; Kouzes and Posner, *Credibility: How Leaders Gain and Lose It, Why People Demand It.*

73 C. Menzies, "Motivation Needs Top-Down Vision," *Australian Financial Review*, June 23, 2000.

74 J.J. Sosik, S.S. Kahai, and B.J. Avolio, "Transformational Leadership and Dimensions of Creativity: Motivating Idea Generation in Computer-Mediated Groups," *Creativity Research Journal*, 11 (1998), pp. 111–21; P. Bycio, R.D. Hackett, and J.S. Allen, "Further Assessments of Bass's (1985) Conceptualization of Transactional and Transformational Leadership," *Journal of Applied Psychology*, 80 (1995), pp. 468–78; W.L. Koh, R.M. Steers, and J.R. Terborg, "The Effects of Transformational Leadership on Teacher Attitudes and Student Performance in Singapore," *Journal of Organizational Behavior*, 16 (1995), pp. 319–33; Howell and Avolio, "Transformational Leadership, Transactional Leadership, Locus of Control, and Support for Innovation."

75 J. Barling, T. Weber, and E.K. Kelloway, "Effects of Transformational Leadership Training on Attitudinal and Financial Outcomes: A Field Experiment," *Journal of Applied Psychology*, 81 (1996), pp. 827–32.

76 A. Bryman, "Leadership in Organizations," in S.R. Clegg, C. Hardy, and W.R. Nord (eds.), *Handbook of Organization Studies* (Thousand Oaks, CA: Sage, 1996), pp. 276–92.

77 Pawar and Eastman, "The Nature and Implications of Contextual Influences on Transformational Leadership."

78 K. Boehnke, A.C. DiStefano, J.J. DiStefano, and N. Bontis, "Leadership for Extraordinary Performance," *Business Quarterly*, 61 (Summer 1997), pp. 56–63.

79 For a review of this research, see House and Aditya, "The Social Scientific Study of Leadership: Quo Vadis?"

80 R.J. Hall and R.G. Lord, "Multi-level Information Processing Explanations of Followers' Leadership Perceptions," *Leadership Quarterly*, 6 (1995), pp. 265–87; R. Ayman, "Leadership Perception: The Role of Gender and Culture," in M.M. Chemers and R. Ayman (eds.), *Leadership Theory and Research: Perspectives and Directions*, (San Diego, CA: Academic Press, 1993), pp. 137–66; J.R. Meindl, "On Leadership: An Alternative to the Conventional Wisdom," *Research in Organizational Behavior*, 12 (1990), pp. 159–203.

81 G.R. Salancik and J.R. Meindl, "Corporate Attributions as Strategic Illusions of Management Control," *Administrative Science Quarterly*, 29 (1984), pp. 238–54; J.M. Tolliver, "Leadership and Attribution of Cause: A Modification and Extension of Current Theory," *Proceedings of the Annual ASAC Conference, Organizational Behaviour Division*, 4, pt. 5 (1983), pp. 182–91.

82 S.F. Cronshaw and R.G. Lord, "Effects of Categorization, Attribution, and Encoding Processes on Leadership Perceptions," *Journal of Applied Psychology*, 72 (1987), pp. 97–106; J.W. Medcof and M.G. Evans, "Heroic or Competent? A Second Look," *Organizational Behavior and Human Decision Processes*, 38 (1986), pp. 295–304.

83 Meindl, "On Leadership: An Alternative to the Conventional Wisdom," p. 163.

84 J. Pfeffer, "The Ambiguity of Leadership," *Academy of Management Review*, 2 (1977), pp. 102–12; Yukl, *Leadership in Organizations*, pp. 265–67.

85 Cronshaw and Lord, "Effects of Categorization, Attribution, and Encoding Processes on Leadership Perceptions," pp. 104–105.

86 The study was conducted by the Conference Board of Canada and was reported in L. Elliott, "Women Switch Jobs to Climb the Power Ladder," *Toronto Star*, June 15, 2000, p. NE1.

87 N. Wood, "Venus Rules," *Incentive*, 172 (February 1998), pp. 22–27; S.H. Appelbaum and B.T. Shapiro, "Why Can't Men Lead Like Women?" *Leadership and Organization Development Journal*, 14 (1993), pp. 28–34; J.B. Rosener, "Ways Women Lead," *Harvard Business Review*, 68 (November–December 1990), pp. 119–25.

88 K. Goff, "The Muscle Behind Martha," *Ottawa Citizen*, October 21, 1999.

89 G.N. Powell, "One More Time: Do Female and Male Managers Differ?" *Academy of Management Executive*, 4 (August 1990), pp. 68–75; K.K. Lush and M.J. Withey, "Gender as a Moderator in the Path-Goal Theory of Leadership," *Proceedings of the Annual ASAC Conference, Organizational Behaviour Division*, 11, pt. 5 (1990), pp. 140–49; and G.H. Dobbins and S.J. Platts, "Sex Differences in Leadership: How Real Are They?" *Academy of Management Review*, 11 (1986), pp. 118–27. In contrast with these studies, one review cites an unpublished study reporting that women demonstrate more people-oriented leadership and are rated higher than men on their leadership. See M.-T. Claes, "Women, Men and Management Styles," *International Labour Review*, 138 (1999), pp. 431–46.

90 A.H. Eagly and B.T. Johnson, "Gender and Leadership Style: A Meta-Analysis," *Psychological Bulletin*, 108 (1990), pp. 233–56.

91 M. Javidan, B. Bemmels, K.S. Devine, and A. Dastmalchian, "Superior and Subordinate Gender and the Acceptance of Superiors as Role Models," *Human Relations*, 48 (1995), pp. 1271–84.

92 A.H. Eagly, S.J. Karau, and M.G. Makhijani, "Gender and the Effectiveness of Leaders: A Meta-Analysis," *Psychological Bulletin*, 117 (1995), pp. 125–45; M.E. Heilman and C.J. Block, "Sex Stereotypes: Do They Influence Perceptions of Managers?" *Journal of Social Behavior & Personality*, 10 (1995), pp. 237–52; R.L. Kent and S.E. Moss, "Effects of Sex and Gender Role on Leader Emergence," *Academy of Management Journal*, 37 (1994), pp. 1335–46; A.H. Eagly, M.G. Makhijani, and B.G. Klonsky, "Gender and the Evaluation of Leaders: A Meta-Analysis," *Psychological Bulletin*, 111 (1992), pp. 3–22.

Chapter Fifteen

1 M. Evans, T. Hamilton, L. Surtees, and S. Tuck, "The Road to a Billion," *Globe and Mail*, January 6, 2000; R. Dyck and N. Halpern, "Team-Based Organizations Redesign at Celestica," *Journal for Quality & Participation*, 22 (September–October 1999), pp. 36–40; "Celestica Nurtures Strong Corporate Culture Within," *Northern Colorado Business Report*, July 16, 1999, p. B5; K. Damsell, "Celestica Escapes from Its Cage," *National Post*, September 1, 1998, p. 9.

 2 J. Bryan, "Economy Booms, Job Stress Looms," *Montreal Gazette*, March 11, 2000; J. McHutchion, "Managing Change Gets Frowns in Business Survey," *Toronto Star*, March 23, 1996, p. C8.

 3 D. Hoewes, "Future Hinges on Global Teams," *Detroit News*, December 21, 1998.

 4 N. Bannister, "Nokia: From Start to Finnish," *The Age* (Melbourne), October 26, 1999; K. Lyytinen and S. Goodman, "Finland: The Unknown Soldier on the IT Front," *Communications of the ACM*, 42 (March 1999), pp. 13–17; S. Baker, "Can CEO Ollila Keep the Cellular Superstar Flying High?" *Business Week*, August 10, 1998, pp. 54–61; J. Dromberg, "Nokia's Line to the Top Slot," *Independent* (London), August 9, 1998, p. 5.

 5 D. Tapscott, A. Lowy, and D. Ticoll (eds.), *Blueprint to the Digital Economy: Creating Wealth in the Era of E-business* (New York: McGraw-Hill, 1998); C. Meyer and S. Davis, *Blur: The Speed of Change in the Connected Economy* (Reading, MA: Addison-Wesley, 1998). For an excellent discussion of how computer networks are changing the world of business, also see K. Kelly, "New Rules for the New Economy," *Wired*, September 1997.

 6 D. Tapscott and A. Laston, *Paradigm Shift* (New York: McGraw-Hill, 1993); W.H. Davidow and M.S. Malone, *The Virtual Corporation* (New York: HarperBusiness, 1992).

 7 D. Tapscott, A. Lowy, and D. Ticoll (eds.), *Blueprint to the Digital Economy: Wealth Creation in the Era of E-Business* (New York: McGraw-Hill, 1998).

 8 T. Keller, "Reinventing the Firm," *National Post Business Magazine*, June 1, 2000, p. 68.

 9 R. Bettis and M. Hitt, "The New Competitive Landscape," *Strategic Management Journal*, 16 (1995), pp. 7–19.

10 "Eight Companies Gear Up to Sell You Electricity," *Toronto Star*, March 1, 2000; S. Laidlaw, "U.S. Sharks Troll Hydro Waters," *Toronto Star*, July 16, 1999, pp. C1, C5; R. Laver, "America on the Line," *Maclean's*, April 5, 1999, pp. 38–43; S. Ellis, "A New Role for the Post Office: An Investigation into Issues Behind Strategic Change at Royal Mail," *Total Quality Management*, 9 (May 1998), pp. 223–34.

11 B. Hill, "Corel Lays Off 21% of Workforce," *Ottawa Citizen*, June 9, 2000; B. Marotte, "CIBC Cuts Costs by \$500M," *Ottawa Citizen*, June 7, 1999; "The Newspaper Wars," *Canoe* (online), March 2, 1999. The survey is reported in Watson Wyatt, "Change Persists in Canadian Workplace," News Release, April 11, 2000.

12 S. Sutel, "The Seagram Saga: A Showbiz Star Is Reborn," *Kitchener-Waterloo Record*, June 21, 2000; G. Patterson, "Investing in High Tech DigIT Interactive Fits into Informission Ring," *Silicon Valley North*, May 2000.

13 K. Goff, "Chapters Online Turns Page on Paperless Books," *Ottawa Citizen*, May 2, 2000; E. Hoare, "Chapters CEO Pens Business Book of His Own," *Halifax Herald*, December 7, 1999; T. Cole, "Larry's Party," *Report on Business Magazine*, September 24, 1999, p. 44.

14 K. Lewin, *Field Theory in Social Science* (New York: Harper & Row, 1951).

15 M. Moravec, O.J. Johannessen, and T.A. Hjelmas, "Thumbs Up for Self-Managed Teams," *Management Review*, 86 (July–August 1997), pp. 42–47.

16 D.A. Nadler, *Champions of Change* (San Francisco, CA: Jossey-Bass, 1998), Chapter 5; P. Strebel, "Why Do Employees Resist Change?" *Harvard Business Review*, May–June 1996, pp. 86–92; R. Maurer, *Beyond the Wall of Resistance: Unconventional Strategies to Build Support for Change* (Austin, TX: Bard Books, 1996); C. Hardy, *Strategies for Retrenchment and Turnaround: The Politics of Survival* (Berlin: Walter de Gruyter, 1990), Chapter 13.

17 C.O. Longenecker, D.J. Dwyer, and T.C. Stansfield, "Barriers and Gateways to Workforce Productivity," *Industrial Management*, 40 (March–April 1998), pp. 21–28.

18 E.B. Dent and S.G. Goldberg, "Challenging 'Resistance to Change,' " *Journal of Applied Behavioral Science*, 35 (March 1999), pp. 25–41.

19 D.A. Nadler, "The Effective Management of Organizational Change," in *Handbook of Organizational Behavior*, ed. J.W. Lorsch (Englewood Cliffs, NJ: Prentice Hall, 1987), pp. 358–69; D. Katz and R.L. Kahn, *The Social Psychology of Organizations*, 2nd ed. (New York: Wiley, 1978).

20 "Making Change Work for You—Not Against You," *Agency Sales Magazine*, 28 (June 1998), pp. 24–27.

21 M.E. McGill and J.W. Slocum, Jr., "Unlearn the Organization," *Organizational Dynamics*, 22(2) (1993), pp. 67–79.

22 R. Katz, "Time and Work: Toward an Integrative Perspective," *Research in Organizational Behavior*, 2 (1980), pp. 81–127.

23 D. Nicolini and M.B. Meznar, "The Social Construction of Organizational Learning: Conceptual and Practical Issues in the Field," *Human Relations*, 48 (1995), pp. 727–46.

24 D. Miller, "What Happens After Success: The Perils of Excellence," *Journal of Management Studies*, 31 (1994), pp. 325–58.

25 T.G. Cummings, "The Role and Limits of Change Leadership," in J.A. Conger, G.M. Spreitzer, and E.E. Lawler III, *The Leader's Change Handbook* (San Francisco: Jossey-Bass, 1999), pp. 301–20.

26 L.D. Goodstein and H.R. Butz, "Customer Value: The Linchpin of Organizational Change," *Organizational Dynamics*, 27 (June 1998), pp. 21–35.

27 J. Juergens, "Corporate Spotlight: ARCNET," *Incentive*, 173 (September 1999), pp. 68–69; G. Brenneman, "Right Away and All at Once: How We Saved Continental," *Harvard Business Review*, September–October 1998, pp. 162–79.

28 A. Gore, "Joel Kocher: Power COO Says It's Time to Evolve," *MacUser*, April 1997.

29 J.P. Kotter and L.A. Schlesinger, "Choosing Strategies for Change," *Harvard Business Review*, March–April 1979, pp. 106–14.

30 O. Edur, "Harnessing Human Power," *National Post*, November 30, 1999, p. F1.

31 M. Kane, "Change Is Fine, Workers Say," *Vancouver Sun*, September 25, 1998, pp. F1, F10.

32 J.P. Walsh and S.-F. Tseng, "The Effects of Job Characteristics on Active Effort at Work," *Work & Occupations*, 25 (February 1998), pp. 74–96; K.T. Dirks, L.L. Cummings, and J.L. Pierce, "Psychological Ownership in Organizations: Conditions Under Which Individuals Promote and Resist Change," *Research in Organizational Change and Development*, 9 (1996), pp. 1–23.

33 "Partners in Honing High-Quality Customer Service Skills," *Training*, 34 (January 1997), pp. S23–S26.

34 B.B. Bunker and B.T. Alban, *Large Group Interventions: Engaging the Whole System for Rapid Change* (San Francisco: Jossey-Bass, 1996); M. Emery and R.E. Purser, *The Search Conference: A Powerful Method for Planning Organizational Change and Community Action* (San Francisco: Jossey-Bass, 1996).

35 T. McCallum, "Vision 2001: Staying Ahead of the Competition," *Human Resource Professional*, November 1996, pp. 25–26.

36 R. Dubey, "The CEO Who Walked Away," *Business Today* (India), May 22, 1998, p. 98.

37 R.E. Purser and S. Cabana, *The Self-Managing Organization* (New York: Free Press, 1998), Chapter 7; "Making Organizational Changes Effective and Sustainable," *Educating for Employment*, August 7, 1998; R. Larson, "Forester Defends 'Feel-Good' Meeting," *Washington Times*, November 28, 1997, p. A9; W. Kaschub, "PECO Energy Redesigns HR, *HR Focus*, 74 (March 1997), p. 3.

38 P.H. Mirvis and M.L. Marks, *Managing the Merger* (Englewood Cliffs, NJ: Prentice Hall, 1992).

39 S. McKay, "The Challenge of Change," *Financial Post Magazine*, April 1992, pp. 43–46.

40 R. Greenwood and C.R. Hinings, "Understanding Radical Organizational Change: Bringing Together the Old and the New Institutionalism," *Academy of Management Review*, 21 (1996), pp. 1022–54.

41 J. Dibbs, "Organizing for Empowerment," *Business Quarterly*, 58 (Autumn 1993), pp. 97–102.

42 G. Brenneman, "Right Away and All at Once: How We Saved Continental," *Harvard Business Review*, September–October 1998, pp. 162–79; G. Flynn, "A Flight Plan for Success," *Workforce*, 76 (July 1997), pp. 72; D. Kramer, "How National Rubber Bounced Back from the Edge of Disaster," *Canadian Occupational Safety*, November–December 1996, pp. 15–16.

43 J. Lublin, "Curing Sick Companies Better Done Fast," *Globe and Mail*, July 25, 1995, p. B18.

44 Nicolini and Meznar, "The Social Construction of Organizational Learning."

45 The importance of systems and structure in reinforcing change is discussed in W.F. Joyce, *MegaChange: How Today's Leading Companies Have Transformed Their Workforces* (New York: Free Press, 1999), Chapters 4 and 5, pp. 477–85.

46 E.E. Lawler III, "Pay Can Be a Change Agent," *Compensation & Benefits Management*, 16 (Summer 2000), pp. 23–26.

47 R.H. Miles, "Leading Corporate Transformation: Are You Up to the Task?" in J.A. Conger, G.M. Spreitzer, and E.E. Lawler III, *The Leader's Change Handbook* (San Francisco: Jossey-Bass, 1999), pp. 221–67; L.D. Goodstein and H.R. Butz, "Customer Value: The Linchpin of Organizational Change," *Organizational Dynamics*, 27 (Summer 1998), pp. 21–34.

48 D.A. Nadler, "Implementing Organizational Changes," in D.A. Nadler, M.L. Tushman, and N.G. Hatvany (eds.), *Managing Organizations: Readings and Cases* (Boston: Little, Brown, and Company, 1982), pp. 440–59.

49 B. McDermott and G. Sexton, "Sowing the Seeds of Corporate Innovation," *Journal for Quality and Participation*, 21 (November–December 1998), pp. 18–23.

50 "CHC Completes Final Step in Rival's Takeover," *St. John's Telegram*, October 29, 1999; CHC Helicopter Corporation, *Annual Report 1999*; C. Flanagan, "Birdman of Newfoundland," *Canadian Business*, August 27, 1999, p. 55.

51 J.P. Kotter, "Leading Change: The Eight Steps to Transformation," in J.A. Conger, G.M. Spreitzer, and E.E. Lawler III, *The Leader's Change Handbook* (San Francisco: Jossey-Bass, 1999), pp. 221–67; J.P. Kotter, "Leading Change: Why Transformation Efforts Fail," *Harvard Business Review*, March–April 1995, pp. 59–67.

52 S. Wetlaufer, "Driving Change: An Interview with Ford Motor Company's Jacques Nasser," *Harvard Business Review*, 77 (March–April 1999), pp. 76–88; S. Zesiger, "Jac Nasser Is Car Crazy," *Fortune*, June 22, 1998, pp. 79–82.

53 M. Beer, R.A. Eisenstat, and B. Spector, *The Critical Path to Corporate Renewal* (Boston, MA: Harvard Business School Press, 1990).

54 J. Childs, "Five Years and Counting: The Path to Self-Directed Work Teams," *Hospital Materiel Management Quarterly*, 18 (May 1997), pp. 34–43.

55 R.E. Walton, *Innovating to Compete: Lessons for Diffusing and Managing Change in the Workplace* (San Francisco: Jossey-Bass, 1987); Beer et al., *The Critical Path to Corporate Renewal*, Chapter 5; R.E. Walton, "Successful Strategies for Diffusing Work Innovations," *Journal of Contemporary Business*, Spring 1977, pp. 1–22.

56 R. Beckhard, *Organization Development: Strategies and Models* (Reading, MA: Addison-Wesley, 1969), Chapter 2. Also see T.G. Cummings and E.F. Huse, *Organization Development and Change*, 4th ed. (St. Paul, MN: West, 1989), pp. 1–3.

57 W.W. Burke, *Organization Development: A Normative View* (Reading, MA: Addison-Wesley, 1987), pp. 12–14.

58 L. Dickens and K. Watkins, "Action Research: Rethinking Lewin," *Management Learning*, 30 (June 1999), pp. 127–40; J.B. Cunningham, *Action Research and Organization Development* (Westport, CN: Praeger, 1993). For a discussion of early applications of action research in Canada, see R. Sommer, "Action Research: From Mental Hospital Reform in Saskatchewan to Community Building in California," *Canadian Psychology*, 40 (February 1999), pp. 47–55.

59 A.B. Shani and G.R. Bushe, "Visionary Action Research: A Consultation Process Perspective," *Consultation: An International Journal*, 6(1) (1987), pp. 3–19.

60 M.L. Brown, "Five Symbolic Roles of the Organizational Development Consultant: Integrating Power, Change, and Symbolism," *Proceedings of the Annual ASAC Conference, Organizational Behaviour Division*, 14, pt. 5 (1993), pp. 71–81; D.A. Buchanan and D. Boddy, *The Expertise of the Change Agent: Public Performance and Backstage Activity* (New York: Prentice Hall, 1992); L.E. Greiner and V.E. Schein, *Power and Organization Development: Mobilizing Power to Implement Change* (Reading, MA: Addison-Wesley, 1988).

61 D.F. Harvey and D.R. Brown, *An Experiential Approach to Organization Development*, 5th ed. (Upper Saddle River, NJ: Prentice Hall, 1996), Chapter 4.

62 M. Beer and E. Walton, "Developing the Competitive Organization: Interventions and Strategies," *American Psychologist*, 45 (February 1990), pp. 154–61.

63 E.H. Schein, *Process Consultation: Its Role in Organization Development* (Reading, MA: Addison-Wesley, 1969).

64 For a case study of poor diagnosis, see M. Popper, "The Glorious Failure," *Journal of Applied Behavioral Science*, 33 (March 1997), pp. 27–45.

65 P. Faiello, "Employee Power," *CA Magazine*, 133 (March 2000), pp. 45–46.

66 Beer, *Organization Change and Development*, pp. 101–102.

67 K.E. Weick and R.E. Quinn, "Organizational Change and Development," *Annual Review of Psychology*, 1999, pp. 361–86.

68 D.A. Nadler, "Organizational Frame Bending: Types of Change in the Complex Organization," in R.H. Kilmann, T.J. Covin, and Associates (eds.), *Corporate Transformation: Revitalizing Organizations for a Competitive World* (San Francisco: Jossey-Bass, 1988), pp. 66–83.

69 T.Y. Choi, M. Rungtusanatham, and J.S. Kim, "Continuous Improvement on the Shop Floor: Lessons from Small to Midsize Firms," *Business Horizons*, 40 (November 1997), pp. 45–50; J.M. Kouzes and B.Z. Posner, *The Leadership Challenge* (San Francisco: Jossey-Bass, 1988), Chapter 10; C. Lindblom, "The Science of Muddling Through," *Public Administration Review*, 19 (1959), pp. 79–88.

70 C.R. Hinings and R. Greenwood, *The Dynamics of Strategic Change* (Oxford, UK: Basil Blackwell, 1988), Chapter 6; D. Miller and P.H. Friesen, "Structural Change and Performance: Quantum versus Piecemeal-Incremental Approaches," *Academy of Management Journal*, 25 (1982), pp. 867–92.

71 P.A. Strassmann, "The Hocus-Pocus of Reengineering," *Across the Board*, 31 (June 1994), pp. 35–38.

72 S.R. Olberding, "Turnaround Drama Instills Leadership," *Journal for Quality & Participation*, 21 (January–February 1998), pp. 52–55.

73 Cummings and Huse, *Organization Development and Change*, pp. 158–61.

74 A.H. Church and W.W. Burke, "Practitioner Attitudes About the Field of Organization Development," *Research in Organizational Change and Development*, 8 (1995), pp. 1–46.

75 A.H. Church, W.W. Burke, and D.F. Van Eynde, "Values, Motives, and Interventions of Organization Development Practitioners," *Group and Organization Management*, 19 (1994), pp. 5–50.

76 E.M. Van Aken, D.J. Monetta, and D.S. Sink, "Affinity Groups: The Missing Link in Employee Involvement," *Organization Dynamics*, 22 (Spring 1994), pp. 38–54; G.R. Bushe and A.B. Shani, *Parallel Learning Structures* (Reading, MA: Addison-Wesley, 1991).

77 D. Whitney and D.L. Cooperrider, "The Appreciative Inquiry Summit: Overview and Applications," *Employment Relations Today*, 25 (Summer 1998), pp. 17–28.

78 D. Whitney and C. Schau, "Appreciative Inquiry: An Innovative Process for Organization Change," *Employment Relations Today*, 25 (Spring 1998), pp. 11–21; F.J. Barrett and D.L. Cooperrider, "Generative Metaphor Intervention: A New Approach for Working with Systems Divided by Conflict and Caught in Defensive Perception," *Journal of Applied Behavioral Science*, 26 (1990), pp. 219–39.

79 G.R. Bushe and G. Coetzer, "Appreciative Inquiry as a Team-Development Intervention: A Controlled Experiment," *Journal of Applied Behavioral Science*, 31 (1995), pp. 13–30; L. Levine, "Listening with Spirit and the Art of Team Dialogue," *Journal of Organizational Change Management*, 7 (1994), pp. 61–73.

80 A. Vido, "Chrysler and Minivans: Are We There Yet?" *CMA Magazine*, November 1993, pp. 11–16.

81 G.A. Neuman, J.E. Edwards, and N.S. Raju, "Organizational Development Interventions: A Meta-Analysis of Their Effects on Satisfaction and Other Attitudes," *Personnel Psychology*, 42 (1989), pp. 461–89; R.A. Guzzo, R.D. Jette, and R.A. Katzell, "The Effects of Psychologically Based Intervention Programs on Worker Productivity: A Meta-Analysis," *Personnel Psychology*, 38 (1985), pp. 275–91.

82 R.J. Long, "The Effects of Various Workplace Innovations on Productivity: A Quasi-Experimental Study," *Proceedings of the Annual ASAC Conference, Personnel and Human Resources Division*, 11, pt. 9 (1990), pp. 98–107.

83 C.-M. Lau, "A Culture-Based Perspective of Organization Development Implementation," *Research in Organizational Change and Development*, 9 (1996), pp. 49–79.

84 R.J. Marshak, "Lewin Meets Confucius: A Review of the OD Model of Change," *Journal of Applied Behavioral Science*, 29 (1993), pp. 395–415; T.C. Head and P.F. Sorenson, "Cultural Values and Organizational Development: A Seven-Country Study," *Leadership and Organization Development Journal*, 14 (1993), pp. 3–7; J.M. Putti, "Organization Development Scene in Asia: The Case of Singapore," *Group and Organization Studies*, 14 (1989), pp. 262–70; A.M. Jaeger, "Organization Development and National Culture: Where's the Fit?" *Academy of Management Review*, 11 (1986), pp. 178–90.

85 For an excellent discussion of conflict management and Asian values, see several articles in K. Leung and D. Tjosvold (eds.), *Conflict Management in the Asia Pacific: Assumptions and Approaches in Diverse Cultures* (Singapore: John Wiley & Sons (Asia), 1998).

86 C.M.D. Deaner, "A Model of Organization Development Ethics," *Public Administration Quarterly*, 17 (1994), pp. 435–46; M. McKendall, "The Tyranny of Change: Organizational Development Revisited," *Journal of Business Ethics*, 12 (February 1993), pp. 93–104.

87 G.A. Walter, "Organization Development and Individual Rights," *Journal of Applied Behavioral Science*, 20 (1984), pp. 423–39.

88 "Perils of Public Sector Work: A Case Study," *Consultants News*, April 1996, p. 5; S. Parker, Jr., "SaskTel Dials the Wrong Number," *Western Report*, February 26, 1996, pp. 14–17.

89 Burke, *Organization Development*, pp. 149–51; Beer, *Organization Change and Development*, pp. 223–24.

Chapter Sixteen

1 J.P. Flintoff, "Keeping Faith in St Luke," *Guardian* (London), September 19, 1998, p. 22; F. Jebb, "Don't Call Me Sir," *Management Today*, August 1998, pp. 44–47; H. Jones, "Selling Space," *Design Week*, April 10, 1998, pp. 18–21; A.R. Sorkin, "Gospel According to St. Luke's," *New York Times*, February 12, 1998, pp. D1, D7; S. Caulkin, "The Advertising Gospel According to St Luke's," *Observer* (London), August 24, 1997, p. 8; M. Carter, "In St Luke's We Trust," *The Independent* (London), April 21, 1997, p. 6.

2 A.G. Bedeian and R.F. Zammuto, *Organizations: Theory and Design* (Hinsdale, IL: Dryden, 1991), pp. 117–18.

3 S. Ranson, R. Hinings, and R. Greenwood, "The Structuring of Organizational Structure," *Administrative Science Quarterly*, 25 (1980), pp. 1–14.

4 "Ford Motor Company Announces Consumer-Focused Organization for the 21st Century," *Auto Channel* (online), October 18, 1999.

5 H. Mintzberg, *The Structuring of Organizations* (Englewood Cliffs, NJ: Prentice Hall, 1979), pp. 2–3.

6 H. Fayol, *General and Industrial Management*, trans. C. Storrs (London: Pitman, 1949); E.E. Lawler III, *Motivation in Work Organizations* (Monterey, CA: Brooks/Cole, 1973), Chapter 7; M.A. Campion, "Ability Requirement Implications of Job Design: An Interdisciplinary Perspective," *Personnel Psychology*, 42 (1989), pp. 1–24.

7 A.N. Maira, "Connecting Across Boundaries: The Fluid-Network Organization," *Prism*, First Quarter 1998, pp. 23–26; D.A. Nadler and M.L. Tushman, *Competing by Design: The Power of Organizational Architecture* (New York: Oxford University Press, 1997), Chapter 6; Mintzberg, *The Structuring of Organizations*, pp. 2–8.

8 C. Downs, P. Clampitt, and A.L. Pfeiffer, "Communication and Organizational Outcomes," in G. Goldhaber and G. Barnett (eds.), *Handbook of Organizational Communication* (Norwood, NJ: Ablex, 1988), pp. 171–211; H.C. Jain, "Supervisory Communication and Performance in Urban Hospitals," *Journal of Communication*, 23 (1973), pp. 103–17.

9 V.L. Shalin and G.V. Prabhu, "A Cognitive Perspective on Manual Assembly," *Ergonomics*, 39 (1996), pp. 108–27; I. Nonaka and H. Takeuchi, *The Knowledge-Creating Company* (New York: Oxford University Press, 1995).

10 A.L. Patti, J.P. Gilbert, and S. Hartman, "Physical Co-location and the Success of New Product Development Projects," *Engineering Management Journal*, 9 (September 1997), pp. 31–37; M.L. Swink, J.C. Sandvig, and V.A. Mabert, "Customizing Concurrent Engineering Processes: Five Case Studies," *Journal of Product Innovation Management*, 13 (1996), pp. 229–44; W.I. Zangwill, *Lightning Strategies for Innovation: How the World's Best Firms Create New Products* (New York: Lexington, 1993).

11 D. Anfuso, "Core Values Shape W.L. Gore & Associates' Innovative Culture," *Workforce*, 78 (March 1999), pp. 48–53; M. Kaplan, "You Have No Boss," *Fast Company*, 11 (November 1997), p. 226; D.M. Price, "Gore-Tex Gets Hip," *Minneapolis Star Tribune*, May 5, 1997, p. D1.

12 Fayol's work is summarized in J.B. Miner, *Theories of Organizational Structure and Process* (Chicago: Dryden, 1982), pp. 358–66.

13 F. Jebb, "Rentokil Initial: A Place for Everyone and Everyone in Their Place," *Management Today*, August 1998, p. 46.

14 J.A. Conger, *Winning 'em Over* (New York: Simon & Schuster, 1998), Appendix A.

15 J.H. Sheridan, "Lessons from the Best," *Industry Week*, February 20, 1995, pp. 13–22.

16 J. Pfeffer, "Seven Practices of Successful Organizations," *California Management Review*, 40 (1998), pp. 96–124.

17 D.D. Van Fleet and A.G. Bedeian, "A History of the Span of Management," *Academy of Management Review*, 2 (1977), pp. 356–72; Mintzberg, *The Structuring of Organizations*, Chapter 8; D. Robey, *Designing Organizations*, 3rd ed. (Homewood, IL: Irwin, 1991), pp. 255–59.

18 B. Simon, "Bank Leads by Example in Transformation," *Business Day* (South Africa), July 30, 1998, p. 17.

19 S. Ellis, "A New Role for the Post Office: An Investigation into Issues Behind Strategic Change at Royal Mail," *Total Quality Management*, 9 (May 1998), pp. 223–34; R.H. Kluge, "An Incentive Compensation Plan with an Eye on Quality," *Quality Progress*, 29 (December 1996), pp. 65–68.

20 T. Peters, *Thriving on Chaos* (New York: Knopf, 1987), p. 359.

21 P. Panchak, "The Future Manufacturing (Interview with Peter Drucker)," *Industry Week*, 247 (September 21, 1998), pp. 96–105. For a thorough critique of delayering, see L. Donaldson and F.G. Hilmer, "Management Redeemed: The Case Against Fads That Harm Management," *Organizational Dynamics*, 26 (Spring 1998), pp. 6–20.

22 "Taking Care of the People," *Canadian Healthcare Manager*, 6 (April–May 1999), pp. 5–9.

23 Mintzberg, *The Structuring of Organizations*, p. 136.

24 The number of layers at Microsoft is inferred from examples in Jebb, "Don't Call Me Sir."

25 P. Galuszka, "Procter's Latest Gamble," *Business Week*, September 14, 1998, p. 58; A. Richards, "Brand New Days; Brand Managers," *Marketing*, December 4, 1997, pp. 26–27.

26 Mintzberg, *The Structuring of Organizations*, Chapter 5.

27 B. Victor and A.C. Boynton, *Invented Here* (Boston: Harvard Business School Press, 1998), Chapter 2; M. Hamstra, "McD Speeds Up Drive-Thru with Beefed Up Operations," *Nation's Restaurant News*, April 6, 1998, p. 3; G. Morgan, *Creative Organization Theory: A Resourcebook* (Newburg Park, CA: Sage, 1989), pp. 271–73; K. Deveny, "Bag Those Fries, Squirt That Ketchup, Fry That Fish," *Business Week*, October 13, 1986, p. 86.

28 T. Burns and G. Stalker, *The Management of Innovation* (London: Tavistock, 1961).

29 Mintzberg, *The Structuring of Organizations*, p. 106.

30 Mintzberg, *The Structuring of Organizations*, Chapter 17.

31 S. Cameron, "Guitarists Worldwide Pick Levy's," *Halifax Chronicle-Herald*, January 2, 2000.

32 Robey, *Designing Organizations*, pp. 186–89.

33 M. Hamstra, "McD's To Decentralize US Management Team," *Nation's Restaurant News*, June 2, 1997, p. 1

34 Robey, *Designing Organizations*, pp. 191–97; Bedeian and Zammuto, *Organizations: Theory and Design*, pp. 162–68.

35 "Tearing Down Silos to Build a Corporate-wide Communication Plan," *PR News*, July 10, 2000.

36 "Cossette Communications Inc.," *Financial Post*, December 16, 1995, p. 21.

37 R.C. Ford and W.A. Randolph, "Cross-Functional Structures: A Review and Integration of Matrix Organization and Project Management," *Journal of Management*, 18 (1992), pp. 267–94.

38 M.F.R. Kets de Vries, "Charisma in Action: The Transformational Abilities of Virgin's Richard Branson and ABB's Percy Barnevik," *Organizational Dynamics*, 26 (Winter 1998), pp. 6–21; D.A. Nadler and M.L. Tushman, *Competing by Design* (New York: Oxford University Press, 1997), Chapter 6; "Tenneco Automotive Realigns for the Future," *PR Newswire*, March 4, 1997.

39 H.F. Kolodny, "Managing in a Matrix," *Business Horizons*, March–April 1981, pp. 17–24; S.M. Davis and P.R. Lawrence, *Matrix* (Reading, MA: Addison-Wesley, 1977).

40 K. Knight, "Matrix Organization: A Review," *Journal of Management Studies*, May 1976, pp. 111–30.

41 C. Herkströter, "Royal Dutch/Shell: Rewriting the Contracts," in G.W. Dauphinais and C. Price (eds.), *Straight from the CEO* (New York: Simon & Schuster, 1998), pp. 86–93.

42 G. Calabrese "Communication and Co-operation in Product Development: A Case Study of a European Car Producer," *R & D Management*, 27 (July 1997), pp. 239–52; J.L. Brown and N.M. Agnew, "The Balance of Power in a Matrix Structure," *Business Horizons*, November–December 1982, pp. 51–54.

43 C.A. Bartlett and S. Ghoshal, "Managing Across Borders: New Organizational Responses," *Sloan Management Review*, Fall 1987, pp. 43–53.

44 Nortel Networks, *Corporate Backgrounder*, July 2000; "A World of Networks: Building the Foundation for the Future," *Telesis*, October 1995; "Nortel Splits Operating Roles," *Globe and Mail*, December 23, 1993, p. B3; L. Surtees, "Power Shifts at Northern Telecom," *Globe and Mail*, February 14, 1991, pp. B1, B2.

45 J. Palmer, "Flight Centre Has an Unusual Team Culture," *Business Day* (South Africa), April 20, 2000, p. 28.

46 J.R. Galbraith, *Competing with Flexible Lateral Organizations* (Boston, MA: Addison-Wesley, 1994); J.B. Rieley, "The Circular Organization: How Leadership Can Optimize Organizational Effectiveness," *National Productivity Review*, 13 (Winter 1993/1994), pp. 11–19; J.A. Byrne, "The Horizontal Corporation," *Business Week*, December 20, 1993, pp. 76–81; R. Tomasko, *Rethinking the Corporation* (New York: AMACOM, 1993); D. Quinn Mills (with G. Bruce Friesen), *Rebirth of the Corporation* (New York: Wiley, 1991), pp. 29–30.

47 L.D. Goodstein and H.R. Butz, "Customer Value: The Linchpin of Organizational Change," *Organizational Dynamics*, 27 (Summer 1998), pp. 21–34.

48 K. Dorrell, "The Right Stuff," *Plant*, December 16, 1996, pp. 18–19; D. Jones, "Robo-Shop," *Report on Business Magazine*, March 1994, pp. 54–62; L. Gutri, "Pratt & Whitney Employees Don't Want to Be Managed: Teams Demand Leadership," *Canadian HR Reporter*, May 2, 1988, p. 8; J. Todd, "Firm Fashions Workplace for High-Tech Era," *Montreal Gazette*, December 12, 1987, p. B4.

49 R. Bettis and M. Hitt, "The New Competitive Landscape," *Strategic Management Journal*, 16 (1995), pp. 7–19; J.R. Galbraith, E.E. Lawler III, and Associates, *Organizing for the Future: The New Logic for Managing Complex Organizations* (San Francisco, CA: Jossey-Bass, 1993).

50 P.C. Ensign, "Interdependence, Coordination, and Structure in Complex Organizations: Implications for Organization Design," *Mid-Atlantic Journal of Business*, 34 (March 1998), pp. 5–22.

51 L.Y. Chan and B.E. Lynn, "Operating in Turbulent Times: How Ontario's Hospitals Are Meeting the Current Funding Crisis," *Health Care Management Review*, 23 (June 1998), pp. 7–18; M.M. Fanning, "A Circular Organization Chart Promotes a Hospital-Wide Focus on Teams," *Hospital & Health Services Administration*, 42 (June 1997), pp. 243–54.

52 W.F. Joyce, V.E. McGee, J.W Slocum, Jr., "Designing Lateral Organizations: An Analysis of the Benefits, Costs, and Enablers of Nonhierarchical Organizational Forms," *Decision Sciences*, 28 (Winter 1997), pp. 1–25.

53 A.M. Porter, "The Virtual Corporation: Where Is It?" *Purchasing*, March 23, 2000, pp. 40–48; J.A. Byrne "The Corporation of the Future," *Business Week*, August 31, 1998, pp. 102–104.

54 C. Baldwin and K. Clark, "Managing in an Age of Modularity," *Harvard Business Review*, 75 (September–October 1997), pp. 84–93; W. Powell, K.W. Koput, and L. Smith-Doerr, "Interorganizational Collabouration and the Locus of Innovation: Networks of Learning in Biotechnology," *Administrative Science Quarterly*, 41 (1996), pp. 116–45; R.E. Miles and C.C. Snow, "The New Network Firm: A Spherical Structure Built on a Human Investment Philosophy," *Organizational Dynamics*, 23(4) (1995), pp. 5–18; R.E. Miles and C.C. Snow, "Causes of Failure in Network Organizations," *California Management Review*, 34 (Summer 1992), pp. 53–72; H.F. Kolodny, "Some Characteristics of Organizational Designs in New/High Technology Firms," in L.R. Gomez-Mejia and M.W. Lawless (eds.), *Organizational Issues in High Technology Management* (Greenwich, CT: JAI Press, 1990), pp. 165–76; W. Powell, "Neither Market nor Hierarchy: Network Forms of Organization," *Research in Organizational Behaviour*, 12 (1990), pp. 295–336.

55 T.W. Malone and R.J. Laubacher, "The Dawn of the E-lance Economy," *Harvard Business Review*, 76 (September–October 1998), pp. 144–52.

56 T. Arsenault, "Return of the Rich Man," *Halifax-Chronicle Herald*, November 5, 1999; J. Hagel III and M. Singer, "Unbundling the Corporation," *Harvard Business Review*, 77 (March–April 1999), pp. 133–41. For a discussion of core competencies, see G. Hamel and C.K. Prahalad, *Competing for the Future* (Boston: Harvard Business School Press, 1994), Chapter 10.

57 D. Egbert, "Label Says 'Nortel,' but Somebody Else Probably Made It," *News and Observer* (Raleigh, NC), June 15, 2000, p. D1. The quotation is found in G. Ip, "Outsourcing Becoming a Way of Life for Firms," *Globe and Mail*, October 2, 1996, p. B8.

58 R. Lieber, "Startups: The 'Inside' Stories," *Fast Company*, 32 (March 2000), p. 284.

59 J. Matthews, "'Baby Bills' Follow Leader to Success," *Baltimore Sun*, August 14, 1998; J.F. Moore, "The Rise of a New Corporate Form," *Washington Quarterly*, 21 (Winter 1998), pp. 167–81.

60 L. Fried, *Managing Information Technology in Turbulent Times* (New York: John Wiley and Sons, 1995); W.H. Davidow and M.S. Malone, *The Virtual Corporation* (New York: HarperBusiness, 1992).

61 G. Morgan, *Imagin-I-Zation: New Mindsets for Seeing, Organizing and Managing* (Thousand Oaks, CA: Sage, 1997); G. Morgan, *Images of Organization*, 2nd ed. (Newbury Park: Sage, 1996).

62 C. Meyer and S. Davis, *Blur: The Speed of Change in the Connected Economy* (Reading, MA: Addison-Wesley, 1998); P.M.J. Christie and R. Levary, "Virtual Corporations: Recipe for Success," *Industrial Management*, 40 (July 1998), pp. 7–11; H. Chesbrough and D.J. Teece, "When Is Virtual Virtuous? Organizing for Innovation," *Harvard Business Review*, January–February 1996, pp. 65–73.

63 Mintzberg, *The Structuring of Organizations*, Chapter 13; D.S. Pugh and C.R. Hinings (eds.), *Organizational Structure: Extensions and Replications* (Farnborough, UK: Lexington Books, 1976).

64 T.A. Stewart, *Intellectual Capital: The New Wealth of Organizations* (New York: Doubleday/Currency, 1997), Chapter 10.

65 Robey, *Designing Organizations*, p. 102.

66 C. Perrow, "A Framework for the Comparative Analysis of Organizations," *American Sociological Review*, 32 (1967), pp. 194–208.

67 Mintzberg, *The Structuring of Organizations*, Chapter 15.

68 Burns and Stalker, *The Management of Innovation*; P.R. Lawrence and J.W. Lorsch, *Organization and Environment* (Homewood, IL: Irwin, 1967); D. Miller and P.H. Friesen, *Organizations: A Quantum View* (Englewood Cliffs, NJ: Prentice Hall, 1984), pp. 197–98.

69 Mintzberg, *The Structuring of Organizations*, p. 282.

70 R.H. Kilmann, *Beyond the Quick Fix* (San Francisco: Jossey-Bass, 1984), p. 38.

71 J. Child, "Organizational Structure, Environment, and Performance: The Role of Strategic Choice," *Sociology*, 6 (1972), pp. 2–22.

72 A.D. Chandler, *Strategy and Structure* (Cambridge, MA: MIT Press, 1962).

73 M.E. Porter, *Competitive Strategy* (New York: The Free Press, 1980).

74 D. Miller, "Configurations of Strategy and Structure," *Strategic Management Journal*, 7 (1986), pp. 233–50.

Chapter Seventeen

1 D. Francis, "Work Is a Warm Puppy," *National Post,* May 27, 2000, p. W20; M. Smith, "Morphing for Dollars," *Report on Business Magazine,* December 31, 1999, p. 33; V. Lu, "The Play Ethic," *Toronto Star,* November 1, 1998, p. F1. Additional information was provided from an interview with ExtendMedia spokesperson Caroline Verboon on September 1, 2000.

2 T.O. Davenport, "The Integration Challenge; Managing Corporate Mergers," *Management Review,* 87 (January 1998), pp. 25–28; E.H. Schein, "What Is Culture?" in P.J. Frost, L.F. Moore, M.R. Louis, C.C. Lundberg, and J. Martin (eds.), *Reframing Organizational Culture* (Beverly Hills, CA: Sage, 1991), pp. 243–53; A. Williams, P. Dobson, and M. Walters, *Changing Culture: New Organizational Approaches* (London: Institute of Personnel Management, 1989).

3 A. Sagie and D. Elizur, "Work Values: A Theoretical Overview and a Model of Their Effects," *Journal of Organizational Behavior,* 17 (1996), pp. 503–14; W.H. Schmidt and B.Z. Posner, Managerial Values in Perspective (New York: American Management Association, 1983).

4 B.M. Meglino and E.C. Ravlin, "Individual Values in Organizations: Concepts, Controversies, and Research," *Journal of Management,* 24 (May 1998), pp. 351–89; C. Argyris and D.A. Schön, *Organizational Learning: A Theory of Action Perspective* (Reading, MA: Addison-Wesley, 1978).

5 P. Brethour, "Software Grunt Follows Unsexy Growth Path," *Globe and Mail,* April 22, 1998, p. B25.

6 S. Baker, "Can CEO Ollila Keep the Cellular Superstar Flying High?" *Business Week,* August 10, 1998, pp. 54–61.

7 M. Brady, "Wellness Program Paying Off in the Poutine Capital," *National Post,* June 12, 2000, p. C19; C. Tremblay, "MDS Nordion 'Happiest, Healthiest Workplace,'" *Ottawa Citizen,* November 15, 1999; "Healthy Workplace Award Reflects a 'Win-Win-Win' Culture," *Canadian Newswire,* October 29, 1999; R. Andrew, "Years of Living Dangerously," *CA Magazine,* March 1999, pp. 26–30.

8 K. Crowley, "RIM Ready to Rev Up Production," *Kitchener-Waterloo Record,* August 9, 2000; G. Crone, "You Know a Company Is Doing Well When Barenaked Ladies Come to Entertain," *National Post,* January 19, 2000, p. C4; S. Chilton, "High-Flying RIM Reaches for the Stars," *Kitchener-Waterloo Record,* May 22, 1999, p. E1.

9   S. Sackmann, "Culture and Subcultures: An Analysis of Organizational Knowledge," *Administrative Science Quarterly,* 37 (1992), pp. 140–61; J. Martin and C. Siehl, "Organizational Culture and Counterculture: An Uneasy Symbiosis," *Organizational Dynamics,* Autumn 1983, pp. 52–64; J.S. Ott, *The Organizational Culture Perspective* (Pacific Grove, CA: Brooks/Cole, 1989), pp. 45–47; T.E. Deal and A.A. Kennedy, *Corporate Cultures* (Reading, MA: Addison-Wesley, 1982), pp. 138–39.

10   A. Sinclair, "Approaches to Organizational Culture and Ethics," *Journal of Business Ethics,* 12 (1993), pp. 63–73.

11   M.O. Jones, *Studying Organizational Symbolism: What, How, Why?* (Thousand Oaks, CA: Sage, 1996); Ott, *The Organizational Culture Perspective,* Chapter 2; J.S. Pederson and J.S. Sorensen, *Organisational Cultures in Theory and Practice* (Aldershot, UK: Gower, 1989), pp. 27–29.

12   "Making Work Fun," *Minneapolis Star Tribune,* August 18, 1998, p. E9.

13   A. Furnham and B. Gunter, "Corporate Culture: Definition, Diagnosis, and Change," *International Review of Industrial and Organizational Psychology,* 8 (1993), pp. 233–61; E.H. Schein, "Organizational Culture," *American Psychologist,* February 1990, pp. 109–19; Ott, *The Organizational Culture Perspective,* Chapter 2; W.J. Duncan, "Organizational Culture: 'Getting a Fix' on an Elusive Concept," *Academy of Management Executive,* 3 (1989), pp. 229–36.

14   J.C. Meyer, "Tell Me a Story: Eliciting Organizational Values from Narratives," *Communication Quarterly,* 43 (1995), pp. 210–24.

15   A. Gordon, "Perks and Stock Options Are Great, but It's Attitude That Makes the Difference," *Globe and Mail,* January 28, 2000.

16   J.Z. DeLorean, *On a Clear Day You Can See General Motors* (Grosse Pointe, MI: Wright Enterprises, 1979).

17   K. Foss, "Isadore Sharp," *Foodservice and Hospitality,* December 1989, pp. 20–30; J. DeMont, "Sharp's Luxury Empire," *Maclean's,* June 5, 1989, pp. 30–33.

18   R. Zemke, "Storytelling: Back to a Basic," *Training,* 27 (March 1990), pp. 44–50; A.L. Wilkins, "Organizational Stories as Symbols Which Control the Organization," in L.R. Pondy, P.J. Frost, G. Morgan, and T.C. Dandridge (eds.), *Organizational Symbolism* (Greenwich, CT: JAI Press, 1984), pp. 81–92; J. Martin and M.E. Powers, "Truth or Corporate Propaganda: The Value of a Good War Story," in Pondy et al. (eds.), *Organizational Symbolism,* pp. 93–107.

19   J. Martin et al., "The Uniqueness Paradox in Organizational Stories," *Administrative Science Quarterly,* 28 (1983), pp. 438–53.

20   P.S. DeLisi, "A Modern-Day Tragedy: The Digital Equipment Story," *Journal of Management Inquiry,* 7 (June 1998), pp. 118–30. Digital's famous shouting matches are also described in E. Schein, "How to Set the Stage for a Change in Organizational Culture," in P. Senge et al, *The Dance of Change* (New York: Currency Doubleday, 1999), pp. 334–44.

21   J.M. Beyer and H.M. Trice, "How an Organization's Rites Reveal Its Culture," *Organizational Dynamics,* 15(4) (1987), pp. 5–24; L. Smirchich, "Organizations as Shared Meanings," in Pondy et al. (eds.), *Organizational Symbolism,* pp. 55–65.

22   L.A. Krefting and P.J. Frost, "Untangling Webs, Surfing Waves, and Wildcatting," in P.J. Frost, L.F. Moore, M.R. Louis, C.C. Lundberg, and J. Martin (eds.), *Organizational Culture* (Beverly Hills, CA: Sage, 1985), pp. 155–68.

23   J.A. Byrne, "How Jack Welch Runs GE," *Business Week,* June 8, 1998.

24   R.E. Quinn and N.T. Snyder, "Advance Change Theory: Culture Change at Whirlpool Corporation," in J.A. Conger, G.M. Spreitzer, and E.E. Lawler III, *The Leader's Change Handbook* (San Francisco: Jossey-Bass, 1999), pp. 162–93.

25   N. Williams, "Office Design Creates 'A Great Place to Work,' " *Toronto Star,* September 9, 1999.

26 J.M. Kouzes and B.Z. Posner, *The Leadership Challenge* (San Francisco: Jossey-Bass, 1995), pp. 230–31.

27 J. Borra, "Working Well," *Chatelaine,* August 1999, p. 34; K. Doler, "Interview: Jeff Bezos, Founder and CEO of Amazon.com Inc.," *Upside,* 10 (September 1998), pp. 76–80; D. Menzies, "What Do You Mean There Are No More Donuts?" *Financial Post Magazine,* December 1996, p. 10.

28 C. Siehl and J. Martin, "Organizational Culture: A Key to Financial Performance?" in B. Schneider (ed.), *Organizational Climate and Culture* (San Francisco: Jossey-Bass, 1990), pp. 241–81; J.B. Barney, "Organizational Culture: Can It Be a Source of Sustained Competitive Advantage?" *Academy of Management Review,* 11 (1986), pp. 656–65; V. Sathe, *Culture and Related Corporate Realities* (Homewood, IL: Irwin, 1985), Chapter 2; Deal and Kennedy, *Corporate Cultures,* Chapter 1. Information about Zero-Knowledge comes from S. Dougherty, "Watch Out for Fast Company," *Montreal Gazette,* May 18, 2000.

29 Adapted from P. Roberts, "The Empire Strikes Back," *Fast Company,* 22 (February–March 1999), pp. 122–31.

30 C.A. O'Reilly and J.A. Chatman, "Culture as Social Control: Corporations, Cults, and Commitment," *Research in Organizational Behavior,* 18 (1996), pp. 157–200.

31 B. Ashforth and F. Mael, "Social Identity Theory and the Organization," *Academy of Management Review,* 14 (1989), pp. 20–39.

32 J. Elliott, "All Work and No Play Can Chase Workers Away," *Edmonton Journal,* February 28, 2000.

33 S.G. Harris, "Organizational Culture and Individual Sensemaking: A Schema-Based Perspective," *Organization Science,* 5 (1994), pp. 309–21; M.R. Louis, "Surprise and Sensemaking: What Newcomers Experience in Entering Unfamiliar Organizational Settings," *Administrative Science Quarterly,* 25 (1980), pp. 226–51.

34 G.S. Saffold III, "Culture Traits, Strength, and Organizational Performance: Moving Beyond 'Strong' Culture," *Academy of Management Review,* 13 (1988), pp. 546–58; Williams et al., *Changing Culture,* pp. 24–27.

35 J.P. Kotter and J.L. Heskett, *Corporate Culture and Performance* (New York: Free Press, 1992); G.G. Gordon and N. DiTomasco, "Predicting Corporate Performance from Organizational Culture," *Journal of Management Studies,* 29 (1992), pp. 783–98; D.R. Denison, *Corporate Culture and Organizational Effectiveness* (New York: Wiley, 1990).

36 E.H. Schein, "On Dialogue, Culture, and Organizational Learning," *Organization Dynamics,* Autumn 1993, pp. 40–51.

37 T. Parker-Pope, "New CEO Preaches Rebellion for P&G's 'Cult,' " *Wall Street Journal,* December 11, 1998.

38 J. Kotter, "Cultures and Coalitions," *Executive Excellence,* 15 (March 1998), pp. 14–15; Kotter and Heskett, *Corporate Culture and Performance.*

39 The features of adaptive cultures are described in W.F. Joyce, *MegaChange: How Today's Leading Companies Have Transformed Their Workforces* (New York: Free Press, 1999), pp. 44–47.

40 M. Acharya, "A Matter of Business Ethics," *Kitchener-Waterloo Record,* March 23, 1999, p. C2. For conceptual discussion on organizational culture and ethics, see S.J. Carroll and M.J. Gannon, *Ethical Dimensions of International Management* (Thousand Oaks, CA: Sage Publications, 1997), Chapter 5; A. Sinclair, "Approaches to Organisational Culture and Ethics," *Journal of Business Ethics,* 12 (1993), pp. 63–73.

41 J. Davidson, "The Business of Ethics," *Working Woman,* 23 (February 1998), pp. 68–71.

42 J. Mizuo, "Business Ethics and Corporate Governance in Japanese Corporations," *Business and Society Review,* March 1999, p. 65; "Shiseido," *Forbes* (supplement), January 11, 1999, p. S6.

43 W. Stueck, "Shared File Leads to Law Firm Merger," *Globe and Mail,* December 20, 1999, p. M1.

44 G.A. Walter, "Culture Collisions in Mergers and Acquisitions," in Frost et al. (eds.), *Organizational Culture,* pp. 301–14; A.F. Buono and J.L. Bowditch, *The Human Side of Mergers and Acquisitions* (San Francisco: Jossey-Bass, 1989), Chapter 6; E.H. Schein, *Organizational Culture and Leadership* (San Francisco: Jossey-Bass, 1985), pp. 33–36.

45 P. Troiano "Post-Merger Challenges," *Management Review,* 88 (January 1999), p. 6.

46 M. Lamey, "Sun Sets for Godfrey," *Montreal Gazette,* June 15, 2000; "The Newspaper Wars," *Canoe* (online), March 2, 1999. For a discussion of how mergers suffer from incompatible corporate cultures, see M.L. Marks, "Adding Cultural Fit to Your Diligence Checklist," *Mergers & Acquisitions,* December 1999.

47 E.H. Schein, *The Corporate Culture Survival Guide* (San Francisco: Jossey-Bass, 1999). A corporate culture audit is also recommended for joint ventures. For details, see K.J. Fedor and W.B. Werther, Jr., "The Fourth Dimension: Creating Culturally Responsive International Alliances," *Organizational Dynamics,* 25 (Autumn 1996), pp. 39–53.

48 D. Buckner, "Nortel versus Cisco," *CBC Venture,* January 4, 2000; R.N. Ashkenas, L.J. DeMonaco, and S.C. Francis "Making the Deal Real: How GE Capital Integrates Acquisitions," *Harvard Business Review,* 76 (January–February 1998), pp. 165–76.

49 K.W. Smith, "A Brand-New Culture for the Merged Firm," *Mergers and Acquisitions,* 35 (June 2000), pp. 45–50; A.R. Malekazedeh and A. Nahavandi, "Making Mergers Work by Managing Cultures," *Journal of Business Strategy,* May–June 1990, pp. 55–57.

50 A. Levy, "Mergers Spread Despite Failures," *Plain Dealer,* August 9, 1998, p. H1.

51 S. Feschuk, "Lean, Mean Anderson Trims Home Oil's Fat," *Globe and Mail,* October 17, 1995, p. B8.

52 "Nortel Uses Acquisition to Transform Role," *Wall Street Journal Europe,* July 26, 2000, p. 13.

53 "Mergers and Acquisitions May Be Driven by Business Strategy—But Often Stumble Over People and Culture Issues," *PR Newswire,* August 3, 1998.

54 J.P. Kotter, "Leading Change: The Eight Steps of Transformation," in J.A. Conger, G.M. Spreitzer, and E.E. Lawler III, *The Leader's Change Handbook* (San Francisco: Jossey-Bass, 1999), pp. 87–99.

55 J. Ball and S. Miller, "DaimlerChrysler Isn't Living Up to Its Promise," *Wall Street Journal Europe,* July 26, 2000; B. Vlasic and B.A. Stertz, "Taken for a Ride," *Business Week,* June 5, 2000, pp. 80–92; B. Klayman, "Year Later, DaimlerChrysler Struggles with Identity," *Toronto Star,* November 13, 1999.

56 "Hitachi to Allow Casual Clothes, Drop Honorifics," *Daily Yomiuri,* April 16, 1999.

57 E.H. Schein, "The Role of the Founder in Creating Organizational Culture," *Organizational Dynamics,* 12(1) (Summer 1983), pp. 13–28.

58 Schein, *Organizational Culture and Leadership,* Chapter 10; T.J. Peters, "Symbols, Patterns, and Settings: An Optimistic Case for Getting Things Done," *Organizational Dynamics,* 7(2) (Autumn 1978), pp. 2–23.

59 I. Sharp, "Quality for All Seasons," *Canadian Business Review,* 17(1) (Spring 1990), p. 22.

60 J. Kerr and J.W. Slocum, Jr., "Managing Corporate Culture Through Reward Systems," *Academy of Management Executive,* 1 (May 1987), pp. 99–107; Williams et al., *Changing Cultures,* pp. 120–24; K.R. Thompson and F. Luthans, "Organizational Culture: A Behavioral Perspective," in Schneider (ed.), *Organizational Climate and Culture,* pp. 319–44.

61 "Get Rich? Work at Home Depot," *Baltimore Sun,* July 27, 1998.

62 W.G. Ouchi and A.M. Jaeger, "Type Z Organization: Stability in the Midst of Mobility," *Academy of Management Review,* 3 (1978), pp. 305–14; K. McNeil and J.D. Thompson, "The Regeneration of Social Organizations," *American Sociological Review,* 36 (1971), pp. 624–37.

63 "A Full Life," *The Economist,* September 4, 1999.

64 M. De Pree, *Leadership Is an Art* (East Lansing, MI: Michigan State University Press, 1987).

65 J.J. Mason, "The Development Phase: Riding Chaos," *ComputerWorld Canada,* April 23, 1999, pp. 18, 20.

66 A.E.M. Van Vianen, "Person-Organization Fit: The Match Between Newcomers' and Recruiters' Preferences for Organizational Cultures," *Personnel Psychology,* 53 (Spring 2000), pp. 113–49; C.A. O'Reilly III, J. Chatman, and D.F. Caldwell, "People and Organizational Culture: A Profile Comparison Approach to Assessing Person–Organization Fit," *Academy of Management Journal,* 34 (1991), pp. 487–516.

67 "Corporate Culture Rivals Company Benefits in Importance to Job Applicants," News Release, Robert Half International, May 1, 1996.

68 M. Siegal, "The Perils of Culture Conflict," *Fortune,* November 9, 1998, pp. 257–62.

69 J. Van Maanen, "Breaking in: Socialization to Work," in R. Dubin (ed.), *Handbook of Work, Organization, and Society* (Chicago: Rand McNally, 1976), p. 67.

70 P. Tam, "Frugal Founder Rewards Employees," *Ottawa Citizen,* November 21, 1999.

Chapter Eighteen

1 P. Luke, "From Secretary to Cyber Queen," *Vancouver Province,* May 14, 2000; A. Daniels, "Virtual Assistant," *Vancouver Sun,* March 27, 2000, p. C10.

2 P. Cappelli, *The New Deal at Work* (Boston, MA: Harvard Business School Press, 1999).

3 B. Callahan, "More Oil, Fewer Workers," *St. John's Telegram,* February 18, 2000.

4 P. Kruger, "Betrayed by Work," *Fast Company,* November 1999, p. 182.

5 E.W. Morrison and S.L. Robinson, "When Employees Feel Betrayed: A Model of How Psychological Contract Violation Develops," *Academy of Management Review,* 22 (1997), pp. 226–56.

6 S.L. Robinson, M.S. Kraatz, and D.M. Rousseau, "Changing Obligations and the Psychological Contract: A Longitudinal Study," *Academy of Management Journal,* 37 (1994), pp. 137–52; D.M. Rousseau and J.M. Parks, "The Contracts of Individuals and Organizations," *Research in Organizational Behavior,* 15 (1993), pp. 1–43.

7 P. Herriot, W.E.G. Manning, and J.M. Kidd, "The Content of the Psychological Contract," *British Journal of Management,* 8 (1997), pp. 151–62.

8 J. McLean Parks and D.L. Kidder, " 'Till Death Us Do Part...' Changing Work Relationships in the 1990s," in C.L. Cooper and D.M. Rousseau (eds.), *Trends in Organizational Behavior,* Vol. 1 (Chichester, UK: Wiley, 1994), pp.112–36.

9 K. Goff, "New Economy, New Standards," *Ottawa Citizen,* September 2, 2000.

10 H.J. Van Buren III, "The Bindingness of Social and Psychological Contracts: Toward a Theory of Social Responsibility in Downsizing," *Journal of Business Ethics,* 25 (June 2000), pp. 205–19; P.R. Sparrow, "Reappraising Psychological Contracting: Lessons for the Field of Human-Resource Development from Cross-Cultural and Occupational Psychology Research," *International Studies of Management & Organization,* 28 (March 1998), pp. 30–63.

11 J. Stevenson, "Technology Driving Massive Change," *London Free Press,* September 15, 1999, p. D12.

12 R. Boudreaux, "Spaniards Are Missing Their Naps," *Los Angeles Times,* March 28, 2000.

13 S.L. Robinson, "Trust and Breach of the Psychological Contract," *Administrative Science Quarterly,* 41 (1996), pp. 574–99. For a discussion of the antecedents of trust, see E.M Whitener, S.E. Brodt, M.A. Korsgaard, and J.M. Werner, "Managers as Initiators of Trust: An Exchange Relationship

Framework for Understanding Managerial Trustworthy Behavior," *Academy of Management Review*, 23 (July 1998), pp. 513–30.

14   R.D. Costigan, S.S. Ilter, and J.J. Berman, "A Multi-Dimensional Study of Trust in Organizations," *Journal of Managerial Issues*, 10 (Fall 1998), pp. 303–17.

15   D.M. Rousseau, S.B. Sitkin, R.S. Burt, and C. Camerer, "Not So Different After All: A Cross-Discipline View of Trust," *Academy of Management Review*, 23 (July 1998), pp. 393–404; R.J. Lewicki and B.B. Bunker, "Developing and Maintaining Trust in Work Relationships," in R.M. Kramer and T.R. Tyler (eds.), *Trust in Organizations: Frontiers of Theory and Research* (Thousand Oaks, CA: Sage, 1996), pp. 114–39.

16   Whitener et al., "Managers as Initiators of Trust"; Bennis and Nanus, *Leaders,* pp. 43–55; Kouzes and Posner, *Credibility: How Leaders Gain and Lose It, Why People Demand It.* Knowledge-based trust is sometimes called "history-based trust" in the psychological literature. See R.M. Kramer, "Trust and Distrust in Organizations: Emerging Perspectives, Enduring Questions," *Annual Review of Psychology*, 50 (1999), pp. 569–98.

17   I. DeBare, "Keeping a Packed Bag at Work," *San Francisco Chronicle*, April 30, 1999.

18   S.L. Robinson and E.W. Morrison, "Psychological Contracts and OCB: The Effect of Unfulfilled Obligations on Civic Virtue Behavior," *Journal of Organizational Behavior*, 16 (1995), pp. 289–98.

19   Canadian Federation of Independent Business, "Study on Workplace Satisfaction in Private, Public Sectors," news release, October 1999. The complete report appeared at www.cfib.ca.

20   D.M. Rousseau, "Changing the Deal While Keeping the People," *Academy of Management Executive*, 10 (February 1996), pp. 50–61.

21   C. Hendry and R. Jenkins, "Psychological Contracts and New Deals," *Human Resource Management Journal*, 7 (1997), pp. 38–44; P. Herriot and C. Pemberton, *New Deals: The Revolution in Managerial Careers* (John Wiley & Sons, 1995), Chapter 3; W.H. Whyte, *The Organization Man* (New York: Simon and Schuster, 1956), p. 129.

22   J.C. Meister, "The Quest for Lifetime Employability," *Journal of Business Strategy* 19 (May–June 1998), pp. 25–28; T.A. Stewart, "Gray Flannel Suit? Moi?" *Fortune,* March 16, 1998, pp. 76–82; A. Rajan, "Employability in the Finance Sector: Rhetoric vs. Reality," *Human Resource Management Journal*, 7 (1997), pp. 67–78.

23   B. Moses, *The Good News About Careers: How You'll Be Working in the Next Decade* (Toronto: Stoddart, 1999); J. Lyon, "How Safe Is Your Job?" *Canadian Banker*, February 1997, pp. 12–15.

24   P. Herriot and C. Pemberton, "Facilitating New Deals," *Human Resource Management* Journal, 7 (1997), pp. 45–56; P.R. Sparrow, "Transitions in the Psychological Contract: Some Evidence from the Banking Sector," *Human Resource Management Journal*, 6 (1996), pp. 75–92.

25   A. Clark and T. Davies, "Young, Impatient and Empowered," *Maclean's*, May 17, 1999, p. A3.

26   Facts about Manpower, Inc. are from its Web site: www.manpower.com. This observation is also noted in T.W. Malone and R.J. Laubacher, "The Dawn of the E-lance Economy," *Harvard Business Review*, 76 (September–October 1998), pp. 144–52.

27   A.E. Polivka, "Contingent and Alternative Work Arrangements, Defined," *Monthly Labor Review*, 119 (October 1996), pp. 3–10. For further discussion of the meaning of contingent work, see S. Nollen and H. Axel, *Managing Contingent Workers* (New York: AMACOM, 1996), pp. 4–9.

28   S. Hipple, "Contingent Work: Results from the Second Survey," *Monthly Labor Review*, 121 (November 1998), pp. 22–35; K. Barker and K. Christensen (eds.), *Contingent Work: American Employment in Transition* (Ithaca, NY: ILR Press, 1998); Sparrow, "Reappraising Psychological Contracting"; G. Edmondson et al., "A Tidal Wave of Temps," *Business Week* (International), November 24, 1997; M. Gibb-Clark, "About 12% of Jobs Temporary, Statscan Finds," *Globe and Mail*, September 11, 1997, p. B4.

29 von Hippel et. al, "Temporary Employment"; A.E. Polivka, "Into Contingent and Alternative Employment: By Choice?" *Monthly Labor Review*, 119 (October 1996), pp. 55–74. A recent U.S. government study revealed that the percentage of contingent workers who want permanent employment is dropping. However, most of these people still prefer permanent employment. See "Gains in Job Security," *Monthly Labor Review*, 121 (March 1998), pp. 74–75.

30 S.B. Gould, K.J. Weiner, and B.R. Levin, *Free Agents: People and Organizations Creating a New Working Community* (San Francisco: Jossey-Bass, 1997); von Hippel, et al., "Temporary Employment," pp. 94–96; W.J. Byron, "Coming to Terms with the New Corporate Contract," *Business Horizons*, January–February 1995, pp. 8–15.

31 P. Gombu and D. Smith, "Day in the Life of a Temp Worker," *Toronto Star*, August 31, 1996, pp. A1, A16.

32 S.J. Hartman, A.C. Yrle, and A.R. Yrle, "Turnover in the Hotel Industry: Is There a Hobo Phenomenon at Work?" *International Journal of Management*, 13 (1996), pp. 340–48; T.A. Judge and S. Watanabe, "Is the Past Prologue? A Test of Ghiselli's Hobo Syndrome," *Journal of Management*, 21 (1995), pp. 211–29.

33 J. Walsh and S. Deery, "Understanding the Peripheral Workforce: Evidence from the Service Sector," *Human Resource Management Journal*, 9 (1999), p. 50; P. Booth, *Contingent Work: Trends, Issues, and Challenges for Employers* (Ottawa: Conference Board of Canada, 1997), p. 5; C. von Hippel, S.L. Mangum, D.B. Greenberger, R.L. Heneman, and J.D. Skoglind, "Temporary Employment: Can Organizations and Employees Both Win?" *Academy of Management Executive*, 11 (February 1997), pp. 93–104.

34 S.F. Matusik and C.W.L. Hill, "The Utilization of Contingent Work, Knowledge Creation, and Competitive Advantage," *Academy of Management Review*, 23 (October 1998), pp. 680–97.

35 J. Larson, "Temps Are Here to Stay," *American Demographics*, 18 (February 1996), pp. 26–30.

36 Malone and Laubacher, "The Dawn of the E-lance Economy."

37 For a recent survey on the complex array of problems and benefits of contingent work, see M. Mallon and J. Duberley, "Managers and Professionals in the Contingent Workforce," *Human Resource Management Journal*, January 2000, p. 33.

38 Beard and Edwards, "Employees at Risk," *Trends in Organizational Behavior*, Vol. 2, pp. 118–19.

39 J. Dionne-Proulx, J.-C. Bernatchez, and R. Boulard, "Attitudes and Satisfaction Levels Associated with Precarious Employment," *International Journal of Employment Studies*, 6(2) (1998), pp. 91–114. The contingencies of contingent work attitudes are reviewed in M. Armstrong-Stassen, "Alternative Work Arrangements: Meeting the Challenges," *Canadian Psychology*, 39 (1998), pp. 108–23. Potential organizational behaviour problems with contingent work are also discussed in J. Pfeffer, *New Directions in Organizational Theory* (New York: Oxford University Press, 1997), pp.18–20.

40 K.M. Beard and J.R. Edwards, "Employees at Risk: Contingent Work and the Psychological Experience of Contingent Workers," in C.L. Cooper and D.M. Rousseau (eds.), *Trends in Organizational Behavior*, Vol. 2 (Chichester, UK: Wiley, 1995), pp. 109–26.

41 D.M. Rousseau and C. Libuser, "Contingent Workers in High Risk Environments," *California Management Review*, 39 (Winter 1997), pp. 103–23; G. LaBarr, "Contingent Worker Safety: A Full-Time Job in a Part-Time World," *Occupational Hazards*, 10 (October 1997), pp. 92–100.

42 "Four Arrested as Campus 'Theft Ring' Is Exposed," *Simon Fraser News*, September 5, 1996.

43 Armstrong-Stassen, "Alternative Work Arrangements"; D.C. Feldman and H.I. Doerpinghaus, "Managing Temporary Workers: A Permanent HRM Challenge," *Organizational Dynamics*, 23 (Fall 1994), pp. 49–63.

44 A.M. Saks, P.E. Mudrack, and B.E. Ashforth, "The Relationship Between the Work Ethic, Job Attitudes, Intentions to Quit, and Turnover for Temporary Service Workers," *Canadian Journal of Administrative Sciences*, 13 (1996), pp. 226–36.

45 A. Czarnecki, "Customer Service Training: More Than an 'Event,' " *Learning for the Workplace* (Supplement to *Canadian HR Reporter*), May 20, 1996, pp. L4–L7; "Markham Stouffville Hospital Wins 1995 Canada Award for Excellence," *Canada NewsWire*, October 3, 1995.

46 J. Van Maanen, "Breaking In: Socialization to Work," in R. Dubin (ed.), *Handbook of Work, Organization, and Society* (Chicago: Rand McNally, 1976), p. 67.

47 C.L. Adkins, "Previous Work Experience and Organizational Socialization: A Longitudinal Examination," *Academy of Management Journal*, 38 (1995), pp. 839–62; T.N. Bauer and S.G. Green, "The Effect of Newcomer Involvement in Work Related Activities: A Longitudinal Study of Socialization," *Journal of Applied Psychology*, 79 (1994), pp. 211–23.

48 E.F. Holton III, "New Employee Development: A Review and Reconceptualization," *Human Resource Development Quarterly*, 7 (Fall 1996), pp. 233–52; G.T. Chao, A. O'Leary-Kelly, S. Wolf, H.J. Klein, and P.D. Gardner, "Organizational Socialization: Its Content and Consequences," *Journal of Applied Psychology*, 79 (1994), pp. 450–63.

49 J.T. Mignerey, R.B. Rubin, and W.I. Gorden, "Organizational Entry: An Investigation of Newcomer Communication Behavior and Uncertainty," *Communication Research*, 22 (1995), pp. 54–85.

50 K. Mieszkowski, "Get with the Program!" *Fast Company*, 13 (February–March 1998), pp. 28–30.

51 B.E. Ashforth and A.M. Saks, "Socialization Tactics: Longitudinal Effects on Newcomer Adjustment," *Academy of Management Journal*, 39 (1996), pp. 149–78; C.D. Fisher, "Organizational Socialization: An Integrative View," *Research in Personnel and Human Resources Management*, 4 (1986), pp. 101–45; N. Nicholson, "A Theory of Work Role Transitions," *Administrative Science Quarterly*, 29 (1984), pp. 172–91.

52 C.C. Pinder and K.G. Schroeder, "Time to Proficiency Following Job Transfers," *Academy of Management*, 2nd ed., Journal 30 (1987), pp. 336–53; N.J. Adler, *International Dimensions of Organizational Behavior* (Belmont, CA: Wadsworth, 1991), Chapter 8.

53 Van Maanen, "Breaking In," pp. 67–130; L.W. Porter, E.E. Lawler III, and J.R. Hackman, *Behavior in Organizations* (New York: McGraw-Hill, 1975), pp. 163–67; D.C. Feldman, "The Multiple Socialization of Organization Members," *Academy of Management Review*, 6 (1981), pp. 309–18.

54 M.K. Gibson and M.J. Papa, "The Mud, the Blood, and the Beer Guys: Organizational Osmosis in Blue-Collar Work Groups," *Journal of Applied Communication Research*, February 2000, p. 68; Ashforth and Saks, "Socialization Tactics"; T.N. Bauer and S.G. Green, "Effect of Newcomer Involvement in Work-Related Activities: A Longitudinal Study of Socialization," *Journal of Applied Psychology*, 79 (1994), pp. 211–23.

55 Porter et al., *Behavior in Organizations*, Chapter 5.

56 "Busy Pork Plant Needs More Workers," *Edmonton Journal*, December 29, 1999.

57 M.R. Louis, "Surprise and Sensemaking: What Newcomers Experience in Entering Unfamiliar Organizational Settings," *Administrative Science Quarterly*, 25 (1980), pp. 226–51.

58 E. Hannan, "Staff Turnover Tops $4B," *The Age* (Melbourne), June 7, 1998. Also see C.A. Young and C.C. Lundberg, "Creating a Good First Day on the Job," *Cornell Hotel and Restaurant Administration Quarterly*, 37 (December 1996), pp. 26–33; S.L. Robinson and D.M. Rousseau, "Violating the Psychological Contract: Not the Exception but the Norm," *Journal of Organizational Behavior*, 15 (1994), pp. 245–59.

59 D.L. Nelson, "Organizational Socialization: A Stress Perspective," *Journal of Occupational Behavior*, 8 (1987), pp. 311–24.

60 Morrison and Robinson, "When Employees Feel Betrayed," p. 251.

61 J.A. Breaugh, *Recruitment: Science and Practice* (Boston: PWS-Kent, 1992), Chapter 7; J.P. Wanous, *Organizational Entry*, 2nd ed. (Reading, MA: Addison-Wesley, 1992), Chapter 3; A.M. Saks and S.F. Cronshaw, "A Process Investigation of Realistic Job Previews: Mediating Variables and Channels of Communication," *Journal of Organizational Behavior*, 11 (1990), pp. 221–36.

62 J.M. Phillips, "Effects of Realistic Job Previews on Multiple Organizational Outcomes: A Meta-Analysis," *Academy of Management Journal*, 41 (December 1998), pp. 673–90.

63 J.P. Wanous and A. Colella, "Organizational Entry Research: Current Status and Future Directions," *Research in Personnel and Human Resources Management*, 7 (1989), pp. 59–120.

64 C. Ostroff and S.W.J. Koslowski, "Organizational Socialization as a Learning Process: The Role of Information Acquisition," *Personnel Psychology*, 45 (1992), pp. 849–74; N.J. Allen and J.P. Meyer, "Organizational Socialization Tactics: A Longitudinal Analysis of Links to Newcomers' Commitment and Role Orientation," *Academy of Management Journal*, 33 (1990), pp. 847–58; F.M. Jablin, "Organizational Entry, Assimilation, and Exit," in F.M. Jablin, L.L. Putnam, K.H. Roberts, and L.W. Porter (eds.), *Handbook of Organizational Communication* (Beverly Hills, CA: Sage, 1987), pp. 679–740.

65 H. Shaw, "Valet of the Malls," *National Post*, August 5, 2000, p. D1; V. Galt, "Lucrative Jobs Seek People," *Globe and Mail*, August 2, 2000, p. M1; J. Pappone, "Eaton Re-opening Attracts 1,000 Prospective Workers," *Ottawa Citizen*, July 20, 2000.

66 E.W. Morrison, "Newcomer Information Seeking: Exploring Types, Modes, Sources, and Outcomes," *Academy of Management Journal*, 36 (1993), pp. 557–89; Fisher, "Organizational Socialization," pp. 135–36; Porter et al., *Behavior in Organizations*, pp. 184–86.

67 D. Francis, "Work Is a Warm Puppy," *National Post*, May 27, 2000, p. W20; R. Maxwell, "Integrate New Employees," *ComputerWorld Canada*, September 10, 1999, pp. 17–18; K. Rowland, "High River's Cargill Foods Is a Home-Grown Success Story," *Calgary Herald*, December 10, 1998, p. 32.

68 S.L. McShane, "Effect of Socialization Agents on the Organizational Adjustment of New Employees," Paper presented at the Annual Conference of the Western Academy of Management, Big Sky, Montana, March 1988.

69 "Employee Loyalty a Fading Virtue," *Canadian Press*, April 9, 2000.

70 M.B. Arthur, D.T. Hall, and B.S. Lawrence, "Generating New Directions in Career Theory: The Case for a Transdisciplinary Approach," in M.B. Arthur, D.T. Hall, and B.S. Lawrence (eds.), *Handbook of Career Theory* (Cambridge, UK: Cambridge University Press, 1989), pp. 7–25.

71 M.B. Arthur, "The Boundaryless Career: A New Perspective for Organizational Inquiry," *Journal of Organizational Behavior*, 15 (1994), pp. 295–306.

72 D.T. Hall, *Careers in Organizations* (Glenview, IL: Scott, Foresman, 1976), pp. 93–97.

73 T. Snyder, "Take This Job and Love It," *Chatelaine*, October 1999, p. 97.

74 J. Holland, *Making Vocational Choices: A Theory of Careers* (Englewood Cliffs, NJ: Prentice Hall, 1973).

75 G.D. Gottfredson and J.L. Holland, "A Longitudinal Test of the Influence of Congruence: Job Satisfaction, Competency Utilization, and Counterproductive Behavior," *Journal of Counseling Psychology*, 37 (1990), pp. 389–98.

76 J. Arnold, "The Psychology of Careers in Organizations," *International Review of Industrial and Organizational Psychology*, 12 (1997), pp. 1–37.

77 For example, see G.R. Cluskey and A. Vaux, "Vocational Misfit: Source of Occupational Stress Among Accountants," *Journal of Applied Business Research*, 13 (Summer 1997), pp. 43–54.

78 R.A. Young and C.P. Chen, "Annual Review: Practice and Research in Career Counseling and Development—1998," *Career Development Quarterly*, December 1999, p. 98.

79 D.T. Hall and J. Richter, "Career Gridlock: Baby Boomers Hit the Wall," *Academy of Management Executive*, 4 (August 1990), pp. 7–22.

80 B. Kaye and C. Farren, "Up Is Not the Only Way," *Training & Development*, 50 (February 1996), pp. 48–53.

81 P. LaBarre, "The Company without Limits," *Fast Company*, 27, p. 160.

82 P. Baker, "A Sideways Move Could Bring You Out of Your Shell," *The Observer*, March 22, 1998, p. 8; "De-Layered Pay Systems Encourage Employees to Move Sideways," *Universal News Services*, January 24, 1997.

83 M. Gibb-Clark, "How Statscan Spreads the Jobs Around," *Globe and Mail*, March 28, 1997, p. B9.

84 A. Davis, "Climbing the Corporate Ladder," *Benefits Canada*, May 1999; S. Nador, "Breaking Down Retention Barriers by Building Up Internal Opportunities," *Canadian HR Reporter*, May 3, 1999, p. 11; G. Salley, "Bank of Montreal's Virtual Career Centre," *Canadian HR Reporter,* November 16, 1998, p. G14; J.C. Meister, "The Quest for Lifetime Employability," *Journal of Business Strategy*, 19 (May–June 1998), pp. 25–28.

85 W.H. Whyte, *Organization Man* (New York: Simon & Schuster, 1956).

86 M.B. Arthur and D.M. Rousseau, *The Boundaryless Career: A New Employment Principle for a New Organizational Era* (New York: Oxford University Press, 1996); M.B. Arthur, "The Boundaryless Career: A New Perspective for Organizational Inquiry," *Journal of Organizational Behavior*, 15 (1994), pp. 295–306.

87 Schmit, "High-Tech Job Hopping"; K. Kelly, "New Rules for the New Economy," *Wired Magazine*, 5 (September 1997). However, for a discussion with the backlash against job hopping, see J. Palmer, "Marry Me a Little," *Barron's*, July 24, 2000, p. 24.

88 Stewart, "Gray Flannel Suit? Moi?"

89 New York Times, *The Downsizing of America* (New York: Times Books, 1996); R.J. Defillippi and M.B. Arthur, "The Boundaryless Career: A Competency-Based Perspective," *Journal of Organizational Behavior*, 15 (1994), pp. 307–24.

90 B. O'Reilly, "The New Deal: What Companies and Employees Owe One Another," *Fortune*, June 13, 1994, pp. 44–52.

91 M. Jarman, "Job Hopping Acceptable," *Arizona Republic*, July 26, 1998.

92 J.P. Sampson, Jr., J.G. Lenz, R.C. Reardon, and G.W. Peterson, "A Cognitive Information Processing Approach to Employment Problem Solving and Decision Making," *Career Development Quarterly*, 48 (September 1999), p. 3.

93 P. Chisholm, "What the Boss Needs to Know," *Maclean's*, May 29, 2000, p. 18.

94 B. Moses, "Give People Belief in the Future," *Workforce*, June 2000, pp. 134–41.

95 P. Allossery, "AGF 'Light Years Ahead' of Most Fund Firms in Branding," *National Post*, May 15, 2000.

96 D. Campbell, "In Charge of a Fire Fight," *Hamilton Spectator*, August 24, 2000.

97 B. Moses, "Career Activists Take Command," *Globe and Mail*, March 20, 2000, p. B6.

98 F.T. McCarthy, "Career Evolution," *Economist*, January 29, 2000.

99 S.E. Sullivan, "The Changing Nature of Careers: A Review and Research Agenda," *Journal of Management*, May 1999, p. 457; Moses, *The Good News About Careers*.

100 N. Beech and A. Brockbank, "Power/Knowledge and Psychosocial Dynamics in Mentoring," *Management Learning*, 30 (March 1999), pp. 7; S.-C. Van Collie, "Moving Up Through Mentoring," *Workforce*, 77 (March 1998), pp. 36–40.

101 H. Handfield-Jones, "How Executives Grow," *McKinsey Quarterly*, January 2000, p. 117.

Appendix A

1 Kerlinger, *Foundations of Behavioral Research* (New York: Holt, Rinehart, & Winston, 1964), p. 11.

2 J.B. Miner, *Theories of Organizational Behavior* (Hinsdale, IL: Dryden, 1980), pp. 7–9.

3 *Ibid.*, pp. 6–7.

4 J. Mason, *Qualitative Researching* (London: Sage, 1996).

5 A. Strauss and J. Corbin (eds.), *Grounded Theory in Practice* (London: Sage Publications, 1997); B.G. Glaser and A. Strauss, *The Discovery of Grounded Theory: Strategies for Qualitative Research* (Chicago, IL: Aldine Publishing Co, 1967).

6 Kerlinger, *Foundations of Behavioral Research,* p. 13.

7 P. Lazarsfeld, *Survey Design and Analysis* (New York: The Free Press, 1955).

8 This example is cited in D.W. Organ and T.S. Bateman, *Organizational Behavior,* 4th ed. (Homewood, IL: Irwin, 1991), p. 42.

9 *Ibid.,* p. 45

10 R.I. Sutton and A. Hargadon, "Brainstorming Groups in Context: Effectiveness in a Product Design Firm," *Administrative Science Quarterly,* 41 (1996), pp. 685–718.